Social
Issues
Primary
Sources
Collection

Medicine, Health, and Bioethics

Essential Primary Sources

Social Issues Primary Sources Collection

Medicine, Health, and Bioethics

Essential Primary Sources

K. Lee Lerner and **Brenda Wilmoth Lerner,** Editors

THOMSON

GALE

Detroit • New York • San Francisco • San Diego • New Haven, Conn. • Waterville, Maine • London • Munich

THOMSON
GALE

Medicine, Health, and Bioethics: Essential Primary Sources

K. Lee Lerner and Brenda Wilmoth Lerner, Editors

Project Editor
Melissa Hill

Editorial
Kathleen J. Edgar, Debra M. Kirby, Kristine Krapp, Paul Lewon, Charles B. Montney, Heather Price, Lemma Shomali

Permissions
Margaret Abendroth, Margaret Chamberlain-Gaston, Jessica Schultz

Imaging and Multimedia
Lezlie Light, Michael Logusz, Christine O'Bryan, Robyn V. Young

Product Design
Pamela A. Galbreath

Composition and Electronic Capture
Evi Seoud

Manufacturing
Rita Wimberley

Product Manager
Carol Nagel

LIBRARY OF CONGRESS CATALOGING-IN-PUBLICATION DATA

Medicine, health, and bioethics : essential primary sources / K. Lee Lerner and Brenda Wilmoth Lerner, editors.
    p. cm. – (Social issues primary sources collection)
    Includes bibliographical references and index.
    ISBN 1-4144-0623-1 (hardcover : alk. paper)
    1. Medical ethics–History–Sources. 2. Bioethics–History–Sources. 3. Medicine–History–Sources. I. Lerner, K. Lee. II. Lerner, Brenda Wilmoth. III. Series.

    R724.M313 2006
    174.2–dc22   2005035526

This title is also available as an e-book.
ISBN 1-4144-0624-X
Contact your Thomson Gale sales representative for ordering information.

Printed in the United States of America
10 9 8 7 6 5 4 3 2

Table of Contents

Advisors and Contributors xv

Acknowledgements xvii

About the Set xxiii

Introduction xxv

About the Entry xxvii

Using Primary Sources xxxiii

Chronology xxxv

1 BIOMEDICAL SCIENCE

Introduction to Biomedical Science 1

The Lancet 2
    Thomas Wakley, 1823

Head and Upper Body 4
    Francesco C. Antommarchi, 1826

Rabies Vaccination in Pasteur's Clinic in Paris 9
    Laurent-Lucien Gsell, 1887

Letter to Lord Chamberlain Hugo Radolinski 11
    Ruldolf Virchow, 1888

Hand with Ring 13
    Wilhelm Conrad Roentgen, 1895

This Day Relenting God 15
    Ronald Ross, 1923

Robert Koch Identifies the Bacteria That Cause
Anthrax, Tuberculosis, and Cholera 17
    K. A. H. Mörner, 1905

The Internal Secretion of the Pancreas 20
Frederick Grant Banting and Charles Herbert Best, 1922

On Individual Differences in Human Blood 23
Karl Landsteiner, 1930

A Strong Nation Is a Healthy Nation 26
N. H. Heiligman, 1940

A Structure for Deoxyribose Nucleic Acid 29
James Dewey Watson and Frances Harry Compton Crick, 1953

Patient Undergoing a CT Scan 32
Anonymous, 1978

Louise Brown and Her Parents 34
Ray Foli, 1979

Pneumocystis Pneumonia—Los Angeles 35
Michael S. Gottlieb, et.al., 1981

Köhler and Milstein Develop Monoclonal Antibodies 39
Hans Wigzell, 1984

Baby Fae Loses her Battle 41
Claudia Wallis, 1984

The Promise of Prozac 45
Geoffrey Cowley, 1990

Animals and Medical Science: A Vision of a New Era 49
David O. Wiebers, 1994

Chorionic Villus Sampling and Amniocentesis 54
Richard S. Olney, 1995

Prions: Newly Identified Infectious Agent 57
Ralf F. Pettersson, 1997

Zoonosis 60
Karen Kasmauski, 2000

The Sequence of the Human Genome 61
John Craig Venter, 2001

Gene Therapy: Promises and Problems 65
Alexander Pfeifer and Inder M. Verma, 2001

What the Heck Is Antibiotic Resistance? 67
John C. Brown, 2002

Stem Cells: Scientific Progress and Future Research Directions . . . 72
Ruth L. Kirchstein and Lana Skirboll, 2001

He Never Gave Up 75
Jeffrey Klugar, 2004

Eulogy for Mattie Stepanek 78
Jimmy Carter, 2004

Can Gene-Altered Rice Rescue the Farm Belt? 82
Alexei Barrionuevo, 2005

Woman Finds Human Finger in Wendy's Chili 85
Dan Reed, 2005

2 CLINICAL MEDICINE

Introduction to Clinical Medicine 89

Case II 90
Horton Howard, 1832

Insensibility During Surgical Operations Produced By Inhalation . . . 91
Henry J. Bigelow, 1846

The Premature Burial 95
Antoine Joseph Wiertz, 1854

Conditions at Bellevue Hospital 97
Anonymous, 1860

Antiseptic Surgery 100
W. Watson Cheyne, 1882

Surgeon Amos Walker Barber, Wyoming Territory 103
Anonymous, circa 1890

Rules for the Prevention of Cholera 106
Anonymous, 1892

Radiation Used to Treat Tumors 110
Emil H. Grubbe, 1902

Origin and Development of Psychoanalysis, First Lecture 113
Sigmund Freud, 1909

Reliable Quinine 116
Anonymous, 1910

Postoperative Insanity 118
John Chalmers Da Costa, 1922

Psychological Consultation Report: Mrs. White and Miss Black . . 120
Corbett H. Thigpen and Hervey C. Cleckley, 1952

Implementation of the Program 124
Douglas B. McKendrick, 1964

Operation: November 29, 1944 126
Alfred Blaylock, 1944

Matthew's New Marrow 129
Matt Clark, 1976

Cholesterol and Heart Disease 131
Nobel Assembly at the Karolinska Institute, 1985

A Developmental Model of Ethnosensitivity in Family Practice Training 136
Jeffrey M. Borkan and Jon Neher, 1991

Outbreak of Ebola Viral Hemorrhagic Fever—Zaire, 1995 139
Centers for Disease Control and Prevention, 1995

Withdrawing Intensive Life-sustaining Treatment 142
Howard Brody, 1997

End-of-Life Issues 147
Frederick Flatow, 1998

Lasers and Fiber Optics Enable Microsurgery and Keyhole Surgery . 150
Robert J. Herko, 2000

BSE Inquiry: The Report, Executive Summary, Key Conclusions . . 152
Committee of the BSE Inquiry, 2000

A Revised System for Reporting Pap Test Results 155
Caroline McNeil and Nicole Gottlieb, 2002

Amy's Story—Anorexia 159
Amy, 2002

X Ray of the Lungs of a Coal Miner 163
Chuck Nacke, 2003

Trends and Results for Organ Donation and Transplantation
in the United States, 2004 166
Scientific Registry of Transplant Recipients, Organ
Procurement and Transplantation Network, 2004

Guide to Children's Dental Care in Medicaid 169
Department of Health and Human Services, 2004

Balancing Act: The Health Advantages of Naturally-Occurring
Hormone Replacement Therapy 173
Barbara Iving, M.D., 2004

Kryptonite 177
Amy Baird, 2004

Telemedicine 180
Jasemian Yousef, 2005

3 WAR AND MEDICINE

Introduction to War and Medicine 185

Disqualifying Diseases 186
Theodoric Romeyn Beck, 1823

A Doctor's Memories 189
Victor C. Vaughan, 1926

Circular Letter No. 36 191
Lieutenant Colonel Earle G. G. Standlee, 1944

Medical Intelligence 196
Robert S. Anderson, 1969

Sorting of Casualties 198
U.S. Department of Defense, 1975

Anthrax as a Biological Weapon: Medical and
Public Health Management 201
Thomas V. Inglesby, 1999

Médecins Sans Frontières (Doctors Without Borders) 203
Lionel Healing, 2006

4 INDUSTRY AND MEDICINE

Introduction to Industry and Medicine 207

Elizabeth Blackwell, First Female Physician 208
  Charles Alfred Lee, 1849

Age First Premarital Petting 210
  Alfred C. Kinsey, 1979

Gentlemen of the Class of 1878 214
  James Summerville, 1983

Nightingale Home and Training School for Nurses,
St. Thomas Hospital 217
  Anonymous, circa 1890

Bayer Pharmaceutical Products 220
  Anonymous, 1900

The Jungle. 223
  Upton Sinclair, 1906

The Flexner Report 227
  Abraham Flexner, 1910

State Registration of Trained Nurses 230
  William Henry Welch, 1903

Letter by Dr. A. S. Calhoun to Franklin D. Roosevelt 232
  Archie S. Calhoun, 1937

Private Health Insurance Originates with Blue
Cross and Blue Shield. 233
  Blue Cross Blue Shield Association, 1954

President Lyndon Johnson Signs Medicare Bill 236
  Lyndon Baines Johnson, 1965

The Belmont Report 238
  U.S. Department of Health, Education, and Welfare, 1979

Product Tampering 243
  Anonymous, 1982

Helicopter Rescue of Air Crash Victims 245
  Anonymous, 1982

Is there a Doctor in the House? 247
  Anonymous, 1986

Shaman Loses Its Magic 249
  Anonymous, 1999

Medical Tourism Companies Luring Americans Abroad
with Surgery-Vacation Trips 252
  Maria M. Parotin, 2004

America, Pull Up A Chair—We've Got Something
Good to Talk About 255
  Centers for Medicare & Medicaid Services, 2005

E-mail from Hurricane Katrina. 260
  James T. Montgomery, 2005

5 PUBLIC HEALTH

Introduction to Public Health 265

John Snow's Map. 266
  John Snow, 1854

Immigrant Girl Receives Medical Exam at Ellis Island 268
  Anonymous, 1905

AAAS Resolution: Death of Dr. James Carroll
from Yellow Fever Experimentation 270
  American Association for the Advancement of Science, 1907

Report on Condition of Women and Child
Wage-Earners in the United States 272
  Charles P. Neill, 1912

Typhoid Mary Has Reappeared 274
  Anonymous, 1915

Sanitation 276
  William Osler, 1921

Preliminary Survey and Current Data 279
  Alabama Department of Public Health, 1937

March of Dimes 282
  Anonymous, 1946

Constitution of the World Health Organization,
Chapters I and II 284
  World Health Organzation, 1947

On the State of Rural Hygiene 287
  Florence Nightingale, 1893

Thalidomide and Congenital Abnormalities 291
  W. G. McBride, 1961

Famine and Public Health 293
  Dempster, 1970

Has Your Child Had a Lead Test Yet? 295
  U.S. Department of Health, Education, and Welfare, 1970

President Nixon Declares "War" on Drugs 297
  Richard M. Nixon, 1971

Marlboro Man; Bob, I've Got Emphysema 300
  Robert Landau, 1976; Scott Houston, 2000

Ali Maow Maalin Survives the Last Endemic Smallpox Case . . . 303
  Anonymous, 1979

Camp Devens Letter 306
  Roy, 1918

Immunization Campaigns 310
California Department of Health Services, circa early 1980s

Community Mental Health Centers Construction Act of 1989 . . . 313
Library of Congress, 1989

A Hand and a Home for Pregnant Addicts 317
Dennis Wyss, 1989

The Clean Air Act, Title 1: Air Pollution Prevention and Control . . . 320
Anonymous, 1990

Motor Vehicle Safety and Public Health 322
Tim Wright, 1998

Pasteurization and Aseptic Processing 325
U.S. Food and Drug Administration, 2001

Bioterrorism at the Salad Bar 328
Bill Frist, 2002

Priority Traffic Safety Laws 330
MADD (Mothers Against Drunk Driving), 2003

Carrier of SARS Made Seven Flights Before Treatment 333
Keith Bradsher, 2003

For a Few Pennies More 338
Television Trust for the Environment, 2004

Drug Recalls 341
David J. Graham, 2004

Alps Still Contaminated by Radiation from Chernobyl 343
Maryann DeLeo, 2004

World Water Crisis 346
Issouf Sanogo, 2005

Fluoridation of Drinking Water to Prevent Dental Caries 347
Centers for Disease Control and Prevention, 1999

Water, Sanitation Key to Disaster Response,
Long-Term Development 351
Erica Bulman, 2005

The Initial Assessment: A Quick Checklist 353
UNICEF, 2005

Memories of Polio 358
Alakananda Mohanty and Martin Pernick, 2005

Outbreak Notice 361
Centers for Disease Control and Prevention, 2005

6 WELLNESS AND HEALTH

Introduction to Wellness and Health 365

Not By Bread Alone 366
Harvey Washington Wiley, 1915

Don'ts in Removing Superfluous Hair 368
    Plym S. Hayes, 1910

Alcoholics and God 370
    Morris Markey, 1939

Conscious Control of our Sex Life 373
    J. Rutgers, 1937

Our Bodies, Ourselves 376
    The Boston Women's Health Book Collective, 1976

A Medical Student in 1867 378
    John Allen Wyeth, 1914

This I Believe 382
    Margaret Sanger, 1953

Remarks on the Youth Fitness Program 384
    John F. Kennedy, 1961

The Complete Book of Running 387
    Jim Fixx, 1977

Americans with Disabilities Act 390
    George H. W. Bush, 1990

A Wake-Up Call 393
    Stanley Coren, 1996

Home Diagnostic Tests: The Ultimate House Call? 395
    Carol Lewis, 2001

Deaths: Preliminary Data for 2003 399
    Donna L. Hoyert, et. al., 2005

Obesity Trends Among U.S. Adults 401
    Centers for Disease Control and Prevention, 2004

America Is Still Working on Its Abs 404
    Alex Williams, 2005

Fresh Faces 408
    Sascha de Gersdorff, 2005

7 ALTERNATIVE MEDICINE

Introduction to Alternative Medicine 413

Yoga and Transcendental Meditation 414
    Genevieve Naylor, 1962

More People Trying Vegetarian Diets 416
    Dixie Farley, 1995

Consensus Statement on Acupuncture 420
    David J. Ramsay, et. al., 1997

Manipulative and Body-Based Practices: An Overview 425
    National Center for Complementary and
    Alternative Medicine, 2004

Echinacea Disappoints: There's Still No Cure
for the Common Cold 428
    Nathan Seppa, 2005

8 BIOETHICS

Introduction to Bioethics 433

Eugenics and Sex Harmony 434
    Winfield Scott Pugh, 1947

Nuremberg Code Establishes the Principle
of Informed Consent 436
    Nuremberg Military Tribunal, 1947

Wilson Memorandum 438
    Charles E. Wilson, 1953

World Medical Association Declaration of Helsinki 440
    World Medical Association, 1964

Survivor of '32 Syphilis Study Recalls a Diagnosis 444
    James T. Wooten, 1972

The Pill: How Is It Affecting U.S. Morals, Family Life? 446
    Anonymous, 1966

Roe v. Wade and the Abortion Debate 450
    Henry A. Blackmun, 1973

On Death and Dying 452
    Elisabeth Kübler-Ross, 1969

Practical Guidelines for Do-Not-Resuscitate Orders 455
    Mark H. Ebell, 1994

The Promised End 459
    George J. Annas, 1996

Tube Is Removed After a Chaotic Day 463
    *William R. Levesque, Anita Kumar, Chris Tisch,
    and Graham Brink, 2005*

Remarks by the President on Medical Privacy 466
    William Jefferson Clinton, 2000

Owning Genetic Information and Gene
Enhancement Techniques 469
    Adam D. Moore, 2000

Organ Donations Increase When Families Have Good
Information about the Donation Process 472
    Agency for Healthcare Research and Quality, 2001

Made-to-order Baby Created in Hopes of Saving Ailing Sister . . . 474
    Margaret Taus, 2000

Screening Creates Disease Free Baby 477
    Anonymous, 2002

Patient Rights and Responsibilities 479
    Johns Hopkins Media Relations Staff, 2004

Human Cloning—Ethical Issues 482
  United Nations, 2005

Monitoring Stem Cell Research 485
  President's Council on Bioethics, 2004

Suffer the Children 488
  Kit R. Roane, 2001

Sources Consulted 493

Index 501

Advisors and Contributors

While compiling this volume, the editors relied upon the expertise and contributions of the following scholars, journalists, and researchers who served as advisors and/or contributors for *Medicine, Health, and Bioethics: Essential Primary Sources*:

Susan Aldridge, PhD
London, United Kingdom

Janet Susan Alred
Medical Science Writer and Journalist
Powell River, British Columbia, Canada

Steven Archambault (PhD Candidate)
University of New Mexico
Albuquerque, New Mexico

William Arthur Atkins, MS
Normal, Illinois

James Anthony Charles Corbett
Journalist
London, United Kingdom

Bryan Davies, JD
Ontario, Canada

Antonio Farina, MD, PhD
Department of Embryology, Obstetrics, and Gynecology, University of Bologna
Bologna, Italy

Sandra Galeotti, MS
São Paulo, Brazil

Larry Gilman, PhD
Sharon, Vermont

Amit Gupta, PhD
Ahmedabad, India

Neil Heims
Writer and Journalist
Paris, France

Brian D. Hoyle, PhD
Microbiologist

Nova Scotia, Canada

Alexandr Ioffe, PhD
Russian Academy of Sciences
Moscow, Russia

Kenneth T. LaPensee, PhD, MPH
Epidemiologist and Medical Policy Specialist
Hampton, New Jersey

Adrienne Wilmoth Lerner (JD Candidate)
University of Tennessee College of Law
Knoxville, Tennessee

Agnieszka Lichanska, PhD
Department of Microbiology and Parasitology, University of Queensland
Brisbane, Australia

Iuri Drumond Louro, MD, PhD
Professor Adjunto, Genética Humana e Molecular; Departamento de Ciências Biológicas; CCHN-UFES; Av Marechal Campos
Vitória, Brazil

Eric v.d. Luft, PhD, MLS
SUNY Upstate Medical University
Syracuse, New York

Pamela V. Michaels, MA
Forensic Psychologist
Santa Fe, New Mexico

Caryn Neumann, PhD
Ohio State University
Columbus, Ohio

Constance K. Stein, PhD
Director of Cytogenetics, Assistant Director of Molecular Diagnostics, SUNY Upstate Medical University
Syracuse, New York

Michael J. Sullivan, MD, PhD, FRACP
Cancer Genetics Laboratory, University of Otago
Dunedin, New Zealand

Melanie Barton Zoltán, MS
Amherst, Massachusetts

Medicine, Health, and Bioethics: Essential Primary Sources is the product of a truly global, multi-lingual group of scholars, researchers, and writers. Despite the span of writers and researchers, the book suffered local delays and disruptions related to Hurricanes Ivan and Katrina while the editors worked and covered stories along the U.S. Gulf Coast. In the aftermath, the sure and steady efforts of the primary copyeditors, Christine Jeryan and Amy Leorch Strumolo, not only added significant accuracy and readability to the text, their efforts also helped to piece back together fragments of texts and sources scattered in both physical and cyberspace.

The editors also wish to commend Adrienne Wilmoth Lerner and Alicia Maria Cafferty for their tireless research skills and effort. The keen eyes and sound judgments of the copyeditors and primary researchers greatly enhanced the quality and readability of the text.

The editors are grateful for the assistance of Thomas Willam, AHIP, Professor and Director, Biomedical Libraries, University of South Alabama, and his kind and knowledgeable staff.

The editors gratefully acknowledge and extend thanks to Peter Gareffa, Carol Nagel, and Debra Kirby at Thomson Gale for their faith in the project and for their sound content advice. Lastly, but perhaps most importantly to a book containing primary source materials, without the tenacious efforts of Project Manager Melissa Hill and the Thomson Gale copyright research staff, quite literally right up to publication deadlines, this book would not have been possible. The editors also wish to acknowledge the contributions of the Thomson Gale Imaging Team, and Marcia Schiff at the Associated Press for their help in securing archival images.

Acknowledgements

Copyrighted Excerpts in *Medicine, Health, and Bioethics: Essential Primary Sources* were reproduced from the following periodicals:

Advancing Global Public Health, 2005 for "Do You Remember...? Tale of a Survivor" by Alakananda Mohanty./ "Do You Remember...? Memoir" by Martin Pernick. Both reproduced by permission of the respective authors.—*Agency for Healthcare Research and Quality*, press release, July 3, 2001. Reproduced by permission.—*American Demographics*, January 6, 1986. Copyright, Crain Communications Inc., 2004. Reprinted with permission.—*American Family Physician*, v. 50, November 1, 1994. Copyright © 1994 American Academy of Family Physicians. Reproduced by permission.—*Annual Review of Genomics and Human Genetics*, v. 2, 2001. Copyright © 2001 Annual Reviews. Reproduced by permission.—*Associated Press*, press release, October 3, 2000. Copyright © 2000 Associated Press. Reprinted with permission of the Associated Press.—*Bioethics*, v. 14, April, 2000. Copyright © 2000 Basil Blackwell Ltd. Reproduced by permission of Blackwell Publishers.—*Boston Magazine*, May 1, 2005. Copyright © *Boston Magazine*/Metro Corp. Reproduced by permission.—*British Medical Journal*, December, 1979. Copyright © 1979 British Medical Association. Reproduced with permission from the BMJ Publishing Group.—*BSE Inquiry: The Report*, v.1, October, 2001. From an Introduction to Findings and Conclusions. HMSO, St. Clements House, 2-16 Colegate, Norwich, NR3 1BQ. Copyright © 2001 Crown. Reproduced by permission.—*The Economist*, February 18, 1999. © 1999 The Economist Newspaper Ltd. All rights reserved. Further reproduction prohibited. *www.economist.com*.—*European Journal of Medical Research*, v. 10, June 22, 2005. Reproduced by permission.—*Family Medicine*, v. 23, March-April, 1991. Copyright © *Family Medicine*. Reproduced by permission of the Society of Teachers of Family Medicine. *www.stfm.org*.—*Fort Worth-Star Telegram*, September 3, 2004. Reproduced by permission.—*Girls' Life*, February-March, 2002. Reproduced by permission.—*The Lancet*, v. 2, 1961 for "Letter to the Editor: Thalidomide and Congenital Abnormalities," by Dr. William McBride. Reproduced with permission of the author.—*Life (film series for television)*, transcript, 2000. Reproduced by permission.—*New England Journal of Medicine*, v. 335, August 29, 1996; v. 336, February 27, 1997. Copyright © 1996, 1997 Massachusetts Medical Society. All rights reserved. Both reproduced by permission.—*New York Times*, July 27, 1972 for "Survivor of '32 Syphilis Study Recalls a Diagnosis" by James T. Wooten. Copyright © 1972 by The New York Times Co. Reprinted by permission of the author./ April 10, 2003; August 16, 2005. Copyright © 2003, 2005 by The New York Times Co. Both reprinted by permission.—*New York Times News Service*, April 6, 2005. Copyright © 2005 by The New York Times Co. Reprinted with permission.—*Newsweek*, May 10, 1976; March 26, 1990. Copyright © 1976, 1990 Newsweek, Inc. Both reproduced by permission.—*San Jose Mercury News*, March 24, 2005. Copyright © 2005, *San Jose Mercury News* (San Jose, California). Republished with permission of *San Jose Mercury News*, conveyed through Copyright Clearance Center, Inc.—*Science*, v. 291, February 16, 2001. Copyright 2001 by AAAS. Reprinted by permission.—*Science News*, v. 168, July 30, 2005. Copyright 2005. Reprinted with permission from *Science News*, the weekly news magazine of science.—*St. Petersburg*

Times, March 19, 2005. Copyright © 2005 *St. Petersburg Times*. Reproduced by permission.—*Sunrise Magazine*, February-March, 1994 for "Animals and Medical Science: Vision of a New Era" by David O. Wiebers. Copyright © 1994 Theosophical University Press. Reproduced by permission of the author.—*Time*, November 26, 1984; v. 133, February 27, 1989; v. 164, October 25, 2004. Copyright © 1984, 1989, 2004 Time, Inc. All rights reserved. All reproduced by permission.—*U.S. News & World Report*, July 11, 1966; December 10, 2001. Copyright 1966, 2001 U.S. News and World Report, L.P. All rights reserved. Both reprinted with permission.—*United Nations Press Release GA/10333*, March 8, 2005. Copyright © 2005 United Nations. The United Nations is the author of the original material. Reproduced by permission.

Copyrighted Excerpts in *Medicine, Health, and Bioethics: Essential Primary Sources* were reproduced from the following books:

Coren, Stanley. From *Sleep Thieves*. The Free Press, a division of Simon & Schuster, 1966. Copyright © 1966 by Stanley Coren. Reprinted by permission of The Free Press, an imprint of Simon & Schuster Adult Publishing Group.—Frist, Bill. From *When Every Minute Counts: What You Need to Know about Bioterrorism from the Senate's Only Doctor*. Rowman & Littlefield, 2002. Copyright © 2002 by Bill Frist. Reproduced by permission.—Heiligman, N. H., From "A Strong Nation Is a Healthy Nation," letter. Lehigh County Tuberculosis Society, Allentown PA, 1940. Copyright © 2006 by the American Lung Association. Reproduced with permission. For more information about the American Lung Association or to support the work it does, call 1-800-LUNG-USA (1-800-586-4872) or log on to *www.lungusa.org*.—Kübler-Ross, Elisabeth. From *On Death and Dying*. Macmillan Publishing Company, Inc., 1969. Copyright © 1969 by Elisabeth Kübler-Ross; copyright renewed © 1997 by Elisabeth Kübler-Ross. Reprinted with the permission of Scribner, an imprint of Simon & Schuster Adult Publishing Group.—Landsteiner, Karl. From *Nobel Lectures: Physiology or Medicine 1901–1970, vol. 2.* Elsevier Publishing Company, Amsterdam, 1965. Copyright © Nobel Foundation. Reproduced with permission.—Morner, K. A. H. From *Nobel Lectures: Physiology or Medicine 1901–1921, vol. 1.* Elsevier Publishing Company, Amsterdam, 1967. Copyright © The Nobel Foundation. Reproduced by permission.—Nightingale, Florence. From "On the State of Rural Hygiene," in *Selected Writings of Florence Nightingale*. Edited by Lucy Ridgely Seymer. The Macmillan Company, 1954. Reproduced by permission of Florence Nightingale Museum, London.—Pettersson, Ralf F. From "Presentation Speech: The Nobel Prize in Physiology or Medicine 1997," in *Les Prix Nobel, The Nobel Prizes 1997*. Edited by Tore Frangsmyr. The Nobel Foundation, 1998. Copyright © The Nobel Foundation. Reproduced by permission.—Ross, Ronald. From *Memoirs with a Full Account of the Great Malaria Problem and Its Solution*. John Murray, London, 1923. Reproduced by permission.—Sanger, Margaret. From *The Margaret Sanger Papers*. Edward R. Murrow's Radio Program Broadcast, 1953. Copyright © The Margaret Sanger Papers. Reproduced by permission of the Literary Estate of Margaret Sanger.—Stepanek, Mattie J. T. From *Journey Through Heartsongs*. Hyperion, 2001. Copyright © 2001 Mattie J. T. Stepanek. All rights reserved. Reprinted by permission of Hyperion.—The Boston Women's Health Collective. *Our Bodies, Ourselves: A Book By and For Women*. Second Edition. Simon & Schuster, 1971. Copyright © 1971, 1973, 1976 by The Boston Women's Health Book Collective, Inc. New material for British edition copyright © Angela Phillips and Jill Rakusen, 1978. All rights reserved. Reprinted with permission of Simon & Schuster Adult Publishing Group. In the UK by permission of Penguin Books Ltd.—UNICEF. From *Emergency Field Handbook: A Guide for UNICEF staff*. United Nations International Childrens' Emergency Fund (UNICEF), 2005. Copyright © 2005 UNICEF. Reproduced by permission.—Vaughan, Victor C. From *A Doctor's Memories*. Bobbs-Merrill, 1926. Copyright © 1926 by The Bobbs-Merrill Company; copyright renewed © 1954 by Warren T. Vaughan. Reprinted with the permission of Scribner, an imprint of Simon & Schuster Adult Publishing Group.—Wigzell, Hans. From *Nobel Lectures: Physiology or Medicine 1981–1990*. World Scientific Publishing, 1993. Copyright © The Nobel Foundation. Reproduced by permission.—World Health Organization. From *Constitution of the World Health Organization*. WHO, 1946. Copyright © World Health Organization (WHO). Reproduced by permission.

Photographs and Illustrations appearing in *Medicine, Health, and Bioethics: Essential Primary Sources* were received from the following sources:

Acupuncture being used to treat a patient's shoulder, Pyongyang, North Korea, July 28, 2004, photograph. © Nayan Sthankiya/Corbis.—Advertisement for Quinine as medication, ca. 1870, photograph. © Bettmann/Corbis.—Alvarez, Nieves, top model, presents her first book, 2001, photograph. © Carrusan/Contifoto/Corbis Sygma.—America's first "Blue Cross Baby" Ann Woodard Reid, is shown holding her own Blue Cross baby, 1954, photograph.—American Red Cross medics tend to a wounded soldier, Normandy, France, June 9, 1944, photograph. AP Images.—Amniocentesis sample, San Juan Capistrano, California, photograph. © Ann Johansson/Corbis.—Anatomical prints of the human body, 1826, illustration by Antommarchi C. Francesco. © The British Library. Reproduced by permission. Further reproduction prohibited.—Anderson, Donald, stands in front of a poster of the 1946 "March of Dimes" campaign, photograph. © Bettmann/Corbis.—Anti-abortion demonstrator argues with abortion rights supporters, San Francisco, 2005, photograph. AP Images.—Anti-crack graffiti, New York City, photograph. © Viviane Moos/Corbis.—Baby Fae, the world's first infant to receive a baboon heart transplant, Loma Linda Medical Center, California, 1984, photograph. © Bettmann/Corbis.—Barber, Ames Walker, photograph. From *Richard Dunlop, Doctors of the American Frontier.* Garden City, NY: Doubleday, 1962. Courtesy American Heritage Center, University of Wyoming.—Bayer aspirin bottle, 1912, photograph. AP Images.—Bayer pharmaceutical advertisement, ca. 1900, photograph. © Bettmann/Corbis.—Beauty pageant contestants, Beijing, China, 2004, photograph. AP Images.—Bellevue Hospital, sick women in ward overrun by rats, 1860, engraving from *Harper's Weekly.* Reproduced by permission of the Museum of the City of New York, *www.mcny.org.*—Best, Charles, and Frederick Banting with one of the dogs that they treated with insulin, photograph. Courtesy of Banting House National Historic Site, Canadian Diabetes Association. Reproduced by permission.—Blackburn, Elizabeth, San Francisco, 2004, photograph. AP Images.—Blackwell, Elizabeth, photograph. © Bettmann/Corbis.—Blackwell, Elizabeth, portrait. © Bettmann/Corbis.—"Blue Baby" Operation. "Surgical Notes: 'Operation, November 29, 1944,'" photograph. The Alan Mason Chesney Medical Archives of The Johns Hopkins Medical Institutions, *www.medicalarchives.jhmi.edu.* Reproduced by permission.—Boesch, Christophe, founder and president of the Wild Chimpanzee Foundation, and Dr. Pierre Formenty study the Ebola virus, Cote D'Ivoire, photograph. © Patrick Robert/Sygma/Corbis.—Bowman, Shane, plays with his old heart, Edmonton, Canada, 2003, photograph. AP Images.—Bradbourne, Phillippa, a thalidomide victim uses her toes to present a bouquet to Princess Anne, London, June 14, 1972, photograph. © Bettmann/Corbis.—Brown, Charles D., fills a vial with BCG, a vaccine against tuberculosis, Albany, N.Y., photograph. AP Images.—Brown, Louise, photograph. UPI/Corbis-Bettmann.—Carter, Jimmy, jogging on the South Lawn of the White House, Washington DC, 1978, photograph. © Bettmann/Corbis.—CDC scientist in the Biosafety Level 4 laboratory, Atlanta, GA., photograph. © CDC/PHIL/Corbis.—Center for Disease Control researcher inspects a deer mouse, Gaeliys, New Mexico, photograph. © Karen Kasmauski/Corbis.—Changing a dressing, illustration by William Cheyne. Wellcome Library, London. Reproduced by permission.—Chanting at the Berkeley Holistic Health Center, California, 1978, photograph. © Roger Ressmeyer/Corbis.—Child Immunization poster, photograph. Courtesy, California Department of Health Services, Immunization Branch, Information and Education Section. Reproduced by permission.—Child lead poisoning, poster from the Department of Health and Human Services. U. S. National Library of Medicine.—Child receiving polio vaccine, Chalco, Mexico, 1992, photograph. © Keith Dannemiller/Corbis.—Chinese herbalist filling prescription, San Francisco, California, ca. 1989, photograph. © Phil Schermeister/Corbis.—Chinese nurse and patients wear masks to ward off pneumonia, Guangzhou, Guangdong province, China, 2003, photograph. © Reuters/Corbis.—Cincinnati Children's Hospital Medical Center billboard ads, 2005, photograph. AP Images.—From a cover of *The Complete Book of Running,* by James Fixx. Cover copyright © 1977 by Random House, Inc. Used by permission of Random House, Inc.—Cord blood samples are processed for cryopreservation, Singapore, 2005, photograph. © Luis Enrique Ascui/Reuters/Corbis.—Crash test vehicle colliding with a stationary object, photograph. © Tim Wright/Corbis.—Crates filled with tofu, photograph. © Michael S. Yamashita/Corbis.—DNA Sequenator at the California Institute of Technology, photograph. © Roger Ressmeyer/Corbis.—Doctors without Borders worker looks after some patients in Dubie, Democratic Republic of the Congo, 2006, photograph. Lionel Healing/AFP/Getty Images.—Draftees being examined by military medical staff, 1940, photograph. © Bettmann/Corbis.—E. P. T. home pregnancy test, photograph. © Bettmann/Corbis.—Early chloroform machine, ca. 1905, photograph. © Bettmann/Corbis.—English Board of Health notice denying burial to cholera victims, 1832, photograph. © Bettman/Corbis.—Extra-Strength Tylenol bottle from the same lot number MC2880, found to have caused cyanide poisoning in three people, photograph. AP Images.—FBI agents outside the American Media Inc. building, Boca Raton, Florida, October 9, 2001, photograph. AP Images.—First cover of *Journal of the American Medical*

Association, July 14, 1883, photograph. AP/Images.—Fleming, Sir Alexander, with Dr. Francis G. Blake and Mrs. Ogden Miller, the first user of penicillin in the United States, Yale University, photograph. AP Images.—Fonda, Jane, doing yoga, 1962, photograph. © Genevieve Naylor/Corbis.—Freud, Sigmund, departs on his first airplane flight, Berlin, Germany, November 9, 1928, photograph. AP Images.—Garbage collection on a Prague street, ca. 1900–1910, photograph. © Scheufler Collection/Corbis.—Gatekeeper secures the entrance to St. Mary's Hospital, where Ebola patients are quarantined, Lacor, 2000 photograph. AP Images.—Genetically modified soybeans, Julio de Castilhos farm, Rio Grande do Sul, 2003, photograph. AP Images.—Girl drinking water at fountain, ca. 1971, photograph. © Stephanie Maze/Corbis.—Good, Gary, Palm Beach County mosquito control analyst, points to larvae of an anopheles mosquito, Lake Worth, Florida, photograph. AP Images.—Great Hall of Ellis Island, where immigrants await for their possible entrance into the United States, New York, photograph. AP Images.—Group practicing yoga, photograph. © Miroslav Zajic/Corbis.—Grubbe, Emil H., ca. 1895, photograph. Copyright Radiology Centennial, Inc.—Health warning sign at the Uniroyal site, Detroit, photograph. AP Images.—Heart transplant operation, 1968, photograph. © Bettmann/Corbis.—Helicopter rescue of victims of the Air Florida 90 crash, 1982, photograph. © Bettmann/Corbis.—Hingson, Ralph, chairman of the Social and Behavioral Science Department at Boston University School of Public Health, photograph. AP Images.—Human prion protein, photograph. AP Images.—Immigrant girl receives medical exam, Ellis Island, 1905, photograph. Picture History.—Indonesian tsunami survivors receive food and water from a U. S. helicopter, Acej Jaya district, January 5, 2004, photograph. © Alres Alia/Reuters/Corbis.—Insensitive/resistant *Staphylococcus* bacteria, photograph. © Lester V. Bergman/Corbis.—Ista, Cynthia, performs acupuncture on a patient at Abbott Northwestern Hospital's Institute for Health and Healing, Minneapolis, 2005, photograph. AP Images.—Kersey, Dr. John, gathers bone marrow for a transplant, photograph. © Ted Spiegel/Corbis.—Klein, Nathan, at a press conference announcing the first gene therapy for Parkinson's disease, Weill Cornell Medical Center, New York, 2003, photograph. AP Images.—Kohler, Ingrid, performs an acupressure therapeutic healing massage, Banda Aceh, Indonesia, photograph. AP Images.—Kübler-Ross, Dr. Elisabeth, 1970, photograph. AP Images.—"L'inhumanation précipitée," painting by Anton Wiertz. © Musees Royaux Des Beaux-Arts de Belgique. Reproduced by permission.—Laser surgery being performed, photograph. © Royalty-Free/Corbis.—*Legionella pneumophilia* bacteria, photograph. © CDC/PHIL/Corbis.—Letter to Lord Chamberlain Hugo Radolinski, January 1, 1888, from Rudolf Virchow. Courtesy of the Clendening History of Medicine Library, University of Kansas Medical Center.—Lewis, Jerry, at the 39th annual Labor Day Weekend Jerry Lewis MDA Telethon, Beverly Hills, September 4, 2005, photograph. © Paul Mounce/Corbis.—Lodesani, Claudia, from Doctors Without Borders checks on a patient, Meulaboh, Indonesia, 2005, photograph. AP Images.—Maalin, Ali Maow, of Merka, Somalia, who has the world's last recorded case of endemic smallpox, 1979, photograph. © Bettmann/Corbis.—McDonald's warns customers about mad cow disease, London, 1996, photograph. © Matt Polak/Corbis Sygma—MADD bumper stickers, Ft. Meade, Florida, 1998, photograph. © Mark Peterson/Corbis.—Manson, Dr. Joann, with results from a study she directed on hormone replacement therapy for women, Boston, 2002, photograph. AP Images.—Marlboro cigarettes billboard, Los Angeles, California, ca. 1976, photograph. © Robert Landau/Corbis.—Matses Indian shaman gathering medicinal plants, Amazon Basin, Peru, photograph. © Alison Wright/Corbis.—McClintock, Barbara, Nobel-Prize-winning geneticist, photograph.© Bettmann/Corbis.—Medical lab technician processes newly donated blood, Community Blood Bank, Lincoln, Nebraska, 2003, photograph. AP Images.—Missett, Judi Sheppard, Jazzercise creator, teaching an exercise class, photograph. © Doug Menuez/Corbis.—Mize, Stephani, and Cody Smith testify before state lawmakers, Oklahoma City, February 28, 2005, photograph. AP Images.—MRI of a human brain is studied at Columbia-Presbyterian Medical Center, New York, 1985, photograph. AP Images.—Navajo medicine man, Hosteen Tso-Begay, performs a ceremonial healing ritual for a four-year-old boy suffering from tuberculosis, Monument Valley, Utah, December 8, 1947, photograph. AP Images.—Nightingale, Florence, portrait. The Library of Congress.—Nun with the Sisters of Notre Dame knits mittens, photograph. © Karen Kasmauski/Corbis.—Obesity trends among U.S. adults, illustration. Centers for Disease Control.—Occluded artery with cholesterol, photograph. © Howard Sochurek/Corbis.—From an illustration in *On the Mode of Communication of Cholera, 2nd ed.*, by John Snow. C. F. Cheffins, Lith, Southampton Buildings, London, England, 1854. Courtesy of Dr. Ralph R. Frerichs, *http://www.ph.ucla.edu/epi/snow/snowmap1_1854_lge.htm*.—Organ bank at Saint Louis Hospital, photograph. © Dung Vo Trung/Corbis Sygma.—Ouazzani, Chafferdine, shows x-rays of a 46-year-old calcified fetus that was removed from a woman's womb, Rabat, 2002, photograph. AP Images.—Papanicolaou, Dr. George, photograph. © Bettmann/Corbis.—Pasteur, Louis, photograph. © Bettman/Corbis.—Patient arrives on the back of a bicycle at a community clinic run by the Kitova Hospital Mobile Program, Uganda, photograph. © Gideon Mendel/Corbis.—Patient in Kiev Hospital is recovering after an operation for thyroid cancer, linked to the Chernobyl disaster, photograph. © Caroline Penn/Corbis.—Patient undergoing a CAT scan, photograph. © Corbis-Bettmann.—PCR machine, Walnut Creek, California, photograph. AP Images.—Petri dishes containing samples of Bacillus cereus and a Bacillus species, Boston, 2001, photograph. AP Images.—Princess Diana with patient at St. Ann's Hospice, Manchester, England, ca. 1985, photograph. © Tim Graham/Corbis.—Priority Traffic Safety Laws, 2003, illustration from MADD brochure. Copyright 2003 Mothers Against Drunk Driving. Brochure is for historical purposes only. All rights reserved. Used by permission.—Prozac, photograph. © Annebicque Bernard/Corbis Sygma—Quinine for the treatment of malaria, advertisement by Ronald Ross. Wellcome Library, London. Reproduced by permission.—Rabies vaccination in Pasteur's clinic, Paris, lithograph by F. Pirodon. Wellcome Library, London. Reproduced by permission.—Radiograph of a hand with a ring, by W. K. Roentgen. Wellcome Library, London. Reproduced by permission.—Reyes, Lilian, a member of the Chilean Movement of Morbid Obese People, Santiago, Chile, 2004, photograph. AP Images.—Richter, Stacey, demonstrates outside a federal courthouse where a hearing opened to decide the fate of physician-assisted suicide law, Portland, Oregon, Friday, 2002, photograph. AP Images.—"Rules for the Prevention of Cholera," photograph. Compliments of The New York Reporter, the home newspaper for the Metropolis. Reproduced by permission of the Museum of the City of New York, www.mcny.org.—Sanger, Margaret, with her sister Ethel Byrne in court, Brooklyn, New York, January, 1917, photograph. AP Images.—Sanger, Margaret, with Mrs. John F. Dryden and Prof. Henry Pratt Fairchild at the opening of the National Conference on Birth Control, Washington, January 15, 1934, photograph. AP Images.—Scientists test bird flu infected chicken samples, National Institute of Hygiene and Epidemiology, Hanoi, Vietnam, 2005, photograph. AP Images.—Senior surfer, photograph. © Mark A. Johnson/Corbis.—Sleep test being performed on a Wesleyan University student, Nebraska, 1995, photograph. AP Images.—Small pox patient, used by the New York State Board of Health anti-disease campaign to encourage the public to vaccinate, photograph. AP Images.—Soldier stands guard in a neighborhood where tsunami victims are slowly returning despite the health threats, Galle, Sri Lanka, 2005, photograph. AP Images.—Starving children in Nigeria, January 21, 1970, photograph. © Hulton-Deutsch Collection/Corbis.—Starzl, Dr. Thomas, performs a liver transplant, University of Pittsburgh Medical Center, Pittsburgh, 1982, photograph. AP Images.—Table 199 in *The Kinsey Data: Marginal Tabulations of the 1938–1963 Interviews Conducted by the Institute for Sex Research* by Paul H. Gebhard and Alan B. Johnson. W.B. Saunders, 1979. Copyright © 1979 by the Institute for Sex Research. Reproduced by permission of The Kinsey Institute for Research in Sex, Gender, and Reproduction, Inc.—Tamper-resistant Tylenol packaging, 1982, photograph. © Bettmann/Corbis.—Tattoos covering heroin needle tracks, photograph. © Ted Streshinsky/Corbis.—Taylor, Cynthia, opens a window in the Mary Elizabeth Inn, San Francisco, 2005, photograph. AP Images.—Teenagers necking in a car, 1954, photograph. © Bettman/Corbis.—Teri Schiavo supporters demonstrate during a news conference outside Woodside Hospice, Pinellas Park, Florida, AP Images.—The Nightingale Home and Training School for Nurses, St. Thomas's Hospital, photograph. Wellcome Library, London. Reproduced by permission.—Tin-roofed shacks in Africa's largest slum, Kibera, 2005, photograph. AP Images.—Train wreckage after a landslide during construction of the Panama Canal, May 29, 1913, photograph. AP Images.—"Up in Smoke" cigarette ad exhibit, New York City, November 29, 2000, photograph. © Scott Houston/Corbis Sygma.—Variola virus, photograph. © CDC/PHIL/Corbis—Venter, Dr. Craig, Celera president at human genome media announcement, Washington DC, February 12, 2001, photograph. © Reuters/Corbis.—Vibratory exercise belt being demonstrated, photograph. AP Images.—Video consultations being used by specialists at the University of Texas to prescribe treatment for prisoners, 1998, photograph. © F. Carter Smith/Corbis Sygma.—Vietnamese women carry a basket of chickens, Hanoi, Vietnam, 2005, photograph. AP Images.—Views of anatomical nomenclature, illustration by Argosy. Thomson Gale.—Vioxx pill, photograph. © Mariana Day Massey/ZUMA/Corbis.—Virchow, Rudolf, photograph. © Bettmann/Corbis.—Washington State Department of Agriculture, organic field inspector conducts a routine annual inspection, 2004, photograph. AP Images.—Watson, James, photograph. AP Images.—Woman carries buckets to collect water, Tahoua, Niger, 2005, photograph. ISSOUF SANOGO/AFP/Getty Images.—Woman using a wheelchair ramp, photograph. © Royalty-Free/Corbis.—Worker checks the labels on vodka bottles, Kristall distillery, Moscow, 1995, photograph. AP Images.—Workers lower the corpse of a boy who died from the Ebola virus into a grave, Mekambo, Gabon, photograph. AP Images.—X ray of the lungs of a coal miner suffering from black lung, 1995, photograph. Chuck Nacke/Time Life Pictures/Getty Images.—Yag laser paparoscopic surgery, photograph. Robert J. Herko/The Image Bank/ Getty Images.

Copyrighted Excerpts in *Medicine, Health, and Bioethics: Essential Primary Sources* were reproduced from the following Web sites:

Blaylock, Alfred, MD, "Surgical Notes: 'Operation: November 29, 1944,'" *www.medicalarchives.jhml.edu.* The Alan Mason Chesney Medical Archives of The Johns Hopkins Medical Institutions, *www.medicalarchives.jhml.edu.* Reproduced by permission.—Brown, John C., "What the Heck is Antibiotic Resistance?" Microbiology at the University of Kansas, "Bugs in the News!" *//people.ku.edu~jbrown/ bugs.html*, January 1, 2002. Copyright © John C. Brown, 2002. Reproduced by permission of the author.—Bulman, Erica, "Water, Sanitation, Key to Disaster Response and Long-term Development," *Associated Press Archive*, March 22, 2005. Copyright © 2005 Associated Press. Reprinted with permission of the Associated Press.—Calhoun, Archie S., "Letter to Franklin D. Roosevelt," *www.fda.gov*, 1937. Reproduced by permission of the literary estate of the author.—Carter, Jimmy, "Eulogy for Mattie Stepanek," *www.cartercenter.org*, June 28, 2004. Reproduced by permission.—Elias, Paul, "Stem Cell Donors," *Associated Press Archive*, March 10, 2005. Copyright © 2005 AP Digital. All rights reserved. Reprinted with permission of the Associated Press.— Johns Hopkins Hospital, "Patient Rights and Responsibilities," *www.hopkinsmedicine.org*, July 16, 2004. Reproduced by permission.—Montgomery, Jim, "Tulane Hospital Evacuation-Jim Montgomery's Story," *www.yahoo.com/group/tulanepsychiatryfaculty/ message/44*, September 5, 2005. Reproduced by permission of the author.—Staff Report, "Screening Creates 'Disease-free' Baby," *www.bbcnews.co.co.uk*, February 27, 2002. Copyright © BBC Enterprises. Reproduced by permission.—Staff Report, "Study: Alps Still Considered Contaminated by Radiation from Chernobyl," *Associated Press Archive*, May 2, 1998. Copyright © 1998, 2003 Associated Press. Reprinted with permission of the Associated Press.—The Nobel Assembly at the Karolinska Institute, "Press Release: The 1985 Nobel Prize in Physiology or Medicine," *www.Nobelprize.org*, October 14, 1985. Copyright © The Nobel Foundation. Reproduced by permission.—World Medical Association, "World Medical Association Declaration of Helsinki: Ethical Principles for Medical Research Involving Human Subjects," *www.ohsr.od.nih.gov*, June, 1964. Copyright 2005, World Medical Association. All rights reserved. Reproduced by permission. *www.wma.net.*

About the Set

Essential Primary Source titles are part of a ten-volume set of books in the Social Issues Primary Sources Collection designed to provide primary source documents on leading social issues of the nineteenth, twentieth, and twenty-first centuries. International in scope, each volume is devoted to one topic and will contain approximately 160 to 175 documents that will include and discuss speeches, legislation, magazine and newspaper articles, memoirs, letters, interviews, novels, essays, songs, and works of art essential to understanding the complexity of the topic.

Each entry will include standard subheads: key facts about the author; an introduction placing the piece in context; the full or excerpted document; a discussion of the significance of the document and related event; and a listing of further resources (books, periodicals, Web sites, and audio and visual media).

Each volume will contain a topic-specific introduction, topic-specific chronology of major events, an index especially prepared to coordinate with the volume topic, and approximately 150 images.

Volumes are intended to be sold individually or as a set.

THE ESSENTIAL PRIMARY SOURCE SERIES

- *Terrorism: Essential Primary Sources*
- *Medicine, Health, and Bioethics: Essential Primary Sources*
- *Environmental Issues: Essential Primary Sources*
- *Crime and Punishment: Essential Primary Sources*
- *Gender Issues and Sexuality: Essential Primary Sources*
- *Human and Civil Rights: Essential Primary Sources*
- *Government, Politics, and Protest: Essential Primary Sources*
- *Social Policy: Essential Primary Sources*
- *Immigration and Multiculturalism: Essential Primary Sources*
- *Family in Society: Essential Primary Sources*

Introduction

The social issues related to medical science are often intimate and spark passionate debate. The primary sources contained in *Medicine, Health, and Bioethics* demonstrate the development, diversity, and nexus of science and ethics as embodied in medical advances, social policy, and law. Most importantly, the articles selected show a complex range of views on topics such as abortion, cloning, and stem cell research that are not always easily characterized as "for" or "against." The intent is not to present the reader with all facets of a topic but rather to provoke critical thinking while providing both a foundation and desire to investigate topics increasingly important in social and political discourse.

The link between science and social issue is well forged. Significant sums of public money go toward biomedical research, and how much is spent on what type of research can engender fractious political and social debate. The fruits of that research bring new temptations and possibilities that beckon some and frighten others.

Since the 1950s, studies of the molecular biology of the gene have provided answers to fundamental questions about the mechanism of inheritance and the relationship between genes and disease. In addition to the articulation of the human genome sequence, the metabolic basis of several hundred inherited disorders is now known and many defective genes resulting in such disorders have already been isolated.

The pace of advance in genetics is daunting, however, and challenges both scientists and non-scientists who must form rational opinions on the social issues related to genetics that seem to arise with equal rapidity. For example, geneticists have developed tools that allow scientists to recreate steps in the evolution of organisms within a laboratory environment. These tools provide the means to carry out experiments that nature alone is incapable of performing. With the techniques of recombinant DNA technology, geneticists have also learned how to transplant genes from one organism to another, thus reshuffling genetic material in ways never experienced in the evolution of life on Earth. Such genetic advances and other research into developmental biology easily leap from the laboratory into the crucible of public discourse regarding "life as we know it" versus "life as we make it."

In turn, issues that were once purely social or ethical issues, such as sexuality or alcoholism, are now understood to be aspects of human behavior and personality, at least in some part, influenced by genetics.

Many of the great successes for medical science are also important social milestones for humanity, especially with regard to the prevention and treatment of infectious disease. Throughout history, microorganisms have spread deadly diseases and caused widespread epidemics that threatened and altered human civilization. In the modern era, civic sanitation, water purification, immunization, and antibiotics have dramatically reduced the overall morbidity and the mortality of disease in advanced nations. Yet, much of the world is still ravaged by disease and epidemics, and new threats constantly appear to challenge the most advanced medical and public health systems.

Without question, advances such as the global eradication of smallpox is a profound achievement in human history. Also, an emphasis on wellness and preventative health measures has allowed physicians to fight a two-front war on disease while returning primary responsibility for health and well-being to the individual.

Regardless, social issues can still arise out of even the most effective and seemingly well-intended of medical advances. For example, although childhood diseases such as measles, mumps, whooping cough, and diphtheria have been effectively controlled by childhood vaccinations, some parents resist or reject vaccinating their own children because they feel that the small personal risk is not mitigated by the larger social benefit of disease control. By opting out of the system by relying on the immunizations of others to reduce the risk of disease, they rely upon the acts of the social group to offer their children personal protection.

The interplay of complex ethical and social considerations is also evident when considering the general rise of infectious diseases that sometimes occurs as an unintended side effect of the otherwise beneficial use of medications. Nearly half the world's population, for example, is infected with the bacterium causing tuberculosis (TB) (although for most people the infection is inactive) yet the organism causing some new cases of TB is evolving toward a greater resistance to the antibiotics that were once effective in treating TB. Such statistics also take on added social dimension when considering that TB disproportionately impacts certain social groups such as the elderly, minorities, and people infected with HIV.

Globalization and the increased contact between societies also raises new biomedical concerns about the potential spread of disease, and sparks social debate regarding the nature and extent of medical cooperation across a varied political landscape. A shrinking global village, beneficial in many cultural and economic aspects, increases the possibility that the terrible loss of life associated with the plagues of the Middle Ages or with the pandemic influenza outbreak of 1918 and 1919 might once again threaten humanity on a worldwide scale.

Lastly, as if the challenges of nature and disease were not sufficient, the political realities at the dawn of the twenty-first century point toward a probability that, within the first half of the century, biological weapons will surpass nuclear and chemical weapons in terms of potential threat to civilization. In such a world, solutions to scientific and public health challenges will spawn new and urgent debate than will span traditional geographic and political boundaries to become truly global social issues.

Because an understanding of the historical development of medical science and the social issues that arise from its advance is increasingly vital, *Medicine, Health, and Bioethics* takes a sweeping view of events over the last 200 years. The articles presented in this volume are designed to be readable and to instruct, challenge, and excite a range of student and reader interests while, at the same time, providing a solid foundation and reference for more advanced study.

K. Lee Lerner and Brenda Wilmoth Lerner,
editors
London, U.K.
March, 2006

About the Entry

The primary source is the centerpiece and main focus of each entry in *Medicine, Health, and Bioethics: Essential Primary Sources*. In keeping with the philosophy that much of the benefit from using primary sources derives from the reader's own process of inquiry, the contextual material surrounding each entry provides access and ease of use, as well as giving the reader a springboard for delving into the primary source. Rubrics identify each section and enable the reader to navigate entries with ease.

ENTRY STRUCTURE

- Primary Source/Entry Title, Subtitle, Primary Source Type
- Key Facts—essential information about the primary source, including creator, date, source citation, and notes about the creator.
- Introduction—historical background and contributing factors for the primary source.
- Primary Source—in text, text facsimile, or image format; full or excerpted.
- Significance—importance and impact of the primary source related events.
- Further Resources—books, periodicals, Web sites, and audio and visual material.

NAVIGATING AN ENTRY

Entry elements are numbered and reproduced here, with an explanation of the data contained in these elements explained immediately thereafter according to the corresponding numeral.

Primary Source/Entry Title, Subtitle, Primary Source Type

[1] # Screening Creates Disease Free Baby

[2] Genetic Selection, Ethical Issues

[3] **News article**

[1] **Primary Source/Entry Title:** The entry title is usually the primary source title. In some cases where long titles must be shortened, or more generalized topic titles are needed for clarity primary source titles are generally depicted as subtitles. Entry titles appear as catchwords at the top outer margin of each page.

[2] **Subtitle:** Some entries contain subtitles.

[3] **Primary Source Type:** The type of primary source is listed just below the title. When assigning source types, great weight was given to how the author of the primary source categorized the source.

Key Facts

[4] **Author:** Anonymous

[5] **Date:** February 22, 2002

[6] **Source:** BBC News. "Screening Creates Disease Free Baby." February 22, 2002. <http://news.bbc.co.uk/1/hi/health/1842932.stm> (accessed December 28, 2005).

[7] **About the Organization:** This news article was written by an unattributed author for the British Broadcasting System (BBC), the United Kingdom's public news service. The BBC provides interactive TV channels, radio networks, and an online news site, all providing local and national news and commentary.

[4] **Author, Artist, or Organization:** The name of the author, artist, or organization responsible for the creation of the primary source begins the Key Facts section.

[5] **Date of Origin:** The date of origin of the primary source appears in this field, and may differ from the date of publication in the source citation below it; for example, speeches are often delivered before they are published.

[6] **Source Citation:** The source citation is a full bibliographic citation, giving original publication data as well as reprint and/or online availability.

[7] **About the Author:** A brief bio of the author or originator of the primary source gives birth and death dates and a quick overview of the person's work. This rubric has been customized in some cases. If the primary source written document, the term "author" appears; however, if the primary source is a work of art, the term "artist" is used, showing the person's direct relationship to the primary source. For primary sources created by a group, "organization" may have been used instead of "author." Other terms may also be used to describe the creator or originator of the primary source. If an author is anonymous or unknown, a brief "About the Publication" sketch may appear.

Introduction Essay
[8] **INTRODUCTION**

Genetics is one of the most rapidly growing specialties in medicine. Since 1980, research in genetics has added immeasurably to the understanding of the etiology of many diseases by identifying biologically important genes and disease-causing mutations. These data have generated large numbers of new clinical diagnostic assays, the majority of which are performed on peripheral blood or bone marrow of children or adults. The information obtained is used to make a specific diagnosis that leads to appropriate treatment for the patient. But when testing is done prenatally, other choices are possible. If the fetus is affected or potentially affected with a debilitating or life threatening disease, pregnancy termination is an option. Although it is not yet possible to create a "designer" baby (a baby with characters chosen by the parents), it is possible to perform prenatal testing for one or more defined characters. This raises concerns about when, and if, it is appropriate to select or deselect a fetus based on certain "desired" criteria.

[8] **Introduction:** The introduction is a brief essay on the contributing factors and historical context of the primary source. Intended to promote understanding and equip the reader with essential facts to understand the context of the primary source.

To maintain ease of reference to the primary source, spellings of names and places are used in accord with their use in the primary source. According names and places may have different spellings in different articles. Whenever possible, alternative spellings are provided to provide clarity.

PRIMARY SOURCE

[9] A woman has chosen to have a genetically selected baby to ensure it does not develop early onset Alzheimer's disease which runs in the family.

The woman, who is thirty and has not been identified, may be unable to recognize or care for her daughter within ten years.

She and her family carry a mutation which causes the onset of Alzheimer's disease before the age of forty.

However, the child, who is now about eighteen months old, did not inherit the tendency to develop the disease.

Early onset Alzheimer's, a very rare condition, is defined as Alzheimer's—a form of dementia—that strikes before the age of sixty-five.

Researchers at the Reproductive Genetics Institute of Chicago said the baby's birth marked the first time preimplantation genetic diagnosis, as the technique is called, has been used to weed out embryos carrying the defect that causes early onset Alzheimer's.

The little girl is thriving, said Yuri Verlinsky, chief author of the report in this week's Journal of the American Medical Association.

Verlinsky said genetic screening has been used more than three thousand times and is often employed to avoid inherited disorders like sickle cell anemia.

His clinic was involved in a case last year where an embryo was chosen to provide stem cells to assist a sibling of the unborn child.

Ethical debate While the child's mother is still healthy, her sister developed early onset Alzheimer's at the age of thirty-eight, her father died at forty-two after suffering psychological and memory problems and one of her brothers began having short-term memory problems at thirty-five.

He said: "I can't speak for the public, but it's a decision of the family and not the public."

In a commentary published in the same journal, Dena Towner and Roberta Springer Loewy of the University of California said the study raised ethical questions.

They said: "Much like her sister, the woman in the report ... most likely will not be able to care for or even recognize her child in a few years."

The two doctors said the mother acted responsibly by ensuring that her child will not have to live with the threat of developing early onset Alzheimer's.

However, they took issue with defining her ethical responsibility "solely in terms of disease prevention" without considering that she may not be able to care for her child.

"The differences between these two interpretations of ethical responsibility are stark, but both rest on assumptions made about reproduction—is it a privilege or it is an unquestionable and inalienable right?" they asked.

[9] **Primary Source**: The majority of primary sources are reproduced as plain text. The primary source may appear excerpted or in full, and may appear as text, text facsimile (photographic reproduction of the original text), image, or graphic display (such as a table, chart, or graph).

The font and leading of the primary sources are distinct from that of the context—to provide a visual clue to the change, as well as to facilitate ease of reading. As needed, the original formatting of the text is preserved in order to more accurately represent the original (screenplays, for example). In order to respect the integrity of the primary sources, content some readers may consider sensitive (for example, the use of slang, ethnic or racial slurs, etc.) is retained when deemed to be integral to understanding the source and the context of its creation.

Primary source images (whether photographs, text facsimiles, or graphic displays) are bordered with a distinctive double rule. Images have brief captions.

The term "narrative break" appears where there is a significant amount of elided (omitted) material with the text provided (for example, excerpts from a work's first and fifth chapters, selections from a journal article abstract and summary, or dialogue from two acts of a play).

Significance Essay
[10] **SIGNIFICANCE**

Ethical issues arise in all areas of medicine, but special attention focuses on genetics, probably because this field explores the transmission of genes within families. In particular, issues associated with prenatal diagnosis seem to be problematic.

Prenatal genetic diagnosis can identify a large number of diseases by evaluation of placental and/or fetal cells. The studies are usually performed between ten and twenty weeks gestation, and the type of study used is based on the parents' age, medical history, and ethnicity. When a known disease or major malformation is identified, the parents have the option of terminating the pregnancy. For a more limited group of diseases, preimplantation genetic diagnosis can be performed. With this technology, eggs removed from the mother are fertilized *in vitro* by sperm from the father, and the resultant zygotes are cultured to the eight to sixteen cell stage. One cell from each is removed and tested, and only "normal" embryos are implanted in the mother's uterus. This technology eliminates the need for termination of an ongoing pregnancy and, thus, is more acceptable to many individuals. Either technique has the effect of selecting a fetus based on specific criteria.

Under what circumstances is this type of selection acceptable? Geneticists use the technology to obtain relevant clinical information on a patient. If the data shows the fetus has a lethal or severely debilitating disorder, termination of pregnancy is considered an acceptable option. Therefore, parents may be offered a choice between continuing or terminating a pregnancy with a confirmed diagnosis of terminal conditions such as anencephaly or trisomy thirteen, or an incapacitating disease such as Tay Sachs, sickle cell disease, or Duchenne muscular dystrophy.

A different dilemma is posed by diseases such as Alzheimer's disease, Huntington's disease, and breast cancer. These are classified as late onset diseases since affected individuals show no signs or symptoms until they are adults. Genetics professionals discourage the use of prenatal diagnosis to select against embryos or fetuses at risk for such disorders since most affected individuals can live a productive life before the disease strikes. However, these diseases are usually progressive, and watching a loved one slowly deteriorate can be devastating for families. Thus, some will chose prenatal diagnosis rather than bringing a child into the world knowing that he or she would have that fate.

An area of genetic selection that is considered unethical by genetics professionals is elective termination of a pregnancy solely because the sex of the fetus is not what the parents desire. This abuse of the system can occur since most prenatal testing provides the sex of the fetus as a courtesy to the parents.

Decisions on what testing to request and how to use the results are often difficult. Geneticists provide counseling, but the final choice rests with the patient. It is critical that all relevant factors be considered before a decision is made. For example, in the case cited above, a question was raised if the mother acted ethically in having a child whom she could take care of for only a few years. But, this should not be an issue if the woman has a partner or family member who participated in the decision to have the child and who will be able to raise the child after the mother becomes incapacitated.

As of January 2006, there are few rules governing genetic selection via prenatal diagnosis, creating a challenge for potential parents and geneticists alike.

[10] **Significance:** The significance discusses the importance and impact of the primary source and the event it describes.

Further Resources

Books

Magill, Gerard, ed. *Genetics and Ethics: An Interdisciplinary Study*. New York: Fordham University Press, 2003.

Verlinsky, Yury, and Anver Kuliev. *Practical Preimplantation Genetic Diagnosis*. New York: Springer, 2005.

Web sites

ADEAR. Alzheimer's Disease Education and Referral Center. National Institute on Aging. <http://www.alzheimers. org/generalinfo.htm> (accessed January 23, 2006).

Genetics and Public Policy Center. <http://dnapolicy.org/index. jhtml.html> (accessed January 23, 2006).

Human Genetics in the Public Interest. The Center for Genetics and Society. <http://www.genetics-and-society.org> (accessed January 26, 2006).

PGD: Preimplantation Genetic Diagnosis. " Discussion by the Genetics and Public Policy Center." <http://dnapolicy. org/downloads/pdfs/policy_pgd.pdf> (accessed January 23, 2006).

[11] **Further Resources:** A brief list of resources categorized as Books, Periodicals, Web sites, and Audio and Visual Media provides a stepping stone to further study.

SECONDARY SOURCE CITATION FORMATS (HOW TO CITE ARTICLES AND SOURCES)

Alternative forms of citations exist and examples of how to cite articles from this book are provided below:

APA Style

Books: Kübler-Ross, Elisabeth. (1969) *On Death and Dying*. New York: Macmillan. Excerpted in K. Lee Lerner and Brenda Wilmoth Lerner, eds. (2006) *Medicine, Health, and Bioethics: Essential Primary Sources*, Farmington Hills, Mich.: Thomson Gale.

Periodicals: Venter, J. Craig, et al. (2001, February 16). "The Sequence of the Human Genome." *Science*, vol. 291, no. 5507, pp. 1304–51. Excerpted in K.

Lee Lerner and Brenda Wilmoth Lerner, eds. (2006) *Medicine, Health, and Bioethics: Essential Primary Sources*, Farmington Hills, Mich.: Thomson Gale.

Web sites: Johns Hopkins Hospital and Health System. "Patient Rights and Responsibilities." Retrieved January 14, 2006 from http://www.hopkinsmedicine.org/patients/JHH/patient_rights.html. Excerpted in K. Lee Lerner and Brenda Wilmoth Lerner, eds. (2006) *Medicine, Health, and Bioethics: Essential Primary Sources*, Farmington Hills, Mich.: Thomson Gale.

Chicago Style

Books: Kübler-Ross, Elisabeth. *On Death and Dying*. New York: Macmillan, 1969. Excerpted in K. Lee Lerner and Brenda Wilmoth Lerner, eds. *Medicine, Health, and Bioethics: Essential Primary Sources*, Farmington Hills, Mich.: Thomson Gale, 2006.

Periodicals: Venter, J. Craig, et al. "The Sequence of the Human Genome." *Science* (2001): 291, 5507, 1304–1351. Excerpted in K. Lee Lerner and Brenda Wilmoth Lerner, eds. *Medicine, Health, and Bioethics: Essential Primary Sources*, Farmington Hills, Mich.: Thomson Gale, 2006.

Web sites: *Johns Hopkins Hospital and Health System.* "Patient Rights and Responsibilities." <http:// www.hopkinsmedicine.org/patients/JHH/patient_ rights.html.> (accessed January 14, 2006). Excerpted in K. Lee Lerner and Brenda Wilmoth Lerner, eds. *Medicine, Health, and Bioethics: Essential Primary Sources*, Farmington Hills, Mich.: Thomson Gale, 2006.

MLA Style

Books: Kübler-Ross, Elisabeth. *On Death and Dying*, New York: Macmillan, 1969. Excerpted in K. Lee Lerner and Brenda Wilmoth Lerner, eds. *Medicine, Health, and Bioethics: Essential Primary Sources*, Farmington Hills, Mich.: Thomson Gale, 2006.

Periodicals: Venter, J. Craig, et al. "The Sequence of the Human Genome." *Science*, 291 (16 February 2001): 5507, 1304–51. Excerpted in K. Lee Lerner and Brenda Wilmoth Lerner, eds. *Medicine, Health, and Bioethics: Essential Primary Sources*, Farmington Hills, Mich.: Thomson Gale, 2006.

Web sites: "Patient's Rights and Responsibilities." Johns Hopkins Hospital and Health System. 14 January 2006. <http://www.hopkinsmedicine.org/patients/ JHH/patient_rights.html.> Excerpted in K. Lee Lerner and Brenda Wilmoth Lerner, eds.

Terrorism: Essential Primary Sources, Farmington Hills, Mich.: Thomson Gale, 2006.

Turabian Style (Natural and Social Sciences)

Books: Kübler-Ross, Elisabeth. *On Death and Dying*, (New York: Macmillan, 1969). Excerpted in K. Lee Lerner and Brenda Wilmoth Lerner, eds. *Medicine, Health, and Bioethics: Essential Primary Sources*, (Farmington Hills, Mich.: Thomson Gale, 2006).

Periodicals: Venter, J. Craig, et al. "The Sequence of the Human Genome." *Science*, 291 (16 February 2001): 5507, 1304–1351. Excerpted in K. Lee Lerner and Brenda Wilmoth Lerner, eds. *Medicine, Health, and Bioethics: Essential Primary Sources*, (Farmington Hills, Mich.: Thomson Gale, 2006).

Web sites: Johns Hopkins Hospital and Health System. "Patient's Rights and Responsibilities." available from http://www.hopkinsmedicine.org/patients/JHH/patient_rights.html; accessed 14 January 2006. Excerpted in K. Lee Lerner and Brenda Wilmoth Lerner, eds. *Medicine, Health, and Bioethics: Essential Primary Sources*, (Farmington Hills, Mich.: Thomson Gale, 2006).

Using Primary Sources

The definition of what constitutes a primary source is often the subject of scholarly debate and interpretation. Although primary sources come from a wide spectrum of resources, they are united by the fact that they individually provide insight into the historical context and environment during which they were produced. Primary sources include materials such as newspaper articles, press dispatches, autobiographies, essays, letters, diaries, speeches, song lyrics, posters, works of art—and in the twenty-first century, Web logs—that offer direct, first-hand insight or witness to events of their day.

Categories of primary sources include:

- Documents containing firsthand accounts of historic events by witnesses and participants. This category includes diary or journal entries, letters, email, newspaper articles, interviews, memoirs, and testimony in legal proceedings.
- Documents or works representing the official views of government leaders. These include primary sources such as policy statements, speeches, interviews, press releases, government reports, and legislation.
- Works of art, including (but certainly not limited to) photographs, poems, and songs, including advertisements and reviews of those works that help establish an understanding of the cultural environment with regard to attitudes and perceptions of events.
- Secondary sources. In some cases, secondary sources or tertiary sources may be treated as primary sources. For example, the article "Implementation of the Program" discusses the evolution of the Red Cross blood donation program across a time span of more than twenty years, from World War II (1938–1945) through the Vietnam War in 1964. The primary source includes recollections of communications exchanged between the U.S. Army and the Red Cross about the need for obtaining large quantities of human blood plasma for use in treating injured soldiers. Ordinarily, an historical retrospective such as this excerpt, published two decades after the initial event, might not be considered a primary source. The fact that the retrospective was written by the general responsible for the Army blood program during World War II, a participant in the initial effort, makes it an illuminating primary source.

ANALYSIS OF PRIMARY SOURCES

The material collected in this volume is not intended to provide a comprehensive overview of a topic or event. Rather, the primary sources are intended to generate interest and lay a foundation for further inquiry and study.

In order to properly analyze a primary source, readers should remain skeptical and develop probing questions about the source. As in reading a chemistry or algebra textbook, historical documents require readers to analyze them carefully and extract specific information. However, readers must also read "beyond the text" to garner larger clues about the social impact of the primary source.

In addition to providing information about their topics, primary sources may also supply a wealth of insight into their creator's viewpoint. For example, when reading a news article about an outbreak of disease, consider whether the reporter's words also indicate something about his or her origin, bias (an irrational disposition in favor of someone or something), prejudices (an irrational disposition against someone or something), or intended audience.

Students should remember that primary sources often contain information later proven to be false, or contain viewpoints and terms unacceptable to future generations. It is important to view the primary source within the historical and social context existing at its creation. If for example, a newspaper article is written within hours or days of an event, later developments may reveal some assertions in the original article as false or misleading.

TEST NEW CONCLUSIONS AND IDEAS

Whatever opinion or working hypothesis the reader forms, it is critical that they then test that hypothesis against other facts and sources related to the incident. For example, it might be wrong to conclude that factual mistakes are deliberate unless evidence can be produced of a pattern and practice of such mistakes with an intent to promote a false idea.

The difference between sound reasoning and preposterous conspiracy theories (or the birth of urban legends) lies in the willingness to test new ideas against other sources, rather than rest on one piece of evidence such as a single primary source that may contain errors. Sound reasoning requires that arguments and assertions guard against argument fallacies that utilize the following:

- false dilemmas (only two choices are given when in fact there are three or more options)
- arguments from ignorance (*argumentum ad ignorantiam*; because something is not known to be true, it is assumed to be false)

- possibilist fallacies (a favorite among conspiracy theorists who attempt to demonstrate that a factual statement is true or false by establishing the possibility of its truth or falsity. An argument where "it could be" is usually followed by an unearned "therefore, it is.")
- slippery slope arguments or fallacies (a series of increasingly dramatic consequences is drawn from an initial fact or idea)
- begging the question (the truth of the conclusion is assumed by the premises)
- straw man arguments (the arguer mischaracterizes an argument or theory and then attacks the merits of their own false representations)
- appeals to pity or force (the argument attempts to persuade people to agree by sympathy or force)
- prejudicial language (values or moral goodness good and bad are attached to certain arguments or facts)
- personal attacks (*ad hominem*; an attack on a person's character or circumstances)
- anecdotal or testimonial evidence (stories that are unsupported by impartial or unreproducable data)
- *post hoc* (after the fact) fallacies (because one thing follows another, it is held to cause the other)
- the fallacy of the appeal to authority (the argument rests upon the credentials of a person, not the evidence)

Despite the fact that some primary sources can contain false information or lead readers to false conclusions based on the "facts" presented, they remain an invaluable resource regarding past events. Primary sources allow readers and researchers to come as close as possible to understanding the perceptions and context of events and, thus, to more fully appreciate how and why misconceptions occur.

Chronology

1779: Domenico Cotugno asserts that cerebrospinal fluid, and not "animal spirit," as previously argued, fills the brain's cavities and ventricles.

1780: Antoine-Laurent Lavoisier and Pierre-Simon Laplace collaborate to demonstrate that respiration is a form of combustion. Breathing, like combustion, liberates heat, carbon dioxide and water.

1780: George Adams devises the first microtome. This mechanical instrument cuts thin slices for examination under a microscope, thus replacing the imprecise procedure of cutting by a hand-held razor.

1780: Lazzaro Spallanzani carries out experiments on fertilization in frogs and attempts to determine the role of semen in the development of amphibian eggs.

1796: Edward Jenner uses cowpox virus to develop a smallpox vaccine. By modern standards, this was human experimentation as Jenner injected healthy eight-year-old James Phillips with cowpox and, after a period of months, with smallpox.

1796: Erasmus Darwin, grandfather of Charles Darwin and Francis Galton, publishes his *Zoonomia*. In this work, Darwin argues that evolutionary changes are brought about by the direct influence of the environment on the organism—an idea primarily associated with Jean-Baptiste Lamarck.

1797: Georges-Léopold-Chrétien-Frédéric Dagobert Cuvier establishes modern comparative zoology with the publication of his first book, *Basic Outline for a Natural History of Animals*. Cuvier studies the ways in which an animal's function and habits determine its form. He argues that form always follows function and that the reverse relationship does not occur.

1798: Government legislation is passed to establish hospitals in the United States devoted to the care of ill mariners. This initiative leads to the establishment of a Hygenic Laboratory that eventually grows to become the National Institutes of Health.

1799: Humphrey Davy suggests nitrous oxide can be used to reduce pain during surgery.

1800: Marie-François-Xavier Bichat publishes his first major work, *Treatise on Tissues*, that establishes histology as a new scientific discipline. Bichat distinguishes twenty-one kinds of tissue and relates particular diseases to particular tissues.

1802: Jean-Baptiste Lamarck and Gottfried Reinhold Treviranus propose the term "biology" to denote a new general science of living beings that would supercede studies in natural history.

1802: John Dalton introduces modern atomic theory into the science of chemistry.

1804: F. W. Serturner discovers how to isolate the chemical morphine from the poppy plant (*Papaver somniferum*).

1810: Franz Joseph Gall lays the basis for modern neurology with his dissections of the brain and his correct suggestions about nerve organization.

1811: Julien-Jean-César Legallois locates the first physiological center in the brain.

1812: Charles Bell differentiates between sensory and motor roots of spinal nerves in his *New Idea of Anatomy of the Brain*. He asserts that each nerve carries either a motor or a sensory stimulus, and not both simultaneously.

1812: Gustav Robert Kirchoff identifies catalysis and mechanisms of catalytic reactions.

1818: William Charles Wells suggests the theory of natural selection in an essay dealing with human color variations. He notes that dark-skinned people are more resistant to tropical diseases than lighter-skinned people.

1820: First United States *Pharmacopoeia* is published.

1821: Jean-Louis Prévost and Jean-Baptiste-André Dumas jointly publish a paper that demonstrates that spermatozoa originate in tissues of the male sex glands. Three years later they publish the first detailed account of the segmentation of a frog's egg.

1822: François Magendie publishes his paper "Functions of the Roots of the Spinal Nerves," that lays the foundation for the Bell-Magendie Law.

1824: Performances at London's West End Aldelphi Theatre entitled "M. Henry's Mechanical and Chemical Demonstrations" showed the effects of nitrous oxide on audience volunteers.

1824: René-Joachim-Henri Dutrochet suggests that tissues are composed of living cells.

1825: Jan Evangelista Purkinje describes the "germinal vesicle," or nucleus, in a hen's egg.

1826: James Cowles Prichard presents his views on evolution in the second edition of his book *Researches into the Physical History of Man*. These ideas about evolution are suppressed in later editions.

1828: Friedrich Wöhler synthesizes urea. This is generally regarded as the first organic chemical produced in the laboratory, and an important step in disproving the idea that only living organisms can produce organic compounds. Work by Wöhler and others establish the foundations of organic chemistry and biochemistry.

1828: In his book *On the Developmental History of Animals*, Karl Ernst von Baer demonstrates that embryological development follows essentially the same pattern in a wide variety of mammals. von Baer's work establishes the modern field of comparative embryology.

1828: Luigi Rolando achieves the first synthetic electrical stimulation of the brain.

1828: Robert Brown observes a small body within the cells of plant tissue and calls it the "nucleus." He also discovers what becomes known as "Brownian movement."

1829: Salicin, the precursor of aspirin, is purified from the bark of the willow tree.

1831: Charles Robert Darwin begins his historic voyage on HMS *Beagle*. His observations during the voyage lead to his theory of evolution by means of natural selection.

1831: Patrick Matthew includes a discussion of evolution and natural selection in his book *On Naval Timber and Arboriculture*. Matthew later claims priority in the discovery of evolution by means of natural selection in an article published in 1860 in the journal *Gardeners' Chronicle*.

1832: Anselme Payen isolates diastase from barley. Diastase catalyzes the conversion of starch into sugar, and is an example of the organic catalysts within living tissue that eventually come to be called enzymes.

1833: Johannes Peter Müller first proposes his law of specific nerve energies. According to this law, every sensory nerve gives rise to one form of sensation, even if it is excited by stimuli outside a normal range.

1836: Félix Dujardin describes the "living jell" of the cytoplasm, which he calls "sarcode."

1836: Theodor Schwann carries out experiments that refute the theory of the spontaneous generation of infusoria. He also demonstrates that alcoholic fermentation depends on the action of living yeast cells. The same conclusion is reached independently by Charles Caignard de la Tour.

1837: René-Joachim Dutrochet publishes his research on plant physiology that includes pioneering work on osmosis. He is the first scientist to systematically investigate the process of osmosis, which he names, and that chlorophyll is necessary for photosynthesis.

1838: Matthias Jakob Schleiden notes that the nucleus first described by Robert Brown is characteristic of all plant cells. Schleiden describes plants as a community of cells and cell products. He helps establish cell theory and stimulates Theodor Schwann's recognition that animals are also composed of cells and cell products.

1839: Jan Evangelista Purkinje uses the term "protoplasm" to describe the substance within living cells.

1839: Theodor Schwann extends the theory of cells to include animals and helps establish the basic unity of the two great kingdoms of life. He publishes *Microscopical Researches into the Accordance in the Structure and Growth of Animals and Plants*, where he asserts that all living things are made up of cells, and that each cell contains certain essential components. He also coins the term "metabolism" to describe the overall chemical changes that take place in living tissues.

1840: Friedrich Gustav Jacob Henle publishes the first histology textbook, *General Anatomy*. This work includes the first modern discussion of the germ theory of communicable diseases.

1840: Justus von Liebig shows that plants synthesize organic compounds from carbon dioxide in the air but take their nitrogenous compounds from the soil. He also states that ammonia (nitrogen) is needed for plant growth.

1840: Karl Bogislaus Reichert introduces the cell theory into the discipline of embryology. He proves that the segments observed in fertilized eggs develop into individual cells, and that organs develop from cells.

1840: Rudolf Albert von Kölliker establishes that spermatozoa and eggs are derived from tissue cells. He attempts to extend the cell theory to embryology and histology.

1841: Anesthetic properties of ether were first used by Dr. Crawford W. Long as he surgically removed two tumors from the neck of an anesthetized patient.

1842: Theodor Ludwig Wilhelm Bischoff publishes the first textbook of comparative embryology, *Developmental History of Mammals and Man*.

1843: Martin Berry observes the union of the sperm and egg of a rabbit.

1844: First recorded use of nitrous oxide in a United States dental practice by Gardner Quincy Colton, a former medical student, and dentist Horace Wells at Hartford, Connecticut.

1844: Robert Chambers anonymously publishes *Vestiges of the Natural History of Creation*, which advocates the theory of evolution. This controversial book becomes a best seller and introduces the general reading public to the theory of evolution.

1845: Karl Theodor Ernst von Siebold is the first scientist to determine protozoa are single-celled organisms.

1845: J. Marion Sims conducts medical experiments on slaves in the United States. Sims becomes the first physician in the United States to have a statue in his honor.

1847: A series of yellow fever epidemics sweeps the American Southern states. The epidemics recur every few years for more than thirty years.

1849: Rudolf Wagner and Karl Georg Friedrich Rudolf Leuckart report that spermatozoa are a definite and essential part of semen, and that the liquid merely keeps them in suspension. They also reject the old hypothesis that spermatozoa are parasites, and argue that spermatozoa are essential for fertilization.

1850–1899

1851: Hugo von Mohl publishes *Basic Outline of the Anatomy and Physiology of the Plant Cell*, in which he proposes that new cells are created by cell division.

1854: George Newport performs the first experiments on animal embryos. He suggests that the point of sperm entry determines the planes of the segmentation of the egg.

1854: Gregor Mendel begins to study thirty-four different strains of peas. He selects twenty-two kinds for further experiments. From 1856 to 1863, Mendel grows and tests over 28,000 plants and analyzes seven pairs of traits.

1854: Rudolf Ludwig Carl Virchow first names the neuroglia, or supportive "glue cells" in the brain.

1855: Alfred Russell Wallace writes an essay entitled "On the Law Which Has Regulated the Introduction of New Species" and sends it to Charles Darwin. Wallace's essay and one by Darwin are published in the 1858 *Proceedings of the Linnaean Society*.

1855: Barolomeo Panizza first proves that parts of the cerebral cortex are essential for vision.

1856: Nathanael Pringsheim observes the sperm of a freshwater algae plant enter the egg.

1857: Louis Pasteur demonstrates that lactic acid fermentation is caused by a living organism. Between 1857 and 1880, he performs a series of experiments that refute the doctrine of spontaneous generation. He also introduces vaccines for fowl cholera, anthrax, and rabies, based on attenuated strains of viruses and bacteria.

1858: Charles Darwin and Alfred Russell Wallace agree to a joint presentation of their theory of evolution by natural selection.

1858: Rudolf Ludwig Carl Virchow publishes his landmark paper "Cellular Pathology" and establishes the field of cellular pathology. Virchow asserts that all cells arise from preexisting cells (*Omnis cellula e cellula*). He argues that the cell is the ultimate locus of all disease.

1859: Charles Darwin publishes his landmark book *On the Origin of Species by Means of Natural Selection.*

1860: Ernst Heinrich Haeckel describes the essential elements of modern zoological classification.

1860: Louis Pasteur carries out experiments that disprove the doctrine of spontaneous generation.

1860: Max Johann Sigismund Schultze describes the nature of protoplasm and shows that it is fundamentally the same for all life forms.

1861: Carl Gegenbaur confirms Theodor Schwann's suggestion that all vertebrate eggs are single cells.

1861: Pierre-Paul Broca first identifies a location in the brain's left hemisphere that, in most people, is associated with speech. It is later called "Broca's area."

1862: Von Hemholtz describes the physiological mechanism of auditory senses (hearing and sound transmission).

1865: An epidemic of rinderpest kills 500,000 cattle in Great Britain. Government inquiries into the outbreak pave the way for the development of contemporary theories of epidemiology and the germ theory of disease.

1865: Franz Schweiger-Seidel proves that spermatozoa consist of a nucleus and cytoplasm.

1865: Gregor Mendel presents his work on hybridization of peas to the Natural History Society of Brno, Czechoslovakia. The paper is published in the 1866 issue of the Society's *Proceedings*. Mendel presents statistical evidence that hereditary factors are inherited from both parents in a series of papers on "Experiments on Plant Hybridization" published between 1866 and 1869. His experiments provide evidence of dominance, the laws of segregation, and independent assortment, although the work is generally ignored until 1900.

1865: Jules-Bernard Luys describes a nucleus in the hypothalamus, forming a part of the descending pathway from the corpus striatum. It becomes known as the "nucleus of Luys."

1865: Claude Bernard publishes *Introduction to the Study of Human Experimentation* that advocates, "never perform an experiment which might be harmful to the patient even if advantageous to science."

1867: Robert Koch establishes the role of bacteria in anthrax, providing the final piece of evidence in support of the germ theory of disease. Koch goes on to formulate postulates that, when fulfilled, confirm bacteria or viruses as the cause of infection.

1868: Thomas Henry Huxley introduces the term "protoplasm" to the general public in a lecture entitled "The Physical Basis of Life."

1869: Johann Friedrich Miescher discovers nuclein, a new chemical isolated from the nuclei of pus cells. Two years later, he isolates nuclein from salmon sperm. This material comes to be known as nucleic acid.

1869: Paul Langerhans discovers irregular islands of cells in the pancreas which produce insulin. Ultimately, the cells become known as the "Isles of Langerhans."

1870: Gustav Theodor Fritsch and Eduard Hitzig discover that electric shocks to one cerebral hemisphere of a dog's brain produce movement on the other side of the animal's body. This is the first clear demonstration of the existence of cerebral hemispheric lateralization.

1870: Lambert Adolphe Jacques Quetelet shows the importance of statistical analysis for biologists and provides the foundations of biometry.

1870: Thomas Huxley delivers a speech that introduces the terms biogenesis (life from life) and abiogenesis (life from non-life; spontaneous generation). The speech strongly supports Pasteur's claim to have refuted the concept of spontaneous generation.

1871: Ferdinand Julius Cohn coins the term bacterium.

1873: Camilo Golgi discovers that tissue samples can be stained with an inorganic dye (silver salts). Golgi uses this method to analyze the nervous system and characterizes the cells known as Golgi Type I and Golgi Type II cells and the "Golgi Apparatus." Golgi is subsequently awarded a Nobel Prize in 1906 for his studies of the nervous system.

1873: Franz Anton Schneider describes cell division in detail. His drawings include both the nucleus and chromosomal strands.

1874: Carl Wernicke discovers the area of the brain associated with word comprehension, eventually to be named "Wernicke's area."

1874: Francis Galton demonstrates the usefulness of twin studies for elucidating the relative influence of nature (heredity) and nurture (environment).

1874: Wilhelm August Oscar Hertwig concludes that fertilization in both animals and plants consists of the physical union of the two nuclei contributed by the male and female parents. Hertwig subsequently carries out pioneering studies of reproduction of the sea urchin.

1875: Eduard Adolf Strasburger publishes *Cell-Formation and Cell-Division*, in which he describes nuclear division in plants. Strasburger accurately describes the process of mitosis and argues that new nuclei can only rise from the division of pre-existing nuclei. His treatise helps establish cytology as a distinct branch of histology.

1875: Ferdinand Cohn publishes a classification of bacteria in which the genus name *Bacillus* is used for the first time.

1875: Theodor Wilhelm Engelmann proves experimentally that the heartbeat is myogenic, which means that it originates in the heart muscle itself, and not from an external impulse.

1876: Edouard G. Balbiani observes the formation of chromosomes.

1876: Robert Koch publishes a paper on anthrax that implicates a bacterium as the cause of the disease, validating the germ theory of disease.

1877: Paul Erlich recognizes the existence of the mast cells of the immune system.

1877: Robert Koch describes new techniques for fixing, staining, and photographing bacteria.

1877: Wilhelm Friedrich Kühne proposes the term enzyme (meaning "in yeast"). Kühne establishes the critical distinction between enzymes, or "ferments," and the microorganisms that produce them.

1878: Joseph Lister publishes a paper describing the role of a bacterium he names *Bacterium lactis* in the souring of milk.

1878: Thomas Burrill demonstrates for the first time that a plant disease (pear blight) is caused by a bacterium (*Micrococcus amylophorous*).

1879: Albert Nisser identifies *Neiserria gonorrhoeoe* as the cause of gonorrhea.

1879: Hermann Fol observes the penetration of the egg of a sea urchin by a sperm. He demonstrates that only one spermatozoon is needed for fertilization and suggests that the nucleus of the sperm is transferred into the egg.

1879: Walther Flemming describes and names chromatin, mitosis, and the chromosome threads. Flemming's drawings of the longitudinal splitting of chromosomes in eukaryotic cells provide the first accurate counts of chromosome numbers.

1880: C. L. Alphonse Laveran isolates malarial parasites in erythrocytes of infected people and demonstrates that the organism can replicate in the cells. He is awarded the 1907 Nobel Prize in Medicine or Physiology for this work.

1880: David Ferrier maps the region of the brain called the motor cortex and discovers the sensory strip.

1880: First attempt at passage of a nationwide food and drug law. Although defeated in Congress, United States Department of Agriculture's findings of widespread food adulteration spur continued interest in food and drug legislation.

1880: The basic outlines of cell division and the distribution of chromosomes to the daughter cells are established by Walther Flemming, Eduard Strasburger, Edouard van Beneden, and others.

1880: The first issue of the journal *Science* is published by the American Association for the Advancement of Science.

1881: Eduard Strasburger coins the terms cytoplasm and nucleoplasm.

1881: Wilhelm Roux, the founder of experimental embryology, publishes *The Struggle of the Parts in the Organism: A Contribution to the Completion of a Mechanical Theory of Teleology*. Roux argues that his experimental approach to embryonic development, based on mechanistic principles, provides evidence that development proceeds by means of self-differentiation.

1882: Angelina Fannie and Walter Hesse in Koch's laboratory develop agar as a solid grow medium for microorganisms. Agar replaces gelatin as the solid growth medium of choice in microbiology.

1882: Edouard van Beneden outlines the principles of genetic continuity of chromosomes in eukaryotic cells and reports the occurrence of chromosome reduction during the formation of the germ cells.

1882: Pierre Émile Duclaux suggest that enzymes should be named by adding the suffix "ase" to the name of their substrate.

1882: Robert Koch discovers the tubercle bacillus and enunciates "Koch's postulates," which define the classic method of preserving, documenting, and studying bacteria.

1882: Wilhelm Roux offers a possible explanation for the function of mitosis.

1883: August F. Weismann begins work on his germ-plasm theory of inheritance. Weismann proposes a theory of chromosome behavior during cell division and fertilization and predicts the occurrence of a reduction division (meiosis) in all sexual organisms.

1883: Edward Theodore Klebs and Frederich Loeffler independently discover *Corynebacterium diphtheriae*, the bacterium that causes diphtheria.

1883: Walther Flemming, Eduard Strasburger and Edouard Van Beneden demonstrate that in eukaryotic cells, chromosome doubling occurs by a process of longitudinal splitting. Strasburger describes and names the prophase, metaphase, and anaphase stages of mitosis.

1883: Wilhelm Roux suggests that chromosomes carry the hereditary factors.

1884: Elie Metchnikoff discovers the antibacterial activity of white blood cells, which he calls "phagocytes," and formulates the theory of phagocytosis. He also develops the cellular theory of vaccination.

1884: Hans Christian J. Gram develops the Gram stain.

1884: Karl Rabl suggests the concept of the individuality of the chromosomes. He argues that each chromosome originates from a preexisting chromosome in the mother cell that is like it in form and size.

1884: Louis Pasteur and co-workers publish a paper entitled "A New Communication on Rabies." Pasteur proves that the causal agent of rabies can be attenuated and the weakened virus can be used as a vaccine to prevent the disease. This work serves as the basis of future work on virus attenuation, vaccine development, and the concept that variation is an inherent characteristic of viruses.

1884: Oscar Hertwig, Eduard Strasburger, Albrecht von Kölliker, and August Weismann independently report that the cell nucleus serves as the basis for inheritance.

1885: Francis Galton devises a new statistical tool, the correlation table.

1885: Louis Pasteur inoculates a boy, Joseph Meister, against rabies. Meister had been bitten by an infected dog. The treatment saves his life. This is the first time Pasteur uses an attenuated germ on a human being.

1885: Theodor Escherich identifies a bacterium inhabiting the human intestinal tract that he names *Bacterium coli* and shows that the bacterium causes infant diarrhea and gastroenteritis. The bacterium is subsequently named *Escherichia coli*.

1886: Adolf Mayer publishes the landmark article "Concerning the Mosaic Disease of Tobacco." This paper is considered the beginning of modern experimental work on plant viruses. Mayer

assumes that the causal agent was a bacterium, although he was unable to isolate it.

1887: Julius Richard Petri develops a culture dish that has a lid to exclude airborne contaminants. The innovation is subsequently termed the petri plate.

1888: Francis Galton publishes *Natural Inheritance*, considered a landmark in the establishment of biometry and statistical studies of variation. Galton also proposes the Law of Ancestral Inheritance, a statistical description of the relative contributions to heredity made by previous generations.

1888: Heinrich Wilhelm Gottfried Waldeyer coins the term "chromosome." Waldeyer also introduces the use of hematoxylin as a histological stain.

1888: Martinus Beijerinck uses a growth medium enriched with certain nutrients to isolate the bacterium *Rhizobium*, demonstrating that nutritionally tailored growth media are useful in bacterial isolation.

1888: The Institute Pasteur is formed in France.

1888: Theodor Heinrich Boveri discovers and names the centrosome (the mitotic spindle that appears during cell division).

1888: Woods Hole Marine Biological Station, which later became the headquarters of the Woods Hole Oceanographic Institution and the Marine Biological Laboratory, is established in Massachusetts.

1889: Richard Altmann develops a method of preparing nuclein that was apparently free of protein. He calls his protein-free nucleins "nucleic acids."

1889: Theodor Boveri and Jean-Louis-Léon Guignard establish the numerical equality of the paternal and maternal chromosomes at fertilization.

1891: Charles-Edouard Brown-Sequard suggests the concept of internal secretions (hormones).

1891: Hermann Henking distinguishes between the sex chromosomes and the autosomes.

1891: Paul Ehrlich proposes that antibodies are responsible for immunity.

1891: Robert Koch proposes the concept of delayed type hypersensitivity.

1891: The Prussian State dictates that even jailed prisoners must give consent prior to treatment (even for tuberculosis).

1892: August Weismann publishes his landmark treatise *The Germ Plasm: A Theory of Heredity*, which emphasizes the role of meiosis in the distribution of chromosomes during the formation of gametes.

1892: Dmitri Ivanowski demonstrates that filterable material causes tobacco mosaic disease. The infectious agent is subsequently shown to be the tobacco mosaic virus. Ivanowski's discovery creates the field of virology.

1892: George M. Sternberg publishes his *Practical Results of Bacteriological Researches*. Sternberg's realization that a specific antibody was produced after infection with vaccinia virus and that immune serum could neutralize the virus becomes the basis of virus serology. The neutralization test provides a technique for diagnosing viral infections, measuring the immune response, distinguishing antigenic similarities and differences among viruses, and conducting retrospective epidemiological surveys.

1892: In a experiment with syphilis, Albert Neisser injects and infects human subjects.

1893: Hans Adolf Eduard Driesch discovers that he could separate sea urchin embryos into individual cells and that the separated cells continued to develop. Driesch concludes that all the cells of the early embryo are capable of developing into whole organisms. Therefore, embryonic cells are equipotent, but differentiated and developed in response to their position within the embryo.

1894: Alexandre Yersin isolates *Yersinia (Pasteurella) pestis*, the bacterium responsible for bubonic plague.

1894: Wilhelm Konrad Roentgen discovers x rays.

1895: Heinrich Dreser, working for the Bayer Company in Germany, produces a drug he thought to be as effective an analgesic as morphine, but without the harmful side effects. Bayer began mass production of diacetylmorphine, and in 1898 began marketing the new drug under the brand name "heroin" as a cough sedative.

1896: Edmund Beecher Wilson publishes the first edition of his highly influential treatise *The Cell in Development and Heredity*. Wilson calls attention to the relationship between chromosomes and sex determination.

1897: John Jacob Abel isolates epinephrine (adrenalin). This is the first hormone to be isolated.

1898: Carl Benda discovers and names mitochondria, the subcellular entities previously seen by Richard Altmann.

1898: Friedrich Loeffler and Paul Frosch publish their *Report on Foot-and-Mouth Disease*. They prove that this animal disease is caused by a filterable virus and suggest that similar agents might cause other diseases.

1898: The First International Congress of Genetics is held in London.

1899: A meeting to organize the Society of American Bacteriologists is held at Yale University. The society will later become the American Society for Microbiology.

1899: Jacques Loeb proves that it is possible to induce parthenogenesis in unfertilized sea urchin eggs by means of specific environmental changes.

1900–1949

1900: Carl Correns, Hugo de Vries, and Erich von Tschermak independently rediscover Mendel's laws of inheritance. Their publications mark the beginning of modern genetics. William Bateson describes the importance of Mendel's contribution in an address to the Royal Society of London.

1900: Hugo Marie de Vries describes the concept of genetic mutations in his book *Mutation Theory*. He uses the term mutation to describe sudden, spontaneous, and drastic alterations in hereditary material.

1900: Karl Landsteiner discovers the blood-agglutination phenomenon and the four major blood types in humans.

1900: Karl Pearson develops the chi-square test.

1900: Paul Erlich proposes the theory concerning the formation of antibodies by the immune system.

1900: Thomas H. Montgomery studies spermatogenesis in various species of Hemiptera. He concludes that maternal chromosomes only pair with corresponding paternal chromosomes during meiosis.

1900: Walter Reed demonstrates that yellow fever is caused by a virus transmitted by mosquitoes. This is the first demonstration of a viral cause of a human disease. Reed injects paid Spanish immigrant workers in Cuba with the agent, paying them if they survive and paying them still more should they contract the disease.

1901: Clarence E. McClung argues that particular chromosomes determine the sex of the individual carrying them. Although his work is done with insects, he suggests that this might be true for human beings and other animals.

1901: Jokichi Takamine and T. B. Aldrich first isolate epinephrine from the adrenal gland. Later known by the trade name Adrenalin, it is eventually identified as a neurotransmitter. This is also the first time a pure hormone has been isolated.

1901: Jules Bordet and Octave Gengou develop the complement fixation test.

1901: William Bateson coins the terms genetics, F1and F2 generations, allelomorph (later shortened to allele), homozygote, heterozygote, and epistasis.

1902: Carl Neuberg introduces the term biochemistry.

1902: Ernest H. Starling and William H. Bayliss discover and isolate the first hormone ("secretin," found in the duodenum).

1902: Santiago Ramon y Cajal first discovers the nature of the connection between nerves, showing that the nervous system consists of a maze of individual cells. He demonstrates that neurons do not touch but that the signal somehow crosses a gap (now called a synapse).

1903: Archibald Edward Garrod provides evidence that errors in genes caused several hereditary disorders in human beings. His 1909 book *The Inborn Errors of Metabolism* is the first treatise in biochemical genetics.

1903: Willem Einthoven invents the electrocardiograph (EKG).

1903: Ernst Ruska develops a primitive electron microscope.

1903: Arne Tiselius offers electrophoresis techniques that become the basis for the separation of biological molecules by charge, mass, and size.

1903: Walter S. Sutton publishes a paper in which he presents the chromosome theory of inheritance. The theory, which states that the hereditary factors are located in the chromosomes, is independently proposed by Theodor Boveri and is generally referred to as the Sutton-Boveri hypothesis.

1905: Nettie Maria Stevens discovers the connection between chromosomes and sex determination. She determines that there are two basic types of sex chromosomes, which are now called X and Y. Stevens proves that females are XX and males are XY. Stevens and Edmund B. Wilson independently describe the relationship between the so-called accessory or X chromosome and sex determination in insects.

1905: William Bateson and Reginald C. Punnett report the discovery of two new genetic principles: linkage and gene interaction.

1906: The United States Congress passes the Pure Food and Drug Act.

1906: Viennese physician and immunological researcher Clemens von Pirquet coins the term "allergy" to describe the immune reaction to certain compounds.

1906: Dr. Richard Strong, a professor of tropical medicine at Harvard, experiments with cholera on prisoners, some of whom die.

1907: Ivan Petrovich Pavlov, investigates the conditioned reflex. A great stimulus for behaviorist psychology, his work establishes physiologically oriented psychology.

1907: William Bateson urges biologists to adopt the term "genetics" to indicate the importance of the new science of heredity.

1908: Godfrey Harold Hardy and Wilhelm Weinberg independently publish similar papers describing a mathematical system that accounts for the stability of gene frequencies in succeeding generations of population. Their resulting Hardy-Weinberg law links the Mendelian hypothesis with population studies.

1908: Margaret A. Lewis successfully cultures mammalian cells *in vitro*.

1908: Thomas H. Morgan publishes a paper expressing doubts about Mendelian explanations for inherited traits.

1909: Jean de Mayer first suggests the name "insulin" for the hormone of the islet cells.

1909: Korbinian Bordmann publishes a "map" of the cerebral cortex, assigning numbers to particular regions.

1909: Phoebus Aaron Theodore Levene discovers the chemical difference between DNA (deoxyribonucleic acid) and RNA (ribonucleic acid).

1909: Sigurd Orla-Jensen proposes that the physiological reactions of bacteria are primarily important in their classification.

1909: Thomas Hunt Morgan selects the fruit fly *Drosophila* as a model system for the study of genetics. Morgan and his co-workers confirm the chromosome theory of heredity and realize the significance of the fact that certain genes tend to be transmitted together. Morgan postulates the mechanism of "crossing over." His associate, Alfred Henry Sturtevant demonstrates the relationship between crossing over and the rearrangement of genes in 1913.

1909: Wilhelm Ludwig Johannsen argues the necessity of distinguishing between the appearance of an organism and its genetic constitution. He invents the terms "gene" (carrier of heredity), "genotype" (an organism's genetic constitution), and "phenotype" (the appearance of the actual organism).

1910: Harvey Cushing and his team present the first experimental evidence of the link between the anterior pituitary and the reproductive organs.

1911: Francis Peyton Rous publishes the landmark paper "Transmission of a Malignant New Growth by Means of a Cell-Free Filtrate." His work provides the first rigorous proof of the experimental transmission of a solid tumor and suggests that a filterable virus is the causal agent.

1912: Casimir Funk coins the term "vitamine." Since the dietary substances he discovers are in the amine group he calls all of them "life-amines" (using the Latin word *vita* for "life").

1912: Paul Ehrlich discovers a chemical cure for syphilis. This is the first chemotherapeutic agent for a bacterial disease.

1912: The United States Public Health Service is established.

1913: Calvin Blackman Bridges discovers evidence of nondisjunction of the sex chromosomes in *Drosophila*. This evidence helps support Thomas H. Morgan's new chromosome theory of heredity.

1914: Edward Calvin Kendall extracts thyroxin from the thyroid gland (in crystalline form).

1914: Frederick William Twort and Felix H. D'Herelle independently discover bacteriophages, viruses which destroy bacteria.

1914: Thomas Hunt Morgan, Alfred Henry Sturtevant, Calvin Blackman Bridges, and Hermann Joseph Muller publish the classic treatise of modern genetics, *The Mechanism of Mendelian Heredity*.

1915: Katherine K. Sanford isolates a single mammalian cell *in vitro* and allows it to propagate to form identical descendants. Her clone of mouse fibroblasts is called L929, because it took 929 attempts before a successful propagation was achieved. Sanford's work is important step in establishing pure cell lines for biomedical research.

1915: United States Public Health Office allows induction of pellagra in Mississippi housed prisoners.

1916: Felix Hubert D'Herelle carries out further studies of the agent that destroys bacterial colonies and gives it the name "bacteriophage" (bacteria eating agent). D'Herelle and others unsuccessfully attempt to use bacteriophages as bactericidal therapeutic agents.

1917: D'Arcy Wentworth Thompson publishes *On Growth and Form*, which suggests that the evolution of one species into another occurs as a series of transformations involving the entire organism, rather than a succession of minor changes in parts of the body.

1918: Calvin B. Bridges discovers chromosomal duplications in *Drosophila*.

1918: Global influenza pandemic kills more people than the number of soldiers who died fighting during World War I. By the end of 1918, approximately 25 million people die from virulent strain of Spanish influenza.

1918: Thomas Hunt Morgan and co-workers publish *The Physical Basis of Heredity*, a survey of the remarkable development of the new science of genetics.

1919: James Brown uses blood agar to study the destruction of blood cells by the bacterium *Streptococcus*. He observes three reactions that he designates alpha, beta, and gamma.

1919: The Health Organization of the League of Nations was established for the prevention and control of disease around the world.

1919: San Quentin doctors perform testicular transplant experiments on hundreds of prisoners.

1920: Frederick Grant Banting, Charles Best, and James B. Collip discover insulin. They develop a method of extracting insulin from the human pancreas. The insulin is then injected into the blood of diabetics to lower their blood sugar.

1921: Otto Loewi discovers that acetylcholine functions as a neurotransmitter. It is the first such brain chemical to be so identified.

1922: Elmer Verner McCollum discovers Vitamin D.

1922: Frederick Banting and Charles Best make the first clinical adaptation of insulin for the treatment of diabetes.

1922: Herbert McLean Evans and colleagues discover Vitamin E.

1923: A. E. Boycott and C. Diver describe a classic example of "delayed Mendelian inheritance." The direction of the coiling of the shell in the snail *Limnea peregra* is under genetic control, but the gene acts on the egg prior to fertilization. Thus, the direction of coiling is determined by the egg cytoplasm, which is controlled by the mother's genotype.

1924: Albert Jan Kluyver publishes *Unity and Diversity in the Metabolism of Micro-organisms*. He demonstrates that different microorganisms have common metabolic pathways of oxidation, fermentation, and synthesis of certain compounds.

Kluyver also states that life on Earth depends on microbial activity.

1925: Johannes Hans Berger records the first human electroencephalogram (EEG).

1926: Bernard O. Dodge begins genetic studies on *Neurospora*.

1926: James B. Sumner publishes a report on the isolation of the enzyme urease and his proof that the enzyme is a protein. This idea is controversial until 1930 when John Howard Northrop confirms Sumner's ideas by crystallizing pepsin. Sumner, Northrop, and Wendell Meredith Stanley ultimately share the Nobel Prize for Chemistry in 1946.

1926: Thomas C. Vanterpool publishes a paper that clarifies the problem of "mixed infections" of plant viruses. His study of the condition known as "streak" or "winter blight" of tomatoes shows that it was the result of simultaneous infection of tomato plants by tomato mosaic virus and a potato mosaic virus.

1927: Hermann Joseph Muller induces artificial mutations in fruit flies by exposing them to x rays. His work proves that mutations result from some type of physical-chemical change. Muller goes on to write extensively about the danger of excessive x rays and the burden of deleterious mutations in human populations.

1927: Thomas Rivers publishes a paper that differentiates bacteria from viruses, establishing virology as a field of study that is distinct from bacteriology.

1928: Alexander Fleming discovers penicillin. He observes that the mold *Penicillium notatum* inhibits the growth of some bacteria. This is the first anti-bacterial, and it opens a new era of "wonder drugs" to combat infection and disease.

1928: Fred Griffith discovers that certain strains of pneumococci could undergo some kind of transmutation of type. After injecting mice with living R type pneumococci and heat-killed S type, Griffith is able to isolate living virulent bacteria from the infected mice. Griffith suggests that some unknown "principle" had transformed the harmless R strain of the pneumococcus to the virulent S strain.

1928: Wilder Graves Penfield first uses microelectrodes to map areas in the human cerebral cortex.

1929: Francis O. Holmes introduces the technique of "local lesion" as a means of measuring the concentration of tobacco mosaic virus. The method becomes extremely important in virus purification.

1929: Frank M. Burnet and Margot McKie report critical insights into the phenomenon known as lysogeny (the inherited ability of bacteria to produce bacteriophage in the absence of infection). Burnet and McKie postulate that the presence of a "lytic unit" as a normal hereditary component of lysogenic bacteria. The "lytic unit" is proposed to be capable of liberating bacteriophage when it is activated by certain conditions. This concept is confirmed in the 1950s.

1929: Willard Myron Allen and George Washington Corner discover progesterone. They demonstrate that it is necessary for the maintenance of pregnancy.

1930: Curt Stern, and, independently, Harriet B. Creighton and Barbara McClintock, demonstrate cytological evidence of genetic crossing over between eukaryotic chromosomal strands.

1930: Max Theiler demonstrates the advantages of using mice as experimental animals for research on animal viruses. Theiler uses mice in his studies of the yellow fever virus.

1930: Ronald A. Fisher publishes *Genetical Theory of Natural Selection*, a formal analysis of the mathematics of selection.

1930: United States Food, Drug, and Insecticide Administration is renamed the Food and Drug Administration.

1931: Alice Miles Woodruff and Ernest W. Goodpasture demonstrate the advantages of using the membranes of the chick embryo to study the mechanism of viral infections.

1931: Joseph Needham publishes his landmark work *Chemical Embryology*, which emphasizes the relationship between biochemistry and embryology.

1931: Phoebus A. Levene publishes a book that summarizes his work on the chemical nature of the nucleic acids. His analysis of nucleic acids seemed to support the hypothesis known as the tetranucleotide interpretation, which suggests that the four bases are present in equal amounts in DNA from all sources. Perplexingly, this indicated that DNA is a highly repetitious polymer that is incapable of generating the diversity that would be an essential characteristic of the genetic material.

1932: Hans Adolf Krebs describes and names the citric acid cycle.

1932: William J. Elford and Christopher H. Andrewes develop methods of estimating the sizes of viruses by using a series of membranes as filters. Later studies prove that the viral sizes obtained by this method were comparable to those obtained by electron microscopy.

1932: At Tuskegee, Alabama, African American sharecroppers become unknowing and unwilling subjects of experimentation on the untreated natural course of syphilis. Even after penicillan comes into use in the 1940s, men remain untreated.

1933: "Regulation on New Therapy and Experimentation" decreeed in Germany.

1933: Twenty-first Amendment to the Constitution repeals Eighteenth Amendment and prohibition laws banning the sale and consumption of alcohol in United States.

1934: J. B. S. Haldane presents the first calculations of the spontaneous mutation frequency of a human gene.

1934: John Marrack begins a series of studies that leads to the formation of the hypothesis governing the association between an antigen and the corresponding antibody.

1935: Wendall Meredith Stanley discovers that viruses are partly protein-based. By purifying and crystallizing viruses, he enables scientists to identify the precise molecular structure and propagation modes of several viruses.

1936: George P. Berry and Helen M. Dedrick report that the Shope virus could be "transformed" into myxomatosis/Sanarelli virus. This virological curiosity was variously referred to as "transformation," "recombination," and "multiplicity of reactivation." Subsequent research suggests that it is the first example of genetic interaction between animal viruses, but some scientists warn that the phenomenon might indicate the danger of reactivation of virus particles in vaccines and in cancer research.

1936: Theodosius Dobzhansky publishes *Genetics and the Origin of Species*, a text eventually considered a classic in evolutionary genetics.

1937: James W. Papez, suggests the name "limbic system" for the old mammalian part of the human brain that produces human emotions.

1937: Marijuana Tax Act effectively criminalizes its use and possession, even for medical reasons.

1937: Richard Benedict Goldschmidt postulates that the gene is a chemical entity rather than a discrete physical structure.

1938: Emory L. Ellis and Max Delbrück perform studies on phage replication that mark the beginning

of modern phage work. They introduce the "one-step growth" experiment, which demonstrates that after bacteriophages attack bacteria, replication of the virus occurs within the bacterial host during a "latent period," after which viral progeny are released in a "burst."

1938: Federal Food, Drug, and Cosmetics Act gives regulatory powers to the Food and Drug Administration.

1938: Hans Adolf Krebs identifies and defines the tricarboxylic acid (TCA) cycle.

1938: Japanese scientists conduct experiments on Chinese prisoners.

1939: Ernest Chain and H. W. Florey refine the purification of penicillin, allowing the mass production of the antibiotic.

1939: Moses Kunitz reports the purification and crystallization of ribonuclease from beef pancreas.

1939: Richard E. Shope reports that the swine influenza virus survived between epidemics in an intermediate host. This discovery is an important step in revealing the role of intermediate hosts in perpetuating specific diseases.

1939: Studies on twins are conducted in Nazi Germany as part of genetic research.

1939: Ishii experiments conducted on Unit 731 inmates at Ping Fan Prison in Manchuria.

1940: Helmuth Ruska obtains the first electron microscopic image of a virus.

1940: Kenneth Mather coins the term "polygenes" and describes polygenic traits in various organisms.

1941: George W. Beadle and Edward L. Tatum publish their classic study on the biochemical genetics entitled *Genetic Control of Biochemical Reactions in Neurospora*. Beadle and Tatum irradiate red bread mold *Neurospora* and prove that genes produce their effects by regulating particular enzymes. This work leads to the one gene–one enzyme theory.

1941: Lipmann describes and identifies the biochemical and physiological role of high energy phosphahates (such as ATP).

1941: Involuntary sterilization experiments and procedures carried out by Nazis at Auschwitz.

1941: Nazi scientists perform experiments exposing Buchenwald and Natzweiler concentration camp prisoners to typhus and, in separate experiments, phosphorus burns.

1942: Jules Freund and Katherine McDermott identify adjuvants (such as paraffin oil) that act to boost antibody production.

1942: Luria and Max Delbruck demonstrate statistically that inheritance of genetic characteristics in bacteria follows the principles of genetic inheritance proposed by Charles Darwin. For their work, the two (along with Alfred Day Hershey) are awarded the 1969 Nobel Prize in Medicine or Physiology.

1942: Selman Waksman suggests that the word "antibiotics" be used to identify antimicrobial compounds that are made by bacteria.

1942: Nazi scientists perform experiments subjecting Dachau concentration camp prisoners to high altitude conditions (freezing and low pressure) and, in other experiments, diseases such a malaria.

1942: Nazi scientists perform experiments on bone regeneration on prisoners at Ravensbrueck concentration camp.

1942: United States military conducts mustard gas experiments on U.S. soldiers.

1943: At University of Cincinnati Hospital experiments are performed using mentally disabled patients.

1944: New techniques and instruments, such as partition chromatography on paper strips and the photoelectric ultraviolet spectrophotometer, stimulate the development of biochemistry after World War II. New methodologies make it possible to isolate, purify, and identify many important biochemical substances, including the purines, pyrimidines, nucleosides, and nucleotides derived from nucleic acids.

1944: At Dachau concentration camp, prisoners are forced to drink only seawater as part of medical experiments.

1944: Oswald T. Avery, Maclyn McCarty, and Colin MacLeod discover the "blueprint" function of DNA (that DNA carries genetic information).

1944: Salvador E. Luria and Alfred Day Hershey prove that mutations occur in bacterial viruses, and develop methods to distinguish the mutations from other alterations.

1944: To combat battle fatigue during World War II, nearly 200 million amphetamine tablets are issued to American soldiers stationed in Great Britain during the war.

1944: Manhattan Project sub program experiments with effects of radioactive implants on U.S. soldiers at Oak Ridge.

1944: United States Public Health Service Act passed.

1944: University of Chicago Medical School professor Dr. Alf Alving conducts malaria experiments on more than 400 Illinois prisoners.

1945: Joshua Lederberg and Edward L. Tatum demonstrate genetic recombination in bacteria.

1945: Max Delbruck organizes the first session of the phage course at Cold Spring Harbor Laboratory. The widely influential phage course, which is subsequently taught for twenty-six consecutive years, serves as the training center for the first two generations of molecular biologists

1946: Nazi physicians and scientists tried by international court at Nuremberg.

1946: Felix Bloch and Edward Mills Purcell develop nuclear magnetic resonance (NMR) as a viable tool for observation and analysis.

1946: Hermann J. Muller is awarded the Nobel Prize in Medicine or Physiology for his contributions to radiation genetics.

1946: James B. Sumner, John H. Northrop, and Wendell M. Stanley are awarded the Nobel Prize in Chemistry for their independent work on the purification and crystallization of enzymes and viral proteins.

1946: Max Delbruck and W. T. Bailey, Jr. publish a paper entitled "Induced Mutations in Bacterial Viruses." Despite some confusion about the nature of the phenomenon in question, this paper establishes the fact that genetic recombinations occur during mixed infections with bacterial viruses. Alfred Hershey and R. Rotman make the discovery of genetic recombination in bacteriophage simultaneously and independently. Hershey and his colleagues prove that this phenomenon can be used for genetic analyses. They construct a genetic map of phage particles and show that phage genes can be arranged in a linear fashion.

1947: Nuremberg Code issued regarding voluntary consent of human subjects.

1948: Barbara McClintock publishes her research on transposable regulatory elements ("jumping genes") in maize. Her work was not appreciated until similar phenomena were discovered in bacteria and fruit flies in the 1960s and 1970s. McClintock was awarded the Nobel Prize in Medicine or Physiology in 1983.

1948: James V. Neel reports evidence that the sickle-cell disease caused by a Mendelian autosomal recessive trait.

1948: Alfred Kinsey publishes *Sexual Behavior in the Human Male*.

1949: Atomic Energy Commission "Green Run" study using intentional release of radiodine and xenon 133 over Hanford, Washington.

1949: John F. Ender, Thomas H. Weller, and Frederick C. Robbins publish "Cultivation of Polio Viruses in Cultures of Human Embryonic Tissues." The report by Enders and co-workers is a landmark in establishing techniques for the cultivation of poliovirus in cultures on non-neural tissue and for further virus research. The technique leads to the polio vaccine and other advances in virology.

1949: Macfarlane Burnet and his colleagues begin studies that lead to the immunological tolerance hypothesis and the clonal selection theory. Burnet receives the 1960 Nobel Prize in Physiology or Medicine for this research.

1949: The role of mitochondria is finally revealed. These slender filaments within the cell, that participate in protein synthesis and lipid metabolism, are the cell's source of energy.

1949: Walter R. Hess receives the Nobel Prize for his experiments involving probes of deep-brain functions. Using microelectrodes to stimulate or destroy specific areas of the brain in experimental animals, he discovers the role played by particular brain areas in determining and coordinating the functions of internal organs.

1949: Atomic Energy Commission studies radioactive isotopes using mentally challenged school children.

1950–1999

1950: Douglas Bevis demonstrates that amniocentesis could be used to test fetuses for Rh-factor incompatibility.

1950: Erwin Chargaff demonstrates that the Tetranucleotide Theory is incorrect and that DNA is more complex than the model that developed by Phoebus A. Levene. Chargaff proves that the nucleic acids are not monotonous polymers. Chargaff also discovers interesting regularities in the base composition of DNA; these findings are later known as "Chargaff's rules." Chargaff discovers a one-to-one ratio of adenine to thymine and guanine to cytosine in DNA samples from a variety of organisms.

1950: Robert Hungate develops the roll-tube culture technique, which is the first technique that allows anaerobic bacteria to be grown in culture.

1950: Ruth Sager's work on the algae *Chlamydomonas* proves that cytoplasmic genes exist and that they can undergo mutation. She shows that such genes

can be mapped on a "cytoplasmic chromosome." Confirmation is provided when other researchers report similar findings in yeast and *Neurospora*. Subsequently the DNA is shown to be associated with cytoplasmic organelles.

1950: Dr. Joseph Stokes of the University of Pennsylvania infects 200 women prisoners with viral hepatitis.

1951: Esther M. Lederberg discovers a lysogenic strain of *Escherichia coli* K12 and isolates a new bacteriophage, called lambda.

1951: Alan Hodgkin, Andrew Huxley, and Bernard Katz offer modern analysis of the mechanisms of nerve impulse transmission.

1951: Rosalind Franklin obtains sharp x-ray diffraction photographs of deoxyribonucleic acid.

1951: University of Pennsylvania under contract with U.S. Army conducts psychopharmacological experiments on hundreds of Pennsylvania prisoners.

1952: Alfred Hershey and Martha Chase publish their landmark paper "Independent Functions of Viral Protein and Nucleic Acid in Growth of Bacteriophage." The famous "blender experiment" suggests that DNA is the genetic material.

1952: James T. Park and Jack L. Strominger demonstrate that penicillin blocks the synthesis of the peptidoglycan of bacteria. This represents the first demonstration of the action of a natural antibiotic.

1952: Karl Maramorosch demonstrates that some viruses could multiply in both plants and insects. This work leads to new questions about the origins of viruses.

1952: Joshua and Ester Lederberg develop the replica plating method that allows for the rapid screening of large numbers of genetic markers. They use the technique to demonstrate that resistance to antibacterial agents such as antibiotics and viruses is not induced by the presence of the antibacterial agent.

1952: Renato Dulbecco develops a practical method for studying animal viruses in cell cultures. His so-called plaque method is comparable to that used in studies of bacterial viruses, and the method proves to be important in genetic studies of viruses. These methods are described in his paper "Production of Plaques in Monolayer Tissue Cultures by Single Particles of an Animal Virus."

1952: Rosalind Franklin completes a series of x-ray crystallography studies of two forms of DNA. Her colleague, Maurice Wilkins, gives information about her work to James Watson.

1952: William Hayes isolates a strain of *E. coli* that produces recombinants thousands of times more frequently than previously observed. The new strain of K12 is named Hfr (high-frequency recombination) Hayes.

1953: James D. Watson and Francis H. C. Crick publish two landmark papers in the journal *Nature*. The papers are entitled "Molecular Structure of Nucleic Acids: A Structure for Deoxyribose Nucleic Acid" and "Genetic Implications of the Structure of Deoxyribonucleic Acid." Watson and Crick propose a double helical model for DNA and call attention to the genetic implications of their model.

1953: Jonas Salk begins testing a polio vaccine comprised of a mixture of killed viruses.

1953: CIA conducts brainwashing experiments with LSD at eighty institutions on hundreds of subjects in a project code named "MKULTRA."

1954: Frederick Sanger determines the entire sequence of the amino acids in insulin.

1954: Seymour Benzer deduces the fine structure of the rII region of the bacteriophage T4 of *Escherichia coli*, and coins the terms cistron, recon, and muton.

1955: Fred L. Schaffer and Carlton E. Schwerdt report on their successful crystallization of the polio virus. Their achievement is the first successful crystallization of an animal virus.

1955: Heinz Fraenkel-Conrat and Robley C. Williams prove that tobacco mosaic virus can be reconstituted from its nucleic acid and protein subunits. The reconstituted particles exhibit normal morphology and infectivity.

1956: Alfred Gierer and Gerhard Schramm demonstrate that naked RNA from tobacco mosaic virus is infectious. Subsequently, infectious RNA preparations are obtained for certain animal viruses.

1956: American Medical Association defines alcoholism as a disease.

1956: Joe Hin Tijo and Albert Levan prove that the number of chromosomes in a human cell is forty-six, and not forty-eight, as argued since the early 1920s.

1956: Mary F. Lyon proposes that one of the X chromosomes of normal females is inactivated. This concept became known as the Lyon hypothesis and helped explain some confusing aspects of sex-linked diseases. Females are usually "carriers" of genetic diseases on the X chromosome because the normal gene on the other chromosome protects them, but some X-linked disorders are partially expressed in female carriers. Based on studies of mouse coat color genes, Lyon proposes that one X chromosome is randomly inactivated in the cells of female embryos.

1956: Vernon M. Ingram reports that normal and sickle cell hemoglobin differ by a single amino acid substitution.

1956–1980: Researchers conduct hepatitis experiments on mentally disabled children at The Willowbrook State School.

1957: Alick Isaacs and Jean Lindemann discover interferon.

1957: François Jacob and Elie L. Wollman demonstrate that the single linkage group of *Escherichia coli* is circular and suggest that the different linkage groups found in different Hfr strains result from the insertion at different points of a factor in the circular linkage group that determines the rupture of the circle.

1957: Francis Crick proposes that during protein formation each amino acid is carried to the template by an adapter molecule containing nucleotides and that the adapter is the part that actually fits on the RNA template. Later research demonstrates the existence of transfer RNA.

1957: The World Health Organization advances the oral polio vaccine developed by Albert Sabin as a safer alternative to the Salk vaccine.

1958: Frederick Sanger is awarded the Nobel Prize in Chemistry for his work on the structure of proteins, especially for determining the primary sequence of insulin.

1958: Matthew Meselson and Frank W. Stahl publish their landmark paper "The replication of DNA in *Escherichia coli*," which demonstrated that the replication of DNA follow the semiconservative model.

1959: Arthur Kornberg and Severo Ochoa are awarded the Nobel Prize in Medicine or Physiology for their discovery of enzymes that produce artificial DNA and RNA.

1959: Rodney Porter begins studies that lead to the discovery of the structure of antibodies. Porter receives the 1972 Nobel Prize in Physiology or Medicine for this research.

1959: Jerome Lejeune, Marthe Gautier, and Raymond A. Turpin report that Down syndrome is a chromosomal aberration involving trisomy of a small telocentric chromosome.

1959: Severo Ochoa and Arthur Kornberg are awarded the Nobel Prize in Medicine or Physiology for their discovery of the mechanisms in the biological synthesis of ribonucleic acid and deoxyribonucleic acid.

1959: Sydney Brenner and Robert W. Horne publish a paper entitled "A Negative Staining Method for High Resolution Electron Microscopy of Viruses." The two researchers develop a method for studying the architecture of viruses at the molecular level using the electron microscope.

1961: Francis Crick, Sydney Brenner and others propose that a molecule called transfer RNA uses a three base code in the manufacture of proteins.

1961: Jacques Miller discovers the role of the thymus in cellular immunity.

1961: Marshall Warren Nirenberg synthesizes a polypeptide using an artificial messenger RNA (a synthetic RNA containing only the base uracil) in a cell-free protein-synthesizing system. The resulting polypeptide only contains the amino acid phenylalanine, indicating that UUU was the codon for phenylalanine. This important step in deciphering the genetic code is described in the landmark paper by Nirenberg and J. Heinrich Matthaei, "The Dependence of Cell-Free Synthesis in *E. coli* upon Naturally Occurring or Synthetic Polyribonucleotides."

1961: Noel Warner establishes the physiological distinction between the cellular and humoral immune responses.

1961: Rachel Carson publishes *Silent Spring* exposing harmful effects of pollutants, including DDT.

1962: James D. Watson, Francis Crick, and Maurice Wilkins are awarded the Nobel Prize in Medicine or Physiology for their work in elucidating the structure of DNA.

1962: After thousands of birth deformities are blamed on the drug, Thalidomide is withdrawn from the market.

1962: FDA requires multiphase human clinical trials before drugs can be released to market.

1963: John Carew Eccles shares a Nobel Prize for his work on the mechanisms of nerve-impulse transmission. He also suggests that the mind is separate from the brain. The mind, he affirms, acts upon the brain by effecting subtle changes in the chemical signals that flow among brain cells.

1963: Ruth Sager discovers DNA in chloroplasts. Boris Ephrussi discovers DNA in mitochondria.

1964: Barbara Bain publishes a classic account of her work on the mixed leukocyte culture (MLC) system that is critical in determining donor-recipient matches for organ or bone marrow transplantation. Bain shows that the MLC phenomenon is caused by complex genetic differences between individuals.

1964: The first Surgeon General's Report on Smoking and Health is released, and the United States government first acknowledges and publicizes that cigarette smoking is a leading cause of cancer, bronchitis, and emphysema.

1964: World Medical Association adopts Helsinki Declaration.

1965: At the height of tobacco use in America, surveys show 52 percent of adult men and 32 percent of adult women use tobacco products.

1965: François Jacob, André Lwoff, and Jacques Monod are awarded the Nobel Prize in Medicine or Physiology for their discoveries concerning genetic control of enzymes and virus synthesis.

1966: Bruce Ames develops a test to screen for compounds that cause mutations, including those that are cancer causing. The so-called Ames test utilizes the bacterium *Salmonella typhimurium*.

1966: FDA and National Academy of Sciences begin investigation of effectiveness of drugs previously approved because they were thought safe.

1966: Marshall Nirenberg and Har Gobind Khorana lead teams that decipher the genetic code. All of the sixty-four possible triplet combinations of the four bases (the codons) and their associated amino acids are determined and described.

1966: United States passes Fair Packaging and Labeling Act.

1966: National Institutes of Health Office for Protection of Research Subjects created.

1966: *New England Journal of Medicine* article exposes unethical Tuskegee syphilis study.

1967: Charles T. Caskey, Richard E. Marshall, and Marshall Nirenberg suggest that there is a universal genetic code shared by all life forms.

1967: Charles Yanofsky demonstrates that the sequence of codons in a gene determines the sequence of amino acids in a protein.

1967: Thomas Brock discovers the heat-loving bacterium *Thermus aquaticus* from a hot spring in Yellowstone National Park. The bacterium yields the enzyme that becomes the basis of the DNA polymerase reaction.

1967: British physician M. H. Pappworth publishes "Human Guinea Pigs," advising "No doctor has the right to choose martyrs for science or for the general good."

1968: FDA administratively moves to Public Health Service.

1968: Lynne Margulis proposes that mitochondria and chloroplasts in eukaryotic cells originated from bacterial symbiosis.

1968: Mark Steven Ptashne and Walter Gilbert independently identify the bacteriophage genes that are the repressors of the lac operon.

1968: Robert W. Holley, Har Gobind Khorana, and Marshall W. Nirenberg are awarded the Nobel Prize in Medicine or Physiology for their interpretation of the genetic code and its function in protein synthesis.

1968: Werner Arber discover that bacteria defend themselves against viruses by producing DNA-cutting enzymes. These enzymes quickly become important tools for molecular biologists.

1969: Jonathan R. Beckwith and colleagues isolate a single gene.

1969: Julius Adler discovers protein receptors in bacteria that function in the detection of chemical attractants and repellents. The so-called chemoreceptors are critical for the directed movement of bacteria that comes to be known as chemotaxis.

1969: Max Delbruck, Alfred D. Hershey, and Salvador E. Luria are awarded the Nobel Prize in Medicine or Physiology for their discoveries concerning the replication mechanism and the genetic structure of viruses.

1969: Stanford Moore and William H. Stein determine the sequence of the 124-amino acid chain of the enzyme ribonuclease.

1970: Controlled Substance Act puts strict controls on the production, import, and prescription of amphetamines. Many amphetamine forms, particularly diet pills, are removed from the over-the-counter market.

1970: FDA requires a patient information package insert in oral contraceptives. The insert must contain information regarding specific risks and benefits.

1970: Hamilton Smith and Kent Wilcox isolate the first restriction enzyme, HindII, an enzyme that cuts DNA molecules at specific recognition sites.

1970: Har Gobind Khorana announces the synthesis of the first wholly artificial gene. Khorana and his co-workers synthesize the gene that codes for alanine transfer RNA in yeast.

1970: Howard Martin Temin and David Baltimore independently discover reverse transcriptase in viruses. Reverse transcriptase is an enzyme that catalyzes the transcription of RNA into DNA.

1970: United States Congress passes Controlled Substance Act.

1971: Christian B. Anfinsen, Stanford Moore, and William H. Stein are awarded the Nobel Prize in Chemistry. Anfinsen is cited for his work on ribonuclease, especially concerning the connection between the amino acid sequence and the biologically active conformation, and Moore and Stein are cited for their contribution to the understanding of the connection between chemical structure and catalytic activity of the active center of the ribonuclease molecule.

1972: Paul Berg and Herbert Boyer produce the first recombinant DNA molecules.

1972: Recombinant technology emerges as one of the most powerful techniques of molecular biology. Scientists are able to splice together pieces of DNA to form recombinant genes. As the potential uses, therapeutic and industrial, became increasingly clear, scientists and venture capitalists establish biotechnology companies.

1973: Annie Chang and Stanley Cohen show that a recombinant DNA molecule can be maintained and replicated in *Escherichia coli*.

1973: Concerns about the possible hazards posed by recombinant DNA technologies, especially work with tumor viruses, leads to the establishment of a meeting at Asilomar, California. The proceedings of this meeting are subsequently published by the Cold Spring Harbor Laboratory as a book entitled *Biohazards in Biological Research*.

1973: First report is made claiming a circadian variation in blood melatonin levels (pineal hormone) in humans. These variations affect mood and may cause the type of depression association with seasonal affective disorder (SAD).

1973: Herbert Wayne Boyer and Stanley H. Cohen create recombinant genes by cutting DNA molecules with restriction enzymes. These experiments mark the beginning of genetic engineering.

1973: Joseph Sambrook and co-workers refine DNA electrophoresis by using agarose gel and staining with ethidium bromide.

1974: Peter Doherty and Rolf Zinkernagl discover the basis of immune determination of self and non-self.

1974: National Research Act establishes "The Common Rule" for protection of human subjects.

1975: César Milstein and George Kohler create monoclonal antibodies.

1975: David Baltimore, Renato Dulbecco, and Howard Temin share the Nobel Prize in Medicine or Physiology for their discoveries concerning the interaction between tumor viruses and the genetic material of the cell and the discovery of reverse transcriptase.

1975: John R. Hughes and others discover enkephalin. This first known opioid peptide, popularly called "brain morphine," occurs naturally in the brain, indicating that the brain's chemicals block the transmission of pain signals.

1975: Scientists at an international meeting in Asilomar, California, called for the adoption of guidelines regulating recombinant DNA experimentation.

1975: Department of Health and Human Services promulgates Title 45 of Federal Regulations titled "Protection of Human Subjects," requiring appointment and utilization of IRBs.

1975: Edward O. Wilson publishes *Sociobiology* proposing interrelation of biology, human behavior, and culture.

1976: FBI warns "crack" cocaine use and cocaine addiction on the rise in the Untied States.

1976: First outbreak of Ebola virus observed in Zaire. More than 300 cases with a 90 percent death rate.

1976: Michael J. Bishop, Harold Elliot Varmus, and co-workers establish definitive evidence of the onco-gene hypothesis. They discover that normal genes could malfunction and cause cells to become cancerous.

1976: New Jersey Supreme Court rules that coma patient Karen Ann Quinlan can be disconnected from her respirator. Quinlan lives in a persistent vegetative state until her death in 1985.

1976: Swine flu identified in soldiers stationed in New Jersey. Virus identified as H1N1 virus causes concern due to its similarities to H1N1 responsible for Spanish flu pandemic. President Gerald Ford calls for emergency vaccination program. More than twenty deaths result from Guillain-Barre syndrome related to the vaccine.

1977: Carl R. Woese and George E. Fox publish an account of the discovery of a third major branch of living beings, the Archaea. Woese suggests that an rRNA database could be used to generate phylogenetic trees.

1977: Frederick Sanger develops the chain termination (dideoxy) method for sequencing DNA, and uses the method to sequence the genome of a microorganism.

1977: Holger Jannasch demonstrates that heat-loving bacteria found at hydrothermal vents are the basis of an ecosystem that exists in the absence of light.

1977: Philip Allen Sharp and Richard John Roberts independently discover that the DNA making up a particular gene could be present in the genome as several separate segments. Although both Roberts and Sharp use a common cold-causing virus, called adenovirus, as their model system, researchers later find "split genes" in higher organisms, including humans. Sharp and Roberts are subsequently awarded the Nobel Prize in Medicine or Physiology in 1993 for the discovery of split genes.

1977: The first known human fatality from H5N1 avian flu occurs in Hong Kong.

1977: The last reported smallpox case is recorded. Ultimately, the World Health Organization declares the disease eradicated.

1978: Scientists clone the gene for human insulin.

1978: Louise Brown, the world's first "test-tube baby," is born.

1979: National Commission issues Belmont Report.

1980: Paul Berg, Walter Gilbert, and Frederick Sanger share a Nobel Prize in Chemistry. Berg is honored for his fundamental studies of the biochemistry of nucleic acids, with particular regard to recombinant-DNA. Gilbert and Sanger are honored for their contributions to the sequencing of nucleic acids.

1980: Researchers successfully introduce a human gene, which codes for the protein interferon, into a bacterium.

1980: Congress passes the Bayh-Dole Act to encourage the utilization of inventions produced under federal funding. The act is amended by the Technology Transfer Act in 1986.

1980: The FDA promulgates 21 CFR 50.44 prohibiting use of prisoners as subjects in clinical trials.

1980: In *Diamond v. Chakrabarty* the United States Supreme Court rules that a genetically modified bacterium can be patented.

1981: Karl Illmensee clones baby mice.

1982: The United States Food and Drug Administration approves the first genetically engineered drug, a form of human insulin produced by bacteria.

1983: *Escherichia coli* O157:H7 is identified as a human pathogen.

1983: Andrew W. Murray and Jack William Szostak create the first artificial chromosome.

1983: Luc Montainer and Robert Gallo discover the human immunodeficiency virus that is believed to cause acquired immunodeficiency syndrome.

1984: Steen A. Willadsen successfully clones a sheep.

1985: Alec Jeffreys develops "genetic fingerprinting," a method of using DNA polymorphisms (unique sequences of DNA) to identify individuals. The method, which has been used in paternity, immigration, and murder cases, is generally referred to as "DNA fingerprinting."

1985: Leroy Hood leads a team that discovers the genes that code for the T cell receptor.

1985: Elizabeth Blackburn and Carol Greider discover the enzyme telomerase, an unusual RNA-containing DNA polymerase that can add to the telomeres (specialized structures found at the ends of chromosomal DNA). Telomeres appear to protect the integrity of the chromosome. Most normal somatic cells lack telomerase, but cancer cells have telomerase activity, which might explain their ability to multiply indefinitely.

1985: Susuma Tonegawa discovers the genes that code for immunoglobulins. He receives the 1986 Nobel Prize in Physiology or Medicine for this discovery.

1985: Kary Mullis, who was working at Cetus Corporation, develops the polymerase chain reaction (PCR), a new method of amplifying DNA. This technique quickly becomes one of the most powerful tools of molecular biology. Cetus patents PCR and sells the patent to Hoffman-LaRoche, Inc. in 1991.

1986: Congress passes the National Childhood Vaccine Injury Act, requiring patient information on vaccines and reporting of adverse events after vaccinnation.

1986: First gene known to inhibit growth is produced by an American team led by molecular biologist Robert A. Weinberg. The gene is able to suppress the cancer retinoblastoma.

1986: Robert A. Weinberg and co-workers isolate a gene that inhibits growth and appears to suppress retinoblastoma (a cancer of the retina).

1986: The United States Food and Drug Administration approves the first genetically engineered human vaccine for hepatitis B.

1986: United States Surgeon General's report focuses on the hazards of environmental tobacco smoke to nonsmokers.

1987: David C. Page and colleagues discover the gene responsible for maleness in mammals. It is a single gene on the Y chromosome that causes the development of testes instead of ovaries.

1987: Maynard Olson creates and names yeast artificial chromosomes (YACs), which provide a technique to clone long segments of DNA.

1987: The United States Congress charters a Department of Energy advisory committee, the Health and Environmental Research Advisory Committee, that recommends a 15-year, multi-disciplinary, scientific, and technological undertaking to map and sequence the human genome. National Institute of General Medical Sciences at the National Institutes of Health begins funding genome projects.

1987: National Institutes of Mental Health concludes that a researcher fabricated and falsified data in a study. The researcher, Steven Breuning, is convicted a year later of defrauding the federal government.

1988: Canadian sprinter Ben Johnson tests positive for anabolic-androgenic steroids at the Seoul Olympic games and must forfeit his gold medal to the second-place finisher, American Carl Lewis.

1988: Harvard University and Dow Chemical patent a genetically engineered mouse with plans to use it in cancer studies.

1988: The Human Genome Organization is established by scientists in order to coordinate international efforts to sequence the human genome.

1989: Cells from one embryo are used to produce seven cloned calves.

1989: Sidney Altman and Thomas R. Cech are awarded the Nobel Prize in Chemistry for their discovery of ribozymes (RNA molecules with catalytic activity).

1989: Office of Scientific Integrity and the Office of Scientific Integrity Review form to investigate scientific misconduct.

1990: Michael R. Blaese and French W. Anderson conduct the first gene replacement therapy experiment on a four-year-old girl with adenosine deaminase (ADA) deficiency, an immune-system disorder. T cells from the patient are isolated and exposed to retroviruses containing an RNA copy of a normal ADA gene. The treated cells are returned to her body where they help restore some degree of function to her immune system.

1990: National Council on Alcoholism and Drug Dependence along with the American Society of Addictive Medicine define alcoholism as a chronic disease that has genetic, psychological, and environmental factors that influence it. Alcoholism is described as a loss of control over drinking; a preoccupation with drinking despite negative consequences to one's physical, mental, and emotional makeup as well as one's work and family life.

1990: Research and development begins for the efficient production of more stable, large-insert bacterial artificial chromosomes.

1990: Supreme Court decision in *Employment Division v. Smith* determines that the religious use of peyote by Native Americans is not protected by the First Amendment.

1990: United States Congress passes Nutrition Labeling and Education Act permitted manufacturers to make some health claims for foods, including dietary supplements.

1991: Mary-Claire King concludes, based on her studies of the chromosomes of women in cancer-prone families, that a gene on chromosome 17 causes the inherited form of breast cancer and also increases the risk of ovarian cancer.

1991: The gender of a mouse is changed at the embryo stage.

1991: The Genome Database, a human chromosome mapping data repository, is established.

1991: World Health Organization announces Council for International Organizations of Medical Sciences guidelines.

1992: American and British scientists develop a technique for testing embryos *in vitro* for genetic abnormalities such as cystic fibrosis and hemophilia.

1992: Congress passes the Prescription Drug User Fee Act requiring the FDA to use product application fees collected from drug manufacturers to hire more reviewers to assess applications.

1992: National Academy of Science publishes *Responsible Science: Ensuring the Integrity of the Research Process*.

1992: Craig Venter establishes the Institute for Genomic Research in Rockville, Maryland. The institute later sequences the genome of *Haemophilus influenzae* and many other bacterial genomes.

1992: Guidelines for data release and resource sharing related to the Human Genome Project are announced by the United States Department of Energy and National Institutes of Health.

1992: The United States Army begins collecting blood and tissue samples from all new recruits as part of a "genetic dog tag" program aimed at better identification of soldiers killed in combat.

1993: An international research team, led by Daniel Cohen of the Center for the Study of Human Polymorphisms in Paris, produces a rough map of all twenty-three pairs of human chromosomes.

1993: French Gépnéthon makes mega-YACs available to the genome community.

1993: George Washington University researchers clone human embryos and nurture them in a petri dish for several days. The project provokes protests from ethicists, politicians, and critics of genetic engineering.

1993: Hanta virus emerges in the western United States in a 1993 outbreak on a Native American reservation. The resulting Hanta pulmonary syndrome (HPS) has a 43 percent mortality rate.

1993: Scientists identify p53, a tumor suppressor gene, as the crucial factor preventing uncontrolled cell growth. In addition, scientists find that p53 performs a variety of functions ensuring cell health.

1994: Biologists discover that both vertebrates and invertebrates share certain developmental genes.

1994: U.S. Department of Energy announce the establishment of the Microbial Genome Project as a spin-off of the Human Genome Project.

1994: Geneticists determine that DNA repair enzymes perform several vital functions, including preserving genetic information and protecting the cell from cancer.

1994: The five-year goal for genetic-mapping is achieved one year ahead of schedule.

1994: The Human Genome Project Information Web site is made available to researchers and the public.

1994: United States Congress passes Dietary Supplement Health and Education Act expressly defining a dietary supplement as a vitamin, a mineral, an herb or other botanical, an amino acid, or any other "dietary substance."

1994: Harvard psychologist Richard Herrnstein and Charles Murray publish *The Bell Curve* that stirs controversey about biology, race, and intelligence.

1995: Peter Funch and Reinhardt Moberg Kristensen create a new phylum, Cycliophora, for a novel invertebrate called *Symbion pandora*, which is found living in the mouths of Norwegian lobsters.

1995: Public awareness of potential use of chemical or biological weapons by terrorist groups increases following the release of sarin gas in a Tokyo subway by Aum Shinrikyo, a Japanese cult, killing a dozen people and sending thousands to the hospital.

1995: Researchers at Duke University Medical Center report that they have transplanted hearts from genetically altered pigs into baboons. All three transgenic pig hearts survive at least a few hours, suggesting that xenotransplants (cross-species organ transplantation) might be possible.

1995: Religious leaders and biotechnology critics protest the patenting of plants, animals, and human body parts.

1995: The sequence of *Mycoplasma genitalium* is completed. *Mycoplasma genitalium*, regarded as the smallest known bacterium, is considered a model of the minimum number of genes needed for independent existence.

1996: Chris Paszty and co-workers successfully employ genetic engineering techniques to create mice with sickle-cell anemia, a serious human blood disorder.

1996: H5N1 avian flu virus is identified in Guangdong, China.

1996: International participants in the genome project meet in Bermuda and agree to formalize the conditions of data access. The agreement, known as the "Bermuda Principles," calls for the release of sequence data into public databases within twenty-four hours.

1996: Researchers Henrich Cheng, Yihai Cao, and Lars Olson demonstrate that the spinal cord can be regenerated in adult rats.

1996: Researchers find that abuse and violence can alter a child's brain chemistry, placing him or her at risk for various problems, including drug abuse, cognitive disabilities, and mental illness, later in life.

1996: Scientists discover a link between autoptosis (cellular suicide, a natural process whereby the body eliminates useless cells) gone awry and several neurodegenerative conditions, including Alzheimer's disease.

1996: Dolly, the world's first cloned sheep, is born. Several European Union nations ban human cloning. United States Congress debates a bill to ban human cloning.

1996: Scientists report further evidence that individuals with two mutant copies of the CC-CLR-5 gene are generally resistant to HIV infection.

1996: South Carolina Supreme Court decides in favor of the Medical University of South Carolina policy to secretly test pregnant patients for cocaine use. The court upheld MUSC's drug testing in an effort to protect the unborn. Cocaine greatly increases the chances of a miscarriage. Low-birth-weight "crack babies" have twenty times as great a risk of dying in their first month of life than normal-weight babies. Those who survive are at increased risk for birth defects.

1996: William R. Bishai and co-workers reports that SigF, a gene in the tuberculosis bacterium, enables the bacterium to enter a dormant stage.

1997: Donald Wolf and co-workers announce that they cloned rhesus monkeys from early stage embryos, using nuclear transfer methods.

1997: Mickey Selzer, neurologist at the University of Pennsylvania, and co-workers, finds that in lampreys, which have a remarkable ability to regenerate a severed spinal cord, neurofilament messenger RNA effects the regeneration process by literally pushing the growing axons and moving them forward.

1997: Oregon voters approve the Death with Dignity Act allowing terminally ill people to receive prescriptions for lethal dosages of drugs to end their lives.

1997: Researchers identify a gene that plays a crucial role in establishing normal left-right configuration during organ development.

1997: Researchers report progress in using the study of genetic mutations in humans and mice to decipher the molecular signals that lead undeveloped neurons from inside the brain to their final position in the cerebral cortex.

1997: The DNA sequence of *Escherichia coli* is completed.

1997: The National Center for Human Genome Research at the National Institutes of Health becomes the National Human Genome Research Institute.

1997: United States passes Food and Drug Administration Modernization Act and reauthorizes the Prescription Drug User Fee Act of 1992. The changes in policy allow for a more rapid review of drugs and delivery devices. The Act also expands FDA regulatory powers over advertising, especially with regard to health claims.

1997: While performing a cloning experiment, Christof Niehrs, a researcher at the German Center for Cancer Research, identifies a protein responsible for the creation of the head in a frog embryo.

1997: William Jacobs and Barry Bloom creates a biological entity that combines the characteristics of a bacterial virus and a plasmid (a DNA structure that functions and replicates independently of the chromosomes). This entity is capable of triggering mutations in *Mycobacterium tuberculosis*.

1998: Dolly, the first cloned sheep, gives birth to a lamb that had been conceived by a natural mating with a Welsh Mountain ram. Researches said the birth of Bonnie proved that Dolly was a fully normal and healthy animal.

1998: Immunologist Ellen Heber-Katz, a researcher at the Wistar Institute in Philadelphia, reports than a strain of laboratory mice can regenerate tissue in their ears, closing holes which scientists had created for identification purposes. This discovery reopens the discussion on possible regeneration in humans.

1998: Scientists find that an adult human's brain can replace cells. This discovery heralds potential breakthroughs in neurology

1998: Scientists in Korea claim to have cloned human cells.

1998: Two research teams succeed in growing embryonic stem cells.

1999: Scientists announce the complete sequencing of the DNA making up human chromosome 22. The first complete human chromosome sequence is published in December 1999.

1999: The public genome project plans to produce a draft genome sequence by 2000.

1999: The National Institutes of Health and the Office for Human Research Protections require researchers conducting or overseeing human subjects to ethics training.

2000–

2000: On June 26, 2000, leaders of the public genome project and Celera announce the completion of a working draft of the entire human genome sequence.

2000: The first volume of *Annual Review of Genomics and Human Genetics* is published. Genomics is defined as the new science dealing with the identification and characterization of genes and their arrangement in chromosomes and human genetics as the

science devoted to understanding the origin and expression of human individual uniqueness.

2000: The National Cancer Institute estimates that 3,000 lung cancer deaths, and as many as 40,000 cardiac deaths per year among adult nonsmokers in the United States can be attributed to passive smoke or environmental tobacco smoke.

2000: United States Congress considers but does not pass the Pain Relief Promotion Act, which would have amended the Controlled Substances Act to say that relieving pain or discomfort—within the context of professional medicine—is a legitimate use of controlled substances. The bill died in the Senate.

2000: United States Congress passes a transportation spending bill including establishment of a national standard for drunk driving for adults at a 0.08 percent blood alcohol level (BAL). States are required to adopt this stricter standard by 2004 or face penalties. By 2001, more than half the states adopt this stricter standard.

2000: United States Drug Addiction Treatment Act allows opioids to be distributed to physicians for the treatment of opioid dependence.

2000: President Bill Clinton signs the Hillary J. Farias and Samantha Reid Date Rape Drug Prohibition Act into law.

2001: In February 2001, the complete draft sequence of the human genome is published.

2001: Scientists from the Whitehead Institute announce test results that show patterns of errors in cloned animals that might explain why such animals die early and exhibit a number of developmental problems. The report stimulates new debate on ethical issues related to cloning.

2001: The company Advanced Cell Technology announces that its researchers have created cloned human embryos that grew to the six-cell stage.

2001: In the aftermath of the September 11 terrorist attacks on the United States, a number of deaths result from the deliberate release of the bacterial agent of anthrax.

2001: The United States announces that the National Institutes of Health will fund research on only sixty-four embryonic stem cell lines created from human embryos.

2001: International Olympic Committee announces that 15–20 percent of the approximately 600 nutritional supplements the agency tested were adulterated with substances that could lead to positive doping tests.

2001: The National Football League joins the National College Athletic Association and the International Olympic Committee in issuing a ban on ephedrine use.

2001: National Institute of Drug Abuse research asserts that children exposed to cocaine prior to birth sustain long-lasting brain changes.

2001: Office of National Drug Control Policy annual report asserts that that approximately 80 percent of Americans abusing illegal drugs use marijuana.

2001: Study entitled *Global Illicit Drug Trends* conducted by the United Nations Office for Drug Control and Crime Prevention, estimates that 14 million people use cocaine worldwide. Although cocaine use leveled off, the United States still maintains the highest levels of cocaine abuse.

2001: The annual Monitoring the Future study, conducted by the University of Michigan and funded by the National Institute on Drug Abuse, found that 17.1 percent of eighth graders had abused inhalants at some point in their lives.

2001: The U.S. military endorses the situational temporary usefulness of caffeine, recommending it as a safe and effective stimulant for its soldiers in good health.

2001: United State Supreme Court ruled 8 to 0 in *United States vs. Oakland Cannabis Buyers' Cooperative* that the cooperatives permitted under California law to sell marijuana to medical patients who had a physician's approval to use the drug were unconstitutional under federal law.

2001: In August, President George W. Bush announces the United States will allow and support limited forms of stem cell growth and research.

2001: Terrorists attack United States on September 11 and kill thousands by crashing airplanes into buildings. Several weeks later, an unknown terrorist sends four letters, including letters to government leaders, that contain anthrax. The anthrax ultimately kills five people.

2002: A company called DrinkSafe Technology announces the invention of a coaster that can be used to test whether a drink has been drugged. If Rohypnol, GHB, or ketamine has been added, the coaster will change color when a drop of the tampered drink is placed on it.

2002: A Florida physician is convicted of manslaughter for prescribing OxyContin to four patients who died after overdosing on the powerful drug. News reports assert that he is the first doctor ever convicted in the death of patients whose deaths were related to OxyContin use.

2002: Following September 11, 2001, terrorist attacks on the United States, the Public Health Security and Bioterrorism Preparedness and Response Act of 2002 is passed in an effort to improve the ability to prevent and respond to public health emergencies.

2002: Health Canada, the Canadian health regulatory agency, requests a voluntary recall of products containing both natural and chemical ephedra.

2002: In June traces of biological and chemical weapon agents are found in Uzbekistan on a military base used by U.S. troops fighting in Afghanistan. Early analysis dates and attributes the source of the contamination to former Soviet Union biological and chemical weapons programs that utilized the base.

2002: Several states, including Connecticut and Minnesota, pass laws that ban teachers from recommending psychotropic drugs, especially Ritalin, to parents.

2002: The Best Pharmaceuticals for Children Act passed in an effort to improve safety and efficacy of patented and off-patent medicines for children.

2002: The planned destruction of stocks of smallpox-causing Variola virus at the two remaining depositories in the United States and Russia is delayed over fears that large scale production of vaccine might be needed in the event of a bioterrorist action.

2002: United States Federal district court judge rejects a Justice Department attempt to overturn Oregon's physician-assisted suicide law. The Justice Department claims that the state law violates the federal Controlled Substances Act.

2003: An unusual pneumonia is reported in Hanoi, Vietnam (later identified as SARS).

2003: World Health Organization officer Carlo Urbani, MD, identifies sudden acute respiratory syndrome or SARS. Urbani later dies of the disease.

2003: Commissioner of Food and Drugs establishes an obesity working group to deal with U.S. obesity epidemic. In March 2004 the group releases "Calories Count: Report of the Obesity Working Group."

2003: Differences in outbreaks in Hong Kong between 1997 and 2003 cause investigators to conclude that the H5N1 virus has mutated.

2003: Food and Drug Administration requires food labels to include trans fat content. This is the first major change to the nutrition facts panel on foods since 1993.

2003: SARS is added to the list of quarantinable diseases in the United States.

2003: The Medicare Prescription Drug Improvement and Modernization Act addresses issues related to making medical information available to the blind and visually impaired.

2003: World Health Organization Global Influenza Surveillance Network intensifies work on development of a H5N1 vaccine for humans.

2004: Anabolic Steroid Control Act of 2004 bans over-the-counter steroid precursors.

2004: Based on recent results from controlled clinical studies indicating that Cox-2 selective agents may be connected to an elevated risk of serious cardiovascular events, including heart attack and stroke, the Food and Drug Administration issues a public health advisory urging health professionals to limit the use of these drugs.

2004: Food and Drug Administration bans dietary supplements containing ephedrine.

2004: Food Allergy Labeling and Consumer Protection Act requires the labeling of food containing a protein derived from peanuts, soybeans, cow's milk, eggs, fish, crustacean shellfish, tree nuts, and wheat that accounts for a majority of food allergies.

2004: Project BioShield Act of 2004 authorizes U.S. government agencies to expedite procedures related to rapid distribution of treatments as countermeasures to chemical, biological, and nuclear attack.

2004: On December 26, the most powerful earthquake in more than forty years occurred underwater off the Indonesian island of Sumatra. The tsunami produced a disaster of unprecedented proportion in the modern era. Less than two weeks after the tsunami impact, the International Red Cross put the death toll at over 150,000 lives and most experts expected that number to continue to climb. Many experts claim this will be the costliest, longest, and most difficult recovery period ever endured as a result of a natural disaster.

2005: H5N1 virus, responsible for avian flu, moves from Asia to Europe. The World Health Organization attempts to coordinate multinational disaster and containment plans. Some nations begin to stockpile antiviral drugs.

2005: Major League Baseball players are subpoenaed to testify before Congress concerning the use of steroids in the sport.

2005: Hurricane Katrina slams into the U.S. Gulf Coast, causing levee breaks and massive flooding to New Orleans. Damage is extensive across the coasts of Louisiana, Mississippi, and Alabama. Federal Emergency Management Agency is widely criticized for a lack of coordination in relief efforts. Three other major hurricanes make landfall in the United States within a two-year period stressing relief and medical supply efforts. Long term health studies begin of populations in devastated areas.

2005: Food and Drug Administration Drug Safety Board is founded.

2005: Death of Theresa (Terri) Schiavo ignites national debate in United States over right to die and ethical treatment practices.

2005: A massive 7.6-magnitude earthquake leaves more than 3 million homeless and without food and basic medical supplies in the Kashmir mountains between India and Pakistan. 80,000 people die.

2006: European Union bans the importation of avian feathers (non-treated feathers) from countries neighboring or close to Turkey.

2006: More than a dozen people are diagnosed with avian flu in Turkey, but United Nations health experts assure public that human-to-human transmission is still rare and only suspected in a few cases in Asia.

2006: Mad cow disease confirmed in Alabama cow as third reported case in the United States.

Biomedical Science

During most of its history, medicine was practiced as an art, rather than on terms now described as science. During the last two centuries, the practice of medicine has become more closely connected to principles drawn from the scientific method, especially with regard to understanding the molecular underpinnings of disease. Since the birth of a research tradition in the modern era, advances in anatomy, physiology, genetics, immunology, and other of scientific subdisciplines increasingly define and extend the reach of modern medicine.

Biomedical science serves medical science by allowing physicians to understand the critical processes associated with infectious diseases caused by bacteria, viruses, protozoans, and other microorganisms; the influence of body physiology and biochemistry on the maintenance of health; and the tolerance or immune-related rejection of transplanted tissues. It also offers a foundation to test a person's blood, urine, or tissue for the presence of disease and to develop new techniques to maintain health.

The legacy of biomedical science is long. Dutch scientist Antonio van Leeuwenhoek (1632–1723) first recognized the existence of cells in the fluids and tissues of the human body. Near the dawn of the nineteenth century, those observations allowed Robert Koch (1843–1910) to demonstrate the bacterial nature of diseases like anthrax, tuberculosis, and cholera. Physicians now understand that many types of bacteria cause disease, ranging from the relatively minor discomfort of gastrointestinal upset to the life-threatening release of toxins into the bloodstream, as in blood poisoning, or septicemia.

Viral diseases, including influenza, avian flu, human immunodeficiency virus (HIV/AIDS), Ebola viral hemorrhagic fever, rabies, and severe acute respiratory syndrome (SARS), also carry significant medical, social, political, and economic impacts. They hold the potential to reshape how modern society adapts to a shrinking global village.

Biomedical science is concerned with detecting diseases by a number of methods. In many diseases, like cancer, early detection can save a person's life. In this regard, the use of noninvasive imaging techniques such as positron emission spectroscopy (PET), magnetic resonance imaging (MRI), and computed tomography (CT) have allowed diagnosis without the need for exploratory surgery.

In 2003, scientists working on the Human Genome Project finished mapping the entire human sequence of genes. This holds great potential to revolutionize the prevention and treatment of illnesses by the use of gene therapy, in which a healthy gene can replace a damaged one in a sick person. A related type of therapy, stem cell therapy, may also hold great potential in the treatment of disease. Fetal stem cells function as a precursor to a variety of tissues in a developing human. Bone marrow and umbilical cord blood contain adult stem cells.

Many social controversies revolve around biomedical science. Stem cell research, for example, is both politically and socially sensitive in many countries, especially in the United States. How to treat millions of people in Africa who are infected with HIV/AIDS, where whole communities are affected and poverty is widespread, is another contentious issue. How humans around the globe deal with these issues will impact the world over the next century.

The Lancet

A Medical Research Tradition is Born

Journal excerpt

By: Thomas Wakley

Date: October 05, 1823

Source: *The Lancet.* Preface. *The Lancet.* first edition, October 5, 1823, 1–2. Available online at <http://www.thelancet.com/about/backfiles> (accessed November 5, 2005).

About the Author: Thomas Wakley was a physician and coroner, practicing medicine in the United Kingdom in the early nineteenth century. He was a well-known advocate of medical reform, who made public commentaries regarding his concerns for the need to share information about the developing profession in a consistent and accessible manner, as well as the necessity to advance the professional stature of medicine.

INTRODUCTION

The first edition of *The Lancet* was published on October 05, 1823. Thomas Wakley, the physician who was *The Lancet*'s creator, sought to provide a forum in which the advances made in the science and practice of medicine could be made easily accessible to the entire medical profession. He also saw the publication as a means of encouraging professional responsibility among his peers. This was accomplished, in part, by highlighting not only advances and new developments, but by offering critiques concerning flaws in the system, and deficits in general medical knowledge and understanding. Wakley covered triumphs and mistakes with equal candor in his journal.

Wakley was the initial editor, as well as the founder and creator of *The Lancet*. He chose the name as a metaphor for what he hoped to accomplish by the inception of the weekly journal; a lancet is a small, two-edged knife used by surgeons to make small deep cuts or punctures. By disseminating weekly editions of the periodical, the medical profession could be kept apprised of current practice, offered a forum in which lectures and symposia could be listed far enough in advance that medical professionals would be afforded the means for ensuring continuing education, and maintaining state-of-the-art knowledge at a time when developments were occurring in medical academics, science, research, and clinical practice at a rapidly increasing rate. Wakley also intended for individual physicians, as well as those in academia or

research, to have a means of sharing case-related information they deemed as having scientific, historical, or social significance.

It was also Wakley's intent to create an avenue for professional disagreement. According to contemporary *Lancet* editor Richard Horton, "Thomas Wakley...aimed to combine publication of the best medical science in the world with a zeal to counter the forces that undermine the values of medicine, be they political, social, or commercial." In Wakley's own words, from the preface to the first edition of *The Lancet*, "We shall be assailed by much interested opposition. But, notwithstanding this, we shall fearlessly discharge our duty."

◼ PRIMARY SOURCE

PREFACE

It has long been a subject of surprise and regret, that in this extensive and intelligent community there has not hitherto existed a work that would convey to the Public, and to distant Practitioners as well as to Students in Medicine and Surgery, reports of the Metropolitan Hospital Lectures.

Having for a considerable time past observed the great and increasing inquiries for such information, in a department of science so pre-eminently useful, we have been induced to offer to public notice a work calculated, as we conceive, to supply in the most ample manner, whatever is valuable in these important branches of knowledge;—and as the Lectures of Sir Astley Cooper, on the theory and practice of Surgery, are probably the best of the kind delivered in Europe, we have commenced our undertaking with the introductory Address of that distinguished professor, given in the theatre of St. Thomas's Hospital on Wednesday evening last. The Course will be rendered complete in subsequent Numbers.

In addition to Lectures, we purpose giving under the head, Medical and Surgical Intelligence, a correct description of all the important Cases that may occur, whether in England or on any part of the civilized Continent.

Although it is not intended to give graphic representations with each Number, yet, we have made such arrangements with the most experienced surgical draughtsmen, as will enable us occasionally to do so, and in a manner, we trust, calculated to give universal satisfaction.

The great advantages derivable from information of this description, will, we hope, be sufficiently obvious to every one in the least degree conversant with medical knowledge; any arguments, therefore, to prove these unnecessary, and we content ourselves by merely showing in what directions their utility will be most active: To the Medical and Surgical Practitioners of this city, whose avocations prevent their personal attendance at the hospitals—To Country Practitioners, whose remoteness from the head quarters, as it were, of scientific knowledge, leaves them almost without the means of ascertaining its progress—To the numerous classes of Students, whether here or in distant universities—To Colonial Practitioners— And, finally, to every individual in these realms. Consequently, we shall exclude from our pages the semi-barbarous phraseology of the Schools, and adopt as its substitute, plain English diction. In this attempt, we are well aware that we shall be assailed by much *interested* opposition. But, notwithstanding this, we will fearlessly discharge our duty. We hope the age of *"Mental Delusion"* has passed, and that mystery and concealment will no longer be encouraged. Indeed, we trust that mystery and ignorance will shortly be considered synonymous. Ceremonies, and signs, have now lost their charms; hieroglyphics, and gilded serpents, their power to deceive. But for these, it would have been impossible to imagine how it has happened that medical and dietetical knowledge, of all others the most calculated to benefit Man, should have been by him the most neglected. He studies with the greatest attention and assiduity the constitutions of his horses and dogs, and learns all their peculiarities; whilst of the nature of his own he is wholly uninformed, and equally unskilled as regards his infant offspring. Yet, a little reflection and application would enable him to avert from himself and family half the constitutional disorders that afflict society; and in addition to these advantages, his acquirements in Medical learning wold furnish him with a test by which he could detect and expose the impositions of ignorant practitioners.

In conclusion—we respectfully observe, that our Columns will not be restricted to Medical intelligence, but on the contrary we shall be indefatigable in our exertions to render "The Lancet" a complete Chronicle of current Literature.

SIGNIFICANCE

The nineteenth and early twentieth centuries were times of rapid changes in the scientific and medical realms. Medical education was beginning to change, with the creation of more university- and hospital-affiliated schools. Medical journals began to proliferate, as the professional community sought to broaden and sharpen the accessible means of disseminating information regarding advances and new discoveries in the science of medicine. All formal reports in *The Lancet* were reviewed by a group of fellow scientists for accuracy, both in the method of collecting data or observations, and for the conclusions presented. This process initiated the peer-review concept that is still standard practice for reporting research results today.

By the middle of the nineteenth century, professional medical organizations were being created, both in the United States and around the world. With improved means of international travel (steamships and safer ocean-going vessels), it became more practical to create international medical congresses, where physicians met for lectures and conference series.

After the American Civil War (1861–1865), with a surge in immigration and the advancing industrial age, came epidemics of deadly infectious diseases, along with problems associated with unsanitary living and working conditions, creating a confluence of events that bespoke the need for a public health system in America. In order to monitor and advance the public health system, it was necessary to create a framework for it, in the form of a system of supporting scientific research laboratories.

Because the shipping industry was America's main venue for import and export of goods and commerce, and because the seaports were the means by which immigrants entered the country before the age of air travel, it was deemed necessary to establish a medical care and monitoring system, called the Marine Hospital Service (MHS). It was responsible for maintaining oversight of the health and well-being of the personnel involved in all aspects of the maritime business. Eventually, it was also given responsibility for ascertaining that passenger ships were not transporting epidemic diseases along with their human cargo. Initially, the only way to carry out that mission was to give each passenger a physical examination and quarantine all those who were visibly ill. Toward the end of the nineteenth century, the germ theory was becoming understood as the key to disease causation, treatment, and prevention. In 1887, the first scientific medical laboratory was opened on Staten Island in New York, and staffed by one scientist, named Joseph Kinyoun, who was an employee of the MHS. He referred to his facility as a "laboratory of hygiene," making a verbal link to the developing public health system in America.

In 1891, the laboratory was relocated to Washington, D.C. and in 1901, the MHS was reclassified in order to give it stature as a public health system; it was renamed the *Public Health and Marine Hospital Service (PH-MHS)*. The research arm of the PH-MHS incorporated new divisions of zoology, chemistry, bacteriology, and pharmacology. The early research program was formalized and given scientific stature and credibility, as it was allocated ongoing funding and tasked with the responsibility for clinical and scientific oversight of pharmaceutical product manufacturing facilities. In 1906, the Pure Food and Drugs Act mandated that the

Journal of the American Medical Association.

Editor: N. S. DAVIS, M.D., LL.D.

THE Official Organ of the American Medical Association. Published weekly in the place of the annual volume of Transactions that was formerly issued. It contains thirty-two pages of reading matter each week, distributed in the following departments: Original Matter; Editorials; Editorial Summary of Progress; Correspondence, Domestic and Foreign; Proceedings of Societies; Association News and Miscellany.

The JOURNAL has a wide circulation, going to all members of the Association and many subscribers in every State and Territory.

Subscription Price, Five Dollars Per Annum.

Address, Journal American Medical Association,

65 RANDOLPH STREET, CHICAGO, ILLINOIS.

The *Journal of the American Medical Association* was first issued on July 14, 1883. The journal began its 123rd year in 2006. AP/WIDE WORLD PHOTOS.

pharmaceutical industry be regulated, this function was also within the purview of the PH-MHS research laboratory facilities.

In 1912, the PH-MHS was again reorganized, and became what it now known as the Public Health Service (PHS), and its research program was again expanded to incorporate the effects of environmental pathogens on the human body, as well as noninfectious (acquired) diseases. In 1930, the laboratory of hygiene was officially renamed the National Institute of Health (NIH), and was afforded sufficient funding to inaugurate the American research education tradition of research and training fellowships and grants. After the end of World War II (1938–1941), there was an explosion in the medical specialty fields, and new research facilities were created to meet the growing knowledge demands. In 1948, the NIH's title was pluralized: it became the National Institutes of Health. By the end of the twentieth century, the NIH had incorporated twenty-seven unique centers and institutes. Its

programs continued to grow and expand, due in large measure to successful collaborations across the nation, and around the world.

The Lancet has been continuously published in excess of 180 years. Currently, over one hundred professional peer-reviewed journals report the latest findings from physicians and research institutions around the world. Research is published in many languages, although due in part to *The Lancet* tradition, English has become the most common and unifying language for reporting the latest news in medical research.

FURTHER RESOURCES

Books

Park, Peter, Mary Brydon-Miller, Budd Hall, and Ted Jackson, eds. *Voices of Change: Participatory Research in the United States and Canada.* Westport, Conn.: Bergin & Garvey, 1993.

Web sites

BBC News: Health. "Vast digital archive opens." <http://news.bbc.co.uk/1/hi/health/3162704.stm> (accessed January 24, 2006).

National Library of Medicine. "Founding of the American Medical Association." <http://www.ama-assn.org/ama/pub/category/12982.html> (accessed January 7, 2006).

National Library of Medicine. "History of Health Services Research Project." <http://www.nlm.nih.gov/hmd/nichsr/intro.html> (accessed January 7, 2006).

Head and Upper Body

Anatomical Prints of the Human Body with Natural Dimensions

Illustration

By: Francesco C. Antommarchi

Date: 1826

Source: British Library Images Online. *Planches anatomiques du corps humain executées d'après les dimensions naturelles, accompagnées d'un texte explicatif ... Publiées par le cte de Lasteyrie.* (Anatomical prints of the human body with natural dimensions). Record number 2076. Shelfmark 1899. h. 24. Page Folio Number 7, 1826.

About the Artist: Francesco C. Antommarchi was the last personal physician to Napoleon Bonaparte during his exile. He arrived on the island of St. Helena on September 10, 1819. Prior to that assignment, Antommarchi spent six years studying anatomy and physiology by dissecting cadavers. He collaborated extensively with the Florentine anatomist Paolo Mascagni, and the artist Antonio Serantoni, resulting in the production of anatomical wax figures that were to be used as teaching tools. There was a growing demand in medical education for the production and use of anatomically accurate, detailed drawings and models.

Upon Mascagni's death, his family entrusted Antommarchi with the final proofreading, editing, and publication of the series of accurate and finely detailed anatomical drawings. He brought them along with him on his journey to St. Helena to attend Napoleon. Possibly as a result of a number of public statements made by Antommarchi about the beauty and detail of the plates, or possibly as a result of his ownership-like actions, Mascagni's heirs severed their relationship with Antommarchi, and resumed ownership of the plates. They delayed publication of the drawings until some emerging advances in printing technology could be instituted.

When Napoleon died, Antommarchi achieved a measure of fame as a result of conducting his postmortem examination and pronouncing that the death had resulted from stomach cancer. This was an issue of considerable public and political speculation at the time. Antommarchi also created a plaster-cast death mask of Napoleon. Upon his return to Paris, Antommarchi was able to have three identical bronze castings of the mask made. Two of the masks have remained on display in a Paris hotel; Antommarchi donated the third to the people of New Orleans, Louisiana. Antommarchi pursued a series of different occupations after his return to Paris. In 1831, he assisted the Polish people in an uprising against the Russians. He fled to Paris to escape the czar's forces. In Paris, he came into possession of a bronze copy of the death mask, and made a series of plaster casts from it. He attempted to sell those casts by mail-order subscription. This was not well received by the French public, and Antommarchi came to believe that France was no longer suitable for him. He immigrated to the New World, and it was during his time in Louisiana that he donated the bronze death mask of Napoleon to the people of New Orleans in 1834. He lived in Mexico for a brief period, and was employed there as an itinerant physician. He then moved for the last time, and settled in Cuba, where he again worked as a physician. Antommarchi became quite adept at performing surgery for the removal of cataracts. He died in Cuba, of yellow fever, in 1838, at the age of 57.

INTRODUCTION

Three and a half centuries before Mascagni's seminal work in anatomy and physiology, Leonardo da Vinci had dramatically advanced the understanding of human anatomy and physiology through his studies of cadavers. He injected hot wax into the cadaver's arteries and veins to better visualize their structures. Paolo Mascagni had studied da Vinci's work, and he employed an updated version of his technique. Mascagni was extremely successful in achieving high levels of vascular definition with it. He had also perfected a procedure for instilling liquid mercury into lymphatic vessels; through his work he was able to demonstrate that the venous and lymphatic systems were anatomically independent.

After Napoleon's death in 1821, Antommarchi returned to Paris, declaring that among Napoleon's last wishes was a desire to have the plates (created by Mascagni) published. He contracted with a Parisian printer to produce a series of full-sized lithographs of the plates. He added some non-anatomical details to them, and published the series under the title *Planches anatomiques du corps humain, executées d'après les dimensions naturelles*, par le Doct. F. Antommarchi, publicées par le C. Lasteyrie, editeur. Mascagni's family was furious, and published a higher quality copper plate set of the original plates, entitled *Anatomia universa P. Mascagni Icones*. A unique characteristic of both sets was the exceedingly fine attention to detail, particularly to that of vascular structures, displayed; this was due to Mascagni's research, and his personal belief system, that vasculature was the transcendent feature of all plant and animal life.

Anatomical drawing had been gaining in both popularity and accuracy since at least the sixteenth century, when Belgian anatomist Andreas Vesalius (1514–1564) completed a series of drawings of partially dissected human beings who were all portrayed in attitudes of slightly bewildered self-contemplation. Over the next three hundred years, the anatomical drawings of flayed (literal translation of the vernacular term used: écorché) figures were shown in a variety of attitudes and poses, from playful to emotional to prayerful to seductive. Artists were able to achieve these effects by utilizing a system of ropes and pulleys with which to manipulate both the cadavers and their human models.

The historical anatomical atlases were intended to be the final statement in physiological accuracy, and to replace the need for cadaver dissection in order to study and understand human anatomy and physiology. At the same time, the atlases were intended as luxury items that reflected the status and wealth of their owners—they were priced so as to be prohibitively expensive to all but the wealthiest individuals. In the introductions to both Antommarchi's and Mascagni's books, there was indication that the accuracy of the drawings was such that dissection was now obsolete,

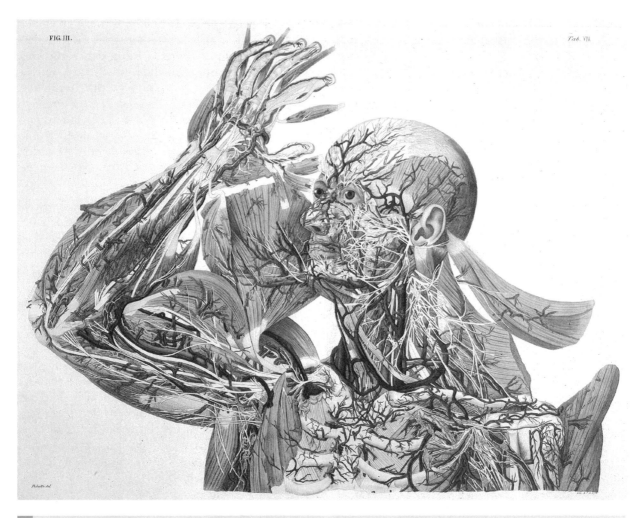

FIG. III.

Tab. VII.

PRIMARY SOURCE

Head and Upper Body: Anatomical Prints of the Human Body with Natural Dimensions. Francesco Antommarchi's drawing showing the head and upper body, part of a collection of anatomical illustrations hailed as detailed enough to render cadaver studies obsolete. BY PERMISSION OF THE BRITISH LIBRARY, 1899.H.24.

and anatomy could be studied without the squeamishness and disgust that accompanied cadaver dissection.

These two parallel atlases were the last major works of their type. This was largely due to the mores and social sensibilities of the time, rather than to the greatness of the works. By the start of the nineteenth century, the art of anatomical drawing from cadavers was becoming obsolete, and cadaver dissections had ceased to be a public event. Dissections came to be carried out in closed laboratory settings, rather than in large theaters, and were primarily for the benefit of students. Throughout the nineteenth century (and continuing to the present day), the science of medicine was fast becoming one of frequent and monumental discoveries; anatomy and biology were

at a crossroads of growing scholarly understanding, and the science of modern physiology was emerging.

PRIMARY SOURCE

HEAD AND UPPER BODY: ANATOMICAL PRINTS OF THE HUMAN BODY WITH NATURAL DIMENSIONS
See primary source image.

SIGNIFICANCE
Work done in the eighteenth century by the Dutch physician Hermann Boerhaave (1668–1738) and his student, Swiss research scientist Albrecht van Haller (1708–1777) was vitally important in developing the

modern science of physiology. They showed that physiology involved more than physical (iatrophysics) reactions or chemical reactions (iatrochemistry), and proposed an integrated model of physiology.

Claude Bernard (1813–1878), a French physiologist, was the nineteenth century's dominant animal physiology researcher and theoretician. He studied carbohydrate metabolism in humans, as well as the many functions of the human autonomic nervous system. His most significant contribution to the science of physiology was his postulate concerning homeostasis: it was his assertion that living organisms are never in a state of rest, but are perpetually undergoing dynamic shifts and changes in order to seek a state of internal equilibrium (homeostasis). It was Bernard's belief that the more successful the organism was at maintaining homeostasis, the healthier it would be.

Sir Charles Bell (1774–1842), a Scottish anatomist who also studied nervous system physiology in the nineteenth century, outlined the functions of the motor and sensory nerves. Another central figure was the French physiologist François Magendie (1783–1855). He detailed the functions of the spinal nerves and studied the mechanisms responsible for swallowing and regurgitation. Marie-Jean-Pierre Flourens (1794–1867), another French physiologist, studied the functions performed by the cerebellum. He was the first researcher to investigate the physiology underlying animal psychology. The German physiologist Peter Müller (1801–1858) postulated that perceptions were determined solely by the sensory organ receiving the sensory/electrophysiological impulse. Ernst Heinrich Weber (1795–1878), a German physiologist, was among the first to determine that the autonomic nervous system is comprised of two distinct nerve systems. He came to this conclusion as a result of his recognition that the heart is stimulated by two different types of nervous activity: one type decreases the heartbeat, while the other increases it. Weber also studied the mechanics of the perceptual processes.

On a microscopic level, the nineteenth century English scientist Robert Brown (1773–1858) was engaged in the study of vegetable cells (orchid epidermis); he was the first to name the cell nucleus, although many scientists had seen it and noted its presence following the discovery of the microscope. The German scientists Matthias Schleiden (1804–1881) and Theodor Schwann (1810–1882) did further research into cell physiology and were able to determine the central role played by the cell nucleus. They proposed cell theory in 1838, the central tenets of which were: all life forms are made from one or more cells;

cells arise only from other, pre-existing, cells; and the cell is the smallest form of life.

Friedrich Gustav Jakob Henle (1809–1885) expanded upon Schleiden's and Schwann's studies, and discovered the ubiquitous nature of cells: they are present in animals and plants, and can be found throughout the structure of the organism. Henle was a German pathologist, anatomist, and physician; his work united the fields of anatomy and biology, and greatly expanded both knowledge and interest in the growing field of physiology. During his early research, he published three anatomical monographs on new animal species; he published papers on the structure and development of hair, on the function and distribution of human epithelial cells, on the physiology and function of immune system-related secretions (mucous, pus, serous matter, etc.), and on the structure of the lymphatic system. Throughout his career, his overriding interests were in the studies of human physiology and pathology: it was his desire to create a compendium of texts that would present all current information in both areas. In 1846, Henle made an outstanding contribution to the world of science: he published the famed *Manual of Rational Pathology*, in which physiology and pathology were treated, for the first time, as two aspects of a single science, and disease was looked at in close relationship to physiology. He discovered and named many anatomical structures, among them Henle's fissure, the loop of Henle, Henle's tubules, Henle's spine, Henle's sheath, Hassall-Henle bodies, and Henle's ampulla.

Henle's second major contribution to the advancement of science took nearly twenty years to come to full fruition: he published the first installment of the *Handbook of Systematic Human Anatomy* in 1855, but the final volume was not published until 1873. The series of texts represented the totality of nineteenth century understanding of anatomy. It was acclaimed for its thoroughness and attention to minute detail as well as for the outstanding nature of its anatomical illustrations, which detailed the anatomy of structures from an almost microscopic level. Accurate anatomical drawing continues to be an integral part of medical science and physiology texts, and Mascagni's and Henle's work continue to stand as gold standards for accuracy and depth of detail.

FURTHER RESOURCES

Books

Porter, Roy. *The Greatest Benefit to Mankind.* New York: W. W. Norton, 1999.

Web sites

Obituaries Today. "Dr. Francesco Antommarchi, Napoleon's Doctor." <http://www.obituariestoday.com/Obituaries/

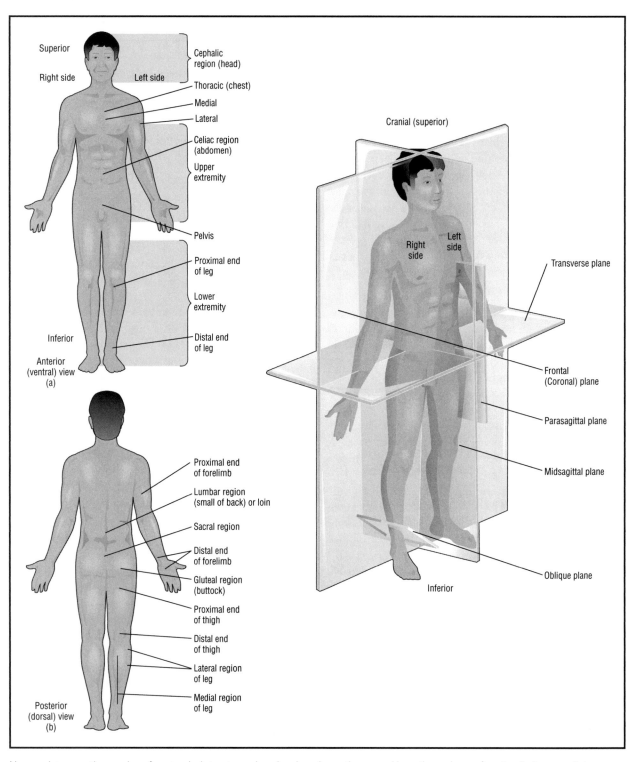

Nomenclature, or the naming of anatomical structures, has developed over the years. Here, three views of anatomical nomenclature are shown: the anterior (or ventral) view; the cranial (or superior) view; and the posterior (or dorsal) view. THE GALE GROUP.

ObitShow.cfm?Obituary_ID=29716&section=pin> (accessed October 19, 2005).

Doyne's Hall of Fame: Faces Behind Ophthalmic Eponyms. "Friedrich Gustav Jacob Henle." <http://www.

mrcophth.com/ophthalmologyhalloffame/henle.html> (accessed October 19, 2005).

UNSW Embryology: A History of Science. "The Beginnings of Modern Science: The Great Anatomists." <http://

embryology.med.unsw.edu.au/History/page2a.htm>
(accessed October 19, 2005).

Journal of the American Medical Association Archives. "Plate
from Planches Anatomiques Volume 286, Number 9,
September 5, 2001." <http://jama.ama-assn.org/cgi/
content/full/286/9/1008> (accessed October 19, 2005).

Rabies Vaccination in Pasteur's Clinic in Paris

Photograph

By: Laurent-Lucien Gsell

Date: 1887

Source: Wellcome Trust Medical Library.

About the Artist: Laurent-Lucien Gsell (1860–1944) was
an artist who painted images of the laboratories
and work of the French microbiologist Louis
Pasteur (1822–1895) on many occasions. This work
is a photograph of one of Gsell's lithographs by
F. Pirodon.

INTRODUCTION

Louis Pasteur had shown that vaccination against
anthrax worked in animals. He used a weakened, or
attenuated, form of a culture of the anthrax bacterium
as the vaccine and found it protected animals against
the disease, compared to control animals who had not
been vaccinated. In 1880, he decided to turn his attention to rabies, a viral infection that attacks the brain
and has a high mortality rate. Rabies could be transmitted to humans through the bite of a rabid animal
and was much feared. Pasteur showed that a vaccine
made from an attenuated form of the rabies virus could
protect dogs that had been bitten by rabid animals. He
hesitated, however, before trying his vaccine on
humans.

Pasteur's first human patient was a young boy
named Joseph Meister who was brought to him from
Alsace on July 6, 1885. Joseph had been bitten fourteen
times by a rabid dog on his hands, legs, and thighs.
Clearly, his life was in danger and Pasteur administered the first dose of vaccine the next day. He used the
dried-out spinal cord from a rabid rabbit as the source
of vaccine. The drying process allowed the virus to lose
much of its virulent character and helped allay safety
fears. The boy was given increasingly strong doses of
vaccine over the next twelve days and was soon able to
return to Alsace in good health, having developed no
symptoms of rabies, nor any ill effects from the
vaccination.

The painting shows a young boy being held by
his mother while one of Pasteur's associates, J. J.
Grancher, holds the syringe and gives the vaccination into his abdomen. Pasteur, in a cap, stands to
the doctor's right, with a letter in his hands. Behind
is a group of fashionably dressed lady observers and,
to the left, an Arab and a Russian patient in national
dress. The work was executed in 1886, a year in
which nearly 2,500 patients, drawn from all over
the world, came to Paris for Pasteur's rabies vaccination. The painting indicates how word of the
rabies treatment had spread rapidly through Paris
and beyond.

▮ PRIMARY SOURCE

RABIES VACCINATION IN PASTEUR'S CLINIC IN PARIS
See primary source image.

SIGNIFICANCE

The development of an effective rabies vaccine
was the final, and most dramatic, success of
Pasteur's long and distinguished career in medicine, chemistry, and microbiology. It established
the germ theory of disease, and vaccination in particular, within the practice of medicine. Today a
vaccine is still used to prevent rabies and it usually
is given after infection because it can take up to
four months for the virus to reach the brain. This
characteristic of the infection is unusual, but fortunate, since there is no cure for the brain infection
that rabies produces. Most other vaccines—for
polio and measles, for instance—are given before
infection takes place.

Vaccination exposes the body to a weakened
form of a pathogen (an organism that causes disease), and this exposure stimulates the immune system to produce antibodies against the pathogen.
Then, when the body is exposed to that pathogen
again, the body's immune system is already primed
to respond. In Pasteur's time, the sheer complexity
of the immune response was not appreciated. Now
much more is known, and the field of vaccines is
one of the most rapidly developing in medicine.
For many years, we have had vaccines against
important diseases, such as polio and tuberculosis.
Indeed, vaccination rid the world of the scourge of
smallpox.

PRIMARY SOURCE

Rabies Vaccination in Pasteur's Clinic in Paris. Lithograph by Laurent-Lucien Gsell showing an associate of Louis Pasteur vaccinating a boy against rabies in 1886. Pasteur stands to the right, holding a letter. WELLCOME LIBRARY, LONDON.

But, there is still much to be done in the fight against infectious diseases. There are still some significant gaps within the vaccine armory. For example, scientists have not yet produced an effective vaccine against AIDS, malaria, or hepatitis C. On the other hand, increased understanding of the immune system has led to the production of vaccines of ever increasing sophistication, such as DNA vaccines. There are also vaccines that can be used against some forms of cancer.

Pasteur's work on rabies led to the establishment of the now world-famous Pasteur Institute in Paris. The institute was funded through public contributions and was initially devoted to rabies vaccination. Since its launch in 1888, the institute has been home to many distinguished scientists, including several Nobel Prize winners.

FURTHER RESOURCES

Books

Dubos, René. *Pasteur and Modern Science.* Berlin: Springer-Verlag, 1988.

Web sites

Institut Pasteur. "Rabies." <http://www.pasteur.fr/recherche/rage/page_seule_english.html> (accessed November 1, 2005).

Pasteur Foundation. "Historic Relations with the United States." <http://www.pasteurfoundation.org/IP-USA.html> (accessed November 1, 2005).

Letter to Lord Chamberlain Hugo Radolinski

Rudolf Virchow and Cellular Pathology

Letter

By: Ruldolf Virchow (translated by Thor Yager, M.D.)

Date: January 1, 1888

Source: Clendening History of Medicine Library. University of Kansas Medical Center.

About the Author: Rudolf Virchow (1821–1902) was a pioneer in pathology and cell biology. He was the first to recognize leukemia, in 1845, and he also investigated thrombosis (blood clots), embolism, cancer, and inflammation. Born in Schivelbein in Prussia, Virchow was educated in medicine at the University of Berlin and took up a position at the Charité teaching hospital in that city. Virchow showed that cells came from other cells, rather than being spontaneously generated, and that diseases, such as cancer, originate within the cells of the body. He was a political liberal who used his influence to draw attention to public health issues such as infection and lack of sanitation.

INTRODUCTION

Rudolf Virchow addresses this letter to Hugo Radolinski, senior aide to Crown Prince Frederick III of Prussia. Radolinksi was an ally of Bismarck, the "Iron Chancellor" to whom Virchow was opposed. The crown prince, referred to here as "His Imperial Highness," had been ill for some time with a growth on his larynx and had been residing in the Italian seaport and health resort of San Remo since November 3, 1887. The printed materials Virchow refers to are pathology reports he had written on biopsy samples taken from the growth. His comments underline the difficulty of making a firm diagnosis of malignancy (cancer) in this case.

The tissue had been taken from the larynx by Dr. Morell Mackenzie who was later knighted by Queen Victoria for his services to the crown prince (who was her son-in-law, having married Victoria, her eldest child). The tumor was thought, by some of his doctors, to be cancerous. However, Virchow was unconvinced

Rudolph Virchow studies a specimen by looking at it through a magnifying glass. ©BETTMANN/CORBIS.

of the diagnosis. The prince, for his part, had refused radical surgery, believing his prognosis to be favorable. His father died on March 10, 1888, and the crown prince became kaiser, returning immediately to Berlin. However, his condition deteriorated and he died on June 15 of that year. A postmortem examination revealed destruction of the larynx by cancer and secondary disease in the lymph glands. Three of Virchow's four reports on the pathology of the tumor were translated into English and published in the journals *The Lancet* and *The British Medical Journal* in late 1887 and early 1888.

▪ PRIMARY SOURCE

Berlin, 1 January 1888

Your Highness,

Today I wanted to express my personal thanks & good wishes for the New Year. Since I missed you at home, I don't want to fail to make up for it in writing.

At the same time, I left behind an envelope with a few small printed materials with the door-keeper, which could

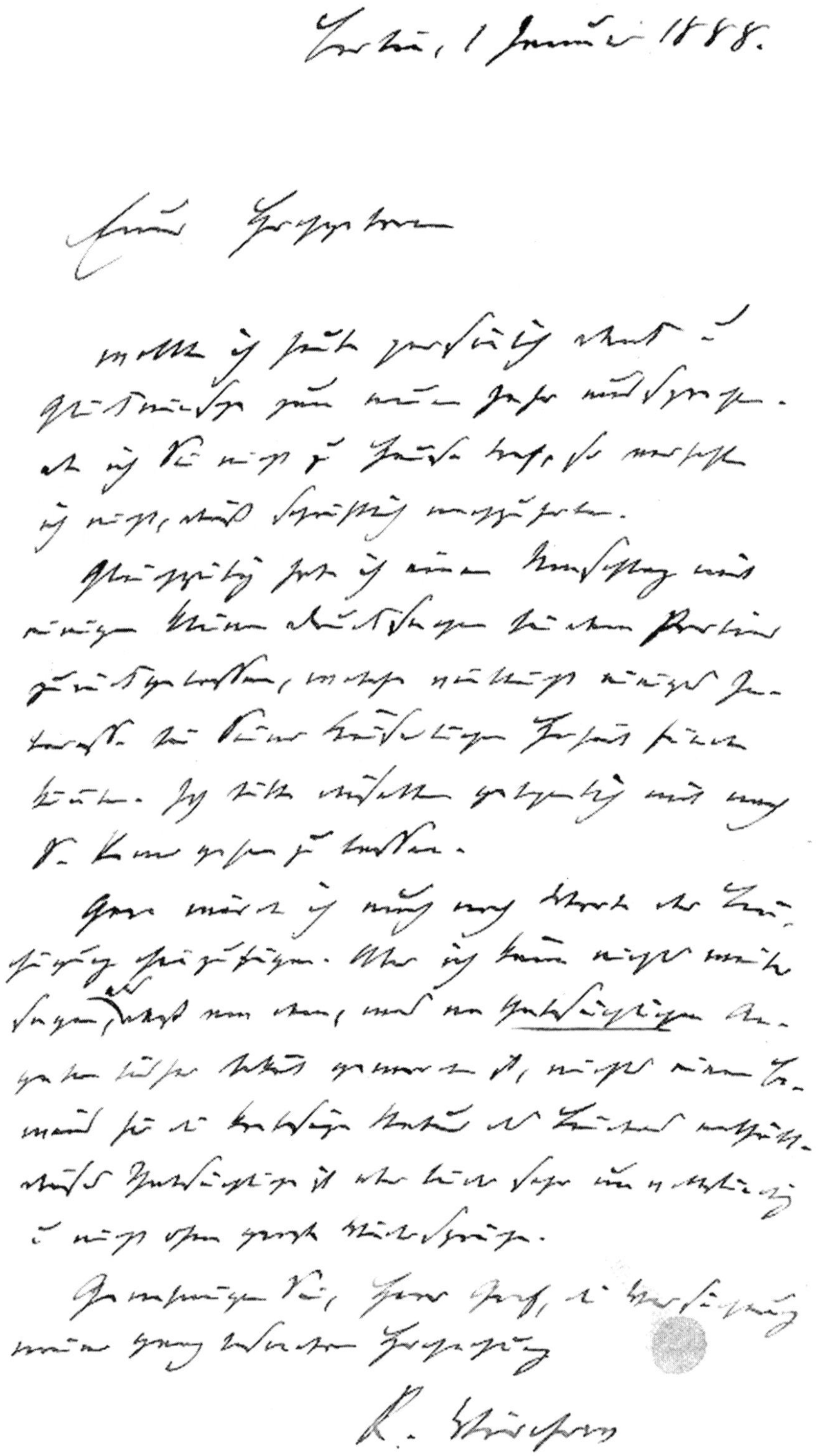

Berlin, 1 Januar 1888.

R. Virchow

PRIMARY SOURCE

Letter to Lord Chamberlain Hugo Radolinski. Handwritten letter, dated January 1, 1888, from Rudolf Virchow to Lord Chamberlain Hugo Radolinski in which Virchow states that although the Crown Prince Frederick III of Prussia's tumor appeared not to be cancerous, the evidence was incomplete. Frederick III died of cancer the same year. COURTESY OF THE CLENDENING HISTORY OF MEDICINE LIBRARY, UNIVERSITY OF KANSAS MEDICAL CENTER.

perhaps be of some interest to His Imperial Highness. I ask the materials be permitted to be taken along to S. Remo at some time.

I would also like to add some words of reassurance. However, I can not say anymore than what in fact other statements have already made known, that so far the evidence does not prove the cancerous nature of the growth. This finding is unfortunately very incomplete & not without great contradictions.

Dear Count, please accept the assurance of my very special high esteem.

R. Virchow

PRIMARY SOURCE

LETTER TO LORD CHAMBERLAIN HUGO RADOLINSKI
See primary source image.

SIGNIFICANCE

Virchow had written a major 1,800-word text on cancer, *Die Krankhalten Geschwülste* (The Tumor Sickness). He also was experienced in the microscopic examination of biopsy material, which been an established method of clinical investigation since the 1830s. He knew that findings could often be misleading because the biopsy sampling could have missed the malignant part of the tumor. In other words, even if the specimen looked normal, there still was no guarantee that the tumor was, in fact, benign.

The German press was highly critical of Dr. Morell Mackenzie, the attending physician, and Virchow, believing that they had misdiagnosed and mishandled Crown Prince Frederick's illness. Mackenzie had been brought over to England to treat the prince at the instigation of his wife, Crown Princess Victoria. Prior to the date of this letter, Virchow had examined biopsies of growths on the prince's larynx that Mackenzie had removed and declared them cancer-free, although, as he points out here, the findings were not definitive. As the prince's illness worsened, Mackenzie was demoted and another physician carried out an emergency tracheotomy. In February 1888, Mackenzie wrote in *The Lancet* that cancer had still not been officially diagnosed in the prince's case. He also felt that the tracheotomy had not been well performed. The prince certainly suffered significant complications from the process and was not well enough to attend his father's funeral. Indeed, the treatment may well have hastened his death. After the prince's death, the German press severely criticized Princess Victoria for having allowed a British physician to treat her husband.

Frederick was succeeded by his son, Wilhelm II, who led Germany into World War I. Had Frederick lived longer, his experience in diplomacy might have averted this catastrophic war and saved millions of lives. But, would he have survived, if Virchow and his other physicians had made a diagnosis of cancer of the larynx earlier? It seems unlikely. In the late nineteenth century, major surgery, such as removal of the larynx, often resulted in the patient's death, either during the procedure or shortly thereafter.

FURTHER RESOURCES
Books
Rather, Lelland J. *A Commentary on the Medical Writings of Rudolf Virchow*. San Francisco: Norman Publishing, 1990.

Web sites
American Academy of Otolarynology Virtual Museum. "Famous Figures: Morell Mackenzie." <http://www.entnet.org/museum/mackenzie.cfm?renderforprint=1> (accessed October 29, 2005).

Hand with Ring

X Rays Discovered by Accident

Photograph

By: Wilhelm Conrad Roentgen

Date: December 22, 1895

Source: Wellcome Trust Medical Library.

About the Photographer: Wilhelm Roentgen (1845–1923) was a German experimental physicist who was educated at Zurich Polytechnic and went on to teach at several universities in Germany. While he was professor of physics at Würzburg, he discovered x rays in 1895. In 1901, he was awarded the first Nobel Prize in physics for this discovery.

INTRODUCTION

It is widely believed that this photograph shows the hand of Roentgen's wife, complete with ring. However, this is an image created by x rays rather than visible light. In 1895, Roentgen had discovered what he described as *eine neuer art von strahlen* (a new kind of ray) completely by accident. He was, at the time, working on the conduction of electricity in gases using a device called a Crookes tube. He noticed that something emitted from the tube created a strange glow on a card coated with a fluorescent chemical.

Quickly, he proceeded to investigate the properties of this new form of radiation, which he called x rays. He found that they traveled in straight lines and could pass through objects that were impervious to light. In fact, x rays penetrate the human body to a greater or lesser extent depending upon tissue density. They pass through skin, fat, blood, and muscle more easily than through bone. So, as the picture here shows, the bones cast a shadow. X-ray images can be captured on a fluorescent screen or upon film. Their ability to help physicians see inside the body was quickly realized by Roentgen and others. As early as March 1896, a doctor in Chicago described x-ray plates showing "bones of the hand and leg and a few coins and keys in a pocketbook."

Roentgen subsequently investigated other properties of x rays. He believed they were a source of electromagnetic radiation, like light and ultraviolet radiation but with a much shorter wavelength. They were produced in the Crookes tube when the electrons emitted from the tube's cathode struck the edge of the tube. Today, x rays are produced when a stream of electrons strikes a heavy metal target.

■ PRIMARY SOURCE

HAND WITH RING

See primary source image.

SIGNIFICANCE

Roentgen's discovery of x rays is a famous example of serendipity—lucky chance—in science. He was not looking for a new form of radiation but when he found it, he dedicated himself to understanding its nature, properties, and applications. Since their discovery, x rays have found increasing use in medicine—from diagnosing broken bones to screening for tuberculosis (TB) and breast cancer. Indeed, one of the earliest applications of x rays was to revolutionize the diagnosis of TB. Before antibiotics, TB was treated by rest in a sanatorium and it was widely thought that early diagnosis was essential if this treatment was to have a good outcome. Using x rays to look for a "shadow" on the lung proved far easier than the traditional method of TB diagnosis—listening for supposedly characteristic chest sounds.

Today, computed tomography (CT) scans are a more sophisticated version of the traditional x ray. To create a CT scan, a series of x-ray images taken from different angles are analyzed by a computer to produce

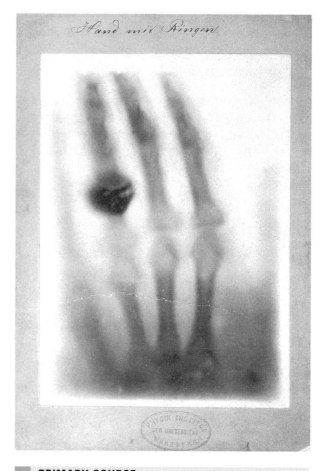

■ PRIMARY SOURCE

Hand with Ring. An early x ray made by German physicist Wilhelm Roentgen in 1895, presumably of his wife's hand. WELLCOME LIBRARY, LONDON.

a cross-sectional picture of the part of the body under examination. CT scans produce more detailed imaging, and they are increasingly used in planning more precise surgeries.

X rays are high-energy radiation and, as such, they can be damaging to healthy tissue with excessive exposure. After Roentgen's discovery, it was soon noted that prolonged exposure to x rays would burn the skin. Many patients and health workers suffered ill effects because the early x-ray machines were used without protection. The damaging effects of x rays, however, were used to advantage as well. Within a year of Roentgen's discovery, a doctor in Vienna had applied x rays to burn a mole off a patient's skin. Today, x rays are still used in one form of radiotherapy for cancer. A beam of x rays, narrowly focused, can destroy tumor tissues. The more precise the targeting of the x rays, the more healthy surrounding tissue is spared their damaging effects.

The British father and son team William (1862–1942) and Lawrence (1890–1971) Bragg used x rays to investigate the three-dimensional structure of molecules and developed a technique known as x-ray crystallography. The Braggs found that x rays are deflected by the electrons in a crystal, creating a pattern on film that is related to the structure of the crystal. X-ray crystallography was used to determine the structure of DNA in 1953, a discovery that lies at the heart of modern biology and genetics. Determining the structure of biological molecules by x-ray crystallography also is increasingly important in drug discovery.

FURTHER RESOURCES
Books

Lock, Stephen, John M. Last, and George Dunea, eds. *The Oxford Illustrated Companion to Medicine.* Oxford: Oxford University Press, 2001.

Porter, Roy, ed. *Cambridge Illustrated History of Medicine.* Cambridge: Cambridge University Press, 1996.

This Day Relenting God

Cause of Malaria Identified

Poem

By: Ronald Ross

Date: 1923

Source: Ronald Ross. Memoirs with a Full Account of the Great Malaria Problem and Its Solution. [London]: John Murray, 1923.

About the Author: Sir Ronald Ross (1857–1932) studied medicine in London before joining the Indian Medical Service in 1881. Throughout his career he focused with a single-minded intensity on the prevention of malaria, and in 1897 discovered the species of mosquito that spreads the disease. His work won him a Nobel Prize in 1902, and he was knighted in 1911. Ross spent the remainder of his life conducting studies in the malarial centers of the world, and forming organizations to combat malaria. He directed the Ross Institute and Hospital for Tropical Diseases, established in his honor in 1926, until his death in 1932. In addition to his medical work, Ross was an acclaimed poet.

INTRODUCTION

Malaria is an ancient killer. It is frequently described in the writings of the Greeks and Romans.

The word itself is Latin, from the Roman word for "bad air," after the fine mist once supposed to cause it.

For hundreds of years, no one knew exactly what caused malaria and, therefore, no one could stop it. In 1880, Charles-Louis-Alphonse Laveran, a French military physician serving in Algeria, identified the plasmodium parasite in the blood of a sick artilleryman. Seventeen years later in India, Captain Ronald Ross extracted a cyst from a dissected female *Anopheles* mosquito and identified malaria as an insect-borne disease.

Malaria is not a single disease in humans. It is a family of four different diseases caused by four different parasites. The parasites are similar in appearance, all belonging to the genus *Plasmodia*. The fevers caused by these four organisms vary enough in their clinical presentations that different labels evolved for their symptoms, even before microbiologists were able to separate them in 1900.

Plasmodium falciparum causes the most severe form of malaria. The victim suffers from intermittent high fevers, with a severe retro-orbital headache, parched throat, and diffuse body aches. The body can be wracked with abdominal cramping, diarrhea, and vomiting. The liver and spleen become enlarged, and if hepatic malfunction reaches a critical level, jaundice may follow. When the parasite reaches a high enough density in the body, it can cause deadly effects by clogging small arteries in the brain and kidneys. The coma of cerebral malaria often comes just before death. Mortality from *falciparum* malaria can range from 20 to 40 percent in untreated victims.

Plasmodium vivax causes a more benign disease. It can kill up to 5 percent of its victims, although mortality is usually lower. Like *falciparum*, it causes a high fever, with skull-splitting headache and icy pains throughout the bones. The body undergoes a change in the thermostat that regulates internal temperature. Sensing incorrectly that the body's temperature is too low, the hypothalamus orders shivering in order to increase the temperature. This creates chills that are so severe that a victim's teeth chatter as the bed shakes.

Both *vivax* and *falciparum* can cause chronic illness in which the victim suffers repeated infection with the parasite. Since red blood cells are destroyed in a malaria attack, the person suffering from repeated attacks becomes anemic, weak, and tired. Malaria patients typically lack the energy for a full workload, in school or on the job. During the reduced immune state of pregnancy, malaria may flare and kill the fetus, mother, or both. *Ovale* and *malariae* are unpleasant but not as deadly as the other two malarial strains.

Mosquitoes can transmit a number of potentially deadly diseases including malaria and the West Nile virus. Mosquito larvae are shown here in water found in a drainage ditch in Florida in 2003. AP/WIDE WORLD PHOTOS.

■ PRIMARY SOURCE

This day relenting God
Hath placed within my hand
A wondrous thing; and God
Be praised. At his command,
Seeking his secret deeds
With tears and toiling breath,
I find thy cunning seeds,
O million-murdering Death.
I know this little thing
A myriad men will save,
O Death, where is thy sting?
Thy victory, O Grave?

SIGNIFICANCE

Malaria has not been eradicated despite Ross's identification of its cause. It is still present in 102 countries and sickens 500 million people per year. In 2005 it was the number-one killer in the world, with HIV/AIDS in second place. Malaria kills three to five million people a year, or about one every 12 seconds, with 90 percent of the deaths occurring in sub-Saharan Africa.

It was once believed that malaria could be eradicated. The draining of marshlands and the use of the pesticide DDT dramatically reduced the six million cases a year that the United States experienced in the first decades of the twentieth century. By 1960, the World Health Organization (WHO) had established antimalarial policies in 100 nations and was confident that the disease could be eradicated.

A number of sociopolitical factors, however, combined to slow the advance of medicine. People became complacent about malaria and public health programs were allowed to falter and lapse. Without outside aid, poor nations did not have the money for malarial control methods. Additionally, countries torn by war focused resources on fighting, not on medical care. Meanwhile, malarial microbes evolved in response to drugs, while the ready availability of air travel brought new strains into areas that lacked immunity to them. Global warming is expected to bring malaria back to northern Europe, and it never completely left southern Europe or the United States. WHO now forecasts a 16 percent growth rate in the disease per year.

FURTHER RESOURCES

Books

Desowitz, Robert S. *The Malaria Capers: More Tales of Parasites and People, Research and Reality.* New York: W. W. Norton, 1993.

Humphreys, Margaret. *Malaria: Poverty, Race, and Public Health in the United States.* Baltimore: Johns Hopkins University Press, 2001.

Robert Koch Identifies the Bacteria that Cause Anthrax, Tuberculosis, and Cholera

Presentation Speech for the Nobel Prize in Physiology or Medicine, 1905

Speech

By: K. A. H. Mörner

Date: December 10, 1905

Source: *Nobel Lectures, Physiology or Medicine 1901–1921.* Amsterdam: Elsevier, 1967. Available online at <http://nobelprize.org/medicine/laureates/1905/press.html> (accessed September 10, 2005).

About the Author: Count K. A. H. Mörner was a chemist, professor, and Rector of the Royal Caroline Institute in Stockholm, Sweden, in 1905 when he presented the Nobel Prize in Medicine or Physiology to Robert Koch.

INTRODUCTION

Along with Louis Pasteur, Robert Koch is regarded as being one of the two founders of bacteriology (the study of bacteria).

It was Koch's training as a physician that led to his seminal research. In 1872, Koch became the District Medical Health Officer in Wollstem, Germany. There, he began to investigate the cause of anthrax. Previous research by Casmir-Joseph Davaine had shown that the occurrence of anthrax in sheep was associated with the appearance of rod-like bodies in the blood.

Koch was able to grow the bodies on a growth medium, now known as *Bacillus anthracis*, demonstrating that they were living organisms. Furthermore, his light microscopy observations of oval translucent bodies inside the organisms represented one of the earliest

descriptions of the dormant spore of the anthrax bacillus (which, in September 2001, became infamous in the United States). Later research by Koch showed that the spores could cause the disease even after being kept in a dried state for years. This work laid the foundation for unraveling the life cycle of anthrax bacillus.

As part of his microscopy studies of bacteria, Koch demonstrated the usefulness of stains such as methyl violet in more definitively revealing the presence of bacteria. This technique, along with his postulates, was crucial in allowing Koch to implicate a bacillus later dubbed *Mycobacterium tuberculosis*, as the cause of tuberculosis in 1882.

Koch also investigated an outbreak of cholera in Egypt, and a later Indian outbreak, where his research implicated a comma-shaped bacillus as the cause of the disease. Future investigators confirmed that this bacterium, *Vibrio cholerae*, was, indeed, the cause of cholera. Koch demonstrated that the microbe could be transmitted from person to person via contaminated drinking water, food, and clothing.

PRIMARY SOURCE

Your Majesty, Your Royal Highnesses, Ladies and Gentlemen.

The Staff of the Royal Caroline Institute takes great pleasure in giving this year's Nobel Prize for Medicine to the man who takes precedence among those now alive as a pioneer in bacteriological research, the prize being awarded to Geheimrat Robert Koch for his work and discoveries concerning tuberculosis.

. . . To make Koch's significance in the development of bacteriology clear, one must take a look at the situation with which Koch was confronted when he made his appearance. Pasteur had indeed already published by then his epochmaking work, which laid the foundations of bacteriology, and medical art had already gathered in one very beneficial fruit which stemmed from this work, namely the antiseptic method of treating wounds proposed by Lister. However, the trail was yet to be blazed, which bacteriological research has followed with such success during recent decades, to discover the causes of individual diseases and to look for the means of combating them. Koch was a pioneer in this.

For two diseases namely anthrax and typhus recurrens in which micro-organisms of a particularly characteristic appearance were relatively easy to demonstrate, it was agreed that the latter were the causes of these diseases. Otherwise the causal relationship between bacteria and diseases was obscure. It is true that there were good grounds for *supposing* that certain other diseases were caused by micro-organisms. But detailed knowledge concerning this was lacking, and experimental findings were very divergent. So, for instance, it was not established whether normal healthy organs contained bacterial germs. This was certainly contested by various prominent investigators, but on the other hand this view was defended by other also prominent authors. Then the question still remained open of whether bacteria observed in a disease were also its cause, or whether their development should rather be considered a result of the pathological process. In addition, in studying one and the same type of disease various investigators looked in vain for bacteria in the organism, while others, however, found them. Moreover, bacteria, which various investigators had observed in a particular disease, were often of a different appearance, so that there was reason for doubting that they were the specific and genuine cause of the disease. On the other hand, in widely differing types of disease, bacteria were met with which, as far as was known, were of one and the same kind, and this gave still more cause for adopting a position of doubt with regard to the causal relationship between these bacteria and the pathological process. It was indeed difficult to imagine that the bacteria discovered had to be regarded as the essential causes of disease, since it looked partly as if the same disease could be caused by different bacteria, and partly as if the same bacteria could produce different diseases. It was easier to suppose that the bacteria all had the property of facilitating the development of the disease by exercising an influence on the organism. The uncertainty was that much greater since the experiments which were carried out often could not demonstrate whether a real bacterial invasion of the organism had taken place.

In 1876 Koch entered the field of bacteriological research with an investigation of anthrax, and two years later he produced his classical investigations into diseases from wound infections. With the views set out there and the way he formulated the questions, he had a fundamental effect on the further development of bacteriology, and the ideas he expressed there recur as a leading motive in his subsequent research and form the foundation of modern bacteriology, as they do of the axioms of hygiene which are derived from it.

He stressed that, if bacteria caused a disease, then they must always be demonstrable in it, and they should develop in a way such that this would account for the pathological process.

He further stressed that the capacity to produce disease could not be a general property of bacteria or one common to them all. On the contrary it should be expected in this respect to find specific properties distinguishing individual bacteria. Even if they resemble other bacteria in their form, etc., they must still be different from one another by virtue of this biological property: in other words, every disease must have its special bacterium, and to combat the

disease, it would be necessary to look for clues in the biology of the bacterium. Koch therefore not only set himself the task of examining the problem of whether diseases were caused by bacteria, but also endeavoured to discover the special micro-organisms of the particular diseases and to get to know more about them: this was a problem which, in the circumstances then prevailing, seemed to offer very little hope of being solved. In the way Koch solved this problem he was just as much, if not more, of a pioneer, then he already was in the abovementioned precision which he had given to the formulation of the problem.

To start with, developing a general methodology is as valuable as finding the correct technique for every special case. Koch's genius has blazed new trails in this respect and has given present-day research its form. To give a detailed description of this is beyond the scope of this account. I only want to mention that he had moreover already given a significant development to techniques in staining and microscopic investigation as well as in the field of experiment in his earliest work. Shortly after this he produced the important method, which is still generally the usual one, of spreading the material under investigation in a solid nutrient medium to allow each individual among the micro-organisms present to develop into a fixed colony, from which it is possible, in further research, to go on to obtain what is known as a pure culture.

Shortly after the publication of his investigations into diseases from wound infections Koch was appointed to the new Institution, the "Gesundheitsamt" (Department of Health), in Berlin. There he started work on some of the most important human diseases, namely, tuberculosis, diphtheria and typhus. He worked on the former one himself. The two latter investigations he left to his first two pupils and assistants, Loeffler and Gaffky. For all three diseases the specific bacteria were discovered and studied in detail. . . .

Through the perfection he gave to methods of culturing and identifying micro-organisms, he has been able to carry out his work with regard to disinfectants and methods of disinfection so important for practical hygiene, and advice concerning the early detection and combating of certain epidemic diseases such as cholera, typhus and malaria.

Now I move over to a brief account of the series of investigations which is the object of the present award.

The idea that tuberculosis is infectious goes back a long way to Morgagni. Already before Koch had started his investigations into this disease, it had been possible to show that tuberculosis may be inoculated into animals. It was not, however, proved that it was caused by a micro-organism, and such an interpretation was contested by very distinguished investigators.

Koch made his first communication concerning his research on tuberculosis in a lecture given on March 24, 1882 to the Physiological Society of Berlin. This lecture

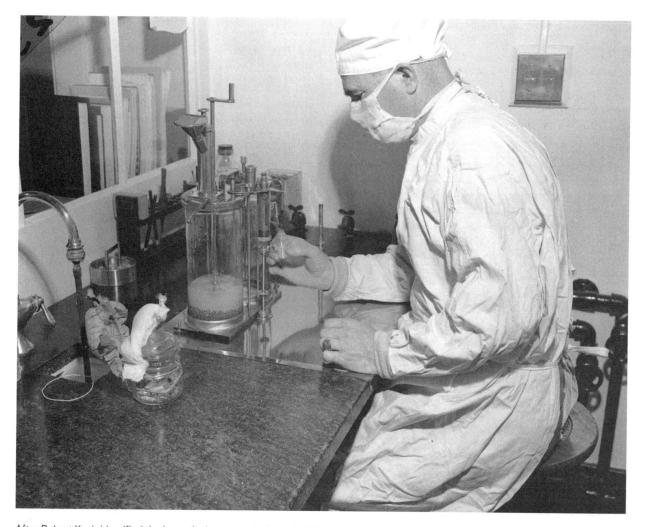

After Robert Koch identified the bacteria that caused tuberculosis in the 1880s, scientists were able to create a vaccine to prevent the disease. Here, a technician fills a vial of vaccine at a New York lab in the 1940s. AP/WIDE WORLD PHOTOS.

covers scarcely two pages of print, yet in it are given the proofs of the discovery of the tubercle bacillus and the description of its chief characteristics. The method for staining it in the affected tissue is described there, its constant occurrence in tuberculous processes in man and beast is mentioned, the procedure for producing pure cultures of it is described, and information is given concerning typical and positive results of inoculating the bacillus in animals. It was emphasized there, in addition, that the bacillus is dependent on the living organism for its development and multiplication, and that hence tuberculous infection is derived primarily from the expectorations of consumptives, and that it can probably also be caused by cattle suffering from "pearl disease." . . .

Seldom has an investigator been able to comprehend in advance with such clear-sightedness a new, unbroken field of investigation, and seldom has someone succeeded

in working on it with the brilliance and success with which Robert Koch has done this. Seldom have so many discoveries of such decisive significance to humanity stemmed from the activity of a single man, as is the case with him. . . .

Geheimrat Robert Koch. In announcing that the Staff of Professors of the Royal Caroline Institute has awarded you this year's Nobel Prize in Medicine for your work and discoveries concerning tuberculosis, I bring you the Staff's homage. . . .

By your pioneering research you have found out the bacteriology of tuberculosis, and written your name for ever in the annals of medicine.

SIGNIFICANCE

Koch's legacy lies in establishing rigorous scientific methods to examine samples, identify the presence of microorganisms, and implicate those bacteria as the cause of a particular disease. His training as a physician and his expertise as a researcher were perfectly suited to the task.

Koch built upon the work of Louis Pasteur, who showed that disease-causing microbes could potentially be grown in cultures outside of the body. Koch perfected what came to be known as the pure culture technique.

Another key achievement was Koch's formulation of a series of rules, or postulates, which, if achieved, were definitive proof of an organism's role in a disease. Koch's postulates stated that an organism was the cause of a disease if: It was always recoverable in every instance of the disease; When obtained from the body, the organism could be maintained in a pure culture for at least several generations; The disease could be reproduced in experimental animals by the introduction of a sample of a pure culture that had not been directly obtained from a disease sample; The organism could be recovered from the sick animal and re-established in pure culture.

While viruses were subsequently found to deviate from these rules, Koch's postulates have proven remarkably adept at pinpointing the cause of diseases, and in guiding the search for cures. By 1900, only a few decades after Koch had developed these research methodologies, twenty-one microorganisms had been identified as the cause of twenty-one different diseases.

FURTHER RESOURCES

Books

Brock, Thomas. *Robert Koch: A Life in Medicine and Bacteriology.* Washington, D.C.: American Society for Microbiology, 2000.

Tracy, Kathleen. *Robert Koch and the Study of Anthrax.* Hockessin, Del.: Mitchell Lane Publishers, 2004.

Web sites

The Nobel Foundation. "The Nobel Prize in Physiology or Medicine, 1905." <http://nobelprize.org/medicine/laureates/1905/index.html> (accessed October 11, 2005).

The Internal Secretion of the Pancreas

Insulin Extracted to Treat Diabetes

Journal article

By: Frederick Grant Banting and Charles Herbert Best.

Date: February 1922

Source: *Journal of Laboratory and Clinical Medicine* 7 (February 1922): 256–271.

About the Author: Canadian scientist Frederick Grant Banting (1891–1941) discovered insulin, along with his colleague Charles Herbert Best (1899–1978). Banting was born in Ontario, Canada, and earned his medical degree and surgical certification from the University of Toronto. Banting began to conduct experiments on the pancreas in the laboratory of a colleague, John Macleod, in 1921. Best, then a graduate student, became Banting's assistant, and the two scientists isolated insulin during the summer of 1921. The Nobel Prize was awarded to Banting and Macleod in 1923 for the discovery of insulin. Banting shared half of his prize with Charles Best, who earned doctorate degrees in both medicine and physiology. Best became a professor of physiology at the University of Toronto, where his further accomplishments included isolating heparin, an anti-coagulant drug.

INTRODUCTION

Insulin is a hormone secreted by the beta cells of the islets of Langerhans (specific groups of cells in the pancreas) as a response to increased glucose (sugar) levels in the blood stream. It promotes the entry of glucose into cells and a drop in blood glucose levels. When the body does not make enough insulin, or when it has difficulty using the insulin that it does make, elevated blood sugar (hyperglycemia) and excess sugar in urine (glycosuria) result—both characteristics of the disease called diabetes mellitus.

Canadian scientists Frederick Grant Banting and Charles Herbert Best were the first to obtain—from extracts of pancreas—a preparation of insulin that could serve to replace a deficiency of the hormone in the human body. In their article, "The Internal Secretion of the Pancreas," published in 1922, they described the successful results of their experiment to treat diabetes in dogs.

Previously, in 1889, scientists had demonstrated the importance of the pancreas in carbohydrate metabolism. They removed the entire pancreas of a dog and observed all the symptoms of severe diabetes in that animal. Subsequently, physiologists and clinicians tried to obtain an internal secretion from the pancreas, now known as insulin, which would be of value in the treatment of diabetes mellitus.

Many researchers tried various forms of pancreatic extracts, using water, saline, alcohol, and glycerin. The extracts obtained were administered by mouth, subcutaneously (injected just beneath the skin), intravenously,

In 1921, Charles Best (left) and Frederick Banting were able to keep a diabetic dog alive using insulin. ©BETTMANN/CORBIS.

or by rectum. These attempts all failed, presumably because the insulin in these extracts was destroyed by trypsin, the proteolytic enzyme of the pancreas found in the digestive juice. Researchers did not know about the action of trypsin on insulin at the time these experiments were carried out.

In 1920, Frederick Banting visited the University of Toronto to speak to John Macleod, the newly appointed head of the department of physiology. Macleod had studied glucose metabolism and diabetes and Banting had a new idea on how to find not only the cause, but also a treatment for the so-called "sugar disease."

While reading the article "The Relation of the Islets of Langerhans to Diabetes, with Special Reference to Cases of Pancreatic Lithiasis" by Moses Barron, Banting had an inspired idea. He suspected that the pancreas's digestive juice was destroying the islets of Langerhans's hormone before it could be isolated. If he could stop the pancreas from destroying the islets, he should be able to isolate insulin. He presented this idea to Macleod, who at first scoffed at it. Banting badgered him until finally Macleod gave him lab space and ten experimental dogs.

On April 14, 1921, Banting began working on this idea in the Physiological Laboratory of the University of Toronto. Professor Macleod allotted him Dr. Charles Best as an associate. The first step was to tie the pancreatic ducts in a number of dogs. At the end of seven weeks these dogs were chloroformed. The pancreas of each dog was removed and all were found to be without trypsin-producing cells. This material was cut into small pieces, ground with sand, and extracted with normal saline. This extract was tested on a dog rendered diabetic by the removal of the pancreas. Following the intravenous injections, the blood sugar of the diabetic dogs was reduced to a normal or subnormal level, and the urine became sugar-free. There was a marked improvement in the general clinical condition of the dogs—they became stronger and more lively, their wounds healed, and their lives were undoubtedly prolonged. Insulin had been isolated.

However, the extract was still impure and could not be injected into humans. In order to obtain a pure insulin extract, J. B. Collip, a biochemist, was brought on board. With his help, the first human patient, Leonard Thompson, was treated with the purified insulin extract in January 1922. The trial resulted in the well-documented revival of the young fourteen-year-old diabetic.

Banting's involvement in the experimental work was less evident during the winter and spring of 1922. However, he did treat diabetic patients, as insulin became more readily available. Sometime in April, with the help of Dr. Joseph Gilchrist and the support of the Department of Soldiers' Civil Reestablishment, Banting established a diabetic clinic at the Christie Street Hospital. He also opened his own practice at 160 Bloor Street West to treat private patients. One of these patients, Jim Havens of Rochester, became the first American citizen to be injected with insulin. In late May, after an agreement was reached with Eli Lilly & Company to distribute insulin on a larger scale, the research entered the clinical testing phase.

Banting and Macleod were awarded the 1923 Nobel Prize in Physiology or Medicine for the discovery of insulin, a prize they later shared with Best and Collip.

PRIMARY SOURCE

The hypothesis underlying this series of experiments was first formulated by one of us in November 1920, while reading an article dealing with the relation of the isles of Langerhans to diabetes. From the passage in this article, which gives a résumé of degenerative changes in the acini of the pancreas following ligation of the ducts, the idea presented itself that since the acinous, but not the islet tissue, degenerates after this operation, advantage might be taken of this fact to prepare an active extract of islet tissue. The subsidiary hypothesis was that trypsinogen or its derivatives was antagonistic to the internal secretion of the gland. The failures of other investigators in this much-worked field were thus accounted for....

In this paper no attempt is made to give a complete review of the literature. A short résumé, however, of some of the outstanding articles, which tend to attribute to the isles of Langerhans the control of carbohydrate metabolism, is submitted.

In 1889 Mering and Minkowski found that total pancreatectomy in dogs resulted in severe and fatal diabetes. Following this, many different observers experimented with animals of various species and found in all types examined, a glycosuria and fatal cachexia after this operation. The fact was thus established that the pancreas was responsible for this form of diabetes....

Lewaschew believed that the islets were modified acinous cells. Laguesse, an anatomist, first suggested that the islets of Langerhans might be the organ of pancreatic internal secretion. He showed that there were comparatively more islets in the fetus and the newborn than in the adult animal. Opie and Sscobolew independently furnished the first clinical foundation for the belief that the islets were involved in pancreatic diabetes.

W. G. MacCallum, in 1909, ligated the pancreatic ducts draining the tail third of the pancreas. After seven months he excised the remaining two-thirds. This was followed by a mild glycosuria. Three weeks later he removed the degenerated tail third. This second operation resulted in an extreme and fatal glycosuria....

Murlin prepared an alkaline extract of pancreatic tissue and after the injection of this solution, a reduction in sugar excreted by a diabetic animal was observed. Kleiner has pointed out that the reduction secured by Murlin might be due to the alkali per se. Kleiner himself has shown that "unfiltered-water extracts of fresh pancreas diluted with 90 percent NaCl when administered slowly usually resulted in a marked decrease in blood sugar." There was no compensating increase in urine sugar, but rather a decrease, which Kleiner suggests may be partly due to a temporary toxic renal effect. Hemoglobin estimations made during the experiment showed that the reduction in blood sugar was not a dilution phenomenon. Paulesco has demonstrated the reducing effect of the whole gland extract upon the amounts of sugar, urea and acetone bodies in the blood and urine of diabetic animals....

From the work of the above-mentioned observers we may conclude: (1) that the secretion produced by the acinous cells of the pancreas are in no way connected with carbohydrate utilization; (2) that all injections of whole-gland extract have been futile as a therapeutic measure in defects of carbohydrate utilization; (3) that the islands of Langerhans are essential in the control of carbohydrate metabolism. According to Macleod there are two possible mechanisms by which the islets might accomplish this control: (1) the blood might be modified while passing through the islet tissue, i.e., the islands might be detoxicating stations and (2) the islets might produce an internal secretion.

We submit the following experiments, which we believe, give convincing evidence that it is this latter mechanism, which is in operation....

METHODS:

The first step was to tie the pancreatic ducts in a number of dogs. At the end of seven weeks these dogs were chloroformed. The pancreas of each dog was removed and all were found to be without trypsin producing cells. This material was cut into small pieces, ground with sand, and extracted with normal saline. This extract was tested on a dog rendered diabetic by the removal of the pancreas. Following the intravenous injection, the blood sugar of the depancreatized dogs was reduced to a normal or subnormal level, and the urine became sugar-free.

RESULTS:

In the course of our experiments we have administered over seventy-five doses of extract from degenerated pancreatic tissue to ten different diabetic animals. Since the extract has always produced a reduction of the percentage sugar of the blood and of the sugar excreted in the urine, we feel justified in stating that this extract contains the internal secretion of the pancreas. Some of our more recent experiments, which are not yet completed, give, in addition to still more conclusive evidence regarding the sugar retaining power of diabetic animals treated with extract, some interesting facts regarding the chemical nature of the active principle of the internal secretion. These results, together with a study of the respiratory exchange in diabetic animals before and after administration of extract, will be reported in a subsequent communication.

We have always observed a distinct improvement in the clinical condition of diabetic dogs after administration of extract of degenerated pancreas, but it is very obvious that the results of our experimental work, as reported in this paper do not at present justify the therapeutic administration of degenerated gland extracts to cases of diabetes mellitus in the clinic.

CONCLUSIONS:

The results of the experimental work reported in this article may be summarized as follows:

Intravenous injections of extract from dog's pancreas, removed from seven to ten weeks after ligation of the ducts, invariably exercises a reducing influence upon the percentage sugar of the blood and the amount of sugar excreted in the urine. . . .

The extent and duration of the reduction varies directly with the amount of extract injected.

Pancreatic juice destroys the active principle of the extract. . . .

The presence of extract enables a diabetic animal to retain a much greater percentage of injected sugar than it would otherwise. . . .

We wish to express our gratitude to Professor Macleod for helpful suggestions and laboratory facilities and to Professor V. E. Henderson for his interest and support.

SIGNIFICANCE

The discovery of insulin for therapeutic use was a milestone in medicine. Before the discovery and extraction of insulin, diabetes was a slow death sentence that usually struck children and adults under thirty. Physicians treated their diabetic patients with a diet low in carbohydrates and sugar and high in fat and protein. People with diabetes often had constant thirst and insatiable appetites, but lost weight when they could not process their food.

There are two major forms of diabetes: insulin-dependent diabetes and insulin-independent diabetes. After Banting's and Best's discovery, people with insulin-dependent diabetes were given cow or pig insulin, which differs very little from the human hormone. Thanks to recombinant (genetic engineering) technology, people with diabetes now are given human insulin.

The isolation of insulin was also a highly publicized medical achievement, and after news of the initial success, the demand for insulin was immediately widespread. Production of insulin was given a high priority after pharmaceutical companies received permission to manufacture insulin without payment of royalties. Scientists hurried to determine proper dosages and to develop manufacturing processes capable of producing sufficient quantities of insulin of consistent strength and purity. By 1923, roughly one year after it was successfully tested in a human, insulin was widely available to a grateful public. One year the disease was an automatic death sentence; the next, people with diabetes—even children—had the hope of living full and productive lives.

FURTHER RESOURCES

Books

Bankston, John. *Frederick Banting and the Discovery of Insulin.* Hockessin, Del.: Mitchell Lane, 2001.

Bliss, Michael. *The Discovery of Insulin.* Chicago: University of Chicago Press, 1982.

Yuwiler, Janice M. *Insulin.* Detroit: Lucent Books, 2005.

Periodicals

Rosenfeld, Louis. "Insulin: Discovery and Controversy." *Clinical Chemistry* 48 (2002): 2270–2288.

Web sites

New Tecumseth Public Library. "Banting Digital Library." <http://www.newtecumseth.library.on.ca/banting/main.html> (accessed April 17, 2005).

Sir Frederick Banting Educational Committee. "The Discovery of Insulin." <http://www.discoveryofinsulin.com> (accessed April 22, 2005).

The Nobel Foundation. "Frederick G. Banting—Nobel Lecture." <http://nobelprize.org/medicine/laureates/1923/banting-lecture.html> (accessed April 16, 2005).

Audio and Visual Media

Diabetes: Towards the Cure, created by Richard Simpson, R. Fraser, and Chris Simpson (Special originally aired on the CanWest Global Network, 2001). BTV Communications, 2001 (VHS).

On Individual Differences in Human Blood

The Discovery of Blood Groups

Lecture

By: Karl Landsteiner

Date: December 11, 1930

Source: *Nobel Lectures, Physiology or Medicine 1922–1941.* Amsterdam: Elsevier, 1965. Also available online at <http://nobelprize.org/medicine/laureates/1930/landsteiner-lecture.html> (accessed May 10, 2005).

About the Author: Karl Landsteiner (1868–1943) was an Austrian physician. After completing a medical degree he worked in biochemistry, investigating the composition of blood ash. He later became interested in immunology and antibodies. Landsteiner contributed significantly to pathological anatomy and immunology, working on polio and the immunology of syphilis. However, it was his lifetime work on blood groups, antigens, and antibodies that brought him fame and the Nobel Prize in Physiology or Medicine in 1930.

Landsteiner did subsequent work on blood groups in New York City where he moved after leaving Vienna.

INTRODUCTION

The Nobel Prize recognizes the most significant achievements in various areas of science. The work recognized by the Nobel Committee has to be highly significant to the scientific community. Scientists awarded the prize must deliver a public lecture on the topic for which they are recognized.

The discovery of the blood groups by Karl Landsteiner in 1901 was very important because it explained why transfusions between different individuals are sometimes successful and sometimes not successful. Unsuccessful transfusions resulted in patients' deaths due to hemolysis (blood cell destruction).

In the years prior to Landsteiner's discovery, numerous trials transfusing blood from person to person and from animals to people were carried out. The first recorded successful blood transfusion was performed by James Blundell in 1818. However, a number of later attempts failed, and the reasons for these failures remained unknown until the beginning of the twentieth century.

Blood is composed of red blood cells (erythrocytes), white blood cells, platelets, and plasma. When blood is spun in a centrifuge, a clear, sticky fluid called serum separates from the red blood cells. Serum was shown to have the ability to induce clustering of the red blood cells, and Landsteiner's studies focused on identifying why this clustering of red blood cells occurred.

Landsteiner discovered that the reaction between two blood types involved antibodies. In his Nobel Prize lecture, he described the research results that led to the discovery of blood groups and attributed the differences among blood groups to non-protein components on the surface of the red blood cells. His lecture also suggested possible practical uses of the blood groups in medicine and forensic science. The use of blood groups in transfusions, as he recommended, became routine during the First World War (1914–1918).

◼ PRIMARY SOURCE

... I selected the simplest experimental arrangements available and the material which offered the best prospects. Accordingly, my experiment consisted of causing the blood serum and erythrocytes of different human subjects to react with one another.

The result was only to some extent as expected. With many samples there was no perceptible alteration, in other words the result was exactly the same if the blood cells had been mixed with their own serum, but frequently a phenomenon known as agglutination—in which the serum causes the cells of the alien individual to group into clusters—occurred.

The surprising thing was that agglutination, when it occurred at all, was just as pronounced as the already familiar reactions which take place during the interaction between serum and cells of different animal species, whereas in the other cases there seemed to be no difference between the bloods of different persons. First of all, therefore, it was necessary to consider whether the physiological differences discovered between individuals were in fact those which were being sought and whether the phenomena, although observed in the case of blood of healthy persons, might not be due to endured illness. It soon became clear, however, that the reactions follow a pattern which is valid for the blood of all humans.... Basically, in fact, there are four different types of human blood, the so-called blood groups. The number of the groups follows from the fact that the erythrocytes evidently contain substances (isoagglutinogens) with two different structures, of which both may be absent, or one or both present, in the erythrocytes of a person. This alone would still not explain the reactions; the active substances of the sera, the isoagglutinins, must also be present in a specific distribution. This is actually the case, since every serum contains those agglutinins which react with the agglutinogens not present in the cells—a remarkable phenomenon, the cause of which is not yet known for certain....

... I—working in conjunction with Levine—obtained significant results by using special immune sera which had been produced by injecting human blood into rabbits; these results led to the discovery of three new agglutinable factors present in all four groups. ... In addition it was shown that weak iso-reactions (Unger, Guthrie et al.; Jones and glynn; Landsteiner and Levine), which do not follow the group rule and which vary in their specificity, are more common than had previously been assumed—irregular reactions, which can indeed easily be distinguished from the typical ones and which in no way affect the validity of the rule of the four blood groups....

... The praecipitin reactions—mentioned at the beginning of this lecture—which revealed the species difference between proteins gave rise to the view that the substrates of all serological reactions were proteins or substances closely related to them. At first this view was shaken by the study of blood antigens. The solubility of specific substances in organic solvents and in particular the investigation into heterogenetic sheep's blood antigen, ... from which a substance specifically binding but not acting directly as an antigen can be separated by extraction with alcohol, led me to the view that the constituents of many cell antigens are not protein-like substances and only as a result of uniting with proteins become antigens, which are appropriately called "complex antigens." This theory was strongly supported by the fact that I was able to restore the antigen action of the specific substance by mixing with protein-containing solutions. . . .

One practical application of the group characteristics which immediately suggested itself was the distinguishing between human blood stains for forensic purposes. . . .

To a far greater extent the group reactions have been used in forensic medicine for the purpose of establishing paternity. The possibility of arriving at decisions in such cases rests on the studies of the hereditary transmission of the blood groups; the principal factural results in this field we owe to the work of von Dungern and Hirszfeld. As a result of their research it became established that both agglutinogens A and B are dominant hereditary character-istics and that transmission of these characteristics fol-lows Mendel's laws. . . .

More important to practical medicine is the use of blood-group reaction in transfusions. . . .

The first blood transfusion in which the agglutinin reaction was taken into account was carried out by Ottenberg, but it was only during the emergencies of the Great War that the method of transfusion with serological selection of donor was widely adopted—a method which has since remained the normal practice. . . .

. . . It should only be mentioned that it is not absolutely necessary to use blood of the same group, but that in stead of this, blood of group O for instance, . . . can also be used. . . . Use of blood from so-called "universal donors" belong-ing to group O can be of great value in emergency cases and for recipients belonging to the rare blood groups. . . .

SIGNIFICANCE

The discovery of ABO blood groups initiated a new era in medicine as successful blood transfusions became possible. After the First World War, transfu-sions became a standard procedure whenever a patient's injuries caused extensive bleeding or a patient required transfusion due to an illness. Typing the blood before a transfusion has virtually eliminated transfusion-associated complications.

In his lecture, Landsteiner mentioned another phenomenon—newborn hemolytic anemia—that he studied with Levine. This type of anemia was shown to have a hereditary basis. At about the same time, another scientist discovered that antibodies raised against Rhesus monkey erythrocytes in rabbits reacted with 85 percent of human samples. These studies led Landsteiner and his colleagues to describe the Rh

A medical lab worker hangs up pouches of newly donated blood. AP/WIDE WORLD PHOTOS.

blood factor. In contrast to blood groups, the Rh factor is only described as positive or negative.

The Rh factor was discovered to cause hemolytic anemia only in cases in which an Rh negative mother and an Rh positive father produced an Rh positive baby. During pregnancy, fetal blood crosses the pla-centa enters the mother's circulation. As a result of this mixing of maternal and fetal blood, antibodies directed against the baby's red blood cells are slowly generated. But, hemolytic anemia of the newborn can be pre-vented by giving the Rh immunoglobulin to pregnant women who are Rh negative. This prevents develop-ment of antibodies in later stages of pregnancy.

Therefore, when a patient is given a blood trans-fusion, the blood that she receives must be compatible not only with her ABO blood group, but also with her Rh factor. The most commonly used blood for trans-fusions is type O and Rh negative. The advantage of type O blood is that its erythrocytes lack both A and B antigens, and thus type O blood cannot be precipitated by anti-A or anti-B antibodies. On the other hand, individuals with type AB can receive blood from any donor, since they have neither anti-A or anti-B anti-bodies in their blood.

Due to uneven distribution of the blood types within a population, blood banks play an important public health role by storing blood donated by volunteers for later use.

The use of blood groups in paternity testing was also suggested by Landsteiner. However, blood groups cannot be used to identify the father, but only to exclude a man as the potential father. This is due to the fact that an individual with type A blood can be either homozygous (AA, carrying two identical blood group gene types), or heterozygous (AO, carrying two different blood group gene types). A person with either of the genotypes will have type A blood. This same pattern is true for blood group B as well.

Currently there are 26 different blood groups known.

FURTHER RESOURCES

Books

Daniels, Geoff. *Human Blood Groups.* Cambridge, Mass.: Blackwell, 1995.

Reid, Marion E., and Christine Lomas-Francis. *The Blood Group Antigens Factsbook.* San Diego: Academic Press, 1997.

Periodicals

Storry, Jill R., and Martin L. Olsson. "Genetic Basis of Blood Group Diversity." *British Journal of Haematology* 126 (2004): 759–771.

Web sites

The Nobel Foundation. "Blood Typing." <http://nobelprize. org/medicine/educational/landsteiner/readmore.html> (accessed May 10, 2005).

O'Neil, Dennis. "ABO Blood Types." <http://anthro. palomar.edu/blood/ABO_system.htm> (accessed May 10, 2005).

A Strong Nation Is a Healthy Nation

Letter

By: N. H. Heiligman

Date: November 1940

Source: *National Library of Medicine.* "A Strong Nation Is a Healthy Nation: Letter from the Lehigh Country Tuberculosis Society." <http://www.nlm.nih. gov/exhibition/ephemera/images/tb21.gif> (accessed December 12, 2005).

About the Author: Tuberculosis societies were voluntary organizations in the United States and elsewhere in the world that were organized to educate the public about the threat of tuberculosis, prevent its spread, and treat the disease. These societies were active in the United States from the end of the nineteenth century into the first few decades of the twentieth century. The physician N. H. Heiligman volunteered for his local tuberculosis society in Pennsylvania when he wrote this letter in 1940. Tuberculosis societies were generally organized under the auspices of the American Lung Association (ALA), which was called the National Association for the Study and Prevention of Tuberculosis when it was founded in 1904. Although its original intent was to prevent the spread of, and facilitate treatment for, tuberculosis, the American Lung Association has greatly broadened its mission to encompass prevention, treatment, and cure of all lung diseases, as well as education about them, both for those who are afflicted with them as well as for the general public. The American Lung Association has also designed a series of educational programs dealing with such topics as smoking cessation, the dangers of secondhand smoke, and the potentially damaging effects of smoking during pregnancy.

INTRODUCTION

Tuberculosis (TB) is an infectious disease that has existed for virtually as long as humans have lived in groups. Indeed, evidence of tuberculosis infection has been documented in Egyptian mummies. Throughout history, there have been periods of time when tuberculosis affected the world's various populations in epidemic proportions, and times when it was less virulent.

Tuberculosis has been called by a variety of names, such as consumption, white plague, and the people's plague. There was a worldwide epidemic of the disease near the end of the nineteenth century, which killed millions and affected many more. Until 1882 when Robert Koch (1843–1910) announced his discovery of the bacterium responsible for tuberculosis, the cause of the disease was unknown and there was neither an effective treatment nor a cure for it. All that was clearly understood was that the disease was contagious. Following Koch's discovery of *Mycobacteriumtuberculosis*, scientific research indicated that the bacterium could live for quite a few hours outside the human body, that it was able to thrive and multiply in warm, moist, dark places, and that the bacterium was spread through the air in sputum or mucus expelled during sneezing or coughing.

In Europe, the disease was viewed as slightly romantic, an illness affecting primarily the rich or privileged classes. In America, it manifested largely in poor and densely populated areas, where the sanitation was likely to be poor, the water suspect or potentially polluted, and the living conditions overcrowded. The move from rural to urban areas following the industrial revolution, as well as the influx of large numbers of immigrants, intensified the severity of the problem. It was impossible to know how many immigrants came to America already exposed to the bacillus, whether actively ill or simply carrying the disease. Unhealthy living conditions fostered the rapid spread of tuberculosis from person to person, due to repeated exposure. By the end of the nineteenth century, tuberculosis was the leading cause of death in the United States. Because both medicine and scientific research in the United States lagged behind the rapid progress being made in Europe and elsewhere in the world at the time, many American physicians at the end of the nineteenth century lacked a clear understanding of the concept of contagion. As a result, they sometimes placed sick people in groups in dark, damp conditions, with little or no ventilation and no sanitary precautions being taken by caregivers. This served as a very effective breeding ground for the bacteria.

Many folk remedies were tried, as well as myriad common-sense approaches, before effective antibiotics were developed in the 1940s. People were prescribed bed rest, varying amounts of activity, confinement indoors, sent outdoors, sent to the seaside, to the mountains, to hot and dry climates, or to cold and snowy areas. Around the turn of the twentieth century, numerous sanatoriums were built across the country (and around the world), to which people with active TB would be sent for rest, relaxation, moderate exercise, and fresh, healthy food, in the hope that they would be cured over time. The sanatoriums were closed by the end of the 1970s, when they were no longer needed.

In the early stages of active illness, people with TB developed fevers and night sweats, decreased appetite and weight loss, and an intermittent cough. As the disease progressed, the cough worsened and increased in frequency. Over time, the individual began to cough up bloody sputum, until the disease progressed to the point where they coughed up fresh blood due to respiratory, esophageal, and tracheal hemorrhages. Although the lungs were the primary organ of involvement, TB could spread throughout the blood and lymphatic systems, and affect the bones and joints, as well as other systems and organs. TB was a deadly disease, but a very small percentage of people did recover from it.

Tuberculosis is now known to be caused by the bacterium called *Mycobacterium tuberculosis*. It is spread by repeated exposure to airborne secretions carried by sneezing, coughing, laughing, talking, spitting, or singing (any forceful expulsion of moist air). Although many people who are exposed to the disease will carry it in a latent form inside their bodies, only those who are actively sick with the disease can transmit it to others. Being exposed to the disease without immediately developing it is not an indication that it will never become active. Latent TB is treated prophylactically to prevent development of the actual illness.

With the development of effective treatments for active TB, prophylactic medications for latent infections, and accurate, effective diagnostic techniques, TB became relatively well-controlled by the middle of the twentieth century, and was nearly eradicated in the United States by the end of the 1970s. As a result, the expansive public health systems that had developed around TB treatment, along with most volunteer tuberculosis societies, were gradually disbanded.

PRIMARY SOURCE

LEHIGH COUNTY
TUBERCULOSIS SOCIETY

719 HAMILOTN STREET, ALLENTOWN, PENNA.
November, 1940

A STRONG NATION
IS A HEALTHY NATION.......

In the days when America is strengthening its defenses against attack from any quarter, the general health of the Nation assumes tremendous importance.

It is not enough that we have a strong Army, Navy, and Air Force, if the Nation that backs up these forces is deficient on bodily vigor and energy. The vitality of a country is the vitality of all its peoples in all classes of society.

Poor health is one of the enemies that bore from within. And tuberculosis must be listed as one of the causes of physical deficiency. Tuberculosis respects no class. It recognizes no national emergencies. Ruthlessly and relentlessly it reaches into the lowliest home and the loftiest mansion and claims more lives between the ages of 15 and 45 than any other cause ... twice as many as the automobile.

Just as Tuberculosis is one of the most vicious enemies of society, so eternal vigilance is the greatest enemy of Tuberculosis. Cure is practically certain if the case is discovered soon enough. Christmas Seals help to make early discovery possible. They provide tuberculin tests, X-rays, rehabilitation service, and assistance in securing employment for recovered patients, not to mention education in the care and prevention of the disease. All this is the program of the Lehigh County Tuberculosis Society, a program that is entirely dependent on the financial support of its contributing members.

Enclosed you will find a Christmas Seal Sale Bond.

Your help in the past has meant much to the success of our work, and we hope you will let us list you once more as one of our contributors.

Gratefully Yours,
N.H. HEILIGMAN, M.D.
President

SIGNIFICANCE

Several seemingly unrelated events occurred in the early 1980s that acted as catalysts for the resurgence of tuberculosis in America and around the world (although the disease had never been close to eradication in many impoverished or undeveloped parts of the globe). In the aftermath of the Vietnam War, large numbers of disenfranchised young adults returned to the United States from Southeast Asia. This occurrence, coupled with the increasing incidence of poverty and overcrowding in urban areas, contributed to an upsurge in poverty and homelessness. Poverty and homelessness tend to breed, among other things, an increase in alcohol and substance abuse in those affected. In the late 1970s and throughout the 1980s, there was a significant increase in the use of injectable drugs. As a result, groups of people with compromised immune systems either shared needles or spent time in close quarters at shelters, homeless centers, and in prisons or jails. It was not uncommon for those individuals to either develop new cases of TB or to have previously latent TB become active.

With the advent affordable air travel, more and more people were able to move around the world quickly and easily. As a result, individuals carrying an active infection could move from one place to another, inadvertently exposing many others in previously unaffected or TB-eradicated areas to the bacteria. In addition, during the early stages of the global HIV and AIDS pandemic in the 1980s, there was a sudden, sharp rise in the number of individuals with impaired immune systems, rendering them vulnerable to acquisition of the tuberculosis bacterium. Once exposed, people with compromised immune systems were far more likely to rapidly develop the illness.

In both of these situations, people with TB symptoms may not have immediately sought medical treatment, since the disease may have either initially appeared to be a cold or a comparatively benign respiratory infection. Because TB was no longer considered a threat in the United States, the general public and the medical profession took some time to recognize its resurgence—particularly in the face of the enormity, both in terms of affected populations and in the number of attendant symptoms and syndromes, of the HIV/AIDS epidemic.

Finally, although there were effective medications for the treatment and prevention of tuberculosis, they required long-term dosing and carried significant side effects. It was quite common for patients to fail to complete the prescribed medication regimen, potentially leading to exacerbation of the symptoms of active TB or to the development of active infection among those with previously latent exposures. This failure to complete prescribed courses of treatment also led to the development of multi-drug resistant tuberculosis, which does not respond to traditional treatment regimens.

According to statistics released by the National Institute of Allergy and Infectious Diseases (NIAID) in 2002, roughly two billion people, or 30 percent of the world's population, were at that time infected with the bacteria that causes tuberculosis. In their report, they stated that eight million people developed active infection, and three million people around the world died from tuberculosis each year. Many of those who die from TB have little or no access to modern medicine or effective infectious disease treatments. The NIAID also estimated that between ten and fifteen million people in the United States carry latent (dormant) TB, and that about 10 percent of them will develop active disease in the future. Since the end of the 1980s, the disease has been gradually declining in incidence in the United States.

The World Health Organization has created several initiatives aimed at the control and eventual eradication of tuberculosis in developing countries. As of 2005, tuberculosis had the highest incidence of occurrence in Southeast Asia, but was most prevalent (highest rate of occurrence for the size of the population) in sub-Saharan Africa. Areas with the highest AIDS-infected populations also had the highest death rates from tuberculosis.

Until the early years of the twenty-first century, one of the greatest difficulties in the effective treatment of active or latent tuberculosis infection was the length of time needed to complete the treatment protocol—up to two full years in some places. The length of treatment, coupled with the burden of the required patient oversight on often fragile health care systems, impeded successful protocol completion. In addition, the long treatment regimen required a greater quantity of expensive medication, placing an additional financial strain on the health systems of poor and economically challenged countries. At the end of 2005, the World Health Organization announced that it had completed the second phase of clinical trials in its Stop TB program with a new combination drug therapy that has the potential to significantly shorten tuberculosis treatment time, possibly by as much as 33 percent. If the next phase of the trials goes as well as the first two have, the new therapies could be available for worldwide distribution by late 2009.

FURTHER RESOURCES

Periodicals

Special topic issue: "Tuberculosis." *JAMA: The Journal of the American Medical Association* 293 (June 8, 2005): 2693–2820.

Web sites

American Lung Association. "HIV and Tuberculosis Fact Sheet." <http://www.lungusa.org/site/pp.asp?c=dvLUK9O0E&b=35433> (accessed December 12, 2005).

American Lung Association. "Multi-Drug Resistant Tuberculosis Fact Sheet." <http://www.lungusa.org/site/pp.asp?c=dvLUK9O0E&b=35815> (accessed December 12, 2005).

American Lung Association. "Tuberculosis Fact Sheet." <http://www.lungusa.org/site/pp.asp?c=dvLUK9O0E&b=35804> (accessed December 12, 2005).

CDC National Center for HIV, STD, and TB Prevention. Division of Tuberculosis Elimination. "Controlling Tuberculosis in the United States: Recommendations from the American Thoracic Society, CDC, and the Infectious Diseases Society of America." <http://www.cdc.gov/mmwr/preview/mmwrhtml/rr5412a1.htm> (accessed December 12, 2005).

Global Health Reporting.org. "Tuberculosis: Overview." <http://www.globalhealthreporting.org/tb.asp> (accessed December 12, 2005).

The Lung Association/L'Association Pulmonaire. "The Story of the Christmas Seals." <http://www.lung.ca/seals/> (accessed December 12, 2005).

A Structure for Deoxyribose Nucleic Acid

Journal article

By: James Dewey Watson

By: Frances Harry Compton Crick

Date: April 2, 1953

Source: J. D. Watson and F. H. C. Crick. "A Structure for Deoxyribose Nucleic Acid." *Nature* (1953): 171, 737–738.

About the Author: James Dewey Watson (1928–) was born in Chicago, Illinois, on April 6, 1928. Watson's early days were spent in Chicago, where he attended Horace Mann Grammar School for eight years and South Shore High School for two years. Immediately after that, he received a tuition scholarship to the University of Chicago and, in the summer of 1943, entered their experimental four-year college. In 1947, he received a B.Sc. degree in zoology. During these years his boyhood interest in bird-watching had matured into a serious desire to learn genetics. Francis Harry Compton Crick (1916–2004) was born on June 8, 1916, at Northampton, England. Crick was educated at Northampton Grammar School and Mill Hill School, London. He studied physics at the University College, London, obtained a B.Sc. in 1937, and started research for a Ph.D., but, in 1939, this academic work was interrupted by World War II. During the war he worked as a scientist for the British Admiralty, where he designed acoustic and magnetic mines for naval warfare. He left the Admiralty in 1947 to study biology. Watson met Crick at the Cavendish Laboratory, Cambridge, England, in 1951, where they discovered their common interest in solving the DNA structure. They thought it should be possible to correctly deduce its structure, given both the experimental evidence generated by Rosalind Franklin (1920–1958) and the careful examination of all possible stereochemical configurations of polynucleotide chains.

INTRODUCTION

Watson and Crick staked their claim for scientific immortality with the introductory sentence: "We wish to suggest a structure for the salt of deoxyribose nucleic acid (D.N.A.)." This could have seemed an audacious sentence, but when put into context it was, indeed, a quite modest way to start a milestone article entitled "Molecular Structure of Nucleic Acids," published in the British journal *Nature* on April 2, 1953.

In the less-than-two-page article, the secret of life was unraveled, revolutionizing many fields of biology, especially genetics, evolution, and medicine. The DNA structure discovery also garnered Watson and Crick, together with their co-worker Maurice H. F. Wilkins (1916–2004), the Nobel Prize in Physiology or Medicine in 1962. But why is such accomplishment so striking? And how did it change our lives?

James Watson stands near a model of the "DNA Double Helix" in 2004. AP/WIDE WORLD PHOTOS.

All living organisms are assembled by a set of commands carried as a linear information string, the DNA molecule. This molecule shares a common line of descent with the first cell that arose on this planet. DNA carries the information of how life is made. DNA's recipe is written in nucleotide (nitrogenous base) sequences, so that amino acids are correctly put together to make proteins. This recipe is uninterruptedly used throughout the lifespan of all organisms.

The DNA molecule is a double-stranded helix that resembles a twisted ladder. Each strand of the helix includes only four different deoxyribonucleotides, adenine (A), thymine (T), cytosine (C), and guanine (G). Nucleotides in the double helix are complementary to each other, so if in one strand there is an A at a particular position, a T is found at the same position in the other strand. The same situation occurs with C and G. The main forces that stabilize the double helix are: hydrophobic interactions, base stacking, and hydrogen bonds. Because the nucleotide interior is hydrophobic, it is pushed away from the aqueous environment and grouped together in order to establish a water-free

core. After this first structural decision, the hydrophobic parts of consecutive nucleotides are stacked on the top of each other making a very strong, but somewhat flexible structure. Finally, complementary nucleotides on opposing strands are aligned correctly by hydrogen bonds. Proteins are synthesized by reading the DNA string in nucleotide triplets, or codons, and translating each triplex into the amino acid it codes for. Several amino acids are linked together to form proteins, which are the molecules necessary for most known functions performed by a living cell.

Furthermore, DNA is a heritable molecule, passed through linear generations. The complementarity of nucleotides provides a means for the transmission of hereditary traits from one generation to the next. Because DNA harbors the code of life and because it also holds information concerning the evolution of all living organisms, the discovery of its structure is one of the most important accomplishments of science.

As envisioned by Ritchie Calder, a British journalist, discovering how these chemical "cards" are shuffled and paired kept scientists busy for fifty years after the golden year of 1953.

■ PRIMARY SOURCE

A STRUCTURE FOR DEOXYRIBOSE NUCLEIC ACID

We wish to suggest a structure for the salt of deoxyribose nucleic acid (D.N.A.). This structure has novel features which are of considerable biological interest.

A structure for nucleic acid has already been proposed by Pauling and Corey. They kindly made their manuscript available to us in advance of publication. Their model consists of three intertwined chains, with the phosphates near the fibre axis, and the bases on the outside. In our opinion, this structure is unsatisfactory for two reasons: (1) We believe that the material which gives the X-ray diagrams is the salt, not the free acid. Without the acidic hydrogen atoms it is not clear what forces would hold the structure together, especially as the negatively charged phosphates near the axis will repel each other. (2) Some of the van der Waals distances appear to be too small.

Another three-chain structure has also been suggested by Fraser (in the press). In his model the phosphates are on the outside and the bases on the inside, linked together by hydrogen bonds. This structure as described is rather ill-defined, and for this reason we shall not comment on it.

We wish to put forward a radically different structure for the salt of deoxyribose nucleic acid. This structure has two helical chains each coiled round the same axis. . . .

... The structure is an open one, and its water content is rather high. At lower water contents we would expect the bases to tilt so that the structure could become more compact.

The novel feature of the structure is the manner in which the two chains are held together by the purine and pyrimidine bases. The planes of the bases are perpendicular to the fibre axis. They are joined together in pairs, a single base from one chain being hydrogen-bonded to a single base from the other chain, so that the two lie side by side with identical z-co-ordinates. One of the pair must be a purine and the other a pyrimidine for bonding to occur. The hydrogen bonds are made as follows: purine position 1 to pyrimidine position 1; purine position 6 to pyrimidine position 6.

If it is assumed that the bases only occur in the structure in the most plausible tautomeric forms (that is, with the keto rather than the enol configurations) it is found that only specific pairs of bases can bond together. These pairs are: adenine (purine) with thymine (pyrimidine), and guanine (purine) with cytosine (pyrimidine).

In other words, if an adenine forms one member of a pair, on either chain, then on these assumptions the other member must be thymine; similarly for guanine and cytosine. The sequence of bases on a single chain does not appear to be restricted in any way. However, if only specific pairs of bases can be formed, it follows that if the sequence of bases on one chain is given, then the sequence on the other chain is automatically determined.

It has been found experimentally that the ratio of the amounts of adenine to thymine, and the ratio of guanine to cytosine, are always very close to unity for deoxyribose nucleic acid.

It is probably impossible to build this structure with a ribose sugar in place of the deoxyribose, as the extra oxygen atom would make too close a van der Waals contact. The previously published X-ray data on deoxyribose nucleic acid are insufficient for a rigorous test of our structure. So far as we can tell, it is roughly compatible with the experimental data, but it must be regarded as unproved until it has been checked against more exact results. Some of these are given in the following communications. We were not aware of the details of the results presented there when we devised our structure, which rests mainly though not entirely on published experimental data and stereochemical arguments.

It has not escaped our notice that the specific pairing we have postulated immediately suggests a possible copying mechanism for the genetic material.

Full details of the structure, including the conditions assumed in building it, together with a set of co-ordinates for the atoms, will be published elsewhere.

We are much indebted to Dr. Jerry Donohue for constant advice and criticism, especially on interatomic distances. We have also been stimulated by a knowledge of the general nature of the unpublished experimental results and ideas of Dr. M. H. F. Wilkins, Dr. R. E. Franklin and their co-workers at King's College, London. One of us (J. D. W.) has been aided by a fellowship from the National Foundation for Infantile Paralysis.

J. D. WATSON F. H. C. CRICK

SIGNIFICANCE

The knowledge about DNA's molecule structure has shed light on the mystery of life and since then, has transformed the way humankind sees itself. In spite of its great significance, the DNA structure story also harbors one of the most famous cases of unsung heroes science has ever known. Her name is Rosalind Franklin, from whom Watson and Crick obtained the DNA X-ray photographs, as acknowledged by Watson. Franklin also was attempting to discover DNA's structure, and almost deciphered the images, when Watson and Crick published their manuscript in 1953. Rosalind Franklin died in 1958, at the age of 37, from ovarian cancer.

Molecular biology and modern genetics have grown dramatically in the past fifty-two years. After cracking the DNA molecule, many advances have been possible through a biotechnological revolution, such as: the sequencing of entire genomes; the laboratory production of many proteins (such as human insulin and growth hormone, which are now obtained from bacteria as a result of recombinant DNA techniques), and the promise of gene therapy for diseases such as cancer. Moreover, DNA information is now assembled in minuscule spaces, so that thousands of genes can be tested simultaneously and effortlessly, creating new promises for the next fifty years of research. Nonetheless, we must learn with this great discovery that science and development must be pursued under the highest principles of integrity, ethics, and respect for life.

FURTHER RESOURCES
Books

Maddox, Brenda. *Rosalind Franklin: The Dark Lady of DNA.* London: Harper Collins, 2002.

Watson, James. *The Double Helix: A Personal Account of the Discovery of the Structure of DNA.* New York: Touchstone, 2001.

Watson, James, and Andrew Berry. *DNA: The Secret of Life.* New York: Knopf, 2003.

Periodicals

Dennis, Carina, and Philip Campbell. "The Eternal Molecule." *Nature* 421 (January 23, 2003): 396.

Gibbs, Nancy, Michael Lemonick, James Watson, et al. "Solving the Mysteries of DNA—The DNA Revolution." *Time* 161 (February 17, 2003).

Web sites

Cold Spring Harbor Laboratory. "James D. Watson: Chancellor." <http://www.cshl.edu/gradschool/jdw_.html> (accessed November 6, 2005).

DNA from the Beginning. "The DNA Molecule is Shaped like a Twisted Ladder." <http://www.dnaftb.org/dnaftb/19/concept/index.html> (accessed November 6, 2005).

Nobel Prize.org. "The Nobel Prize in Physiology or Medicine 1962." <http://nobelprize.org/medicine/laureates/1962/index.html> (accessed November 6, 2005).

Time. "Scientists & Thinkers: James Watson & Francis Crick." <http://www.time.com/time/time100/scientist/profile/watsoncrick.html> (accessed November 6, 2005).

Audio and visual media

DNA: The Amazing Double Helix, produced by Educational Video Network, Inc., 2000 (DVD).

DNA: The Secret of Life, created by the Moorehead Planetarium and Science Center. Windfall Films, 2003 (DVD).

Understanding DNA, produced by Educational Video Network, Inc., 2004 (DVD).

WGBH. *Nova.* "Cracking the Code of Life." Available from <http://www.pbs.org/wgbh/nova/genome/program.html> (with video link; accessed December 14, 2005).

Patient Undergoing a CT Scan

Medical Imaging: PET Scanner, CT, and MRI Replace Many Exploratory Surgeries

Photograph

By: Anonymous

Date: April 9, 1978

Source: Corbis Corporation

About the Photographer: An unknown photographer contributed this photograph to Corbis, a media agency headquartered in Seattle, Washington.

INTRODUCTION

Medical imaging—the ability to look inside the human body without cutting into it—began with the discovery of x rays by Wilhelm Roentgen (1845–1923) in 1895. X rays pass through skin, fat, blood and muscle more easily than through bone. The shadow cast by the bones can be captured upon film and such x-ray images have long been used for diagnostic purposes—to assess a bone fracture, for instance. However, conventional x rays reveal little of the anatomy of soft tissue, such as tendons, blood vessels, and nerves. It is the air in the lungs which allows detail to be seen in a chest x ray, which is still a useful way of diagnosing lung cancer or tuberculosis.

Another limitation of conventional x rays is that a three-dimensional structure is being compressed onto a two-dimensional film which can make interpretation difficult. Nor can conventional x rays distinguish between variations in the density of different tissues. The South African researcher Allan Cormack (1924–1998) addressed this last issue by working out the mathematics of the variation in tissue density, which he published in 1963 and 1964. But there was no practical way of putting this to use until the British engineer Godfrey Hounsfield (1919–2004) developed the first computerized tomography (CT) scanner in 1972, known as the EMI scanner.

As shown in the photograph below, the scanner directs an x ray from a tube on a rotating ring into the patient's body to be picked up by a detector at the other side of the ring. In this way, the x-ray beam can, with computer assistance, create a cross-sectional image of the human body. For the first time, the brain could be seen clearly with white and gray matter, and cavities, all being revealed. Later developments allowed visualization of other parts of the body. The CT scanner proved a milestone in the non-invasive diagnosis of conditions such as cancer and head injury. In 1979, shortly after the photograph below was taken, Hounsfield and Cormack shared the Nobel Prize for Medicine for the invention of the CT scanner.

PRIMARY SOURCE

PATIENT UNDERGOING A CT SCAN
See primary source image.

SIGNIFICANCE

CT scanning has eliminated the need for most exploratory surgery by allowing doctors to examine most parts of the body to pinpoint signs of disease. Conventional CT scanning is, however, limited by the need for the rotating ring to return to its original position once an image of a one centimeter slice of the patient's

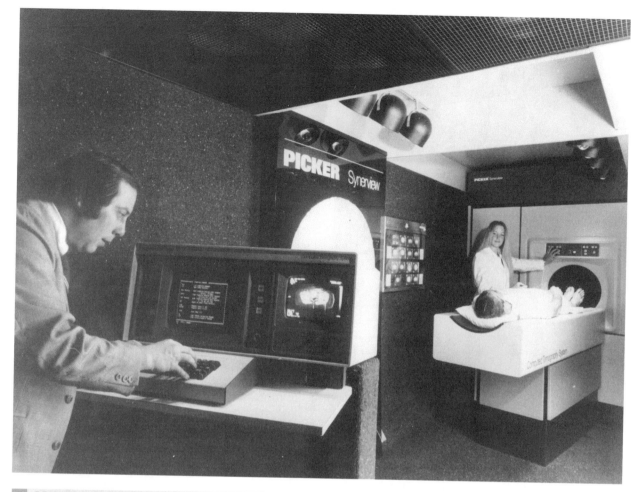

Patient undergoing a CT scan. An early computerized tomography (CT) scanner is shown here. The scanner rotates to take pictures of the patient, and creates computer-aided images of the internal organs. CT and later scanning technologies reduced the need for many exploratory surgeries. ©BETTMANN/CORBIS.

body has been created. The patient is moved gradually into the scanner while many such slice images are gathered. In spiral CT, which was developed in the late 1980s, the scanner can move continuously over the patient, scanning a volume of tissue rather than a series of slices. This is faster and gives clearer images. Small lesions are thus less likely to be missed. In many hospitals, conventional scanners are used for routine examinations of the head, for stroke or head injury, while the spiral scanner is reserved for more complex diagnostic work.

An even more recent advance is the multislice scanner—a spiral CT scanner which uses multiple rows of detectors, rather than a single row. It is fast, taking less than a second to image a volume of tissue and gives an excellent quality of image. New applications such as vascular, cardiac, and colonic imaging have been made possible with the advent of multislice spiral scanners.

But they are costly and generate a great deal of data, raising implications for storage and interpretation.

The patient receives a higher dose of x rays from a multislice scanner, and even a conventional CT scan exposes the patient to some radiation. There has been concern that the over use of CT scans may, therefore, increase a patient's risk of cancer. For instance, some patients opt to have a whole-body CT scan as a form of medical check-up to detect problems early, even when they have no symptoms. The health benefit of the whole-body CT scan has not been proven to outweigh the risks. Similarly, the value of screening smokers for early signs of lung cancer by spiral CT is also not yet established.

Magnetic resonance imaging (MRI) does much the same job as CT, but without any exposure to radiation. In MRI, the patient is exposed to a magnetic field that

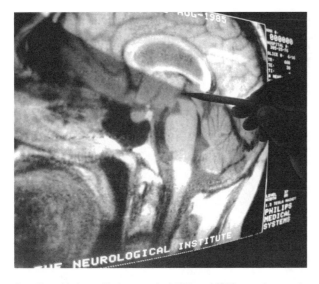

At a New York medical center in 1985, an MRI is used to study anatomical detail within a human brain. AP/WIDE WORLD PHOTOS.

About the Photographer: Ray Foli contributed this photograph to Corbis, a media agency headquartered in Seattle, Washington, that supplies photographs and other images to magazines, newspapers, television, and advertising concerns.

INTRODUCTION

Failure to conceive is not uncommon—between one in six and one in twenty couples are affected by infertility in either the male or female partner. The British gynecologist and obstetrician Patrick Steptoe (1913–1988) had long been interested in both laparoscopy, the process of looking into the abdominal cavity through a tiny incision in the umblicus, and infertility. He joined with Robert Edwards, a physiologist at Cambridge University, to investigate the possiblility of *in-vitro* fertilization (IVF)—that is, creating an embryo by fertilizing an egg with sperm in the laboratory. The embryo would then be placed back in the mother's uterus in the hope that a pregnancy would be established.

After a decade of research, involving some unsuccessful clinical trials, IVF claimed its first success with the birth of Louise Joy Brown in Oldham District Hospital, England, on July 25, 1978. Mother Lesley had been told she had only a one in a million chance of conceiving naturally because of blocked fallopian tubes. Her egg was fertilized with husband John's sperm in a glass dish—or petri dish—in the laboratory and replaced in Lesley's uterus for a relatively uneventful pregnancy.

Of course, Louise Brown's appearance in the world was no ordinary birth. While her appearance on *Phil Donahue*, depicted below, shows her as a normal, healthy child, she has had to spend years explaining to people that she was not actually born in a laboratory. Misunderstandings no doubt arose by the "test tube baby" shorthand that was used from the beginning to describe the IVF approach.

interacts with hydrogen atoms within the tissues of the body. Signals are thus generated which can be used to build an image of the tissue. CT is thought better at imaging organs in motion—the lungs and bowel—while MRI is often preferred for imaging the pelvis and diagnosing neurological disorders like multiple sclerosis. For solid organs such as the liver, spleen, pancreas, and kidneys, either CT or MRI can be used.

FURTHER RESOURCES

Books

Porter, Roy, ed. *Cambridge Illustrated History of Medicine.* Cambridge, UK: Cambridge University Press, 1996.

Periodicals

Garvey, Conall J., and Rebecca Hanlon. "Computed Tomography in Clinical Practice." *British Medical Journal* 324 (2002): 1077–1080.

Web sites

Nobelprize.org. "The Nobel Prize in Physiology or Medicine 1979." <http://nobelprize.org/medicine/laureates/1979/presentation-speech.html> (accessed December 21, 2005).

Louise Brown and her Parents

Assisted Reproduction

Photograph

By: Ray Foli

Date: September 7, 1979

 PRIMARY SOURCE

LOUISE BROWN AND HER PARENTS

See primary source image.

SIGNIFICANCE

Louise Brown was guest of honor at a twenty-fifth birthday celebration at Bourn Hall, which has become one of Britain's main IVF centers. She is a normal and healthy young woman; however, whether there are long-term health effects from being born by IVF

Louise Brown and Her Parents. Louise Brown, the first infant born as a result of *in-vitro* fertilization, appears with her parents on the *Phil Donohue* television program in 1979. ©BETTMANN/ CORBIS.

remains to be seen from ongoing research. A few years later, sister Natalie was also born by IVF and since 1978, well over one million other IVF babies have been born to infertile couples around the world.

Originally seen as a treatment for blocked fallopian tubes, the indications for IVF are now far wider and the technology has become more advanced. However, success rates remain at between 20 to 30 percent. For infertile men, intracytoplasmic sperm injection (ICSI)—where sperm that do not move properly or fail to penetrate the egg—has proved to be a particularly valuable form of IVF. ICSI involves the direct injection of a sperm into the egg and it has about the same success rate as IVF.

More controversially, perhaps, IVF allows the separation of egg, sperm and uterus, allowing for unconventional pregnancies to be established. Donor sperm and donor egg can be used to create an embryo that can be implanted in the uterus of a third person. This happened in 1995, when a Los Angeles couple recruited a woman to act as a surrogate mother for such an embryo, creating uncertainty about issues of parental rights. And, infrequently, lab mix-ups have occurred where an embryo has been transferred to a woman that was intended for another.

Post-menopausal women, who would not be able to conceive naturally, could also have an embryo made from donor sperm and egg implanted into their uterus. IVF also offers the possibility of parenthood to homosexual couples. Meanwhile, babies have also been born from frozen eggs, taken from women whose fertility was otherwise threatened from illness, and from the sperm of a dead man. Clearly, IVF now offers parenthood to many people other than the physically infertile.

The laboratory setting of IVF has also led to the screening of embryos for genetic disease. Today's fast DNA analysis technology means it is possible to take just one cell from an eight-celled embryo, prior to placing it in the uterus, and test it for genetic defects. Typically, the woman undertaking IVF receives drugs that allow the production of more than one egg so that several embryos are produced. In so-called preimplantation diagnosis, each embryo can be screened for faulty genes and only healthy ones placed in the uterus. Then the parents can continue with the pregnancy, confident that a healthy child will be born. For many, this procedure is preferable to chorionic villus testing during pregnancy followed by the option of termination if a genetic problem is encountered. However, this was not the original purpose of IVF. The ethical issues around IVF which are brought up by genetic testing or third party involvement clearly need careful assessment and control.

FURTHER RESOURCES

Books

Porter, Roy, ed. *Cambridge Illustrated History of Medicine.* Cambridge, UK: Cambridge University Press, 1996.

Web sites

BBC News. "Profile: Louise Brown. A quarter-century on, and the clamour surrounding 'test tube baby' Louise Brown has barely died down." <http://news.bbc.co.uk/ 1/hi/health/3056141.stm> (accessed December 21, 2005).

BBC News. "Fertility Milestones." <http://news.bbc.co.uk/1/ hi/health/3056141.stm> (accessed December 21, 2005).

Pneumocystis Pneumonia—Los Angeles

Journal article excerpt

By: Michael S. Gottlieb, et al.

Date: June 5, 1981

Source: M. S. Gottlieb, et. al. "*Pneumocystis* Pneumonia—Los Angeles," *Moridity and Mortality Weekly report* (June 5, 1981): (30) 21, 1–3. Available online at <http://www.cdc.gov/mmwr/preview/mmwrhtml/june_5.htm> (accessed January 21, 2006).

About the Author: Michael S. Gottlieb was an assistant professor of medicine at the University of California at Los Angeles (UCLA) in 1981, when he submitted the featured report as its lead author. In 1985, Gottlieb co-founded the American Foundation for AIDS Research. He maintains a private medical practice in Los Angeles.

INTRODUCTION

Within an eight-month period in 1980–1981, five young men were hospitalized in the Los Angeles area with a rare, severe form of pneumonia caused by the pathogen (disease-causing microorganism) *Pneumocystis carinii*. In reporting the outbreak to the Centers for Disease Control and Prevention (CDC), the physician Michael S. Gottlieb and his colleagues first documented in medical literature (in the report below) the disease that was to become known as AIDS.

The report jarred physicians in New York and San Francisco, who noticed a handful of similar cases occurring at about the same time. In another unusual occurrence, eight young men in the New York area with Kaposi's sarcoma had recently died. Kaposi's sarcoma is a form of skin cancer that was usually seen mainly in elderly persons. Suspecting a new or emerging disease among young men, the CDC formed a task force to investigate the outbreaks.

All of the young men with both *Pneumocystis* pneumonia and Kaposi's sarcoma were actively homosexual, and early on, the task force considered the disease likely to be confined to the community of homosexual males. By the end of 1981, it became clear that that the newly recognized disease affected other population groups, when the first cases of *Pneumocystis* pneumonia were reported in drug users who injected their drugs. It also became clear that the disease was not confined to the United States, when similar cases were found within a year in the United Kingdom, Haiti, and in Uganda, where the disease was called "slim."

In 1982, scientists at the CDC linked the transmission of the disease to blood, and coined the term AIDS, describing the viral disease as an acquired immune deficiency syndrome. The CDC's editorial response to Gottlieb's report describing the initial assumption that the disease resulted in an alteration in the immune system proved to be correct. The infectious nature of AIDs, however, remained unconfirmed until 1984, when scientists at both the Pasteur Institute in Paris and the National Cancer Institute identified the virus eventually known as the Human Immunodeficiency Virus (HIV) that causes AIDS.

◼ PRIMARY SOURCE

EPIDEMIOLOGIC NOTES AND REPORTS

In the period October 1980–May 1981, 5 young men, all active homosexuals, were treated for biopsy-confirmed *Pneumocystis carinii* pneumonia at 3 different hospitals in Los Angeles, California. Two of the patients died. All 5 patients had laboratory-confirmed previous or current cytomegalovirus (CMV) infection and candidal mucosal infection. Case reports of these patients follow.

Patient 1: A previously healthy 33-year-old man developed *P. carinii* pneumonia and oral mucosal candidiasis in March 1981 after a 2-month history of fever associated with elevated liver enzymes, leukopenia, and CMV viruria. The serum complement-fixation CMV titer in October 1980 was 256; in May 1981 it was 32. The patient's condition deteriorated despite courses of treatment with trimethoprim-sulfamethoxazole (TMP/SMX), pentamidine, and acyclovir. He died May 3, and postmortem examination showed residual *P. carinii* and CMV pneumonia, but no evidence of neoplasia.

Patient 2: A previously healthy 30-year-old man developed *P. carinii* pneumonia in April 1981 after a 5-month history of fever each day and of elevated liver-function tests, CMV viruria, and documented seroconversion to CMV, i.e., an acute-phase titer of 16 and a convalescent-phase titer of 28 in anticomplement immunofluorescence tests. Other features of his illness included leukopenia and mucosal candidiasis. His pneumonia responded to a course of intravenous TMP/SMX, but, as of the latest reports, he continues to have a fever each day.

Patient 3: A 30-year-old man was well until January 1981 when he developed esophageal and oral candidiasis that responded to Amphotericin B treatment. He was hospitalized in February 1981 for *P. carinii* pneumonia that responded to TMP/SMX. His esophageal candidiasis recurred after the pneumonia was diagnosed, and he was again given Amphotericin B. The CMV complement-fixation titer in March 1981 was 8. Material from an esophageal biopsy was positive for CMV.

Patient 4: A 29-year-old man developed *P. carinii* pneumonia in February 1981. He had had Hodgkins disease 3 years earlier, but had been successfully treated with radiation therapy alone. He did not improve after being given intravenous TMP/SMX and corticosteroids and died in March. Postmortem examination showed no evidence of Hodgkins disease, but *P. carinii* and CMV were found in lung tissue.

Patient 5: A previously healthy 36-year-old man with clinically diagnosed CMV infection in September 1980 was seen in April 1981 because of a 4-month history of fever, dyspnea, and cough. On admission he was found to have *P. carinii* pneumonia, oral candidiasis, and CMV retinitis. A complement-fixation CMV titer in April 1981 was 128. The patient has been treated with 2 short courses of TMP/SMX that have been limited because of a sulfa-induced neutropenia. He is being treated for candidiasis with topical nystatin.

The diagnosis of *Pneumocystis* pneumonia was confirmed for all 5 patients antemortem by closed or open lung biopsy. The patients did not know each other and had no known common contacts or knowledge of sexual partners who had had similar illnesses. Two of the 5 reported having frequent homosexual contacts with various partners. All 5 reported using inhalant drugs, and 1 reported parenteral drug abuse. Three patients had profoundly depressed in vitro proliferative responses to mitogens and antigens. Lymphocyte studies were not performed on the other 2 patients.

Editorial Note: *Pneumocystis* pneumonia in the United States is almost exclusively limited to severely immunosuppressed patients (1). The occurrence of pneumocystosis in these 5 previously healthy individuals without a clinically apparent underlying immunodeficiency is unusual. The fact that these patients were all homosexuals suggests an association between some aspect of a homosexual lifestyle or disease acquired through sexual contact and *Pneumocystis* pneumonia in this population. All 5 patients described in this report had laboratory-confirmed CMV disease or virus shedding within 5 months of the diagnosis of *Pneumocystis* pneumonia. CMV infection has been shown to induce transient abnormalities of *in vitro* cellular-immune function in otherwise healthy human hosts (2,3). Although all 3 patients tested had abnormal cellular-immune function, no definitive conclusion regarding the role of CMV infection in these 5 cases can be reached because of the lack of published data on cellular-immune function in healthy homosexual males with and without CMV antibody. In 1 report, 7 (3.6%) of 194 patients with pneumocystosis also had CMV infection' 40 (21%) of the same group had at least 1 other major concurrent infection (1). A high prevalence of CMV infections among homosexual males was recently reported: 179 (94%) had CMV viruria; rates for 101 controls of similar age who were reported to be exclusively heterosexual were 54% for seropositivity and zero fro viruria (4). In another study of 64 males, 4 (6.3%) had

positive tests for CMV in semen, but none had CMV recovered from urine. Two of the 4 reported recent homosexual contacts. These findings suggest not only that virus shedding may be more readily detected in seminal fluid than urine, but also that seminal fluid may be an important vehicle of CMV transmission (5).

All the above observations suggest the possibility of a cellular-immune dysfunction related to a common exposure that predisposes individuals to opportunistic infections such as pneumocystosis and candidiasis. Although the role of CMV infection in the pathogenesis of pneumocystosis remains unknown, the possibility of *P. carinii* infection must be carefully considered in a differential diagnosis for previously healthy homosexual males with dyspnea and pneumonia.

SIGNIFICANCE

From the relative obscurity of a handful of cases among the male homosexual community in the early 1980s, AIDS has mushroomed to become a pandemic involving ever-increasing millions. The disease, now accepted as being the result of the effects of infection by one of several types of the Human Immunodeficiency Virus (HIV), is suspected to have originated in Central Africa, where a similar strain of the virus was present in a sub-group of chimpanzees. AIDS knows no boundaries of sexual orientation, gender, or age.

In 2004, more than three million people worldwide died from AIDS. As of 2005, nearly forty million people are infected with HIV; approximately double the population of Australia. Nearly two-thirds (approximately twenty-five million) live in sub-Saharan Africa. The increase in the number of cases in this region has been particularly marked, as has the involvement of women, who now comprise nearly half all infected adults worldwide.

The Joint United Nations Program on HIV/AIDS (UNAIDS) and the World Health Organization regard AIDS in Africa as not one single epidemic, but of a series of outbreaks. Beginning in the late 1970s, HIV spread across the breadth of the continent from West Africa to the Indian Ocean. The epidemic then spread southward, where it is now most pronounced.

According to 2004 figures from UNAIDS, South Africa is the world's hotbed of AIDS, representing almost 65 percent of the world's cases. The prevalence of the disease has remained fairly stable. However, this may reflect the near equal number of new cases (3.1 million in 2004) and deaths (2.3 million in 2004).

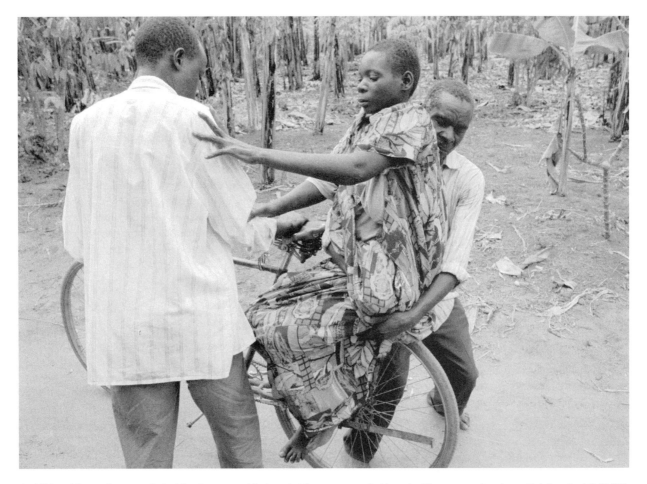

An HIV-positive patient travels by bicycle to a mobile hospital for treatment in Uganda. The country has been fighting the HIV/AIDS epidemic since 1982. ©GIDEON MENDEL/CORBIS.

The Caribbean is the second-worst-affected region. The prevalence of HIV in the population is at or above 3 percent in the Bahamas, Trinidad and Tobago, and Haiti.

Over 400,000 Latin American women are infected with HIV. However, the bulk of those who are infected are men who have sex with men and those who inject illicit drugs. A particularly grim example is provided by Brazil, where some 60 percent of drug users in major cities are estimated to be infected.

As of 2005, the HIV infection rate is growing most quickly in Asia. From 2002 to 2004, there was a 50 percent increase in infections in East Asia, with 56 percent of these being in women. This sharp increase was fueled by epidemics in China, Indonesia, and Vietnam. Epidemics are also erupting in several states in India.

Affluence is no guarantee of safety from HIV/ AIDS. In both the United States and Europe, the number of HIV infections is increasing. However, the wider affordability of antiretroviral therapy is decreasing the overall death rate from the disease. The increasing numbers of people who are surviving longer with HIV is proving taxing to many local health care systems. In developed countries, unprotected sex between heterosexuals is now a major cause of AIDS.

In the 1980s and 1990s researchers proved that the principle target for AIDS-related maladies is the immune system. Much research has since focused on clarifying the changes in the infected human immune system, and in trying to prevent, slow or even reverse these changes.

A type of T cell called the CDC4+ T cell aids in the destruction of virus-infected host cells. But, in HIV infection the number of CDC4+ cells declines over time, allowing the viral infection to proceed. The resulting decline in the immune system impairs a person's ability to fight off foreign organisms leaves the person vulnerable to life-threatening illnesses that normally would be routinely dispatched.

If the reasons for the accelerated loss of the T cells can be determined, perhaps the loss can be prevented. This would better equip patients to fight the infection.

In the 1990s, the use of Highly Active Anti-Retroviral Therapy (HAART), consisting of a "cocktail" of drugs targeted to the AIDS virus, has shown promising results in delaying the onset of symptoms. The drug mixture typically contains a nucleoside analog, which blocks genetic replication, and inhibitors of two enzymes that are critical enzyme in the making of new virus (protease and reverse transcriptase).

The benefits achieved by HAART comes at the expense of side effects that can often be severe. Also, the treatment is expensive, which blunts the use of this approach in the areas of the world most at need. Research published toward the end of 2001 indicates that the use of HAART in a systematic but periodic fashion achieves the benefits but lessens the occurrence of side effects and decreases treatment cost.

What lies ahead? Estimates of the number of people living with HIV in 2020 vary from approximately forty million, according to UNAIDS, to 200 million, according to the International AIDS society. As the majority of those affected of young to middle aged adults, the economic consequences of the removal of the vital part of the work force could be catastrophic.

FURTHER RESOURCES

Books

Barnett, Tony, and Alan Whiteside. *AIDS in the Twenty-First Century: Disease and Globalization* Waynesboro: Marlowe & Company, 2003.

Bourke, Dale Hanson. *The Skeptics Guide to the Global AIDS Crisis: Tough Questions, Direct Answers*. New York: Norton, 2003.

Ghosh, Jayait, et. al., *HIV ans AIDS in Africa: Beyond Epidemiology*. Oxford: Blackwell Publishers, 2003.

Grodeck, Brett, and Daniel S Berger. *The First Year-HIV: An Essential Guide for the Newly Diagnosed*. New York: Norton, 2003.

Web sites

AIDSinfo. U.S. Department of Health and Human Services. <http://aidsinfo.nih.gov/> (accessed January 30, 2006).

Centers for Disease Control and Prevention (CDC). "HIV/AIDS." <http://www.cdc.gov/hiv/> (accessed January 20, 2006).

Köhler and Milstein Develop Monoclonal Antibodies

Presentation Speech for the Nobel Prize in Physiology or Medicine, 1984

Speech

By: Hans Wigzell

Date: 1984

Source: *Nobel Lectures, Physiology or Medicine 1981–1990*. Singapore: World Scientific, 1993. Available online at <http://nobelprize.org/medicine/laureates/1984/presentation-speech.html> (accessed September 10, 2005).

About the Author: Hans Wigzell is a professor at the Karolinska Institute, the largest medical university in the world, and was the institute's president from 1995–2003. In 2002, Wigzell was appointed chair for the World Health Organization-United Nations AIDS Vaccine Advisory Committee.

INTRODUCTION

The ability of the immune system to recognize foreign compounds and living organisms, and to produce proteins that react with them, is one of the crucial means by which the body defends itself against disease.

The production of antibodies (proteins that react with antigens) is specific; a certain antibody forms towards a certain antigen (the foreign invader that produces an immune response in the body). In a typical immune response, however, many different kinds of antibodies will be produced, as many different antigenic targets are present.

The ability to target a single antigen can be valuable in disease therapy. Until the development of monoclonal antibodies, this ability was not clinically achievable. Monoclonal antibodies are antibodies directed towards the same antigen that are produced by the same type of cells (plasma cells). The cells are able to grow indefinitely.

Normally, this unchecked cell growth is called a myeloma, and is the root of cancer. Georges Köhler and César Milstein were successful in combining the infinite growth of myeloma cells with the exquisitely specific antibody formation ability of immune cells obtained from the spleen cells of mice.

In the scientists' pioneering research, for which they were recipients of the 1984 Nobel Prize in Physiology or Medicine, myeloma cells were fused with the antibody-secreting spleen cells of mice that had been exposed to certain antigens. The technique, called somatic cell hybridization, produced a series of combination cells called hybridomas. Each hybridoma was immortal (it could grow and divide indefinitely) and each particular hybridoma produced and secreted a particular antibody. So, each hybridoma was a factory for the production of a single (or monoclonal) antibody.

▮ PRIMARY SOURCE

Your Majesties, Your Royal Highnesses, Ladies and Gentlemen,

It is typical for the human mind that little thought goes to the functions of our body when we are healthy, yet acute interest frequently develops in times of disease. The immune system is a somewhat anonymous, talented and well-trained cellular society within ourselves which must function properly to maintain our health. The immune defence has the inherent capacity to rapidly recognize foreign material and can subsequently remember this contact for decades, thus creating the basis for vaccination. Through a clever usage of genetic material and large numbers of cells, the immune system within a single human being is able to produce defence molecules, antibodies, in billions of different shapes. The Nobel prize winners in physiology or medicine this year have all worked with the capacity of the immune system to produce specific antibodies.

… In order to fully understand the importance of Georges Köhler's and César Milstein's discoveries we should first take some steps back. Sera from intentionally immunized animals or humans constitute very important tools in the hospitals as well as in research laboratories. They are used to diagnose infectious diseases, as well as to determine the concentration of a particular hormone in a sample. But every one of these immune sera contains a unique mixture of antibodies produced by a large number of different cells and their progeny and the various antibodies react in a similar yet distinctly different manner. Thus, each immune serum has to be tested to determine the special features of that particular serum with regard to its ability to distinguish between two related hormones, different bacteria, etc. Regardless of whether the immune serum is close to being perfect or not, it will always be used up, and it is then necessary to start again trying to produce a similar kind of serum. International standardizations of tests using immune sera have thus been greatly hampered.

The discovery and development of principles for production of the so-called monoclonal antibodies by the hybridoma technique by Georges Köhler and César Milstein have largely solved all the above major problems. And the story of the discovery of the technique also contains the moral of a saga, where the evil is put into the service of the good. How did this discovery take place? César Milstein is a highly prominent biochemist working for a long time in Cambridge in England. A major interest in his research has been to explore various facets of antibody production. Milstein used tumor cells which had arisen in cells of a type that normally produce antibodies. Such tumors also produce proteins which in all respects look like antibodies, although it is difficult to find suitable foreign structures to which they can bind. Milstein wanted amongst other things to study what would happen if two different tumor lines were allowed to fuse, e.g. what would happen to the production of the antibody-like proteins if for instance the tumor cells came from different species? Milstein constructed tumor cell lines allowing only hybrid cells between the two tumor cells to grow in certain defined tissue culture solutions. The systems worked and the hybrid cells produced large quantities of the antibody-like proteins, some of which at the molecular level could be shown to be hybrid molecules as well.

At the same time the young researcher Georges Köhler struggled in Basel in Switzerland to study normal antibody-producing cells in tissue culture. His research was in part frustrating as he could only get very few cells to survive for short periods of time. Köhler knew of the important studies of Milstein, and it seemed logical to see if normal antibody-forming cells could be fused with tumor cells to produce long-lived hybrid cell lines. If this was indeed possible the experiments of Milstein would indicate that they should then continue to produce their antibodies. At the same time the normally evil feature of tumor cells, the capacity to proliferate for ever, would now be turned into a very beneficial feature. Köhler went to Milstein's laboratory and together they wrestled with the problems and managed to solve them in a hectic two year period, 1975–1976. By that time they had succeeded to develop a technique allowing them at will to fish up exactly those rare antibody-producing cells that they wanted from a sea of cells. These cells were fused with tumor cells creating hybrid cells with eternal life and capacity to produce the very same antibody in high quantity. Köhler and Milstein called these hybrid cells hybridomas, and as all cells in a given hybridoma come from one single hybrid cell, the antibodies made are monoclonal.

Köhler's, and Milstein's development of the hybridoma technique for production of monoclonal antibodies have in less than a decade revolutionized the use of antibodies in health care and research. Rare antibodies with a tailor-made-like fit for a given structure can now be made in large quantities. The hybridoma cells can be stored in tissue banks and the very same monoclonal antibody can be used all over the world with a guarantee for eternal supply. The precision in diagnosis is greatly improved, and entirely new possibilities for therapy have been opened up via the hybridoma technique. Rare molecules present in trace amounts in complex solution can now be purified in an efficient manner using monoclonal antibodies. In all, it is therefore correct to describe the hybridoma technique discovered by Georges Köhler and César Milstein as one of the major methodological advances in medicine during this century.

Dr. Jerne, Dr. Köhler and Dr. Milstein,

On behalf of the Nobel Assembly of the Karolinska Institute I would like to congratulate you on your outstanding accomplishments and ask you to receive the Nobel Prize in Physiology or Medicine from the hands of His Majesty the King.

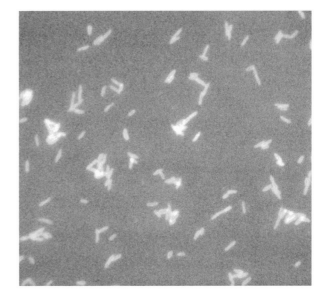

Legionella pneumophila causes illnesses such as Legionnaires' disease and Pontiac fever. Here, the bacteria are tagged with a monoclonal antibody containing dye and then viewed in ultraviolet light. ©CDC/PHIL/CORBIS.

SIGNIFICANCE

Monoclonal antibodies have become widely used in the diagnosis and study of diseases. For example, a monoclonal antibody can be combined (tagged) with a fluorescent molecule to allow scientists to visualize the disease target when tissue samples are obtained and examined. As well, a therapeutic agent, such as a radioactive atom or an antibiotic, can be tagged to the monoclonal antibody to specifically deliver the treatment to the target.

The use of monoclonal antibodies in human applications, however, has been slower to develop, and monoclonal antibody-based drugs remain more promise than clinical reality. The major stumbling block involves rejection, as monoclonal antibodies are raised in mice, and mice antibodies are themselves recognized as foreign by the human immune system. Thus, before the beneficial monoclonal antibodies have a chance to act, they are destroyed by the human immune system.

Raising monoclonal antibodies in humans would circumvent this problem. But, ethical restrictions prevent this approach, since humans would need to be deliberately exposed to the harmful agents that are the eventual target of the therapy. Instead, laboratory-based approaches, where combinations of mouse and human antibodies are being tried, aim to make the therapeutic antibody tolerable when given to a person. Transgenic mice, which produce human antibodies against the target antigen, are a promising avenue of research.

Some examples of commercially available formulations of monoclonal antibodies include preparations to help block the host-mediated (autoimmune) rejection of organs following transplantation of pancreatic cells in type 1 diabetes mellitus, to ease the progression of rheumatoid arthritis (another autoimmune disease), to target and kill some cancer cells, and to help block allergic asthma reactions.

FURTHER RESOURCES
Books

Shepard, Philip S., and Christopher Dean. *Monoclonal Antibodies: A Practical Approach*. Oxford: Oxford University Press, 2000.

Simmons, Marie A. *Monoclonal Antibodies: New Research*. New York: Nova Biomedical Books, 2005.

Baby Fae Loses her Battle

The Baboon Heart Fails but a Doctor Defends the Transplant

Magazine article

By: Claudia Wallis

Date: November 26, 1984

Source: Claudia Wallis. "Baby Fae Loses Her Battle: The Baboon Heart Fails But a Doctor Defends the Transplant." *Time* 124 (November 26, 1984): 88–89.

About the Author: Claudia Wallis is a former managing editor of *Time*, the oldest weekly news magazine in the United States. *Time* was founded by Briton Hadden and Henry Luce of the *Yale Daily News*, the longest running daily college newspaper in America. It offers comprehensive and lively coverage of politics, economics, entertainment, medicine, and science. *Time* has a worldwide circulation of about 5.4 million and is distinguished by the red border around its cover.

INTRODUCTION

The first human-to-human heart transplant was carried out in South Africa by Dr. Christiaan Barnard (1922–2001) in 1967. The recipient was a middle-aged man. For infants, however, heart transplantation has always been more difficult. A baby's heart weighs, typically, about one ounce and is about the size of a walnut. An adult's heart would be too large to transplant into a baby and few babies die under conditions that make their organs suitable for transplantation. Nevertheless, the first human-to-human heart transplant in the United States was performed on an infant, using an infant donor. The surgeon was Dr. Adrian Kantrowitz (1918–) and the operation took place in New York just three days after Dr. Barnard's operation. Unfortunately, the child died soon after the surgery was performed.

For babies born with a congenital condition known as hypoplastic left-heart syndrome (HLHS), which affects one child in 12,000 born in the United States, transplantation would appear to be a good solution. The left side of the heart cannot work properly because of the malformation and it is common for infants with HLHS to die within a few days of birth. There is so-called palliative surgery available, but it is difficult and has a limited success rate.

Dr. Leonard Bailey (1942–) of Loma Linda Medical Center, California, had spent much of his career in pediatric cardiac surgery and had a special interest in HLHS. By 1984, transplant surgery had advanced to the point that he thought an animal-to-human transplant was possible and, indeed, desirable given the shortage of human hearts for infants. The drug cyclosporin could prevent the rejection of the new heart by the immune system. In addition, the infant immune system is not yet fully developed, making rejection less likely.

Xenotransplantation is the technical term for organ transplantation between species, such as from a baboon to a human. In the 1960s, there had been a few operations involving transplants of kidneys and hearts from baboons and chimpanzees to humans, but with little success. The species barrier created additional problems with rejection. However, by 1984, Dr. Bailey thought the time might be right to try a xenotransplant operation to treat a baby with HLHS. When "Baby Fae," as she was known, was born with the condition, her parents agreed to let Dr. Bailey and his team go ahead with a baboon transplant.

■ PRIMARY SOURCE

After 21 days of battling to preserve a fragile life, Dr. Leonard Bailey was visibly spent. His voice trembled and broke with emotion last Friday as he faced the press at Loma Linda University Medical Center in California to provide the epitaph for the dark-haired infant known as Baby Fae. "Today we grieve the loss of this patient's life," said the 41-year-old heart surgeon. That life, he insisted, had not been in vain. "Infants with heart disease yet to be born will some day soon have the opportunity to live, thanks to the courage of this infant and her parents. We are remarkably encouraged by what we have learned from Baby Fae." So ended an extraordinary experiment that had captured the attention of the world and made medical history. For three weeks the 5-lb. infant had survived with the heart of a baboon—more than two weeks longer than any previous recipient of an animal heart.

Her brief life was marked by more than its share of controversy. Doctors challenged the wisdom of using an animal heart when a human organ might have been preferable; animal lovers protested the sacrifice of a healthy monkey for what they saw as medical sensationalism; and others questioned the circumstances under which Fae's parents had consented to so drastic a procedure. Nonetheless, Fae's struggle for survival converted many skeptics and won the hearts of millions of people. Her progress and setbacks—virtually every beat of her simian heart—were avidly followed. Hundreds of Americans sent cards, flowers, even money to the infant as gestures of support and sympathy.

Though no one expected Fae's survival to be easy, her death last Thursday night came as a surprise. The child, who was born with a fatal defect called hypoplastic left heart, had received the heart of a seven-month-old female baboon on Oct. 26 and made steady progress for the next two weeks. In a touching videotape made just four days after surgery, Baby Fae was seen yawning and stretching, seemingly a normal infant in every respect. By the second week she was no longer dependent on a supplementary oxygen supply or intravenous feeding.

According to her doctors, problems did not arise until the 14th day after surgery, when a battery of tests revealed

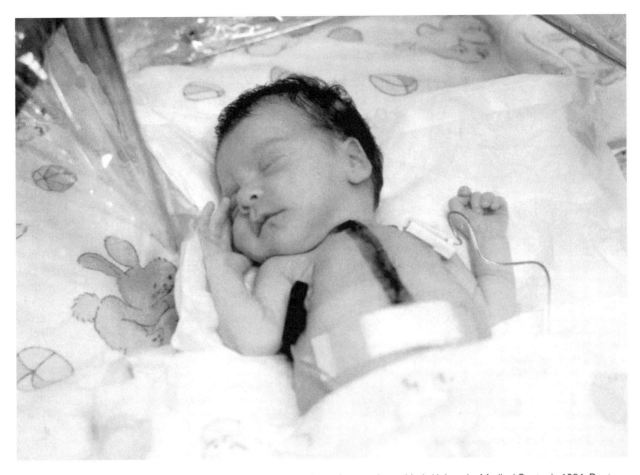

Baby Fae, the world's first infant to receive a baboon heart transplant, sleeps at Loma Linda University Medical Center in 1984. Doctors at Loma Linda said they were initially "elated" with the child's progress, but Baby Fae died 21 days after the controversial transplant. October 30, 1984. ©BETTMANN/CORBIS.

that the infant's body was beginning to reject the alien heart. Over the next five days, doctors increased her dosages of the antirejection drugs, supplemented her weakening heart with digitalis, eased the strain on her breathing with a respirator and resumed intravenous feeding. By Wednesday of last week Surgeon David Hinshaw told a packed auditorium of reporters at Loma Linda that "she is in the process of turning around. Signs of rejection are reversing right down the line. Baby Fae is holding her own."

As late as 7 p.m. Pacific time on Thursday, just two hours before she died, a hospital spokesman was reporting that the child was "hanging in there." In fact, Baby Fae was experiencing kidney failure. For several days, the child's urine output had been declining—an indication that the kidneys were not functioning properly. This put other organs in jeopardy and ultimately contributed to heart failure, Bailey explained at the press conference. It was not clear if Fae's kidney problem was due to her drug regimen, the surgery or rejection, which can trigger the

failure of a number of organs. Most likely, it was a combination of factors. Though doctors had discussed the possibility of a second transplant—either from a human donor or another baboon—the child's weakened condition made this impossible. At 10:30 p.m. the hospital released a tersely worded death announcement: despite "intensive efforts" to restore her heart, "Baby Fae died at 9 p.m. Her parents were with her as much as possible during this period and are receiving support from chaplains and the physicians."

In response to questions last week, Bailey said that Baby Fae suffered little pain in her final hours. "I believe she suffered a great deal more before I saw her than after," he insisted. "The best days of her short life were after her transplant." The parents, he maintained, had no regrets about the experiment: "They felt that it was an enriching experience."

Despite the hospital's efforts to protect the identity of the parents, information about the mother, Teresa, 23, began to seep out last week. Baby Fae's unmarried parents are an impoverished couple who moved from Kansas to Barstow, Calif., 90 miles northeast of Los Angeles, about two years ago. According to an NBC report, both parents had brushes with the law in their home state: the mother for passing bad checks, the father for disorderly conduct. Though the couple had lived together for five years and had a 2-1/2-year-old son, the father deserted Teresa a week before the birth of Baby Fae. She then turned to a close friend, Henry Raedel, 28, who was with her when she entered Barstow's small hospital on Oct. 14. Less than three hours later Baby Fae was born. The child was three weeks premature and suffering from a seriously underdeveloped heart; her real name was said to be Stephanie Fae.

According to her hospital roommate, Teresa is a tall, thin, outgoing blond and a heavy smoker who worried about her daughter. The newborn was transferred to the Loma Linda medical center, a Seventh-day Adventist institution with an excellent reputation in pediatric cardiology. Doctors there explained to Teresa that the baby would probably die within a few days and that she could either leave her at the hospital or take her home. Raedel tearfully told the Los Angeles Times that after a sleepless vigil, "watching her to make sure she was breathing," they took the child home to die.

The hospital called Fae's mother within the next two days and, as Bailey explained, proposed the baboon heart transplant. A friend recalls that Teresa "decided she had to do anything possible to try and save her baby's life." Barstow residents who are close to the mother say that she was well aware of the experimental nature of the operation and was not pressured into agreeing to it.

Even so, many questions have been raised about the way in which consent was obtained. The hospital's refusal to release the text of the form signed by Fae's parents fueled the controversy. This document "is crucial," says Arthur Caplan, a medical ethicist at the Hastings Center in Hastings-on-Hudson, N.Y. "Were the parents informed about the possibility of a human heart?" Others felt that Bailey may have misrepresented the facts about the "Norwood procedure," a surgical treatment recently developed to help infants with hypoplastic heart. Indeed, in his public statements, Bailey understated the success rate of this alternative.

The medical world will be reflecting on the case of Baby Fae for a long time. While a number of physicians considered the experiment premature, most were impressed and surprised by the infant's record-setting survival. "This has been a success," says Dr. Donald Hill, chief of cardiovascular surgery at Pacific Presbyterian Medical Center in San Francisco. "They have demonstrated that there is a window early in life where the

opportunity to make a successful transplant from a baboon to a human exists." But neither Hill nor other doctors foresaw any possibility of using simian hearts as a permanent solution to heart disease. "I think these transplants might be used to bide time until a human heart can be found," says Dr. Michael DeBakey, the pioneering Houston heart transplant surgeon.

Such stopgap measures are desperately needed. "There is a tremendous shortage of donor organs for infants," says Dr. Thomas Starzl, a leading liver transplant surgeon at Pittsburgh's Children's Hospital. He estimates that eleven out of twelve of his infant patients who are now waiting for liver transplants will die before suitable donors can be found. Baby Fae has already had one salutary effect. According to Barbara Schulman, coordinator for the Regional Organ Procurement Agency at UCLA, over the past three weeks the number of prospective infant donors referred to the agency has soared.

Bailey and his team believe that the lessons of Baby Fae will pave the way for future baboon heart transplants, and he is convinced that the next time "we will be able to diagnose rejection earlier." The surgeon was vague about when the next time might be. "I plan to attempt it again by-and-by," he told reporters. Fae's mother, he noted, had encouraged his efforts. "The last thing she said to me was to carry on and not to let it be wasted."

SIGNIFICANCE

The Baby Fae case was controversial and there have been few animal-to-human organ transplants since that time. Bailey was accused by some medical and ethics experts of foolhardy experimentation and even child abuse. Animal rights activists complained of the sacrifice of a healthy baboon. There were questions, too, over whether a human heart transplant or palliative surgery might have been possible in this case. In short, had the parents and Baby Fae been exploited for the sake of pushing forward the boundaries of science? Many within the medical community did support the work, however, arguing there can be no advances without risk, and Baby Fae would surely have died without this intervention.

From a clinical point of view Baby Fae's case was interesting, since she survived for twenty-one days, which is longer than some recipients of human-to-human heart transplants survived at that time. Given that the latter is almost routine these days, thanks to advances in anti-rejection therapy and better understanding of immunology, perhaps xenotransplantation is now a feasible prospect? Scientists have been working to develop pig hearts for transplant, using genetic modification of the pigs to overcome rejection issues. However, there are still ethical and safety barriers to be crossed before those awaiting a transplant can be offered a pig's heart. Receiving an organ from another species may not be the main issue, since pig heart valves have been successfully transplanted into humans for some years now. With other organs, however, the risks have not yet been shown to be outweighed by the benefits.

The Baby Fae case may have done nothing, directly, to advance the cause of xenotransplantation. But it did have other benefits. First, it raised awareness of the tragedy of HLHS and led to further research. Second, more human-to-human heart transplants were carried out in infants. In November 1986, the Loma Linda team celebrated the first birthday of "Baby Moses"—the first successful newborn human heart transplant. Without Baby Fae it is unlikely that Baby Moses would have survived.

FURTHER RESOURCES

Periodicals

Donnelley, Strachan. "The Heart of the Matter; Using Primate Hearts as Human Heart Transplant Bridges." *The Hastings Center Report* 1 (January 1, 1989): 26–28.

Web sites

The Center for the Study of Technology and Society. "Today in Technology History." <http://www.tecsoc.org/pubs/history/2001/oct26.htm> (accessed November 5, 2005).

LLUMC Legacy. "Baby Fae." <http://www.llu.edu/info/legacy/Legacy3.html> (accessed November 5, 2005).

The Promise of Prozac

Neuropharmacology

Magazine article

By: Geoffrey Cowley

Date: March 26, 1990

Source: G. Cowley, K. Springen, E. A. Leonard, K. Robins, and J. Gordon. "The Promise of Prozac." *Newsweek* (March 26, 1990): 38–41.

About the Author: Geoffrey Cowley is a senior editor for *Newsweek* magazine. After earning a B.A. in English from Lewis and Clark College in Portland, Oregon, and an M.A. in English from the University of Washington, Cowley worked as a reporter and feature writer at *The Seattle Times*, then an editor at *The*

Sciences. He joined *Newsweek* in 1988, where he has written extensively about global health trends.

INTRODUCTION

"The Promise of Prozac" was published in *Newsweek* in 1990, about four years after the 1986 market launch of Prozac, the first antidepressant medication in the selective serotonin reuptake inhibitor (SSRI) group. The article outlines theories about Prozac's mechanism of action in relieving depression and how this proposed mechanism altered the public's perception of mental illnesses, such as depression, phobias, and obsessive compulsive disorder (OCD), so they were seen as physical illnesses rather than character flaws.

The *Newsweek* article outlines Prozac use grew rapidly because it is generally better tolerated by most patients for long-term treatment than are older antidepressant drugs, such as tricyclics and monoamine oxidase inhibitors (MAOIs). With the launch of Prozac, the authors explain, it became possible for most people to use a pharmaceutical treatment for depression indefinitely, with few or no side effects. Since Prozac relieves depression in about 60 percent of patients taking it, the only drawback for the overwhelming majority using the drug has been its cost, which has often been covered by health insurance.

The article ends by raising possibilities regarding the ways in which psychopharmacology might not only treat diagnosed mental illness, but also equip people to cope more effectively with the stresses of ordinary life, including relationships and work. At the outset, the authors note that such use by "healthy" people could result in unintended long-term negative consequences, including certain drug side effects. Nevertheless, the article concludes that the relatively benign safety profile of Prozac has encouraged speculation regarding how pharmaceuticals could alter personality in ways that could benefit people and society.

■ PRIMARY SOURCE

Susan A. has spent most of her adult life fighting with people—her parents, her neighbors, her co-workers, her husband. The 39-year-old Seattle woman has suffered bouts of depression and bulimia, abused drugs and alcohol, and twice tried to kill herself. She once sought relief in an antidepressant called doxepin, but she didn't like the way it made her feel.

Two years ago her therapist, Dr. Michael Norden, suggested she try a new drug called Prozac. She did. Within a month, Susan had given up psychotherapy in favor of school and a full-time job. She had also given up tranquilizers and street drugs. "I feel 1,000%," she said in a written note. "I actually like Mom & Dad now, I'm well liked at work, I don't ruminate on the negatives, I don't have murderous rages, my marriage is five times better."

Richard Lane likes Prozac, too. He sells it, at $1.60 per capsule, out of his pharmacy in Boston's Beacon Hill neighborhood. But brisk sales are only part of its appeal. "Most of these people used to come in here and complain," he says of his Prozac customers. "Now they're saying, 'I never felt better!'" Lane just hopes the effect lasts. "I can't tell when someone's on medication," he says, "but I sure can tell when they're off."

Prozac, now the nation's most prescribed antidepressant, hit the market in December 1987. Sales reached $125 million in 1988 and soared to $350 million in 1989 (more than was spent on *all* antidepressants just two years earlier). Market analysts expect the drug to pull in $500 million this year and to top $1 billion by 1995. The big numbers are partly a product of price—Prozac costs about 20 times as much as a generic antidepressant—but they also reflect a demand. An estimated 15 million Americans suffer from clinical depression, and physicians are writing or renewing 650,000 Prozac prescriptions every month.

Good press: Nearly everyone has something nice to say about the new treatment. It looks like a "wonder drug" to *New York* magazine, a miracle diet pill to the *National Enquirer.* The drug has had such good press that even healthy people have started asking for it. "Our phone rings off the hook every time someone does a story about Prozac," says Dr. David Hellerstein, head of psychiatric outpatient services at Manhattan's Beth Israel Medical Center. "People want to try it. If you tell them they're not depressed they say, 'sure I am!'"

Though Eli Lilly markets it only as a treatment for depression, doctors are using Prozac to treat anxiety, addictions, bulimia and obsessive-compulsive disorder. When it works, it can change people's lives—sometimes even their names. Dr. Peter D. Kramer, a Rhode Island therapist who writes a column for *The Psychiatric Times,* recently described running into one of his patients in the local market.

"I have a new name," she told me, beaming.

"Oh?" I said, thinking she had married.

"Yes," she said. "I call myself Ms. Prozac."

Fluoxetine, as Prozac is known in the literature, is just the first of a new generation of antidepressants now headed for the market. A half-dozen related compounds are still in clinical trials. Together, these breakthrough drugs may change the lives of millions—not because they're inherently more effective in treating depression

(they're not), but because they're far easier to tolerate and have a broader range of applications. Prozac is not without side effects—scattered case reports have described severe adverse reactions—and its long-term risks are unknown. A wide range of people from the suicidal to the mildly depressed, are receiving the drug, but it is simply too early to know if Prozac is the answer for all of them. Some experts fear it is being passed out too freely, much as Valium was in the '70s. Yet even skeptics agree that Prozac and its cousins are casting new light on the nature of mental illness and expanding the potential of psychiatry.

For 30 years antidepressants have come in two basic varieties: tricyclics (such as Elavil and Tofranil) and monoamine oxidase inhibitors, or MAOIs (Nardil, Parnate). No one knows quite how any of these drugs relieve depression, but they all have at least one key feature in common. They bolster the action of serotonin and norepinephrine, two of the chemicals that transmit impulses through the nervous system. The tricyclics work by blocking reabsorption of these messengers by the nerve cells that release them; the MAOIs interfere with enzymes that break the messengers down. Prozac works on the same principle as the tricyclics (it keeps a neurotransmitter in circulation by blocking reabsorption) but it works exclusively on serotonin. "Instead of using a shotgun," says Dr. James Halikas, a professor of psychiatry at the University of Minnesota, "you're using a bullet."

The scattershot character of the old tricyclics makes them very tricky to administer. Instead of starting out on a flat, standard dose, a patient spends several weeks taking larger and larger amounts of the drug. The physician uses blood tests to determine which dose yields the right serum concentration....

Even at the optimal doses, the old drugs have an array of unpleasant side effects. The MAOIs can become deadly if taken with pickles, dairy products, red wine, beer or allergy medications. The tricyclics can cause low blood pressure and heart disturbances—real hazards for elderly patients. And they are notorious for causing sluggishness, dizziness, blurred vision, constipation and weight gain. Given those alternatives, some patients opt for depression. Others fall into a vicious cycle of using a drug until they're feeling better and then stopping, only to fall deeper into the abyss.

...Prozac has quite a different character. Though the drug typically takes three weeks to become effective, a daily dose of one or two 20-milligram capsules is generally sufficient. That means patients escape the ordeal of blood monitoring. There is far less risk of overdose (only one patient has succeeded at committing suicide with the drug alone—and that person took 7,000 mg, nearly 100 times the maximum daily dose). With Prozac, says Dr. Jan

Fawcett, chairman of psychiatry at Chicago's Rush Presbyterian St. Luke's Medical Center, "you're not putting such a weapon in someone's hands."

As for side effects, the most common include headaches, nausea, insomnia, jitteriness and weight loss. But many Prozac users are only too happy to shed a few pounds. And most vastly prefer being slightly wired to feeling sluggish. The bottom line is that people who went years without relief are now getting it.

Consider the case of Ellen M. The 48-year-old editor has been enduring depressions and experimenting with different treatments since she was 11 years old. First it was sleeping pills to get her through the night. Later she tried Sinequan, a tricyclic, but the drug exacerbated her glaucoma. So she tried an MAOI, which did her no good, and then switched to another nontricyclic called Desyrel. The Desyrel improved her mood, but each dose put her directly to sleep—and she had to take it three times a day. Finally she switched to Prozac. "I feel so normal that I have to use tricks to remember whether I've taken it," she says. "I don't feel drugged. I don't feel euphoric. I'm just euphoric that I'm not depressed."

In light of Prozac's many virtues—its specificity, its low toxicity, the convenience with which doctors and patients can use it—the excitement it generates is not hard to fathom. But as Lilly itself concedes, there are good reasons for handling Prozac with care. All drugs have the potential for adverse reactions, and none works for everyone who takes it. Prozac is no exception. And because it's so new, some therapists argue that it shouldn't be the treatment of first resort. They say patients should get Prozac only after they've tried the traditional alternatives. By using such a new drug so frequently, says Dr. Ed Schweizer of the University of Pennsylvania Medical School, "doctors are throwing caution to the wind."

...One concern is that therapists, not to mention family doctors, may be giving the drug to people without fully diagnosing their problems. Because the tricyclics can be so dangerous, psychiatrists rarely hand them out without first performing a complete physical and psychological exam, notes Hellerstein, of Beth Israel. That work-up may show that the depression stems from some hidden illness—cancer, hypothyroidism, AIDS—or from a job or marriage problem that no drug can possibly solve. Because Prozac is perceived as safe, the temptation is to prescribe first and ask questions later....

A small minority of patients don't simply fail to get better on Prozac—they get worse. Some develop what's known as caffeine syndrome. "They feel restless, grit their teeth, sometimes have tremors," says Dr. John Baker of San Francisco, who has used the drug to treat depression in AIDS patients. Both men and women have complained of decreased sexual interest and a loss or delay of orgasm while on the drug. There is also a slight risk of seizures (12 cases were reported among 6,000 patients in worldwide clinical trials).

In rare cases, Prozac users have become manic, violent or suicidal. A research team headed by Dr. Martin H. Teicher of Harvard Medical School recently reported that six previously nonsuicidal patients developed "intense, violent suicidal preoccupation after 2–7 weeks of fluoxetine treatment." "In our own experience," the team wrote, "this side effect has occurred in 3.5% of patients receiving fluoxetine." Lilly is aware of such findings, but says "the overall experience with Prozac indicates that it is a safe and effective medication." ...

...Caveats aside, the evidence to date suggest that Prozac is a big improvement over the older treatments. Moreover, therapists keep finding other promising uses for it. The older tricyclics have never been much good for treating obsessive-compulsive disorder (OCD), a biologically based syndrome afflicting an estimated 4 million Americans. But studies consistently show that Prozac and two other new compounds—fluvoxamine and a novel tricyclic called cloripramine—work as well against OCD as they do against depression....

...The new antidepressants' other possible uses have been less thoroughly documented, but the case reports are intriguing. Last fall, for instance, researchers at Boston's McLean Hospital reported that they'd used Prozac or a combination of two other serotonin enhancers (trazodone and tranylcypromine) to treat three women who had suffered from both bulimia and kleptomania. All three got relief from the drugs—and their compulsions to binge and to steal returned whenever the treatments were withdrawn. Prozac has also shown some promise as a treatment for such diverse problems as obesity, addiction and "borderline personality disorder," Susan A.'s now manageable condition.

As Prozac's success stories mount, so does the sense that depression and other mental disorders are just that—treatable illnesses, not failings of character. The stigma is receding, and the search for still better treatments is accelerating. Sooner or later, notes Dr. Peter Kramer, the Rhode Island therapist who treated "Ms. Prozac," there may even be a drug that can "change people in ways they want to be changed—not just away from illness but toward some desirable psychological state." We're only beginning to fathom the mind's exquisite chemistry. As our knowledge expands, so will the possibilities for enhancing our mental states. Who knows? Maybe wit and insight will eventually come in capsule form. For now, the good news is that afflicted people are escaping their torment.

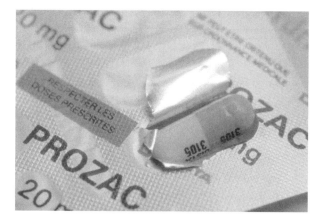

Prozac, which is widely prescribed to treat depression, affects neurotransmitters in the brain. ©ANNEBICQUE BERNARD/CORBIS SYGMA.

SIGNIFICANCE

Although the *Newsweek* article "The Promise of Prozac" was written several years ago, the issues raised in the article are still cogent. One of the psychiatric experts cited in the article, Peter Kramer, went on to write about many of the themes explored in the article. In 1993, he published *Listening to Prozac*, which became a best seller, and in 2005, he published *Against Depression*, a polemic against the tendency to find virtue or value in depression. Kramer's ideas are now at the center of controversy over the nature of depression.

The significance of "The Promise of Prozac" lies in its characterization of depression and other disorders, as well as ordinary personality traits, as biological conditions that can be altered with psychopharmacology. The article does not explore the origins of depression or other mental qualities such as wit or insight, but their origin seems to be of little consequence. Whatever factors are involved in the development of depression, the article suggests that the biochemical state of the brain might be altered using drugs such as Prozac to improve mental and emotional functioning. This improved functioning could include greater powers of concentration and attention to detail, enabling people to better fulfill social roles in work and interpersonal relationships. Drugs might also produce greater emotional resilience in people, helping them to fix problems creatively without being overwhelmed by negative feelings about past failures or traumas.

The publicity exemplified by the *Newsweek* article and Kramer's books about new generation antidepressants—mainly selective serotonin reuptake inhibitors (SSRIs), such as Prozac (fluoxetine) and Paxil (paroxetine)—led to an explosion in the use of these drugs. A report by the U.S. Department of Health and Human Services in 2000 revealed that by 1998, SSRIs had captured 62 percent of the massive Medicaid market for antidepressants, a market which grew 40 percent from 1995 to 1998. Most of this growth was due to SSRI prescriptions, which did not supplant the older antidepressants (tricyclics and monoamine oxidase inhibitors). Rather, SSRIs expanded the demand for antidepressant treatment.

Many of the patients using SSRIs might not have been prescribed drug treatment five years earlier and would only have received psychotherapy. A large part of this growth in SSRI prescriptions is due to the ease with which family doctors are able to prescribe them, since these medications come in a standard dose. Prescribing the older antidepressant drugs, which require the dosage to be precisely adjusted for each patient, is usually the province of psychiatric specialists.

Many of the issues raised in the *Newsweek* article and the books of Peter Kramer are philosophical in nature and have not been tested—and, indeed, would be difficult to test—in clinical trials. The U.S Food and Drug Administration (FDA) has not approved the use of the SSRIs to "improve emotional resilience" or "enhance concentration," except in the context of clinical depression. There is, as yet, no evidence beyond the anecdotes and testimonials mentioned in "The Promise of Prozac" and Kramer's books that such drugs can improve peoples' personalities when the individuals taking them do not meet the criteria for clinical depression.

Furthermore, the use of SSRIs for depression is "empirical." Physicians prescribe them because they have been shown to be effective in treating depression, but the mechanism by which they work is still not known. There is increasing evidence that prolonged, untreated depression results in a loss of brain cells, increased physical illness, higher death rates, and other deleterious biological consequences. However, there currently is no evidence for the way in which depression might produce these effects.

There is a corresponding lack of evidence in experimental psychology for claims that Prozac or other drugs improve activities of daily living in people not diagnosed as depressed (or as having other mental disorders, such as phobias, attention disorders, anxiety, etc.). Yet the pressures on people in contemporary Western society may cause more and more of them to ask their physicians to prescribe drugs that might boost their ability to perform successfully.

In 2004, the FDA required manufacturers of Prozac and other antidepressants to include a "black box" warning statement (the FDA's strongest warning) on their packaging and labeling. This warning states:

Antidepressants increase the risk of suicidal thinking and behavior (suicidality) in children and adolescents with major depressive disorder (MDD) and other psychiatric disorders. Anyone considering the use of [Drug Name] or any other antidepressant in a child or adolescent must balance this risk with the clinical need. Patients who are started on therapy should be observed closely for clinical worsening, suicidality, or unusual changes in behavior. Families and caregivers should be advised of the need for close observation and communication with the prescriber."

FURTHER RESOURCES

Books

Kramer, Peter. *Against Depression.* New York: Viking, 2005.

———. *Listening to Prozac.* New York: Penguin Books, 1993.

Shank, Joshua Wolf. *Lincoln's Melancholy.* Boston: Houghton Mifflin, 2005.

Web sites

U.S. Department of Health and Human Services. "Access and Utilization of New Antidepressant and Antipsychotic Medications, Chapter VI, Patterns of Antipsychotic and Antidepressant Utilization in Medicaid, 1995–1998." <http://aspe.hhs.gov/health/reports/Psychmedaccess/chap06.htm> (accessed October 30, 2005).

Animals and Medical Science: A Vision of a New Era

Magazine article

By: David O. Wiebers

Date: 1994

Source: David O. Wiebers. "Animals and Medical Science: Vision of a New Era." *Sunrise Magazine.* February/March (1994).

About the Author: David O. Wiebers is the Director of Neurology and a Professor of Neurology at the Mayo Clinic College of Medicine. He is also a Consultant in Neurology and Clinical Epidemiology at the Mayo Clinic in Rochester, Minnesota. His particular areas of interest are stroke prevention and epidemiology, intracranial aneurysms, diagnosis and treatment of stroke and related disorders, natural history and management of carotid occlusive disease, and the treatment of intracranial vascular malformations. He has been credited with nearly 150 scholarly publications.

INTRODUCTION

There has always been considerable controversy around the use of animals in research laboratories. The degree of disagreement between those in favor and those opposed varies with the subject area: there is slightly less discord in the medical research realm than there is in the cosmetic and other consumer product testing arenas. As a rule, it is the research protocols that involve causing pain and suffering to animals that are the most contentious. When the outcome of the study will be of significant and measurable benefit to humankind and there will be minimal and promptly addressed pain or suffering caused to the experimental animals, research shows moderate public support of the process. Many research scientists whose opinions are published in the animal research literature state that they would prefer it if their work could be done without the use of experimental animals, they purport to use the smallest possible number of laboratory animals, and to use the most humane methods possible, within the confines of study requirements. Legislation and public policy dictate guidelines for the use and treatment of animals in the laboratory setting, and the United States Department of Agriculture conducts oversight of research facilities using animal subjects in order to ascertain that the requirements of the Animal Welfare Act are followed.

Animals are used in medical research for a variety of reasons: many disease processes can best (or only) be studied in living organisms; it is universally considered impractical and unethical to expose healthy humans to disease protocols or to unproven techniques and interventions in order to study a disease process or to develop effective medical or surgical interventions; many types of animals are sufficiently biologically similar to humans in their disease susceptibility to be used for study of processes in humans; and animals have shorter lives, so intervention outcomes can be studied over the course of a lifespan. In carrying out research projects, scientists often seek to control as many environmental and physiological variables as possible, in order to be certain that any changes they see in the organism are due to their intervention and not to some environmental or extraneous influences. With animals, it is more possible to control temperature, food and fluid intake, lighting, and other aspects of their environment during research studies.

When scientists develop potentially effective new pharmaceuticals, surgical techniques, or other medically related techniques or interventions, they must first be tested for efficacy and safety in animals. When the animal testing results can be demonstrated to be unequivocally positive, they may then be piloted in human volunteers who could derive substantial

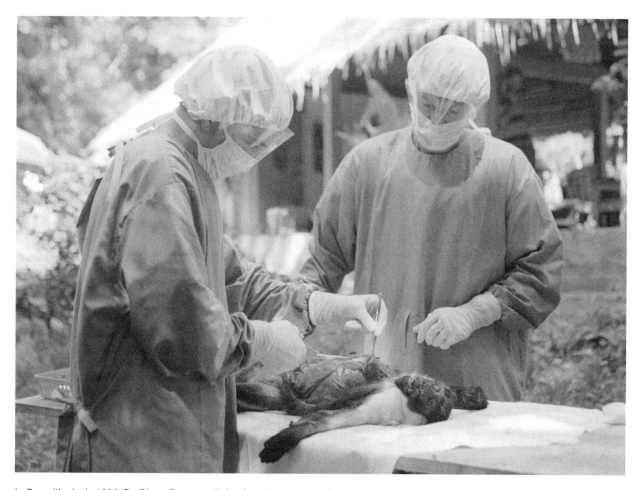

In Cote d'Ivoire in 1996, Dr. Pierre Formenty (left) of the World Health Organization (WHO) works with ethnologist Christophe Boesch of the Wild Chimpanzee Foundation to learn more about the effects of the Ebola virus. ©PATRICK ROBERT/SYGMA/CORBIS.

potential benefit from the interventions. Those human studies are called clinical trials.

Some examples of research involving animals that have had very beneficial outcomes for humans have occurred in studies of heart disease, cancer therapies, and treatments for bacterial infections. Among the techniques that have been developed as a result of laboratory animal research are: electrocardiography, cardiac catheterization, angiograms, techniques for measurement of cardiac blood flow, angioplasty, cardiac bypass surgery, and heart transplant techniques and technologies.

Many different types of animals have been used to study the ways in which viruses can cause tumors, and the ways in which tumors and various forms of cancer grow and spread. Chemotherapy protocols, radiation therapies, and many types of surgical interventions were developed as a result of laboratory animal research.

Early studies of antibiotics, particularly the use and efficacy of penicillin, were carried out with the use of rodents. They are still used in order to determine the effectiveness of targeted antibiotics with specific bacterial organisms, as well as to study efficacy, toxicity, side effects, and potential dosing protocols for newly developed pharmaceuticals.

PRIMARY SOURCE

The use of animals in biomedical research is perhaps the most volatile and controversial of all the issues facing the animal protection and medical communities.

As a physician, I have a great interest in the advancement of medical science to improve the health of humans and other living beings, but I also have a great interest in the protection of animals, and I can tell you that it has not always been easy or pleasant to reconcile the priorities of these two communities when it comes to this issue.

A number of animal-research advocates have called upon physicians everywhere to "defend medical science" and have been highly critical of physicians who seriously question practices within the field of medicine in regard to animal research, testing, and education. In the course of discussing so-called "extremists" and "radicals" in the animal movement, many animal-research advocates have begun to apply these terms not only to the few individuals engaged in violent, unlawful tactics but also to anyone who would advocate any change from the status quo, no matter how small.

With many of the voices currently emanating from the medical community so adamantly opposed to animal protectionists, and with the public and lawmakers historically having looked to the medical community as the primary source for defining public policy in this area, all of us who are seeking any type of change may feel a bit overwhelmed at times. Indeed, although it is very encouraging to see immense progress in many areas of animal protection over the past decade or two, in the area of biomedical research and testing, relatively little progress has occurred over the past century. All of this may logically lead you to ask: in the face of such overwhelming opposition to change, is it really possible to accomplish anything substantive in this area?

My answer to this is a resounding "yes." I am convinced that substantive progress can and will occur in this and many other areas because of the power in the underlying motivation of those involved in animal protection. The power of love and compassion for all life, combined with the ability to recognize the deeper identity of other sentient beings, instills within the human spirit an enduring and unfailing energy to protect and care for nonhuman as well as human life. Simple as this may seem, none of us should underestimate the power of this motivation.

There are other reasons for optimism on a more tangible level, not the least of which is that there are a growing number of physicians and scientists, including individuals at academic institutions, who simply do not buy the status quo in this area.

In addition, I would contend that physicians and scientists, including those presently opposed to animal protectionists, are for the most part otherwise caring, loving individuals and that this characteristic provides them with a strong potential to awaken to the importance of recognizing a higher priority for animals, given the proper circumstances.

In the meantime, however, the situation has become so sufficiently charged that many animal research advocates are resorting to rather extreme statements in order to sway opinions within the medical community and general public.

There are a number of fallacies being perpetuated that need to be challenged by those who truly give a high priority to the well-being of animals and want to see some kind of balance in the presentation of this information.

The first of these is that human health and animal welfare are incompatible. A number of organizations and individuals within the medical community have been telling the public and their legislators that *any* modifications in the current animal research and testing process would be too threatening to human health to justify the risk. This simply is not the case. There are substantial opportunities to incorporate the mainstays of HSUS policy in biomedical research, testing, and education, including the three Rs of refinement of techniques, reduction of the numbers of animals used, and replacement of animal methods with other techniques. Indeed, I would submit that the current volume of animal use in biomedical research, testing, and education could be substantially reduced without any ill effect on human health whatsoever.

A second fallacy is that animal protection groups threaten the future of medical science. Challenging the status quo is seldom easy. Usually those who profit from or strongly identify with a given institution will react defensively and with incredulity when someone questions the established order. This has led to a perceived dichotomy and adversarial relationship between the scientific and animal protection communities. Yet, I would contend that animal protection organizations can and should have a *positive* impact upon the scientific community (and upon society) by serving as a stimulus for changes that would otherwise be unlikely to occur.

Among these are advances in legislation such as the Animal Welfare Act, which, despite its many shortcomings, represented a step in the right direction, as is now acknowledged by both the animal protection and medical communities. Prior to the original act and its subsequent revisions passing into law, most organizations and individuals in the medical community advocating animal research were strongly opposed to these changes; now many of these same scientists and organizations cite the legislation as beneficial but oppose any further changes. Yet, 75 to 90 percent of the animals used for research in this country are not even covered by the Animal Welfare Act, and provisions applicable to performing the research procedures themselves are minimal.

The animal protection community can and should also serve as a positive stimulus for the development of alternatives to the use of animals in research and testing, and I think the Russell and Burch Award is a good example of this. (Annual award bestowed by HSUS on a member of the scientific community who has made a significant contribution towards the study of research methods not requiring animal testing.)

In challenging the status quo, I would challenge my colleagues in the medical community—if we have a genuine priority for the well-being of animals, the medical community should be *embracing* the animal protectionists' concerns rather than rebuffing them. We should delight in finding and implementing solutions which accommodate these concerns and welcome the opportunity to do so.

A third fallacy involves the recurring theme put forth by animal research advocates that all—or virtually all—major medical advances have relied upon and occurred because of animal experimentation. This is an important consideration because, if one accepts the premise, one is led to the conclusion that animal research may be the only means at our disposal to advance medical science. It is understandable that animal researchers and academic scientists would tend to value the significance of animal research, and there is certainly substantial basis in fact for recognizing the contributions of scientists and science based upon the use of animals in research. However, to generalize from the facts and claim that all or even most biomedical knowledge of significance is derived from research using animals is a sizable distortion of the truth and reflects poorly upon those propagating it. It also sells short the myriad of clinicians and clinical researchers who, over the years, have made incredible contributions to medical knowledge without the use of animals.

Let me make a few comments about alternatives to animal research. Most physicians and scientists would agree that the development of alternatives to using live animals in research is desirable. Indeed, some encouraging progress is being made in this area with regard to the use of tissue cultures and other *in vitro* testing, as well as mathematical and computer models. However, we should not be under any false illusions that all of the findings of animal research can be reproduced in a computer model or tissue culture given our current level of technology and understanding. It is disappointing that a number of animal research advocates have taken this a step further and all but dismissed alternatives as severely limited while criticizing animal protectionists for exaggerating their potential. Some have expressed alarm at the idea that animal protection groups would *hope* for the day when the use of animals in research could be completely abolished, stating that this reveals the underlying "radical" nature of these groups.

Yet it is many of these same scientists who, despite their scientific knowledge, fail to think more broadly about the concept of alternatives.

Even though there are many instances where we cannot produce a specific piece of information without using live animals, we need to be open to the possibility that that piece of information may not be needed to solve the clinical problem we are addressing. In this circumstance, the "alternatives" concept becomes somewhat broader and focuses upon the end result rather than specific types of information.

Seeing this issue through the eyes of both a medical researcher and animal protectionist has taught me that the priority and motivation for finding alternatives to the use of animals differ considerably among individuals involved in these disciplines, and this undoubtedly accounts for at least some of the lack of progress in developing alternative methods. In addition, there has been very little incentive to physicians and researchers to develop these methods from the standpoints of available funding and academic career development. One of the things that we who are involved in animal protection need to do more of is to think of ways to motivate and inspire physicians and animal researchers to utilize their scientific knowledge and innovativeness to develop other means to address health problems.

Perhaps the time has come for all of us to recognize that humankind's greatest goal, which outweighs lengthening life through medical advancements, is to evolve spiritually and that in order to do this there is a need for us as a species to learn to think of other beings as ends rather than means. I would hate to think that being a physician or scientist meant that one could not care deeply about the well-being of sentient beings other than human beings. For those involved in animal protection, a deep caring implies more than lip service. It implies placing a high priority on securing humane conditions for animals as well as humans, even in the face of incurring substantial extra cost. It involves a careful and critical look at projects and areas in which animal research is highly unlikely to benefit human or animal health, and/or is grossly inhumane, and a cessation of those projects. It implies a high priority for the development of alternatives to the use of animals in research testing, and education. We should be devoting considerably more time and resources to the development of such alternatives. The main reasons we are not doing so involve convenience, extra cost, the ease of using previously learned methods as opposed to developing new ones, and the lack of enough true concern about other sentient beings besides human beings.

The title of this talk included the phrase, "vision of a new era." I have already indicated to you today that I am convinced that we are on the verge of an era where things will change more substantively in this area. This will come about either with cooperation between the medical and animal protection communities or without such cooperation, through increasing pressure from public and governmental sources. The latter circumstance would take longer, and the ultimate result would be far less congenial to the medical profession. Fortunately, I think there are enough intelligent and compassionate members of both the animal protection and medical communities to warrant optimism that a cooperative effort will constitute the road we travel.

The primary mission of the medical profession is to alleviate human suffering, the achievement of which is often enhanced by various advancements in medical knowledge including the development of new technologies and treatments. The animal protection community simply wishes to extend this alleviation of suffering to other beings besides human beings.

I am convinced we can have both.

I am convinced we *must* have both in order for us to evolve as a species.

This then constitutes the beginning of a new era when both the animal protection and scientific communities realize that many of their goals are the same and that society and medical science can work toward improving human health while also working to eliminate the need for the use of animals in biomedical research, testing, and education.

In the image of this era, I see a day where the initiatives of the animal-protection community are welcomed by the scientific community and where all of us begin to come to the conscious realization that it is compassion for all life rather than scientific achievement that represents the pinnacle of human existence.

I see a day when all medical schools and veterinary schools require ethics courses with substantive discussions about animals, not merely as objects for humans to utilize in any way that may presumably benefit our species, but rather as independent sentient beings.

I see a day when medical schools and research facilities clearly recognize that it is their obligation to *humanity* as well as animals to develop nonanimal research methods to advance human health and that, yes, it *can* be done because they have the will and the desire to do it.

I see a day when human vanity and convenience are no longer sufficient to justify the suffering and killing of other species and the use of animal testing for the cosmetics and household-products industries can be eliminated.

I see a day when scientific investigators are so moved by compassion that their brilliance and ingenuity are directed toward thinking about and developing innovative alternatives to animal research and testing rather than innovative ways to avoid changing the status quo.

Some may call all of this wishful thinking—and certainly I don't claim to have a crystal ball or to be able to put some precise time frame on any of this. However, there are a number of factors which make the coming of this era inevitable.

I have already alluded to the power of the underlying motivation of "compassion for all life" which drives the animal-protection movement. It is also important to recognize that all humans have within them the potential to awaken to this motivation and that we as a species have an underlying need to do so in order to evolve spiritually.

Thirdly, and perhaps most revealing, is the observation that this is indeed a one-way street. For those individuals who have awakened to the virtue and necessity of a "compassion for all life" ethic, there is no turning back. Rather, these individuals continue to evolve toward perfecting this ethic in their own lives and in the world around them. The evolution of our species will mirror that of its individual members. As with other significant changes in social attitudes throughout history, the opposition will be formidable; the process will be cumbersome, costly, and frustrating; the means to achieving change will be varied; and the road will be trying and sometimes discouraging. But, the result will be glorious—think about it: a world that will foster not only harmony between humans and other animals, but also between humans and other humans.

SIGNIFICANCE

Research involving animals is likely to continue as long as there is no acceptable or reliable alternative. That being the case, there is a movement toward ensuring that laboratory research animals suffer as little as possible in the process, through the use of the three R's: Reduction, Refinement, and Replacement. Reduction involves using as few animals as necessary for a particular research purpose. Rather than replicating the same result numerous times, a scientist advocating reduction might determine that a much smaller number of replications of a particular result would allow for confidence in a particular scientific conclusion.

Refinement has to do with finding the least painful and stressful means of carrying out a particular research protocol. For example, the technique of *capture and restraint* is felt to be stressful and frightening for animals, and is often followed by painful injections or blood draws, adding pain and injury to stress and trauma. A tether and jacket system, in which a catheter and rubber tube are inserted into the vein of an anesthetized laboratory animal and then fastened into place, so the animal has some freedom of movement, and does not have to be caught or restrained in order for the substance to be injected or blood to be drawn, is considered a significant refinement. By using refinements, scientists are able to cause the animals less pain, trauma, and stress.

Replacement is when research that had historically used animals is carried out by other, alternative, means. For instance, cell cultures or computer simulations and modeling are now used in place of live animals for certain types of research.

The United States Department of Agriculture creates regulations, and the National Institutes of Health sets guidelines for the uses of animals in laboratory and medical research. Research institutions, whether they are academic or commercial, are required to have Institutional Animal Care and Use Committees (IACUCs), whose function it is to interpret, carry out, and enforce humane policies for laboratory animal treatment based on the regulations and guidelines set for them by the UDSA and the NIH, as well as their own state, local, and institutional policies and procedures.

Utilizing the three R's in animal research should advance the goals of science while increasing efficiency and cost-effectiveness, minimizing pain, suffering, and trauma, using the fewest possible animals, and employing the most humane possible treatment. There is general consensus among research scientists that animal research must continue until scientifically appropriate alternatives are available, but that the least possible harm must be inflicted while so doing.

FURTHER RESOURCES

Books

Carbone, Larry. *What Animals Want: Expertise and Advocacy in Laboratory Animal Welfare Policy.* Oxford: Oxford University Press, 2004.

Web sites

BBC News. "Head-to-Head: Animal Testing." <http://news.bbc.co.uk/1/hi/uk/1124524.stm> (accessed December 9, 2005).

Coalition for Consumer Information on Cosmetics. "About Us: Who We Are and What We Do." <http://www.leapingbunny.org/about_us.htm> (accessed December 9, 2005).

Humane Society of the United States. "Animal Testing." <http://www.hsus.org/animals_in_research/animal_testing/> (accessed December 9, 2005).

Nuffield Council on Bioethics. "The Ethics of Research Involving Animals." <http://www.nuffieldbioethics.org/go/ourwork/animalresearch/introduction> (accessed December 9, 2005).

Chorionic Villus Sampling and Amniocentesis

Recommendations for Prenatal Counseling

Journal article

By: Richard S. Olney

Date: July 21, 1995

Source: Richard S. Olney, et al. "Chorionic Villus Sampling and Amniocentesis: Recommendations for Prenatal Counseling." *Morbidity and Mortality Weekly Report* 44 (July 21, 1995): 1–12.

About the Author: Richard S. Olney is a physician and scientist at the Centers for Disease Control and Prevention, National Center for Environmental Health, Division of Birth Defects and Developmental Disabilities, Birth Defects and Genetic Diseases Branch, in Atlanta, Georgia.

INTRODUCTION

Prenatal diagnosis uses a tiny sample of cells from the fetus to detect chromosomal abnormalities and some single gene disorders, such as cystic fibrosis, sickle cell anemia, and Tay-Sachs disease. The techniques most often used are chorionic villus sampling (CVS) and amniocentesis, and these are described in some detail in the article below. Prenatal diagnosis must always be accompanied by appropriate counseling so that the prospective parents can make an informed decision.

Counseling for prenatal diagnosis explores two different aspects of risk. First the risk of the fetus actually having the genetic condition or chromosomal abnormality being tested for needs to be discussed. Family history and the state of medical knowledge have a bearing here. As with all health risks, there is a degree of uncertainty involved and the parents need to be made aware of this. They also need to know how likely the test is to give an accurate result. Modern technology and good laboratory practice means that accuracy rates may approach 100 percent—but the possibility of an incorrect result can never be ruled out.

The article below was prompted by reports in 1991 that babies born after CVS were more likely to have birth defects—mainly shortened or missing fingers or toes but also, occasionally, abnormalities of the tongue and jaw. Prenatal diagnosis and counseling aim to provide parents at risk of having a child with a genetic disorder with as much information as possible. With this information they are equipped to make the right decision for them—termination, continuing the pregnancy, or, in some cases, choosing to not undergo the prenatal test.

PRIMARY SOURCE

Chorionic villus sampling (CVS) and amniocentesis are prenatal diagnostic procedures that are performed to detect fetal abnormalities. In 1991, concerns about the relative safety of these procedures arose after reports were published that described a possible association between CVS and birth defects in infants. Subsequent

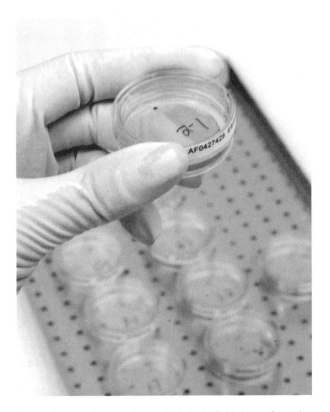

An amniocentesis procedure, which tests fluid drawn from the sac around the fetus, checks for genetic problems, lung development, and spinal cord defects, among other health issues. ©ANN JOHANSSON/CORBIS.

studies support the hypothesis that CVS can cause transverse limb deficiencies. Following CVS, rates of these defects, estimated to be 0.03%–0.10% (1/3,000–1/1,000), generally have been increased over background rates. Rates and severity of limb deficiencies are associated with the timing of CVS; most of the birth defects reported after procedures that were performed at greater than or equal to 70 days' gestation were limited to the fingers or toes.

The risk for either digital or limb deficiency after CVS is only one of several important factors that must be considered in making complex and personal decisions about prenatal testing. For example, CVS is generally done earlier in pregnancy than amniocentesis and is particularly advantageous for detecting certain genetic conditions. Another important factor is the risk for miscarriage, which has been attributed to 0.5%–1.0% of CVS procedures and 0.25%–0.50% of amniocentesis procedures. Prospective parents considering the use of either CVS or amniocentesis should be counseled about the benefits and risks of these procedures. The counselor should also discuss both the mother's and father's risk(s) for transmitting genetic abnormalities to the fetus.

INTRODUCTION

Chorionic villus sampling (CVS) and amniocentesis are prenatal diagnostic procedures used to detect certain fetal genetic abnormalities. Both procedures increase the risk for miscarriage. In addition, concern has been increasing among health-care providers and public health officials about the potential occurrence of birth defects resulting from CVS....

CVS utilizes either a catheter or needle to biopsy placental cells that are derived from the same fertilized egg as the fetus. During amniocentesis, a small sample of the fluid that surrounds the fetus is removed. This fluid contains cells that are shed primarily from the fetal skin, bladder, gastrointestinal tract, and amnion. Typically, CVS is done at 10–12 weeks' gestation, and amniocentesis is done at 15–18 weeks' gestation. In the United States, the current standard of care in obstetrical practice is to offer either CVS or amniocentesis to women who will be greater than or equal to 35 years of age when they give birth, because these women are at increased risk for giving birth to infants with Down syndrome and certain other types of aneuploidy. Karyotyping of cells obtained by either amniocentesis or CVS is the standard and definitive means of diagnosing aneuploidy in fetuses. The risk that a woman will give birth to an infant with Down syndrome increases with age. For example, for women 35 years of age, the risk is 1 per 385 births (0.3%), whereas for women 45 years of age, the risk is 1 per 30 births (3%). The background risk for major birth defects (with or without chromosomal abnormalities) for women of all ages is approximately 3%.

Before widespread use of amniocentesis, several controlled studies were conducted to evaluate the safety of the procedure. The major finding from these studies was that amniocentesis increases the rate for miscarriage (i.e., spontaneous abortions) by approximately 0.5%. Subsequent to these studies, amniocentesis became an accepted standard of care in the 1970s. In 1990, more than 200,000 amniocentesis procedures were performed in the United States.

In the 1960s and 1970s, exploratory studies were conducted revealing that the placenta (i.e., chorionic villi) could be biopsied through a catheter and that sufficient placental cells could be obtained to permit certain genetic analyses earlier in pregnancy than through amniocentesis. In the United States, this procedure was initially evaluated in a controlled trial designed to determine the miscarriage rate. The difference in fetal-loss rate was estimated to be 0.8% higher after CVS compared with amniocentesis, although this difference was not statistically significant. Because that study was designed to determine miscarriage rates, it had limited statistical power to detect small increases in risks for individual birth defects.

CVS had become widely used worldwide by the early 1980s. The World Health Organization (WHO) sponsors an International Registry of CVS procedures; data in the International Registry probably represent less than half of all procedures performed worldwide. More than 80,000 procedures were reported to the International Registry from 1983–1992; approximately 200,000 procedures were registered from 1983–1995. CVS is performed in hospitals, outpatient clinics, selected obstetricians' offices, and university settings; these facilities are often collectively referred to as prenatal diagnostic centers. Some investigators have reported that the availability of CVS increased the overall utilization of prenatal diagnostic procedures among women greater than or equal to 35 years of age, suggesting that access to first-trimester testing may make prenatal chromosome analysis appealing to a larger number of women. Another group of obstetricians did not see an increase in overall utilization when CVS was introduced. The increase in CVS procedures was offset by a decrease in amniocentesis, suggesting that the effect of CVS availability on the utilization of prenatal diagnostic testing depends on local factors. In the United States, an estimated 40% of pregnant women greater than or equal to 35 years of age underwent either amniocentesis or CVS in 1990.

Although maternal age-related risk for fetal aneuploidy is the usual indication for CVS or amniocentesis, prospective mothers or fathers of any age might desire fetal testing when they are at risk for passing on certain mendelian (single-gene) conditions. In a randomized trial conducted in the United States, 19% of women who underwent CVS were 35 years of age. (DNA-based diagnoses of mendelian conditions, such as cystic fibrosis, hemophilia, muscular dystrophy, and hemoglobinopathies, can be made by direct analysis of uncultured chorionic villus cells (a more efficient method than culturing amniocytes). However, amniocentesis is particularly useful to prospective parents who have a family history of neural tube defects, because alphafetoprotein (AFP) testing can be done on amniotic fluid but cannot be done on CVS specimens.

When testing for chromosomal abnormalities resulting from advanced maternal age, CVS may be more acceptable than amniocentesis to some women because of the psychological and medical advantages provided by CVS through earlier diagnosis of abnormalities. Fetal movement is usually felt and uterine growth is visible at 17–19 weeks' gestation, the time when abnormalities are detected by amniocentesis; thus, deciding what action to take if an abnormality is detected at this time may be more difficult psychologically. Using CVS to diagnose chromosomal abnormalities during the first trimester allows a prospective parent to make this decision earlier than will amniocentesis. . . .

RECOMMENDATIONS

An analysis of all aspects of CVS and amniocentesis indicates that the occasional occurrence of CVS-related limb defects is only one of several factors that must be considered in counseling prospective parents about prenatal testing. Factors that can influence prospective parents' choices about prenatal testing include their risk for transmitting genetic abnormalities to the fetus and their perception of potential complications and benefits of both CVS and amniocentesis. Prospective parents who are considering the use of either procedure should be provided with current data for informed decision making. Individualized counseling should address the following:

Indications for procedures and limitations of prenatal testing:

1. Counselors should discuss the prospective parents' degree of risk for transmitting genetic abnormalities based on factors such as maternal age, race, and family history.
2. Prospective parents should be made aware of both the limitations and usefulness of either CVS or amniocentesis in detecting abnormalities.

Potential serious complications from CVS and amniocentesis:

1. Counselors should discuss the risk for miscarriage attributable to both procedures: the risk from amniocentesis at 15–18 weeks' gestation is approximately 0.25%–0.50% (1/400–1/200), and the miscarriage risk from CVS is approximately 0.5%–1.0% (1/200–1/100).
2. Current data indicate that the overall risk for transverse limb deficiency from CVS is 0.03%–0.10% (1/3,000–1/1,000). Current data indicate no increase in risk for limb deficiency after amniocentesis at 15–18 weeks' gestation.
3. The risk and severity of limb deficiency appear to be associated with the timing of CVS: the risk at 10 weeks' gestation (0.20%) is higher than the risk from CVS done at greater than or equal to 10 weeks' gestation (0.07%). Most defects associated with CVS at greater than or equal to 10 weeks' gestation have been limited to the digits.

Timing of procedures:

1. The timing of obtaining results from either CVS or amniocentesis is relevant because of the increased risks for maternal morbidity and mortality associated with terminating pregnancy during the second trimester compared with the first trimester.
2. Many amniocentesis procedures are now done at 11–14 weeks' gestation; however, further controlled

studies are necessary to fully assess the safety of early amniocentesis.

SIGNIFICANCE

Medical counseling has to be continually updated in the light of new research and advances in science. Concern over birth defects among babies whose mothers underwent CVS prompted the recommendations outlined above. This concern also led to further studies, which produced conflicting results. Some found that CVS was not linked to birth defects, while others found that it was, both before and after ten weeksof pregnancy. A 1999 study from the World Health Organization's ongoing CVS Registry found no increased risk of birth defects in the babies of more than 200,000 women who had undergone the procedure.

Since the report excerpted above was issued, the science of prenatal diagnosis has provided new options to future parents. In-vitro fertilization (IVF) was once seen only as a treatment for infertility. It involves mixing the man's sperm and the woman's egg in a glass dish and implanting the resulting embryo in the woman's womb. It is now possible to create embryos in this way and then screen them for genetic disorders, such as cystic fibrosis, by analyzing the DNA of a single cell taken from the embryo. This is made possible thanks to a technique, now well-established, called polymerase chain reaction (PCR), which allows the amplification of DNA from a sample as tiny as a single cell. With enough DNA, a genetic analysis can be ready within days.

With pre-implantation diagnosis, only healthy embryos are placed in the mother's womb. She can continue with the pregnancy knowing that her child does not carry the genetic defect that was screened for. Pre-implantation diagnosis has been welcomed by those whose religious beliefs do not permit them to terminate a pregnancy. However, it is still a specialized technique that is available only at selected facilities.

Moreover, IVF does not always lead to pregnancy, even in a fertile woman. There is still a place for prenatal diagnosis following natural conception. Researchers have evidence that some fetal cells circulate in the mother's blood supply. In the future, they hope that this can be the basis of non-invasive prenatal diagnosis, which involves testing the mother's blood. This would eliminate the slight risk of harm to the fetus that is posed by both CVS and amniocentesis.

FURTHER RESOURCES

Web sites

March of Dimes. "Medical References: Chorionic Villus Sampling." <http://www.marchofdimes.com/profess ionals/681_1165.asp> (accessed November 24, 2005).

Medline Plus. "Chorionic Villus Sampling." <http:// www.nlm.nih.gov/medlineplus/ency/article/ 003406.htm> (accessed November 24, 2005).

Prions: Newly Identified Infectious Agent

Speech

By: Ralf F. Pettersson

Date: December 10, 1997

Source: Presentation speech for the Nobel Prize in Physiology or Medicine at the Karolinska Institute, delivered by Ralf F. Pettersson during the 1997 Nobel Prize in Physiology or Medicine ceremony in Stockholm, Sweden. Available online at <http://nobel-prize.org/medicine/laureates/1997/presentation-speech.html> (accessed September 20, 2005).

About the Author: Ralf F. Pettersson is a professor of microbiology and head of the Ludwig Institute for Cancer Research in Stockholm, Sweden.

INTRODUCTION

Prions, whose name stems from the designation "proteinaceous infectious particles" (abbreviated PrPs), are proteins that are by themselves infectious. The discovery of prions and confirmation of their infectious nature was revolutionary and controversial in microbiology. This is because it overturned a long-held dogma that infections were caused by intact organisms, particularly microorganisms such as bacteria, fungi, parasites, or viruses, which contained genetic material in the form of either deoxyribonucleic acid (DNA) or ribonucleic acid (RNA). Because proteins lack genetic material, the prevailing attitude was that any protein alone was incapable of causing disease.

Prions were discovered, along with their role in the degeneration of brain tissue, by American physician Stanley Prusiner. This work earned him the 1997 Nobel Prize in Physiology or Medicine.

In contrast to infectious agents that are not normal residents of a host, prion proteins are normally present in brain tissue in humans and all mammals studied thus far. Research published in 2004 detected prions in other sites in the body of animal models, leading to the suggestion that prions may be more widespread than previously proposed.

A prion is normally a protein constituent of the membrane that surrounds the cells in the brain. The protein is small, only some 250 amino acids in length, and contains regions that have a helical conformation and other regions that adopt a flat, zigzag arrangement of amino acids.

The prion's normal function is still mysterious. Studies using mutant mice that are deficient in prion manufacture indicate that the protein may help protect the brain tissue from destruction that occurs with increasing frequency as someone ages. Specifically, prions may aid in the survival of brain cells known as Purkinje cells, which predominate in the cerebellum, a region of the brain responsible for movement and coordination.

The prion theory states that the protein is the sole cause of the prion-related diseases, and that these diseases result when a normally stable prion is flipped into a different shape. Regions that are helical and zigzag are still present, but their locations in the protein are altered. This confers a different three-dimensional shape to the protein.

The change in conformation of one prion somehow triggers a shape change in its neighboring prions. Over time, this accumulating altered conformation destroys the structure (and so function) of brain tissue.

PRIMARY SOURCE

Your Majesties, Your Royal Highnesses, Ladies and Gentlemen

This year's Nobel Prize in Physiology or Medicine has been awarded to Stanley B. Prusiner for his discovery of prions - a new biological principle of infection.

What is a prion? It is a small infectious protein capable of causing fatal dementia-like diseases in man and animals. It has been known for approximately a century that infectious diseases can be caused by bacteria, viruses, fungi and parasites. All these infectious agents possess a genome, the hereditary material that provides the basis for their replication. The ability to replicate is essential for the manifestation of the diseases they cause. The most remarkable feature of prions is that they are able to replicate themselves without possessing a genome; prions lack hereditary material. Until prions were discovered, duplication without a genome was considered impossible. This discovery was unexpected and provoked controversy.

Although the existence of prions was not known until the work of Stanley Prusiner, many prion diseases have been previously documented. On Iceland, scrapie, a disease affecting sheep was first described in the eighteenth century. In the 1920s, the neurologists Hans Creutzfeldt and Alfons Jakob discovered a similar disease in man. During the 1950s and 60s, Carleton Gajdusek studied kuru, a disease that was spread through cannibalistic rituals practiced by the Fore people in New Guinea. Presently attention is focused on mad cow disease, which has affected approximately 170,000 cows in Britain. These diseases exhibit common pathologies. They are inevitably fatal due to the destruction of the brains of infected individuals. The incubation times may last for several years, during which the affected regions of the brain become gradually spongy in appearance. Gajdusek discovered that kuru and Creutzfeldt-Jakob disease could be transmitted to monkeys, demonstrating that these diseases are contagious. In 1976, when Gajdusek received his Nobel Prize, the nature of the infectious agent was completely unknown. At this time, these diseases were assumed to be caused by a new unidentified virus, termed a slow or unconventional virus. During the 1970s, no significant advances regarding the nature of the agent were made, that is, not until Stanley Prusiner took on the problem.

Prusiner set out to purify the infectious agent, and after ten years of hard work, he obtained a pure preparation. To his great surprise, he found that the agent consisted only of a protein, which he named prion, a term derived from proteinaceous infections particle. Strangely enough, he found that the protein was present in equal amounts in the brains of both diseased and healthy individuals. This discovery was confusing and it was generally concluded that Prusiner must have arrived at the wrong conclusion. How could a protein cause disease if it was present both in diseased and healthy brains? The answer to this question came when Prusiner showed that the prion protein from diseased brains had a completely different three-dimensional conformation. This led Prusiner to propose a hypothesis for how a normal protein could become a disease-causing agent by changing its conformation. The process he proposed may be compared to the transformation of Dr. Jekyll to Mr. Hyde—the same entity, but in two manifestations, a kind innocuous one, and a vicious lethal one. But how can a protein replicate without a genome? Stanley Prusiner suggested that the harmful prion protein could replicate by forcing the normal protein to adopt the shape of the harmful protein in a chain reaction-like process. In other words, when a harmful protein encounters a normal protein, the normal protein is converted into the harmful form. A remarkable feature of prion diseases is that they can arise in three different ways. They can occur spontaneously, or be triggered by infection, or occur as a consequence of hereditary predisposition.

The hypothesis that prions are able to replicate without a genome and to cause disease violated all conventional conceptions and during the 1980s was severely criticized. For more than ten years, Stanley Prusiner fought an uneven battle against overwhelming opposition. Research during the 1990s has, however, rendered strong support for the correctness of Prusiner's prion hypothesis. The mystery behind scrapie, kuru, and mad cow disease has finally been unraveled. Additionally, the discovery of prions has opened up new avenues to better understand the pathogenesis of other more common dementias, such as Alzheimer's disease.

Stanley Prusiner,

Your discovery of the prions has established a novel principle of infection and opened up a new and exciting area in medical research. On behalf of the Nobel Assembly at the Karolinska Institute, I wish to convey to you my warmest congratulations and I now ask you to step forward to receive your Nobel Prize from the hands of His Majesty the King.

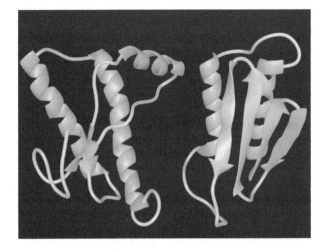

In this computer-generated image, a normal human prion protein is shown on the left and a diseased prion protein appears on the right. AP/WIDE WORLD PHOTOS.

SIGNIFICANCE

How a normally functioning prion is first triggered to become infectious is not yet understood by scientists, but is central to efforts to control the progression of neurological diseases. One theory, known as the virino hypothesis, proposes that the infectious form of a prion is formed when the protein associates with the nucleic acid from some infectious organism. Efforts to find prions associated with nucleic acid, however, have so far been unsuccessful.

If the origin of the infectious prion is unclear, the nature of the infectious process following the creation of the infectious form of the prion is becoming clearer. The altered protein somehow is able to stimulate a similar structural change in surrounding prions. The change in shape is assumed (but not yet proven) to result from the direct contact and binding of the altered and infectious prion with the unaltered and still-normally functioning prions. The altered proteins also become infective and encourage other proteins to undergo the conformational change. The cascade produces proteins that literally clog up the brain cells. The affected cells lose their ability to function and die.

The death of the affected regions of the brain cells produces holes in the tissue. This appearance led to the designation of the disease as spongiform encephalopathy.

It is now generally acknowledged that prion diseases of animals, such as scrapie in sheep and bovine spongiform encephalopathy (popularly dubbed mad cow disease) can cross the species barrier to humans. In humans, the progressive loss of brain function is clinically apparent as Creutzfeldt-Jakob disease, kuru, and Gerstmann-Sträussler-Scheinker disease. Other human diseases that are suspected candidates for a prion origin include Alzheimer's disease and Parkinson's disease.

A prion-like protein has been discovered in yeast. There, it does not have a neurological degeneration. The microorganism is able to transfer genetic information to the daughter cell by means of a shape-changing protein rather than by the classical means of a gene. This finding indicates that prions may be a ubiquitous feature of many organisms, where they may serve vital roles not associated with disease.

FURTHER RESOURCES
Books

Nestle, Marion. *How the Cows Turned Mad: Unlocking the Mysteries of Mad Cow Disease*. Berkeley: University of California, 2004.

Prusiner, Stanley. *Prion Biology and Diseases (Cold Spring Harbor Monograph Series)*. Cold Spring Harbor, N.Y.: Cold Spring Harbor, 2003.

Sheen, Barbara. *Mad Cow Disease (Diseases and Disorders)*. New York: Lucent, 2004.

Yam, Philip. *The Pathological Protein: Mad Cow, Chronic Wasting, and Other Deadly Prion Diseases*. Chichester, UK: Copernicus, 2003.

Zoonosis

Photograph

By: Karen Kasmauski

Date: July 3, 2000

Source: Corbis Corporation.

About the Photographer: Karen Kasmauski has worked on twenty major stories for *National Geographic* since 1984, and is a photographer-in-residence. She is known for her photographs of complex social issues, which have been finalists for the National Magazine Awards. She also works on newspapers, and has published a book of her photographs, *Hampton Roads,* and contributed the images to *Impact: Dispatches from the Front Lines of Global Health* with text by Peter Jaret.

INTRODUCTION

A zoonosis is an infectious disease such as rabies or plague that can be transferred from wild or domestic animals to humans. Humans can contract zoonoses, the plural of zoonosis, from mammals, birds, fish, amphibians, reptiles, and even insects. Depending on the disease, humans contract zoonotic diseases in different ways, including direct contact or close proximity with an animal, or by sharing an animal's water source.

Epidemiologists and other scientists who study diseases describe the transmission of zoonotic diseases in terms of hosts and vectors. A host organism is an animal that is infected with or carries a bacterial, viral, or parasitic disease. The disease can be transferred directly from the host to a person via a mechanism such as the exchange of fluid, or through a vector organism that is an intermediary between a human and the host. An example is the deer tick vector for the well-known illness, Lyme disease. The tick picks up the disease while feeding on an infected mouse or other small mammal. The tick carries the bacterial disease in its gut, and can pass it to a new host during a later feeding. Normally, Lyme disease is transmitted between small mammals, but a human can contract Lyme disease if bitten by the infected tick vector. Although deer do not become infected with Lyme disease, they are responsible for carrying and transporting ticks. There are some diseases which humans contract from animal vectors that are not classified as zoonoses; such as the transmission of malaria by mosquitoes. To complete their life cycle these non-zoonotic diseases require a human host. A true zoonotic disease is capable of being transferred to humans

PRIMARY SOURCE

Zoonosis. A CDC researcher inspects a deer mouse trapped in a study of hantavirus in the Four Corners area of New Mexico. The deer mouse is a carrier of this dangerous virus. The study tracks population changes with the mice and infection rates. ©KAREN KASMAUSKI/CORBIS.

from animals, but does not need a human body in order to survive.

The Hantavirus Pulmonary Syndrome (HPS) is an often fatal zoonotic disease contracted by humans who breathe in the aerosolized virus transmitted by the urine, droppings, or saliva of infected rodents. This deadly pulmonary illness was unknown when it appeared in May of 1993, in the so-called "Four Corners" region of the United States, where the states of New Mexico, Utah, Arizona, and Colorado meet. Initially, it was unclear what was able to quickly kill healthy adults in this region. Virologists from the Center of Disease Control (CDC) used techniques that allow an analysis of a virus at the molecular level, to link the pulmonary illness to a previously unknown type of hantavirus, which was later named *Sin Nombre* (Spanish for "Without Name").

PRIMARY SOURCE

ZOONOSIS

See primary source image.

SIGNIFICANCE

Scientists are learning about HPS through the study of rodent populations, which often requires the trapping and collection of various mice species. Research in the Southwestern United States has linked the years having higher levels of precipitation with a larger population of rodents, as the moisture leads to a greater supply of food for rodents, as well as higher vegetation growth, which provides ample habitat and protection for the rodents. Due to the weather phenomenon El Niño in 1991 and 1993, there was much more rain in the Southwest. The population density of deer mice in New Mexico grew from one deer mouse per hectare to twenty to thirty per hectare during that time period. It is thought that this large population of mice led to the first outbreak of HPS in May 1993. Although rare, HPS has since been found throughout the United States. Rodent control around the household is the primary defense against the hantavirus.

There are some rare zoonotic diseases for which the host is still unknown. Ebola, for example, has several very deadly forms that periodically infect communities in Central Africa. Once a human is infected with Ebola, the disease can spread rapidly from human to human through the direct contact of bodily fluids. Research has shown that perhaps primates, elephants, or bats, could be responsible for carrying Ebola and transmitting it to humans. One hypothesis is that the disease spreads to a human who handles or ingests meat from an infected primate. Bats are considered possible vectors, since they do not die from Ebola, and could therefore be a host that maintains the disease in tropical forests. A much less dangerous form of Ebola is found in the Asia Pacific region.

One zoonotic disease, tularemia, which is similar to plague and found in rodents, is highly infectious. In its aerosolized form, it has been considered a possible biological weapon as far back as World War II, since it takes a very small amount of the bacteria to infect an individual. It is naturally spread by a type of biting flies, contaminated water, and through handling infected animal carcasses. These bacteria can survive in low-temperature water and soil. The United States is said to have maintained stocks of tularemia bacteria until the 1970s.

FURTHER RESOURCES

Books

Preston, Richard. *The Hot Zone: A Terrifying True Story*. New York: Anchor, 1995.

Periodicals

Bunk, S. "Weathering Hantavirus: Ecological Monitoring Provides Predictive Model." *The Scientist*. (1999): 13(14)14.

"Tularemia." *Journal of Environmental Health* (April 2003): 65(8)31.

Web sites

Centers for Disease Control and Prevention. "Ebola hemorrhagic fever." <http://www.cdc.gov/ncidod/dvrd/spb/mnpages/dispages/ebola.htm> (accessed January 16, 2006).

Centers for Disease Control and Prevention. "Hantavirus Pulmonary Syndrome (HPS)" <http://www.cdc.gov/ncidod/diseases/hanta/hps/> (accessed January 19, 2006).

Centers for Disease Control and Prevention. "Lyme disease." <http://www.cdc.gov/ncidod/dvbid/lyme/index.htm> (accessed January 16, 2006).

Disease Control and Environmental Epidemiology Division, Colorado Department of Public Health and Environment. "Zoonotic Diseases." <http://www.cdphe.state.co.us/dc/zoonosis/zoonosis.asp> (accessed January 16, 2006).

World Health Organization. "Ebola." <http://www.who.int/mediacentre/factsheets/fs103/en/index.html> (accessed January 16, 2006).

The Sequence of the Human Genome

Journal article

By: John Craig Venter

Date: February 16, 2001

Source: J. C. Venter, et. al. "The Sequence of the Human Genome." *Science* 291(Feb. 2001): 5507, 1304–51.

About the Author: J. Craig Venter was involved in genomic studies first as researcher at the National Institutes of Health. In 1992, Venter co-founded The Institute for Genomic Research (TIGR). At TIGR, his group sequenced the first bacterial genome of the virus *Haemophilus influenzae* by a method known as shotgun sequencing, the method that he later used to sequence other genomes. After becoming a president of Celera Genomics in 1998, Venter and his team sequenced the fruit fly, mouse, rat, and human genomes. In 2003, Venter undertook a global expedition to obtain and study microbes from the Earth's varying environments. This work is carried out by the J. Craig Venter Institute, formed in 2004.

INTRODUCTION

The sequencing of the human genome, that is, finding the order of the building blocks of the nucleic acids that make up the entire genetic material of a human, was first proposed in 1985. In 1988, the Human Genome Organization was established to coordinate the international efforts to sequence the genome. While the United States was the largest contributor to the project, other countries such as Japan, Germany, the United Kingdom, France, and China established their own human genome projects, and also contributed to the global sequencing effort.

In 1991, the Human Genome Project was started in the U.S. with the aim of sequencing the entire human genome composed of 2.9 billion base pairs (two building blocks, or nucleotide bases, that connect DNA into a double strand) in fifteen years.

One obvious challenge facing scientists involved in the project was how to sequence (map) the huge number of base pairs and collate all of the sequencing data. In the mid-1980s, small-scale sequencing was routine. However, it was expected that a large project like the human genome sequence would require novel approaches, or it would require much more time than the goal of fifteen years. New techniques that were essential for success were the development of a sequencing method that used fluorescent dyes to tag different bases, high-throughput sequencing, which read DNA sequences about twelve times faster than older technology, and computing tools able to compile the data into one sequence.

The first step in the process of establishing the sequence was to subdivide the genome into manageable pieces, and this was achieved by cloning its fragments. Cloning was performed by inserting the fragments of human DNA into small DNA molecules known as plasmids, or vectors. These molecules are able to multiply in a cell. The inserted fragments were sequenced and their sequences were combined with the data from genetic maps to eventually create a full genome sequence.

A full human genetic map was constructed by using polymorphic markers (gene sequences that have variant forms) that were evenly spaced close together in the genome. The Human Genome Project generated over 10,000 polymorphic markers to create a framework map. Previously cloned and mapped human genes were also placed on the framework.

The Human Genome Organization project was publicly funded and the sequences were made public on a regular basis. At the same time, commercial companies also began sequencing the genome, often taking advantage of publicly available data for use in their genome sequencing projects. Among the commercial competitors to the public human genome project the most prominent was J. C. Venter's Celera Corporation.

Dr. Craig Venter, President of Celera Genomics Corp., addresses members of the media in Washington DC February 12, 2001 during a news conference announcing the public release of the map of the human genetic code (rear). ©REUTERS/ CORBIS.

The Celera approach to the genome sequencing was very different from the map-based public efforts. They proposed to use shotgun sequencing (sequencing of DNA that has been randomly fragmented into pieces) of the genome and subsequently putting it together. This approach was widely criticized and was generally expected to be unsuccessful. The ability to order the large number of sequences in the correct manner was seen as the main obstacle of this approach. However, it was shown to be successful after Celera sequenced the genome of the fruit fly *Drosophila melanogaster* in 2000 using this method.

The shotgun sequencing method relied on generating high-quality DNA clone libraries, from which all of the inserts were sequenced without the localization of the DNA fragments to the chromosomes at this stage. The sequences were subsequently assembled by combining shorter fragments into longer ones, generating overlapping fragments of sequence, called contigs. The average fragments assembled in that way by Celera were 1000–10,000 base pairs long. These larger contigs were then localized to the chromosomes and eventually formed a full genome sequence.

Venter announced in April 2000 that his group had finished sequencing the human genome during testimony before Congress on the future of the Human Genome Project. After mapping the genome was complete, his article "The Sequence of the Human Genome" was published in *Science* ten months later.

PRIMARY SOURCE

A 2.91-billion base pair (bp) consensus sequence of the euchromatic portion of the human genome was generated by the whole-genome shotgun sequencing method. The 14.8-billion bp DNA sequence was generated over 9 months from 27,271,853 high-quality sequence reads (5.11-fold coverage of the genome) from both ends of plasmid clones made from the DNA of five individuals. Two assembly strategies—a whole-genome assembly and a regional chromosome assembly—were used, each combining sequence data from Celera and the publicly funded genome effort.

…Decoding of the DNA that constitutes the human genome has been widely anticipated for the contribution it will make toward understanding human evolution, the causation of disease, and the interplay between the environment and heredity in defining the human condition. A project with the goal of determining the complete nucleotide sequence of the human genome was first formally proposed in 1985 (1). In subsequent years, the idea met with mixed reactions in the scientific community (2). However, in 1990, the Human Genome Project (HGP) was officially initiated in the United States under the direction of the National Institutes of Health and the U.S. Department of Energy with a 15-year, $3 billion plan for completing the genome sequence. In 1998, we announced our intention to build a unique genome sequencing facility, to determine the sequence of the human genome over a 3-year period. Here we report the penultimate milestone along the path toward that goal, a nearly complete sequence of the euchromatic portion of the human genome. The sequencing was performed by a whole-genome random shotgun method with subsequent assembly of the sequenced segments….

…It has been predicted for the last 15 years that complete sequencing of the human genome would open up new strategies for human biological research and would have a major impact on medicine, and through medicine and public health, on society. Effects on biomedical research are already being felt. This assembly of the human genome sequence is but a first, hesitant step on a long and exciting journey toward understanding the role of the genome in human biology. It has been possible only because of innovations in instrumentation and software that have allowed automation of almost every step of the process from DNA preparation to annotation. The next steps are clear: We must define the complexity that ensues when this relatively modest set of about 30,000 genes is expressed. The sequence provides the framework upon which all the genetics, biochemistry, physiology, and ultimately phenotype depend. It provides the boundaries for scientific inquiry. The sequence is only the first level of understanding of the genome. All genes and their control elements must be identified; their functions, in concert as well as in isolation, defined; their sequence variation worldwide described; and the relation between genome variation and specific phenotypic characteristics determined. Now we know what we have to explain. Another paramount challenge awaits: public discussion of this information and its potential for improvement of personal health. Many diverse sources of data have shown that any two individuals are more than 99.9% identical in sequence, which means that all the glorious differences among individuals in our species that can be attributed to genes falls in a mere 0.1% of the sequence. There are two fallacies to be avoided: determinism, the idea that all characteristics of the person are "hard-wired" by the genome; and reductionism, the view that with complete knowledge of the human genome sequence, it is only a matter of time before our understanding of gene functions and interactions will provide a complete causal description of human variability. The real challenge of human biology, beyond the task of finding out how genes orchestrate the construction and maintenance of the miraculous mechanism of our bodies, will lie ahead as we seek to explain how our minds have come to organize thoughts sufficiently well to investigate our own existence.

SIGNIFICANCE

Along with Venter's group, the human genome sequence was reported at the same time by the International Human Genome Sequencing Consortium in an article in the journal *Nature*. Both papers described in detail how each group sequenced and analyzed the structure of the genome. Thus, the two papers hailed the finish of the sequencing race between the public and private human genome sequencing groups.

The comparison of the sequences produced by the two groups revealed that there are still quite large stretches of unknown sequence gaps in the assembly of the genomes. The public Human Genome Project sequence had more numerous, but shorter gaps than the Celera genome. Moreover, some known large genes have not been found on a single contig. In

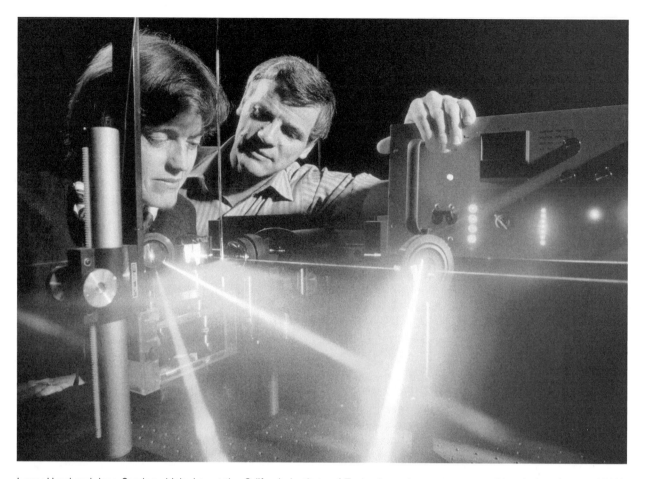

Leroy Hood and Jane Sanders, biologists at the California Institute of Technology, demonstrate a machine designed to read DNA sequences. The sequenator uses lasers, and is hundreds of times faster than human sequencers. ©ROGER RESSMEYER/CORBIS.

addition, analysis of sequences using DNA fragments synthesized in the laboratory revealed that about 0.14 percent of sequences are not shared by the two genomes. In 2003, the Human Genome Project published (and made available on the Internet) their final, more complete version of the human genome, along with a database of variations in the most common gene sequences that distinguish one individual from another.

Now that the first phase of understanding the sequence of human genome is complete, scientists are beginning to learn the function of individual genes. An important aim of research in genetics is to understand how DNA is regulated, especially in relation to disease development. Since the genome was published, scientists have identified errors or mutations in genes that play a major role in the development of complex diseases, such as Parkinson's disease and some prostate and colon cancers. In the future, many diseases caused by gene mutations will be curable, as gene therapy will replace malfunctioning genes with normally functioning versions.

Completion of the human genome sequence also initiated a series of ethical discussions on the use of genetic information. The main areas of concern are the potential use of knowledge to discriminate against a person due to their genetic makeup, and the use of the genome to design genetically superior babies.

The international collaborative effort that resulted in sequencing the human genome provided a fundamental base for a biomedicine in the twenty-first century. Additionally, that fundamental base has yielded clues about the evolution of humans as a species. Scientists studying the 2003 human genome sequence identified about 1000 new genes that became part of the human genome when humans diverged from smaller mammals, about 75 million years ago.

FURTHER RESOURCES

Books

Dennis, Carina, and Richard Gallagher, eds. *The Human Genome*. New York: Palgrave Macmillan, 2002.

Periodicals

International Human Genome Sequencing Consortium. "Initial Sequencing and Analysis of the Human Genome." *Nature*, vol. 409 (2001): 860–921.

Web sites

Nature. "Genome Gateway." <http://www.nature.com/genomics/human/index.html> (accessed September 15, 2005).

Science. "Functional Genomics: The Human Genome." <http://www.sciencemag.org/feature/plus/sfg/human/index.shtml> (accessed September 15, 2005).

Gene Therapy: Promises and Problems

Journal article

By: Alexander Pfeifer

By: Inder M. Verma

Date: 2001

Source: *Annual Review of Genomics and Human Genetics* 2 (2001): 177–211.

About the Author: Alexander Pfeifer, professor of medicine at the Ludwig-Maximilians University in Munich, Germany, was a researcher at the Salk Institute for Biological Studies in La Jolla, California, at the time this article was published. Inder M. Verma is a professor of molecular biology and researcher at the Salk Institute.

INTRODUCTION

Genetics is the ultimate life science frontier for the understanding of the innermost mechanisms regulating the origin and evolution of all life forms on Earth, from the simplest unicellular organisms to highly complex multicellular mammals. The remarkable advances of the last twenty years in molecular biology, cytogenetics, and biochemistry, as well as the development of new biotechnologies, have led to the deciphering of the genetic code of several species, including humans. These advances shed new light on the physiology of organisms and on the laws of inheritance of genetic traits from one generation to the next.

The Human Genome Project, an international research consortium initiated in 1990 involving research centers on almost every continent, and Celera Genomics of Rockville, Maryland, a private enterprise, succeeded in sequencing the DNA of human chromosome 21 by 2000. (The genome is the total set of DNA sequences encoded by genes that characterize a given organism.) In 2002, the Human Genome Project completed the sequencing of all human chromosomes, thus opening the way for the next step in molecular genetics, known as proteasomics or proteomics, the characterization of all proteins encoded by human genes.

Proteins are the structural and functional products of genetic activity, responsible for the development of organisms, tissue repair, and cell functioning. Errors either in gene sequences or in protein synthesis are at the root of a great number of diseases, whether inherited or acquired after birth. Research in molecular genetics already has led to the development of new classes of medications, such as molecular-targeted anticancer drugs (agents that interfere with cancer cell proliferation in a selective manner). Several drugs of this class can be taken orally. The adverse effects they cause are fewer and milder than those caused by traditional chemotherapy, and these drugs also are more effective in controlling several types of cancer. However, gene therapy offers a much bolder therapeutic approach for cancer and other diseases involving gene deregulation or mutation. Gene therapy aims to identify defects in a specific gene or the absence of a given gene associated with a specific dysfunction and to transfer therapeutic genetic material to that segment of DNA to restore normal function.

The article, "Gene Therapy: Promises and Problems," presents a thorough review of the state of the art in gene therapy research. It relies on research from the Salk Institute laboratories and other important seminal research that contributed to the design and development of several approaches to gene therapy.

■ PRIMARY SOURCE

ABSTRACT

. . . Gene therapy can be broadly defined as the transfer of genetic material to cure a disease or at least to improve the clinical status of a patient. One of the basic concepts of gene therapy is to transform viruses into genetic shuttles, which will deliver the gene of interest into the target cells. Based on the nature of the viral genome, these gene therapy vectors can be divided into RNA and DNA viral vectors.

Parkinson's sufferer Nathan Klein, standing with his wife, Claire Hamilton, right, and fourteen-year-old twin children Jackie and Eric Klein, addresses a press conference announcing the first gene therapy for Parkinson's disease, at the New York Weill Cornell Medica Center in New York City August 20, 2003. Klein is the first patient to receive this historic procedure after nearly fifteen years of research. AP/WIDE WORLD PHOTOS.

... The majority of RNA virus-based vectors have been derived from simple retroviruses like murine leukemia virus. A major shortcoming of these vectors is that they are not able to transduce nondividing cells. This problem may be overcome by the use of novel retroviral vectors derived from lentiviruses, such as human immunodeficiency virus (HIV). The most commonly used DNA virus vectors are based on adenoviruses and adeno-associated viruses. Although the available vector systems are able to deliver genes in vivo into cells, the ideal delivery vehicle has not been found. Thus, the present viral vectors should be used only with great caution in human beings and further progress in vector development is necessary.

... Biologists will remember Monday, June 19, 2000, as an historic day. Flanking Bill Clinton, the 42nd President of the United States of America, were Francis Collins of the National Institutes of Health (NIH), leader of the publicly funded Human Genome project, and Craig Venter, CEO of Celera Genomics of Rockville, Maryland, to announce the near-completion of the sequencing of the human genome. Imagine: The entire 3 billion nucleotides of our genome are decoded—an impossible task just a few years ago. The estimate of the number of genes ranges from a low of 35,000 to a high of more than 100,000. What a bonanza for gene therapy. The science of gene therapy relies on the introduction of genes to cure a defect or slow the progression of the disease and thereby improve the quality of life. Therefore, we need genes. Suddenly, we have tens of

thousands of them at hand. Though gene therapy holds great promise for the achievement of this task, the transfer of genetic material into higher organisms still remains an enormous technical challenge. Presently available gene delivery vehicles for somatic gene transfer can be divided into two categories: viral and nonviral vectors. Viruses evolved to depend on their host cell to carry their genome. They are intracellular parasites that have developed efficient strategies to invade host cells and, in some cases, transport their genetic information into the nucleus either to become part of the host's genome or to constitute an autonomous genetic unit. The nonviral vectors, also known as synthetic gene delivery systems (45), represent the second category of delivery vehicles and rely on direct delivery of either naked DNA or a mixture of genes with cationic lipids (liposomes). In this review, we focus on viral vectors and highlight some examples of their use in clinical trials. A complete, constantly updated list of human gene therapy trials in the United States is available at the Office of Biotechnology Activities, NIH (http://www4.od.nih.gov/oba/rdna.htm).

SIGNIFICANCE

Gene therapy aims to correct or slow the progression of certain diseases by supplying the involved tissues with the necessary missing genes or with other regulatory genes that control a given gene expression. In spite of the elegance of the theory behind gene therapy, technical difficulties and safety issues involving the best systems to deliver genetic material to cells remain. Two delivery systems initially were considered: the use of modified viruses as transporters (vectors) and the use of non-viral vectors, known as "synthetic gene delivery systems."

Viruses depend on their host cells' genetic machinery to replicate themselves. They have developed the ability to invade host cells where they sequester certain cellular organelles to replicate their genetic information and, in some cases, to transport and integrate the viral sequences into the host DNA. Approximately 50 percent of the sequences present in human DNA consist of residues of integrated viral sequences. Long tandem repeats (LTRs) are one example. Viral vectors fall into two categories: 1) integrating viral vectors such as retroviruses and adeno-associated virus (AAV), which have the potential to provide life-long expression of the delivered genes (known as transgenes); and 2) non-integrating viruses, such as adenoviruses. Since these non-integrating viruses have medium-size, single or double DNA strands that are bigger than the single or double RNA strands of retroviruses and AAVs, they can transport human transgenes with longer sequences than retroviruses can.

However, a long list of obstacles must be overcome before viral vectors can be safely and efficiently used to deliver transgenes on a regular basis. Gene therapy researchers are studying with such obstacles as: 1) tissue specificity; 2) inserting transgenes in safe, site-specific DNA regions; 3) averting the risk of blood disorders, such as leukemia or other cancers due to uncontrolled gene expression; 4) viral infections; and 5) overcoming a systemic (throughout the body) immune response against viral proteins. In addition, transgenes must be delivered to a great number of targeted cells to effect a cure or to arrest disease progression.

In order to optimize the safety and efficiency of viral vectors, researchers have identified the function of each gene in the genome of vector viruses and have also studied the properties of its proteins and enzymes. Scientists have manipulated the genome of several viruses to knock out those genes that produce disease and, in some cases, have also manipulated specific gene sequences in vector viruses to enhance the ability of the transgenes to integrate into targeted cells.

Gene therapy using vectors other than viruses has presented other initial difficulties, including poor efficiency in delivering transgenes to cells and the fact that an inability to sustain transgene expression within the target. In recent years, this approach is gaining a new impetus thanks to advances understanding of viral genomics and to new bioengineering technologies. The utilization of certain viral enzymes in synthetic delivery systems, instead of viral vectors, has led to the production of new vectors that soon may be used to promote the safe integration of transgenes in specific genomic locations. For example, Rep integrase, an enzyme isolated from AAV was able to promote the integration of a transgene into a safe site on human chromosome 19 without the use of a viral vector. This is just one example of the promising non-viral vectors presently under development, thanks to the extensive research of viral genomes in recent years. In the near future, it is hoped that other advances will make long-term therapeutic gene integration and expression in human cells possible, without the risks posed by viral vectors.

The spectrum of diseases that can be targeted by gene therapy is immense, including several neurodegenerative diseases, cancers, diabetes, hyperlipemias, and X-linked severe combined immunodeficiency (X-SCID). In fact, X-SCID is the only disease for which clinical trials with viral vectors have been successful since 1999. At least seventeen children have been cured thus far, but unfortunately three children also have died due to leukemia-like disorders related to the vectors used.

The National Institutes of Health and the U.S. Food and Drug Administration have established strict guidelines for gene therapy research and for clinical trials to ensure the protection of volunteers enrolled in trials and the quality of such experimental therapies.

FURTHER RESOURCES
Periodicals

Glover, D. J., H. J. Lipps, and D. A. Jans. "Towards Safe, Non-Viral Therapeutic Gene Expression in Humans." *Nature Reviews Genetics* 6 (April 2005): 299–310.

Kaiser, Jocelyn. "Gene Therapy—Panel Urges Limits on X-SCID Trials." *Science* 307 (March 11, 2005): 1544–1545.

Somia, Nikunj, and Inder M. Verma. "Gene Therapy: Trials and Tribulations." *Nature Reviews Genetics* 1 (November 2000): 91–99.

Wilson, Natalie. "Gene Therapy: Heartening News." *Nature Reviews Genetics* 4 (October 2003): 756.

What the Heck Is Antibiotic Resistance?

Online article

By: John C. Brown

Date: January 2002

Source: *University of Kansas, Department of Molecular Sciences.* "What the Heck is Antibiotic Resistance?" <http://people.ku.edu/~jbrown/resistance.htm> (accessed October 6, 2005).

About the Author: John C. Brown is an immunologist and professor of microbiology at the University of Kansas. Brown's current research involves the molecular and genetic mechanisms involved in the disease systemic lupus erythematosus.

INTRODUCTION

The ability to adapt is a crucial aspect to the survival of bacteria. Bacteria can adapt to challenges by altering their structure and metabolism. Some of these alterations occur only as long as the challenge is imposed. Other adaptations require changes in the genetic material of the bacteria that can be passed on to succeeding generations. Such heritable changes are the basis of the emergence of bacterial resistance to antibiotics.

The first known antibiotic, penicillin, was discovered in 1929. Since then many more naturally produced antibiotics have been discovered or chemically synthesized. When these agents were first used, the prospect of complete control of troublesome bacteria was readily envisioned. However, within a few decades of the introduction of penicillin, bacterial resistance to the antibiotic appeared.

Once resistance appears, its spread can be rapid. For example, by the mid 1990s, almost 80 percent of all strains of *Staphylococcus aureus* had acquired resistance to penicillin.

Bacterial antibiotic resistance can occur in two ways. One is inherent (or natural) resistance. Gram-negative bacteria such as *Escherichia coli* are often naturally resistant to penicillin, for example. This is because these bacteria are surrounded by two membranes. The outer membrane makes it more difficult for an antibiotic like penicillin to reach its target inside the cell. In addition, enzymes located in the gap between the outer and inner membranes can dissolve some antibiotics as they reach the gap. Sometimes, bacterial resistance to an antibacterial agent arises when a change in the outer membrane restricts the inward movement of the antibiotic. Such a change represents adaptation.

Resistance can also be acquired, and is almost always due to a change in the genetic make-up of the bacterial genome. The genomic change can occur because of a random mutation or as a directed response by the bacteria to the selective pressure imposed by the antibacterial agent. Once the genetic alteration that confers resistance is present, it can be passed on to subsequent generations. In this way, the resistance can quickly spread as succeeding generations of bacteria develop.

PRIMARY SOURCE

WHAT ARE ANTIBIOTICS?

Antibiotics are chemical substances that inhibit the growth of (bacteriostatic) or kill (bactericidal) bacteria. These substances are produced naturally by a variety of organisms such as bacteria and fungi. You are likely familiar with antibiotics such as erythromycin or penicillin and its chemical derivatives (Ampicillin). Erythromycin (a member of the macrolide family of antibiotics) is produced by the bacterium *Streptomyces erythraeus*. One of the laboratory-produced variations of this antibiotic is Clindamycin. Penicillin, a member of the beta-lactam antibiotics, is produced by the fungus, *Penicillium*.

HOW DOES AN ANTIBIOTIC WORK?

Various antibiotics work in different ways. If you think about it, there are several ways that a bacterium could be prevented from growing or living.

- Prevent the bacterial cell wall from forming properly. The cell wall of bacteria is required to prevent the cell from rupturing. Water flows across membranes into regions where the concentration of salts is higher (inside of a bacterial cell). If the cell wall weren't there, the cell would fill with water to the point that the membrane ruptured.

- Prevent protein synthesis. New proteins, both those involved in structure as well as chemical reactions (enzymes) must be made continuously or the bacterial cell will die. Old proteins are damaged relatively quickly and soon cease to function—also—new proteins are needed for the new cells produced by cell division (bacterial growth).

- Interfere with DNA synthesis. The chromosome of the cell must be replicated continuously in order for cell division to take place. If this process is disrupted, the cells not only cannot increase in number, the cells will die because a fundamental process has been jeopardized.

- Disrupt plasma and/or outer membrane (in the case of Gram-negative bacteria) function. The cell's plasma membrane, made of two layers of fat (lipids) and many different proteins surrounds all of the bacterial cell's contents. With the two exceptions of water and gases, ALL other nutrient constituents required by the cell must enter the cell across the plasma membrane by specific transport proteins. Too, the energy-producing system of many bacteria (the electron transport system) resides within the plasma membrane. Consequently, any disruption of plasma membrane function will kill the cell.

The antibiotics listed and briefly described below, act on one of these fundamental systems required by bacteria for life.

- Prevent the cell wall (made of cross-linked polymers of peptidoglycan) from being formed properly. The beta-lactam antibiotics such as penicillin and penicillin derivatives as well as the cephalosporins, work in this way. Some examples of the penicillin antibiotics are Ampicillin and Methicillin, and the cephalosporin antibiotics, Cefoxitin and Cefoperazone. Vancomycin is another antibiotic, different from the penicillins and cephalosporins, that is also a very important bacterial cell wall synthesis inhibitor.

- Disruption of the ability of bacteria to make proteins (protein synthesis inhibitors). These antibiotics include those known as tetracyclines, examples of which are aureomycin and tetracycline, those known as aminoglycosides, such as streptomycin, and those known as macrolides such as Erythromycin.

- Interfere with chromosome replication, i.e., DNA synthesis. These antibiotics are designed completely in the laboratory and have never been observed to naturally occur. These antibiotics are the quinolones, an example of which is Ciprofloxacin. You may be familiar with this antibiotic and its use to kill the bacteria responsible for anthrax.
- Bacterial membrane disruption antibiotics also exist, but cannot be taken internally by humans. Our cell membranes are very similar to bacterial cell membranes. Thus, disruption of the bacterial plasma membrane will also disrupt our own cells' plasma membrane. Such antibiotics, the example of which is Polymyxin B. Such antibiotics will be found in creams and are for topical (surface of skin) use, only.
- Interference with fundamental metabolism—the overall chemical systems in bacteria. These antibiotics are things like the sulfa drugs, an example of which is sulfanilamide. Another metabolism inhibitor is Trimethoprim. These kinds of antibiotics interfere with metabolic systems that bacteria alone, possess.

WHAT IS ANTIBIOTIC RESISTANCE?

Antibiotic resistance is the ability of a bacterial cell to resist the harmful effect of an antibiotic. This resistance may be represented by several different systems, and a given bacterial cell may have one or more of these systems available.

- The bacterium may have a system that prevents entry of the antibiotic into the cell.
- The bacterium may have a system that destroys the antibiotic if the antibiotic gains entry into the cell.
- The bacterium may have a system that associates with the antibiotic inside the cell and therefore blocks the action of the antibiotic.
- The bacterium may have a system that pumps the antibiotic back out of the cell before the antibiotic can act within the cell.

Any one or more of these systems possessed by a bacterium can prevent a particular antibiotic from working. It is rare for a given bacterium to have either one or more of these systems that prevents the action of every single antibiotic available against that bacterium. However, it looks like this situation is changing. For example, there are strains of the organism that causes tuberculosis, *Mycobacterium tuberculosis,* that are resistant to all of the present antibiotics available to kill this dangerous bug.

HOW IS ANTIBIOTIC RESISTANCE ACQUIRED?

In the absence of human involvement, bacteria in the wild do not usually have resistance to antibiotics. In order for a bacterium to gain resistance to a given antibiotic, there must be either a natural mutation in a gene within the bacterial chromosome (less common), or, the system that leads to resistance must be acquired. Acquisition of antibiotic resistance occurs when genetic material is taken up by the bacterial cell and either incorporated into the chromosome, or, that is able to exist in a stable form independent of the chromosome. Such stable genetic elements that can not only exist but that can replicate independently of the chromosome, are known as plasmids. If the genetic information encoded by a plasmid leads to resistance against a particular antibiotic, this plasmid is known as a resistance plasmid. The bacterium that acquired the new genetic information that leads to resistance, is now known as an antibiotic-resistant *strain* of that bacterial species. Examples of such bacterial strains include Vancomycin Resistant enterococci (VRE) and Methicillin Resistant *Staphylococcus aureus* (MRSA).

IF ONE CELL OF A BACTERIAL SPECIES IS RESISTANT TO A GIVEN ANTIBIOTIC, ARE ALL BACTERIAL CELLS OF THAT SPECIES RESISTANT TO THE SAME ANTIBIOTIC?

No; only that strain and subsequent offspring of that strain will be resistant to that antibiotic. For example, if a bacterial cell acquires a system that destroys penicillin or methicillin, all other cells of that species may still be sensitive to the killing action of the antibiotic. However, the cell that acquired resistance to methicillin will usually be able to pass on this resistance in the form of stable genetic information to all of the progeny of that one cell. Since bacterial cells can divide every 20 minutes, in a very short time there can be many, many cells of the new, resistant strain that will no longer be killed by methicillin.

WHAT DIFFERENCE DOES IT MAKE IF A BACTERIAL CELL OR TWO ACQUIRES ANTIBIOTIC RESISTANCE?

The overwhelming majority of bacteria are not only helpful to us but necessary for our good health. This preponderance of good bacteria means that there are fewer spaces available for harmful (pathogenic—disease causing) bacteria to occupy and enormous competition for the limited nutrients available. Consequently, it's tough for bad bacteria to gain a foothold and to exist in large numbers—special conditions must usually occur in order for such a thing to happen. One such special condition is the loss of competition for space and food. Since antibiotics kill both good and bad bacteria alike, if there is a disease-causing bacterial cell that happens to be resistant to an antibiotic, and most of the good bacteria are killed—this antibiotic resistant bad bacterium now has a significantly better competitive advantage. This strain may now increase in number, gain a foothold and cause disease—and all members of this strain will be resistant to at least one antibiotic that could kill them, to boot.

UNDER WHAT CONDITIONS DO BACTERIA MOST EASILY ACQUIRE RESISTANCE TO A GIVEN ANTIBIOTIC?

When bacteria are in a limited geographic environment with routine, consistent exposure to antibiotics—such as a hospital—or within a single individual on long-term antibiotic therapy—or within farm animals treated with low, non-therapeutic doses of antibiotics for weight gain. If antibiotics are used extensively, there is an increased likelihood of selection of a bacterial cell that is resistant to the effects of a given antibiotic. Look at it this way—if there were 100 people in a room and only one individual had an umbrella, spraying water from the ceiling would select that one person for dryness—resistance to getting wet. If this person and their umbrella divided every 20 minutes, soon, the room would be filled only with individuals who had umbrellas and all could remain dry. That individual would represent a strain of bacterium, resistant to an antibiotic, and allowed to increase in number and to perhaps become the predominant occupant of the room.

Another situation that encourages selection for antibiotic resistance is indiscriminate usage of antibiotics. If an antibiotic isn't needed to treat a disease, such as a disease caused by a virus (antibiotics work only on bacteria), the use of antibiotics in this situation increases the opportunity to select a bacterial strain that is resistant to that antibiotic. One particularly troublesome situation in this area is the routine use by the animal food industry of low, non-therapeutic dosage levels of antibiotics. These antibiotics are either the same or very similar to the antibiotics used for human health. Non-therapeutic use of antibiotics means that the animals are not treated simply to prevent spread of an ongoing disease, but healthy animals are treated to prevent spread of disease and to also increase weight gain. It is not yet understood how low levels of antibiotics cause the animals to gain weight. However, the widespread use in this manner of several different antibiotics is thought to increase the risk of development of antibiotic resistance among bacteria dangerous to human health. Antibiotic-resistant bacteria would have a significantly higher chance under such conditions of being selected as survivors.

IS ANYONE DOING ANYTHING ABOUT THIS ISSUE?

There is increasing awareness of what we are doing to increase the presence of antibiotic-resistant strains of disease-causing bacteria—both in the medical community and in the animal food industry. There are many more discussions and recommendations being made that is resulting in less indiscriminate use of antibiotics.

However, this issue is a world-wide problem and continuous efforts are being made to reduce this threat to human health. One recent success appears to have occurred in Europe. A recent article in the journal *Science* attests to the effect of a ban on use of the antibiotic, Avoparcin, in animal feed on the prevalence of antibiotic resistance in human hospital patients.

Studies had shown that bacteria isolated from the intestines of animals that were resistant to Avoparcin were also resistant to Vancomycin. Both of these antibiotics work by preventing the cell wall of bacteria to form properly—without cell wall integrity, bacterial cells will rupture and die. As mentioned above, Vancomycin-resistant enterococci exist and are a significant concern for surgery patients who may become infected with these bacteria. Scientists felt that reduction of the use of Avoparcin might eventually reduce the prevalence of Vancomycin-resistant bacteria.

The concern that antibiotics in animal feed could eventually select for antibiotic resistant bacterial strains, and that these strains could enter the human intestines through the food chain, caused the European Union to reach an important decision—that is, to ban in 1997 any further use of Avoparcin in livestock feed. Researchers in Europe have been monitoring the effects of this ban. Since the ban was instituted a significant decrease in Vancomycin-resistant enterococci has been observed in bacteria isolated from chickens, pigs and in chicken meat in stores. Perhaps most importantly, in an Antwerp, Belgium hospital patient study in June, 2001, an approximate ten-fold decrease in Vancomycin-resistant enterococci were observed relative to when the ban was begun. Since the use of Vancomycin in Belgian hospitals had not changed since 1997, this decrease in Vancomycin resistance appears to be clearly associated with the decrease in use of the similar antibiotic, Avoparcin, in farm animals. In the United States, the U.S. Food and Drug Administration (FDA) has recommended that two different antibiotics be banned from use in livestock feed. The final decision on such a ban has not yet been made.

SIGNIFICANCE

Acquired adaptation of bacteria to many antibiotics has become a problem since the early 1990s. For example, many hospitals now must cope with the presence of methicillin-resistant *Staphylococcus aureus* (MRSA), which displays resistance to almost all currently used antibiotics. Dealing with infections caused by MRSA and other resistant organisms requires increased hospital staff hours, increased supplies, and can restrict the availability of hospital beds when

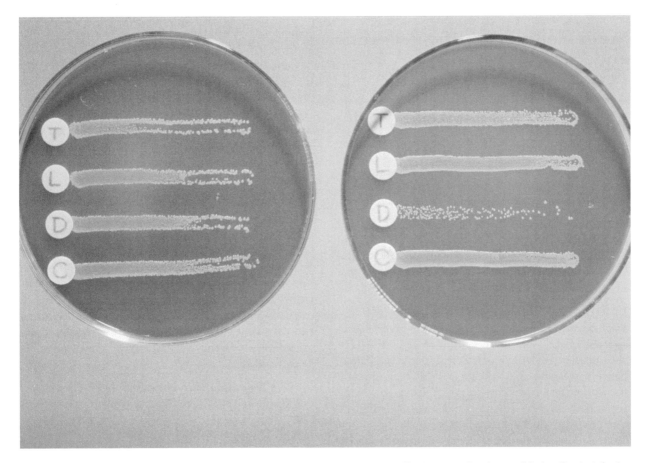

Researchers put swabs of *Staphylococcus* bacteria on petri dishes to measure the effectiveness of various antibiotics. On the left, the *Staphylococcus* is being treated with penicillin; on the right, with a penicillin derivative. ©LESTER V. BERGMAN/CORBIS.

cohorting (grouping together patients with the same disease) or isolation is necessary.

The few antibiotics to which antibiotic-resistant bacteria do respond tend to be expensive, with few options for delivery. For example, the drug meropenum is sometimes prescribed for persons with pneumonia, meningitis, or serious skin infections that are caused by organisms that are resistant to common antibiotics. Meropenum can be delivered by intravenous injection or infusion only, and is two to three times more expensive than the commonly prescribed antibiotics for these conditions.

Additionally, disease-causing organisms can sometimes adapt so that they are able grow and multiply on solid surfaces. This mode of growth is called a biofilm. A biofilm environment induces many changes in growing bacteria, many involving the expression of previously unexpressed genes and deactivation of actively expressing genes. The structure of the biofilm and these genetic changes often make the bacteria extraordinarily resistant to many antibiotics. Biofilms sometimes occur on some hospital surfaces, and in implanted devices such as artificial joints and long-term intravenous access catheters.

Complicating the picture, the pattern of gene expression may not be uniform throughout the biofilm. Evidence from studies where intact and undisturbed biofilms have been studied has shown that the bacteria living near the top of the biofilm, and so closer to the outside environment, are very different from their counterparts located deeper in the biofilm. This arrangement functions to make the bacterial population very hardy when confronted with antibiotics and other threats to their survival.

FURTHER RESOURCES
Books

Shnayerson, Michael, and Mark J. Plotkin. *The Killers Within: The Deadly Rise of Drug-Resistant Bacteria*. New York: Little, Brown, 2002.

Walsh, Christopher. *Antibiotics: Actions, Origins, Resistance*. Washington, DC: ASM Press, 2003.

Stem Cells: Scientific Progress and Future Research Directions

Government document

By: Ruth L. Kirchstein

By: Lana Skirboll

Date: 2001

Source: R. L. Kirchstein and L. Skirboll. *Stem Cells: Scientific Progress and Future Research Directions.* Washington, D.C.: U.S. Department of Health and Human Services, 2001. Available online at <http://stemcells.nih.gov/info/scireport> (accessed August 20, 2005).

About the Author: Ruth Kirchstein is a former acting director of the National Institutes of Health (NIH). She obtained her Doctor of Medicine degree at Tulane University School of Medicine in 1951. Subsequently she worked as a researcher in experimental pathology at the Division of Biologics Standards. Following the change of the division to a bureau of the Food and Drug Administration in 1972, she became a deputy director. In 1974, she became the first woman institute director at the NIH. One of her achievements relates to the promotion of the Sabine polio vaccine. She was also involved in the AIDS campaign at the beginning of the epidemic. Lana Skirboll is the director of Office of Science Policy at the NIH. She advises the NIH director and the NIH institutes on the policies and procedures for safe conduct of biological research. Among other activities, she is also responsible for development of the NIH's guidelines for research using human stem cells.

INTRODUCTION

The National Institutes of Health (NIH) are a part of the U.S. Department of Health and Human Services. The NIH, which is comprised of twenty-seven institutes and centers in the United States, conduct and support medical research in this country and in other parts of the world.

The NIH have compiled information on stem cells themselves, the areas in which they are used, and protocols used for obtaining, growing, manipulating, and transplanting them. All research on stem cells performed in any of the institutes of the NIH or any other federal institution must comply with the Federal Stem Cell Policy.

Federally funded research on human embryonic stem cells only can be performed on the cell lines that are in the NIH stem cell registry. Other cell lines can be submitted to the registry provided that they fulfill the eligibility criteria. The most important criterion is that the process of removal of cells from the embryo must have been initiated before August 9, 2001. The other criteria are: 1) the stem cells were obtained from an embryo generated for reproductive purposes that is no longer needed for that purpose; 2) an informed consent was obtained from the donor; 3) the donor received no financial compensation for the donation.

All of the cell lines in the cell registry are accompanied by a detailed description of the markers, karyotype, passage, and conditions used for growing, thus providing the potential researcher with all of the important information needed for their use. Currently a limited number of lines is available due to an on-going derivation process, and also due to the fact that some of the cell lines initially registered are unusable because they have failed to expand into undifferentiated cells.

While mouse embryonic stem cells have been used in research since 1981, the first human embryonic stem cells were isolated and grown in culture in 1998 by James Thomson at the University of Wisconsin. Research on the mouse stem cells has revealed the ways in which their development can be manipulated to form cells of various tissues. It was discovered that, under the appropriate conditions, these stem cells could form any cell type found in the body, such as neurons, blood, muscle, or bone cells. Therefore, embryonic stem cells are considered pluripotent, meaning that they are able to generate any tissue and cell type in the body.

Subsequent studies in adult animals and humans showed the presence of stem cells in adult tissues. The most commonly isolated adult stem cells are the hematopoietic stem cells. However, the numbers of stem cells in adult tissues are much lower than in embryonic tissues and generally they are more limited in the types of cells they can form. Yet, adult stem cells still exhibit some level of plasticity—the ability to differentiate into cells of different tissue types.

Researchers believe that embryonic stem cells may be of particular use in the treatment of neurological diseases, such as Parkinson's disease or Alzheimer's disease. These stem cells also may be useful for research in regeneration of damaged nerves, heart muscle, and other tissues. Another emerging area of study involves the use of the stem cells in combination with gene therapy. The ease of manipulation of embryonic stem cells may be important for delivering targeted gene therapy.

In the search for human embryonic stem cells, the stocks of unimplanted embryos in fertility clinics became a target for researchers who wanted to generate lines of these cells for use in future treatments. However, the use of these embryos quickly raised ethical and legal questions. Moreover, a number of practical and safety issues relating to the use of such cells also emerged.

The NIH report on stem cells was compiled at the request of the Secretary of Health and Human Services, T. G. Thompson. It provides basic information about stem cells derived from all possible sources—embryonic tissues, fetal tissues, and adult tissues. This report was written in such a way that it is useful both to the general public and to scientists. It includes general information about stem cells, their derivation, and their possible applications in the treatment of a number of diseases. However, it makes no recommendations regarding the research on stem cells. The report also does not address the legal and ethical issues involved in the use of stem cells for research.

PRIMARY SOURCE

A stem cell is a cell that has the ability to divide (self replicate) for indefinite periods—often throughout the life of the organism. Under the right conditions, or given the right signals, stem cells can give rise (differentiate) to the many different cell types that make up the organism. That is, stem cells have the potential to develop into mature cells that have characteristic shapes and specialized functions, such as heart cells, skin cells, or nerve cells. . . .

Most scientists use the term pluripotent to describe stem cells that can give rise to cells derived from all three embryonic germ layers—mesoderm, endoderm, and ectoderm. These three germ layers are the embryonic source of all cells of the body. . . .

Unipotent stem cell, a term that is usually applied to a cell in adult organisms, means that the cells in question are capable of differentiating along only one lineage. . . .

The embryonic stem cell is defined by its origin—that is from one of the earliest stages of the development of the embryo, called the blastocyst. . . . The embryonic stem cell can self-replicate and is pluripotent—it can give rise to cells derived from all three germ layers.

The adult stem cell is an undifferentiated (unspecialized) cell that is found in a differentiated (specialized) tissue; it can renew itself and become specialized to yield all of the specialized cell types of the tissue from which it

Cord blood samples are processed for cryopreservation at a Singapore laboratory, August 26, 2005. Since 1988, stem cells have been used to treat an increasing number of diseases, including blood and metabolic disorders, immunodeficiency ailments, and autoimmune diseases. ©LUIS ENRIQUE ASCUI/REUTERS/CORBIS.

originated. Adult stem cells are capable of self-renewal for the lifetime of the organism. Sources of adult stem cells have been found in the bone marrow, blood stream, cornea and retina of the eye, the dental pulp of the tooth, liver, skin, gastrointestinal tract, and pancreas. . . .

A hematopoietic stem cell is a cell isolated from the blood or bone marrow that can renew itself, can differentiate to a variety of specialized cells, can mobilize out of the bone marrow into circulating blood, and can undergo programmed cell death, called apoptosis. . . .

Ultimately, stem cell gene therapy should allow the development of novel methods for immune modulation in autoimmune diseases. One example is the genetic modification of hematopoietic stem cells or differentiated tissue cells with a "decoy" receptor for the inflammatory cytokine interferon gamma to treat lupus. For example, in a lupus mouse model, gene transfer of the decoy receptor, via DNA injection, arrested disease progression....

Efforts to develop stem cell based therapies for Parkinson's Disease provide a good example of research aimed at rebuilding the central nervous system. As is the case with other disorders, both the cell-implantation and the trophic-factor strategies are under active development. Both approaches are promising. This is especially true of cell implantation, which involves using primary tissue transplanted directly form developing fetal brain tissue....

The partial repair of the damaged heart muscle suggests that the transplanted mouse hematopoietic stem cells responded to signals in the environment near the injured myocardium. The cells migrated to the damaged region of the ventricle, where they multiplied and became "specialized" cells that appeared to be cardiomyocytes....

Transplanted human stem cells are dynamic biological entities that interact intimately with—and are influenced by—the physiology of the recipient. Before being transplanted, cultured human stem cells are maintained under conditions that promote either the self-renewing expansion of undifferentiated progenitors or the acquisition of differentiated properties indicative of the phenotype the cells will assume. After incompletely differentiated human stem cells are transplanted, additional fine-tuning occurs as a consequence of instructions received from the cells' physiologic microenvironments within the recipient.

Assessing human stem cell safety requires the implementation of a comprehensive strategy. Each step in the human stem cell development process must be carefully scrutinized. Included in this global assessment are the derivation, expansion, manipulation, and characterization of human stem cell lines, as well as preclinical efficacy and toxicity testing in appropriate animal models. Being able to trace back from the cell population prepared for transplantation to the source of the founder human stem cells also allows each safety checkpoint to be connected, one to the other....

In addition, hematopoietic stem cells "home," or migrate, to a number of different spots in the body—primarily the bone marrow, but also the liver, spleen, and lymph nodes. These may be strategic locations for localized delivery of therapeutic agents for disorders unrelated to the blood system, such as liver diseases and metabolic disorders such as Gaucher's disease....

SIGNIFICANCE

The ability to use stem cells in disease treatments by simple transplantation makes them a feasible therapeutic approach. It is possible to use a patient's own stem cells for treatment or to utilize a line of embryonic stem cells that have been isolated from other individuals and stored.

In the majority of current and possible future treatments, stem cells are differentiated in the laboratory to generate cells similar to those that are intended for replacement. These manipulated cells are then transplanted into the patient's target organs. It is essential to standardize the methods for isolation, manipulation, and transplantation of the cells to ensure patient safety.

Screening for antigens (foreign substance that can induce an immune response) is one of the most important issues confronting the therapeutic use of stem cells. (Such screening is routinely done in traditional organ transplantation procedures.) In addition, the cells must be examined for pathogens (disease-causing organisms) to ensure that the patient is not given an infectious disease along with the stem cells.

Hematopoietic stem cells already have been used in treating leukemias, and are part of a reasonably well established and accepted method of treatment. They are the only stem cells currently used to treat diseases.

The use of other stem cells, especially human embryonic stem cells, is under development. There are three main areas that require further study. The first area concerns the development of methodologies to differentiate the stem cells into the cells required in a particular tissue. The second research area involves the development of a system or systems to deliver the cells into the tissues. Finally, ways to prevent the rejection of stem cells by the recipient also require more study.

With a limited supply of organs for transplants, stem cells are increasingly viewed as an attractive alternative for treating failing organs. However, much more research is needed and clinical trials are essential before human embryonic stem cells become a viable and accepted treatment.

FURTHER RESOURCES

Books

Thomson, Alison, and Jim McWhir, eds. *Gene Targeting and Embryonic Stem Cells (Advanced Methods)*. Oxford: BIOS Scientific Publishers, 2004.

Periodicals

Kaufman, D. S., and J. A. Thomson. "Human ES Cells—Haematopoiesis and Transplantation Strategies." *Journal of Anatomy* 200 (2002): 243–248.

Li, X., et al. "Specification of Motoneurons From Human Embryonic Stem Cells." *Nature Biotechnology* 23 (2005): 215–221.

Prelle, K., N. Zink, and E. Wolf. "Pluripotent Stem Cells— Model of Embryonic Development, Tool for Gene Targeting, and Basis of Cell Therapy." *Anatomia, Histologia, Embryologia* 31 (2002): 169–186.

Thomson, J. A., et al. "Embryonic Stem Cell Lines Derived From Human Blastocysts." *Science* no. 5391 (1998): 1145–1147.

Yoon, Y., et al. "Clonally Expanded Novel Multipotent Stem Cells From Human Bone Marrow Regenerate Myocardium After Myocardial Infarction." *Journal of Clinical Investigation* 115 (2005): 326–338.

Web sites

The National Institutes of Health. "Stem Cell Information." <http://stemcells.nih.gov/info/> (accessed June 15, 2005).

He Never Gave Up

What Actor and Activist Christopher Reeve Taught Scientists About the Treatment of Spinal Cord Injury

Magazine article

By: Jeffrey Klugar

Date: 2004

Source: Jeffrey Klugar. "He Never Gave Up: What Actor and Activist Christopher Reeve Taught Scientists About the Treatment of Spinal-Cord Injury." *Time*, (Obituary). October 10, 2004.

About the Author: Jeffrey Klugar (sometimes spelled Kluger) is a senior writer for *Time*, for which he has written several cover stories. He has also authored two books on space and space travel, *Apollo 13*, and *Journey Beyond Selene*. He has received several honors and awards for his journalism. Prior to joining the staff of *Time*, he wrote for several other periodicals.

INTRODUCTION

Christopher Reeve, an actor well-known for his portrayal of the title character in the *Superman* movies, was also an accomplished athlete with a passion for horseback riding. On May 27, 1995, Reeve was involved in a gymkhana equestrian event when his horse balked at a jump, throwing his rider over his head. Reeve's hands became tangled in the reins, and he landed on his head, fracturing his top cervical vertebrae and causing a spinal cord injury (SCI). The immediate outcome of this injury was a total loss of function below the level of the fracture; because the damage to his spinal cord was severe, Reeve lost immediate movement from the neck down, as well as the ability to breathe voluntarily. The severity of his injuries was extreme, immediate, complete, and permanent.

In a complete injury, there is total loss of function below the level of the SCI, resulting in absolute loss of voluntary movement and sensation. In an incomplete injury, there is some functional ability remaining; there may be some voluntary movement or sensation remaining below the level of the SCI. In a complete injury, both sides of the body are affected to the same degree; that is not necessarily the case for individuals with incomplete injuries. In an incomplete injury, the voluntary movement and level of sensation need not be equivalent; that is, there may be feeling in areas that have no movement, as well as the reverse. One side or area of the body may be affected differently than the other.

When the spinal cord injury affecting the uppermost cervical vertebrae occurs, as was the case for Christopher Reeve, there is loss of ability to breathe voluntarily, necessitating supported respiration by mechanical means, such as a ventilator or respirator.

There are three key components that determine degree of recovery and rehabilitation from SCI at present. They are: location of injury and degree of compression of the spinal cord, time until aggressive medical treatment occurs, and type of rehabilitation facility or nature of rehabilitation undertaken. The closer to the top of the spinal column the injury occurs, the greater the area of the body affected, In addition, the degree of compression of the spinal cord determines the severity of the SCI: the more compression of the cord, the more likely the damage will be permanent and complete. In the past, the first course of treatment in a spinal cord injury involved stabilization of the site, and complete bed rest until the spinal swelling diminished enough to enable medical professionals to determine the extent of the injuries. Current research suggests that prompt and aggressive medical and, when necessary, surgical intervention can decrease swelling intensity and duration, and may ameliorate some of the secondary damage, possibly even preventing axonal death. A corticosteroid called Prednisolone has been shown to have the ability to reverse some damage, and to have some protective ability for the spinal cord, if it is administered within eight hours of the occurrence of the injury.

When making decisions about rehabilitation facilities, it is crucial to choose one that has significant experience with spinal cord injuries, one in which SCI patients are housed near one another for comfort and support, and one in which the techniques employed are state of the art. It is imperative that non-physical aspects of the SCI are dealt with as well: spinal cord injuries are sudden, cataclysmic, and life-altering. The injured person often has to redefine him/herself in terms of abilities and level of independence.

▪ PRIMARY SOURCE

In public, Christopher Reeve usually played the stoic, silently enduring the indignities of paralysis. In private, he was more candid. He had vowed, shortly after the 1995 horseback-riding injury that left him a quadriplegic, that he would walk again by his fiftieth birthday. That milestone came—and went—in 2002. "I'm tired of being noble," he confessed shortly afterward in a long conversation with *TIME*. "I try to go about this with as much dignity as I can, but not a day goes by when I don't make some effort to get out of this situation."

Dignity and effort are good words to describe how Reeve lived the final nine years of his life, which ended last week with his death from heart failure at age 52. While the actor most famous for playing Superman was never as close to walking again as he perhaps believed, he none-theless spent his immobile years in constant motion, raising money for paralysis research, speaking out for stem-cell funding, offering hope to other paralysis suf-ferers, even using his body as a proving ground for new therapies. At least partly through his efforts, paralysis research accelerated in that time—small consolation to the family he leaves behind, but a real gift for researchers still laboring in the field.

Within months of Reeve's injury, he became active in an advocacy group that eventually became the Christopher Reeve Paralysis Foundation, which has so far raised $47 million for spinal-cord research. One of the first things Reeve came to appreciate was that healing a damaged cord is monstrously hard. Unlike nerves in, say, the skin, spinal nerves don't regenerate. Even a small wound can cut off the signals that enable the body to move, feel and draw breath.

Scientists had been wrestling with that problem long before Reeve was hurt, but he helped drive their research. An area of study that his foundation funds involves so-called Schwann cells, which play a role in helping nonspinal nerves to regenerate. In animal studies, Schwann cells grafted to the damaged part of the spine encourage nerve cells to grow into the graft but not, so far, to connect downstream. "They fail to bridge the cord," says Dalton Dietrich, scientific director of the Miami Project to Cure Paralysis.

Scientists are trying to get around that by fortifying Schwann grafts with cells from the olfactory bulb, a bun-dle of nerve tissue in the nasal cavity. Olfactory cells regenerate well, and when they are combined with Schwann cells in animals, spinal tissue does a better job of reconnecting.

Another approach the Reeve Foundation has helped fund involves treating the spinal cord with a drug called rolipram, which stops injured tissue from breaking down. Paralyzed rats treated with Schwann cells and rolipram have shown a 70% improvement in mobility. Elsewhere, researchers are working on ways to neutralize growth inhibitors, proteins in the body that—for reasons known only to nature—block the healing of spinal tissue. By synthesizing other proteins that inhibit the inhibitors, spinal cells may be freed to grow.

For all the heat generated over stem cells, that science still requires a great deal of work. Senators John Kerry and John Edwards have both invoked Reeve's advo-cacy of embryonic stem-cell funding in their campaign against the Bush Administration, which restricts research on religious grounds. But scientists must first coax stem cells to develop into nerve cells before they can begin to put them to work in the spine.

Perhaps most tantalizing, if only because it's available now, is the power of exercise. In 2002, Reeve stunned the medical world with the news that he had regained some sensation over 70% of his body and could move most of his joints underwater. His doctors credited the turnaround to long hours of assisted exercise, particularly a regime of electrical stimulation that causes rhythmic contractions of muscles, allowing patients to ride a stationary bicycle and operate other equipment. Paralyzed animals show growth in spinal nerves after electrical exercise, and that may be what happened in Reeve's body.

Reeve readily acknowledged that he was not a paraly-tic Everyman. With his high profile and ample funds, he had access to the best possible care. For that reason, he was often criticized for creating false hope. But a lack of any hope at all is something many paralyzed people already have in abundance. Reeve made it his mission to offer them something more. That and the foundation he created are a legacy that endures.

▪

SIGNIFICANCE

Christopher Reeve was an activist for political freedoms and human rights long before the 1995 acci-dent that left him paralyzed. He was a liberal Democrat who devoted considerable time and atten-tion during the pre-accident phase of his life to poli-tical activism concerned with the environment, the concerns of children, funding for the arts, and first amendment rights; after the incident that left him quadriplegic, his advocacy was directed at medical research concerning spinal cord injury. He and his wife, Dana, founded the Christopher Reeve Paralysis Foundation (CRPF), the CRPF Research Consortium, and the Christopher and Dana Reeve Paralysis Resource Center, devoted to education, advocacy, and the advancement of research aimed at curing spinal cord injuries. After making a difficult decision to continue his life after the horseback riding accident, Reeve became determined to use his celebrity and recognizable name to advocate for broader and deeper research into the treatment and cure of paralysis. He attended Senate and Congressional hearings, lobbied, and personally met with law- and policy-makers, in an effort to give a *face* to spinal cord injuries.

Until recently, it was assumed that a damaged spinal cord could not either rebuild itself or be repaired. Current research is aimed at understanding the cellular mechanisms underlying the original growth and development of axons and neurons in the central nervous system, with the goal of creating means in which they can be re-grown subsequent to SCI. Ethical and responsible stem cell research has great promise in this area; embryonic stem cells have been used with some success in regeneration research involving lower animals.

When the spinal cord is injured, two types of cellular destruction occur: primary damage occurs at the time of the event, and secondary damage is caused by the swelling of the spinal cord and the buildup of fluid around the site of the injury, cutting off the blood supply to the spinal neurons and axons, and causing cellular death. Current research is aimed both at minimizing primary damage and at preventing secondary damage.

Another very large area of research focus concerns efforts at encouraging regeneration of axons. One way in which this is studied is by long-term observation of the development of immature nervous systems in young, developing animals. A variety of mechanisms are being studied at present, with one central goal being the development of a way to overcome a paradoxical physiological process in adult humans: axons and neurons in the central nervous system do possess the capacity to regenerate and re-grow after injury, but are prevented from doing so by a number of inhibitory processes. It appears that the inhibitory factors are present in order to prevent CNS damage by cellular overgrowth—but this protective mechanism effectively prevents re-growth when there is a need for it to occur. Research scientists have documented the

presence of at least three proteins that inhibit or prevent growth in the CNS; they are studying them in order to map out their exact mechanisms of action. When they have discerned exactly what makes them function as they do, they may have uncovered the keys to either reversing their action or to *turning them off*. Axonal regeneration is a highly specific process: the axons must grow only in certain directions, and to specific lengths, and they must make exactly the correct neuronal and biochemical connections in order to function properly.

Burgeoning technology and advancing computer sophistication has led to another avenue of rehabilitation, involving the development of adaptive and prosthetic devices. Computers are being used to create a connection between physiology and physical therapy technology. One result of this research is called FES, or functional electrical stimulation. This technology was used by Chris Reeve in the form of a stationary bicycle: electrodes were placed on the muscles of his legs and attached to a computer, which he or his assistant could control. He was placed on a specially adapted stationery bicycle, and the muscles were stimulated in such a way that his legs would move and he could turn the pedals of the bike—keeping his large muscles from deteriorating, and providing a degree of aerobic conditioning that would otherwise be extremely difficult for a person with limb paralysis to obtain.

Christopher Reeve was able to use the power of his famous name to both encourage and to fund research in all of the developing areas of spinal cord injury treatment. He was absolute in his belief that a cure for paralysis was on the horizon; as a result, he was able to advance the knowledge and technology with which spinal cord injury research progressed by enormous amounts during the nine years after his accident.

FURTHER RESOURCES

Web sites

AAPM&R: American Academy of Physical Medicine and Rehabilitation. "Advances Made in Treatment of Spinal Cord Injuries." <http://www.aapmr.org/condtreat/injuries/sciadvance.htm> (accessed December 23, 2005).

Christopher Reeve Homepage. "Without Pity: A Film About Abilities." <http://www.nlm.nih.gov/hmd/about/collectionhistory.html> (accessed December 23, 2005).

MayoClinic.com. "Spinal Cord Injury." <httphttp://www.mayoclinic.com/health/spinal-cord-injury/DS00460/DSECTION=8> (accessed December 23, 2005).

The National Academies. "The Promise of Stem Cells: From Research to Medical Therapies." <http://www

.christopherreeve.org/atf/cf/{219882E9-DFFF-4CC0-95EE-3A62423C40EC}/stem%20cell%208-pager%20 final%20rev%207-3.pdf> (accessed December 23, 2005).

National Institute of Neurological Disorders and Stroke. "Spinal Cord Injury: Hope Through Research." <http://www.ninds.nih.gov/disorders/sci/detail_sci.htm> (accessed December 23, 2005).

Eulogy for Mattie Stepanek

Speech excerpt

By: Jimmy Carter

Date: 2004

Source: *The Carter Center.* "Eulogy for Mattie Stepanek." <http://www.cartercenter.org/printdoc.asp? docID=1791&submenu=news> (accessed December 20, 2005).

About the Author: Jimmy Carter, born James Earl Carter, Jr., was the thirty-ninth president of the United States. He was born in Plains, Georgia, on October 1, 1924, into a peanut-farming family. He has been married to Rosalynn Smith Carter since 1946; they have three sons and a daughter. Among his main areas of focus during his presidency were global human rights and efforts at creating a lasting peace in the Middle East. Since leaving the presidency, Jimmy Carter has remained actively involved in a number of worldwide educational, human rights, and peace-keeping efforts. He is a recipient of the Nobel Peace Prize.

INTRODUCTION

Mattie Stepanek was born on July 17, 1990, and died just under fourteen years later, on June 22, 2004. He was a prolific writer and poet, public speaker, and activist for peace. He was born with a form of muscular dystrophy known as dysautonomic mitochondrial myopathy. His sister and two brothers, all of whom died before him, had the same disease, as does his mother, who has the adult form of the disorder. Mattie published five books of poetry during his brief life. Because he was able to achieve a great deal of public recognition and visibility as a result of his best-selling books and the attendant public appearances, he was made a spokesperson for the Muscular Dystrophy Association and elected as a Goodwill Ambassador in 2002 (a title he retained until his death in 2004).

Muscular dystrophy is the umbrella term given to a diverse array of inherited neuromuscular diseases that affect more than one million people in the United States alone. Some commonalities among the varied diseases are the gradual wasting and loss of muscle tissue, coupled with increasing muscular weakness and eventual loss of motor function. There is, as yet, no cure for any of the forms of muscular dystrophy, although there is much active and ongoing medical and scientific research. The goals for treatment include providing stabilization and increasing mobility and independence, reducing curvatures and deformities caused by weakening and wasting of muscle tissue (over time, muscle dissolves and is replaced by fatty tissue), and maximizing functional quality of existence across the life span. As technology and available life-enhancing treatments have developed, the life span for persons with muscular dystrophy that first develops in infancy or early childhood has gradually increased, extending through the late teens and sometimes into young adulthood.

For a disease to be inherited, one or both parents must carry the defective gene. When a disorder requires only one copy of the defective gene to develop, it has a dominant mode of inheritance. If this gene is carried on one of the twenty-two non-sex human chromosomes, it is called an autosomal dominant gene. When a disorder requires two copies of the same defective gene in order to be expressed in the next generation, it has a recessive mode of inheritance. In that case, a child must receive one copy of the gene from each parent in order to develop the disease. A parent who carries a single copy of the defective gene does not have the disease, but may pass the disease to his/her children.

■ PRIMARY SOURCE

When I was running for governor a number of years ago, my wife and I didn't have much money so we traveled around the state and we estimated later that we shook hands personally with 600,000 people.

Later I ran for president, as some of you may remember, and campaigned in all 50 states. Subsequently, I traveled around the world. In fact, since I left the White House, my wife and I have been to more than 120 nations. And we have known kings and queens, and we've known presidents and prime ministers, but the most extraordinary person whom I have ever known in my life is Mattie Stepanek.

I didn't know Mattie until about three years ago when Make-A-Wish Foundation sent me a letter and said there was a little boy who only had a few more days to live and his final request was to meet Jimmy Carter. I was surprised and honored and within a few days, as a matter of fact, the *Good Morning America* program arranged for Mattie to be interviewed and for me to come there as a surprise to meet with him. He later told his mother, Jeni, that when I walked in the room he thought it was a presidential impersonator. And later, when it proved to be me, he told Jeni, and Jeni told me, that that was the first time in his life, and maybe the only time, when Mattie was speechless. But we exchanged greetings and formed, I would say, an instantaneous bond of love. . . .

That meeting and our subsequent relationship have literally changed my life for the better. Mattie said that day that I had been his hero for a long time and I was sure that he was just joking and he could tell on the ABC program that I didn't really quite believe him. And so to prove that, he sent me a video, a 20-minute-long video that he had made when he was 6-years-old, explaining the life of Jimmy Carter. And for the different segments in the video, he dressed appropriately.

So, it started out I was a little farm boy and Mattie had on ragged clothes and he spoke with what Rose (Rosalynn) and I thought was an atrocious Southern accent. And then later I was a naval officer and then later I came back to be a farmer and then ultimately was president, so he changed clothes every time. And then while I was president, he gave an appeal to human rights and peace and things of that kind and while the camera was on him, he realized later, his toes kept wiggling, he was barefoot, so for a long time he apologized to me that he should have done that segment over and at least put on shoes to be president.

He sent me another video, which I would like for all of you to try to see. It's a video of his competition as a black belt in martial arts for the ultimate prize in that intense and demanding sport. It was incredible to see the agility of that young boy and the strength in his body.

Mattie and I began to correspond. After his death, Jeni gave me the honor of letting me come and do this speech. I had my secretary get out our correspondence. It's that thick, on every possible subject. He was always in some degree of anguish, and I think embarrassment, when his books on the *New York Times* list were always above mine. And he would sympathize with me and say, "Well, you know maybe poetry just has less competition than what you are writing about." But he was very sensitive to my feelings.

We also were close enough for Mattie to share some of his problems with me in his private messages. He talked about when he and Jeni were not well off and some local churches, I'm sure not the one represented here this morning, would take up a food collection and send it to them. Mattie used to examine the labels on the food and quite often he said he would find that the date had expired and that people were giving poor people inferior food that they didn't want to use themselves. And Mattie said, "If my books make a lot of money, we're going to get food that's brand new and make sure that poor people get the best food, even if we have to eat the old, outdated food in our house."

He was very proud of the fact that he and his mother could move into a place that had windows.

I've thought a lot about Mattie's religious faith. It's all-encompassing, to include all human beings who believe in peace and justice and humility and service and compassion and love. The exact characteristics of our Savior Jesus Christ. He was still a boy, although he had the mind and the consciousness and the awareness of global affairs of a mature, philosophical adult.

One of his prime goals in life was to see the movie "Return of the King" seven times and I hope he was able to accomplish his goal. I'm not quite sure. But that was the kind of thing that he had as his ambitions.

He was as proud as I was when I won the Nobel Peace Prize, which has already been mentioned. As soon as the ceremony was over at the hall in Oslo, I went by myself to the top of a little hill right behind the place and I found a rock and I inscribed on it and I sent it to Mattie, because I felt that he shared the honor that I had received.

The last few days, I have been re-reading some of Mattie's statements that he wrote to me, I've re-read the correspondence. One thing he said was, "I choose to live until death, not spend the time dying until death occurs."

Jeni told me about one occasion when Mattie was supposed to be a main part of the program which he helped prepare to raise funds for muscular dystrophy, but when the time approached he was in the intensive care unit. They announced at first that Mattie could not attend the event that meant so much to him, in which he had helped in its preparation. He insisted on coming. When he got there and began to say his lines, he announced, "I'm out of breath. I can't speak." Mattie loved to dress up and to wear fancy clothes and his favorite kind of clothes, as some of you may surmise, was a tuxedo. So Jeni and Mattie arranged for him to put on a tuxedo and he said, "When I have a tuxedo on, I can talk." So he went back with his tuxedo.

Mattie said he wanted to be, as an ultimate goal in his life, an ambassador of humanity and a daddy. Mattie had already named his first seven children and had even given personal idiosyncrasies and characteristics to the first four. He wanted to leave a human legacy and family descendents, but Mattie's legacy, obviously, is much greater than that.

As has already been quoted, he said, "I want to be a poet, a peacemaker and a philosopher who played." Mattie was deeply aware of international affairs and shared a lot of his thoughts with me. He was once again in the intensive care unit when the war in Iraq began and Mattie burst into uncontrollable sobs of grief and anger. Jeni said he had never cried nearly so much about his own health or his own problems. . . .

I spent seven years earlier in my life writing a book of poems about which Mattie was graciously complimentary. Poetry seemed to flow out of Mattie, kind of like an automatic stream, directed by inspiration through Mattie's hands for the enjoyment of hundreds of thousands, maybe millions of people. I want to read just a few of them with which many of you are familiar, because he combined humor with serious thoughts. All of them I would say are unique, surprising when you read them.

One of them is titled "About Angels" and he honored me by letting me write the foreword to this book, called *Journey Through Heartsongs.*

About Angels
Do you know what angels wear?
They wear
Angel-halos and Angel-wings, and
Angel-dresses and Angel-shirts under them, and
Angel-underwear and Angel-shoes and Angel-socks, and
On their heads
They wear
Angel-hair—
Except if they don't have any hair.
Some children and grownups
Don't have any hair because they
Have to take medicine that makes it fall out.
And sometimes,
The medicine makes them all better.
And sometimes,
The medicine doesn't make them all better,
And they die.
And they don't have any Angel-hair.
So do you know what God does then?
He gives them an
Angel-wig.
And that's what Angels wear.

And another one that he wrote:

I Could. . .if They Would
If they would find a cure when I'm a kid . . .
I could ride a bike and sail on rollerblades, and
I could go on really long nature hikes.
If they would find a cure when I'm a teenager . . .
I could earn my license and drive a car, and
I could dance every dance at my senior prom.
If they would find a cure when I'm a young adult . . .
I could travel around the world and teach peace, and
I could marry and have children of my own.
If they would find a cure when I'm grown old . . .
I could visit exotic places and appreciate culture, and
I could proudly share pictures of my grandchildren.
If they would find a cure when I'm alive . . .
I could live each day without pain and machines, and
I could celebrate the biggest thank you of life ever.
If they would find a cure when I'm buried into Heaven . . .
I could still celebrate with my brothers and sister there, and
I could still be happy knowing that I was part of the effort.

And the last poem I will read is titled:

When I Die (Part II)
When I die, I want to be
A child in Heaven.
I want to be
A ten-year-old cherub.
I want to be
A hero in Heaven,
And a peacemaker,
Just like my goal on earth.
I will ask God if I can
Help the people in purgatory.
I will help them think,
About their life,
About their spirits,
About their future.
I will help them
Hear their own Heartsongs again,
So they can finally
See the face of God,
So soon.
When I die,
I want to be,
Just like I want to be
Here on earth.

Well, it's hard to know anyone who has suffered more than Mattie. Sandy sent us almost daily reports about his bleeding, internally and from his fingers. I doubt that anyone in this great auditorium has ever suffered so much except his mother, Jeni, and our Savior Jesus Christ, who is also here with us today. I always saw the dichotomy between Mattie as a child and with the characteristics and intelligence and awareness of an adult. Just as we see the dichotomy of Jesus Christ who was fully a human being at the same time as truly God.

I would say that my final assessment is that Mattie was an angel. Someone said that to him once and he said, "No, no." He was very modest. But really in the New Testament language, angel and messenger are the same and there's no doubt that Mattie was an angel of God, a messenger of God.

He was concerned about his legacy, wanting to have seven children and talking about his grandchildren, but Mattie's legacy is forever because his Heartsongs will resonate in the hearts of people forever. I thank God that he is no longer suffering and that he's with the Prince of

Peace, getting big hugs in Heaven and maybe wearing a tuxedo.

SIGNIFICANCE

As the study of the makeup of DNA and the genetics of disease becomes more sophisticated, it will become possible to identify the genetic abnormalities that are associated with each of the various forms of muscular dystrophy. Each form of the disease is caused by a specific genetic defect, or improperly constructed protein. That protein has been identified in Duchenne and Becker Muscular Dystrophies, and it is called dystrophin. In Myotonic Dystrophy, the genetic defect is on chromosome number 19, and the enzyme coded on that gene is called myotonin protein kinase. A flawed gene located on chromosome number 14 has been linked to Oculopharyngeal Muscular Dystrophy. Limb-Girdle Muscular Dystrophy is thought to be a constellation of several subtypes of the disorder, as it can be caused by imperfectly constructed genes located on chromosomes 2, 13, 15 (the enzyme calpain 3) and 17 (muscle protein adhalin) in its autosomal recessive form, and in its autosomal dominant form on chromosome number 5.

Although there are a great many forms of muscular dystrophy, nine of them are more prevalent than the others, according to the Muscular Dystrophy Association. They are: Duchenne Muscular Dystrophy (DMD), Myotonic Dystrophy (also called DM or Steinert's Disease), Becker Muscular Dystrophy (BMD), Emery-Dreifuss Muscular Dystrophy (EDMD), Facioscapulohumeral Muscular Dystrophy (also called either FSH or Landouzy-Dejerine Disease), Congenital Muscular Dystrophy (CMD), Oculopharyngeal Muscular Dystrophy (OPMD), Limb-Girdle Muscular Dystrophy (LGMD), and Distal Muscular Dystrophy (DMD).

The most promising avenue for developing treatments for muscular dystrophy involves targeted gene therapy, where a beneficial gene is substituted for the gene that is responsible for the disease. Developing a useful gene therapy is challenging, as scientists search for a way to deliver the beneficial gene into enough cells of the body to effectively treat the disease. In 2005, scientists used a virus called the adeno-associated virus 8 (AAV8) to effectively deliver a gene to all the skeletal muscles of the body of rodents. If this gene-delivery technique is shown to work the same way in humans, this virus-based gene therapy may be the first effective gene therapy for muscular dystrophy.

In the meantime, the most common treatments for the muscular dystrophies involve orthopedic and other

Comedian and host Jerry Lewis at the 39th annual Labor Day Weekend Jerry Lewis Muscular Dystrophy Association (MDA) Telethon held at the Beverly Hills Hilton. September 4, 2005. ©PAUL MOUNCE/CORBIS.

assistive devices, braces, supports, and other mobility aids. Physical and occupational therapy are common, and speech and language therapy are employed as necessary. For those forms of MD associated with seizures or muscle stiffening, antiseizure medications are typically prescribed. Corticosteroids are often employed as a means of slowing the progression of the disease, preserving muscle strength, and increasing comfort.

The entertainer Jerry Lewis's name has been associated with charitable and fund-raising work for the Muscular Dystrophy Association since 1955. During that year, the very first MDA Telethon was hosted by Lewis at Radio City Music Hall during the month of June. Beginning in 1966, the annual MDA Telethon was held over Labor Day weekend, and was televised. It was the first time that fund-raising had been accomplished on such a large-scale during a single event. The 2004 Telethon was dedicated to the memory of Mattie Stepanek, and raised $54.9 million for the research and treatment of muscular dystrophy and related diseases.

FURTHER RESOURCES

Web sites

MayoClinic.com. "Diseases and Conditions: Muscular Dystrophy." <http://www.mayoclinic.com/health/muscular-dystrophy/DS00200> (accessed December 20, 2005).

Medline Plus. "Muscular Dystrophy." <http://www.nlm.nih.gov/medlineplus/musculardystrophy.html> (accessed December 20, 2005).

Muscular Dystrophy Association. <http://www.mdausa.org/> (accessed December 20, 2005).

Schneider Children's Hospital. "What is Muscular Dystrophy?" <http://www.schneiderchildrenshospital.org/peds_html_fixed/peds/orthopaedics/musdys.htm> (accessed December 20, 2005).

Can Gene-Altered Rice Rescue the Farm Belt?

Crops Engineered to Help Alleviate Hunger

Newspaper article

By: Alexei Barrionuevo

Date: August 16, 2005

Source: New York Times

About the Author: Alexei Barrionuevo is a contributor to the *New York Times*, a daily newspaper with a circulation of over one million readers worldwide.

INTRODUCTION

In theory, any organism—bacteria, plant, or animal—can be modified by genetic engineering. The technique involves the transfer of a gene of interest from one species to another, creating a combination of genes not found in nature. Since genes are the blueprints for proteins, the aim of a genetic engineering experiment is usually to have the modified host species manufacture a protein that belongs to another species. These proteins have many applications—in medicine, in the food industry, and in research. For example, bacteria modified with the human insulin gene can act as a host for the manufacture of this essential drug for diabetes treatment. Other medicines made in this way include human growth hormone, erthyropoietin (a treatment for anemia), and "clotbuster" drugs (used to treat strokes and heart attacks). Without genetic engineering, these proteins would only be available in tiny amounts or not at all.

Agriculture engineer Amadeu Faco holds genetically modified soybeans seeds at a Julio de Castilhos' farm, in the southern Brazilian state of Rio Grande do Sul, Dec. 1, 2003. AP/WIDE WORLD PHOTOS.

Genetically modified (GM) crops such as soy, rice, and tobacco, are planted and used in many countries. The first examples were crop plants engineered to contain a toxin from the bacterium *Bacillus thuringiensis* (bt). Because the bt toxin attacks insects—by perforating their gut—such GM plants are more resistant to predators than non-modified plants and yields from these crop are higher. Such technology could, say its supporters, help feed the world. But GM plants have always been controversial. Critics fear that ingesting "foreign" genes might create a health hazard. There are also concerns, as described in the article below, that GM crops might contaminate the environment through gene transfer.

Despite the protests, which have included destruction of GM crops by environmental activists and bans on GM food by restaurants, research on plant genetic engineering has continued. The article reproduced below describes an application where genetic modification is used not to improve the plant—as in the bt example—but to create a kind of factory to manufacture proteins that could benefit human health by helping to alleviate world hunger.

■ PRIMARY SOURCE

WATSON, Mo.— Like an expectant father, Jason Garst stood in calf-deep water and studied the three-foot-high rice plants growing in a flooded field.

It was a curious sight in northwest Missouri, where the growing season is considered to be too short for rice. Mr. Garst, a sixth-generation farmer, is hoping at least one of the 12 varieties on his test plot will sprout this fall. If one does, he will start growing rice plants that have been genetically engineered to produce proteins found in human milk, saliva and tears. Once converted into a powder form, those proteins would be used in granola bars and drinks to help infants in developing countries avoid death from diarrhea.

"I know in my heart that this will be better than anything else we are doing," said Mr. Garst, 35, who also farms soybeans and potatoes.

The rice project is backed by a private company called Ventria Bioscience but also has the support of the state and a local university, which are hoping to reverse the long decline in the area's farm economy. But the project has run into opposition from environmental groups and even the beer giant Anheuser-Busch amid fears about the health effects of genetically engineered crops, making Mr. Garst's little rice paddy a piece of a larger battlefield.

The economic and academic ambitions of the Missouri project make it unique, but the arguments echo those heard in similar disputes in Europe and, increasingly, in the United States. Critics of Ventria's plans are concerned that the gene-altered rice could contaminate regular rice crops and pose a health risk to consumers, scaring off buyers. Ventria and its academic partner in the project, Northwest Missouri State University, say they can control the potential for contamination. And they say the risks are minimal when balanced against the potential for the special rice to help cut the costs of drugs and save lives.

The debate has a certain urgency in the Farm Belt because it highlights the challenge facing much of the region's economy: finding new products that will reduce farmers' reliance on commodity crops. As equipment has become more efficient and foreign competition has stiffened, farms have consolidated and profit margins have shrunk, forcing farmers to plant ever more acres to squeeze out a living. The genetic engineering work that Ventria and other companies are doing can add value to products like rice, offering farmers a more stable income that does not rely on steep government subsidies.

"There is no question that this represents a chance to transform the economy of the region," said Mark Drabenstott, director of the Center for the Study of Rural America at the Federal Reserve Bank of Kansas City. "For regions like northwest Missouri, there is not a long list of economic alternatives."

Despite opposition, Ventria's plans to grow genetically engineered rice—eventually to commercial scale—are going forward. The company began growing rice in North Carolina this summer after getting approval from the Agriculture Department. Once Ventria decides where it will grow rice in Missouri, it will have to apply for a permit from the department, a process expected to take two to three months.

Dean L. Hubbard, president of Northwest Missouri State, persuaded Ventria last year to move its operations from Sacramento to new buildings planned for the Northwest campus in Maryville, about 90 miles north of Kansas City.

Seeking a way to reverse the area's slide in population, Dr. Hubbard teamed up with Melvin D. Booth, a Northwest Missouri alumnus who previously ran two large biotechnology companies. The two approached Ventria about making it part of the university's plan to form joint ventures with young biopharmaceutical companies.

Ventria was already considering similar offers from universities in Georgia, Louisiana and North Carolina, but Scott E. Deeter, Ventria's chief executive, agreed to visit the university last August. Mr. Deeter said that on the ride from the Kansas City airport, he was intrigued when Dr. Hubbard described the university's program to heat and cool the campus using bio-fuel derived from paper and wood chips.

At the meeting, Mr. Garst presented him with a research paper he had prepared on what it would take to grow rice in northern Missouri. "It was very impressive," said Ning Huang, Ventria's vice president for research and development, who was there.

Finally it came down to whether Ventria scientists would agree to move to Maryville, population 10,000, from California. Next year 13 will move, including Dr. Huang.

Under the agreement reached last November, Ventria will pay farmers more than double what they make on their most profitable crop, and pay Northwest Missouri $500 an acre for crops grown on university land. The university is spending about $10 million to help build a production and teaching complex, and the state is kicking in another $10 million.

Atchison County, Mo., where Mr. Garst's farmland is, has lost more than 1,000 people, or 14 percent of its population, since 1990. The town of Watson, once a thriving rural hub with three grocery stores and an opera house, has just over 100 people and no place to buy a soda. Most buildings have been boarded up.

"To reverse the population slide, you have to make it profitable to farm," Dr. Hubbard said. "My dream is that 10 years from now, this rural economy has been transformed, that it is vibrant again and people are renovating their downtowns."

The fate of Mr. Garst's experimental rice plot has loomed larger since Ventria encountered resistance to planting its rice in the southern part of the state, where rice has traditionally been grown.

When the company was considering Missouri as a place to grow its rice, it talked to Anheuser-Busch, which uses Missouri rice in its beer. Mr. Deeter said Anheuser-Busch initially did not raise any opposition to the project. But when Ventria tried to plant rice in southern Missouri this spring, the beer maker threatened not to buy any rice grown in the state. The company feared a consumer backlash if people thought gene-altered rice could end up in their bottles of Bud.

For Missouri's farm economy, the risk of growing pharmaceutical rice is high. More than half of Missouri's rice is sent abroad, to the European Union and Caribbean countries that are especially sensitive about genetically modified products.

"We are still having to make statements to our customers that the rice we export is not genetically modified," said Carl Brothers, the vice president for marketing at Riceland Foods, which markets more than half of Missouri's rice. "We are concerned longer term that if Ventria and others get involved that will get harder to say."

The two companies reached a truce in April: Ventria agreed not to grow genetically modified rice within 120 miles of commercial rice crops. "We can continue to purchase rice grown and processed in Missouri as long as Ventria's growing areas remain sufficiently far from commercial rice production," said Francine Katz, a spokeswoman for Anheuser-Busch.

That deal suddenly made four test plots in the northern part of the state, including Mr. Garst's, all the more important, since Ventria's agreement with Northwest Missouri State calls for the company to grow 70 percent of its rice in the state.

To prove to its customers that it would have a diverse supply base, Ventria must grow in at least one other location in North America, and is also searching for a growing area in the Southern Hemisphere to be able to produce year-round. In June, Ventria planted 70 acres of genetically modified rice in North Carolina. There, environmentalists continue to attack the company, saying the rice poses a threat to other crops and the human food chain.

Ventria's rice fields are just a few miles from a rice-seed-screening research center and are also close to two wildlife refuges with large populations of migrant birds and swans that environmentalists contend could transport Ventria's rice seeds into wild areas. Storms and floods, environmentalists say, could also lead to rice contamination.

"Just washing away in a big rain-storm is enough," said Margaret Mellon, director of the food and environment program at the Union of Concerned Scientists in Washington. Scientists at Ventria, which is yet to make any money from its bio-rice, say rice is among the safest crops for genetic engineering. Rice stalks pollinate themselves, so the altered genes, which are synthetic versions of human genes, cannot be easily transferred to plants in other fields. And Ventria requires farmers to employ a "closed system," using dedicated equipment and a production process where the seed is ground into a powder before it leaves the farm.

But critics say that there is no way to guarantee that the farmers will follow all the government regulations and Ventria's rules, and that they are worried about the risk of contamination because it would be hard to detect. "We simply wouldn't know if a contamination event took place," said Craig Culp, a spokesman for the Center for Food Safety, in Washington.

Dr. Hubbard acknowledged that there are risks, but he said he believed that they were minimal.

Federal regulations have been tested before, most notably in 2002, when drug-producing corn made by ProdiGene began sprouting in soybean fields near its Iowa and Nebraska sites. The Agriculture Department seized 500,000 bushels of soybeans and assessed the company nearly $3 million in fines and disposal costs. Earlier, in 2000, a gene-altered variety of corn that was approved for animal feed but not for human consumption was found in taco shells and other grocery items, prompting recalls.

Mr. Garst is a modern breed of farmer with a master's degree and a healthy interest in science. And he himself has done whatever he can to wring more from his commodity crops, even trying out a $300,000 tractor that steers automatically using a global-positioning satellite to till straighter rows.

"Obviously, you will not see pharmaceutical crops from here to Kansas City," he said of Ventria's project. "But there will be pockets in this area where you will see development. If you keep two more farmers in this area it is huge—there are four of us now."

SIGNIFICANCE

The protein products being made by the Ventria GM rice "factories" include lactoferrin and lysozyme. Both are natural human proteins with many potential applications. Lactoferrin is found in tears, saliva, and breast milk. It has anti-viral, anti-fungal, and anti-bacterial properties and boosts the immune system. As such, it forms one of the body's natural defenses against infection. Given that there is a rise in resistance to many antibiotics, there is an urgent need for

Barbara McClintock, who won a Nobel Prize for her research on the genetics of corn. ©BETTMANN/CORBIS.

new drugs that can help fight infection—still the leading cause of death worldwide. Lactoferrin may be able to take on this role. Lysozyme has similar properties and, indeed, research has shown that it also can enhance the effects of lactoferrin.

Many other companies are using plants like rice, tobacco, or corn to make therapeutic proteins to treat a range of diseases. While some of these molecules, like insulin, can be made in genetically-modified bacteria or yeast, more complex molecules need more complex hosts. For instance, monoclonal antibodies, which are being used in the treatment of cancer and inflammatory diseases like rheumatoid arthritis, are usually made in cells derived from hamsters. These cell-based production systems involve fermenting cell cultures in giant stainless steel vessels under sterile conditions. One limitation of this approach is often the cost—these new drugs can be very expensive—and there is an ongoing search for cheaper and higher-yield production systems.

Using whole plants, like rice, tobacco, or corn, as production systems may provide a cost advantage and,

as the article points out, it also provides the farmer with a useful alternative crop that can be sold. The use of genetically modified animals, such as pigs and rabbits, which secrete the therapeutic protein in their milk is another approach under development. So far, no drugs made in this way using genetically-modified plants or animals have reached the marketplace, although many are at the advanced clinical trial stage. GM plants have long been controversial. But if scientists can finally prove that their benefit to humanity outweighs the risk, then GM plants may make a valuable contribution.

FURTHER RESOURCES

Books

Pinstrup-Andersen, Per, and Ebbie Schioler. *Seeds of Contention: World Hunger and the Global Controversy Over GM Crops.* Washington, D.C.: International Food Policy Research Institute, 2001.

Periodicals

Giddings, Glynis, Gordon Allison, Douglas Brooks, and Adrian Carter. "Transgenic Plants as Factories for Biopharmaceuticals." *Nature Biotechnology* 18 (2000): 1151–1155.

Humphrey, Brooke D., Ning Huang, and Kirk D. Klasing. "Rice Expressing Lactoferrin and Lysozyme Has Antibiotic-like Properties When Fed to Chicks." *Journal of Nutrition* 132 (2002): 1214–1218.

Web sites

BBC News. "Study Finds Benefits in GM Crops." November 29, 2004. <http://news.bbc.co.uk/1/hi/sci/tech/4046427.stm> (accessed November 20, 2005).

Woman Finds Human Finger in Wendy's Chili

Forensic Medicine Identifies Hoax

Newspaper article

By: Dan Reed

Date: March 24, 2005

Source: *San Jose Mercury News*

About the Author: Dan Reed is a contributor to the *San Jose Mercury News,* a weekly newspaper serving the Silicon Valley area of California. It has a circulation of over 800,000.

INTRODUCTION

According to the U.S. Department of Labor's Bureau of Labor Statistics, industrial accidents lead to thousands of severed fingertips each year. Only a minority of these incidents occur in the food or leisure industry. One such case did occur in mid-2005, when a piece of index finger, severed at the first knuckle, was found in a pint of frozen chocolate custard purchased at a shop in North Carolina. It happened that an employee of the custard manufacturer had accidentally put his finger into the machine that beats the custard mixture. Fellow employees tried to help him and in the meantime, an attendant unknowingly scooped out custard containing the body part and served it to a customer.

The frozen custard incident arose from a genuine accident. Most cases of body parts being found in food are cases of mistaken identity—the item may look like a finger but turns out to be something else—or are in fact hoaxes, perpetrated in the hope of financial gain. In the story reproduced below, police soon suspected a hoax, when part of a finger was found in a portion of Wendy's chili. After all, none of the Wendy's employees was missing a finger and the offending body part had not been "simmering" for a lengthy time, so had probably not come from the kitchen. Police suspected that the finger might have been planted, and tests used in forensic medicine confirmed their suspicions.

PRIMARY SOURCE

SAN JOSE, Calif.—Wendy's chili is not made out of people—well, it is, but just a little bit.

Santa Clara County health officials confirmed Wednesday that the thing a woman bit on when enjoying her chili at a Monterey Highway Wendy's was, in fact, a human finger. They're not sure whose. It was about an inch-and-a-half, with a longish, nicely groomed nail.

And while it gave the woman—Anna Ayala, 39, of Las Vegas—a bad case of the willies, it likely caused no physical illness, officials said.

That's because the finger was safely cooked, simmering along at 170 degrees with more traditional chili ingredients, such as tomatoes, beef and beans.

At about 7:20 p.m. Tuesday, Ayala, in town with her family to drop off her in-laws who live in San Jose, scooped up a mouthful of chili.

It was her first visit to a Wendy's. "I'm more of a Carl's Jr. person," she said Thursday night.

"Suddenly something crunchy was in my mouth," she said, "and I spit it out."

After much examination, she and her tablemates realized just what the special ingredient was. Then the vomiting commenced.

Police and county health officials were called to the Wendy's, but no one there was missing any digits.

"We had everyone kind of show us they had 10 fingers, and everything was OK there," said Ben Gale, director of the county's Department of Environmental Health.

In confirming it was a finger, the county medical examiner also found that it wasn't badly decomposed and had a solid set of fingerprints. Conceivably, officials said, police could lift a print and perhaps match it to a partially fingered person through a database. Then ask, what happened?

For now, officials figure—since it was a jagged cut—it may have happened on a meat grinder.

In any case, the county shut the Wendy's for a while and impounded all the remaining chili and all the ingredients used to make it, which is whipped up on site. They hope to track all the fixings to try to find the source of the finger.

It is, of course, possible it was planted by someone who wants to cash-in on a gross-out civil suit.

"That's certainly plausible," said Medical Examiner Joseph O'Hara, "but then where would she have gotten the finger?"

All involved say they've never experienced anything like it. And Wendy's spokesman Bob Bertini said never in the fast-food chain's 35 years has a body part showed up in the food.

Wendy's founder Dave Thomas always used to say, "Quality is our recipe."

Maybe so, but they might want to rejigger the chili recipe.

SIGNIFICANCE

Anna Ayala quickly hired a lawyer to put in a compensation claim against Wendy's, which aroused the suspicion of police investigating the case. A woman from the town of Pahrump, sixty miles west of Las Vegas, came forward and said she had lost a fingertip in an encounter with a leopard a month before the Wendy's incident. She'd last seen it packed in ice in a Las Vegas emergency room, after doctors failed to re-attach it. Neither she, nor the hospital, knew what had happened to the fingertip and thought it possible that, somehow, it had ended up in the chili. DNA testing was discussed but not carried out, as the woman's fingertip sounded as if it was much smaller than the one under investigation.

Meanwhile, Wendy's sales were down by millions of dollars because of the unfavorable publicity and workers had to be laid off in some of its restaurants in northern California. The company wanted the case settled fast and offered a reward for information. This led to a tip off that identified the owner of the finger as a co-worker of Ayala's husband, a construction worker who had had an industrial accident.

On April 21, Ayala was arrested on charges of attempted grand larceny. The fingertip had allegedly been sold by its owner to settle a debt and ended up in Ayala's possession. She then planted it in her Wendy's meal in an attempt to get money from the company. Investigators discovered she had filed thirteen similar claims in the past in either her own name or in those of her children's, none of which appears to have been successful. Her husband was, at the time, in jail for identity theft charges, but he has also been implicated in the Wendy's case. In September, the pair pleaded guilty to the charges against them. It is clear that there was no link between Wendy's and the severed finger, but it still took months for sales to recover.

Forensic medicine, the application of medical principles to aid in solving a crime or to present legal testimony, is a growing medical specialty in the United States and was paramount in confirming the hoax perpetrated on Wendy's. In forensics laboratories, genetic material (DNA, deoxyribonucleic acid) can be analyzed from a variety of human samples including blood, semen, saliva, urine, hair, buccal (cheek) cells, tissues, or bones. DNA extracted from these samples is analyzed in a lab and results from these studies are compared to DNA analyzed from known samples. DNA extracted from a sample obtained from a crime scene (such as the finger in the chili at Wendy's) is then compared and with DNA extracted from the victim or suspect. In this case, the finger was confirmed by DNA testing to match the co-worker's DNA. Forensic pathologists also use DNA comparison methods to identify human remains in disaster situations.

FURTHER RESOURCES
Web sites

ABC News. "Despite Finger, Body Parts in Food Rare." <http://abcnews.go.com/US/print?id=726139> (accessed November 19, 2005).

Riley, Donald E. "DNA Testing: An Introduction For Non-Scientists." *Scientific Testimony.* <http://www.scientific.org/tutorials/articles/riley/riley.html> (accessed November 20, 2005).

USA Today. "Finger in Wendy's Chili Traced to Husband's Co-Worker." <http://www.usatoday.com/money/industries/food/2005-05-13-wendys-finger_x.htm> (accessed November 19, 2005).

Clinical Medicine

Clinical medicine is the branch of medicine in which a physician works directly with patients to promote health and cure illness. This involves direct observation, diagnosis, treatment, and clinical research on human subjects. Clinical medicine is usually practiced in a doctor's office or a hospital setting.

Over the last two hundred years, the way physicians have treated patients has changed dramatically. The scientific understanding of the course of diseases and the nature of human health are vastly improved. Near the mid-nineteenth century, it was not known that germs caused diseases, and that simple preventive steps, like having physicians wash their hands and wear gloves or other protective clothing, could prevent the spread of infections. At that time, surgical operations typically resulted in the death of about half of all patients, mostly due to post-surgical infections.

Joseph Lister (1827–1912) was the first physician to use an antiseptic on wounds. His carbolic acid spray kept wounds free from microorganisms (a strategy that became known as antiseptic surgery) and dramatically reduced the number and severity of surgically related infections. Lister's discovery is often cited as the dawn of modern clinical medicine.

Since then, clinical medicine has continued to evolve. The development of many specialized medicines, especially antibiotics, has changed the treatment of disease, drastically reducing deaths from diseases like tuberculosis, which once killed millions of people. Imaging technology, such as ultrasound, computed tomography (CT) scans, and positron emission tomography (PET) scans, have revolutionized the diagnosis of many disorders. Research into new surgical techniques and information transmission now make some remote treatments possible, with the patient and physician sometimes separated by hundreds or thousands of miles.

Still, in spite of the most sophisticated diagnosis and treatment methods, many diseases and injuries are still fatal. There is also some risk in just treating disease, especially with surgery, and, as with transplant surgery, the initial treatment attempts sometimes fail. In addition, physicians are discovering the ways that a patient's body and mind share a common and inseparable biochemistry, and that sometimes the best treatments sometimes involve not only the body, but the mind as well.

Patient counseling is an important aspect of clinical medicine, especially when a physical ailment has a psychological component, for example, with eating disorders like anorexia. An emerging medical and social issue involves the care of increasing numbers of elderly patients suffering both the cumulative debilitating effects of physical ailments, but also from mental deficiencies, like dementia and Alzheimer's disease. Many medical schools have recognized the importance of the physician-patient relationship, and include behavior training as a part of the medical education curriculum.

As medical science continues to advance, the applications of clinical medicine will continue to give rise to social concerns and issues. The challenge to practitioners is how to create the best balance of treating the patient's mental and physical health, using the best available technologies, but also maintaining a personal connection with patients.

Case II

Midwifery in the 1830s

Book excerpt

By: Horton Howard

Date: 1832

Source: Horton Howard. *A Treatise on the Complaints Peculiar to Females: Embracing a System of Midwifery; the Whole in Conformity with the Improved System of Botanic Medicine.* Columbus, Ohio: Horton Howard, 1832.

About the Author: William Ripley, a physician whose notes on one woman's labor and delivery are reprinted in the excerpt below, was part of a movement in the early nineteenth century to replace female midwives with male physicians.

INTRODUCTION

Midwives provided most obstetrical and gynecological care for women until the 1800s. Birth was largely regarded as a natural process that did not require specialized medical knowledge, although an experienced midwife's skills were considerable. Anyone who had borne several healthy children and observed several births was considered qualified by these experiences to assist other women through pregnancy and delivery.

Midwives usually provided mostly moral support as nature took its course during pregnancy, although they were capable of providing some assistance, such as attempting to turn a fetus in the womb to enable a better presentation for birth. Intervention during labor was uncommon, and was usually undertaken only in the case of an impossible delivery or the death or near death of the mother or fetus. Midwives did not use forceps, which were reserved for physicians, nor did they possess the instruments necessary for performing an embryulcia (extraction of the fetus from the uterus) in the event of fetal death or high risk of maternal death. They did not engage in bloodletting, purging, or other complicated procedures. Nevertheless, they probably (and unwittingly) contributed significantly to maternal deaths by delivering a series of children in the course of a day without washing their hands. Unaware of the dangers of germs, both midwives and physicians spread puerperal (childbed) fever, a common infection of the reproductive organs that often proved fatal.

Traditional midwifery began to disappear in urban centers in favor of medical obstetrics between 1760 and 1820 as a consequence of both new medical technology and physician's strong opposition to midwives. With their forceps and opiates, physicians promised a safer and more comfortable delivery. Pregnant women believed that the superior training of these men meant safer and shorter labor. In reality, it did not. Mothers faced an increasing threat of infection from the use of unwashed forceps as well as a possible anesthesia overdose or damage from forceps. Only after 1940 did medicine achieve the record of safety that it had promised to women in earlier centuries.

White midwives gradually disappeared in the United States by the mid-nineteenth century, as (male) physicians took over their practices. The few who remained worked essentially as physician's assistants. Birth became a medical event to be managed by interventionist attendants. The situation among the black population was markedly different. Africans Americans generally lacked the money to pay physicians fees. This combination of economics and racial prejudice allowed black midwives to maintain thriving practices into the twentieth century, long after their white colleagues had vanished.

The following passage from *A Treatise on the Complaints Peculiar to Females Embracing a System of Midwifery* illustrates, in one laboring woman's case, the initial role of the midwife, and the ensuing consultation of two physicians.

■ PRIMARY SOURCE

On the 12th day of Oct. 1830, at 9 o'clock, P.M. I was called on by Jesse Adams to see his wife, who was attacked with puerperal convulsions. She had been in hard labor about fourteen hours, with very little progress. A midwife was called in at first, but when she was attacked with convulsions Dr. Ramsay was called, who was then President of the Medical College of Ohio. When Dr. R. arrived, she lay in a state of total insensibility, and could not be aroused. The Doctor, after an examination, said his engagements were such that he could not undertake her case, as it might detain him a longer time than he could spare, and advised that another doctor should be sent for immediately, and left her. I arrived about two hours after he left; but there was no material change in her condition, excepting that she could be roused a little, and she swallowed some medicine, viz: a tea of raspberry leaf and valerian, and a little of the third preparation of Dr. Thomson; after which she soon revived, and labor came on. On examination, I found the os tineæ (mouth of the womb) dilated, and the child's head at the inferior strait of the pelvis. The pains were regular, with regular intervals, effectual but not severe. She was in this condition when I had been there about twenty minutes, and Dr. Ramsay came in again. He inquired of me how long I had been there; I told him about twenty minutes: he then inquired of the midwife how she had been in his absence; and on being informed, he asked me what I thought was the prospect. I told him I thought it favorable, and I did not apprehend any difficulty. He staid by while she had several pains, and then advised to give the ergot tea. I told him I thought we could do without it. He then took his leave; but as he went out, several women who were present went out with him to learn what was his opinion of the case. He answered them freely, that he thought it a very bad case, and very dangerous; and said he was much mistaken if she got through safely. However, the child was born within about fifteen minutes after his departure, and the woman had a very comfortable night; and she and the child are both well at this time, it being the 9th of February, 1832.

WILLIAM RIPLEY.

SIGNIFICANCE

By the late 1960s, and spurred by the scientific advances of the germ theory of disease, midwives had largely vanished from the landscape of American medicine. The women's health movement spawned by feminism in the early 1970s prompted many to challenge some aspects of traditional modern medicine. Male obstetricians typically practiced a patriarchal style of medicine with the patient expected to follow orders. Midwifery, with its focus on women caring for women, offered a less hospital-centered and more informed, supportive birth experience.

When physicians replaced midwives, their holistic approach vanished as well. Midwives traditionally supported women throughout labor by explaining the physical process, offering words of encouragement, and helping to lessen their patients' fears. Focused almost entirely on delivering a healthy baby, physicians did not always consider the mother's needs and concerns.

Modern midwives are often advanced practice nurses with master's degrees who can prescribe medication, so some of the old advantages offered by physicians no longer apply. Nurse midwives additionally provide gynecological services such as annual exams, contraception information, and menopause care that some women prefer to receive from another woman.

In the first decade of the twenty-first century, coaches who provide physical and emotional support for laboring mothers called *doulas* enjoyed a resurgence in popularity. The term, which means "wise women," dates to ancient Greece; a modern doula fulfills all the duties of a midwife except for actually delivering the baby. Although the number of doulas nationwide remained quite small at 5,000 in 2004, the steadily increasing popularity of such helpers reflected the trend toward a more patient-centered delivery.

FURTHER RESOURCES

Books

Walzer Leavitt, Judith. *Brought to Bed: Childbearing in America, 1750 to 1950.* New York: Oxford University Press, 1986.

Periodicals

Robinson, Sharon A. "A Historical Development of Midwifery in the Black Community, 1600–1940." *Journal of Nurse Midwifery* 29, no. 4 (1984): 247–250.

Insensibility During Surgical Operations Produced By Inhalation

Anesthesia Gives Rise to Modern Surgery

Journal article

By: Henry J. Bigelow

Date: 1846

Source: Henry J. Bigelow. "Insensibility During Surgical Operations Produced By Inhalation." *Boston Medical and Surgical Journal* 35 (1846): 309–317.

About the Author: Henry J. Bigelow (1818–1890) was a clinical pharmacologist and surgeon, who wrote many essays based on his observations, research, and experience with the early use of anesthesia in the performance of surgical procedures. Among his best known publications is the extended essay entitled *A History of the Discovery of Modern Anesthesia.* It was Dr. Bigelow's assertion that the optimal agent for surgical anesthesia should result in safe, total, and sustainable insensibility throughout the course of the entire procedure. Although he did not believe ether to be completely perfect as an agent of insensibility, as it was flammable, he deemed it adequate for the performance of successful surgeries. Indeed, it is the use of ether during operative procedures that has been credited with the inception of the anesthetic revolution and the dawn of the modern surgical era. Throughout his career, Henry J. Bigelow wrote extensively on various anesthetic preparations and techniques, most notably on the use of ether and of chloroform for induction of insensibility.

INTRODUCTION

Before the introduction of modern methods of anesthesia, surgery was a rare, and often life-threatening, event. Before insensibility-causing agents were discovered, a variety of non-pharmaceutical methods were employed, including the use of mandrake root, henbane, opium, jimsonweed, cannabis, datura, coca, and hemp as means of clouding consciousness. Ingestion of large amounts of alcohol was also used for this purpose. None of these methods were particularly satisfactory, as they did not completely prevent the perception of pain, and all had unpredictable side effects, including possible death.

Surgery was considered a treatment of last resort, and the agony endured by surgical patients was substantial. Typically, a large and brawny surgical assistant was employed for the purpose of holding down the patient who was tightly strapped to the table. Patients screamed in fear and pain throughout the procedure, and were considered fortunate if they fainted from pain early on in the proceedings. The operation was necessarily extremely quick, taking not more than a few minutes from start to finish, in order for the patient to survive. As a result, accuracy was often lacking and complications such as postoperative bleeding and infection were common.

Hypnosis, or mesmerism, was sometimes used as a means of altering consciousness, as was acupuncture. Other non-pharmacological methods used included the application of a mixture of cold and salt to the surgical site, compression of blood flow to the area, concussion (usually a sharp blow to the jaw) in an effort to mechanically induce a state of unconsciousness, compression of blood flow through the carotid arteries in the neck, bleeding or blood-letting, and the use of counterirritants as a means of distraction (rubbing the patient elsewhere on the body with stinging nettles, for example).

In 1846, Henry J. Bigelow read a local newspaper article concerning dentist William Morton's painless surgical removal of an ulcerous tooth through the use of inhaled ether. Bigelow met Morton, and arranged for him to demonstrate his painless surgical technique at the Massachusetts General Hospital, where Bigelow was a junior surgeon. Dr. John Collins Warren, head surgeon at the Massachusetts General Hospital, agreed to perform the operation, with Morton providing the anesthesia. Henry J. Bigelow's account of several similar proceedings follows.

■ PRIMARY SOURCE

It has long been an important problem in medical science to devise some method of mitigating the pain of surgical operations. An efficient agent for this purpose has at length been discovered. A patient has been rendered completely insensible during an amputation of the thigh, regaining consciousness after a short interval. Other severe operations have been performed without the knowledge of the patients. So remarkable an occurrence will, it is believed, render the following details relating to the history and character of the process, not uninteresting.

On the 16th of Oct. 1846, an operation was performed at the hospital upon a patient who had inhaled a preparation administered by Dr. Morton, a dentist of this city, with the alleged intention of producing insensibility to pain. Dr. Morton was understood to have extracted teeth under similar circumstances, without the knowledge of the patient. The present operation was performed by Dr. Warren, and though comparatively slight, involved an incision near the lower jaw of some inches in extent. During the operation the patient muttered, as in a semi-conscious state, and afterwards stated that the pain was considerable, though mitigated; in his own words, as though the skin had been scratched with a hoe. There was, probably, in this instance, some defect in the process of inhalation, for on the following day the vapor was administered to another patient with complete success. A fatty tumor of considerable size was removed, by Dr. Hayward, from the arm of a woman near the deltoid muscle. The operation lasted four or five minutes, during which time the patient betrayed occasional marks of uneasiness; but upon subsequently regaining her consciousness, professed not only to have felt no pain, but to have been insensible to surrounding objects, to have known nothing of the operation, being only uneasy about a child left at home. No doubt, I think, existed, in the minds of those who saw this operation, that the unconsciousness was real; nor could the imagination be accused of any share in the production of these remarkable phenomena.

I subsequently undertook a number of experiments, with the view of ascertaining the nature of this new agent, and shall briefly state them, and also give some notice of the previous knowledge which existed of the use of the substances I employed.

The first experiment was with sulphuric ether, the odor of which was readily recognized in the preparation employed by Dr. Morton. Ether inhaled in vapor is well known to produce symptoms similar to those produced by the nitrous oxide. . . .

It remains briefly to describe the process of inhalation by the new method, and to state some of its effects. A small two-necked glass globe contains the prepared vapor, together with sponges to enlarge the evaporating surface. One aperture admits the air to the interior of the globe, whence, charged with vapor, it is drawn through the second into the lungs. The inspired air thus passes through the bottle, but the expiration is diverted by a valve in the mouth piece, and escaping into the apartment is thus prevented from vitiating the medicated vapor. A few of the operations in dentistry, in which the preparation has as yet been chiefly applied, have come under my observation. The remarks of the patients will convey an idea of their sensations.

A boy of sixteen, of medium stature and strength, was seated in the chair. The first few inhalations occasioned a quick cough, which afterwards subsided; at the end of eight minutes the head fell back, and the arms dropped but owing to some resistance in opening the mouth, the tooth could not be reached before he awoke. He again inhaled for two minutes, and slept three minutes, during which time the tooth, an inferior molar, was extracted. At the moment of extraction the features assumed an expression of pain, and the hand was raised. Upon coming to himself he said he had had a "first rate dream—very quiet," he said, "and had dreamed of Napoleon—had not the slightest consciousness of pain—the time had seemed long;" and he left the chair, feeling no uneasiness of any kind, and evidently in a high state of admiration. The pupils were dilated during the state of unconsciousness, and the pulse rose from 130 to 142.

A girl of sixteen immediately occupied the chair. After coughing a little, she inhaled during three minutes, and fell asleep, when a molar tooth was extracted, after which she continued to slumber tranquilly during three minutes more. At the moment when force was applied she flinched and frowned, raising her hand to her mouth, but said she had been dreaming a pleasant dream and knew nothing of the operation.

A stout boy of twelve, at the first inspiration coughed considerably, and required a good deal of encouragement to induce him to go on. At the end of three minutes from the first fair inhalation, the muscles were relaxed and the pupil dilated. During the attempt to force open the mouth he recovered his consciousness, and again inhaled during two minutes, and in the ensuing one minute two teeth were extracted, the patient seeming somewhat conscious, but upon actually awaking he declared "it was the best fun he ever saw," avowed his intention to come there again, and insisted upon having another tooth extracted upon the spot. A splinter which had been left, afforded an opportunity of complying with his wish, but the pain proved to be considerable. Pulse at first 110, during sleep 96, afterwards 144; pupils dilated.

The next patient was a healthy-looking, middle-aged woman, who inhaled the vapor for four minutes; in the course of the next two minutes a back tooth was extracted, and the patient continued smiling in her sleep for three minutes more. Pulse 120, not affected at the moment of the operation, but smaller during sleep. Upon coming to herself, she exclaimed that "it was beautiful— she dreamed of being at home—it seemed as if she had been gone a month." These cases, which occurred successively in about an hour, at the room of Dr. Morton, are fair examples of the average results produced by the inhalation of the vapor, and will convey an idea of the feelings and expressions of many of the patients subjected to the process. Dr. Morton states that in upwards of two hundred patients, similar effects have been produced. The inhalation, after the first irritation has subsided, is easy, and produces a complete unconsciousness at the expiration of a period varying from two to five or six, sometimes eight minutes; its duration varying from two to five minutes; during which the patient is completely insensible to the ordinary tests of pain. The pupils in the cases I have observed have been generally dilated; but with allowance for excitement and other disturbing influences, the pulse is not affected, at least in frequency; the patient remains in a calm and tranquil slumber, and wakes with a pleasurable feeling. The manifestation of consciousness or resistance I at first attributed to the reflex function, but I have since had cause to modify this view.

It is natural to inquire whether no accidents have attended the employment of a method so wide in its application, and so striking in its results. I have been unable to learn that any serious consequences have ensued. One or two robust patients have failed to be affected. I may mention as an early and unsuccessful case, its administration in an operation performed by Dr. Hayward, where an elderly woman was made to inhale the vapor for at least half an hour without effect. Though I was unable at the time to detect any imperfection in the process, I am inclined to believe that such existed. One woman became much excited, and required to be confined to the chair. As this occurred to the same patient twice, and in no other case as far as I have been able to learn, it was evidently owing to a peculiar susceptibility. Very young subjects are affected with nausea and vomiting, and for this reason Dr. M. has refused to administer it to children. Finally, in a few cases, the patient has continued to sleep tranquilly for eight or ten minutes, and once, after a protracted inhalation, for the period of an hour. . . .

Two recent cases serve to confirm, and one I think to decide, the great utility of this process. On Saturday, the 7th Nov., at the Mass. General Hospital, the right leg of a young girl was amputated above the knee, by Dr. Hayward, for disease of this joint. Being made to inhale the preparation, after protesting her inability to do so from the pungency of the vapor, she became insensible in about five minutes. The last circumstance she was able to recall was the adjustment of the mouth piece of the apparatus, after which she was unconscious until she heard some remark at the time of securing the vessels—one of the last steps of the operation. Of the incision she knew nothing, and was unable to say, upon my asking her, whether or not the limb had been removed. She refused to answer several questions during the operation, and was evidently completely insensible to pain or other external influences. This operation was followed by another, consisting of the removal of a part of the lower jaw, by Dr. Warren. The patient was insensible to pain of the first incision, though she recovered her consciousness in the course of a few minutes.

The character of the lethargic state, which follows this inhalation, is peculiar. The patient loses his individuality and awakes after a certain period, either entirely unconscious of what has taken place, or retaining only a faint recollection of it. Severe pain is sometimes remembered as being of a dull character; sometimes the operation is supposed by the patient to be performed upon somebody else. Certain patients, whose teeth have been extracted, remember the application of the extracting instruments; yet none have been conscious of any real pain. . . .

SIGNIFICANCE

The successful public use of inhaled ether and chloroform for the performance of surgical procedures heralded the start of the modern anesthetic era. The senior Oliver Wendell Holmes, who was both a physician and a poet, wrote a letter to William Morton, in which he first made use of the words anaesthetic and anaesthesia for inhaled agents producing insensibility to pain. Anesthetic and anesthesia were derived from Greek words, and meant "without (an) sensibility (esthesia)."

In addition to the production of unconsciousness, ether served to stabilize cardiovascular function. As a result, ether has remained a model for the synthesis of myriad inhaled anesthetic agents until the present day.

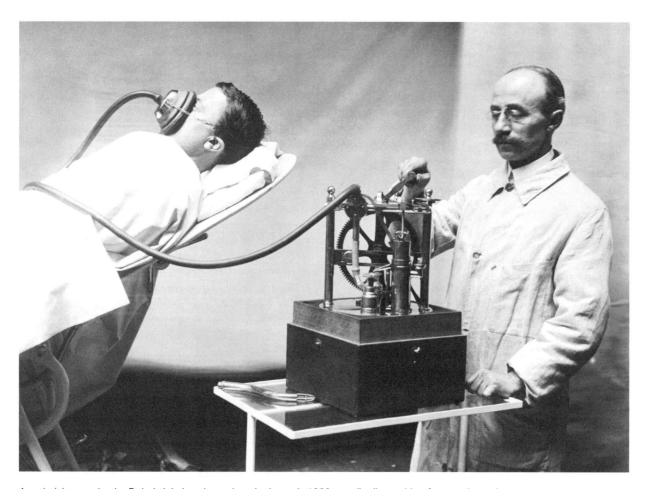

A technician cranks the Dubois inhaler, shown here in the early 1900s, to distribute chloroform to the patient. ©BETTMANN/CORBIS.

Anesthetics had been used sporadically since the early 1840s, but were not widely recognized until October 16, 1846, when William T. G. Morton, at the Massachusetts General Hospital, assisted Dr. John C. Warren in the removal of a tumor from the neck of Gilbert Abbot, by providing the inhalation agent sulfuric ether.

The use of ether as an inhaled anesthetic quickly spread to Europe. Dental surgeon James Robinson was the first to administer anesthesia by ether in England on December 19, 1846. On January 19, 1847, Sir James Young Simpson, professor of obstetrics at the University of Edinburgh, was the first to employ the use of ether during labor. In November of the same year, Dr. Simpson first used chloroform as an anesthetic agent. Although it was considered to be more potent, it also could cause major side effects, such as severe, late-onset liver damage and could even result in death. It enjoyed a substantial degree of popularity because it was both effective and easier to use than ether.

Sulfuric ether was first used in wartime on March 29, 1847. Edward H. Barton used it in Vera Cruz, Mexico, in order to perform an amputation.

Local anesthesia was developed in 1877. This was a monumental scientific breakthrough as well, because it led to the development of infiltration anesthesia, spinal, and epidural anesthesia, and nerve blocks. By the start of the twentieth century, stabilization and protection of the airways during surgery became possible through the development and implementation of breathing tubes placed in the trachea during surgical procedures.

By the second decade of the twentieth century, the use of intravenous induction methods of anesthesia had been standardized; these permitted the patient to fall asleep in a more relaxed and normal manner. In the 1940s, muscle relaxants were developed.

Anesthesiologists are now highly trained physicians, often aided by nurse anesthetists and other skilled paraprofessionals. Anesthesia is no longer used simply for inducing unconsciousness during surgery, it is also used in labor and delivery, trauma and emergency medicine, for the induction of therapeutic coma in critical care, for extensive treatments such as burn debridement, and for the management of chronic and severe pain syndromes. Anesthesiologists can now adjust anesthetic agents to produce varying levels of consciousness or sedation in their patients, allowing for a safer surgery or treatment procedure.

FURTHER RESOURCES
Web sites

Anesthesia Nursing and Medicine. "Dr. Bigelow." <http://www.anesthesia-nursing.com/bigelow.html> (accessed October 19, 2005).

Anesthesia Nursing and Medicine. "Ether—Part II." <http://www.anesthesia-nursing.com/ether2.html> (accessed October 19, 2005).

Anesthesia Nursing and Medicine. "The Unusual History of Ether." <http://www.anesthesia-nursing.com/ether.html> (accessed October 19, 2005).

Massachusetts General Hospital: Neurosurgical Service. "The Evolution of Ether: Today's Anesthesiology." <http://neurosurgery.mgh.harvard.edu/History/evolve.html> (accessed October 19, 2005).

The Premature Burial

Painting

By: Antoine Joseph Wiertz

Date: 1854

About the Artist: Antoine Wiertz (1806–1865) was a relatively obscure painter of the Romantic school. In 1832, he won a paid fellowship called the Prix de Rome, which enabled him to paint in Rome. At the conclusion of the fellowship, he returned to his native Belgium, where he was moderately successful. He made several unsuccessful attempts to submit his work to the Paris Salon. In 1852, the Belgian government offered to build him a studio in exchange for a series of works of art.

INTRODUCTION

Prior to the advent of modern medicine, which renders the possibility of incorrect pronouncement of death—and premature burial—quite unlikely, there were few definitive means of determining death. As a result, it was not unheard of for an extremely ill person to fall into a coma or a stupor and to appear to observers to be dead. Bodies were often quickly buried, particularly in times of plague or cholera. There have been numerous tales, dating back to very early history, of the apparently dead spontaneously reviving and living on for extended periods of time. One such story is that of Marjorie Halcrow Erskine of Chirnside, Scotland. She was reported to have died in 1674 and was buried in a rather shallow grave by the village sexton, who planned to rob her grave and steal her jewelry. As the sexton attempted to cut off the woman's finger in order to obtain one of her rings, she suddenly revived. Ms. Erskine was able to return home, and she lived a full life, giving birth to and raising two sons.

In the seventeenth through nineteenth centuries, in times of plague, cholera, and smallpox epidemics, a substantial number of premature burials were reported. A nineteenth century researcher named William Tebb published a book in 1896 entitled *Premature Burial and How It May Be Prevented*. In it, he detailed 219 instances of near premature burial, 149 cases of genuine premature burial, ten cases of dissection before actual death, and two cases in which embalming began before death had occurred.

Wiertz's paintings tended to be larger than life, and many of them had morbid themes. Some examples of this morbidity in his artwork include: *The Premature Burial* (1854), *The Two Beauties: La Belle Rosine* (1847), *The Suicide* (1854), and the triptych *The Last Thoughts and Visions of a Decapitated Head* (1853). The latter painting was intended to be a strong statement in opposition to the death penalty. Like many of his contemporary Romantic artists, Wiertz was opposed to the use of capital punishment, both from a political and a humanitarian perspective. Wiertz drew some of his inspiration from the popular literature of his day. *The Last Thoughts and Visions of a Decapitated Head* probably was inspired, at least in part, by Victor Hugo's 1828 novel entitled *Le Dernier Jour D'Un Condamne* (The Last Day of a Condemned Man/Convict). *The Premature Burial* was inspired by American writer Edgar Allan Poe's 1850 short story of the same name.

 PRIMARY SOURCE

THE PREMATURE BURIAL
See primary source image.

SIGNIFICANCE

During the eighteenth and nineteenth centuries, various methods were employed to ensure that an individual was, in fact, dead. In one method, a hot poker was applied to the patient's rectum, while another involved pouring warm urine into the patient's mouth. Yet another creative strategy required the attending physician to stick the finger of the apparently deceased into his (the physician's) ear in an effort to feel the *buzz* or *hum* of life. In 1846, a French physician named Eugene Bouchut suggested that the stethoscope be used to determine when the heart stopped beating in order to determine that death had occurred.

The most extreme measures for preventing premature burial occurred in Germany between 1790 and 1860. There, roughly fifty centers called *Leichenhäuser*, or waiting mortuaries, were built. In these buildings, corpses were kept in warm rooms. Each corpse had strings wrapped around fingers and toes, with the other ends of the strings attached to bells. The bells were meant to be rung by the awakening person, but there is no report of a bell ever ringing. The bodies were maintained until evidence of putrefaction was unequivocally present (complete with requisite stench). Some of the waiting mortuaries had luxury and common rooms—some were even open for public observation. A later Leichenhaus in Vienna utilized an electronic bell system.

Individuals went to elaborate lengths to prevent premature burial. Some requested that their heads be severed. Others wanted their arteries slashed (Danish writer Hans Christian Andersen, 1805–1875), their bodies dissected (Polish composer Frédéric Chopin, 1810–1849), or their bodies embalmed. All these measures were designed to ensure with absolute certainty that the individual was dead before he or she was buried.

In 1896, Count Karnice-Kamicki, a chamberlain to the Russian czar, invented a device to be affixed to a coffin in order to avoid premature burial—or, rather, to provide a means of correcting that unfortunate situation. His mechanism was comprised of a tube running from the inside of the coffin to an airtight box several feet above the ground. A spring, which ran the length of the tube, was attached to a glass sphere sitting on the chest of the body. The slightest movement of the body would trigger the spring, causing the lid of the airtight box to pop open, thus allowing light and air to into the interior of the coffin via the connecting tube. The box above the grave also contained a flag, a bell or a buzzer, and a light that could be seen and heard from a considerable distance.

Modern medicine has devised a variety of methods for determining death. For example, an electroencephalogram can show an absence of electrical activity in the brain and a cardiac monitor can verify the absence of efficient electrical activity in the heart. Core temperature recorders also can reveal a drop in core body temperature below that found in a living person. Angiography and certain brain scans also can confirm that no blood is circulating in the brain. When the death occurs outside the hospital setting, the typical guidelines for determining that death has occurred include: 1) more than five minutes have elapsed since the person's last breath, and 2) the person has no pulse.

FURTHER RESOURCES
Books

Bondeson, Jan. *Buried Alive: The Terrifying History of Our Most Primal Fear*. New York: W. W. Norton, 2001.

Iserson, Kenneth. *Death to Dust: What Happens to Dead Bodies?* Tucson: Galen Press, 1994.

■ **PRIMARY SOURCE**

The Premature Burial. Fears of premature burial, such as those expressed in this 1854 painting by Antoine Wiertz, were sensationalized in mid-nineteenth century art and literature, often in the aftermath of outbreaks of cholera and other epidemic diseases. "L'INHUMANATION PRÉCIPITÉE" BY ANTON WIERTZ. INV.NR. 1968.©MUSEES ROYAUX DES BEAUX-ARTS DE BELGIQUE.

Taylor, Troy. *Beyond the Grave.* Decatur, Ill.: Whitechapel Press, 2001.

Tebb, William, and Edward Vollum. *Premature Burial and How It May Be Prevented.* London: S. Sonnenschein, 1896.

Web sites

Forbes.com. "A Fate Worse Than Death." <http://www.forbes.com/free_forbes/2001/0305/193.html> (accessed February 5, 2005).

Conditions at Bellevue Hospital

Illustration

By: Anonymous

Date: 1860

Source: Anonymous engraving. *Harper's Weekly,* 1860. (Image also appears in A. S. Lyons and R. J. Petrucelli. *Medicine: an Illustrated History.* New York: Abrams, 1978.)

About the Artist: *Harper's Weekly* was launched in 1857 by Fletcher Harper, one of the four brothers who owned Harper & Brothers, the largest book publisher in the United States at that time. It was Fletcher Harper's second successful foray into magazine publishing following *Harper's Monthly,* which he had created in 1850 and modeled on the *London Illustrated News.* By 1860 the circulation of *Harper's Weekly* had reached 200,000.

INTRODUCTION

New York's Bellevue Hospital, while technically not the oldest hospital in the United States, is a lineal descendant of the original infirmary for soldiers and slaves established in New Amsterdam (now the city of

New York) by Jacob Varrenvanger, surgeon to the Dutch West India Company, in 1658. Soon after the English took over the colony, the infirmary was moved and merged with a "public almshouse and house of correction" that was constructed at the site of the present New York City Hall. In 1794, after a yellow fever epidemic broke out along the U.S. eastern seaboard, the facility was moved to Chambers Street. However, the new premises proved inadequate to deal with the epidemic, so the institution was moved again to a mansion on a farm—"Belle View"—outside the then city limits, its present location. The grounds and buildings of the combination hospital, almshouse, and penitentiary institution were gradually expanded over the next forty years; the hospital itself was completed in 1826. New York citizens objected to the continuation of the almshouse and jail at the site, and these components were removed from the hospital grounds in 1847. From that time until well into the twentieth century, Bellevue emerged as one of the premier hospitals and medical schools in the United States.

Bellevue conjures many negative images in popular imagination, particularly regarding its highly publicized unsanitary conditions in the nineteenth century—exemplified by the engraving below—and its psychiatric facilities to which many citizens were involuntarily committed. However, the history of Bellevue reflects many innovations in American medicine. These include the first lying-in ward in New York; the first formal course for midwives; the development of modern public health practices; the first hospital-based ambulance service; the first school of nursing, and the first hospital outpatient department. On a less positive note, the institution was also the first hospital in the United States to establish its own cemetery, in which many patients and staff were buried. Currently Bellevue is the largest city hospital in the United States, treating 26,000 inpatients and handling 400,000 outpatient clinic visits annually. It provides physical and mental health emergency services for New York City, and continues as a teaching hospital and School of Medicine under the auspices of New York University.

In the nineteenth century, sanitary conditions and patient treatment at Bellevue stand out as objectionable. The problems at Bellevue were reported and illustrated in the local press, such as *Harper's Weekly*, as the reproduced illustration shows. However, it was Bellevue's size and location in the emerging metropolis of New York City that made it the target of investigative reporting and advocacy for indigent and psychiatric patients. Doubtless many institutions in

smaller cities exhibited conditions as bad as or worse than those at Bellevue, but these cities lacked the journalistic fervor that has existed in New York. The story of Bellevue is a prominent case study in how the American hospital system, under pressure from watchdogs in the press, local humanitarian organizations, and the medical profession, gradually incorporated rules of compassion and accountability in the treatment of patients. Many of these rules are now incorporated into municipal, state, and federal laws that govern patient care in American health care institutions.

PRIMARY SOURCE

CONDITIONS AT BELLEVUE HOSPITAL
See primary source image.

SIGNIFICANCE

Early in the nineteenth century, staffing levels at Bellevue Hospital were extremely inadequate and the hospital was managed by incompetent political appointees. A handful of doctors had charge of a burgeoning population of hundreds and then thousands of hospitalized patients. Dedicated staff physicians at Bellevue shared the fate of many of its patients: twenty-seven staff physicians died from diseases contracted on the job at the institution between 1825 and 1884, mainly from typhus, cholera, puerperal fever, and yellow fever. The farm on which the institution had been built was neglected and produced little food. Conditions were appalling and hospital supplies were plundered wholesale. The institutional mortality rate averaged 20 percent per year in those years. An 1837 account from a history of Bellevue describes patients abandoned by nurses and servants due to concerns of typhus, lying with open wounds in filthy blankets without sheets and pillows.

Reports of these harsh conditions, such as the account in *Harper's Weekly* from which this illustration was taken, began to stir the conscience of laypersons and medical professionals in New York and beyond. The first step toward improving conditions was taken in 1847, when the prison inmates and the smallpox patients were transferred to Blackwell's Island. The mentally ill also were removed to Blackwell's Island. The almshouse was not moved until ten years later. Around that time, the elite among New York's medical profession began to take seats on the institution's governing board, ending the hospital's mismanagement by political cronies. Physician education in the form of clinical lectures on

PRIMARY SOURCE

Conditions at Bellevue Hospital. Illustration appearing in the magazine *Harper's Weekly* in 1860 depicting the unsanitary conditions at New York's Bellevue Hospital. MUSEUM OF THE CITY OF NEW YORK.

medical and surgical topics was initiated in the middle of the nineteenth century, bringing about a remarkable improvement in the quality of care and reducing the death rate to just over 9 percent by 1853.

The American Civil War (1861–1865) dealt a blow to staffing and conditions at Bellevue. Almost all of the younger doctors volunteered for service and six of the remaining physicians died in yet another typhus epidemic. However, in a more positive development, Bellevue surgeon Dr. Edward P. Dalton, who had organized a vast horse-drawn ambulance service for the Army, created a hospital ambulance service based on the efficient and successful service he had set up for the military.

Although Bellevue made great strides in increasing its capacity, modernizing its facilities, upgrading the physician staff, and introducing antisepsis and sanitation, the poor quality of its nursing staff continued to

hurt patient outcomes. Bellevue nurses, attendants, and helpers were originally furnished by the penitentiary. Many of them worked for room and board only, and lacked training, education, and competence. In 1872, Louisa Lee Schuyler, responding to persistent reports of squalor and substandard conditions at Bellevue, established a visiting committee of educated and socially connected women. When these women first toured the facility, they found gloom, poor lighting, lingering unsanitary conditions, and abysmal staffing levels. This committee publicized the shortcomings of patient conditions and care at the institution, leading at last to a flow of taxpayer funding and charitable donations that began to markedly improve patient treatment and illness outcomes.

As mentioned above, the mentally ill were transferred from Bellevue to Blackwell's Island in the late 1840s. This raises a question regarding the conditions and treatment of the mentally ill in New York in the middle of the nineteenth century. Did New Yorkers remove a problem from Bellevue Hospital only to relocate the same problem to a more remote and less visible part of the city? An anonymous account of the "Lunatic Asylum" on Blackwell's Island that appeared in *Harper's New Monthly Magazine* in 1866 seems to put that concern to rest. The following excerpt provides insight into local attitudes toward the insane as well as into the conditions that were maintained for them at that time.

> In the construction of ordinary asylums attention is given more to the homelike comforts than to the great strength of the establishment. It is the moral power that holds the patients more effectually than strong rooms, and probably there is no asylum in the country, except that at Auburn, from which a sane man could not readily escape. In the Asylum on Blackwell's Island there are no rooms really stronger than the usual sleeping-rooms of the hotels in the city, and the only appearance of extra strength is in the cast-iron sashes of the windows, which might be readily broken. They are well adapted, however, to common cases of insanity, but are insecure for the criminal insane with dangerous propensities...One of the unhappiest results of the reception of this class is, that the other insane feel truly degraded by the association, and are fearful that their own lives are endangered. Many of the patients are exceedingly sensitive, and feel deeply any real or fancied injury or injustice. It becomes with them a matter of complaint that murderers even occupy the same halls with them and sit at the same table. Expressions of feeling arouse a spirit of ill-will and antagonism, and serious quarrels and difficulties result. (Anonymous. Harper's New Monthly Magazine, vol. 32, no. 249, February 1866.)

This passage reveals much sympathy and compassion for the "lunatics" at Blackwell's Island. The article, while thorough in pointing out the shortcomings of care in the institution, expresses a benign attitude toward the care of the mentally ill. It also points out the lack of sensitivity for the patients' concerns shown by the institutional staff. The article further notes that the insane were housed on a separate part of the island from the prisoners. The asylum was located near an area of considerable natural beauty and by a neighborhood of mansions built by wealthy New Yorkers. Thus, while the treatment of psychiatric patients in the early nineteenth century at Bellevue reflected the devastating neglect that all of the patients and inmates suffered there, it appears that transferring the insane to Blackwell's Island was motivated by a desire to improve conditions, not only at Bellevue itself, but also for the mentally ill. By the mid-nineteenth century, therefore, public attitudes toward the mentally ill

had already begun to be transformed from punitive to treatment-oriented. Today the overwhelming majority of the mentally ill at Bellevue are treated on an outpatient or emergency basis. The 1994 book *Crazy All the Time: On the Psych Ward of Bellevue Hospital* provides a vivid contemporary description of these services from the perspective of a Bellevue staff psychologist.

A review of the history of Bellevue supports a largely optimistic assessment of the progress of institutional medical practice in the United States, despite flawed political systems and negligent or malicious officials and employees. Accounts of the hospital's vicissitudes and struggles are gripping and raw. However, the Bellevue of today represents a triumph of the health care professions and the New York community over the extreme adversity of financial neglect and waves of epidemics. Perhaps, the greatest adversity that was conquered, however, was the devastating ignorance on the part of the general public concerning conditions at Bellevue, an ignorance that the vigilance of journalists and the social conscience of citizens finally banished.

FURTHER RESOURCES

Books

Covan, Frederick L., and Carol Kahn. *Crazy All the Time: Life, Lessons, and Insanity on the Psych Ward of Bellevue Hospital*. New York: Simon & Schuster, 1994.

Web sites

Bellevue Hospital Center. <http://www.nyc.gov/html/hhc/html/facilities/bellevue.shtml> (accessed November 20, 2005).

History Magazine. "Bellevue Hospital." <http://history-magazine.com/bellevue.html> (accessed November 20, 2005).

NYC 10044. "Blackwell's Island Lunatic Asylum." <http://nyc10044.com/timeln/asylum/lunatic.html> (accessed November 20, 2005).

Antiseptic Surgery

Method of Changing a Psoas Abscess Dressing

Illustration

By: W. Watson Cheyne

Date: 1882

Source: Antiseptic Surgery: Method of Changing a Psoas Abscess Dressing. Figure 38 in *Antiseptic*

Surgery: Its Principles, Practice, History and Results, by W. Watson Cheyne. London: Smith, Elder, 1882.

About the Author: William Watson Cheyne (1852–1932), a Scottish physician and surgeon famed for his pioneering work with British surgeon Joseph Lister (1827–1912) on the development of antiseptic surgery, was educated at King's College in Aberdeen and at Edinburgh University, from which he graduated in 1875. After a brief stay in Vienna, he was appointed house surgeon to Joseph Lister, who was then a professor of clinical surgery at the Edinburgh Royal Infirmary. At the same time, Cheyne was appointed to the position of demonstrator of anatomy at Edinburgh University, a post he occupied from 1876 to 1877. In 1877, Cheyne was promoted to the position of Lister's first house surgeon at King's College Hospital. After accepting positions of progressively increasing responsibility, Cheyne was appointed assistant surgeon and teacher of practical surgery in 1880; he became a surgeon with care of outpatients in 1887, surgeon and teacher of operative surgery in 1889, and professor of the principles and practice of surgery in 1902. He was a fellow or member of several prestigious royal and professional societies, including Fellow of the Royal Society (1902), Fellow of the Royal College of Surgeons (1879), Hunterian Professor at the Royal College of Surgeons (1888 and 1890–1892), and President of the Royal College of Surgeons (1914–1916). He held civilian military appointments, including civil consulting surgeon to British forces during the Anglo-Boer War between 1899 and 1902, and consulting surgeon to the Royal Navy in 1915. He was made a Knight Commander of the Order of St. Michael and St. George in 1916, elected a member of Parliament for the University of Edinburgh and St. Andrews in 1917, and was made a member of Parliament for the Combined Scottish Universities from 1918 to 1922. He was a prolific scholarly writer, and published textbooks, most of which were concerned with infections and infectious diseases. One of his most well-known works was *Antiseptic Surgery: Its Principles, Practice, History and Results,* published by Smith, Elder in London in 1882.

INTRODUCTION

Prior to the late 1800s, there were varying assumptions about the causes of disease. The predominant theory was that of spontaneous generation—the idea that many types of living matter could be spontaneously produced from non-living matter. For example, it was commonly believed that rotting meat could give rise to maggots.

The invention of the microscope by the Dutch scientist Anton van Leeuwenhoek (1832–1723) in the 1670s only served to reinforce the belief in spontaneous generation, since it allowed the observer to see many new forms of matter. The theory held that many new organisms, too tiny to be seen with the naked eye, could be produced spontaneously. For example, a small stem of hay, when initially observed under the microscope, looked like a simple hay stem. However, when left in water for a few days and then re-examined, the hay was observed to have produced many *animalcules.* Over time, spontaneous generation as the means of production of many organisms became the prevailing theory. This theory further held that air was necessary in order for this spontaneous generation of organisms to occur.

In the 1840s, shortly before the French bacteriologist Louis Pasteur's (1822–1895) groundbreaking work, Hungarian physician Ignaz Semmelweis (1818–1865) made an important contribution to the future development of germ theory. He concluded that handwashing before delivering a baby prevented the spread of childbed fever (infection after childbirth). Before Semmelweis developed his theory, physicians often moved directly from performing autopsies on women who had recently died of childbed fever to attend the next live birth. Semmelweis noted that this practice resulted in the new mothers contracting a virulent form of the fever, which often caused their deaths while still in the hospital. He was able to demonstrate that simple hand washing before deliveries prevented childbed fever. This was a crucial link in the experimental chain leading to the synthesis of germ theory.

Also in the 1840s, German anatomist Jakob Henle's (1809–1885) work led him to conclude that disease was caused by living particles that acted like parasites in human beings. In an attempt to identify the parasites, Henle set forth three postulates for the transmission of disease in human beings: 1) the parasite must be consistently present in someone who is sick; 2) the parasite can be isolated; and 3) the parasite can reproduce the disease when transmitted or administered to a healthy person. This provided another critical link to the development of germ theory.

In 1859, the young French chemist Louis Pasteur entered a contest sponsored by the French Academy of Sciences, in which the best experiment proving or disproving the theory of spontaneous generation would set the course for the future of science. Pasteur designed an experiment in which meat broth was boiled in a flask, and the neck of the flask was heated and bent into an s-shape. His belief was that air could reach the surface of the broth, but airborne microorganisms would be trapped in the neck of the flask by the effects of gravity. Pasteur discovered that no microorganisms grew in his broth. However, when the flask was tilted so that the broth reached the low spot in the neck where he postulated that the microorganisms had settled, the broth quickly became cloudy with microorganisms attaching themselves to the broth and beginning to reproduce. While it was already known that boiling killed microorganisms, it had not been known that air alone was insufficient to initiate contamination. Pasteur's experiment showed that the air was simply the transport mechanism for the contaminants. Pasteur won the contest. He definitely and simultaneously disproved the theory of spontaneous generation, and also proved that microorganisms exist in air.

As a result of further work, Pasteur also discovered that some microorganisms needed air in order to grow (aerobes), while others could grow without it (anaerobes). Finally, in 1864, Pasteur postulated his theory that infectious diseases are caused by living organisms called "germs." This was the first explication of germ theory, one of the most important contributions ever made to medical science.

Joseph Lister studied the work of Semmelweis, Henle, and Pasteur, and developed a series of theories and techniques for the prevention and control of infection during surgical procedures. He called these techniques the antiseptic method, or antisepsis. Antiseptic methods are universal in health care today for preventing the occurrence and spread of infection.

PRIMARY SOURCE

ANTISEPTIC SURGERY
See primary source image.

SIGNIFICANCE

Sir Joseph Lister is the seminal figure in the development of antiseptic surgery. He was in charge of the surgical wards at the Glasgow Infirmary in Scotland. Lister was quite horrified by the conditions he found at the infirmary, and even more so by the enormous post-surgical mortality rate. Gangrene and sepsis, both typically fatal, were common after surgical procedures due to the general lack of hygiene common in medical facilities at that time (the early 1860s). Both gangrene and sepsis are attributable to a lack of cleanliness in the wound area.

In 1865, Lister read one of Pasteur's scientific papers concerning the germ theory of disease. He theorized that if germs caused infection and disease, the best way of preventing disease would be to kill the germs before they could come into contact with the surgical wound site. Lister called the technique of killing microbes before they could cause infection (sepsis) the "antiseptic principle." He tried applying carbolic acid to open wounds to see if that prevented the development of infection. In addition, he used an apparatus that sprayed a carbolic acid mist continuously on the surgical area during operations. He found that both of these techniques were extremely successful and wrote about them at length in his famous text, *Antiseptic Principle of the Practice of Surgery*.

Lister instituted stringent antiseptic principles and procedures into the hospital routine, as well as in the operating room. He required all staff to wash their hands before operations and to use clean instruments and wound dressings. As a result of the use of Lister's techniques, the rate of wound infections and postoperative fatalities decreased dramatically. Word of his successes spread throughout the medical and scientific communities, and both his fame and the use of his antiseptic techniques increased. Lister's name now is synonymous with the initiation of hygienic conditions in hospitals and with the development of early theories of antiseptic surgery.

The progression of scientific knowledge from spontaneous generation to the discovery of microbes, the germ theory of disease, and the development of the antiseptic method paved the way for modern medical and surgical techniques, the control of infection, and modern public health measures to curtail the spread of disease.

FURTHER RESOURCES
Web sites

Access Excellence. "The Slow Death of Spontaneous Generation (1668–1859)." <http://www.accessexcellence.org/ RC/ AB/BC/Spontaneous_Generation.html> (accessed October 20, 2005).

Bayer Pharmaceuticals Corporation. "A Brief History of Infectious Disease: Causes of Infection." <http://www.bayerpharma-na.com/healthcare/hc0107.asp#henle> (accessed October 20, 2005).

Bayer Pharmaceuticals Corporation. "A Brief History of Infectious Disease: The Germ Theory of Disease and the Beginning of Bacteriology." <http://www.bayerpharma-na.com/healthcare/hc0108.asp> (accessed October 20, 2005).

Bayer Pharmaceuticals Corporation. "A Brief History of Infectious Disease: Germs (Bacteria & Viruses)." <http://www.bayerpharma-na.com/healthcare/hc0109.asp> (accessed October 20, 2005).

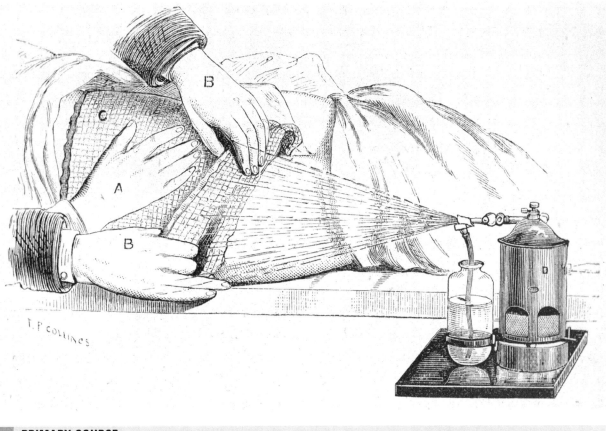

Antiseptic Surgery: Method of Changing a Psoas Abscess Dressing. Figure 38 in W. Watson Cheyne's *Antiseptic Surgery: Its Principles, Practice, History and Results,* showing an antiseptic method for changing the dressing of an abscessed wound. WELLCOME LIBRARY, LONDON.

Science and Technology. "Joseph Lister & Antiseptic Surgery." <http://web.ukonline.co.uk/b.gardner/Lister.html> (accessed October 20, 2005).

Surgeon Amos Walker Barber, Wyoming Territory

Frontier Medicine

Photograph

By: Anonymous

Date: Circa 1890

Source: Richard Dunlop. *Doctors of the American Frontier.* Garden City, N.Y.: Doubleday, 1962.

About the Author: Amos Walker Barber was born in Bucks County, Pennsylvania, on April 16, 1861.

He studied literature and medicine at the University of Pennsylvania. After graduating from medical school, Dr. Barber worked as a staff physician at the Pennsylvania Hospital from 1883 until 1885. In 1885, he moved to the Wyoming Territory to accept a position as surgeon in charge of the military hospital at Fort Fetterman. Not long after, Barber was promoted to acting surgeon in the U.S. Army, and he accompanied General Crook's expedition to Arizona. Upon his return from that expedition, Barber was assigned to Fort D. A. Russell. After resigning from military service, Amos Walker Barber opened up a private medical practice in Cheyenne, Wyoming. He joined the Republican political party, and was elected Secretary of State in Wyoming in 1890. He served in that position from 1890 until January 1895, at which time he became Acting Governor. He rejoined the U.S. Army during the Spanish American War, and was appointed Assistant Surgeon in 1898. He returned to Cheyenne and resumed his medical practice after the war's end. Amos Walker Barber died on May 19, 1915, and was buried in Cheyenne.

INTRODUCTION

Frontier doctors during the nineteenth century did not have access to many of the scientific techniques and clinical knowledge being developed at medical schools in Europe. In fact, many frontier doctors never attended a formal medical school of any kind. Although there were three forms of medical education prevalent until near the close of the nineteenth century (university schools, proprietary schools, and the apprenticeship method), none of them placed significant emphasis on clinical or laboratory studies. Anatomy was studied via the dissection of cadavers; physiology was largely theoretical due to the lack of laboratory facilities at most schools. Medicine was still fairly primitive in the United States, and students wishing to obtain an education with greater emphasis on medical science, research, or clinical practice, were forced to go to Europe to further their academic studies. The age of rapid scientific and technological breakthroughs had not yet dawned, germ theory was not well understood, sanitary methods were not routinely employed, and effective medications were scarce. All in all, the practice of medicine throughout much of the nineteenth century relied more on pragmatic skills and a compassionate manner than on sound scientific principles. Because there were relatively few physicians for the overall population—and even fewer hospitals, particularly in the southwest and western frontier areas—physicians had to be prepared to handle any sort of emergency alone. They were often called out in the middle of the night or in harsh weather conditions, and they had little emergency training and even less equipment.

There were few effective medications or techniques with which to treat most ailments; strong emetics, purgatives, blistering, and bloodletting were still commonly practiced—none of which were clinically effective. Pain was treated with morphine, opium, and laudanum (a mixture of alcohol and opium). Broken bones were treated by splinting and, if the fracture was severe, by amputation. Surgery was performed in the home, as was the delivery of babies—although that was largely the province of midwives unless the delivery was extremely complicated and required medical intervention. Payment for services rendered rarely involved an actual exchange of money, and was often given in the form of food, clothing, livestock, or personal services, such as yard or farm work. Highly contagious diseases, such as cholera and typhoid, were treated largely by isolating the sick from the well, and cleaning the areas (environments) of outbreak as much as possible.

■ **PRIMARY SOURCE**

SURGEON AMOS WALKER BARBER, WYOMING TERRITORY
See primary source image.

SIGNIFICANCE

Frontier medicine, although reliant on minimal instrumentation and equipment, paved the way for many practical advances in medicine, such as the need for sanitation and the development of hospitals and emergency transportation. Frontier doctors also did much to advance and perfect many medical tools and techniques, such as the stethoscope, the thermometer, surgical tools, anesthesia, and the use of antiseptic conditions.

The southwestern and western frontier areas were affected severely by contagious diseases, since these areas tended to have small, rather dense population centers separated by large unpopulated regions. As a result, diseases spread rapidly from one household to another. The living conditions were often harsh, the sanitary facilities were minimal, and the ability to contain epidemics nonexistent. Among the more virulent of the contagious diseases affecting the frontier were tuberculosis, smallpox, measles, pneumonia, diptheria, dysentery, septicemia, cholera, and typhoid. Port areas also experienced outbreaks of pneumonic and bubonic plague, carried by flea-infested rats leaving ships (trading, military, and other maritime vessels). The rodents carried the bacteria-infested fleas to livestock and domestic animals. The livestock were slaughtered and used for food, under unsanitary conditions, thus transmitting the disease to humans. At that point, it could be further spread by direct human-to-human contact. The diseases prevalent among the frontier settlers were even more lethal to the Native American population, because the Native Americans had no immunity to the diseases. Measles, smallpox, and tuberculosis were especially devastating to the Native Americans that came into contact with the frontier settlers.

In general, epidemics and outbreaks of highly contagious diseases had a high fatality rate, particularly among babies and young children. The hardships of life on the frontier, coupled with the lack of "modern" medical care, reduced the life span of many settlers. At the end of the nineteenth century, the average life span for a Caucasian male was only forty-seven years. Life spans did not lengthen appreciably until the advent of vaccines and antibiotics, technical advances in wound care, surgery, and emergency medicine, and publicly

PRIMARY SOURCE

Surgeon Amos Walker Barber, Wyoming Territory. Surgeon Ames Walker Barber, stationed at Fort Fetterman in Wyoming Territory, poses with his horse and dog—a saddlebag doctor's best friends. COURTESY AMERICAN HERITAGE CENTER, UNIVERSITY OF WYOMING.

mandated use of sanitation in homes and business establishments.

In more remote frontier areas, settlements were so isolated that epidemics were less frequent, but more likely to be lethal. Cholera was the chief source of contagion. Medical care was less readily available, since the local doctor might have to travel great distances between populated areas. Whisky was the commonly used anesthetic, sanitary conditions were minimal, and vermin—particularly lice—were rampant. Settlers sometimes fought with Native Americans. When a settler was struck with an arrow, a frontier doctor typically removed the projectile by cutting off the arrowhead and pulling the shaft back out through the body. Infections were common. Pain

was often treated by a topical application of opium powder or morphine directly on the wound. Severely mutilated limbs were amputated, and doctors worked to hone their skills so that they could complete an amputation within two to three minutes.

Wagon trains seldom included doctors. Most often, the wagon master carried a kit of basic first aid supplies and patent medicines. Anyone who became sick on the trail was laid inside a wagon, usually on top of supplies that became contaminated by the patient. The combined effects of exposure to the elements and jerky wagon movements frequently killed individuals who fell sick during the journey. Cholera was the most common contagious disease on the trail, and it was typically both acquired and transmitted through the drinking of stagnant or contaminated water along the route.

Mining camps, common in the southwest and western territories, were often violent places. Doctors spent much of their time removing bullets, repairing lacerations, and splinting or amputating broken limbs. Many traumas were sustained within the mines as well—typically crush injuries, blast burns, and fractures from falls down shafts. In mining towns, alcohol-related injuries were common and sexually transmitted diseases (STDs)—particularly syphilis—were rampant. Influenza and upper respiratory infections were quite common in mining towns, since the men spent their days exposed to cold water and their nights consuming alcohol in very crowded saloons. Snake bite, another hazard of frontier living, was treated by washing the site and packing it with potassium permanganate.

On ranches, doctors frequently treated cowboys who had sustained horse-related injuries. Broken legs, concussions, and dislocated shoulders were common. Complicated fractures often necessitated amputation of the limb. Chloroform was the usual anesthetic. Since surgical instruments were in short supply, any sharp saw or knife that was readily available and appropriately sized became the surgical instrument.

With the coming of the railroads near the end of the nineteenth century, doctors treated many steam-induced burns and scalds. They amputated arms, hands, and fingers crushed in couplers. However, on a more positive note, doctors also made good use of the available steam and plentiful hot water to improve sanitary conditions and prevent wound infections.

Medical care was better for those in military service than for virtually anyone else living on the frontier, because military surgeons were among the most highly trained in the country. Military doctors were required to have graduated from an "accredited" medical school. In addition, they had to pass an examination testing not only their medical knowledge, but also their understanding of geography, history, languages, literature, and other general information in order to receive a commission. Physicians accompanied every military expedition outside of the western and southwestern forts and encampments. Battlefield injuries and traumas were relatively few, but many soldiers were infected with contagious diseases. Fevers, dysentery, rheumatism, and upper respiratory tract infections were the most prevalent illnesses. Smallpox was largely prevented by inoculation of all soldiers with cowpox; tuberculosis was rare, because anyone with tuberculosis symptoms was prevented from enlisting.

Sexually transmitted diseases were rare at isolated forts, although not uncommon at forts near densely populated towns. Pneumonia, accidental gunshot wounds, and homicide were the most common causes of death among the soldiers. The larger forts had infirmaries and hospitals that provided the most advanced medical care available at the time.

FURTHER RESOURCES
Books

Bethard, Wayne. *Lotions, Potions, and Deadly Elixirs: Frontier Medicine in America.* Lanham, Md.: Roberts Rinehart Publishers, 2004.

Dunlop, Richard. *Doctors of the American Frontier.* Garden City, N.Y.: Doubleday, 1965.

Ludmerer, Kenneth M. *Learning to Heal: The Development of American Medical Education.* Baltimore, Md.: Johns Hopkins University Press, 1996.

Rothstein, William G. *American Physicians in the Nineteenth Century: From Sects to Science.* Baltimore, Md.: Johns Hopkins University Press, 1972.

Rutkow, Ira. *Bleeding Blue and Gray: Civil War Surgery and the Evolution of American Medicine.* New York: Random House, 2005.

Smith, James J. *Looking Back, Looking Ahead: A History of American Medical Education.* Chicago, Ill.: Adams Press, 2003.

Steele, Volney. *Bleed, Blister, and Purge: A History of Medicine on the American Frontier.* Missoula, Mont.: Mountain Press, 2005.

Web sites

fredrickboling.com. "A Tribute to the Frontier Doctor." <http://www.fredrickboling.com/frontier%20medicine.html> (accessed November 10, 2005).

Rules for the Prevention of Cholera

Public health notice (photograph)

By: Anonymous

Date: August 14, 1892

Source: New York Board of Health.

About the Author: The New York Board of Health was set up in 1806 and moved control of health affairs from the state to the city. However, for the first sixty years of its existence, the Board confined its activities to fighting epidemics of diseases such as cholera and did little other public health work. In 1866, the Board was organized more formally and in 1870 it became the

Health Department, which was divided into the Sanitary Bureau and the Bureau of Records. The former was further divided into four divisions: Contagious Diseases, General and Special Sanitary Inspection, Plumbing and Ventilation, and Offensive Trades and Food Inspection. In 1890, the Division of Contagious Diseases divided New York City into eleven districts, each headed by a medical sanitary inspector who was a physician responsible for general sanitary conditions in the district.

INTRODUCTION

Cholera is an acute bacterial infection whose causative agent, *Vibrio cholerae*, was identified by the German bacteriologist Robert Koch (1843–1910) in 1883. The disease had existed in Southeast Asia for many centuries and began to spread to Europe and America from the early nineteenth century through trading and immigration. Epidemic cholera reached England in 1831 and North America in 1832. The disease was much feared because of its mortality rate of up to 40 percent. Death from cholera was caused by massive dehydration, which led to kidney failure, with low blood pressure and low blood glucose being complicating features. It was initially believed that cholera was caused by a miasma or "bad air," until the germ theories of Koch and Louis Pasteur (1822–1895) were established during the second half of the nineteenth century.

The New York Board of Health had already experienced some success in fighting the 1866 cholera outbreak. This success was used as a springboard to make much-needed improvements in public health, such as reporting and investigating cases of infectious disease and emphasizing disinfection as a means of control. The "Rules for the Prevention of Cholera" would not be out of place in New York City today. The mention of germs shows an awareness of the new theory of disease. It was known that infection occurs through ingestion of contaminated food and water and that *V. cholerae* is destroyed by boiling. Therefore, the advice to avoid unboiled water and raw, uncooked foods is sensible, as is the guidance on handwashing and personal hygiene.

■ PRIMARY SOURCE

RULES FOR THE PREVENTION OF CHOLERA
See primary source image.

■ PRIMARY SOURCE

RULES FOR THE PREVENTION OF CHOLERA
As Officially Recommended by the N.Y. Board of Health.Health Department, New York, Aug. 11, 1892.

PREVENTION OF CHOLERA EASIER THAN CURE. HOW CAUGHT.

Healthy persons "catch" cholera by taking into their systems through the mouth, as in their food or drink, or from their hands, knives, forks, plates, tumblers, clothing, etc., the germs of the disease which are always present in the discharges from the stomach and bowels of those sick with cholera.

Thorough cooking destroys the cholera germs; therefore:

> DON'T eat raw, uncooked articles of any kind, not even milk.
> DON'T eat or drink to excess. Use plain, wholesome, digestible food, as indigestion and diarrhoea favor an attack of cholera.
> DON'T drink unboiled water.
> DON'T eat or drink articles unless they have been thoroughly and recently cooked or boiled, and the more recent and hotter they are the safer.
> DON'T employ utensils in eating or drinking unless they have been recently put in boiling water; the more recent the better.
> DON'T eat or handle food or drink with unwashed hands, or receive it from the unwashed hands of others.
> DON'T use the hands for any purpose when soiled with cholera discharges. Thoroughly cleanse them at once.

Personal cleanliness and cleanliness of the living and sleeping rooms and their contents, and thorough ventilation, should be rigidly enforced. Foul water closets, sinks, Croton faucets, cellars, etc., should be avoided, and, when present, should be referred to the Health Board at once, and be remedied.

PRECAUTIONARY MEASURES OF TREATMENT.

The successful treatment and the prevention of the spread of this disease demand that its earliest manifestations be promptly recognized and treated; therefore,

> DON'T doctor yourself for bowel complaint, but go to bed and send for the nearest physician at once. Send for your family physician; send to a dispensary or hospital; send to the Health Department; send to the nearest police station for medical aid.
> DON'T wait, but send at once. If taken ill in the street, seek the nearest drug store, dispensary, hospital

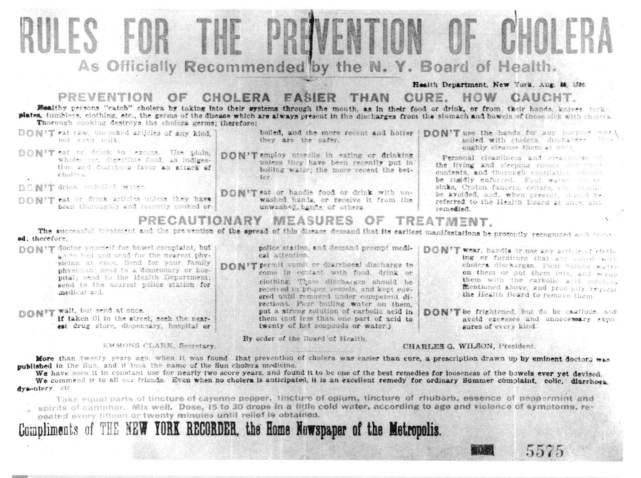

RULES FOR THE PREVENTION OF CHOLERA

As Officially Recommended by the N. Y. Board of Health.

Health Department, New York, Aug. 16, 1892.

PREVENTION OF CHOLERA EASIER THAN CURE. HOW CAUGHT.

Healthy persons "catch" cholera by taking into their systems through the mouth, as in their food or drink, or from their hands, knives forks, plates, tumblers, clothing, etc., the germs of the disease which are always present in the discharges from the stomach and bowels of those sick with cholera. Thorough cooking destroys the cholera germs; therefore:

DON'T eat raw, uncooked articles of any kind, not even milk.

DON'T eat or drink to excess. Use plain, wholesome, digestible food, as indigestion and diarrhoea favor an attack of cholera.

DON'T drink unboiled water.

DON'T eat or drink articles unless they have been thoroughly and recently cooked or boiled, and the more recent and hotter they are the safer.

DON'T employ utensils in eating or drinking unless they have been recently put in boiling water; the more recent the better.

DON'T eat or handle food or drink with unwashed hands, or receive it from the unwashed hands of others.

DON'T use the hands for any purpose when soiled with cholera discharges thoroughly cleanse them at once.

Personal cleanliness and cleanliness of the living and sleeping rooms and their contents, and thorough ventilation should be rigidly enforced. Foul water in the sinks, Croton faucets, cellars, etc., should be avoided, and, when present, should be referred to the Health Board at once, and remedied.

PRECAUTIONARY MEASURES OF TREATMENT.

The successful treatment and the prevention of the spread of this disease demand that its earliest manifestations be promptly recognized and treated; therefore,

DON'T doctor yourself for bowel complaint, but go to bed and send for the nearest physician at once. Send for your family physician; send to a dispensary or hospital; send to the Health Department; send to the nearest police station for medical aid.

DON'T wait, but send at once. If taken ill in the street, seek the nearest drug store, dispensary, hospital or police station, and demand prompt medical attention.

DON'T permit vomit or diarrhoeal discharge to come in contact with food, drink or clothing. These discharges should be received in proper vessels, and kept covered until removed under competent directions. Pour boiling water on them, put a strong solution of carbolic acid in them (not less than one part of acid to twenty of hot soapsuds or water.)

DON'T wear, handle or use any article of clothing or furniture that are soiled with cholera discharges. Pour boiling water on them or put them into, and scrub them with the carbolic acid solution mentioned above, and promptly request the Health Board to remove them.

DON'T be frightened, but do be cautious, and avoid excesses and unnecessary exposures of every kind.

By order of the Board of Health.

EMMONS CLARK, Secretary.   CHARLES G. WILSON, President.

More than twenty years ago, when it was found that prevention of cholera was easier than cure, a prescription drawn up by eminent doctors was published in the Sun, and it took the name of the Sun cholera medicine.

We have seen it in constant use for nearly two score years, and found it to be one of the best remedies for looseness of the bowels ever yet devised.

We commend it to all our friends. Even when no cholera is anticipated, it is an excellent remedy for ordinary Summer complaint, colic, diarrhoea, dysentery, etc.

Take equal parts of tincture of cayenne pepper, tincture of opium, tincture of rhubarb, essence of peppermint and spirits of camphor. Mix well. Dose, 15 to 30 drops in a little cold water, according to age and violence of symptoms, repeated every fifteen or twenty minutes until relief is obtained.

Compliments of THE NEW YORK RECORDER, the Home Newspaper of the Metropolis.

5575

PRIMARY SOURCE

Rules for the Prevention of Cholera. New York Board of Health notice indicating measures necessary to prevent the European cholera epidemic of 1892 from spreading to the city of New York. ©MUSEUM OF THE CITY OF NEW YORK.

or police station and demand prompt medical attention.

DON'T permit vomit or diarrhoeal discharge to come in contact with food, drink or clothing. These discharges should be received in proper vessels, and kept covered until removed under competent directions. Pour boiling water on them, put a strong solution of carbolic acid in them (not less than one part of acid to twenty of hot soapsuds or water.)

DON'T wear, handle or use any article of clothing or furniture that are soiled with cholera discharges. Pour boiling water on them or put them into and scrub them with the carbolic acid solution mentioned above, and promptly request the Health Board to remove them.

DON'T be frightened, but do be cautious, and avoid excesses and unnecessary exposures of every kind.

By order of the Board of Health.
EMMONS CLARK, Secretary
CHARLES G. WILSON, President

More than twenty years ago, when it was found that prevention of cholera was easier than cure, a prescription drawn up by eminent doctors was published in the Sun, and it took the name of the Sun cholera medicine.

We have seen it in constant use for nearly two score years, and found it to be one of the best remedies for looseness of the bowels ever yet devised.

We commend it to all our friends. Even when no cholera is anticipated, it is an excellent remedy for ordinary Summer complaint, colic, diarrhoea, dysentery, etc.

Take equal parts of tincture of cayenne pepper, tincture of opium, tincture of rhubarb, essence of peppermint and spirits of camphor. Mix well. Dose, 15 to 30 drops in a little cold water, according to age and violence of symptoms,

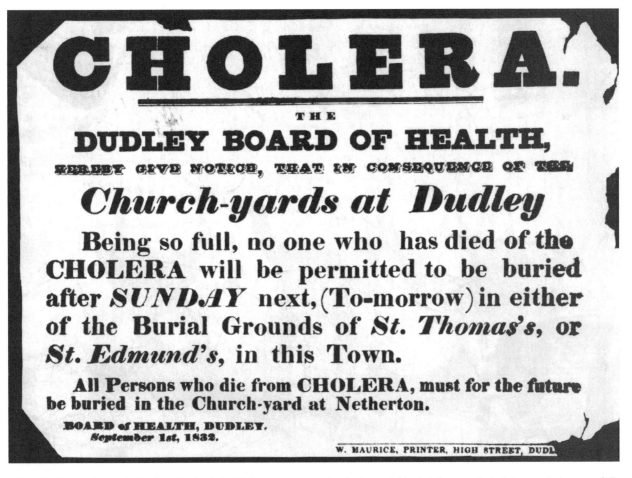

CHOLERA.

THE DUDLEY BOARD OF HEALTH,

HEREBY GIVE NOTICE, THAT IN CONSEQUENCE OF THE

Church-yards at Dudley

Being so full, no one who has died of the CHOLERA will be permitted to be buried after *SUNDAY* next, (To-morrow) in either of the Burial Grounds of *St. Thomas's,* or *St. Edmund's,* in this Town.

All Persons who die from CHOLERA, must for the future be buried in the Church-yard at Netherton.

BOARD of HEALTH, DUDLEY.
September 1st, 1832.

W. MAURICE, PRINTER, HIGH STREET, DUDL

When cholera broke out in Dudley, England, in 1832, so many people died so quickly that the town's burial grounds became full. ©BETTMAN/CORBIS.

repeated every fifteen or twenty minutes until relief is obtained.

Compliments of the THE NEW YORK RECORDER, the Home Newspaper of the Metropolis.

SIGNIFICANCE

In 1890, Jacob Riis (1849–1914), a police reporter for the *New York Tribune,* published an influential book titled *How the Other Half Lives,* which highlighted the steps still necessary to improve public health and sanitation in the city. Meanwhile, a fifth cholera pandemic was underway in China, Japan, Egypt, Russia, and Germany. In late August 1892, there was news of an outbreak in Hamburg and infected passengers on a ship from that city were headed for New York, bringing with them the threat of contagion. Quarantining of these passengers, and other efforts by the Boards of Health, stopped the pandemic spreading to the U.S.

Hermann M. Biggs, a physician who was well acquainted with the pioneering work of Koch and Pasteur, had become consultant pathologist to the New York Department of Health in 1888 and was influential in the fight against cholera in the city. With the threat of a new epidemic, Biggs was able to obtain funds to set up a bacteriological laboratory under his leadership. It was, perhaps, the first laboratory in the world to be used for the routine diagnosis of disease using the latest scientific methods, and it provided a valuable model for governments elsewhere to follow. Laboratory results were used to show instances of pollution in the local water supply, and this led to preventive legislation. The laboratory's work also led to the chlorination of the water supply in 1911 and the pasteurization of milk in 1912, both important advances in the fight against infectious diseases, such as cholera. For many years, the municipal bacteriological laboratory in New York was the leading medical research center in the country.

FURTHER RESOURCES

Books

Crisci, Madeline. *Public Health in New York City in the Late Nineteenth Century.* Bethesda: U.S. Department of Health and Human Services, 1990.

Lock, Stephen, John M. Last, and George Dunea, eds. *The Oxford Illustrated Companion to Medicine.* Oxford: Oxford University Press, 2001.

Periodicals

Baumgartner, Leona. "One Hundred Years of Health: New York City, 1866–1966." *Bulletin of the New York Academy of Medicine* 45 (1969): 555–575.

Radiation Used to Treat Tumors

Journal article

By: Emil H. Grubbe

Date: 1902

Source: Emil H. Grubbe. "Emil H. Grubbe on the X-Ray." *Medical Record*, 1902.

About the Author: Emil Grubbe was born in Chicago, Illinois, to parents who were German immigrants, on January 1, 1875. By the age of thirteen, he had become a full-time worker. His first job was washing bottles and running errands at a drugstore. At his next job, working as an office boy at Marshall Field's, he piqued the interest of Marshall Field, who encouraged Grubbe to go back to school and study science and medicine. By the time he was fifteen years old, Grubbe had decided to attend medical school; however, because of his lack of formal education, it was necessary for him to complete his basic education before he could gain acceptance. He studied at the Northern Indiana Normal School (in Valparaiso) during the day and worked as a watchman at night. In 1895, he entered Hahnemann Medical College of Chicago. His facility for the study and teaching of science soon came to the fore, and he was given an academic teaching appointment in physics and chemistry while he was, himself, a student. Grubbe was fascinated by Roentgen's discovery of X rays in November of

1895—so much so that he immediately set about acquiring his own vacuum discharge tube. The remainder of his life was dedicated to the study and utilization of X rays. Grubbe, Edison, and many of their contemporaries began studies designed to specify the varying uses of the Roentgen rays. Rather early on, Grubbe developed extensive dermatitis of the hands and neck, which he immediately surmised to be a result of the application of the rays. His peers strongly encouraged him to begin experimenting with the use of his radiation apparatus in the treatment of cancer. His clinical work was quite successful, and, in February 1896, he opened the very first radiation therapy facility in Chicago. He continued in the active practice of medicine until 1947 and died of complications resulting from multiple malignancies in 1960.

INTRODUCTION

Dr. Emil H. Grubbe (1875–1960) is one of the American pioneers of radiation therapy. While a student at Hahnemann Medical College in Chicago, Illinois, he developed a fascination with Roentgen's discovery of radiation; this passion guided Grubbe's entire professional career. By the end of 1895, Grubbe had acquired a vacuum discharge tube and had begun a series of experiments on the ray's fluoroscopic capabilities and their medical implications. While researching the rays, Grubbe developed dermatitis of the hands and neck and believed that the dermatitis was related to his unprotected use of radiation. As a result, Grubbe and his colleagues made the cognitive leap to practical use of the rays for curative purposes and undertook studies of the rays' effects on patients who had various types of carcinomas. He reported great success and, in February 1896, opened the first radiation therapy facility in Chicago at South Cottage Grove Avenue.

Grubbe continued his medical studies and graduated from Hahnemann in 1899. He accepted a faculty position and rose to the position of chair of electrotherapeutics and radiography, a position that he held until 1919. By the early 1900s, he was teaching at four universities and colleges in Chicago, as well as maintaining a medical therapy practice. Grubbe was a prolific writer, and published nearly one hundred scholarly articles during the course of his professional career. Although he was initially a medical generalist, his main interest was in the use of radiation to treat disease, and he gradually focused his practice more and more in that arena. By the second decade of the twentieth century, he had restricted his medical practice exclusively to radiation therapy. Grubbe continued the private practice of radiation therapy until his retirement in 1947. Throughout nearly his long professional career, Grubbe struggled with radiation dermatitis and anemia—eventually resulting in the amputation of his left hand in 1929.

Grubbe was considered by many colleagues to be challenging, grandiose, and self-important. In the earliest days of his career, he reported that he was too busy to publish the results of his radiation studies—a delay that led to professional contentions that he was not quite as much of a pioneer as he purported to be. However, from a historical standpoint, he is considered to be among the first American radiation therapists.

PRIMARY SOURCE

We have a number of other patients who have taken x-ray treatment, and who have remained free from recurrence for periods ranging from six months to a year and a half. Many other cases could be cited, but time and space forbid.

In conclusion, we wish to submit the following deductions:

1. The x-ray is the most remarkable therapeutic agent of the decade.
2. In properly selected cases of so-called "incurable conditions" the x-ray has brought about remarkable results.
3. Relief from pain is one of the most prominent features of the treatment.
4. Retrogressive changes are noticed in all primary cancer or tuberculous growths.
5. The x-ray has a pronounced effect upon internal cancers.
6. The greatest value of the x-ray is obtained in treating post-operative cases to prevent recurrences.
7. The proportion of clinical cures by this treatment is greater than that obtainable by any other method of treatment.
8. We are positively justified in assuming an idiosyncrasy to x-rays.
9. The peculiarities of each case must be studied in order toget the best results, i.e. no strict rules for treatment can be laid down.
10. Dermatitis, if properly produced, is within certain limits a desirable feature of x-ray treatment.
11. Since the vacuum of an ordinary x-ray tube changes constantly, such tubes are useless for radio-therapeutic work, and only tubes which allow of [sic] perfect control of vacuum should be used.
12. The x-ray has a selective influence on cells of the body; abnormal cells being affected more readily than the normal.
13. Hemorrhages and discharges are decidedly lessened and, ultimately, cease in the majority of cases.

14. Even in the hopeless, inoperable cases, the x-ray prolongs life, makes the patient comfortable, and the last hours free from pain.

The use of the x-ray is, without doubt, a very valuable addition to the therapeutics of malignant disease, and cannot demand too much attention from the progressive physician.

SIGNIFICANCE

The discovery of radiation was followed swiftly by extensive research and practical application of its myriad therapeutic uses—evolving into the study and practice of radiation oncology. These therapeutic uses of radiation have had a profound impact on human life. Shortly after Roentgen discovered the "new light"— which he subsequently named X rays—in 1895, scientists such as Emil H. Grubbe began to do research on and develop practical and therapeutic uses for the rays, which were touted as nothing short of miraculous. Almost simultaneously, it was discovered that Roentgen's X rays could penetrate flesh to illuminate the bone beneath and also could cure malignancies and other disorders.

Roentgen discovered the X ray quite by accident— he was researching light phenomena and other emissions using an evacuated glass tube (the cathode ray tube). He is purported to have looked at his hand as he held different substances between the tube and a screen, and been astonished to have seen the bones of his hand. When he publicly announced the results of his work, others grasped quickly the potential implications of such a discovery.

X rays soon were used to cure both surface and deeply embedded malignancies and other health maladies. Although Grubbe and others also quickly discovered the negative side effects of exposure to the rays—such as dermatitis and burns—the curative and life-lengthening effects of the X rays were believed to far outweigh any negative side effects.

Emil Grubbe reportedly undertook the first systematic use of radiation therapy for the treatment of cancer on January 29, 1896, when he began work with a patient who had advanced and recurrent breast cancer. He treated her with a series of eighteen daily one-hour doses of radiation. This treatment appeared to have a locally curative effect, however, the patient died of metastatic carcinoma soon after the end of her treatment.

Thomas Edison, whose research with X rays resulted in the development of the fluoroscope, expanded upon the work of Grubbe and his

Emil H. Grubbe in his lab, 1895. ©RADIOLOGY CENTENNIAL, INC.

contemporaries. He suspended his work with radiation when his assistant and friend, Clarence Dally, experienced radiation burns and died in 1904.

In the late 1890s, a Boston dentist named William Rollins designed shielding devices that dramatically reduced the number and degree of radiation burns. This led to an exponential rise in the use of radiation technology. In 1907, Clyde Snook developed and implemented a high-voltage power supply. The development of this power supply eliminated the need to use chemical or mechanical interrupters and large induction coils and dramatically improved the speed of radiation therapy delivery. In 1913, William Coolidge invented the hot-cathode X ray tube; his invention made X rays widely available for use by the medical community for the first time.

The exponential development and implementation of radiation—and radiation oncology—technology has continued through the twentieth and into the twenty-first century. Roentgen's rays and Grubbe's low-voltage prolonged exposure radiotherapy have evolved into modern radiological treatment and diagnostic procedures such as angiography, ultrasonography, CT (computed tomography), MRI (magnetic resonance imaging), SPECT (single photon emission computed tomgraphy), and PET (positron emission tomography) scanning.

FURTHER RESOURCES

Books

Hodges, Paul C. *The Life and Times of Emil H. Grubbe.* Chicago: University of Chicago Press, 1964.

Periodicals

Grubbe, E. H. "Priority in the Therapeutic Use of X-rays." *Radiology* 21 (August 1933b): 156–162.

Grubbe, E. H. "Who Was the First to Make Use of the Therapeutic Qualities of the X-ray?" *Radiological Review* 22 (August 1933a): 184–187.

Web sites

American Society for Therapeutic Radiology and Oncology. "One Hundred Years of Radiation Oncology." <http://www.astro.org/pdf/History/hundred.pdf> (accessed September 1, 2005).

IMPAC Medical Systems. "Intensity Modulated Radiation Therapy—The Shape of Things to Come?" <http://www.impac.com/company/pressroom/ind_arts/lpr01042.html> (accessed September 1, 2005).

X-Ray Accessory Corporation. "The Amazing Powers of the Rays." <http://soyeeproductsny.com/The%20Amazing

Sigmund Freud (right) and his theories greatly impacted the study of psychology and how psychoanalysts view the science today. AP/WIDE WORLD PHOTOS.

%20Powers%20Of%20The%20Rays.htm> (accessed September 1, 2005).

X-Ray Accessory Corporation. "New Avenues of Advertising." <http://www.soyeeproductsny.com/ New%20Avenues%20For%20Advertising.htm> (accessed September 1, 2005).

Origin and Development of Psychoanalysis, First Lecture

Lecture excerpt

By: Sigmund Freud

Date: September 1909

Source: Lecture delivered September, 1909. Revised by Freud and reprinted in the *American Journal of Psychology* (September 1910): 21 (2) 181–218.

About the Author: Sigmund Freud (1856–1939), born Sigismund Schlomo Freud, is the founder of the psychoanalytic movement worldwide. He has long been considered among the most influential psychological theorists of the twentieth century.

INTRODUCTION

Sigmund Freud was born in Freiburg, Moravia, to Jewish parents. His father, Jakob Freud, was a wool merchant; his mother was Amalia Nathanson. She was Jakob's second wife (although some sources list her as his third wife), and was twenty years younger than her husband. Amalia gave birth to Sigmund, the first of her seven children, when she was twenty-one years old. Jakob had two older sons by a previous marriage. When Sigmund was about four years old, the family moved to Vienna, Austria, where he spent most of his life. The family moved to Vienna because laws allowing discrimination against Jewish people had been vacated in the late 1850s.

Freud was an exceptional student throughout his entire academic career. He began medical studies at the University of Vienna in 1873, and engaged in physiological research for six years with Ernst Brucke (1819–1892), who was the director of the physiology laboratory at the university. Freud's initial concentration was in biology; from there he specialized first in physiology and then in neurology. Freud graduated from medical school in 1881 and became engaged to Martha Bernays in 1882.

From 1882 until 1885, Freud completed his residency and worked at the General Hospital in Berlin, where he directed a children's program. Freud went to France from 1885 to 1886 to pursue postgraduate work in psychiatry and neurology. He first studied with the famed psychiatrist Jean Charcot (1825–1893) in Paris, and then with his colleague and rival Hippolyte Bernheim (1840–1919) in Nancy. Both psychiatrists were doing research on the use of hypnosis in working with patients suffering from hysteria and other psychological abnormalities.

Upon his return from France in 1886, Freud married Martha Bernays. They had six children together, the youngest of whom, Anna, became a well-known psychoanalyst. Sigmund Freud set up a private practice in neuropsychiatry in Vienna, which he dedicated to the treatment of psychological disorders. Although he had been quite impressed with the successes of Charcot and Bernheim, Freud did not believe that the effects of hypnosis were long lasting and set about finding a more permanent form of treatment.

Earlier in his medical studies, Freud had also been influenced by the work of his friend and colleague,

Josef Breuer (1842–1925), who encouraged his patients to talk at length about their past experiences while under the influence of hypnosis. Freud began to work in conjunction with Breuer, and they encouraged their neurotic patients to talk uninhibitedly and without any internal (self-imposed) or external restrictions about their earliest memories of symptom occurrence. They discovered that this process often led to gradual amelioration of symptoms and greatly improved overall functioning. During his work with Breuer, Freud originated and developed the theory that many neuroses, defined as phobias, hysterical paralysis, psychosomatic complaints, and some forms of paranoia, originated with severe traumas occurring in early life that were later forgotten or removed from consciousness. The goal of treatment was to facilitate the patient's ability to recall the experience to consciousness. Once the early traumatic memory was recalled, the patient could deeply confront or re-experience it both emotionally and intellectually. In the course of the confrontation, the trauma's emotional power could be "discharged," which would serve to remove the underlying psychological roots of the psychopathological symptoms and manifestations. This experience was called catharsis.

In 1895, Freud and Breuer co-authored the book *Studies in Hysteria*—based on the case of "Anna O."—which explained their theory in some detail. Not long after the publication of this book, Freud and Breuer parted ways; Breuer contended that Freud placed excessive emphasis on the sexual origins and content of neuroses. Freud continued to refine and develop both his theories and the practice of psychoanalysis; he also began an in-depth self-analysis that lasted for several years.

Freud shared details about the origins of psychotherapy in the following lecture delivered at the celebration of the twentieth anniversary of the opening of Clark University in Worcester, Massachusetts, in September, 1909.

▇ PRIMARY SOURCE

Ladies and Gentlemen:

It is a new and somewhat embarrassing experience for me to appear as a lecturer before students of the New World. I assume that I owe this honor to the association of my name with the theme of psychoanalysis, consequently it is of psychoanalysis that I shall aim to speak. I shall attempt to give you in very brief form an historical survey of the origin and further development of this new method of research and cure.

Granted that is a merit to have created psychoanalysis, it is not my merit. I was a student, busy with passing of my last examinations, when another physician of Vienna, Dr. Joseph Breuer, made the first application of this case and its treatment, which can be found in detail in *"Studien über Hysterie,"* later published by Dr. Breuer and myself.

But first one word. I have noticed, with considerable satisfaction, that the majority of my hearers do not belong to a medical profession. Now do not fear that a medical education is necessary to follow what I shall have to say. We shall now accompany the doctors a little way, but soon we shall take leave of them and follow Dr. Breuer on a way which is quite his own.

Dr. Breuer's patient was a girl of twenty-one, of a high degree of intelligence. She had developed in the course of her two years' illness a series of physical and mental disturbances which well deserved to be taken seriously. She had a severe paralysis of both right extremities, with anesthesia, and at times the same affection of members of the left side of the body; disturbance of eye-movements, and much impairment of vision; difficulty in maintaining the position of the head, an intense *Tussis nervosa*, nausea, when she attempted to take nourishment, and at one time for several weeks a loss of the power to drink, in spite of tormenting thirst. Her power of speech was also diminished, and this progressed so far that she could neither speak nor understand her mother tongue; and, finally, she was subject to states of "absence," of confusion, delirium, alteration of her whole personality. These states will later claim our attention. . . .

The illness first appeared while the patient was caring for her father, whom she tenderly loved, during a severe illness which led to his death, a task which she was compelled to abandon because she herself fell ill. [Dr. Breuer] gave his patient sympathy and interest, although at first he did not understand how to help her. It had been noticed that the patient, in her states of 'absence,' of psychic alteration, usually mumbled over several words to herself. These seemed to spring from associations with which her thoughts were busy. The doctor, who was able to get these words, put her in a sort of hypnosis and repeated them to her over and over, in order to bring up any associations that they might have. The patient yielded to his suggestion and reproduced for him those psychic creations which controlled her thoughts during her 'absences,' and which betrayed themselves in these single spoken words.

These were fancies, deeply sad, often poetically beautiful, day dreams, we might call them, which commonly took as their starting point the situation of a girl beside the sick-bed of her father. Whenever she had related a number of such fancies, she was, as it were, freed and restored to her normal mental life.

The doctor soon hit upon the fact that through such cleansing of the soul more could be accomplished than a temporary removal of the constantly recurring mental 'clouds.' Symptoms of the disease would disappear when in hypnosis [when] the patient could be made to remember the situation and the associative connections under which they first appeared, provided free vent was given to the emotions which they aroused. . . .

She was talking one day during hypnosis about her English governess, whom she disliked, and finally told, with every sign of disgust, how she had come into the room of the governess, and how that lady's little dog, that she abhorred, had drunk out of a glass. [At the time] out of respect for conventions, the patient had remained silent. Now, after she had given energetic expression to her restrained anger, she asked for a drink, drank a large quantity of water without trouble, and woke from hypnosis with the glass at her lips. The symptom thereupon vanished permanently.

. . .When, a number of years later, I began to use Breuer's researches and treatment on my own patients, my experiences completely coincided with his.

. . .Ladies and gentlemen, if you will permit me to generalize, as is indispensable in so brief a presentation, we may express our results up to this point in one formula: *Our hysterical patients suffer from reminiscences.*

. . .This fixation of the mental life on the pathogenic traumata is an essential, and practically a most significant characteristic of the neurosis.

. . .So we are forced to the conclusion that the patient fell ill because the emotion developed in the pathogenic situation was prevented from escaping normally, and that the essence of the sickness lies in the fact that these 'imprisoned' emotions undergo a series of abnormal changes.

SIGNIFICANCE

By 1896, Freud had coined the term psychoanalysis for the type of clinical work he was doing. In his system, he replaced hypnosis, which had received early recognition as a means of facilitating recall, with "free association." Free association involved the patient's lying upon a couch in Freud's office, achieving a highly relaxed state of mind, and talking about whatever came to mind, without censorship or regard to content in a stream of consciousness manner. Meanwhile, Freud sat behind the patient, listened, took extensive notes, and made interpretations of the underlying meanings in what was said. Freud interpreted not only what was said, but also the connections and associations between thoughts expressed near one another in time. It was his belief that free association was a viable means of uncovering the contents of the unconscious, recalling forgotten or repressed memories, and coming to understand the reasons that they had been removed from consciousness.

In 1900, Freud published what has frequently been considered his greatest work, *The Interpretation of Dreams.* By so doing, he firmly established the legitimacy and importance of the psychoanalytic movement. At that time, the general belief was that dreams were a biological manifestation of random electrical impulses in the brain. Freud, however, asserted the very controversial hypothesis that dreams actually represented the disguised manifestations of repressed sexual desires. Psychoanalytic theory did make a distinction between the concrete (literal, also called the manifest content) and the symbolic (abstract, also called latent) content of the dream. The latent content was deemed the important material, since Freud believed that it represented repressed conflictual material for the dreamer.

In 1901, Freud published *The Psychopathology of Everyday Life.* In 1902, he was appointed to an associate professorship at the University in Vienna. He began to attract a following and, also in 1902, he founded the Psychological Wednesday Society, which was later (1908) renamed the Vienna Psychoanalytic Society. This society grew into the International Psychoanalytic Association (1910) and included Alfred Adler (1870–1937) and Carl Jung (1875–1961) among its members. Freud's loyal followers formed the core of the psychoanalytic movement—although many chose to split off from classical psychoanalysis and form their own theoretical schools over time.

Freud published *Three Essays on the Theory of Sexuality* in 1905. His early work excited great controversy and was not well received due, in large part, to its emphasis on sexuality. His importance in the field of psychological theory began to be recognized in 1908, when the first International Psychoanalytic Congress was held in Salzburg, Austria, gaining Freud considerable international acclaim. His international stature was further heightened in 1909, when he was invited to deliver a series of lectures in the United States. He traveled to America with Carl Jung, and they met such American luminaries as the philosopher and psychologist William James (1842–1910). The course of lectures evolved into the 1916 text, *Five Lectures on Psychoanalysis.* Freud's association with Jung lasted just until 1913, when they had a falling out over Freud's exclusively sexual interpretation of the concepts of libido and incest. Jung's publication of *Symbols of Transformation* in 1912 led to their theoretical and personal, final rift.

Although Freud was deeply affected when any of his followers split off to pursue other philosophical avenues, he also recognized that this was a common occurrence in the early days of a new science. He continued to work, to write, and to publish prolifically, until his death in 1939. In 1923, Freud developed mouth cancer, a disease that he battled until his death. He underwent a series of operations that left him unable to appear in public. At that time, his philosophical and theoretical writings began to take on a new direction—*Group Psychology and the Analysis of the Ego*, published in 1921, *The Future of an Illusion*, published in 1927, and *Civilization and its Discontents*, published in 1929, all dealt with broad cultural issues.

When Adolf Hitler (1889–1945) began his rise to power, the work of psychoanalysis ceased in Germany, and Freud's books were publicly burned in Berlin. The League of Nations requested that Freud and Albert Einstein collaborate on the creation and publication of *Why War?* in 1933. When the Nazis invaded Austria, Freud and his family were able to secure (by means of a large financial transaction) safe passage to England, where he lived until his death in 1939. His final book *Moses and Monotheism*, was completed in England and published shortly before he died. Freud's death was unusual for its time, since he was an early proponent of physician-assisted suicide. Since he had terminal mouth cancer and was in great pain, Freud requested that his physician administer a lethal dose of morphine, which was done on September 23, 1939.

Psychoanalytic theory was poorly received at first, due primarily to its emphasis on sexuality. It has remained controversial through the years and generally has at least as many vigorous detractors as adherents. The enormity of the unconscious in Freud's theoretical model has been challenged. Modern psychological theorists postulate that the motivations and problems associated with the unconscious are far less than was held by classical analytic theory, and that the unconscious is far less "busy" than Freud believed. Those theoretical schools that utilize the concept of the unconscious tend to view it as that aspect of the mind that holds whatever it is that an individual does not need or want to hold in consciousness.

Despite its flaws and its detractors, Freud's psychoanalytic theory has made many important and lasting contributions to the field of psychology. First, Freud pointed out that much behavior is motivated by biology, especially in early life, and that society has an enormous impact on the development of expressed behavior. Second, Freud proposed the theory that early psychological trauma can lead to problems in later life—although that is not always true, it is a well-accepted concept. Third, Freud's naming and description of the various ego defenses has held up well through time and is still largely accepted. Finally, Freud set the standard for psychotherapy. The "talking cure" remains useful, although modern psychiatry emphasizes the role of brain chemistry in psychiatric diseases and pharmacological drugs to treat them. Today, most psychiatric patients spend less time talking about themselves in detailed conversations with the medical doctor (and very little time in free association) than when Freudian psychoanalysis was at its peak. For the most part, clinical psychologists have assumed the role of therapeutic counselor. Although the concept of transference has lost some popularity, most psychotherapists agree that the development of a close and trusting relationship between therapist and client is essential for the success of the therapeutic process.

FURTHER RESOURCES

Books

Freud, Sigmund. *The Interpretation of Dreams*. Oxford: Oxford University Press, 2000.

Web sites

Freud Museum London. "Freud's Library." <http://www.freud.org.uk/fmlibe.htm> (accessed November 20, 2005).

The New York Freudian Society. "Freud Abstracts." <http://nyfreudian.org/abstracts/> (accessed November 15, 2005).

The New York Psychoanalytic Society and Institute. "The Abraham A. Brill Library." <http://www.psychoanalysis. org/resources-library.html> (accessed November 15, 2005).

Personality Theories. "Sigmund Freud." <http://www.ship.edu/%7Ecgboeree/freud.html> (accessed November 16, 2005).

Reliable Quinine

Quinine Permits Exploration, Colonization

Advertisement

By: Anonymous

Date: 1910

Source: Burroughs Wellcome advertisement for Quinine Bisulphate, 1910.

About the Author: The pharmaceutical firm of Burroughs Wellcome was established in London in 1880 by two Americans, Silas Burroughs and Henry Wellcome. The company was known for high standards of quality control and for innovative (for the time) uses of advertising. In addition, it established its own research laboratories to develop new drugs and vaccines.

INTRODUCTION

Quinine, the first effective treatment for malaria, was also the first disease-specific medicine in the Western medical arsenal. Unlike earlier medicines that only masked or relieved the symptoms of diseases, quinine was capable of bringing about either a temporary or permanent cure, depending upon the type of malarial infection.

Quinine first cured a European of malaria in 1638 when the wife of the viceroy in Lima, present-day Peru, was given a northern Andean remedy to save her life. Quinquina, as it was known in the Andes, came from the bark of a native tree. Upon her return to her estate in Spain, the Countess of Cinchon

Reliable Quinine

For the treatment of malaria.
Of exceptional purity and alkaloidal value.

TRADE MARK 'TABLOID' BRAND

Quinine Bisulphate

Famed throughout the world for its purity, accuracy, convenience and palatability.

Supplied as follows: gr. 1/2, in bottles of 50 and 100; gr. 1, in bottles of 36 and 100; gr. 2, gr. 3, gr. 4, gr. 5, gr. 10, 0·1 gm., 0·25 gm. and 0·5 gm., in bottles of 25 and 100. Issued *plain* or *sugar-coated*, except gr. 10 and 0·5 gm., which are *plain* only.

TRADE MARK 'WELLCOME' BRAND

Quinine Sulphate

Attains a much higher standard of purity than required by the British Pharmacopœia.

Supplied in "Compact Crystals" and "Large Flake" (the ordinary form), both being identical in composition. Issued in bottles and tins of convenient sizes.

Prices and supplies of all B. W. & Co.'s fine Quinine Products obtainable of Pharmacists in all parts of the world.

BURROUGHS WELLCOME & CO., LONDON
NEW YORK   MONTREAL   SYDNEY   CAPE TOWN
XX 190   MILAN   SHANGHAI   *Copyright*

■ PRIMARY SOURCE

Reliable Quinine. Advertisements for quinine manufactured by the London-based Burroughs Wellcome pharmaceutical firm promised an effective treatment for the dreaded disease of malaria.

employed the ground-up bark to contain and cure the malaria around Cinchon, a few miles southeast of Madrid. However, no one quite understood why quinine was effective or how the patient was cured. In 1820, the French chemists Pierre-Joseph Pelletier and Jean-Bienaimé Caventou isolated two alkaloids from the bark of the cinchona tree. They named the white crystal quinine, and the brown liquid cinchonine.

Malaria was so widespread throughout the world that there was an enormous demand for a cure. In the course of the 1820s, chemical manufacturing firms sprang up to produce quinine and cinchonine. The latter became known as the poor man's quinine because it sold for a fraction of quinine's price. Quinine gained an international reputation as the effective cure for malaria. The high demand for it led to robust profits, with many of the modern pharmaceutical corporations tracing their roots to the quinine industry.

Quinine was easily portable. European colonists regularly consumed it as prophylaxis (prevention), permitting them to carry on explorations, missionary work, and military activity in areas where malaria was endemic. Unfortunately, the taste of quinine was repugnant, even to British taste buds. The British government recommended that quinine be taken in a mixture to disguise the taste. In India, the British took quinine dissolved in water, with gin added, thereby creating the famed drink of gin and tonic.

Beginning in the twentieth century, quinine was employed in mass public health campaigns, known as quininization, in an effort to stop the misery caused by malaria. The policy was first adopted in Italy, with considerable success. Unfortunately, quininization was expensive and quinine could not prevent relapses for all forms of malaria. Governments decided instead to switch their funds to efforts to eradicate the female *Anopheles* mosquito, the animal vector responsible for the spread of malaria.

■ PRIMARY SOURCE

RELIABLE QUININE
See primary source image.

■

SIGNIFICANCE

Cinchona bark is not easy to obtain and this difficulty made quinine a challenge to produce. In 1944, synthetic quinine was developed by American scientists. When synthetic quinine proved to be very effective against malaria with fewer side effects, the need for natural quinine subsided.

As mosquito control efforts became more sophisticated, scientists expected that the combination of quinine and fewer malaria-spreading mosquitoes would eradicate malaria. However, governments scaled back malaria control efforts before the mosquito was eliminated, partially due to evidence that insecticides containing the chemical DDT, while effective against the mosquitoes that cause malaria, also killed fish and birds. Additionally, the mosquito evaded door-to-door spraying efforts by avoiding indoor walls and ceilings, and instead, bit workers in the field. The ease of global travel brought malaria-infected travelers to countries that had not seen a malaria outbreak in decades. In South Africa, malaria returned in 1997, after a fifty-year absence.

Complicating the situation, forms of the malaria parasite that are not affected by synthetic quinine and other anti-malarial drugs emerged in Southeast Asia in the 1990s. Scientists forecast that quinine-resistant malaria could spread to Africa, where ninety percent of the world's cases of cerebral malaria occur. The death rate from malaria in Africa could double to seven million per year as a result. A Chinese herbal medicine, artemether, that can treat resistant malaria was discovered by Western scientists in the mid-1990s, but it is not readily available.

Drug firms have been slow to develop artemether because they cannot apply for patents on a drug that is already used in traditional Chinese medicine and has already been described in the scientific literature. Therefore, no firm would have the sole rights to the drug that would guarantee healthy profits. One French company currently manufactures the drug from scrub wormwood extracts, however, the cost of the drug is twice as much as quinine. In poverty-stricken African countries, few could afford artemether.

In late 2005, the Bill and Melinda Gates Foundation announced a $258 million gift for fighting malaria in the developing world. Almost one third of the money will support efforts to develop a vaccine to protect children against a severe form of malaria, while the remaining funds will be used to speed the development of new drugs to treat people that are already infected with the disease and to develop effective new pesticides. Scientists also have returned to pesticides containing DDT for use against mosquitoes in limited areas in some African countries where malaria is endemic (naturally occurring).

In this advertisement from the 1870s, customers are assured that this quinine-based product is "ready for use" whenever they need it. ©BETTMANN/CORBIS.

FURTHER RESOURCES

Books

Hobhouse, Henry. *Seeds of Change: Five Plants That Transformed Mankind.* New York: Harper & Row, 1986.

Humphreys, Margaret. *Malaria: Poverty, Race, and Public Health in the United States.* Baltimore: Johns Hopkins University Press, 2001.

Rocco, Fiametta. *Malaria and the Quest for a Cure that Changed the World.* New York: HarperCollins, 2003.

Postoperative Insanity

Book excerpt

By: John Chalmers Da Costa

Date: 1922

Source: Albert J. Ochsner. *Surgical Diagnosis and Treatment*. Philadelphia: Lea & Febiger, 1922.

About the Author: John Chalmers Da Costa (1863–1933) was born in Philadelphia, Pennsylvania, and trained in medicine at Jefferson Medical College. In 1907, he became head of the Department of Surgery and in 1910 became the first Samuel D. Gross Professor at the college.

INTRODUCTION

Da Costa is an important figure in the history of surgery in the United States. His skills as a teacher were renowned and his book *Modern Surgery: General and Operative* (1894) became a classic text in medical schools throughout the country, running to ten editions (the last edition appeared in 1931). Da Costa also served as editor of the 1905 U.S. edition of *Gray's Anatomy* and of the English edition of Zuckerman's *Operative Surgery*. His association with Jefferson Medical College began in 1887, when he took up a post as assistant in the surgical outpatient department and as assistant demonstrator in anatomy, and was to last for over forty years.

During World War I, Da Costa rose to the rank of commander in the Navy. In 1919, he tended to the often-ailing President Woodrow Wilson onboard the *George Washington* during peace treaty and League of Nations negotiations. He also had a long-standing interest in the fire service and would often ride out with the chief of the Philadelphia Fire Department to assist injured firefighters. Da Costa was involved in psychological medicine as well, since he was a physician at the Pennsylvania Hospital for the Insane before moving to Jefferson. In the following book excerpt, his interests in insanity and surgery come together in a discussion on postoperative insanity.

■ PRIMARY SOURCE

POSTOPERATIVE INSANITY

Varioius states of mental disturbance may become manifest after a surgical operation. For instance: hysterical excitement, delirium, amnesia, confusion, impulses, hypochondria, mental depression, obsessions, especially morbid fears, illusions, hallucinations or actual insanity. Real insanity is rare.

It has been estimated that out of one thousand abdominal operations four will go insane. If we except from cosideration operations upon the ovaries, insanity is no more frequent after abdominal than after other operations. . . .

The anasthetic has a certain depressing influence; in fact, it may actually seem to poison a person. The operation produces shock and loss of blood. The brilliant investigations of Crile, of Cleveland, have shown how brain cells suffer from the influence of shock and how subconscious causes of brain exhaustion are actually at work even when consciousness is abolished by ether or chloroform. Afte an operation a patient may suffer from pain, sleeplessness, worry, fear of death or deformity and from homesickness. Cases of postoperative insanity, except those due to head injury, have possessed predisposition, hereditary or acquired. The surgical operation is an exciting cause acting upon an unstable nervous system. Such patients were predisposed to insanity. . . .

Some years ago, in a paper on the diagnosis of postoperative insanity, I made the following statement:

"The normal, stable, healthy brain will probably never go insane after an operation, unless that operation touched the brain, removed the testicles, or removed the ovaries."

The insanity may come on at once after an operation. In such a case the surgeon is apt to regard the anesthetic as causal. According to Savage, of London, in such a case the patient is insane upon waking up from the anesthetic. I have seen no such case. The usual period of the onset of insanity is from three to ten days after the operation. Acute insanities are apt to come on in a day or two. Certain insane conditions, for instance, states of fixed and limited delusions, may come on much later, even as late as two or three weeks after an operation. . . .

The two most active exciting elements of postoperative insanity are undoubtedly fear and worry. . . . The immense power of fear in causing physical trouble and mental disaster is well known. Fear may be responsible for miscarriage, paralysis agitans, syncope, grayness of the hair, jaundice, diabetes, epilepsy, and other conditions.

It is well known that it can sober a drunk man, make a mother's milk poison her baby, induce catalepsy, aphasia, amnesia, and various other things.

It need scarcely be a matter of surprise that fear may cause insanity. As I have said, "An anti-operation fear may become a postoperative phobia."

I do not believe, however, that fear or that the sudden and violent manifestation of fear, we call fright, is very often responsible for postoperative insanity.

Of course, most people when they are badly frightened refuse to be operated on. I have found in my surgical experience that people usually come to the operation with calmness and courage, and some of them with actual satisfaction that the moment has come to rid them of pain, or a danger to life, or a harassing disease.

I believe worry is the most common exciting factor. Many surgical cases are terribly worried for a long period before an operation. Worry brought with it apprehension and depression, which hung upon them until they finally decided to have the operation done. Now and then a person will come to an operation expecting to die. Such prophets of evil are always bad patients. Many who, before operation expect to have terrible pain and suffering, morbidly magnify the prospect. We all know the serious condition worry may induce, how it spoils the appetite, impairs the digestion; interferes with sleep; lessens the resisting power; causes loss of flesh and frequently an actual hysterical condition. People thus worried are irritable, highly suspicious, and difficult to deal with, and not unusually are very homesick. Morbid worry is a real cause of insanity....

The treatment of postoperative insanity is to be directed entirely by the alienist. In certain cases we find the patient has been sick for a sufficient length of time to convince us that the attack of insanity is not going to be a very brief one, and we must decide whether or not to commit him to an institution for the insane. It is not possible to care for such cases in a general hospital. We must never make the mistake of sending someone to an institution for the insane when the attack is very temporary, because we wrong a man, and injure all his prospects to let him have the repute of having been a patient in a hospital for the insane, no matter how brief the time he remained there. But a prolonged attack necessitates care in a hospital for the insane.

SIGNIFICANCE

The postoperative insanity that Da Costa refers to is now known as postoperative delirium. Derived from the Latin word meaning "off the tracks," delirium is a state of acute confusion where the person affected may suffer memory loss and hallucinations and may appear agitated or drowsy in turn. It was known to the great Greek physician Hippocrates (460–370 BCE) and described by physicians in the nineteenth century. Delirium is considered a medical emergency and, if left untreated, it prolongs hospital stays, leads to other complications, and increases the risk of mortality. With treatment, however, postoperative delirium is reversible, typically persisting for around a week.

Although delirium is most commonly a side effect of medication, there are many other causes and it is often observed after surgery, as Da Costa points out. Surveys show that between 5 and 10 percent of surgical patients suffer from postoperative delirium and figures as high as 42 percent are sometimes observed following orthopedic surgery. Older people are more at risk of postoperative delirium, although it can occur at any age.

Da Costa's theory that fear and worry are the prime causes of postoperative delirium is interesting;

in fact, postoperative delirium is not well understood, but is thought to arise from a profound and reversible change in brain chemistry. He is correct to emphasize the profound interaction between mind and body, but mistaken in his earlier statement that only brain operations or those involving removal of the testicles or ovaries lead to insanity. Any kind of surgery can lead to postoperative delirium.

Sometimes a person with postoperative delirium will need to remain temporarily hospitalized for their own safety. Da Costa was correct to be concerned about the stigma of confining a person with temporary insanity to an asylum—no doubt he is drawing on his experience as a doctor in such an institution. Clearly he is trying to promote a more enlightened view of the condition. Today, postoperative delirium can be treated with a number of medications, including benzodiazepine tranquilizers, antidepressants, and melatonin. The latter can normalize sleep-wake cycles; it is believed that disruption of these cycles, arising from the disturbance in brain chemistry, may play a role in this type of delirium. Full recovery from delirium—including the postoperative kind—is common, given prompt diagnosis and treatment. But in Da Costa's day, some patients with delirium spent the rest of their lives in institutions for the mentally ill.

FURTHER RESOURCES

Books

Lipowski, Zbigniew J. *Delirium: Acute Confusional States.* New York: Oxford Uiversity Press, 1990.

Porter, Roy. *Madness: A Brief History.* Oxford: Oxford University Press, 2003.

Web sites

Thomas Jefferson University. "Notable Jefferson Alumni of the Past." <http://jeffline.tju.edu/SML/archives/exhibits/notable_alumni/john_chalmers_dacosta.html> (accessed November 18, 2005).

Psychological Consultation Report: Mrs. White and Miss Black

Mental Illness Awareness

Book excerpt

By: Corbett H. Thigpen and Hervey C. Cleckley

Date: 1952

Source: Corbett H. Thigpen and Hervy C. Cleckley. *The Three Faces of Eve*. New York: Bantam, 1998.

About the Author: Hervey C. Cleckley was a professor of psychiatry and neurology at the Medical College of Georgia, as well as Chief of Psychiatry and Neurology at University Hospital. Hervey Cleckley, along with Corbett Thigpen, became famous for his work with multiple personality disorder when the non-fiction best-selling book *The Three Faces of Eve* was published in 1952, based on the two physicians's work with their patient Christine Costner Sizemore. Cleckley later wrote another text, *The Mask of Sanity*, concerning psychopathy and sociopathy. Corbett H. Thigpen was a Clinical Professor of Psychiatry at the Medical College of Georgia. Along with Hervey C. Cleckley, he became well known in both scientific and popular press circles with the publication of *The Three Faces of Eve*. Along with his long and distinguished career in the practice and teaching of psychiatry, Thigpen had an abiding fondness for magic, and was an adroit amateur magician.

INTRODUCTION

Dissociative identity disorder (DID), formerly called multiple personality disorder (MPD) is thought to have existed since very early humans first experienced trauma. Since at least the eighteenth century, there have been detailed clinical and scientific records in which DID/MPD was considered a form of psychopathology. The first modern scholarly description of multiplicity was published in 1791 by Eberhardt Gmelin, who described a young woman living in Stuttgart who suddenly began speaking and acting as though she were a French aristocrat, even speaking her native German with a heavy French accent. It is noteworthy that this behavior occurred during the French Revolution, during which many members of the French aristocracy fled to Stuttgart. Of clinical interest is that when she was the "French Woman," she could remember everything that had occurred as either persona; the "German Woman" denied any knowledge of the existence of the "French Woman."

Early American physician Benjamin Rush (1745–1813) collected a number of case histories of persons exhibiting symptoms consistent with DID/MPD during the late eighteenth and early nineteenth centuries. Rush wrote the first American psychiatry text, entitled *Medical Inquiries and Observations Upon Diseases of the Mind*, published in 1812. He believed that that dissociation was a doubling of consciousness, and was caused by a cerebral hemisphere disconnection.

In 1816, the case of Mary Reynolds was published by the physician Samuel Latham Mitchell. This was the first time that a clinical report of DID/MPD was in the popular press, and it attracted significant media and public attention, with stories about her appearing in *Harper's New Monthly Magazine* in 1860. Mary Reynolds published an autobiography in which she detailed her experiences: at nineteen, she said that she took to her bed for nearly three months; during that time she was blind and deaf for a period of five weeks. After recovery from the temporary sensory loss, she had an episode in which she slept for more than a day; when she awakened, she reported having no recollection of her former life. She spent the next several weeks relearning many of her previous skills, with the exception of handwriting: she often used mirror writing (writing in reverse, from right to left). Her "new" personality was considered far more fun-loving and outgoing than her prior self. After more than a month, she had another long period of sleep, and woke as her former self, with amnesia for the intervening time. For the next fifteen years, her personalities alternated frequently until, when she reached her mid-thirties, the second personality remained in control of her consciousness, and she did not shift again. She died at age sixty-one.

French physician, psychiatrist, and philosopher Pierre Janet (1859–1947) studied DID/MPD extensively, and published numerous case studies during the late nineteenth and early twentieth centuries. In 1906, Morton Prince, founder of the *Journal of Abnormal Psychology*, published his account of the case of Christine Beauchamp, entitled *The Dissociation of a Personality;* Miss Beauchamp exhibited three different personalities, in addition to her waking self. The Beauchamp case has been cited in psychology and psychiatry texts as recently until the present day, both because of the clinical aspects of the case and because Prince stated his belief that the disorder was caused iatrogenically (caused by therapists, typically through hypnotism). Currently, there continues to be a significant cadre of mental health professionals as well as laypersons, who assume that DID/MPD is akin to false memory syndrome, and can be situationally caused. There has not yet been conclusive evidence presented in the scientific or scholarly literature that has attributed causality for MPD/DID.

In 1954, Cleckley and Thigpen published their case report of work with Christine Costner Sizemore in the *Journal of Abnormal Psychology*, and interest in DID/MPD was again piqued in the mental health community. In 1957, the case achieved wide popular acclaim through the publication of their nonfiction book, *The Three Faces of Eve*. In brief, the details of the case are as follows: the patient was referred for treatment by her spouse, as a result of severe and blinding headaches, reported by the patient to be followed by blackouts. Her psychiatrists were puzzled by her amnesia for a recent trip, and utilized hypnosis, which cleared the blocked memory. Shortly thereafter, they received a letter from the patient that included a paragraph apparently written in a different handwriting than the rest of the missive. The patient denied sending the letter, although she reported having started and then thrown it away. During the course of therapy, she admitted hearing voices, and then appeared to experience a sharp headache. Moments later, she shifted into another personality, who had very different mannerisms and body language; she also referred to herself by a different name. The book (and the movie) is based on some fourteen months of therapy and interviews with the patient and her two "alters."

▮ PRIMARY SOURCE

PSYCHOLOGICAL CONSULTATION REPORT

This twenty-five year-old married female patient was referred for psychological examination with a provisional diagnosis of dual personality. Two complete psychological examinations were requested, one of the predominant personality, Mrs. White, the other,…of the secondary personality, Miss. Black.

The patient is the oldest of three siblings, having twin sisters. She quit school two months before graduation form high school. She was employed as a telephone operator. She has been married six years and has a girl four years old. Patient states that she did things recently she cannot remember having done, and expresses serious concern about this condition. The following psychological tests were administered in both examinations:

Wechsler-Bellevue Intelligence Scale
Wechsler Memory Scale
Drawings of Human Figures
Rorschach

Test Behavior Patient was neat, friendly, and cooperative. However, while Mrs. White was more serious, more conscientious, and displayed more anxiety, Miss Black appeared somewhat less anxious and was satisfied with giving more superficial responses. Still the basic behavior pattern was very similar in both personalities, indicating that inhibitory forces were not markedly abolished even in the role of the desired personality. Speech was coherent, and there were no distortions in ideation or behavior according to the assumed personality. No psychotic deviations could be observed at the present time.

Test Results While Mrs. White is able to achieve an IQ of 110 on the Wechsler-Bellevue Intelligence Scale, Miss Black attains an IQ of 104 only. There is evidence that the native intellectual endowment is well within the bright normal group; however, in Mrs. White's case anxiety and tenseness interfere, in Miss Black's superficiality and slight indifference as to achievement are responsible for the lower score. While Mrs. White shows more obsessional traits, Miss Black shows more hysterical tendencies in the records. It is interesting to note that the memory function in Miss Black is on the same level as her Intelligence Quotient, while Mrs. White's memory function is far above her IQ, although she complained of a disturbance of memory. The only difficulty encountered by both personalities is on recall of digits, a performance in which telephone operators usually excel! On the other hand, the Rorschach record of Miss Black is by far healthier than the one of Mrs. White. In Miss Black's record a hysterical tendency is predominant, while Mrs. White's record shows constriction, anxiety, and obsessive compulsive traits. Thus Miss Black is able to conform with the environment, while Mrs. White is rigid and not capable of dealing with her hostility.

Personality Dynamics A comparison of the projective tests indicates repression in Mrs. White and regression in Miss Black. The dual personality appears to be the result of a strong desire to regress to an early period of life, namely the one before marriage. Miss Black is actually the maiden name of Mrs. White. Therefore, there are not two different personalities with completely dissimilar ideation, but rather one personality at two stages of her life. As is characteristic for this type of case, the predominant personality is amnesic for the existence, activities, or behavior of the secondary or subordinate system, while the secondary personality is aware and critical of the predominant personality's activities and attitudes. The latter reaction is quite similar to the ego-conflict in obsessive compulsive disturbances.

Mrs. White admits difficulty in her relation with her mother, and her performance on the Rorschach and drawings indicate conflict and resulting anxiety in her role as a wife and mother. Only with strong conscious effort can she compel herself to subject herself to these roles. The enforced subjection results in ever increasing hostility. This hostility, however, is not acceptable to her, and activates a defense mechanism of regression to avoid severe guilt feelings, by removing the entire conflictual situation form conscious awareness. At the same time, the new situation (in which she plays the role of Miss Black) permits her to discharge some of her hostility towards Mrs. White. Miss Black on the other hand has regained her previous status of freedom from marital and maternal conflicts, and thus has liberated herself from the insoluble situation in which Mrs. White found herself through her marriage. In addition, she can avert the—in her conviction—inevitable spiritual loss of her child. Thus, it is not surprising that she shows contempt for Mrs. White who permitted herself to become involved in such a situation because of her lack of foresight, as well as her lack of courage to forcefully solve the dilemma.

Actually, the problem started at a much earlier period of life, with a strong feeling of rejection by her parents, especially after the birth of her twin sisters. Mrs. White loves them dearly, Miss Black despises them. After quitting school to help support the family, she (that is to say Mrs. White) sent home money to be used for overcoats for her twin sisters, denying herself a badly wanted wristwatch. When the money was used to buy them two wristwatches instead of overcoats, she reacted with strong, but repressed, hostility. Significantly, she removed her wristwatch while examined as Mrs. White, stating that she doesn't like jewelry. There are several illustrations of her strong sense of rejection as well as sibling rivalry in her records.

Leopold Winter, Ph.D.
Clinical Psychologist
U. S. Veteran's Administration Hospital
Augusta, Georgia
July 2, 1952

SIGNIFICANCE

Dissociative Identity Disorder (formerly Multiple Personality Disorder), as defined (in part) by the *Diagnostic and Statistical Manual of Mental Disorders*, is characterized by the presence of two or more distinct identities or personality states that recurrently take control of the individual's behavior accompanied by an inability to recall important personal information that is too extensive to be explained by ordinary forgetting.

The disorder is diagnosed far more frequently in the United States than elsewhere in the world, and three to nine times more frequently in females than in males. Females are also typically found to have more "alters," or distinctive personalities than males.

Although the overall population estimates vary, it is reported that up to 1 percent of American adults have some form of this chronic disorder. There is some suggestion in recent evidence for genetic linkage; and for development of the disorder as a result of recurrent and severe abuse or major trauma in early childhood. The disorder remains controversial, with clinician opinion ranging from those who liken DID to false memory syndrome and accept as true iatrogenic causality (occurring as the result of treatment by a health professional), to those who believe that the disorder occurs in 8 to 10 percent of the general population. Most clinicians report viewing dissociation on a very broad continuum, with nearly everyone having some experiences of being lost in a daydream, reverie, book, or movie, and relatively few having the experience of complex and chronic dissociative experiences resulting in functional impairment.

Mental illness, in sharp contrast to disorders with purely physical causation, has long been fraught with stigma. Until just a few generations ago, it was common to hide people with chronic or severe mental illness in institutions, or to lock them away in attics or basements. People with minor psychopathology (disorders in which they are not psychotic, and retain some ability to function in society while actively experiencing symptoms) often denied their illnesses, again for fear of social reprisals. By presenting mental illness in a way that was both acceptable and understandable to the general public, *The Three Faces of Eve* was instrumental in raising public awareness of psychopathology, as well as giving it an appealing face by having a young and attractive actress portray Eve (who was described positively in the book as well). Over the next few decades, mental illness was made more and more a subject for popular viewing and discussion. Several books, fiction and nonfiction, became bestsellers and were made into films (either for commercial release or for television broadcast, notably *Sybil* and *One Flew Over the Cuckoo's Nest*, leading to a spate of films and books describing various disorders from the patient perspective. The popularization of the neurotic as hero (or, at least, as sympathetic or lovably bumbling persona) spawned a film and directorial career for the writer/actor Woody Allen, whose ability to portray the nobility of the fragile psyche made it acceptable (and even trendy) to visit a therapist.

FURTHER RESOURCES

Books

American Psychiatric Association. *Diagnostic and Statistical Manual of Mental Disorders*, Fourth Edition, Text Revision (DSM-IV-TR). Washington, D.C: American Psychiatric Association, 2000.

Sizemore, Chris Costner, and Elen Sain Pittillo. *I'm Eve.* Garden City, N.Y.: Doubleday, 1977.

Periodicals

Becker-Blease, K. A., K. Deater-Deckard, et al. "A Genetic Analysis of Individual Differences in Dissociative Behaviors in Childhood and Adolescence." *Journal of Child Psychology and Psychiatry.* 45 (3) (2004): 522–532.

Web sites

Allegheny College. "Mary Reynolds (1793–1854): The First Known Case of Multiple Personality Disorder." <http://merlin.alleg.edu/employee/a/adale/maryr/Home%20Page.htm> (accessed November 21, 2005).

ISSD World. "The International Society for the Study of Dissociation: Diagnostic Tools." <http://www.issd.org/world/isworld_5.html> (accessed November 21, 2005).

ISSD World. "The International Society for the Study of Dissociation: Guidelines for Treating Dissociative Identity Disorder in Adults." <http://www.issd.org/indexpage/treatguide1.htm> (accessed November 21, 2005).

Paul R. McHugh. "Multiple Personality Disorder (Dissociative Identity Disorder)." <http://www.psycom.net/mchugh.html> (accessed November 21, 2005).

Prepublication version of the Journal of Traumatic Stress. "Dissociation: An Insufficiently Recognized Major Feature of Complex PTSD." <http://www.onnovdhart.nl/articles/jts_complex_%20ptsd.pdf> (accessed November 21, 2005).

Implementation of the Program

Blood Banks Established

Book excerpt

By: Douglas B. McKendrick

Date: 1964

Source: Douglas B. McKendrick. *Blood Program in World War II.* Washington, D.C.: U.S. Government Printing Office, 1964.

About the Author: Brigadier General Douglas B. Kendrick was the officer responsible for the Army blood program during World War II and much of the Korean War. The book was published by the Office of Medical History, which is part of the U.S. Surgeon General's Office. The mission of the Office of Medical History is to support the men and women of the U.S. Army Medical Department through publications that recognize their contribution in conflicts such as World War II.

INTRODUCTION

In 1900, the Austrian immunologist Karl Landsteiner (1868–1943) showed that blood serum from a donor often caused the red blood cells of the recipients to clump together, indicating some fundamental incompatibility. He went on to discover the A, B, O blood group system, which laid the foundations for the science of blood banking and transfusions. Then, at the start of World War I, in 1914, it was shown that the addition of citrate, along with refrigeration, helped preserve blood donations for transfusion. Although there are no figures for the number of transfusions carried out in World War I, there is evidence that it was widely used and was regarded as the most important medical development of the conflict.

Between the two World Wars (1918–1939), major strides in the large scale banking and transfusion of blood were made. For instance, in 1935, a group of doctors at the Mayo Clinic in Rochester, Minnesota, became the first to build on their experience of blood transfusion by beginning to store citrated blood. This "banked" blood was utilized for transfusion in a hospital setting.

Then, in August 1936, Federico Duran-Jorda established the Barcelona Blood Transfusion Service. He and his team collected blood, tested it, and pooled it by blood group before storing it under refrigeration. The blood could then be transported in refrigerated vehicles to the front line in the Spanish Civil War. This was the kind of experience that set the scene for the appeals for blood, described in the excerpt, to help wounded soldiers in World War II.

■ PRIMARY SOURCE

The Surgeons General of the Army and the Navy sent identical letters to Mr. Davis on 7 January 1941, requesting the cooperation of the American Red Cross in the collection of blood for plasma, as follows:

The national emergency requires that every necessary step be taken as soon as possible to provide the best medical service for the expanded armed forces. Even though the need for proper blood substitutes may not be immediate, there seems every reason to take steps now which shall provide in any contingency for an adequate supply of these substances for use in individuals suffering from hemorrhage, shock, and burns.

To this end, in order to assure this adequate supply of the blood substitutes for the use of the United States Army, I am asking the American Red Cross and the Division of Medical Sciences, National Research Council, to organize a cooperative undertaking which shall provide the armed services with human blood plasma. In this cooperative effort, I request the American Red Cross to secure voluntary donors in a number of the larger cities of this country, to provide the necessary equipment, to transport the drawn blood rapidly to a processing center, to arrange for separating the plasma and for storing the resulting product in refrigerated rooms.

I am also requesting the Division of Medical Sciences, National Research Council, to assume general supervision of the professional services involved in this collection and storage of blood plasma, and to provide competent professional personnel, both for a national supervising group and for the local collecting agencies. I am also urging that the National Research Council continue to encourage investigation of the various methods of preparation of blood substitutes, preferably in dried form.

While it is impossible to estimate the requirements of the armed forces at the present time, because of the uncertainties of the international situation, I feel strongly that a large quantity, a minimum of 10,000 pints, of blood plasma should be placed and maintained in refrigerated storage. This feeling is based upon the fact that not only will the plasma be of greatest service if a military emergency arises, but also of ultimate use in any national catastrophe.

I am also writing to the National Research Council making this identical request, and am expressing the hope that the cooperative undertaking may receive approval, with prompt organization of the whole enterprise.

On 9 January 1941, Mr. Davis replied as follows:

The American Red Cross will be glad, as requested in your letter of January 7th, to cooperate with the Division of Medical Sciences of the National Research Council and the Army and the Navy in providing the armed services with human blood plasma.

Representatives of the Red Cross will confer with representatives of the National Research Council and the Army and the Navy immediately in order to formulate the necessary plans for getting the project underway.

On 7 January 1941, Maj. Gen. James C. Magee and Vice Adm. Ross T. McIntire, MC, USN, wrote Dr. Lewis H. Weed, Chairman, Division of Medical Sciences, NRC, requesting the cooperation of his agency in this project.

On 9 January, Dr. Weed replied as follows:

I wish to acknowledge receipt of your letter of yesterday requesting that the American Red Cross and the Division of Medical Sciences, National Research Council, cooperate in an undertaking which will lead to the procurement of large quantities of human blood plasma.

I can assure you at once that the Division of Medical Sciences will do everything possible to make this cooperation effective. In fact, I am sure that I speak for the members of the Division in telling you that every effort will be made to accelerate the whole mechanism of obtaining and processing the necessary blood.

The Division of Medical Sciences has already taken the initial steps leading to the formation of an operating subcommittee under the general Committee on Transfusions and will probably select Dr. C. P. Rhoads of Memorial Hospital as the chairman of this committee. No time will be lost in undertaking the necessary organization so that a supply of human plasma may be in storage for the use of the armed forces.

SIGNIFICANCE

In 1941, when the United States first entered the war, it was felt that blood plasma, rather than whole blood, would be the most appropriate treatment for soldiers suffering from shock caused by blood loss. However, it became apparent that British physicians were saving more lives through the use of whole blood transfusions. By 1944, whole blood was being transported by air from the U.S. to help soldiers in European and the Pacific theaters of the war.

Thus, in response to the demands of the world war, the U.S. military had built the first national blood donation program. In all, more than 13 million pints of whole blood were drawn by the American Red Cross during World War II for direct use or for the preparation of plasma. Only some of this was used by the military, and the rest was diverted to civilian purposes. After the war, the national blood program declined and it was rebuilt as a localized civilian program.

The U.S. entered the Korean War in 1950 without a national blood program in place and no blood was shipped to Korea during the first seventy days of the conflict. A program was assembled in due course, drawing on the experience of World War II, and 400,000 units were used in the next three years. A certain amount of blood was wasted, which led to the development of plastic blood bags for better storage.

Beginning in 1965, the Vietnam War required a military blood program for almost ten years, and many useful lessons were learned from the experience. For instance, studies sponsored by the military enabled whole blood to be stored for four or five weeks, depending on the citrate formula used. Packed red blood cells and fresh-frozen plasma also were used for the first time. Frozen red blood cells also were used briefly in Vietnam and were re-introduced in the Gulf War of 1990–1991. Blood also has been used in more recent conflicts such as those in Bosnia, Kosovo, and Iraq.

Experience shows that blood is used less efficiently in a war situation than it is for civilian purposes. For instance, in the Bosnian War, 5,600 units of red blood cells were supplied, but only 79 were used. The remainder was not all wasted—some was given to Bosnian hospitals in desperate need and the U.S. civilian supply did not suffer. In the Gulf War, there were fewer casualties than had been anticipated, so much of the blood requisitioned was never used. War is, inevitably, unpredictable. Over the last century, medical experience in military conflicts has led to the establishment of a national blood banking system that not only covers the uncertainties of war, but also provides for the needs of the civilian population.

FURTHER RESOURCES

Web sites

International Trauma, Anesthesia and Critical Care Society. "Blood Use in War and Disaster: The U.S. Experience." <http://www.itaccs.com/traumacare/archive/05_01_Winter_2005/blooduse.pdf#search='Blood%20Program%20in%20World%20War%20II'> (accessed November 23, 2005).

Public Broadcasting Service (PBS). "Red Gold: The Epic History of Blood. Blood History, 1920–1949, The Impact of War." <http://www.pbs.org/wnet/redgold/history/timeline4.html> (accessed November 23, 2005).

Operation: November 29, 1944

The "Blue Baby" Operation and Heart Surgery

Surgical notes

By: Alfred Blaylock

Date: November 29, 1944

Source: Alan Mason Chesney Medical Archives of the Johns Hopkins Medical Institutions. The operative note by Alfred Blalock was first published in 1966 before enactment of the Health Insurance Portability and Accountability Act (HIPAA) and has been republished in various publications over the years. The citation for the original publication is as follows: Ravitch, Mark M., editor. *The Papers of Alfred Blalock.* 2 vols. Baltimore: Johns Hopkins Press, 1966. Vol. 1:xli,xliii.

About the Author: Alfred Blalock (1899–1964) was born in Culloden, Georgia, and earned his medical degree from Johns Hopkins University in 1922. Afterwards, he became the first surgical resident of the new Vanderbilt University Hospital in Nashville,

Tennessee. There, Blaylock did pioneering work on reversing hemorrhagic and traumatic shock. In 1941, he returned to Johns Hopkins as surgeon-in-chief and director of the department of surgery in the medical school. He remained in these posts until his retirement in 1964.

INTRODUCTION

Blalock demonstated that shock (inability of the body to supply enough oxygen to meet tissue requirements) could be brought on by loss of blood and that transfusion of plasma or whole blood could be an effective treatment. This approach saved the lives of thousands of casualties during World War II (1938–1945). Blalock and his surgical technician, Vivian Thomas, carried out work on dogs while researching shock. Though Thomas had little formal education, his skill in the operating theater was legendary and the two men developed a formidable partnership that was to last over thirty years. In 1938, they performed an anastomosis (surgical joining) between the left subclavian artery (which supplies blood to the neck and arms) and the left pulmonary artery in one animal. The experiment was intended to produce pulmonary hypertension, a condition where there is raised blood pressure in the blood vessels supplying the lungs. The experiment failed in this respect, but the surgical procedure was to prove vital in later research.

On his return to Johns Hopkins, accompanied by Thomas, Blalock turned his attention to heart surgery. Here he met Helen Brooke Taussig (1898–1986), the head of the children's heart clinic. Taussig had an interest in congenital heart defects, including a condition called Tetralogy of Fallot. As the name suggests, this condition involves four different defects—narrowing of the pulmonary artery that serves the lungs, a hole in the wall between the two ventricles (the lower chambers of the heart), enlargement of the right ventricle, and defective positioning of the aorta, the main artery to the body. Tetralogy of Fallot results in severely impeded blood flow to the lungs. The blood cannot be properly oxygenated and children born with Tetralogy of Fallot are very weak, with a bluish tinge to their skin, known as cyanosis, which is due to insufficient oxygen in their blood. Thus, these children often were described as "blue babies."

Blalock and Taussig considered that the anastomosis procedure described above might offer a cure for Tetralogy of Fallot by allowing the blood a chance to oxygenate and bypassing the malformations. Their first patient was fifteen-month-old Eileen Saxon and the course of the operation is described in Blalock's notes reproduced below. The surgical team was very much reliant on their manual dexterity and their determination, since there was little in the way of high-tech equipment available. The role played by Vivian Thomas was especially praised by eyewitnesses to the operation, which was pronounced a success when the child gradually became less and less blue during the days following the surgery. Her mother later recalled "When I saw Eileen for the first time, it was like a miracle…I was beside myself with happiness."

PRIMARY SOURCE

OPERATION: Nov. 29, 1944
Dr. Alfred Blaylock
Ether - Oxygen - Dr. Harmel

ANASTAMOSIS OF LEFT PULMONARY ARTERY TO LEFT SUBCLAVIAN ARTERY This patient was an undernourished child who had cyanosis on frequent occasions. The diagnosis was pulmonary stenosis.

Under ether and oxygen, administered by the open method, an incision was made in the left chest extending from the edge of the sternum to the axillary line in the third interspace. The second and third costal cartilages were divided. The pleural cavity was entered. The left lung looked normal. No thrill was felt in palpating the heart and pulmonary artery. The left pulmonary artery was identified and was dissected free of the neighboring tissues. The left pulmonary artery seemed to be of normal size. The superior pulmonary vein, on the other hand, seemed considerably smaller than normal to me. I had hoped that the artery to the left upper lobe might be sufficiently long to allow an anastamosis, but this did not appear to be the case. The left subclavian artery was then identified and was dissected free of the neighboring tissues. The vertebral artery and the branches of the thyrocervical axis were doubly ligated and divided. The subclavian was so short that there would not have been sufficient length for our purpose, had this not been done. The subclavian artery as then ligated distal to the thyrocervical trunk. A bulldog clip was placed on the subclavian artery at a point just distal to its origin from the aorta. The subclavian artery was then divided just proximal to the ligature. Two bulldog clips were then placed on the left pulmonary artery, the first clip being placed at the origin of the left pulmonary artery, and the second clip being placed just proximal to the point where the artery entered the lung. There was ample space between these two clips for our purpose. A small transverse incision was then made in the wall of the pulmonary artery. By the use of china beaded silk on fine needles, an anastamosis was then performed between the end of the left subclavian artery and the side of the left pulmonary artery. A posterior row of sutures was placed first. There was practically no bleeding following the removal of the bulldog clips.

The anastamosis seemed to be a satisfactory one, and the main point of worry comes from the small size of the left subclavian artery. I was disturbed because I could not feel a thrill in the pulmonary artery after the clips were removed. I do not believe that this was due to any clot in the subclavian artery, because it seemed to pulsate vigorously. It is possible that it was due to a low pressure in the systemic circulation. I do not actually know what the systemic pressure was. Another possibility was that it might have been due to spasm of the subclavian artery. My only regret was that the subclavian artery was not bigger. It is possible that the increased red cell count in this patient may have predisposed to thrombosis.

Sulfanilamide was placed in the left pleural cavity. This was followed by closure of the incision in the chest wall. The third and fourth ribs were approximated by two encircling sutures of braided silk. The soft tissues of the wall were closed in layers with silk sutures.

The patient stood the procedure better than I had anticipated. It is interesting that the cyanosis did not appear to increase very greatly from the temporary occlusion of the left pulmonary artery. It is also of interest that the circulation in the nail beds of the left hand appeared to be fairly good at the completion of the operation.

I did not attempt to visualize the left common carotid artery. It is possible thatthis would have been bigger than the left subclavian. This child was very small and I am confident that the subclavian artery would be more easily dealt with in a larger child.

(Dr. Blaylock)

ms

PRIMARY SOURCE

OPERATION: NOVEMBER 29, 1944
See primary source image.

SIGNIFICANCE

Blalock and Taussig's "blue baby" operation marks the beginning of modern cardiac surgery and of pediatric cardiology in particular. Prior to this time, there often was little hope for babies born with a congenital heart defect. In 1944, Blalock also pioneered a bypass procedure for another congenital abnormality called coarctation of the aorta. In 1948, he launched an operation to correct transposition of the great blood vessels, a further congenital defect in which the pulmonary artery and the aorta are incorrectly connected.

PRIMARY SOURCE

Operation: November 29, 1944. Surgical notes of Alfred Blaylock explaining his pioneering operation in 1944 to correct the heart defect known as Tetralogy of Fallot in fifteen-month-old Eileen Saxon. THE ALAN MASON CHESNEY MEDICAL ARCHIVES OF THE JOHNS HOPKINS MEDICAL INSTITUTIONS.

Meanwhile, the "blue baby" operations continued. The third case, a cyanotic six-year-old boy who could no longer walk, was particularly memorable. Even as the final sutures were put in place, the small patient was acquiring what Taussig described as "lovely normal pink lips." He went on to become an active boy.

At the same time in both theaters of World War II, surgeons were faced with large numbers of casualties with traumatic injuries to the heart (bullets or shrapnel fragments lodged in heart tissues). One U.S. Army surgeon, Dwight Harken, devised a technique for cutting into the wall of a beating heart, locating the shrapnel, and removing it with a finger. In 1952, Walton Lillehei and John Lewis, two surgeons at the University of Minnesota, corrected the heart defect of a five-year-old girl after cooling her body to 81°F (27.2°C), a technique that allowed the body to survive without a pumping heart for ten minutes. True open-heart surgery was perfected after the 1958 invention of the heart bypass machine, which takes over the function of both the heart and lungs during surgery. Shortly thereafter, a drug was invented to stop the heart during surgery, allowing surgeons to correct structural defects and perform complex operations, such as bypass grafts and valve replacements, on an unbeating heart.

In the years that followed the blue baby operation, thousands of "blue babies" were cured by the technique. In 1952, Taussig reported results on the first 1,000 patients. Doctors from all over the world traveled to Johns Hopkins to learn the operation from Blalock and Taussig. Both physicians were honored nationally and internationally as word of their ground-breaking work spread through the medical community.

FURTHER RESOURCES

Books

Acierno, Louis J. *The History of Cardiology*. London: Parthenon Publishing, 1994.

Westaby, Stephen. *Landmarks in Cardiac Surgery*. Oxford: Isis Medical Media, 1997.

Web sites

Alan Mason Chesney Medical Archives of the Johns Hopkins Medical Institutions. "The Blue Baby Operation." <http://www.medicalarchives.jhmi.edu> (accessed November 1, 2005).

Matthew's New Marrow

HLA and Bone Marrow Transplantation

Magazine article

By: Matt Clark

Date: May 10, 1976

Source: *Newsweek.*

About the Author: Based in New York, the magazine *Newsweek* is known for its coverage of global issues in politics, economics, medicine, science, and the arts. Founded by Thomas J. C. Martyn, former foreign editor of *Time*, the first *News-Week*, as it was then called, appeared on February 17, 1933, and cost ten cents. Today, *Newsweek* has a worldwide circulation of more than four million and has won many prestigious awards for its journalism. Matt Clark was born in Chicago, Illinois, in 1930. He was the medical editor of *Newsweek* when he wrote "Matthew's New Marrow." Clark has received a number of awards for science journalism including the Albert Lasker Medical Journalism Award (1964, 1967) and the American Heart Association's Howard W. Blakeslee Award (1965, 1968, 1973, 1983).

INTRODUCTION

Bone marrow transplant (BMT) involves the infusion of bone marrow into a person whose lymphocytes (white blood cells) are deficient or absent. The bone marrow is the source of these cells, and a transplant is potentially life-saving for people with leukemia, immune deficiency disorders, and other conditions arising from lymphocyte dysfunction.

Doctors knew the role of bone marrow in leukemia and anemia as long ago as the nineteenth century and tried giving bone marrow by mouth to affected patients. Such experiments failed, but research in animals suggested BMT could be a real therapeutic possibility. In 1958, French researcher Jean Dausset (1916–) made a major advance when he described human leukocyte antigens (HLAs), proteins on the surfaces of all cells in the body that allow the immune system to distinguish foreign from non-foreign cells.

That is, because invading bacteria, viruses, and even organ transplants have different HLAs on their surfaces, the immune system will reject them. In the context of BMT, it is important that the HLAs of the recipient match the HLAs of the bone marrow donor. Dausset was awarded the 1980 Nobel Prize for Physiology or Medicine in recognition of this work.

Ideally, therefore, the donor should be an identical twin of the recipient. Since identical twins are genetically identical, they have the same HLAs. In 1956, Dr. E. Donnall Thomas (1920–) of Cooperstown, New York, performed the first successful BMT on a patient with leukemia, using an identical twin as donor. Along with Dr. Joseph E. Murray (1919–), Thomas went on to win the Nobel Prize for Physiology or Medicine in 1990 for work on organ and cell transplantation.

In 1968, the first bone marrow transplant for severe combined immune deficiency (SCID) was performed on a four-month-old boy at the University of Minnesota. SCID is a rare inherited disorder that leaves a child completely vulnerable to infection, since the patient's immune system lacks lymphocytes and cannot make antibodies against invading organisms. To survive, affected children must live in a sealed environment—hence the name "bubble boy" given to this young patient. The donor was the boy's sister; the extended family had already lost eleven children to SCID. The BMT was successful and the boy is now grown-up, fully employed, and a father himself.

However, only a minority of those who could benefit from BMT have an identical twin or a suitable sibling as donor. Doctors wanted to make BMT more widely available by finding unrelated donors with HLAs that matched those of the potential recipients. Matthew Ruffer's case, described here, is the first in which a non-related donor took part in a successful BMT. Matthew was found at birth to have SCID and the BMT was carried out at Memorial Sloan-Kettering Cancer Center in New York, using bone marrow from a donor in Sweden. Matthew had already lost a sister to SCID after doctors had tried a BMT using their father as a donor.

■ PRIMARY SOURCE

Matthew Ruffer was born in July 1973, but he was unable to go home with his parents until two months ago. That's because the blond, blue-eyed youngster came into the world without the normal ability to fight off even slight infections. Shortly after birth, he was placed in a special sterile room at New York's Memorial Sloan-Kettering Cancer Center awaiting a lifesaving bone-marrow transplant. But now the wait is over. Matthew has gone home in good health, and has also marked a milestone in medical history: he is the first person ever to survive with a marrow transplant from an unrelated donor.

Matthew's case is a happy illustration of the important strides that have been made in tissue transplantation in just a few years. It began in 1970, when Roger and Connie Ruffer of Bryan, Ohio, had their first child, a girl. Shortly after birth, the infant developed a series of infections, and tests disclosed that she was suffering from a rare inherited disorder called combined immune deficiency disease. Because of this genetic defect, she lacked lymphocytes, the white blood cells that attack invading viruses and bacteria and also make antibodies. Since nearly all blood cells are derived from the bone marrow, Dr. Robert Good of the University of Minnesota tried to remedy the baby's defect by transplanting bone marrow from her father. But the attempt failed and the child died at the age of eighteen months.

The failure, though tragic, wasn't entirely surprising because bone-marrow transplantation presents the most serious problems of any type of tissue graft. With kidney transplants, for example, the major question is whether the recipient's immune system will recognize the donor organ as foreign and reject it. But with marrow transplants there is a twofold danger. Even with his sharply limited resistance, the patient may reject the graft. Or the transplanted bone morrow—because it is the source of the very lymphocytes that are involved in immune reactions—may reject the patient. The result is graft-versus-host disease, or GVH, which can produce fatal bone-marrow and liver damage.

Match: Because of the risk of GVH, almost all bone-morrow transplants done to date have involved patients with brothers or sisters whose tissues closely match their own. Dr. E. Donnall Thomas and his team at the University of Washington in Settle have done more than 200 such transplants for patients with leukemia or aplastic anemia, a condition in which the marrow produces neither red nor white cells. About 30 leukemics and 50 patients with anemia who received marrow from matched siblings have survived for up to five and a half years. But many children with these blood disorders don't have suitable siblings, so researchers are trying to make marrow transplants between unrelated individuals both safe and effective.

When Connie Ruffer became pregnant again, Good knew that her child had a one-in-four chance of having immune deficiency and blood tests performed after Matthew was born confirmed the worst. Soon, he was taken to Sloan-Kettering, where Good had become research director. There the child was kept in a sterile room and tended by personnel in masks and spotless garb. Good and his associates set about finding a donor.

Samples of what few lymphocytes Matthew's system did produce were sent to Cophenhagen's Rigshospitalet, where a typing lab keeps tabs on thousands of Danish blood donors for possible participation in organ transplants. Sloan-Kettering's Dr. Bo Dupont had worked on a similar case there. Tissue typing involves matching blood cells by their reaction to antibodies as well as by mixing donor and recipient lymphocytes in cultures. Starting with 800 prospective donors for Matthew, Dupont and Dr. Arne Svejgaard spent six months and performed 40,000 culturing procedures to narrow the search down to Mrs. Lis Larsen, a 46-year-old agricultural lab technician with two children of her own. In Denmark, donation of blood without pay is a tradition, and even though bone-marrow extraction is more complicated, Mrs. Larsen readily agreed to donate to Matthew.

On four occasions, between December 1973 and July 1974, Mrs. Larsen was anesthetized and marrow was extracted from inside her hip bone by means of a 4-inch needle. The marrow was flown to New York. There it was injected into Matthew's bloodstream, which carried it to the bone-marrow cavities. It was given in small amounts to avoid GVH. But each of the four transplants failed shortly afterward, and Matthew developed a slight rash, the sign of a mild GVH reaction.

Reasoning that the marrow cells may have been damaged somehow during the transatlantic flights, Dr. Richard O'Reilly, who had supervised the marrow injections, asked Mrs. Larsen to come to New York in January 1975, for a fresh donation.

This time, Matthew was given a large amount of marrow cells, together with a drug called Cytoxan to prevent rejection of the marrow transplant. The results were better. Matthew began to produce functioning lymphocytes, but after his exposure to the outside world, a more severe GVH reaction set in and he developed aplastic anemia.

Lethal: Back in his sterile room, Matthew was given antibiotics to wipe out the bateria he had picked up. In November, Mrs. Larsen returned to New York to donate marrow. This time, O'Reilly and his associates infused 1 billion cells into Matthew's veins, after giving him a potentially lethal dose of Cytoxan to prevent rejection. "Every time we had to make a move," says Good, "we were moving into the unknown." But finally the graft took, and large doses of the steroid prednisone prevented severe GVH disease. By last January, Matthew's body was producing normal levels of red and white blood cells....

Two months ago, Matthew was able to go to his parents' present home in Fort Lee, N.J., and now he comes to the hospital only once a week for a checkup. He takes no drugs, hasn't had any infections and shows no untoward effects from his many months in the sterile room, except one. Matthew is only now just beginning to talk. He has been slow in this respect, his doctors think, because for so much of his life he never saw anyone's mouth forming words. They were all wearing surgical masks.

SIGNIFICANCE

Matthew Ruffer's bone marrow transplant was far from simple. He received multiple infusions of bone marrow and, in fact, needed seven in all before his blood count became normal. He also suffered various complications, including graft-versus-host disease (GVH), where the transplanted bone marrow reacts against the host and produces potentially fatal responses, including liver failure. Matthew's eventually successful procedure opened the door to more widespread BMT, especially as doctors began to understand more of the HLA system—that three specific HLAs, i.e. HLA-A, HLA-B, and HLA-DR, were the most important in determining a match between donor and recipient. GVH continues to be an issue in BMT and is a very active area of research.

The next major development in bone marrow transplantation was the creation of a database of HLA-type volunteers who could act as donors. This was driven by researchers at the Fred Hutchinson Cancer Research Center, an early pioneer in BMT, who searched for a donor for a young girl with leukemia in 1979. The operation was successful, but she died later from a recurrence of her disease. Her family campaigned for the creation of HLA-typed databases of volunteers and these were established in several U.S. cities over the next few years. In 1984, the U.S. Congress passed the National Organ Transplant Act, which set the scene for the establishment of the National Bone Marrow Donor Program (NMDP). In 1987, the first donor was identified and gave two years of extra life to a girl with acute leukemia. By 1996, there were two million potential donors participating in the NMDP and 5,000 transplants had taken place. By then, peripheral and umbilical cord blood were also being used as sources of lymphocytes for transplant. The NMDP is now global and 40 percent of BMTs involve a U.S. patient receiving cells from an international donor or vice versa.

FURTHER RESOURCES
Books
Carrier, Ewa. *100 Q&A About Bone Marrow and Stem Cell Transplantation.* Boston: Jones and Bartlett, 2003.

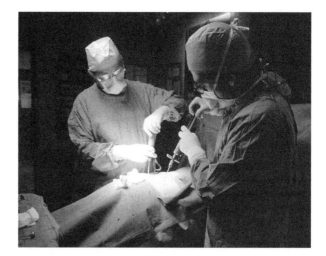

Dr. John Kersey, a leader in bone marrow transplant (BMT) research, gathers bone marrow from a patient at the University of Minnesota. ©TED SPIEGEL/CORBIS.

Web sites
Seattle Cancer Care Alliance. "What is a Bone Marrow Transplant." <http://www.seattlecca.org/patients andfamilies/adultCare/transplant/WhatIsBoneMarrow Transplant.htm> (accessed November 5, 2005).

National Marrow Donor Program. "The History of Marrow and Blood Cell Transplants." <http://www.marrow. org/NMDP/history_of_transplants.html> (accessed November 5, 2005).

University of Minnesota Cancer Center. "Transplant Biology & Therapy. Historical Overview." <http://www. cancer.umn.edu/page/research/trsplant/bmthist.html> (accessed November 5, 2005).

Cholesterol and Heart Disease

Press Release for the 1985 Nobel Prize in Physiology or Medicine

Press release

By: Nobel Assembly at the Karolinska Institute

Date: October 14, 1985

Source: Nobel Assembly at the Karolinska Institute. Press Release: The 1985 Nobel Prize in Physiology or Medicine. <http://nobelprize.org/medicine/laureates/ 1985/press.html> (accessed December 11, 2005).

About the Author: The Nobel Assembly at the Karolinska Institute has awarded the Nobel Prize annually since 1901 for achievements in physics, chemistry, physiology or medicine, literature, and peace.

INTRODUCTION

The Karolinska Institute's 1985 press release announced the awarding of the Nobel Prize in Physiology or Medicine to two American researchers at the University of Texas—Michael S. Brown and Joseph L. Goldstein—for their discoveries in the regulation of cholesterol. The main purpose of the press release was to outline the discoveries in cholesterol physiology and their significance to science and medicine. The release recounts Brown's and Goldstein's finding that receptors on cellular surfaces mediate the uptake of circulating low-density lipoprotein (LDL), a substance of fundamental importance in building cellular membranes, synthesizing hormones, and many other physiological functions. The researchers discovered that abnormalities in these receptors result in their inability to take up circulating LDL. As a result, high LDL levels in the bloodstream can accumulate in hard plaques on arterial walls. These plaques narrow and harden the arteries (atherosclerosis), leading to reduced blood circulation in cardiac and peripheral arteries. Advanced cases result in ischemic heart disease and myocardial infarctions or heart attacks in which sections of the heart muscle are starved of oxygen and die.

The immediate medical application of this discovery was to cases of familial hypercholesterolemia, an inherited disorder that results in circulating LDL of up to five times normal levels. Brown and Goldstein discovered that cells from individuals that were homozygous for this trait had no capacity to bind and absorb circulating LDL, while far more common heterozygous cases had impaired capability due to reduced numbers of receptors to bind LDL.

Understanding the physiology of cholesterol regulation paved the way for drug treatment of milder hypercholesterolemia cases, which constitute the vast majority of patients with elevated cholesterol. Treatments for high cholesterol now comprise the largest drug expenditure category for the U.S. health care system.

■ PRIMARY SOURCE

The Nobel Assembly at the Karolinska Institute has today decided to award the Nobel Prize in Physiology or Medicine for 1985 jointly to

Michael S. Brown and Joseph L. Goldstein

for their discoveries concerning "the regulation of cholesterol metabolism."

SUMMARY

Michael S. Brown and **Joseph L. Goldstein** have through their discoveries revolutionized our knowledge about the regulation of cholesterol metabolism and the treatment of diseases caused by abnormally elevated cholesterol levels in the blood. They found that cells on their surfaces have receptors which mediate the uptake of the cholesterol-containing particles called low-density lipoprotein (LDL) that circulate in the blood stream. Brown and Goldstein have discovered that the underlying mechanism to the severe hereditary familial hypercholesterolemia is a complete, or partial, lack of functional LDL-receptors. In normal individuals the uptake of dietary cholesterol inhibits the cells own synthesis of cholesterol. As a consequence the number of LDL-receptors on the cell surface is reduced. This leads to increased levels of cholesterol in the blood which subsequently may accumulate in the wall of arteries causing atherosclerosis and eventually a heart attack or a stroke. Brown and Goldstein's discoveries have led to new principles for treatment, and prevention, of atherosclerosis.

CHOLESTEROL—AN IMPORTANT SUBSTANCE

The cholesterol debate during the last decade may have given the public the impression that cholesterol is something you have to avoid to survive. This is, however, neither possible nor desirable: cholesterol is present in all our tissues and is produced in the body. Cholesterol is also vitally important for several of the normal processes in the body.

Cholesterol originates from two main sources—from within through biosynthesis predominantly in the liver, and from without through fat in the food. In the liver as well as in the intestine cholesterol is packeted into particles in such a way that it can be transported in the blood and lymphatic fluid. These particles are called lipoprotein—a combination of fat and proteins. There are different kinds of lipoproteins and they are classified on the basis of their density as determined by ultracentrifugation: Low Density Lipoproteins (LDL), Very Low Density Lipoproteins (VLDL) and High Density Lipoproteins (HDL). The particles transporting cholesterol circulating in the blood are LDL. . . .

A normal healthy person has approximately 2 g cholesterol per liter plasma. The highest abnormal values, approximately 10 g per liter, are found in persons with a severe disease called familial hypercholesterolemia (FH), which is an inborn error of metabolism.

CHOLESTEROL IS FOUND IN CELL MEMBRANES AND IS CONVERTED TO HORMONES AND BILE ACIDS

Cholesterol has two main functions in the body. It constitutes a structural component in cell membranes, and it is converted to certain steroid hormones and bile salts. More than 90 per cent of the cholesterol in the body is found in cell membranes.

Each cell is surrounded by a membrane, the cell or plasma membrane. Its function is not only to be a protective coat. It also serves as a border control determining which substances are allowed to enter or leave the cell. This function is sometimes facilitated by the presence of specific receptors whereby certain molecules are efficiently trapped and taken up by the cell.

The cells either produce their own cholesterol or take up LDL circulating in the blood stream. The discovery of the LDL-receptor by Brown and Goldstein in 1973 was a milestone in cholesterol research.

Several hormones are produced from cholesterol like estrogen and testosteron, cortison and aldactone. Cholesterol is stored in cells of the adrenals and gonads and can be utilized as soon as there is a requirement for these hormones.

Cholesterol also takes part in the synthesis of vitamin D, which prevents development of rickets. Vitamin D is produced in the skin when exposed to the sun's ultraviolet light.

Another vital function of cholesterol is associated with food intake. Cholesterol is converted into bile acids in the liver and is transported via the bile to the upper intestine where the bile salts emulsify the dietary fat making it absorbable. The bile salts then return to the blood stream and are taken up by the liver and again secreted into the upper intestine. This recycling of bile acids normally limits the liver's need for cholesterol.

EXCESS CHOLESTEROL ACCUMULATES IN THE WALLS OF ARTERIES

As stated above cholesterol is of vital importance for the body. Thus, cholesterol deficiency, a rare disease, causes severe damage particularly in the nervous system. However, the most common abnormality in the cholesterol metabolism is of the opposite kind. Excess cholesterol accumulates in the walls of arteries forming bulky plaques that inhibit the blood flow until a clot eventually forms, obstructing the artery and causing a heart attack or stroke.

The accumulation of cholesterol in the arterial walls is a slow process lasting over decades. Among factors contributing and accelerating this process are high blood pressure, a high intake of animal fat in the food, smoking, stress and genetic factors.

Studies on patients with familial hypercholesterolemia (FH) by Michael S. Brown and Joseph L. Goldstein constitute founding stones for our present knowledge concerning the cholesterol metabolism. FH exists in different forms and is inherited as a monogenic dominant trait.

Individuals who carry the mutant gene in double dose (homozygotes) are severely affected. Their serum cholesterol levels are five times higher than in healthy persons, and severe atherosclerosis and coronary infarction is seen already in adolescence, or even earlier. Individuals who have inherited only one mutant gene (heterozygotes) develop symptoms later in life—at 35 to 55 years of age. Their cholesterol levels are approximately 2–3 times higher than in normal people.

PATIENTS WITH FH LACK FUNCTIONAL LDL-RECEPTORS

Brown and Goldstein studied cultured human cells (fibroblasts) from healthy individuals and individuals with FH. Like all animal cells cultured fibroblasts need cholesterol in their cell membranes. Cholesterol—in the form of LDL—was found to be taken up by highly specific receptor molecules on the cell surface—the LDL-receptor. The revolutionizing discovery was then made that fibroblasts from patients with the most severe form of FH completely lacked functional LDL-receptors. Fibroblasts from patients with the milder form of FH had fewer LDL-receptors than normal—a reduction by half.

Brown and Goldstein also discovered that the synthesis of cholesterol in normal fibroblasts was inhibited when LDL-containing serum was added to the cell culture. Fibroblasts from homozygous patients with FH were not inhibited since they lacked functional LDL-receptors. Consequently their intracellular synthesis could not be influenced.

In later studies Brown and Goldstein showed that LDL which had bound to the receptor was taken up by the cells as a LDL-receptor complex. One effect of the uptake of cholesterol is that it inhibits the manufacture of new LDL-receptors on the cell surface. A reduced number of LDL-receptors leads to a diminished LDL uptake. LDL then remains in the blood stream with the risk of accumulation in the arterial walls.

Brown and Goldstein have discovered a new, and unexpected way of regulation of cholesterol metabolism. Normally cells have a high capacity to synthesize their own cholesterol. With a low availability of cholesterol (LDL) in the blood circulation the cells increase the number of LDL-receptors on their surface. The concentration of LDL in the blood is thereby diminished. The more LDL there is in the blood circulation the easier it is for the cells to acquire it. With a high dietary fat intake an excess of LDL circulates in the blood.

THE DISCOVERIES HAVE RESULTED IN NEW APPROACHES FOR THE TREATMENT OF ATHEROSCLEROSIS

The discovery of the LDL-receptor has broadened our understanding of cholesterol metabolism considerably and explained the mechanism behind familial hypercholesterolemia.

Brown and Goldstein have used modern molecular biology techniques to show that the LDL-receptor is a glycoprotein located in the cell membrane.... The LDL-receptor defect can be one of several different kinds: in some cases the receptor is completely lacking, in others LDL binds poorly, or not at all, to receptor and in still others LDL is bound to the receptor but the LDL-receptor complex is not internalized....

The severe form of FH (homozygous) is rare, about one in a million people. The milder form of FH (heterozygous) is much more common, about one in 200–500 people. This means that in a city like Stockholm several thousand inhabitants have the disease with its associated risks of atherosclerosis and heart infarction.

Brown and Goldstein have introduced entirely new principles for treatment of FH based on their discovery of the LDL-receptor. In individuals with the milder heterozygous form of FH the number of LDL-receptors has been increased using drugs—cholestyramine and mevinolin. Such treatment has been found to lower blood cholesterol levels. In the more severe homozygous form of FH, where functional LDL-receptors are missing, medication is no therapeutic alternative. There liver transplantation has been tried. A severely ill 6 year old girl, who already had suffered several heart attacks, was given a new liver and heart simultaneously. More than six months after the operation her blood cholesterol levels were in the range of 3 g per liter compared to 12 g per liter before the liver transplantation.

The discoveries made by Brown and Goldstein have drastically widened our understanding of the cholesterol metabolism and increased our possibilities to prevent and treat atherosclerosis and heart attacks. But their discoveries have even more far-reaching implications. Coronary infarction is a major cause of death in most industrialized countries. The disease is caused by hereditary and environmental factors, which together cause a reduction of the number of LDL-receptors. This increases the blood levels of LDL and thereby the risk for atherosclerosis. Brown and Goldstein's revolutionary results have widened our horizon and holds promise for future fascinating developments. They speculate themselves about therapy with drugs that increase the number of LDL-receptors simultaneous with a lesser demand for dietary regimens...."it may one day be possible for many people to have their steak and live to enjoy it too."

SIGNIFICANCE

Brown and Goldstein received the 1985 Nobel Prize in Physiology or Medicine in recognition of work that led to widespread treatment of elevated cholesterol, which is credited with the prevention of millions of deaths and cases of disability from cardiovascular disease. Few other medical discoveries rival the understanding of cholesterol physiology in terms of fostering secondary preventive pharmaceutical treatment.

The Centers for Disease Control and Prevention (CDC) estimates that approximately 20 percent of adults in the United States suffer from hypercholesterolemia. The prevalence of high cholesterol increases with age, with the highest incidence observed in women between the ages of sixty-five and seventy-four. According to the World Health Organization (WHO), hypercholesterolemia is implicated in 56 percent of coronary heart disease cases globally, resulting in 4.4 million deaths annually. The female death rate due to high cholesterol is marginally higher than the male death rate.

When hypercholesterolemia is diagnosed, doctors generally advise patients to reduce circulating LDL cholesterol by reducing dietary cholesterol (avoiding the consumption of foods containing animal fats) and increasing exercise. This "lifestyle change" regimen can lead to weight loss, which also reduces circulating LDL cholesterol. If lifestyle modifications are not effective in reducing cholesterol levels, then drug therapy is prescribed. New guidelines issued by the Institute of Medicine in 2001 lowered the limit for what was considered to be "healthy" cholesterol levels and nearly tripled the number of Americans who are candidates for cholesterol-lowering drugs.

While there are three other classes of cholesterol-lowering drugs—niacin, fibrates, and bile acid sequestrants—HMG-CoA reductase inhibitors (so-called statin drugs, such as Lipitor, which can lower LDL cholesterol by 25 percent or more) are the most effective and well-tolerated cholesterol reducing drug class. By 2001, they comprised about 90 percent of the cholesterol-lowering drug market. Currently, statin drugs comprise either the largest or second-largest drug class in terms of expenditures for most health insurance plans. In 2005, the sales of Lipitor, the market leading statin drug, are expected to hit $10 billion. Total sales for the drug class could reach $20 billion.

Clinical trials have demonstrated that statin therapy significantly reduces the risk of coronary events for patients with elevated cholesterol levels. A study by the National Center for Health Statistics (NHCS) using data from the National Ambulatory Medical Care Survey (NAMCS) and the National Hospital Ambulatory Medical Care Survey (NHAMCS)

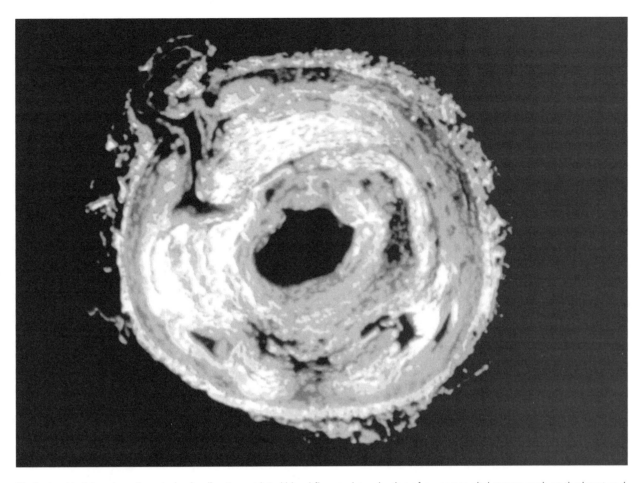

Cholesterol buildup clogs the arteries leading to restricted blood flow and a reduction of oxygen to vital organs such as the heart and brain. ©HOWARD SOCHUREK/CORBIS.

examined statin drug utilization by age, sex, race, or ethnicity, and selected diagnoses. The NCHS study found that between 1960 and 2000 the percent of adults with high cholesterol decreased from 33 percent to 18 percent, partly due to an increase in drug therapy, and partly due to reduced intake of animal fats among other factors. During this time the rate of statin prescriptions in ambulatory care visits tripled from 1995 to 2001 among those aged forty-five and older.

Despite a cascade of clinical trial results confirming the role of cholesterol in heart disease, such a role and the increasingly heavy use of statin drugs is still not universally accepted. The International Network of Cholesterol Skeptics (THINCS), which represents a group of physicians and medical researchers, questions the interpretation of clinical trial results by groups such as the American Heart Association and the pharmaceutical industry showing an association of cholesterol levels with incidence of heart disease. They maintain that the statistical association between

cholesterol reduction using statin drugs and reduced heart attack deaths exists because of characteristics of the drugs not associated with cholesterol reduction. For example, statins appear to reduce inflammation in the arteries of the heart that can cause the buildup of atherosclerotic plaques.

Statin drugs are generally considered to be well-tolerated. However, they are associated with rhabdomyalysis (breakdown of muscle tissue), reductions in Coenzyme Q-10 (a naturally occurring antioxidant), and liver damage, particularly when taken with alcohol, non-steroidal anti-inflammatory drugs, and acetaminophen.

In spite of continuing controversy and some side effects, the treatment of hypercholesterolemia and even moderately elevated or "normal" cholesterol levels appears likely to grow further. The Nobel Prize press release reported that Brown and Goldstein themselves speculated that cholesterol treatment might allow people to eat steak without facing greater risk of dying from heart disease. As with other emerging types of drug treatment, such as the utilization of selective serotonin re-uptake inhibitors (SSRI antidepressants), conjecture abounds that pharmaceuticals could eventually be taken by people with few or no signs and symptoms of disease. At the same time, third-party payers will carefully examine such use by low-risk patients to determine if it is cost-effective in terms of preventing future complications that result in hospitalization.

FURTHER RESOURCES

Books

Beers, M. H., and R. Berkow, eds. *The Merck Manual of Diagnosis and Therapy.* Centennial Edition. Whitehouse Station, N. J.: Merck Research Laboratories, 1999.

Web sites

American Public Health Association. "Statin Drug Use: Age and Gender Differences." <http://apha.confex.com/apha/132am/techprogram/paper_81482.htm> (accessed November 3, 2005).

Cardiology Channel. "High Cholesterol." <http://www.cardiologychannel.com/hypercholesterolemia/> (accessed November 3, 2005).

The International Network of Cholesterol Skeptics. "Concerned Scientists Dispute New Cholesterol-Lowering Guidelines." <http://www.thincs.org/pressrelease82004.htm> (accessed January 11, 2006).

A Developmental Model of Ethnosensitivity in Family Practice Training

Journal article

By: Jeffrey M. Borkan and Jon Neher

Date: March-April 1991

Source: Jeffrey M. Borkan. "A Developmental Model of Ethnosensitivity in Family Practice Training." Family Medicine (March-April 1991).

About the Author: Trained as a family physician, Jeffrey Borkan works in both family medicine and medical anthropology. He has split his career between the United States and Israel, working as a researcher, educator and clinician. Borkan has been influential in guiding medical education curricula and health policy decisions, and is a recognized authority in mixed method research (using both qualitative and quantitative analysis methods in the same study). As of 2005, Borkan is Professor and Chair of the Department of Family Medicine and Physician in Chief for Memorial Hospital of Rhode Island/Brown Medical School. Jon Neher holds the positions of Clinical Professor at the University of Washington and Assistant Director for Curriculum at Valley Medical Center's Family Medicine department in Washington. He has spent his career working in medical education and curriculum development. He is regarded for his work in promoting residency training and enjoys the pressure of opening up his practice to residency review.

INTRODUCTION

Family physicians are one of the first medical professionals the public contact when concerned about their health care. As most societies in North America have a diverse cultural population, the patient walking into the doctor's office could be from any number of ethnic backgrounds. Research in the United States, Canada, United Kingdom, and New Zealand has shown that the visible minority population receives a lower standard of health care than that of the western Caucasian population. Borkan and Neher ask why that is the case and what can be done from a family physician's training point of view.

Language barriers, spiritual beliefs, cultural differences, income, residential situation and location, are all cited as being challenges to receiving appropriate medical care. Borkan and Neher assert that cross-cultural medicine is a natural and important part of family practice.

It is not possible to anticipate every cultural exposure a physician will incur during the life of his or her practice. Medical schools have taken some steps to implement ethnosensitivity training into their curriculum. Mostly, such training occurs during the first or second year of medical school and can last from a three-hour discussion to a year-long immersion into different cultures. Practice-based learning sessions, small group discussions, role-playing, video analysis, and multicultural presenters are popular ways to teach cross-cultural sensitivity. Although medical schools can try to include ethnosensitivity training in their curricula, there is a lack of consistency in educational quality.

PRIMARY SOURCE

ABSTRACT

Cross-cultural medicine is a normal and important part of family practice. Unfortunately, its acceptance and

Navajo medicine man, Hosteen Tso-Begay, performs a ceremonial healing ritual for a four-year-old boy suffering from tuberculosis in Monument Valley, Utah in 1947. The boy is seated in the middle of a sandpainting while his body has been annointed with a potion of herbs. Later he will be given a medicine of corn pollen and water to drink. AP/WIDE WORLD PHOTOS.

implementation into family practice training programs has been limited. . . .

Cross-cultural medicine has been introduced into academic family medicine repeatedly over the last ten years, yet it has not taken hold in any substantial way. . . .

The barriers are many: the core family medicine curriculum is already quite full, cross-cultural literature often appears too exotic or to romanticized to apply to the "usual" doctor-patient encounter, and Western medicine continues to be primarily focused on pathophysiology rather than the patient's experience of illness and the biopsychological model. An additional problem with implementing any standard curriculum is that trainees have varying capacities both to accept cultural differences and to integrate cross-cultural tools and insights into practice. . . .

. . .The authors' goals were to create a system that evaluates a trainee's level of cross-cultural sophistication, minimizes jargon, normalizes ethnicity as a part of every doctor-patient encounter, and can easily be implemented by family medicine faculty. . . .

Ethnosensitivity is desirable in family practice for several reasons. Not only does it support the stated goals of integrating appreciation for the whole person and the behavioral sciences into clinical practice, but it also advances doctor-patient communication and presumably patient satisfaction. . . .

Cognitive strategies useful in combating denial [of cultural insensitivity] are first aimed at fostering the simple awareness of cultural differences and then helping trainees make finer distinctions within ethnic or cultural groups. For example, rather than just recognizing an individual as "Latino," they should be able to identify the social and cultural attributes of Mexicans, as opposed to Puerto Ricans or El Salvadorians. Methods might include lectures from authorities, educational cultural events focusing on a specific ethnic group in the community (such as "Native American Day"), games, demonstrations, and even home visits. A particularly appropriate simulation game is "Baf'a Baf'a." Easily modifiable to medical situations, this game encourages participants to examine cross-cultural differences in communication and meaning.

In a more interpretive fashion, the medical trainee needs to be aware that everyone has ethnicity. Such differences are often not apparent on the surface. Because a patient's looks somewhat like a provider and speaks the same language does not imply that they share the same worldview. . . .

Superiority In the superiority stage, trainees admit to the presence of other cultures and of cultural differences but tend to rank them according to their own value systems. Usually this results in their own culture being seen as the most advanced and other worldviews as being somewhat flawed. Negative stereotyping is perhaps the most obvious manifestation of this stage. In addition, such trainees may hold rigidity to the precepts of their "provider culture," Western biomedicine. Members of other provider cultures, such as chiropractors, homeopaths, and midwives, may be denounced as holding traditional health care systems may be scoffed at. These condescending attitudes may drive patients into cowed silence or out of the healthcare center altogether.

Occasionally someone will come to view another culture as superior and attempt to wholly adopt it in a process of "reversal." "Going native" is a common occupational hazard among anthropologists, foreign service agents, and others who work in an isolated manner in a diverse spectrum of cultures. This involves identification with a group's attitudes, beliefs, and practices to the exclusion of one's own. In family practice, this phenomenon is commonly seen in first year residences who return from their internal medicine or surgery rotations with scowling disapproval of family practice and its weaknesses. Although reversal may seem to be more developmentally advanced than simple cultural superiority, it in fact implies denigration of one's own culture.

Several cognitive strategies exist for dealing with superiority. The main goal is to make the trainee aware of the relative strengths and weaknesses of each system, including his or her own. Similarities, rather than differences, between cultures, value systems, and ethnic groups are to be stressed during this stage. . . .

Minimization Minimization involves acknowledging that cultural differences do exist but viewing them as unimportant against a backdrop of basic human similarities. This is an extremely seductive attitude for trainees, since it is reinforced by dominant American and Western medical views. The "melting pot" concept minimizes the importance of ethnic differences and devalues immigrant cultural practices and beliefs, promoting "pan-Amercanisms" instead. Most medical training emphasizes the reductionist model, stressing biochemistry and pathophysiology while de-emphasizing the medical effects of personality, family structure, and socio-cultural factors. Nonphysiologic attributes are seen as marginal, exotic, or quaint.

The same reductionist model that purports that "we are all the same under the skin" gives a false sense of efficiency and clarity to the trainee who can treat all individuals without need of lengthy history taking or without acknowledging confounding psychological variables. The standard presentation of patients, "A seventy-two-year-old male with X, Y, and Z," strips the individual of nearly all identifying social characteristics, including name. . . .

Relativism At this stage, ethnic and cultural differences are at last acknowledged and respected. The worldviews of other cultures are no longer seen as threatening and their value is intellectually accepted. Ethnocentric biases are put aside, and the trainee is able to view other cultures without ego-salvaging distortions. In effect, the trainee says, "I know that people have cultural differences and that those differences are important in understanding their behavior." An actual knowledge of specific cultural differences, however, is not implied. . . .

There are two major problems encountered by trainees in the stage of cultural relativism. The first is being over-whelmed by the sheer mass of cultural information they assume they have to absorb and integrate. In a training process that stresses complete mastery over detail, it is little wonder that residents may exclaim, "I'm not even comfortable with my level of knowledge in biochemistry, physiology, and neuroanatomy. I don't have time to learn Chinese herbalism and acupuncture too!" . . .

The second major problem encountered in the stage of cultural relativism is wrongly ascribing important data about physical, emotional, and social illness to ethnicity rather than pathology. This occurs because the trainee is unaware of the value system of the patient. . . .

Empathy Empathy involves the trainee's ability to shift his or her frame of reference so as to experience events as a patient might. Vital to this process is an understanding of the patient's value system and worldview. It is a much more sophisticated response than "sympathy." . . .

Empathy may facilitate communication between practitioner and patient, thereby enhancing diagnostic accuracy, compliance, and patient satisfaction. . . .

Strategies for promoting empathy and advancing the trainee into the stage of integration are basically experiential. Cultural immersion is essential. A year in a Navajo hospital, an afternoon at a flop house, or a few hours wearing a blindfold and having to be escorted are all appropriate techniques. . . .

Integration Cultural integration is the most advanced level of physician awareness. The culturally integrated practitioner is a multicultural individual who has cognitively, emotionally, and socially meshed with several cultures. The successful integrator stands both inside and outside a culture, having both deep understanding and a critical viewpoint. The integrating physician is able to "balance a consideration of universal norms, specific norms, and individual norms in (a) differentiating between normal and abnormal behavior, (b) considering etiologic factors, and (c) implementing appropriate interventions. . . .

. . .The ability to accept, empathize, and contextually evaluate are goals which are consistent with the highest values of family practice and in keeping with the art of healing within our specialty. . . .

SIGNIFICANCE

In 1991, Borkan and Neher published an assessment guide to anticipate the level of ethnosensitivity of graduating family doctors. Their guide stipulates seven learning levels that can be exhibited by trainees and builds upon earlier work conducted by M. J. Bennett published in 1986. They note that such levels would vary with the different ethnic group the trainee encounters.

At the most basic level of cultural sensitivity, the trainee could be perceived as being fearful of the encounter with a person from a different race. This fear could preclude the trainee's provision of medical care. Denial of any cultural difference could lead to misunderstandings and discontinuity of care. A perception that the trainee's race is superior to the patient's engenders negative stereotypes. Understanding the benefits and disadvantages of each culture, including their own, would help the trainee draw similarities upon which to build a doctor-patient relationship. With the superiority comes minimization and the belief that differences are unimportant in a medical relationship. However, minimizing differences may lead to a loss of the patient's identity, background and lifestyle and the patient becomes a condition rather than an individual person.

As trainees start to understand the differences in cultural relationships, relativism—acknowledging that ethnic and cultural differences exist and should be respected—comes into play. The trainee's frame of reference can then change to empathy and an ability to relate the patient's decision-making and cultural influences. Finally, integration is the level at which a trainee can acknowledge and understand the multicultural aspect of society and meets the goal of societal healing set forth for the role of family physician.

In the United States, there are still problems with racial disparity in relation to the provision of health care. In their update of health disparities literature, published in the *Annals of Internal Medicine* in 2004, Judith Long and her colleagues state that "black patients receive fewer appropriate medical services than white people." In one program in New Zealand, physician educators are combating the effects of racism through a cultural immersion medical education program. In a 2002 issue of *Academic Medicine*, they suggest "the principles of cultural immersion, informed by the concept of cultural safety, could be adapted to indigenous and minority groups in urban settings to provide medical students with the foundations for a lifelong commitment to practicing medicine in a culturally safe manner."

Borkan and Neher's assessment guide provides a framework upon which to assess a physician's preparation for working in a multicultural society. However, since Borkan and Neher's paper was published in 1991, few medical school curricula cover ethnosensitivity training in depth. The culturally sensitive physician, therefore, tends to be more a product of career learning and lifestyle choice rather than training before graduation.

FURTHER RESOURCES
Books

Culhane-Pera, Kathleen A., D. E. Vawter, P. Xiong, B. Babbitt, and M. M. Solberg.*Healing by Heart: Clinical and Ethical Case Stories of Hmong Families and Western Providers*. Nashville, Tenn: Vanderbilt University Press, 2003.

Periodicals

Kagawa-Singer, M., and L. J. Blackhall. "Negotiating Cross-Cultural Issues at the End of Life." *Journal of the American Medical Association*, vol. 286, no. 23, (2001):2993–3001.

Long, J. A., V. W. Chang, S. A. Ibrahim, and D. A. Asch. "Update on the Health Disparities Literature." *Annals of Internal Medicine*, vol. 141, (2004):805–812.

Loudon, R. F., P. M. Anderson, P. S. Gill, and S. M. Greenfield. "Educating Medical Students for Work in Culturally Diverse Societies." *Journal of the American Medical Association*, vol. 282, no. 9, (1999):875–880.

Outbreak of Ebola Viral Hemorrhagic Fever—Zaire, 1995

Report excerpt

By: Centers for Disease Control and Prevention (CDC)

Date: May 19, 1995

Source: Centers for Disease Control and Prevention. "Outbreak of Ebola Viral Hemorrhagic Fever-Zaire, 1995." *Morbidity and Mortality Weekly Report* (2005): May 19;44(19):381–2.

About the Author: The Centers for Disease Control and Prevention is a federal government agency that provides health and safety information for United States citizens and international health professionals. It reports accurate and timely information regarding health issues, and develops and applies disease prevention and control measures. The CDC is also involved in health promotion and education.

INTRODUCTION

An emergent disease can be a disease which appears suddenly and for the first time, or a known and previously controllable disease that again becomes problematic. An example of the latter is tuberculosis. An example of the former is Ebola.

Ebola is a viral disease. The Ebola virus is one of two members of a family designated as the Filoviridae. The name of the virus comes from a river in the Democratic Republic of the Congo, where the first outbreak of the disease occurred.

Ebola produces a high fever, headache, muscle aches, abdominal pain, tiredness, and diarrhea within a few days of infection. Bloody diarrhea and vomiting of blood can also occur. At this stage recovery is possible. But, for most the disease quickly progresses to produce copious internal bleeding, shock, and death. The infection is lethal in over 90 percent of cases. As well, the disease is highly contagious. Thus, an outbreak can quickly devastate a community, often to die out just as quickly, since death can occur before the virus has been transmitted to another host.

As of 2005, four species of Ebola virus have been identified. The speciation is based on immunological differences and variation in genetic sequences. Three of the species—Ebola-Zaire (isolated in 1976), Ebola-Sudan (also isolated in 1976), and Ebola-Ivory Coast (isolated in 1994)—cause disease in humans. The fourth species, Ebola-Reston (named for the United States military primate research facility where the virus was isolated, during a 1989 outbreak of the disease), causes the disease in primates. The Ebola Reston strain (type of the virus) can be transmitted from primates to humans, but does not seem capable of causing disease in humans.

The source of the Ebola virus is still unknown. However, its structural and symptomatic similarities to filovirus, which establish a latent (slow to grow or dormant) infection in African monkeys, macaques, and chimpanzees, make it very conceivable that the Ebola virus likewise normally resides in an African primate. However, as of 2006, this possibility has not been confirmed. Indeed, recent evidence indicates that fruit bats or elephants may also be a reservoir for the virus.

Almost all confirmed human cases of Ebola have occurred in Africa, although two laboratory workers in England and Russia developed Ebola fever as a result of a laboratory accident in which the workers' skin was punctured by a needle contaminated with the virus.

Person-to-person spread of the virus likely requires immediate contact. The possibility of airborne transmission of the virus is debatable. In the Reston outbreak, the primate Ebola strain may have spread via the air distribution system, since some of the monkeys that were infected were never in physical contact with the other infected monkeys. However, this has never been confirmed, nor has a similar method of spread been documented with the pathogenic human strains.

The CDC responded to an outbreak of hemorrhagic fever in Zaire in May 1995 that was found to be Ebola. The CDC team collected blood samples from victims and suspected cases, cared for persons with Ebola, monitored personal contacts of the victims for signs of infection, tracked the cause and origins of the outbreak, and helped with containment measures. The following excerpt is taken from a preliminary report during the investigation.

PRIMARY SOURCE

Outbreak of Ebola Viral Hemorrhagic Fever—Zaire, 1995

On May 6, 1995, CDC was notified by health authorities and the U.S. Embassy in Zaire of an outbreak of viral hemorrhagic fever (VHF)-like illness in Kikwit, Zaire (1995

population: 400,000), a city located 240 miles east of Kinshasa. The World Health Organization and CDC were invited by the Government of Zaire to participate in an investigation of the outbreak. This report summarizes preliminary findings from this ongoing investigation.

On April 4, a hospital laboratory technician in Kikwit had onset of fever and bloody diarrhea. On April 10 and 11, he underwent surgery for a suspected perforated bowel. Beginning April 14, medical personnel employed in the hospital to which he had been admitted in Kikwit developed similar symptoms. One of the ill persons was transferred to a hospital in Mosango (seventy-five miles west of Kikwit). On approximately April 20, persons in Mosango who had provided care for this patient had onset of similar symptoms.

On May 9, blood samples from fourteen acutely ill persons arrived at CDC and were processed in the biosafety level four laboratory; analyses included testing for Ebola antigen and Ebola antibody by enzyme-linked immunosorbent assay, and reverse transcription-polymerase chain reaction (RT-PCR) for viral RNA. Samples from all fourteen persons were positive by at least one of these tests; eleven were positive for Ebola antigen, two were positive for antibodies, and twelve were positive by RT-PCR. Further sequencing of the virus glycoprotein gene revealed that the virus is closely related to the Ebola virus isolated during an outbreak of VHF in Zaire in 1976.

As of May 17, the investigation has identified ninety-three suspected cases of VHF in Zaire, of which eighty-six (ninety-two percent) have been fatal. Public health investigators are now actively seeking cases and contacts in Kikwit and the surrounding area. In addition, active surveillance for possible cases of VHF has been implemented at thirteen clinics in Kikwit and fifteen remote sites within a 150-mile radius of Kikwit. Educational and quarantine measures have been implemented to prevent further spread of disease. Reported by: M Musong, MD, Minister of Health, Kinshasa, T Muyembe, MD, Univ of Kinshasa; Dr. Kibasa, MD, Kikwit General Hospital, Kikwit, Zaire. World Health Organization, Geneva. Div of Viral and Rickettsial Diseases, and Div of Quarantine, National Center for Infectious Diseases; International Health Program Office, CDC.

EDITORIAL NOTE

Editorial Note: Ebola virus and Marburg virus are the two known members of the filovirus family. Ebola viruses were first isolated from humans during concurrent outbreaks of VHF in northern Zaire and southern Sudan in 1976. An earlier outbreak of VHF caused by Marburg virus occurred in Marburg, Germany, in 1967 when laboratory workers were exposed to infected tissue from monkeys imported from Uganda. Two subtypes of Ebola

The body of a five-year-old Ebola victim is buried by workers dressed in protective gear in Mekambo, Gabon, in 2001. The child was one of five family members who contracted the deadly virus. AP/WIDE WORLD PHOTOS.

virus—Ebola-Sudan and Ebola-Zaire—previously have been associated with disease in humans. In 1994, a single case of infection from a newly described Ebola virus occurred in a person in Cote d'Ivoire. In 1989, an outbreak among monkeys imported into the United States from the Philippines was caused by another Ebola virus but was not associated with human disease.

Initial clinical manifestations of Ebola hemorrhagic fever include fever, headache, chills, myalgia, and malaise; subsequent manifestations include severe abdominal pain, vomiting, and diarrhea. Maculopapular rash may occur in some patients within five to seven days of onset. Hemorrhagic manifestations with presumptive disseminated intravascular coagulation usually occur in fatal cases. In reported outbreaks, fifty percent to ninety percent of cases have been fatal.

The natural reservoirs for these viruses are not known. Although nonhuman primates were involved in the 1967 Marburg outbreak, the 1989 U.S. outbreak, and the 1994 Cote d'Ivoire case, their role as virus reservoirs is unknown. Transmission of the virus to secondary cases occurs through close personal contact with infectious blood or other body fluids or tissue. In previous outbreaks, secondary cases occurred among persons who provided medical care for patients; secondary cases also occurred among patients exposed to reused needles. Although aerosol spread has not been documented among humans, this mode of transmission has been demonstrated among nonhuman primates. Based on this information, the high fatality rate, and lack of specific treatment or a vaccine, work with this virus in the laboratory setting requires biosafety level four containment.

CDC has established a hotline for public inquiries about Ebola virus infection and prevention ({800} 900-0681). CDC and the State Department have issued travel advisories for persons considering travel to Zaire. Information about travel advisories to Zaire and for air passengers returning from Zaire can be obtained from the CDC International Travelers' Hotline, (404) 332-4559.

SIGNIFICANCE

There is no cure for the infection caused by the Ebola virus. However, near the end of an outbreak of the virus in 1995 in Kikwit, Africa, blood products from survivors of the infection were transfused into those actively experiencing the disease. Of those eight people who received the blood products, only one person died. Whether or not the transfused blood conveyed some protective factor could not be determined.

The devastating nature of an Ebola infection is remarkable given the very small size of the viral genome. Fewer than a dozen genes have been detected. How the virus establishes an infection and evades the host immune system armed with so few proteins is still mysterious, and the subject of ongoing study.

Teams of scientists from the Special Pathogens Branch at the CDC continue to investigate outbreaks of emerging diseases including Ebola, along with teams from the World Health Organiztion. In the latest Ebola outbreak that occurred in April 2005 in a forested area of the Cuvette-Ouest region that borders Gabon, more than twenty people died before the outbreak dissipated.

Ebola and other emergent diseases are also significant because they may be indicative of a shifting natural ecological balance. In the case of Ebola, the increasing encroachment of humans into previously pristine territory may have brought our species into contact with hitherto un-encountered microbes. Alternately, agricultural practices such as the use of poultry "factory farms", housing millions of birds, may have created conditions conducive to the rapid spread of avian influenza. The avian influenza has so far established disease in few humans. Yet, the highly mutable genome of the virus (which is similar in sequence to that of the influenza virus that caused the devastating epidemic of 1918) makes adaptation of the virus to a human host a foreseeable possibility.

FURTHER RESOURCES

Books

Lashley, Felissa R., and Jerry D. Durham. *Emerging Infectious Diseases: Trends and Issues.* New York: Springer Publishing Company, 2002.

Fong, I. W. *Infections and the Cardiovascular System: New Perspectives (Emerging Infectious Diseases of the 21st Century).* New York: Plenum, 2003.

Palladino, Michael A., and Stuart Hill. *Emerging Infectious Diseases (The Benjamin Cummings Special Topics in Biology Series).* New York: Benjamin Cummings, 2005.

Preston, Richard. *The Hot Zone: A Terrifying True Story.* New York: Anchor, 1995.

Withdrawing Intensive Life-sustaining Treatment

Recommendations for Compassionate Clinical Management

Journal article

By: Howard Brody

Date: 1997

Source: H. Brody, et al. "Withdrawing Intensive Life-sustaining Treatment: Recommendations for Compassionate Clinical Management." *New England Journal of Medicine* 336 (1997): 652–657, 1304–1351.

About the Author: Howard Brody obtained both a bachelor's degree in biochemistry and a doctoral degree in philosophy from Michigan State University. His medical degree was earned at Michigan State University College of Human Medicine. He is board-certified in family medicine, and his particular areas of interest include medical ethics and physician-patient communication. Between 1985 and 2000 he was director of the Center for Ethics and Humanities in the Life Sciences at Michigan State University. Brody is a board member of the American Society for Bioethics and Humanities.

In addition, he is author of several books and numerous book chapters and scholarly articles regarding medical ethics.

INTRODUCTION

Death, along with the process of dying, has been studied, written about in scholarly, popular, and spiritual works, contemplated by philosophers and clerics, and fought against universally. Medical science and technology have created new means of achieving, sustaining, prolonging, and transforming the quality of life, but have seen less success in preventing death. A few generations ago, death was the expected outcome for individuals who suffered significant trauma or serious infection. Less than half a century ago, a diagnosis of cancer or heart disease was considered a brief prelude to death. Today, technology and medical expertise can frequently prolong life for people with stroke, heart disease, cancer, dementia, chronic obstructive pulmonary disease (COPD), emphysema, pneumonia, AIDS, and a host of other formerly (rapidly) terminal diseases. Much of the time, but certainly not always, the added months or years of life are of high quality and functionality.

End-of-life care is an emerging and growing multidisciplinary specialty within the broader practice of medicine. Although most of this type of care takes place in a hospice setting, it also may occur in hospitals, skilled nursing facilities, nursing homes, and in the home of the dying patient. Palliative care is a central component of end-of-life treatment, although it is used in other situations, such as chronic pain, severe trauma, and burn care treatment, as well. In essence, palliative care involves the elimination or substantial relief of pain or suffering, and the promotion of the highest possible quality of life throughout the dying process. The goal of high quality end-of-life care is the promotion of positive experiences for the patient and family or support system.

Beginning in 1997, with start-up funding provided by the Robert Wood Johnson Foundation, the American Medical Association began an intensive training program, the goal of which was the development and implementation of a comprehensive program of Education on Palliative and End-of-Life Care (EPEC) for physicians. EPEC was designed to broaden the clinical competencies necessary for the provision of high-quality, caring, compassionate, and appropriate care for the dying patient. Since 2000, EPEC has moved beyond the AMA to professional and paraprofessional societies and organizations and has been adopted by a broad spectrum of physical and behavioral health care programs as the educational standard for end-of-life care.

Communication is a key aspect of end-of-life care: the patient must be given honest, understandable information, delivered in a manner that facilitates informed and appropriate decision-making. It is imperative that the patient and family or support system feel they have been given dignity, respect, and a voice throughout the process. It also is important for them to know that everything possible was done to facilitate the highest possible quality of life for the dying patient. An open communication and trust system must exist, in which the palliative care wishes and preferences of the patient can be heard. The physician should engage in a discussion with the patient and the involved care givers/family members, in which the possible treatment options and likely outcomes are discussed, along with the symptoms and disabilities associated with each. The patient is given the opportunity to state what he or she does and does not wish to experience. Health care proxies, advance directives, living wills, and emergency/heroic or life-prolonging options are discussed, the patient's wishes are legally documented, and copies are attached to the medical chart. It is at this point that the patient is given the opportunity to discuss personal preferences regarding the limits of care, the degree of consciousness desired during the final stages of the dying process, where he or she wishes to die, and after-death arrangements. This is also the time to discuss organ and transplant donor options.

■ PRIMARY SOURCE

Despite an ethical and legal consensus regarding the right of patients or their surrogates to refuse life-prolonging therapy, surveys show that dying patients in hospitals in the United States frequently receive unwanted interventions. One reason for this may be a lack of training among physicians and nurses in the clinical aspects of withdrawing intensive life support. Staff members are highly skilled in aggressive life-extending treatment, and some hospitals now have services specializing in palliative care for patients forgoing life-extending treatment. But there may be no one specifically trained in managing the transition from one style of care to the other. Forced to choose between what they were trained to do and what they were never trained to do, physicians and nurses may continue aggressive therapy well beyond the point at which patients or families (or the health care professionals themselves) would prefer to stop. Moreover, well-intentioned but unskilled cessation of treatment may cause distressing symptoms, leading physicians to conclude incorrectly that

the withdrawal of treatment necessarily increases suffering. Such negative experiences may influence the way physicians counsel patients and families about therapeutic options.

We address two essential aspects of good clinical care for dying patients—technical issues in the compassionate withdrawal of life-prolonging therapy, and counseling and emotional support for patients, families, and staff during this process. The specific treatments addressed (mechanical ventilation, dialysis, and artificial nutrition and hydration) were identified by physicians in one survey as those most likely to cause patients discomfort when withdrawn. With careful symptom management, such discomfort need not occur.

DETERMINING TREATMENT GOALS

Compassionate withdrawal of treatment requires moving from a tactical approach (focusing on each intervention) to a strategic approach (aiming at defined goals). Dying patients and their families may have many different goals, including promoting the comfort of the patient and the family, maintaining (or achieving) the patient's ability to communicate, withdrawing interventions judged to be particularly burdensome, or allowing death to occur with rapidity or certainty. The desired goals, not the availability of any specific technology, should dictate the plan of care.

As goals are better identified, a comparison of benefits and burdens is useful in negotiating and refining a plan of palliative care. Any intervention that the patient finds more burdensome than beneficial, given the overall goals of treatment, should be limited or eliminated. . . .

There are many routine interventions that may cause unnecessary discomfort to hospitalized dying patients, including daily laboratory tests, regular radiographic examinations, frequent determination of vital signs and weight, aggressive pulmonary hygiene, frequent turning, and debridement of pressure sores. These procedures frequently escape attention simply because they are so commonly ordered in the hospital.

Pain and discomfort require immediate attention. The patient's subjective report of the presence and degree of distress should guide treatment. For patients who cannot speak, signs of distress such as restlessness, moaning, and agitation (and to a lesser extent tachypnea and tachycardia) may suggest a need for better pain management. Even if they are unable to confirm distress, there is no sound rationale for withholding adequate analgesia or sedation from such patients.

Physicians sometimes worry about administering analgesics and sedatives, especially opioids, to dying patients, because the risk of respiratory depression might violate the rule, "Do no harm." There is, however, ample justification for the liberal use of these drugs in the care of the dying. Empirical data suggest that respiratory depression is distinctly uncommon. Patients from whom intensive life support is withdrawn and who are given large doses of opioids for comfort live as long on average as patients not given opioids, suggesting that the underlying disease process, not the medication, usually determines the time of death.

The patient's goals should determine the timing and sequence of withdrawing interventions. . . .

SPECIFIC AGENTS AND SYMPTOMS

Opioids are the most useful drugs for relieving pain in terminally ill patients. Morphine is widely available and is well absorbed from a variety of routes, and its metabolism is uncomplicated. . . .Morphine also reduces dyspnea.

The optimal dose of morphine for relief of pain or dyspnea is determined by increasing the dose until the patient responds. Patients who have not previously received opioids should initially be given low doses, which should be rapidly increased until symptoms are relieved. For patients with particularly severe or acute symptoms, rapid titration requires that an experienced clinician be at the bedside. Most opioids, including morphine, hydromorphone, and fentanyl, have no maximum dose; the ceiling, if any, is determined by side effects such as excessive sedation or, rarely, respiratory depression, not by an arbitrary number of milligrams.

Benzodiazepines should be the first pharmacologic treatment for anxiety during the dying process. . . .Most anxiety can be relieved by pharmacotherapy accompanied by brief supportive counseling, relaxation and distraction techniques, and simple touch. Altering the environment with music, reduced lighting, and decreased noise is often helpful.

Some antimicrobial drugs promote comfort (e.g., for thrush or perirectal herpes). If the patient has no distress from infection—as is often the case with bacteremia—antibiotics may only prolong dying while adding to the patient's distress by requiring the maintenance of intravenous access. If high fevers cause discomfort, antipyretic drugs can be given every two hours, with acetaminophen given alternately with aspirin or other nonsteroidal drugs. Hypothermia blankets, ice packs, and alcohol baths usually cause more discomfort than the fever itself. Nausea and vomiting can generally be reduced by the aggressive use of antiemetics. Other palliative care techniques may be used to manage symptoms, such as haloperidol for intractable nausea and vomiting and antiarrhythmic drugs for neuropathic pain that is resistant to opioids.

MECHANICAL VENTILATION

Physicians and nurses view the withdrawal of mechanical ventilation as more problematic than the withdrawal of other interventions. Critical care physicians rated ventilator withdrawal as substantially more likely to cause patient discomfort than the discontinuation of any other life-prolonging treatment.

Some physicians (and families) elect not to withdraw ventilators from dying patients, but instead to stop other treatments in the hope that death will occur while the patient is still on the ventilator. They may assume that the patient will be more comfortable dying in this fashion or that withdrawing mechanical ventilation is more morally troublesome than withdrawing other interventions. In a survey of critical care physicians, 15 percent reported that they almost never withdraw ventilator support from dying patients who are forgoing life-sustaining treatment, and 26 percent believed there was a moral difference between not initiating treatment with a ventilator and withdrawing one already in use. However, discontinuing mechanical ventilation falls squarely within the patient's or proxy's right to refuse unwanted treatment and does not differ morally from forgoing dialysis, chemotherapy, or resuscitation. . . .

Before mechanical ventilation is withdrawn, the attending physician, nurse, and other involved staff members should discuss the procedure, strategies for assessing and ensuring comfort, and the patient's expected length of survival with the family (and the patient, if competent). . . .

Regardless of the method [of withdrawing mechanical ventilation], frequent assessment of the patient's comfort during and after withdrawal of the ventilator is mandatory. . . .

DIALYSIS

Dialysis may be discontinued by the patient's choice or if death appears nearly certain in critically ill persons with multisystem failure. Patients may survive for hours or weeks; studies have reported a mean length of survival of eight to nine days.

In one small series, about 65 percent of 19 patients seemed to have comfortable deaths after dialysis ceased; this was particularly likely in patients with concomitant diseases. . . .

ARTIFICIAL NUTRITION AND HYDRATION

It has been relatively difficult to convince health care professionals that it is appropriate to withdraw artificial nutrition and hydration, despite ethical guidelines and court decisions that support the practice. Many think these therapies occupy a unique niche, as both life-extending and palliative. This assumption is unwarranted, however, both because death after the withdrawal of artificial nutrition and hydration will usually be comfortable and because continued treatment may cause considerable discomfort from fluid overload or when restraints are required.

Although there are numerous case reports and few controlled studies, the emerging consensus suggests that seriously ill or dying patients experience little if any discomfort upon the withdrawal of tube feedings, parenteral nutrition, or intravenous hydration—perhaps because of the release of endogenous opioids or the analgesic effects of ketosis. . . .

COUNSELING AND SUPPORT

As medical personnel gain skill in managing the compassionate withdrawal of life-prolonging therapy, they will become more comfortable caring for dying patients. Staff members who are proficient in the technical aspects of care can make themselves available for the emotional support of patients and families. The confidence of medical personnel, coupled with tangible attention to the comfort of patients, will help alleviate families' unwarranted fears that their decision to withdraw treatment will be viewed as constituting cruelty or abandonment.

Patients and families can be further reassured by staff members' frequent attendance at the bedside. Because treatment must be individualized and doses carefully titrated to symptoms, caring for patients this way will prevent any perception that the patient is being abandoned just because aggressive life support is no longer being employed. Because spending more time at the bedside may be difficult for physicians, it is advantageous to employ a team approach involving nurses and other staff members. But physicians ought not to use "busyness" and the presence of a team as excuses to abdicate their responsibilities for comprehensive, compassionate care of dying patients. The concerned attending physician who spends extra time at the bedside becomes an invaluable exemplar in teaching institutions.

Families' questions about uncomfortable symptoms should be answered candidly. Plans to monitor for signs of discomfort and the medications to be given if such signs appear should be explained. A commitment to treat discomfort presumptively may provide further reassurance. Families can help physicians and nurses distinguish patients' random movements from signs of true distress.

The family often wishes to know how long the patient will live. Family members who wish to maintain a bedside vigil must deal with work and home responsibilities as well as with the stress of witnessing the impending death. Staff members should understand how difficult uncertainty is for the family, interpret for them any signs that indicate the probable length of time remaining, and offer practical assistance, while gently reminding family members of the impossibility of firm predictions. Families vary in their need to be present at the time of death. Although it is tempting to suggest that exhausted family members leave the hospital for respite, promising that they will be contacted in time to return before the patient dies, such a promise is almost impossible to keep. Hospitals should have space available nearby where families can get rest and nourishment.

A quiet environment, with soft lighting and music, that allows physical contact with the patient may promote calm for the patient and the family alike. Some have proposed that new palliative care sites should be attached to intensive care units. Others have managed to create a quiet, supportive environment even within a busy unit. Staff members may confer with families on whether religious or other cultural observances would be comforting, and they should be as flexible as possible in facilitating these practices.

The hospice movement has stressed that not only patients and families, but also heath care professionals, need emotional support in dealing with death. Caring for dying patients and their families exacts a serious toll on physicians and nurses. Feelings of frustration, loss, and emotional exhaustion are not signs of weakness but predictable results of this difficult work, especially when staff members extend themselves beyond the mere physical care of the patient. Clinicians need to be aware of these reactions and be willing to seek constructive ways of dealing with them.

The therapeutic principles we have described will go a long way toward making the management of dying after the withdrawal of treatment a rewarding rather than a debilitating or distressing experience. Ensuring at the outset that all members of the medical team understand the goals of management and concur with the treatment plan helps prevent negative emotions later. Even those who disagree with a decision will often be more comfortable in the end if colleagues listen to their concerns and acknowledge their feelings.

If these management strategies are understood and applied by physicians and other care givers, patients and their families may again think of hospitals as sources of comfort to both the living and the dying, instead of places where one must all too often struggle to exercise the right to determine one's own fate.

SIGNIFICANCE

When death is a prolonged process, rather than an abrupt occurrence, it is important to carefully choose the attending physician or health care professional.

Among the factors important in this selection process are: 1) the experience the individual has with the death and dying process; 2) the setting in which the individual works (home, hospital, skilled nursing facility, nursing home, hospice, etc.) and how this setting matches the desires by the patient; 3) how well the individual understands the process of palliative care and his or her willing to fully and promptly address each symptom as it arises; 4) the familiarity of the individual with agency, program, and community support systems such as home health care, occupational and physical therapy, dietary and nutritional services, etc.; 5) the individual's knowledge of and contacts with the appropriate specialty consultants; and, 6) most importantly, the relationship between the health care professional and the dying person, which must be based on trust and respect.

In deciding on a treatment plan and system of care, it is important to consider the means by which the patient's care will be paid for. In the United States, it is important that the health care team understand the limits and provisions of the patient's health insurance policy (private payment, public payor such as Medicare or Medicaid, catastrophic insurance, long-term care insurance, or no insurance). Quite often, a medical social worker, care manager, or case manager can help the patient and family find the best possible system of care given the individual circumstances, and can help the patient and family members understand and navigate the benefits system.

When deciding among available treatment options, there is sometimes a difficult choice to be made between aggressive therapies and less aggressive therapies or no therapy. Aggressive therapies may prolong life, but often have potentially devastating side effects that compromise quality of life. Less aggressive therapies or no therapy at all may result in greater quality of life and comfort in the time remaining to the patient, although this time may be shorter than if a more aggressive therapy was chosen. It is critical that the patient and family be fully informed of the overall prognosis and not given false or misleading hope of a different outcome. As a patient nears the end of life, it is important that palliative care focus fully on relieving pain and preventing discomfort of any kind. This may be challenging for some medical professionals, since, quite often, they are trained to give lower doses of medication that do not completely alleviate the pain because of fears of addiction.

An essential component of the treatment decision process must be the consideration of spiritual, religious, philosophical, and cultural beliefs and norms of the patient. Those existential beliefs often play into the patient's feelings about advance directives, decisions about resuscitation, artificial nutrition and hydration, and other death-postponing measures.

Another important decision for end-of-life care is the setting in which the patient wishes to spend the last days of life. If it is the preference of patient and family to prepare for death in the intimate familiarity of home, it is critical that the attending physician be sensitive and supportive of that request and make the necessary preparations a part of the palliative care plan.

Organ donation is an option open to most people, even those dying of a prolonged or degenerative illness. In those circumstances, it is typically the corneas, skin, and bone that can be harvested. In the case of an individual who dies suddenly, more organs, including the heart, liver, lungs, and kidneys, as well as corneas, skin, and bone, can usually be donated to save the lives of others. In either situation, the individual may have decided to become an organ donor in advance, and may carry a standard organ donor card. It is best if the individual is able to communicate those wishes in advance to family members, as well as to the health care team. Some of the cultural concerns around organ donation can be easily allayed by the medical social worker or a member of the patient's behavioral health care team. The appearance of the body is not affected, so organ donation will not impact the ability to conduct a traditional funeral. In addition, there is no cost to the donor or family, and organ donation does not occur until after death (or brain death, in the event of trauma or violent death).

Although there is a tendency for the medical profession and the caretaking community to focus on the physical aspects of dying, it is of equal importance to attend to the individual's emotional and psychological needs during the dying process. People nearing the end of life often experience a wide range of emotions, from anger to fear to anxiety to anticipatory grief and bereavement to reactive, and sometimes clinical, depression. A goal of multidisciplinary palliative care is to assist the patient and family in finding meaning in both the living and the dying processes. It is essential to focus equally on all aspects of the individual's living and dying—to address the physical, the emotional, the spiritual, and the social. In addition to the practical aspects of caring for a person who is nearing the end of life, social and cultural beliefs about illness and death will impact all aspects of the process, as will the practicalities of taking care of a dying person. Any of these can place enormous stress on an already fragmented or fragile care or support system. The social work member of the palliative care team can provide professional support and assistance in managing the cascade of emotions and circumstances surrounding the impending death.

Palliative care providers view death as an integral part of life and strive to assist the dying patient and family with identifying, communicating openly about, and meeting physical, spiritual, and social/practical needs. Palliative care teams are multidisciplinary and are typically comprised of medical and nursing specialists and care providers, social workers and behavioral health care providers, physical and occupational therapists, pharmacists, and clergy. Not every discipline is necessarily represented on every palliative care team, as care plans are predicated on the needs of the individual over time. Among the aims of the team is to assist the patient with non-physical concerns, such as the creation of the patient's goals for the dying process, offering counseling, emotional, and spiritual support. The palliative care team also affords 24/7 access, so needs can be promptly and thoroughly met, and questions immediately addressed. The work of the team does not end with the death of the patient. They also offer help, support, and counseling to the bereaved caregivers.

FURTHER RESOURCES
Books

Kuebler, Kim K. *End of Life Care: Clinical Practice Guidelines.* Philadelphia: W. B. Saunders, 2001.

Web sites

American Family Physician. "Hospice Care in the Nursing Home." <http://www.aafp.org/afp/980201ap/keay. html> (accessed November 2, 2005).

American Journal of Critical Care. "Development of the American Association of Critical-Care Nurses' Sedation Assessment Scale for Critically Ill Patients." <http://ajcc.aacnjournals.org/cgi/content/short/14/6/ 531> (accessed November 2, 2005).

American Psychological Association. "Culturally Diverse Communities and End-of-Life Care." <http:// www.apa.org/pi/eol/fsculturallydiverse.pdf> (accessed November 2, 2005).

MEDSCAPE from WebMD. "Impact of a Proactive Approach to Improve End-of-Life Care in a Medical ICU." <http://www.medscape.com/viewarticle/447781> (accessed November 2, 2005).

On Our Own Terms—Moyers on Dying. "Final Days: The Dying Experience." <http://www.thirteen.org/onour ownterms/final/index.html> (accessed November 2, 2005).

The Robert Wood Johnson Foundation. "A Record of Accomplishment in End-of-Life Care." <http:// www.rwjf.org/newsroom/

featureDetail.jsp?featureID=886&type=> (accessed November 2, 2005).

TransWeb.org. "Non-Heart Beating Organ Donors: A Medical, Legal, and Ethical Overview." <http:// www.transweb.org/news/calendar/archive/ nhbd_text.html> (accessed November 2, 2005).

End-of-Life Issues

The Hospice Movement

Meeting minutes

By: Frederick Flatow

Date: June 2, 1998

Source: *National Cancer Institute. Division of Extramural Affairs.* "President's Cancer Panel Meeting Minutes. June 2, 1998, New Haven, Connecticut." <http:// deainfo.nci.nih.gov/advisory/pcp/archive/pcp0698/ minutes.htm> (accessed January 7, 2006).

About the Author: Frederick Flatow, the Medical Director of the Connecticut Hospice, addressed the President's Cancer Panel (PCP) meeting on the subject of the hospice movement. The PCP is a group of three experts appointed by the president, whose role is to advise the National Cancer Program, which aims to reduce the burden of cancer on the Unites States population. The panel is supported by the National Cancer Institute, and its meetings address issues of importance in cancer care. All the meetings are open to the public.

INTRODUCTION

Dame Cicely Saunders (1918–2005), the British physician who founded the modern hospice movement, considered death as natural as birth. She campaigned to relieve the physical and emotional suffering that so often accompanies the end of life or, put simply, to make death a life-affirming and peaceful process. Trained as a nurse, she drew inspiration from a Polish man, David Tasma, who was dying of cancer. The two became close and he left her £500 in his will to found a hospice—that is, a home or hospital that would be dedicated to the care of the dying. Nearly twenty years later, the dream was realized when St. Christopher's Hospice, in south-east London, opened its doors. The hospice now cares for around 1,600 patients and their families each year, and the hospice movement has become international.

Cicely Saunders trained in medicine and became the first doctor to devote her whole career to the care of the dying. Soon after qualifying she began research into pain control, working at St. Joseph Hospice in London where nursing care was provided for the dying. She developed the idea of anticipating and preventing pain through the detailed understanding of the various analgesic drugs so that patients could receive effective doses that would leave them alert. Saunders was also very aware of the link between physical and mental suffering. This recognition was the beginning of palliative care—the holistic care of those with advanced and progressive illness. Although the focus of medicine remained—and still does—on the curative side, by the late 1950s, Saunders was one of a handful of doctors on either side of the Atlantic who pushed ahead with development of palliative care. A deeply religious woman, Saunders did not believe in euthanasia. She held strongly that palliative care could give quality of life until its end, and that, perhaps, if palliative care were more widely available, as a right, the desire for euthanasia would dwindle. The excerpt given below was presented by Frederick Flatow at a President's Cancer Panel meeting. It describes the importance of palliative care in the United States and explains some of the challenges that remain in this area.

PRIMARY SOURCE

BACKGROUND

The Connecticut Hospice, Inc. located in Branford, Connecticut, is an active institution providing palliative care and end of life care to a large segment of the state's population. Palliative care seeks to prevent, relieve, reduce, or soothe the symptoms of a disease or disorder, but without curative intent. It attends to the emotional, spiritual, and practical needs and goals of patients and those close to them. It encompasses hospice care and end of life care, but is not necessarily restricted to those who are dying. Although dying is a fact of life, end of life care is inadequate in this country.

The hospice movement dates to the Middle Ages in Europe where hospices provided a place of shelter, sustenance, and care for travelers. In the 19th century, hospices served the dying, especially those with cancer. The modern hospice movement began in England in 1967 with the establishment of St. Christopher's Hospice in London by Dame Cecily Saunders.

The Connecticut Hospice, Inc. was the first hospice in the United States and was established as a home care hospice. In 1979, the first freestanding hospice was built in Branford as a companion to the home-based program.

With 52 beds, the freestanding hospice serves 1,200 patients per year. An equal number of patients are served in the home care program; approximately 250 patients per day receive care through the home-based program, representing 80 percent of total patient days.

In hospice care, the family and the patient together comprise the unit of care. As such, they are all involved in developing and implementing the care plan and in particular, in setting care-related goals. Care is provided by an interdisciplinary team that includes physicians, nurses, pastoral care, and the arts, among others. Bereavement care is provided to the family for one year following the death of the patient.

The mission of hospice is to provide care for the patient, giving comfort through relief of pain and symptom control and to provide emotional and spiritual support, it attempts neither to prolong life nor hasten death.

KEY POINTS

- Although studies of end of life care have been performed (such as the Institute of Medicine's study "Approaching Death and Improving Care at the End of Life") and a growing number of foundations are involved providing palliative care, there still is a great deal to be accomplished.
- In 1984, hospice care was added to the list of covered Medicare benefits; under the benefit, a physician must certify that the patient suffers from a terminal illness and has a life expectancy of six months or less. Addition of the hospice benefit eased the financial burden of end of life care for many Medicare patients over 65 years old; this population represents approximately two-thirds of patients at the Connecticut Hospice. Many patients under 65 years, however, lack insurance coverage for hospice care and resources available through the Medicaid program are constrained.
- Late referrals for hospice care pose persistent problems. In the inpatient unit at Connecticut Hospice, 22 percent of patients do not survive more than three days following admission. In such cases, the patient and family are deprived of valuable care and support.
- The skills used in the hospice care of cancer patients are applicable to the care of patients with other chronic illnesses and end-stage diseases, and the clinical profile of hospice populations is changing. Cancer-related hospice admissions in Connecticut have remained constant, but their percentage relative to total hospice admissions has declined from 90 percent to approximately 70 percent as admissions of patients with other illnesses have steadily increased.

- As a result of shortened acute hospital stays, patients and families often do not have adequate time to learn about the cancer diagnosis, prognosis, and the anticipated course of the illness. They are also deprived of time to contemplate the illness and begin to prepare for what lies ahead. Many patients, therefore, arrive at hospice care requiring a great deal of support and teaching, and they are often in a state of transition and denial.

- To better address patients' needs in the current health care environment, an intermediate level of hospice care should be developed. Patients are currently accepted into hospice care while they are receiving peritoneal dialysis, ventilator support, intravenous therapies with fluids and antibiotics, and total parenteral nutrition. With teaching and emotional and spiritual support in the face of terminal illness, patients and families usually realize the futility of such measures. These therapies are gradually terminated and good symptom control can be achieved.

- Of the approximately 2.4 million deaths in the United States each year, approximately 60 percent die in the hospital, often in intensive care units; 17 percent die in nursing homes and other chronic care facilities, some with limited staff and family support. Most of the remainder die at home and approximately 20 percent of these patients have hospice contact; this represents only 14 or 15 percent of total deaths. Although this percentage is growing, it remains inadequate.

- Most patients who die without hospice care experience poor pain control because their health care providers have limited knowledge of opiate pharmacology and poor pain assessment skills; further, communication with patients about pain tends to be inadequate. Many providers fear governmental oversight and restrictions related to prescribing controlled substances.

- According to findings from the Study to Understand Prognoses and Preferences for Treatment (SUPPORT) trial, funded by the Robert Wood Johnson Foundation and reported in the *Journal of the American Medical Association*, attempts to improve communication and information flow between physicians, patients, and families through the use of skilled nurse facilitators had little effect on major outcomes. Outcomes assessed included do-not-resuscitate (DNR) orders, days spent in the intensive care unit in futile states, pain control (approximately 50 percent of the patients were not comfortable), and poor use of hospital resources. Study results demonstrated that improved communication was inadequate to change established medical practice.

- End of life care is inadequately addressed in medical education. In 1994, only five of 126 medical schools provided a separate course on the care of the dying and only 25 percent of residency programs included courses on the medical and legal aspects of end of life care. Only 17 percent of training programs offered a hospice rotation, and many of these were elective.

- Physicians have a great deal of difficulty communicating bad news to patients and families. As a result, they may not always be the patient's advocate when the futility of active therapy becomes obvious. Sometimes physicians believe that a little more treatment will offer a little more hope and allay fear, but often the patient suspects otherwise. At this point, treatment goals should be refocused to include good supportive care, good symptom control, maintenance of independence for as long as possible, control of financial burdens to the extent possible, and reassurance that the patient will not be abandoned by the physician. Providers must never say that nothing more can be done for a patient. Although treatment with curative intent may be futile, a great deal can be done to make the patient more comfortable in the dying process.

- It is also true that the pursuit of active care in a futile situation can be a result of patient and family demands. Given the constant barrage of media coverage regarding medical successes and technologic advances, the public has an unrealistic view of what caregivers can accomplish. This is a major problem for our society.

- It is difficult to practice palliative medicine and acute care medicine simultaneously. In its purest form, the curative model concentrates on the goal of cure; clinical problems are approached as puzzles to be solved. The objective of the analysis is to identify and ameliorate the disease process itself and symptoms are treated as clues to the diagnosis. Multiple laboratory tests and imaging studies are primary, and subjective experiences become secondary. By contrast, in the palliative model, symptoms are phenomena and in their own right are worthy of treatment. The goal under this model is symptom control and the relief of suffering for the patient. Cure is admirable and the curative model is wholly appropriate when medicine is capable of restoring health completely. But the majority of medical problems fall between these extremes, requiring an approach that includes the multiple goals of medicine: health restoration, life preservation, rehabilitation, prevention, comfort, and caring.

- Medical education today overemphasizes the curative model; we need to regain a more compassionate and humanistic approach to care. The SUPPORT trial results suggest that the major efforts to change this balance should come early in the educational process. In this way, future physicians may be better skilled in both curative care and palliation, and be able to apply both models within a continuum of care.

An elderly patient at a hospice in Manchester, England, receives a visit from Princess Diana in the mid-1980s. ©TIM GRAHAM/CORBIS.

SIGNIFICANCE

Today 7,000–8,000 palliative care initiatives in more than 100 countries around the world are dedicated to relieving the end-of-life suffering of millions of patients. They are found in a number of settings—independent hospices offering community-based care and day care, in-patient facilities integrated in a hospital setting, and specialist teams who go out into the community offering their services. Many are supported by non-governmental organizations and charities, others by the health systems of the country involved.

There are many different aspects of hospice work. Symptom control is key—whether it is pain relief or treatment of problems such as breathlessness. Complementary therapies, such as art therapy and aromatherapy, offer both physical and mental benefit to the patient. Many hospices also offer education, research, and training to the medical community so that palliative care theory and practice can be more widely disseminated. Bereavement services are particularly important, since death raises many issues of a practical, social, financial, and emotional nature. Above all, the patient must be helped to die with comfort and dignity in the place of their choosing, which is, more often than not, their own home.

It is not just the patient that can benefit from hospice care. The needs of the family and carers must also be met. They may need training in simple nursing procedures, information about the patient's illness, and support to look after their own physical and mental health. The hospice is also a place where spiritual values are addressed, as these are central to the dying process. Whether or not individuals are religious, they will have spiritual concerns that they may wish to discuss and express through whatever means is appropriate.

The ideas of palliative care are now firmly established, but their practice is not as widespread as it should be. Everyone, surely, has a right to die pain-free and with dignity. Palliative care should, ideally, be free and easy to access. Indeed, demand will grow as the population ages and more people require end-of-life care. However sophisticated the latest scientific advances are, medicine will never be able to cure everything and eventually death will come to everyone. People often associate palliative care with cancer but, in fact, there are many other severe conditions for which it is also appropriate. In particular, there is an urgent need to relive the end-of-life suffering of those with HIV/AIDS, most of whom live in developing countries where palliative care provision is patchy, at best.

FURTHER RESOURCES

Books

Andreae, Christine. *When Evening Comes: The Evolution of a Hospice Volunteer*. New York: Thomas Dunne Books, 2000.

Clark, David. *Cicely Saunders*. Oxford: Oxford University Press, 2002.

Web sites

Hospice Information. "Facts and Figures." <http://www.hospiceinformation.info/factsandfigures.asp> (accessed January 7, 2006).

Lasers and Fiber Optics Enable Microsurgery and Keyhole Surgery

Photograph

By: Robert J. Herko

Date: 2000

Source: YAG Laser Laparoscopic Surgery. Getty Images. 2000.

About the Photographer: Robert J. Herko is a professional photographer who works with many large commercial, state government, and corporate clients. He utilizes thirty-five millimeter, medium, and large format photography equipment, as well as digital cameras and software to accomplish assignments. He has written several books on the techniques and practice of (commercial) photography.

INTRODUCTION

Prior to the last quarter of the twentieth century, virtually all surgical procedures were open, meaning that they involved an incision in the vicinity of the surgical site. Major surgeries, such as cholecystectomy (removal of the gall bladder), hysterectomy (removal of the uterus, with or without oophorectomy, or removal of the ovaries), organ transplants, or orthopedic procedures typically necessitated an incision that was a minimum of several inches long, often along with the use of muscle paralyzing agents in order to split the necessary muscle layers. The risk of infection was considerable, because of the exposed surface area for the duration of the procedure, postoperative pain was often debilitating, hospital stays were lengthy, and recovery was a several-week to several-month process. In addition, surgeries, because of their extensiveness, were lengthy procedures, increasing the risk and trauma to the patient by requiring prolonged periods of anesthesia.

With the evolution of the surgical microscope, as well as the adaptation of jeweler's tools for use in the operative setting, it became possible to perform microsurgery. Pioneered in the mid-1960s in California, microsurgery offered the opportunity to perform surgery on minute or fragile structures, such as blood vessels. In its early stages, it was often used to reattach partially (or completely) severed digits, toes, and, eventually, limbs. From precision and technically intricate surgery, it was a relatively short technological and evolutionary step to laparoscopic microsurgery, in which small incisions (typically less than one centimeter in length) are made in the skin, fine instruments, surgical microscopes and camera equipment are utilized to perform invasive surgery through the use of several small incisions (for tools and viewing equipment), dramatically reducing surgical risk, vastly shortening surgical procedure time, and significantly minimizing postoperative complications, recovery time, and hospital stays. Laparoscopic surgery, also called keyhole surgery, also enables the use of sedation and local anesthesia in place of general anesthesia in many cases. There has been considerable research on the safety and efficacy of keyhole surgery, and one of many the interesting findings from a German study has concerned post-surgical immune system function. The German team discovered that patients who had undergone keyhole surgery, when compared with patients who had the same procedures performed using traditional open methods, had a more intact general immune system after the procedure. In other words, although

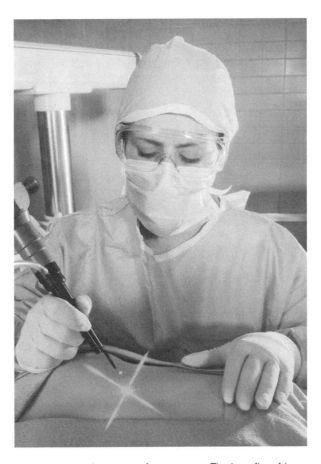

A doctor uses a laser to perform surgery. The benefits of laser surgery include less swelling, less bleeding, less pain, and quicker healing and recovery. ©ROYALTY-FREE/CORBIS.

there is always a systemic inflammatory response to any invasive procedure, there was less trauma to the overall immune system subsequent to the less invasive laparoscopic procedure. This suggests that the rate of infection among patients with laparoscopic procedures is likely to be less than for those with open surgical procedures.

Toward the end of the twentieth century, the construction and development of various types of lasers progressed to the point where they began to be used in the medical and surgical realm, where they have represented a significant technological advancement of the use of electrosurgical techniques.

PRIMARY SOURCE

LASERS AND FIBER OPTICS ENABLE MICROSURGERY AND KEYHOLE SURGERY

See primary source image.

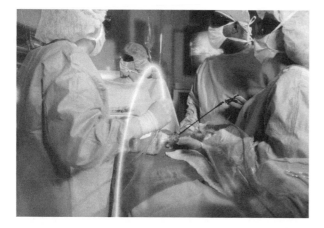

PRIMARY SOURCE

Lasers and Fiber Optics Enable Microsurgery and Keyhole Surgery. Photograph enhanced to show the laser beam during laparoscopic laser surgery. Laser and fiber optic technology enable physicians to visualize and perform many surgeries on internal organs with less damage to surrounding tissues than previous surgical techniques, resulting in smaller incisions and less recovery time. ROBERT J. HERKO/THE IMAGE BANK/GETTY.

SIGNIFICANCE

Laser surgery essentially involves the use of a focused beam of moving light energy in a manner akin to the use of an electronic scalpel or a cautery. The light energy heats the targeted tissue, and can cause it to vaporize. It is used to ablate or remove lesions, tumors, scars, and other types of masses, as well as to shrink or seal blood vessels. When used as a surgical scalpel, it cauterizes while it ablates, minimizing bleeding in most instances. Currently, there are several types of medical and surgical lasers being employed, each of which performs different types of functions. One of the most striking characteristics and distinct advantages of the use of the laser in surgery is precision. It is able to target a specific type or area of tissue, and leave the surrounding structures undisturbed. As a result, it is very useful in sealing blood vessels, removing small lesions and tissue structures and leaving intact surgical margins (cleanly removing all of the desired tissue)—thereby preventing the spread of tumors by leaving stray cells behind which can seed. Lasers are also used to ablate nerve endings in order to eliminate sources of chronic pain, to provide palliative relief in patients who are chronically or terminally ill, or to diminish postoperative pain. Lasers, particularly the argon type, are commonly used to correct vision defects (in place of corrective lenses or the now passé radial keratotomy procedure). In addition, surgical lasers are used for the removal

of unwanted body hair and to make cosmetic improvements in appearance (plastic or cosmetic surgery). Lasers are now used to vaporize benign and malignant lesions, skin growths, fibroid tumors, gallstones, endometrial cysts (endometriosis), and kidney stones. Lasers are now being used to treat dysfunctions of virtually every organ system, as well as to perform complicated bone and muscle (orthopedic) surgeries.

In the field of neurosurgery, the newest technological advance involves completely non-invasive surgery, through utilization of the gamma knife stereotactic radiosurgical procedure. Quite often, brain lesions and lesions of the central nervous system are either not amenable to surgery by virtue of their location, or their invasive surgical removal poses a risk that outweighs any potential benefit. The gammaknife is created by the precise intersection of 201 (high dose) gamma rays, causing the targeted lesion to dissipate and eventually dissolve. It is a single exposure radiation procedure.

FURTHER RESOURCES

Books

Townes, Charles H. *How the Laser Happened: Adventures of a Scientist.* New York, NY: Oxford University Press, 2002.

Web sites

American Society for Laser Medicine and Surgery. "History of ASLMS." <http://www.aslms.org/aslms/history.html> (accessed January 16, 2006).

BBC News. "Keyhole surgery 'boosts' organ donation." <http://news.bbc.co.uk/1/hi/health/705376.stm> (accessed January 16, 2006).

Shutterbug Software Tips. "Robert Herko: The Pro Goes Digital." <http://www.shutterbug.net/refreshercourse/software_tips/0603toppro/index.html> (accessed January 16, 2006).

BSE Inquiry: The Report, Executive Summary, Key Conclusions

Britain Investigates Mad Cow Disease and Variant Creutzfeldt-Jakob Disease

Government document

By: Committee of the BSE Inquiry

Date: 2000

Source: Committee of the BSE Inquiry. *Return to an Order of the Honourable the House of Commons dated October 2000 for the Report, Evidence and Supporting Papers of the Inquiry into the Emergence and Identification of Bovine Spongiform Encephalopathy (BSE) and Variant Creutzfeldt-Jakob Disease (vCJD) and the Action Taken in Response to it up to 20 March 1996.* London: Minister of Agriculture, Fisheries, and Food, 2000.

About the Author: The Committee of the BSE (commonly known as mad cow disease) Inquiry consisted of a judge, Lord Phillips of Worth Matravers, assisted by June Bridgeman, an expert in public administration, and pathologist Professor Malcolm Ferguson-Smith. The inquiry was announced in 1997 and began work the following year.

INTRODUCTION

Creutzfeldt-Jakob disease (CJD) is one of a rare group of fatal diseases known as the transmissible spongiform encephalopathies (TSEs). TSEs affect the brains of both humans and other animals, such as sheep and cattle. These diseases cause progressive loss of brain tissue, leading to a typical spongy appearance that is evident on post-mortem examination of the brain. CJD causes dementia and a range of neurological symptoms, including unsteadiness and jerky movements. It has always been present in humans and scientists have identified four different forms of the disease. Sporadic CJD primarily affects individuals over fifty and is of unknown cause. Familial CJD is inherited, and is characterized by a younger age of onset and a longer disease course than sporadic CJD. Iatrogenic (acquired through medical treatment) CJD occurs through contamination of the brain and nervous system with infected tissue via medical procedures, such as treatment with human growth hormone.

Finally, variant CJD (vCJD) is the form of the disease that emerged in Britain in the mid–1990s. It affects mainly younger people and has a longer course than other forms—an average of fourteen months between onset of symptoms and death. Early symptoms are often psychiatric, such as anxiety and depression, and there may be persistent pain, with odd sensations in the face and limbs. These are followed by more obvious neurological symptoms and progressive dementia.

The vCJD outbreak in Britain echoed the emergence in the 1950s of a strange and invariably fatal condition called kuru (meaning "trembling with fear") among the Fore people of New Guinea. After years of living among the group, American doctor Carlton Gajdusek (1923–)—who went on to win the

Nobel Prize for Medicine or Physiology in 1976—came to the conclusion that the disease was transmitted in the ritualistic eating of the brains of the deceased, a Fore funeral custom. He suspected that one of these brains, at least, must have belonged to someone with sporadic or familial CJD. There were some striking parallels between the emergence of vCJD and its links with the earlier epidemic bovine spongiform encephalopathy (BSE or mad cow disease), a TSE found in cattle. The latter prompted a public enquiry to investigate the cause of the outbreak and the main issues addressed are summarized in the excerpt below.

■ PRIMARY SOURCE

1. INTRODUCTION

1. In December 1986 a new animal disease was discovered by the State Veterinary Service. It quickly became known as Bovine Spongiform Encephalopathy or BSE. It caused irreversible 'spongy' changes to the brains of cattle and was invariably fatal. The public called it 'mad cow disease.'

2. For ten years the Government told the people:

- there is no evidence that BSE can be transmitted to humans;
- it is most unlikely that BSE poses any risk to humans; and
- it is safe to eat beef.

3. Then, on 20 March 1996, Mr Stephen Dorrell, the Secretary of State for Health, stood up in Parliament and announced that ten young people had contracted a new variant of the harrowing, and invariably fatal, Creutzfeldt-Jakob disease—vCJD—and that it was probable that they had caught BSE. Further cases of vCJD were to follow. By September 2000 there had been over 80 cases and the frequency with which they were being reported seemed to be growing.

4. For nearly three years we have been examining all that is known about the history of BSE and vCJD and looking at how these diseases were handled by the Government and by others in the period between December 1986 and 20 March 1996. This Report sets out what we have found.

5. In 1986 the United Kingdom had a worldwide reputation for competence and efficiency in animal health and welfare matters, and in the handling of outbreaks of serious animal diseases. Its skilled veterinarians and scientists, with the State Veterinary Service and veterinary laboratories in the forefront, operated established processes to identify, contain and eradicate animal diseases. They worked closely with farmers, veterinarians in private practice, public health professionals and the relevant industrial sectors.

They raised awareness, gave advice, and recommended statutory regulation where appropriate and compensation if need be. The process required well-established communication between advisers and practitioners, effective systems of animal surveillance and information-gathering, programmes of research, and detailed shared understanding of the links between animal and human health in all its aspects, including the food chain.

6. The UK also had highly regarded public health processes of long standing to handle outbreaks of human disease. These included surveillance, preventive action, such as immunisation and advice, and treatment. The health of the nation was at the heart of the remit of the Health Ministers and the professional responsibility of the four Chief Medical Officers, one for each part of the UK, who advised the Government.

7. What went wrong after the new fatal degenerative brain disease of cattle, BSE, emerged in 1986? Why did the announcement in 1996 that humans had probably been struck down by this particular brain disease find the guardians of public health and the world at large so shocked, and apparently unprepared, and leave the public so disillusioned? Our remit does not extend to the frantic diplomatic activity and other events after that date, but the consequences are still bearing heavily on the British economy and have inflicted tragedy on some families and left blighting uncertainty and fear hanging over many more.

8. The full extent and effects of the human disease will not be discernible for many years to come. Baffling questions include the unusual nature of Transmissible Spongiform Encephalopathies (TSEs), the reasons why specific people have become prey to the human version of BSE, and the extent to which others, particularly those exposed to the agent in the 1980s, may yet develop it. These difficult and still unresolved questions have hampered and bedevilled the whole course of events. What we do know is that as of September 2000, shortly before publication of this Report, over 80 victims of vCJD, most of them young, had had their lives destroyed and their families' happiness and hopes had been irreparably damaged.

9. BSE has been a peculiarly British disaster. Almost all the victims of vCJD have been in the United Kingdom. Only four other human victims of vCJD have been diagnosed elsewhere. Over 170,000 cattle have been diagnosed with BSE here compared with fewer than 1,500 abroad, mostly it would appear traceable to British-sourced animals or infected feed at the beginning of the British epidemic. So far, over 4.7 million British cattle have had to be slaughtered, and their carcasses burned or buried as potentially dangerous waste. A thriving high-quality cattle and meat export industry has been wiped out. The livelihood of thousands of farmers and businesses has been damaged. Even at this tail-end of the animal epidemic there were still over 2,000 cases of BSE notified in 1999 and cases continue to be reported as we write.

10. Small wonder that people want to know why it happened and whether it was handled wisely and well. In particular:

- What was the cause of BSE emerging and spreading country-wide? Was it as a result of intensive modern farming practices? Was it a result of inadequate regulation or lowered standards? Why is it so overwhelmingly the UK that has been afflicted?
- Seventy-four victims, mostly young people, have died of a new variant of CJD. Is it certain that they contracted this dreadful disease as a result of some form of connection with BSE? If so, why was it that they were struck down?
- Was the emergence of BSE and its threat to human health effectively handled by those whose responsibility it was to do so?
- Did individuals respond as they should have done, having regard to the state of knowledge at the time?
- Was the truth about the nature of BSE and the threat it posed concealed from the public? Has there been a cover-up?
- Did we make proper use of our scientists?
- Did our health and welfare services adequately cater for the special needs of those who contracted vCJD and their families?
- What lessons does the catastrophic course of events hold for public policy and the way we do things in the future?

11. These questions have been very much in our minds throughout this Inquiry, as we have explored exactly what happened day by day during the ten years that led up to the announcement of 20 March 1996 that BSE had probably generated a new and fatal human disease. Some questions, such as the numbers who are likely to succumb to the human disease, we are not in a position to answer. Our remit is to report to Ministers on the course of events and the adequacy of the responses to them in the light of knowledge at the time. We have sought to do so thoroughly and fairly. We have reviewed not only the years since BSE first emerged, but the events that led up to it. We have read a large number of scientific publications. We have sifted 3,000 files of documents, and have studied 1,200 statements and many contributions from the public, whom we have sought to keep fully up to date with every stage of our proceedings. We have listened to 138 days of public oral evidence from 333 witnesses.

SIGNIFICANCE

The BSE Inquiry was comprehensive, thorough, and open (proceedings being updated daily on the

A poster at a McDonald's in London, England, informs customers in 1996 that it will no longer be serving British beef. ©POLAK MATT/CORBIS SYGMA.

Internet). It was complex in that it dealt with an interaction between agricultural, veterinary, and medical practice, as well as government policy. Scientists assume that TSEs are caused by an entity known as a prion, which is a corrupted form of a normal brain protein. The diseases are less well understood than infections caused by bacteria or viruses, which made analysis of the science behind the BSE and vCJD epidemics especially challenging.

The picture that emerged from the inquiry was, briefly, that vCJD is, indeed, the human form of BSE (mad cow disease). The inquiry concluded that infected material—either from sheep infected with scrapie (a sheep TSE) or from BSE-infected cattle—was incorporated into cattle feed. Further, it was found that changes in the processing of carcasses used for animal feed were the likely cause of this contamination. Products, such as burgers and pies, made from so-called mechanically rendered meat (MRM) were contaminated with BSE because MRM typically will contain traces of nervous system tissue such as

brain or spinal cord. People consuming these MRM-containing products had then become infected with vCJD. Fortunately, the epidemic, though tragic for the victims and their families, was limited by steps such as the wholesale slaughtering of infected cattle and a ban on imports of British beef.

The inquiry led to a variety of developments. For example, in an attempt to restore public confidence, a Food Standards Agency was set up in the United Kingdom to advise on food safety issues. Regulatory authorities are moving towards eliminating animal products from the manufacture of medicines and other items destined for human consumption. The BSE Inquiry also led to changes in the supply of blood and blood products, in an attempt to screen out donors that are, unknowingly, carrying vCJD. Typically, TSEs have a long incubation time—in the case of kuru, up to forty years. As a result, it is not clear whether more cases of vCJD will emerge. The BSE episode highlighted the problem of zoonotic disease—that is, the transmission of disease from animals to humans. The recent outbreak of "bird flu" suggests that this is a continuing concern, and the lessons learned from the BSE Inquiry will not be forgotten.

FURTHER RESOURCES
Books
Ridley, Rosalind M., and Harry F. Baker. *Fatal Protein. The Story of CJD, BSE, and Other Prion Diseases*. Oxford: Oxford University Press, 1998.

Periodicals
Brown, Paul. "Bovine Spongiform Encephalopathy and variant Creutzfeldt-Jakob Disease." *British Medical Journal* 322 (2001): 841–844.

Web sites
U.S. Food and Drug Administration. "Bovine Spongiform Encephalopathy (BSE)." <http://www.fda.gov/oc/opacom/hottopics/bse.html> (accessed November 10, 2005).

A Revised System for Reporting Pap Test Results

Early Detection of Cancer through Screening

Magazine article

By: Caroline McNeil and Nicole Gottlieb

Date: April 24, 2002

The "pap" test is named for Dr. George N. Papanicolaou, who devised the procedure. ©BETTMANN/CORBIS.

Source: Caroline McNeil and Nicole Gottlieb. "Bethesda 2001: A Revised System for Reporting Pap Test Results." *BenchMarks* 2 (April 24, 2002). <http://www.cancer.gov/newscenter/benchmarks-vol2-issue4> (accessed February 21, 2006).

About the Author: This article was written by contributors to *BenchMarks*, the magazine of the U.S. National Cancer Institute (NCI). The NCI is a component of the National Institutes of Health (NIH), one of eight agencies that compose the Public Health Service (PHS) in the Department of Health and Human Services (DHHS). Established under the National Cancer Act of 1937, it is the federal government's principal agency for cancer research and training.

INTRODUCTION

The cervical smear was introduced by the Greek-American pathologist George Papanicolaou (1883–1962) (hence the name 'Pap' smear). In the 1920s, Papanicolaou began to study cellular abnormalities in samples taken from women with cancer of the cervix (the neck of the uterus). The technique that Papanicolaou developed for taking a cervical smear has changed little since his time. The physician or nurse spreads the walls of the vagina using an instrument called a speculum and then takes a sample of cells from the cervix by inserting a wooden spatula or brush through the speculum. The sample is then "smeared" onto a glass slide and examined under a microscope for abnormalities in the cells. Sometimes these abnormalities are slight and if the smear is repeated the cells are found to have reverted to a normal appearance. At other times the abnormality reveals a pre-cancerous condition that needs treating or even cancer itself—which has a much greater chance of being cured if found at this early stage.

In 1943, Papanicolaou published an account of his work in *Diagnosis of Uterine Cancer by the Vaginal*

Smear. Following this publication, the cervical smear started to become a routine health screening test for women both in the U.S. and elsewhere. Before this, cervical cancer was once of the most common causes of cancer death among American women. The number of cases began to fall sharply once screening for cervical cancer with the Pap smear became well established. Cervical cancer is now considered rare. American Cancer Society statistics indicate about 10,000 new cases per year of cervical cancer occur; up to 4,000 of which will prove fatal. Women who have never been screened are most at risk of death from cervical cancer.

No screening test is 100 percent accurate. Cervical smears are examined by pathology technicians under a microscope, so there is inevitably an objective element in the result. Faulty handling or inadequate sampling also may contribute to inaccuracy. In addition, there is sometimes confusion as to how results should be interpreted. Thus, a few women receive either a false positive or a false negative result. A false positive means a woman is thought to have pre-cancer or cancer when she is, in fact, healthy. False-positive test results can cause a great deal of anxiety and unnecessary medical investigation. A false negative means that a cancer has been missed, and this may place a woman's life at risk if the missed cancer spreads. The article below describes recommendations, called the Bethesda 2001 System, for the manner in which pathologists should describe smear results.

▌ PRIMARY SOURCE

BenchMarks interviewed Diane Solomon, M.D., of the Division of Cancer Prevention at the National Cancer Institute (NCI), who is the first author on the *JAMA* article titled "The 2001 Bethesda System: Terminology for Reporting Results of Cervical Cytology." Dr. Solomon has worked extensively in the field of cervical cytology and coordinated the development of The Bethesda System in 1988, as well as its revision in 1991 and the current 2001 revision. Dr. Solomon talked to *BenchMarks* about the changes included in Bethesda 2001 and what the revised system will mean for women and their doctors.

Why is the publication of these two papers considered a "milestone"?

Dr. Solomon: This is a milestone because it's the first time, to my knowledge, that we have collaborative development of terminology that the lab uses and management guidelines for clinicians based on that terminology. I think that in this collaborative development, each process improved the other—there was cross-fertilization. The involvement of clinicians in the revisions to the Bethesda terminology as well as the participation of pathologists in

the development of clinical guidelines will result in better communication between the laboratory and clinicians because both groups are invested in the terminology and the guidelines.

How, specifically, will these publications improve care of patients with Pap test abnormalities?

Dr. Solomon: It will improve the care of women because these guidelines are based on the most up-to-date information we have from research and clinical trials in the area of cervical abnormalities.

A specific example would be in the area of ambiguous test results. We have information from a clinical trial sponsored by the National Cancer Institute that identified a group of women with ambiguous test results that are at higher risk of having an underlying high-grade lesion, or abnormality, that needs to be treated. That finding led to a new term in the new 2001 Bethesda System called "atypical squamous cells cannot exclude HSIL" (ASC-H), which identifies this small number of women.

The guidelines, in turn, recommend that these women be managed differently based on this increased risk. That would be an example of how we have research coming together to inform terminology, and which then becomes the basis for the development of clinical management guidelines.

In addition, the terminology clarifies the communication between the laboratory and the clinician, so that there's less confusion about what the Pap test findings mean— their clinical significance. For instance, in the previous version of Bethesda, there was a category known as benign cellular changes. This caused a lot of confusion amongst clinicians who really weren't quite sure whether this was "Negative" or whether this reflected something that really required management—was this woman at increased risk? In the 2001 version of Bethesda, benign changes are more clearly identified as negative for atypical cervical changes. Even if there's inflammation that's causing some cellular changes, the findings are categorized as negative. Hopefully this will reduce concern and confusion in communications between the laboratory and clinician.

The fact that this is a uniform terminology that has been adopted by the vast majority of laboratories in the United States means that no matter where a woman is undergoing cervical screening, the terms will be the same.

Are you confident that most laboratories will use the new system?

Dr. Solomon: If past versions of The Bethesda System are any guide, over 90 percent of laboratories in the United States will use some form of the 2001 Bethesda System....

How does Bethesda 2001 reflect our current knowledge of the biology of cervical cancer?

Dr. Solomon: We've learned a lot over the past 10 to 15 years about the biology of cervical cancer. We know that cervical cancer is clearly related to infection with a virus known as human papillomavirus, or HPV. While HPV is the main cause of cervical cancer, having an HPV infection does not necessarily lead to cervical cancer. In fact, HPV infection is very, very common, while cervical cancer is not. We understand that most people who are infected with HPV have the infection, but only transiently—it goes away on its own. The person's immune system responds to the presence of the virus and, over the course of a year or so the infection resolves and the virus is no longer found. In some small number of cases the virus persists and cell changes occur that may lead to a precursor lesion to cancer. If not treated such precursor lesions may eventually lead to cancer.

The Bethesda terminology reflects our understanding of the role of HPV and cellular changes in the development of cervical cancer by emphasizing the fact that there is a dichotomy of low-grade lesions and high-grade lesions in the spectrum of squamous cell changes. Low-grade lesions are, by and large, transient infections with HPV that may cause some cellular changes. But in most cases the infection will go away on its own.

Uncommonly, HPV persists and you may have more abnormal cell changes known as a high-grade squamous intraepithelial lesion, or HSIL. This indicates that the HPV infection has not gone away on its own. This is the lesion that needs to be recognized and treated so that cancer never even develops.

The low-grade and high-grade dichotomy in the spectrum of squamous changes is not something new in Bethesda 2001. It actually was introduced in earlier versions of Bethesda but there has been controversy as to whether this was the proper categorization of the spectrum of squamous changes. What we've learned over the past ten years is that yes, the low-grade/high-grade dichotomy is actually the best way to translate what we know about the development of cervical cancer precursors and cervical cancer into terminology for cervical cancer screening. So sometimes we use knowledge to change things and sometimes our new findings actually just reinforce what we had before. In this case, our new knowledge has confirmed the terminology in earlier versions of Bethesda.

Were there concerns about previous Bethesda Systems?

Dr. Solomon: The original Bethesda System introduced a term known as "Atypical Squamous Cells of Undetermined Significance," which is a very long way of saying that the laboratory is not quite sure what the findings represent. This term has been shortened to an acronym known as ASCUS, which clinicians as well as laboratories have found very frustrating because it's not quite clear how to manage women who have this ambiguous ASCUS result.

And in fact the National Cancer Institute sponsored a clinical trial of women who have ASCUS, as well as low-grade squamous findings, to ask the question "What is the best way to manage women with these types of test results?" We've certainly learned a lot based on ALTS [ASCUS/LSIL Triage Study], which in fact has now informed the development of guidelines for managing women with these findings. So this is a case where the Bethesda terminology really prompted a clinical trial that has provided data that in turn was used in the development of clinical management guidelines.

It's a frustrating fact for laboratorians, clinicians, doctors, and women that there are limitations to any medical test. No screening test is perfect, and one of the limitations in terms of the Pap test, or cervical cytology, is that the findings are not always crystal clear. There are cell changes that are ambiguous and we have to recognize that. We have to try to reduce that ambiguous category to the lowest possible number, but we also have to acknowledge that that's one of the limitations of the test. I think the ALTS findings help us deal with that reality of the limitation of cervical screening.

Do you foresee another revision of The Bethesda System?

Dr. Solomon: Not immediately! However, it is true that The Bethesda System is a living document, and that means that it is flexible and can incorporate new developments or new findings based on research. But I think that with this third revision that we have reached a point where we have incorporated all that we currently know about HPV, about the development of cervical precancers and cancers. But I think it's also important to recognize that should there be new data that comes to light, The Bethesda System is ready to evolve and incorporate new findings....

What do you see as the next steps related to cervical cancer screening?

Dr. Solomon: We need to continue efforts to reach women who have not been screened. Unscreened women are among those at highest risk for cervical cancer.

We also need to reevaluate screening recommendations for how often women should have Pap tests done, when they should begin having Pap tests done, and if they ever reach a point at which Pap tests are no longer needed. I think one of the key areas that we need to address with regard to screening, is the question of how we incorporate new technologies into new cervical cancer screening recommendations.

What do you see as the next steps in terms of research in cervical cancer screening?

Dr. Solomon: I think one of the most exciting areas in cervical cancer research is the work on developing vaccines against human papillomavirus, or HPV, which we know is the cause of cervical cancer. I think that this is extremely promising and has the potential for having a tremendous impact in terms of women's health—both in the United States, as well as worldwide.

In the United States we're fortunate to have a strong cervical cancer screening infrastructure, where women have, by and large, access to Pap testing. But in many parts of the world that lack such an infrastructure, cervical cancer is the number one cause of cancer deaths among women. Development of a vaccine would have a significant impact on reducing deaths due to cervical cancer worldwide.

SIGNIFICANCE

The Pap smear was the earliest example of cancer screening, and it is now possible to screen for various other cancers. However, the value and applicability of screening varies with the type of cancer. Many experts agree that breast and colon cancer screening should be recommended to the general population, while screening for ovarian cancer is best applied to higher risk groups. Prostate cancer screening using the prostate specific antigen (PSA) test is popular with the public and some physicians recommend it, but there is some debate over its value in predicting disease when no symptoms are present.

Screening is a means of detecting cancer early, before symptoms arise. Tests are, therefore, given to many people who do not actually have cancer and will not develop it. It is important that screening tests are as non-invasive as possible to minimize any health risk from the test and also to encourage people to receive them. Some tests rely on physical examination and pose no risk to the patient (unless an inaccurate result is given). For instance, a dentist should always check for oral cancer during a routine exam, and physicians and nurses can check a woman's breasts for lumps that may indicate that cancer is present.

Some screens depend upon imaging techniques, such as mammography for breast cancer and computed tomography for lung cancer. Colon cancer screening can be done by a lab test known as the fecal occult blood test or by colonoscopy, where the colon is examined by inserting a thin tube equipped with a miniature camera. This carries a small risk of perforating the colon, and may eventually be superseded by "virtual" colonoscopy where computed tomography images of the colon are collected.

Laboratory screening tests are generally based on measuring levels of cancer-related substances in the blood called biomarkers. The best known is the PSA test for prostate cancer risk. Another is the CA125 test for women at risk of ovarian cancer, which is usually combined with ultrasound imaging. Many biomarker tests are under development for bladder and other cancers. The estimates of the number of cancers that can be avoided by screening vary between 3 and 35 percent. More research is still needed to determine the optimal frequency of screening and to develop new and more accurate tests.

FURTHER RESOURCES
Periodicals

Solomon, D., et al. "The 2001 Bethesda System: Terminology for Reporting Results of Cervical Cytology." *Journal of the American Medical Association* 287 (2002): 2114–2119.

Web sites

American Cancer Society. "Overview: Cervical Cancer. How Many Women Get Cancer of the Cervix?" <http://www.cancer.org/docroot/CRI/content/CRI_2_4_1X_What_are_the_key_statistics_for_cervical_cancer_8.asp?rnav=cri> (accessed December 3, 2005).

National Cancer Institute. "Cancer Screening Overview. Health Professional Version." <http://www.cancer.gov/cancertopics/pdq/screening/overview/healthprofessional> (accessed December 3, 2005).

Amy's Story-Anorexia

Newspaper article

By: Amy

Date: 2002

Source: "Amy's Story-Anorexia." *Girl's Life.* Baltimore: Monarch Avalon, February-March, 2002.

About the Author: Amy is a young woman from East Lansing, Michigan, who describes her experience of anorexia and her recovery in therapy at the Renfrew Center in Philadelphia, which is dedicated to the treatment of people with eating disorders and depression. She is a talented artist who has exhibited and sold paintings. Amy won a scholarship to Savannah

Model Nieves Alvarez overcame anorexia and later wrote a book about her experience. ©CARRUSAN/CONTIFOTO/CORBIS SYGMA.

College of Art and Design, but had to give up her place because of her illness. Amy attended Michigan State University and hopes to eventually return to art school.

INTRODUCTION

Anorexia nervosa is an eating disorder involving severe food restriction. The German psychiatrist Hilde Bruch, who moved to the United States in the 1930s, began to raise awareness of the condition with her classic text *Eating Disorders: Obesity, Anorexia Nervosa and the Person Within* written in 1973. Before this, the disorder tended to go unrecognized. However, anorexia probably has a long history. The medieval mystics believed that self-starvation would bring them closer to God. One notable example was St. Catherine of Siena (1347–1380) who was said to have gone without solid food for eight years.

Public awareness of anorexia probably began with the death of the American singer Karen Carpenter in 1983 from heart failure brought on by the condition. After years of self-starvation, for which she would eventually receive treatment, Carpenter weighed 108 pounds when she died. Amy describes that she understood the dangers of anorexia. Indeed, she had hung posters around her school for Eating Disorders Awareness Week. But, as she admits, denial is a hallmark of the condition and recovery is only possible once the individual admits what she is doing to herself.

Amy's story is a confessional that is intended to help other young women who may recognize her experience. Anorexia is a disease that affects primarily young females (whites are affected more often than women of other ethnicities) who are often exposed to tremendous media pressures to be thin. Thus, in the girls' magazine, Amy's story targets the primary correct demographic audience at risk for anorexia.

PRIMARY SOURCE

Anorexia is like you're running down a hill, and all this wind is going through your hair, and it's exciting. But all of a sudden, you're going too fast and start to spiral out of control. You fall. Then you're just sitting on the ground, shocked, with all these bruises.

If you knew me in high school, you'd never think I had any problems. I was the girl who had it all—a near-perfect GPA, the lead in the school play and an editorial position on the school newspaper. I was also involved in several clubs and activities, like Students for Environmental Action, Student Congress and yearbook. I even had a cool boyfriend—everyone in school said we were "the perfect couple."

I'm also a painter. I've won several school and state art awards. My work has been displayed in local galleries, as well as the Art Institute of Chicago. I've even sold some of my paintings for hundreds of dollars.

My friends saw me as a stable, happy-go-lucky girl—the one everyone went to for help with their problems. But I hardly ever talked to my friends about my problems, mainly because I didn't have any—or at least none I could admit.

For as long as I can remember, I've wanted to do everything under the sun—and be the best at it. If I got a C, I'd be really hard on myself— much harder than my parents were on me. But by fall 2000—the first semester of my senior year—I was totally exhausted and burnt out. In addition to keeping up my GPA and extracurricular activities, I was under a tight deadline to get out numerous art school applications and put together a portfolio of my paintings. My parents made it pretty clear they wanted me to get a scholarship, since paying for college would be a challenge.

Plus, things weren't so great at home. I'd always had a terrible relationship with my dad. I felt like he ignored me most of the time. He could also be pretty scary. He screamed at me for little things, like leaving crumbs on the kitchen counter after making a snack. I'd tell him when he hurt my feelings, but he'd just walk away and slam the door. On top of it all, he and my mom were fighting a lot, too.

But the thing is, I didn't want to burden my friends with my family problems because most of their parents are divorced. I felt lame complaining about my bickering parents—at least they were still together.

It was hard to be at school and even harder to be at home. As a result, I began eating less. I'd be too upset to eat at home because my parents were always bickering at the dining room table. I didn't eat much outside the house either because I was rushing around all the time. Starving myself wasn't my actual goal at first—just more of a response to everything going on in my life. But I started losing weight.

I didn't even realize I was shedding pounds until my friends and family began telling me how great I looked. Even my dad complimented me, which felt so good. So I made a conscious effort to keep my weight down by only eating low-fat foods. Soon, my clothes got even looser. Then I became vegetarian, also cutting out all foods with chemicals and preservatives. I lost even more. I felt I had finally found something I could completely control—my weight. I could restrict what I ate, how much I ate and when I ate. Even though my life felt crazy, I could do this one thing very well and, initially, I got a high from this accomplishment. I weighed myself all the time. Gaining or losing a single pound determined my mood for the whole day.

For a month or so, everyone kept complimenting me. But before long, my clothes were like sacks. By spring, jeans that fit perfectly in the fall were hanging off my hips. My mother told me I looked too skinny and that she was worried about how much weight I had lost. My friends said the same thing.

But, rather than admitting there was a problem, I lied. I told everyone—my family, my friends, even my boyfriend—that I'd lost weight because of this winter flu I couldn't shake. Of course, the reason I was sick was because I hadn't eaten much in four months. But I assured everyone I was fine. I made a special effort to eat snacks around friends and family, pretending it was no big deal. Then I'd eat nothing else for the rest of the day.

Looking back, I can't believe I was such a liar. I'd always been a terrible liar, never able to keep a straight face. But I quickly became a master of deception because I didn't want to give up my food restrictions. That's the only thing I felt I could count on.

What's weird is that I grew up totally aware of the dangers of anorexia. My mom taught me all the warning signs of eating disorders and how important it is to have a good body image. I read magazine articles and saw TV shows about eating disorders. I remember watching a movie in health class about the dangers of anorexia. I even hung warning posters around school during Eating Disorder Awareness Week. But I never connected my own weight loss to anorexia. Denial, of course, is a symptom of the disease.

By second semester of my senior year, I had totally stopped listening to my body's signals. I ignored my grumbling belly and hunger pangs. I was exhausted from not having enough nutrients in my body. I barely had enough energy to dance (I love to dance) or do my artwork. It all just felt like it took too much effort. I was always freezing cold because my body lacked the necessary fat to keep me warm. People thought I wore heavy layers to hide my body, but it was mostly because I was just so darn cold!

I knew the calorie count of practically everything, and would typically only have an apple and some water for each meal. A voice in my head kept telling me the less food I let touch my lips, the more stable and safe I would be.

But my body was far from safe. My friends and family kept telling me I was too skinny, but no one could force me to eat. And, to be honest, it made me feel powerful that I could ignore their pleas and starve myself.

It got to a point that I couldn't even pretend to be happy anymore. While I was rehearsing for the school play, I got really sick and had to see a doctor. Both he and the nurses told me I was too thin, but I lied and told them I was going to gain the weight back. "Not a problem," I told them.

Having an eating disorder is so lonely—losing weight is the only thing that really matters. I forgot all about my passions and interests, friends and family. All I had was the ability to make myself sicker.

Still, I scored a scholarship to the Savannah College of Art and Design and went despite my parents' concerns about my health. By this time, I was only 90–some pounds. Even as my bones poked out from under my skin, I could not admit to anyone—including myself—how incredibly sick I was. I couldn't concentrate on lectures. I couldn't remember a thing I had read moments after reading it. Just climbing a set of stairs made my heart race. I was always exhausted. I didn't even want to paint—the reason I had worked so hard to attend Savannah in the first place.

I cried myself to sleep each night, wanting to get better but knowing I was in way over my head. When I would finally doze off, I believed there was a chance I wouldn't wake up in the morning.

One afternoon, while riding the local bus in Savannah, a stranger told me I'd better start taking care of myself. That was the moment I totally broke down. I knew I needed help. I told my parents to come get me. I felt like the ultimate failure.

As I packed, I found a photo of myself at age 15, before the disorder. I was taking classes at an art institute in Chicago, and I was with two friends in the picture. I was covered in paint, and I was glowing because I was so happy—I knew exactly who I was and what I wanted. I suddenly realized how unfamiliar those feelings of joy had become to me. I wanted them back. I wanted to live.

My parents brought me home and took me to The Renfrew Center in Philadelphia, a national institute dedicated to educating and treating people with eating disorders and depression. The morning I left for Renfrew, I stood shaking in the shower. I made a bargain with God. I promised to love life again if he would help me get through this.

Those first days at the center were incredibly painful. I had spent so much time lying to myself and everyone else. Then, all of a sudden, I was forced to be honest. I had to see a therapist every other day and open up about my sickness for the first time. I knew I had to be truthful because I had reached a point where I could really understand how bad off I was. I wanted to change.

I spent a lot of time in group therapy, too. I'd talk about how lonely and upsetting the past year had been. Confiding in the other patients helped me begin to heal. It was like we'd known each other forever. We'd all been through so many of the same experiences. It was like having a bunch of sisters who unconditionally loved me. I finally felt comfortable asking for help. I could say, "I'm having a rough day. Could you help me?" and these girls would hug me without any questions.

At Renfrew, we were forced to finish everything on our plates. We were weighed every morning to make sure we were gaining weight. If not, we were switched to a meal plan with even more food. I wanted to eat, but I couldn't. My body wasn't used to eating, and it was incredibly difficult. Food came back up my throat right after I swallowed.

My meal plan was increased again and again until I was up to 4,000 calories a day. The food shocked my system. I had no idea how much internal damage I had done to my body. All of my organs—heart, brain, liver—were starving.

But I forced myself to eat and, gradually, was able to keep food down. I kept at it and, much to my surprise, I felt better once my body accepted the food. I smiled for the first time in a year and even joked with the other girls. I=remembered what joy felt like.

Patients' families were required to get counseling, too. It was time for my family to deal with our issues. After a particularly rough therapy session, my father said to me, "You don't have to be sick for me to notice you," and asked me to forgive him. He was crying, and I realized I wanted to forgive him. That was huge. I also realized that, in many ways, my anorexia was an attempt to find out if

my family, friends, and boyfriend would still love me even if I weren't perfect. As it turns out, starving myself was a calculated way for me to get attention without asking for it.

After three weeks at Renfrew (the average stay), I returned home. I now have my own nutritionist and a meal plan I follow to make sure my weight stays stable. Once a week, I go to both a family therapist and my own therapist. Eating still isn't easy, especially since my body was so messed up that I had to eat tons of food to gain even a few pounds. But it helps that I stay in close touch with my friends from the center, and we exchange letters of inspiration.

It's around Christmas now, and I've been in recovery for three months. I know I have a long way to go. Anorexia doesn't just go away. That's why experts refer to "recovery" rather than a "cure." The truth is, 40 percent of anorexics relapse within four years.

I got so used to seeing my body a certain way that sometimes I get anxious about gaining weight. But I'm trying to change the way I look at the added pounds. Rather than thinking, "I'm gaining weight," or "getting fat," I think "I deserve to take up space and make a place for myself."

Physically, I'm pretty lucky. My vital signs are good. I sleep soundly and feel calm. However, I do worry that I have done permanent damage to my body. My menstrual cycle stopped during my weight loss. I just got it back but the doctors don't know if I'll be able to have kids. I really want children, so not having them is a sad and scary thought.

I'm taking small steps toward my future. I'm attending Michigan State University next semester rather than going back to Savannah. I don't want any major changes in my life while I'm trying to get healthier. But, I do hope to eventually transfer back into an art school. At Renfrew, I was painting again, mostly as a form of therapy. And now that I am eating, my energy is back, as well as my desire to create.

Not all of my old high school friends stuck by me, but my closest friends have. They are thrilled I'm in treatment. I feel terrible for all the lies and for shutting them out. As for my boyfriend, he supported me even at my worst, and I consider him my best friend.

My dad and I are still working on our relationship. He deals with his own issues in therapy, and it helps him better relate to me. We hang out at coffee shops, museums or CD stores. I never thought I'd say this, but I enjoy spending time with him. We make time daily to share our concerns.

So far, my life has not turned out at all as I expected. But I'm tons stronger than I thought I was. And I know it's OK, even necessary, to ask for help when you're struggling. So many girls with eating disorders are caretakers; pretending things are fine in their own lives. But if you are suffering, you have to admit things aren't fine. You owe it to yourself to be honest and to be your best.

SIGNIFICANCE

There are aspects to Amy's story which will be very familiar to health professionals dealing with anorexia. Her weight falls below 100 pounds due to chronic self-starvation. It is usual for those with anorexia to fall below eighty-five percent of their ideal body weight. She is always cold, tired, and hungry (it is not true that anorexics do not feel hunger). Anorexia can lead to organ failure from the stress of starvation, and mortality rates are up to twenty percent. Amy may not have suffered permanent damage, but she is worried about infertility, which is a common complication of the condition.

Losing weight makes Amy feel confident and in control of her surroundings. This is a common feature among anorexics. A disturbed body image, where she still sees herself as overweight even though she becomes thinner, is also common. People with anorexia are often talented, high achieving perfectionists, like Amy. However, lack of self esteem is a problem, and there are often family tensions and conflicts present.

Therapy, both family and individual, is often helpful to an anorexic, along with a careful re-feeding program under direct medical supervision. However, relapse rates can be as high as forty percent within four years, which is why recovering anorexics need continuing medical and psychiatric therapy. It is interesting that anorexia is far more common in Western cultures where fashion models, pop stars, and actresses are often very thin. These famous women are often seen as role models by impressionable girls. What makes the issue even more complex is that many Western-developed nations are also battling the problem of obesity, and publicity is often directed at methods of combating overeating.

FURTHER RESOURCES

Books

Gottlieb, Lori. *Stick Figure*. New York: Penguin Group, 2001.

Periodicals

Striegel-Moore, Ruth H., and Cynthia M.Bulik. "Anorexia Nervosa. Special Issue." *International Journal of Eating Disorders*. 37 (2005):S1–S104.

Web sites

MayoClinic.com. "Eating Disorders." <http://www.mayo clinic.com/health/eating-disorders/DS00294> (accessed November 1, 2005).

X Ray of the Lungs of a Coal Miner

Occupational Fatalities Decline

Photograph

By: Chuck Nacke

Date: November 17, 2003

Source: *Time&Life* Pictures/Getty Images. "An X-Ray of the Lungs of a Coal Miner Suffering From Black Lung." Submitted 17 November 2003.

About the Photographer: Chuck Nacke is a photographer and photojournalist who began his career at age 15, when he began submitting pieces to a newspaper in his home town. He has traveled the globe as an industrial, corporate, and commercial photographer.

INTRODUCTION

The United States Department of Labor (DOL) was created in 1913;its goals were "to foster, promote, and develop the welfare of working people, to improve their working conditions, and to enhance their opportunities for profitable employment." From the outset, it had a federal mandate to improve workplace safety and to decrease occupational fatalities. During the first year that the DOL was in existence, the total workforce numbered between 30 and 40 million, and there were a total of approximately 23,000 occupational fatalities. It has been nearly a century since the DOL embarked on its mission of improved workplace safety, and occupational fatalities have decreased dramatically—a fact that is even more meaningful when considering the increase in the nation's workforce (individuals who are employed either within or outside of the home).

At the turn of the century, roughly 140 million Americans were gainfully employed, representing an increase of one hundred million workers. In 1913, the workforce contained a significant number of children who worked full-time (counted by the DOL for statistical purposes so long as they were at least age ten); by the twenty-first century, youth below the age of sixteen were prohibited from employment by the majority of industries, and could seldom be employed full-time except during vacations from school. During the

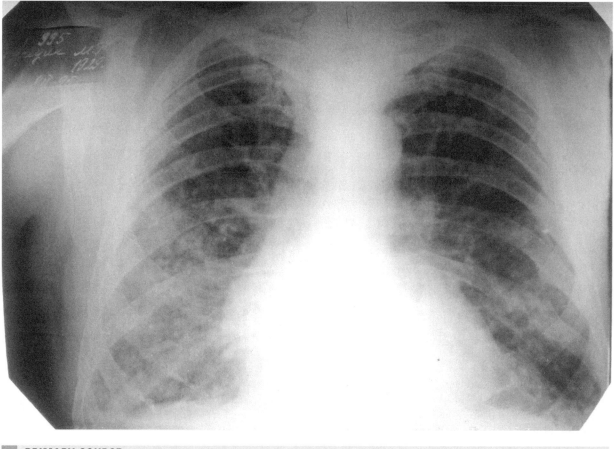

PRIMARY SOURCE

X Ray of the Lungs of a Coal Miner. An x ray showing the lungs of a coal miner suffering from coal worker's pneumoconiosis, often called black lung disease. The Occupational Safety Health Administration enforced regulations that drastically reduced injury and death from black lung disease and other occupational hazards during the twentieth century. CHUCK NACKE/TIME LIFE PICTURES/GETTY IMAGES.

early days of the DOL, near 40 percent of those employed were involved in agriculture; that has declined to less than five percent of the total workforce currently. Construction, mining, railroad work, and manufacturing of goods have declined from more than 30 percent to less than 20 percent of those employed. There were few safeguards for workers in the early years of the twentieth century, and working conditions were often quite hazardous. The mining industry was largely unregulated at the start of the twentieth century, and fatal accidents numbered between one thousand to two thousand per year. By the start of the twenty-first century, that number has dropped to less than forty deaths annually.

Black lung disease (or coal worker's pneumoconiosis), as shown in the photograph of a coal miner' lungs, was once a common result of working in the coal mining industry. The disease was caused by minute particles of coal dust present in the air of coal mines, that caused irritation and tissue damage to miner' lungs when inhaled. The severity of black lung disease was often a function of the amount of exposure to coal dust over time. By their fifties, miners were often short of breath, and had the telltale black areas present upon lung x ray or tissue examination. Severe cases resulted in death from heart failure, when the right side of the heart became enlarged and strained due to chronic lung disease.

PRIMARY SOURCE

X RAY OF THE LUNGS OF A COAL MINER
See primary source image.

SIGNIFICANCE

The incidence of black lung disease has decreased markedly since the late 1960s. In 1969, the Federal Coal Mine Health and Safety Act was passed, mandating that dust levels be kept at a level of not more than 2.0mg per cubic meter (down from the prior allowable rate of 8.0mg per cubic meter). Although a slight risk of dust exposure remains even with the use of modern respirators by the miners, the reported incidence of the disease has significantly diminished.

Technological advances have greatly contributed to increased workplace safety: heating and cooling, lighting, electrical power with back up generators, air and water filtration, ventilation and environmental purification techniques, availability of reliable communication systems, and the vast advances made possible by computer technology have all contributed enormously to increasing the safety of the work environment, and to vastly improving the ability to respond expeditiously and appropriately during a job site crisis or disaster, decreasing fatalities in those situations.

Between 1980 and the present day, occupational fatalities have continued to decline steadily, at a rate of slightly more than three percent per year (per OSHA). Among all age groups, the single greatest change has occurred among workers who are between the ages of sixteen and twenty years old (about 7 percent). Unintentional injuries have declined at a greater rate than workplace homicides (just under 4 percent versus slightly less than 1 percent). Overall, the Southern and Western regions of the United States started out with the highest occupational fatality rates in 1980, and have seen the most significant annual percentage drops, particularly among unintentional injuries.

In considering changes in occupational fatalities, it is relevant to note that not all work-related fatalities occur on the jobsite. The Occupational Health and Safety Administration (OSHA) estimates that about 50,000 people die annually as a result of cumulative hazardous exposures on the job, and that another six million experience work-related injuries. All of these statistics represent significant decreases during the course of the century, but OSHA, in partnership with the Mine Safety and Health Administration (MHSA) are committed to continuing efforts aimed at identifying potential risk factors to employee health and safety, and ameliorating or eradicating them.

In 2004, there were a total of 5,703 workplace fatalities reported in the United States. Of those, 2,494 occurred in the manufacturing (459), construction (1,224), and mining and natural resources (811) industries. Of the remainder, the majority occurred in the trade, transportation, and utilities industry (1,455) and in professional and business services realm (448).

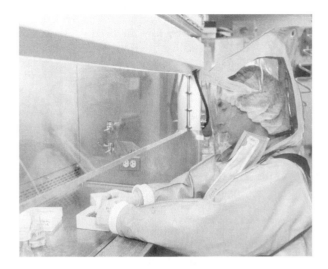

A scientist with the Centers for Disease Control and Prevention (CDC) wears protective clothing as he works in a biosafety laboratory in Atlanta, Georgia. ©CDC/PHIL/CORBIS.

In line with its efforts directed at increasing workplace safety, efficiency, and productivity, OSHA has created a set of ergonomic guidelines (guidelines for correct posture and positioning of the body while at work) aimed at preventing on-the-job hazards. The aim of the guidelines is to create a set of uniform standards for various employment types and job locations that can be implemented on-site, increasing workplace safety, identifying possible mechanisms of injury, and outlining ways in which the potential risks or hazards can be managed or eliminated. This embodies a strong pro-active approach to decreasing workplace injuries and fatalities.

FURTHER RESOURCES

Periodicals

Loomis, D., D. B. Richardson, J. F. Bena and A. J. Bailer. "Deindustrialization and the long term decline in fatal occupational injuries." *Occupational and Environmental Medicine*. 61 (2004): 616–621.

Loomis, D., J. F. Bena and A. J. Bailer. "Diversity of trends in occupational injury mortality in the United States, 1980–1996." *Injury Prevention*. 9 (2003): 9–14.

Web sites

CDC National Institute for Occupational Safety and Health. "Fatality Assessment and Control Evaluation (FACE) Program." <http://mentalhealth.about.com/gi/dynamic/offsite.htm?site=http://www.cdc.gov/niosh/homepage.html> (accessed January 17, 2006).

chucknacke.com. "Photojournalism and About me." <http://chucknacke.com/aboutme.html> (accessed January 17, 2006).

United States Department of Labor: Bureau of Labor Statistics. "Census of Fatal Occupational Injuries Summary, 2004." <http://stats.bls.gov/news.release/cfoi.nr0.htm> (accessed January 17, 2006).

Trends and Results for Organ Donation and Transplantation in the United States, 2004

Government document

By: Scientific Registry of Transplant Recipients, Organ Procurement and Transplantation Network

Date: 2004

Source: U.S. Department of Health and Human Services. "2004 Annual Report of the U.S. Organ Procurement and Transplantation Network and the Scientific Registry of Transplant Recipients: Transplant Data 1994–2003." Washington, D.C.: U.S. Government Printing Office, 2004.

About the Author: The U.S. Department of Health and Human Services (DHHS) is the Government agency responsible for protecting the health of all Americans and providing essential services, especially to those least able to help themselves. The Organ Procurement and Transplantation Network (OPTN), which deals with the supply and distribution of organs for transplant, is administered by the United Network for Organ Sharing (UNOS) under contract to the DHHS. The OPTN was set up by the U.S. Congress under the National Organ Transplant Act of 1984.

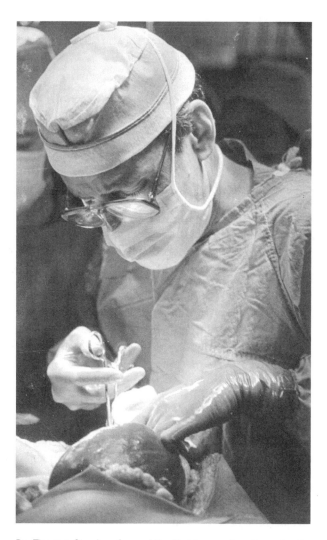

Dr. Thomas Starzl performed the first human liver transplant in 1963 at the University of Colorado. He performed the first successful liver transplant four years later. AP/WIDE WORLD PHOTOS.

INTRODUCTION

It is now over half a century since the surgeon Joseph E. Murray (1919–) carried out the world's first kidney transplant in Boston, Massachusetts. In 1967, Christiaan Barnard (1922–2001) performed the first human heart transplant in Cape Town, South Africa, and, in the same year, Thomas Starzl (1926–) reported the first liver transplant at the University of Colorado Health Sciences Center in the U.S. Although Dr. Murray received the Nobel Prize for Physiology or Medicine in 1990 for his work, organ transplantation was controversial for many years. Many saw it as risky and unethical. Today, organ transplantation has become almost routine thanks to advances in both science and logistics, as well as to changes in public opinion.

In the early days, people receiving new kidneys, hearts, and livers were often extremely sick and not expected to survive without a new organ. This alone could, perhaps, justify the risks of surgery. However, even if the patient did survive the operation, the graft often did not survive because the body, naturally, rejected it as "foreign." A good deal of new research was needed to better understand the rejection process and to develop methods to persuade the recipient's body to accept the transplanted organ.

The introduction of the drug cyclosporine in 1978 changed the face of organ transplantation. Cyclosporine is an immunosuppressant. As the name suggests, it is able to suppress the immune system sufficiently to stop transplant rejection. However, interfering with the immune system is potentially dangerous, because this system normally protects the body from infection and cancer. Therefore, the dosage of cyclosporine post-transplant must be precise—too little and the new organ will be rejected, too much and the patient is vulnerable to infection, cancer, and other complications.

The other major development that brought organ transplantation into mainstream medicine was the establishment, in the U.S., of the United Network for Organ Sharing (UNOS). This network resulted from the enactment of the National Organ Transplant Act in 1984, the law that set a legal framework for organ transplantation. UNOS handles the logistics of the donor organ supply and matches organs to suitable recipients through the Organ Procurement and Transplantation Network (OPTN). It brings together medicine, science, public policy, and technology to facilitate every organ transplant performed in the U.S. Its research department collects regular statistics on organ transplantation and produced the report extracted here.

PRIMARY SOURCE

INTRODUCTION

...This publication is intended to be useful for patients, the transplant community, the public, and the Federal Government; its goal is to improve patient care and enhance equitable access to transplantation. . . .

SUMMARY STATISTICS FOR 2002–2003 ON TRANSPLANTATION IN THE UNITED STATES

During 2003, more than 25,000 organs were transplanted in the United States—over 18,000 from deceased donors and almost 7,000 from living donors. Compared to data from the prior year (2002), these numbers reflect an increase in the number of deceased donor transplants by 2.2% overall and by 1.9% for deceased donors; a greater increase was noted for living donors (2.9%). During the same period, more than 7,000 patients were reported to have died while waiting for a transplant. The number of deaths on the waiting list did not change substantially from 2002 to 2003; however, there was a decrease in the overall death rate because of the increase in waiting list size.

The waiting list for deceased donor transplants has increased at more than twice the rate of increase in the number of transplants during the past year, by 5.1% versus 1.9%. This large increase is a continuation from earlier years and provides a strong indication of the ever-increasing demand for organs. The total number of patients on the waiting list reached almost 86,500 in 2003. . . . When the number of patients waiting for a transplant increases, it demonstrates that the demand exceeds the supply—more patients are added to the list than are removed from it. Hopefully these removals occur because of transplantation, but they also represent death and (occasionally)

recovery from organ failure. The . . . demand for kidney and pancreas transplants increased steeply; lung and liver transplant demand also increased, though to a lesser degree. By contrast, the number of patients awaiting heart, heart-lung and intestine transplants decreased in 2003 compared to the prior year. Longer time trends for the past decade are demonstrated for each organ in the organ-specific chapters that follow.

As a consequence of the steeply increasing demand for transplants and slowly increasing supply of organs, the waiting list is getting longer and the waiting times for transplant candidates, which are already long, are getting longer. The urgent need for more donor organs is suggested by many of the chapters in this report; it is particularly pronounced for kidneys, pancreata, and livers.

Evaluation of the number of transplants performed by organ in 2003 compared with the prior year reveal large differences. Kidney transplantation leads organ transplantation, and living donor kidney transplants accounted for 44% of all kidney transplants in 2003. Liver transplantation too continues to show a substantial growth (6%). By contrast, the number of living donor liver transplants decreased by 11% to 320 during the recent year. Living donor liver transplantation accounts for only 6% of all liver transplants. Heart transplantation decreased by 4.2% to 2,024 transplants in 2003. Lung transplants number just over 1,000 per year, and showed a 3.7% increase since 2002. Living lung transplants account for less than 2% of all lung transplants. Pancreas transplantation for Type 1 diabetics is most commonly performed simultaneously with kidney transplantation. It showed a reduction in 2003 compared to the prior year, which is consistent for all types of pancreas transplants. In 2003 there were 52 small intestine transplants, which suggests a substantial recent increase.

Two critical measures describe key outcomes after transplantation: the function of the transplanted graft and survival of the transplant recipient. Patient survival after transplantation has been generally improving over time. . . . One-year patient survival for kidney and pancreas transplants were around 95%–97%; corresponding survival rates were about 86% for liver and heart, about 80% for lung and intestine, and lowest for combined heart-lung recipients.

Functional survival of the transplanted organ, i.e. graft survival, has improved substantially over the past decade and has been relatively stable in recent years. . . . Compared to the data for patient survival, figures for graft failure are usually lower. This is due to the fact that patients may survive a graft failure by receiving a timely second transplant, by returning to dialysis (for kidney transplant recipients), or by returning to insulin therapy (for pancreas transplant recipients). More detailed trends over longer time spans are provided in the organ-specific chapters of this report. . . .

CONCLUSION

This report provides a great deal of information on the current state of transplantation in the United States. The observed time trends over the past decade and most recent two years give important perspectives on many areas of organ donation, immunosuppression, organ-specific issues, and overall outcomes. Numerous impressive improvements are documented in this report, as are areas that need to be addressed with great urgency—such as enhancing organ donation to reduce the annually increasing gap between available organs and the growing need for life-saving transplantation.

SIGNIFICANCE

The report highlights the increase in the waiting list for organ transplants and, consequently, the growing gap between demand and supply. Clearly, the waiting list is growing faster than donor organs become available for transplant. There are various reasons to explain the growth in the number of patients awaiting an organ transplant. First, the skill and experience of transplant surgeons and doctors, both in performing these operations and in caring for the recipients, has increased dramatically over the last decade. Once seen as the last option for the desperately sick, a kidney, heart, or liver transplant is now seen as a realistic and cost-effective alternative to ongoing medical treatment, such as kidney dialysis.

In addition, the population is aging rapidly. At one time, physicians would not consider doing a transplant on a recipient over the age of fifty-five. Now that barrier has been crossed because research has shown that older recipients, if carefully selected, can do as well as younger ones. This means that there are now many older people on the transplant waiting list and the number is bound to increase in the future.

The growth of the waiting list has led to efforts to increase the supply of donor organs. Just as surgeons are now operating on older recipients, they also are accepting older donors. At one time, the typical organ donor was a young, healthy man or woman who had been killed in a traffic accident. Now there is a wide range of donors—including the living (for livers and kidneys). There has been an increase in the use of living donors—usually, but not always, a relative of the recipient. Needless to say, this has raised ethical questions, since taking a healthy organ from a living person, however willing that person is, does harm.

A 12-year-old heart transplant patient is shown tossing his old heart (weighing about 555 grams) into the air. The boy's old heart was enlarged to more than 2.5 times its normal size due to a virus. AP/WIDE WORLD PHOTOS.

This impact on the living donor has to be carefully balanced against the benefit to the recipient.

Ongoing study of transplant recipients is another major development in the field of organ transplantation. At one time, the main goal of the transplant operation was the survival of the recipient and the new organ. Now that thousands of transplant recipients have survived for many years, there has been the opportunity to study their health, both physical and psychological. Transplant recipients are vulnerable to a number of health problems, many of which arise from the use of immunosuppressants, which must be taken for life by transplant recipients. As a result, posttransplant medication regimes have been fine-tuned and many advances have been made to improve the health care of transplant recipients.

FURTHER RESOURCES

Books

Lock, Stephen, John M. Last, and George Dunea, eds. *The Oxford Illustrated Companion to Medicine.* Oxford: Oxford University Press, 2001.

Web sites

United Network for Organ Sharing. "Organ Donation and Transplantation." <http://www.unos.org> (accessed November 22, 2005).

Guide to Children's Dental Care in Medicaid

Booklet excerpt

By: Department of Health and Human Services

Date: October 2004

Source: Department of Health and Human Services USA. "Guide to Children's Dental Care in Medicaid." Available online at <http://www1.cms.hhs.gov/MedicaidEarlyPeriodicScrn/Downloads/EPSDTDentalGuide.pdf> (accessed January 5, 2006).

About the Author: The United States Department of Health and Human Services (DHHS) is a federal agency tasked with protecting the health and welfare of all persons residing in the United States, and with assuring that they receive, or have access to, all necessary human services. DHHS is charged with oversight or administration of more than three hundred discrete programs. Although it is a federal agency, it works very closely with state and local governments to assure the adequate provision of public, and public health, services.

INTRODUCTION

There are written (on papyrus scrolls) descriptions of primitive attempts at dentistry dating back to 3700 BCE. Diseases of the mouth, teeth, and gums predate history: evidence of dental caries (tooth decay, or dental cavities) were found in mummies in the pyramids of Giza. Little has changed through time, and the most common ailments of the mouth are still related to dental caries and gum disease (periodontal disease).

The earliest dentists to mention preventive dentistry (in concept, not in terminology) in their scholarly writings were from Bologna, Italy. In 1400, a dentist named Giovanni de Arcoli, advised his patients against the excessive eating of sugary sweets, told them to avoid foods at the extremes of temperature (very cold or very hot), and was an advocate of keeping the mouth, gums, teeth, and oral cavity clean. The toothbrush was invented in China, just before the start of the sixteenth century. In 1766, the British dentist Thomas

Berdmore published a textbook in which he stated that there existed a relationship between the ingestion of excessive amounts of sugar and the development of dental problems. In 1819, Levi Spear Parmly published a book entitled *A Practical Guide to the Management of the Teeth*, in which he described a technique for flossing the teeth with waxed silk thread. He stated that this, along with daily cleaning of the teeth using a brush and tooth cleaner, would completely prevent the development of dental caries and periodontal disease. Economics was a significant factor hampering the widespread practice of adequate oral hygiene: dental brushes were very costly, tooth cleaners and silk thread were prohibitively expensive. It was not until the development of cost-effective nylon products during World War II that toothbrushes and dental floss became affordable for the general public. Even then, few people found the concept of flossing after meals viable.

Until the 1940s, dentistry was viewed primarily as a reactive and healing-oriented profession: people went to the dentist only when they were in pain or had difficulty eating. American culture did not have a norm for preventive dentistry. The first large-scale public health efforts at preventive dentistry concerned the introduction of fluoride into public water supplies. The American Dental Association determined that the regular drinking of fluoridated water could decrease the likelihood of developing cavities by up to 40 percent. It was also discovered that the ingestion of fluoride could reverse early signs of dental decay.

Tooth brushing after meals was well-known to clean teeth, and to remove decay-causing oral bacteria. The addition of fluoride to commercially available toothpastes bolstered the preventive effects of brushing at least twice daily. Components of modern oral hygiene, practiced in the home setting are: brushing teeth after meals, flossing at least once daily, eating few processed sugar-laden foods, limiting between meal and late-night snacking, and eating healthy foods.

Modern preventive dentistry has several components, differing according to age group. For very young children, the ingestion of fluoride, either through the commercial water supply or in the form of daily oral supplements or oral rinses and bolstered with semi-annual applications of fluoride directly to the teeth, is recommended. In addition, a thin plastic coating called a *sealant* is often painted on the primary teeth of young children, particularly on the biting surfaces of the molars. This is believed to diminish the likelihood of decay, and to aid in the retention of primary teeth until the adult teeth are ready to descend naturally. During the last two decades of the twentieth century, significant attention was focused on the tendency of babies who were put to sleep while drinking a bottle (which they were permitted to retain) to develop decay in the front teeth. As a result, the use of a bottle after the first year, as well as the use of milk or formula as a sleep aid, was strongly discouraged. Parents were encouraged to use a soft cloth to wipe out babies' mouths after they ate or drank, even prior to the eruption of teeth. A first visit to the dentist has been recommended as soon as most of the first teeth have descended, followed by routine twice-yearly appointments.

It is now considered a standard practice to have twice yearly dental visits, with thorough examinations, bitewing x rays annually, full mouth x rays every two-to-three years, and semi-annual teeth cleaning performed by an oral hygienist.

PRIMARY SOURCE

In the mid-1970's, the Centers for Medicare & Medicaid Services (CMS) (formerly the Health Care Financing Administration), published *"A Guide to Dental Care: EPSDT/Medicaid."* That guide was intended to complement, supplement and expand upon policy information contained in CMS' State Medicaid Manual (SMM)....
The guide was developed for the use of state Medicaid agencies, dental and other health care providers, and national, state and local policy makers involved in organizing and managing oral health care for children under Medicaid's Early and Periodic Screening, Diagnostic and Treatment (EPSDT) service....

Over the past two decades dramatic changes have occurred in dental science and technology, in public policy approaches to dental care delivery, and in the Medicaid program itself....

Consequently, CMS issued a contract to the American Academy of Pediatric Dentistry (AAPD) for the purpose of reviewing the original Guide and developing a revision for use by stakeholders concerned about children's oral health in Medicaid....

The Guide is intended to serve as a resource of current information on clinical practice, evolving technologies and recommendations in dental care. The guide is not intended to change current Medicaid policies, nor is it intended to impose any new requirements on states....

DENTAL CARIES IN U.S. CHILDREN

Among the many dental conditions affecting children, dental caries (tooth decay) is the preeminent concern in the context of Medicaid services because of their substantial prevalence in the low-income population. Tooth decay continues to be the single most common chronic disease among U.S. children, despite the fact that it is highly preventable through early and sustained home care and regular professional preventive services.

The prevalence and severity of tooth decay in U.S. children has changed considerably over the past several decades. Once a disease of nearly universal occurrences for nearly all children, tooth decay is now generally distributed in the pediatric population to the point that roughly 80 percent of caries in permanent teeth is concentrated in 25 percent of U.S. children. Also, minority and low-income children disproportionately experience decay in their primary teeth. The high-risk, high-prevalence, high-severity group, which currently represents nearly 20 million children, is largely comprised of low-income children (nearly all of whom are eligible for Medicaid or SCHIP), with higher levels of caries found in African-American and Hispanic groups at all ages.

Dental caries generally is considered to be reversible or capable of being arrested in the earliest stages through a variety of proven interventions. Beyond the early stages, the decay process generally tends to advance and become more difficult and costly to repair the longer it remains untreated. Hence, treatment initiated early in the course of dental caries development will almost always be easier for both child and dentist, less expensive, and more successful than treatment begun at a later time.

Prevalence and Risk Data from recent national surveys reaffirm the persistence of dental caries as the single most prevalent chronic disease of childhood. Roughly half of U.S. children experience dental caries by age nine; and the proportion rises to about 80 percent by age 17. Overall, national epidemiological surveys show that nearly one-in-five (18.7%) U.S. children two to four years of age have visually evident tooth decay.... Tooth decay is closely tied to socioeconomic levels, with children from low-income families more likely to develop caries. Preschoolers in households with incomes less than 100% of the federal poverty level (FPL) are three to five times more likely to have cavities than children from families with incomes equal to or above 300 percent of the FPL. The Third National Health and Nutrition Examination Survey (NHANES III) found visible decay in 30 percent of two to five year-old children in poverty and 24 percent of near-poor children (100%–200% of the FPL). Caries was present in only 12 percent of middle-income youngsters and 6 percent were from families with the highest income levels.

Severity Within the highest-risk, lowest-income group, roughly one-quarter or four to five million children experience more severe levels of the disease, often with associated pain, infection and disruption of normal activities. These children generally acquire the disease early in childhood and often present as infants with multiple teeth in advanced stages of decay (a condition now referred to as "early childhood caries" or "ECC," and known previously as "baby bottle caries"). Children living in households below 200 percent of the poverty level—roughly half of U.S. children—have three and one half times more decayed teeth than do children in more affluent families.

Unmet Treatment Needs Dental care is the most common unmet treatment need in children. Lower-income children have more untreated dental disease than more affluent children who obtain care on a regular periodic basis. Reasons for this disparity include the fact that low-income children are more likely to experience dental disease and frequently only access care on an episodic or urgent basis when decayed teeth cause pain or swelling. NHANES III, the most recent national survey, found that nearly 80 percent of the decayed teeth of poor two to five year olds and 40–50 percent of the decayed permanent and primary teeth in six to fourteen year-olds were unfilled (untreated).

Consequences The consequences of severe, untreated dental disease and poor oral health in millions of American children are evident in many dimensions. Biologically, untreated dental disease can lead to pain, infection and destruction of teeth and surrounding tissues with associated dysfunction. Untreated tooth decay may lead to delayed overall development among young children affected with severe forms of the disease. Dental diseases have been shown to be associated with systemic health conditions. Socially, affected children have problems with school attendance and performance, and are often stigmatized because of their appearance. Potential consequences to the health system as a result of poor dental health care would include: frequent visits to emergency departments (often without definitive resolution of the presenting problem); hospital admissions; and treatment provided in operating rooms for conditions that are either largely preventable or amenable to less costly care had they been treated earlier.

CONTEMPORARY DENTAL CARE FOR CHILDREN

Emphasis on Early Initiation of Oral Health Care Science has provided a clear understanding that tooth decay is an infectious, transmissible, destructive disease caused by acid-forming bacteria acquired by toddlers from their mothers shortly after their first teeth erupt (generally around six months of age). In its early stages, the effects of dental caries are largely reversible through existing interventions (e.g., fluorides) that promote replacement of lost minerals from the outer layer of the tooth (enamel). These findings, combined with epidemiological data on the occurrence of tooth decay in infants and young children, suggest that true primary prevention must begin in the first to second year of life. This evidence also suggests that particular attention should be paid to the oral health of expectant and new mothers.

In early childhood there is tremendous growth and development of the face and mouth, with dentition-associated disturbances that may require the attention of dental professionals. Other common oral conditions of childhood (in addition to tooth decay) include: gingivitis and mucosal (soft tissue) infections; accidental and intentional trauma; developmental disturbances associated with teething or tooth formation; poor alignment of teeth or jaws; and craniofacial abnormalities (including clefts of the lip and/or palate). Additionally, parents frequently request information on a diverse array of concerns including: sucking habits; fluoride usage; tooth alignment; timing and order of tooth eruption; and discolored teeth....

Successful Models for Achieving Oral Health *"Dental Primary Care"*
Professional guidelines (and Medicaid statutory requirements) for addressing pediatric oral health needs are predicated on early and periodic clinical examinations to assess for evidence of pathologic changes or developmental abnormalities, diagnoses to determine treatment needs, and follow-up care for any conditions requiring treatment. These recurring periodic oral assessments ("dental check-ups") are generally coupled with routine preventive services (self-care instructions, fluoride applications, dental sealants, etc.) and increasingly seek to incorporate assessments of risk factors that elevate the likelihood of destructive changes if allowed to persist. This pattern of periodic assessments, preventive services, and necessary follow-up care also generally applies for adults, who collectively are more susceptible to the development of periodontal disease, oro-pharangeal cancers, and other soft tissue abnormalities. A large and growing proportion of the U.S. population that has adopted this pattern of care faces relatively few barriers to accessing services because of household income levels and/or private dental insurance. They enjoy unprecedented levels of oral health status. However, access for low-income children remains a challenge....

Critical Clinical Elements of Dental Services This section provides an overview of several critical clinical issues regarding children's dental services, as well as further elaboration of topics introduced in prior sections. Dental care includes diagnostic services, preventive services, therapeutic services and emergency services for dental disease which, if left untreated, may become acute dental problems or may cause irreversible damage to the teeth or supporting structures. Dental diseases and conditions of primary concern during childhood include dental caries (tooth decay) and problems or anomalies related to disturbances of growth and development. Periodontal diseases and other conditions affecting so-called soft tissues within the mouth and underlying bone, often related to systemic health problems, also affect oral health in a smaller percentage of children.

Because children remain at varying levels of risk for dental diseases and developmental disturbances, and because the best outcomes are achieved when these conditions are detected and treated early, periodic examinations at intervals commensurate with levels of risk are recommended for all children starting at an early age and continuing throughout childhood and adolescence. The often insidious onset of dental diseases require that practitioners responsible for children's oral health understand underlying disease processes and have the training, experience, and equipment necessary to accurately diagnose and manage common dental diseases and, when necessary, provide a range of therapeutic services to restore damaged structures.

SIGNIFICANCE

As with nearly all health care related concerns, there is a direct relationship between socioeconomic status and likelihood of engaging in preventive dentistry (or preventive medicine). In America, there is also a clear association between racial and ethnic minority group membership and poverty. The poorer one is, the less likely she is to have either profitable employment or a job that provides adequate medical or dental insurance, and to have ready access to reliable transportation. In rural and frontier communities, the challenges are compounded by geography and demographics: few health care professionals choose to locate in areas of poverty and sparse population. Often, isolated areas lack either access to public transportation or a public transit system.

Although fluoridated water has been shown to be highly effective at strengthening tooth enamel and thereby reducing the likelihood of developing caries, only about half of the public water supplies in the United States utilize it. In areas where there is no fluoride in the water, the most impoverished people are likely to have the highest number of cavities, as well as the greatest incidence of emergency room visits for the treatment of pain associated with cavities, gum disease, dental abscesses, or oral infections. There is also a disproportionate relationship between poverty and poor diet (routine intake of low quality food, containing high concentrations of fats, preservatives, chemical additives, and processed sugars.

Individuals and families with limited income are significantly less likely to go to a dentist on a routine (non-emergent) basis than those whose incomes are well above the poverty level. Although many children and families living at or below the poverty level in the United States are entitled to receive Medicaid benefits, many do not apply. Of those who do obtain benefits, not all will be able to manage the requirements of well-child or preventive medical or dental visits. For many people living in poverty, particularly those who are geographically isolated, it has been virtually impossible to obtain dental (and medical) care unless it is an emergency. In part, this is because of the scarcity of dental providers who are willing to accept Medicaid patients. The public health system has been working to change this situation by increasing reimbursements for routine dental services (as well as urgent and emergent treatments), and attempting to streamline the cumbersome paperwork (claims) and administrative burdens of Medicaid providers. With ever-advancing technology, computer systems have become far more affordable for even the smallest of businesses, lending to the feasibility of electronic billing systems to further simplify and expedite the claims submission and negotiation processes. Several states have now passed legislation that prevents dentists (and some other types of health care providers) from being accepted as providers for private insurers (HMOs, PPOs, etc.); others are offering incentives such as location pay and loan forgiveness programs in order to attract qualified dental professionals to impoverished, rural, or frontier areas. The goal of the American Dental Association, as well as that of the American Public Health System (Medicaid, Medicare, etc.) is to guarantee access to excellent dental and medical care for all people, regardless of geographic location or socioeconomic status, in order to ensure "well" and preventive visits on a routine basis.

FURTHER RESOURCES
Books
Dunning, James M. *Dental Care for Everyone: Problems and Proposals*. Lincoln, Neb.: iUniverse, 1999.

Web sites
American Dental Association. "Preventive Dentistry Costs Less." <http://www.ada.org/prof/resources/pubs/ada news/adanewsarticle.asp?articleid=1100> (accessed January 5, 2006).

American Dental Association. "State and Community Models for Improving Access to Dental Care for the Underserved—A White Paper (October 2004)." <http://www.ada.org/prof/resources/topics/topics_access_whitepaper.pdf> (accessed January 5, 2006).

Canadian Diabetes Association. "Dental Care: Tooth or Dare." <http://www.diabetes.ca/Section_About/dental.asp> (accessed January 5, 2006).

CDC: Department of Health and Human Services. "Oral Health: Preventing Cavities, Gum Disease, and Tooth Loss." <http://www.cdc.gov/nccdphp/publications/aag/oh.htm> (accessed January 5, 2006).

Children's Defense Fund. "Oral Health: Dental Problems Warrant Serious Concern." <http://www.childrens defense.org/childhealth/oralhealth.aspx> (accessed January 5, 2006).

Balancing Act: The Health Advantages of Naturally-Occurring Hormone Replacement Therapy

Testimony excerpt

By: Barbara Alving, M. D.

Date: July 22, 2004

Source: United States House of Representatives. "Testimony Before the Subcommittee on Human Rights and Wellness Committee on Government Reform." <http://reform.house.gov/UploadedFiles/HHS%20alving.pdf> (January 16, 2006).

About the Author: Barbara M. Alving is a physician who has specialized in hematology. Through the course of her professional career, she has served as investigator in the blood and blood products division of the Food and Drug Administration, served as Chief of the Department of Hematology at the Walter Reed Army Medical Center, directed the hematology and oncology unit at Washington Hospital Center before accepting a position at the National Heart, Lung, and Blood Institute (NHLBI). She served as Acting Director of NHLBI for approximately four years before joining the National Center for Research Resources, as Director, in 2005. She is a part holder of two patents, has edited several scholarly books, and has authored more than one hundred academic and scholarly works.

INTRODUCTION

Historically, menopause has been defined as the time in a woman's life when she ceases to menstruate monthly. The age at which this is occurs varies a great deal by individual, but it typically happens somewhere between the mid-forties and early fifties for most women. For several years prior to actual cessation of menses (typically defined as a period of at least twelve months without menstruation), many women experience cycle changes, with erratic or missed menses.

There are three primary circumstances in which menopause occurs: naturally, when hormone levels decrease over time and menstruation gradually ceases according to the rhythms of the body, surgically, when the uterus and one or both ovaries are removed, and medically, when the ovaries are damaged or chemically destroyed (also called chemical ablation) by radiation or chemotherapy for the treatment of cancer.

In the past, it was called the change of life, referring to the shift in lifestyle that happens when women can no longer bear children. The myriad of associated symptoms experienced by many (although certainly not all) women were considered highly subjective and therefore prone to distortion—particularly by male physicians—and quite unavoidable. The conventional wisdom suggested that menopausal discomfort, as a purely natural component of the aging process, was simply a phase of life to "suffer through and endure."

Symptoms associated with hormonal reductions (estrogen and progesterone) associated with menopause have included: irregular or missed menses; night sweats; hot flashes; emotional lability and mood swings; depression or mood disorder; headaches; weight gain; fluid retention (sometimes accompanied by swelling in the joints or in the extremities); markedly decreased libido (loss of interest in sex); sore or tender breasts—sometimes accompanied by an increase in cystic masses of the breasts, ovaries, or uterus; irritability or moodiness; fatigue or diminished energy level; confusion or difficulty making decisions; temporary thinking or memory changes; vaginal dryness; urinary incontinence; insomnia or sleep pattern changes; muscle or joint pain or stiffness; and other physical, emotional, or psychosocial signs and symptoms. More recently, concerns began to be raised regarding the possibility of a temporal association between menopause and onset of osteoporosis or loss of bone density and the development of heart disease (no implication of association between osteoporosis and heart disease is herein implied).

In the mid-1920s, a form of estrogen synthesized from the urine of pregnant women was first used as a treatment for the symptoms of menopause. By the

Dr. JoAnn Manson with a printout from a study she directed on hormone replacement therapy for women at her office in Boston, December 12, 2002. Manson, chief of preventive medicine at Harvard's Bringham and Women's Hospital, said researchers found long-term hormone replacement does not prevent heart attacks, as many thought, and increases the risk of breast cancer. AP/WIDE WORLD PHOTOS.

1940s, it had been determined that a biosimilar substance could be made from the urine of pregnant mares (adult female horses), a much more plentiful and less costly supply. The patented formulation resulting from this discovery became very widely prescribed for the treatment of menopausal symptoms, beginning in 1943. By the mid-1970s, Premarin was one of the most frequently prescribed pharmaceuticals in the United States. Things began to change in 1975, when the first report linking synthetic estrogens (Premarin and similar drugs) to an increase in the development of uterine cancer (also called endometrial cancer). In the 1980s, progesterone was added to the former estrogen-only hormone replacement therapies, in an effort to prevent endometrial cancers.

During the latter half of the twentieth century, the burgeoning women's movement began to focus the attention of the medical and biomedical research establishment in America (and elsewhere in the developed world) on a large number of women's health issues. For the first time, close scrutiny concerning etiology was focused on breast, cervical, uterine, and ovarian cancers; on osteoporosis; on the incidence and prevalence of heart disease; on arthritis and connective tissue diseases; and on memory changes first evidenced at midlife. The following testimony was provided to Congress by a scientist participating in the Women's Health Initiative, a long-term study examining the benefits and risks of hormone replacement therapy for women.

PRIMARY SOURCE

Testimony Before the Subcommittee on Human Rights and Wellness
Committee on Government Reform
United States House of Representatives *Balancing Act: The Health Advantages of Naturally Occurring Hormones in Hormone Replacement Therapy*

Statement of Barbara Alving, M.D., MACP Acting Director National Heart, Lung, and Blood Institute National Institutes of Health, U.S. Department of Health and Human Services

I am pleased to appear before this Committee in my capacity as Acting Director of the National Heart, Lung, and Blood Institute (NHLBI) and director of the NIH Women's Health Initiative (WHI), which has been administered by the NHLBI since 1997. I am here, first, to tell you what we learned from the WHI with regard to hormone therapy using conjugated equine estrogen and, second, to comment on alternative therapies that are now receiving attention.

The WHI began in 1991 to investigate approaches that might be helpful to older women in preventing common chronic diseases—coronary heart disease, breast and colorectal cancers, and osteoporosis. Estrogen "replacement" therapy is one such approach. For much of the twentieth century, popular thinking was that restoring levels of estrogen, which ebb during middle age, would enable women to remain "forever young." Although estrogen was initially prescribed to alleviate troublesome menopausal symptoms, a number of epidemiological studies provided evidence that women who took estrogen experienced a lower incidence of disease, particularly cardiovascular disease (CVD), and enjoyed better health overall than women who did not. Data from many basic science investigations provided plausible explanations for the observed CVD benefit, and an NHLBI-supported clinical trial documented improvements in CVD risk factors (e.g., cholesterol levels) that might account for such a benefit.

But, the observation that women who took estrogen tended to enjoy better health did not prove causality, and important questions remained. Does estrogen make women healthy? Or...does being healthy (or, at least, health-conscious) make women take estrogen? The WHI hormone trial was designed to address these questions. It recruited about 27,000 healthy postmenopausal women, 50-79 years of age, and divided them into one of two groups according to whether they had still had a uterus. Those who had a uterus were assigned to take either a pill containing estrogen and progestin (0.625 mg of conjugated equine estrogen plus 2.5 mg medroxyprogesterone acetate—Prempro) or a placebo; those who had undergone a hysterectomy took an estrogen pill (0.625 mg of conjugated equine estrogen—Premarin) or a placebo.

It is worth noting that at the outset of the WHI trial, many interested parties believed that an outcome favoring estrogen was a foregone conclusion. Indeed, some doctors and researchers argued that such a trial was unethical because it would require half of the participating women to take placebos and thereby deny them the presumed benefits of hormones. Nonetheless, arguments in favor of randomized, placebo-controlled, clinical trials prevailed—and, as we now know, they were justified.

The WHI trial of estrogen plus progestin was halted in 2002 after an average follow-up of 5.2 years. Compared with women who took a placebo pill, women taking the hormones experienced an excess risk of breast cancer and more episodes of heart attack, stroke, and blood clots. Although the hormone-treated women had lower rates of colorectal cancer and fractures, and overall death rates were equal, it was concluded that the hormone combination should not be recommended as a health-promoting regimen. Moreover, the WHI Memory Study (WHIMS), which focused on women aged 65 years and older, found an increased risk of dementia and no effect on cognitive impairment among recipients of estrogen plus progestin.

Subsequently, in the spring of 2004, the WHI estrogen-alone trial also was halted upon determination that the hormone therapy had no effect on coronary heart disease risk but increased the risk of stroke. The study also found that estrogen-alone therapy significantly increased the risk of deep vein thrombosis, had no significant effect on the risk of breast or colorectal cancer, and reduced the risk of hip and other fractures. Findings from the WHIMS, published just last month, indicated that estrogen therapy did not reduce incidence of dementia and had an adverse effect on cognitive function.

In light of the WHI and WHIMS findings, the Food and Drug Administration (FDA) offers the following recommendations (updated April 19, 2004):

- Estrogens and progestins should not be used to prevent memory loss, heart disease, heart attacks, or strokes.
- Estrogens provide valuable therapy for many women, but carry serious risks, and therefore postmenopausal women who use or are considering using estrogen or estrogen with progestin treatments should discuss with their physicians whether the benefits outweigh the risks.
- For hot flashes and significant symptoms of vulvar and vaginal atrophy, these products are the most effective approved therapies. These products are also options for women whose significant risk of osteoporosis outweighs the risks of treatment; other treatments for prevention of postmenopausal osteoporosis are available.
- Estrogens and progestins should be used at the lowest doses for the shortest duration to reach treatment goals, although it is not known at what dose there may be less risk of serious side effects. Women are encouraged to talk to their health care provider regularly about whether treatment is still needed.
- There is a higher incidence of abnormal mammograms which require medical attention.
- Each woman's individual medical situation needs to be carefully discussed with her health care provider to make the best decision for her.

For prescription hormone formulations other than those studied in the WHI, the FDA advises the following: "Although...other estrogens and progestins were not studied, it is important to warn postmenopausal women who take estrogens and progestins about the potential risks, which must be presumed to be the same."

In the aftermath of the WHI findings, increased attention has been focused on the use of complementary and alternative medicine (CAM) to manage symptoms associated with the menopausal transition. Dietary supplements, including botanicals, are the most commonly used CAM modality for menopausal symptoms.

The National Center for Complementary and Alternative Medicine (NCCAM) supports basic and clinical research on the safety and efficacy of botanicals such as soy, black cohosh, and red clover in alleviating hot flashes, osteoporosis, and cognitive and affective problems. Other studies are generating laboratory data that are vital to understanding mechanism of action, characterizing the botanicals, identifying active constituents, and preparing standardized supplements. For example, two ongoing basic studies are looking at the effect of black cohosh extract on human breast tissue and its role as a serotonin modulator, and other research is looking at the effect of soy on breast and endometrial tissue as well as bone. In addition to individual research project grants, the NCCAM supports several research centers on women's health.

The National Institute on Aging (NIA) is supporting a 4-year, randomized, controlled trial to evaluate the efficacy and safety of phytoestrogen-based approaches (black cohosh, and a multibotanical preparation given with and without soy diet counseling) for treating vasomotor symptoms in perimenopausal and postmenopausal women.

Toxicity of black cohosh and other herbals and phytoestrogens is being evaluated by the National Institute of Environmental Health Sciences as part of an overall effort to establish the safety of herbal medicines.

The scientific literature on CAM therapies for menopause is equivocal, due to problems with small trials, short duration of treatment, large placebo effects, and imprecise measures for critical outcomes such as hot flashes. Investigations of the efficacy of soy to prevent cognitive changes, for example, have produced conflicting results, with the latest study (published in the July 7, 2004, issue of the *Journal of the American Medical Association*) finding no effect. The NCCAM has contracted with the Agency for Healthcare Research and Quality to conduct a review and assessment of the literature to provide a clearer picture of what is known about soy.

Clearly, additional research will be needed to provide safety and efficacy information on the range of CAM modalities being used by women to manage menopausal symptoms. The NIH is working to improve the rigor of future studies in this area. In collaboration with eight other NIH components, the NCCAM convened a working group of scientists to assess the quality of hot flash measurements currently in use and to make recommendations for research needed to improve these measurements. In addition the NCCAM, the NIA, and others at the NIH will co-sponsor a state-of-the-science meeting in March 2005 on the management of menopause-related symptoms.

Women are eagerly awaiting the outcome of federal efforts to uncover new approaches to address menopausal symptoms. Moreover, in discussions with gynecologists in the community, we have learned that women are seeking natural (biologically identical) hormone therapies via entities such as the Women's International Pharmacy (http://www.womensinternational.com/about.html).

Thank you for the opportunity to address these issues of great importance to women. I would be pleased to answer any questions the committee may have.

SIGNIFICANCE

The boom of perimenopausal, menopausal, and postmenopausal women taking estrogen-only replacement abruptly reversed after the publication of the 1975 scientific research report linking markedly increased risk of uterine cancer associated with synthetic estrogen use. In the 1980s, progesterone was combined with the estrogens, in order to more closely approximate the human body's natural hormonal activity. It was assumed, both among the medical and the lay communities, that hormone replacement therapy not only relieved the myriad symptoms associated with menopause, but afforded some protection or decreased the incidence of osteoporosis. Traditional hormone replacement therapy for a women who had undergone surgical removal of the uterus (and were therefore not at risk for uterine cancer) was estrogen alone; for women with an intact uterus, it was a combination of estrogen and progesterone, either in a single administration, or taken cyclically (to mimic the body's natural hormonal fluctuations).

The Women's Health Initiative (WHI) a large-scale long-term study initially anticipated finding that there was substantial benefit to be derived, for postmenopausal women, in utilizing conventional hormone replacement therapy (HRT). A summary of the findings published by WHI and the FDA is as follows: study participants who were given combination hormone therapy, when compared to study participants given placebo, were found to be at greater risk for stroke, breast cancer, heart attack, and the development of blood clots. Contrary to prior hypotheses, HRT was not found to diminish cognitive changes sometimes associated with menopause; it was found to increase the risk for early onset of dementia. The two significant benefits of combination HRT were a reduction in fractures, suggesting some protective benefit against osteoporosis, and decreased likelihood of developing rectal or colon cancer. For study participants who were given estrogen-only HRT: when compared with those receiving placebo, they were at greater risk of stroke or for developing blood clots; no between groups difference was found for heart attack risk or for the development of colon or rectal cancers. The effect on incidence of breast cancer was considered uncertain, and there was a definite protective effect against fractures associated with osteoporosis. While still evaluating the study results, and continuing some aspects of the project, it is the overall recommendation of WHI that synthetic HRT not be a treatment of first resort, that it be used only in the event of severe and life-impacting symptoms not amenable to any other treatment, and the used for the briefest possible duration.

Rather than immediately utilizing synthetic HRT, there is benefit in adopting healthy lifestyle and dietary habits long before the onset of menopause. If menopausal symptoms are severe or life impacting, some physicians advise considering bio-identical (sometimes called natural hormone therapy) hormones created from plant-based phytoestrogens and progesterones. They are extracted from plant products and combined with hydrocarbons in a laboratory setting, in order to render them identical to hormones occurring naturally in the human body. These preparations can be tailored to the individual biochemistry of the person for whom they are prescribed, by a health care professional working in concert with a compounding pharmacist. Considerable research is currently in progress in this area, as well as in other areas of complementary and alternative treatments for the symptoms of menopause.

FURTHER RESOURCES

Books

Lee, John R., and Virginia Hopkins. *What Your Doctor May Not Tell You About Menopause: The Breakthrough Book on Natural Hormone Balance.* New York: Time Warner Book Group, 2004.

Wiley, T. S., and Julia Taguchi. *Sex, Lies and Menopause: The Shocking Truth About Synthetic Hormones and the Benefits of Natural Alternatives.* New York: HarperCollins, 2004.

Web sites

Holistic online.com. "Menopause and HRT." <http://www.ncrr.nih.gov/about_ncrr/ncrr_director.asp> (accessed January 16, 2006).

National Center for Research Resources. "The Director's Page." <http://www.ncrr.nih.gov/about_ncrr/ncrr_director.asp> (accessed January 16, 2006).

Women's Health Initiative. "Questions and Answers About the WHI Postmenopausal Hormone Therapy Trials." <http://www.nhlbi.nih.gov/whi/whi_faq.htm> (accessed January 16, 2006).

Kryptonite

Alzheimer's Disease

Poems

By: Amy Baird

Date: 2004

Source: Amy Baird. "Kryptonite." *Alzheimer's Association.* <http://www.alz.org/Resources/poems/abaird.asp>; <http://www.alz.org/Resources/poems/abaird2.asp> (accessed October 20, 2005).

About the Author: Amy Baird is a contributor to the Alzheimer's Association Web site. She writes of her experiences with her father and his Alzheimer's disease.

INTRODUCTION

Alzheimer's disease, the most common form of dementia, is not a normal part of aging. It is a progressive neurodegenerative (degeneration or deterioration of the brain's ability to function) disease. Over time, Alzheimer's disease destroys the individual's ability to learn, to think, to remember, to make decisions, to exercise good judgment, to communicate with words, and to carry out the activities of daily living (such as dressing, using the toilet, brushing teeth, and self-feeding). Alzheimer's disease is ultimately fatal, although the course of the illness varies widely. It can progress over periods as short as two or three years to periods as long as twenty years. Family members of individuals with Alzheimer's disease often say that the personality of their loved one has "disappeared" or that the loved one "has lost all personality or resemblance to the person she once was."

People with Alzheimer's disease (AD) experience behavioral, emotional, and personality changes. They may become hostile, suspicious, anxious, agitated, combative, or emotionally labile, and they may sometimes experience delusions or hallucinations that may cause them to appear mentally ill. They often experience sleep difficulties, confusion, restlessness (coupled with a tendency to wander), and depression. The primary risk factor for the development of AD is advancing age. The number of people with the disease doubles for every five years beyond the age of sixty-five.

On nuclear scans, the brains of people with AD are shown to have abnormal clumps (called amyloid plaques) and tangled bundles of fibers (termed neurofibrillary tangles) that are composed of misplaced proteins. Research has uncovered three genes that cause early onset (familial or inherited) AD. Age-related AD is believed to be caused by genetic mutations that cause displacement and build up of amyloid proteins.

The Alzheimer's Association has created a checklist of ten common warning signs that may indicate that an individual is suffering from AD. Often, the initial sign is memory loss characterized by forgetting recently learned information. This forgetfulness worsens over time, and the individual also loses the ability to recall the information at a later time. Another AD sign is loss of the ability to carry out the steps necessary to complete a familiar task, such as preparing a familiar recipe, playing a board game, going through the process of paying and mailing off a recurring bill, for example. It is quite common for people with AD to experience difficulties with the use of language. In verbal and written communication, they may substitute one word for another or use words in an anachronistic way, making it very difficult to understand what they are trying to express. People with AD sometimes combine a tendency toward restlessness and wandering off with disorientation for time and place. That is, they may wander away from home, become lost in their own immediate neighborhood, lose track of where they are and how they got there, and be quite unable to find their way home. Judgment is often impaired. Individuals with AD are more likely to dress inappropriately for local weather conditions or to be easy prey for scams, con artists, or telemarketers. Persons with AD gradually lose the ability for abstract thought. They may be unable to discern shades of meaning or to understand facial expressions or voice tones. They may be unable to manipulate information mentally, to interpret nuances, or even to understand humor. Individuals with AD often misplace everyday items by putting them in unusual or illogical locations (putting the house keys in a potted plant or a wallet in the toilet tank). They may experience rapid and dramatic mood swings with no precipitating events. For example, they may suddenly begin to weep, laugh uncontrollably, or explode in rage—all within a brief period of time and for no discernible reason. Finally, people with AD tend to slow way down. They may sleep for excessive periods of time, sit passively in front of the television from morning until night, or lose all interest in the world around them.

Nearly every person knows someone with AD, or knows someone who is affected by it—a caregiver, family member, friend, neighbor, or co-worker. Alzheimer's disease is overwhelming: to the individual, to the family, to the caregivers. It has devastating effects on the individual's entire social system. Since there is no treatment available to halt the progression of the disease, care and support remain the primary issues for the individual and family members. The Alzheimer's Foundation of America (AFA) estimates that for every one person who lives with AD, there are one to four caregivers dealing with the effects of the disease twenty-four hours a day, seven days a week.

PRIMARY SOURCE

Kryptonite

I'm twenty years old,
Far too young to be dealing
With this.

This is something that
Forty-year-old mothers discuss
With their balding husbands as they try to sleep.

It doesn't seem real,
Seems like a nightmare, a whirling, steaming
Unreality.

My Father is getting old.
He's been going bald since before I was born.

He's always had a hard time
Remembering and now, it seems,
He can't hear or think.

The doctor suspects it could be Alzheimer's.
That nasty word that turns
Strong men into drooling children.

I've seen it happen many times before.
My aunt and uncle both lived with the disease
For a few years before they died, their spirits
Leaving weak and emancipated bodies behind.

It's the most heartbreaking thing that I have ever seen.
The blank stare that never seems to comprehend
Who you are or what you are doing there.
All of this waiting for me just over the horizon.

I can already see him growing younger,
Less strong and it makes my heart ache.
He is my super hero slowly being led to kryptonite.

Kryptonite II

Two years later and the lethal kryptonite
Has its hold.
My daddy sits in diapers,
Drooling in a wheelchair
As nurses wipe off his face.

My mother and I take turns
Feeding him ice cream.
We catch the spit out parts
With a spoon and feed him
Like an infant.

He calls me mother because
He can't remember my name.
Although he calls to me
In the midst of his daydreams.
Always telling me to not forget to lock the door.

The strong man can no longer
Save the world. He can't even walk.
The world passes by without
Him even noticing.
I pass by without him noticing.

The eyes look blankly out into
The world (which only he can see).
His world is filled with parties and
Working outside. In reality it is only
Filled with stark white walls and dirty linoleum.

My mother lives alone.
Alone in a big house with a dog.
She visits him twice a day
And cries every night.
I try to go about my daily life.

The pain is starting to dull.
I watch him as the kryptonite
Slowly takes away everything that
He was and is.

Damn kryptonite.

SIGNIFICANCE

There is currently no cure for Alzheimer's disease, but there are a number of promising treatments that may serve to lessen some symptoms during the progression of the disease. Adequate palliative care and support, for both the person with the disease and for the caregivers, can greatly improve the quality of life for all involved.

At the start of the twenty-first century, five million Americans were estimated to have Alzheimer's disease (based on the results of the 2000 U.S. Census). This is more than twice the number that were reported to have the disease in 1980, and the number of cases is expected to triple by 2050. One in ten Americans who are sixty-five or older have Alzheimer's disease, and half of those ages eighty-five or older have (or will develop) it.

As the country's, and the world's, citizens grow older and live longer, the situation grows progressively more acute. With the number of individuals experiencing the symptoms of AD growing exponentially, the issue of their care becomes a major health and social concern. Based on the assumption that there are one to four caregivers closely involved with each patient suffering from AD, there were roughly 10 to 25 million Americans dealing with AD on a daily basis at the start of the twenty-first century, and between 30 and 75 million will be burdened with it by 2050. The economic impact alone, in terms of lost wages and work time for caregivers, is staggering. According to the AFA, the yearly cost of caring for individuals with Alzheimer's disease in the United States is around $100 billion. Each family spends about $18,000 to $36,000 per year to care for their loved one with AD. In addition, the annual cost to businesses, for lost time by primary caregivers, insurance costs, and loss of revenues from decreased productivity, is more than $60 billion per year.

There are some relatively new models of support for primary caregivers, enabling them to maintain quality of life while caring for a loved one, lowering cost of care, and reducing the need to miss work and family time. One such model is the AFA's "Together for Care" model. According to the AFA's Web site, the goals of this program are: 1) to fund the start up and expansion of programs and services at national and local levels in order to better provide the optimal care

In a landmark research project, the University of Kentucky studied nuns from the Sisters of Notre Dame to learn more about aging and Alzheimer's disease. ©KAREN KASMAUSKI/CORBIS.

families deserve; 2) to give grants to families to offset the cost of caring for their loved ones; and 3) to fund programs and services at organizations nationwide to help them offer resources either without cost or at a modest fee to families. The "Together for Care" philosophy supports the individual, the caregivers, the community, and society as a whole.

Another such model is The Eden Alternative, and its associated program, The Green House Project. The Eden Alternative is designed to promote positive changes in the ways in which communities live and work, and to create an inherent reward system for the delivery of excellent care. Its philosophy and goals focus on helping others create community environments for elders, in which they are supported, cognitively stimulated, and empowered. Elders are encouraged to live in a growth-facilitating system. Close and ongoing contact with nature, young people, and companion animals are integral parts of the model. The love and companionship of animals and children diminish or eliminate the feelings of loneliness, boredom, and isolation so common in elders living alone. Medical and supportive care are designed to be adjuncts to daily life, rather than the central focus of an individual's existence. Both of these programs offer comprehensive, humane care to the individual living with AD—as do a number of other programs—but, in addition, they focus on empowerment, support for the extended caregiver network, and the creation of a community environment. These are unique and exciting new approaches that can offer real hope for the future.

FURTHER RESOURCES

Books

Mace, Nancy L., and Peter V. Rabins. *The 36-Hour Day. A Family Guide to Caring for Persons With Alzheimer Disease, Related Dementing Illnesses, and Memory Loss in Later Life.* New York: Warner, 2001.

Periodicals

Hebert, L. E., et al. "Alzheimer's Disease in the U.S. Population: Prevalence Estimates Using the 2000 Census." *Archives of Neurology* 60 (August 2003): 1119–1122.

Web sites

Alzheimer's Association. "Common Tests." <http://www.alz.org/AboutAD/Diagnosis/Tests.asp> (accessed October 19, 2005).

Alzheimer's Association. "Standard Prescriptions for Alzheimer's." <http://www.alz.org/AboutAD/Treatment/Standard.asp> (accessed October 19, 2005).

Alzheimer's Foundation of America. "About Alzheimer's." <http://www.alzfdn.org/alzheimers/index.shtml> (accessed October 24, 2005).

The Eden Alternative. "What is Eden?" <http://www.edenalt.com/about.htm> (accessed October 24, 2005).

National Institute of Neurological Disorders and Strokes. "NINDS Alzheimer's Disease Information Page." <http://www.ninds.nih.gov/disorders/alzheimersdisease/alzheimersdisease.htm> (accessed October 19, 2005).

Telemedicine

Validation of a Real-time Wireless Telemedicine System, Using Bluetooth Protocol and a Mobile Phone, for Remote Monitoring Patient in Medical Practice.

Journal article

By: Jasemian Yousef

Date: June 22, 2005

Source: Jasemian Yousef. "Validation of a Real-time Wireless Telemedicine System, Using Bluetooth Protocol and a Mobile Phone, for Remote Monitoring Patient in Medical Practice." Abstract. *European Journal of Medical Research* 10 (June 2005): 254–262.

About the Author: Jasemian Yousef is a biomedical engineer and is affiliated with the Center for Sensory-Motor Interaction at Aalborg University in Aalborg, Denmark.

INTRODUCTION

Telemedicine has been in conceptual development since the 1920s. At the same time that the first televisions were being developed, the engineers at AT&T Bell Laboratories were creating picture telephones (that is, telephones that would allow both sender and receiver to see one another while talking— not the digital picture-transmitting telephones of the twenty-first century). The first live demonstration of a two-way video telephone conference occurred in April 1930. Two individuals, at different geographic locations, sat in sound- and light-proof booths with their picture telephones. The images were displayed to each speaker by means of a neon lamp reflecting to a receiving disk. The speakers looked into photoelectric cells that captured and transmitted the images, and their faces were illuminated by blue light. They spoke through desk-mounted microphones, and listened through loudspeakers. Although the demonstration was considered highly successful, and it received very favorable press, AT&T did not release a video telephone product for several more decades.

Contemporary telemedicine incorporates a variety of technologies: standard and fiber-optic telephone service coupled with high-speed, wide-bandwidth transmission of digitized signals utilizing computers, fiber optics, and satellite transmission systems, enhanced by sophisticated peripheral equipment, software, and the use of the Internet. The National Library of Medicine (NLM) acts as the telemedicine clearinghouse for the United States. It collects and disseminates cutting-edge information about telemedicine, and it funds and administratively supports research and development of technology related to telecommunications applications for medicine.

The goals of the burgeoning science of clinical telemedicine are three-fold: 1) to facilitate diagnosis; 2) to provide consultation; and 3) to deliver health services in areas where there is limited access to medical care. This is of particular importance in rural and frontier areas, which may be hundreds of miles distant

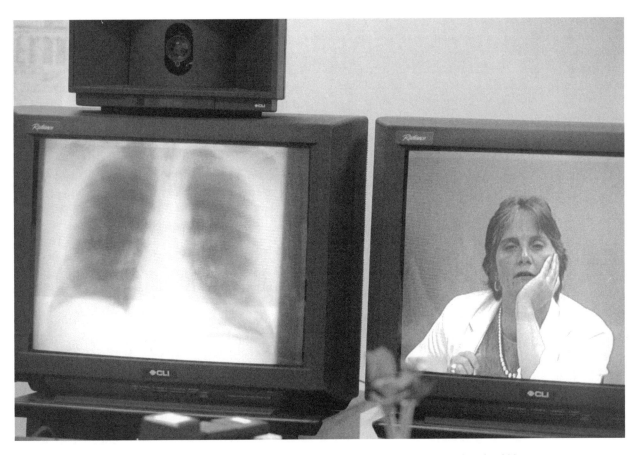

Specialists at the University of Texas prescribe treatment for prisoners following video consultations in 1998. ©F. CARTER SMITH/CORBIS SYGMA.

from specialty medical providers. The three most common ways of using telemedicine are: 1) for tele-consulting, where a patient is in a medical office with an examining provider and a distant provider is available online or by video for a real-time office visit and medical/diagnostic opinion or consultation (provider with patient to distant provider); 2) tele-monitoring (similar to care management or visiting nurse care), where a health care professional at a distant site has a visual and auditory link with a patient who is at home, and either interviews the patient or uses electronic monitoring equipment to determine health status (provider to patient); and 3) store-and-forward tele-medicine, in which an electronic record is created for a specific patient, containing data and test results (often pathology, radiology, or CT/MRI/PET/SPECT scan film/data as well), and a distant health care specialist acts as a reviewer and consultant for diagnostic or treatment planning purposes. Telemedicine is also used for teleconferencing and for distance learning purposes.

PRIMARY SOURCE

This paper validates the integration of a generic real-time wireless telemedicine system utilising Global System for Mobile Communications (GSM), BLUETOOTH protocol and General Packet Radio Service (GPRS) for cellular network in clinical practice. In the first experiment, the system was tested on 24 pacemaker patients at Aalborg Hospital (Denmark), in order to see if the pacemaker implant would be affected by the system. In the second experiment, the system was tested on 15 non-risky arrhythmia heart patients, in order to evaluate and validate the system application in clinical practice, for patient monitoring. Electrocardiograms were selected as the continuously monitored parameter in the present study. The results showed that the system had no negative effects on the pacemaker implants. The experiment results showed, that in a realistic environment for the patients, the system had 96.1% up-time, 3.2 (kbps) throughput, 10(-3) (packet/s) Packet Error Rate and 10(-3) (packet/s) Packet Lost Rate. During 24 hours test the network did not respond for 57 minutes, from which 83.1% was in the range of 0-3 minutes, 15.4% was in the range of 3–5 minutes, and only 0.7% of the down-time was > or = 5 and < or = 6 minutes. By a subjective evaluation, it was demonstrated that the system is applicable and the patients as well as the healthcare personnel were highly confident with the system. Moreover, the patients had high degree of mobility and freedom, employing the system. In conclusion, this generic telemedicine system showed a high reliability, quality and performance, and the design can provide a basic principle for real-time wireless remote monitoring systems used in clinical practice.

SIGNIFICANCE

In rural and frontier regions, and in typically underserved or difficult to reach areas, such as prisons, areas of military troop deployment, and commercial maritime vessels, provision of adequate health care has long been a challenge. In those settings, the medical system is often quite fragile. Providers are isolated and lack a peer community. They are often stressed due to high demands on their time with little or no back-up assistance. In addition, they often are underpaid and clinic settings are typically under-funded. (Rural and frontier communities are often poorer than more urban or suburban settings, so they may be more dependent of publicly paid health care, which typically is reimbursed to the provider at a lower rate than commercial third-party payers; in addition, community and ancillary programs for patient participation generally are lacking.) A similar situation exists for health care providers assigned to prison, military troop locations, and maritime vessels. Several access issues generally are common to each of these settings including: 1) geography (large distances between providers, between patients and providers, or between patients and health care facilities); 2) a lack of available and appropriate health care service or program options; 3) a lack of public or accessible transportation systems; 4) low or fixed income; 5) public insurance payment (and therefore limited options and lower reimbursement rates); and 6) possibly, a cultural norm suggesting that health care is not sought except in the most dire emergency.

With the advent of telemedicine, health care providers can literally be in two places at once. They can fill those service gaps without traveling great distances and can use resources with far greater efficiency and effectiveness than previously would have been possible. In each of these environments, the availability of telehealth/telemedicine services provides increased access to general and specialty health care, and provides this care with greater efficiency and effectiveness. Telemedicine can dramatically shorten the waiting time for general and specialty care. In addition, it can facilitate and enhance professional communication, support, and continuing education, and can potentially yield significant cost savings by eliminating lost revenues for transportation, emergency medical care, and missed appointments.

Along with the rapid evolution of the technology necessary to foster the advancement of telemedicine, has come the equally exponential growth and development of the Internet. Consumers are making greater and greater use of electronic technology to gather information and become educated. They use this electronic technology to do research, look up information, gather diagnostic information, order and receive diagnostic tests and protocols, and purchase pharmaceuticals. This parallel growth provides an ideal partnership for the technologically astute consumer, who is far more likely to be confident about the reliability and authenticity of telehealth resources accessed through the Internet than through other means.

There are other trends that make telemedicine a progressively more viable and potentially important tool. The population is aging and people are living longer. Older adults may not be sufficiently mobile to make frequent trips to medical offices or clinics for routine monitoring or for oversight of equipment, such as cardiac, blood pressure, and other vital sign monitors. In addition, increasing numbers of older adults live on fixed incomes. To pay for their medical care, they are dependent on Medicare, pensions, and limited health care insurance. These factors are fueling a shift in the most common sites of health care delivery. Fewer people will be admitted to hospitals, in part because of limited reimbursement, and fewer older adults will seek medical services at health care clinics and medical offices, for both economic and practical reasons (limited mobility of an aging and poorer population). The health care delivery site of choice will become the home. An additional benefit of the use of computer technology for patient monitoring will be the electronic patient record. This electronic record will facilitate consolidation of care and may prevent service duplication and over-prescribing of medications.

FURTHER RESOURCES
Web sites

The American Telemedicine Association. "ATA Newsroom." <http://www.atmeda.org/news/newres.htm> (accessed November 3, 2005).

The Changing Face of Medical Practice. "Tomorrow's Telemedicine Today." <http://telemed.medicine

.uiowa.edu/TRCDocs/slides/ttt/sld001.htm> (accessed November 3, 2005).

National Laboratory for the Study of Rural Telemedicine. "Final Report." <http://telemed.medicine.uiowa.edu/TRCDocs/Pubs/FinalReport/nlm1final.html> (accessed November 3, 2005).

Office for the Advancement of Telehealth. "2001 Report to Congress on Telemedicine—Executive Summary." <http://telehealth.hrsa.gov/pubs/report2001/exec.htm> (accessed November 3, 2005).

Office for the Advancement of Telehealth. "Welcome: Imagine a World Where No Matter Who You Are or Where You Are, You Can Get the Health Care You Need When You Need It." <http://telehealth.hrsa.gov/welcome.htm> (accessed November 3, 2005).

United States National Library of Medicine. National Institutes of Health. "Fact Sheet: Telemedicine Related Programs." <http://www.nlm.nih.gov/pubs/factsheets/telemedicine.html> (accessed November 3, 2005).

War and Medicine

The following section regarding war and medicine touches on a special subdivison of clinical medicine, the treatment of soldiers, and war-related injuries and diseases. War is inherently destructive: knives, bullets, bombs, and radiation exposure all wound and maim. These injuries often require immediate emergency medical attention in the form of surgery.

In the chaos of combat, medical care can be difficult to provide. Then, as now, a key task for physicians and nurses is the sorting of casualties by priority of treatment (triage), so that medical resources can be used most effectively and the most lives saved. In some conflicts, as was the case in the Spanish-American War, the toll from disease can be higher than that caused by battle.

Soldiers are not the only casualties of war. Civilians are often unintended victims as well. Additionally, war often results in large numbers of refugees that live in crowded, makeshift conditions that help breed disease. *Medecins Sans Frontiers* (Doctors Without Borders), an international aid organization founded in 1971 (and which received the 1999 Nobel Peace Prize) continues to provide medical services worldwide to victims of war or internal conflicts, as well as in the wake of natural disasters.

War has spurred the development of significant advances in medical techniques and medicines. For example, penicillin was first mass produced for troops during World War II (1938–1945). Also during that war, dried plasma, which could be preserved longer than the liquid version, was used for the first time, saving the lives of thousands of allied soldiers. Since the Second World War, significant military resources have been devoted to "medical intelligence," understanding the medical and health needs of soldiers in the field.

While biomedical science has been used to save lives at risk due to war injuries, it has also been used to create weapons of war. The use of disease-causing (pathogenic) bacteria and other microorganisms as weapons of war has been practiced for centuries. However, beginning in World War I (1915–1918), their use became more sophisticated. Microorganisms that can be easily dispersed in the air are potential biological weapons, especially microbes such as *Bacillus anthracis* (the cause of anthrax) that form structures called spores. Spores can persist in the environment for extended periods (at least a century) and, when inhaled or exposed to a wound, can germinate into the growing and pathogenic form of the organism. These conveyers of anthrax have been a biological weapon for centuries, but, as occurred in the aftermath of the September 11, 2001 terrorist attacks in the United States, can now be deployed in a much more directed and sophisticated way.

The genetic era has also influenced war and medicine. In countries that include the United States, dedicated military research facilities currently work on the genetic aspects of microbial diseases. In the case of the United States, this research is presently aimed mostly at developing vaccines, although in the past, countries including the United States, Britain, and Canada maintained offensive biological warfare programs.

Disqualifying Diseases

Medicine and Military Recruitment

Book excerpt

By: Theodoric Romeyn Beck

Date: 1823

Source: Theodoric Romeyn Beck. *Elements of Medical Jurisprudence, Volume I of II*. Albany, NY: Webster and Skinner, 1823.

About the Author: Theodoric Romeyn Beck was a nineteenth-century physician, medical professor, manager of a psychiatric facility (then called a lunatic asylum) and private school principal. He was active in the New York State Medical Society. He wrote and researched in several medical areas, particularly on issues concerning deaf-mutism and on psychopathology (the two were unrelated); his best-known body of work was the two-volume book text entitled *Elements of Medical Jurisprudence*, co-authored with his brother John Broadhead.

INTRODUCTION

During the late eighteenth and much of the nineteenth centuries, the general population of the United States did not have a cultural commitment to the pursuit of physical fitness, as everyday life was rigorous and physically demanding enough for most people—particularly those in rural and frontier areas, which comprised much of the country at that time.

During the Industrial Revolution and after the American Civil War (1861–1865), two major shifts in American life changed the nation's overall level of health and fitness: Developing technologies replaced many of the most labor-intensive jobs, so people didn't have to work as hard physically, and rural settlers moved to the cities for higher-paying jobs, shifting to an urban lifestyle that required far less walking and exertion. As a result, the general fitness level of the population declined considerably.

With America's entry into World War I in 1917, hundreds of thousands of men were drafted into the military. Conscription data indicated that nearly half of all deferrals, that is, those not accepted for active duty but reserved for call-up as needed, and one-third of all men drafted were considered to be "unfit for combat." Many were categorized as "highly unfit" prior to their military training. Of those draftees who received deferrals for possible service at a later date, the three most frequently cited reasons were large numbers of dental caries (commonly called dental cavities), flat feet, and venereal disease. After World War I, legislation was passed that required better school-based physical education programs.

In the World War II (1941–1945) draft, nearly half of all men registering were again either rejected for military service or given noncombat classifications. Since this conflict, like the previous World War, was a low-tech ground and air war, basic fitness for combat was necessary. During World War II, the primary categories for rejection were displayed symptoms of mental illness, chronic and life- or mobility-impacting physical illness, observable physical disabilities that interfered with mobility or weapons use, rashes and skin diseases, and stated homosexuality. During World War II, particularly, there was a social stigma in being and classified 4F (unfit for duty), and recruits often did not disclose chronic health conditions to examiners, or often sought assignment in stateside organizations that supported the war effort.

■ PRIMARY SOURCE

Of disqualifications for military service.

In every state, however despotic, there are certain classes of individuals exempted from military duty. This is in fact deemed indispensable, even with those who consider the male population merely as the material for armies. There must remain some to renew the waste of war—some to support the females and children of the nation, and others to protect them from injury.

The Jewish lawgiver, in his statutes, mentions several classes who were exempted from this duty, and in particular, all married persons during the first year of their marriage. And similar provisions are to be traced in the laws or customs of all countries.

In the United States, by a law of congress, all persons under eighteen years of age and above forty-five, are exempted. The importance of this regulation in time of war is incalculable, since it prevents the destruction of such whose strength is not yet matured, as well as those who are already feeling the advances of age. It is also understood, that there are many diseases which disqualify and exempt from military duty. The law of the state of New York directs, that the age and ability to bear arms of every enrolled person, shall be determined by the commandant of the company, with the right of appeal to the commanding officer of the regiment; and it adds, what indeed must now appear superfluous, *"that the certificate of a surgeon or surgeon's mate shall not be conclusive evidence of the inability of any person to bear arms."* ...

Before being inducted into the U.S. military during World War II (1939–1945), draftees and volunteers were required to pass a medical examination. They could be disqualified from service for having poor vision, bad teeth, flat feet, heart problems, mental illness, and various diseases. © BETTMANN/CORBIS.

The military system of France being more perfect than that of any other nation, it might be expected that rules on this subject would be formed; and accordingly we find that such were promulgated at an early period after the revolution. . . .

Among the preliminaries necessary to obtain an exemption, are the following: Every conscript who pleads bad health or bodily inability, must appeal in the first instance to his municipal administration; and he is not entitled to present himself for this purpose, unless he brings a certificate from a health officer, that he is really affected with a disease which appears to him to authorise an application. He is then to be examined by a health officer in presence of the administration, if he is capable of attending, or in presence of a delegate from it, if he be totally unable to attend in person. Before any dispensation

be granted, the commission of the executive directory must be heard; and he may, if any doubts be entertained, require a counter-examination. When the municipal administration consider any appeal to be without foundation, the conscript is obliged to join the army without delay. When they consider themselves incompetent to decide upon the appeal, the conscript is allowed to present himself immediately before the central administration, for their decision. And the municipal administration can only grant *definitive* dispensations in cases of palpable and notorious infirmities. They may allow *provisional* ones, not exceeding three months, when acute diseases or accidents prevent the conscript form presenting himself.

All the decisions of the municipal, must be sent to the central administration, for their approbation or rejection; and if they refuse to ratify them, the conscript must again be examined. Lastly, then they confirm a dispensation, it is sent to the minister of war, who forwards an exemption to the conscript, or annuls the dispensation. . . .

The officers of health, in giving their opinion, are directed to regulate themselves by the following tables:

TABLE 1. *Evident infirmities, implying absolute incapability of military service, and which are left to the decision of the municipal administrations of the canton.*

1. Total privation of sight. 2. The total loss of the nose. 3. Dumbness; permanent loss of voice; complete deafness. If there be any doubt of the existence of these infirmities, or if they do not exist in a great degree, the decision is to be reserved for the central administration. 4. Voluminous and incurable goitres, habitually impeding respiration. 5. Scrophulous ulcers. 6. Confirmed phthisis pulmonalis, i.e. in the 2d or 3d degrees. Care should be taken to report the symptoms characterizing this state; and as they are but too evident, they ought to procure an absolute dispensation. But for commencing phthisis, asthma, and haemoptisis, the municipal administration ought to grant only a provisional dispensation, if the person is incapable of presenting himself before the central administration; the decision in these different cases being reserved to the latter. 7. The loss of the penis, or of both testicles. 8. The total loss of an arm, leg, foot, or hand. The incurable loss of motion of these parts. 9. An aneurism of the principal arteries. 10. The curvature of the long bones; rickets and nodosities sufficient evidently to impede the motion of the limbs. Other diseases of the bones, although great and palpable, are sometimes liable to doubt, and therefore are reserved for the judgment of the central administration. 11. Lameness (claudication) well marked, whatever be the cause; this must be precisely stated. The same is the case with considerable and permanent retraction of the flexor or extensor muscles of a limb, or paralysis of these, or a state of relaxation impeding the free exercise of the muscular movements. 12. Atrophy of a limb, or decided marasmus, characterised by marks of hectic and wasting, which should be stated in the report.

SIGNIFICANCE

The use of a selective service system, or military draft process, began during the American Civil War in both the Union and Confederacy. It was also employed during World Wars I and II, the Korean War in the early 1950s, and for the Vietnam War in the 1960s.

During the war in Vietnam, the draft lottery and selective service systems were used at different times. In both cases, it was relatively easy to obtain a deferment, simply by being a college student who received passing grades. In retrospect, some sociologists consider the deferment process used during Vietnam biased in favor of those who could afford higher education. Legislative reforms have made the current draft law considerably more equitable: college students are deferred only until the end of the current semester (seniors until the end of the academic year; local boards must be culturally, ethnically, and racially representative of the communities in which they were located; and a random lottery determines the order of call to duty). At present, there is no military draft system in active use in the United States.

Historically, induction centers have functioned similarly: an inductee receives a letter informing him of a time and place to appear for induction. The inductee must arrive at the designated time and place prepared to leave for basic training/"boot camp." Upon arrival, the inductee is given an aptitude test or interview, undergoes a physical examination, and is classified according to fitness for service. Because of the sheer numbers of people being moved through the system during a military draft, processes are streamlined as much as possible. The job of the staff at the induction center is simply to see whether the inductee is "fit" for military service; this designation generally extends for a period of two years. Prior to leaving for basic training, the inductee is given any necessary vaccinations or inoculations, and undergoes any other medical regimens necessitated by the assigned field of duty (deployment location and combat classification, or military job).

Because there is no draft for service in the armed forces of the United States as of January 2006, military enlistment is considered voluntary. When an applicant is being considered for military duty, the three primary areas examined are: aptitude for military service, background screening and evaluation (also called a background investigation), and physical qualifications. The overall medical standards are the same across all branches of service for enlisted, appointed, inducted, or accessed (reservists) troops, and they appear in Military Entrance Processing Station (MEPS) Regulation 40-1.

Essentially, they state that the recruit neither actively has nor is a carrier for a communicable disease, is physically and psychologically able to meet the demands and hardships of basic training, is sufficiently adaptable to relocate wherever s/he is sent by the selected branch of the service, can adapt to the environmental, physical and geographic demands of deployment location, and can carry out all of the requisites of military duty and troop assignment without significantly aggravating or worsening any pre-existing deformities, conditions or defects.

There is an extensive list of disqualifying medical conditions, many of which can be recommended for an official waiver by an examining physician at the time of the military induction physical. The (examining) physician must belong to the branch of the service to which the recruit has applied; each waiver is individually determined, based on the recommendation of the medical profile (MEPS) officer, the specific situation, and the current needs and mandates of that particular service branch.

In discussion of most chronic or inherited systemic diseases, disorders, or the consequences thereof, the questions to be considered pertain to whether the condition is progressive; could be worsened or aggravated by military service; might preclude satisfactory completion of required training and subsequent duty assignment; and could potentially constitute an undue hazard to the recruit or to others, particularly in time or place of combat.

All potential military applicants must complete an aptitude and placement test called the CAT-ASVAB (typically unless they are recruited for a specific medical service position type such as physician, nurse, psychologist, or social worker); meet height and weight standards; pass vision and hearing examinations; undergo urine and blood tests, obtaining results that fall within normal limits; have clean drug and alcohol screening tests; successfully complete visible muscle group and joint range-of-motion maneuvers (in undergarments); and have a satisfactory physical examination and health history interview. Female applicants are also given a pregnancy test.

In terms of actual numbers of individuals processed through induction centers during the major conflicts of the twentieth century, a total of 2,810,296 American men were inducted into military service during World War I; 10,110,104 men during World War II; 1,529,539 draftees were processed into the armed forces for the Korean War; and the Vietnam War saw 1,857,304 men drafted, processed, and inducted into military service.

For the most part, although modern military conflicts are technologically oriented and involve less physical combat, that possibility always exists, so an overall high level of health, fitness, and physical agility are still required for entrance into military service.

FURTHER RESOURCES

Books

Rice, Emmett A. *A Brief History of Physical Education.* New York: A.S. Barnes, 1926.

Web sites

Department of Defense Instruction Number 6130.4. "SUBJECT: Criteria and Procedure Requirements for Physical Standards for Appointment, Enlistment, or Induction in the Armed Forces." <http://www.dtic.mil/whs/directives/corres/pdf2/i61304p.pdf/> (accessed November 28, 2005).

Office of the Surgeon General. "Office of Medical History: Infectious Diseases & General Medicine." <http://history.amedd.army.mil/booksdocs/wwii/internalmedicinevolIII/frameindex.html> (accessed November 28, 2005).

United States Army Regulation 40-501. "Medical Service Standards of Medical Fitness." <http://usmilitary.about.com/gi/dynamic/offsite.htm?site=http://www.usapa.army.mil/pdffiles/r40%5F501.pdf> (accessed November 28, 2005).

Veterans for Peace. Military Draft. <http://www.veteransforpeace.org/Military_draft_102403.htm> (accessed November 29, 2005).

World War II History. African-Americans in World War II. "Physical Fitness." <http://www.world-war-2-history.com/books/1/11> (accessed November 28, 2005).

A Doctor's Memories:

The Spanish-American War

Book excerpt

By: Victor C. Vaughan

Date: 1926

Source: Victor C. Vaughan. A Doctor's Memories. Indianapolis: Bobbs-Merrill, 1926.

About the Author: Victor C. Vaughan became dean of the University of Michigan Medical School in 1891. When the Spanish-American war erupted he took a leave from the university to become a surgeon with the Michigan Volunteer Infantry. Immediately after the conflict ended, he worked with Walter Reed to investigate typhoid fever outbreaks in military barracks. After his work on the typhoid board ended, he returned to his position as dean, where he stressed science-based, research-oriented teaching and study of medicine.

INTRODUCTION

In 1898, the United States fought a four-month war with Spain, which began as a result of brutal Spanish policy toward its colony of Cuba. Termed the "Splendid Little War" by John Milton Hay, then U.S. Ambassador to Great Britain, the conflict cost less lives in battle than anticipated at 345 dead, but cost the lives of more than 2,500 men from disease.

In the mid-1890s, Cubans attempted to gain their freedom from Spain by fighting a war for independence. Sympathy for the Cuban cause grew in the United States, especially after the Spanish began using concentration camps that killed thousands of Cuban civilians. Sensationalist American newspapers often distorted Cuban events in their bid for readership, which further inflamed anti-Spanish feelings. Emotions reached a fever pitch on February 15, 1898, when the U.S.S. *Maine* sank after a mysterious explosion in Havana harbor, killing 260 sailors. Americans blamed Spain for the loss, the yellow press thundered "Remember the *Maine*," and on April 25, 1898, the United States declared war on Spain.

The conflict was one-sided. The Spanish fleet arrived in Santiago de Cuba on May 19, 1898 only to be blockaded by American forces later that month. When the Spanish ships tried to escape in July, the fleet was destroyed. Meanwhile, 17,000 American troops were sent in to capture Santiago. The Spanish forces, though weak, managed to put up a strong resistance before being overwhelmed. The war effectively ended when Santiago surrendered on July 17, 1898.

Hostilities formally ceased with the Treaty of Paris on December 10, 1898, which gave Cuba independence from Spain, although the island remained under American control. Spain also ceded Puerto Rico, the Philippines, and Guam to the United States. This established an American presence in both the Caribbean and Asia.

PRIMARY SOURCE

The Spanish-American War

After the sinking of the *Maine* in the harbor at Havana, the proclamation of war against Spain, and the call for volunteers, I was anxious to enlist; but having a wife and five children dependent upon me, I could not conscientiously do so. There was quite an outbreak of enthusiasm for enlistment among the students of the University of Michigan. President Angell was then in Constantinople as United States Ambassador to Turkey, and President Hutchins, who later became permanent President, was acting in that capacity. One day he came to me and said that the students were all astir about the war, wanted to hold a mass meeting with speeches, and might be stampeded into enlistment. He advised that the mass meeting be permitted, that representatives of the students be invited to talk, and that the older and wiser members of the Faculty pour the oil of caution upon the troubled waters of youth. As dean of the Medical School I was asked to attend the meeting and to do my part in allaying and cooling the enthusiasm and patriotism of the students. Reluctantly I consented to do my small share in this work.

University Hall was crowded. Even the students who made speeches, for the most part at least, evidently had been selected from among those most likely to be moderate in speech. I sat on the platform and listened to talk after talk by my older and wiser colleagues. One admonished the students that their first duty was to their parents, that they should not enlist without consulting them, and that they had parents distributed from the Atlantic to the Pacific. Another said that the student's first duty was to the University, that if he enlisted he interrupted his course of study, would probably not be able to regain his place in his class, and would suffer delay in graduation. A third told the students that there were enough unemployed in this country to fill the quota called for by the President, advised waiting until the unemployed had enlisted, and if it appeared that the ranks were not filled by these, enlistment by the students might be considered. I had promised President Hutchins that I would be at least moderate in my speech and I went to the meeting fully determined that I would comply with my promise. I have long known that in speaking I labor under a serious defect, but I had no realization until that night of the extent to which this defect dominates and determines my actions. Whatever I may intend to say, when I am to make a speech, when I actually begin to talk, I always give expression to my convictions. Many a time I have gone before an audience intending by my words to palliate and to compromise, but after I begin to talk I have always been led by my convictions rather than by my intentions. At the mass meeting I was called upon to follow the colleague who had spoken of filling the ranks with the unemployed. This drove me into a mental frenzy, and standing before the audience, I said: "God pity the country whose tramps must fight its battles; it is true that you are here to acquire an education with the purpose of fitting yourself for the work of life; but I would rather see these walls crumble into dust than to see you hesitate to go when your country calls. You have duties towards your parents, but your first duty is to serve your country." Along this line I rushed on in a verbal flood until my time limit was reached.

The next afternoon Governor Pingree, in his office at Lansing, called me by telephone, informed me that he had read my speech, had signed my commission, and that I would report for duty at Camp Alger, Virginia, without delay. Some enlist because they like the soldier's life, some for patriotic reasons, but I received my commission at the outbreak of the Spanish-American War because I talked too much.

On the third or fourth evening after my arrival at Camp Alger we had had our mess, and were sitting in front of Colonel Boynton's tent and listening to an Irish officer from a nearby Massachusetts regiment read Mr. Dooley on the war, when an orderly from brigade headquarters rode up and handed the Colonel a piece of paper. Finishing the reading Colonel Boynton arose and said, "We strike tents to-morrow morning at seven o'clock, entrain at Dun Loring, go to Alexandria and there take boat for Old Point Comfort. To-morrow we will be on our way to Cuba." This order applied to the brigade consisting of the 33rd and 34th Michigan and the 7th Massachusetts under command of General Duffield.

At this point I perpetrated my first blunder in military affairs. I sent my orderly to the office of the division surgeon, Colonel A. C. Girard, with a note saying that up to that time my brigade had received no medical supplies and that I protested against going to Cuba without full medical equipment. I was subsequently told by one who was with the colonel that he was indignant when he read my notes and as I appreciated later, he had a right to be angry. In an incredibly short time the colonel's orderly rode up to my tent and handed me the piece of paper I had sent and on the back was written: "First endorsement, sir: To protest to a superior officer is unmilitary; you should have requested. However, five ambulances are now on their way to your regiment with more supplies than you can possibly need in Cuba." I may say that the excess disappeared long before those wounded at the Battle of Santiago had been dressed. . . .

SIGNIFICANCE

Despite its brevity and low casualty rate, the Spanish-American War had a significant impact upon American military medicine. It was one of the first major wars fought after the medical establishment had accepted the germ theory of disease.

After the war, Vaughan, Reed, and their colleagues on the typhoid fever board established the importance of both human contact and flies in the spread of typhoid fever. They developed the concept of healthy typhoid carriers as agents of infection and eliminated "typhomalarial fever" as a diagnosis by identifying the two diseases with distinguishing blood tests. Perhaps of greatest importance for the welfare of common soldiers, they showed that line officers were often

responsible for typhoid epidemics that ravaged the army in 1898.

Medical officers, although commissioned, were outside of the military hierarchy and needed the cooperation of regular officers to implement any sanitary procedures. Even though physicians regularly warned that poor sanitation and fecal contamination helped spread typhoid, line officers continued to design latrines as they always had. As a result, typhoid fever killed more men in the war than any other cause, with 20,738 cases reported and 1,590 deaths.

Luckily, physicians did not need line officers' approval to treat the wounded, and they took immediate steps to ensure sanitation. They saved lives and limbs with antiseptic first aid on the battlefield and aseptic surgical techniques in the operating theater. As a result, the mortality of wounded American soldiers was the lowest in military history to date.

After the war, the military establishment enacted a number of innovations to minimize future deaths from disease. The Department of Military Hygiene was established at West Point in 1905 to instruct line officers in the fundamentals of military hygiene and camp sanitation. In 1911, typhoid immunization became compulsory for all U.S. soldiers. With this decision, the U.S. Army became the first in the world to adopt an inoculation against typhoid.

FURTHER RESOURCES
Books

Cirillo, Vincent J. *Bullets and Bacilli: The Spanish-American War and Military Medicine*. New Brunswick, N.J.: Rutgers University Press, 2004.

Cosmas, Graham A. *An Army for Empire: the United States Army in the Spanish-American War*. Columbia: University of Missouri Press, 1971.

Circular Letter No. 36

Penicillin Treats Bacterial Infections

Government document

Date: July 1, 1944

Source: E. Standlee. Report From Army Headquarters, Office of the Surgeon. North African Theater of Operations. Circular Letter No. 36. Available online at: *Office of Medical History.* <http://history.amedd. army.mil/default_index2.html> (accessed November 20, 2005).

About the Author: In 1942, Army Lieutenant Colonel Earle G. G. Standlee was designated chief medical purchasing and contracting officer for the Army Chief Surgeon's Office, European Theater of Operations. Within a year, he was reassigned to a similar position in North Africa, where he participated in writing Circular Letter No. 36. Standlee later retired from the Army as a major general and frequently reviewed military medical history publications for the Office of the Surgeon General.

INTRODUCTION

Antibiotics are naturally formed or synthetically made compounds that specifically kill bacteria. Viruses, whose structure differs from bacteria and which require the transcription machinery of bacteria or other host cells, are not affected by antibiotics. There are many different antibiotics that target different structures on the surface or inside of bacteria, or which disrupt select biochemical facets of bacterial operation.

Naturally occurring antibiotics are produced by bacteria and various eukaryotic organisms like plants. Their function is to allow the organism to outcompete other organisms for an ecological niche or to protect the organism from bacterial infection. Such compounds are detected by screening natural samples for antibacterial potency. In modern times this screening has been automated, enabling thousands of samples to be screened each day.

There are different classes of antibiotics, based on their structural chemistry and mode of action. Penicillin, for example, is a beta-lactam antibiotic, named for the ring structure that is a constituent of the molecule. Tetracyclines, aminoglycosides, rifamycins, quinolones, and sulphonamides are other classes of antibiotics.

Reflecting their different chemistries, the mode of action of the various antibiotics is different. Beta-lactam antibiotics disrupt the manufacture of peptidoglycan (the main stress-bearing meshwork in the bacterial cell wall) by blocking the construction of the peptidoglycan building blocks or preventing their incorporation into the existing peptidoglycan. Aminoglycoside antibiotics kill bacteria in a different way—by binding to a subunit of the ribosome and blocking the manufacture of protein. Aminoglycosides also can retard the movement of essential molecules from the outside to the inside of a bacterium. As a final example, quinolone antibiotics act by blocking the ability of an enzyme to uncoil the DNA double helix. This

stops the DNA from replicating and is lethal to the bacterium.

Some antibiotics—known as narrow-spectrum antibiotics—act on only a few types of bacteria. Other antibiotics kill many kinds of bacteria, and so are described as having a broad-spectrum of activity.

Bacteria can be killed or weakened by agents other than antibiotics. Antiseptics, for example, are compounds that were originally conceived to control bacterial infections of the blood (sepsis; hence their name). Antiseptics prevent the growth of pathogenic (disease-causing) microorganisms. Organisms that are weakened by antiseptics can be rendered more susceptible to the defense mechanisms of the host.

The use of antimicrobial compounds dates back thousands of years. The black eye makeup—known as kohl—used by the ancient Arabs and Egyptians is an antiseptic mixture of copper and antimony. Indeed, present day treatment for trachoma (blindness caused by infection of the eyes by the bacterium *Chlamydia trachomatis*) utilizes medicine that is very similar to kohl.

While studying influenza viruses in his laboratory in 1928, the Scottish physician Alexander Fleming (1881–1955) noticed that a mold was growing by chance on a culture plate containing a staphylococcus bacteria, and that the mold had created a zone on the plate where the bacteria was not growing. With further experimentation, Fleming found that the mold contained a powerful anti-bacterial agent that could prevent the growth of staphylococci even when highly diluted. He named the agent penicillin. Over a decade later, in 1941, Oxford researchers Howard Florey (1898–1968) and Ernst Chain (1906–1979) found a way to purify and stabilize enough penicillin to administer to a human. All three scientists won the 1945 Nobel Prize in physiology or medicine for this accomplishment.

The Unites States Army made immediate use of penicillin in World War II (1941–1945). In hospitals near the front, the new therapeutic agent saved thousands of soldiers from post-battlefield wound infections, and proved an effective agent in treating many cases of syphilis and gonorrhea among the troops. American and British military hospitals served as a large-scale proving ground for the drug, and military physicians helped standardize dosage and administration procedures for penicillin. The following Army report summarizes the indications and usage for penicillin in treating soldiers wounded in North Africa in World War II.

**HEADQUARTERS
NORTH AMERICAN THEATER OF OPERATIONS
OFFICE OF THE SURGEON
APO 534
1 JULY 1944
CIRCULAR LETTER NO. 36**
SUBJECT: PENICILLIN THERAPY IN WOUND MANAGEMENT, SURGICAL DISEASE, BURNS, AND ANAEROBIC INFECTIONS

1. *General.* a. In World War II, two quite different policies have governed the use of chemotherapeutic agents in the management of wounds. Chemotherapy has been recommended: (1) as a substitute for adequate wound surgery, seeking to delay and minimize operative procedures; (2) as an adjunct to established and progressive surgical measures designed to achieve better results within an increased margin of safety. The latter has been and will continue to be the policy governing the management of the wounded in this theater.

b. The use of penicillin as an adjunct to surgery outlined in this circular is defined as *therapy* rather than *prophylaxis*. Routine immunization of troops with tetanus toxoid is a *prophylactic* measure. Administration of penicillin for contaminated wounds and established infection is a therapeutic measure. As with all therapy, if the desired goal is to be achieved, intelligent and precise professional supervision of every detail is essential.

2. *Scope of Penicillin Therapy.* a. Penicillin is accepted as the best available antibacterial agent for gram-positive bacteria and gram-negative diplococci. It is ineffective for gram-negative bacilli.

b. Penicillin does not sterilize dead, devitalized or avascular tissue, nor does it prevent the septic decomposition of contaminated blood clot. There is no evidence that it can neutralize preformed bacterial exotoxins or inhibit the locally necrotizing bacterial enzymes in undrained pus. These limitations demand that surgical wound management retain the principles of excision of devitalized tissue, dependent drainage of residual dead space, evacuation of pus and delayed or staged closure of contaminated wounds (see Circular Letter No. 26, Office of the Surgeon, Hq. NATOUSA).

c. The use of penicillin in an individual patient is based upon the decision that infection is probable or present.

d. It is recommended that parenteral administration be the basis of penicillin therapy. The local or topical use of penicillin is a supplement to systemic therapy only in lesions of the central nervous system, serous cavities and joints. The diffusion of the drug into these areas appears slow and limited.

3. *Penicillin Therapy in Relation to Sulfonamide Therapy.* a. Topical and oral administration of sulfonamides as first aid measures will be continued.

b. Intravenous sulfonamide prior to initial surgery will be replaced by parenteral administration of penicillin (par. 6, a).

c. At the conclusion of the initial wound operation, the decision will be made either to institute a postoperative course of penicillin therapy or to maintain chemotherapy with sulfonamides. It is recommended that the agents be used individually and not concomitantly. If a course of penicillin is elected, topical frosting of the wound with sulfonamide is omitted. The following observations will serve as a guide in this decision:

1. Clinical experience with penicillin has been greatest with wounds of the extremities and the thorax. The drug is recommended for these injuries.
2. The value of penicillin in craniocerebral wounds is well established, but an extensive experience has not been accumulated.
3. Cleanly debrided soft part wounds uncomplicated by fracture, extensive tissue destruction, or retained missiles are adequately handled by sulfonamide therapy.
4. Preliminary evaluation of penicillin therapy for fecal contamination of the peritoneal cavity is encouraging but at the present time is inadequate for comparison with sulfonamide therapy. In view of the difficulties in maintaining a fluid intake adequate to safeguard sulfonamide therapy in this group of cases, substitution of penicillin may be made at the discretion of time surgeon. Forcing of fluids is not necessary solely because of penicillin therapy and in fact, reduces the effective concentration of the drug by rapid urinary excretion.

4. *Routes of Penicillin Administration.* a. Intramuscular. This is the standard route for administration. The deltoid, gluteus and thigh muscles are recommended as the sites for injection. The same area may be used repeatedly. Subcutaneous administration is to be avoided.

b. Intravenous. The intravenous route is reserved for patients with shock or immediately life endangering infection. A single intravenous injection provides a therapeutic concentration of the drug that lasts for two hours. If intravenous therapy is indicated to span a longer period, the injection is repeated or constant drip administration instituted.

5. *Dosage.* a. Systemic therapy. Current practice dictates a dosage of 200,000 units in 24 hours, given as 25,000 units every three hours by the intramuscular route. Larger initial dosage or greater 24 hourly dosage have no demonstrable merit. Maintenance of full dosage schedules throughout the course of therapy is better than a graded terminal decrease in dosage.

b. Local therapy. The powdered sodium salt of penicillin is slightly acid and provokes a burning pain and serous discharge if applied to an open wound. A solution containing 10,000 units per c.c. is well tolerated as an intramuscular injection but may produce headache, meningismus and pleocytosis of the spinal fluid after intrathecal injection. The maximal effective local concentration is 250 to 500 units per c.c. The usual concentration employed chemically varies between 500 and 5,000 units per c.c. with predominate usage of a solution containing 1,000 units per c.c. The following dosage schedules are recommended for local instillation:

1. Intrathecal space: 7,500 units
2. Pleural cavity: 25,000 units
3. Peritoneal cavity: 50,000 units
4. Knee joint: 10,000 unitsLocal instillation of penicillin may be repeated at intervals of 12 to 48 hours in accordance within clinical indications. Needle aspiration and injection is preferable to inlying tubes.

6. *Use of Penicillin in Mobile Hospitals*. The following recommendations are made on the basis of procedures that have been found practical in Evacuation Hospitals:

a. Upon arrival in the shock or preoperative ward, the wounded will receive 25,000 units of penicillin intramuscularly, unless the wound is certainly of a trivial nature. If shock is present, an additional 25,000 units will be given intravenously.

b. Preoperative dosage is continued at 3 hourly intervals. It is more practical to give penicillin to every patient in a preoperative ward at the same time, than to keep each patient on a dosage schedule based on the time of arrival. There is no objection to a time interval of less than 3 hours between the first two injections.

c. The decision to continue penicillin or to substitute sulfonamide in the postoperative period is made when the operation is concluded and the nature and extent of the injury evaluated (see par. 3 c).

d. No patient will be held in a mobile hospital solely for the purpose of continuing penicillin therapy. The usual criteria based on the condition of the patient will determine the suitability for evacuation. In general, the drug is continued for 2 to 3 days beyond the period of clinical recovery from the hazard or subsidence of infection. A course of therapy may be associated with slight fever which disappears after the drug is stopped. Suitable periods of therapy are:

1. Soft part wounds: 5 to 7 days
2. Compound fractures: 10 to 12 days
3. Thoracic wounds: 8 to 10 days
4. Abdominal wounds: 8 to 10 days
5. Craniocerebral wounds: 8 to 10 days
6. Joint wounds: 7 to 14 days

e. Patients evacuated prior to completion of a course of therapy will carry a notation "On Penicillin" in the space provided under the designation "Special attention needed in transit, or other remarks" on the jacket of the Field Medical Record (Form 52d). This will indicate the need for continuation of therapy in holding stations, hospital ships and fixed hospitals.

7. *Use of penicillin in Holding Stations or Hospital Ships*. a. Form 52d will be examined in each case upon admission to identify those patients receiving penicillin therapy (par. 5 e).

b. 25,000 units of penicillin will be administered intramuscularly every 3 hours to all such designated patients.

8. *Use of Penicillin in Fixed Hospitals*. a. Patients designated as "On Penicillin" will have time course continued on admission to time hospital. Discontinuance of therapy will be time responsibility of a medical officer after lie has reviewed the status of time patient.

b. Secondary suture of cleanly debrided soft part wounds does not require penicillin therapy. Soft part wounds requiring delayed debridement or secondary debridement or within established infection may properly receive penicillin.

c. Reparative surgical procedures on wounds complicated by skeletal, joint, nerve, tendon or vascular injury require penicillin therapy.

d. Established wound infection is an indication for penicillin therapy.

e. Early secondary reparative operations through recently healed wounds require penicillin therapy.

9. *Surgical Disease*. a. Acute or chronic infections such as furuncles, carbuncles, felons, desert sores, tenosynovitis, etc. should be treated with penicillin whenever it is judged that loss of time from duty can be shortened. . . .

For the SURGEON:
(S) E. STANDLEE
E. STANDLEE, Colonel, MC., Deputy Surgeon.

SIGNIFICANCE

Although penicillin was initially considered a war asset and war secret in the U.S. and Britain, by the end of 1945, commercial manufacturing plants were capable of producing enough penicillin so that physicians also could prescribe it to their civilian patients. Treatment protocols and dosage regimes that were perfected during wartime served

Anne Miller (center) is believed to be the first person to use penicillin in the United States. Here, she meets Alexander Fleming (right), who discovered penicillin, and Francis G. Blake of the Yale Medical School. AP/WIDE WORLD PHOTOS.

the civilian population at the war's end. Penicillin was labeled a "miracle drug" after it also demonstrated its effectiveness in curing other bacterial infections including scarlet fever, meningitis, diphtheria, and bacteremia or septicemia (commonly known as blood poisoning).

In the decades following the discovery of penicillin, a flood of naturally occurring antibiotics was discovered, refined, and marketed. Antibiotics quickly became (and still are) a vital part of the treatment for infections and one of the major medical innovations of the twentieth century. Indeed, antibiotics were so effective that, by the 1970s, the conventional wisdom held that the threat of bacterial infectious diseases was ebbing. However, this heady hope proved to be

shortsighted, and bacterial resistance to antibiotics began to concern scientists in the late 1980s.

Antibiotic development has become a race. New or altered antibiotics need to be developed to at least keep pace with the resistance acquired by clinically important bacteria. One strategy to keep antibiotics sensitive to the organisms they are intended to fight is to modify an existing antibiotic to restore its potency. Modifying an antibiotic slightly, such as by the addition of a different chemical group to alter the three dimensional structure of the compound, can work. Unfortunately, bacteria relatively quickly tend to develop resistance to the modified compound.

Misuse or overuse of antibiotics contributes to the development of bacterial resistance. For example, treatment of viral illnesses, such as a cold or the flu, with an antibiotic is a useless strategy, since antibiotics are ineffective against viruses. Yet, exposing any bacteria resident in the patient to the antibiotic can prompt the development of a more resistant and hardy bacteria.

Incomplete antibiotic therapy also is an example of misuse. If an antibiotic is used properly to treat an infection (i.e., taken as directed for the full length of time), the infectious bacterial population should be completely eliminated. However, the use of too low a concentration of an antibiotic or ending therapy too soon can leave bacterial survivors, which have the capacity to acquire resistance. If the resistance is governed by a genetic alteration, the genetic change may be passed on to subsequent generations of bacteria who also have resistance to the antibiotic.

As one example, many strains of the bacterium that causes tuberculosis are now resistant to one or more of the antibiotics routinely used to control this lung infection. Also, some strains of *Staphylococcus aureus*, a bacteria responsible for common infections, are resistant to almost all antibiotics.

FURTHER RESOURCES

Books

Shnayerson, Michael, and Mark J. Plotkin. *The Killers Within: The Deadly Rise of Drug-Resistant Bacteria.* New York: Little, Brown, 2002.

Walsh, Christopher. *Antibiotics: Actions, Origins, Resistance.* Washington, D.C.: ASM, 2003.

Web Sites

Wellcome Trust. "The Medicine Chest: History of Antibiotics." <http://www.wellcome.ac.uk/doc_WTX026108. html> (accessed November 20, 2005).

Medical Intelligence

Book excerpt

By: Robert S. Anderson

Date: 1969

Source: Robert S. Anderson, COL. MC. *Preventive Medicine in World War II, Volume IX.* Washington, D.C.: Office of the Surgeon General: U.S. Army, 1969.

About the Author: Robert S. Anderson attained the rank of colonel in the United States Army Medical Corps.

He served as the Director of Historical Unit of the Medical Service Corps during the 1960s.

INTRODUCTION

As defined in the Military Intelligence Professional Bulletin, medical intelligence is *that category of intelligence resulting from the collection, evaluation, analysis, and interpretation of foreign medical, biotechnological, and environmental information that is of interest to strategic and military medical planning.* The Armed Forces Medical Intelligence Center (AFMIC) is a "field production activity" of the Defense Intelligence Agency. The AFMIC is housed at Fort Detrick, located in Frederick, Maryland. Its mission is a very broad one, extending from assessment and evaluation of bioterrorism capabilities of extremist groups, known terrorists, and foreign governments, to medical and environmental conditions for troops deployed worldwide, to global surveillance of infectious diseases, to anticipated medical needs for American troops as well as refugees, detainees, and potential prisoners of war worldwide, to potential biological and environmental hazards in military theaters, to cooperative efforts with world health agencies aimed at sharing of disease and potential bioterrorism surveillance information. Within the armed forces, the data gathered by medical intelligence efforts is used in many ways, among the most salient of which involve pre-planning of medical needs, and making advance preparations in an effort to anticipate probable strategic responses "on the ground" when troops are to be deployed to a specific area. In many ways, the process of gathering and utilizing medical intelligence data is akin to risk management in the civilian sector.

For the past thirty or forty years, most of the military actions in which American military forces have been locally involved (troops stationed in the immediate area) have been markedly different in terms of terrain, culture, environment, sanitary and hygiene systems, medical and health concerns (endemic diseases) and biohazards, than the United States. By having medical intelligence about local conditions likely to be encountered, it is possible for the military planners to create the most realistic and appropriate possible infrastructure, in order to enhance the efficiency of the military action. As well, military intelligence can be utilized to create a series of potential scenarios for use in potential disaster or emergency response situations, such as anticipation of possible homeland terrorist acts, or planning adequate responses to natural disasters such as floods or hurricanes.

PRIMARY SOURCE

By 1 January 1944, when it was reestablished on a divisional basis, Medical Intelligence Division had grown from its original one officer and one clerk to a staff of eleven officers, six civilians of professional rank, and sixteen clerks and stenographers. The staff had a remarkably broad linguistic coverage, and a suitably qualified public health engineer. Capt. George O. Pierce, SnC, had been added to the staff to assume responsibility for the collection of information on water supplies and sewage disposal facilities.

Intelligence documents were being collected and added to the file at the rate of almost 1,000 a month, and those of special value to other offices were being distributed on loan in accordance with a planned distribution system. Surveys of most areas of immediate military significance had been revised or were scheduled for revision, and a formal plan for distribution recognized by the Joint Chiefs of Staff as the agency to contribute the medical section of the newly created JANIS (Joint Army and Navy Intelligence Studies) which had replaced the War Department Strategic Surveys. Three medical intelligence officers were on duty overseas, and plans were under development for the assignment of others. . . .

JANIS series.—The development of the JANIS series marked also a forward step in dissemination of medical intelligence. In the War Department Strategic Surveys, the medical section had been but a brief paragraph in a chapter devoted to "The Population and Social Conditions." The original JANIS plan perpetuated this very minor position, but as a result of a series of conferences with the JANIS board, the outline was changed, and the medical section became one of a series of 15 coordinate chapters.

This event, which passed unnoticed except in the divisional semi-monthly report, merited greater attention than was accorded it, for it marked the first time that the military services had recognized the Medical Department as a major contributor to the intelligence planning of a military operation. It signified acceptance of the fact that full knowledge of medical facilities and hazards is of major concern, parallel in importance with knowledge of weather and terrain. Medical intelligence had actually assumed its rightful role in the intelligence field, and the division had become the source to which other parts of the Armed Forces were to turn for their information. . . .

Enemy equipment collection.—The year 1944 also saw the establishment of an orderly program for the collection of enemy equipment and its return to the Zone of Interior for study purposes, and the beginning of the program for the collection of information on German scientific progress during the war period. As the ultimate defeat of Germany became a foregone conclusion, War Department attention was focused on the formulation of a program to make certain that the German scientific and technologic advances would be learned and made available to the United States. The program was to be a matter of major concern to medical intelligence for the next year, requiring much time and skilled personnel. It again emphasized the fact that an intelligence program, if it is to function properly, must be broader than the confines of preventative medicine or any other field of medicine. . . .

The spring of 1945 saw the maximum expansion of medical intelligence. The programs for the collection of enemy equipment and scientific data in Germany were operating at full strength. In all other respects, medical intelligence interest in Washington had shifted from Europe to the Pacific. . . .

SIGNIFICANCE

The AFMIC was originally commissioned with the objective of gathering, interpreting, and appropriately distributing information regarding the medical, hygienic, and sanitary conditions and facilities on nations involved in World War II. It was initially created (in April of 1941) as a stand-alone division called the United States Army Medical Intelligence Office,; it was made a field production activity of the Defense Intelligence Agency on January 1, 1992.

As currently conceptualized within the defense Intelligence Agency, the AFMIC has four major objective areas, in addition to its overarching primary missions of provision of health care and essential medical support to outbound deployed troops, to enhance homeland security against bioterrorist threats, and to provide *stat* medical intelligence information on an as-needed emergent basis. The four objectives concern: the oversight of medical and biotechnological research and development, operationalization, and global sharing of relevant international medical resources; maintaining current data regarding infectious and communicable diseases, biohazards, and environmental vectors that could pose a threat to world health; tracking global advances in biotechnology, nanotechnology, biological and pharmaceutical advances and potential threat agents, medical science developments, and any other medical intelligence issues that might be of interest to the American military defense system; and the collection and dissemination of gathered medical intelligence data regarding the global effects (to include civilian and military populations) of pandemics (such as HIV/AIDS, tuberculosis, and influenza)and debilitating or potentially lethal diseases (diarrheal diseases, cholera, malaria, etc.), the nature and capabilities of worldwide medical care provision systems, global research and development in the pharmaceutical and biological realms, and biomedical research and development—via published reports, relational databases, briefings, position papers, conferences and educational activities, and the like.

Since the creation of an alliance between the Centers for Disease Control and Prevention (CDC) and the Medical Intelligence community in 1997, a significant joint effort has entailed cooperative information gathering, educational programming, research, technological advancement, and sharing of resources in a humanitarian effort to enhance provision of health care and afford significant and lasting improvement of quality of life for the world's citizens. The AFMIC has well-developed capabilities in creation and management large-scale health care systems, which can be effectively combined with the CDC's expertise in the areas of data gathering and analysis, statistical tracking and trending, and synthesis of the gathered information into creation of evidence-based clinical practices. The goal of the collaboration is both military and humanitarian: to optimize systems for timely and effective health care in the developing (and developed) world, and to create an efficient and comprehensive infectious disease surveillance and medical and bioterrorism threat-monitoring system that will bolster the capabilities of homeland security.

FURTHER RESOURCES

Books

Headquarters, Department of the Army. *AR 381-26 Army Foreign Material Exploitation Form*. Washington, D.C.: Department of the Army, 1987.

Richelson, Jeffey T. *The U.S. Intelligence Community (4th Edition)*. Boulder, Colo.: Westview Press, 1989.

Wolfowitz, Paul. *Department of Defense Directive Number 6420.1*. Washington, D.C.: Department of Defense, 2004.

Web sites

Government Health IT. "DOD builds health library for deployed troops." <http://govhealthit.com/article 89869-08-11-05-Web> (accessed January 20, 2006).

Government Health IT. "Senate passes pandemic bill to help developing countries." <http://govhealthit.com/article 91830-12-29-05-Web> (accessed January 20, 2006).

iHealthBeat. "Senate passes global disease surveillance bill." <http://www.ihealthbeat.org/index.cfm?Action=dspItem &itemID=117776> (accessed January 20, 2006).

Military Intelligence Professional Bulletin. "Medical Intelligence: A Case Study of Azerbaijan." <http://www.fas.org/irp/agency/army/mipb/1996-1/wolowicz.htm> (accessed January 20, 2006).

Sorting of Casualties

Military Medicine and Triage

Book excerpt

By: U.S. Department of Defense

Date: 1975

Source: U.S. Department of Defense. *Emergency War Surgery*. Washington, D.C., 1975.

About the Author: The U.S. Department of Defense provides the country with the military forces needed to deter war and protect the national security. These military forces include the Army, Navy, Marine Corps, and Air Force—about 1.4 million men and women on active duty. In addition, about 1.3 million individuals belong to the Reserve and the National Guard. Under the President of the United States, the Secretary of Defense exercises authority, direction, and control over the department.

INTRODUCTION

Advances in medical knowledge and medical techniques often accompany wars. The number of casualties created by combat necessarily forces innovations in treatment and care. These innovations, rather than being abandoned at the end of a conflict, are incorporated into civilian medicine for the benefit of the general public. Emergency medical services and trauma care systems are two areas of medical care that have been greatly influenced by military medicine.

The term triage—from the French word *trier*, meaning to sort—originated about 1916 during World War I. It refers to a medical team's task of deciding which casualties to treat first. However, the sorting of casualties began during the American Civil War. At the first battle of the war, Bull Run in 1861, injured men were forced to find their way to safety on their own, or with only their comrades to help them. At the second Battle of Bull Run, 3,000 wounded were not picked up for at least three days and 600 remained on the field for a week.

After one fiasco in which men with minor illnesses, such as colds, were sent North ahead of men with life-threatening injuries, the Union reformed its system of medical care. The army set up an ambulance service and a systematic chain of evacuation to remove wounded men from the battlefield. Patients were triaged according to the severity of their wounds. Both the Union and Confederate armies gradually evolved a process whereby a secondary hospital was

In June 1944, many Allied soldiers were killed and wounded as they stormed the beaches of Normandy in France. The invasion, a pivotal campaign in World War II, found medics from the Army and American Red Cross tending to the wounded amid intense fighting. AP/WIDE WORLD PHOTOS.

formed, further back from the battlefield. The wounded were examined at the regimental hospital, sent to this secondary hospital, and only days later evacuated to the system of general military hospitals.

By the turn of the twentieth century, medical organization had improved dramatically. In the twentieth century, each military conflict in which the United States has been involved has seen a progressive decline in mortality rates. The death rate for wounded American soldiers during World War I was roughly 8 percent; World War II was less than 5 percent; the Korean War was just over 2 percent; and the Vietnam War was 2 percent. The military's approach to trauma care helped to reduce wartime mortality rates. The same concepts and approaches that the military uses have been successfully adapted and applied to civilian trauma care, including field triage, patient packaging, radio communications, and rapid patient transport. By adapting these skills, there has been a decrease in civilian morbidity and mortality rates as well.

PRIMARY SOURCE

SORTING OF CASUALTIES

Sorting, or triage, implies the evaluation and classification of casualties for the purposes of treatment and evaluation. It is based on the principle of accomplishing the greatest good for the greatest number of wounded and injured men in the special circumstances of warfare at a particular time. . . .

GENERAL CONSIDERATIONS

No task in the medical service requires more informed judgment than casualty sorting. The officer responsible for sorting has very heavy responsibilities. He must exercise sound judgment as he decides which patients need immediate resuscitation, which require resuscitation and surgery simultaneously, and which can tolerate delay in surgery. Of equal importance, after the initial surgery, sound surgical judgment is needed in deciding which patients should be evacuated to other hospitals.

The care of the wounded in any battle zone is always influenced by the prevailing tactical situation. These same considerations are reflected along the entire system of evacuation. They eventually affect the type of care rendered in even the generalized or specialized treatment hospital.

Military surgery, however, represents no crude departure from accepted surgical standards. A major responsibility of all military surgeons is to maintain these principles and practices as fully as possible, even under adverse physical conditions. Ideally, all the adjuvants of surgery, including whole blood, plasma, other fluids, chemotherapeutic and antibiotic agents, and anesthetic agents, are available well forward and should be employed in the same judicious manner as in civilian practice. In short, although certain compromises may be necessary, it is indefensible, even in forward areas, not to carry out correct initial measures. If this policy is not observed sedulously, later reparative surgery cannot be performed with the greatest possible benefit to the casualty. . . .

The availability of rapid transportation by air does not alter in any way the necessity for the correct application of surgical principles. Speed in evacuation and comfort during transportation from the fighting front are highly desirable. Reduction in the timelag from wounding to initial wound surgery will almost always mean the salvage of life and limb, shortening of the period of recovery and rehabilitation, and reduction of functional disability. . . .

SORTING AT THE BATTALION AID STATION

In the Vietnam conflict, the battalion aid station, for the most part, was bypassed with direct evaluation from the battlefield to clearing stations or definitive surgical hospitals. All efforts were expended to resuscitate the critically injured. No patient was immediately considered unsalvageable. After evaluation, only the most severe head wounds were placed in this category. If helicopter evacuation cannot be utilized directly from the battlefield to a definitive surgical hospital, the following criteria will apply:

Group 1. Those whose injuries are so slight that they can be managed by self-help or so-called buddy care. These casualties can be returned promptly to their units for full duty.

Group 2. Those whose wounds require medical care but are so slight that they can be managed at the battalion aid station or in the divisional area. These casualties can be returned to duty after being held for only a brief period.

Group 3. Those whose injuries demand surgical attention (a) immediately, (b) after resuscitation, or (c) as soon as practicable.

Group 4. Those mortally wounded or dead on arrival.

As a practical matter, sorting begins with the casualty himself. His wound may be such that he can elect to continue fighting or can walk to the aid station himself, or it may be so serious that he must summon aid. . . .

At the battalion aid station, the casualty is examined by a medical officer or his assistant. Disposition of casualties in groups 1, 2, and 4 may be made quickly. The medical officer should spend most of his time with those in group 3, where treatment will most likely influence the outcome.

SORTING AT THE LEVEL OF INITIAL WOUND SURGERY

At this level, priorities for surgery must be decided. The primary decisions concern the urgency or permissive delay in the provision of supportive therapy and surgical care. These are decisions which cannot be delegated to inexperienced personnel. The officer who makes them must be familiar with the effects of anesthesia and surgery in the special wounds to be treated; with the patient's probable response to resuscitation and operation; with the optimal timing of this operation; and with the immediate postoperative problems. . . .

PRIORITIES OF TREATMENT

With these considerations in mind, the following priorities for surgical intervention are recommended. Injuries not included in these listings are dealt with according to the indications of the individual case.

1. *First Priority:*

   a. asphyxia, respiratory obstruction from mechanical causes, sucking chest wounds, tension pneumothorax, and maxillofacial wounds in which asphyxia exists or is likely to develop.
   b. Shock caused by major external hemorrhage, major internal hemorrhage, visceral injuries or evisceration, cardiopericardial injuries, massive muscle damage, major fractures, multiple wounds, and severe burns over 20 percent. As shock is likely to occur in any of these injuries, it is

well to institute treatment to forestall it before it develops.

2. *Second Priority:*

   a. Visceral injuries, including perforations of the gastrointestinal tract; wounds of the biliary and pancreatic systems; wounds of the genitourinary tract; and thoracic wounds without asphyxia.
   b. Vascular injuries requiring repair. All injuries in which the use of a tourniquet is necessary fall into this group.
   c. Closed cerebral injuries with increasing loss of consciousness.
   d. Burns under 20 percent of certain locations, for example, face, hands, feet, genitalia, and perineum.

3. *Third Priority:*

   a. Brain and spinal injuries in which decompression is required.
   b. Soft-tissue wounds in which debridement is necessary but in which muscle damage is less than major.
   c. Lesser fractures and dislocation.
   d. Injuries of the eye.
   e. Maxillofacial injuries without asphyxia.
   f. Burns of other locations under 20 percent.

SIGNIFICANCE

Injury, especially from accidents, is the leading cause of death and disability among children and young adults. Innovations in trauma care begun in military settings have reduced these numbers. While the emotional cost of trauma cannot be estimated, the financial costs include medical care, rehabilitation, and lost wages and productivity of those injured and killed. The sorting of injured persons by triage during a natural or manmade disaster also brings prompt, organized care that can maximize the number of lives saved. Besides those persons involved in military medicine, community physicians and nurses, along with police and persons working with aid organizations, such as the Red Cross, are often trained in the concept of triage.

There is no universally accepted system for categorizing a patient's injuries. Injury classifications are defined by the triage instruments used by the local system. Many systems use color codes, numbers, or symbols to denote the broadly defined medical needs of patients.

In the years since 1975, triage has expanded to a five-tier system. For patients with green or fourth priority, minor transport can be delayed since the patient is likely to survive even if care is delayed for hours or days. For patients with yellow or third priority, urgent care is needed but the patient is likely to survive if care is initiated within a few hours. For blue or second priority patients, their injury is catastrophic and they are unlikely to survive or will need complicated medical treatment within minutes. For red or first priority patients, their condition is critical and urgent care is needed to ensure survival. These persons are likely to survive if care is initiated. Black is the designation for persons who are dead at the scene or on arrival at the hospital. Triage mandates the proper allocation of resources and an integrated trauma system. Without an integrated trauma system, the ability of emergency medical services to provide for the needs of a community is greatly diminished. The military led the way in showing the importance of such organization.

FURTHER RESOURCES

Books

Cowdrey, Albert E. *Fighting for Life: American Military Medicine in World War II*. New York: The Free Press, 1994.

Naythons, Matthew. *The Face of Mercy: A Photographic History of Medicine at War*. New York: Random House, 1993.

Anthrax as a Biological Weapon: Medical and Public Health Management

Journal article

By: Thomas V. Inglesby

Date: May 12, 1999

Source: Thomas V. Inglesby, et. al. "Anthrax as a Biological Weapon: Medical and Public Health Management." *Journal of the American Medical Association*. (1999): 281, 1735–1745.

About the Author: Thomas V. Inglesby is a physician and Chief Operations Officer of the Center for Biosecurity at the University of Pittsburgh Medical Center in Pittsburgh, Pennsylvania, where he also serves as an associate professor of medicine and adjunct professor of public health.

INTRODUCTION

Anthrax is a pulmonary disease caused by the bacterium *Bacillus anthracis*. While the disease has gained recent prominence since the deliberate spread of the bacterium in the United States in the autumn of 2001, anthrax has been present for millennia.

The description of the sooty "morain" in the book of Exodus is reminiscent of anthrax, and the disease is probably the "burning wind of plague" in Homer's *Iliad*. The mass death of horses and cattle (the primary targets of anthrax infection, along with sheep) during the Eurasian campaign of the Huns in 80 CE was also likely due to anthrax.

Accompanying the antiquity of anthrax is the exploitation of the disease as a weapon. Hundreds of years ago, diseased bodies were dumped into wells to poison the enemy's drinking water supply, or were launched over the barricading walls of the fortified cities of the enemy. In modern times, the weaponization of anthrax was a research priority during both world wars. Indeed, during World War II (1939–1945), Britain produced five million anthrax cakes at the Porton Down facility, intended for air-dropping over Germany to infect the food supply.

Human anthrax can occur when the bacterium enters the body via a cut, the ingestion of contaminated food or water, and, most in its most lethal form, when inhaled.

The inhalation form of anthrax typically involves a metabolically dormant form of the organism known as a spore. The spore is designed to protect the genetic material of the bacterium during hibernation during times when nutrients are scare or conditions are harsh. When conditions are better, such as when the spore arrives in the lungs, the spore resuscitates and the bacterium resumes normal growth and division. The anthrax spore is tiny and so can be easily inhaled. As well, few spores are needed to cause anthrax disease.

The dangers of an airborne release of anthrax spores are well known, both historically and in contemporary times. British open-air testing of anthrax weapons in 1941 on Gruinard Island in Scotland made the island toxic for humans and animals even to the present day. In 1979, an accidental release of anthrax spores from a bioweapons facility near the Russian city of Sverdlovsk killed sixty-eight people and sickened at least seventy-nine others who were four kilometers downwind of the accident.

Most recently, beginning on September 18, 2001, letters containing anthrax spores were sent through the United States postal system to media outlets and the offices of two U.S. senators. Inhalation of the spores when letters were opened caused the death of five

FBI agents wearing biohazard suits pour liquid into a yellow drum outside the American Media Inc. building in Boca Raton, Fla., Oct. 9, 2001 after an employee died of the rare disease. The Anthrax virus was found in an employee's nose and on a computer keyboard Oct. 8, 2001. AP/WIDE WORLD PHOTOS.

people. As of 2005, the individual or group responsible for the bioterrorist attack has not been identified.

The report "Anthrax as a Biological Weapon: Medical and Public Health Management" was written almost two years before the September 2001 anthrax attacks, and reflects the difficulty in predicting and preventing a bioterrorist attack using anthrax. Nations and groups that are known to have weaponized anthrax are revealed, and scenarios of attacks in urban areas, including estimated casualties, are outlined.

PRIMARY SOURCE

INTRODUCTION

Of the numerous biological agents that may be used as weapons, the Working Group on Civilian Biodefense has identified a limited number of organisms that could cause disease and deaths in sufficient numbers to cripple a

city or region. Anthrax is one of the most serious of these diseases.

High hopes were once vested in the Biological Weapons and Toxins Convention, which prohibited offensive biological weapons research or production and was signed by most countries. However, Iraq and the former Soviet Union, both signatories of the convention, have subsequently acknowledged having offensive biowarfare programs; a number of other countries are believed to have such programs, as have some autonomous terrorist groups. The possibility of a terrorist attack using bioweapons would be especially difficult to predict, detect, or prevent, and thus, it is among the most feared terrorist scenarios.

Biological agents have seldom been dispersed in aerosol form, the exposure mode most likely to inflict widespread disease. Therefore, historical experience provides little information about the potential impact of a biological attack or the possible efficacy of postattack measures such as vaccination, antibiotic therapy, or quarantine. Policies and strategies must therefore rely on interpretation and extrapolation from an incomplete knowledge base. The Working Group on Civilian Biodefense reviewed the available literature and expertise and developed consensus recommendations for medical and public health measures to be taken following such an attack. . . .

HISTORY OF CURRENT THREAT

For centuries, anthrax has caused disease in animals and, uncommonly, serious illness in humans throughout the world. Research on anthrax as a biological weapon began more than 80 years ago. Today, at least 17 nations are believed to have offensive biological weapons programs; it is uncertain how many are working with anthrax. Iraq has acknowledged producing and weaponizing anthrax.

Most experts concur that the manufacture of a lethal anthrax aerosol is beyond the capacity of individuals or groups without access to advanced biotechnology. However, autonomous groups with substantial funding and contacts may be able to acquire the required materials for a successful attack. One terrorist group, Aum Shinrikyo, responsible for the release of sarin in a Tokyo, Japan, subway station in 1995, dispersed aerosols of anthrax and botulism throughout Tokyo on at least 8 occasions. For unclear reasons, the attacks failed to produce illness.

The accidental aerosolized release of anthrax spores from a military microbiology facility in Sverdlovsk in the former Soviet Union in 1979 resulted in at least 79 cases of anthrax infection and 68 deaths and demonstrated the lethal potential of anthrax aerosols. An anthrax aerosol would be odorless and invisible following release and would have the potential to travel many kilometers before disseminating. Evidence suggests that following an outdoor aerosol release, persons indoors could be exposed to a similar threat as those outdoors.

In 1970, a World Health Organization (WHO) expert committee estimated that casualties following the theoretical aircraft release of 50 kg of anthrax over a developed urban population of 5 million would be 250,000, 100,000 of whom would be expected to die without treatment. A 1993 report by the US Congressional Office of Technology Assessment estimated that between 130,000 and 3 million deaths could follow the aerosolized release of 100 kg of anthrax spores upwind of the Washington, DC, area—lethality matching or exceeding that of a hydrogen bomb. An economic model developed by the Centers for Disease Control and Prevention (CDC) suggested a cost of $26.2 billion per 100,000 persons exposed....

SIGNIFICANCE

"Anthrax as a Biological Weapon: Medical and Public Health Management" provided recommendations that were utilized during the 2001 anthrax attacks by public health officials, including recognizing and treating anthrax disease in patients, decontaminating an environment after contamination with anthrax, and preventing the disease in those exposed to anthrax. Inglesby and his colleagues, then at the Johns Hopkins Center for Civilian Biodefense Strategies in Baltimore, Maryland,revised the article after the 2001 anthrax attacks to include new information, including diagnostic clues, updated vaccination recommendations, judgments about environmental surveillance and decontamination, future research, and newer antibiotic treatments.

Anthrax infections are difficult to treat because the initial symptoms are similar to other, less serious, infections such as the flu. By the time the true nature of the threat is realized, the infection is well established and may be too advanced to treat.

Three components of *Bacillus anthracis* cause anthrax. A protective capsule that surrounds the bacterium blunts recognition of the invading bacterium by the body's immune system and lessens the antibacterial action of antibodies and immune cells that do respond to the infection. This protection early in infection can allow the organism to grow to large numbers. The capsule also contains a so-called protective antigen that allows the bacterium to protrude through membrane of host cells, and burrow away from the hosts' immune defenses. Finally, a component called edema

factor disables a host molecule called calmodulin, which is used to regulate many chemical reactions in the body. In anthrax, edema factor causes fluid to accumulate at the site of infection.

As the infection proceeds, toxins produced by the bacteria enter the bloodstream and circulate throughout the body. The resulting cell death and tissue destruction can be lethal.

A vaccine to anthrax does exist, but the possibility of serious side effects has restricted its general use. As of 2005, the vaccine is restricted to those deemed to be at high risk (soldiers, workers in meat processing plants, anthrax research scientists). Among the candidate targets of a safer vaccine are the edema factor and the protective antigen of the bacterium's capsule. The latter is crucial for the entry of the bacterium into host cells. Its compromise would thwart the ability of the invading bacteria to hide inside host cells, and so they would be more effectively killed by the immune reaction and applied antibiotics.

FURTHER RESOURCES
Books

Cole, Leonard A. *The Anthrax Letters: A Medical Detective Story.* Washington: National Academy of Science, 2003.

Guillemin, Jeanne. *Anthrax: The Investigation of a Deadly Outbreak.* New York: Norton, 2003.

Holmes, Chris. *Spores, Plagues, and History: The Story of Anthrax.* Dallas: Durban House Publishing, 2003.

Web sites

Centers for Disease Control and Prevention (CDC). "Anthrax." 2003. <http://www.bt.cdc.gov/agent/anthrax/index.asp> (accessed September 21, 2005).

Médecins Sans Frontières (Doctors Without Borders)

Photograph

By: Lionel Healing

Date: January 19, 2006

Source: Getty Images

About the Photographer: Lionel Healing is a London-based reporter and photographer who contributes regularly to Agence France-Press, a worldwide news organization headquartered in Paris.

INTRODUCTION

Médecins Sans Frontières (MSF), known in English as Doctors Without Borders, is an international, independent humanitarian organization designed to provide assistance in emergency situations caused by war, drought, famine, epidemics, disasters (either natural or man-made), or lack of available health care. It was established in 1971. Among the characteristics that distinguish MSF from other charitable organizations are its independence from government funding (it relies on primarily private donations and is very successful at fundraising) and its ability and willingness to make public opinion statements. Currently, MSF has branches in nearly twenty countries around the world. Roughly 80 percent of its funding comes from public and private donations; the remaining 20 percent is received from governmental and international humanitarian agencies.

MSF is staffed by physicians, nurses, health care providers, logisticians, technicians, technical and non-medical personnel, sanitation and water experts, and administrative workers. There is a small core of paid staff, a large number of volunteer workers, and a significant number of local staffers hired at each major site. MSF participates in an average of nearly 4,000 medically related missions each year.

MSF's primary tasks are the provision of basic and emergency physical and mental health care on-site at hospitals and clinics (either existent or created locally by MSF staff); the performance of surgery; the provision of vaccinations and immunizations; and the operation of feeding centers, primarily for children and mothers of babies. MSF also employs experts who are able to dig and construct wells or bring in potable (safe to drink) water, in order to establish a means of supplying clean drinking water. When necessary, MSF also assists in creating temporary shelters and can supply blankets and plastic sheeting materials.

In addition to their emergency operations, MSF operates longer-term projects to treat infectious and communicable diseases such as HIV/AIDS, tuberculosis, and sleeping sickness, and to provide physical and mental health treatment for marginalized groups and street children. MSF also has an expert epidemiology section, and it has been utilized around the world to diagnose, treat, monitor, and contain epidemics of cholera, meningitis, and measles, among other diseases.

By traveling in small teams and enlisting local resources, MSF teams have penetrated war zones and reached refugee groups and epidemic epicenters. The photograph below shows a makeshift refugee camp in the Democratic Republic of Congo set up by MSF in

PRIMARY SOURCE

Doctors Without Borders. A Médecins Sans Frontières (Doctors Without Borders) worker delivers health care in a refugee camp in Dubie, Katanga, Democratic Republic of Congo. LIONEL HEALING/AFP/GETTY IMAGES.

January 2006 after over 18,000 people fled conflict between the Congolese Army and Mai Mai rebels.

PRIMARY SOURCE

DOCTORS WITHOUT BORDERS
See primary source image.

SIGNIFICANCE

Because of its size, well-trained staff, and ability to hire significant numbers of local people in order to meet personnel needs, MSF is generally able to respond extremely quickly to emergencies. They utilize highly specialized kits and equipment packs that enable them to carry all needed supplies with them when they mobilize, so they are literally able to "hit the ground running," with no delay before they are able to begin emergency operations.

Their field kits are tailored to be an exact match for the type of emergency situation, geographic conditions, terrain, environmental conditions, and estimated patient population size. They can set up portable operating theatres, clinics, and hospitals immediately upon arrival in an affected area. They have created myriad treatment and response protocols that are customized to fit any necessary situation; their kits and protocols have been adopted by emergency and relief organizations worldwide.

Because MSF is an independent international organization, it has no political ties or limitations to prevent it from responding to any situation believed likely to benefit from its assistance. It was not designed to become involved in international governmental affairs. For those involved in the local response of MSF, the effort is a humanitarian one. Traveling staff are primarily volunteers (although their personal expenses are paid and they may receive a small stipend) who are willing to make themselves available with very little notice; they are typically deployed in an area for six to twelve months. Assigned locations may be remote and dangerous. MSF hires local staff and provides them with training and materials, and all personnel (MSF core and local staff) work in cooperation with other local and international emergency and relief organizations.

One of the unique aspects of MSF, in contrast to nearly all other relief and aid organizations, is its commitment to combining humanitarian medical care with outspoken opinion on the causes of worldwide suffering. It is equally vocal on perceived impediments to the provision of effective medical care. For example, MSF has spoken publicly against pharmaceutical companies that refuse to manufacture pediatric dosages of AIDS-related drugs or to provide affordable and appropriate medications to African countries hardest hit by the AIDS pandemic. MSF has sought (and received) audiences with the United Nations, various international and governmental organizations, and the worldwide media, in an effort to communicate both the needs of their various patient groups and to educate the world on violations of international humanitarian doctrines that they have witnessed or that they believe have been perpetrated across the globe. Researchers, academics, and scientists associated with MSF publish scholarly articles,

create media campaigns, engage in public education programs, and offer presentations and exhibits at local and international conferences, in an effort to create public awareness of medical and living conditions in underserved, impoverished, and war-torn areas of the world. MSF has launched a major initiative called the Campaign for Access to Essential Medicines, through which they are trying to help underserved or marginalized populations obtain safe, effective, affordable treatments for such diseases as HIV/AIDS, tuberculosis, and malaria.

Médecins Sans Frontières was awarded the Nobel Peace Prize in 1999.

FURTHER RESOURCES

Books

Bertolotti, Dan. *Hope in Hell: Inside the World of Doctors Without Borders.* Tonawanda, N.Y.: Firefly Books, 2004.

Médecins Sans Frontières, eds. *In the Shadow of Just Wars: Violence, Politics, and Humanitarian Action.* Translated by Fabrice Weissman and Doctors Without Borders. Ithaca, N.Y.: Cornell University Press, 2004.

Web sites

Campaign for Access to Essential Medicines. "Companies Not Selling New AIDS Drugs in Africa." <http://www.accessmed-msf.org/index.asp> (accessed December 8, 2005).

Médecins Sans Frontiers/Doctors Without Borders. "About Us." <http://www.doctorswithoutborders.org/aboutus/index.cfm> (accessed December 8, 2005).

Network for Good. "Doctors Without Borders USA." <http://partners.guidestar.org/controller/searchResults.gs?action_gsReport=1&partner=networkforgood&ein=13-3433452> (accessed December 8, 2005).

Nobelprize.org. "The Nobel Peace Prize 1999: Médecins Sans Frontières." <http://nobelprize.org/peace/laureates/1999/index.html> (accessed January 31, 2005).

Industry and Medicine

Medicine is the second largest industry in the United States, and the medical industry continues to broaden its modern social, economic, and cultural importance on a global scale.

Oversight of programs designed to regulate the medical industry and to facilitate access to health care requires large and complex governmental agencies. In most Western countries, such agencies both administer and consume significant economic resources. In the United States, for example, the Department of Heath and Human Services (DHHS) accounts for approximately twenty-five percent of all federal spending.

The medical industry has roots that extend back more than a century. Many companies that began with another purpose are now primarily associated with health care and/or the manufacture of pharmaceuticals. Bayer, now known globally as the leading manufacturer of Aspirin (acetylsalicylic acid), existed as a marketer of chemicals related to dyes in 1880, but by the turn of the twentieth century, had broadened into a pharmaceutical maker. Bayer's sales of the "wonder drug" aspirin generated considerable revenue for the company, and paved the way for modern mass-produced and mass-marketed drugs.

Especially in an age of heightened awareness of terrorism, quality control of drugs is a high priority for the pharmaceutical industry. In 1982, after over-the-counter medicine was deliberately contaminated with lethal amounts of cyanide, resulting in deaths in the United States, recalls and packaging laws were quickly enacted to reduce the risk of further incidents. Such acts and oversight inextricably link and draw the medical industry into a close relationship with government and other social institutions.

The influence of pharmaceutical companies over legislators and oversight groups has been a matter of concern. Other contentious social issues that involve the medical industry include the training of physicians and nurses, the provision of health insurance by private companies, and issues related to the public image of the medical industry, especially as reflected, even indirectly, through advertising as discussed in "Is there a Doctor in the House?" Also at issue is the inclusion within the medical industry of women and minorities, where diversification regarding race and gender is still considered by some a transition in progress.

Access to health care has perhaps been the most highly-debated issue in recent decades. In some countries, access to heath care is considered a fundamental human right and therefore provided by nationalized services. In the United States, financial assistance for health care is provided by government programs such as Medicare and Medicaid as well as private insurers. Medicare is the largest health insurer in the United States (processing more than $1 billion in claims per year) and Medicare and Medicaid combined provide health insurance for twenty five percent of U.S. citizens. Others are covered by private insurance, either through their employers or through individual purchase. However not all employers provide this benefit and many not covered through government programs or employers cannot afford the cost of individual coverage, leaving more than forty million Americans without health insurance.

Elizabeth Blackwell, First Female Physician

Valedictory Address to the Graduating Class of Geneva Medical College at the Public Commencement

Speech

By: Charles Alfred Lee

Date: January 23, 1849

Source: Charles Alfred Lee. *Valedictory Address to the Graduating Class of Geneva Medical College at the public commencement, January 23, 1849, Published by request of the class* Buffalo: Jewett Thomas, 1849. The selection includes an important footnote, included in the published version, that Lee did not mention at the ceremony.

About the Author: As Dean of the Faculty of Geneva Medical College from 1847 to 1853, Charles Alfred Lee, a physician, presented the valediction at the world's first conferral of a regular medical degree upon a woman.

INTRODUCTION

Elizabeth Blackwell was born in Bristol, England, on February 3, 1821, and immigrated with her family to America in 1832 when her father's sugar business collapsed. In her 20s, she earned her living as a schoolteacher, mostly in poverty, and studied medicine on her own with the support of a few open-minded physicians in Asheville, North Carolina, in Charleston, South Carolina, and in Philadelphia, Pennsylvania. Liberal Quaker physicians in Philadelphia urged her to apply to medical school to break the gender barrier in medicine.

The faculty of one of these schools, Geneva Medical College in upstate New York, decided to curry favor among the students by leaving the presumed rejection of Blackwell's application to them, stipulating that their decision must be unanimous. The assembled students preferred to play a practical joke on the faculty and admit her, which they did after physically persuading the lone holdout. The faculty found itself honor-bound to allow Blackwell to enroll for the fall term in 1847.

Blackwell's presence civilized her rowdy classmates; her superior intellect shamed them into becoming serious students; and her humility inspired them to do their best. They soon recognized that she was more qualified than most of the men. She consistently ranked at the head of her class. She was not the first

In an era with limited career opportunities for women, Elizabeth Blackwell became the first female doctor in the United States. ©BETTMANN/CORBIS.

woman to practice medicine, hold an M.D. degree, or be recognized as a physician, but on January 23, 1849, she became the first woman in the world to earn a regular M.D. degree from an accredited medical school by satisfying the normal requirements of a full course of study.

PRIMARY SOURCE

An event connected with the proceedings of this day deserves some notice on this occasion, calculated as it is to excite curiosity and comment, and to be held up as an example for other institutions to imitate or condemn. I mean the conferring of the degree of M.D. upon one of that sex which is generally supposed to be wanting in the physical, if not moral qualifications necessary for the successful practice of the Healing Art. So far as I am informed, this is the first instance, in this country, or any other, where a female has graduated in medicine, after having gone through the regular prescribed course and term of study; and in the present instance, it is my duty to add, without the omission, or the slighting of any branch of study, and that too, in so thorough a manner, as to leave nothing unattempted, or unattained, which it is necessary for one to know, who expects to practice with honor and success in every department of our profession.

Such an instance of self-sacrificing devotion to science; of perseverance under difficulties, and obstacles next to insurmountable—of unremitting, unrelaxing toil, in pursuit of that knowledge, so important to, and yet so rarely possessed by her sex—and all this for the purpose of mitigating human misery, relieving the sick, and extending her sphere of usefulness in the world, this, I say, deserves as it will receive, the heart-felt approbation of every generous and humane mind. This event will stand forth hereafter as a memorable example of what woman can undertake and accomplish, too, when stimulated by the love of science and a noble spirit of philanthropy. Why should medical science be monopolized by us alone? Why should woman be prohibited from fulfilling her mission as a ministering angel to the sick, furnished not only with the softer and kindlier attributes of her sex, but with all the appliances and resources of science? If she feels called to this life of toil and responsibility, and gives evidence of her qualifications for such a calling, in humanity's name, let her take her rank among the disciples of Aësculapius, and be honored for her self-sacrificing choice. Such cases must ever be too few, to disturb the existing relations of society, or excite any other feeling on our part than admiration at the heroism displayed, and sympathy, for the sufferings voluntarily assumed! God speed her, then, in her errand of mercy, and crown her efforts with abundant success!*

*Since the above discourse was delivered, an article has appeared in the Boston Medical and Surgical Journal, condemning in very severe terms, the conduct of the Faculty of Geneva College, in allowing Miss B. admission to their courses of lectures, and of the Trustees in conferring upon her the degree of M.D.

The writer, while he acknowledges the validity of the argument, so far as it is founded on the general physical disqualifications of the sex for the medical profession, and the incompatibility of its duties, with those properly belonging to the female portion of society, believes, nevertheless, that instances occasionally happen, where females display such a combination of moral, physical, and intellectual qualifications for discharging creditably and skillfully the duties belonging to our calling, that it would seem equally unwise and unjust, to withhold from them those advantages and those honors, which are open to nearly all others, whether deserving of them or not. While he holds this opinion, he at the same time feels bound to say, that the inconveniences attending the admission of females to all the lectures in a medical school, are so great, that he will feel compelled on all future occasions, to oppose such a practice, although by

so doing, he may be subjected to the charge of inconsistency.

SIGNIFICANCE

The leading American medical journal of the era, the *Boston Medical and Surgical Journal*, which later became the *New England Journal of Medicine*, reported the facts of Blackwell's graduation, without editorializing, in an anonymous announcement, "Doctress in Medicine," on February 7, 1849. Reaction was swift and almost entirely negative. The journal published two pseudonymous attacks, "The Late Medical Degree to a Female" by "D. K." on February 21, 1849, and "The Late Medical Degree at Geneva" by "Justus." on February 28. As "D. K." is pronounced like the Greek *dikê*, both pseudonyms are puns on the word "justice."

D. K.'s main argument was that a woman's entry into the medical profession was unnatural and unnecessary. Not as vitriolic as D. K., Justus admitted D. K.'s point that womankind is generally unfit for medicine, but argued that occasionally some women are called to it. He suggested that the profession should find places for "masculine women" as obstetricians and gynecologists. Lee's opinion that Blackwell should be both the first and the last woman physician was between D. K.'s conservative and Justus's somewhat liberal points of view. Among the other arguments then put forth against women in medicine were that they were physiologically, psychologically, and morally incapable of functioning objectively under the rigors of clinical practice; that their brains were smaller and therefore, they were not intelligent enough; that dealing with medical issues threatened their delicacy and offended their modesty; and that their appearance as professionals outside the home undermined the ethical fabric of society.

Blackwell could not find an internship in the United States, so she went to Europe for postgraduate medical training, first at La Maternité in Paris, then at St. Bartholomew's in London. Her dream of becoming a surgeon ended in November 1849 in Paris, when an accidental infection from a pediatric case of purulent ophthalmia blinded her left eye. She then turned toward the social aspects of medicine, building her career on writing, teaching, administration, and reform. Blackwell shuttled across the Atlantic for two decades before settling in her native England in 1869. Besides being the first woman doctor in America, she was also, by virtue of being listed in the *British Medical Register* in 1858, the first in Great Britain. She established a small practice in

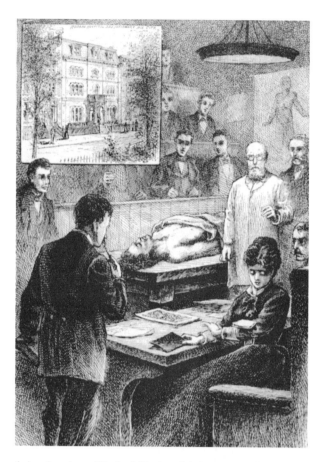

A drawing shows Elizabeth Blackwell during an operating class at the Women's Hospital and Infirmary in New York City. ©BETTMANN/CORBIS.

London and taught gynecology at the London School of Medicine for Women from 1875 until she retired in 1907. She died at home in Hastings, England, on May 31, 1910.

The earliest women doctors struggled to find patients. Men refused to see them and women were at first reluctant. Only after the success of such ventures as Elizabeth Blackwell's and Marie Elizabeth Zakrzewska's New York Infirmary and Dispensary for Women and Children, founded in 1857, and Zakrzewska's New England Hospital for Women and Children, founded in 1862, did women patients begin to recognize the benefits of having women physicians on the staffs of hospitals and clinics. The advent of female physicians allowed medicine to overcome the uneasiness of male delicacy and modesty in the presence of female bodies and thus provided more thorough, more compassionate, and more empathetic health care for female patients. By 2005, roughly half of all students in medical schools in the United States were female.

FURTHER RESOURCES
Books

Blackwell, Elizabeth. *Pioneer Work in Opening the Medical Profession to Women: Autobiographical Sketches.* London: Longmans, 1895.

Boyd, Julia. *The Excellent Doctor Blackwell: The Life of the First Female Physician.* Stroud, Gloucestershire: Sutton, 2005.

Hays, Elinor Rice. *Those Extraordinary Blackwells: The Story of a Journey to a Better World.* New York: Harcourt, 1967.

Web sites

Hobart and William Smith Colleges. "Elizabeth Blackwell, M.D., the First Female Medical Doctor, Educated at Geneva Medical College." <http://campus.hws.edu/his/blackwell/> (accessed September 9, 2005).

National Library of Medicine. "That Girl There Is Doctor in Medicine." <http://www.nlm.nih.gov/hmd/blackwell/> (accessed September 9, 2005).

Upstate Medical University. "Historical Collections." <http://www.upstate.edu/library/history/> (accessed September 9, 2005).

Age First Premarital Petting

Kinsey Reports

Table

By: Alfred C. Kinsey

Date: 1979

Source: Paul H. Gebhard and Alan B. Johnson. *The Kinsey Data: Marginal Tabulations of the 1938–1963 Interviews Conducted by the Institute for Sex Research.* Philadelphia: W. B. Saunders Company, 1979.

About the Author: Alfred C. Kinsey graduated magna cum laude from Bowdoin University with bachelor's degrees in biology and psychology in 1916, and earned a doctorate in biology from Harvard University in 1919. After teaching zoology and botany at Harvard for a short while, he began his professional career as an assistant zoology professor at Indiana University in 1920. In 1938 he was asked to develop a course on marriage, and during his research for this course he discovered the relative paucity of published information about human sexuality. Soon his research overtook his interest in teaching the class, an undertaking that occupied the remainder of his professional career. He began by gathering the sexual behavior histories of his students, eventually expanding his database to include a large-scale nationwide study that eventually encompassed more than 18,000 interviews. Kinsey and his colleagues published *Sexual Behavior in the Human Male* in 1948 and *Sexual Behavior in the Human Female* in 1953.

INTRODUCTION

In 1938, Indiana University zoology professor Dr. Alfred Kinsey was asked to develop a course about sex and marriage for female students and their spouses or fiancés. Kinsey did extensive research in preparation, and quickly discovered the dearth of published material on human sexual behavior in the medical, biological, and psychological literature.

Kinsey was keenly interested in the continuum of human sexual behavior. This was in stark opposition to the political climate in which he was operating—extremely repressive and conservative, with a pervasive taboo against the open discussion of sexuality. Given the tenor of the times, his work was highly controversial from the outset.

Deciding that the most efficient and effective means of data gathering was by interview and case history, he began to collect the sexual histories of students in his marriage classes. This formed the foundation of his master database. Seeking to broaden the scope of his data, he designed a series of 350 questions around which to frame his interviews; this gave him extremely detailed, accurate, and comprehensive data.

As the scope and intensity of his project grew, along with no small degree of controversy, Kinsey was asked to choose between continuing to work as a university professor and devoting himself to his research full time. He chose the latter, and began to seek grants and outside support to increase the scope of his research while still maintaining an affiliation with Indiana University.

By 1940 his work was funded by the National Research Council (NRC), which was in turn funded by the Rockefeller Foundation. This enabled Kinsey to hire a team of research scientists and clinical interviewers, who spread out across the country to acquire even more diverse data. Less than a decade after he had begun interviewing students, Alfred Kinsey and his staff had collected more than 10,000 sexual histories spanning the demographic continuum. These formed the basis of the extensive collection of books, articles, and other media now known as Kinsey Institute for Research in Sex, Gender, and Reproduction. The institute is also a nationwide center for research programs and a repository for the (now electronic) sex research database.

The first data compilation was published in 1948 as *Sexual Behavior in the Human Male*. It contained much that was considered startling and enormously controversial: According to the book, more than 90 percent of the 9,000 males interviewed admitted that they had masturbated; and more than a third said they had experienced some form of homosexual encounter. The book was filled with data tables and statistical analyses—a bestseller that was extremely technical and difficult to read.

The second volume, *Sexual Behavior in the Human Female*, was similarly received. Of the 6,000 women interviewed in the book, half had not been virgins when they married, one-quarter had engaged in extramarital affairs, and 9 percent reported never having experienced an orgasm. The second book's notoriety eclipsed even that of the first. The figures on pre- and extramarital behavior were scandalous, and conflicted directly with conventional views of women at the time.

◼ PRIMARY SOURCE

TABLE 199. AGE FIRST PREMARITAL PETTING
See primary source image.

SIGNIFICANCE

By publishing these two books, Kinsey effectively ended the secrecy and misinformation surrounding human sexual behavior, created a venue for ongoing research, and opened a forum for public discussion. According to his data, not only had 37 percent of American male and 13 percent of American female interviewees had homosexual experiences, 62 percent of female and 92 percent of male respondents acknowledged that they masturbated. Premarital sex was reported to be a fairly common occurrence, and many married couples (50 percent of the responding males and 25 percent of the responding females) had engaged in extramarital relationships. It is important to recognize not only the social and cultural climate in which these studies were published, but the political and legal one as well: Nonmarital sex was illegal nationwide, and even within the confines of marriage many states had outlawed oral and anal sex.

From the start, there were those who felt that the sample was biased, and that people might exaggerate their sexual histories; those issues continue to be debated. Some clergy and political conservatives believed that Kinsey's openness about his own bisexuality encouraged overreporting of homosexual behavior. One of the most inflammatory and enduring criticisms of the data concerned the discussion of sexual behavior in children. Critics alleged that this research

TABLE 199. AGE FIRST PREMARITAL PETTING

AGE	MALE			FEMALE		
	White		Black	White		Black
	College	Non College	College	College	Non College	College
	%	%	%	%	%	%
-10	0.4	0.7	1.2	0.3	0.3	0.5
11	1.1	1.8	2.3	0.8	0.8	0.5
12	5.4	9.4	4.7	3.0	3.4	5.1
13	12.1	20.5	25.7	7.6	7.8	7.4
14	16.8	22.6	19.3	11.7	13.4	14.3
15	14.5	14.7	19.9	15.8	16.2	23.5
16	17.4	9.9	10.5	19.8	21.1	20.7
17	11.5	7.3	7.6	14.9	12.4	13.4
18	7.6	5.2	2.3	11.2	11.0	7.4
19	4.4	1.8	2.3	4.6	4.7	1.8
20	2.6	2.4	2.3	3.1	2.7	2.3
21	1.6	1.3	0	2.2	2.3	0.9
22	1.1	0.1	1.2	1.1	0.9	0.9
23	1.0	0.4	0	0.8	1.1	0
24	0.7	0.1	0	0.6	0.8	0
25	0.4	0.6	0	0.8	0.3	0.9
26	0.5	0.3	0.6	0.3	0.4	0
27	0.3	0	0	0.2	0	0.5
28	0.1	0.3	0	0.3	0.1	0
29	0.1	0	0	0.2	0.1	0
30	0.1	0	0	0.2	0.1	0
31	0.1	0	0	0.2	0	0
32	--	0	0	--	0	0
33	--	0.1	0	--	0	0
34	0.1	0	0	--	0	0
35	--	0.1	0	--	0	0
36+	--	0	0	0.2	0.1	0
Known N	4547	668	171	4184	995	217
Unknown N	35	14	1	10	4	0
Inapplicable N	112	84	5	164	29	6
Card and column	13/8-9			12/8-9		

STANDARD QUESTION: "How old were you the first time there was any hugging, kissing or petting—anything more than a goodnight kiss?"

NOTE: The inapplicable N consists of those without petting experience.

NOTE: The petting is postpubertal.

PRIMARY SOURCE

Table 199. Age First Premarital Petting. This table, from *The Kinsey Data: Marginal Tabulations of the 1938–1963 Interviews Conducted by the Institute for Sex Research*, shows the age, sex, race, and education level at which people first experienced premarital petting. ©1979 BY THE INSTITUTE FOR SEX RESEARCH.

paved the way for a dramatic increase in child sexual abuse; his defender, however, believed that his work actually encouraged, for the first time in history, the reporting of adult-child sexual activity. Kinsey publicly and repeatedly stated that no children were directly involved in the research project, and that much of the data came from a sample of nine men, primarily located in one prison facility, who were admitted pedophiles.

Kinsey's book on female sexuality was published during the McCarthy era, a period in the 1950s of intense suspicion in the United States, further heightening the controversy surrounding its release. Kinsey's grant funding and public support dwindled, and the institute was forced to seek new funding. Kinsey's health deteriorated, and he died in August 1956. Paul Gebhard, an anthropologist who had played a central role in the project, assumed leadership, intending to maintain a lower public profile for the institute while aggressively seeking funding to continue the research. By the 1960s, the political, cultural, and social climate in the United States had become less restrictive, and funding from NIMH was secured. The institute undertook a series of projects on homosexuality, which had been planned by Kinsey before his death and were encouraged by the NIMH. In the 1970s a much more interdisciplinary approach to sexual behavior research was adopted, and the Institute's library and archival collections were opened to qualified scholars.

At a conference commemorating the twenty-fifth anniversary of Kinsey's death and in deference to his considerable scientific contributions, the institute was renamed the Alfred C. Kinsey Institute for Sex Research. When June Machover Reinisch became director in 1982, its name changed again to the Kinsey Institute for Research in Sex, Gender, and Reproduction. Dr. Reinisch broadened the institute's mission to include biomedical and psychobiological methods, and extended its scope to incorporate multidisciplinary approaches. She initiated a large-scale public-awareness campaign, as well as an internationally syndicated newspaper column entitled "The Kinsey Report," that answered readers' questions on sexuality and sexual behavior.

When Reinisch retired in 1983; Stephanie Sanders served as interim director until John Bancroft assumed leadership in 1995. Bancroft sought to further Reinisch's research agenda, but worked to educate the scientific community and withdraw the institute's name from the public forum. He contended that a prevailing air of fear still surrounds sex research, and that the religious right and conservative politicians fuel the ongoing controversy. Bancroft believed that the Institute should work to inform and educate policy

Teenagers Estelle and Brandon necking in a car in 1954 at a dusk until dawn prom party. ©BETTMAN/CORBIS.

makers, address the reluctance to study sexuality scientifically, and foster a truly interdisciplinary approach to the scholarly study of gender and sexuality. Julia Heiman became director of the Kinsey Institute in June 2004. Her research interests included the study of sexual dysfunction in women and the relationship between early abuse and development of adult sexual behavior.

Gebhard and Johnson reanalyzed all the research data originally collected by Kinsey and his staff using modern statistical methods and found very few significant differences from the original results. They published *The Kinsey Data Marginal Tabulations of 1938–1963 Interviews Conducted by the Institute for Sex Research* in 1979. More than fifty years after the data was collected, it's used by social science and other researchers as a basis for comparison with contemporary studies.

Kinsey's contributions to the study of human sexual behavior were enormous—not only did he disprove the mythology of the day, he created a framework for the scientific study of sex. He developed a heterosexual–homosexual rating scale, showing that sexuality did not have to be exclusively either one or the other—that sexual behavior existed on a continuum. He also broke new ground by proving that American adults engaged in a wide variety of sexual acts and behaviors.

FURTHER RESOURCES
Books

Jones, James H. *Alfred C. Kinsey: A Public/Private Life*. New York: W. W. Norton, 1997.

Pomeroy, Wardell Baxter. *Dr. Kinsey and the Institute for Sex Research*. New York: Harper & Row, 1972.

Periodicals

Bancroft, John. "Kinsey and the Politics of Sex Research." *Annual Review of Sex Research* 15 (2004): 1–39.

Bancroft, John, Erik Janssen, Lori Carnes, et al. "Sexual Activity and Risk-Taking in Young Heterosexual Men: The Relevance of Personality Factors." *Journal of Sex Research* 41, no. 2 (2004): 181–192.

Bancroft, John, and Z. Vukadinovic. "Sexual Addiction, Sexual Compulsivity, Sexual Impulse Disorder or What? Towards a Theoretical Model." *Journal of Sex Research* 41, no.3 (2004): 225–304.

Bullough, Vern L. "Sex Will Never Be the Same: The Contributions of Alfred C. Kinsey." *Archives of Sexual Behavior* 33, no. 3 (2004): 277–286.

———. "Alfred Kinsey and the Kinsey Report: Historical Overview and Lasting Contributions." *Journal of Sex Research* 35, no. 2 (1998): 127–131.

Graham, C. A., J. A. Catania, R. Brand, et al. "Recalling Sexual Behavior: A Methodological Analysis of Memory Recall Bias via Interview Using the Diary as the Gold Standard." *Journal of Sex Research*. 40, no. 4 (2003): 325–332.

Web sites

The Kinsey Institute. "About the Institute." <http://www.indiana.edu/~kinsey/about> (accessed November 25, 2005).

National Geographic News. "Could Kinsey's Sex Research Be Done Today? Part 1." <http://news.nationalgeographic.com/news/2004/11/1116_041116_sex_research.html> (accessed November 25, 2005).

National Geographic News. "Could Kinsey's Sex Research Be Done Today? Part 2." <http://www.news.nationalgeographic.com/news/2004/11/1116_041116_sex_research.html> (accessed November 25, 2005).

Gentlemen of the Class of 1878

Minority Medical Education

Book excerpt

By: James Summerville

Date: 1983

Source: James Summerville. *Educating Black Doctors: A History of Meharry Medical College.* Tuscaloosa, Ala.: University of Alabama Press, 1983.

About the Author: The Nashville, Tennessee, author James Summerville was born in 1947. He has written a number of nonfiction and young adult books, many concerning the American South and Southern history.

Throughout his career, in addition to writing, he has held several public and private business-related positions.

INTRODUCTION

Prior to the reforms catalyzed by Abraham Flexner (1886–1959), there was virtually no uniformity in American medical education. One aspect, however, was quite standard—African Americans were not admitted to the vast majority of United States medical schools. There were a small number of medical schools in the northern regions of the country that allowed entrance to free African American men before the American Civil War (1861–1865). Some Southern medical schools did not graduate their first African American until the second half of the twentieth century, after the enactment of desegregation laws. Even if they were permitted to gain entrance to university-affiliated medical schools, few (if any) African Americans had enough formal education to be able to succeed in a university setting.

Both enslaved and free African Americans had very limited access medical care, since most white physicians preferred not to treat African Americans. On the whole, African Americans lived in conditions of poverty and squalor, and their mortality rates, as well as their susceptibility to communicable diseases, were high. Because they had little ability to obtain traditional medical care, folk remedies were prevalent in African American communities.

African Americans were considered inferior in every way to whites, and were consistently treated as such in many parts of the United States, particularly before the advent of the Civil Rights Movement in the mid-twentieth century. A significant body of historical data indicates that African Americans were used as uninformed subjects in medical and experimental scientific research, and that their bodies were often used as dissection cadavers after death. The Emancipation Proclamation, followed by the conclusion of the Civil War, guaranteed some rudimentary rights to African Americans, but did nothing to prohibit segregation and institutionalized racism.

James Derham was the first African American to be trained as a physician, using the apprenticeship model. He was born a slave in Philadelphia, Pennsylvania, in 1757 and was owned by a series of physicians, whose work he was permitted to observe. After working to save enough money to purchase his freedom, Derham opened an independent medical practice.

James McCune Smith was the first African American to graduate from a medical school. He completed his medical degree at Scotland's University of Glasgow in 1837. He returned to America after completing his education and opened a medical practice. He was well-known, not only for his medical acumen, but for his work as a writer and an outspoken abolitionist. He also owned two pharmacies during the course of his medical career.

The first African American to graduate from a U.S. university-affiliated medical school was David Jones Peck, who graduated from Rush Medical College in 1847. Prior to gaining entrance to medical school, Peck apprenticed and studied under Dr. Joseph Gazzam—a white physician who was opposed to slavery. He practiced medicine in the United States for a brief time before moving to Central America.

During the last half of the nineteenth century and into the beginning of the twentieth century, there was a brief proliferation of medical schools for African Americans. By the end of the first quarter of the twentieth century, two remained (and they are still in existence): Meharry Medical College in Nashville, Tennessee, and Howard University School of Medicine in Washington, D.C. A third, Morehouse School of Medicine in Atlanta, Georgia, opened in 1975. The following speech was delivered at the graduation of the Meharry Medical College class of 1878.

PRIMARY SOURCE

Gentlemen of the Class of 1878:

I congratulate you tonight, first, because you are recognized as men. You were born slaves, the recognized property of others. . . . Tonight you are on your own; no fetters bind your limbs, no human manacles your intellect, no earthly master has the keeping of your conscience. . . . I hail you as *men*.

Your position here tonight is the trumpet voice of encouragement to the poor young men who have a desire to secure a thorough education. Your example tells them that they need not wait for others if they will use the powers God has given. . . .

Your school days are about to end, but not your student life. . . . Know what is in your books; as soon as possible, get the best and dated works on medicine; read the best medical journals you can find. Be married to your books and dare allow to think for yourselves. Study your patients, notice carefully the various forms of disease, the effects of every prescription, the surroundings of the sick. . . . Remember that internal remedies will not remove dirt on the skin, or tonics overcome the destructive influences of bad ventilation, dampness, and filthiness. Get your mind filled with the idea of healthy surroundings for your patients, and labor to secure everywhere observance of the laws that will prevent disease as well as heal the sick. . . .

You cannot go to Africa as a people, and it is doubtful if that would be best. Your home is here, and you are no carpetbagger. Generations in the future will find your people here. Cultivate for these generations the friendliest relations with your professional brethren; and others of the Anglo-Saxon race, and by your diligence in study, modesty in deportment, fidelity, and kindness to your patients, and your earnest efforts to promote the highest welfare of your people, demand the respect of the entire community. . . .

SIGNIFICANCE

Prior to publication of the Flexner Report in 1910, there were three distinct forms of medical education: the apprenticeship, the proprietary school, and the university-affiliated medical school. The American Medical Association sought to standardize educational programs and shift to a solely university-affiliated model. This plan met with limited success until the research that became the Flexner Report was undertaken. At the start of the twentieth century, there were nearly 150 medical schools in the United States. At the end of the medical school reform movement, ninety-five remained, two of which were the aforementioned African American medical schools.

African American physicians faced a number of challenges. White hospitals were not typically open to them as training institutions, nor as work places. In addition, white patients did not wish to be treated by African American doctors. Most white hospitals did not admit African American patients—although some hospitals did have segregated *colored wards*. The rare African American patients in white-run hospitals could not be treated by African American physicians. Eventually, this system led to the development of hospitals owned and administered by African Americans. The first large-scale hospital dedicated to the provision of medical care for African Americans was the Freedman's Hospital in Washington, D.C. It was designed to offer care to freed slaves. The facility still exists and is now called Howard University Hospital. Provident Hospital, the first medical facility owned and managed by African Americans, was opened by a physician named Daniel Hale Williams in 1891 in Chicago, Illinois. It was also a nurse's training school.

By the middle of the twentieth century, there were nearly 125 hospitals across the United States dedicated specifically to the provision of medical care for African

Americans. However, less than one-fifth of those hospitals were fully approved by the American College of Surgeons. By the start of the twenty-first century, only three African American hospitals remained open: Howard University Hospital in Washington, D.C., Norfolk Community Hospital in Norfolk, Virginia, and Riverside General Hospital in Houston, Texas.

The 1960s and early 1970s witnessed another significant change in American medical education, but this shift was initiated by the student populations themselves. The country was awash with student activism and protests throughout most of the 1960s. By the end of the decade, some of those activists entered medical school, and the student mindset shifted (however briefly) away from quiet conservatism to more vocal activism and liberalism. Students made their feelings publicly known on a variety of political issues. They protested the lack of resources available in local economically disadvantaged communities, as well as to traditionally underserved groups. In addition, they organized to promote reform of admissions and academic policies that were discriminatory toward women and racial minorities (particularly African Americans and Hispanic Americans), who were statistically under-represented in the medical student populations.

After World War II, more students than ever before entered medical school. However, the increased student population did not reflect the demographics of the American population, particularly in terms of the numbers of racial and ethnic minorities and women gaining admission. For African Americans, the statistics were particularly discouraging—although roughly 10 percent of the U.S. population identified as African American, less than 3 percent of students entering medical school were African American. Of those that matriculated, many were unable to obtain residencies, fellowships, hospital staff positions, or faculty appointments upon graduation from medical schools that were not predominantly African American (and affiliated with African American hospitals). Several medical schools, particularly those in the southern or southeastern United States, remained segregated until the end of the 1960s when they were legally required to change their policies.

In response to both student activism and growing political pressure to eliminate racism in medical schools, the Association of American Medical Colleges (AAMC) created an Office of Minority Affairs in 1969, and organized a task force to address the issue of under-representation of minorities in medicine the following year. The task force stated that the percentage of minority group members practicing as physicians should approximate their percentages in the overall population. As a result, American medical schools were charged with the responsibility of increasing their minority student admissions from less than 3 percent in 1970 to 12 percent by 1976.

Affirmative action programs were created at nearly all post-secondary institutions, beginning in the late 1960s. Affirmative action ensured not only a more favorable admissions process for minority students, but it afforded ongoing support and enrichment programs throughout the educational process. Students in the affirmative action programs might be offered supplementary or remedial tutoring programs, ongoing academic counseling, longer academic terms and summer programs, peer support groups, and a variety of supportive and supplemental activities, all aimed at increasing the likelihood of academic success and eventual graduation or program completion.

Financial aid was a central part of the most successful affirmative action programs; scholarship funds were increased considerably through funding from several major philanthropic and grant foundations. The National Medical Foundation, which was at that time the primary source for minority student private scholarships, increased from $195,000 in 1968 to $2,280,000 in 1974.

Another paradox was created as a result of affirmative action programs. The better funded schools were able to offer highly competitive financial aid and funding packages to the top African American scholars, and were, therefore, able to outcompete the smaller, less richly funded, traditionally African American schools. As a result, African American and smaller medical schools had a very difficult time attracting a sufficient number of appropriately qualified students. These schools either left places unfilled or were forced to admit less qualified students in order to meet admissions percentages (smaller, racially diverse schools) or to stay financially solvent (traditionally African American schools).

Uneven admission standards presented another conundrum. Less qualified students were admitted to medical schools whose graduation standards had not been relaxed to match their entrance standards. As a result, students were admitted who had very low probability of either academic success or probable program completion and graduation. In an effort to increase the likelihood of academic success, some medical schools provided significant academic support, intensive tutoring, course repetition as needed, or allowed students to spread coursework out over a longer time period (six years rather than four, for example). Although a significant proportion of minority students or students from disadvantaged academic or socioeconomic backgrounds required academic assistance or support during the first half of medical school, they were found to be essentially on par with their peers during the clinical years.

African American hospitals were hit very hard by the effects of affirmative action. Although African American students had difficulty obtaining internships and residencies in prior decades, this was much less likely to occur after the inception of affirmative action. As a result, many African American physicians were able to secure positions at larger (integrated) and better funded teaching hospitals, leaving positions unfilled at African American hospitals. As a consequence of affirmative action, many African American hospitals were forced to close due to insufficient staffing and financial resources.

By the end of the first phase of affirmative action in 1974, minority student enrollments had increased to approximately 10 percent. Overall, the greatest increases were shown by Native Americans, students from the mainland of Puerto Rico, and Mexican Americans. The percentage of African American students rose from just under 3 percent to roughly 7.5 percent. Over the next decade, these enrollment percentages remained relatively static, while the minority percentages in the overall American population rose significantly. In effect, by remaining stable, the minority enrollment percentages dropped significantly (because they did not keep up with changes in the larger population). Because the enrichment and affirmative action programs took place at and above the post-secondary school, and no nationwide programs were created to increase the overall quality of academic instruction and preparation at the lower levels (elementary, middle school, and high school), the qualified applicant pool effectively shrank or, at least, failed to grow.

In recognition of the continuing difficulty in obtaining qualified applicants from all sectors of the American population, the AAMC created a program entitled "Project 3000 in 2000," in 1990. The centerpiece of the program was the development of partnerships between medical schools and elementary, middle, and high schools, as well as colleges, in their local communities. It was hoped that this program would lead to global improvement in the quality of education delivered, resulting in an enlarged pool of well qualified minority applicants. Although some viable and ongoing partnerships were created, the program fell far short of its stated goal—having 3,000 minority students enrolled in American medical schools in the year 2000. In 2000, although minority group members comprised more than 21 percent of the overall population, the enrolled medical student population included less than eleven percent minority students.

FURTHER RESOURCES

Books

Barzansky, Barbara, and Norman Gevitz, eds. *Beyond Flexner: Medical Education in the Twentieth Century.* New York: Greenwood Press, 1992.

Buckler, Helen. *Doctor Dan: Pioneer in American Surgery.* Boston: Little, Brown and Company, 1954.

Gamble, Vanessa Northington. *Making a Place for Ourselves: The Black Hospital Movement, 1920–1945.* New York: Oxford University Press, 1995.

Moldow, Gloria. *Women Doctors in Gilded-Age Washington: Race, Gender, and Professionalization.* Urbana, Ill.: University of Illinois Press, 1987.

Morais, Herbert. *The History of the Negro in Medicine.* New York: Publisher's Company for the Association for the Study of Negro Life and History, 1967.

Periodicals

Beardsley, E. H. "Good-bye to Jim Crow: The Desegregation of Southern Hospitals." *Bulletin of the History of Medicine* 60 (1986): 367–386.

———. "Making Separate, Equal: Black Physicians and the Problems of Medical Segregation in the Pre-World War II South." *Bulletin of the History of Medicine* 57 (1983): 382–396.

Savitt, T. L. "Entering a White Profession, Black Physicians in the New South." *Bulletin of the History of Medicine* 61 (1987): 507–540.

Nightingale Home and Training School for Nurses, St. Thomas Hospital

Florence Nightingale Organizes Modern Nursing

Photograph

By: Anonymous

Date: ca. 1890

Source: The Nightingale Home and Training School for Nurses, St. Thomas's Hospital. Photograph in *A History of Nursing: The Evolution of Nursing Systems from the Earliest Times to the Foundation of the First English and American Training Schools for Nurses*, by Adelaide Nutting. Vol.2. New York: G. P. Putnam's Sons, 1907–1912.

About the Author: Mary Adelaide Nutting (1858–1948) is chiefly remembered for her contributions to nursing education, including the establishment of the department of nursing at Teachers College, Columbia University, and her authorship of the four-volume *A History of Nursing: The Evolution of Nursing Systems from the Earliest Times to the Foundation of the First English and American Training Schools for Nurses.*

INTRODUCTION

Nursing originated as one of the maternal crafts, a service traditionally performed by women with little or no training who served from a sense of duty or kindness, and expected no compensation. Later, nursing became a charitable occupation chiefly for nuns. When the Reformation during the sixteenth century closed Roman Catholic religious orders in England, few nuns were left to care for the sick. In order to fill the nursing ranks, women were recruited from numerous sources, including the jails. By the nineteenth century, nursing still lacked organization, professionalism, and standards of practice.

Florence Nightingale remedied this problem and structured nursing into a profession. Born on May 12, 1820, in Florence, Italy, to British parents on a European tour, Nightingale received the best education available for a young girl in the early nineteenth century. In the Victorian era, women of Nightingale's elite social class did not seek careers. Nightingale believed, however, that she had a calling from God to become a nurse. She studied nursing in a three-month course at the Institution of Protestant Deaconesses at Kaiserswerth, Germany, and then traveled to Paris to study with the Sisters of Charity.

When the Crimean War began in 1853, there were no organized nurses to care for wounded British soldiers. Nightingale traveled to the front with the permission of the secretary of war. Assigned to a filthy, cholera-ridden, overcrowded hospital, Nightingale and the nurses under her command quickly established order. They scrubbed the hospital, set up kitchens to provide balanced meals, put up screens to give the patients privacy, and set up recreational activities for recuperating soldiers. When Nightingale arrived in the Crimea, the death rate at her hospital was fifty to sixty percent. Within six months, the mortality rate among the wounded had dropped to two percent. As most deaths occurred at night, Nightingale made nighttime rounds carrying an oil lamp to illuminate her way. Afterwards, Nightingale was often referred to as "The Lady with the Lamp."

Returning to Britain, Nightingale opened the Nightingale Home and Training School for Nurses at St. Thomas Hospital in London on June 24, 1860. She believed that the focus of a training school should be nursing education rather than nursing service. While other training schools offered courses lasting only a few weeks or a few months, Nightingale enrolled students in a year-long program that included coursework on anatomy, surgical nursing, physiology, chemistry, food sanitation, ethics, and professionalism. Stressing compassion and empathy, she insisted that the patient be treated as a whole person and not simply as a disease. The Nightingale school is considered the first modern school of nursing and its foundation marked the beginning of nursing as an organized profession.

Nightingale spent the remainder of her life working to better nursing education. She focused on improving hospital care for the poor and attempted, without success, to persuade the military to hire female nurses as the backbone of hospitals.

PRIMARY SOURCE

NIGHTINGALE HOME AND TRAINING SCHOOL FOR NURSES, ST. THOMAS HOSPITAL

See primary source image.

SIGNIFICANCE

In the nineteenth century, medical science was developing rapidly, particularly after the tentative acceptance of the germ theory for causing wound infections and disease in general. The potential for saving many lives existed, but could not yet be realized because the structure to support the new measures for antisepsis (such as cleanliness of instruments and in care giving methods) was not in place. Physicians were frustrated in their efforts to provide good health care because hospital facilities and the personnel that staffed them were inadequate. Although the problems were well-known, no remedies were proposed until Florence Nightingale offered them.

Nightingale launched the modern nursing movement by setting standards for nursing education. As Nightingale realized, nurses played a vital role as the foundation of hospital care. Physicians did not see patients as often as the nurses, and physicians did not typically concern themselves with matters such as cleanliness and diet that were crucial to a patient's recovery. It was left to the on-duty nurse to spot problems and to remedy them before a patient suffered. However, despite the growing importance of nursing, most nurses before Nightingale's era were taught only

PRIMARY SOURCE

Nightingale Home and Training School for Nurses, St. Thomas Hospital. The Nightingale Home and Training School for Nurses in St. Thomas's Hospital, London, ca. 1890, the first organized school for nurses. WELLCOME LIBRARY, LONDON.

a few simple procedures by doctors or their assistants. After nursing education was standardized, they were fully prepared to participate in the medical revolution.

The nineteenth century changes in medical care that enabled people to live longer, healthier lives were the result of scientific and educational advances. However, patients avoided hospitals in the first half of the century, as they were often considered filthy, disease-ridden places where skilled care was lacking

and death was common. Nightingale's nurses helped transform the public's perception of hospitals; they became institutions where care was delivered by capable, clean hands.

Today, professional nurses receive standardized education and clinical training, pass examinations administered by a state board of examiners, are maintained on a registry, seek continuing education, and abide by set standards of practice.

FURTHER RESOURCES

Books

Baly, Monica E. *Florence Nightingale and the Nursing Legacy.* London: Croom Helm, 1986.

Dossey, Barbara Montgomery. *Florence Nightingale: Mystic, Visionary, Healer.* Springhouse, Pa.: Springhouse, 2000.

Bayer Pharmaceutical Products

Technology Allows for Medicines to Be Developed in Quantity

Advertisement

By: Anonymous

Date: 1900

Source: Anonymous advertisement. *Harper's Weekly,* 1900. (Image also appears in A. S. Lyons and R. J. Petrucelli. *Medicine: An Illustrated History.* New York: Abrams, 1978.)

About the Author: *Harper's Weekly* was launched in 1857 by Fletcher Harper, one of the four brothers who owned Harper & Brothers, the largest book publisher in the United States at that time. It was Fletcher Harper's second successful foray into magazine publishing following *Harper's Monthly,* which he had created in 1850 and modeled on the *London Illustrated News.* By 1860 the circulation of *Harper's Weekly* had reached 200,000.

INTRODUCTION

The Bayer company is one of the world's oldest drug manufacturing firms. It began as an industrial chemical company in the German city of Wuppertal in 1863 and became a pharmaceutical company, Farbenfabriken vorm. Friedr. Bayer & Co., in 1881. Bayer's development of industrial chemical processes and adaptation of these processes to the bulk manufacturing of pharmaceuticals laid the foundation for the modern pharmaceutical industry. The company established a scientific laboratory in the 1880s that was primarily focused on industrial research and development. These research efforts gave rise to numerous intermediates, dyes, and pharmaceuticals, including the "drug of the century"—aspirin—which was launched in 1899.

The promotional illustration reproduced here shows the portfolio of products manufactured by Bayer Pharmaceuticals and distributed in the United States around the turn of the century. It presents the company's entire product offering in a compact format.

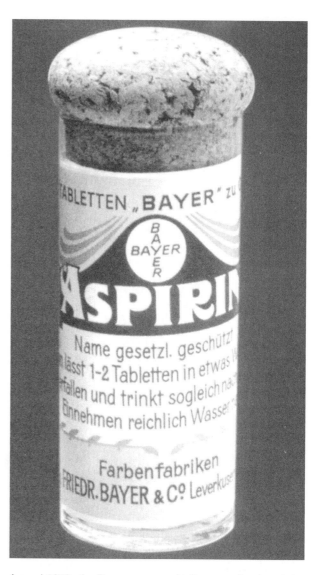

Around 1912, the Bayer company in Germany developed the technology to create aspirin in tablet form (bottle shown here). Prior to that, it was available as a powder. AP/WIDE WORLD PHOTOS.

Prominent illustration panels are devoted to the four most widely used and heavily promoted products: Aspirin for pain and fever, Lycetol for gout, Heroin for cough suppression, and Salophen for arthritis. In addition to these "blockbuster" products, sixteen specialty or "niche" products share smaller panels in the illustration. These include Sycose, a homeopathic remedy, Europhen, an herbal medication, Somatose for providing nutrition to typhoid patients, Hemicranin for migraine headaches, Protargol for the staining of laboratory samples, and Phenacetin, formerly used to ease pain or fever, but now withdrawn from use because of its link to high blood pressure, heart attacks, cancer, and kidney disease.

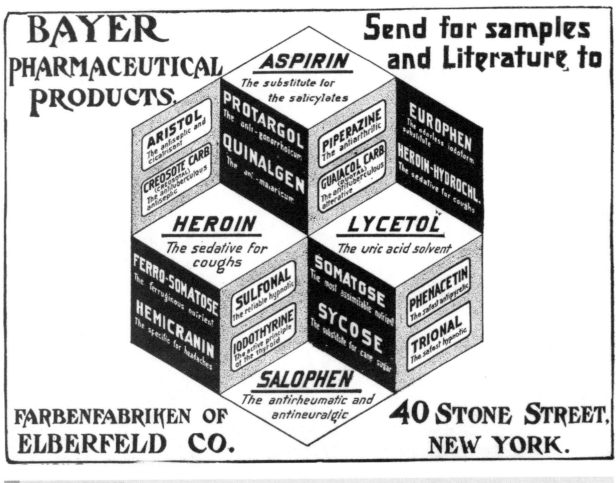

Bayer Pharmaceutical Products. Bayer Pharmaceutical Products promotion, ca. 1900, advertising its "wonder drug" aspirin, along with heroin and others. ©BETTMANN/CORBIS.

While safety concerns soon emerged for several of these products, Bayer's production and promotion of heroin as a "non-addictive" substitute for morphine and codeine stands out as one of the most dramatic mistakes in the medical use of dangerous substances. The Bayer promotional illustration comes from an era when pharmaceutical products were not systematically tested for efficacy, side effects, and long-term safety. Discovery of the medical use of these products, and the discovery of the drawbacks to their use, was based largely on anecdotal evidence from physician case reports describing the results of treating small numbers of patients or even based simply on folk wisdom. Bayer's main concern in those days was that the products be chemically stable, pure, and standardized, since the company's industrial chemical production methods made possible their manufacture in quantities sufficient for worldwide distribution.

BAYER PHARMACEUTICAL PRODUCTS
See primary source image.

SIGNIFICANCE

Bayer's application of industrial chemical methods to the manufacturing of pharmaceutical products gave rise to a business sector that now dominates scientific innovation in health care worldwide. From the late 1800s until very recently, the structure of the pharmaceutical sector was based on the model created by Bayer, consisting of vertically integrated medium-sized and large companies that discovered drugs, tested them in the laboratory and on patients, developed processes for their mass production, and commercialized them. (Only recently have small bio-technology firms taken the lead away from the large integrated firms in drug discovery and initial human testing.) This integration of discovery, research and development (R&D), and commercialization made the pharmaceutical industry one of the two large-scale forces in the health care industry. The other major player is the third-party medical payment system, largely a private industry in the United States and mainly a taxpayer-funded government function in other industrial nations. Despite attempts to achieve economies of scale through hospital systems and physician group practices, health care providers, including both hospitals and physician practices, have remained mostly locally focused and relatively small scale operations by comparison.

From its inception, however, suspicions about the purity, quality, safety and efficacy of the pharmaceutical industry's products led to its intensive regulation by government. One needs only to look at the Bayer product portfolio and its inclusion of heroin to realize the stakes involved. The history of the pharmaceutical industry is inextricably bound to the history of its regulation, and this regulation has shaped both the medical and financial direction of the industry over the past century. In 1902, the American Pharmaceutical Association set up a drug laboratory intended to assist with standardizing pharmaceuticals and analytical test results. An expert in the detection of drug adulteration was appointed director of the laboratory and started testing operations in 1903.

The drug laboratory spent its first years searching for ways to make pharmaceutical analyses more accurate. This work alerted the public to problems with the drug supply. Publicity over these findings led to journalist campaigns to pass the Pure Food and Drug Act of 1906.

The Pure Food and Drug Act prohibited inter-state commerce of wrongly labeled and adulterated drugs and food, and placed responsibility for monitoring compliance with the drug laboratory. The law established units for drug inspection, essential oils, synthetic products, and pharmacology units, all of which focused on the investigation and analysis and efficacy claims for products sold as therapies. The drug inspection unit was given enforcement powers. After scrutinizing hundreds of domestic and imported drugs during the first year of enforcement, it recommended prosecution for manufacturers of about five percent of the samples.

Given the industrial and financial interests at stake, major challenges to drug regulation were soon mounted. In 1910, the investigation unit recommended

prosecution of "Johnson's Mild Combination Treatment for Cancer" as "worthless." The government lost the case at trial when enforcement of the veracity of claims was ruled outside the scope of the Pure Food and Drug Act. Congress then issued the Sherley Amendment in 1912, which brought therapeutic claims under the jurisdiction of the act, but required that such claims would have to be proven "false and fraudulent" before they could be outlawed.

Although the regulation of drug efficacy claims was established under the Sherley Amendment, drug safety was still unregulated. Reports of deaths from the administration of anesthesia, the use of a weight loss drug (dinitrophenol), and, in 1937, the use of an anti-freeze analogue as an elixir, which killed many children, prompted the passing of the Federal Food, Drug and Cosmetic Act in 1938. This act required that new drugs be tested for safety and have adequate labeling before marketing to the public. It also established the Food and Drug Administration (FDA), now the world's foremost regulatory agency controlling safety, efficacy, and manufacturing standards for pharmaceutical products. It was not until 1951 that a clear line was established between prescription and non-prescription or over-the-counter drugs, adding another layer of safety and efficacy verification before a patient could use a product claiming to be therapeutic.

Despite the regulation of drug safety came decades after the regulation of efficacy claims, the rationale and standards for safety monitoring are significantly less controversial than those for drug efficacy. Few opinion leaders are willing to protest FDA's safety monitoring requirements because safety concerns are more clear-cut and immediate than concerns over inadequately supported efficacy claims. The latter depend on the interpretation of population-based, inferential statistical analysis, particularly clinical trials. Periodically the *Wall Street Journal* editorial page faults the FDA for bureaucratically delaying or frustrating the development of drugs that could save the lives of cancer and other terminally ill patients. Some physicians would reserve the decision to allow treatment with specific drugs to an agreement between doctor and patient, with no government (or third-party payer, for that matter) second-guessing.

Familiarity with the history of fraud and lack of concern for public health on the part of a small, but persistent, minority of manufacturers appears to justify regulatory oversight of the pharmaceutical industry. If regulators did not require very expensive and often lengthy thorough scientific efficacy and safety testing before marketing, it is difficult to imagine that pharmaceutical firms would have established impartial and effective oversight on their own, given the history briefly recounted here. This oversight and the clinical trial regimen that it has spawned have provided the basic statistical evidence—admittedly just a "starting point" for deciding on therapy—on which physicians and patients rely in choosing products. This regulation-generated evidence standard is certainly not adequate for deciding treatment for every idiosyncratic patient case, because the results of clinical trials represent the average of the population's (or major subgroups') response to treatment. Thus, concerns over the fairness and accuracy of efficacy regulation for particular patient subgroups or patients with rare conditions will continue to arise.

In recent years, the news media have carried many predictions of the manufacture of individually tailored medicines based on matching the diversity of the human genome. Under this scenario, specific medications will be targeted to specific patient genotypes for reliably safe and effective treatment. If these predictions prove true, the current population-based statistical methodology used by FDA would need to be changed to become more sensitive to potential individual responses to treatments. Already the agency is reaching out to pharmaceutical and biotechnology firms in an attempt to jointly fashion new evidentiary standards that would be more appropriate for genomic-based medicine development. While current standards of proof of safety and efficacy are imperfect and should be modified as pharmaceutical technology progresses, the relationship between regulation and industry has been symbiotic and beneficial both for industry prosperity and public health. Given the history of drug development and marketing, the burden of proof rests with those asserting that physicians and companies by themselves could and would adequately protect human life and stick to evidence-based efficacy claims without government regulation.

FURTHER RESOURCES
Books

Kleinke, J. D. *Oxymorons: The Myth of a U.S. Health Care System*. San Francisco: Jossey-Bass, 2001.

Piantadosi, Stephen. *Clinical Trials: A Methodologic Perspective*. New York: Wiley Interscience, 1997.

Smith, Mickey, et al. *Pharmaceutical Marketing: Principles, Environment and Practice*. New York: Pharmaceutical Products Press (Haworth Press), 2002.

Periodicals

Calliff, R. M. "Defining the Balance of Risk and Benefit in the Era of Genomics and Proteomics." *Health Affairs* 23 (January-February 2004): 77–87.

Cockburn, I. M. "The Changing Structure of the Pharmaceutical Industry." *Health Affairs* 23 (January-February 2004): 10–22.

Kleinke, J. D. "Access Versus Excess: Value-Based Cost Sharing for Prescription Drugs." *Health Affairs* 23 (January-February 2004): 34–47.

"A Morally Repugnant Cancer Drug Policy." *Wall Street Journal* (November 25, 2005): A11.

Web sites

Bayer. "Company History." <http://www.bayer.com/about-bayer/history/page701.htm> (accessed November 23, 2005).

U.S. Food and Drug Administration. Center for Drug Evaluation and Research. "A Brief History of the Center for Drug Evaluation and Research." <http://www.fda.gov/cder/about/history/default.htm> (accessed November 27, 2005).

The Jungle

Inspections Yield Safer Food Supply

Book excerpt

By: Upton Sinclair

Date: 1906

Source: Upton Sinclair. *The Jungle*. New York: The Jungle Publishing Co., 1906.

About the Author: Upton Sinclair, a writer and reformer, was born in Baltimore, Maryland, in 1878. After attending graduate school at Columbia University, he began to publish novels. Sinclair ran for public office several times as a Socialist candidate, including runs for a U.S. Senate seat from New Jersey and the governorship of California. In 1934, as a Democrat, he was nearly elected governor of California by promising government-owned factories an elaborate pension plan. In addition to *The Jungle*, Sinclair wrote two other muckraking novels. In 1943, he won the Pulitzer Prize for the novel, *Dragon's Teeth*, that addressed the rise of Adolf Hitler. He died in New Jersey in 1968.

INTRODUCTION

The Meat Inspection Act of 1906 mandated federal inspection of all livestock (cattle, swine, sheep, goats, and horses, but not poultry) destined to be sold overseas or in another state. The legislation is generally credited to public disgust at the meatpacking processes that were revealed in the pages of Upton Sinclair's *The Jungle*.

The novel provided readers with stomach-churning descriptions of the unhealthy and corrupt conditions in the Chicago meatpacking industry. Sinclair's protagonist is Jurgis Rudkis, a Lithuanian immigrant who firmly believes that hard work will lead him to success in America. He perseveres despite one setback after another before finally becoming disillusioned. Rudkis comes to see that the forces of the meatpacking industry are too massive to be overcome by one individual. He becomes a Socialist.

Sinclair expected the novel to promote Socialism. Most Americans paid little attention to the book's political message because they were too horrified by descriptions of what went into sausages and cans of lard. According to Sinclair, canned meat products contained rats, rat droppings, expectorations, floor filth, and the occasional unfortunate worker who fell into a vat. As Sinclair himself declared, "I aimed at the public's heart and hit it in the stomach."

Despite Sinclair's claim and the oft-told story of *The Jungle* converting President Theodore Roosevelt into a supporter of an inspection law, the book is not solely responsible for the 1906 inspection law. The United States had been moving towards some sort of wide-ranging federal meat inspection legislation for some years prior to the publication of *The Jungle*; however, the book brought the issue to the forefront of American consciousness.

The first meat regulation appeared in Boston in 1692. These early regulations were not aimed at protecting the consumer from bad meat. Instead, slaughterhouses, with their noise and pollution, were public nuisances. The regulations aimed to stop or reduce these nuisances. By the late nineteenth century, increasing knowledge about bacteria led to an attempt to understand the causes of disease. This development prompted the rapid expansion of municipal health departments in the early twentieth century. However, these departments were badly understaffed and the few inspectors they employed were not professionally trained.

Meanwhile, the first federal meat inspection act passed on August 30, 1890. It mandated the inspection of salted pork and bacon intended for export. The law was a response to strict European import laws aimed at diseased American meat. On March 3, 1891, in reaction to continued European restrictions, Congress approved a law that mandated inspection of all cattle, sheep, and swine prior to slaughter only if the meat was to be shipped in interstate commerce. Goats, horses, and poultry were not included, since such animals were rarely sold by processors.

Congress did not protect the local meat buyer and did not guarantee the quality of meat after the initial inspection of the live animal. As Sinclair discovered, human food was prepared under the most revolting conditions. Meat inspectors sent to Chicago in 1906 by President Roosevelt after the publication of *The Jungle* discovered numerous processing problems. Workers, categorized by inspectors as "indescribably filthy," would typically climb over diseased carcasses thrown on the floor and stand with dirty shoes upon tables used to process meat. Supervisors were unconcerned with such unsanitary practices, indicating that the practices were common.

■ PRIMARY SOURCE

And shortly afterward one of these, a physician, made the discovery that the carcasses of steers which had been condemned as tubercular by the government inspectors, and which therefore contained ptomaines, which are deadly poisons, were left upon an open platform and carted away to be sold in the city; and so he insisted that these carcasses be treated with an injection of kerosene—and was ordered to resign the same week! So indignant were the packers that they went farther, and compelled the mayor to abolish the whole bureau of inspection; so that since then there has not been even a pretense of any interference with the graft. There was said to be two thousand dollars a week hush money from the tubercular steers alone; and as much again from the hogs which had died of cholera on the trains, and which you might see any day being loaded into boxcars and hauled away to a place called Globe, in Indiana, where they made a fancy grade of lard.

Jurgis heard of these things little by little, in the gossip of those who were obliged to perpetrate them. It seemed as if every time you met a person from a new department, you heard of new swindles and new crimes. There was, for instance, a Lithuanian who was a cattle butcher for the plant where Marija had worked, which killed meat for canning only; and to hear this man describe the animals which came to his place would have been worthwhile for a Dante or a Zola. It seemed that they must have agencies all over the country, to hunt out old and crippled and diseased cattle to be canned. There were cattle which had been fed on "whisky-malt," the refuse of the breweries, and had become what the men called "steerly"—which means covered with boils. It was a nasty job killing these, for when you plunged your knife into them they would burst and splash foul-smelling stuff into your face; and when a man's sleeves were smeared with blood, and his hands steeped in it, how was he ever to wipe his face, or to clear his eyes so that he could see? It was stuff such as this that made the "embalmed beef" that had killed several times as many United States soldiers as all the bullets of the Spaniards; only the army beef, besides, was not fresh canned, it was old stuff that had been lying for years in the cellars.

Then one Sunday evening, Jurgis sat puffing his pipe by the kitchen stove, and talking with an old fellow whom Jonas had introduced, and who worked in the canning rooms at Durham's; and so Jurgis learned a few things about the great and only Durham canned goods, which had become a national institution. They were regular alchemists at Durham's; they advertised a mushroom-catsup, and the men who made it did not know what a mushroom looked like. They advertised "potted chicken,"—and it was like the boardinghouse soup of the comic papers, through which a chicken had walked with rubbers on. Perhaps they had a secret process for making chickens chemically—who knows? said Jurgis' friend; the things that went into the mixture were tripe, and the fat of pork, and beef suet, and hearts of beef, and finally the waste ends of veal, when they had any. They put these up in several grades, and sold them at several prices; but the contents of the cans all came out of the same hopper. And then there was "potted game" and "potted grouse," "potted ham," and "deviled ham"—de-vyled, as the men called it. "De-vyled" ham was made out of the waste ends of smoked beef that were too small to be sliced by the machines; and also tripe, dyed with chemicals so that it would not show white; and trimmings of hams and corned beef; and potatoes, skins and all; and finally the hard cartilaginous gullets of beef, after the tongues had been cut out. All this ingenious mixture was ground up and flavored with spices to make it taste like something. Anybody who could invent a new imitation had been sure of a fortune from old Durham, said Jurgis' informant; but it was hard to think of anything new in a place where so many sharp wits had been at work for so long; where men welcomed tuberculosis in the cattle they were feeding, because it made them fatten more quickly; and where they bought up all the old rancid butter left over in the grocery stores of a continent, and "oxidized" it by a forced-air process, to take away the odor, rechurned it with skim milk, and sold it in bricks in the cities! Up to a year or two ago it had been the custom to kill horses in the yards—ostensibly for fertilizer; but after long agitation the newspapers had been able to make the public realize that the horses were being canned. Now it was against the law to kill horses in Packingtown, and the law was really complied with—for the present, at any rate. Any day, however, one might see sharp-horned and shaggy-haired creatures running with the sheep and yet what a job you would have to get the public to believe that a good part of what it buys for lamb and mutton is really goat's flesh!

There was another interesting set of statistics that a person might have gathered in Packingtown—those of the various afflictions of the workers. When Jurgis had first inspected the packing plants with Szedvilas, he had marveled while he listened to the tale of all the things that were made out of the carcasses of animals, and of all the lesser industries that were maintained there; now he found that each one of these lesser industries was a separate little inferno, in its way as horrible as the killing beds, the source and fountain of them all. The workers in each of them had their own peculiar diseases. And the wandering visitor might be skeptical about all the swindles, but he could not be skeptical about these, for the worker bore the evidence of them about on his own person—generally he had only to hold out his hand.

There were the men in the pickle rooms, for instance, where old Antanas had gotten his death; scarce a one of these that had not some spot of horror on his person. Let a man so much as scrape his finger pushing a truck in the pickle rooms, and he might have a sore that would put him out of the world; all the joints in his fingers might be eaten by the acid, one by one. Of the butchers and floorsmen, the beef-boners and trimmers, and all those who used knives, you could scarcely find a person who had the use of his thumb; time and time again the base of it had been slashed, till it was a mere lump of flesh against which the man pressed the knife to hold it. The hands of these men would be criss-crossed with cuts, until you could no longer pretend to count them or to trace them. They would have no nails,—they had worn them off pulling hides; their knuckles were swollen so that their fingers spread out like a fan. There were men who worked in the cooking rooms, in the midst of steam and sickening odors, by artificial light; in these rooms the germs of tuberculosis might live for two years, but the supply was renewed every hour. There were the beef-luggers, who carried two-hundred-pound quarters into the refrigerator-cars; a fearful kind of work, that began at four o'clock in the morning, and that wore out the most powerful men in a few years. There were those who worked in the chilling rooms, and whose special disease was rheumatism; the time limit that a man could work in the chilling rooms was said to be five years. There were the wool-pluckers, whose hands went to pieces even sooner than the hands of the pickle men; for the pelts of the sheep had to be painted with acid to loosen the wool, and then the pluckers had to pull out this wool with their bare hands, till the acid had eaten their fingers off. There were those who made the tins for the canned meat; and their hands, too, were a maze of cuts, and each cut represented a chance for blood poisoning. Some worked at the stamping machines, and it was very seldom that one could work long there at the pace that was set, and not give out and forget himself and have a part of his hand chopped off. There were the "hoisters," as they were called, whose task it was to press the lever which lifted the dead cattle off the floor. They ran along upon a rafter, peering down through the damp and the steam; and as old Durham's architects had not built the killing room for the convenience of the hoisters, at every few feet they would have to stoop under a beam, say four feet above the one they ran on; which got them into the habit of stooping, so that in a few years they would be walking like chimpanzees. Worst of any, however, were the fertilizer men, and those who served in the cooking rooms. These people could not be shown to the visitor,— for the odor of a fertilizer man would scare any ordinary visitor at a hundred yards, and as for the other men, who worked in tank rooms full of steam, and in some of which there were open vats near the level of the floor, their peculiar trouble was that they fell into the vats; and when they were fished out, there was never enough of them left to be worth exhibiting,—sometimes they would be overlooked for days, till all but the bones of them had gone out to the world as Durham's Pure Leaf Lard!

A meat inspector checks a side of beef. After a cow in Washington state was found to have mad cow disease in late 2003, many consumers turned to organic beef, such as that processed at this plant near Bow, Washington. AP/WIDE WORLD PHOTOS.

SIGNIFICANCE

The Meat Inspection Act of 1906 provided for a post-mortem inspection of carcasses, banned dyes or chemicals in prepared foods, prohibited false labeling, permitted the destruction of condemned meat, and provided for sanitary inspection of all establishments involved in meat processing. By 1939, two-thirds of the nation's meat supply came under federal inspection. The new law did not cover farmers, small retail butchers, or small meat dealers. To address this gap, many cities adopted legislation to protect the health of their citizens. By 1923, nearly all large cities had a uniform system of meat inspection. The inspection laws had both economic and public health implications. The legislation protected the growing American export market, while also preventing the spread of diseases caused by the consumption of bad meat.

While the U.S. meat inspection laws were once widely regarded as the best in the world, weaknesses have become apparent over time. The sheer numbers of animals slaughtered each year makes it impossible for the federal Food Inspection Service to carefully examine each carcass. A typical plant in Nebraska slaughters 3,000 cattle a day. Deadly pathogens, such as *E. coli*, from improperly cleansed meat have on several occasions killed meat consumers and led to major recalls.

However, it is the emergence of mad cow disease or bovine spongiform encephalopathy (BSE) that has led many scientists to conclude that meat processors must increase their vigilance in guarding the food supply. Mad cow disease is a brain-wasting illness that is believed to be spread in cattle by tainted animal feed. Eating contaminated meat from infected animals can cause a fatal human variant of BSE that has been blamed for the deaths of at least 150 people, mostly in England, since BSE was first reported in the 1980s. In 2003, Japan temporarily banned imports of American meat. Before the ban, Japan had been the biggest buyer of U.S. beef. In 2004, the U.S. enacted new inspection regulations to prevent the spread of BSE. The measures provide for the destruction of all internal organs of cattle more than thirty months old and require that the meat from older animals must be sold without bones. Public interest groups have since reported a number of meat safety violations, but meatpacking plants insist that they are largely in compliance.

FURTHER RESOURCES
Books

Eby, Clare Virginia, ed. *The Jungle: An Authoritative Text, Contexts, Backgrounds, and Criticism.* New York: Norton, 2003.

Marcus, Alan I. *Cancer from Beef: DES, Federal Food Regulation and Consumer Confidence.* Baltimore: Johns Hopkins University Press, 1994.

The Flexner Report

Standardizing Medical Education in the United States
and Canada

Report

By: Abraham Flexner

Date: 1910

Source: Abraham Flexner. *Medical Education in the United States and Canada: A Report to the Carnegie Foundation for the Advancement of Teaching.* Bulletin Number Four. New York: The Carnegie Foundation, 1910.

About the Author: Abraham Flexner (1886–1959) was born in Louisville, Kentucky. He attended Johns Hopkins University and graduated in 1886 with a degree in education. He spent nineteen years as a secondary school teacher and a principal before seeking a graduate education at Harvard University and the University of Berlin. In 1908, he was employed by the Carnegie Foundation for the Advancement of Teaching and, in 1910, issued the groundbreaking and controversial *Medical Education in the United States and Canada*, commonly called *The Flexner Report.* In his report, Flexner analyzed the status of American medical education and deemed it sorely lacking. The outcome of this body of work was full-scale reform and re-tooling of the medical education system in the United States—from admission standards and academic institution organization to standardization of curriculum across the schools and clinical training of physicians-in-training. Between 1912 and 1925, Flexner was a member of the General Education Board and served as its secretary from 1917 to 1925. He founded the Institute for Advanced Study at Princeton University with Louis Bamberger. Abraham Flexner acted as the head of the institute from 1930 to 1939. He also published numerous treatises on education. The most notable among them were: *A Modern School* (1916), *The Gary Schools* (co-authored with F. B. Bachman in 1918), *The Burden of Humanism* (delivered also as the Taylorian Lecture at Oxford University in 1928), and the well-known *Universities: American, English, German* (1930).

INTRODUCTION

Abraham Flexner is one of the most well-known names in the history of medical education, since he is considered to have been the catalyst for the transformation and standardization of American medical studies.

During much of the nineteenth century, it generally took little effort to become a physician in the United States. There were three different types of medical education in the America during most of the nineteenth century: an apprenticeship system in which students received direct and practical training from a local physician; a proprietary school system in which groups of students attended lectures given by physicians who owned the schools; and university systems in which students were given training that was both didactic (lecture style) and clinical, through university and hospital affiliations. The latter group received training in a variety of areas of medicine, including scientific, osteopathic, chiropractic, homeopathic, physiomedical, botanical, Thomsonian, and eclectic.

The proprietary schools generally had no formalized entrance requirements, other than an ability to pay tuition. Courses were both brief and general: the typical curriculum entailed two sixteen-week semesters, the second of which was merely a repetition of the first. Instruction was in lecture and text format, with no appreciable academic clinical or laboratory practice. The typical proprietary medical school faculty numbered seven or eight. They usually owned the school and operated it as a profitable venture, hence the name "proprietary school." As a rule, proprietary medical schools had no university or hospital affiliations.

American students seeking a more comprehensive or scientifically based medical education were forced to study in Europe, where the curricula were far more in-depth, and focused more on the scientific and clinical realms. Most American students going abroad chose medical schools in England, Scotland, Germany, or France.

American-trained physicians, because of the lack of standardization in education and training, varied widely in their medical knowledge, therapeutic techniques, philosophies, and abilities to successfully treat illness and injury. There were few licensing examinations and even fewer requirements in order to engage in the practice of medicine.

During the second half of the nineteenth century, the American Medical Association (AMA) was engaged in public efforts to standardize American medical education. Their campaign met with minimal success, since most Americans doubted that any one form of medical education and training was significantly better than another. In addition, the American political philosophy discouraged national regulation of any of the professions.

By the beginning of the twentieth century, clinical and scientific laboratory research had unquestionably proven that previously accepted "medical treatments," such as purging, blistering, and bleeding, were ineffective. There was growing acceptance of public sanitation, the efficacy of vaccination, and the utility of antiseptic surgery in the prevention and treatment of disease.

At the same time, faculty at university-affiliated medical schools asserted that the skills necessary for the practice of scientifically based medicine could not be learned by simple memorization of texts and passive listening to lectures, but could only be gained by the diligent application of the scientific method throughout several years of academic and clinical medical training and education. It was their belief that medical students should be equally schooled in bedside care, laboratory work, and academic studies in order to become skilled physicians.

The AMA undertook a campaign aimed at the closure of all American medical schools that did not move to the new educational standards. In 1904, the AMA created the Council on Medical Education (CME) in order to advance the reorganization of American medical education. The CME created two major goals for implementation: 1) standardization of specific academic and educational prerequisites for medical school entry; and 2) nationwide adoption of the *ideal* academic medical curriculum. This curriculum involved an initial two years of rigorous training in the laboratory sciences, followed by another two years spent in clinical rotations at a teaching hospital.

In 1908, the CME proposed a complete survey of all American medical schools in order to disseminate information concerning the proposed educational reforms and to gather preliminary data on the various teaching methods currently employed. The CME engaged the Carnegie Foundation for the Advancement of Teaching to conduct the survey. Henry S. Pritchett, then president of the Carnegie Foundation, selected Abraham Flexner to lead the survey.

▮ PRIMARY SOURCE

The striking and significant facts which are here brought out are of enormous consequences not only to the medical practitioner, but to every citizen of the United States and Canada; for it is a singular fact that the organization of medical education in this country has hitherto been such as not only to commercialize the process of education itself, but also to obscure in the minds of the public any discrimination between the well trained physician and the physician who has had no adequate training whatsoever. As a rule, Americans, when they avail themselves of the services of a physician, make only the slightest inquiry as to what his previous training and preparation have been. One of the problems of the future is to educate the public itself to appreciate the fact that very seldom, under existing conditions, does a patient receive the best aid which is possible to give him in the present state of medicine, and that this is mainly due to the fact that a vast army of men is admitted to the practice of medicine who are untrained in sciences fundamental to the profession and quite without a sufficient experience with disease. A right education of public opinion is one of the problems of future medical education.

The significant facts revealed by this study are as follows:

(1) For twenty-five years past there has been an enormous over-production of uneducated and ill trained medical practitioners. This has been in absolute disregard of the public welfare and without any serious thought of the interests of the public. Taking the United States as a whole, physicians are four or five times as numerous in proportion to population as in older countries like Germany.

(2) Over-production of ill trained men is due in the main to the existence of a very large number of commercial schools, sustained in many cases by advertising methods through which a mass of unprepared youth is drawn out of industrial occupations into the study of medicine.

(3) Until recently the conduct of a medical school was a profitable business, for the methods of instruction were mainly didactic. As the need for laboratories has become more keenly felt, the expenses of an efficient medical school have been greatly increased. The inadequacy of many of this school may be judged from the fact that nearly half of all our medical schools have incomes below $10,000, and these incomes determine the quality of instruction that they can and do offer.

Colleges and universities have in large measure failed in the past twenty-five years to appreciate the great advance in medical education and the increased cost of teaching it along modern lines. Many universities desirous of apparent educational completeness have annexed medical schools without making themselves responsible either for the standards of the professional schools or for their support.

(4) The existence of many of these unnecessary and inadequate medical schools has been defended by the argument that a poor medical school is justified in the interest of the poor boy. It is clear

that the poor boy has no right to go into any profession for which he is not willing to obtain adequate preparation; but the facts set forth in this report make it evident that this argument is insincere, and that the excuse which has hitherto been put forward in the name of the poor boy is in reality an argument in behalf of the poor medical school.

(5) A hospital under complete educational control is as necessary to a medical school as is a laboratory of chemistry or pathology. High-grade teaching with a hospital introduces a most wholesome and beneficial influence into its routine. Trustees of hospitals, public and private, should therefore go to the limit of their authority in opening hospital wards to teaching, provided only that the universities secure sufficient funds on their side to employ as teachers men who are devoted to clinical science.

In view of these facts, progress for the future would seem to require a very much smaller number of medical schools, better equipped and better conducted than our schools now as a rule are; and the needs of the public would equally require that we have fewer physicians graduated each year, but that these should be better educated and better trained. With this idea accepted, it necessarily follows that the medical school will, if rightly conducted, articulate not only with the university, but with the general system of education. . . .

SIGNIFICANCE

Over a period of eighteen months, Abraham Flexner visited a total of 155 medical schools across the United States. For each institution, he examined five specific areas in depth: 1) the entrance requirements; 2) the size and specific training of the faculty; 3) the extent of both the endowment and the amount of tuition charged per student; 4) the quality and sufficiency of the laboratory facilities; and 5) the availability and affiliation with a teaching hospital whose medical staff would function as clinical faculty. He found very few medical schools possessing the necessary combination of skilled and educated academic and clinical teaching faculty, appropriate hospital and laboratory facilities, and financial resources necessary to support the AMA's CME proposed reform for medical education. Flexner stated, "We have indeed in America medical practitioners not inferior to the best elsewhere; but there is probably no other country in the world in which there is so great a distance and so fatal a difference between the best, the average, and the worst."

Flexner was of the opinion that it would be impossible to raise the performance of the schools most lacking in the five essential areas to the standards of the best equipped institutions He felt that it was better to close the inferior medical schools and concentrate on those showing the most promise for the delivery of a superior education. Flexner said, "The point now to aim at is the development of the requisite number of properly supported institutions and the speedy demise of all others."

One of Flexner's greatest impacts in the support of reform for American medical education lay in his public health approach. It was his contention that the values and ethics inherent in a progressive system of scientific medical education were incompatible with the proprietary approach. Flexner stated, "Such exploitation of medical education is strangely inconsistent with the social aspects of medical practice. The overwhelming importance of preventive medicine, sanitation, and public health indicates that in modern life the medical profession is an organ differentiated by society for its highest purposes, not a business to be exploited."

Shortly after the Flexner Report was published, state licensing boards across the country began to emerge. They required medical schools to implement significantly more arduous pre-admission requirements and far more rigorous curriculum standards. In 1912, the Federation of State Medical Boards was created, and it agreed to utilize the AMA's (CME's) academic standards as its basis for academic accreditation. During this time period, philanthropic foundations began to create large financial endowments aimed at furthering medical education and research at various medical institutions. By 1940, proprietary medical schools no longer existed, and the rigorous medical curriculum desired by the AMA's CME and espoused by Flexner had become the norm.

FURTHER RESOURCES
Books

Ludmerer, Kenneth M. *Time to Heal: American Medical Education from the Turn of the Century to the Era of Managed Care.* New York: Oxford University Press, 1999.

Rothstein, William G. *American Physicians in the Nineteenth Century: From Sects to Science.* Baltimore: Johns Hopkins University Press, 1972.

Starr, Paul. *The Social Transformation of American Medicine.* New York: Basic Books, 1982.

Wheatley, Steven C. *The Politics of Philanthropy: Abraham Flexner and Medical Education.* Madison: University of Wisconsin Press, 1988.

Periodicals

Beck, Andrew H. "The Flexner Report and the Standardization of American Medical Education." *Student JAMA [Journal of the American Medical Association]* 291 (2004): 2139–2140.

Billings, J. S. "Ideals of Medical Education." *Science* 18 (1891): 1–4.

State Registration of Trained Nurses

Speech

By: William Henry Welch

Date: 1903

Source: William Henry Welch. *Papers and Addresses by William Henry Welch*, vol. III. Baltimore: Johns Hopkins Press, 1920.

About the Author: William Henry Welch (1850–1934), a pathologist and bacteriologist, helped raise the level of medical instruction in the United States. After pursuing medical studies in Germany, he returned to the U.S. to organize the first teaching laboratory for pathology at Bellevue Hospital. The first professor appointed to the new Johns Hopkins University Medical School in 1884, he helped institute new admission standards for medical students that included a bachelor's degree with appropriate courses in the sciences. In 1903, at the time of this speech, Welch was president of the Maryland Board of Health and dean of the medical faculty at Johns Hopkins. He would later serve as the president of the American Medical Association and as the president of the National Academy of Sciences. The discoverer of the bacillus causing gas gangrene, he is also responsible for helping to spread knowledge of bacteria among medical scientists.

INTRODUCTION

The nursing profession's quest for status as a health care profession began in the late nineteenth century with the formation of the American Nurses' Association (ANA). The organization aimed to raise the standards of nursing, initially by pushing for state registration of nurses that would mandate standardization of training. In 1903, William Henry Welch spoke to the newly formed Maryland state chapter of the ANA about state registration of nurses.

Nursing in the twentieth century was a woman's profession. Along with careers in teaching, libraries, and social work, nursing provided personal satisfaction and met the criteria for women's work. A nursing career drew on years of socialization and a consciousness bred to serve. Women who took up nursing could assume a social role consistent with the home. Nurses remained subordinate to (mostly male) doctors, served others, and had limited possibilities for advancement. This pattern of subservience and female submissiveness led to an undervaluing of the contributions of nurses.

To develop nursing as a profession, the ANA had to attach it in the public mind with competence in a distinguished field. ANA members believed that registration would force schools of nursing to improve the quality of training offered to students. Some of these schools were barely worthy of being called educational establishments. Typically attached to a hospital in this era, too many of these schools simply existed to provide inexpensive, menial labor for the hospital. As an indication of the lack of status of nursing, one Kansas hospital expected its nurses to provide patient care and mow the hospital lawn.

Determined to make the public view of nursing as a worthy partner to medicine, the ANA pushed for state registration. It had long been a requirement that medical practitioners meet certain fixed educational standards and become licensed. It seemed logical to many in the health care professions to expect nurses to also adhere to fixed standards.

PRIMARY SOURCE

. . . I hope, therefore, that in this state you will aim to secure such standards as are equal to the best. If that is not possible, get what you can, but, if possible, set up a standard that will be recognized not only here but in all the states of the country, so that a nurse who is a registered nurse in the state of Maryland shall by that very fact be recognized as qualified to practice her profession in any state of the union. I do not know that you will encounter the question that we have in the medical profession, that is, the great problem of reciprocity between the different states, but it is a matter for you to consider. The underlying difficulty has been just what I have stated, that the qualifications have been so little uniform in the different states that as a result a physician who has passed his examination and has been perhaps for a number of years practicing in a given state finds great difficulty in changing his residence and engaging in practice in another state; he may no longer be able to pass the requisite examination. . . .

You are only endeavoring to secure for your profession what has already been secured for other professions. You are not therefore asking for anything that is novel, that is experimental, or the application of any new principles of legislation whatever. The conditions differ little as regards nurses than as regards physicians, or pharmacists, or dentists, or lawyers, all of whose professions are amply protected now by the law. It is not for the present and doubtless it will never be considered judicious to prescribe that those who do not meet your qualifications shall be hindered from the practice of nursing. Judge Harlan has explained, that is not contemplated. It is clear that such a purpose would encounter an overwhelming opposition. You ask for nothing of the kind. Everyone is permitted to practice the art of nursing. You simply ask that some definite meaning shall be attached to the term trained and registered nurse, that meaning implying that those qualified to register have had a certain definite training. Now if all training schools in the country had high standards of education, similar periods of study and equal facilities or giving practical training, it might be questioned whether there was any urgent necessity for this registration of nurses. In the earlier days very likely such a need did not exist, but now the very fact that this movement has arisen and obtained in these three or four years since it began such momentum indicates that there is need for making clear in what the qualifications of a trained nurse really should consist.

The art of nursing, as Judge Harlan has stated, is a profession that is of the highest rank. It is one eminently fitted for women, it is one that requires a long period of training, one that requires special qualifications in the way of education on the part of the nurse, and I may say that I consider, although I am not a practitioner of medicine, that there is no improvement in modern medicine which outranks in importance, in its value in the prevention and cure of disease, the introduction of the system of trained nurses. One can put one's finger on great discoveries in medicine, the relation of bacteria, we will say, to the causation of disease, which is of the greatest interest in the progress of medicine, but so far as the treatment of disease is concerned the applications of the system of trained nursing counts for as much, if not more than any scientific discovery in medicine. So important is it that it is the main factor in the treatment and management of a number of the important and prevalent diseases. The benefits, therefore, which will come from the passage of this law in a measure are to you as a body of trained nurses, but in larger measure to the medical profession and in still larger measure to the whole community, to the general public. Therefore it seems to me that all the enlightened forces of society should be interested in the furtherance of this great movement on your part.

SIGNIFICANCE

The first registration laws for nurses adopted in the U.S. were permissive laws. People who satisfied the legal standards were permitted to register and use the title, "Registered Nurse." However, students who failed the licensure examination were merely referred to as graduate nurses and they continued to work as professional nurses. State nurse practice acts typically defined professional nursing as the performance for compensation of professional services requiring the application of scientific knowledge and nursing skills in the care of the sick. Unqualified nurses who did not claim to be registered nurses did not break the law. By 1923, all of the states had nursing licensure laws but these laws meant little in practice.

Nursing schools were able to avoid meeting the legal guidelines set down in the permissive licensure laws. Where schools lacked the resources to upgrade their programs, they often chose to forego the legal requirements. As registration was not mandatory, this decision had no serious consequences for hospitals, since they could hire the graduates of their own schools of nursing rather than the more expensive registered nurses. Hospital management justified their support of low entrance requirements for the profession of nursing on the grounds that it was in the public interest to have many nurses.

Following the 1923 Rockefeller Foundation survey of nurse education and the 1926–1934 Grading of Nursing Schools study, legislators in various states began to consider revising nursing licensure laws. The new legislation aimed to safeguard the health of the public from incompetent members of a health care team and aid nurses by establishing a fair field of competition. In 1938, New York became the first state to require licenses of all who nursed for hire. The dramatic and sudden increase in the nurse supply occasioned by World War II (1941–1945) forced the suspension of the law and it did not come into full effect until 1949. Other states followed the example of New York with licensure becoming standard in the 1950s.

Along with licensure and education requirements, today's nurses are bound to specific standards of practice that are law within each state. The nursing profession also contains several licenses and levels of practice, according to established educational requirements. Practical or vocational nurses provide direct patient care, registered nurses provide patient assessment, deliver specialized and direct care, and fill supervisory and administrative roles. Advanced practice nurses make diagnoses, deliver specialized care, and have limited authority to prescribe medications.

FURTHER RESOURCES

Books

Johnstone, Megan-Jane. *Nursing and the Injustices of the Law.* Sydney: W. B. Saunders, 1994.

Melosh, Barbara. *"The Physician's Hand": Work Culture and Conflict in American Nursing.* Philadelphia: Temple University Press, 1982.

Websites

Johnson and Johnson: The Nursing Profession. "Discover Nursing—Nursing: The Basics." <http://www.discovernursing.com/jnj-sectionID_2-pageID_8-dsc-landing.aspx> (accessed January 13, 2006).

Letter by Dr. A. S. Calhoun to Franklin D. Roosevelt

Food, Drug, and Cosmetic Act of 1938

Letter excerpt

By: Archie S. Calhoun

Date: October 22, 1937

Source: "Letter by Dr. A. S. Calhoun to Franklin D. Roosevelt." Available online at U.S. Food and Drug Administration. Ballantine, Carol. "Taste of Raspberries, Taste of Death." <http://www.fda.gov/oc/history/elixer.html> (accessed January 30, 2006).

About the Author: Archie S. Calhoun was a medical doctor who practiced family medicine in the early decades of the twentieth century.

INTRODUCTION

Beginning in the first decade of the twentieth century the United States Food and Drug Administration (FDA) enacted a series of legislations and acts that have imposed measures to control the quality of food items and medicine. For example, in 1906, the FDA (which at that time was known as the Bureau of Chemistry) passed the Food and Drugs Act. Under this act, certain food items as well as drugs were determined to be unsafe and their use was illegal. However, within a few decades, the shortcomings of the act became apparent. Some drugs were found to have no therapeutic value. One example is a diabetes drug marketed as Banbur. Even more ominously, some cosmetics were found to be harmful. A then-popular eyelash dye known as Lash-Lure caused blindness in some users.

By the early 1930s, it was apparent that the Food and Drugs Act needed to be revamped in order to provide more current, forceful, and stable legislation pertaining to the use of food, cosmetics, and drugs. A new bill proposing to completely revise this law was introduced into the Senate in the year 1933. At first, the proposal was not regarded as urgent by the Senate and after four years, action had yet to be taken.

In 1937, more than one hundred Americans, many of them children, died after taking a medicine intended to treat streptococcal infections and marketed as Elixir Sulfanilamide. The active ingredient in the preparation was dissolved in diethylene glycol in order to make a liquid form of the drug. The diethylene glycol in the mixture was toxic to humans. However, because the drug was not illegal under the existing Food and Drugs Act, its use was permitted. Furthermore, at that time there was no requirement for drug testing prior to marketing.

The physician Archie Calhoun was motivated in 1937 to write to then President Franklin D. Roosevelt to recount the deaths of patients under his care due to the use of medicines that were at that time not subject to legislated quality control. At that time the Food, Drug, and Cosmetic Act was being formulated. The letter was influential in convincing Roosevelt of the need for the legislation.

■ PRIMARY SOURCE

Nobody but Almighty God and I can know what I have been through these past few days. I have been familiar with death in the years since I received my M.D. from Tulane University School of Medicine with the rest of my class of 1911. Covington County has been my home. I have practiced here for years. Any doctor who has practiced more than a quarter of a century has seen his share of death.

But to realize that six human beings, all of them my patients, one of them my best friend, are dead because they took medicine that I prescribed for them innocently, and to realize that that medicine which I had used for years in such cases suddenly had become a deadly poison in its newest and most modern form, as recommended by a great and reputable pharmaceutical firm in Tennessee: well, that realization has given me such days and nights of mental and spiritual agony as I did not believe a human being could undergo and survive. I have known hours when death for me would be a welcome relief from this agony. (Letter by Dr. A. S. Calhoun, October 22, 1937)

SIGNIFICANCE

Not surprisingly, the public outcry was resounding. In response, the Food, Drug, and Cosmetic Act of 1938 was singed into law on June 25 of that year. This act required drug manufacturers to test and demonstrate to the FDA (who, then as now, administer the act) the safety of any new drug prior to its sale. The act also included a more comprehensive list of drugs that were unsafe, and so illegal for sale.

Another aspect of the act that has proven to be important was the requirement for labeling of ingredients and safe dosage levels. This legislation formed the foundation for modern-day food and drug regulation. Over the years, there have been periodic amendments to the Food, Drug, and Cosmetics Act of 1938. However, the FDA still uses the rigorous provisions of this act to ensure food and drug safety.

Aspects of the act such as labeling and safe dose guidelines have proven to be important and paved the way for labeling of other consumer products. As well, the mandated requirement for the demonstration of product safety prior to marketing has been fundamentally important in protecting consumers. This safety-first approach has been adopted by other countries and is a vital part of health protection legislation.

In 2005, the FDA announced the creation of a new and independent Drug Safety Oversight Board to oversee the management of drug safety issues, and to provide new information in an easily accessible format to health care providers and patients about the risks and benefits of medicines.

FURTHER RESOURCES

Periodicals

Wax, P. M. "Elixir sulfanilamide-Massengill revisited." *Veterinary and Human Toxicology* (December 1994): 36(6):561–2.

Web sites

U.S. Food and Drug Administration. "Consumer Education: What You Should Know About Buying and Using Drug Products." <http://www.fda.gov/cder/consumerinfo/DPAdefault.htm> (accessed January 29, 2006).

U.S. Food and Drug Administration. "The 1938 Food, Drug, and Cosmetic Act." <http://www.fda.gov/oc/history/historyoffda/section2.html> (accessed May 5, 2005).

Private Health Insurance Originates with Blue Cross and Blue Shield

Photograph

By: Blue Cross Blue Shield Association

Date: 1954

Source: *Blue Cross Blue Shield Association.* "History of Blue Cross® Blue Shield®." <http://www.bcbs.com/history/bluebeginnings.html> (accessed October 20, 2005).

About the Author: The Blue Cross Blue Shield Association is an umbrella organization representing state and regional Blue Cross and Blue Shield health plans across the United States. It provides public relations, research, and infrastructure services to the individual plans.

INTRODUCTION

Prior to 1920, expenditures on hospital and medical services were relatively low for most Americans, as physicians and hospitals had far fewer technological tools and drug therapies at their disposal with which to treat their patients. The loss of income from disability due to illness often had greater economic impact than paying for medical care, and people often purchased "sickness insurance" similar to contemporary disability insurance rather than health insurance to protect income. A 1918 government survey found that people spent less than eight percent of their incomes on medical expenses.

At the same time, commercial life insurance companies did not believe that they had the expertise and understanding of health risk to offer health insurance. They feared they would be financially victimized by "adverse selection," in which people with serious illnesses or engaged in the riskiest behaviors would purchase insurance, while the healthiest and safest people would forego health coverage.

During the 1920s, the training of physicians became more scientific, emphasizing knowledge of bacteriology, infectious agents, diagnostic testing, pharmaceutical treatment, and disease prevention with vaccines. Doctors became more professionalized and began to charge higher fees. The demand for clean, well-equipped hospital facilities with room to care for patients outside the home increased with growing urbanization and the lack of room in city dwellings to care for the sick. The economic burden of illness began to grow, making financial preparation for its eventuality prudent. As the decade of the 1920s progressed, the cost of medical care became a topic of growing concern and public debate.

It was logical that employers in high-risk occupations, such as mining, and schools employing many women (for whom high maternity expenses could be expected) would see the economic value of purchasing insurance for medical care to ensure that patients could pay their bills. Such pre-paid employer health plans were originally contracts between specific employers and hospitals or physician associations. During the early 1930s, these agreements became so widespread that the American Hospital Association (AHA) encouraged its members with pre-paid health plans to coalesce under the Blue Cross moniker. The AHA's motivation was both to encourage the development of programs that protected the economic well-being of the population and to reduce price competition among the hospitals.

A similar amalgamation occurred among physician programs under the Blue Shield name. Physicians were not so averse to price competition and price discrimination, but worried that intensifying national concern over medical costs would lead to government regulation. Also, they worried that the hospitals under the Blue Cross system would begin to offer insurance for medical services as well. They protected their interests by organizing into Blue Shield plans and preempting both Blue Cross and advocates for establishing national compulsory health insurance. Initially, Blue Shield plans covered medical and surgical expenses while patients were hospitalized, but later they covered physician office visits and services as well.

The photograph of the first person whose birth was financed by Blue Cross is part of the Blue Cross and Blue Shield Association's effort to educate the American public about the origins of the complex U.S. private health care financing system. When the photograph was taken in 1954, the Blue Cross system had already been in existence for more than twenty years. The story of the picture takes a twist when the caption explains that the first "Blue Baby" is not the baby in the picture, but the mother. This underscored the increasingly critical role that Blue Cross programs had come to assume in the financing of health and maternity expenses for a widening group of Americans.

Blue Cross programs arose during the hard economic times of the Depression (1929–1939) when hospital expenses were beginning to be of material concern to families. Blue Shield programs, which pay for physician services, had a nearly simultaneous, but

independent origin that was fostered by efforts of workers engaged in difficult and risky labor to finance medical care that was often the result of job-related injuries and chronic illnesses. Employers paid for both hospital and medical care under the Blue Cross Blue Shield system. Thus, the story of the origins of private health insurance in the United States is also the story of the conception and growth of contemporary employer-paid health insurance.

PRIMARY SOURCE

PRIVATE HEALTH INSURANCE ORIGINATES WITH BLUE CROSS AND BLUE SHIELD

See primary source image.

SIGNIFICANCE

The original Blue Cross and Blue Shield plans were not-for-profit organizations that were required to offer patients free choice of physicians and hospitals. They secured state legislation exempting them from carrying insurance reserves such as were required of commercial insurance companies. Instead, hospitals agreed to provide care for patients when the plans lacked funds for reimbursement. Freedom from burdensome reserve requirements helped to keep costs down and further contributed to growing health insurance sales.

The Blue Cross and Blue Shield plans grew rapidly, insuring over 20 million Americans by 1940. By that time, the commercial insurance companies began to show interest in health insurance once the "Blues" had pioneered the concept, defined the "medical necessity" of treatments, and established the financial viability of employer-group health coverage. Commercial coverage helped fuel further rapid growth of health insurance. By 1950, both commercial and Blue Cross Blue Shield plans had enrolled more than 140 million members.

The U.S. employer-based health insurance system is characterized by a multitude of optional policy features, some of which can be elected by an employer in behalf of its entire insured group and others which are elected by individual employees. Employees generally pay extra for optional coverage, and this can increase their contributions to thirty percent or more of the total insurance premium. The employees' contributions are deducted from their paychecks.

One of the enduring controversies regarding group health insurance involves community rating

PRIMARY SOURCE

Private Health Insurance Originates with Blue Cross and Blue Shield. America's first "Blue Cross Baby" was born in Durham, North Carolina. Her birth was the first in America to be covered by a health insurance family certificate that included maternity benefits. The entire cost of her delivery and her mother's ten-day hospital stay totaled $60. Actually, it is the mother in this picture who was the first "Blue Cross Baby." She is holding her own "Blue Cross Baby" born in 1954. COPYRIGHT HOLDER UNKNOWN.

versus experience rating. Under community rating, the cost of insuring sick people is spread across a large population of mostly healthy people, as in a state. Under experience rating, the cost of a policy depends on the health-insurance-claims experience of people in a defined group, such as a company. Companies often question why they should subsidize the health care costs of people in the larger community that may be older and sicker than their employees. This reluctance to accept cost spreading has resulted in a breakdown of community rating so that older, sicker groups pay higher premiums than younger, healthier groups for the same benefits. One consequence of experience rating is that the health experience (and the insurance premium) for any particular group fluctuates over time around an average cost closely related to its average age (group experience "regresses to the mean"). There is constant "churning" of health plan membership as companies get good rates based on several years of often fortuitously low health care insurance claims, then get "blown off the books" by insurance underwriters as their claims inevitably get worse in succeeding years. Actuarial analysis shows that three good years during which members enjoy better than average health tend

to be followed by three bad years during which the group experiences more illness claims and worse than average health. This is the so-called health insurance "underwriting cycle." This churning in membership based on short-term experience has, in turn, led to an undervaluing of illness prevention in the U.S. There is less incentive to encourage healthy lifestyles among plan members, if they are going to be with another plan in less than five years. Churning also results in more employers dropping employee medical coverage as they are faced with premium increases that they can't afford; hence, the large number of employed, uninsured persons in the United States.

In the 1960s, it became clear that employer-based insurance left many retired and elderly people without health coverage at a time when they require more health services. Medicare, public health care financing for people over sixty-five, was established in 1965. Increasingly critical prescription drug coverage will be added to Medicare in 2006. Also, the U.S. has a substantial population of mostly poor women and their children who are not employed and cannot participate in an employer plan. In 1966 Congress passed the Medicaid law establishing a state-federal partnership to provide health care financing for persons in poverty without access to other health care coverage. These two programs provided a health care "safety net" that addressed two major weaknesses in the employment-based health insurance system, and pre-empted system critics who advocated a national health insurance program similar to those found in other industrialized countries.

The evolution of the U.S. public-private health insurance system has been incremental in that glaring gaps in coverage have been addressed with public insurance programs such as Medicare and Medicaid. Expenditures on these public programs now account for about one-third of all U.S. health care expenditures. The cost of health care for both public and private health insurance programs is growing at a rate that has outpaced general inflation in the U.S. economy for decades. Health care comprises an ever-increasing proportion of the nation's total economic output. It currently is about fifteen percent of the total U.S. economic output—the highest of any of the Organization for Economic Cooperation and Development (OECD) industrialized countries. In spite of this enormous expenditure, about 40 million Americans do not have health insurance and receive uncompensated care on an emergency basis. The U.S. also has the highest rate of health care cost increases among these industrialized nations. These trends are driven by rapidly advancing medical technology, the insulation of consumers from the true costs of health care by their insurance plans, and, according to some economists and insurance executives, a lack of cost-effectiveness in U.S. health care.

The remarkable and unparalleled growth of private health insurance coverage in the U.S. presents a mixture of advantages and problems. The U.S. system continues to foster the highest degree of innovation in medical technology and pharmaceutical treatment as well as in financing mechanisms. Recent examples of such financing schemes include managed health care plans in which payers intervene in medical treatment with guidelines (usually devised by medical societies), restrictions, and incentives for certain patterns of care. Another innovation is the so-called consumer-driven plan in which patients encounter the true costs of healthcare as they deduct reimbursements to health care providers from a tax-exempt health care savings account (HSA). Health care expenditures in the U.S. are not subject to a national budget that can be cut back, and individuals have discretion regarding how much they can spend on health care, and when and where they can get services.

Some of the problems with U.S. health care and health care financing include the huge population of uninsured persons, the lack of incentives for illness prevention, and the absence of interest in applying cost-effectiveness analysis to health care interventions. Both public and private payers often pay significantly higher prices for new treatments that are only incrementally effective for relatively narrow patient groups. These treatments often have been prescribed instead of older treatments that are equally effective for most patients. For example, a patient with transient headache pain might be prescribed a cox-2 inhibitor drug, such as Vioxx, that costs dollars per dose, when an aspirin, costing pennies per dose, might be equally effective.

The lack of cost-effectiveness accountability in U.S. health care arises because both public and private health insurance programs have been effectively prevented from applying cost-effectiveness criteria to the coverage of medical products and services by consumer and taxpayer pressure on businesses and the government. The risk of high health care inflation appears to be greater under a private system than under a public system because prices for health care products and services under government-run systems are usually severely constrained. On the other hand, such constraints appear to reduce investment in research and development for medical technology, as witnessed by the fact that most pharmaceutical research and development activity now takes place in the United States.

After more than eighty years of private, largely employer-based U.S. health insurance, companies are finding that funding health care puts them at a disadvantage in global economic competition. They are shifting an ever larger proportion of the cost of care and insurance premiums to employees, who are paying more either out-of-pocket at the pharmacy or clinic or out of their paychecks. Health economists, such as Uve Reinhardt of Princeton, maintain that employees have been paying for health care all along in reduced long-term income growth. The U.S. now appears to be moving toward a health care system in which consumers—perhaps with employer guidance and infrastructure for negotiating with providers and increasing protective regulation from government—will become the primary payers for their own care.

FURTHER RESOURCES

Books

Dranove, David. *The EconomicEvolution of American Health Care.* Princeton: Princeton University Press, 2000.

Kleinke, J. D. *Oxymorons: The Myth of a U.S. Health Care System.* San Francisco: Jossey-Bass, 2001.

Periodicals

Thomasson, Melissa A. "From Sicknessto Health: The Twentieth-Century Development of U.S. Health Insurance." *Explorationsin Economic History* 39 (July 2002): 233–253.

Web sites

Blue Cross Blue Shield Association. "History of Blue Cross® Blue Shield®." <http://www.bcbs.com/history/bluebeginnings.html> (accessed October 20, 2005.)

President Lyndon Johnson Signs Medicare Bill

Speech excerpt

By: Lyndon Baines Johnson

Date: July 30, 1965

Source: "President Lyndon B. Johnson's Remarks with President Truman at the Signing in Independence of the Medicare Bill." *Public Papers of the Presidents of the United States: Lyndon B. Johnson, 1965.* Volume II, entry 394, pp. 811–815. Washington, D.C.: Government Printing Office, 1966.<http://www.lbjlib.utexas.edu/johnson/archives.hom/speeches.hom/650730.asp> (accessed February 1, 2006).

About the Author: Lyndon B. Johnson (1908–1973) served as the thirty-sixth president of the United States from 1963 to 1969.

INTRODUCTION

Until the early 1960s, elderly citizens in the United States were burdened with high medical expenses. Those citizens with low incomes or pensions were often hard-pressed to pay medical bills, and benefits provided by the Social Security Act of 1935 did not include certain medical coverage. The Medicare Bill—title XVIII of the Social Security Act, was passed in 1965 to ensure a comprehensive health insurance plan for the elderly. The act, which was signed into law by then president Lyndon B. Johnson, provided health coverage to most citizens aged sixty-five years and more.

Under the structure of Medicare, employees contributed a determined and relatively small portion of their salary towards health insurance. Employers also contributed. The accumulated sum over time enabled those reaching sixty-five years of age to be provided with hospital care, diagnostic care, and post-hospital home visits for certain periods, depending on the nature of the illness and/or care required.

Medicare consists of two main sections. The first section is known as Hospital Insurance (HI), or part A, which provides benefits during hospitalization. The second section is Supplementary Medical Insurance (SMI), or part B, which provides benefits for physician services, physical and occupational therapy, and some home health care.

Part A is generally provided automatically and free of premiums to persons age sixty-five or over who are eligible for Social Security benefits. Part A ensures pay for care in hospitals, skilled nursing homes, home health agencies, and hospice care. The period of care and benefits available vary depending on the type of care. For example, hospital care includes costs of a semi-private room, meals, regular nursing services, operating and recovery rooms, intensive care, inpatient prescription drugs, laboratory tests, x rays, psychiatric hospitals, and inpatient rehabilitation.

Part B of Medicare covers doctors' bills, outpatient medical care, and many other medical services not covered under Part A. These services include, as some examples, physician services, laboratory and other diagnostic tests, x-ray therapy, home dialysis supplies and equipment, ambulance services, flu, pneumonia, and hepatitis vaccinations. In addition, Part B also covers certain equipment that is certified to be medically necessary including wheelchairs, oxygen, and mobility aids such as a wheel chair.

All citizens enrolled under Part A are eligible for benefits under Part B on a voluntary basis, provided all services are either medically necessary or one of several prescribed preventive benefits. Any one who wishes to avail of these benefits must pay a monthly premium.

■ PRIMARY SOURCE

PRESIDENT LYNDON B. JOHNSON'S REMARKS WITH PRESIDENT TRUMAN AT THE SIGNING IN INDEPENDENCE OF THE MEDICARE BILL JULY 30, 1965

. . . It was a generation ago that Harry Truman said, and I quote him: "Millions of our citizens do not now have a full measure of opportunity to achieve and to enjoy good health. Millions do not now have protection or security against the economic effects of sickness. And the time has now arrived for action to help them attain that opportunity and to help them get that protection."

Well, today, Mr. President, and my fellow Americans, we are taking such action—twenty years later. And we are doing that under the great leadership of men like John McCormack, our Speaker; Carl Albert, our majority leader; our very able and beloved majority leader of the Senate, Mike Mansfield; and distinguished Members of the Ways and Means and Finance Committees of the House and Senate—of both parties, Democratic and Republican.

Because the need for this action is plain; and it is so clear indeed that we marvel not simply at the passage of this bill, but what we marvel at is that it took so many years to pass it. And I am so glad that Aime Forand is here to see it finally passed and signed—one of the first authors.

There are more than 18 million Americans over the age of sixty-five. Most of them have low incomes. Most of them are threatened by illness and medical expenses that they cannot afford.

And through this new law, Mr. President, every citizen will be able, in his productive years when he is earning, to insure himself against the ravages of illness in his old age.

This insurance will help pay for care in hospitals, in skilled nursing homes, or in the home. And under a separate plan it will help meet the fees of the doctors.

Now here is how the plan will affect you.

During your working years, the people of America, you, will contribute through the social security program a small amount each payday for hospital insurance protection. For example, the average worker in 1966 will contribute about one dollar and fifty cents per month. The employer will contribute a similar amount. And this will provide the funds to pay up to ninety days of hospital care for each illness, plus diagnostic care, and up to one hundred home health visits after you are sixty-five. And beginning in 1967, you will also be covered for up to one hundred days of care in a skilled nursing home after a period of hospital care.

And under a separate plan, when you are sixty-five—that the Congress originated itself, in its own good judgment—you may be covered for medical and surgical fees whether you are in or out of the hospital. You will pay three dollars per month after you are sixty-five and your Government will contribute an equal amount.

The benefits under the law are as varied and broad as the marvelous modern medicine itself. If it has a few defects—such as the method of payment of certain specialists—then I am confident those can be quickly remedied and I hope they will be.

No longer will older Americans be denied the healing miracle of modern medicine. No longer will illness crush and destroy the savings that they have so carefully put away over a lifetime so that they might enjoy dignity in their later years. No longer will young families see their own incomes, and their own hopes, eaten away simply because they are carrying out their deep moral obligations to their parents, and to their uncles, and their aunts. . . ."

SIGNIFICANCE

Medicare, when first implemented in early 1966, covered most people with the age of sixty-five or more. However, by 1973, it was modified to include all people over sixty-five. Although the Medicare bill has undergone modifications since it was passed, the basic structure of the act remains the same. Beginning in January 2006, Medicare also offered a new prescription drug benefit program.

Medicare has become the largest health insurance program in the United States, and is often regarded as a significant success story in health care around the world. According to the Centers for Medicare and Medicaid Services (CMS), four million eligible citizens received hospital care totaling $2.4 billion under Medicare during the first year following implementation of the program, and 200,000 people also received home health services. As of 2006, according to the CMS, 95 percent of the sixty-five-plus population of the United States, or over thirty million people, are covered by Medicare.

By the year 2030, the amount of Medicare recipients in the United States is estimated to reach seventy-one million people, twice the current 2006 amount. As the Baby Boom population (babies born from 1945–1960) becomes eligible for Medicare and medical costs continue to rise, projected burdens on the system will challenge the ability of the Medicare system to provide its mandated services. Efforts to strengthen and

modernize the Medicare system are underway and include streamlining paperwork, encouraging marketplace competition from private health plans, and improving health care quality and efficiency.

FURTHER RESOURCES
Books

CCH Health Law Editors. *Medicare Explained*. Riverwoods, Ill.: CCH Incorporated, 2005.

Fenten, John H. and J. Stenken. *All About Medicare 2005*. Cincinnati, Ohio: National Underwriter Co., 2005.

Web sites

Centers for Medicare and Medicaid Services. "Medicare: A Brief Summary." <http://www.cms.hhs.gov/publications/overview-medicare-medicaid/default3.asp> (accessed July 15, 2005).

The White House. "Strengthening Medicare: A Framework to Modernize and Improve Medicare." <http://www.whitehouse.gov/infocus/medicare> (accessed July 15, 2005).

The Belmont Report

Ethical Principles and Guidelines for the Protection of Human Subjects

Government document

By: United States Department of Health, Education, and Welfare. National Commission for the Protection of Human Subjects of Biomedical and Behavioral Research

Date: April 18, 1979

Source: National Commission for the Protection of Human Subjects of Biomedical and Behavioral Research. *The Belmont Report: Ethical Principles and Guidelines for the Protection of Human Subjects of Research*. Washington, D.C.: U.S.G.P.O., 1979.

About the Author: Congress passed the National Research Act of 1974 in the wake of negative publicity for both the government and the scientific community regarding the cruel treatment of some medical research subjects. Among the consequences of this act was the Department of Health, Education, and Welfare (DHEW) creating the National Commission for the Protection of Human Subjects of Biomedical and Behavioral Research, which met at the Belmont House in Elkridge, Maryland, beginning in February 1976.

INTRODUCTION

In the 1960s, the concept of human individual autonomy rose to the forefront of political discourse throughout the Western world. One part of this discourse that continues its crescendo at the beginning of the twenty-first century concerns the rights of patients and biomedical research subjects. Two gradual disclosures in the late 1960s and early 1970s were the major impetus for passing the National Research Act, for founding the Office for Protection from Research Risks (OPRR) in 1972, and ultimately for writing the Belmont Report.

From 1932 to 1972, the United States Public Health Service (USPHS) studied the full natural course of syphilis among 399 poor African American men in Tuskegee, Alabama. The USPHS lied to these men about the purpose of the study, deceived them about the nature of their disease, and deliberately withheld curative treatment from them even after penicillin was proved effective against syphilis in the 1940s. From 1955 to 1972, New York State sponsored experiments on hepatitis among mentally retarded children at Willowbrook State School for the Retarded, Staten Island. These incompetent research subjects were exploited without the informed consent of their parents or legal guardians. Shortly after the press published these stories, the federal government took decisive action to prevent the further undermining of public trust in science and medicine.

■ PRIMARY SOURCE

ETHICAL PRINCIPLES AND GUIDELINES FOR THE PROTECTION OF HUMAN SUBJECTS OF RESEARCH

Part B: Basic Ethical Principles The expression "basic ethical principles" refers to those general judgments that serve as a basic justification for the many particular ethical prescriptions and evaluations of human actions. Three basic principles, among those generally accepted in our cultural tradition, are particularly relevant to the ethics of research involving human subjects: the principles of respect of persons, beneficence and justice.

1. Respect for Persons. Respect for persons incorporates at least two ethical convictions: first, that individuals should be treated as autonomous agents, and second, that persons with diminished autonomy are entitled to protection. The principle of respect for persons thus divides into two separate moral requirements: the requirement to acknowledge autonomy and the requirement to protect those with diminished autonomy.

An autonomous person is an individual capable of deliberation about personal goals and of acting under the direction of such deliberation. To respect autonomy is to give weight to autonomous persons' considered opinions and choices while refraining from obstructing their actions unless they are clearly detrimental to others. To show lack of respect for an autonomous agent is to repudiate that person's considered judgments, to deny an individual the freedom to act on those considered judgments, or to withhold information necessary to make a considered judgment, when there are no compelling reasons to do so.

However, not every human being is capable of self-determination. The capacity for self-determination matures during an individual's life, and some individuals lose this capacity wholly or in part because of illness, mental disability, or circumstances that severely restrict liberty. Respect for the immature and the incapacitated may require protecting them as they mature or while they are incapacitated.

Some persons are in need of extensive protection, even to the point of excluding them from activities which may harm them; other persons require little protection beyond making sure they undertake activities freely and with awareness of possible adverse consequences. The extent of protection afforded should depend upon the risk of harm and the likelihood of benefit. The judgment that any individual lacks autonomy should be periodically reevaluated and will vary in different situations.

In most cases of research involving human subjects, respect for persons demands that subjects enter into the research voluntarily and with adequate information. In some situations, however, application of the principle is not obvious. The involvement of prisoners as subjects of research provides an instructive example. On the one hand, it would seem that the principle of respect for persons requires that prisoners not be deprived of the opportunity to volunteer for research. On the other hand, under prison conditions they may be subtly coerced or unduly influenced to engage in research activities for which they would not otherwise volunteer. Respect for persons would then dictate that prisoners be protected. Whether to allow prisoners to "volunteer" or to "protect" them presents a dilemma. Respecting persons, in most hard cases, is often a matter of balancing competing claims urged by the principle of respect itself.

2. Beneficence. Persons are treated in an ethical manner not only by respecting their decisions and protecting them from harm, but also by making efforts to secure their well-being. Such treatment falls under the principle of beneficence. The term "beneficence" is often understood to cover acts of kindness or charity that go beyond strict obligation. In this document, beneficence is understood in a stronger sense, as an obligation. Two general rules have been formulated as complementary expressions of beneficent actions in this sense: (1) do not harm and (2) maximize possible benefits and minimize possible harms.

The Hippocratic maxim "do no harm" has long been a fundamental principle of medical ethics. Claude Bernard extended it to the realm of research, saying that one should not injure one person regardless of the benefits that might come to others. However, even avoiding harm requires learning what is harmful; and, in the process of obtaining this information, persons may be exposed to risk of harm. Further, the Hippocratic Oath requires physicians to benefit their patients "according to their best judgment." Learning what will in fact benefit may require exposing persons to risk. The problem posed by these imperatives is to decide when it is justifiable to seek certain benefits despite the risks involved, and when the benefits should be foregone because of the risks.

The obligations of beneficence affect both individual investigators and society at large, because they extend both to particular research projects and to the entire enterprise of research. In the case of particular projects, investigators and members of their institutions are obliged to give forethought to the maximization of benefits and the reduction of risk that might occur from the research investigation. In the case of scientific research in general, members of the larger society are obliged to recognize the longer term benefits and risks that may result from the improvement of knowledge and from the development of novel medical, psychotherapeutic, and social procedures.

The principle of beneficence often occupies a well-defined justifying role in many areas of research involving human subjects. An example is found in research involving children. Effective ways of treating childhood diseases and fostering healthy development are benefits that serve to justify research involving children—even when individual research subjects are not direct beneficiaries. Research also makes it possible to avoid the harm that may result from the application of previously accepted routine practices that on closer investigation turn out to be dangerous. But the role of the principle of beneficence is not always so unambiguous. A difficult ethical problem remains, for example, about research that presents more than minimal risk without immediate prospect of direct benefit to the children involved. Some have argued that such research is inadmissible, while others have pointed out that this limit would rule out much research promising great benefit to children in the future. Here again, as with all hard cases, the different claims covered by the principle of beneficence may come into conflict and force difficult choices.

3. Justice. Who ought to receive the benefits of research and bear its burdens? This is a question of justice, in the sense of "fairness in distribution" or "what is deserved." An injustice occurs when some benefit to which a person is entitled is denied without good reason or when some burden is imposed unduly. Another way of conceiving the principle of justice is that equals ought to be treated equally. However, this statement requires explication. Who is equal and who is unequal? What considerations justify departure from equal distribution? Almost all commentators allow that distinctions based on experience, age, deprivation, competence, merit and position do sometimes constitute criteria justifying differential treatment for certain purposes. It is necessary, then, to explain in what respects people should be treated equally. There are several widely accepted formulations of just ways to distribute burdens and benefits. Each formulation mentions some relevant property on the basis of which burdens and benefits should be distributed. These formulations are (1) to each person an equal share, (2) to each person according to individual need, (3) to each person according to individual effort, (4) to each person according to societal contribution, and (5) to each person according to merit.

Questions of justice have long been associated with social practices such as punishment, taxation and political representation. Until recently these questions have not generally been associated with scientific research. However, they are foreshadowed even in the earliest reflections on the ethics of research involving human subjects. For example, during the nineteenth and early twentieth centuries the burdens of serving as research subjects fell largely upon poor ward patients, while the benefits of improved medical care flowed primarily to private patients. Subsequently, the exploitation of unwilling prisoners as research subjects in Nazi concentration camps was condemned as a particularly flagrant injustice. In this country, in the 1940's, the Tuskegee syphilis study used disadvantaged, rural black men to study the untreated course of a disease that is by no means confined to that population. These subjects were deprived of demonstrably effective treatment in order not to interrupt the project, long after such treatment became generally available.

Against this historical background, it can be seen how conceptions of justice are relevant to research involving human subjects. For example, the selection of research subjects needs to be scrutinized in order to determine whether some classes (e.g., welfare patients, particular racial and ethnic minorities, or persons confined to institutions) are being systematically selected simply because of their easy availability, their compromised position, or their manipulability, rather than for reasons directly related to the problem being studied. Finally, whenever research supported by public funds leads to the development of therapeutic devices and procedures, justice demands both that these not provide advantages only to those who can afford them and that such research should not unduly involve persons from groups unlikely to be among the beneficiaries of subsequent applications of the research.

Part C: Applications Applications of the general principles to the conduct of research leads to consideration of the following requirements: informed consent, risk/benefit assessment, and the selection of subjects of research.

1. Informed Consent. Respect for persons requires that subjects, to the degree that they are capable, be given the opportunity to choose what shall or shall not happen to them. This opportunity is provided when adequate standards for informed consent are satisfied. While the importance of informed consent is unquestioned, controversy prevails over the nature and possibility of an informed consent. Nonetheless, there is widespread agreement that the consent process can be analyzed as containing three elements: information, comprehension and voluntariness.

Information. Most codes of research establish specific items for disclosure intended to assure that subjects are given sufficient information. These items generally include: the research procedure, their purposes, risks and anticipated benefits, alternative procedures (where therapy is involved), and a statement offering the subject the opportunity to ask questions and to withdraw at any time from the research. Additional items have been proposed, including how subjects are selected, the person responsible for the research, etc.

However, a simple listing of items does not answer the question of what the standard should be for judging how much and what sort of information should be provided. One standard frequently invoked in medical practice, namely the information commonly provided by practitioners in the field or in the locale, is inadequate since research takes place precisely when a common understanding does not exist. Another standard, currently popular in malpractice law, requires the practitioner to reveal the information that reasonable persons would wish to know in order to make a decision regarding their care. This, too, seems insufficient since the research subject, being in essence a volunteer, may wish to know considerably more about risks gratuitously undertaken than do patients who deliver themselves into the hand of a clinician for needed care. It may be that a standard of "the reasonable volunteer" should be proposed: the extent and nature of information should be such that persons, knowing that the procedure is neither necessary for their care nor perhaps fully understood, can decide whether they wish to participate in the furthering of knowledge. Even when some direct benefit to them is anticipated, the subjects should understand clearly the range of risk and the voluntary nature of participation.

A special problem of consent arises where informing subjects of some pertinent aspect of the research is likely to impair the validity of the research. In many cases, it is sufficient to indicate to subjects that they are being invited to participate in research of which some features will not be revealed until the research is concluded. In all cases of research involving incomplete disclosure, such research is justified only if it is clear that (1) incomplete disclosure is truly necessary to accomplish the goals of the research, (2) there are no undisclosed risks to subjects that are more than minimal, and (3) there is an adequate plan for debriefing subjects, when appropriate, and for dissemination of research results to them. Information about risks should never be withheld for the purpose of eliciting the cooperation of subjects, and truthful answers should always be given to direct questions about the research. Care should be taken to distinguish cases in which disclosure would destroy or invalidate the research from cases in which disclosure would simply inconvenience the investigator.

Comprehension. The manner and context in which information is conveyed is as important as the information itself. For example, presenting information in a disorganized and rapid fashion, allowing too little time for consideration or curtailing opportunities for questioning, all may adversely affect a subject's ability to make an informed choice.

Because the subject's ability to understand is a function of intelligence, rationality, maturity and language, it is necessary to adapt the presentation of the information to the subject's capacities. Investigators are responsible for ascertaining that the subject has comprehended the information. While there is always an obligation to ascertain that the information about risk to subjects is complete and adequately comprehended, when the risks are more serious, that obligation increases. On occasion, it may be suitable to give some oral or written tests of comprehension.

Special provision may need to be made when comprehension is severely limited—for example, by conditions of immaturity or mental disability. Each class of subjects that one might consider as incompetent (e.g., infants and young children, mentally disable patients, the terminally ill and the comatose) should be considered on its own terms. Even for these persons, however, respect requires giving them the opportunity to choose to the extent they are able, whether or not to participate in research. The objections of these subjects to involvement should be honored, unless the research entails providing them a therapy unavailable elsewhere. Respect for persons also requires seeking the permission of other parties in order to protect the subjects from harm. Such persons are thus respected both by acknowledging their own wishes and by the use of third parties to protect them from harm.

The third parties chosen should be those who are most likely to understand the incompetent subject's situation and to act in that person's best interest. The person authorized to act on behalf of the subject should be given an opportunity to observe the research as it proceeds in order to be able to withdraw the subject from the research, if such action appears in the subject's best interest.

Voluntariness. An agreement to participate in research constitutes a valid consent only if voluntarily given. This element of informed consent requires conditions free of coercion and undue influence. Coercion occurs when an overt threat of harm is intentionally presented by one person to another in order to obtain compliance. Undue influence, by contrast, occurs through an offer of an excessive, unwarranted, inappropriate or improper reward or other overture in order to obtain compliance. Also, inducements that would ordinarily be acceptable may become undue influences if the subject is especially vulnerable.

Unjustifiable pressures usually occur when persons in positions of authority or commanding influence—especially where possible sanctions are involved—urge a course of action for a subject. A continuum of such influencing factors exists, however, and it is impossible to state precisely where justifiable persuasion ends and undue influence begins. But undue influence would include actions such as manipulating a person's choice through the controlling influence of a close relative and threatening to withdraw health services to which an individual would otherwise be entitled.

SIGNIFICANCE

The Belmont Report prompted much new legislation and regulation in the decades following. In 1991, the Department of Health and Human Services (DHHS) codified the "Federal Policy for the Protection of Human Subjects." This policy is called the "Common Rule" because, even though created by DHHS, it applies equally to all federal departments and agencies that grant money for scientific research that involves human subjects. Among other provisions, it strengthened the 1974 mandate that every institution receiving federal funds for research must have its own Institutional Review Board (IRB) to approve all research protocols. In 2000, the OPRR, now within DHHS, became the Office for Human Research Protections (OHRP).

Legal and ethical issues surrounding informed consent and informed refusal remain in a state of flux and continue to be a major concern of the federal government. In 1998, the National Bioethics Advisory Commission issued a report called *Research Involving Persons with Mental Disorders that may Affect Decisionmaking Capacity*. Abuses, carelessness, and deaths still occur, even at the most prestigious American academic research institutions. Eighteen-year-old Jesse Gelsinger died during experimental gene therapy for his rare metabolic disease in 1999 at the University of Pennsylvania. Twenty-four-year-old Ellen Roche, a healthy volunteer, died of a reaction to an experimental medication for asthma in 2001 at Johns Hopkins University. In such cases federal agents immediately intervene, scrutinizing the IRB, the principal investigator, and the protocols. The government retains the authority to suspend funding and even to shut down the whole research enterprise of the institution.

FURTHER RESOURCES
Books

Berg, Jessica W., Paul S. Appelbaum, Charles W. Lidz, and Lisa S. Parker. *Informed Consent: Legal Theory and Clinical Practice*. 2nd edition. New York: Oxford University Press, 2001.

Doyal, Len, and Jeffrey S. Tobias, eds. *Informed Consent in Medical Research*. London: BMJ Books, 2001.

Getz, Kenneth, and Deborah Borlitz. *Informed Consent: The Consumer's Guide to the Risks and Benefits of Volunteering for Clinical Trials*. Boston: CenterWatch, 2003.

Periodicals

Beauchamp, Tom. "The Legacy and the Future: 30 Years after the Belmont Report." *Protecting Human Subjects*. vol. 10 (2004): 1–3.

Cassell, Eric J. "The Principles of the Belmont Report Revisited: How Have Respect for Persons, Beneficence, and Justice Been Applied to Clinical Medicine?" *Hastings Center Report*. vol. 30, no. 4 (July-August 2000): 12–21.

Web sites

Georgetown University. "The Birth of the Belmont Report." <http://www.georgetown.edu/research/nrcbl/nbac/transcripts/jul98/belmont.html> (accessed January 15, 2006).

Kent State University. "ISB National Research Act." <http://www.kent.edu/rags/Compliance/IRB-National-Research-Act.cfm> (accessed January 15, 2006).

National Institutes of Health. "Regulations and Ethical Guidelines." <http://ohsr.od.nih.gov/guidelines/belmont.html> (accessed January 9, 2006).

United States Department of Health and Human Services. "Code of Federal Regulations, Title 45, Public Welfare, Part 46, Protection of Human Subjects, Revised June 23, 2005, Effective June 23, 2005." <http://www.hhs.gov/ohrp/humansubjects/guidance/45cfr46.htm> (accessed January 9, 2006).

United States Department of Health and Human Services, Office for Human Research Protections. "Belmont Report."

<http://www.hhs.gov/ohrp/belmontArchive.html> (accessed January 9, 2006).

United States Department of Health and Human Services, Office for Human Research Protections. "Policy Guidance." <http://www.hhs.gov/ohrp/policy/> (accessed January 9, 2006).

Product Tampering

The Tylenol Scare

Photograph

By: Anonymous

Date: 1982

Source: Corbis Corporation.

Photograph

About the Photographer: Associated Press Worldwide

Date: 1982

Source: Associated Press Worldwide Photographs.

About the Photographer: The Associated Press (AP), one of the world's largest news acquisition and distribution organizations, is owned by a group of more than 1,500 newspapers. It utilizes multiple media resources, ranging from digital and visual film and photography to radio reports and written articles appearing in newspapers or electronic media. In addition, AP maintains an extensive archival collection of photographs.

INTRODUCTION

Prior to 1982, when seven people in Illinois died after ingesting Extra-Strength Tylenol capsules that had been treated with a cyanide compound, few in the general population was familiar with the concept of product tampering. The adulterated capsules came from four different production lots (MC2880, MA1891, MB2738, and MD1910). Victims purchased the over-the-counter (OTC) medications from five different stores in the greater Chicago area; two additional cyanide-tainted Extra-Strength Tylenol bottles were recovered unopened from a sixth store. The police investigation of the murders concluded that the medication bottles had each been previously removed from the stores and opened. The capsules they contained were treated with the cyanide compound, and then the bottles were resealed and returned to store shelves over a period of weeks or months before the first poisoning and death occurred. The number of cyanide-laced capsules varied from bottle

Product Tampering: The Tylenol Scare. Close-up of tamper-resistant Tylenol packaging. This new kind of packaging was introduced as a result of a 1982 incident in which Extra Strength Tylenol capsules were laced with cyanide after production. ©BETTMANN/CORBIS.

to bottle; in no case were the entire contents of a bottle poisoned. In each of the bottles recovered after the deaths, the adulterated capsules had been completely emptied of their original contents and refilled with the cyanide mixture.

Although there was an enormous amount of publicity and media attention given to these murders, no perpetrator was ever arrested or indicted for the crimes. Several "copycat" product tamperings, resulting in additional deaths, occurred over the next decade. Three of those took place in 1986 and involved Excedrin, Lipton Cup-A-Soup, and Tylenol. Additional episodes occurred in 1991 with Sudafed and in 1992 with Goody's Headache Powder.

As a direct result of the 1982 Extra-Strength Tylenol poisonings, legislation was enacted that mandated tamper-proof packaging for most over-the-counter medications and some cosmetic products. The Poison Prevention Packaging Act, originally passed in 1970, provides a series of guidelines and requirements for products that are likely to be stored in the average

American household. It is designed to protect the safety of all individuals, but is particularly geared to children. It is designed to safely contain items such as cleaning products, assorted chemicals designed to be used in the home or immediate outside environment, and various types of household fuels. It also applies to safety packaging for certain foods, prescribed and over-the-counter medications, and some cosmetics.

PRIMARY SOURCE

PRODUCT TAMPERING: THE TYLENOL SCARE
See primary source images.

SIGNIFICANCE

Subsequent to the Extra-Strength Tylenol and copycat product-tampering murders, much media attention was focused on ensuring that the over-the-counter medications purchased by the public were safe. As a result, the Consumer Product Safety Commission (CPSC) and the Food and Drug Administration (FDA) required that tamper-resistant packaging regulations be mandated and implemented for all over-the-counter, and some cosmetic, preparations. The exceptions to this requirement include skin products (lotions, creams, some ointments), items used for dental care (toothpastes, dental floss, and various dental adhesives), and insulin containers.

In contrast to the colloquial use of the term, the FDA interprets the term "cosmetic" to mean a substance generally considered desirable, but that is neither medically prescribed nor deemed absolutely essential for the adequate maintenance of good health or for the purposes of ensuring personal hygiene. Substances such as mouthwash, non-prescribed douches, and vaginal deodorants are all considered cosmetics by the Food and Drug Administration.

Each product subject to the tamper-resistant packaging requirement must be labeled to indicate that it has tamper-resistant packaging. This packaging must be immediately visible when the container is inspected. The package must also carry an illustrated statement describing the nature and appearance of the tamper-resistant features. The labeling must be designed to remain intact if the product is, in fact, interfered with in any way—so that it is immediately obvious to the consumer that this interference has occurred.

The FDA suggests that two different barrier systems be used in order to further decrease the

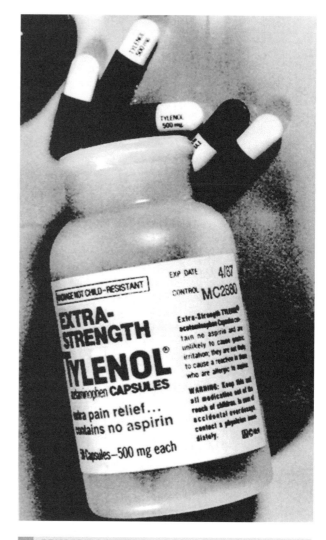

PRIMARY SOURCE

Product Tampering: The Tylenol Scare. Photograph of a bottle of Extra-Strength Tylenol from Lot MC2880, one of the lots involved in the 1982 product-tampering case that resulted in seven death. AP/WIDE WORLD PHOTOS.

likelihood of tampering. For example, a bottle of an over-the-counter pain reliever may have a plastic seal completely affixing cap to bottle and a mylar sheet sealing the top of the bottle under the lid. If the packaging has been disturbed in any way, the potential consumer will notice it. In a world of increasing technological sophistication, no package can be considered absolutely tamper-proof. The goal of tamper-resistant packaging is to protect consumers to the greatest degree possible from either intentional or inadvertent product packaging safety breaches.

In addition to tamper-resistant product packaging for the general public, household products that are considered either hazardous or potentially unsafe for children must have specific types of child-resistant packaging. There is a two-part requirement in this area of product packaging. The package must present a substantial and prolonged barrier to a child under the age of five who is attempting to breach it, and it must simultaneously be possible for an elder adult to open the package with a reasonable degree of ease. It is possible for some products, particularly those marketed specifically to older adults, to be produced without child-safety packaging, so long as those products carry a visible and obvious statement, such as: "This product or package is only intended for purchase by households NOT containing young children," or "This package is NOT child-resistant."

FURTHER RESOURCES

Web sites

Consumer Product Safety Commission. "Poison Prevention Packaging Act." <http://www.cpsc.gov/businfo/pppa.pdf> (accessed December 18, 2005).

FACSNET. "Product Tampering: The Legal Framework of Product Tampering." <http://www.facsnet.org/tools/nbgs/ref_tutor/tampering/framework.php3> (accessed December 19, 2005).

FACSNET. "Product Tampering: The Proliferation of Product Tampering." <http://www.facsnet.org/tools/nbgs/ref_tutor/tampering/prolif.php3> (accessed December 19, 2005).

Foreignborn.com. "Tamper-Resistant Packaging." <http://www.foreignborn.com/self-help/medical/medicine/3-packaging.htm> (accessed December 19, 2005).

Helicopter Rescue of Air Crash Victims

Aeromedical Transport

Photograph

By: Anonymous

Date: January 13, 1982

Source: "Helicopter Rescue of Air Crash Victims." Bettmann Collection. Corbis Corporation.

INTRODUCTION

Aeromedical transport usually occurs for one of several reasons. Medical transport may be required from the scene of an accident that occurred in a location that is difficult or impossible to access via ground transportation (traditional ambulance) in a safe or timely manner. A medical facility that lacks specialized equipment or technology required for a specific patient emergency often uses an air ambulance to transport the patient to a hospital that is able to provide the needed services. When time is of the essence, as in severe trauma, an air ambulance is often used. Finally, medical air transport is often the most efficient way to repatriate a patient, meaning moving the ill or injured person from an initial facility to one that is closer to home for reasons of cost or convenience.

There are currently two types of air ambulance: fixed-wing aircraft and rotary-wing aircraft. Fixed-wing aircraft are traditional airplanes, and can range from military transport planes to small jets to propeller-driven aircraft. Emergency medical transport helicopters (rotary-wing aircraft) can vary in size as well, but typically only transport one, or at most two, patients per trip.

The first significant use of fixed-wing air medical transport is generally considered to have occurred during World War II (1938–1941), when troop transport planes were used to evacuate injured Allied soldiers from near the battlefield to military and field hospitals. During the conflict in Korea in the early 1950s, the United States pioneered the use of helicopters for evacuating wounded troops in the battlefield. By the Vietnam War in the mid-1960s, helicopters were widely used to transport injured troops from the field directly to military trauma centers.

Currently, there are hundreds of aeromedical transport (AMT) companies operating worldwide. In the United States, they are typically affiliated either with federal or state government agencies (including the military), hospitals and medical centers, or are owned by private companies. Many medical transport operators have a fleet that includes ground transport ambulances, fixed wing and rotary wing aircraft. Some also offer medical assistance for patients who are able to use commercial flights services, but need minor medical assistance en route (such as those recovering from major surgery and being transported to rehabilitation or step-down medical facilities). In many cases, AMT providers are able to offer worldwide "bed to bed" transport, with ambulance transport from the sending facility to the fixed wing aircraft (equipped with specialized equipment, technology, and staff normally found in the intensive care unit of a medical facility), met by a waiting ambulance at the

PRIMARY SOURCE

Helicopter Rescue of Air Crash Victims. Rescue workers load a victim of the 1982 Air Florida Flight 90 Crash into a helicopter in Washington, D.C. The plane crashed into the Potomac River and the medical helicopter served as both rescue vehicle and ambulance. ©BETTMANN/CORBIS.

receiving airport for transport to the receiving medical facility.

At the initial scene of an aviation accident in January 1982, an early Park Service helicopter ambulance was the sole official responder to the disaster, after Air Florida Flight 90 crashed into the 14th Street bridge and then plunged into the Potomac River in Washington, D.C. Crowded, icy highways made it impossible for ground ambulances to respond in time to reach the few survivors who clung to the aircraft tail section floating in the river. The nearest Coast Guard vessel was occupied with another search-and-rescue mission at a distance downriver. The Park Service helicopter with one paramedic on board managed to arrive at the scene and serve as both rescue vehicle and ambulance for all but one of the survivors of the crash. Modern aeromedical transport organizations are continuously available, operating twenty-four hours daily, seven days per week.

PRIMARY SOURCE

HELICOPTER RESCUE OF AIR CRASH VICTIMS
See primary source image.

SIGNIFICANCE

Although both fixed- and rotary-wing transport are quite commonly used modes of patient transport, fixed-wing (plane) transport has been determined to be the safer and more cost-effective of the two in non-emergency situations. Helicopter transports are used most for short distance transports, for those where time is a critical factor for patient survival, or to evacuate patients from trauma scenes in which either the terrain or circumstance prohibits approach by ground vehicles, as in the case of a mountaineering accident occurring on a steep, roadless slope, or a battlefield evacuation of wounded troops. In those circumstances, the abilities of a helicopter to touch down without a fixed landing strip or to achieve a vertical take-off would be essential. In transporting individuals with spinal cord injury, helicopters are often used both for speed of transport and to ensure the smoothest possible ride, thereby minimizing the possibility of incurring additional central nervous system (CNS) trauma. In medical parlance, there is a time known as *the golden hour*, which is the first sixty minutes after an individual sustains a major trauma, a stroke, or a cardiac event. If access is gained to a major medical center within this timeframe, the likelihood of a successful outcome is substantially increased.

Nearly all fixed-wing air medical transport services are equipped with advanced life support (ALS) technologies, due to their use for longer distance, higher altitude transports. Many companies providing fixed-wing air medical transports are able to cover much in a single transport: for example, an American citizen goes to Geneva on business, gets involved in a motor vehicle accident, and sustains multiple and severe injuries. She is initially hospitalized in Geneva, given emergency treatment and undergoes orthopedic surgeries. She is stabilized, but needs several weeks of traction and relative immobilization, and then will need many months of recuperation, followed by a lengthy physical rehabilitation process. Her health insurer pays for the emergency and stabilizing treatments, and then requests that she be transferred to a medical facility in her home area for long-term treatment. An air medical transport could be arranged to provide bedside-to-bedside services; it would have all necessary equipment and personnel on board to be able to treat her en route, as well as to deal with any potential medical emergencies during the flight.

Emergency interim medical care is often available on rotary-wing transports. Some are utilized primarily for rapid trauma transport, and carry a physician, nurse, or emergency medical technician on board, as well as life-sustaining equipment and medications for emergency use. Others are operated as inter-hospital facilities, and provide continuous care from pick-up at one facility to arrival at the (destination) facility.

The evolution of the air medical transport model has greatly expanded the reach and the capacity of emergency and critical care medicine. It is now possible to pick up individuals who are injured or ill at isolated settings, and to rapidly transport them to an urgent care setting, providing emergency care en route. In this way, the likelihood of assuring medical intervention during the golden hour after a stroke, spinal cord injury, accident, or cardiac event is greatly enhanced.

FURTHER RESOURCES

Periodicals

Varon, Joseph, Robert E. Fromm, and Paul Malik. "Hearts in the Air: The Role of Aeromedical Transport." *Chest.* 124(5) (2003): 1636–1637.

Web sites

CAMTS: Commission on Accreditation of Medical Transport Systems. "Accreditation FAQs." <http://www.camts.org/index.php?option=content&task=view&id=4&Itemid=27> (accessed December 29, 2005).

The Internet Journal of Emergency and Intensive Care Medicine. "Aeromedical Transport: Facts and Fiction." <http://www.ispub.com/ostia/index.php?xmlFilePath=journals/ijeicm/vol1n1/aeromed.xml> (accessed December 29, 2005).

Is there a Doctor in the House?

Some Health Care Ads are in Such Bad Shape, They Need Emergency Treatment

Magazine article

By: Anonymous

Date: January 6, 1986

Source: *American Demographics, Advertising Age,* Crain Communications

About the Author: This article was published without attribution or a byline, and was written by a staff writer for *American Demographics* now part of *Advertising Age,* the weekly magazine about trends in the advertising industry.

INTRODUCTION

Advertising health care services directly to the consumer, whether it be a hospital, a diagnostic test or a prescription drug, at its best increases patient power by raising awareness. At its worst, it undermines the physician's authority and exploits the patient in the interest of profit. The United States is the only industrialized nation so far that has pushed direct-to-consumer (DTC) health care prescription drug advertising. Other countries, such as New Zealand and Canada, have come out against such advertising. In 2002, the European Parliament voted not to allow DTC advertising for drugs for asthma, AIDS, and diabetes.

DTC advertising has long been a contentious issue. Governments everywhere are obliged to do what they can to encourage business for the sake of their country's prosperity. Advertising increases the income of advertising, pharmaceutical, health care, media, and, naturally, advertising companies, while increasing the workload of physicians. The health care expenditure of patients, insurance companies, and employers are also increased by demand arising from DTC advertising. These increased profits and costs could perhaps be justified if there was a clear benefit to the health of the population and resulting in a decrease of unmet medical needs.

The very nature of DTC advertising in the broadcast and print media, however, is often contradictory to raising awareness in those areas where it is most needed. Advertisements are often too short to convey much meaningful information; and research in the industry has shown that they are likely to confuse or worry the patient. As the following article illustrates, DTC advertisements are often misleading and tend to focus on areas such as cosmetic surgery, where health promotion is not the key issue.

Marketing executive Phyllis Goodman displays two billboard ads for Cincinnati Children's Hospital Medical Center at the hospital in Cincinnati. Goodman is overseeing the hospital's television and billboard campaign to attract new patients. AP/WIDE WORLD PHOTOS.

PRIMARY SOURCE

A menacing photo of a glistening scalpel is the centerpiece for an ad from the Health Insurance Association of America on how to cut rising hospital costs.

A billboard sporting the bulging profile of a very pregnant woman urges expectant mothers to "Have it your way" at Chicago's Hinsdale Hospital.

A newspaper ad for a chiropractor makes a pitch for new accident victims by using a disturbing drawing of a man who has bashed his head against the steering wheel of his wrecked car.

Some health-care advertising is enough to make you sick. Although most ads for hospitals, doctors and clinics are in good taste, a disturbing amount of money is being spent on remarkably insensitive ads that prey on consumers' insecurities, ignorance or fears.

And, unfortunately, we're likely to see more. Since the ban on ads by professional medical organizations was lifted by a 1979 Supreme Court decision, health-care ad expenditures have skyrocketed to nearly $60 million a year. There are several reasons for the boom: Hospital occupancy is the lowest it's been in decades; a doctor glut is forcing many physicians to scramble for new patients; and today's you've-got-to-look-good-at-any-price attitude has made plastic-surgery clinics as popular as McDonald's.

Part of the trouble for some health-care ads is built in. Trying to explain complicated medical problems such as alcohol or drug addiction in a minute or less almost guarantees failure. "People want pat solutions to health problems," says Michael Castleman, managing editor of *Medical Self-Care* magazine. "It's little surprise so many health-care ads come on with foolproof remedies."

A California TV ad for Schick Shadel Hospital's alcohol-abuse program, for example, plays like a soap opera. Wifey comes home and finds hubby with his head buried in his hands. He confesses he drank too much the night before. His drinking ruins everything, she replies. He tells her he's going into Schick's alcohol treatment program. "Schick helps you lose the craving for alcohol," he says. And, "it only takes ten days with a couple of follow-up visits." The ad seems to promise that alcoholism is no harder to get rid of than ring around the collar.

Some of the most troublesome of the bunch are the pitches for plastic-surgery clinics. TV ads for New York outfits like Personal Best, Profiles and Contours and Park East Plastic Surgery Center seem to promise that a little lift here and a neat tuck there can make life a dream. The viewer is led to believe that cosmetic surgery will supply not only a new look, but the kind of new outlook on life that can presumably solve other problems.

But some of these clinics haven't been able to work the same makeover magic on their ads. In one of the least effective, for Profiles and Contours, the camera slowly pans down a long line of people, as if to give the viewer a choice of model noses and chins. Next, the screen is filled with a slim and shapely female torso that rotates for inspection—like a toaster on display in a shop window. There is nothing appealing about these people—in fact, the ad conjures uncomfortable images reminiscent of scenes in the movie "Invasion of the Body Snatchers."

Health-care advertising consultant Greg Korneluck defends these plastic-surgery commercials. "They're product specific and get the phones ringing," he says. That may be the case, but these kinds of ads have a responsibility to do more than just sell a service. The decision to have plastic surgery is a complicated and difficult one, and consumers are entitled to more information and less soft sell. Whether for a hospital, a private doctor or a special clinic, health-care ads always require serious treatment.

SIGNIFICANCE

Health care is a complex issue, and the advertising industry's consumer-targeted approach continues to evolve. Since 1986, when the article above was written, governments have provided little guidance to the public about DTC advertising. With the spread of the Internet, where regulatory issues are more difficult, DTC advertisements are commonplace, often stemming from countries outside the United States, and advertising medications to be available without a prescription. The consumer bears the responsibility for purchasing online medications from reliable suppliers and observing all local laws regarding their distribution.

The American College of Physicians (ACP) has expressed ideas about the control of DTC advertising that could form the basis of new policies. According to the ACP, ads to the consumer should, like those in medical journals aimed at physicians, do more to disclose benefits and harms alike of a treatment or service. More evidence-based data should be included. In particular, ads should be directed towards supporting those with real medical needs, rather than creating a need where one did not previously exist.

Physicians are becoming proactive on the issue of DTC advertising and are often prepared for the patient who has obtained information from ads, either in the print or broadcast media or from the Internet. The advertising can indeed, as its advocates suggest, be of benefit, because it gives the physician a starting point for a potentially useful dialog with the patient. Physicians are also increasingly refusing to yield to a patient who has been overly influenced by advertising.

While the Food and Drug Administration (FDA) does have guidelines on DTC marketing of prescription drugs, which lay down the type of information that should be included and how it should be presented, there is no requirement for companies to have ads cleared by the FDA before they appear. Meanwhile, the ACP's Ethics Manual says that

physicians and health care institutions should not make statements that are unsubstantiated, false, deceptive or misleading, including statements that mislead by omitting relevant information.

FURTHER RESOURCES

Periodicals

Mansfield, Peter R., Barbara Mintzes, Dee Richards, and Les Toop. "Direct to consumer advertising." *British Medical Journal* 330 (2005): 5–6.

Web sites

American College of Physicians. "Consumer ads: How Should You Handle the Pressure?" <http://www.acponline.org/ethics/casestudies/consumerads.htm> (accessed November 11, 2005).

Nurseweek. "Hospitals Use Advertising to Reach the Masses." <http://www.nurseweek.com/features/99-2/promotion.html> (accessed November 11, 2005).

Shaman Loses Its Magic

Ethnobotany and Drug Discovery

Newspaper article

By: Anonymous

Date: February 18, 1999

Source: "Shaman Loses Its Magic," *The Economist,* February 18, 1999.

About the Author: This article, published without attribution or byline, was written by a staff writer for the *The Economist,* a weekly London newspaper with a circulation of over one million readers worldwide, over half in the United States.

INTRODUCTION

Fossil remains identified in northern Iraq reveal that the use of medicinal plants may date from the middle Paleolithic age some 60,000 years ago. Even today many significant drugs, including morphine, aspirin, and quinine are plant based. Still more come from other natural sources—many cholesterol-lowering drugs and antibiotics, for instance, are extracted from bacteria and fungi. In addition, natural products can often be chemically adapted to produce semisynthetic versions. In total, close to half of all drugs now in use come directly or indirectly from natural sources.

There are an estimated quarter-million plant species on earth, of which only around 6 percent have been investigated scientifically for their medicinal properties. An early approach to drug discovery—extracting useful medicines from plants—was English physician William Withering's extraction of the cardiac drug digitalis from the foxglove plant *(Digitalis purpurea)* in 1785. The following article describes how Shaman Pharmaceuticals, a company based in San Francisco, tried to bring modern science to ethnobotany, which studies a culture's botanical knowledge and use of local plants for food, medicine, clothing, and in religious ritual.

■ PRIMARY SOURCE

SHAMAN LOSES ITS MAGIC

IT WAS a tree-hugger's dream. Save the rainforests. Respect and honour the knowledge of the people who live there. And still make money for your shareholders. Unfortunately, it doesn't look as though it is going to work. Earlier this month, Shaman Pharmaceuticals, the leading proponent of the "ethnobotanical" approach to drug discovery—an attempt to identify the active molecules in folk remedies, in order to turn them into modern prescription medicines—threw in the towel.

Shaman's failure to convert old-wives' tales into drugs (though it is still pursuing the idea in the less rigorously regulated field of herbal dietary supplements) probably marks the end of the sort of selective "botanising " that started the pharmaceutical industry, when the pain-killing properties of willow bark led to the invention of aspirin. Merck, one of the world's biggest drug companies, spent ten years trying to extract and develop the active principles from Chinese herbal remedies. It failed too. Other firms are downgrading the role of traditional medicine when screening plants for useful substances. Instead, they prefer the automated mass-screening techniques originally developed to deal with the artificial products created in vast numbers by modern combinatorial chemistry.

It is a popular misconception, probably generated by such pharmaceutical celebrities as quinine, and fed by environmentalists keen to preserve rainforests, that those forests abound with billion-dollar blockbuster drugs just waiting to be discovered. The facts are different. Between 1960 and 1982, America's National Cancer Institute (NCI) and Department of Agriculture (DOA) collected 35,000 samples of roots, fruits, and bark from 12,000 species of plants. Only three significant products were discovered in them.

Taxol, Camptothecin, and homoharringtonine have all proved useful as anticancer drugs, but they do not suggest that the forests are teeming with pharmaceutical opportunities. And more recent collections by the NCI and DOA (gathered between 1986 and 1996 from South America)

have been even more disappointing. As yet, not a single drug has emerged from them.

Shaman tried hard. It sent teams of physicians and botanists into the rainforests of more than 30 countries in Asia, Africa, and South America. They collaborated with local healers to identify plants with medicinal properties. And the firm abided by the standards laid down in the Convention on Biological Diversity signed in Rio de Janeiro in 1992. This sought to highlight the economic value of regions rich in species and ensure that local people benefited.

That meant that, in exchange for the knowledge it received, Shaman provided a payment of up to $8,000 (or the equivalent in goods and services) to the healer's community. It also promised long-term benefits if a drug was actually developed from one of the plants concerned.

But although short-circuiting the screening process by starting with medically proven plants may have looked a smart move ten years ago, screening technology has got better and better. It will soon be possible to check molecules for promising biological activity at a rate of 100,000 a day. It may look more elegant to ask the locals, but screening everything, regardless, is now faster and cheaper.

On top of that, the folk healers' concerns are not necessarily those of drug companies. The former are frequently preoccupied with curing parasitic infestations unknown in the rich countries that provide the companies with their markets. They are much less adept at diagnosing and treating diseases such as cancer, where the real money is to be made.

There are some areas of overlap, however. Shaman had seemed to be making good progress on type II diabetes (which is untreatable with insulin). Diabetes is a disease that is recognised in many cultures because sufferers, whose blood-sugar levels are out of control, tend to pass sugar-rich urine. By using ethnobotany to provide the raw materials, Shaman's researchers were able within four years to isolate 30 compounds that lowered blood-sugar levels enough to make them look promising as anti-diabetes drugs.

Whether any of those molecules would have made it through the regulatory process will probably never be known, but it was that process that eventually brought things to a halt. The drug in question, Provir, was actually intended as an antidiarrhoeal treatment (diarrhoea being another problem that the rich and poor worlds share).

Provir was particularly designed for AIDS patients. That did not save it. When the Food and Drug Administration, which approves medicinal drugs in America, told Shaman it would have to conduct a further series of clinical trials on the stuff, it gave up. The trials would have delayed things by 18 months, and cost tens of millions of dollars that the company could not afford.

The end of Shaman's adventure does not, however, mean that the rainforests have lost their allure completely. Merck, for example, has a long-standing arrangement with Costa Rica to prospect for drugs in that country's forests. The firm also collaborates with the New York Botanical Gardens to collect plants from all over the world. But the wisdom of the ages will not be coming with them. Modern technology has won.

SIGNIFICANCE

In the pharmaceutical industry, failure is more common than success when it comes to finding drugs that actually work in real patients. So the demise of Shaman's business is not surprising. But while their difficulties do not entirely doom the chances that new drugs will be discovered from natural resources, it is a cautionary tale, highlighting some of the issues involved in ethnobotany.

There are two main kinds of drugs, classified according to their chemical structure. Small molecules, like aspirin, can be made either in the laboratory or extracted from plants and other natural resources. Biologics, such as insulin, are generally produced by fermentation or culturing genetically modified cells. These are large-protein molecules, normally given by injection. Advances in genetic technology have put biologics on the ascendant, providing new treatments for cancer, inflammatory disease, and other conditions. Small-molecule drugs still hold an important place in the pharmacological armory, especially as they can often be given in tablet form. But the advent of biologics means the process of drug discovery has changed and approaches to natural products must be revised.

Chemists searching for new small-molecule drugs now have technology that can screen thousands of natural compounds for biological activity in a short time, allowing the myriad compounds in the plant and microbial worlds to be studied with high-throughput methods. Once found, however, obtaining these extracts may prompt legal questions of compensation, intellectual property rights, and environmental protection in the country of origin. The 1992 United Nations Convention on Biological Diversity established guidelines under which such natural resources may be exploited, including protecting delicate biological environments, fair compensation, and

Shamans, also called healers or medicine men, use a variety of herbs and medicinal plants in their healing rituals and ceremonies. ©ALISON WRIGHT/CORBIS.

minimizing potentially harmful impacts upon indigenous cultures.

Besides the regulatory issues, there are practical ones. Plants often contain hundreds of different compounds and much chemical analysis may be needed to identify the active ingredients. Some such botanical extracts—mixtures of compounds used as medicine—have been evaluated clinically. Saint-John's-wort, for example, has been touted in the treatment of mild to moderate depression; some studies claim it is as effective conventional antidepressant drugs; other claims remain unproven. Many botanical extracts are available and can often be bought without a prescription, but consumer's cannot always be as sure of content or quality as they can with a pharmaceutical drug.

The demise of Shaman Pharmaceuticals does not mean the end of ethnobotany. Taxol, originally produced from the bark of Pacific yew trees (*Taxus brevitola*), is one of the most effective cancer drugs. A synthetic version allowing for mass production was introduced in 1994. Meanwhile, researchers in Norway and Australia are searching the marine environment for new antibiotics and cancer drugs. Researchers cannot afford to overlook any resource, either natural or synthetic, when it comes to the discovery of new medicines. Adding technology to the search should help speed up the process.

FURTHER RESOURCES

Books

Schultes, Richard Evans, and Siri von Reis, eds. *Ethnobotany: Evolution of a Discipline.* Portland, Ore.: Dioscorides Press, 1995.

Periodicals

Fabricant, Daniel S., and Norman R. Farnsworth. "The Value of Plants Used in Traditional Medicine for Drug Discovery." *Environmental Health Perspectives* 109, Supplement 1 (2001): 69–75.

Web sites

Amazonia. "Shaman Pharmaceutical's Response to an Article in The Economist (Feb. 20th–26th)." <http://www.amazonia.net/Articles/197.htm> (accessed November 18, 2005).

Medical Tourism Companies Luring Americans Abroad with Surgery-Vacation Trips

Newspaper article

By: Maria M. Parotin

Date: September 3, 2004

Source: *Fort Worth Star–Telegram*

About the Author: This article was written by a contributor to the *Fort Worth Star–Telegram*, a daily newspaper based in Fort Worth, Texas.

INTRODUCTION

Medical tourism is travel to other countries for surgical, dental, or medical treatment, often in combination with a vacation. The phenomenon has been fueled by the growth of cheap international travel, the Internet, and better standards of medical technology and care in many countries. In addition, common medical procedures are sometimes much less costly and more readily available than they are at home.

The vast majority of medical tourists come from the United States, Canada, Great Britain, Western Europe, Australia, or the Middle East—all countries where vacationing is common and there is a high demand for plastic and elective surgery. The most frequent destinations are India, South America, Greece, Turkey, and Eastern Europe. Sometimes the flow of traffic is reversed, and medical tourists visit Great Britain to take advantage of the United Kingdom's free or low-cost National Health Service. With the expansion of the European Union and unrestricted travel between countries, this trend is likely to intensify.

Some countries are both a source of medical tourists and a destination for them; in Germany, for instance, robot-assisted minimally invasive surgery is offered at one center; dental services and plastic surgery are offered at Munich Airport as part of a "fly in, fly out" package.

The article below describes the experience of two fairly typical medical tourists—women who visited Mexico for plastic surgery. They welcomed the chance to recover from their face-lifts in private and pleasant surroundings, a factor that drives many to seek rhinoplasty (nose remodeling), liposuction, breast reduction, and dental procedures abroad.

PRIMARY SOURCE

MEDICAL TOURISM COMPANIES LURING AMERICANS ABROAD WITH SURGERY-VACATION TRIPS

Byline: Maria M. Perotin Fort Worth, Texas—Carolynne Bond Kent and her cousin Patsy embarked on a vacation getaway to the mountains of central Mexico three years ago.

There, the women strolled along cobblestone streets, sampled restaurant dishes, and relaxed in a quaint hacienda.

They also recuperated from the face-lifts that were the real purpose of their trip. Both 69 at the time, the pair traveled to Mexico to have plastic surgery—joining the ranks of "medical tourists" who are venturing outside the United States for cosmetic surgery and other procedures.

The women found a surgeon online at www.facelift-mexico.com, which promotes a 10-day vacation–surgery package in historic San Miguel de Allende, Mexico. And they paid a fraction of the price that doctors would have charged at home.

"I've done a lot of traveling in my life. I wasn't nervous at all," said Patsy, a Texas resident who asked that her last name be withheld. (She wouldn't want people to know she's had a face-lift, after all.)

Although statistics are not available, businesses that market medical trips are turning up all over the globe. Many tout the low price of treatments, boast luxurious accommodations, and advertise attention-grabbing packages—such as "surgeon and safari" expeditions in South Africa or "breast implants and tango" trips to Argentina.

That concerns some U.S. doctors, who worry about the credentials of the foreign surgeons, the sanitary conditions of their operating rooms, and patients' access to follow-up care.

The risks can be significant.

In June, the national Centers for Disease Control and Prevention warned that 12 women had bacterial infections after traveling to the Dominican Republic for "tummy tucks," liposuction, and breast surgeries.

The women—from New York, Massachusetts, North Carolina, Rhode Island, and Puerto Rico—had been treated at various surgery centers in that country's capital city over 10 months. Nine of them became so badly infected that they were later hospitalized.

"People want to go for the deal. They want to go abroad because, quote unquote, 'They can get the same surgery for a reduced price.' Therein is the fallacy," said Rod Rohrich, president of the American Society of Plastic Surgeons. "America has the best health care system in the world."

Kent, of Birmingham, Ala., counters that many countries have well-trained doctors and clean facilities. And she preferred her stint in a Mexican hospital to an outpatient procedure in the United States, she said.

"This was a three-day hospital stay, where you are monitored and all of that constantly," Kent said. "I thought that just sounded a whole lot better." . . .

For Kent, the trip to Mexico had one notable advantage beyond the low price—discretion.

Kent was able to recover far from home and curious acquaintances when her discolored post-surgery face looked its worst. By the time she returned to Alabama, she was able to hide the remaining bruises with makeup, she said.

"When I finally went out, nobody even noticed," Kent said. "And I didn't tell anybody."

That's a prevalent selling point for many medical tourism packages, which highlight the ease with which patients can disguise their surgeries.

"Why should anyone else have to know or need to know?" asks one travel company that offers cosmetic surgery in Malaysia. "With Beautiful Holidays . . . you just go away on holiday and return having never looked better before."

Rohrich said some patients return from surgery vacations only to face severe medical complications, including infections from unsterilized surgical equipment, slipped breast implants and loss of skin.

Rohrich receives about a dozen calls each year from victims of botched foreign cosmetic surgeries or from hospital emergency rooms where patients have sought help, he said.

Those patients sometimes must spend more money to undo the damage of the previous procedures, he said. And they often have to persuade U.S. doctors to tackle the complications of another physician's surgery.

"You're putting yourself and your body and your life at incredible risk. Is it worth saving $500 on your face-lift if it could kill you?" Rohrich said. "There are excellent surgeons in Mexico and all these countries. But I can tell you most of them don't have these fly-in, fly-out deals."

Luiz Toledo, a surgeon in Brazil who is active in the International Society of Aesthetic Plastic Surgery, said patients generally look outside their own countries for better-quality services, cheaper prices, or a combination of the two. But he warned against seeking treatment from "cowboys."—untrained doctors with different specialties who perform cosmetic procedures for quick profits.

"A patient may travel to Brazil, Mexico, South Africa, or Costa Rica and have top-quality surgery with a cheaper price, due to the exchange rate or to economic differences between countries," Toledo said in an e-mail. "It is wrong, however, and it should not be encouraged, to travel for surgery only because it is cheap."

Medical tourism companies provide varying amounts of information about their doctors for clients who want to check out the qualifications of their surgeons. Some offer resumes and references from previous clients, while others provide little more than a doctor's name.

While most of the vacation–surgery packages emphasize cosmetic procedures, sponsors of medical tourism promote other services too—including fertility treatments in Barbados, LASIK eye surgery in Malaysia, and heart bypass surgery in Costa Rica.

Plenitas, a 1-year-old company in Argentina, offers more than 20 medical specialties, including cardiology, ophthalmology, dentistry and plastic surgery.

Chief Executive Officer Roberto Gawianski said the company has targeted U.S. clients most aggressively but also draws patients from Canada, Great Britain, Spain and other countries.

So far, Plenitas serves about 10 to 12 patients monthly and has plans to expand further, Gawianski said.

While low-cost plastic surgery—as cheap as $1,000 for liposuction—is most in demand, dental care and gastric banding services are big sellers too, Gawianski said. The company's most popular package: a seven-day "breast implants and tango" trip that includes private Spanish and dance lessons for patients.

One Plenitas client from Los Angeles, who asked to be identified only as Nancy, said she spent the days before her surgery last month skiing, then went sightseeing in Buenos Aires and at Iguazu Falls near the Argentina-Brazil border.

"I was looking to combine the procedure with travel," she said. "I only get so many days off in a year, and I didn't want to spend them laid up in a hotel room."

The 37-year-old executive secretary—who had liposuction of the inner thighs, arms, abdomen and waist—traveled to Thailand for a nose job last year.

This time, she said, she considered returning there or having surgery in Japan or Tijuana, Mexico. But she opted for Plenitas' package because the $2,400 fee was far cheaper than elsewhere.

She didn't contemplate any California surgeons at all.

"Given my income, it would've been prohibitively expensive to do it here in Los Angeles," she said. "So I took to the Internet, like a lot of people do."

Nancy tried to conduct research about her surgeon and the operating facilities before the procedure, but admits she learned little more than his name.

"It was a leap of faith, because I must tell you there wasn't a whole lot of information available on the doctor," she said.

Nonetheless, she said she's satisfied with the results of her surgery—especially because colleagues haven't guessed the true reason for her visit to Argentina this summer.

"Nobody at my office knows. They haven't noticed. They just think I lost a few pounds," she said. "I've got so many pictures taken at Iguazu Falls and taken in front of the presidential palace. People don't suspect that I had time to go into a hospital." . . .

SIGNIFICANCE

Plastic surgery is still the most common reason people travel abroad for medical treatment. But as the industry expands so, too, do the indications: LASIK surgery (which uses laser treatment to correct vision), infertility treatment, and dental work have become popular choices for medical tourists. Some also travel for more urgent treatments such as joint replacements and heart bypass surgery, often because of long waiting lists for these procedures in the home country. British patients have even been encouraged by

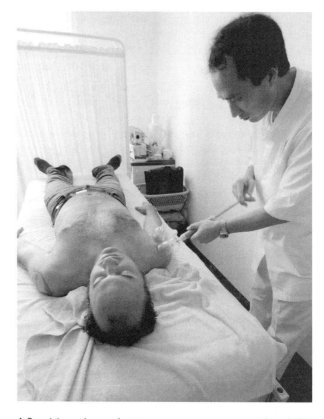

A Spanish tourist receives acupuncture treatment at a hospital in North Korea. The patient is also undergoing a procedure called cupping, in which glass jars are placed on the skin to bring toxins to the surface. ©NAYAN STHANKIYA/CORBIS.

their doctors to have joint replacements in France where there is spare capacity. This may save months, if not years, of pain and disability; for many, this makes it worth the cost.

Medical tourism is now a global industry, but its long history began with the pilgrimages made by the ancient Greeks to the famous temple of Asklepios (Asclepius) the healing god, in Epidaurus. Roman Britons traveled to the spa at Bath, and wealthy Europeans have been drawn to spas in Germany, Hungary, and Slovenia since the nineteenth century. Indeed, the spa holiday, a close cousin to medical tourism, is becoming increasingly popular, with far-flung destinations in Sri Lanka and Thailand.

Countries that actively promote medical tourism include Cuba, Costa Rica, Hungary, India, Israel, Jordan, Lithuania, Malaysia, and Thailand. Others, such as Belgium, Poland, and Singapore have begun to develop their own destinations. Some countries offer specialized packages that reflect their culture and heritage: South Africa, for example, promotes "medical safaris": plastic surgery and a chance to see wildlife. Israel offers infertility treatment along with a tour of religious sites.

India is, however, the leading destination for medical tourism. Under its national health policy, medical treatment for foreign patients is considered an export and eligible for all financial incentives extended to export earnings. The country has also moved into a related area, medical outsourcing, in which subcontractors provide medical services for overstretched systems in other countries. Research suggests that medical tourism could earn India one to two billion U.S. dollars by 2012. The industry is boosted by a large supply of well qualified medical staff and continuing advances in medical technology. One of India's largest centers treated around 60,000 medical tourists between 2001 and 2004.

Naturally, medical tourism has minuses as well as pluses. Tourists may find, for example, that their medical insurance does not cover their treatment, which forces them to pay out of pocket. Many choose to do this for elective or plastic surgery, particularly if the trip costs no more than a regular vacation and insurance would not cover the procedure even if it were performed at home. When serious medical conditions are involved, the investment may be worthwhile in terms of improved health even without help from insurance. This must be weighed, however, against the possible lack of aftercare in some foreign centers, particularly since health systems in foreign countries may not treat complications that arise. In addition, the return trip could pose the danger of deep vein thrombosis (blood clots) if lengthy air travel is attempted too soon after surgery. Many medical tourist destinations also have weaker malpractice systems than the United States and so redress, if things go wrong, is far less likely.

Medical tourism and medical outsourcing sometimes draw resources from the destination country, and may even restrict treatments to the local population. Some medical tourism centers counter this by offering free or low-cost services to locals alongside those for foreigners. As with other Internet-driven international ventures, medical tourism is difficult to regulate. As the industry expands, some countries have set guidelines and regulations for both patients and medical practitioners, while others allow the industry to operate with little oversight.

FURTHER RESOURCES
Periodicals

Bhattacharjee, S. "Noor Fatima, and Medical Tourism." *Journal of the Indian Medical Association*. (August 2003): 101(8) 497.

Web sites

CBC News Indepth. "Medical Tourism: Need Surgery, Will Travel." <http://www.cbc.ca/news/background/healthcare/medicaltourism.html> (acccessed November 19, 2005).

Medical Tourism. "Destinations." <http://www.medicaltourism.com/destinations.aspx> (accessed November 19, 2005).

America, Pull Up A Chair— We've Got Something Good to Talk About

Medications Made Available to Seniors

Government document

By: Centers for Medicare & Medicaid Services

Date: 2005

Source: *Medicare: The Official U.S. Government Site for People with Medicare*. "America, Pull Up a Chair— We've Got Something Good To Talk About." <http://www.medicare.gov/medicarereform/drugbenefit.asp> (accessed November 18, 2005).

About the Author: Originally called the Health Care Financing Administration (HCFA), the Centers for Medicare & Medicaid Services (CMS) is a federal agency housed within the U.S. Department of Health and Human Services (DHHS). The mission of DHHS is protecting the health of, and providing essential human services to, all Americans. Although it is an agency of the U.S. government, DHHS works closely with state and county agencies and with private sector grant recipients. It has administrative oversight of more than 300 programs, ranging from health and social science research, disease prevention, wellness promotion, and improving maternal and infant health to prevention and treatment of substance abuse and domestic violence, comprehensive health care services for Native Americans, financial assistance and services to low-income and needy families, Head Start programs, emergency and disaster medical preparedness, and the Medicaid and Medicare Programs. In addition to the administrative oversight it provides, DHHS facilitates the collection of national health, epidemiological, and other essential data. The DHHS oversees and administers numerous federal and block grant programs, as well as the financial aspects of Medicare and Medicaid. The combined budget for DHHS represents about 25 percent of all federal spending. Medicare is the nation's largest health insurer; it processes more than $1 billion in claims per year. Medicare and Medicaid provide health insurance for approximately one quarter of the entire U.S. population.

INTRODUCTION

The Medicare and Medicaid programs were enacted as Title XVIII and Title XIX, respectively, of the Social Security Act. President Lyndon Baines Johnson signed them into law on July 20, 1965. By so doing, he gave health care coverage to nearly all Americans aged 65 or older, as well extended health care services and benefits to low-income children deprived of parental support, their caretaking relatives, the blind, and to individuals with disabilities. Senior citizens were the largest single population group living in poverty, and less than half had any access to insurance coverage prior to the initiation of Medicare. By mid-1966, Medicare had been implemented and had more than 19 million enrollees. At that time, the Social Security Administration (SSA) was the government body responsible for the oversight of Medicare, and the Social and Rehabilitation Service (SRS) was charged with oversight of the Medicaid. Both of those agencies were within the U.S. Department of Health, Education, and Welfare (HEW).

In 1967, the Early and Periodic Screening, Diagnosis, and Treatment (EPSDT) benefit, a comprehensive health services program, was established for all Medicaid recipients below the age of twenty-one. In 1972, the Medicare benefit was extended to individuals below the age of sixty-five who were diagnosed with end stage renal (kidney) disease (ESRD) and to those with permanent disabilities. Medicaid eligibility for elderly, blind, and disabled residents of particular states could, for the first time, be linked to the new federal Supplemental Security Income program (SSI). Medicare was authorized to conduct demonstration programs for the first time.

In 1977, the Health Care Financing Administration was established within HEW. HCFA was given responsibility for the coordination of Medicare and Medicaid, although the SSA retained beneficiary enrollment and payment processing. In 1980, HEW was divided into two agencies: the Department of Education and the Department of Health and Human Services. HCFA fell under the auspices of DHHS. In 2001, DHHS Secretary Tommy Thompson changed the name of HCFA to the Centers for Medicare and Medicaid Services.

CMS administers the federal Medicare program and works in conjunction with the states to provide administrative oversight of the Medicaid program, the State Children's Health Insurance Program (SCHIP), and health insurance portability standards. CMS also has administrative oversight responsibility for the administrative simplification standards from the Health Insurance Portability and Accountability Act of 1996 (HIPAA), the quality standards for long-term care and skilled nursing facilities via its survey and certification processes, and the quality standards for clinical laboratories under the auspices of the Clinical Laboratory Improvement Amendments.

The single most significant legislative change to Medicare since its creation in 1965 occurred on December 8, 2003, when President George W. Bush signed the Medicare Prescription Drug, Improvement, and Modernization Act (MMA) into law. The 2003 legislation adds an outpatient prescription drug benefit to Medicare (Medicare Part D), improves health care access for Americans living in rural areas, and expands health care options to include such services as flu shots and mammograms.

The MMA created a prescription drug discount card that could be used until 2006; it also allows for competition among health plans. This competition encourages the different plans to be innovative in their programming and benefits and to offer greater flexibility of coverage. MMA covers new preventive benefits (among them the flu shots and mammograms previously mentioned) and institutes other broad changes. The major innovation, Medicare Part D (prescription drug plan), goes into effect on January 1, 2006. It is a voluntary outpatient prescription drug benefit and will be available to beneficiaries who participate in private drug plans as well as to those who choose Medicare Advantage Plans. Employers and retirement plans offering (retiree) drug coverage that is comparable to Medicare Part D will be eligible for a federal subsidy. A significant aspect of Medicare Part D is the consideration of beneficiary income in coverage determination. Beneficiaries whose incomes are less than 150 percent of the federal poverty limit will be eligible for financial assistance (subsidies) with the Part D program; those with higher incomes will pay premiums for Part D and will pay a higher share of the Medicare Part B premiums starting in 2007.

PRIMARY SOURCE

Because this new coverage is so important, the Centers for Medicare & Medicaid Services (CMS) wants to promote a national conversation to make sure that all people with Medicare, and those who care for them, understand this new coverage. This conversation will take place in many different places and in many different ways—it will occur across the kitchen table, in senior centers, at churches, between friends, neighbors, parents and their children, pharmacists and their customers. Because this new coverage is a vital addition to Medicare that will help people save money and live better, healthier lives, it's important to have information about it. It will extend the promise of modern drug treatment to everyone with Medicare. If you have Medicare, we strongly urge you to learn more about this new coverage. Right now, you can talk about this with many different people and start thinking about the coverage you want. And, if you have family and friends with Medicare, we ask that you help them learn more about it, too.

People are talking about Medicare prescription drug coverage right now in many different settings. To provide additional help and places for these conversations to occur, the Centers for Medicare & Medicaid Services (CMS) has created more than 140 community-based education networks and is working with nearly 10,000 local partners including the State Health Insurance Programs (SHIP) and Area Offices on Aging all across the country. These networks and partners provide a variety of services, from distributing materials to educational meetings to personalized counseling for people with Medicare. To help these groups and to help you, CMS has developed a variety of resources such as consumer brochures, on-line tools, and educational materials.

All of the CMS materials and on-line tools are available now. They are listed below as part of a four-step process to help you understand the process of choosing Medicare prescription drug coverage. . . .

FOUR STEPS TO GET MEDICARE PRESCRIPTION DRUG COVERAGE

To help people with Medicare take advantage of the new Medicare prescription drug coverage, there are four steps you can think about while making a decision:

1. Getting Started The decision to get Medicare prescription drug coverage depends on how you pay for your drugs now and how you get your Medicare coverage. Most people with Medicare pay for drugs and get their Medicare in one of five ways:

- Original Medicare only, or Original Medicare and a Medigap ('supplement') Policy without drug coverage. The new Medicare drug coverage will cover half of the costs for you if you have this kind of coverage now. Enhanced options are available that provide more coverage.
- Original Medicare and a Medigap ('supplement') Policy with drug coverage. The new Medicare drug

coverage will generally provide much more comprehensive coverage at a lower cost.
- Retiree or union coverage. In most cases, people with good retiree or union coverage can continue to get it, with new financial support from Medicare.
- Medicare Advantage Plan (like an HMO or PPO) or other Medicare Health Plan, which already include drug coverage and other extra benefits.
- Dual coverage from Medicare with Medicaid drug coverage. These people will automatically get comprehensive prescription drug coverage from Medicare, starting on January 1.

NOTE: If you have limited income and resources, but you don't have Medicaid, you may qualify for extra help that may pay for about 95% of your drug costs. . . .

Because the way that Medicare drug coverage works depends on your current coverage, Medicare has specific information available to help you no matter what type of coverage you have. . . .

2. Determining what matters most and reviewing plan options Once you decide that you want prescription drug coverage, think about what matters most to you. There are a range of plan options available, so you can focus on the kind of coverage you prefer. There are two ways you can get your Medicare drug coverage. You can add drug coverage to the traditional Medicare plan through a "stand alone" prescription drug plan. Or you can get drug coverage and the rest of your Medicare coverage through a Medicare Advantage plan, like an HMO or PPO, that typically provides more benefits at a significantly lower cost through a network of doctors and hospitals. No matter what type of plan you choose, you can choose a plan that reflects what you want in terms of cost, coverage and convenience.

- **Cost:** What you pay for the coverage, including premiums, deductible, and payments for your drugs.
- **Coverage:** What benefits are provided (like coverage in the "coverage gap" and other coverage enhancements), which drugs are covered and the rules (like prior authorization) for getting those drugs.
- **Convenience:** Which pharmacies are part of the plan and whether the plan has a mail-order option.

The Centers for Medicare & Medicaid Services has created an online resource, *Landscape of Local Plans*. This resource helps you find Medicare prescription drug plans by state or Medicare Advantage plans with prescription drug coverage by county. It lets you see the plans in your area that offer drug coverage, including basic information to help you find ones that meet your needs based on cost, coverage, and convenience.

This is the first week that you can see drug plan data. Some of the features of the Medicare Prescription Drug

Plan Finder are not yet available. These features will allow you to further personalize your search for a drug plan that meets your needs. These features will be available well before you can choose to enroll in a plan on November 15. Right now, it is important to get ready to choose a plan by making a note of the drugs you take, the coverage features most important to you, and any specific pharmacies you prefer to use. The Landscape of Local Plans is a good resource for finding out about the plans in your area to get ready to make a choice.

3. Choosing a plan Beginning on November 15, people with Medicare can choose a prescription drug plan. There are many ways to choose a plan. You may rely on advice from people you know or trust, or choose a plan you are already familiar with, or use the Landscape of Local Plans located on medicare.gov to find a plan that meets your needs. All of the plan options must meet or exceed Medicare's standards for coverage, including coverage for medically necessary drugs.

If you want to make more specific plan comparisons based on what matters to you, you can get personalized information from the Medicare Prescriptions Drug Plan Finder....

...The Landscape of Local Plans is a good resource for finding out about the plans in your area to get ready to make a choice.

Once the Medicare Prescription Drug Plan Finder is fully operational, it will help you to personalize your search for a drug plan, and look at a side-by-side, personalized comparison of up to three plans at a time so you can find one that meets your needs. This list of plans provides a view of important plan information so you can compare plans based on cost, coverage and convenience.

- **Cost:** The Medicare Prescription Drug Plan Finder will show you a list of drug plans in your area, sorted by the plan with the lowest total cost for the drugs you take now. It can also help you narrow down the choices based on deductibles or premiums.
- **Coverage:** The Medicare Prescription Drug Plan Finder makes it easy for you to see what kind of coverage each plan offers and it gives you personalized information on plans that might meet your needs for you based on the coverage they offer and their other features.
- **Convenience:** The Medicare Prescription Drug Plan Finder can identify plans that are accepted by your preferred pharmacy and other nearby pharmacies, and plans that provide mail-order prescriptions.

The Medicare Prescription Drug Plan Finder will also help you if you aren't sure whether:

- You qualify for extra help paying for a Medicare drug plan,
- Your employer/union is continuing your current coverage with a Medicare subsidy, or
- You are already enrolled in a Medicare Advantage Health Plan or in a Medicare drug plan.

4. Enroll You can enroll in a plan starting November 15. Medicare will have an online Enrollment Center available on that date.... Coverage begins January 1, 2006 if you join a plan by December 31, 2005. The deadline to enroll to get coverage next year is May 15, 2006.

Other important information: If you work on behalf of a group of people with specific drug needs (like people with Lupus), Medicare has another tool that can help you. The Formulary Finder lets you enter a typical combination of drugs used by people with a certain condition to find out which plans in an area have formularies that cover these drugs.

SIGNIFICANCE

As of January 1, 2006, every person who has Medicare should be able to utilize the new Medicare Part D prescription benefit; the new benefit may serve not only to significantly lower out-of-pocket prescription costs for senior citizens and other Medicare beneficiaries in 2006, but may help to protect against higher prescription drug costs in the future. Each beneficiary can choose a drug plan (although the number of available plans varies from state to state, the average is at least a dozen choices). The Medicare Prescription Drug Coverage is an insurance plan, for which Medicare members will pay a monthly premium. This premium, too, varies—and is dependent upon income. People who live at or below the poverty level in their state are eligible for subsidies, reduced premiums, or programs in which they pay no premiums. It is important that individuals sign up for specific drug plans during the initial enrollment period, since penalties may be assessed for late enrollment.

There are two types of insurance plans offering Medicare Prescription Drug coverage. The first type is through Medicare Advantage Plans and other Medicare Health Plans, which enables people to get all of their (Medicare) health care services/coverage through a single plan. The second type of plan involves the Original Medicare Plan, some Medicare Cost Plans, and Medicare Private Fee-for-Service Plans. All of those programs are administered by insurance companies or other private payors who have been approved by, and contracted with, Medicare.

Although there are monthly premiums and prescription co-pays assessed by the new Medicare Part D, there are two extremely important differences from traditional insurance premiums. First, people with limited incomes and resources will be eligible for financial help in the form of reduced rates, subsidies and waivers, or no cost prescription drug coverage. Second, this insurance benefit coverage is not in any way impacted by the beneficiary's health status or the number of prescriptions used. No person will be denied coverage due to health status or ability to pay—a milestone in American prescription drug coverage.

The typical beneficiary nationally will pay about $32.20 per month for prescription drug coverage, ranging from a low of $3–4 to a high of nearly $100 monthly. Individuals can choose to pay monthly premiums by having them deducted directly from their social security checks, by electronic debit directly from a bank account, or by direct billing. A beneficiary will have the pay the first $250 of prescription medication costs per year—the universal deductible. Medicare will then pay 75 percent of the next $2,000 worth of prescription medications on the plan's formulary. After that, there is a gap in coverage that has come to be called the "donut hole," in which beneficiaries will be responsible for 100 percent of the costs for all prescription medications until they have paid another $2,850 in out-of-pocket costs. After that point, Medicare will begin paying approximately 95 percent of the costs for all remaining prescription drugs for the rest of the calendar year. This is known as catastrophic coverage. The total out-of-pocket costs for drugs on the plan's list is capped at $3,600 per year.

All drug plans will be required to provide coverage that is at least as comprehensive as the standard coverage set by Medicare. Plans may use their own discretion in creating extended or enhanced plans, with broader or more inclusive covered drug lists. Those plans also may charge a higher standard monthly premium for their coverage. Individuals who have certified (by Medicare) comparable coverage via their employers or a retirement plan may not need to join a Medicare Prescription Drug Plan.

The Medicare Drug Plans will cover generic and brand name drugs, but they will only cover drugs available by prescription, biologicals, and insulin. Over-the-counter medications will not be covered. The plans also will cover all medical supplies associated with the injection of insulin, such as syringes, needles, alcohol wipes, and gauze pads. Medicare-covered prescription drugs must available only by prescription, be approved by the Food and Drug Administration (FDA), be used and sold in the United States, and be used for medically accepted indications. Not all Medicare "covered drugs" will be covered by any one prescription drug plan (PDP) or Medicare Advantage Prescription Drug (MA-PD) plan, as each plan is responsible for developing its own formulary (list of preferred drugs covered by the plan). Medicare has placed specific requirements on the plan formularies. They must be developed by a Pharmacy and Therapeutics Committee, the majority of whose members must be either physicians or practicing pharmacists, and the formulary must include drugs in each therapeutic category and covered drug class.

There are some types of prescription medications that are completely excluded from Medicare Part D coverage. These medications also are excluded under the Medicare-approved drug discount card. They are excluded by statute, and they are drugs used for: anorexia; weight loss; weight gain; fertility; cosmetic purposes; hair growth; symptomatic relief of coughs and colds; prescription vitamins and mineral products with the exception of prenatal vitamins and fluoride preparations; non-prescription, or over-the-counter, drugs; barbiturates; and benzodiazepines.

Plans may choose to cover any or all of the excluded drugs at their own cost, or they may choose to share the cost with their enrollees. There is another group of non-covered drugs—the medications and biologicals covered under Medicare Part A or Part B (unless the individual enrollee does not meet the coverage requirements under Medicare Part A or Part B). Some examples of pharmaceuticals or biologicals in this category are post-transplant immunosuppressive drugs, certain oral anti-cancer drugs, and hemophilia clotting factors.

As of January 1, 2006, roughly 42 million Americans will be eligible for Medicare's Part D Prescription Drug Coverage. The belief, and the expectation, is that the competition among prescription drug plans will both drive down the cost of prescription medications and keep the costs from spiraling upward in the future. Although there will be premiums assessed for these plans, there will be financial assistance and zero-cost coverage available for those minimally or unable to afford premium costs. The program is designed to deliver discounted drug prices and to pay all but 5 percent of prescription drug costs in excess of $3,600 per calendar year. Federal Medicare officials believe that the new Medicare Part D will save enrollees an average of $1,200 on their prescription drug purchases during 2006.

FURTHER RESOURCES

Web sites

Center for Medicare Advocacy, Inc. "Medicare Part D: Prescription Drug Coverage." <http://www.medicareadvocacy.org/CHOICES/ChoicesPartD.htm#howsitwork> (accessed November 19, 2005).

Centers for Medicare & Medicaid Services. "CMS/HCFA History." <http://www.cms.hhs.gov/about/history/> (accessed November 17, 2005).

The New York Times on the Web. "Confusion is Rife About Drug Plan as Sign-Up Nears." <http://www.nytimes.com/2005/11/13/national/13drug.html> (accessed November 13, 2005).

SeniorAmericanInsurance. "Medicare Part D Prescription Coverage for Seniors." <http://www.seniorlifeinsurance.net/medicare_part_d.html?OVRAW=medicare%20part%20d&OVKEY=medicare%20part%20d&OVMTC=standard> (accessed November 15, 2005).

washingtonpost.com. "Medicare's Part D as Plan B." <http://www.washingtonpost.com/wp-dyn/content/article/2005/11/12/AR2005111200173.html> (accessed November 13, 2005).

E-mail from Hurricane Katrina

Delivering Medical Care During Crisis

E-mail

By: James T. Montgomery

Date: September 5, 2005

Source: *Yahoo! Groups. Tulane Hospital Evacuation-Jim Montgomery's Story.* <http://groups.yahoo.com/group/tulanepsychiatryfaculty/message/44> (January 01, 2006).

About the Author: James T. Montgomery is the president and chief executive officer of Tulane University Hospital and Clinic (TUHC) in New Orleans, Louisiana.

INTRODUCTION

On August 29, 2005, Hurricane Katrina made landfall in New Orleans, Louisiana. Officials had previously ordered the entire city evacuated, but many residents were either unable or unwilling to comply with the directive. Many of those living in New Orleans' lowest-lying neighborhoods or parishes (some were two yards or more below sea level) were poor, sick, or elderly; this meant they were physically or financially unable to travel, lacked transportation, were chronically or seriously ill, or had no place to go.

Others were in skilled nursing facilities or hospitals, still others in jails or penitentiaries. The city, like virtually all cities in hurricane-prone coastal states, had hurricane, emergency preparedness, evacuation, and disaster-response plans. New Orleans' levees were purportedly constructed to be able to withstand the force of a category four hurricane.

When the rains started and the winds hit, however, the force of the storm proved too much for the levees, and portions began to crumble. Within fewer than twenty-four hours, according to U. S. news and government reports, approximately 80–85 percent of the city was flooded, more than 1,000 people were dead, and the city's resources were largely paralyzed. The water rose so swiftly that many people had no time to leave, others drowned as they fell on their way to roofs or other high ground. Some were bedridden and could not escape, others survived the hurricane and subsequent flooding only to die while waiting for help to arrive.

In hospitals and medical centers many patients were too ill to be transported to other facilities before the storm hit. Some were on ventilators or other life-sustaining medical equipment, others were medically unstable, or were undergoing treatments that could not easily be interrupted. Some were brought in as casualties of the hurricane or its aftermath; others arrived at the hospital in labor.

Because hospitals are equipped with redundant power systems, typically backup generators capable of powering all necessary electrical equipment, it was assumed that the New Orleans hospitals would be able to get through the hurricane and its immediate aftermath without undue difficulty. James T. Montgomery weathered hurricane Katrina at the facility Tulane University Hospital and Clinic.

■ PRIMARY SOURCE

From: Randall Legeai *Date:* Thu Sep 8, 2005 4:45 pm *Subject:* Tulane Hospital Evacuation—Jim Montgomery's Story Dr. Winstead asked that I forward the attached writeup by Jim Montgomery that details his experiences at Tulane Hospital following the hurricane.

I thought it might be easier to compose an e-mail to all of you at once that tells some of the story of the past few days. First and foremost I felt your prayers and heard your concerns that were registered with Donna and others and they comforted me and kept me calm which was essential in this time.

In Dylan's song, "A Hard Rain's a-Gonna Fall," the singer is asked the questions of where have you been, what did you see, what did you hear, who did you meet, and what'll you do now, my blue-eyed son, to which he answers with a collage of images of his experience that attempts to answer each question. In this crisis the images were moving so fast that I think it'll take awhile to put it together but here's an attempt to do so.

This storm as of noon Friday the 25th didn't seem like it would be muchof an event, but by 5 pm things began to look different. We met as a group on Saturday to begin our routine preparations for a hurricane. Donna left for her brother's home and I went home to put things together there. I started to think what do I absolutely not want to lose in case the house would be swept away and the answer only revealed the photos of the family thru the years so that and few clothes was all I took.

The Storm: God's Natural World has an awesome power. From the small observation windows from our tallest floors, we observed awnings being blown off, a blinding rain and a general sense [that] if God's ever angry we're going to lose big. Our first inspections revealed little damage. A few broken windows and some roof damage but the building held up well. In fact, if you were in the inner core of the facility you only vaguely heard it. We even walked around late in the afternoon since there was only limited flooding no worse than a heavy thunderstorm. Overconfident, we even stated we had absorbed the best punch that nature could throw and we seemed intact.

At 1:30 am on Tuesday morning began the biggest crisis and challenge of my life and in the life of Tulane and no doubt New Orleans. I was awakened by my COO who told me the water in the boiler room was rising a foot an hour since midnight and if it continued at that rate at best we had only another two to three hours before we would lose all power since we already were on emergency power since early Monday morning. We had only 7 ventilator patients whose lives would be in jeopardy, and we had to move fast to get them out. We had no boat and no helicopter pad. Houston we have a problem.

I called Acadian Ambulance (who I know well) but had no business connection to our hospital and asked their immediate help. We have a parking deck connected to the hospital that we had evaluated as sturdy enough to support helicopter flight, but it had four light poles in the middle. I want to tell you what happened in the next four hours was nothing short of a miracle. Our maintenance group got the light poles down; Acadian agreed to pick our patients up, we made arrangements with our other HCA [Corporate operator of hospitals and health systems] hospitals to take them. Our staff and physicians got their patients ready, and most importantly, the water rise began to slow to an inch/hr and a little after the sun came

up copters were on the roof and patients began to be transported.

Early on Tuesday morning we met with our key managers who were at the hospital. We prayed for support and comfort and guidance for what we knew was going to be a difficult period. We talked about what we knew, and what we didn't know, which was considerable because we had no contact from FEMA or the Mayor's office. We had no idea why the water was rising and from what limited facts we had, no one did. We had to assume that it would keep rising and we would lose power and then we would have no power at all. Thus, no light, no ac [airconditioning], suction, oxygen, elevators, phones ie [sic]. Everything that is precious to good care. We had to get out so we hatched a plan and I tried to stay out of the way and let our physicians and nurses triage patients; others determined what vital supplies we needed replenishing; HCA was working frantically to coordinate a transportation effort to pick up patients and eventually, our staff. How many people? Good question. At least 1,200, which included a total of 160 patients, employees, and physicians and their families and 76 dogs and cats that I didn't know about at the time.

Tuesday: The looting began. We witnessed people, dozens of them, wading in front of the hospital with bag after bag of stuff from different stores in the vicinity. Bandits took over two hotels adjacent to us and forced out many of our employees' families who had been housed there, forcing them back to the hospital [and] creating further complications.

That night our people on the roof evacuating patients heard gunshots in the air but they continued their work. The lawlessness and insurrection certainly was a distraction but our Tulane Police were great, and they are very capable. Late in the day we ran out of fuel so our generators shut down and the building began to get hot. The last of the ventilator patients had to go up six stories by way of pickup trucks since the elevators shut down and our ambulance was too tall to squeeze to the top. During the day, I had a conversation with a patient's father who told me that the parking deck pad would hold big helicopters. How did he know? Because he was a Blackhawk pilot. Ok. Then there appeared out of nowhere this guy, John Holland, who was sent in by HCA to be our Flight Coordinator—whatever that is. "The man" had arrived who would communicate with the birds in the air and boy is that important because our patients had begun to fly away.

Wednesday: If you would like to know if we slept, here's a little experiment: Try heating the bedroom up to about 90–95 degrees. First, you're hot and then you sweat and get cold and then the cycle repeats. Daybreak and I tell you patients are being moved into a queue to move. I saw our staff, residents, and faculty move sick patients with a grace and dignity that was most impressive. This was our third day and the stress on our people began to show. Everyone was asking when, where, & how were we going to get out. The city sewer system was obviously backing up and spilling out and creating an acrid smell that over the next few days made it almost impossible to breathe. With no water pressure you can't bathe.

But here's a general observation: If everyone smells the same you really don't notice it, you just feel unclean. On this day, the La. Wildlife and Fisheries Department showed up to help us move some patients that we had inherited from the Superdome on Sunday night. Yes, over 60 extra medically needy people with chronic conditions. So by boat we sent them and their loved ones away. I met a woman whose most valuable possession was her pillow and her radio that I personally promised her to protect. It's in my office now.

The Big Birds began to fly. Blackhawk's down. Instead of one or two patients they could move up to four with some additional staff. Beautiful sight but there was more to come. By the end of the day we had moved all but about twenty patients including two who weighed more than 400 lbs and one artificial heart assist-device patient, which was the challenge of the week since the device itself weighed more than 500 lbs. So imagine hauling this weight three to four floors down a dark stairwell at 90-plus degrees. It was a young man's job and it was done.

Let me tell you that the coordination from the patient's room to the staging area to the helipad into the helicopter was a work of art composed by many painters. It truly was a thing of beauty and it touched everyone who was there.

By the end of day, HCA had constructed an extraction plan for the remaining staff. Helicopter to the airport, buses to pick up and take to Lafayette. Sounds good but there were lots of needs and who knows what the government may decide to do.

Thursday: Line up and get ready. Have a little breakfast. We basically were living on Strawberry Pop-Tarts, honey oat bars, and for dinner a little protein, tuna fish. Fortunately, I like all of them but I'm sure I lost ten lbs or so. Anyway, the line was formed and I personally counted 700 hundred people. Our staff, physicians, theirchildren and spouses, and just to top it off 76 dogs and cats. Holy God. How are we going to deal with that? So we relegated them immediately to second-class citizenship to another line and pray we don't have to put the pets to sleep if no one will haul them.

At first there were just a few small copters and we had some patients to move and it was slow. Moving through the line people were calm with a few exceptions but overall they managed their plight well. Then a situation developed. A frantic medical director of critical care showed up by boat from Charity. Major problem. Charity was in a meltdown. He had 21 critical care patients many being hand ventilated for two days and he couldn't get any help from the state. You may have heard this story reported by CNN. Their version and ours differ but raise your hand if you think the media gets it right all the time. Can you help me he asked? This was a tough question, but it had only one answer. We would give them access to the small aircraft, which wasn't going to help us move our staff anyway. So that process began much to the chagrin of our nonprofessional staff and family. They just didn't understand it. Our nurses and doctors did, but it increased the crowd's intensity. Midday and it was moving slow. It didn't look good. Then from 3 to 5 things happened.

A Chinook helicopter is big. Two rotors and it carries about 50–60 people. It moves with a slow deliberate confidence that is hard to describe. But one showed up. We had questions about could it land so we asked "the man, John" and he said yes but nothing else could be on the pad when it did due to the turbulence. I want to tell you as it approached cheers broke out from below and people thought they had a chance. So for a few hours we made progress and then it stopped. No more big birds, big problem. What happened? Don't know. I called my daughter Megan where Donna was staying and she seemed elated. "You're back." "What?" I asked. She tells me Gov. Blanco had just announced that Tulane had totally been evacuated. According to my account she was about 400 people short in her analysis. But we now had a new problem. They think we're not here. Better let someone know.

I called the La. Nat'l Guard. Guess who answered, Brad Smith, the patient's father I spoke of earlier. He had gotten a ride back with some of the Wildlife boys and was now flying sorties into New Orleans. He quickly got a hold of the Office of Emergency Preparedness and let them know we still needed help. So maybe Friday we'd get out. People were remarkably calm when we told them they'd be there another day. They just sat down and began to prepare to go to bed.

We left the hospital and remained in the parking deck. One it was cooler, two there would be less confusion in the morning, and three it was safer since there was less territory for our Tulane Police to patrol. I know the media has played up the anarchy, and no doubt there was some concern, but I always thought we were safe.

So imagine trying to fall asleep on your concrete driveway without a pad or pillow. It's kind of tough. Then throw in an unexpected helicopter landing at 1 am. The wind is a little dicey. The bird dropped off 50 percent of the Marines in New Orleans. One guy needed to go to Charity so we had to take him over. Next event for the evening: at 4 am we were treated to a massive explosion at a warehouse on the river several miles away. I happened to be looking directly at it at the time. It must have reached a 1,000 ft in the air. Then by the end of the evening we began actually to get cold. But it finally ended.

Friday: The end is pretty anticlimatic. At 8 o'clock unexpected Chinooks began showing up taking 60 people at a time. I wonder if our pilot friend in the Guard had anything to do we it but I haven't asked him yet. So in a matter of 2 1/2 hrs. everyone was gone but our police and the last remnants of management. So after attempts to arrange a coordination with Charity to use the helipad, we left for home sweet home.

Obviously, this is only phase one of a complicated recovery for New Orleans. Each of you no doubt is praying for this recovery. So many people have lost so much and it reaches far beyond New Orleans. I talked to the Chairman of the Board of HCA yesterday upon returning and told him it was the worst and most difficult challenge I have ever been personally involved with but at the same time I don't think I've ever felt as great a sense of accomplishment from anything I've been involved with. Our staff performed like clockwork and it was a beautiful thing to observe. Our success in this week is simply measured by the fact that we didn't lose a patient during this trying time.

Jim

P.S. This event is just below a nuclear catastrophe in its degree of magnitude, and it's clear we're not ready and if we don't do better the next time a really hard rain's a-gonna fall.

SIGNIFICANCE

In the aftermath of Hurricane Katrina, many New Orleans hospitals have closed either temporarily or permanently. Several have been condemned. Initially, military and civilians worked side-by-side in an outdoor tented facility set up across the street from University Hospital, designed to render low-level medical, dental, and pharmacy services. A military field hospital was set up at the Convention Center to handle more serious medical or surgical concerns. It had a maximum stay of two days before patients were transported to one of the three remaining fully functioning New Orleans hospitals.

During the crisis (the hurricane surge and ensuing flooding), there were many unexpected heroes. Shelters were set up in neighboring areas (both within the hurricane-affected states of Louisiana, Alabama, Florida, and Mississippi and in other states, both bordering and distant from the Gulf Coast region), and thousands of people offered to shelter displaced persons or families in their homes. Relief organizations received large donations of money and supplies. Volunteers from across the nation, and from other countries such as Mexico, Israel, Germany, and Georgia, helped with search and rescue efforts, medical care, power restoration, and general crisis management; and they brought in massive quantities of first aid, medical and pharmaceutical supplies, and clean drinking water.

Many local citizens, who were themselves profoundly affected by the storm: losing property, homes, personal possessions, pets, or, worst of all, family members, worked tirelessly to assist others. They used boats (their own or those they "borrowed" from boatyards) to rescue people who were stranded, and to move the sick and disabled from damaged or powerless medical or nursing facilities to functioning sites. Health care providers remained at their posts in hospitals and medical centers for several days without relief. When generators became flooded or ran out of fuel many staff members spent hours hand-ventilating patients who could not breathe on their own. Staff carried patients up or down many flights of stairs, often accompanied by heavy medical equipment and supplies, to get them to locations from which they could be transported to receiving facilities. Lifesaving work continued under unimaginable conditions: no running water, no lights, no air-conditioning amid temperatures verging on 100 degrees Fahrenheit; sewage systems failed; and food and water were scarce. By all available reports, people in the medical settings acted with a profound sense of dedication, doing their best to save lives.

When some hospitals that had been seriously damaged by the storm began to reach critical shortages, staff went to other local facilities to summon help. Physicians, nurses, emergency medical technicians, and other physical and behavioral health care workers (both professionals and paraprofessionals) volunteered to come to the hardest-hit areas to aid in rescue and relief efforts. Cadres of ambulances, air medical transport equipment, and mobile hospitals were brought in from around the country, often before they could even be requested. Eventually, all of the severely damaged hospitals were evacuated, patients were safely transported to other facilities, and staff members were finally able to leave. Despite the critical shortages, unsanitary and primitive conditions, few lives were lost among the hospital patients.

FURTHER RESOURCES

Web sites

EMSNETWORK.org. "Hurricane Katrina: Our Experiences by Paramedics Larry Bradshaw and Lorrie Beth Slonsky." <http://www.emsnetwork.org/artman/publish/article_18427.shtml> (January 1, 2006).

Meadowcrest Hospital, Tenet, Louisiana. "A Disaster Beyond Comparison." <http://www.meadowcresthosp.com/CWS Content/meadowcresthosp/aboutUs/phillipsowakatrina. htm> (January 1, 2006).

USINFO.STATE.GOV. "Acts of Kindness, Heroism Reported in the Wake of Hurricane." <http://usinfo.state.gov/gi/ Archive/2005/Sep/02-225769.html> (January 1, 2006).

USINFO.STATE.GOV. "U.S. Launches Massive Response to Aid Hurricane Katrina Victims." <http:// usinfo.state.gov/gi/Archive/2005/Sep/02-225769.html> (January 1, 2006).

USINFO.STATE.GOV. "World Community Offers Support to Victims of Hurricane Katrina." <http://usinfo.state.gov/ gi/Archive/2005/Sep/06-611544.html> (January 1, 2006).

Public Health

Public health encompasses legislation, medical surveillance, health care delivery, and other means that aim to safeguard the public from disease, and to maintain and improve the general health of the population. Ongoing public health efforts address the health and safety of the workplace, public, and home environments. Public health initiatives and policies often must balance the collective good with individual rights. Hygiene standards, noise abatement laws, traffic safety laws, water fluoridation, and equipment safety standards are just some of the areas where public safety measures may be regarded as an infringement on personal liberty.

In order to be effective, public health initiatives must come into direct contact with the population they are intended to benefit. The annual wintertime vaccination campaign against influenza, for example, is targeted to the elderly and those who are least able to resist infection. Broader approaches include publicity campaigns that encourage the adoption of more healthy diets and lifestyles, and legislation that prohibits cigarette smoking in public buildings.

Another example of public health legislation involves water quality standards and testing criteria that exist in many developed countries, which have helped to reduce the contamination of water by pathogenic (disease-causing) microorganisms and nonbiological material. In the United States, adoption of water quality guidelines has almost eliminated outbreaks of typhoid, a bacterial disease spread through contaminated water. Elsewhere in the world, however, as summarized in the "World Water Crisis" report from the United Nations, access to clean water is still a problem in the spread of disease.

Although the threat from infectious diseases has eased tremendously in developed countries, the same is not true for many underdeveloped countries, where access to health care may be limited. At the global level, agencies such as the World Health Organization (WHO) and the United Nations Children's Fund (UNICEF) provide help through such efforts as vaccination and nutritional campaigns that seek to combat diseases such as polio and improve overall health.

When disease outbreaks occur investigative teams from groups like the WHO and the U.S. Centers for Disease Control and Prevention (CDC) fan out across the globe to determine the cause and possible spread of the outbreak. These efforts to track and control disease are especially important to developing and underdeveloped nations. Both direct testing and mathematical models are used to predict the spread of diseases such as SARS and the emerging avian flu viruses. If a public threat is evident, mandated restrictions (such as quarantine) may be imposed on animals and humans. The power to monitor and impose such restrictions across politically diverse boundaries is set to become one of the most critical of social and political issues in the modern era where diseases can leap continents in a few jet-age hours.

Food safety is another public health issue that can sometimes have global ramifications. Restrictions are sometimes placed on agricultural products, including bioengineered food and beef from countries where Bovine Spongiform Encephalopathy (Mad Cow Disease) has been detected. Additionally, in the era of bioterrorism, food and water supplies must be safeguarded from deliberate contamination.

John Snow's Map

Epidemiological Investigation Solves London Epidemic

Photograph

By: John Snow

Date: 1854

Source: John Snow. Map 1, in *On the Mode of Communication of Cholera*. 2nd. ed. London: 1855. Available online at: Ralph R. Frerichs, MD. UCLA. Department of Epidemiology /School of Public Health. "John Snow's Map 1" (Broad Street Pump Outbreak, 1854). <http://www.ph.ucla.edu/epi/snow/snowmap1_1854.html> (accessed October 30, 2005).

About the Author: John Snow (1813–1858) was an English physician who made great advances in the understanding of both anesthetics and the spread of disease, especially cholera.

INTRODUCTION

Although the Asian form of cholera may have existed in India since 400 CE, it was not until the nineteenth century that it was known in Europe. The first pandemic, which reached Great Britain in 1831, caused as much fear and panic as tuberculosis did in the early twentieth century and HIV/AIDS does today. The death rate from cholera was over 50 percent and medical opinion was sharply divided as to the cause. At that time, John Snow was a doctor's apprentice gaining his first experience with the disease, noting its symptoms of diarrhea and extreme dehydration.

The germ theory of disease, which holds that viruses and bacteria are the causative infectious agents of diseases such as yellow fever, smallpox, typhoid, cholera, and others, was in its infancy at this time. Some doctors believed in *contagion*, in which disease spreads from one person to another. Others assumed that *miasmata*, or toxins in the air, spread disease. Given the dire state of personal and public hygiene in the mid-nineteenth century, either theory held merit at the time.

Snow first began a serious scientific investigation of cholera transmission during the 1848 London epidemic. In his classic essay, *On the Mode of Communication of Cholera*, published on August 29, 1849, he postulated that polluted water was a source of cholera—especially water contaminated by the waste of an infected person, a not-uncommon occurrence at the time. When an outbreak erupted a few years later in central London at the end of August 1854, close to

where Snow himself lived, he resumed his research. The map, published in 1855 as a second edition of his earlier pamphlet, shows how he linked the local cases, shown as dark blocks, to their source—a water pump in Broad Street.

PRIMARY SOURCE

JOHN SNOW'S MAP

See primary source image.

SIGNIFICANCE

John Snow's research, detailed on his famous map, is an early example of epidemiology, the scientific study of the occurrence, distribution, and control of disease. Snow's map traced the 1854 cholera outbreak to the Broad Street pump. However, the claim that he removed the pump handle himself—which would, of course, have stopped exposure to the contaminated water—may be false. He recommended its removal, but this was probably done by the local curate, Henry Whitehead, several days after the outbreak began and when, according to collected data, it was already on the wane.

It is partially thanks to John Snow's work in the Broad Street area that Britain suffered fewer major outbreaks of cholera after this time. An influential figure in medical circles, he had been elected president of the Medical Society of London in 1855. Fortunately for British public health, the successful proof of his theory on the transmission of cholera—from person to person via contaminated water—took hold, and the "environmental" theory eventually died away. Although the actual causative agent, the bacterium *Vibrio cholerae*, would not be identified until 1883, Snow's preventive methods worked. Indeed, they are still effective today, for despite the advent of vaccination and antibiotics, handwashing and the avoidance of contaminated food and water are still fundamental ways of preventing infection.

Because Snow based his investigation on the idea of germ theory, which French microbiologist Louis Pasteur (1822–1895) would later prove, he used a scientific approach and epidemiological study of cholera victims to validate his hypothesis. As his case notes amply demonstrate, much of his research was driven by his patients' visible suffering.

Today epidemiologists work in a similar, although more sophisticated, manner. As causes of most infections are now understood, today's puzzles include chronic conditions such as diabetes, cancer,

■ **PRIMARY SOURCE**

John Snow's Map. Map showing the area of central London where English physician John Snow documented cholera cases in 1854 (shown by dark bars), and linked them with contaminated water from a public pump in Broad Street, one of the first examples of investigating a disease outbreak using principles of epidemiology. COURTESY, DR. RALPH R. FRERICHS, <HTTP://WWW.PH.UCLA.EDU/EPI/SNOW.HTML>.

and heart disease. Infection claimed so many lives in Snow's day that there was hardly a chance to investigate these longer-term medical problems. The twenty-first century equivalent of John Snow's Broad Street pump are lifestyle and genetics, which current research indicates are the major cause of chronic disease. The careful scientific approach that produced John Snow's map still inform the best kind of epidemiology today, with enormous potential to improve human health.

FURTHER RESOURCES

Books

Shephard, David A. E. *John Snow: Anaesthetist to a Queen and Epidemiologist to a Nation.* Cornwall, Prince Edward Island, Canada: York Point, 1995.

Web sites

UCLA Department of Epidemiology. School of Public Health. "John Snow." <http://www.ph.ucla.edu/epi/snow.html> (accessed November 11, 2005).

Immigrant Girl Receives Medical Exam at Ellis Island

Photograph

By: Anonymous

Date: 1905

Source: Immigrant Girl Receives Medical Exam at Ellis Island. Picture History, LLC.

About the Photographer: Officials at Ellis Island photographed the processing of immigrants at Ellis Island on several occasions to reassure Americans that the government was taking measures to protect the nation from the threats posed by unchecked immigration.

PRIMARY SOURCE

Immigrant Girl Receives Medical Exam at Ellis Island. A line of immigrant women await their turn as a young woman receives a medical examination at Ellis Island. PICTURE HISTORY.

INTRODUCTION

The decades after the American Civil War (1861–1865) witnessed a shift in the attitudes of Americans toward immigrants. A spirit of acceptance changed to one of suspicion and fear. This escalating xenophobia can be traced to the vast numbers of immigrants who poured into the United States within a few decades. Between 1880 and 1920, more than twenty million immigrants entered the U.S., with almost fourteen million of them arriving in the twentieth century. Even more disturbing to native-born Americans, many of these immigrants were not Anglo-Saxon, practiced unusual customs, followed the Catholic, Jewish, or other faiths, did not speak English, and were unfamiliar with democratic traditions.

In response to the flood of strangers, Americans demanded immigration restrictions. In 1892, the Ellis Island Immigration Station opened its doors in New York in the shadow of the Statue of Liberty. By the time that it closed in 1954, about twelve million of the "huddled masses" first touched American soil there. At its peak in 1907, the center processed about 5,000 people per day. These were mostly European immigrants who arrived crammed into steerage compartments of ships. Asian immigrants were processed at Angel Island near San Francisco. Those immigrants who could afford first- and second-class cabins did not have to visit Ellis Island. Instead, they were examined aboard ship and most of them simply walked down the gangway onto the streets of Manhattan.

Ellis Island existed to weed out dangerous immigrants. An army of inspectors, doctors, nurses, and public officials questioned, examined, and documented the newcomers. Immigrants were poked and prodded for signs of infectious disease or debilitating handicaps. Although some who were sick or lame were detained for days or weeks, the vast majority of immigrants received stamps of approval and were on their way to their new homes after three or four hours.

Only 2 percent of immigrants were denied entry altogether. These immigrants were identified as criminals, anarchists, or carriers of contagious diseases such as tuberculosis or trachoma, an eye disease resulting in blindness. These people were placed back on the ship for transport, usually back to Europe.

Immigrants wait at Ellis Island in New York City to see if U.S. officials will allow them to enter the country. Between 1892 and 1924, about one in five immigrants were not allowed into the country due to poor health or political reasons. AP/WIDE WORLD PHOTOS.

■ **PRIMARY SOURCE**

IMMIGRANT GIRL RECEIVES MEDICAL EXAM AT ELLIS ISLAND

See primary source image.

■

SIGNIFICANCE

Ellis Island was not the first effort to stop the entry of disease-carrying immigrants, although it is the best-known and largest attempt. The posting of medical officers at ports dates to the epidemic of bubonic plague in the fourteenth century. In the 1970s, the eradication of smallpox and other communicable diseases made it appear as if screening of immigrants was no

longer necessary. However, in response to twenty-first century plagues, medical officers are again being stationed at ports of entry.

In 2002, cases of severe acute respiratory syndrome or SARS were seen among international travelers entering the U.S. In response, Congress and the Centers for Disease Control reinvigorated the practice of stationing medical officers at ports. The threat of the rapid spread of SARS combined with fears of exotic diseases like the Ebola virus and the dangers of bioterrorism to prompt more stringent medical screening. The quarantine system, which includes most major airports, is designed to stop microbial threats at the borders.

By 2005, the U.S. had medical officers at 474 sites, including airports, seaports, and land border crossings, to screen people entering the country for communicable diseases. The officers are particularly concerned about travelers with symptoms of H5N1, the deadly avian flu virus that began in Asia. The Los Angeles immigration station is typical with one or two reports received per week from international airlines reporting passengers with flu-like symptoms. The medical officer examines the travelers, asks where they have been and whether they had contact with live birds. No cases of bird flu have been discovered in the U.S. as of January 2006, but a person arriving with a suspected case would be referred to a local hospital. No one would be quarantined. The officers also identify high-risk diseases that could potentially come into the U.S. through such cargo as bush meat, pelts, and exotic animals.

It is doubtful that a highly communicable human disease such as avian flu could be stopped at the border. Medical officers expect that they may stop some infected people early, but they do not assume that increased surveillance will stop every infected traveler.

FURTHER RESOURCES
Books

Coan, Peter M. *Ellis Island Interviews: In Their Own Words.* New York: Facts on File, 1997.

Pitkin, Thomas. *Keepers of the Gate: A History of Ellis Island.* New York: New York University Press, 1975.

AAAS Resolution: Death of Dr. James Carroll from Yellow Fever Experimentation

Professional society resolution

By: American Association for the Advancement of Science

Date: December 30, 1907

Source: American Association for the Advancement of Science, Washington, D.C.

About the Author: Founded in 1848, the American Association for the Advancement of Science (AAAS) is the world's largest scientific society, serving ten million individuals. It is affiliated with 262 scientific societies and academies around the world. Its mission is to promote the understanding of science nationally and globally through education, leadership, and acting

as spokesperson. AAAS publishes the weekly journal *Science*, as well as many books, reports and newsletters.

INTRODUCTION

Yellow fever is an acute, infectious viral disease that is transmitted by the bite of two species of female mosquito, *Aedes aegypti* and *Hemogogus*. Now rare, but not unknown, yellow fever originated in central Africa. The slave trade and increased commerce brought it to the New World beginning in the fifteenth century through to the nineteenth century. In the United States, there were thirty-five epidemics occurring between 1702 and 1800, and from 1800 to 1879 there was an epidemic almost every year. In 1878, the U.S. Marine Hospital Service, the forerunner of today's U.S. Public Health Service, was charged with collecting data on yellow fever and other infectious diseases. The service also had responsibility for introducing quarantine methods at ports of entry to stop the introduction and spread of these diseases into the United States.

Yellow fever can be mild or so severe as to be potentially fatal. In mild cases, the symptoms are similar to those of influenza. More severe cases are marked by internal bleeding and liver and kidney damage. Jaundice may occur, which gives the disease its name. Mortality can be as high as 50 percent in populations that have no immunity to the disease, which is why it hit the Spanish, French, and English armies invading the New World so hard.

Opinion was divided over the causes of yellow fever. Some thought it was bacterial. Others favored the fomite theory—that items such as clothing and bedding touched by an infected person were contagious. A Cuban doctor, Carlos Juan Finlay (1833–1915), believed mosquitoes spread the disease. He put this idea forward as early as 1881 but was not taken seriously.

The Spanish-American War of 1898 led to a U.S. Army presence in the Carribean and Cuba. An epidemic of yellow fever in Cuba led to the infection of 1,200 soldiers in 1900. Something had to be done and the Army Surgeon General George Miller Sternberg (1838–1915) set up the Yellow Fever Commission in Havana, headed by Major Walter Reed (1851–1902), to investigate the cause and prevention of yellow fever. Surgeon James Carroll (1854–1907) was his second-in-command and the two proceeded to work with a group of other doctors, including Finlay who gave them mosquito larvae to use in experiments. Carroll was one of the volunteers who put himself forward to be bitten by a mosquito "loaded" with yellow fever to see if he would contract the disease. He did contract the

During the construction of the Panama Canal (1880–1914), many workers succumbed to diseases such as malaria and yellow fever. AP/ WIDE WORLD PHOTOS.

disease, but seemed to recover. However, he died of heart valve disease, thought to be a late complication of the yellow fever, in 1907. The resolution below describes a call for a pension to be given to his widow, Jennie, to help her support their seven children, in recognition of her loss and Carroll's contribution to medical science.

▮ PRIMARY SOURCE

AAAS RESOLUTION: DEATH OF DR. JAMES CARROLL FROM YELLOW FEVER EXPERIMENTATION

Whereas, The late Major James Carroll, M.D., USA, was the first to submit voluntarily to the bite of an infected stegomyia, and from the bite of this mosquito, suffered a severe attack of yellow fever, the effects of which led to his ultimate death, and

Whereas, This was the first experimentally produced case of yellow fever leading to the present knowledge of this

disease, which has practically enabled its complete control, therefore, be it

Resolved, That the American Association for the Advancement of Science now in session in Chicago, Illinois recommends to the Senate and House of Representatives of the United States of America the passage of a bill securing to Mrs. Jennie Carroll, widow of the late Major James Carroll of the Yellow Fever Commission, of the United States Army, a special pension for the support of herself and her seven children.

[*Adopted by the AAAS Council, December 30, 1907.*]

▮

SIGNIFICANCE

Carroll's widow was awarded a pension of $125 a year by the government from the date of his death. So, too, was the widow of Dr. Jesse Lazear (1866–1900), another member of the board, who contracted and died of yellow fever early on in the investigation.

Fortunately, none of the recruited volunteers died during the experiments with the mosquitoes.

The work of the Yellow Fever Board established that mosquitoes were the vector (intermediate insect or animal that transmits a disease to humans) for the transmission of yellow fever. Their findings led to the control of mosquitoes in Havana from 1901, and yellow fever was soon all but eradicated from Cuba. This was the first example in history of preventing a disease through control of its vector. Soon mosquito control measures were similarly applied in Panama. Both malaria and yellow fever were thus brought under control, opening the way for the construction of the Panama Canal.

Although the board's experiments were risky, they were commended for the ethical way in which they sought informed consent from all the volunteers (who were, in turn, praised for their courage). Reed and Carroll began the U.S. Army's tradition of medical research, which aims to protect the health of the military. Today the Army investigates both infectious and non-infectious disease, and is involved in vaccine research. Other programs cover blood products, trauma medicine, and surgical techniques.

FURTHER RESOURCES

Books

Lock, Stephen, John M. Last, and George Dunea, eds. *The Oxford Illustrated Companion to Medicine*. Oxford: Oxford University Press, 2001.

Periodicals

Pierce, John R., and James V. Writer, eds. "Solving the Mystery of Yellow Fever: The 1900 U.S. Army Yellow Fever Board." *Military Medicine* 166 supplement (2001): 1–82.

Report on Condition of Women and Child Wage-Earners in the United States

Maternal, Infant Mortality in the U.S. Decreases During the Twentieth Century

Book excerpt

By: Charles P. Neill

Date: 1912

Source: Charles P. Neill. *Report on Condition of Women and Child Wage-Earners in the United States*. Vol XII.

Washington; Government Printing Office, 1912, pages 11–16.

About the Author: Charles P.("C. P.") Neill held a PhD in Economics from Johns Hopkins University, and was the Commissioner of Labor for the United States government from 1905 to 1913. After leaving the federal government, he worked as an arbitrator for several railroad companies, and fought for injury and workman's compensation laws for laborers.

INTRODUCTION

As the government and the private sector initiated and completed Progressive Era reforms in the United States—such as improved public health campaigns, better labor laws, sanitation systems, and anti-poverty programs—an underlying assumption that infant mortality rates would improve was shattered by turn of the century government reports and progressive literature that documented extremely high mortality rates for children under twelve months of age.

Most writings for the public consisted of sensationalistic exposes, designed to familiarize the middle class with the plight of the poor. Government reports, however, were designed for bureaucrats, public health officials, and politicians; as time passed, the results of these reports were benchmarks for determining progress.

Charles P. Neill (1865–1942), United States Commissioner of Labor and author of the following excerpt, ordered the creation of a series of reports on the conditions of women and children laborers in the United States. These reports, published from 1910 to 1912, investigated and catalogued laborers' age, hours of labor, term of employment, health, illiteracy, sanitary conditions, and other industry matters pertaining to public health and safety. Although infant mortality rates did later drop sharply as a result of intensive maternity health and infant care education campaigns, this series was the driving force behind such programs; as this document reveals, one out of every six children born in "registered" states died before the age of one in the United States at the time of these reports.

PRIMARY SOURCE

IMPORTANCE OF DEATH RATE UNDER ONE YEAR AS COMPARED WITH GENERAL DEATH RATE Infant mortality, or the deaths of children under twelve months of age, is generally recognized as one of the most complex social problems of the present day. The first fact which entitles it to a place among our most serious social problems is its magnitude as compared with the general death rate. Despite the lack of mortality records for the whole United States, and the many and serious defects of those for many of the registration States, the registration area of the Twelfth Census was sufficiently large to produce in its figures an approximate index of the mortality of the country at large. Checked up as are these figures of mortality in various age groups by those of England and Wales, France, and various other foreign countries with established systems of registering vital statistics, they probably record with approximate accuracy the death rate under age one, as compared with the ratio of deaths at other ages. In a recent statistical study of this subject, [Edward B. Phelps: A Statistical Study of Infant Mortality. Quarterly Publications of the American Statistical Association, new series, No. 83 (September, 1908), pp. 266–268] it was shown (the figures being restricted to the registration States and omitting the registration cities in nonregistration States in order to eliminate the abnormally high mortality of the colored population in the registration cities of the South) that the rate of deaths per one thousand living population under age one, in the registration States in 1900, apparently was 159.3, as contrasted with a death rate of only 14.1 per one thousand population over age one. In other words, the death rate of the census year 1900, in the registration States, in the case of infants under one year of age was more than eleven times as high as at all other ages of childhood and adult life, as measured by the ratio of deaths to living population in both age groups. This comparison is probably approximately correct, though the returns of all censuses of population under age one are somewhat unreliable owing to the carelessness of parents in reporting as "one-year-old" babies within a few months, under or over, that age.

2 MORTALITY AND EMPLOYMENT OF MOTHERS: STABILITY OF DEATH RATE UNDER ONE YEAR The second fact concerning infant mortality which has attracted the attention of those who have investigated the subject is, that the infant death rate as compared with that at higher ages has shown so little improvement during a long period. It has not responded adequately to improvements in public sanitation and medical practice. A recent English writer on the subject has commented on this aspect of the problem: "Whilst during the last half century, a time of marvellous growth of science and of preventive medicine, human life has been saved and prolonged, and death made more remote for the general population, infants still die every year much as they did in former times. Indeed, in many places it appears that they die in greater numbers, and more readily than in the past." In many cities and in some countries there apparently has been a decrease in the infant death rate of late years, but this decrease has not been sufficiently widespread or extended through a sufficiently long period of years to lessen the seriousness of the situation.

INFANT MORTALITY RATE DEFINED Before proceeding further, it is necessary to explain the method by which the infant mortality rate is usually computed, and the difference between that rate and an ordinary death rate. By the infantile mortality rate is meant "the proportion which the deaths of such infants bear to every one thousand births. An ordinary death rate is the proportion which the total deaths of a community bear to one thousand of the population in such a community. But it is clear that a more accurate death rate for infants is obtained if we compare the total number of infant deaths not to one thousand of the general population, but to one thousand births in the same year." In the presentation of infantile mortality rates, stillbirths are usually excluded, and this practice has been followed in the present case. The only exception in this study to the above method of expressing the infant death rate is in the statement above from the United States Census, in which the infant death rate for the registration area for 1900 is stated as 159.3 per one thousand living population under age one.

It has frequently been argued that a high infant mortality has a selective influence; in other words, that it acts as a "weeding-out process," and hence tends to reduce mortality at later ages. Doctor Newshoime, with the records of the registrar-general of births, deaths, and marriages as a basis, concludes as follows: Infant mortality is the most sensitive index we possess of social welfare and of sanitary administration, especially under urban conditions. A heavy infant mortality implies a heavier death rate up to five years of age; and right up to adult life the districts suffering from a heavy child mortality have higher death rates than the districts whose infant mortality is low. A careful study of the death rate in England and Wales during the last fifty years, at each of the first five years of life, leaves it doubtful whether any appreciably greater selection or "weeding out' is exercised by a heavier than by a lighter infantile mortality. Any such effect, if it exists, is concealed behind the over-whelming influence exerted by the evil environment to which children are exposed in districts of high infant mortality. It is strictly correct, therefore, to say that a high infant mortality implies a high prevalence of the conditions which determine national inferiority.

SIGNIFICANCE

Although the single largest factor in reducing the rate of maternal deaths from childbirth occurred after the germ theory of disease was elucidated in the 1860s, when physicians and midwives attending births began to wash their hands and sanitize equipment, infant mortality rates decreased at a slower pace. As the report documents, the commonly held assumption that high infant mortality rates would leave only the hardiest in a population to survive, therefore leading to lower mortality rates at later ages, was false. High mortality rates in infancy among a population led to high mortality rates across all ages within a specific group. The alarming statistic—nearly one in six dead before the age of one—gave progressives the proof they needed to fight harder for an intensive public health campaign aimed at reducing infant mortality rates.

Neill's final statement in this excerpt is a direct stab at factory owners and industrialists who claimed that wage slavery, factory conditions, pollution, and poverty in urban centers with high concentrations of immigrants were all simply part of economic progress and capitalism. In addition, the focus of this Report on Wage Earners was to examine the impact of mothers' factory work on infant mortality; by linking labor to infant deaths, the report not only gave an objective, statistical viewpoint on the relationship between mothers' labor and child deaths, but also provided progressives with a moral tool to use against industrialists.

In 1912, the same year this report was issued, the Children's Bureau was formed, to help infants and children via improvements in the environment, housing standards, nutrition, education, and medical services. By 1949, infant mortality rates had declined 49 percent; by 1997, eighty-five years after this report, infant mortality for children under twelve months in the United States had dropped to one in 140. The Children's Bureau was eliminated in 1969, largely a function of bureaucratic reorganization; by this time maternal and child health was treated as part of a wider public health campaign, with programs such as Women, Infants and Children (WIC) and Children's Health Insurance Programs (CHIP) helping to improve infant mortality and morbidity rates.

FURTHER RESOURCES
Books
McGerr, Michael. *A Fierce Discontent; The Rise and Fall of the Progressive Movement in America, 1870–1920.* New York: Free Press, 2003.

Periodicals
Almgren, Gunnar, Susan Kemp, and Alison Eisinger. "Appraising the Legacy of Hull House: The Role of the United States Children's Bureau in the American Mortality Transition." *Center for Studies in Demography and Ecology Working Papers (University of Washington)* (1999) No. 99-11.

Typhoid Mary Has Reappeared

Quarantine and Public Health

Newspaper article

By: Anonymous

Date: April 4, 1915

Source: "'Typhoid Mary' Has Reappeared: Human Culture Tube, Herself Immune, Spreads the Disease Wherever She Goes." *New York Times* (April 4, 1915): SM3.

About the Author: This unattributed article was written by a staff writer for the *New York Times*, a daily newspaper with a circulation of over one million readers worldwide.

INTRODUCTION

Mary Mallon, a known carrier of typhoid, refused to stop behaving in ways that risked spreading the disease and forced the government to jail her to protect the public health. The first person in North America to be identified as a healthy typhoid carrier, Mallon was an Irish-born cook who worked for wealthy New Yorkers. In 1906, she was employed in the rented summer home of banker Charles Henry Warren in Oyster Bay, Long Island, when typhoid fever struck six people in the household of eleven. The owners of the rental house hired investigators to determine the source of the epidemic. The detectives traced forty-seven cases of typhoid and three deaths to Mallon.

A contagious bacterial disease, typhoid had a fatality rate of 10 percent, although milder cases also occurred. Typhoid bacteria remain in the intestine, liver, and bile ducts until they are transmitted via urine and feces. Victims suffer fever, chills, headaches, malaise, severe cramping, and diarrhea or constipation. The symptoms often continue for over a month. While sick, persons with typhoid weaken and became susceptible to complications such as dehydration or intestinal bleeding.

As a single, working class woman, Mallon needed to work in order to support herself. She was reputedly an excellent cook, but was unaware of the germ theory of disease and of the simple measures, such as hand washing, necessary to prevent spreading disease. Investigators discovered that 30 percent of the bacteria excreted by Mallon in her urine were the bacteria that cause typhoid.

In March 1907, New York City health officials literally dragged Mallon kicking and screaming into a city ambulance. They deposited her in a small cottage on North Brother Island that formed part of the grounds of an isolation hospital. Although she was released for brief periods, Mallon died in captivity in 1938 at the age of sixty-nine, after spending twenty-six years in her island prison.

■ PRIMARY SOURCE

"TYPHOID MARY" has reappeared. With her has come the usual epidemic of the fever to which she is immune. This time she brought her apparently inexhaustible supply of typhoid bacilli to no less extended a field than the Sloane Maternity Hospital, where, under an assumed name, she had obtained a position as cook.

Here she was dispensing germs daily with the food served up to the patients, employees, doctors, and nurses of the hospital—a total of 281 persons. Twenty-five of this number were attacked by typhoid before the epidemic could be checked....

...At present she is back on North Brother Island, from which she was released nearly three years ago....

...Thanks to the untiring sleuthing of Dr. George A. Soper, sanitary expert of this city, Mary Mallon's case had been called to the attention of the health authorities and rapidly became famous the world over.

This "human culture tube," herself immune to typhoid, but a peripatetic breeding ground for the bacilli, was proved by Dr. Soper to have been responsible for at least seven typhoid epidemics and she has since produced some more. After considerable skirmishing, the authorities landed Mary in 1907 at North Brother Island, against which confinement she vigorously protested. She appealed to the courts and brought a suit for her release and another suit for $50,000, neither of which was successful.

She was finally released on parole. The conditions of her release were that she should report at frequent intervals to the Board of Health and should, under no circumstances, engage in her former profession as cook. For a short time she complied. But after about three months she returned with the complaint that her profession being taken from her, she had lost her chances of making a living for herself, and the city should be responsible. So a position was obtained for her as laundress, but it was only a short time before "Typhoid Mary" had vanished, parole notwithstanding.

This was over two years ago. The Department of Health had heard nothing of her until the investigation of the sudden epidemic in January at the Sloane Hospital... Dr. Soper was called in and soon had the disease under control....

[Soper says:] "Mary Mallon is said to feel that she is the victim of an unjust punishment. I think that if she could get rid of the idea that she is being persecuted and would answer some questions concerning her history, that I might be able to help her in various ways. As it is, I'm afraid that liberty is an impossible privilege to allow her. This, however, is a matter for the Board of Health to decide, and I have no desire to pass my view upon it."

"What is to be done about all the other carriers of whose existence we are for the most part unaware? Shut them up? Isolate them, as in the case of Mary Mallon? No, not if they will act intelligently. But something must be done if typhoid is to be stamped out in this country. And typhoid must be exterminated. It is the last of the filth diseases which formerly ran like wildfire through the civilized world."...

SIGNIFICANCE

The case of Mary Mallon raised serious constitutional questions. The Bill of Rights protects Americans from being seized by the government and held without a jury trial. Mallon's case never came to trial because she committed no crime according to the existing legal statutes. While it may have been morally wrong to transmit typhoid, no law made it illegal to do so. Additionally, no law allowed New York City to confine Mallon indefinitely.

Typhoid Mary also represented a clear-cut case of the necessity to sometimes infringe upon individual rights in order to protect the public. By the beginning of the twentieth century, most Americans agreed that the government should act to prevent disease even when such action occasionally infringed upon the liberty of those who might have stood in the way of such disease prevention. Quarantines were viewed as the price some individuals had to pay to ensure the health of the majority.

The case of Typhoid Mary also represented a turning point for the field of public health. The identification of Mallon gave support to the progressive idea of better living through science. Mallon's case demonstrated that it was possible for humans to conquer disease through the new process of testing for bacteria. Finding Mallon showed that science could identify ostensibly healthy people who could potentially spread disease to the general public.

After Mallon's case, authorities did indeed track down hundreds of New Yorkers who were accused of harboring typhoid bacilli and transmitting the germs to susceptible people. While not all of these typhoid carriers were cooperative with government officials, no other person suffered the treatment that Mallon experienced. Typhoid Mary is unique in American history as the only person to be quarantined indefinitely as a public health menace.

Federal quarantine legislation was first passed by Congress in 1878 in an effort to contain the yellow fever epidemics that occurred in the later nineteenth century. The Public Health Service Act of 1944 clearly defined federal control of quarantine. Traditionally, state health departments were charged with enacting quarantines and compliance by citizens was usually voluntary. Quarantines were used in the twentieth century to help stem the spread of diseases, including typhoid fever, measles, tuberculosis, influenza, and polio, within the United States. Diseases from abroad were held at bay by establishing quarantine stations at every major U.S. port, airport, and border crossing. The term quarantine was clarified to mean separation of a vehicle, person, animal, or material suspected of exposure or carrying a contagious disease, while the term isolation was clarified to mean exclusion of a person or animal who is ill with a disease.

When the Centers for Disease Control and Prevention (CDC) assumed responsibility for quarantine in 1967, the focus broadened to include surveillance of disease outbreaks worldwide. In the modern era, air travel and transport has the potential to spread communicable diseases rapidly. As a result, quarantine has again come to the forefront of scientific concern. In 2004, after the emergence of severe acute respiratory syndrome (SARS) in Asia, President George W. Bush added SARS to the list of diseases included in an executive order for which quarantine can be used. The list also includes include cholera, diphtheria, infectious tuberculosis, plague, smallpox, yellow fever, and viral hemorrhagic fevers such as the disease caused by the Ebola virus. In 2005, public health officials considered the potential necessity for quarantine measures in the event of a pandemic of avian (H5N1) influenza.

When contagious diseases such as Ebola break out among the population, health care workers must quarantine the sick to keep the infection from spreading to others. AP/WIDE WORLD PHOTOS.

Web sites

Centers for Disease Control and Prevention. "Isolation and Quarantine." <http://www.cdc.gov/ncidod/dq/sars_facts/ isolationquarantine.pdf>(accessed October 17, 2005).

NOVA. "History of Quarantine." <http://www.pbs.org/ wgbh/nova/typhoid/quarantine.html> (accessed October 17, 2005).

FURTHER RESOURCES

Books

Leavitt, Judith Walzer. *Typhoid Mary: Captive to the Public's Health.* Boston: Beacon, 1996.

Markel, Howard. *Quarantine!: East European Jewish Immigrants and the New York City Epidemics of 1892.* Baltimore: Johns Hopkins, 1999.

Sanitation

William Osler and Public Health

Book excerpt

By: William Osler

Date: 1921

Source: William Osler, "Sanitation," in *The Evolution of Modern Medicine*. New Haven, Ct.: Yale University Press, 1921.

About the Author: William Osler (1848–1919) was "the best known physician in the English-speaking world at the turn of the [twentieth] century." Appointed physician and chief at the Johns Hopkins Hospital in 1888, William Osler revolutionized modern medical education in the United States based on principles used to train physicians in England and Germany. He initiated the practice of teaching physicians about disease by bringing them to the patient's bedside, believing that they learned best by doing.

INTRODUCTION

This excerpt from the medical educator and policy-maker William Osler's book on the evolution of modern medicine uses a famous example of the importance of public health measures to society by showing its crucial role in a massive public works project—the building of the Panama Canal. Endemic diseases such as yellow fever, plague, and malaria had frustrated early attempts to build a canal through the Isthmus of Panama by disabling and killing thousands of project workers and managers. Osler described the work of Dr. William Crawford Gorgas (1854–1920), chief of sanitary affairs for the project, who made the canal possible by organizing public health and sanitation efforts. (Earlier, Gorgas had protected the health of U.S. soldiers with sanitary measures during the Spanish-American War.) Osler pointed out that it was not ignorance of public health principles that had doomed earlier efforts to build the canal, but a lack of effective public health organization and the thorough implementation of disease control measures.

Osler went on to further point out that it was not ignorance of the science regarding the value of sanitation that had resulted in typhoid fever epidemics in the U.S. and Canada in the early years of the twentieth century. Instead it was the lack of public health infrastructure and organization in an otherwise sophisticated and "sensible" society. This lack of infrastructure, he argued, was fostered by a corresponding lack of a sense of common purpose and interest in the common good where public health was concerned.

Osler lived and taught medicine according to practical principles emphasizing organization and implementation. He applied these principles in using health knowledge in the service of broader social progress and public good.

Trash collection helped to reduce people's exposure to disease-ridden bacteria and fungus. In the days before garbage trucks, men loaded trash into carts and hauled it away. ©SCHEUFLER COLLECTION/CORBIS.

PRIMARY SOURCE

When, in 1904, the United States undertook to complete the Canal, everyone felt that the success or failure was largely a matter of sanitary control. The necessary knowledge existed, but under the circumstances could it be made effective? Many were doubtful. Fortunately, there was at the time in the United States Army a man who had already served an apprenticeship in Cuba, and to whom more than to anyone else was due the disappearance of yellow fever from that island. To a man, the profession in the United States felt that could Dr. Gorgas be given full control of the sanitary affairs of the Panama Zone, the health problem, which meant the Canal problem, could be solved. There was at first a serious difficulty relating to the necessary administrative control by a sanitary officer. In an interview which Welch and I had with President Roosevelt, he keenly felt this difficulty and promised to do his best to have it rectified. It is an open secret that at first, as was perhaps only natural, matters did not go very smoothly, and it took a year or more to get properly organized. Yellow fever recurred on the Isthmus in 1904 and in the early part of 1905. It was really a colossal task in itself to undertake the cleaning of the city of Panama, which had been for centuries a pest-house, the mortality in which, even after the American occupation, reached during one month the rate of 71 per thousand living. There have been a great many brilliant illustrations of the practical application of science in preserving the health of a community and in saving life, but it is safe to say that, considering the circumstances, the past history, and the extraordinary difficulties to be overcome, the work accomplished by the Isthmian Canal Commission is unique. The year 1905 was devoted to organization; yellow fever was got rid of, and at the end of the year the total mortality among the whites had fallen to 8 per thousand, but among the blacks it was still high, 44. For three years, with a progressively increasing staff which had risen to above 40,000, of whom more than 12,000 were white, the death rate progressively fell.

Of the six important tropical diseases, plague, which reached the Isthmus one year, was quickly held in check. Yellow fever, the most dreaded of them all, never recurred. Beri-beri, which in 1906 caused sixty-eight deaths, has gradually disappeared. The hookworm disease, ankylostomiasis, has steadily decreased. From the very outset, malaria has been taken as the measure of sanitary efficiency. Throughout the French occupation it was the chief enemy to be considered, not only because of its fatality, but on account of the prolonged incapacity following infection. In 1906, out of every 1000 employees there were admitted to the hospital from malaria 821; in 1907, 424; in 1908, 282; in 1912, 110; in 1915, 51; in 1917, 14. The fatalities from the disease have fallen from 233 in 1906 to 154 in 1907, to 73 in 1908 and to 7 in 1914. The death rate for malarial fever per 1000 population sank from 8.49 in 1906 to 0.11 in 1918. Dysentery, next to malaria the most serious of the tropical diseases in the Zone, caused 69 deaths in 1906; 48 in 1907; in 1908, with nearly 44,000, only 16 deaths, and in 1914, 4. But it is when the general figures are taken that we see the extraordinary reduction that has taken place. Out of every 1000 engaged in 1908 only a third of the number died that died in 1906, and half the number that died in 1907.

In 1914, the death rate from disease among white males had fallen to 3.13 per thousand. The rate among the 2674 American women and children connected with the Commission was only 9.72 per thousand. But by far the most gratifying reduction is among the blacks, among

whom the rate from disease had fallen to the surprisingly low figure in 1912 of 8.77 per thousand; in 1906 it was 47 per thousand. A remarkable result is that in 1908 the combined tropical diseases—malaria, dysentery and beri-beri—killed fewer than the two great killing diseases of the temperate zone, pneumonia and tuberculosis—127 in one group and 137 in the other. The whole story is expressed in two words, *effective organization,* and the special value of this experiment in sanitation is that it has been made, and made successfully, in one of the great plague spots of the world....

One disease has still a special claim upon the public in this country. Some fourteen or fifteen years ago, in an address on the problem of typhoid fever in the United States, I contended that the question was no longer in the hands of the profession. In season and out of season we had preached salvation from it in volumes which fill state reports, public health journals and the medical periodicals. Though much has been done, typhoid fever remains a question of grave national concern. You lost in this state in 1911 from typhoid fever 154 lives; every one sacrificed needlessly, every one a victim of neglect and incapacity. Between 1200 and 1500 persons had a slow, lingering illness. A nation of contradictions and paradoxes—a clean people, by whom personal hygiene is carefully cultivated, but it has displayed in matters of public sanitation a carelessness simply criminal: a sensible people, among whom education is more widely diffused than in any other country, supinely acquiesces in conditions often shameful beyond expression. The solution of the problem is not very difficult. What has been done elsewhere can be done here. It is not so much in the cities, though here too the death rate is still high, but in the smaller towns and rural districts, in many of which the sanitary conditions are still those of the Middle Ages.

SIGNIFICANCE

William Osler has been the subject of several biographies aimed at showing how one individual can have such sweeping influence on the development of an entire profession. As vitally important as was his contribution, to the current generation he is essentially a "medical icon" whose work is now embedded in the everyday learning and practice of medicine. The essence of Osler's contribution was in his comprehensive, holistic, and empathetic interest in human health, which developed during a simpler time when a single thinker was able to span much of medical knowledge. Medicine is now scientific, compartmentalized, and technical, and dominated by specialists. Some physicians have lamented that a broad and influential career such as Osler's is "no longer available" to contemporary physicians.

Public health, however, remains a very broad and multifaceted field that is somewhat congenial to generalists and medical activists. With his multifactorial outlook on life and health, Osler was keenly interested in public health and the organization of society to deal with health threats. In the excerpt, he admires the way in which the U.S. government confronted such threats in Cuba and Panama. He seems puzzled by the lack of motivation of civilian society to take strong preventive action in dealing with unsanitary conditions that result in disease outbreaks. He expresses impatience with the complacency of society in not moving to eradicate obvious threats, such as typhoid fever, that could be alleviated with simple sanitary environmental practices.

Osler's critique of the public health and sanitation practices common in the U.S. and Canada are interesting because it remains relevant to contemporary society. Currently we have the knowledge to understand the spread of epidemics from AIDS to SARS, and appreciate the need to deal proactively with potential threats from bioterrorism to avian influenza. Yet it seems that when public health threats can be couched in either military or economic terms, policymakers begin to strongly focus on improving public health infrastructure and fully funding disease monitoring and control capabilities such as the U.S. Public Health Service and the Centers for Disease Control and Prevention. Expert knowledge about dire threats to human life by itself has historically not galvanized politicians to act in the interest of public health.

For example, with regard to a potential avian influenza (bird flu) outbreak, it became clear to economic analysts in early 2005 that an epidemic on the scale of the 1918 influenza epidemic could bring about a collapse in the globally integrated economy. After that analysis, there was suddenly a great increase in discussion, planning, and establishment of contingency supplies of vaccines and antiviral medications. Yet, expert predictions of another flu pandemic similar to the one in 1918 have been routinely issued periodically by world health authorities ever since the 1918 catastrophic outbreak occurred.

In 2001, a bioterrorist attack on the U.S. with anthrax electrified the country and caused federal, state, and local officials to review public health infrastructure and local capabilities to deal with another attack. Only a few people died from anthrax in that assault, yet the military nature of the attack outraged policymakers and brought about a general improvement in funding and organization of U.S. public health. In this case, bioterrorism warnings had frequently been issued by experts long before 2001, but it took a real attack to make bioterrorism more than a hypothetical possibility and spur resolute action.

Having seen the effective way in which people could come to grips with health threats when economic and military issues were at stake, as in the invasion of Cuba and the Panama Canal construction, Osler wanted to channel the same kind of concerted action and energy into confronting the public health issues of everyday life. Perhaps a short supply of Osler's characteristic energy and empathy explains the inaction of the society of his time and ours, in the face of health threats and suffering that have befallen others, but have not yet hit home.

FURTHER RESOURCES

Books

Bliss, Michael. *William Osler: A Life in Medicine.* Oxford: Oxford University Press, 1999.

Cushing, Harvey. *Life of Sir William Osler.* London: Oxford University Press, 1925.

Osler, William. *The Principles and Practice of Medicine.* 6th edition. New York: D. Appleton, 1906.

Periodicals

Groen, Frances K. "Three Who Made an Association: I. Sir William Osler, 1849–1919, II. George Milbry Gould, 1848–1922, III. Margaret Ridley Charlton, 1858–1931, and the Founding of the Medical Library Association, Philadelphia, 1898." *Bulletin of the Medical Library Association* 84 (July 1996): 311–319.

Web sites

University of Medicine and Dentistry of New Jersey. "Sir William Osler." <http://www4.umdnj.edu/camlbweb/osler.html> (accessed December 3, 2005).

Preliminary Survey and Current Data

Public Health Reaches Counties

Official document

By: Alabama Department of Public Health

Date: 1937

Source: Alabama Department of Public Health. *Manual for the Conduct of County Health Departments.* Wetumpka, Ala.: Wetumpka Printing, 1937.

About the Author: Alabama's Department of Public Health was created by the state legislature in 1875. County health departments were established the following year.

INTRODUCTION

When it was first settled, the territory that became the United States was quite rural: Population was sparse; settlements were made up of groups of homesteads, farms, and the like that were, for the most part, widely separated. Life in the New World was hard and filled with physical labor. Life expectancy was short by contemporary standards, averaging only forty to fifty years. Disease, even when epidemic or transmitted by animals or insects, tended to concentrate in areas of dense population and rarely jumped from one location to another. Small settlements kept outbreaks of illness relatively confined.

As the Industrial Revolution spread from Europe to America, major demographic shifts began to occur. People moved away from rural areas and into cities, where jobs were plentiful. There they mixed with an influx of immigrants, who also flocked to burgeoning industrial areas. People worked long hours in crowded factories and lived in decrepit, tightly clustered, poorly ventilated dwellings. There was no indoor plumbing, drinking water was often unclean, sewage and trash were dumped on the streets, and food often spoiled while it was transported from farm to city.

These conditions created a growing health crisis, forcing governments to address the problems of disease, pollution, violence, and the conditions under which they flourished. This was the dawn of the public health system in the United States, when state legislatures began to collect and monitor data about the population to assess needs and implement appropriate remedies. At the same time, scientific and medical research were rapidly improving public hygiene and discovering new ways to treat and even eradicate some major diseases of the time.

By the 1930s, health departments were organizing at the county level. The following document outlines instructions for a county health officer to assess the resources and needs of a local population.

▮ PRIMARY SOURCE

PRELIMINARY SURVEY AND CURRENT DATA

133. **Foreword:** The county health officer, upon assuming his duties, should spend the first few weeks visiting the various parts of the county, during which time he should begin collecting the information suggested below. As time goes on, the missing items and those of lesser importance can be secured. At all times, the data should be kept current and as accurate as possible. As far as practicable, the information should be collected through personal contact. The collection of this information offers an excellent entree, and an opportunity to explain the purpose and work of a county health department.

134. **General:**

Pertinent facts in history of county.

Area in square miles.

Topography and character of soil.

Political subdivisions and natural community groupings of population, government and county, civil districts, incorporated and unincorporated communities.

Name, position and address of public officials.

Principal industries and number of persons employed.

Assessed valuation—real, personal, corporations— total.

Public revenue—county, improvement districts, schools, cities, and special tax, if any.

Income—per capita, per family.

Expenditures chargeable to public revenue.

135. **Statistics:**

Population—total, and by towns, civil districts, or other political subdivisions.

Number native white, colored, and foreign-born by nationalities.

Population figures should include last two federal censuses and estimate for current years.

Morbidity, mortality, and birth statistics for last 5 years.

Name and address of local registrars.

136. **Rural Districts:**

Population—total, by political subdivisions, and by rural community groupings.

Number of homes.

General housing conditions and economic status.

Number of home owners.

Number of homes with safe water supply.

Number of homes with sanitary excreta disposal.

Number of homes effectively screened.

Principal farm pursuits and products.

137. **Cities (each city and village):**

General:

Population figures analyzed as indicated.

Brief description and pertinent facts in history.

Principal industries and number of persons employed.

Number of homes.

Number of home owners, tenants.

General housing conditions and economic status.

Form of government; officials—name, position and address.

Copy of sanitary code.

Public revenue, expenditures chargeable to public revenue.

Special:

(a) Public Water Supply:

Source, method of purification, operating control, sanitary analyses.

Number of connections, percentage of population served.

(b) Private Water Supplies:

Number, population served.

Sanitary quality.

(c) Excreta Disposal:

Public sewerage system—number connected, disposal of effluent.

Cesspools—number, population using.

Privies—number, types, population using.

Scavenger service—type, population served.

(d) Garbage:

Method storage, collection, disposal, percentage of population served.

(e) Milk Supply:

Quantity consumed; amount raw; amount pasteurized, sanitary quality of each.

Number of cows tuberculin tested.

Number of dairy farms in good sanitary condition.

Copy of milk ordinance.

(f) Morbidity, mortality, and birth statistics for last five years.

138. **School System:**

Population—school age, enrollment, daily attendance, total.

School districts—number rural, number town, total.

School buildings—number rural, number town, total.

Safe water supply—number rural, number town, total.

Sanitary drinking facilities—number rural, number town, total.

Sanitary lavatory facilities—number rural, number town, total.

Safe excreta disposal—number rural, number town, total.

Proper heating, lighting and seating facilities—number rural, number town, total.

Name and address of teachers, school board members.

Health service, health education, recreation.

139. **Churches:**

Safe water supply—number.

Safe excreta disposal—number.

Name and address of pastors.

140. **Institutions:**

Hospitals—type, bed capacity, requirements for admission.

Sanatoria—type, bed capacity, requirements for admission.

Charity homes—type, capacity, population, requirements for admission.

Others—type, capacity, population, requirements for admission.

141. **Health Service (past and present):**

Cities and County—personnel, budget, program, activities, accomplishments.

Schools—personnel, budget, program, activities, accomplishments.

142. **Physicians:**

Number in active practice, name and address.

Professional organizations—officers, name, address.

Public health activities.

143. **Dentists:**

Number in active practice, name and address.

Professional organizations—officers, name, address.

Public health activities.

144. **Organizations:**

Private, civic, commercial, community, or other organizations: Number, purpose, officers, name, address.

Note: The above data should be recorded on cards and cross-indexed for ready reference.

145. **Laws and Ordinances:** The health officer should become acquainted with the principal state health laws and should secure a copy of all state health regulations and local health ordinances. State health laws and regulations are contained in the Compilation of Public Health Laws, available to all county health departments.

146. **Individual Homes:** Time should not be taken in the beginning for a detailed survey, but the family folder should be completed when the home is visited for any other purpose.

SIGNIFICANCE

The need for a public health system to curb epidemics was reflected in Civil War casualty statistics:

disease killed roughly twice as many soldiers as wounds from battle. Among the primary causes of death were typhoid, malaria, (often indistinguishable in the years before blood tests and called "typhomalaria"), measles, respiratory infections, and diarrheal diseases.

The very first public health efforts, enacted locally, were aimed at reducing the infectious diseases that arrived with immigrants—particularly smallpox and measles. Local regulations were established to inspect ships as they arrived and to quarantine those on vessels where infection was found.

In rural areas, smaller-scale systems drafted local regulations regarding sanitation and hygiene. Inspectors traveled to dwellings and businesses in their assigned areas, making visual inspections and gathering data, assessing fines and penalties for those out of compliance.

Beyond the local loosely organized public health commissions and inspectors, however, was a great need for the development of a broader system—America was expanding rapidly and developing a host of social and medical problems as a result. Not only did epidemics erupt in rapidly growing cities and industrialized areas, there were increased outbreaks of violence, increasing use of alcohol, poor working conditions, and widespread child labor.

As women entered the workforce, they worked to earn suffrage and began to agitate for political, social, and health reforms. Schools of nursing and public health clinics were established, producing public health nurses who helped reform maternal and infant care, dramatically decreasing mortality for mothers and infants.

There was also a growing recognition of the need to standardize disparate local public sanitation programs and to train public health officers. Other professionals also played important roles: physicians and research scientists to diagnose illness and develop treatments; civil engineers to create public sewage, trash, and drinking water systems; public health nurses to oversee health, wellness, and nutrition programs; local health inspectors and surveyors; and legislators and government officials to draft and enforce regulations.

By the early decades of the twentieth century, the public health system had become part of America's social fabric. Using media campaigns to educate people about immunizations and illness-prevention programs, it was a driving force in controlling tuberculosis, diphtheria, polio, and rubella. Public health agencies created wellness centers, developed maternal and infant clinics, and created educational programs. With the Social Security Act of 1935, the public health system became even more stable, and remains an integral part of the American health system.

FURTHER RESOURCES

Books

Gostin, Lawrence O. *Public Health Law and Ethics: A Reader.* Berkeley, Calif.: University of California Press, 2002.

Periodicals

"Achievements in Public Health, 1900–1999: Changes in the Public Health System." *MMWR: Morbidity and Mortality Weekly Report* 48, no. 50 (December 24, 1999): 1141–1147.

"Achievements in Public Health, 1900–1999: Healthier Mothers and Babies" *MMWR: Morbidity and Mortality Weekly Report* 48, no. 38 (October 1, 1999): 849–858.

"Achievements in Public Health, 1900–1999: Safer and Healthier Foods" *MMWR: Morbidity and Mortality Weekly Report* 48, no. 40 (October 15, 1999): 905–913.

"Ten Great Public Health Achievements" *MMWR: Morbidity and Mortality Weekly Report.* 48, no. 12 (April 2, 1999): 241–243.

Web sites

Jefferson County Department of Health. "History: Public Health Before 1917." <http://www.jcdh.org/default. asp?ID=10> (accessed November 11, 2005).

March of Dimes

Portrait of Donald Anderson

Poster

By: Anonymous

Date: January 8, 1946

Source: "Portrait of Donald Anderson." March of Dimes.

INTRODUCTION

The charitable medical organization now known as the *March of Dimes* was created by President Franklin Delano Roosevelt in 1937. It was originally called the National Foundation for Infantile Paralysis; its original mission was to generate funds for the treatment of polio. The nickname March of Dimes was the result of a play on words by a comedian named Eddie Cantor. He altered the name of a well known newsreel called *The March of Time* and called the fundraising campaign for which he was a celebrity spokesperson the *March of Dimes*, suggesting that every person in America send a dime to President Franklin Roosevelt at the White House, to pledge their support for the fight to conquer polio. This suggestion was so widely adopted that nearly two million dollars were raised by the charity within about a week, and nearly one sixth of that was sent directly to the president. The National Foundation for Infantile Paralysis adopted a multi-pronged approach to eradication of polio: it funded research on the types and etiology of the disease, on determination of the modes of transmission and incubation of the virus, on the viruses' epidemiology, and on its treatment. The foundation also trained and recruited health care professionals to respond to local outbreaks and epidemics, much like a contemporary emergency and disaster relief organization.

One of the unique aspects of the fundraising methodology for the National Foundation (referred to interchangeably as the National Foundation and the March of Dimes) was its humanity and directness: it targeted the average citizen, acknowledging that a contribution of even a dime would have a positive impact on the fight against polio. Rather than seeking corporate donors or soliciting the wealthy, the March of Dimes sought to empower the general population, carrying out their agenda on a grassroots level. Collection buckets were even passed through the audiences at movie theaters. This was also the first time that fundraising campaigns used celebrity spokespeople. By the early 1940s, the March of Dimes had begun using a poster campaign as a means of encouraging contributions; they used images of happy, healthy children who had genuinely benefited from the work of the charity. In 1954, the March of Dimes helped to spearhead the largest clinical trial ever conducted (at that time) in America. Jonas Salk (1914–1995), whose research had received funding from the National Foundation, had created a vaccine that was hoped to prevent polio, and it was widely field tested. In 1955, the National Foundation announced the successful result of the clinical trial, and the vaccine's ability to prevent polio. After this success, the National Foundation shifted focus, and began to study birth defects and premature births in the United States.

PRIMARY SOURCE

PORTRAIT OF DONALD ANDERSON
See primary source image.

PRIMARY SOURCE

Portrait of Donald Anderson. Five-year-old Donald Anderson poses in front of a 1946 March of Dimes poster that featured his successful battle with infantile paralysis. The poster, with the headline, "Your dimes did this for me!," appeared in magazines, clinics, and other settings. ©BETTMANN/CORBIS.

SIGNIFICANCE

The March of Dimes "poster child" campaign successfully carried the organization's message until 1986, when children chosen to participate in promotions were re-designated March of Dimes National Ambassadors.

The March of Dimes has remained steadfast in its commitment to ensuring the health and well being of children, and of eliminating causes of death among the very young. At present, the focus of the March of Dimes is threefold: to prevent birth defects, to eliminate premature births, and to dramatically lower the rate of infant mortality. It seeks to accomplish its goals by funding and supporting research, by creating grassroots educational campaigns, by conducting activities on the local level, and by engaging actively in advocacy at the state and federal levels. One of their large, ongoing programs regarding the elimination of birth defects concerns the use of folic acid as a means of preventing neural tube defects. The March of Dimes is engaged in an active educational campaign informing women of the need to take an appropriate dose of folic acid daily, beginning before pregnancy and continuing through early gestation. According to data published by the Centers for Disease Control and Prevention, nearly three quarters of all neural tube defects could be prevented by this one simple measure (taking a daily 400mcg dose of folic acid before conception and during the first trimester of pregnancy).

In addition to the prevention of neural tube defects, the March of Dimes is engaged in the process of determining the etiology (cause or origin) of birth defects caused by either genetics or the environment. Many birth defects are caused by exposure to environmental teratogens (substances or conditions capable of causing birth defects), such as tobacco or alcohol use, many types of prescription or over-the-counter medications, and some types of chemicals to which a person may become exposed. Birth defects can be manifested by any of several different means: the infant may have a physiological defect or abnormality, such as missing limbs or digits, cleft lip or soft palate malformation, neural tube defects, heart, circulatory, organ, or bodily system malformations; there may be an endocrine or metabolic abnormality, such as phenylketonuria (PKU); a developing embryo could be exposed to rubella (also called German measles), cytomegalovirus (also called CMV), HIV/AIDS, or any of several sexually transmitted diseases through its mother during the early stages of gestation.

As a result of ever-advancing technology, it is now possible to identify a significant number of birth defects during the early stages of gestation. In families where there is a risk of inherited disorder or in those in which there is an absence of family history (as in the case of a parent who was adopted and knows no history of biological origins), pre-pregnancy genetic counseling and screening may be recommended. For those who are already pregnant and present with risk factors such as potential heritability, lack of historical data, advanced maternal age, presence of a child in the family with an inherited disorder or other form of birth defect, people with teratogen exposure, women with a prior history of birth complications or miscarriages, or women who have an abnormal ultrasound or blood test associated with the pregnancy, further testing may be recommended in order to rule out birth defects.

The March of Dimes also advocates passage of the PREEMIE Act (S.707/H.R. 2861) before the U.S. Congress, that would authorize the National Institutes of Health and the Centers for Disease Control and Prevention to expand research into the causes of premature birth and develop strategies to prevent it, along with providing additional health services for those at risk for preterm birth.

FURTHER RESOURCES
Books
Black, Kathryn. *In the Shadow of Polio: A Personal and Social History*. Reading, MA: Addison-West, 1996.

Web sites
March of Dimes. "Study Finds Markers for Premature Birth Risk at the Molecular Level." <http://www.marchofdimes.com/aboutus/14458_14991.asp> (accessed January 18, 2006).

MayoClinic.com."Prenatal Testing: What's Involved and Who Should Consider It?" <http://www.mayoclinic.com/health/prenatal-testing/PR00014> (accessed January 18, 2006).

OTIS: Organization of Teratology Information Specialists. "Fact Sheets." <http://otispregnancy.org/otis_fact_sheets.asp> (accessed January 18, 2006).

OTIS: Organization of Teratology Information Specialists. "Teratology, Information Specialists, and OTIS." <http://otispregnancy.org/otis_about_us.asp> (accessed January 18, 2006).

Constitution of the World Health Organization, Chapters I and II

Journal article

By: World Health Organzation, Interim Commission

Date: October 1947

Source: World Health Organization, Interim Commission. "Constitution of the World Health Organization." *Chronicle of the World Health Organization* 1, no. 1/2 (October 1947): 29–30.

About the Author: The Commission of the World Health Organization (WHO) was established in 1946 to assume the functions of previous international health organizations and to oversee the transfer of their powers into the WHO. The commission organized the first World Health Assembly in 1948, with representatives and advisors from eighteen nations: Australia, Brazil, Canada, China, Egypt, France, Great Britain, India, Liberia, Mexico, Norway, the Netherlands, Peru, Ukraine, U.S.A., USSR, Venezuela, and Yugoslavia. The commission was retired on August 31, 1948, after the establishment of the WHO.

INTRODUCTION

The idea of international cooperation in public health dates to 1851, when the first in a series of international sanitary conferences was held in Paris. The inaugural convention sought to establish rules for the inspection and isolation, if necessary, of cargo ships and their crews. In response to rising concern over the spread of infectious diseases such as typhoid, yellow fever, and, especially, cholera, delegates argued the relative merits of quarantine over sanitation, and debated whether the most likely route of infection was person-to-person contagion or "miasmata"— toxic, airborne vapors. Although a consensus on quarantine policy was reached, the agreement was never officially adopted.

In 1903 the eleventh conference laid the groundwork for the first global health organization, the Office Internationale d'Hygiène Publique (OIHP), which was finally established in 1907. The League of Nations launched its Health Organization in 1920, and the two groups joined forces during World War II as the United Nations Relief and Rehabilitation Administration (UNRRA), headquartered in Washington, D.C. After the war their work was taken over by WHO and the United Nations International Children's Emergency Fund (UNICEF).

WHO emerged from the International Health Conference in 1946 and its constitution was signed on July 22 of that year. The First World Health Assembly convened on June 24, 1948, and its constitution was enacted on April 7, an anniversary now celebrated as World Health Day.

▮ PRIMARY SOURCE

ANNEX 1.
CONSTITUTION OF THE WORLD HEALTH ORGANIZATION

THE STATE parties to this Constitution declare, in conformity with the Charter of the United Nations, that the following principles are basic to the happiness, harmonious relations, and security of all peoples:

Health is a state of complete physical, mental and social well-being, and not merely the absence of disease or infirmity.

The enjoyment of the highest attainable standard of health is one of the fundamental rights of every human being without distinction of race, political belief, economic, or social condition.

The health of all peoples is fundamental to the attainment of peace and security and is dependent upon the fullest co-operation of individuals and States.

The achievement of any State in the promotion and protection of health is of value to all. Unequal development in different countries in the promotion of health and control of disease, especially communicable disease, is a common danger.

Healthy development of the child is of basic importance; the ability to live harmoniously in a changing total environment is essential to such development.

The extension to all peoples of the benefits of medical, psychological and related knowledge is essential to the fullest attainment of health.

Informed opinion and active co-operation on the part of the public are of the utmost importance in the improvement of the health of the people.

Governments have a responsibility for the health of their peoples which can be fulfilled only by the provision of adequate health and social measures.

ACCEPTING THESE PRINCIPLES, and for the purpose of co-operation among themselves and with others to promote and protect the health of all peoples, the contracting parties agree to the present Constitution and hereby establish the World Health Organization as a specialized agency within the terms of Article 57 of the Charter of the United Nations.

Chapter I—Objective
Article 1

The objective of the World Health Organization (hereinafter called the Organization) shall be the attainment by all peoples of the highest possible level of health.

Chapter II—Functions
Article 2

In order to achieve its objectives, the functions of the Organization shall be:

(a) to act as the directing and co-ordinating authority on international health work;

(b) to establish and maintain effective collaboration with the United Nations, specialized agencies, governmental health administrations, professional groups, and such other organizations as may be deemed appropriate;

(c) to assist governments, upon request, in strengthening health services;

(d) to furnish appropriate technical assistance and, in emergencies, necessary aid upon the request or acceptance of governments;

(e) to provide or assist in providing, upon the request of the United Nations, health services and facilities to special groups, such as the peoples of trust territories;

(f) to establish and maintain such administrative and technical services as may be required, including epidemiological and statistical services;

(g) to stimulate and advance work to eradicate epidemic, endemic, and other diseases;

(h) to promote, in co-operation with other specialized agencies where necessary, the prevention of accidental injuries;

(i) to promote, in co-operation with other specialized agencies where necessary, the improvement of nutrition, housing, sanitation, recreation, economic, or working conditions, and other aspects of environmental hygiene;

(j) to promote co-operation among scientific and professional groups which contribute to the advancement of health;

(k) to propose conventions, agreements, and regulations, and make recommendations with respect to international health matters and to perform such duties as may be assigned thereby to the Organization and are consistent with its objective;

(l) to promote maternal and child health and welfare and to foster the ability to live harmoniously in a changing total environment;

(m) to foster activities in the field of mental health, especially those affecting the harmony of human relations;

(n) to promote and conduct research in the field of health;

(o) to promote improved standards of teaching and training in the health, medical and related fields;

(p) to study and report on, in co-operation with other specialized agencies where necessary, administrative and social techniques affecting public health and medical care from preventive and curative points of view, including hospital services and social security;

(q) to provide information, counsel, and assistance in the field of health;

(r) to assist in developing an informed public opinion among all peoples on matters of health;

(s) to establish and revise as necessary international nomenclatures of diseases, of causes of death and of public health practices;

(t) to standardize diagnostic procedures as necessary;

(u) to develop, establish, and promote international standards with respect to food, biological, pharmaceutical, and similar products;

(v) generally to take all necessary action to attain the objective of the Organization.

SIGNIFICANCE

The WHO Constitution is an ambitious document, one that lays down a program of action for an interest common to all nations—public health. While WHO has a mission to aid developing countries, it is hampered by a limited budget and the inability to impose its will on member states. In addition, WHO does not provide health services directly, but advises, trains, researches, and funds a range of health programs within the dictates of its constitution. In its early days, the organization's focus was stratified into priorities. First were malaria, maternal and child health, tuberculosis, sexually transmitted diseases, nutrition, and sanitation; followed by improving public health administration; parasitic diseases; viral diseases; and finally, mental illness.

By 1968, WHO's focus had shifted somewhat. Because many newly independent nations, who had joined WHO as member states, were clearly in need of such support, WHO began providing more education and training to health staff, and gave more direct assistance to countries to enable them to develop their own public health programs. The group's initial priorities were—and continue to be—important.

WHO's most spectacular success has been the Intensified Smallpox Eradication Programme, a system of mass vaccinations launched in 1967. After a decade of intense international effort, the last naturally occurring case was recorded in Somalia in 1977. Similar programs for the eradication of diseases such as onchocerciasis (river blindness) and polio have made major progress as well. The malaria eradication program established in 1955, however, has been far less successful because of the lack—to date—of an effective vaccine.

New health challenges and priorities continue to emerge. In 1987, WHO and other UN organizations became part of the Joint United Nations Programme on HIV/AIDS, a concerted international effort to confront and contain the global epidemic. The need for focus on noncommunicable diseases, especially those caused by tobacco and obesity, has become apparent as well. Finally, continuing inequalities in health care around the world prompted the organization to advance its "Health for All by the Year 2000" agenda in 1978, a program whose success, clearly, has been limited.

Critics say that WHO, like many large organizations, is inefficient and run badly. And at times, it is true, the group has sorely needed inspired leadership and sound management. Nevertheless, it has achieved much in its almost six decades of existence, and much work remains if they are to meet ongoing challenges in global public health.

FURTHER RESOURCES

Books

Beigbeder, Yves, with Mahyar Nashat, Marie-Antoinette Orsini, and Jean-François Tiercy. *The World Health Organization.* The Hague: Martinus Nijhoff, 1998.

Web sites

Public Broadcasting Service. "The World's Doctor" (Air date: September 29, 2998). <http:// http://www.pbs.org/ newshour/bb/health/july-dec98/who_9-29.html> (accessed December 14, 2005).

University of Toronto. Faculty of Information Studies. "The World Health Organization Smallpox Eradication Programme." <http://choo.fis.utoronto.ca/fis/courses/ lis2102/KO.WHO.case.html> (accessed February 21, 2006).

World Health Organization. "WHO HIV/AIDS Programme." <http://www.who.int/hiv/en> (accessed December 14, 2005).

On the State of Rural Hygiene

Public Health System Provides Health Care to Rural Areas

Essay

By: Florence Nightingale

Date: 1893

Source: Lucy Ridgeley Seymer, ed. *Selected Writings of Florence Nightingale.* New York: Macmillan, 1954.

About the Author: Florence Nightingale (1820–1915)— nurse, pioneer of hospital reform, and humanitarian—was born in Florence, Italy, on May 12, 1820. She was raised in Derbyshire, England, and was tutored at home by her father. At the age of 29, she journeyed throughout Europe, with the intention of studying European hospital systems. In 1850, she began nursing school in Alexandria, Egypt, at the Institute of Saint Vincent de Paul. She concluded her nursing studies at the Institute for Protestant Deaconesses in Kaiserwerth, Germany. By 1853, she had completed her schooling and had accepted a position as Superintendent of London's Hospital for Invalid Gentlewomen. During the Crimean War, Florence Nightingale served as Director of Nursing for the war effort; she had great success in instituting sanitary methods, and in limiting the growth and spread of infection among the sick and wounded. After the war ended, in 1860, she founded the Nightingale School and Home for Nurses at Saint Thomas' Hospital in London. Florence Nightingale pioneered professional nursing education. In addition, she wrote the first widely published textbook on nursing, *Notes on Hospitals*, in 1860. Nightingale was a prolific writer and she has had a profound impact on the fields of nursing and medicine, on hospital reform, and on the development of the rural public health system. Florence Nightingale dedicated her life to the betterment of life circumstances for her fellow citizens and was given many awards, both within her country and internationally, for her efforts. In 1907, Nightingale became the first female to be awarded the British Order of Merit. In 1915, the Crimean Monument in London's Waterloo Place was built and dedicated to honor her memory.

INTRODUCTION

In the early decades of the 1800s, the concept of public health in the United Kingdom was largely an oxymoron, particularly for the socioeconomically disadvantaged, and especially so for those living in urban settings, where crowded housing conditions were (and are until the present day) the norm.

Trash and raw sewage were commonly dumped out of the windows of dwellings, and piled in yards, on public streets, and wherever there was empty space. Wells were relatively scarce, and were often contaminated, with the result that numerous families might share the same polluted water source. In 1831, there was an epidemic of cholera in Asia and Europe, although this was attributed by many scientists of the day to air and atmospheric conditions rather than to bacteria spread though tainted water.

In 1838, the Poor Law Commissioners created, and widely published, a report on the effects of rampant epidemic diseases on the poor of London's Bethnal Green and Whitechapel. Edwin Chadwick, a socially prominent proponent of social justice reform and the need for instituting sanitary conditions as a normal part of life for the poor and underprivileged classes, spent several years as the Secretary of the Poor Law Commission. It was his contention that poverty, disease, and living in squalor were inextricably intertwined. This did not imply that the wealthy were living under appreciably more sanitary conditions. They were merely able to afford somewhat cleaner living conditions and were less likely to share contaminated well water. In 1840, Chadwick conducted his own research on the prevalent environmental settings among the poor, and in 1842 the Poor Law Commissioners published his report on the *Sanitary Conditions of the Labouring Population of Great Britain*. The report attributed the rampant spread of disease to "atmospheric impurities" brought about by the decomposition of vegetable and animal wastes in open trash heaps, dampness, filth, and close and overcrowded housing and working situations. In addition to laying out the causes of the health problems among the poor and oppressed in Great Britain, Chadwick proposed solutions to minimize the spread of infection and disease. He recommended the creation of adequate drainage and water systems, and proposed that a plan be created for regular waste and trash removal from homes, yards, alleys, and streets.

The Poor Law Commissioners were able to induce the British House of Commons to create a work group tasked with the investigation of health problems in urban areas. The group recommended the creation and institution of a variety of regulations aimed at improving the sanitary conditions of dwellings and worksites. They also recommended the passage of a Sewerage Act and the opening of offices of the Board of Health in every town. The Board of Health would be charged with the regulation of the cleanliness and availability of water systems, as well as with the disposal of waste and prevention of vermin infestation. There was also an attempt to legislate the construction of homes and neighborhoods. Because people worked very long hours and there was a scarcity of public transportation—particularly for those who earned only subsistence wages—homes were built as close as possible to the workplace. As a result, homes also were built very close together, people and homes were overcrowded, and streets were narrow. The further result of this type of mass construction was a lack of adequate airflow and proper ventilation, leading to the widespread proliferation of airborne infection-causing contaminants.

Florence Nightingale read her essay on the state of rural hygiene at the Conference of Women Workers in Leeds, England, in 1893. It is excerpted below.

PRIMARY SOURCE

We will now deal with the PRESENT STATE OF RURAL HYGIENE, which is indeed a pitiful and disgusting story, dreadful to tell.

For the sake of giving actual facts,—it is no use lecturing upon drainage, watersupply, wells, pigsties, storage of excrement, storage of refuse, etc., etc., *in general*; they are dreadfully concrete,—take leave to give the facts of one rural district, consisting of villages and one small market town, as described by a Local Government Board official this year; and I will ask the ladies here present whether they could not match these facts in every county in the kingdom. Perhaps, too, the lady lecturers on Rural Hygiene will favour us with some of their experiences.

A large number of the poor cottages have been recently condemned as "unfit for human habitation," but though "unfit" many are still "inhabited," from lack of other accommodation.

Provision for conveying away surface and slopwater is conspicuous either by its absence or defect. The slopwater stagnates and sinks into the soil all round the dwellings, aided by the droppings from the thatch. (It has been known that the bedroom slops are sometimes emptied out of window.) There *are* inside sinks, but the wastepipe is often either untrapped or not disconnected.

It is a Government Official who says all this.

Watersupply almost entirely from shallow wells, often uncovered, mostly in the cottagegarden, not far from a pervious privy pit, a pigsty, or a huge collection of house refuse, polluted by the foulness soaking into it. The liquid manure from the pigsty trickles through the ground into the well. Often after heavy rain the cottagers complain that their wellwater becomes thick.

The water in many shallow wells has been analysed. And some have been closed; others *cleaned out*. But when no particular impurity is detected, no care has been taken to stop the too threatening pollution, or to prohibit the supply. In one village which *had* a pump, it was so far from one end that a pond in an adjoining field was used for their supply.

It may be said that, up to the present time, *practically* nothing has been done by the Sanitary Authorities to effect the removal of house refuse, etc.

In these days of investigation and statistics, where results are described with microscopic exactness and tabulated with mathematical accuracy, we seem to think figures will do instead of facts, and calculation instead of action. We remember the policeman who watched his burglar enter the house, and waited to make quite sure whether he was going to commit robbery with violence or without, before interfering with his operations. So as we read such an account as this we seem to be watching, not robbery, but murder going on, and to be waiting for the rates of mortality to go up before we interfere; we wait to see how many of the children playing round the houses shall be stricken down. We wait to see whether the filth will really trickle into the well, and whether the foul water really will poison the family, and how many will die of it. And then, when enough have died, we think it time to spend some money and some trouble to stop the murders going further, and we enter the results of our "masterly inactivity" neatly in tables; but we do not analyse and tabulate the saddened lives of those who remain, and the desolate homes in our "*sanitary* districts."

Storage of Excrement in These Villages. This comes next. And it is so disgustingly inefficient that I write it on a separate sheet, to be omitted if desired. But we must remember that if we cannot bear with it, the national health has to bear with it, and especially the children's health. And I add, as a fact in another Rural District to the one quoted above, that, in rainy weather, the little children may play in the privy or in the so-called "bam" or small outhouse, where may be several privies, several pigs, and untold heaps of filth. And as the little faces are very near the ground, children's diarrhœa and diseases have been traced to this miasma.

Cesspit Privies. The *cesspits are excavations* in the ground; often left unlined. Sometimes the privy is a wooden sentrybox, placed so that the fœcal matter falls directly into a ditch. Cesspits often very imperfectly or not at all covered. Some privies with a cubic capacity of 18 or 20 feet are emptied from once to thrice yearly. But we are often told that all the contents "ran away," and that therefore emptying was not required!

These privies are often close to the well—one within a yard of the cottagers' pump.

Earth closets are the exception, cesspit privies the rule. (In another place 109 cesspit privies were counted to 120 cottages. And, as might be expected, there was hardly a pure well in the place.)

In one, a market town, there *are* waterclosets, so called from being without water.

Storage of Refuse and Ashes. Ashpits are conspicuous by their absence. Huge heaps of accumulated refuse are found piled up near the house, sometimes under the windows, or near the well, into which these refuse heaps soak. Where there *are* ashpits, they are piled up and overflowing. Privy contents are often mixed up with the refuse or buried in a hole in the refuseheap.

As to the final disposal, in most cases the cottagers have allotments, but differing in distance from but a few yards to as much as two miles from their homes. Their privy contents and ash refuse are therefore valuable as manure, and they would "strongly resent" any appropriation of it by the Sanitary Authority.

And we might take this into account by passing a byelaw to the effect that house refuse must be removed at least once a quarter, and that if the occupier neglected to do this, the Sanitary Authority would do it, *and would appropriate* it. This amount of pressure is thoroughly legitimate to protect the lives of the children.

Health Missioners might teach the value of cooperation in sanitary matters. For instance, suppose the hire of a sewagecart is 1s. the first day, and sixpence every other day. If six houses, adjacent to each other, subscribed for the use of the sewagecart, they would each get it far cheaper than by single orders.

The usual practice is to wait until there is a sufficient accumulation to make worth while the hiring of a cart. The ashes, and often the privy contents too, are then taken away to the allotments. A statement that removal takes place as much as two or three times a year is often too obviously untrue.

But, as a rule, the occupiers have sufficient garden space, i.e., curtilage, for the proper utilisation of their privy contents. (I would urge the reading of Dr. Poore's "Rural Hygiene" on this particular point.)

Often the garden is large enough for the utilisation of ashes and house refuse too. But occupiers almost always take both privy and ashpit contents to their allotments. Thus hoardingup of refuse matters occurs. In some cases the cost of hiring horse and cart—the amount depending on the distance of the allotment from the dwelling—is so serious a consideration that if byelaws compelled the occupiers to remove their refuse to their allotments, say every month, either the value of the manure would be nothing, or the scavenging must be done at the expense of the Sanitary Authority. From the public health point of view, the Sanitary Authority should of course do the scavenging in all the villages.

The health Economy of the Community demands the most profitable use of manure for the land. Now the most profitable use is that which permits of least waste, and if we could only regard economy in this matter in its true and broad sense, we should acknowledge that the Community is advantaged by the frequent removal of sewage refuse from the houses, where it is dangerous, to the land, where it is an essential. And if the Community is advantaged, the Community should pay for that advantage. The gain is a double one—safety in the matter of health, increase in the matter of food, besides the untold gain, moral as well as material, which results from the successful cultivation of land.

There are some villages without any gardens—barely room for a privy and ashpit. But even in these cases the occupiers generally have allotments.

Plenty of byelaws may be imposed, but byelaws are not in themselves active agents. And in many, perhaps in most, cases they are impossible of execution, and remain a dead letter.

SIGNIFICANCE

The Public Health Act of 1848 led to the creation of a Central Board of Health, as well as many Local Boards of Health, each imbued with its own duties and responsibilities. Although the Central Board of Health only lasted until 1854, the work that it had accomplished, along with that of Edwin Chadwick, Robert Peel, and Florence Nightingale eventually raised sufficient public and governmental ire and concern to cause local authorities to turn their attention to issues of public health. Between 1854 and 1871, particularly during the time that Sir John Simon served as Chief Medical Officer for the Board of Health, sanitary processes underwent dramatic improvements. There were several acts passed in Parliament, leading to the development of adequate drainage and sewer systems across many areas of the country. The Local Government Board replaced the Central Board of Health in 1871, paving the way for modernization of the public health system progressing through the end of the nineteenth and into the twentieth century and beyond. In 1872, the Public Health Act transferred responsibility for rural sanitation to the Boards of Guardians; and in 1875 the Disraeli Public Health Act was passed. In effect, the 1875 Act shifted the power and responsibility for oversight of public health, in both urban and rural areas, from central back to local government—finally ensuring that rural public health would be at the forefront of the local public consciousness.

As public methods of regulating drainage, containing sewage, and preventing contamination of the land and water systems continued to improve, the spread of disease markedly diminished. This made cities far safer and more appealing to inhabit, particularly as they typically formed the centers for industry and commerce and, therefore, were where the highest paying jobs were located. With the advent of the Industrial Revolution, leading to a burgeoning *technical* job market, more and more people flocked to the cities in hopes of learning and advancing trades, and earning significantly more money than ever before.

In addition, health care became centered in cities and more densely populated suburban areas—larger hospitals were built, and medical practitioners of all types moved to areas where more money could be

Florence Nightingale was called "The Lady with the Lamp" because she carried a lantern when tirelessly tending the sick and wounded during the Crimean War. ©BETTMANN/CORBIS.

earned. This led to a the rise of health practitioner groups, clinics, and more specialized practice of medicine—and resulted in a dearth of adequate care in outlying, less densely populated areas.

The Hospital Survey and Construction Act, commonly known as the Hill-Burton Act of 1947, attempted to address the growing health facility disparities in the United States. At the start of the Second World War, there were 3,076 named counties in the U.S.—of those, 1,282 counties had no community hospitals. There were 1,794 existent community hospitals, and a significant proportion of those were grossly inadequate or outdated. In 1944 and again in 1945, President Roosevelt declared a pressing need for adequate and appropriate health care for all people in America. In response, Senators Lister Hill and Harold Burton sponsored the above-mentioned bill, which led to a comprehensive plan in which the location, size, and type of health care and hospital facilities were determined for each state in the nation. For the first time in many areas, hospital licensure laws were created and implemented. Hospital construction plans were created and approved by the U.S. Public Health Service, and local communities were able to receive large-scale funding in order to construct clinics, health centers, and hospitals. This was of great benefit to the poorest and most rural areas, which typically had no health care whatsoever. Although most of the construction was for general health care facilities, increasing attention was also paid to specialized facilities for tuberculosis, psychiatric and chronic illness units in general hospital facilities, as well as development of rural and public health centers. Between 1947 and 1975, the last year in which Hill-Burton monies were expended, 6,900 hospitals received funding. By the middle of the 1970s, the nationwide average for community hospital beds had risen from fewer than 3 per thousand people to 4.5 per thousand. For the first time, many rural areas had access to health care and hospital facilities.

Although the Hill-Burton Act has had a tremendous and lasting impact on medical care in the U.S., the problem of ensuring adequate and appropriate access to health care for the poorest of the poor in rural and outlying areas remains. In rural areas, particularly in sparsely populated or largely impoverished regions, it is difficult to attract and retain health care providers. Generally, there is often a lack of available public transportation and a scarcity of people who can afford to access care. Some indigent people without significant education or ready transportation in rural areas often find it difficult to manage the requirements for remaining on the rolls of public health care systems, such as Medicaid. Without sufficient paying customers to ensure an adequate cash flow, there is little incentive for health care providers to locate their offices in rural areas.

FURTHER RESOURCES

Web sites

A Web of English History: The Peel Web. "Public Health: Inadequate Cleansing." <http://www.historyhome.co.uk/peel/p-health/clean.htm> (accessed August 29, 2005).

A Web of English History: The Peel Web. "Public Health: No Waste Disposal." <http://www.historyhome.co.uk/peel/p-health/dirt.htm> (accessed August 29, 2005).

The Internet Modern History Sourcebook. "Florence Nightingale: Rural Hygiene." <http://www.fordham.edu/halsall/mod/nightingale-rural.html> (accessed August 29, 2005).

Thalidomide and Congenital Abnormalities

Letter

By: W. G. McBride

Date: December 16, 1961

Source: McBride, W. G. "Thalidomide and Congenital Abnormalities." Letter to the Editor. *The Lancet* 2 (December 16, 1961): 1358.

About the Author: Born in Sydney, Australia, in 1927, gynecologist and obstetrician William G. McBride brought the link between the drug thalidomide and birth defects to the attention of the medical world. In 1962, he was designated "Australian of the Year" for this achievement. Other honors followed and he used some of his prize money to set up Foundation 41, a research institute for the study of birth defects. However, in 1987, he was accused of scientific fraud over his claims that another drug, Debendox, causes birth defects and was struck off the medical register. Later, his position as an obstetrician was restored.

INTRODUCTION

Thalidomide was first synthesized in 1953 and became popular as a sedative prescribed for the morning sickness often associated with pregnancy. By 1958, thalidomide was being heavily advertised and promoted around the world. However, in April 1961, obstetrician William McBride began to notice cases of a rare birth defect involving shortened or absent limbs in babies whose mothers had used thalidomide in pregnancy. At the Crown St. Women's Hospital in Sydney, Australia, where McBride practiced, he soon persuaded the hospital to stop using the drug and wrote of his concerns to Distillers, the company that sold the drug in Australia. At about the same time, pediatrician and geneticist Widukind Lenz noted many similar cases in Germany, where thalidomide was available without prescription.

At this time, physicians assumed that the placenta was impervious to any drugs the expectant mother ingested—unless the drug actually killed her. This belief persisted despite experimental evidence to the contrary. Since thalidomide was not fatal in overdose, it was deemed safe. When thalidomide was approved, drugs were not tested in pregnant animals for their teratogenic effect—that is, for their ability to cause developmental abnormalities in the fetus. McBride wrote the letter below to a leading medical journal,

The Lancet, to alert the medical community to the dangers of thalidomide.

■ PRIMARY SOURCE

THALIDOMIDE AND CONGENITAL ABNORMALITIES

Sɪʀ,—Congenital abnormalities are present in approximately 1·5% of babies. In recent months I have observed that the incidence of multiple severe abnormalities in babies delivered of women who were given the drug thalidomide ('Distaval') during pregnancy, as an anti-emetic or as a sedative, to be almost 20%.

These abnormalities are present in structures developed from mesenchyme—i.e., the bones and musculature of the gut. Bony development seems to be affected in a very striking manner, resulting in polydactyly, syndactyly, and failure of development of long bones (abnormally short femora and radii).

Have any of your readers seen similar abnormalities in babies delivered of women who have taken this drug during pregnancy?

Hurstville, New South Wales.

W. G. McBʀɪᴅᴇ.

SIGNIFICANCE

McBride's warning concerning the teratogenic effects of thalidomide saved countless babies from being born with birth defects. However, the drug remained on the market for some time following McBride's warning, which accounts for the fact that there are still some 8,000 thalidomide survivors in the world today.

The observations of McBride and Lenz were to have far-reaching effects on the pharmaceutical industry. They were astute enough to notice rare and unusual conditions occurring in their patients and to spot patterns and connections with factors such as drug exposure. After thalidomide, it became mandatory to test new drugs on pregnant animals. Doctors became far more aware of the potential teratogenic effect of drugs and were more careful about the drugs they prescribed to pregnant women.

In general, the drug regulatory authorities acquired more sweeping powers after the thalidomide tragedy. One important development was the establishment of systems for post-market drug surveillance. That is, once a drug is on the market, it is monitored for any new side effects that emerge in the general population. These new side effects are reported through the physician. As a result of these post-

A young thalidomide victim, born without arms, clutches a bouquet with her toes as she presents it to Princess Anne of Great Britain in 1972. ©BETTMANN/CORBIS.

marketing surveillance efforts, several drugs have been withdrawn on safety grounds. Unanticipated drug side effects still occur and they still harm or even kill vulnerable people. However, tighter regulation has undoubtedly improved patient safety.

Meanwhile, thalidomide has enjoyed something of a resurgence as a treatment for leprosy and multiple myeloma. However, it is no longer prescribed to women who are pregnant or who may become pregnant. Scientists now know that other drugs are as dangerous to an unborn child as thalidomide is. One such drug is isotretinoin, which is used in the treatment of severe acne. A woman actually needs to provide proof of a negative pregnancy test before she can be prescribed isotretinoin, according to the U.S. Food and Drug Administration. While on the drug, she must use an effective method of contraception. The fetus is most vulnerable to medication exposure through the placenta in the first three months of pregnancy. In the thalidomide case, one in five women who had taken the drug between thirty-seven and fifty-four days of pregnancy gave birth to a child with birth defects.

FURTHER RESOURCES
Books
Lock, Stephen, John M. Last, and George Dunea, eds. *The Oxford Illustrated Companion to Medicine.* Oxford: Oxford University Press, 2001.

Web sites
James Lind Library.org. "Thalidomide: An Unexpected Adverse Effect." <http://www.jameslindlibrary.org/trial_records/20th_Century/1960s/mcbride/mcbride_commentary.html> (accessed November 21, 2005.

Famine and Public Health

Picture

By: Dempster

Date: January 21, 1970

INTRODUCTION

Famine is the extreme lack of food and nutrients, often resulting in widespread disease and death. A particularly large number of famines occurred during the 1900s, and into the twenty-first century, despite the world's extensive social, economic, and technical advances during the same time period. Although efforts have been made to combat and prevent famines, food shortages around the globe, due to such factors as war, drought, and ill-focused political decisions, continue to take a toll on the lives of some of the world's most impoverished inhabitants.

Acute hunger can cause people to die of starvation directly, but there are many more individuals who may survive famine, only to be faced with the health problems that often accompany undernourishment and vitamin and mineral deficiencies. Common effects of malnutrition include stunted growth, weakness, and susceptibility to disease. People who are malnourished often have poor concentration, which exacerbates the problem of hunger, as it is difficult for hungry people to work in fields, or earn money for buying food. Pregnant women, those who are breast-feeding newborns, and children are the most vulnerable to hunger related problems. Over 150 million children, worldwide, below the age of five, are said to be underweight. Eleven million children under the age of five die each year, with over half of the deaths directly related to malnutrition. Typically these children do not die from starvation itself, but rather from the diseases that strike

a weak and vulnerable body, whose immune system is likely unable to put up a defense. The four most common childhood illnesses in developing countries are diarrhea, respiratory illness, malaria, and measles.

All parts of the globe are known to have experienced famine. The blockade of German trade ships by Britain and France, along with a harsh winter in 1916–1917, left several hundred thousand Germans dead prior to the start of World War I. Five to eight million people in Ukraine died from famine during the 1930s, when the Soviet Union seized agriculture outputs in hopes of exporting more food to bring in money for industrialization. The Chinese famine between 1958–1962 is considered one of the worst in history, with estimates of up to thirty million people dying as China's leader, Mao Ze-dong, implemented a plan of rapid industrialization in rural areas.

Famines occurring in Africa have received the most extensive international publicity. During Nigeria's civil war with Biafra between 1968–1970, at least one million civilians died from hunger and fighting. The world was shocked by photographs of starving children with distended stomachs caused by protein deficiency. Between 1984–1985, drought throughout Ethiopia impacted 120 million people, with scenes of starvation seen on television sets throughout the western world. Fundraising events all over the world led to the arrival of some emergency food aid to Ethiopia, but bottlenecks at the ports, and poor quality roads slowed down relief efforts. Throughout the 1990s and into the twenty-first century, civil war between the Arab and black Sudanese have led to food crises, particularly in the Darfur region of Sudan, where 3.4 million, or half of the region's population have been forced from their homes and farmlands. Throughout various regions of Africa, ongoing political unrest, unreliable rainfall, and poverty keep millions of people at risk of hunger.

PRIMARY SOURCE

FAMINE AND PUBLIC HEALTH
See primary source image.

SIGNIFICANCE

The United Nations (UN) classifies 1.2 billion people below the international poverty line, living on less than one dollar per day. Many of these people experience regular food shortages, while others are just barely able to meet their daily food requirements. All families under the poverty line are vulnerable to shocks such as droughts, earthquakes, and wars, all

PRIMARY SOURCE

Famine and Public Health. Nigerian children are seen here during the famine resulting from the Nigeria/Biafra War in the 1970s.
©HULTON-DEUTSCH COLLECTION/CORBIS.

which are likely to further hamper the ability of impoverished people to eat adequate levels of food. Those people, who have difficulty meeting food requirements, and those who are barely able to survive, are considered to have low levels of food security.

The condition know as kwashiorkor results from protein deficiency, and is responsible for the swollen abdomen that often appears in malnourished children during a famine. Absolute starvation usually results in body tissue and fluid wasting, and ultimately, kidney failure or heart failure brought on by an imbalance of electrolytes (minerals and salts) in the body. Other diseases that often threaten a population vulnerable to famine include cholera, measles, and pneumonia.

Despite the availability of food throughout the developed world, reaching people who need food is not a simple task. Poor infrastructure can make the transportation of food difficult. Also, the necessary political will of developed countries to assist poorer nations

must be present. There are many different international bodies with mission statements regarding the decreasing of hunger, malnutrition, and poverty. Eradicating hunger is the first of the twenty-first century's Millennium Development Goals (MDGs), set at the United Nations (UN) Millennium Summit in 2000. There are three UN agencies directly involved in food assistance and agriculture: the World Food Program (WFP), the Food and Agriculture Organization (FAO), and the International Fund for Agriculture Development (IFAD). WFP is the agency responsible for coordinating and distributing food aid provided by the United States, European Union, Japan, and other countries. WFP's operations bring food to people displaced by war, those who cannot grow food due to drought, and WFP helps schools and hospitals distribute more nutritious meals. FAO and IFAD deal more with agriculture development, and with helping communities produce larger quantities of food more efficiently.

FURTHER RESOURCES

Books

Lappé, Frances Moore, Joseph Collins, and Peter Rosset. *World Hunger: 12 Myths.* New York: Grove Press, 2001.

Runge, Carlisle Ford, et al. *Ending Hunger in our Lifetime: Food Security and Globalization.* Baltimore: John Hopkins University Press, 2003.

Web sites

Bread for the World Institute. "Famine." <http://www.bread.org/learn/global-hunger-issues/famine.html> (accessed January 16, 2006).

Philips, B. *BBC.* "Biafra: Thirty Years On." <http://news.bbc.co.uk/2/hi/africa/596712.stm> (accessed January 16, 2006).

United Nations Children Fund. "Darfur: Children Facing Severe Food Shortages." <http://www.unicef.org/emerg/darfur/index_30529.html> (accessed January 16, 2006).

Watson, F. *Institute of Child Health—NutritionWorks.* "One Hundred Years of Famine—A Pause for Reflection." <http://www.ennonline.net/fex/08/ms20.html> (accessed January 16, 2006).

Has Your Child Had a Lead Test Yet?

Poster

By: U.S. Department of Health, Education, and Welfare

Date: 1970

Source: "Has Your Child Had a Lead Test Yet?" Poster available online at the National Library of Medicine. <http://www.nlm.nih.gov/exhibition/visualculture/environmental01.html> (accessed December 2, 2005).

About the Author: The Cabinet-level Department of Health, Education and Welfare (HEW) was created in 1953, during the Eisenhower administration. In 1979, the Department of Education Organization Act was signed into law. It created a separate Department of Education, and HEW officially became the Department of Health and Human Services on May 4, 1980. The Department of Health and Human Services is the United States government's principal agency for protecting the health of all Americans and providing essential human services, especially for those who are least able to help themselves.

INTRODUCTION

Lead poisoning in children was first discovered in Australia in the late nineteenth century. In 1904, J. L. Gibson discovered the cause of such poisoning. He traced it to the repeated ingestion of peeling and chipping lead-based paint in old, dilapidated homes by children with pica, an appetite for non-food items. In subsequent years, little effort was made to prevent childhood exposure to lead. No alternative to lead in paint had been discovered and poor and minority children—who were the major victims of such poisoning—attracted comparatively little media and government attention.

The natural concentration of lead in humans is extremely small. Lead has no useful function in the body and damages both children and adults. However, children, especially those under the age of six, are more susceptible to lead poisoning because their bodies are still developing. Children are exposed to lead from many sources—food, water, car emissions, ceramics, cosmetics, dust, soil, and paint. While lead-based paint is the principal high-dose source available to children, these other sources contribute to the total body burden of lead and reduce the margin of safety to a level where only slight exposure to lead in paint may result in health problems.

Lead damages the nervous and renal systems as well as the formation of blood cells. Since lead poisoning first affects blood cells, blood is tested to determine exposure to lead. High levels of lead in the blood can cause a lower IQ, learning disabilities, attention deficit disorder, behavioral problems, stunted growth, impaired hearing, and kidney damage. Damage to the brain and nervous system from lead poisoning is irreversible.

The replacement of lead by titanium oxide in the 1940s led many Americans to mistakenly believe that lead poisoning was a problem of the past. They did not realize that the hazardous paint still remained in millions of older homes. Adding to the danger, lead poisoning appears gradually and can easily be overlooked. In the 1960s, a widespread effort at public education by government agencies and citizens' groups began to screen children for lead exposure.

■ PRIMARY SOURCE

HAS YOUR CHILD HAD A LEAD TEST YET?
See primary source image.

Little children like to put things in their mouths. Some like the taste of paint that peels from walls and wood-work. When children eat chips of old paint and plaster they are in real danger. Old paint contains lead, and lead is poison!

Little children can poison themselves by eating paint chips.
You can find out if your children are getting lead poisoning…before they get sick. By testing a small amount of blood, the doctor can tell whether your child has too much lead in his body.

The doctor can help children who have too much lead in their bodies…if he finds out before it's too late. So don't delay: *Ask the doctor or nurse how to get a free lead test for your children.*

U.S. Department of Health, Education, and Welfare
Health Services and Mental Health Administration
Bureau of Community Environmental Management

PRIMARY SOURCE

Has Your Child Had a Lead Test Yet? The U.S. Department of Health, Education, and Welfare distributed posters in the 1970s to persuade parents of the importance of testing children for lead exposure. U.S. NATIONAL LIBRARY OF MEDICINE.

SIGNIFICANCE

The efforts by public and private agencies to educate the public about lead poisoning proved to be successful. The numbers of children found with lead in their blood resulted in a general realization that lead poisoning was still taking a high toll on children. In 1970, the Surgeon General shifted the focus from identification and treatment of overt lead poisoning to prevention through mass screening and early identification of children with high levels of lead absorption.

Congressional hearings led to passage of the 1971 Lead-Based Paint Poisoning Prevention Act. Among other things, the act authorized federal financial assistance to help communities develop and carry out screening and treatment programs as well as programs to eliminate the cause of lead-based paint poisoning. It funded the Childhood Lead-Based Paint Poisoning Prevention Program, which conducted mass screenings.

Scientists assumed that only pre-World War II (1941–1945) homes contained hazardous levels of lead. The mass screenings revealed that even houses constructed in the 1960s contained lead-based paint. Lead poisoning also occurred in children living in homes under renovation and remodeling.

Cases of lead poisoning have declined steadily in the U.S., since the 1978 federal ban on lead-based paint in housing. Yet, other sources of lead exposure remain. In 2005, the Environmental Protection Agency (EPA) asked companies engaged in home renovation and remodeling to adopt protective measures voluntarily. Under a 1992 law, the EPA was to have issued new regulations covering such activities as the tearing out of ceilings, walls, and other fixtures covered with lead-based paint. However, the regulations were never issued. The EPA issued the voluntary measures in the belief that they would be less expensive for businesses to implement. It believed, in 2005, that about 1.4 million children under the age of seven in 4.9 million households were at risk of lead exposure due to unsafe repair and renovation work.

FURTHER RESOURCES

Books

Cherry, Flora Finch, ed. *Childhood Lead Poisoning Prevention and Control: A Public Health Approach to an Environmental Disease*. New Orleans: Maternal and Child Health Section, Office of Health Services and Environmental Quality, Department of Health and Human Resources, 1981.

Web sites

National Center for Environmental Health, Centers for Disease Control. "Childhood Lead Poisoning Prevention Program." <http://www.cdc.gov/nceh/lead/lead.htm> (accessed December 2, 2005).

President Nixon Declares "War" on Drugs

Speech

By: Richard M. Nixon

Date: June 17, 1971

Source: The American Presidency Project

About the Author: Richard Milhous Nixon (1913–1994) was the thirty-seventh president of the United States. He was a Republican who was first elected in 1968 and re-elected in 1972. The famous Watergate scandal involving irregularities during the re-election campaign came to light shortly after that campaign, and Nixon resigned in 1974.

INTRODUCTION

Drug use and abuse have been common in societies worldwide for thousands of years. But it is only in the last 200 years that governments have begun to try to tackle drug abuse with a view to reducing some of the associated health problems and criminal activities.

The Harrison Narcotic Act, passed in 1914, was one of the first formal attempts to control drug abuse in the United States. It put strict controls on the prescription, sale, and possession of opium, morphine, heroin, and cocaine (but not marijuana). Thousands of physicians, pharmacists, and users were arrested as a result of the Act. But America is perhaps best known for Prohibition, which began in 1919 and forbade people to buy or drink alcohol. Many Americans saw this as an intrusion into their private lives. The legislators accepted that there would be a certain amount of illicit use of alcohol, but they could never have anticipated how widespread it would be. Prohibition, which came to an end in 1933, saw the start of organized and large-scale crime in the United States.

In 1932, alcohol was illegal, while marijuana was not. Five years later, the situation was reversed when the Marijuana Tax Act was passed. This effectively outlawed marijuana. During the 1960s, there was a huge upsurge in illicit drug use, both among soldiers serving in the Vietnam War and at home. Many began to talk of decriminalization or even legalization of drugs. It was against this background that Richard Nixon came to power. He had been elected on a "law and order" platform and his "War on Drugs" was part of this platform. Nixon delivered these remarks to press representatives in the briefing room of the White House on June 17, 1971.

▮ PRIMARY SOURCE

Ladies and gentlemen:

I would like to summarize for you the meeting that I have just had with the bipartisan leader which began at 8 o'clock and was completed 2 hours later.

I began the meeting by making this statement, which I think needs to be made to the Nation: America's public enemy number one in the United States is drug abuse. In order to fight and defeat this enemy, it is necessary to wage a new, all-out offensive.

I have asked the Congress to provide the legislative authority and the funds to fuel this kind of an offensive. This will be a worldwide offensive dealing with the problems of sources of supply, as well as Americans who may be stationed abroad, wherever they are in the world. It will be government wide, pulling together the nine different fragmented areas within the government in which this problem is now being handled, and it will be nationwide in terms of a new educational program that we trust will result from the discussions that we have had.

With regard to this offensive, it is necessary first to have a new organization, and the new organization will be within the White House. Dr. Jaffe, who will be one of the briefers here today, will be the man directly responsible. He will report directly to me, and he will have the responsibility to take all of the Government agencies, nine, that deal with the problems of rehabilitation, in which his primary responsibilities will be research and education, and see that they work not at cross-purposes, but work together in dealing with the problem.

If we are going to have a successful offensive, we need more money. Consequently, I am asking the Congress for $155 million in new funds, which will bring the total amount this year in the budget for drug abuse, both in enforcement and treatment, to over $350 million.

As far as the new money is concerned, incidentally, I have made it clear to the leaders that if this is not enough, if more can be used, if Dr. Jaffe, after studying this problem, finds that we can use more, more will be provided. In order to defeat this enemy which is causing such great concern, and correctly so, to so many American families, money will be provided to the extent that it is necessary and to the extent that it will be useful.

Finally, in order for this program to be effective, it is necessary that it be conducted on a basis in which the American people all join in it. That is why the meeting was bipartisan; bipartisan because we needed the support of the Congress, but bipartisan because we needed the leadership of the Members of the Congress in this field.

Fundamentally, it is essential for the American people to be alerted to this danger, to recognize that it is a danger that will not pass with the passing of the war in Vietnam which has brought to our attention the fact that a number of young Americans have become addicts as they serve abroad, whether in Vietnam, or Europe, or other places. Because the problem existed before we became involved in Vietnam; it will continue to exist afterwards. That is why this offensive deals with the problem there, in Europe, but will then go on to deal with the problem throughout America.

One final word with regard to Presidential responsibility in this respect. I very much hesitate always to bring some new responsibility into the White House, because there are so many here, and I believe in delegating those responsibilities to the departments. But I consider this problem so urgent—I also found that it was scattered so much throughout the Government, with so much conflict, without coordination—that it had to be brought into the White House.

Consequently, I have brought Dr. Jaffe into the White House, directly reporting to me, so that we have not only the responsibility, but the authority to see that we wage this offensive effectively and in a coordinated way.

The briefing team will now be ready to answer any questions on the technical details of the program.

▮

SIGNIFICANCE

President Nixon's "War on Drugs" speech set the scene for the establishment of the Drug Enforcement Agency and the National Institute for Drug Abuse. His attitude toward drug users was not wholly punitive; he set aside money for research and treatment as well. Jerome Jaffe, who is mentioned in the speech, began the "Drug Czar" position as head of the Special Action Office for Drug Abuse. One of his first tasks was to deal with soldiers who had become addicted to heroin in Vietnam. Addicted soldiers were not released from the service until they had undergone treatment; this program resulted in many formerly addicted soldiers maintaining their sobriety when they returned home.

President Ronald Reagan continued the war on drugs in the 1980s, and slogans such as "Just Say No" and "Zero Tolerance" became popular. With the advent of AIDS, which can be spread by drug use,

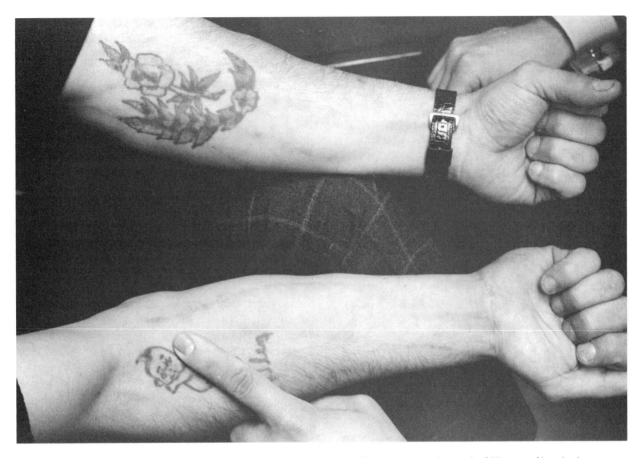

An addict uses tattoos in an attempt to hide needle track marks on his arms. The scars were the result of 20 years of heroin abuse. ©TED STRESHINSKY/CORBIS.

and the highly addictive crack cocaine, tough new penalties were introduced and incarcerations for drug offenses began to soar.

At the start of the twenty-first century, however, there were signs of a shift back towards the medical model of drug addiction. The state of California passed an act in 2000 that offered treatment instead of punishment for those convicted of minor drug offenses. This echoes the more pragmatic approach to drug policy adopted in the United Kingdom and some other European countries like The Netherlands. The policies in these countries emphasize harm reduction, decreasing demand, and offering treatment for abuse problems.

In the United States, the Office of National Drug Control Policy establishes policies, priorities, and objectives for the nation's drug control program. Statistics relating to drug usage in the U.S. are gathered by the Substance Abuse and Mental Health Services Administration, and the National Institute on Drug Abuse (a part of the National Institutes of Health) studies and disseminates information on drug abuse and addiction, prevention, and treatment. While the use of certain drugs, such as crack cocaine, and hallucinogens, such as LSD, were reduced by the turn of the twenty-first century, new drugs, such as synthetic morphine and codeine, "club" drugs, such as ecstasy and methamphetamines, contributed to a resurgence in drug use among older teens and young adults.

FURTHER RESOURCES

Books

Goldstein, Avram. *Addiction: From Biology to Drug Policy.* New York: W. H. Freeman, 1994.

United Nations Drug Control Program. *World Drug Report 2000: United Nations Office for Drug Control and Crime Prevention.* New York: Oxford University Press, 2001.

Web sites

Office of National Drug Control Policy. "Healing America's Drug Users: Getting Treatment Resources Where They Are Needed." February 2005. <http://

www.whitehousedrugpolicy.gov/publications/policy/ ndcs05/healing_amer.html> (accessed November 24, 2005).

The Addiction Doctor. "History of Drug Laws." <http:// www.addictiondoctor.com/pages/NixonsWar.htm> (accessed November 24, 2005).

Marlboro Man; Bob, I've Got Emphysema

Tobacco, Cultural Icon, Recognized as Health Hazard

Photograph

By: Robert Landau

Date: 1976

Source: Marlboro Cigarettes Billboard. Corbis Stock Photography Image. 1976.

About the Photographer: Robert Landau, the photographer who captured the famed Marlboro Man on a Pacific Outdoor billboard set against an urban Los Angeles streetscape, is a graduate of the California Institute of the Arts. Among his favorite subjects is his native Los Angeles, which he has been photographing for nearly a quarter of a century. Museums and art galleries around the world have displayed his photographic work, and he is the author of two best-selling books of his work: *Billboard Art* and *Outrageous L. A.*, both published by Chronicle Books. He has traveled the globe extensively, and has photographed luminaries, dignitaries, and heads of countries.

Photograph

By: Scott Houston

Date: 2000

Source: Bob, I've Got Emphysema. Corbis Stock Photography Image. 2000.

About the Photographer: Professional photographer Scott Houston took this Marlboro Man look-alike image for the Tobacco Control Section of the California Department of Health Services anti-smoking campaign in 2000.

INTRODUCTION

Tobacco and cigarette smoking has been as much a cultural practice as a personal habit and addiction for millions of people across the globe. For many years, it was glamorized in film, print media, television, and signage (billboard and poster advertisements) across the United States and around the world. Long after the first speculations—and even after clinical research indicated definitive proof—that tobacco use was deleterious to health, it remained a cultural norm. Even after the data indicated that second-hand smoke also was deadly, the social norm remained. Cultural icons, such as movie stars and international royalty, were all identified with cigarette smoking—often even with specific brands. Viewers of American cinema associated such legendary figures as Marilyn Monroe, Humphrey Bogart, Mae West, the members of the Rat Pack, James Dean, and John Wayne with cigarette smoking. Indeed, it seems impossible to envision the creation of a pictorial or visual history of contemporary global culture without many images of pipes, cigars, and cigarettes.

Cigarette smoking, in particular, was glamorized in American popular culture during at least the first half of the twentieth century. In posters and advertising campaigns for both World War I and World War II, brave, rugged, handsome soldiers were portrayed with cigarettes dangling form their mouths. In the 1920s, women first began to be shown by the media as cigarette smokers. These and other similar images were interpreted as testaments to the strength and freedom inherent in America. In the mid-twentieth century, things began to change. In 1957, *Reader's Digest* published an article suggesting a link between smoking and lung cancer. In 1964, the first Surgeon General's Report on Smoking and Health was published, in which a relationship was first made explicit between smoking and health hazards. In the late 1960s and early 1970s, progressively more legislation designed to restrict advertising for cigarettes and other tobacco products was enacted, with a particular emphasis on discouraging youth from starting to smoke cigarettes.

No other American brand of cigarettes has had as successful and universal an iconic symbol as the Marlboro Man. The Marlboro Man was first introduced in 1955 in a series of ads featuring men engaged in a variety of occupations, all of whom had tattoos on their hands, wrists, or forearms. A Philip Morris Marlboro advertisement read: "Man-sized taste of honest tobacco comes full through. Smooth-drawing filter feels right in your mouth. Works fine but doesn't get in the way. Modern Flip-top box keeps every cigarette firm and fresh until you smoke it." The advertising campaign achieved unprecedented success: within eight months of the appearance of the Marlboro Man, sales had increased by 5,000 percent. Public response to each of the male characters in the ads was

PRIMARY SOURCE

Marlboro Man. Manufacturers of cigarettes were required by law to remove advertisements such as this billboard featuring Marlboro cigarettes after a 1998 class action suit settlement. ©ROBERT LANDAU/CORBIS.

measured, and the cowboy was found to be overwhelmingly favored. For the next forty years, the Marlboro icon was the cowboy. Philip Morris never used actors or models in their Marlboro Man advertisements—they always used real cowboys, going about their normal cowboy lives.

The Marlboro Man's persona became so widely recognized, along with the familiar rectangular red and white cigarette box, that copy was no longer necessary. The sight of the cowboy riding his horse through pristine mountainous landscape (Marlboro Country), either alone or with one of his trusted friends, became symbolic of freedom in America—or, at least, the freedom to smoke Marlboro cigarettes.

PRIMARY SOURCE

MARLBORO MAN

See primary source image.

PRIMARY SOURCE

BOB, I'VE GOT EMPHYSEMA

See primary source image.

SIGNIFICANCE

In 1971, tobacco advertisements were banned from television. At that point, the Marlboro Man was so firmly entrenched as an American icon that sales did not suffer in any way. A new sales campaign was begun—a combination of print ads and vast billboards. The Marlboro Man grew even larger than life. Billboards over sixty-feet-tall showing the cigarette smoking cowboy dominated the outdoor advertising landscape.

Seventeen years after advertisements touting cigarette smoking were banned from television, the tobacco industry lost its first major lawsuit and had to pay a settlement to the widow of a cigarette smoker. In

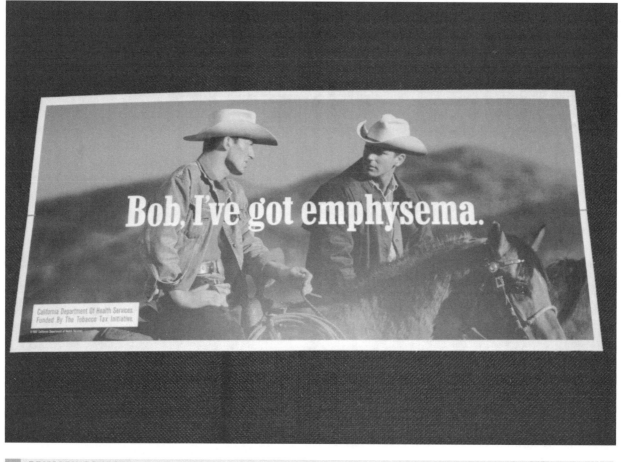

PRIMARY SOURCE

Bob, I've Got Emphysema. A 2000 California Department of Health Services anti-smoking message parodies the historically well-known Marlboro cigarette advertisements. ©SCOTT HOUSTON/CORBIS SYGMA.

November 1998, a $206 billion class action settlement was reached between the major tobacco manufacturers and forty-six states. As a result, in April 1999, all of the tobacco advertising billboards in America had to be removed. The large tobacco companies were required to continue paying their leases until their expiration dates, and anti-smoking billboards were erected in their stead. The tobacco companies involved in the suit were R. J. Reynolds/Nabisco, Brown and Williamson, Lorillard, and Philip Morris. The ban on advertising included: prohibition of all outdoor advertising of tobacco products, including billboards on roadsides, stadiums, arenas, and shopping malls. Tobacco advertisers were no longer permitted to put their logos on clothing or merchandise like backpacks, bags, caps, and T-shirts. In addition, they were banned from employing cartoons in either advertising or pro-duct packaging. As a concession of sorts, the tobacco companies were permitted to post ads of no more than

fourteen square feet in stores that sold tobacco products.

Many states, the Centers for Disease Control and Prevention, the Food and Drug Administration, and the National Cancer Institute designed anti-smoking billboards to be paid for by the tobacco companies. Some of the ads look remarkably, and intentionally, like the ads previously posted by the cigarette/tobacco manufacturers. One such series features the familiar-looking cowboys on horseback. In one ad, the caption reads "Bob, I've got emphysema;" another said, "Bob, I miss my lung." Others addressed the fact that long-term tobacco use can be fatal.

The tobacco manufacturers were far from daunted by the new restriction. By the mid- to late 1980s, they began moving toward other effective forms of deliver-ing their message to the public. They spent large amounts of money on magazine and other print advertising, increased the use of retail store displays and direct mail promotions, and hosted special (specific brand) smoking-related events at bars and clubs.

In stepping up their anti-smoking campaigns, the states and the various health-related industries took a three-pronged approach. First, they tried to convince people that the tobacco industry lies and misleads the public, especially youth, into believing that tobacco use is not harmful. Second, they tried to make people understand and believe that nicotine is addictive. And third, they sought to educate the public about the dangers of second-hand smoke—that it kills, just like the act of smoking does.

Two former Marlboro Men, both long-time smokers, died of lung cancer and their deaths received a great deal of media attention. Wayne McLaren died of lung cancer in 1992 at age fifty-one. After learning that he had lung cancer McLaren became an anti-smoking activist. He appeared before the Massachusetts legislature in support of a bill to increase the tax on cigarette purchases in order to fund health education for youth. He spoke at the annual Philip Morris shareholders meeting, making an appeal to the corporation to limit its advertising. At the end of his life, McLaren appeared in a very powerful anti-smoking commercial. It featured a montage of images of a young, healthy, rugged McLaren in a Stetson hat, intercut with images of the ravaged and dying man in his hospital bed. In the voice-over, McLaren's brother derides the tobacco companies for their statements about smoking being equated with an independent lifestyle and asks, "Lying there with all those tubes in you, how independent can you really be?"

David McLean, a longtime Marlboro Man, died of cancer in 1995. Ten years before his death, the longtime smoker developed emphysema. Two years before he died, he was diagnosed with lung cancer. After his death, his wife and son filed a wrongful death suit against Philip Morris, alleging that he had been made to smoke several packs of cigarettes daily while posing for advertisements, that he was given packs of Marlboros as gifts, and that he was often mailed cartons of the cigarettes. They allege that McLean did not believe his former employer would ever intentionally do anything to hurt him.

Ironically, there is a massive, well-financed public industry devoted to promoting a product that volumes of scientific research indicate could kill those who use it. Tobacco use is one of the primary preventable killers worldwide, yet people continue to smoke and to chew tobacco, and many more start using tobacco products every day. Worldwide, smoking-related illnesses cost billions of dollars annually, yet there is little regulation of the industry in some countries. The addictive, and the potentially fatal, drug nicotine is not considered a controlled substance anywhere in the world. It is estimated that half of all long-time smokers will die of a tobacco-related illness.

FURTHER RESOURCES

Books

Sloan, Frank A., et al. *The Price of Smoking*. Cambridge, Mass: MIT Press, 2004.

Periodicals

Boffi, R., R. Mazza, and A. Ruprecht, et al. "The Tobacconist Boutique, An Inviting (and Misleading) Marriage Between Smoking and Culture." *Tumori* 90 (2004): 161.

Web sites

ASH: Action on Smoking and Health. "Smoking Health Facts." <http://no-smoking.org/june03/06–19-03-6.html> (accessed October 18, 2005).

Boston.com News/ The Boston Globe. "Ashes to Ashes: Smoking Bans Have Triumphed from Boston to Bhutan. But They're Unlikely to Snuff Out the Centuries-old Culture of Smoke." <http://www.boston.com/news/globe/ideas/articles/2005/05/15/ashes_to_ashes?pg=full> (accessed October 18, 2005).

The Foundation for a Smoke Free America. "The Truth About Tobacco." <http://www.anti-smoking.org/children.htm> (accessed October 18, 2005).

International Tobacco. "In Italy, Smoking Curbs Face an Uphill Battle." <http://lists.essential.org/pipermail/intl-tobacco/2000q3/000222.html> (accessed October 18, 2005).

International Tobacco. "Smoking Culture in Russia." <http://lists.essential.org/pipermail/intl-tobacco/2000q3/000223.html> (accessed October 18, 2005).

Trevor Pateman Selected Works. "How is Understanding an Advertisement Possible?" <http://www.selectedworks.co.uk/advertisement.html> (accessed October 19, 2005).

Tobacco Survivors United. "Philip Morris Image a Tough Sell." <http://www.selectedworks.co.uk/advertisement.html> (accessed October 19, 2005).

Ali Maow Maalin Survives the Last Endemic Smallpox Case

World Health Organization Declares Smallpox Eradicated

Photograph

By: Anonymous

Date: 1979

Source: "Last Endemic Smallpox" Bettmann Collection. Corbis Corporation.

INTRODUCTION

The World Health Organization (WHO) played a major part in the global eradication of smallpox by coordinating an international vaccination effort that led to the absence of the disease in humans. The role of the WHO was especially important in remote areas with poor infrastructure and inadequate health care facilities that often lacked medical personnel capable of delivering the vaccines.

Smallpox, or variola virus, is an Orthopoxvirus and a member of the Poxviridae family of viruses. Smallpox has two main forms, variola minor and variola major. The two forms of smallpox varied in the mortality they caused. Variola minor resulted in death in only about 1 percent of cases, while variola major was fatal about 40 percent of the time. Variola major caused four subtypes of the disease, ranging from a relatively mild form of smallpox to the severe form that often leads to hemorrhaging (uncontrolled bleeding) and death.

Despite the existence of viruses that are closely related to smallpox, such as cowpox, camelpox, and monkeypox, there is no animal reservoir of smallpox. Close contact with an infected person is usually necessary for smallpox transmission, as smallpox is spread by saliva droplets containing the virus. There are also no carriers of the disease that are without symptoms. These characteristic factors made the job of eradicating smallpox more straightforward than controlling other more easily transmitted viruses, such as influenza.

Smallpox requires seven to seventeen days to incubate. This symptomless and non-infectious stage is followed by the onset of flu-like symptoms, usually accompanied by high fever. After two to three days, fever decreases and a rash appears, first in the mouth and tongue, then on the face. Over the next three days, the rash becomes raised bumps filled with pus (vesicles), which later develop into typical bellybutton-shaped vesicles. These then give rise to firm pustules. Over the following days, pustules eventually form crusts and become scabs, which then heal and fall off, leaving pockmarks. A person with smallpox remains infectious until the scabs clear.

Smallpox has taken the lives of millions of people throughout history. Its victims are estimated to number 300 million in the twentieth century alone. People with smallpox who did not die were often left disfigured with pockmarks. Another common complication of smallpox was blindness. Smallpox epidemics ranged across the social strata. Along with millions of common citizens, Queen Mary II of England (1662–1694), King Luis I of Spain (1707–1724), Tsar Peter II of Russia (1715–1730) and King Louis XV of France (1710–1774) all died of smallpox.

The variola virus most likely originated in Africa. Evidence of smallpox has been found in ancient Egyptian mummies and in descriptions of apparent outbreaks of the disease. From Africa, smallpox spread to India and China with traveling traders. During the eleventh and twelfth centuries, it came to Europe with returning crusaders. The Americas were free of the virus until the arrival of European settlers in 1500s. The death toll from smallpox in Mexico alone (mostly among natives) is estimated to be ten million during the first ten years of Spanish rule.

In the Middle Ages, there was no prevention against the disease in Europe. Measures to control the spread of smallpox consisted of isolating the sick and burning their clothing and personal effects. In Africa, China, and India, however, a form of inducing immunity to smallpox called variolation developed. Variolation relied on inoculating a healthy person with pus isolated from the pocks of a person with smallpox. Variolation was usually followed by a mild form of smallpox, which prevented a serious case of the illness. However, people inoculated by variolation were infectious for some time, and there were cases of death as a result of variolation and ensuing smallpox. Despite the drawbacks, variolation was the first active preventative measure taken against the disease.

Variolation remained common outside Europe for centuries, and was introduced to Europe and North America in the 1700s by the English writer and socialite Lady Mary Wartley Montagu (1689–1782), who herself suffered from smallpox. In 1796, British physician Edward Jenner (1749–1823) used cowpox virus to induce immunity against smallpox. His invention arose from the observations he made during a smallpox outbreak in Gloucestershire, England, in 1788. Jenner noted that people working closely with cattle, especially dairymaids who contracted the milder disease cowpox, were not affected by smallpox. Jenner used material from the pocks of a dairy maid's hand to test his vaccine on an eight-year-old boy, who later demonstrated immunity to smallpox.

Despite initial resistance by the medical community, the discovery led to the inoculation of over 100,000 people by beginning of the 1800s in England. After Jenner published his findings on vaccination against smallpox, the practice spread to the European continent and to the Americas, and the

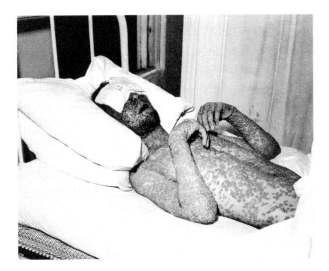

"This man was never vaccinated against smallpox." That is the warning given by the New York State Board of Health to citizens in 1941 during a vaccination campaign. AP/WIDE WORLD PHOTOS.

first mass inoculations began. Although the numbers of cases in Europe then decreased, there were endemic (naturally occurring) areas in Africa and Asia where the virus was spreading.

At the eleventh World Health Assembly (WHA) meeting in 1958, the Soviet Union delegation proposed the goal of eradicating naturally occurring smallpox throughout the globe. It took until 1967, however, for the WHO to finally launch an intensified eradication program. The program involved setting up regional WHO offices and teams of vaccinators, along with surveillance officers and volunteers to gather data. Teams vaccinated people in the areas immediately surrounding outbreaks first, and then expanded the vaccination target areas outward. In the remote areas in particular, rewards were offered to people who reported cases of smallpox to health workers. Persons in developed countries routinely received smallpox vaccinations, usually in childhood.

In all, over 200,000 people worked on the smallpox eradication effort worldwide. The estimated cost was about 300 million dollars, and over one billion doses of vaccine were administered. The mass inoculations were initially performed with a jet injector, which was replaced in 1968 with a bifurcated (two-pronged) needle. The bifurcated needle reduced the amount of vaccine needed for inoculation to only a tiny drop, and could be better administered in the field.

During the early 1970s, individual countries began to report that they were free of smallpox. The last known case of endemic (naturally-occurring) smallpox occurred in Merka, Somalia, in 1977, where Ali Maow

Maalin, a hospital cook, came down with the disease. Maalin is shown in the accompanying photograph after he recovered in 1979.

Before the final victory over smallpox was declared, a special system for certification of smallpox eradication was established. The International Commission for Certification, consisting of international teams of public health, epidemiologists (scientists who track disease outbreaks), and virology experts, was established by the WHO. Areas with endemic smallpox were visited by the Commission two years after the last case of the disease was reported, and based on the reports of the regional authorities, issued certificates when an area was declared smallpox free. Officially, the eradication of smallpox was declared at the thirtieth World Health Assembly meeting in 1980, in Geneva, Switzerland.

PRIMARY SOURCE

ALI MAOW MAALIN SURVIVES THE LAST ENDEMIC SMALLPOX CASE

See primary source image.

SIGNIFICANCE

Eliminating smallpox was one of the major public health success stories of the twentieth century. This effort demonstrated that international cooperation on important health issues could be achieved. Moreover, it also demonstrated that it is possible to eradicate an infectious disease with an effective vaccination program, and that vaccination is a useful preventative method in the fight against infectious diseases.

The smallpox vaccine, although highly successful in preventing the disease, showed some side effects. The most common side effects were eczema, mild smallpox-like disease, and in rare cases, encephalitis. Deaths attributed to the vaccine were rare; estimates showed that one death per million was associated with smallpox inoculations. Significantly, not all people can be given the vaccine, especially those with some autoimmune conditions such as eczema, or with weakened immune systems due to illness or immunosuppressive therapy.

As a result of smallpox eradication, routine smallpox vaccination was officially halted in all countries in 1986. Some scientists voiced hesitation about routine vaccination, as claims were made that smallpox could make a comeback, or a similar animal poxvirus could mutate to where it could infect humans. Monkeypox virus infections have been occasionally identified in humans, but cases have not significantly spread.

PRIMARY SOURCE

Ali Maow Maalin Survives the Last Endemic Smallpox Case. Ali Maow Maalin, of Merka, Somalia, who had the world's last recorded case of endemic smallpox in 1977, is shown after his recovery two years later. ©BETTMANN/CORBIS.

People who received the smallpox vaccine retain immunity for at least ten years. Even if exposed to smallpox later than ten years after vaccination, a vaccinated person will likely produce fewer viruses and is much less likely to spread the disease. The exact time interval of effective smallpox vaccine protection has not been determined with certainty, but it is clear that since the immunization ceased, immunity against the disease has diminished in the general population.

After the eradication of smallpox, stocks of the virus were retained in six laboratories in China, Holland, South Africa, the former USSR, the United Kingdom, and the United States. These stocks were later reduced to just two, one in Russia and another in the United States. All smallpox virus stocks were scheduled to be destroyed in 1999, however, both Russia and the U.S. refused to comply with the deadline, stating that a small stock should be maintained for future study, including genetic engineering of the smallpox virus. Later, a World Health Organization scientific committee recommended temporary retention of the remaining stocks of the smallpox virus for research purposes, with the eventual goal remaining for their destruction. Those against the retention of

smallpox stocks point to the possibility of a laboratory accident that could release the smallpox virus to the public, or to the possibility that smallpox could be used by terrorists as a biological weapon.

Current research is aimed at producing a safer, longer-lasting vaccine using modern manufacturing techniques that will produce immunity even in individuals unable to receive the standard vaccine. Researches working with the smallpox virus also aim to develop new and improved anti-viral drugs.

The WHO also recommended in 2004 that 200 million doses of smallpox vaccine should be maintained by the organization, as well as a supply of bifurcated needles.

FURTHER RESOURCES
Books

Fenner, Frank, et.al. *Smallpox and Its Eradication.* Geneva: World Health Organization, 1988.

Plotkin, Stanley A., and Walter A. Orenstein, eds. *Vaccines.* Philadelphia: W.B. Saunders, 1999.

Periodicals

Arita, I. "Can We Stop Smallpox Vaccination?" *World Health*, no. 5 (1980): 27–29.

Fenner, Frank. "How Can We Be Sure?" *World Health*, no. 5 (1980): 35–39.

Henderson, D. A. "A Victory for All Mankind." *World Health*, no. 5 (1980):3–5.

———— "Smallpox as Biological Weapon: Medical and Public Health Management." *JAMA*, no. 22 (1999): 2127–2137.

Web sites

Centers for Disease Control and Prevention (CDC). "Smallpox." <http://www.bt.cdc.gov/agent/smallpox/index.asp> (accessed September 9, 2005).

Flight, Collette. *BBC Science and Discovery.* "Smallpox: Eradicating the Scourge." <http://www.bbc.co.uk/history/discovery/medicine/smallpox_01.shtml> (accessed May, 9, 2005).

Camp Devens Letter

Influenza Pandemic of 1918

Letter

By: Roy

Date: September 29, 1918

Source: "Camp Devens Letter." *British Medical Journal* (December 22–29, 1979).

About the Author: The writer of this letter, known only as "Roy," was an army physician assigned to Camp Devens, Massachusetts, during the influenza pandemic of 1918.

INTRODUCTION

The influenza pandemic of 1918 killed more people than any other epidemic in recorded history, including the bubonic plague pandemic of the fourteenth century known as the Black Death. Although it apparently originated in China as a variation of the influenza virus, the 1918 flu was generally known as the Spanish flu because of the large number of deaths it caused in Spain in early 1918.

The Spanish flu moved too quickly for public health authorities to adequately respond. The disease, nicknamed the "purple death," caused the skin to turn the color of wet ashes and sparked sudden nosebleeds. It struck suddenly—a healthy person could become deathly ill within one to two hours. The fever that accompanied this flu often reached 105 °F. Aches also were characteristic of the disease with sufferers commonly describing themselves as feeling as if they had been bruised or beaten all over their bodies. A cough, dripping nose, and sore throat completed the diagnosis of influenza. Those in the grip of the disease were typically delirious and occasionally were found wandering in the streets. Pneumonia was a common complication of the Spanish flu and contributed to the high death rate. Many who survived the flu were so weakened by their illness that they fell prey to bronchitis and pleurisy. As the symptoms of the flu subsided, weakness and depression often lingered.

Although the viral strain responsible for the Spanish flu was a particularly virulent one, the worldwide impact of the disease was intensified by the fact that it broke out in the last year of World War I (1914–1918). The massive worldwide movements of troops and shifts of civilian populations during the conflict provided the best possible opportunity for the spread of airborne germs. In the United States, influenza first appeared in early 1918 in the chief embarkation port of New York City. The U.S. Army lost almost as many soldiers from the illness as they lost in combat, snarling attempts to reinforce divisions already in battle and significantly influencing the conduct of the war.

In both military and civilian life, hospital resources were strained by the sheer number of persons sick with influenza. Physicians and nurses were overwhelmed and in short supply. Quarantine measures were enacted, but did little to stem the spread of the disease. Mortuaries were overcrowded. One Army physician, known only as "Roy," documented his observations of the epidemic at the base hospital at Camp Devens, Massachusetts. The letter was found years later and now resides in the archives at the University of Michigan.

■ PRIMARY SOURCE

Camp Devens, Mass.
Surgical Ward No 16
29 September 1918
(Base Hospital)

My dear Burt,

It is more than likely that you would be interested in the news of this place, for there is a possibility that you will be assigned here for duty, so having a minute between rounds I will try to tell you a little about the situation here as I have seen it in the last week.

As you know I have not seen much Pneumonia in the last few years in Detroit, so when I came here I was somewhat behind in the niceties of the Army way of intricate Diagnosis. Also to make it good, I have had for the last week an exacerbation of my old "Ear Rot" as Artie Ogle calls it, and could not use a Stethoscope at all, but had to get by on my ability to "spot" 'em thru my general knowledge of Pneumonias. I did well enough, and finally found an old Phonendoscope that I pieced together, and from then on was all right. You know the Army regulations require very close locations etc.

Camp Devens is near Boston, and has about 50,000 men, or did have before this epidemic broke loose. It also has the Base Hospital for the Div. of the N. East. This epidemic started about four weeks ago, and has developed so rapidly that the camp is demoralized and all ordinary work is held up till it has passed. All assembleges of soldiers taboo.

These men start with what appears to be an ordinary attack of LaGrippe or Influenza, and when brought to the Hosp. they very rapidly develop the most viscous type of Pneumonia that has ever been seen. Two hours after admission they have the Mahogany spots over the cheek bones, and a few hours later you can begin to see the Cyanosis extending from their ears and spreading all over the face, until it is hard to distinguish the coloured men from the white. It is only a matter of a few hours then until death comes, and it is simply a struggle for air until they suffocate. It is horrible. One can stand it to see one, two or twenty men die, but to see these poor devils dropping like flies sort of gets on your nerves. We have been averaging about 100 deaths per day, and still keeping it up. There is no doubt in my mind that there is a new mixed infection here, but what I dont know.

My total time is taken up hunting Rales, rales dry or moist, sibilant or crepitant or any other of the hundred things that one may find in the chest, they all mean but one thing here—Pneumonia—and that means in about all cases death.

The normal number of resident Drs. here is about 25 and that has been increased to over 250, all of whom (of course excepting me) have temporary orders—"Return to your proper Station on completion of work." Mine says "Permanent Duty," but I have been in the Army just long enough to learn that it doesnt always mean what it says. So I dont know what will happen to me at the end of this.

We have lost an outrageous number of Nurses and Drs., and the little town of Ayer is a sight. It takes Special trains to carry away the dead. For several days there were no coffins and the bodies piled up something fierce, we used to go down to the morgue (which is just back of my ward) and look at the boys laid out in long rows. It beats any sight they ever had in France after a battle. An extra long barracks has been vacated for the use of the Morgue, and it would make any man sit up and take notice to walk down the long lines of dead soldiers all dressed and laid out in double rows. We have no relief here, you get up in the morning at 5.30 and work steady till about 9.30 P.M., sleep, then go at it again. Some of the men of course have been here all the time, and they are TIRED.

If this letter seems somewhat disconnected overlook it, for I have been called away from it a dozen times the last time just now by the Officer of the Day, who came in to tell me that they have not as yet found at any of the autopsies any case beyond the Red. Hepatitis. stage. It kills them before they get that far.

I dont wish you any hard luck Old Man but I do wish you were here for a while at least. Its more comfortable when one has a friend about. The men here are all good fellows, but I get so damned sick o Pneumonia that when I go to eat I want to find some fellow who will not "Talk Shop" but there aint none nohow. We eat it, live it, sleep it, and dream it, to say nothing of breathing it 16 hours a day. I would be very grateful indeed if you would drop me a line or two once in a while, and I will promise you that if you ever get into a fix like this, I will do the same for you.

Each man here gets a ward with about 150 beds, (Mine has 168) and has an Asst. Chief to boss him, and you can imagine what the paper work alone is—fierce—and the Govt. demands all paper work be kept up in good

shape. I have only four day nurses and five night nurses (female) a ward-master, and four orderlies. So you can see that we are busy. I write this in piecemeal fashion. It may be a long time before I can get another letter to you, but will try.

This letter will give you an idea of the monthly report which has to be in Monday. I have mine most ready now. My Boss was in just now and gave me a lot more work to do so I will have to close this.

Good By old Pal,
"God be with you till we meet again"
Keep the Bouells open.
(Sgd) Roy.

SIGNIFICANCE

By the end of 1919, the influenza pandemic had run its course. However, influenza continues to be a serious disease, causing many deaths worldwide each year. Even in a year when only a mild form of influenza circulates and despite the availability of vaccines, an estimated one to one and one-half million people die from influenza infections or from complications related to the disease. Generally, the very old, the very young, and those with compromised immune systems are more vulnerable to complications from the flu. During the 1918 influenza pandemic, an exaggerated immune response to the virus occurred in otherwise young, healthy adults and led to the severe lung inflammation that caused death.

The influenza pandemic of 1918 killed more people—mostly otherwise healthy young adults—than any other disease of similar duration in world history. Exact numbers of those struck by influenza are unknown. In 1919, a U.S. Public Health Service survey of eleven cities and towns discovered that about 280 out of 1,000 persons had influenza during the pandemic, yielding an estimated national infection rate of over 25 million afflicted Americans in 1918–1919. Deaths worldwide were estimated at 30 million to 75 million, or about 2.5 to 5 percent of the world's population in 1918.

In 2005, scientists announced that they had sequenced the genetic structure of the virus responsible for the 1918 influenza pandemic. By analyzing tissue samples recovered from a 1918 flu victim found frozen in the Alaskan tundra, along with preserved lung tissue samples from affected World War I soldiers, scientists were able to determine that the virus is a variety of avian (bird) influenza, known as the H1N1 strain.

In March 2005, two women wear masks as they carry a basket of diseased chickens in Vietnam. The chickens are suspected of having the "bird flu," which has killed humans in countries such as Cambodia, China, Indonesia, Thailand, Turkey, and Vietnam. AP/WIDE WORLD PHOTOS.

Influenza epidemics tend to occur about every thirty years, and recent events have significantly heightened concern among scientists that another deadly pandemic may be on the horizon. In 2005, the World Health Organization warned that the H5N1 avian influenza strain (commonly known as the "bird flu"), which recently emerged in Asia, may lead to the next global influenza pandemic. Evidence suggests that the H5N1 flu is genetically similar to the virus that caused the 1918 pandemic. Although it is difficult for the H5N1 flu virus to be spread from person to person, mutations in the virus could alter this disease-transmission picture. If the virus changes so that it can be easily spread in airborne droplets, such as from a cough or sneeze, a global pandemic could result. In 2005, the world's population totals about 6.5 billion people—more than three times greater than the 1918 population. An influenza pandemic with mortality rates similar to those seen in the 1918 epidemic could kill an estimated 150 million people.

Strategies to counter a future avian influenza pandemic include tracking wild birds that host avian flu viruses, culling infected domestic birds, quarantining birds and poultry in trade, producing more antiviral drugs, and developing a vaccine to target the H5N1 influenza virus.

FURTHER RESOURCES

Books

Crosby, Alfred W. *America's Forgotten Pandemic.* New York: Cambridge University Press, 2003.

Kirsty Duncan. *Hunting the 1918 Flu: One Scientist's Search for a Killer Virus.* Toronto: University of Toronto Press, 2003.

Web sites

PBS American Experience. "Influenza 1918." <http://www.pbs.org/wgbh/amex/influenza/index.html> (accessed October 20, 2005).

Immunization Campaigns

How Many Immunizations Does It Take To Protect Your Child?

Poster

By: California Department of Health Services

Date: The poster first appeared in the early 1980s as part of a public health campaign. The exact date is uncertain.

Source: California Department of Health Services. *National Library of Medicine.* "How Many Immunizations Does It Take To Protect Your Child?" Available online at <http://profiles.nlm.nih.gov/VC/B/B/C/G/> (accessed June 2, 2005).

About the Author: As with most state health agencies, the California Department of Health Services (CDHS), also previously known as the California department of Health, is charged with the mission to protect and improve the health of citizens. The department promotes public health through programs that offer direct care and education. Services offered by the CDHS include medical care, public health education, preventive medical services, environmental health programs, and special needs programs.

INTRODUCTION

Public health is a branch of preventative medicine concerned with the physical, mental, social, and environmental health of the community as a whole. From everyday lifestyle needs such as food and workplace safety to proper childhood care, public health professionals apply scientific principles to analyze a community environment and institute measures that promote community well-being.

Most developed countries support national public health institutions that research current health trends, and rely on information provided to them by smaller, local public health centers throughout the country to help predict future trends. For instance, the Centers for Disease Control and Prevention (CDC) in the Unites States, among its other functions, collect and analyze data provided by state and local health departments. Special methods of information gathering regarding disease prevalence, along with methods to recognize patterns and institute control measures for significant findings, form the basis of epidemiology. Epidemiologists use statistics to find relationships between the incidence of disease and correlating factors, such as diet, lifestyle patterns, and the environment.

Actual health care and many public education programs designed to prevent illness are operated by state and local health agencies. Regardless of the level of the organization, public health agencies assist the government involved to enact temporary measures, or pass legislation to protect the health of the population at large.

Vaccination helps the immune system prepare defenses that protect against specific severe or lethal diseases. Both medically and socially significant, vaccines offer protection from a range of diseases.

Vaccination specifically refers to a procedure in which the presence of an antigen (a foreign substance that stimulates an immune response) stimulates the formation of antibodies that are designed to destroy the antigen. In a properly functioning immune system, the exposure to a less potent (also known as attenuated) form of an antigen in a vaccine helps the immune system prepare antibodies that can then attack more potent forms of the antigen (or the antigen carrier, such as a virus). Antibodies act to protect the host from future exposure to the antigen.

Techniques of vaccination have been practiced since early in the eighteenth century when a common practice in Turkey was to expose uninfected individuals to scrapings of a lesion from those infected with smallpox. This exposure to the antigen allowed the buildup of immunity that in many cases protected the vaccinated individual from contracting the disease. Subsequently, in 1796, the English physician Edward Jenner (1749–1823) refined the technique and produced a vaccine for cowpox.

In addition to medical significance, the advancement of vaccines has carried significant social impact. For example, poliomyelitis, commonly known as polio, an infectious viral disease of childhood that often resulted in severe muscle paralysis, created a lingering atmosphere of fear in the United States during the first half of the twentieth century. Mothers isolated their children from both playmates and public locations to prevent exposure to the disease. By 1954, American physician Jonas Salk (1914–1995) tested his polio vaccine made from the killed virus, and Americans eagerly waited in lines at public health centers (many of these were makeshift sites in schools or auditoriums) by the thousands to inoculate their children. Polio is now on the brink of global extinction, with vaccination routine in the developed world, and efforts to vaccinate those in remote areas continuing.

The schedule at which a vaccine is administered is important for its effectiveness. Often, vaccines require a series of inoculations given at specific intervals. The need to follow a specific vaccination schedule represents the main thrust of the poster illustrated, and is found as a common component of many such public health awareness posters.

The poster titled, "How Many Immunizations Does It Take To Protect Your Child?" represents a class of publications promoted by public health officials who are charged with protecting and improving the physical, mental, social, and environmental health of the community.

Public education programs, exemplified by the poster, are designed to prevent illness and to protect the health of the population at large.

PRIMARY SOURCE

IMMUNIZATION CAMPAIGNS
See primary source image.

SIGNIFICANCE

During the late 1970s and early 1980s, the rise of individualism and the popularity of self-help movements in the United States and Western Europe provided a new challenge to public health officials. Individuals began to take control of their own heath care and, in essence, some control and responsibility was wrested away from the physician and other health care workers. This presented a special challenge to public health agencies who now had to turn from campaigns that simply encouraged people to see their physician (or warned them against certain behaviors), to public awareness campaigns that provided specific and detailed information such as the course of childhood vaccinations and the schedule for those vaccinations.

Public health agencies used posters to appeal to a population increasingly dependent on visual media as a format that could inexpensively capture attention and convey vital information.

The development of vaccines that offer protection from a range of diseases, including polio, smallpox, and measles, is considered among the most significant of accomplishments of medical science. Current research continues to develop vaccines against diseases such as acquired immune deficiency syndrome (AIDS), additional types of influenza, and certain types of cancer.

Vaccination is currently carried out by a variety of methods, such as injection, inhalation, or oral ingestion.

The material used for vaccination can be divided into four classes.

Vaccines with living, but weakened, viruses are termed attenuated vaccines. The attenuated virus does not cause a severe infection, but does present the body with sufficient challenge to mount and thus "learn" an immune response. The MMR vaccine (the common abbreviation for the measles, mumps, and rubella vaccine), such as mentioned in the poster, is an example of an attenuated vaccine.

Vaccination can also involve the use of dead viruses and bacteria. The antigen, usually a specific molecule that resides on the surface of the cell, is sufficient alone to provoke an immune response that subsequently provides protection against live bacteria or virus carrying the same surface molecule.

The third type of vaccination uses toxin produced by the living bacterium, but not the bacteria themselves. Diphtheria and tetanus vaccines are examples of toxoid vaccines promoted by the poster.

The fourth class of vaccine is engineered, or uses a chemical compound formed from the fusion of portions of two antigens. The *Haemophilus influenzae* type b (Hib) vaccine, promoted in the poster, is such a biosynthetic vaccine.

The emphasis on proper vaccinations for children is especially important because during the first two years of life, it is important to develop immune protection against a number of viral and bacterial diseases, including, polio, hepatitis B, MMR, pertussis (also called whooping cough), diphtheria, tetanus, *Haemophilus influenzae* type b, and certain pneumococcal infections.

Often, a single exposure or vaccination will not produce the desired level of immune protections and so repeated exposure is provided by following an optimal vaccination schedule. For example, the vaccination against diphtheria, tetanus, and pertussis (DTP) is typically administered, as depicted in the poster, at two, four, and six months of age, again at fifteen to eighteen months, then at four to six years of age.

The duration of protection from disease varies according to the disease. In some cases there is lifelong immunity, but others such as tetanus require repeated exposure via "booster" vaccinations. Although vaccination carries a slight risk of complications ranging from soreness at the injection site to, rarely, illness and death, the risks of not being vaccinated are shown statistically as far more dangerous.

In addition to oversight of adequate production and distribution of vaccines, public health officials at the local, national, and international level are charged with the responsibility to educate the public regarding vaccines available, and the proper course of administration. Public health achievements such as the

How Many Immunizaitons Does It Take To Protect Your Child? "How Many Immunizations Does It Take To Protect Your Child?" a California Department of Health Services poster promoting childhood immunizations, was featured in California public health facilities in the 1980s. COURTESY, CALIFORNIA DEPARTMENT OF HEALTH SERVICES, IMMUNIZATION BRANCH, INFORMATION AND EDUCATION SECTION.

promotion of vaccination through health education programs have benefited millions throughout the world. As a result of global vaccination efforts, eighty percent of the world's children are vaccinated against major childhood diseases such as diphtheria, pertussis, measles, polio, and tetanus, and, globally, child mortality has decreased since 1980.

The political realities of the twenty-first century create new concerns for public health officials and vaccination education programs. For example, the last known case of smallpox occurred in Africa in 1977, and smallpox vaccinations are no longer routinely necessary as the disease is considered eradicated. However, recent concerns regarding the potential for deliberate use of smallpox virus as a bioterror weapon force government and public health officials to continue to prepare for a smallpox outbreak. The stockpile of smallpox vaccine in the United States in 2005 was estimated at only 15 million doses. Even if diluted to minimal levels that provide clinical effectiveness, the vaccine supply would be sufficient for less than half the population of the United States. In case of mass exposure to smallpox or an outbreak, the current strategy calls for using the vaccine supply for those affected and to create a ring of protection in the population surrounding the outbreak. The level of protection still offered to older Americans by virtue of their own childhood smallpox vaccination remains a question of scientific interest and debate.

FURTHER RESOURCES

Books

Hopkins, D. R. *The Greatest Killer: Smallpox in History.* Chicago: University of Chicago Press, 2002.

Koop, C. Everett. *Critical Issues in Global Health.* Hoboken, N.J.: John Wiley & Sons, 2002.

Link, Kurt, *The Vaccine Controversy: The History, Use, and Safety of Vaccinations.* Westport, Conn.: Praeger, 2005.

Preston, Richard. *The Demon in the Freezer.* New York: Random House, 2002.

Periodicals

Henderson, D. A., et al. "Smallpox as a Biological Weapon: Medical and Public Health Management." *Journal of the American Medical Association* 281 (1999): 2127–2137.

Rosenthal, S. R., M. Merchlinsky, C. Kleppinger, et. al. "Developing New Smallpox Vaccines." *Emerging Infectious Diseases* 7 (2001): 920–926.

Web sites

Centers for Disease Control and Prevention. "Smallpox Factsheet: Vaccine Overview." Public Health Emergency Preparedness and Response. December 9, 2002. <http://

www.bt.cdc.gov/agent/smallpox/vaccination/facts.asp> (accessed June 2, 2005).

National Library of Medicine. "History of Medicine." <http://www.nlm.nih.gov/hmd/index.html> (accessed June 2, 2005).

Community Mental Health Centers Construction Act of 1989

Official document

By: Library of Congress

Date: January 23, 1989

Source: *Library of Congress. THOMAS.* "Community Mental Health Centers Construction Act of 1989. One hundred and first Congress, first session. S. 225 IS." <http://thomas.loc.gov/cgi-bin/query/z?c101:S.225.IS> (accessed November 12, 2005).

About the Author: The Community Mental Health Centers Construction Act of 1989 was introduced by New York senator Daniel Patrick Moynihan (1927–2003) and passed by the 101st Congress of the United States.

INTRODUCTION

The treatment of persons who are severely and chronically mentally ill has undergone several revolutions in the United States. Prior to the widespread availability of hospitals and other facilities in which to house such patients, they were cloistered at home, often confined to attics or basements, and kept locked away from other people. There was enormous social and cultural stigma associated with "insanity," due in part to confusion about its causes. Much fear and superstition reigned, with varying beliefs that such conditions might be due to a curse or spell, possession by demons or evil spirits, or even the nefarious influence of the moon, which gave rise to the term "lunacy." Because no one understood its genesis, and there were no effective treatments, mentally ill patients were either left to suffer or subjected to harsh, extreme measures intended to drive the source of the illness from the patient: exorcism, purging, bleeding, near-drowning, and freezing. There was neither widespread belief in nor expectation of recovery in mentally ill patients until at least the mid-twentieth century.

The Mary Elizabeth Inn in San Francisco, California, provides shelter and services for women who are trying to overcome situations such as abuse, addiction, homelessness, financial problems, and mental health issues, among others. AP/WIDE WORLD PHOTOS.

In the middle of the eighteenth century, facilities to house individuals unable to care for themselves began to appear, particularly in urban areas. The development of such institutions was due in large measure to societal changes wrought by the industrial revolution: As demand for a ready workforce grew, fewer people were left at home to care for those unable to live independently. This led to the growth of orphanages, alms- and poorhouses, as well as asylums for the mentally ill, cognitively challenged, and physically impaired. These facilities warehoused large groups of people for long periods of time, often with minimal care—because there was no real concept of treatment or rehabilitation. Through the end of the eighteenth century, the institutionalized mentally ill were often chained or shackled, restrained in beds or cell-like rooms, and generally incarcerated like the most hardened and dangerous criminals.

During the nineteenth century, "moral management" therapy, begun in England by William Battie (1703–1776), was introduced in the United States. In this model, the mentally ill were no longer chained or sequestered. Although still institutionalized, they were put in calm and familiar settings, with the belief that such surroundings increased the likelihood of a cure. Early treatment was encouraged, in the belief that this

greatly increased the possibility of remediation. For those who were not severely ill or did not suffer from a psychotic disorder, this treatment was sometimes helpful, allowing them to return to some measure of normalcy.

Unfortunately, moral management was not at all effective for severe mental illnesses; in fact, its lack of restraints led to a sharp increase in aggressive behavior among patients. Furthermore, a large, new, and frequently aggressive segment was added to the severely and chronically mentally ill population after the American Civil War, when a syndrome emerged among returning soldiers that would likely be characterized today as posttraumatic stress disorder.

In the twentieth century the advent of the public health system produced a proliferation of asylums, which dispensed a disturbingly wide spectrum of care, along with an increasing patient population. In 1963 President John F. Kennedy (1917–1963) signed the Community Mental Health Centers Act, which was intended to end human warehousing; fund, create, and build a system of community mental health centers to provide comprehensive mental health services nationwide; and to ensure timely, efficient, and effective treatment of mental illness in outpatient settings. The act, amended in 1989, is excerpted below.

■ PRIMARY SOURCE

Community Mental Health Centers Construction Act of 1989 (Introduced in Senate)
S 225 IS

101st CONGRESS

1st Session

S. 225

To amend title XIX of the Public Health Service Act to provide for the construction of community mental health centers, and for other purposes.

IN THE SENATE OF THE UNITED STATES

January 25 (legislative day, JANUARY 3), 1989

Mr. MOYNIHAN introduced the following bill; which was read twice and referred to the Committee on Finance

A BILL

To amend title XIX of the Public Health Service Act to provide for the construction of community mental health centers, and for other purposes.

Be it enacted by the Senate and House of Representatives of the United States of America in Congress assembled,

SECTION 1. SHORT TITLE.

This Act may be cited as the 'Community Mental Health Centers Construction Act of 1989'.

SEC. 2. FINDINGS AND PURPOSE.

(a) FINDINGS– Congress finds that—

(1) in 1955 Congress established a Joint Commission on Mental Illness and Health to provide an 'objective, thorough, and nationwide analysis and reevaluation of the human and economic problems of mental illness', and at that time three out of every four individuals treated for mental illness were institutionalized with a total of some five hundred and fifty-nine thousand individuals in public mental hospitals;

(2) in 1960, the Joint Commission report, 'Action for Mental Health', recommended that the mentally ill be cared for in the community, and that Federal financial assistance be provided to the States to accomplish this;

(3) in 1962, President Kennedy established the Interagency Task Force on Mental Health, and the Task Force recommended that Federal aid should be provided to assist States in constructing a nationwide network of such centers;

(4) in 1963 the Kennedy Administration recommended before Congress that a goal, by 1980, of one community mental health center per one hundred thousand individuals, or two thousand such centers nationwide, be established, and the Mental Retardation Facilities and Community Mental Health Centers Construction Act of 1963 began the Federal commitment to build this nationwide network of community mental health centers;

(5) in 1967 Congress specifically reaffirmed the goal of having a nationwide network consisting of two thousand community mental health centers in place by 1980;

(6) the mentally ill were to receive treatment, not from large institutions, but from community mental health centers to be built with the assistance provided as a result of the Mental Retardation Facilities and Community Mental Health Centers Construction Act of 1963 and subsequent legislation;

(7) however, the total number of community mental health centers, which could provide mental health services in the community, that have been built with the help of the Federal Government up to the present time is only seven hundred and sixty-eight;

(8) even so, from 1963 to 1980 the number of residents in public mental hospitals declined from five hundred and five thousand in 1963 to one hundred and fifty thousand in 1980; and

(9) even so, as a result of the Federal Government's failure to meet its commitment to build two thousand community mental health centers by 1980, many of the Nation's mentally ill individuals cannot be adequately cared for in the community, and today such individuals comprise at least 1/3 of the homeless population of the United States.

(b) PURPOSE– It is the purpose of this Act to—

(1) restate the commitment began by the Mental Retardation Facilities and Community Mental Health Centers Construction Act of 1963 to build one community mental health center for every one hundred thousand individuals;

(2) provide the funding necessary to meet the commitment to build a community mental center for every one hundred thousand Americans; and

(3) provide mental health services to homeless mentally ill and chronically mentally ill individuals.

SEC. 3. MENTAL HEALTH CONSTRUCTION BLOCK GRANTS.

Title XIX of the Public Health Service Act (42 U.S.C. 201n et seq.) is amended by adding at the end thereof the following new part:

'PART D—MENTAL HEALTH CONSTRUCTION BLOCK GRANTS

'Sec. 1930. Definitions.

'As used in this part:

'(1) COMMUNITY MENTAL HEALTH CENTER– The term 'communnity mental health center' means a facility providing services for the prevention or diagnosis of mental illness, or care and treatment of mentally ill patients, including homeless mentally ill and chronically mentally ill patients, or rehabilitation of such persons, which services are provided principally for persons residing in a particular community or communities in or near which the facility is situated.

'(2) CONSTRUCTION– The term 'construction' includes construction of new buildings, expansion, remodeling, and alteration of existing buildings and the initial equipment of any such buildings (including medical transportation facilities, and architect's fees), but excludes the cost of off-site improvements and the cost of the acquisition of land.

'(3) STATE– The term 'State' includes the District of Columbia, the Virgin Islands, the Commonwealth of Puerto Rico, Guam, American Samoa, the Commonwealth of the Northern Mariana Islands, and the Trust Territory of the Pacific Islands.

'Sec. 1931. Community Mental Health Center Construction Grants.

'(a) IN GENERAL– For each of the fiscal years 1990 through 1994, the Secretary, in consultation with the National Institute of Mental Health, shall make allotments to States from the sums appropriated under subsection (f), to assist such States in constructing community mental health facilities.

'(b) Allotments–

'(1) IN GENERAL– The Secretary shall allot to each State an amount that bears the same ratio to the total amount available as the number of individuals residing in a State, bears to the total number of individuals residing in all States.

'(2) MINIMUM AMOUNT– No State shall receive an allotment of less than $250,000.

'(3) USE OF AMOUNT– Funds allotted to a State under this subsection shall be used for the purpose of–

'(A) building or renovating structures that shall be used as community mental health centers; and

'(B) providing for the adequate staffing and maintenance of community mental health centers that have been constructed or renovated using funds provided under this section.

'(4) LIMITATION– At least 75 percent of the funds allotted to a State under this subsection shall be used to provide services for the homeless mentally ill and chronically mentally ill.

'(5) MATCHING FUNDS– In order to be eligible for an allotment under this subsection the State must certify that it will provide matching funds in an amount equal to such amount.

'(6) DATA– The Secretary shall obtain from the Bureau of the Census, and any other appropriate Federal agency, the most recent data and information necessary to determine the allotments provided for in this subsection.

'(c) Application–

'(1) IN GENERAL– In order to receive an allotment for a fiscal year under this section each State shall submit an application to the Secretary.

'(2) FORM– An application submitted under this subsection shall be in such form, contain such information, and be submitted by such date as the Secretary shall require.

'(d) REALLOTMENTS– Any portion of the allotment to a State under subsection (b) that the Secretary determines is not used by a State in the period that the allotment is made available, shall be reallocated by the Secretary to other States in proportion to the original allotment to such States.

'(e) DISTRIBUTION OF FUNDS– The Secretary shall make the State allotment available to the Governor of such State who shall distribute such funds.

'(f) AUTHORIZATION OF APPROPRIATIONS– There are authorized to be appropriated to carry out this section such sums as are necessary in each of the fiscal years 1990 through 1994.

'(g) ADMINISTRATION– A State shall not use more than 10 percent of the funds allotted to such State under this section for administrative expenses.'

SIGNIFICANCE

In large measure, the practice of warehousing the chronically mentally ill continued into the twentieth century, although available treatment options continued to expand and improve, particularly for those able to benefit from psychotherapy. In the 1930s the now-controversial practice of lobotomy came into vogue, followed shortly by electroconvulsive therapy (ECT), or shock treatment.

After World War II, the institutionalized patient population rose again; this increase, however, was tempered slightly by the 1946 National Mental Health Centers Act, which introduced the community mental health center paradigm and promoted the idea of outpatient treatment. The use of psychotropic drugs began in 1954 with the use of Thorazine to treat psychotic disorders. This was followed by a virtual explosion of psychotropic drugs. For the first time, it appeared that severely mentally ill patients might be treated successfully with medication and eventually be able to leave institutions. Hospital stays began to decrease, and patients were treated more effectively and humanely while they were there.

The Community Mental Health Centers Act heralded the era of "deinstitutionalization," which reduced the nationwide psychiatric inpatient population from a high in excess of one-half million in 1960 to fewer than one hundred thousand by the mid 1980s. A year later the 1964 Comprehensive Mental Health Bill and the Medicare, followed by the Medicaid Acts of 1966, made sweeping changes in the ways federal, state, and local governments paid for mental health care.

Although outpatient treatment centers have been tremendously successful and effective in many ways, their advent has had a significant downside as well. Because most inpatient facilities no longer provide long-term care, options to treat severe or chronic mental illnesses are often limited. Many communities, particularly those that are impoverished or isolated, lack sufficient means to provide comprehensive services. As a result, individuals often end up homeless and wandering; living in shelters, bus, or train stations; or simply existing in the outdoors. It is also quite common for the mentally ill to be victims of violent crime, or to be arrested. Many end up in prison, where they may or may not receive adequate care.

The model envisioned by the original Community Mental Health Centers Act has yet to be created: a truly nationwide, comprehensive, multidimensional system that provides medication, housing assistance, physical health care, education, job training, support programs, care management, and wraparound services. The act's 1989 amendment is one step toward realizing that vision.

FURTHER RESOURCES
Periodicals

Drake, R. E., A. I. Green, K. T. Mueser, and H. H. Goldman. "The History of Community Mental Health Treatment and Rehabilitation for Persons with Severe Mental Illness." *Community Mental Health Journal* 39, no. 5 (2003): 427–440.

Web sites

National Mental Health Association. "NMHA and the History of the Mental Health Movement." <http://www.nmha.org/about/history.cfm> (accessed January 5, 2006).

Treatment Advocacy Center. <http://www.psychlaws.org/default.htm> (accessed January 5, 2006).

A Hand and a Home for Pregnant Addicts

Crack Cocaine Impacts Society

Magazine article

By: Dennis Wyss

Date: 1989

Source: Dennis, Wyss. "Mandela House: A Hand and a Home for Pregnant Addicts." *Time* 133 (February 27, 1989).

About the Author: Dennis Wyss worked as a staff writer for *Time* magazine.

INTRODUCTION

Crack cocaine emerged rapidly in the mid–1980s, becoming a major national concern within a year. Crack offered a new way to deliver cocaine to the system by smoking it instead of snorting or injecting it. The crack epidemic was unusual and disturbing in that it occurred during a long-term downward trend in overall drug use in the United States. Crack use was centered in the nation's urban areas among African Americans, and it was associated to an unusual degree with violent crime.

The first reported use of crack cocaine was in the Bahamas in 1983. By 1985, it was readily available on the streets of New York City and spreading to other parts of the United States. As it reached each community, its rapid and intense high and its addictive capacity instantly marked crack as a very dangerous drug.

The hallmark of crack cocaine, perhaps more than any other drug, is its ability to induce persistent, intensive drug-seeking behaviors. A drug absorbed through the lungs after smoking quickly reaches the brain, rapidly producing the sought-after high. Cocaine taken through the nose attains a peak high in ten to fifteen minutes and lasts about an hour, while cocaine injected into the blood peaks in three to five minutes and lasts thirty to forty-five minutes. In sharp contrast, a crack cocaine high is achieved in ten to fifteen seconds and lasts about fifteen minutes. Crack users typically smoke repeated doses or "hits" of the drug to extend the high, sometimes for many hours.

The reinforcing properties of cocaine are enormous. The drug user experiences a powerful craving that leads him or her to abandon all else in a compulsion to obtain more of the drug. Heavy crack users often forego food and sleep to stay high. They frequently suffer malnutrition and exhaustion as a result of such behavior.

Crack affects the user's personal relationships and responsibilities in a range of ways. Long-time psychological effects of crack use include behavior and personality changes such as impulsive, often violent behavior and paranoia. Medical effects of crack use include chronic respiratory problems (usually a persistent cough), chronic fatigue, and insomnia. The overall result of crack use is a rise in crime and violence and, usually, the collapse of the user's family relationships. The article, "Mandela House: A Hand and a Home for Pregnant Addicts," discusses the relationship between crack-addicted mothers and their babies, and one project that offered help in Oakland, California.

PRIMARY SOURCE

The day after welfare checks arrive in her East Oakland, Calif., neighborhood, Minnie Thomas sees the ghosts of mothers shuffling in the winter chill. They are emaciated from crack-cocaine binges, and their hair is wrapped in rags to hide patches where clumps have fallen out. Thomas sees them glance at the children draped carelessly on their hips, then down at the sidewalk. "A woman's eyes are a window to her soul," she says. "Those eyes tell you clear as day that they've blown their check on crack."

Nestled in a tidy, working-class area just three miles away is Mandela House, a residential program founded by Thomas over a year ago for crack-addicted pregnant women. In a cozy five-bedroom home that smells of baby powder and food cooking on the stove, fingers that recently clutched glass crack pipes now rest upon distended bellies. From a back room floats the sound of a baby's cry and a soft, throaty voice singing, "Runaway child, runnin' wild, / . . . go back home where you belong./ You're lost in the great big city."

In the four years since crack hit U.S. streets like hard rain, hospitals have experienced an epidemic of sick, undersized newborns. Crack affects the fetus by constricting the baby's blood vessels and restricting passage of nutrients and oxygen. Even one "hit" can cause fetal damage. At Oakland's Highland General Hospital, doctors say about 18% of some 2,400 births in 1988 were crack-afflicted babies.

The problem of pregnant crack-addicted women is relatively recent, and programs aimed at treating them are scarce. Thomas, a counselor to ex-offenders in Oakland for eleven years, had no model when she began her program in December 1987. But with the dramatic increase of crack-contaminated infants, she did not wait for someone else to show the way. "There was a void in the system," she explains. "People who needed help the most were being ignored." Thomas received her inspiration from the ex-offender mothers she had worked with, who fought to turn their lives around. Her plans received support from officials who knew and respected her work. She named her program for Winnie Mandela, wife of imprisoned South African black leader Nelson Mandela.

Mandela House these days is home to four mothers and their babies and three mothers-to-be. Residents receive prenatal care, drug counseling, classes in child development, personal finances and career guidance. They also share child care, housecleaning and cooking. "Mine is reality treatment," says Thomas. "I'm trying to put some order in their lives." Women are referred to Mandela House from jail, court and county protective services. The program is funded by the county, a private grant and donations.

On a typical Monday morning, the neatly dressed mothers gather on living-room sofas for a counseling session led by Thomas. Longtime residents express unfettered affection for their tall, slim mentor, dressed today in a red jumpsuit, brown tweed jacket, black high heels and silver bracelets. "She doesn't judge you from what others say, she judges you from what you say and do," says Monique Gray, a Mandela House veteran of one year. "You can't fool Minnie," four-month resident Patricia Rodgers admits.

When Beverly Dynes, now seven months pregnant, had been in Mandela House for only one month, she confided, "I keep asking myself, 'If I was back out on the streets and offered some rocks, what would I say?' Before, my answer would be 'yes!' But now it's 'probably.' God, that's a big step." Another woman responded, "Amen." But Thomas' steady message, then as now, is "You say you're better, but just how much better are you?" She tells the groups, "You've got to remind yourself every day why you're here because the closer you come to leaving, the closer you'll come to temptation time."

Mothers at Mandela House have more than addiction in common. They're mostly poor and black. All have other children in family and foster homes. Beatings by boyfriends and husbands were regular. What brought their world crashing down was an out-of-control lust for the intense feelings of power and well-being that flow from a hit of crack. "Crack has taken away these women's pride," says Thomas. "By the time they find their way here, they'll beg, steal and trade their bodies to the dope man for more." The mothers uneasily deny that their babies were affected by crack, but Thomas says all the children have shown signs of their mothers' drug use.

Thomas, 55, illustrates her lessons with examples from her own life of trials. Her husband was killed in a fire at his foundry job, leaving her with three young children. While working full time, she earned a degree in sociology from San Francisco State University. Several years later, she was almost killed in a fire that destroyed her house. Today, living in the neighborhood that many of her mothers come from, she is often awakened at night by dopers going to and from a "rock house" across the street. "I tell the women constantly that I'm part of them," Thomas says, remembering her own youthful wildness, pain and disorder. "I tell them, 'I was you.'"

Thomas' rules are as unforgiving as the deadly streets of East Oakland. Drugs, violence and profanity are outlawed. Mothers cannot leave the Mandela House grounds during their first 30 days; trips to doctors' appointments or

Alerting people to the dangers of crack cocaine, a graffiti artist expresses the impact that the inexpensive, yet powerful drug has had on society: "Crack Kills." ©VIVIANE MOOS/CORBIS.

court dates must be made with Thomas or one of her small staff. Residents are randomly tested for drugs. Eventually, women can earn short leaves, phone calls and family visits. School and jobs follow when the resident and Thomas agree it's time.

Many of the women have a lifetime of experience to overcome. Rodgers' earliest childhood memory was watching her heroin-addict mother stick a needle in her arm. Until recently, Rodgers was lost in a haze of cocaine smoke and subsisted on leftovers pilfered from a fast-food restaurant. Now she sits in the Mandela House kitchen, which is rich with the smell of baking meat loaf.

"The first time I hit the pipe, I thought, 'Wow! Home run!'" says Rodgers, a beautiful but hardened 29-year-old former dealer who is pregnant with her eighth child. Beneath her gold-tinged curls, a small metal plate covers a hole smashed in her skull with a board swung by an angry boyfriend. Her dark eyes glitter when she speaks of crack. Then she looks weary, confused and angry. "When I came here, I figured I'd get a place to sleep and some food, and then split and get an abortion and get high once in a while,"

she says. "But I was just lying to myself, lie after lie after lie."

Several women have been expelled or have bolted from Mandela House. One was a mother whose legs Thomas held in the hospital all night while she was giving birth. Two weeks later, the woman suddenly left with her baby. "I felt like I'd been kicked in the stomach," Thomas says. "For the first time, I cried."

But others, proud, and more than a little scared, are preparing to graduate. One is Gray, 27, who is attending college, lining up a job and planning to leave with her eleven-month-old son. "All my life I was told I was nothing but dirt," says Gray. "Minnie made me believe I wasn't dirt and could do anything I wanted and that I didn't need drugs to do it."

Mandela House has more than 60 women waiting to take Gray's place. The task is monumental, but Thomas perseveres even when mothers she loves desert her and return to the seductive glow of the crack pipe. "If they don't hear me now, they'll hear me later," she says. "Some will leave, start smoking rocks again and sink back to the gutter. But even when they're down there, they'll keep hearing Minnie. And they'll be back." It is a blessing that Minnie Thomas will be waiting.

SIGNIFICANCE

By the 1990s, the media was filled with images of crack houses, crack babies, and the black crack user. A largely urban drug, crack seemed to be something that would remain safely away from largely white, suburban areas, but would cause enormous damage to the inner-city African American communities. The impact of crack has since shifted.

It is now possible to find crack anywhere in the United States. It is no longer an urban problem. Seeing an opportunity for new customers and more money, crack dealers moved to the suburbs, bringing crime and social disruption with them.

The most disturbing casualties of the crack trade are the crack babies. In the 1980s and 1990s, the crack baby epidemic was highlighted through pictures of tiny newborns who were believed to have lifelong health problems. Health and education activists feared a new generation of urban tragedies. However, unlike fetal alcohol syndrome, which has physical effects that interfere with a child's development, the symptoms associated with crack-exposed babies appear to be connected to their environment. Crack addicts simply do not devote much attention to their babies and tend to abandon the children to relatives and other caregivers while pursuing the next hit. Such neglect often leaves children with language and interpersonal difficulties; often these difficulties can be remedied.

The history of drug abuse indicated that as the use of crack cocaine diminished over time it was likely to be replaced with another potent drug. In the 1990s, crack was replaced by methamphetamine as the new, "in" drug. Now considered the greatest drug problem in the United States, "meth" is much like crack in that it is highly addictive and is typically smoked. However, it is far easier to obtain, since it can be made from inexpensive, over-the-counter ingredients.

FURTHER RESOURCES
Books

Cooper, Edith Fairman. *The Emergence of Crack Cocaine Abuse.* New York: Novinka Books, 2002.

Erickson, Patricia, et al. *The Steel Drug: Cocaine and Crack in Perspective.* New York: Lexington Books, 1994.

Williams, Terry. *Crackhouse: Notes from the End of the Line.* Reading, MA: Addison-Wesley, 1992.

The Clean Air Act, Title 1: Air Pollution Prevention and Control

Part A: Air Quality and Emissions Limitations, Section101: Findings and Purposes

Legislation

By: Anonymous

Date: November 15, 1990

Source: United States Environmental Protection Agency.

About the Author: The U.S Environmental Protection Agency (EPA) was established by President Richard Nixon in 1970 to draft, administer, and enforce national standards for air and water purity. The EPA enforces laws like the Clean Air Act, carries out environmental research, and sponsors various pollution prevention programs and energy conservation efforts.

INTRODUCTION

The Clean Air Act (CAA) was passed in 1970, the year the EPA was created. The act marked the launch of a vigorous and ambitious campaign to improve air quality by requiring federal, state, and local governments to work together to administer environmental legislation like the CAA.

Air pollution is the contamination of air with substances that can harm human health or cause environmental damage. Much of the CAA's purview involves identifying pollutants and setting maximum concentration levels, standards above which exposure is more likely to lead to harm. The CAA identifies two types of standards: primary standards, which are intended to protect human health; and less-stringent secondary standards, which protect property and the environment, including wildlife.

The CAA monitors ground-level ozone, nitrogen oxides, sulfur dioxide, lead, volatile organic compounds (VOCs), and carbon monoxide and dioxide, as well as particulate matter. Their effects are complex and varied, depending upon the level and duration of exposure. Exposure to air pollution can lead to asthma and other lung diseases, cardiovascular disease, heart attack, cancer, and brain damage.

Vehicle emissions and the combustion of fossil fuels are the two main sources of air pollution. With remedies imposed by the CAA, nearly four decades after it was enacted, emissions have been greatly reduced, thanks to cleaner cars, factories, and homes. The CAA amendments of 1990, excerpted below, intensified and renewed the provisions of the CAA, building upon the achievements of its first two decades.

■ PRIMARY SOURCE

THE CLEAN AIR ACT
TITLE I : AIR POLLUTION PREVENTION AND CONTROL
Part A—Air Quality and Emission Limitations
FINDINGS AND PURPOSES
Sec. 101 (a) The Congress finds—

(1) that the predominant part of the Nation's population is located in its rapidly expanding metropolitan and other urban areas, which generally cross the boundary lines of local jurisdictions and often extend into two or more States;

(2) that the growth in the amount and complexity of air pollution brought about by urbanization, industrial development, and the increasing use of motor vehicles, has resulted in mounting dangers to the public health and welfare, including injury to agricultural crops and livestock, damage to and the deterioration of property, and hazards to air and ground transportation;

(3) that air pollution prevention (that is, the reduction or elimination, through any measures, of the amount of pollutants produced or created at the source) and air pollution control at its source is the primary responsibility of States and local governments; and

(4) that Federal financial assistance and leadership is essential for the development of cooperative Federal, State, regional, and local programs to prevent and control air pollution.

(b) The purposes of this title are—

(1) to protect and enhance the quality of the Nation's air resources so as to promote the public health and welfare and the productive capacity of its population;

(2) to initiate and accelerate a national research and development program to achieve the prevention and control of air pollution;

(3) to provide technical and financial assistance to State and local governments in connection with the development and execution of their air pollution prevention and control programs; and

(4) to encourage and assist the development and operation of regional air pollution prevention and control programs.

Industrial facilities can have a major impact on the environment. Here, at a Uniroyal site in Detroit, Michigan, a warning sign alerts people that the area contains hazardous substances. AP/WIDE WORLD PHOTOS.

(c) Pollution Prevention.—A primary goal of this Act is to encourage or otherwise promote reasonable Federal, State, and local governmental actions, consistent with the provisions of this Act, for pollution prevention.

[42 U.S.C. 7401]

■ SIGNIFICANCE

Ten years after the introduction of the CAA amendments, a panel of economists, scientists, and public health experts analyzed computer models to estimate what health gains might be expected from controlling air pollution. Setting their sights on the year 2010, they predicted the legislation would prevent 23,000 premature deaths and nearly two million asthma attacks a year. In addition, as many as 22,000 hospital admissions for lung disease, 42,000 for heart disease and 5,000 emergency room visits for asthma could be avoided with cleaner air.

A 2005 review suggested that the Acid Rain Program inaugurated by the amendments had been particularly successful, having reduced sulfur dioxide emissions by five million tons and nitrogen oxide emissions by three million tons from 1990 levels. The resultant decline in acid deposition has reduced damage to buildings, trees, and lakes.

Most U.S. cities and communities have much cleaner air, with total emissions of major air pollutants reduced by more than 50 percent. Three-quarters of the country now meets the National Air Quality Standards stipulated by the amendments. In addition, stricter controls on vehicle emissions have significantly reduced emissions of hydrocarbons, carbon monoxide, nitrogen oxides, and particulate matter.

Of course, much remains to be done. A major issue is global warming—the increase in Earth's temperature, which may correspond to levels of so-called "greenhouse gases" (such as carbon dioxide) that result from burning fossil fuels. Scientists disagree over the causes of global warming and if action can be taken to prevent it. The CAA alone cannot cure all of the planet's environmental concerns—although it can improve the health of Americans and their immediate environment.

FURTHER RESOURCES
Web sites

Climate Ark—Climate Change Portal. "Benefits of Clean Air Act Amendments Tallied." <http://www.climateark.org/articles/1999/benclen.htm> (accessed December 5, 2005).

Department of Energy Environmental Policy and Guidance. "Clean Air Act." <http://www.eh.doe.gov/oepa/laws/caa.html> (accessed December 5, 2005).

Environmental Protection Agency. "15th Anniversary of the Clean Air Act Amendments of 1990." <http://www.epa.gov/air/cleanairact/> (accessed December 5, 2005).

National Safety Council. A Division of the National Safety Council. "Section 1: Background on Air Pollution." <http://www.nsc.org/ehc/mobile/acback.htm> (accessed December 5, 2005).

Motor Vehicle Safety and Public Health

Photograph

By: Tim Wright

Date: September 4, 1998

Source: Insurance Institute for Highway Safety. Corbis. September 4, 1998.

About the Photographer: Tim Wright is a photographer and photojournalist whose photographic and written work has appeared in numerous popular and new magazines for over twenty years. In addition to his extensive magazine work, both in the United States and around the world, Wright has completed extensive corporate and advertising professional assignments.

INTRODUCTION

According to the National Center for Statistics and Analysis, a division of the National Highway Traffic Safety Administration (NHTSA), motor vehicle accidents (MVAs) represented the single greatest cause of death in the United States in the year 2002, for all persons between the ages of three and thirty-three years old (43,005 deaths). In 2003, 42,884 people lost their lives as a result of highway fatalities. According to the NHTSA published statistics for the year 2004, there were 42,636 people killed in automobile accidents, and motor vehicle accidents remained the number one killer for persons between the ages of three and thirty-three. For all age groups, motor vehicle accidents consistently rank among the top ten causes of death (often placed under the category of unintentional injury).

Although the statistics for roadway fatalities have maintained an overall downward trend since reaching a high of 116,385 in 1969 in terms of overall numbers, the results have remained consistent in terms of the ranking of roadway-based fatalities among leading causes of death. The great overall decrease in highway deaths has been due, in large measure, to the use of seatbelts (which now includes both lap belts and shoulder harnesses), child safety restraint systems, airbags, stringent laws regarding motor vehicle safety and construction, and significantly improved highway and traffic safety law—including the enforcement of speed limits and driving-under-the-influence or driving-while-intoxicated (DWI/DUI) laws.

One of the central figures in the institution and enforcement of changes in motor vehicle and roadway/highway safety has been an activist and advocate named Ralph Nader. In 1965, Nader published the first edition of the now legendary book *Unsafe at Any Speed*, which was a condemnation of the automotive industry for its lack of mechanical safety standards. The book, as well as media attention drawn from Nader's advocacy and activism, eventually resulted in a spate of automobile safety laws, beginning the following year (1966). With the passage of the National Traffic and Motor Vehicle Safety Act of 1966, the motor vehicle industry became subject to federal

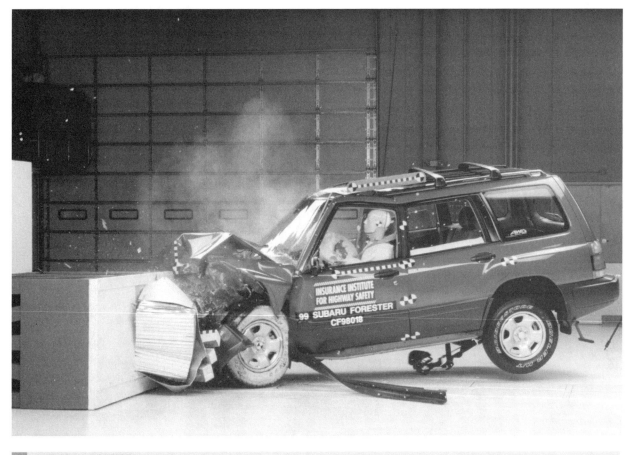

Motor Vehicle Safety and Public Health A Subaru Forester is tested during a front-impact crash conducted by the Insurance Institute for Highway Safety near Charlotesville, Virginia. As motor vehicle accidents are the number one cause of death among young Americans ages 15–24, both industry and the government are evaluating and attempting to improve automobile safety design. ©TIM WRIGHT/CORBIS.

regulations for the first time. His work led to standards in automobile safety manufacturing that permitted, for the first time, the creation of industry standards and data collection that allowed for recall and repair of defective groups of automobiles (for example, recalling a particular year, make, and model of vehicle for repair of defective accelerator system construction). He was also responsible for the creation of the Center for Auto Safety, and the creation of what has come to be known as the Lemon Law, which affords protection to purchasers of used cars.

■ **PRIMARY SOURCE**

MOTOR VEHICLE SAFETY AND PUBLIC HEALTH
See primary source image.

■

SIGNIFICANCE

As motor vehicle safety standards became more stringent, it became necessary to find a means of testing the claims of manufacturers, in order to ascertain whether they were truthful in their advertising, and whether the vehicles really did perform as described. The Insurance Institute for Highway Safety (IIHS) has created a Vehicle Research Center (also called the VRC), designed to accomplish that function. Although the federal government does large-scale testing through the NHTSA, it is generally the data released by the VRC that attracts the most media attention. The goals of the two agencies, while compatible, are slightly different; the IIHSVRC is a not-for-profit research center whose sole purpose is to reduce the number of fatalities attributed to automobile accidents, by rendering cars better able to withstand serious collisions. The VRC not only crash tests

If all motorists in Massachusetts wore Safety Belts there would be

- 75-100 fewer traffic deaths each year; and

- 15,000 fewer injuries.

At a press conference, Ralph Hingson of Boston University's School of Public Health urges motorists to buckle up. Studies show that when drivers and passengers wear safety belts, they are less likely to suffer injuries or die in car crashes. AP/WIDE WORLD PHOTOS.

individual makes and models of motor vehicles, it also performs crash testing with two moving vehicles having front-and side-impact collisions, and can crash test at higher speeds (up to fifty miles per hour). Crash simulations are also done with "crash-test dummies" to examine individual components and their protective efficacy, such as seat belts, driver, passenger and side curtain air bags, child restraint systems, headrests, and the like. They do this in order to assess the performance of the individual component or system independent of the damage to the rest of the vehicle during a collision. The data gleaned by both agencies' research and testing is submitted to the motor vehicle manufacturers, with safety ratings and recommendations for specific improvements.

Crash-test dummies have been created in a range of the configurations likely to occur in the average motor vehicle using population: six-month-old infant, twelve-month-old toddler, three-year-old and six-year-old children, small female, medium-sized male, and large male. They are constructed so as to be as biomechanically similar to humans as possible; that is,

they must conform to the height, weight, body posture, and movement on impact of the humans that they are emulating, and are affixed with sensors to record the nature and types of forces and impact effects on various areas of the body during a collision.

There are a number of intervening factors that have contributed to the continuation of motor vehicle accidents as a leading cause of death among younger Americans. The NHTSA collects fatality data from various locations around the country, and uses it to make inferences about the factors contributing to fatal motor vehicle accidents in America annually. Although virtually the entire country has seat belt laws, not every area consistently enforces them, and a significant number of deaths are caused by injury or by ejection arising from failure to use seatbelts or child restraints, or from using them improperly. In 2004, nearly 40 percent of the vehicle occupants involved in fatal automobile or truck collisions were not wearing restraints, and nearly three-fourths of those in fatal accidents who were completely ejected from the vehicle had not worn restraints.

Substance abuse, particularly the use of alcohol, is a determining factor in many MVAs. The NHTSA estimates that nearly 17,000 people died in alcohol-related collisions in 2004, representing nearly 40 percent of all fatal MVAs; of those, thirty percent involved a driver had a blood alcohol concentration (BAC) at or above the legal limit for intoxication. Of those 2004 MVAs involving drivers who were legally intoxicated, one third were less than twenty-four years old, nearly 30 percent were between twenty-five and thirty-four years old, and slightly more than 20 percent were between thirty-five and forty-four. Among those who were at or above the legal level for intoxication, many had either been involved in previous MVAs, had prior DWI convictions—some involving license suspensions or revocations, or had prior speeding convictions. Alcohol, youth, and speeding are a particularly deadly combination. Thirty percent of all fatal crashes in 2004 involved drivers who were traveling at excessive speed for the roadway conditions; thirty-eight of those who were less than twenty years old were speeding when their fatal accidents occurred. Forty percent of the intoxicated drivers were speeding at the time of their fatal MVAs. Overall, the group with the greatest likelihood of being involved in a fatal MVA, particularly one involving alcohol, speeding, failure to employ restraints, or some combination of these, was males under the age of twenty-four. The NHTSA statistics reported that young males died in MVAs in 2004 three times more frequently than did females; they represented nearly seventy percent of all traffic or pedestrian deaths.

FURTHER RESOURCES

Books

Nader, Ralph. *Unsafe At Any Speed, 25th Anniversary Edition*. Massachusetts: Knightsbridge Publishing Company, 1991.

Periodicals

Mcdonald, Kevin M. "Shifting Out of Neutral: A New Approach to Global Road Safety." *The Vanderbilt Journal of Transnational Law* 38, no. 3 (2005): 743–790.

Web sites

Insurance Institute for Highway Safety. "FAQ." <http://www.hwysafety.org/faq.html> (accessed January 16, 2006).

The Nader Page. "Ralph Nader Biographical Information." <http://www.nader.org/enbio.html> (accessed January 16, 2006).

Tim Wright Photography. "About Tim Wright." <http://www.timwrightphoto.com/about.php> (accessed January 16, 2006).

United States National Highway Traffic Safety Administration. "Traffic Safety Facts: 2004 Data." <http://www-nrd.nhtsa.dot.gov/pdf/nrd-30/ncsa/TSF2004/809911.pdf> (accessed January 16, 2006).

Pasteurization and Aseptic Processing

Grade "A" Pasteurized Milk Ordinance

Ordinance excerpt

By: U.S. Food and Drug Administration

Date: 2001

Source: "Item 16p. Pasteurization and Aseptic Processing." in U.S. Food and Drug Administration. *Grade "A" Pasteurized Milk Ordinance*, 2001 Revision. pages 62–63. Available online at: <http://www.cfsan.fda.gov/~acrobat/pmo01.pdf> (accessed January 25, 2006).

About the Author: The U.S. Food and Drug Administration is a federal agency responsible for ensuring the safety and regulation of food, drugs, cosmetics, medical devices, animal feed, and radiation-emitting products such as cell phones, lasers, and microwave ovens.

INTRODUCTION

Pasteurization is the term for a process where milk is heated to reduce the numbers of microorganisms (bacteria, molds, and yeast) that would otherwise spoil the milk and possibly pose a health threat to those drinking the milk or eating the milk product. The temperature used is not, however, harsh enough to alter the taste or appearance of the milk.

Pasteurization does not necessarily kill all the microbes in the milk. However, the numbers of organisms become so few that they pose no threat to milk quality or health, assuming the product is used by a certain date (the expiration date).

Pasteurization accomplishes two goals. First, the milk is rendered safe from microbial contamination. Second, because the pasteurized milk is packaged in clean containers and kept away from contact with air (which also contains microorganisms that could recontaminate the milk), the milk will stay fresher for a longer period of time. This allows milk to be transported greater distances to the supermarket shelf, and to be sold for a longer period of time.

The temperature and time conditions used in pasteurization were determined following experiments that utilized a variety of microorganisms. Of particular concern is *Coxiella burnettii*, a type of bacteria that is resident in some barnyard animals, and so can be transmitted to milk, and which is resistant to the protein-coagulation activity of heat. By selecting conditions of temperature and time that kill this bacterium, other, less heat-tolerant microbes will also be killed or greatly reduced in number.

Pasteurization is accomplished in one of two ways; the batch method or the continuous method. In the batch method, milk is added to a vat that is surrounded by a jacket of water or steam. The milk is heated to the desired temperature for the determined time and then either cooled down or transferred to another container for cooling. This process is used more for milk products such as ice cream than for liquid milk.

Far more commonly, liquid milk is pasteurized using the continuous flow method, in which the milk is pumped past heated stainless steel plates into a tank where it cools and finally into another tank where the milk is packaged into jugs or cartons. Because the process involves the continuous flow of milk, a greater volume can be pasteurized in a given time than in the batch method.

The continuous method has been modified such that the milk is exposed to a higher temperature at a greater flow rate. This process—known as high-temperature, short-time pasteurization (HTST)—allows even greater quantities of milk to be treated in a given time without compromising quality of the final product.

With proper technique, high-temperature, short-time pasteurization reduces the number of microorganisms by 0.00001 times the original number. A final form of pasteurization is called ultra-high temperature (UHT) method involves heating the product at 138 degrees Celsius (280.4 degrees Fahrenheit) for a minimum of only two seconds.

Ensuring the safety and quality of milk is one of the U.S. Public Health Service's oldest activities, as it first enacted standards for pasteurization in 1924. Then called the *Standard Milk Ordinance*, numerous revisions have been made under the auspice of the Food and Drug Administration.

PRIMARY SOURCE

ITEM 16P. PASTEURIZATION AND ASEPTIC PROCESSING

Pasteurization shall be performed as defined in Section 1, Definition X of this *Ordinance*. Aseptic processing shall be performed in accordance with 21 CFR 113, 21 CFR 108 and the Administrative Procedures of Item 16p., C, D, and E of this Section.

PUBLIC HEALTH REASON Health officials unanimously agree upon the public health value of pasteurization. Long experience conclusively shows its value in the prevention of disease that may be transmitted through milk. Pasteurization is the only practical, commercial measure, which, if properly applied to all milk, will destroy all milkborne disease organisms. Examination of lactating animals and milk handlers, while desirable and of great value, can be done only at intervals and; therefore, it is possible for pathogenic bacteria to enter the milk for varying periods before the disease condition is discovered. Disease bacteria may also enter milk accidentally from other sources, such as flies, contaminated water, utensils, etc. It has been demonstrated that the time-temperature combinations specified by this *Ordinance*, if applied to every particle of milk, will devitalize all milkborne pathogens. Compilations of outbreaks of milkborne disease by the PHS/FDA, over many years, indicate that the risk of contracting disease from raw milk is approximately fifty (50) times as great as from milk that has been "pasteurized."

A note of caution is in order. Although pasteurization destroys the organisms, it does not destroy the toxins that may be formed in milk when certain staphylococci are present, as from udder infections, and when the milk is not properly refrigerated before pasteurization. Such toxins may cause severe illness. Aseptic processing has also been conclusively demonstrated to be effective in preventing outbreaks from milkborne pathogens.

Numerous studies and observations clearly prove that the food value of milk is not significantly impaired by pasteurization.

ADMINISTRATIVE PROCEDURES The pasteurization portion of this Item is deemed to be satisfied when:

1. Every particle of milk or milk product is heated in properly designed and operated equipment to one of the temperatures specified in the following table and held continuously at or above that temperature for at least the time specified:

Pasteurization Temperature vs. Time

Temperature	Time
63°C (145°F)	* 30 minutes
72°C (161°F)	*15 seconds
89°C (191°F)	1.0 second
90°C (194°F)	0.5 seconds
94°C (201°F)	0.1 seconds
96°C (204°F)	0.05 seconds
100°C (212°F)	0.01 seconds

*If the fat content of the milk product is 10 percent (10%) or more, or if it contains added sweeteners, the specified temperature shall be increased by 3 °C (5 °F).

Provided, that eggnog shall be heated to at least the following temperature and time specifications:

69°C (155°F) 30 minutes
80°C (175°F) 25 seconds
83°C (180°F) 15 seconds

Provided further, that nothing shall be construed as barring any other pasteurization process, which has been recognized by FDA to be equally efficient and which is approved by the Regulatory Agency.

2. The design and operation of pasteurization equipment and all appurtenances thereto shall comply with the applicable specifications and operational procedures of Subitems (A), (B), (D) and (E).

SIGNIFICANCE

Pasteurization protects consumers from the health hazards that would otherwise result from the consumption of raw milk. Milk is an abundant source of nutrients for bacteria and other microorganisms. Thus, if not handled properly, milk can become contaminated. Without pasteurization, milk could not be transported long distances to market, or be held on the supermarket shelves for very long. Pasteurization, therefore, has made possible the current conventional selling of milk and other dairy products. Pasteurization also can ensure the quality and safety of other products, including fruit juices, cider, honey, and beer.

The process of pasteurization was named after its discoverer, Louis Pasteur. In addition to pasteurization, Louis Pasteur made a number of other discoveries in the nineteenth century concerning microorganisms that fundamentally changed the world. In one series of investigations, Pasteur demonstrated absolutely that the growth occurring in a liquid food source was due to the presence of microorganisms, and not to the spontaneous appearance of life (a theory called spontaneous generation). Pasteur ingeniously designed a flask with a long neck that bent downward and then upward. Sterile growth medium in the flask did not become cloudy with growth, even when left exposed to the air, since the microbes that entered the neck settled out in the lower portion of the S-shaped neck. But, when the neck was broken to eliminate the curved portion, growth quickly developed in the medium.

This line of experimentation peaked Pasteur's interest in fermentation, the microbial alteration of a

Louis Pasteur is shown working in his lab. He conducted various experiments that ultimately led to the discovery known as pasteurization. ©CORBIS.

nutrient source that occurs under certain environmental conditions. His studies led to the demonstration that wine and milk could be heated to kill spoilage bacteria and mold. In particular, his work with wine was hailed, as spoilage of grapes was a significant problem in the French winemaking industry. The process was later called pasteurization in his honor.

FURTHER RESOURCES
Books

Debre, Patrice, and Elborg Forster. *Louis Pasteur*. Baltimore: Johns Hopkins University Press, 2000.

Robbins, Louise. *Louis Pasteur And the Hidden World of Microbes (Oxford Portraits in Science)*. Oxford: Oxford University Press, 2001.

Web sites

Embassy of France in Canada. "Louis Pasteur." <http://amba france-ca.org/HYPERLAB/PEOPLE/_pasteur.html> (accessed April 25, 2005).

Shearer, J. K., K. C. Bachman, and J. Boosinge. *University of Florida, Institute of Food and Agricultural Sciences.* "The Production of Quality Milk" <http://edis.ifas.ufl.edu/DS112> (accessed January 22, 2006).

Bioterrorism at the Salad Bar

Book excerpt

By: Bill Frist

Date: 2002.

Source: Bill Frist. *When Every Moment Counts: What You Need to Know about Bioterrorism, from the Senate's Only Doctor.* Lanham, Md.: Rowman & Littlefield, 2002.

About the Author: Senator Bill Frist is a Republican from Tennessee who became Senate Majority Leader in 2002. He serves on the Finance and Rules committees in addition to the Health, Education, Labor and Pensions (HELP) committee. Prior to entering politics, he was a cardiothoracic (heart and lung) surgeon.

INTRODUCTION

Senator Bill Frist first used his medical training to explain the threat of bioterrorism after the anthrax attacks in the final months of 2001. His book *When Every Moment Counts* is part of a personal campaign that included a series of public speeches to raise awareness of specific bioterrorist threats, especially anthrax and smallpox. Political cynics have observed that Frist, in attempting to identify himself with the cause of fighting bioterrorism, might also have been trying to raise his public profile. Be that as it may, the threat of bioterrorism against the nation's food supply certainly merits public attention, particularly because it is not just hypothetical but, as Frist points out in the following excerpt, a reality that the country has already confronted. The 1984 salmonella attack on restaurants near The Dalles, Oregon, had largely faded from popular memory by 2002 when Frist wrote his book, so it seemed clear that the United States needed a refresher course in the lessons learned from that attack.

Frist emphasizes that bioterrorism uses fear as a weapon, and to counter this, he makes a considerable amount of information accessible, even to nonspecialist readers, in a coherent, knowledgeable way. According to him, this could reduce the nation's vulnerability to future attacks by building popular support for maintaining the public health infrastructure, which is particularly valuable in motivating people to support enhanced public health preparedness across the board. He makes the case that increased spending on public health and scientific research is an important component in the fight against bioterrorism because it can provide some confidence that an outbreak can be controlled.

■ PRIMARY SOURCE

BIOTERRORISM AT THE SALAD BAR: THE THREAT TO OUR FOOD AND WATER SUPPLY

For the United States, a bioterrorist attack on our food supply is not merely hypothetical. It has already happened here.

In September 1984 an outbreak of food poisoning caused by the bacterium *Salmonella typhimurium* swept through the community of The Dalles, the quiet county seat of Wasco County, Oregon. A total of 751 people became ill, though none died. It was the largest outbreak of foodborne disease in the United States that year.

Public health and law enforcement officials were baffled. Their investigation found links to at least ten of the town's thirty-eight restaurants. Most of the restaurants where people had eaten before coming down with food poisoning had salad bars, but there was no common supplier. There didn't appear to be any pattern that connected all the cases—until the criminal investigation turned up the truth a year later.

Followers of Indian guru Bhogwan Shree Raineesh had built a huge international headquarters and commune in Wasco County and were locked in a zoning dispute with the local government. So commune members came up with a plan: If they could make enough voters sick on election day, they could influence the outcome in their favor.

In September, two months before the election, they had a test run of their plan. They prepared cultures of *Salmonella typhimurium* bacteria in their secret lab on the commune, and then commune members poured the bacteria loaded items in salad bars and, in some restaurants, into coffee creamers.

Two commune members eventually pleaded guilty and went to prison for the attack.

The Oregon attack taught us several hard lessons. It exposed our vulnerability to the deliberate contamination of food in public places. The salmonella culture used in the attack is easily obtained from raw foods bought in a grocery store, and it can be produced in large quantities with simple equipment and little expertise. Residents of The Dalles were fortunate that the cult didn't use a more lethal agent, such as botulinum toxin or even anthrax or tularemia.

The attack also underscored the need for health care providers and laboratories to cooperate and coordinate with local and state public health departments so that any future outbreaks can be detected more quickly.

And The Dalles case changed the way we look at public health emergencies. At the time, back in 1984, it never occurred to investigators that a group would deliberately contaminate food in several restaurants in an effort to advance their political or religious agenda.

Now we know that if a mysterious outbreak of infectious disease occurs that fits no known pattern and doesn't seem to have any common link, the possibility of intentional contamination must be considered, and law enforcement should be called in immediately to investigate.

Since the anthrax attacks of 2001 in the United States, public health officials keep a closer watch for signs of bioterrorism. Here, a microbiologist examines *Bacillus cereus*, which causes food poisoning. AP/WIDE WORLD PHOTOS.

SIGNIFICANCE

Twenty-one years after the first bioterrorism attack on salad bars in Oregon and four years after the 2001 anthrax attacks, it is both fortunate and remarkable that there has been no large-scale biological attack.

News stories published around the time of the anthrax attacks recalled the impact of the salad bar contamination at The Dalles, and noted that the town had not recovered economically from the bioterrorism incident. This publicity opened old wounds in the struggling Oregon community, which had recently seen local aluminum factories close and a downturn in the cherry market, both of which cost hundreds of local jobs. The psychological and economic impact of the attack was much more serious than its health impact, since everyone that was infected recovered quickly.

Because the salmonella attacks occurred in a rural area and were perpetrated by a small fanatical cult, the incident quickly faded from national attention. Nevertheless the incident may provide a glimpse of how the United States might respond to a more widespread and concerted bioterrorism attack. On one hand, people in The Dalles became afraid to go out in public, becoming prisoners in their own homes. On the other hand, however, they voted heavily in ensuing local elections to prevent cult members, who had already taken over the city council of neighboring Antelope, from taking over the whole county politically.

The confrontation was a classic case of bullying in which the aggressor crossed a line far enough to provoke determined resistance from ordinary citizens as well as both county and federal officials. After the mystery had been solved and the cult dispersed under pressure from law enforcement, the citizens of Antelope sent a bronze statue of an antelope to The Dalles, which now stands in front of the county courthouse. The statue displays a plaque that reads, "In order for evil to prevail, good men should do nothing."

The salmonella poisoning had actually been the culmination of growing hostilities between the local population and cult members, who had incorporated themselves into a municipality and created a large and threatening police force. Perhaps the most chilling aspect of the incident was the shock that local people felt from the disruption of the safety and comfort in which they lived, and when they realized that they faced aggression from opponents determined to impose their will by fear and force.

Frist believes America's cocoon of prosperity and security may require additional taxpayer support for the public health infrastructure. As often happens when providing for the common good, unfortunately, it is difficult to marshal financial support when everyday threats such as epidemics and safety hazards are perceived to threaten "other" people. Bioterrorism, however, can be directed at anyone, and such a threat could generate enough support for extraordinary expenditures and open-ended investment in the public health system.

The salmonella and anthrax attacks in the U.S. both had psychological effects that far outweighed the physical. This has led some to argue that the magnitude of bioterrorism has been exaggerated and that it does not justify the time and expense of medication stockpiling and government preparedness. Actually, biodefense, unlike other aspects of public health, devotes considerable resources for a potential future catastrophe instead of existing health threats. It is similar to proposed programs to stockpile medicines to combat bird flu, should that virus mutate and create a human pandemic. Small numbers of people have been victimized by both threats already; they remain, however, potential catastrophes.

When might political promotion of bioterrorism preparedness cross the line from a rational response to a real threat to a strategy intended to cow people into acceptance of a political agenda or raise a politician's profile as a bioterrorism expert? While all of these motivations may operate simultaneously, the ultimate result should be to marhsal people's desire for self-preservation to solve a problem that many would just as soon not think about. Just as the U.S. space program and military research benefited the civilian economy, allocating resources to biodefense has already buttressed public health preparedness, and might produce additional benefits in drug discovery as well. As a result, the nation should be better able to withstand a real large-scale bioterrorism attack.

FURTHER RESOURCES

Books

Frist, Bill. *When Every Moment Counts: What You Need to Know about Bioterrorism from the Senate's Only Doctor.* Lanham, Md.: Rowman & Littlefield, 2002.

Miller, Judith. Stephen Engelberg. and William J. Broad. *Germs: Biological Weapons and America's Secret War.* New York: Simon and Schuster, 2001.

Periodicals

Elmer-Dewitt, Philip. "America on Guard: America's First Bioterrorism Attack." *Time*, October 8, 2001.

Web sites

South Coast Today, "Oregon Town has Never Gotten over Its 1984 Bioterrorism Scare." <http://www.s-t.com/daily/10-01/10-20-01/a02wn011.htm> (accessed December 21, 2005).

When Every Moment Counts. <http://www.wheneverymomentcounts.com> (accessed December 21, 2005).

Priority Traffic Safety Laws

Mothers Against Drunk Driving (MADD)

Pamphlet

By: MADD (Mothers Against Drunk Driving)

Date: 2003

Source: Mothers Against Drunk Driving. *MADD TEA-21 Reauthorization Brochure.* Washington, D.C.: MADD, 2003.

About the Author: In 1980, Candace Lightner's thirteen-year-old daughter Cari was walking on a neighborhood street when she was killed in a hit-and-run collision by a person who was driving while intoxicated. The driver of the vehicle had four previous convictions for driving while intoxicated (DWI), and was out on bail for an alcohol-related motor vehicle accident that had taken place two days previously. Despite this dangerous history, he still had a valid California driver's license (the state in which the fatality occurred). Although he was convicted in Cari Lightner's death, he received only a two-year sentence, which was served outside of a prison setting. This was not an unusual occurrence at the time, as DWI convictions were not treated as serious offenses, even when they resulted in fatalities. Candace Lightner was deeply distraught about the relative lack of legal repercussions for the driver who was responsible for her daughter's death. She decided to seek positive changes in the way drunk driving was viewed by the media and by the criminal justice system. Her efforts led to the creation of the organization originally called Mothers Against Drunk Drivers (MADD). Her initial goals were to raise public consciousness concerning the potential consequences of driving while intoxicated, to raise awareness of the frequency with which that occurred, and to significantly modify the existing laws concerning driving while intoxicated.

INTRODUCTION

In 1979, Cindi Lamb and her five-month-old daughter Laura were involved in a motor vehicle accident in Maryland, caused by an intoxicated driver who hit their vehicle head on while traveling at an excessive speed (reported at more than 100 miles per hour). Laura Lamb suffered a spinal injury that left her a paralyzed quadriplegic. Then, in 1980, Candace Lightner's daughter was killed by a drunk driver. Lightner and Lamb began to work together, and MADD began to grow. Initially, most chapters were formed by victims of DWIs and their families. A television movie about Candace Lightner's life airing in 1983 focused national attention on MADD, dramatically accelerating the growth of the organization. By the early 1990s, MADD reported having more than 400 chapters in thirty-two states in America, as well as branches in Australia, New Zealand, the United Kingdom, and Canada.

By raising public awareness of the relationship between driving while intoxicated, MADD aims to reduce traffic fatalities through several means: increasing penalties and other consequences for DWI; decreasing public complacency about the magnitude of the problem of DWI in America; giving an authentic face to the consequences of driving while intoxicated, by their quite visible and outspoken presence as victims and family members of those affected by drivers who were intoxicated; providing a mechanism for the creation of educational programs about the dangers of DWI aimed at youth; and decreasing public tolerance regarding drinking and driving. The National Highway Traffic Safety Administration (NHTSA) was an early ally for MADD, and awarded them a development grant.

MADD's success was unprecedented. Drunk driving deaths declined steadily and dramatically, so much so that a twenty-year goal of reducing alcohol-related fatalities by one fifth (20 percent) was achieved three years early.

There is an important distinction to be made between alcohol-related accidents, and a drunk driving accident or DWI accident (also called DUI, or driving while under the influence). An alcohol-related accident means that a person who is involved in the crash, whether driver or passenger, has ingested an alcoholic beverage prior to the collision, but does not have a blood alcohol level at or above the legal limit (the national standard for intoxication is a blood alcohol content or BAC of 0.08 mg/ml.). In a DWI, the driver of one or more of the vehicles (typically the one responsible for causing the collision) has a blood alcohol content of at least 0.08 mg/ml.

MADD also campaigned for extending transportation laws known as the TEA-21 (Transportation Equity Act for the 21st Century), which provided for increased highway safety measures and enforcement of driving while intoxicated laws. The following brochure calls for extended TEA-21 measures, and increased awareness of highway safety.

PRIMARY SOURCE

PRIORITY TRAFFIC SAFETY LAWS

See primary source image.

SIGNIFICANCE

The Transportation Equity Act for the Twenty-first Century (TEA-21) expired on September 30, 2003, but was extended several times. MADD continued its campaign for further extensions of the law, and advocated for increased funding for education and

DWI prevention measures in future versions of transportation acts. On August 10, 2005, President George W. Bush signed the Safe, Accountable, Flexible, Efficient Transportation Equity Act into law, which extends most of the TEA-21 framework until 2009.

In 1984, MADD's name was changed from *Mothers Against Drunk Drivers* to *Mothers Against Drunk Driving*. One reason for the name change was as a means of drawing greater attention to the concept of criminality inherent in the act of driving while intoxicated. It has always made victim advocacy a central goal, and has been instrumental in giving those whose lives were affected by DWI a public voice and a comprehensive support system. MADD has created a wraparound network of victim support services ranging from "warm lines" offering telephone support by trained staff; to public education and information brochures, campaigns, and curricula; to local advocate offices with staff that can provide in-person support to those victims engaged in the legal justice process; to magazine and Web sites for victims and concerned others.

Almost from the start, MADD focused considerable educational programming and media attention on the seriousness of underage drinking, and was instrumental in raising the federal standard for legal drinking age to twenty-one. It has had many strong and successful campaigns aimed at the prevention of underage drinking.

Among its many assets in MADD's high-visibility and recognizability campaigns, bumper stickers and MADD-emblazoned red ribbons on motor vehicles serve as potent reminders of the potential devastation caused by driving while intoxicated. In fact, the red ribbon, emblematic of MADD's *Tie One On For Safety* has been in use since 1986. The road sign consisting of a key across a martini glass inside the universal symbol for "No" or "Stop" has become synonymous with the mission of MADD and is recognized virtually worldwide.

MADD has had an enormous impact on legislation concerning drinking and driving, at the local and state as well as at the federal levels. By raising the minimum legal drinking age to twenty-one across the United States, many thousands of lives have been saved. Adjudicating the maximum blood level content for legal definition of intoxication at 0.08 has saved at least as many lives. MADD's campaigns against underage drinking, coupled with their promotion of the *designated driver* concept for those of legal drinking age, has helped to create a nationwide climate of awareness of the devastating potential of drinking alcohol and driving. In addition, MADD supports a

Priority Traffic Safety Laws

Higher-Risk Driver Standard

Higher-risk drivers fall into three categories: repeat offenders, offenders with a blood alcohol concentration (BAC) of .15 or higher, or offenders convicted of driving on a suspended license when the suspension was the result of driving under the influence. Nationally, one-third of all drivers arrested or convicted of driving while intoxicated are repeat offenders and in 2000, 58 percent of the alcohol-related traffic fatalities involved drivers with a BAC of .15 or above. A national standard must be enacted to ensure that higher-risk drivers are subject to consistent and aggressive detection, arrest and prosecution.

Key Action Items:

◆ Restrict vehicle operation by suspending licenses, impounding or immobilizing vehicles and requiring alcohol ignition interlock devices on offenders' vehicles.

◆ Require compensation to the community through fines, mandatory incarceration and financial restitution to crash victims.

◆ Promote recovery programs through mandatory alcohol assessment and treatment, intensive probation and attendance at victim impact panels.

◆ States that do not enact the national higher-risk driver standard would face the loss of highway construction funds.

Primary Seat Belt Standard

The best defense against an impaired driver is a seat belt. According to NHTSA, for every percentage point increase in seat belt usage, 280 lives can be saved.

Key Action Item:

◆ Establish a national primary seat belt standard. States would be eligible for "jumbo" financial incentives for three years. States that have not enacted a primary seat belt standard after three years would face the loss of highway construction funds.

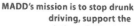

Mothers Against Drunk Driving (MADD) is a 501(c) (3) non-profit grass roots organization with more than 600 chapters nationwide.

MADD's mission is to stop drunk driving, support the victims of this violent crime, and prevent underage drinking.

4

Open Container Standard

Open container laws separate the consumption of alcohol from the operation of a vehicle. A common-sense measure, banning open containers in the passenger compartment of a vehicle will decrease the likelihood that drinking and driving will occur.

Key Action Item:

◆ Enact a national ban on open containers in the passenger compartment of motor vehicles. States that do not enact a ban on open containers would face the loss of highway construction funds.

.08 BAC Standard

Since the passage of the national .08 per se BAC standard in 2000, 18 states have passed this important legislation, bringing the total number of states in compliance to 38 and the District of Columbia (as of early May 2003).

Key Action Items:

◆ MADD will continue to work to ensure .08 BAC is the standard in every state.

◆ MADD will vigorously oppose any attempt to repeal the national .08 BAC standard.

PRIMARY SOURCE

Priority Traffic Safety Laws. Brochure published by MADD advocating reauthorization of the nation's surface transportation laws. The content in this brochure is to be used for purposes of historical documentation. MOTHERS AGAINST DRUNK DRIVING (MADD).

Bumper stickers from the group MADD (Mothers Against Drunk Driving) warn people of the dangers of driving under the influence of alcohol. ©MARK PETERSON/CORBIS.

nationwide prohibition of open containers in vehicles, creation and enforcement of nationwide standards governing the oversight of what they term "higher risk drivers": those who have multiple DWI arrests, those who drive on suspended or revoked licenses resulting from DWIs, and those with very high BAC at time of arrest (defined as BAC of 0.15 or greater). They also endorse strict federal standards mandating seat belt and child safety restraint system usage in all motor vehicles.

Based on reports published by MADD, some 300,000 lives have been saved since they began their work more than a quarter of a century ago. They state that although alcohol-related motor vehicle accidents resulting in fatalities have declined more than 40 percent during their first twenty-five years of operation, between 15,000 and 20,000 people are still killed in motor vehicle accidents in which alcohol is a causative factor. MADD's membership, and its management

have become increasingly diverse as it has grown. In 2005, MADD's new national president took office: for the first time, the organization is being led by a person of color, who also happens to be male. Glynn Birch's twenty-one month old son was killed by a drunk driver in 1988; his attorney encouraged him to enlist MADD's assistance in writing a victim impact statement that was pivotal in obtaining the maximum allowable prison sentence for the driver of the vehicle. Birch was active at the local, state, and federal levels before his election to the MADD national presidency.

FURTHER RESOURCES

Periodicals

Usdan, S. L. "Drinking Locations Prior to Impaired Driving Among College Students: Implications for Prevention." *Journal of American College Health*. (Sep-Oct 2005): 54(2): 69–75.

Web sites

MADD online. "Have a Ball, Baby!: MADD Safe Party Guide." <http://www.madd.org/madd_programs/ 0,1056,4841,00.html> (accessed January 8, 2006).

MADD online. "Stats and Resources." <http://www.madd. org/stats/> (accessed January 8, 2006).

Carrier of SARS Made Seven Flights Before Treatment

Globalization and Health

Newspaper article

By: Keith Bradsher

Date: April 10, 2003

Source: Keith Bradsher. "Carrier of SARS Made Seven Flights Before Treatment." *New York Times* (April 10, 2003): 5507, 1304–51.

About the Author: Keith Bradsher, the son of a Polk Award winning journalist and reporter for the *Washington Star*, was also the recipient of a George Polk Award for his series on the dangers posed by sport utility vehicles (SUVs). He was a finalist for the Pulitzer Prize in journalism and won the 2003 New York Public Library Helen Bernstein Book Award for Excellence in Journalism. Bradsher attended the University of North Carolina on a Morehead Scholarship. While he was in graduate school, earning a public policy master's degree from Princeton University's Woodrow Wilson School, he filed more than 140 business stories with the

Los Angeles Times. He became a staff writer for the *New York Times* (NYT) in 1989, at the age of twenty-five. In 1996, he became the Detroit Bureau Chief for the NYT. It was in Chicago that he became involved with the automotive industry, and he began the series of stories on SUVs that spawned a book and much critical and professional acclaim, while also raising the ire of the industry. Bradsher was the Detroit Bureau Chief from 1996 to 2001, and has been the Hong Kong Bureau Chief for the NYT since 2001.

INTRODUCTION

Before the development of mass forms of transportation, the spread of diseases was relatively confined within geographic areas; humans could only spread disease among their immediate neighbors. Other transmission vectors, such as insects, rodents, and birds, were limited in their ability to cross vast open terrain (mountains, canyons, deserts, etc.) or large bodies of water. This provided a type of natural barrier for the distant spread of disease. Beginning with the early explorers and followed by trade and transport vessels, things began to change, as diseases were carried from one continent to another. Columbus and his sailing crews, for example, spread syphilis from the Old World to the New World.

With the advent of intercontinental air travel, the planet became one large global community. In this global community, diseases can be transmitted within a matter of hours, well within the incubation period of nearly every virus and bacterium.

Throughout recorded history, the spread of disease has been facilitated by vessels of transportation, as well as by large population movements. It is not uncommon for armies, which typically operate under crowded, stressful, and disease-prone conditions (lack of sleep, diminished sanitary conditions, foreign and unpredictable environmental conditions, irregular, and often, insufficient nutrition), to incubate communicable diseases within their ranks and spread them to the communities in which they are stationed during times of military conflict. Because armies (or other military groups) are mobile, it is easy for them to spread diseases common to one region to the population of another region that had been previously unaffected.

In early efforts to establish disease control and to prevent the spread of plagues, European countries established a period of forty days in which troops and ships, among others, were maintained outside of population areas in sanitary zones. This control mechanism was called quarantine (from the Latin root word

quanta, meaning forty), and it was practiced from the first century CE through the seventeenth century.

With the development of steamship trade, followed by the development of large-scale railroad systems, the spread of disease beyond continental boundaries increased tremendously. Cholera outbreaks became epidemic. In an effort to develop cooperative means of preventing mass spread of disease, the First International Sanitary Conference was held in Paris in 1851. The concept of quarantine was deemed ineffective, and a decision was made to institute international standards regarding hygiene and sanitation for international commerce and transport. In 1907, the International Office of Public Health was established in Paris.

Management or elimination of disease spread by maritime shipments has long been a concern as well. Vectors, such as rats, mice, fleas, cockroaches, lice, bedbugs, flies, and mosquitoes, tend to be plentiful in waterfront, container, and port areas. Because rodents, insects, and vermin may access ships in port, it is necessary to maintain stringent vector control measures to suppress or prevent infestation during the time that ships are docked. Typically, shipping companies employ infestation and infection control officers who are charged with conducting frequent and thorough inspections of the ships, dock areas, and all shipping containers. There are three major risk areas for vector contamination of ships. In port, disease vectors have easy, direct access to ships. In addition, ports provide multiple entry points for disease vectors, since goods (and people) from all over the world move through them. Also, the movement of containers, the loading and unloading of food, and the direct handling of food in port areas, offer the potential for vector attraction or exposure. The second area of risk is posed by those aboard ships that are in passage. Ships typically have limited medical staff or facilities, rendering diagnosis and adequate treatment at sea quite difficult. Finally, the dense population on board a ship and the difficulty of isolating infection pose serious health risks for passengers and crew, as well as for those in the port areas where the ship docks.

During the first third of the twentieth century, the burgeoning use of transcontinental and international air travel raised new concerns about global disease transmission. The first sanitary convention concerned with air travel was held in 1933, using the existent international maritime laws of infection control as a model. The convention focused on developing and implementing means of medical inspection and control of disease transmission during air travel. It laid the foundation for the creation of the World Health

Organization Committee on Hygiene and Sanitation in Aviation, the agency responsible for ensuring the safety of the world community by preventing the spread of disease via commercial or military air travel or transport.

Improvements in aircraft design have increased speeds and decreased travel times. As a result, an individual can move from virtually any population center on the globe to any other within twenty-four hours. This situation leads to a number of potentially disastrous health consequences. First, many types of disease-causing bacteria can live in a host for more than twenty-four hours before symptoms of an illness appear, increasing the likelihood of unwitting disease transmission. Second, an individual may have been exposed to an illness and may develop symptoms after arriving at his or her destination, thereby introducing the illness to a new location. Third, an individual may not feel sick, but may still be able to transmit the disease to others, thereby potentially infecting fellow passengers (as well as others once he arrives at his destination). Fourth, an actively sick individual can expose flight staff and fellow passengers, as well as individuals at his destination. In addition, insects are common disease vectors and may be inadvertently transported in luggage, cargo, or food.

The design of the current air traffic system facilitates disease transmission. Airlines operate largely on a "hub and spoke" system. In this system, passengers travel from their home airports to large, crowded "hub" airports. From the hub airports, they then travel to smaller "spoke" airports. Nearly every flight that moves inter- or transcontinentally has one or more intermediate stops, thereby increasing the potential for bacterial or disease exposure exponentially. Before ever reaching his or her final destination, an infected passenger has multiple opportunities to expose not only the passengers and crew on his/her own flight, but multiple passengers and flight crews moving through crowded airports. The worldwide movement of a number of specific diseases—penicillin-resistant gonorrhea, cholera, rubella, hemorrhagic fever, influenza, AIDS (in the United States), and, more recently, SARS—has been linked to, or facilitated by, air travel.

▮ PRIMARY SOURCE

HONG KONG, April 10—Health officials announced here tonight that a man infected with a new respiratory disease had flown from Hong Kong to Munich, Barcelona, Frankfurt, London, Munich again, Frankfurt again and then back to Hong Kong before entering a hospital.

The Hong Kong Department of Health appealed for passengers and air crews from all seven flights to consult medical professionals. A health department spokeswoman said it was not yet known whether the man, who is 48, had infected anyone else on the flights with the disease—severe acute respiratory syndrome, or SARS.

All the flights were on Lufthansa. The airline said in a statement tonight that it had disinfected all the planes and was contacting the air crews and passengers. It said the chances of anyone's having become infected during the flights were "very remote."

Airlines have been saying that the filters aboard modern planes do a good job of removing viruses from the air. But according to the health department here, at least 13 people have fallen ill with SARS so far after they shared a flight from Hong Kong to Beijing last month with an elderly man who had been infected with the disease while visiting his brother in a hospital here.

Tonight's appeal for the Lufthansa crews and passengers to come forward follows nearly a dozen such calls by health officials and by airlines operating flights in and out of Hong Kong. Travelers have continued to board planes while feeling ill despite strenuous warnings from the World Health Organization and national health agencies that they not do so.

In the case that was announced tonight, the man flew on Lufthansa Flight 731 on March 30 from Hong Kong to Munich, and traveled the next day on Flight 4316 to Barcelona, according to an itinerary that was released here by the health department. He developed symptoms while in Barcelona.

The man then traveled on Flight 4303 to Frankfurt on April 2 and on to London the same day on Flight 4520. He went to Munich the next day on Flight 4671, then headed for Frankfurt on April 4 on Flight 265. He connected with Flight 738 the same day back to Hong Kong, arriving on April 5.

The man checked into a hospital here on April 8 and was confirmed today to have SARS.

Doctors do not yet know how infectious, if at all, people are in the early stages of SARS. Increasingly, doctors suspect that some people may be able to transmit the disease before the symptoms become evident. But Hong Kong's health secretary, Dr. Yeoh Eng-kiong, warned tonight that doctors here had become infected from people who had not yet shown the full symptoms identified by the World Health Organization.

Dr. Yeoh suggested that even someone with just diarrhea could be infectious.

The sick man's nationality was a mystery tonight. The health department's statement did not specify it, while the airline's statement described the man as "Chinese." A

Lufthansa official said the company had been told by the health department only that the man was Chinese. The department spokeswoman, in turn, said that the man seemed to be of Chinese descent but that the agency had been unable to determine his nationality.

"He travels a lot," the spokeswoman said. "We don't know his passport."

Hong Kong, which is a special administrative region of China, still issues separate passports from mainland China, a legacy of its days as a British crown colony. Officials here sometimes refer to people as Chinese if they are from Taiwan, which Beijing regards as a renegade province, or if they are people of any nationality who happen to be of Chinese descent.

The infected man's travels could not come at a worse time for Hong Kong, as countries have begun limiting the entry of people traveling from here or imposing quarantines on them.

Malaysia stopped issuing visas today to practically all holders of passports from Hong Kong and mainland China. Cathay Pacific Airways, Hong Kong's main airline, said tonight that it had suspended all flights to Kuala Lumpur, the Malaysian capital, because there were few passengers.

Regina Ip, Hong Kong's security secretary, met with Malaysia's consul general here to protest the decision. "There is no reason why the mobility of Hong Kong residents who do not have any close contact with infected persons should be restricted," she said afterward.

Singapore also imposed a 10-day quarantine on all foreign workers earning less than $24,000 a year who have recently been in a SARS-affected country or territory. Employers must pay costs of the quarantine. Singapore has been trying for years to lure high-income employees in financial services and other lucrative industries, while making it harder for lower-income workers to go there and do jobs that less-educated Singaporeans might otherwise do.

Hong Kong's economy depends heavily on its role as Asia's transportation hub, the place from which businesses can control and coordinate factories and other businesses spread across the continent. Hong Kong has the world's busiest container port for sea freight, the world's busiest airport for international cargo shipments and what was, until recently, Asia's busiest airport in terms of international air passenger departures.

But the availability of flights here is withering as many governments have warned citizens not to visit and many businesses have ordered their employees not to travel here.

Cathay Pacific has canceled a quarter of its daily flights here. Dragonair, an affiliated carrier that dominates the skies between Hong Kong and cities in mainland China,

has stopped operating almost half its flights. Continental Airlines canceled its daily nonstop flight from Hong Kong to New York this week for lack of passengers.

The airport authority here said that a third of all flights originally scheduled to operate today had been canceled for various reasons.

Health officials have said that the virus causing SARS can probably survive no more than several hours outside the body, so that air and sea cargo shipments from Hong Kong, as well as mail, do not pose a risk to recipients.

SIGNIFICANCE

The Federal Aviation Administration estimates that, worldwide, more than 1.6 billion people travel by commercial air transportation every year. This statistic suggests that virtually any communicable disease can be moved from one region, country, or continent or another in less than twenty-four hours. Whether or not passengers traveling with a disease-carrying individual become sick varies according to: 1) the way in which the disease is transmitted (in sputum or mucosal secretion, by airborne particles in a sneeze or a cough, by skin to skin contact, or blood or other bodily fluid exchange); 2) the level of communicability of the disease (how easily it is passed from one person to another); and 3) the general health or level of hardiness of the persons who come into contact with the carrier.

The air on board jetliners is typically a mixture of filtered outside and recirculated air. It is not considered to be any more conducive to disease transmission than the air in any other crowded environment. The air circulation system on board the typical jet aircraft is quite sophisticated. The manner in which the air is filtered and exchanged with outside air provides for a total change of cabin air fifteen to twenty times every hour. The recirculated air passes through high-efficiency particulate air (HEPA) filters that trap bacteria, particulate matter, fungi, and most viruses. This degree of air filtering is far greater than that which occurs in most high occupancy office buildings. The major concern, therefore, is not disease spread within the aircraft itself, but the transmission of diseases from one region to another by infected individuals.

It is possible for a person with a highly contagious, active illness to transmit it to those sitting in close proximity. This risk increases with the length of the flight or with extended waiting on runways when the air circulation systems are turned off.

The potential for the outbreak and global transmission of avian influenza (bird flu) is of enormous concern to the World Health Organization (WHO). Avian flu has killed more than fifty people in Asia since 2003, where it is widespread in both birds and humans. The present strain of the virus, which causes an extremely severe respiratory disease associated with a high death rate in humans, is not capable of sustained human to human transmission. However, the WHO is investigating scenarios that might occur if the virus mutates into a more contagious form. Since people would have no immunity to this new form of the virus, there is the possibility that a global pandemic (an epidemic that occurs over a wide geographic area, crosses international boundaries, and affects a large number of individuals) could result.

The WHO has strongly suggested that all countries develop, or update, their internal influenza pandemic preparedness plans. Specifically, every country should be prepared to respond to a rapidly moving contagious disease and the vast socioeconomic disruptions that could result if large numbers of citizens are sick or dying. To minimize the risk of disease transmission—both from person to person and from region to region—the WHO also recommends that anyone who is actively sick not fly on commercial airlines.

The WHO administers the International Health Regulations (IHR). These regulations are the legal, global protocol to prevent the international spread of infectious diseases. They provide a single, unified, codified set of policies, procedures, and protocols for the prevention of pathogen transmission and are equally applicable to air, train, and maritime transport. The IHR, in force since 1969, underwent revisions and updates during 2004 and 2005, following intergovernmental negotiations attended by more than 150 countries.

The IHR provide an essential tool for facilitating and expediting the sharing of urgent, critical epidemiological information on the transboundary spread of communicable diseases. Among the goals of the revised regulations are: 1) bolstering the global community's collective defenses against the spread of infectious diseases; 2) increasing the efficiency of the WHO's outbreak alert and response protocols; 3) ensuring transmission of timely and accurate data concerning potential international public health concerns; and 4) providing all necessary direct technical assistance to outbreak affected areas.

The Global Outbreak Alert and Response Network (GOARN), with administrative oversight from the WHO, is a collaborative effort among hundreds of technical, health-related, and academic institutions. Its mission is to ensure the rapid pooling and deployment of technical resources for the purpose of swift identification, confirmation, and appropriate response to disease outbreaks of international import. GOARN combines the infrastructure and expertise of such diverse organizations as the International Federation of Red Cross and Red Crescent Societies, UNICEF, the U.N. High Commissioner for Refugees (UNHCR), the U.S. Centers for Disease Control and Prevention, and international medical, epidemiological, disease surveillance, and laboratory initiatives. GOARN provides technical assistance, leadership, and coordination on site (in the field), while continuously transmitting information to the international community concerning the international outbreak threat level. The overall goals of GOARN include global disease surveillance, immediate reporting, and effective containment of outbreaks in order to prevent an international pandemic. It is critical that local, state, industry, and international agencies cooperate and collaborate in order to minimize threats to public health.

FURTHER RESOURCES

Books

DeHart, Roy L., ed. *Fundamentals of Aerospace Medicine.* Philadelphia: Lea and Febinger, 1985.

Last, John M., ed. *Maxcy-Rosenau Public Health and Preventive Medicine.* New York: Appleton-Century-Crofts, 1980.

Web sites

BBC News. "Air Travel 'Fuelled SARS Spread'." <http://news.bbc.co.uk/2/hi/asia-pacific/3329483.stm> (accessed October 27, 2005).

Disease/Infection News. "Better Air Onboard Reduces Spread of Disease on Aircrafts." <http://www.news-medical.net/print_article.asp?id=8352> (accessed October 27, 2005).

Journal of Multicultural Nursing and Health. "The Role of Aircraft in the International Transmission of Disease." <http://www.findarticles.com/p/articles/mi_qa3919/is_200001/ai_n8896335> (accessed October 27, 2005).

News Target.com. "U.S. Health Agencies Working to Deal With Diseases Spread by Air Travel." <http://www.newstarget.com/006872.html> (accessed October 27, 2005).

Preventing Pandemics. "Federal Health and Airline Officials Outline New Cooperative Efforts to Prevent Spread of Infectious Diseases on Commercial Air Travel." <http://www.house.gov/transportation/press/press2005/release29.html> (accessed October 27, 2005).

UCLA School of Public Health, Department of Epidemiology. "A Germ Has a Ticket to Ride, and Airlines Can't Stop It." <http://www.ph.ucla.edu/EPI/bioter/germhasticket.html> (accessed October 27, 2005).

For a Few Pennies More

Salt Fortification with Iodine

Television transcript

By: Television Trust for the Environment

Date: 2004

Source: *Television Trust for the Environment.* "For a Few Pennies More." Lifeonline, <http://www.tve.org/life-online/index.cfm?aid=1127> (accessed November 4, 2005).

About the Author: Television Trust for the Environment (TVE) in an independent non-profit organization dedicated to raising global awareness of the environment, development, human rights, and health issues through television broadcasts. TVE was set up in 1984 with the support of the Worldwide Fund for Nature, the United Nations Environment Program, and Central TV.

INTRODUCTION

In the 1980s, Kodyat B. Djokomoelyanto, an Indonesian physician and hormone expert, investigated the problem of iodine deficiency among the people living on the slopes of Mount Merapi, one of the region's most active volcanoes. It is not uncommon for the soil in volcanic areas to be deficient in iodine, which may have serious implications for the health of those living there. Djokomoelyanto found cretinism, a condition marked by bulging eyes, a low hairline, and stunted growth, among many individuals here and treated them with iodine-infused oil. This program looks at one of his patients, Kahmidi, who went on to marry and have two healthy children after his treatment.

Djokomoelyanto's work highlighted the problem of iodine deficiency and the solution. But it is easier to supplement salt with iodine than to give individuals iodine treatment. The program "For a Few Pennies More" reveals that the iodized salt program is not being properly put into practice in the Mount Merapi area. Researchers looked at families where the children had goiter, a swelling of the thyroid gland that is a hallmark of iodine deficiency. When the salt they used was analyzed, it had had little or no iodine in it. The salt producers, although obliged to add iodine by law, were cutting costs by leaving it out. This was a false economy, since the World Bank shows that lack of nutrients, such as iodine, can lead to a drop in gross domestic product of up to 5 percent. People lacking iodine miss out not just on work productivity, but on quality of life. The program highlights the need to enforce the iodized salt legislation at a national and local level, for the sake of the health and happiness of the people.

PRIMARY SOURCE

COMMENTATOR: Mount Merapi on the island of Java... Merapi is Indonesia's most active—and dangerous—volcano. But despite the danger, the slopes below Merapi are intensively farmed. Java's volcanoes have created some of the most fertile agricultural land on earth. With 120 million people, Java is the world's most densely populated island. Yet it's self-sufficient in food—the fertile soil allows farmers two to three harvests a year with little or no need for fertilizer. But in spite of this natural abundance, there's a vital ingredient missing from Java's soil. It's only needed in minute quantities—but for millions of Indonesians it can mean the difference between health and happiness or a lifetime of handicap and misery....

Dwi Asnawan is three years old. But he cannot yet walk or talk. He's sick because he's not getting enough iodine in his food. Iodine is a trace element usually present in tiny amounts in soil and water. Because it's missing from his parents' land, his food is also missing it. This morning two other children suspected of having the same problem have come to this clinic—which specializes in iodine deficiency disorders. Dr Untung is director of the clinic.

DR UNTUNG (translation): Iodine deficiency kills children. The most serious damage happens in the womb and in the first three months of life. Without iodine, children suffer from a range of illnesses we call Iodine Deficiency Disorders—or IDD. There may be 3 million children here with IDD, and we don't have the money to do expensive lab tests, so we have to rely on visual observations like this....

COMM: Dwi's mother Mahmuda has had a swelling on her throat since her early teens. It's a strong sign of lack of iodine. Iodine is needed by the thyroid gland—normally invisible—to make hormones needed to control vital bodily functions. When there's not enough it has to work harder and expands, producing this telltale swelling, known as goitre. So it's no surprise that her child is also unwell. All three mothers have come from the village of Sengi at the foot of Mt. Merapi. While goitre's the best known sign of iodine deficiency, the most serious damage goes unseen. It takes place in the months before and after birth. Damage done at this stage of a child's development is irreversible. In areas where iodine deficiency is endemic a high proportion of babies are born seriously underweight. And there are many stillbirths.

Mahmuda's neighbour Sryani is about to go into labour.

SRYANI (translation): Those with goitre are generally weak and in poor health . . . you sometimes see people with swollen limbs . . . but the worse thing is when children are sick.

COMM: With three of her neighbours' children sick, Sryani feels her unborn child is at risk. An extreme effect of iodine deficiency is cretinism. Cretins suffer from severe and irreversible mental and physical retardation. They're usually very short and may be partially deaf.

DR UNTUNG WIDODO, Director of IDD Research Centre, Borobudur (translation): How old are you? Eh? How old?

OLD MAN: I'm 66.

DR UNTUNG: Do you have children?

OLD MAN: Nah.

DR UNTUNG: Are you married?

OLD MAN: No, no I'm not married.

DR UNTUNG: Don't you want to?

OLD MAN: No.

COMM: Goitre and cretinism are only the most visible sign of the far wider, more devastating impacts of iodine deficiency. IDD can seriously damage the brain, slowing mental responses and impairing intelligence levels. Even moderate IDD can lead to a drop of 10 to 20 points in the IQ performance of sufferers.

DR UNTUNG (translation): Children suffer most—they're slower and less intelligent. Then as adults they will be weaker and unable to work as well . . . and they'll be less productive and won't have the same quality of life. In fact it's like losing a huge part of your life, never getting the chances you should have had.

COMM: Where people lack the iodine their bodies need there are untold stories of lost opportunities in life. But for Kahmidi, who suffers from severe cretinism, life changed completely 20 years ago. A distinguished endocrinologist came to Sengi, and took a personal interest in him.

PROFESSOR DJOKOMOELYANTO: When I saw him he was so lonely under the tree. He doesn't work at all. But he was classified as an endemic cretin.

COMM: Giving iodine supplements can't reverse existing brain damage but it can revitalize sufferers.

PROFESSOR DJOKOMOELYANTO: Next year . . . when I came back there he was so different in appearance and he decided to marry somebody. It seems that he married a woman, a taller woman, who was also classified as an endemic cretin.

GINAH & KAHMIDI (Translation): Before I got that injection I couldn't use my brain . . . I couldn't understand anything.

He just couldn't use his brain.
And it wasn't only my brain I couldn't use. . . . I just couldn't do anything.
He couldn't do anything.
But the injection made me feel stronger. That's when I decided I wanted a wife. . . . It was the iodine treatment that did the trick.

COMM: Women with IDD are particularly vulnerable—and are more likely to have stillbirths, miscarry, or have low birth-weight babies with permanent brain damage or cretinism.

GINAH (translation): When we got married, I was so happy. . . . Now we were like everyone else. . . . But to be honest . . . I was worried that if I had a baby, I wanted it to be normal like other people's babies. . . .

COMM: Professor Djokomoelyanto also injected Ginah with the iodised oil, to increase the chance that any children she and Kahmidi had would be normal. Soon, Ginah and Kahmidi did conceive, and to their great relief and joy, they had a son AND he was entirely normal. Their son, Rame, is now 18 and well above average intelligence. The doctor who treated his parents decided to sponsor Rame's education. Rame is the first member of his family ever to attend university. He's majoring in chemistry—for a particular reason. . . .

RAME (translation): If I get to become a good scientist I'd like to find ways of helping people like my Dad. I hope no more generations are being born in the future having to suffer like my Dad did. When I was a kid I used to dream of discovering some kind of cure to make him normal . . . of course I know now that that's not possible. Since I was a kid I wished my Dad could be as tall as other kids' Dads . . . and think normally and talk normally with other people.

QUESTION: Was Kahmidi ever badly treated by other villagers because of his condition?

GINAH (translation): No he was always well treated and the villagers were very understanding. In fact his father loved him better than his other children because of his condition.

Because my husband can't speak properly, we've developed our own special language in the family. So if outsiders can't understand what he's trying to say, we do—even if he uses the wrong words. . . .

RAME (Translation): Who did you say is having a baby?

GINAH: It's Syrani up the road.

RAME: Ah. . . . How are her tomatoes doing?

KAHMIDI: They're good!

RAME: Why don't we grow tomatoes too then?

KAHMIDI: We do. . . . We're growing them ourselves too!

RAME: What? Those that came in the plastic bag?

KAHMIDI: Ha ha ha!

RAME: You're having me on! You didn't grow them yourself! (laughing)

KAHMIDI: We bought them from a neighbour who needed cash. No we didn't grow them.

KAHMIDI: I want my sons to get good jobs so they can be "real" people. I'm proud of them!

COMM: Rame's family's story is vivid proof that all that's needed to end the scourge of IDD is a consistent dosage of iodine—provided it's given soon enough and in the right quantities. . . .

COMM: Across the world, vast areas of land don't contain enough iodine—and a billion people remain at risk from IDD. Treating entire populations with regular iodine supplements—in the way that Kahmidi and Ginah were—is impractical. A simpler option is to fortify salt with small amounts of iodine. Salt is an ideal carrier because everyone needs it in fairly constant daily doses. In conjunction with many governments UNICEF has long advocated the universal iodisation of salt. In Indonesia, salt producers are legally obliged to add iodine to salt. This salt factory on Java's northern coastline is typical of Indonesia's many salt producers, adding the specified amount of iodine. It's added through a dispensing nozzle before being thoroughly mixed in. But, if, officially, most of the salt in Indonesia is already being iodised, why are so many people still suffering from IDD?

Part 2

DR UNTUNG: Hello Mahmuda!

MAHMUDA: Hello.

DR UNTUNG: Can we go inside?

MAHMUDA: Yes please come in.

DR UNTUNG: He's not still crying is he? I'd like to take a look at the salt you're using.

MAHMUDA: Sorry about the mess in here.

DR. UNTUNG (Sync): Let's take a look at this salt then. . . . If the salt is good, it will turn deep blue. Just look at this . . . this is not good at all. It has absolutely no iodine in it. It says on the pack that it's iodised—but it's not! You're being cheated! . . .

COMM: . . . The successful experience of many other countries confirms that iodising salt is by far the most effective way to combat IDD—but it needs to be properly enforced. As a result, most people here aren't getting enough iodine supplements. Dr Untung is outraged. . . .

COMM: As a result of sub-standard salt being sold as iodised, untold numbers of children will never have the chance to live their lives to the full. Back in the village of Sengi, Sryani has had her baby, a normal healthy boy.

Dr UNTUNG: All this adds to the problem of development in our country. IDD is a simple problem which we know how to fix—cheaply and effectively. But for the relative cost of just a few pennies we haven't done it. Instead our country is being held back with a much more serious and costly problem.

KAHMIDI: Even though I'm poor, short, and ugly, and let's face it, my wife isn't exactly pretty, . . . it doesn't matter, because we are proud to have two good strong and healthy children. . . .

SIGNIFICANCE

The problems of iodine deficiency are well known. The thyroid gland needs iodine to make hormones that influence growth and mental functioning. Iodine deficiency makes the thyroid swell because it has to work harder. The enlarged thyroid is easily recognizable as a condition called goiter. Women with goiter are vulnerable to miscarriage or to producing babies with brain damage.

Food fortification refers to the addition of nutrients to a food, whereas supplementation means the addition of nutrients to a food that already contains smaller amounts of that nutrient. Salt has been fortified with iodine in the United States and most other developed countries since the early 1900s. Other fortifications or supplementations include iron, niacin, and B vitamins added to flour and rice, milk with vitamins A and D added, and infant formulas fortified with iron.

The World Bank says that iodine deficiency is one of many vitamin and mineral deficiencies that impact the output and quality of life in developing countries. To address these problems, they advocate a mixture of education, distribution of supplements, and the fortification of common foodstuffs, like salt, or water. These solutions have proven to be effective and inexpensive. What is missing is robust adherence to legislation on fortification by industry, as seen in the Mount Merapi example, and awareness of the problem among the population.

Meanwhile, the World Health Organization (WHO) is committed to the elimination of iodine deficiency. WHO says that the problem affects 740 million people a year in 130 countries and is the single greatest cause of preventable brain damage in fetuses and infants. WHO plans to monitor the iodine status of vulnerable populations and investigate the quality of iodized salt. The current campaign is building on some success, for the number of countries with iodized salt has increased from forty-six to ninety-three in the period 1990–1998.

UNICEF (United Nations Children's Fund) also campaigns against iodine deficiency. It is working with the public, salt producers, and decision-makers, pointing out the toll that inaction will exact on a nation's health. In 2003, UNICEF organized a salt testing experiment involving children in Uzbekistan, which showed that 55 percent of samples were iodized. This is not good enough, but it is better than the 19 percent that a similar experiment revealed in 2000. UNICEF says that neither the Russian Federation nor Ukraine is going to be able to eliminate iodine deficiency in the near future. Lost productivity as a result of children born with iodine deficiency will cost the Federation about 1.3 billion Euro. Only 30 percent of Ukrainian households are consuming iodized salt. There is, as "For a Few Pennies More" points out, still much more to be done.

FURTHER RESOURCES
Web sites
UNICEF. "Iodine Deficiency." <http://www.unicef.org/ceecis/iodine_deficiency> (accessed November 4, 2005).

World Bank. "Enriching Lives: Overcoming Vitamin and Mineral Malnutrition in Developing Countries." <http://www.worldbank.org/html/extdr/hnp/nutrition/enrich.htm> (accessed November 4, 2005).

World Health Organization. "World Health Organization Sets Out to Eliminate Iodine Deficiency Disorder." <http://www.who.int/inf-pr–1999/en/pr99-wha17.html> (accessed November 4, 2005).

Drug Recalls

Risk of Acute Myocardial Infarction and Sudden Cardiac Death in Patients Treated with COX-2 Selective and Non-Selective NSAIDs

Memorandum

By: David J. Graham

Date: September 30, 2004

Source: David J. Graham. "Risk of Myocardial Infarction and Sudden Cardiac Death in Patients Treated with COX-2 Selective and Non-Selective

NSAIDs" (memorandum) U.S. Food and Drug Administration. September 30, 2004. Available online at <http://www.fda.gov/cder/drug/infopage/vioxx/vioxxgraham.pdf> (accessed October 1, 2005).

About the Author: David J. Graham is Associate Director for Science and Medicine at the Unted States Food and Drug Administration (FDA) Office of Drug Safety. As both a physician and public health expert, Graham has participated in research that has led to the removal of ten drugs from the pharmaceutical market that were deemed unsafe.

INTRODUCTION
The U.S. Food and Drug Administration (FDA) is an agency within the Department of Health and Human Services and consists of eight divisions, including the Center for Drug Evaluation and Research (CDER). The CDER promotes and protects the health of Americans by assuring that all prescription and over-the-counter drugs are safe and effective. Its jurisdiction encompasses most food products other than meat and poultry, human and animal drugs, therapeutic agents of biological origin, medical devices, radiation-emitting products for consumer, medical, and occupational use, cosmetics, and animal feed. Agency scientists evaluate applications for new human drugs and biologics, complex medical devices, food and color additives, infant formulas, and animal drugs.

Produced by Merck & Co., Vioxx belongs to a class of selective nonsteroidal anti-inflammatory drugs, or NSAIDs, called COX-2 inhibitors. Cycloogygenase is an enzyme that produces mediators that cause pain and inflammation in the body, and exists in two forms, known as COX1 and COX2. COX-2 inhibitors reduce inflammation and pain, while minimizing undesired gastrointestinal adverse effects, such as stomach ulcers, that are sometimes associated with other anti-inflammatory drugs.

In the clinical trials conducted before approval of Vioxx, the drug showed a significant therapeutic advantage over existing approved drugs due to fewer gastrointestinal side effects, including bleeding. Because of its advantages and wide potential, the review and approval of Vioxx was made a fast-track priority. Vioxx was approved by the FDA in 1999, and COX-2 inhibitors soon dominated the prescription-drug market for NSAIDs. The drug was marketed in more than eighty countries and its sales had reached $2.5 billion in 2003.

Several studies published after the approval of Vioxx, however, showed that the drug could cause

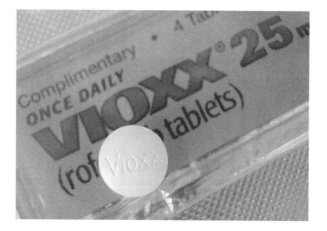

A 25-mg pill of Vioxx, made by Merck & Co., is shown, in Los Angeles, CA. Vioxx, was withdrawn in September after a study showed patients taking it for 18 months had double the risk of heart attacks and strokes. ©MARIANA DAY MASSEY/ZUMA/CORBIS.

increased blood pressure, a known risk factor for cardiovascular disease, and also increased blood clotting in some people taking the drug. A long-term clinical study conducted by David J. Graham at the FDA showed that people taking the medicine for more than eighteen months exhibited an increased risk for development of serious cardiovascular problems, including heart attacks and blood clots. This study also found that patients taking the highest recommended daily dosage of Vioxx had three times the risk of heart attack and sudden cardiac death compared to those not taking it. Graham summarized his findings in the following memo to Paul Seligman, the FDA's Director of Drug Safety.

■ PRIMARY SOURCE

MEMORANDUM
DEPARTMENT OF HEALTH AND HUMAN SERVICES
PUBLIC HEALTH SERVICE
FOOD AND DRUG ADMINISTRATION
CENTER FOR DRUG EVALUATION AND RESEARCH
DATE: September 30, 2004
FROM: David J. Graham, MD, MPH
Associate Director for Science, Office of Drug Safety
TO: Paul Seligman, MD, MPH
Acting Director, Office of Drug Safety
SUBJECT: Risk of acute myocardial infarction and sudden cardiac death in patients treated with COX-2 selective and non-selective NSAIDs

The following report describes the study we performed to investigate the cardiovascular risk of the COX-2 selective

NSAIDs rofecoxib and celecoxib, and a variety of non-selective, traditional NSAIDs. . . .

BACKGROUND

Cyclooxygenase-2 (COX-2) selective nonsteroidal anti-inflammatory drugs (NSAIDs) are prescribed for the treatment of arthritis and other musculoskeletal complaints because of their reduced gastrointestinal toxicity compared with traditional, non-selective NSAIDs. Questions about cardiovascular risk with these newer agents were raised by the finding of a 4-fold difference in incidence of acute myocardial infarction (AMI) between patients treated with rofecoxib (Vioxx) 50 mg/day compared to naproxen 1000 mg/day in a large randomized clinical trial. Given the high utilization of COX-2 agents in the US, even a small difference in cardiovascular risk between members of this class would have substantial public health impact.

A series of observational studies have examined the questions of cardiovascular risk with rofecoxib. A cohort study found nearly a 2-fold increased risk of serious coronary heart disease (AMI [acute myocardial infarction, or heart attack] and sudden cardiac death, SCD) among users of high-dose rofecoxib (>25 mg/day) compared to non-users. Another cohort study found no increase in risk but did not look at high-dose rofecoxib separately. A case-control study found an increased risk of hospitalized AMI in patients treated with rofecoxib compared with celecoxib use or no current use of other NSAIDs at both high- and standard-doses of rofecoxib. . . .

METHODS

Study setting. Kaiser Permanente is an integrated managed care organization providing comprehensive health care to over 6 million residents in the state of California. . . .

Base cohort. From January 1, 1999 through December 31, 2001, all patients from age 18 to 84 years who filled at least one prescription for a COX-2 selective or non-selective NSAID were identified. Patients with at least 365 days of health plan coverage prior to the date of that first NSAID prescription were entered into the study cohort if they had no diagnoses of cancer, renal failure, liver failure, severe respiratory disease, organ transplantation, or HIV/AIDS during the screening interval. Cohort members were followed from this entry date until the end of the study period, occurrence of an AMI or death, whichever came first.

Study design. Within this NSAID-treated cohort, a nested case-control study was performed. The primary study question was: is the risk of AMI and SCD increased in patients taking rofecoxib at standard (=25 mg/day) or high (>25 mg/day) doses compared with a) remote use of any NSAID or b) current use of celecoxib.

Study outcome. The study outcome of interest was a serious cardiac event, defined as hospitalized AMI or out-of-hospital SCD. . . . Outpatient deaths were classified as SCD if the underlying cause of death listed conditions previously associated with this outcome including hypertensive heart disease, ischemic heart disease, conduction disorders, dysrhythmias, heart failure, atherosclerotic heart disease, sudden death, or death from an unknown cause. . . .

DISCUSSION

Our data suggest that risk of serious coronary heart disease is increased in patients treated with rofecoxib compared with celecoxib use. High-dose rofecoxib conferred a 3.7-fold increase in risk and standard-dose a 1.5-fold increase compared with celecoxib, the most frequently prescribed COX-2 selective agent. . . .

CONCLUSIONS

Rofecoxib increases the risk of serious coronary heart disease defined as acute myocardial infarction and sudden cardiac death. High-dose rofecoxib increased risk by 3.7-fold and standard-dose rofecoxib increased risk by 1.5-fold compared to celecoxib use. . . .

The population impact of rofecoxib's increased risk is great because of the widespread exposure to the drug. This illustrates the effect that even a relatively small increase in risk can have if you're dealing with a serious outcome that is not rare in the general population, such as is the case with AMI and SCD. . . .

Prior to today, my conclusions regarding rofecoxib were that high-dose use of the drug should be ended and that lower-dose rofecoxib should not be used by physicians or patients. If lower-dose rofecoxib remained on the market, physicians and patients needed to understand that risk of AMI and SCD was substantially increased and that there were safer alternatives.

SIGNIFICANCE

Also on September 30, 2004, Merck, the manufacturer of Vioxx, announced a voluntary worldwide withdrawal of the drug. In the days following the announcement, Merck's shares lost value and the Vioxx story was front-page news across the United States.

A recall is a voluntary withdrawal from the market of products that may cause health problems, usually done by the manufacturer or distributor with the intention to protect the public. Drug recalls are possible when serious adverse effects are identified after approval either in post-marketing long-term clinical trials or through spontaneous reporting of adverse events. In the case of Vioxx, however, some scientists criticized the FDA and Merck for rushing an unsafe drug to market and leaving it there too long.

Graham testified before Congress in November 2004 (six weeks after writing this memo) about the dangers of the drug Vioxx and the state of the FDA's drug approval process. The Vioxx case also led to a storm of criticism from members of Congress, medical journals, and even scientists from within the FDA, and fuelled fierce debate about how to reorganize the agency's system of monitoring approved drugs. As the dust from the withdrawal of Vioxx began to settle, one consideration became clear: the views of society regarding the balance between the risks and benefits of medicines has shifted, and pharmaceutical companies, regulators, and scientists are considering higher standards of safety that new products could be required to demonstrate before they are brought to market.

FURTHER RESOURCES
Books

Ng, Rick. *Drugs From Discovery to Approval.* Indianapolis: Wiley-Liss, 2003.

Periodicals

Oberholzer-Gee, F. Inamdar, SN. "Merck's Recall of Rofecoxib—a Strategic Perspective." *New England Journal of Medicine.* 18 (2004): 2147–2149.

Web sites

U.S. Food and Drug Administration. "Vioxx (Rofecoxib) Questions and Answers." <http://www.fda.gov/cder/drug/infopage/vioxx/vioxxQA.htm> (accessed September 13, 2005).

Alps Still Contaminated by Radiation from Chernobyl

Chernobyl Aftermath

Article

By: Maryann DeLeo

Date: 2004

Source: Associated Press International "Report: Alps still contaminated by radiation from Chernobyl." Associated Press Archive. (May 2, 1998).

About the Author: The Associated Press (AP), one of the world's largest news-gathering and -disseminating organizations, is owned by more than 1,500 newspapers around the world. Its resources include digital, visual, aural, and electronic media. In addition, the AP maintains an extensive archive of photographs, articles, reports, and speeches.

INTRODUCTION

When the Chernobyl nuclear power plant exploded on April 26, 1986, four reactors were in operation, and two more were under construction. Fatigued and inadequately trained employees, operating without adequate safety precautions, were testing the reactor core system's stability during a power shutdown when a chain of events overheated the reactor, causing an explosion and core fire that killed thirty-two people outright and spewed massive amounts of radioactive material into the air for nine days.

Because much of the debris settled in the area immediately around Chernobyl,—Belarus, Russia, and Ukraine—these countries were the most heavily contaminated, a catastrophe that affected about seven million people. Shifting winds, however, carried nuclear particles and contaminated dust to Scandinavia, northern France, the United Kingdom, the southern regions of Germany, Switzerland, Poland, and the Baltic states.

Effects of the Chernobyl explosion were far-reaching and long-lasting. The leaking "sarcophagus," of reactor 4 gave off vast amounts of more than one hundred radioactive contaminants, three of which were predominant: strontium-90, which has a radioactive half-life of twenty-nine years, cesium-137, with a half-life of thirty years; and iodine-131, which has a half-life of eight days. This means that high levels of cesium and strontium will remain in the environment for the foreseeable future. (Half-life is the length of time required for half of the atoms in an element to dissipate.)

Although most of the radioactive iodine decayed quickly, other contaminants were readily absorbed by the creatures living in areas affected by the radiation cloud, sharply increasing their risk of developing leukemia as well as thyroid and other forms of cancer. In addition, radiation was absorbed by soil, water, plants, and trees. Contaminated grains and crops were eaten by animals and humans, leading to the ingestion of more radioactive materials, both in foodstuffs and dairy products. As animals and humans both drank the water, and fish swam in it, still more radioactive materials were consumed. Radiation in the atmosphere was absorbed by clouds, which literally rained down onto the earth again, increasing contaminants in water and sewage systems still further.

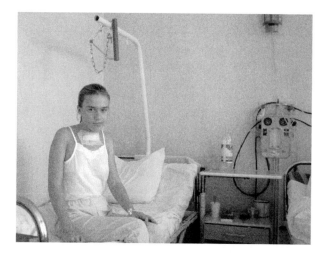

Fourteen-year-old Anya is recovering in hospital after an operation for thyroid cancer, linked to the Chernobyl disaster. ©CAROLINE PENN/CORBIS.

■ PRIMARY SOURCE

Study: Alps Still Contaminated by Radiation from Chernobyl—Paris (AP) The peaks of the Alps still contain radiation from the 1986 Chernobyl nuclear disaster, according to a study released Saturday.

Campers, shepherds, park wardens, mushroom lovers, and others who frequent the mountainous heights could be at risk and should be warned, the report said. The Paris-based Center for Research and Independent Information on Radioactivity based its conclusions on tests conducted in 1996 and 1997 in the French, Italian, Swiss, and Austrian Alps.

The Alps were particularly affected by radiation from the explosion at the Chernobyl nuclear plant because of their height and the trajectory of the toxic cloud the blast produced, the study said.

Scientists took soil samples in the Alps from 40 places at heights ranging from 5,000 to 9,000 feet.

They found soil contaminated with Cesium-137, a radioactive isotope with a half-life of 30 years, as well as Americium-241, a radioactive substance that disperses much more slowly than cesium.

The center intends to submit its findings to the French Environment Ministry on Monday.

Chernobyl's reactor No. 4 exploded during a test April 26, 1986, killing at least 32 people in the immediate aftermath and spewing a deadly radioactive cloud across large parts of the former Soviet Union and Europe.

SIGNIFICANCE

In Belarus, where more than 50 percent of the radioactive fallout came to rest, about one-quarter of the farmland has been contaminated and is no longer usable. In Ukraine, where forestry and related industries are extremely important components of the country's economy, 40 percent of the forests have been contaminated.

A surprising amount of partially contaminated agrarian land is still in use, although the governments of Belarus and Ukraine have tried to limit the amount of radiation in the food chain with programs that teach farmers the safest ways to manage their farmland and by providing "clean" food for livestock. While this helped large commercial agrarian establishments, it did little for the thousands of subsistence farmers who keep livestock and grow crops for their own consumption and small-scale market trade.

In Ukraine the timber industries have been devastated, as have food and living environments for countless birds and small animals. As yet, no published studies have documented the long-term impact of this contamination on rural communities that depend on the forests as a source of food—birds, small game, berries, and mushrooms—and construction materials.

In the explosion's immediate aftermath, an area spanning eighteen kilometers (roughly thirty miles) around the reactor was deemed fully contaminated and uninhabitable. Residents were eventually evacuated from this area and forced to relocate, but their lives were changed irrevocably. Having been exposed to radioactive contamination, they had to anticipate potential future health concerns such as the development of leukemia as well as thyroid and other types of cancer.

Although people were eventually forced to move, the government initially underplayed the magnitude of the disaster and did not evacuate people in the hardest-hit areas rapidly enough; neither did authorities ensure that all affected citizens were given iodine to diminish the risk of thyroid cancer. Taken together, the forced relocations, lack of adequate emergency health management, and economic losses have been enormous. Not surprisingly, the incidence of depressive disorders and alcohol abuse has also increased dramatically in the regions affected most by Chernobyl.

Yet another aspect of life after Chernobyl has become even more complex and abstract: Millions must learn how to live in a world filled with insidious radiation, which cannot be seen, heard, or felt in any direct way. Livestock that have eaten plants and grains grown on irradiated soil taste no different than those that were not; children look healthy until they develop cancer. The emotional and psychological effects are devastating: Not only do people live knowing that radiation is present, they're uncertain about their long-term health, and have lost faith in their leaders.

Although public reports tried to minimize the severity of the disaster's effects, people could see dramatic increases in leukemia, thyroid cancer—particularly among children and young adults, and birth defects, which have risen 250 percent since the explosion, according to the Chernobyl Children's Project International (CCPI) and statistics released by the Belarus government.

Due to the paucity of trained local care providers and the very extensive needs of these children, many of them are institutionalized. The Vesnova Orphanage, a facility with poor sanitary conditions and inadequate health care that houses many of them, was dragged into the limelight of global media by the CCPI. This helped bring about a major construction project and secured greater professional staffing at the facility, markedly improving the quality of care there.

Because regions farther away from Chernobyl—much of Europe and, eventually, the entire world—were exposed to significantly less radiation, the effects on long-term health have been more difficult to assess. The World Health Organization has estimated that the increased incidence of thyroid and other types of cancer (various forms of leukemia and solid tumor cancers) may be difficult to distinguish from other factors. It is known that soil in areas exposed to fallout registered elevated levels of radiation more than a decade after the incident. This suggests that people have been exposed to at least low-level radiation over that time, either by ingestion or direct exposure, thereby increasing the possibility of long-term health effects.

FURTHER RESOURCES

Periodicals

Jacob, P., T. I. Bogdanova, E. Buglova, et. al. "Thyroid Cancer Risk in Areas of Ukraine and Belarus Affected by the Chernobyl Accident." *Radiation Research* 165, no. 8 (January 2006): 1–8.

Web sites

Chernobyl.info. "The International Communications Platform on the Longterm Consequences of the Chernobyl Disaster." <http://www.chernobyl.info/> (accessed December 18, 2005).

Greenpeace International. "Whitewashing Chernobyl's Impacts." <http://www.greenpeace.org/international/press/releases/whitewashing-chernobyl-s-impac> (accessed December 18, 2005).

International Atomic Energy Agency. "Chernobyl: The True Scale of the Accident." <http://www.iaea.org/

NewsCenter/Focus/Chernobyl/index.shtml> (accessed December 18, 2005).

World Nuclear Association. "Chernobyl Accident: September 2005." <http://www.world-nuclear.org/info/chernobyl/inf07.htm> (accessed December 18, 2005).

World Water Crisis

United Nations World Water Assessment Program

Photograph

By: Issouf Sanogo

Date: July 5, 2005

Source: Getty Images

About the Photographer: Issouf Sanogo photographs news and sport events in Africa, and has been a contributor for over five years to *Agence France Presse*, a worldwide news agency headquartered in Paris.

INTRODUCTION

Lack of access to clean water has many consequences; one of the most important is the impact on human health. People need access to between five and eight gallons (about twenty-to-fifty liters) of clean water per day for drinking, cooking, and washing. At present, a child born in the developed world consumes thirty to fifty times as much water resources as one in the developing world—an inequity which, ultimately, has an adverse affect on both societies—as this is a global, rather than national, issue.

The United Nations World Water Assessment Program (WWAP) is a project seeking a better understanding of processes and policies that will improve the supply and quality of freshwater resources around the globe. WWAP's goals include assessment of the world's freshwater resources and ecosystems and identification of critical issues and problems.

WWAP was set up in 2000 in recognition that only an integrated approach can help solve the global water crisis. The program works across all relevant UN agencies and in partnership with national governments and has emerged from discussions at various milestone meetings on environment and development, such as the 1992 Rio Earth Summit. Since then, there has been a growing recognition that lack of access to clean water is threatening the stability, security and environmental sustainability of the developing nations and this has resulted in a number of specific targets for

PRIMARY SOURCE

World Water Crisis. A woman carries buckets a long distance to collect water near Tahoua, Niger, in July 2005. Niger, one of the world's poorest countries, faces an emergency after locust swarms and five years of virtual drought destroyed crops. ISSOUF SANOGO/AFP/GETTY IMAGES.

action. For example, the United Nations Millennium Declaration calls for a reduction by half in the number who do not have sustainable access to safe drinking water by 2015.

PRIMARY SOURCE

WORLD WATER CRISIS
  See primary source image.

SIGNIFICANCE

The first challenge of the WWDR is improving access to a safe water supply. Water causes disease when it is contaminated by microorganisms, chemicals, and parasites. Lack of sanitation and basic hygiene compounds these problems. The numbers of illnesses caused by contaminated water are many, but the World Health Organization (WHO) has singled out diarrheal diseases, malaria, and shistosomiasis (also known as bilharziasis) as being particularly worrying. Each day, diarrheal disease (including cholera) kills more than 6,000 children around the world. Most of this could be prevented, for almost 90 percent of cases are linked to unsafe water, inadequate sanitation, and poor hygiene.

Malaria claims over one million lives a year. The mosquitoes which carry the malaria parasite breed in stagnant water and the disease has been linked to poorly managed water projects such as irrigation and dam building. As many as 500 million people are at risk of schistosomiasis, a parasitic disease causing blindness. Lack of clean water for washing the face is a major factor in schistosomiasis. Meanwhile, between twenty-eight and thirty-two million people in Bangladesh are exposed to drinking water with toxic levels of arsenic. In China, twenty-six million people have tooth problems, and one million have bone problems, because there is too much fluoride in their drinking water.

WHO has complied figures that reveal the scale of the water crisis. Nearly one person in five, 1.1 billion people, living in the world today does not have access to safe water, and nearly two thirds of these people live in Asia. Nearly half the world's population does not have access to adequate sanitation. In the last decade, almost two billion people were affected by floods and droughts that threatened the water supply. Each time there is a natural disaster, warnings about the spread of disease are generally issued within a few days. Prompt planning and action to safeguard water in these situations is essential.

The WWAP seeks to address the water crisis, and its health implications, through many actions: assessment of the scale of the problem, looking at practices for water management that work, and disseminating these through national governments through education and training. It has carried out sixteen detailed case studies in Senegal, France, Thailand, Peru, and elsewhere to gain a more thorough understanding of key aspects of water management.

The second UN World Water Development Report is scheduled to be published in 2006–2007. Preliminary reports state that many countries are still not on track to meet the millennium goal of improving access to safe water. Meanwhile, water pollution and destruction of ecosystems continue to increase. However, the report offers the most comprehensive survey ever of the state of the world's freshwater and present many examples of best practices that can help governments and people manage their most precious resource—water.

FURTHER RESOURCES

Books

United Nations/World Water Assessment Programme. *UN World Water Development Report: Water for People, Water for Life.* Paris, New York, and Oxford: UNESCO (United Nations Educational, Scientific and Cultural Organization) and Berghahn Books, 2003.

Web sites

UNESCO. "World Water Assessment Programme." <http://www.unesco.org/water/wwap/> (accessed February 3, 2006).

World Health Organization. "Water-Related Disease." <http://www.who.int/water_sanitation_health/diseases/en/> (accessed February 3, 2006).

Fluoridation of Drinking Water to Prevent Dental Caries

Journal article

By: Centers for Disease Control and Prevention

Date: October 22, 1999

Source: Division of Oral Health, National Center for Chronic Disease Prevention and Health Promotion, Centers for Disease Control and Prevention. "Achievements in Public Health, 1900–1999: Fluoridation of Drinking Water to Prevent Dental Caries." *Morbidity and Mortality Weekly Report* 48 (October 22, 1999): 933–940.

About the Author: The Centers for Disease Control and Prevention (CDC) is part of the U.S. Department of Health and Human Services. It was founded in 1946 to help control malaria. Today, its mission is to improve public health by preventing, investigating, documenting, and controlling chronic and emergent disease, injuries, workplace hazards, disabilities, and environmental health threats.

INTRODUCTION

Campaigns to improve the health of the public, instituted by organizations such as the CDC and the World Health Organization (WHO), can take many forms. They may seek to educate and inform, or they may offer a specific service, such as vaccination against smallpox or measles. Sometimes campaigns lead to a change in the law. For example, many countries have moved beyond merely advising people to quit smoking towards banning it in public places.

To be successful, a public health campaign must be supported by sound science and it must have broad support among the population. The latter is vital, given that some public health measures may involve a certain amount of intrusion on people's individual liberties. For instance, many people who smoke feel their rights are violated by anti-smoking legislation and remain unconvinced of the dangers of secondary smoke.

In the journal article that follows, the CDC describes the fall in tooth decay due to the fluoridation of drinking water and the accompanying improvement in public health as one of the biggest public health success stories of the twentieth century. The underpinning science appears convincing and fluoridation won the support of most doctors, dentists, and policy makers.

■ PRIMARY SOURCE

Fluoridation of community drinking water is a major factor responsible for the decline in dental caries (tooth decay) during the second half of the 20th century. The history of water fluoridation is a classic example of clinical observation leading to epidemiologic investigation and community-based public health intervention. Although other fluoride-containing products are available, water fluoridation remains the most equitable and cost-effective method of delivering fluoride to all members of most communities, regardless of age, educational attainment, or income level.

DENTAL CARIES

Dental caries is an infectious, communicable, multifactorial disease in which bacteria dissolve the enamel surface of a tooth. Unchecked, the bacteria then may penetrate the underlying dentin and progress into the soft pulp tissue. Dental caries can result in loss of tooth structure and discomfort. Untreated caries can lead to incapacitating pain, a bacterial infection that leads to pulpal necrosis, tooth extraction and loss of dental function, and may progress to an acute systemic infection. . . .

At the beginning of the 20th century, extensive dental caries was common in the United States and in most developed countries. No effective measures existed for preventing this disease, and the most frequent treatment was tooth extraction. . . .

HISTORY OF WATER FLUORIDATION

The identification of a possible etiologic agent for mottled enamel led to the establishment in 1931 of the Dental Hygiene Unit at the National Institute of Health headed by Dr. H. Trendley Dean. Dean's primary responsibility was to investigate the association between fluoride and mottled enamel. . . .

The hypothesis that dental caries could be prevented by adjusting the fluoride level of community water supplies from negligible levels to 1.0–1.2 ppm was tested in a prospective field study conducted in four pairs of cities (intervention and control) starting in 1945: Grand Rapids and Muskegon, Michigan; Newburgh and Kingston, New York; Evanston and Oak Park, Illinois; and Brantford and Sarnia, Ontario, Canada. After conducting sequential cross-sectional surveys in these communities over 13–15 years, caries was reduced 50%–70% among children in the communities with fluoridated water. . . .

The effectiveness of community water fluoridation in preventing dental caries prompted rapid adoption of this public health measure in cities throughout the United States. As a result, dental caries declined precipitously during the second half of the 20th century. For example, the mean DMFT among persons aged 12 years in the United States declined 68%, from 4.0 in 1966–1970 to 1.3 in 1988–1994 (CDC, unpublished data, 1999) The American Dental Association, the American Medical Association, the World Health Organization, and other professional and scientific organizations quickly endorsed water fluoridation. Knowledge about the benefits of water fluoridation led to the development of other modalities for delivery of fluoride, such as toothpastes, gels, mouth rinses, tablets, and drops. Several countries in Europe and Latin America have added fluoride to table salt.

EFFECTIVENESS OF WATER FLUORIDATION

Early studies reported that caries reduction attributable to fluoridation ranged from 50% to 70%, but by the mid-1980s the mean DMFS scores in the permanent dentition of children who lived in communities with fluoridated water were only 18% lower than among those living in communities without fluoridated water. A review of studies on the effectiveness of water fluoridation conducted in the United States during 1979–1989 found that caries reduction was 8%–37% among adolescents (mean: 26.5%).

Since the early days of community water fluoridation, the prevalence of dental caries has declined in both communities with and communities without fluoridated water in the United States. This trend has been attributed largely to the diffusion of fluoridated water to areas without fluoridated water through bottling and processing of foods and beverages in areas with fluoridated water and widespread use of fluoride toothpaste. Fluoride toothpaste is efficacious in preventing dental caries, but its effectiveness depends on frequency of use by persons or their caregivers. In contrast, water fluoridation reaches all residents of communities and generally is not dependent on individual behavior.

Although early studies focused mostly on children, water fluoridation also is effective in preventing dental caries among adults. Fluoridation reduces enamel caries in adults by 20%–40% and prevents caries on the exposed root surfaces of teeth, a condition that particularly affects older adults.

Water fluoridation is especially beneficial for communities of low socioeconomic status. These communities have a disproportionate burden of dental caries and have less access than higher income communities to dental-care services and other sources of fluoride. Water fluoridation may help reduce such dental health disparities.

BIOLOGIC MECHANISM

Fluoride's caries-preventive properties initially were attributed to changes in enamel during tooth development because of the association between fluoride and cosmetic changes in enamel and a belief that fluoride incorporated into enamel during tooth development would result in a more acid-resistant mineral. However, laboratory and epidemiologic research suggests that fluoride prevents dental caries predominately after eruption of the tooth into the mouth, and its actions primarily are topical for both adults and children. These mechanisms include 1) inhibition of demineralization, 2) enhancement of remineralization, and 3) inhibition of bacterial activity in dental plaque.

Enamel and dentin are composed of mineral crystals (primarily calcium and phosphate) embedded in an organic protein/lipid matrix. Dental mineral is dissolved readily by acid produced by cariogenic bacteria when they metabolize fermentable carbohydrates. Fluoride present in solution at low levels, which becomes concentrated in dental plaque, can substantially inhibit dissolution of tooth mineral by acid.

Fluoride enhances remineralization by adsorbing to the tooth surface and attracting calcium ions present in saliva. Fluoride also acts to bring the calcium and phosphate ions together and is included in the chemical reaction that takes place, producing a crystal surface that is much less soluble in acid than the original tooth mineral.

Fluoride from topical sources such as fluoridated drinking water is taken up by cariogenic bacteria when they produce acid. Once inside the cells, fluoride interferes with enzyme activity of the bacteria and the control of

intracellular pH. This reduces bacterial acid production, which directly reduces the dissolution rate of tooth mineral.

POPULATION SERVED BY WATER FLUORIDATION

By the end of 1992, 10,567 public water systems serving 135 million persons in 8573 U.S. communities had instituted water fluoridation. Approximately 70% of all U.S. cities with populations of greater than 100,000 used fluoridated water. In addition, 3784 public water systems serving 10 million persons in 1924 communities had natural fluoride levels greater than or equal to 0.7 ppm. In total, 144 million persons in the United States (56% of the population) were receiving fluoridated water in 1992, including 62% of those served by public water systems. However, approximately 42,000 public water systems and 153 U.S. cities with populations greater than or equal to 50,000 have not instituted fluoridation. . . .

SAFETY OF WATER FLUORIDATION

Early investigations into the physiologic effects of fluoride in drinking water predated the first community field trials. Since 1950, opponents of water fluoridation have claimed it increased the risk for cancer, Down syndrome, heart disease, osteoporosis and bone fracture, acquired immunodeficiency syndrome, low intelligence, Alzheimer disease, allergic reactions, and other health conditions. The safety and effectiveness of water fluoridation have been re-evaluated frequently, and no credible evidence supports an association between fluoridation and any of these conditions.

21ST CENTURY CHALLENGES

Despite the substantial decline in the prevalence and severity of dental caries in the United States during the 20th century, this largely preventable disease is still common. National data indicate that 67% of persons aged 12–17 years and 94% of persons aged greater than or equal to 18 years have experienced caries in their permanent teeth.

Among the most striking results of water fluoridation is the change in public attitudes and expectations regarding dental health. Tooth loss is no longer considered inevitable, and increasingly adults in the United States are retaining most of their teeth for a lifetime. For example, the percentage of persons aged 45–54 years who had lost all their permanent teeth decreased from 20.0% in 1960–1962 to 9.1% in 1988–1994 (CDC, unpublished data, 1999). The oldest post-World War II "baby boomers" will reach age 60 years in the first decade of the 21st century, and more of that birth cohort will have a relatively intact dentition at that age than any generation in history. Thus, more teeth than ever will be at risk for caries among persons aged greater than or equal to 60 years. In the next century, water fluoridation will continue to help prevent caries among these older persons in the United States.

Most persons in the United States support community water fluoridation. Although the proportion of the U.S. population drinking fluoridated water increased fairly quickly from 1945 into the 1970s, the rate of increase has been much lower in recent years. This slowing in the expansion of fluoridation is attributable to several factors: 1) the public, some scientists, and policymakers may perceive that dental caries is no longer a public health problem or that fluoridation is no longer necessary or effective; 2) adoption of water fluoridation can require political processes that make institution of this public health measure difficult; 3) opponents of water fluoridation often make unsubstantiated claims about adverse health effects of fluoridation in attempts to influence public opinion; and 4) many of the U.S. public water systems that are not fluoridated tend to serve small populations, which increases the per capita cost of fluoridation. These barriers present serious challenges to expanding fluoridation in the United States in the 21st century. To overcome the challenges facing this preventive measure, public health professionals at the national, state, and local level will need to enhance their promotion of fluoridation and commit the necessary resources for equipment, personnel, and training.

The fluoridation of community drinking water led to a reduction in tooth decay during the second half of the 20th century. ©STEPHANIE MAZE/CORBIS.

SIGNIFICANCE

With the widespread availability of fluoride toothpaste and more awareness of the importance of dental care, tooth decay is no longer such a big issue in oral health. Attention has shifted to the problem of gum disease, which can also lead to tooth loss and which plays a role in other diseases. So, does the fact that fluoridation, despite its success in improving the nation's oral health, is not—and never has been—universal, still matter?

As the American Dental Association (ADA) celebrated sixty years of fluoridation, it also pointed out, with regret, that one-third of the U.S. population still does not have access to a fluoridated public water supply. Along with the ADA, the CDC and many other medical and dental opinion makers still firmly believe that fluoridation of the water supply is the most democratic and cost-effective way of reducing inequities in oral health. Water is a vital part of the diet and the public supply is available to all, whatever their socioeconomic status. People do not necessarily have such equal access to dental care or even fluoride toothpaste.

The global picture echoes the American one, with the World Health Organization pressing for more widespread adoption of fluoridation. Of course, it must be done properly and to the right level, which is between 0.7 to 1.2 parts per million (about one milligram per liter), at a certified water treatment plant. Too much fluoride can mark the teeth, a condition called dental fluorosis. Excess fluoride can also lead to skeletal fluorosis, which may weaken the bones. However, reports that fluoride can cause cancer and other health problems have not been substantiated. And excess fluoride can readily be removed from the water supply.

There remain, however, those who are opposed to fluoridation and many cities have voted not to have their water fluoridated. Partly this arises from a belief that fluoride is truly harmful to health. It is true that the chemicals that are added to the water supply, such as hexafluorosilicic acid, are corrosive and need handling with care. However, they are much diluted in the water. Fluoride in water is odorless, tasteless, and colorless, and only is detectable by specialized tests. The other main reason for opposing fluoridation is that there is a strong belief that water should be "pure"; fluoride is seen as a form of pollution. Furthermore, being forced to take in fluoride in our drinking water because the government thinks it is "good" for us is seen as an invasion of personal liberty and privacy. The same arguments apply to food that is fortified with vitamins or minerals, as well as to the chlorination of drinking water to prevent waterborne diseases. Such public health measures always balance public good against individual freedom. To be credible, they must, of course, be backed by the best scientific studies.

FURTHER RESOURCES
Web sites

American Dental Association. "After 60 Years of Success in Fighting Dental Decay, Water Fluoridation Still Lacking in Many Communities." <http://www.ada.org/public/media/presskits/fluoridation/index.asp> (accessed November 21, 2005).

World Health Organization. "World Water Day 2001: Oral Health." <http://www.who.int/water_sanitation_health/oralhealth/en/> (accessed November 21, 2005).

Water, Sanitation Key to Disaster Response, Long-Term Development

2004 Indian Ocean Tsunami

News article

By: Erica Bulman

Date: 2005.

Source: Erica Bulman. "Water, Sanitation Key to Disaster Response, Long-term Development." Associated Press Archive. (March 22, 2005).

About the Author: Erica Bulman is a journalist who works for the Associated Press International. She has been affiliated with Associated Press bureaus around the world during the last decade, and has written on subjects ranging from sports to politics to war to natural disasters. She is currently posting sports stories and reports from Austria and Switzerland.

INTRODUCTION

On the morning of December 26, 2004, at about seven o'clock local time, an earthquake measuring 9.0 on the Richter scale occurred in the floor of the Indian Ocean about one hundred miles from the western coast of the Indonesian island of Sumatra. The earthquake set into motion a series of tsunamis that struck eleven countries along the Indian Ocean's coast, leaving an estimated 200,000 people dead or unaccounted for. Although there is an international tsunami warning system that alerts countries along the Pacific Rim of an impending tsunami, countries bordering the Indian Ocean had no such system in place in 2004.

The first warning that people had of the impending tsunamis was when they saw the enormous waves approaching the shore. When tsunamis are created, generally far out at sea, they travel at tremendous speeds (several hundred miles per hour), and are extremely long. As they approach the land, they slow down and increase greatly in size and power. Immediately before the first wave reaches the shore, the breakwater is suddenly pulled back from the shore by the force of the tsunami. When the tsunamis struck on December 26, 2004, on the Indian Ocean coastal areas, they swept across large areas of land, washing away entire villages and cities. Many bodies were left along the beaches; others swept away and never recovered. Not only were homes, businesses, schools, and commercial buildings destroyed, the ecosystems that existed in the affected areas were decimated as well. Many of the affected coastal areas were impoverished, some had long histories of political or economic instability. The low-lying areas had limited amounts of clean drinkable water, and wells were typically close to the soil surface. The tsunamis washed salt water over the topography, destroying crops and gardens, and contaminating the ground and well water, leaving humans and animals with no available source of water for drinking, cooking, or bathing. It also destroyed septic and sanitary systems, and flooded the existing water systems with sewage as well as saline.

Among the first priorities of the relief and emergency response agencies was the rapid establishment of large-scale sanitation systems, (along with removal and disposal of tens of thousands of bodies), and the provision of clean and drinkable water. After a disaster of the magnitude of the 2004 tsunamis, an urgent concern was the prevention of potentially fatal diseases spread by contaminated water and exposure to raw sewage.

▮ PRIMARY SOURCE

The lack of any major outbreak of disease in areas hit by the Dec. 26 tsunami is largely due to the rapid deployment of clean water and sanitation teams, the international Red Cross said Tuesday.

In a statement marking World Water Day, the International Federation of Red Cross and Red Crescent Societies said the response provided a dramatic demonstration of the need for clean water. But the resource is also essential for longer-term chronic shortages in the developing world, the federation and other international organizations said.

A soldier stands guard next to a pool of stagnant water where bodies lay earlier this week, in a neighborhood where residents are slowly returning despite the health threats involved by living in unsanitary conditions in downtown Galle, southern Sri Lanka January 2, 2005. AP/WIDE WORLD PHOTOS.

The United Nations says more than 1.1 billion people around the world lack safe water and 2.4 billion have no access to sanitation, leading to over 3 million deaths every year.

"People who can turn on a tap and have safe and clean water to drink, to cook with and to bathe in often take it for granted, and yet more than 1 billion of our fellow human beings have little choice but to use potentially harmful sources of water," said Dr. Lee Jong-Wook, head of the World Health Organization.

The Red Cross federation said it had deployed 7 emergency response units in Indonesia and Sri Lanka, providing clean water to nearly 500,000 people.

It was its largest deployment of water and sanitation teams since it set up the emergency response system of its national societies 10 years ago, the federation said.

"After a major catastrophe, populations are particularly vulnerable to waterborne diseases, and our ability to produce large quantities of safe water and provide adequate sanitation quickly has been crucial in ensuring that these communities were not subjected to a second disaster," said Markku Niskala, secretary-general of the federation.

This year's World Water Day marks the launching of the "Water for Life" decade, during which the United Nations and governments are seeking to halve the number of people without access to safe drinking water and basic sanitation by 2015.

Ministers and government representatives are scheduled to meet next month at the Commission for Sustainable Development's thirteenth session in New York to take policy decisions on practical measures to ensure access to water for people worldwide.

"We need to increase water efficiency, especially in agriculture. We need to free women and girls from the daily chore of hauling water, often over great distances," U.N. General Secretary Kofi Annan said.

The plan also aims to safeguard water for the future of the Earth's ecosystems, crucial for protecting and preserving biodiversity in freshwater lakes and rivers, mountain landscapes, wetlands, estuaries, coastal zones and oceans.

SIGNIFICANCE

The damage on December 26 was actually two-fold: the earthquake out in the Indian Ocean caused a great deal of subterranean damage, fracturing pipelines and destroying well structures; the tsunamis devastated the land areas and destroyed water and sanitation systems over large land areas in eleven different countries, essentially simultaneously. Aid efforts were swiftly organized in order to deliver drinking water, and were effective in preventing large outbreaks of cholera and other waterborne diseases.

Among the initial major tasks of the first responders was the creation of massive water purification and distribution systems, both to preserve life and to prevent the outbreak or spread of waterborne, and potentially fatal, illnesses (such as cholera, malaria, and the diarrheal diseases). Because of the magnitude of the disaster and resultant crises, and the need to immediately bring in sufficient quantities of water to support the populations and to sustain the relief and rebuilding efforts—and a goal was to create a sustainable water supply method for the projected several years that would be needed (at a minimum) to rebuild the ravaged areas—massive water containment systems were set up on various sites in which the contaminated water was piped in and treated to make it clean and safe for consumption. The water was then trucked to local relocation and distribution sites daily. At the same time, relief agencies began to train local workers in appropriate methods for cleaning and decontaminating wells—a process which takes a prolonged period to accomplish completely. Local workers are also trained in the operation of the water decontamination systems, as these are to remain in place until the safe water systems have been completely restored or created (in some cases). In addition to the large-scale water treatment facilities, smaller decontamination systems have been erected in many areas where the entire ground well system is likely to remain contaminated for prolonged periods—this represents another effort at restoring some sense of normalcy and independence in gradually recovering villages and towns.

By training local citizens in the maintenance and oversight of these systems, autonomy is restored—and the groundwork (so to speak) for future crisis response is set in place—which is especially important in areas likely to experience similar future events. The livelihoods of many thousands of people were lost with the tsunamis, along with their homes and families. By providing training and education, people were able to begin recreating a sense of economic and personal stability, a critical element of the long-term recovery process.

Much of the prior living area was destroyed, causing many thousands of people to be displaced and relocated. They are living in makeshift or temporary housing, typically with few amenities (although their lives were generally quite spare to begin with). Businesses no longer exist, families have been decimated, social structures have been lost, and homes are gone. Survivors need to have the necessities of life available in a dependable manner, so having a ready supply of clean water for drinking and washing is paramount.

Of nearly equal importance is the construction and maintenance of sanitary facilities such as latrines and solid waste disposal systems. The worldwide relief agencies are engaged in not only creating a temporary system for use until permanent shelters and overall reconstruction efforts are completed, but in the establishment of a stable infrastructure that will support healthy future development. A long term goal of all relief efforts is forward movement: creating a dynamic system that encourages independent future growth and development, and provides a basis for ongoing stability.

FURTHER RESOURCES
Web sites

CDC.com. "Safe Water System (SWS): Where Has The SWS Been Used?" <http://www.cdc.gov/safewater/where_pages/where_tsunami.htm#> (accessed January 6, 2006).

CNN.com: Science & Space. "Tsunami Centers To Go On 24-Hour Alert." <http://www.cnn.com/2006/TECH/science/01/05/seismic.alaska.ap/index.html> (accessed January 6, 2006).

World Health Organization. "Water Safety Plans: Managing Drinking Water Quality from Catchment to Consumer." <http://www.who.int/water_sanitation_health/dwq/wsp170805.pdf> (accessed January 6, 2006).

The Initial Assessment: A Quick Checklist

Delivering Aid Amid Disaster

United Nations document

By: UNICEF

Date: 2005

Source: UNICEF Staff. *Emergency Field Handbook: A Guide for UNICEF Staff.* New York: UNICEF, 2005.

About the Author: In December 1946, the United Nations created the United Nations International Children's Emergency Fund (UNICEF) to act as a children's disaster relief agency following World War II. Its first mission was to provide for the health and welfare of war-affected children in Europe, who were in need of health care services, clothing, and food (among other things). Although the initial focus was on providing life-sustaining services and eradicating treatable diseases in children, UNICEF rapidly broadened focus to consider the assurance of basic human rights for all of the world's children: sufficient healthy food, adequate shelter, education, and safety from violence or exploitation. UNICEF was awarded the Nobel Peace Prize in 1965. More recently, UNICEF sponsored the World Summit for Children in 1990, delineating a United Nations endorsed ten-year program designed to improve the quality of life for the world's children. It has taken an in-depth look at the effects of armed children on children, and launched a global campaign for the betterment of children's lives, entitled Say Yes For Children in 2001. In 2002, a United Nations Special Session on Children set precedent by allowing children to act as delegates to the session. Through its many programs, UNICEF continues to positively impact the lives of all of the world's children.

INTRODUCTION

There are typically four components of general disaster response: planning or preparedness before the occurrence of the disaster/crisis; crisis or disaster response; immediate recovery and preliminary reconstruction; and long-term rehabilitation and rebuilding. In the planning or preparing for a disaster stage detailed plans of likely disasters are created, along with response scenarios. Nonperishable items critical for quick response may be stockpiled or sources of rapid supply may be identified. Of course, this planning is only effective for foreseeable disasters. For example, if a town is located on the coast in a hurricane-prone area, it is reasonable to have a hurricane preparedness plan. Many urban and densely populated areas have disaster plans in place in the event of a terrorist attack. In the United States, local, city, and state governments have a variety of disaster plans in place. The federal government has created the Department of Homeland Security's Federal Emergency Management Agency (FEMA) to anticipate and prepare for disasters involving the United States or its population (on American soil or elsewhere).

If an impending disaster is predicted—such as a hurricane, flood, tsunami, or tornado—and there is both sufficient preparation time and an adequate communication system, there may be a warning period prior to the disaster. The appropriate disaster plan may be implemented including evacuation of the highest risk areas, closure and boarding up of buildings, and instructions to the public via public radio and television stations. During the crisis or disaster itself, efforts are focused either on mitigating the effects of the crisis or on reacting to immediate needs for rescue or the provision of food and clean water. The immediate post-disaster period includes rescue, search and recovery, determination of a hierarchy of needs, notifying appropriate agencies and mobilizing resources, and gathering and sharing information. Among the first actions following a disaster are the provision of emergency medical assistance, triaging and transporting the injured to medical facilities, setting up and implementing a communications system, and a preliminary assessment of physical, material, and structural damage. Long-range recovery and rehabilitation take the concepts of the initial recovery phase and extend them across time. Among the priorities of this phase are: educating those affected regarding the changes in their environment or life circumstances; providing support and reconstruction services for those affected; restoring all lost services and infrastructure; and planning for the future development of the area.

◼ PRIMARY SOURCE

This checklist is a tool to help guide UNICEF's initial rough assessment, before a more formal rapid assessment by sector can take place. It can be used by non-specialists to get a basic understanding of areas where people might need assistance.

WHAT TO DO

Rapidly obtain the following information through initial field visits with other UN partners, if possible, and from contacts with UNICEF field and sub-offices, and partners in government, non-governmental organizations (NGOs) and other UN agencies.

Characteristics of the crisis and baseline data

- What is happening? What do you know about what is happening? What do you not know about what is happening?
- Where is the problem occurring? Include latitude and longitude, if possible.
- What is the geographic extent of the affected area?
- What are the physical and ecological characteristics of the affected area?
- What is the severity of the crisis in different localities?
- What appears to be the major dynamic of this crisis? Is there an expected end to the crisis? When?
- Who has the most reliable and accurate information about what is going on?
- What is the impact of the crisis on the government? What is the expected response of the government and local authorities, if any?
- What was the population in the area before the disaster (size, economic status and location of communities)?
- What political and administrative structures still exist in the affected area?
- What type of development or other aid programmes were or are operating in the area?
- Is there a regional dimension to the emergency? Is there more than one country involved?

Number and status of affected people.

- What is the approximate number of people affected by the crisis (with a rough percentage of women, children and children under five)?
- What are the reported numbers of dead, injured and missing persons?
- Are there especially vulnerable groups? Who are they and what are their numbers?
- Have families become separated? What percentage?
- Do most people have shelter, clothing? What percentage?
- What are the ethnic and cultural characteristics of the different groups (language, average family size, typical household living arrangements)?
- What are people doing to help themselves?
- What, if anything, are women doing differently than men to cope?
- Are youth groups and organizations active in development initiatives? If so, what is their role in normal circumstances and are they able to help local communities in this emergency?
- Are traditional coping mechanisms operating? If not, why not?

- Are there coping mechanisms in place that UNICEF could easily support?
- What is the government and its partners (bilateral or multilateral, civil society or NGO) doing to mitigate the impact of the emergency?

Displacement

- Have people been displaced? If so, from where? What is the cause?
- What is the approximate number of children in the displaced population?
- Is the displaced population growing or expected to grow? Are numbers of children likely to change?
- Are people likely to move farther?
- If so, where are they likely to go and when?
- Is the host community assisting or able to assist those who are displaced?
- Is there enough space for all those likely to arrive?
- What type and quantity of possessions have people brought with them? Did they bring domestic items?

Access, security and threats

- Has the UN done a risk and threat assessment? What phase?
- Is there year-round access to the affected population?
- If not, what is preventing access?
- What are the security threats for the affected population and humanitarian actors? Is there continued fighting? Are there landmines, banditry, blockades, rioting, natural risks, etc.?
- Are people threatened because of their gender or ethnic, political, religious or national identity?
- Are non-state actors involved? Are they recognized by the government?
- Has movement been restricted by the government or by non-state actors?
- Is UNICEF already engaging non-state actors? How? In what circumstances?

Health and nutrition

- What are the immediate and obvious health problems (wounds, respiratory infections, gastrointestinal diseases and parasites, malaria, measles)?
- Are health facilities functioning?
- Where are the health centers and hospitals? If possible, use GPS to locate and facilitate mapping of available resources.
- Are there adequate health workers for the facilities?
- Have there been disruptions in supply of medicines, medical equipment or in the cold chain? Of what magnitude?
- Are any groups without food?
- If so, is this because food is unavailable or because the people lack purchasing power?

- Are households able to prepare food?
- Are there visible signs of malnutrition—children too thin or with oedema (swollen belly)?
- In a quick check using a mid upper-arm circumference strip, are there children who classify as moderately or severely malnourished? What percentage of those sampled?
- Do people have shelter? Is it cold enough to need blankets?

Water and sanitation

- Do people have access to water?
- Where are the water points? If possible, use GPS to locate and facilitate mapping of available resources.
- Is water sufficient for all beneficiaries?
- Is the water safe for drinking?
- Do people have adequate containers to safely store and transport water?
- Are hygienic items (soap, sanitary protection) available?
- What sanitation facilities are people, especially women, using?
- How are people disposing of excreta?

Child protection

- Are there reports or evidence of children being killed, deliberately targeted or caught in the crossfire?
- Are there reports or evidence of separated or unaccompanied children?
- Are there reported cases of rape and sexual abuse?
- Are there reports or evidence of traumatized children?
- Is there anybody in the affected community who is monitoring andresponding to these protection issues?
- Are traditional childcare arrangements functioning?
- Are there indications of stigma against any particular group of children? If so, what?
- Are there children orphaned by AIDS among those affected by the crisis?
- Are there reports or knowledge of landmines in the affected area?
- Are there landmine victims? How many? Of what age?

Education

- Are the schools functioning? Are alternate learning spaces available? Are children going to school? What percentage are in primary and secondary levels?
- Are there facilities and community structures for care of preschool-age children?
- Where are the schools? If possible, use GPS to locate and facilitate mapping of available resources. Is there any disparity in attendance between boys and girls? Why?

- Are there teachers in the affected community? Are there customarycaregivers for younger children?
- Is there damage to school facilities? How much? Are there alternative places for children to learn?
- Are there other factors hindering school attendance (fear, threats, violence, mines, natural risks, sociocultural factors)?

HIV/AIDS

- Are there reported cases of rape and sexual abuse?
- What are the normal patterns of behaviour in the community relating to HIV/AIDS affected and infected groups, and is there any sign of stigma and discrimination?
- What is the HIV-prevalence rate in the area or among the affected group? Rapidly collect secondary data from existing sources, including hospitals, NGOs, surveys, health management information systems, etc.
- Is HIV prevalence particularly high within certain population groups affected by the emergency?
- Are minimum universal precautions available (safe blood supply, sterilization or disposal of sharps, gloves, condoms, etc.)?
- Are there groups such as impoverished or displaced people, illegal migrants, children and women (especially unaccompanied) or people depending on food aid or the distribution of other items, that are at particularly high risk of sexual exploitation or violence because of the situation?

Partners

- Which local or international organizations have a presence in the affected area, and what are their fields of expertise?
- Could these organizations become implementing partners, if necessary?
- Which organizations have good local contacts and counterparts?

Logistics and operations

- What is the weather expected to be like in the short- and medium-term? Are weather conditions and seasonal changes likely to affect public health or the delivery of assistance?
- How is the affected area best accessed? What are the road conditions to and in the affected area?
- Are UNICEF's usual local suppliers operating? Would they be able to increase their provision of supplies, if needed?
- What means of transport are locally available (trucks, aircraft, animals, boats)?
- Are telecommunications systems functioning?

- Are banking and financial systems functioning in the local area? Are they functioning nationally?

SIGNIFICANCE

Although the general response to disaster and crisis situations remains the same regardless of population, children present a greater cause for concern, due in part to their inability to be self-sufficient at an early age. Once the initial event has occurred and immediate medical concerns have been addressed, child welfare and protection becomes paramount. Children are often separated from family members in a crisis or disaster, and they may be orphaned or lose one or more immediate family members or caregivers. If children have lost parents or caregivers, it is critical to ensure safety, shelter, and protection for them, in order to provide for their basic survival needs. Even in intact families, homes are often lost or left during a disaster. One of the early goals of child-focused agencies is to register children who have been separated from their families. Then the agencies seek ways to reunite families or attempt to find stable placement for children who have lost their families. Children who are orphaned or separated from their families are particularly vulnerable to abuse or exploitation, so it is essential to protect them from further trauma and harm.

In the wake of a crisis, normal routines are lost, schedules and daily activities no longer exist, and the world of a child becomes frightening and unstable. Following a disaster, most child relief agencies quickly focus on the creation of centralized, child-safe spaces, either in schools, child activity centers, or day care centers. In those facilities, there are generally programs of grief and trauma work, psychotherapy, stress management, and trust-building activities, to aid children (and adults) in coping with the grief, loss, trauma, and changes in their lives. Schools are rebuilt early in the reconstruction process, both to give a semblance of normalcy to children's lives and to provide a place for job and vocational training (often necessary when the disaster damages or destroys the economic infrastructure of the region).

Nutrition and hydration are essential for supporting and maintaining life. Relief agencies focus not only on bringing in adequate food and clean drinkable water, but also work with local agencies and in-country resources to create long-term means of providing water and nourishment. Such efforts often include supporting the creation of a new infrastructure by

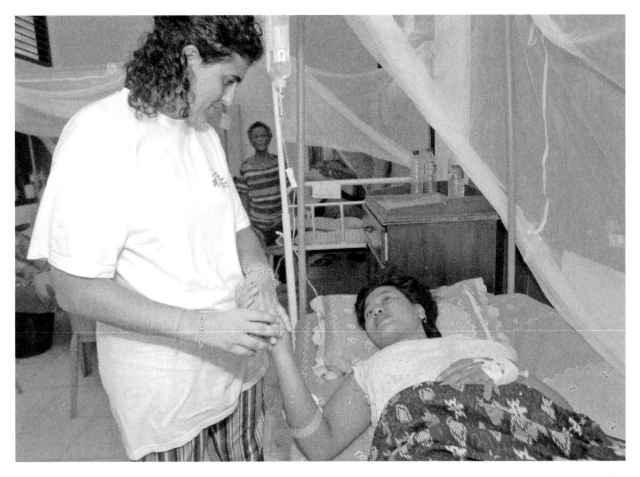

In January 2005, a physician from Doctors without Borders, a medical humanitarian aid organization, helps a patient in Indonesia who suffered injuries during the tsunami disaster. AP/WIDE WORLD PHOTOS.

bringing in livestock and the means to establish agricultural system, setting up water purification facilities, and creating sanitation programs.

In the aftermath of a disaster, conditions are often created that can lead to large-scale health issues, such as outbreaks of cholera, malaria, and typhoid. These health issues are the result of the loss of sanitation, contaminated food and water, and possible vermin or rodent infestations in the affected areas, or in areas where large groups of displaced people are crowded into temporary shelters. Medical relief workers bring in vaccines, institute prophylactic measures, and work with local (sometimes newly trained) professionals and paraprofessionals to create public health systems.

Not infrequently, disasters and crises occur in areas that are already stressed due to political instability, civil unrest, drought, famine, pandemics (such as AIDS or tuberculosis), or geological conditions (areas

prone to earthquakes or flooding). In those circumstances, it is necessary for relief agencies not only to rebuild what has been lost in the immediate event, but to work with local agencies and governments to create infrastructures, social networks, and economic systems. This creates longer term stability and provides the population with a means to sustain itself and develop over time.

FURTHER RESOURCES
Web sites

Direct Relief International. "Focus Areas: Focusing on Mothers and Children." <http://www.directrelief.org/ sections/our_work/focus_areas.html> (accessed January 5, 2006).

Federal Emergency Management Agency. "A Guide to the Disaster Declaration Process and Federal Disaster Assistance." <http://www.fema.gov/rrr/dec_guid. shtm> (accessed January 5, 2006).

The Sphere Project. "The Sphere Project Handbook—Humanitarian Charter and Minimum Standards in Disaster Response." <http://www.sphereproject.org/handbook/index.htm> (accessed January 5, 2006).

UNICEF. "Millenium Development Goals: About the Goals." <http://www.unicef.org/mdg/28184_28230.htm> (accessed January 5, 2006).

World Health Organization. "Health Action in Crisis." <http://www.who.int/hac/en/index.html> (accessed January 5, 2006).

Memories of Polio

Memoir

By: Alakananda Mohanty

By: Martin Pernick

Source: "Do you Remember?" in *Advancing Global Public Health.* University of Michigan. Available online at <http://www.polio.umich.edu/history/memories.html> (accessed on December 10, 2005).

About the Authors: The writers of two these pieces contributed to the University of Michigan's fiftieth-anniversary celebration of a safe and efficacious polio vaccine.

INTRODUCTION

Poliomyelitis (polio or infantile paralysis) is a viral illness which has been known since the time of the ancient Egyptians some 3,000 years ago. It was further described by doctors at the end of the eighteenth century. In many of those infected, polio causes only mild symptoms. But in some cases the virus destroys nerve cells in the spinal cord and the base of the brain, causing a devastating illness and potentially fatal paralysis.

Polio epidemics have occurred throughout history. At the end of the nineteenth century, 50,000 people a year would be affected by epidemics in the United States. Franklin Roosevelt (1882–1945) was disabled by an attack in 1921; in 1938 he established the National Foundation for Infantile Paralysis, dubbed by American comedian Eddie Cantor (1892–1964) as the "March of Dimes," which was dedicated to fighting polio. Meanwhile, Harvard researchers Philip Drinker (1894–1972) and Louis Agassiz Shaw (1886–1940) developed an artificial respirator known as the iron lung to help those whose breathing muscles had been paralyzed by polio.

Thomas Francis (1900–1969) was a virologist who joined the new School of Public Health at the University of Michigan in 1941, where he established and directed a research laboratory for viral diseases. That same year, Jonas Salk (1914–1995) became a postgraduate student at the university, studying vaccine development with Francis. Later in the decade, Francis turned his attention to enteric viruses, with an intense focus on polio, while Salk went on to develop a polio vaccine at the University of Pittsburgh Medical School. Francis ran the field trials for his former student, and on April 12, 1955, pronounced Salk's vaccine "safe, effective, and potent."

In the articles that follow, Pernick describes his participation in this trial; survivor Mohanty tells what it is like to suffer from a severe case of polio.

I was a second-grade student at the Hewlett Primary School in Hewlett, Long Island, outside New York City, when my parents enrolled me in the Salk Field Trials. I remember them explaining to me that some kids would get real vaccine and some kids would get water, in order to test whether it worked. I remember being bussed to some other site to get the shots and that the shots did not hurt as much as I expected.

I particularly remember the day the results were announced. My parents sat me down to tell me that the vaccine was the greatest discovery of my lifetime, that I had played a role in history, and that I was one of the lucky ones to get the real vaccine. My memories of that good news are also closely associated with my memory of my parents solemnly sitting me down in the same chair a few days later to tell me of a great loss to science—the death of Albert Einstein. In retrospect, I think perhaps those events had something to do with my becoming a professor of the history of medicine.

In the fall of 1955, I changed schools, moving to PS 66 in the New York City borough of Queens. Shortly after that, the NYC public schools began mass immunizations with the new vaccine. I remember refusing to take the shots, because I had already had them. Neither my teacher nor the principal believed me. The principal all but accused me of lying to avoid the pain of a shot, and sent a note home requiring my parents to come to school if they wanted me to not get the shot. In retrospect I suspect that (unlike the field trial) this school simply vaccinated everyone without asking or notifying parents, since if my parents had gotten some kind of consent form to sign they would have been able to explain my situation in advance.

I'm not sure, but I think my family pediatrician gave me one or two annual "booster" shots in the years immediately after the field trial series of three injections. I recall being told that was because no one knew yet how long the initial immunity lasted.

Before the vaccine my parents and friends were very aware of the polio epidemics of the early '50s. I remember before the vaccine being warned not to eat food that had fallen on the floor because if I did I'd "get polio." (After the vaccine I was still not allowed to eat food that fell on the floor, but the explanation switched to "germs" rather than specifically "polio.")

Martin Pernick

Professor of History

University of Michigan

Ann Arbor, MI

Tale of a Survivor It was the end of the summer of 1960 and my family and I had just returned from a rather tedious vacation from my ancestral village. I was getting ready to start school and I was extremely excited about wearing new clothes and meeting new friends. I was out in front of my home when I first experienced what seemed like flu symptoms. What bad timing—school starting and I was getting sick.

The next couple of days were a blur—our doctor visiting me at the house, family and medical personnel whispering in hushed tones. It was extremely difficult to sit up and I couldn't turn or bend my neck without a great deal of pain. Unimaginable pain began to take over my back. Polio never entered my mind.

As a precaution, my mother informed me, I was to have a spinal tap. And there it was . . .not even a margin-lined diagnosis. Polio. I must tell you, this was not a sympathetic disease in any sense of the word. The next few days were a nightmare and I don't mind telling you that when somebody asked me to participate here with my story, it brought back a flood of memories that I had suppressed. Once the word was out our neighbourhood went into immediate panic. Pools were drained. My family were shunned. Quarantine signs went up around my house and my brother was not allowed to go to school.

When I arrived at City's largest hospital with hundreds of others, I was strapped to a gurney and lined up in the queue, as there were no beds available. My parents were literally dragged away to avoid any contact with me.

As I recall, when I was lifted into a bed it was with a medical staff clothed in long smock, masks and gloves . . . again no contact. I was wheeled into a ward with others.

If you asked me what was my worst experience while battling this disease, I would have to say the pain: constant intensified, horrific physical pain. There was a nurse who had worked with polio patients and developed a treatment procedure that involved massage, exercises, and wrapping affected limbs to reduce muscle spasms and the resultant pain. When I tell you I counted the hours in between these treatments, it is not an exaggeration and my entire torso was wrapped. As a result of these treatments, I was left with blisters, but the submission of pain temporarily was worth it.

After the first few days, I had visitors. First to see me were my parents. You could tell by their eyes they were horrified as to what I must have looked like. So went my days, sobbing parents, and the constant pain. . . .

My best recollection is that perhaps two weeks after I entered the hospital, the pain subsided, and I was to be released to go home. My disabilities not yet compiled, nonetheless, I was deemed not contagious and with many stipulations set free. Keep in mind, I had not had the opportunity to try and walk during my stay and the doctors told my parents that I might never walk again without crutches. How I must have looked: my curly locks all matted, [thin] as a rail all curled up in a wheelchair being pushed to my parents. I still remember as I approached them, I asked the nurse to stop and I stood up and took a few steps into the arms of my father.

My follow-up visits were to be at the hospital for physical therapy and regular visits to orthopaedic department. My residual disabilities were limited to the left side of my body. One leg was shorter and my spine had a curvature. I also had a muscle weakness in my lower back, which has stayed with me.

The road back is never easy, but with the love and support of family and friends, the stigma of polio affliction was soon forgotten. I now approach the over-40 time of my life, and some of the old aches and pain occur once again.

The bottom line is that polio survivors are just that—survivors. We did what we had to do then and we have to make the best of what comes along now. We live with polio every day of our lives, be it a bad memory, a nagging pain, or a fear of a limb that may decide to give up. . . . But we go on. Being a part of the Polio Immunisation program seems right to me. If my involvement can spare just one child from the agonies of this dreadful disease, then it will be worth recounting the past. Now you can go and say, "I met someone today who survived polio." I thank you for your time, patience, compassion, and most of all your friendship.

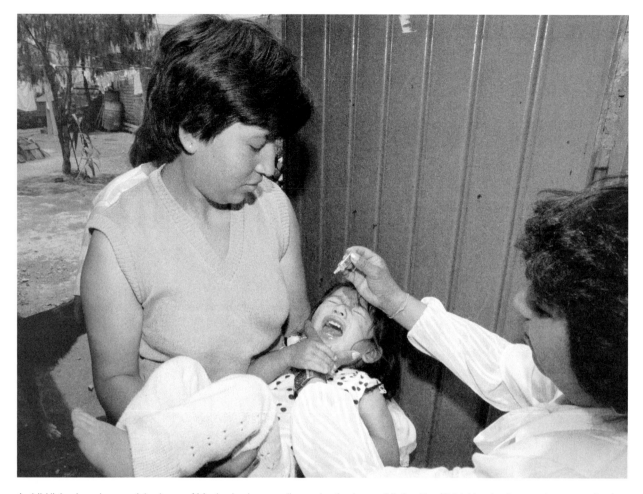

A child living in an impoverished area of Mexico is given a polio vaccination by a public health official. Vaccinations are key to eradicating the crippling disease worldwide. ©KEITH DANNEMILLER/CORBIS.

Alakananda Mohanty

Communications Associate

Rotary International PolioPlus Program

New Delhi, India

SIGNIFICANCE

Alfred Sabin (1906–1993) developed an oral polio vaccine in the mid-1950s. Although an oral vaccine is always preferable to an injectable, like the Salk vaccine, early trials of the Sabin vaccine were problematic. His vaccine was a weakened form of polio virus, while the Salk vaccine was an attenuated, or "killed" version. Some healthy volunteers actually developed polio as a result of having taken the Sabin vaccine because the virus in it became active in their bodies. Sabin modified his vaccine and there were further clinical trials between 1958 and 1960. The Sabin vaccine then superseded the Salk in the United States and elsewhere and paved the way for the eradication of polio in the Western hemisphere in 1994.

Polio can be a devastating disease, especially for the young, and the World Health Organisation (WHO) has committed itself to eradicating it in same way as it has smallpox. This goal has not yet been achieved, although good progress has been made. The eradication involves mass vaccination and this has proved difficult in areas affected by conflict. However, WHO manages to negotiate a temporary cease-fire on occasion to hold a mass vaccination day. In a conflict, both sides have an interest in eradicating disease among their populations, so this is a feasible way forward, so long as the appropriate negotiations take place. There have been outbreaks in recent years in Somalia, Yemen, and Sudan, but action is being focused now upon these countries. These outbreaks are thought to have arisen by transmission from Nigeria, where polio is still endemic, as it is in

Pakistan and Afghanistan, although there are few cases. As of late 2005, the total number of cases of polio, globally, was about 1,500.

Meanwhile, Western countries cannot be complacent. Where people refuse vaccination for their children, polio outbreaks can still occur, as happened in The Netherlands in 1993. The Sabin polio vaccine, while convenient and effective, keeps the virus in circulation, albeit in a weakened form. Furthermore, people with compromised immunity, such as those with HIV/AIDS, could act as a potential reservoir for the poliovirus. Therefore, scientists encourage continued vaccination against polio at the present time, even though the disease has been greatly diminished.

FURTHER RESOURCES

Books

Lock, Stephen, John M. Last, and George Dunea, eds. *The Oxford Illustrated Companion to Medicine*. Oxford, UK: Oxford University Press, 2001.

Web sites

Advancing Global Public Health. "Thomas Francis." <http://www.polio.umich.edu/history/francis.html> (accessed November 23, 2005).

University of Virginia. Historical Collections at the Claude Moore Health Sciences Library. "Iron Lung." <http://historical.hsl.virginia.edu/ironlung> (accessed January 4, 2006).

Outbreak Notice

Avian Influenza (H5N1)

Bulletin

By: Centers for Disease Control and Prevention

Date: December 29, 2005

Source: Centers for Disease Control and Prevention. "Notice about Avian Influenza A (H5N1) in Asia and Travel during the Lunar New Year."December 29, 2005. Available online at <http://www.cdc.gov/travel/other/avian_flu_lunar_newyear_2006_english.htm> (accessed February 2, 2006).

About the Author: The Centers for Disease Control and Prevention (CDC) is a federal government agency that provides health and safety information for United States citizens and international health professionals. It reports accurate and timely information regarding health issues, and develops and applies disease

prevention and control measures. The CDC is also involved in health promotion and education.

INTRODUCTION

The influenza (flu) virus has always been a major threat to human health. It is highly infectious and, therefore, has the potential to cause epidemics. There are three types of influenza virus, known as A, B, and C. Influenza A is the most worrying to health officials, as it is responsible for most epidemics and pandemics (world-wide epidemics). Indeed, the influenza pandemic of 1918 killed 15–20 million people, more than twice as many as had died in World War I (1915–1918). Influenza A affects both people and animals, such as birds, pigs, horses, seals, and whales. Influenza B affects humans only and causes epidemics within a population, but not pandemics. Influenza C is also confined to humans and usually causes only mild illness.

Influenza A is classified into sub-types depending on the nature of two proteins on the surface of the virus. There are sixteen types of the hemagluttinin (H) surface protein and nine of the neuraminidase (N) protein. This leads to many different H and N combinations, known as subtypes, of influenza A. Subtypes can be further classified into strains, which vary as to how pathogenic, or dangerous, they are.

Avian influenza (bird flu) is common because wild birds are natural hosts for various subtypes of influenza A, including the highly pathogenic H5N1 subtype that is currently causing worldwide concern among public health officials. The virus does not normally make the wild birds sick, but they can transmit it through their saliva and feces. Poultry—domesticated birds like chickens, ducks, and turkeys—can catch influenza from wild birds and, in contrast, the domesticated birds do become sick. Outbreaks of H5N1 bird flu occurred in eight Asian countries—Cambodia, China, Indonesia, Laos, South Korea, Thailand, Japan, and Vietnam—in 2003 and 2004, killing up to 100 percent of some of the flocks affected. Bird flu can spread to humans through contact with infected birds and there have been an increasing number of human cases reported since 1997, with an accompanying mortality rate of more than 50 percent.

CDC is naturally concerned at the prospect of the spread of avian flu to the United States. International travel has always posed a potent risk of spreading disease. If avian flu does enter the country, it will most likely be from someone traveling from a country where they have become infected. Thus, CDC has a duty to warn travelers to take adequate precautions, as detailed in the advice below.

Vietnamese scientists test bird flu infected chicken samples at a respiratory virus laboratory, at the National Institute of Hygiene and Epidemiology in Hanoi, Vietnam in 2005. Poultry farmers need to adopt strict hygiene standards to curb Asia's deadly bird flu virus, a top Vietnamese official said on the eve of an international conference on fighting the disease. AP/WIDE WORLD PHOTOS.

PRIMARY SOURCE

Outbreak Notice

Notice about Avian Influenza A (H5N1) in Asia and Travel during the Lunar New Year

Released: December 29, 2005

Updated: January 18, 2006

This notice in other languages:

- Chinese (traditional)
- Vietnamese
- Thai
- Indonesian

The Centers for Disease Control and Prevention (CDC) has issued a specific Outbreak Notice for travel during the Lunar New Year to countries reporting human infection with avian influenza A (H5N1) viruses. Because of increased travel to and from countries reporting human infection with H5N1 during the Lunar New Year, and increased preparation and consumption of poultry for the holiday, this notice provides information to travelers about where H5N1 outbreaks are occurring, health measures to take before travel, and what to do if illness occurs during or after travel. CDC issues various levels of notification about disease outbreaks. Currently, CDC and the World Health Organization (WHO) do not recommend restrictions for travel to any of the countries affected by H5N1.

Avian influenza A (H5N1) viruses usually affect wild birds but since 2003 have been associated with serious, widespread disease among poultry, such as chickens, in parts of Asia and Europe. During 2005, outbreaks of H5N1 infection among poultry and other birds have been confirmed in Cambodia, China, Croatia, Indonesia, Kazakhstan, Mongolia, Romania, Russia, Thailand, Turkey, Ukraine, and Vietnam. Poultry outbreaks were also reported in Malaysia and Laos during 2004.

While human infections with H5N1 viruses have been rare, more than 130 human cases have been confirmed by WHO since January 2004. All reported human cases have occurred in Vietnam, Thailand, Cambodia, Indonesia, and China, with more than half of the cases resulting in death. For information about avian influenza and the current number of human cases, please see the World Health Organization (WHO) website at <ttp://www.who.int/csr/disease/avian_influenza/en/>.

Most cases of H5N1 infection in humans have been linked to direct or close contact with infected poultry in the affected countries. Therefore, when possible, individuals should take care to avoid contact with live, well-appearing, sick, or dead poultry and with any surfaces that may have been contaminated by poultry or their feces or secretions. Transmission of H5N1 viruses to two persons through eating uncooked duck blood may also have occurred in Vietnam in 2005. Individuals should never eat uncooked poultry or poultry products, including blood.

CDC collaborates closely with WHO and other partners to closely monitor the H5N1 situation in countries reporting human cases and poultry outbreaks. CDC also works with other U.S. agencies, state and local governments, and private organizations to maintain a high level of surveillance for H5N1 and other potential influenza threats domestically. At this time, neither human cases of avian influenza A (H5N1) nor animal infections have been reported in the United States.

The following are recommendations for travel to areas reporting avian influenza A (H5N1).

Before any international travel to an area affected by H5N1 avian influenza

- Visit CDC's Travelers' Health website at <http://www.cdc.gov/travel> to educate yourself and others who may be traveling with you about any disease risks and CDC health recommendations for international travel in areas you plan to visit. For other information about avian influenza, see CDC's avian influenza website: <http://www.cdc.gov/flu/avian/index.htm>.
- Be sure you are up to date with all your routine vaccinations, and see your doctor or health-care provider, ideally 4–6 weeks before travel, to get any additional vaccinations, medications, or information you may need.

- Put together a travel health kit containing basic first aid and medical supplies. Be sure to include a thermometer and alcohol-based hand gel to clean your hands. See the Travelers' Health Kit page in Health Information for International Travel for other suggested items.
- Before your trip, find a doctor or clinic in the country you will be visiting in case you get sick.
- Check your health insurance plan to see if it covers illness abroad. Consider the purchase of supplemental insurance, as well as trip cancellation insurance or medical evacuation insurance. A list of medical evacuation services is provided on the U.S. Department of State web page Medical Information for Americans Traveling Abroad, at <http://travel.state.gov/travel/tips/health/health_1185.html>.

During travel to an affected area

- Do not have direct or close contact with poultry, including touching well-appearing, sick, or dead chickens and ducks. Stay away from places such as poultry farms and bird markets where live poultry are raised or kept, and avoid handling surfaces contaminated with poultry feces or secretions.
- As with other infectious illnesses, one of the most important preventive practices is careful and frequent handwashing. Cleaning your hands often with soap and water removes potentially infectious material from your skin and helps prevent disease transmission. Waterless alcohol-based hand gels may be used when soap is not available and hands are not visibly soiled.
- Influenza viruses are destroyed by heat; therefore, all foods from poultry, including eggs and poultry blood, should be thoroughly cooked.
- If you become sick with symptoms such as a fever accompanied by a cough, sore throat, or difficulty breathing or if you develop any illness that requires prompt medical attention, a U.S. consular officer can assist you in locating medical services and informing your family or friends. Inform your health care provider of any possible exposures to avian influenza. See Seeking Health Care Abroad in Health Information for International Travel for more information about what to do if you become sick while abroad. You should not travel until you are free of symptoms, unless your travel is health-related.

When Preparing Food

- Separate raw meat from cooked or ready-to-eat foods. Do not use the same chopping board or the same knife for preparing raw meat and cooked or ready-to-eat foods.

- Do not handle either raw or cooked foods without washing your hands in between.
- Do not place cooked meat back on the same plate or surface it was on before it was cooked.
- All foods from poultry, including eggs and poultry blood, should be cooked thoroughly. Egg yolks should not be runny or liquid. Because influenza viruses are destroyed by heat, the cooking temperature for poultry meat should reach 70°C (158°F).
- Wash egg shells in soapy water before handling and cooking, and wash your hands afterwards.
- Do not use raw or soft-boiled eggs in foods that will not be cooked.
- After handling raw poultry or eggs, wash your hands and all surfaces and utensils thoroughly with soap and water.

After your return:

- Monitor your health for 10 days.
- If you become ill with a fever plus a cough, sore throat, or trouble breathing during this 10-day period, see a doctor. **Before you visit a doctors office or clinic, tell them: 1) your symptoms, 2) where you traveled, and 3) if you have had direct contact with poultry or close contact with a very sick person. This way the doctor can be aware that you have traveled to an area reporting avian influenza.**
- Do not travel if you are sick, unless it is for medical care. Limiting contact with others as much as possible can help prevent the spread of infections.

SIGNIFICANCE

The CDC advice is applicable not only in the context of avian influenza, but to travel health in general. It has much to say, too, about avoiding infection in everyday life. If all travelers heeded simple hygiene rules such as frequent handwashing and taking extra care in food preparation, there would be fewer cases of infection of any kind. When it comes to preventing bird flu the rules for prevention are clear. People catch bird flu by contact with infected poultry. Transmission of the virus from one person to another is rare, although not unknown.

The question now is whether the bird flu virus could undergo genetic changes in humans that would make it more easily transmissible from person to person, possibly resulting in a pandemic. Many public health experts assume that a pandemic is likely in the near future and they believe that urgent action is now needed to stop it from occurring. The first line of defense begins with containing outbreaks in domestic chickens, as well as monitoring the movement of ducks, swans, or other migratory birds that can harbor the virus.

Antigenic shift is a far more abrupt change in the composition of H and N, which creates a new subtype of virus. The immune system would offer no protection against the new virus and so it could spread very rapidly, creating a pandemic. As of early 2006, World Health officials continued to express fear that there will be more cases of H5N1 bird flu in humans and that the virus will undergo antigenic shift to become a more pathogenic and infectious type. Following such a mutation H5N1 will no longer be classified as an avian virus but rather as a human influenza virus.

There are two weapons against a pandemic of bird flu—vaccination and anti-viral drugs. Scientists are working on a vaccine, but the "new" virus needs to have emerged and be identified before this vaccine will be ready. It will also need to be produced on a large scale to protect enough people to stop a pandemic. There are two anti-viral drugs that can treat bird flu—Tamiflu (oseltamivir) and Relenza (zanamivir)—but it is not certain that there will be sufficient doses available in time to protect everyone at risk.

The general public must be made aware of the potential dangers of a pandemic. The popular media too often spread panic and worry about health matters. The CDC, in this travel advice, seeks to educate and inform. Infection is a major public health issue which is not confined to concern about avian influenza. The more we can learn about preventing and fighting infection, the more lives will be saved, both in the United States and around the world.

FURTHER RESOURCES

Web sites

Centers for Disease Control and Prevention. "Information about Avian Influenza (Bird Flu) and Avian Influenza A (H5N1) Virus." <http://www.cdc.gov/flu> (accessed November 16, 2005).

World Health Organization. "Avian Influenza." <http://www.who.int/mediacentre/factsheets/avian_influenza/en/print.html> (accessed November 16, 2005).

Wellness and Health

Health and wellness is a phrase that first gained popularity in the 1970s. It refers to self-motivated actions taken by those who wish to improve their physical health and/or appearance, mental or spiritual outlook, or protect themselves from disease. The pursuit of physical fitness and a healthy lifestyle has since become an important part of many people's lives, encompassing exercise, diet, mental health, disease prevention, and sexuality.

In 1970, the Boston Women's Health Book Collective published *Our Bodies, Ourselves*, which provided health and medical information, and promoted an activist approach to guiding health policy. The book was somewhat controversial at the time, particularly for its approach to a women's right to abortion, and health/sexuality issues.

Today, the idea of individuals taking responsibility for their own health and wellness is fairly mainstream, with many books, magazines, and newspaper sections as well as websites and television shows devoted to the subject.

In addition to the various media resources people can access, organizations like Alcoholics Anonymous (AA) and Weight Watchers also provide support. These types of groups stress self-analysis and behavioral change.

Personal responsibility in the form of physical exercise programs have gained popularity over the years and have helped many people become more physically fit. In the 1970s, for example, the aerobics movement founded by the American physician Kenneth Cooper was a driving force behind the increased popularity of aerobics. Running was popularized by authors such as Jim Fixx, whose book *The Complete Book of Running* sold millions of copies.

In addition to aerobics, a plethora of fitness programs and equipment are now available. Many have proven value, while others make sensational claims and are more dubious. Although the approach adopted by organizations like Weight Watchers has shown that a balanced diet combined with exercise can improve and maintain fitness over time, Americans continue to embrace products and plans that promise rapid change. Fad diets, for example, encourage rapid weight loss, but are usually accompanied by weight gain once the diet is ended. Weight reduction products aimed at the overweight and clinically obese generate sales in the billions of dollars annually in the United States alone. The regulation and policing of the lucrative diet industry can generate intense legal, social, and political controversy.

Many people associate a certain physical appearance with robust health. In "America Is Still Working on Its Abs," this obsession with a muscular body is examined. The desire for a younger-looking body has led to a surge in cosmetic surgeries and procedures such as liposuction and botox injections.

Today, health and wellness also encompasses disease detection and prevention. "Home Diagnostic Tests: The Ultimate House Call?" looks at commercially available home testing. Pregnancy test kits have been available for several decades. But now, home-based tests can even be done for diseases such as acquired immunodeficiency syndrome (AIDS). Although not intended to replace examination and consultation by a physician, home tests offer privacy, and often immediate results.

In terms of mental health, approaches such as biofeedback, psychoanalysis, and counseling have become popular.

Not By Bread Alone:

The Principles of Human Nutrition

Book excerpt

By: Harvey Washington Wiley

Date: 1915

Source: Harvey Washington Wiley. *Not by Bread Alone: The Principles of Human Nutrition.* New York: Hearst's International Library, 1915.

About the Author: Harvey Washington Wiley served as the commissioner of the Bureau of Chemistry—the precursor to the U.S. Food and Drug Administration—from 1905 to 1912. A trained medical doctor and chemist, Wiley was a pioneer in the study of sugars and chemical preservatives in food. Credited with authoring the Pure Food and Drugs Act of 1906, Wiley's work during the previous two decades on food preservatives and sugar helped him in passing the act. Wiley resigned from his position as FDA commissioner in 1912 to work with *Good Housekeeping* magazine; he developed the "Good Housekeeping Seal of Approval," a continuation of his work in nutrition and consumer protection.

INTRODUCTION

The Progressive Movement moved from the nineteenth into the twentieth century with a strong faith in scientific progress as the answer to social, moral, medical, economic, and public health problems. The Industrial Revolution had brought great economic strengths to the country as a whole, but with these strengths came problems, such as overcrowding in urban areas, disease, industrial accidents and deaths, and extreme poverty. As cities and towns applied progressive reforms to such public health and social matters as prostitution, sanitation, child labor, and women's health, scientists like Harvey Washington Wiley applied new techniques and ideas to the human condition as a whole.

Because many Americans equated science with progress, an industrial or scientific approach to any problem or issue was generally considered superior. From the development of artificial baby milk formulas to patent medicines that claimed to cure a wide range of ailments, any product or procedure that was called "scientific" was "progressive" and therefore better. However, critics began to expose problems with mechanical food production, labor systems in factories, and other complications that were created

by scientific processes; Upton Sinclair's novel from this era, *The Jungle*, is a scathing indictment of the meat-packing industry, its lax health standards, and the role that wage slavery and immigrant exploitation played in American industry's economic success.

Harvey Washington Wiley gained fame for his experiments in feeding Borax and other chemical preservatives to humans. His famous "poison squad" of fourteen volunteers ingested Borax at every meal for months on end (they also ingested chemicals such as formaldehyde and benzoates during subsequent experiments) to test the effects of such dangerous chemicals on the body. Wiley's experiments continued for more than five years, and revealed to the public that not only were these chemicals harmful, but that restrictions on manufacturers in using these chemicals in foods and tonics was mandatory. As a result of Wiley's work, basic reforms, such as food labeling, banning of certain poisons, and placing the burden of proof for the use of certain chemicals on the manufacturers, became commonplace.

Wiley's experiments and pro-regulation views angered manufacturers, but a surprising ally emerged in the pure food and drug movement—women. Although women in the United States did not yet have the federal vote, Wiley's pure food movement appealed to mothers and wives who sought, in the interest of scientific efficiency and progress, to feed their families better, purer food.

In 1906 the Pure Food and Drug Act was passed, and it became law in 1907. Wiley's work did not stop at legal progress; in an era of efficiency engineers and perfection through education, Wiley continued to author books for experts in chemistry, but also wrote for the general reading public. *Not By Bread Alone* is a treatise on the need for better appreciation of the role of proper eating habits, basic nutrition, and the role of dietetics in overall health.

PRIMARY SOURCE

The greatest industry in any community is eating. This is not an industry confined to a particular class of people; it embraces every individual of the community. There are no child-labor laws regulating this industry. Infants engage in it immediately after birth. Old people continue the industry to the brink of the grave. The magnitude of the industry is not appreciated as it should be. If we count the time spent in eating alone, it is of considerable extent. If one should live sixty years, which is considerably above the average, and eat as he should eat according to the principles of Fletcher and his school, he would spend almost three hours a day at the table. This is one-eighth of his life, and in sixty years would amount to seven years and a half. This is probably an exaggerated time compared with actual work at the table, but including the time of preparing for the dinner in a proper way and the time consumed in a proper way in social intercourse at the table it may be regarded as approximately correct.

TIME SPENT IN EATING

The time spent at the table, however, is not by any means all the time spent in this great industry. We must have something to eat and have it properly prepared. There is no way of getting exact data on this point, but it is probable that after reaching the age of service the average man or woman spends four hours a day either in getting something to eat or in preparing it to be eaten. In forty-four years of adult life one-sixth of the time may properly be ascribed to these efforts. In round numbers, seven years and a half of the allotted time of adult life in sixty years of living, namely, forty-four years, is devoted to getting food and preparing it to be eaten. But this is not all of the time which we devote to this industry. Sleep is intimately connected with nutrition. It is during sleep that the numberless carpenters and masons that build the body and repair its waste are chiefly busy. During sleep new particles are built into the body and the old particles are taken out, thus completing the work which was commenced at the table. We should sleep eight hours a day. One-third of our time is spent at complete rest or asleep. In sixty years this would amount to twenty years. Add that to the fifteen years which we spend sitting at the table and getting something to eat and preparing it to be eaten, and we have a total of thirty-five years of the sixty years we live devoted to this one great industry.

It is consequently a matter which should engage our closest attention. We should be trained, if possible, to engage in this industry with the maximum of skill and benefit. Do we do this? No. Here is one great industry in which there are few skilled laborers. Everyone is a common day laborer with no idea of the nature of the business in which he is engaged and with no special skill to perform the duties of that business with effectiveness and benefit. Not being skilled laborers, nor experts, we may expect to draw the minimum salary. That minimum salary is paid to us in diminished years of life and in diminished efficiency while we live.

It is true that there are now quite a large number of persons who have made the subject of dietetics a study. The number of persons who are engaging in this study is daily increasing.

Instead of being a mere theory, the tenets of nutrition are now assuming scientific form and accuracy. One-third of a century ago there was probably not a medical college in the country that taught any scientific theory of diet. Today one of the armaments of the physician most prized is to know something of the philosophy of foods. All over the country there are established schools of domestic science which, among other things, teach the principles of human nutrition. Even in the public schools our children are beginning to be taught something of that which is most essential to their welfare, namely, how to live. We are beginning to realize that the feeding of man is of more consequence than the feeding of pigs or steers. Yet there are a hundred people in this country today who know how to feed pigs and steers where there is one who knows how to feed children or grown people.

SIGNIFICANCE

Wiley's book is a call-to-arms for progressives and the public to focus on nutrition as a public health matter. The "Gospel of Efficiency" that was part of the Progressive Movement comes through in Wiley's detailed breakdown of the hours that should be devoted to various activities: eating, sleeping, and seeking and preparing food, for example. This meticulous deconstruction is meant to show the reader, through scientific precision, the logic of the author's argument, and therefore a need for action.

As chemists made great strides from the 1880s to the 1930s, isolating vitamins, glucose, fats, and understanding metabolic processes, Wiley wished to connect laboratory discoveries with the daily diet of Americans. *Not By Bread Alone* called not only for a change in the average American's food consumption and preparation habits, but also for widespread education in medical colleges on the role of proper nutrition in improving public health.

Wiley authored more than seventy books during his lifetime, many of which detailed his studies on food additives, such as saccharin, and their harmful effects on the body. Wiley's legacy extended through the 1930s with the passage of the 1938 Food, Drug, and Cosmetic Act, which took up the Pure Food and Drugs Act and strengthened it, protecting consumers from deadly additives, such as formaldehyde and sulfanilamide, and helping to shape the food industry and the American diet.

FURTHER RESOURCES
Books

McGerr, Michael. *A Fierce Discontent; The Rise and Fall of the Progressive Movement in America, 1870–1920.* New York: Free Press, 2003.

Sinclair, Upton. *The Jungle*. New York: The Jungle Publishing Co., 1906.

Web sites

U.S. Food and Drug Administration. "The Story of the Laws Behind the Labels. Part I: 1906 Food and Drugs Act." <http://www.cfsan.fda.gov/~lrd/history1.html> (accessed November 20, 2005).

Don'ts in Removing Superfluous Hair

Electricity and Medicine

Book excerpt

By: Plym S. Hayes

Date: 1910

Source: Plymmon Sanford Hayes. *Electricity and the Methods of its Employment in Removing Superfluous Hair and Other Facial Blemishes*. Hammond, Ind.: Frank S. Betz Co., 1910.

About the Author: Plymmon Sanford Hayes (1850–1894) was a physician who was particularly interested in dermatology, as well as in gynecology. He wrote fairly extensively on the use of electrosurgical methods in treatment of skin lesions and for removal of excessive facial hair growth. He was a professor of chemistry and toxicology at the Women's Medical College, professor of analytical chemistry at the Chicago College of Pharmacy, and professor of gynecology and of electro-therapeutics at the Chicago Polyclinic.

INTRODUCTION

Since the beginning of recorded history, people have been trying to improve their facial appearance. The ancient Egyptians used arsenic to treat skin cancer, and animal oils, salt, alabaster, and curdled milk to soften and smooth the skin. The Greeks and Romans combined pumice, tree resins, frankincense, and myrrh to lighten skin and to remove blemishes, lesions, and scarring. In Turkey, fire was used to slightly singe the skin, as an exfoliant; and in Indian, women used a mixture of pumice and urine for the same purposes. By the late 1800s, dermatologists had begun to use a variety of chemical compounds to reduce scarring and facial wrinkles.

The ancient Egyptians utilized sandpaper as a mechanical method for removing facial blemishes and eliminating scars. As recently as the early 1900s, dermatologists were using sandpaper in conjunction with motorized dermabrasion to remove scarring and improve skin texture.

The first scholarly mention of the use of electrolysis for hair removal was in 1875. Charles Michel, an ophthalmologist practicing in St. Louis, Missouri, had been searching for a way to treat his patients' ingrown eyelashes, which were both painful and a deterrent to clear vision. Michel tried a new technique in which he attached a surgical needle to a live electrical wire from a dry-cell battery, and inserted the needle down the length of the hair shaft to the follicle, where it remained for a period of several minutes. The follicle was destroyed, the strand came out easily, and the hair did not grow back. Michel coined the term electrolysis for this procedure, a term that remains in use today. The early machinery was crude, and the process was both slow and somewhat painful.

Electrosurgery, as it is more commonly called in modern times, has been used to destroy and to remove benign and malignant skin lesions since the early 1900s. The most common complications of surgery performed with electricity at that time were burns, shocks, and infection.

PRIMARY SOURCE

I cannot close without again emphasizing the fact that too often too strong a current is used, especially by those who are beginning the use of electrolysis in the treatment of facial blemishes. Remember that too strong a current may leave indelible marks behind, and that too weak a current may only necessitate your having to do a part of your work over again.

DON'TS

in Removing Superfluous Hair

Don't use a sharp-pointed needle.

Don't attach the needle to the positive pole.

Don't use too strong a current.

Don't continue the current long enough to leave a visible scar.

Don't remove two hairs in close proximity to each other.

Don't attempt the removal of a hair near an acne pustule.

In Removing Other Facial Blemishes by Means of Electrolysis

Don't use a blunt-pointed needle.

Don't use too weak a current.

Don't attempt the removal by electrolysis of a rapidly growing vascular nævus of more than one-third of an inch in diameter.

SIGNIFICANCE

After Willem Einthoven's (1860–1927) invention of the electrocardiograph in 1906, scientists and others quickly became fascinated with potential uses for electricity in medicine and health maintenance. Galvanic spectacles delivered a current across the bridge of the nose intended to stimulate the optic nerve and improve vision. Galvanic dumbbells delivered an electric current to help muscles contract while exercising, and led to later generations of electric exercise machines intended to accomplish the exercise for the user. "Electrotherapy" was used to treat conditions ranging from hysteria to circulation disorders, often in combination with massage therapy. For the first half of the twentieth century, the public struggled with determining which electric devices were actually therapeutic, and which stemmed from quackery.

In the present day, most significant skin problems are treated by dermatologists and dermatologic surgeons, who specialize in the treatment of diseases and disorders of the skin, hair, nails, veins, and surrounding tissues. Dermatologists are trained in the treatment and management of benign and malignant skin growths and skin cancers; they are able to offer palliative and restorative treatments for aging and sun-damaged skin; and they also are able to implement desired cosmetic improvements of the skin. The two most common forms of treatment for skin diseases, scarring, and lesions are electrosurgery and laser treatment.

Although people use a wide variety of home and other remedies for removing unwanted hair, the most common methods are electrolysis and laser treatment. Of the two, only electrolysis is able to advertise permanent hair removal by destruction and obliteration of the hair follicle.

Electrosurgery is used to destroy benign and malignant lesions, to control or eliminate bleeding, and to cut or excise unwanted tissue. There are four major electrosurgical modalities: electrodessication, fulguration, electrocoagulation, and electrosection. The electrical power used is determined by the desired results—so the general rule is to start out with low power and increase the output power until the desired result is obtained. In electrodessication, a live electrode is placed against, or inserted beneath, the skin in order to destroy the tissue immediately. In fulguration, the tip of the electrode is held just far enough away from the skin to produce a spark that travels to the skin's surface, producing shallow tissue destruction. Electrocoagulation is used to seal blood vessels. This technique is used to treat skin lesions caused by small blood vessels clustering near the surface of the skin. In electrosection, the electrode is used in place of a scalpel; the tip of the electrode is moved through the lesion in order to remove it in its entirety.

The potential complications of electrosurgery remain the same as they were a century ago: burns, shock, and infection. However, the incidence of complications is now very low, since the surgical process is sterile and precise. The equipment is built with redundant warning devices, and surgeons fine tune the current used to the desired outcome and to the physiologic responses of the individual. Wound care is accomplished with suturing, as necessary, and standard antiseptic treatment.

Lasers have been used in medicine since the 1960s, with increasingly more precision and technical advancement over time. Wave 3 lasers, in use since 1979, were first used for the removal of ingrown eyelashes (as a means of unwanted hair removal); they were found to be of some benefit. These lasers are most effective for treatment of some vascular and skin lesions, and for some types of tattoo removal. Lasers are not currently considered effective as a permanent means of hair removal, although laser treatment may reduce or delay the re-growth of unwanted hair. The laser light creates heat as it passes through the outer surface of the skin, and it targets melanin, the darker pigment found in both the follicle and the hair shaft. If the follicle is in an active growth phase when it is heated—even if it is still beneath the surface of the skin—it is no longer able to produce hair. The laser typically targets thousands of shafts of hair at any one time. According to the American Society for Dermatologic Surgery, some laser-treated areas have remained free of new hair growth for up to two years. Laser treatment is non-invasive and has minimal side effects if properly administered.

Electrolysis continues to be popular as a means of permanently removing unwanted hair. Invasive electrolysis involves the insertion of a sterile probe along the hair shaft to the base of the dermal papilla (the "root" of the hair). A low level electrical current is applied, the dermal papilla and its surrounding regenerative cells are destroyed, and the hair follicle is loosened and removed with a forceps. The hair is permanently destroyed. Although a considerable number of hairs can be destroyed during the course of a single session (depending on the patient's tolerance), multiple sessions are generally needed in order to remove a significant amount of hair. In addition, an electrologist can only remove visible hairs, so the treatment needs to occur over a period of time because of differing hair growth cycles and alternating periods of activity and dormancy within any single hair follicle.

FURTHER RESOURCES

Web sites

American Family Physician. "Electrosurgery of the Skin." <http://www.aafp.org/afp/20021001/1259.html> (accessed November 28, 2005).

American Society for Dermatologic Surgery. "Laser Applications." <http://www.asds-net.org/Patients/FactSheets/patients-Fact_Sheet-lasers.html> (accessed November 27, 2005).

American Society for Dermatologic Surgery. "Laser Hair Removal." <http://www.asds-net.org/Patients/FactSheets/patients-Fact_Sheet-laser_hair_removal.html> (accessed November 27, 2005).

ValleyLab. "Principles of Electrosurgery." <http://www.valleylab.com/education/poes/poes_02.html> (accessed November 25, 2005).

Alcoholics and God

Alcoholism Gives Rise to Twelve-Step Behavioral Therapy

Magazine article

By: Morris Markey

Date: September 30, 1939

Source: Morris Markey. "Alcoholics and God." *Liberty* (September 1939).

About the Author: Morris Markey was a well-known journalist in the first half of the twentieth century. He was acquainted with Charles Towns, the owner of Towns' Hospital in New York, for many years. Markey was intrigued by what Towns told him about Alcoholics Anonymous (A.A.), the self-help fellowship that had been co-founded by a patient at the hospital. Markey approached Fulton Oursler for a commission to write a story about Alcoholics Anonymous. Oursler was the editor of *Liberty*, a magazine with a religious orientation. The story appeared as a cover feature in the September 1939 issue.

INTRODUCTION

Alcoholics Anonymous (A.A.) was formed in Akron, Ohio, in 1935 as a result of a meeting between two self-confessed alcoholics, Bill W., a New York stockbroker (the Towns Hospital patient), and Dr. Bob S., a surgeon in Akron. Bill had been impressed with his hospital treatment. It taught him that alcoholism is a disease over which he had no control. Both men had also had contact with the Oxford Groups in America, who tried to promote spirituality in everyday living. This approach had helped Bill with his drinking problem, but not Bob.

A.A. groups were set up at Akron's City Hospital and, later in 1935, in New York. A third group was formed in Cleveland in 1939. Bill and Bob were committed to remaining sober and helping others achieve the same goal. Early in 1939, they published the A.A. philosophy in a textbook titled *Alcoholics Anonymous*. They now wanted publicity to develop the A.A. project. Markey's magazine article, which describes the A.A. approach in detail, was the first national coverage of the fellowship. It was followed by a series of articles in the *Cleveland Plain Dealer*, which were highlighted by a positive editorial. The response was dramatic. *Liberty* received over 800 urgent pleas for help, and the A.A. team responded personally to every one. Following the Cleveland articles, A.A. membership in that city grew to 500. The idea of A.A. was now poised to spread through the United States.

PRIMARY SOURCE

IS THERE HOPE FOR HABITUAL DRUNKARDS? A CURE THAT BORDERS ON THE MIRACULOUS—AND IT WORKS!

For twenty-five or thirty cents we buy a glass of fluid which is pleasant to the taste, and which contains within its small measure a store of warmth and good-fellowship and stimulation, of release from momentary cares and anxieties. That would be a drink of whisky, of course—whisky, which is one of Nature's most generous gifts to man, and at the same time one of his most elusive problems. It is a problem because, like many of his greatest benefits, man does not quite know how to control it. Many experiments have been made, the most spectacular being the queer nightmare of prohibition, which left such deep scars upon the morals and the manners of our nation. Millions of dollars have been spent by philanthropists and crusaders to spread the doctrine of temperance. In our time the most responsible of the distillers are urging us to use their wares sensibly, without excess.

But to a certain limited number of our countrymen neither prohibition nor wise admonishments have any meaning, because they are helpless when it comes to obeying them. I speak of the true alcoholics, and before going any further I had best explain what that term means.

For a medical definition of the term, I quote an eminent doctor who, has spent twenty-five years treating such people in a highly regarded private hospital: "We believe . . . that the action of alcohol in chronic alcoholics is a manifestation of an allergy—that the phenomenon of craving is limited to this class and never occurs in the average temperate drinker. These allergic types can never safely use alcohol in any form at all." . . .

Among physicians the general opinion seems to be that chronic alcoholics are doomed. But wait! Within the last four years, evidence has appeared which has startled hard-boiled medical men by proving that the compulsion neurosis can be entirely eliminated. Perhaps you are one of those cynical people who will turn away when I say that the root of this new discovery is religion. But be patient for a moment. About three years ago a man appeared at the hospital in New York of which our doctor is head physician. It was his third "cure." Since his first visit he had lost his job, his friends, his health, and his self-respect. He was now living on the earnings of his wife.

He had tried every method he could find to cure his disease: had read all the great philosophers and psychologists. He had tried religion but he simply could not accept it. It would not seem real and personal to him.

He went through the cure as usual and came out of it in very low spirits. He was lying in bed, emptied of vitality and thought, when suddenly, a strange and totally unexpected thrill went through his body and mind. He called out for the doctor. When the doctor came in, the man looked up at him and grinned.

"Well, doc," he said, "my troubles are all over. I've got religion."

"Why, you're the last man . . ."

"Sure, I know all that. But I've got it. And I know I'm cured of this drinking business for good." He talked with great intensity for a while and then said, "Listen, doc. I've got to see some other patient—one that is about to be dismissed."

The doctor demurred. It all sounded a trifle fanatical. But finally he consented. And thus was born the movement which is now flourishing with almost sensational success as Alcoholics Anonymous.

Here is how it works:

Every member of the group—which is to say every person who has been saved—is under obligation to carry on the work, to save other men.

That, indeed, is a fundamental part of his own mental cure. He gains strength and confidence by active work with other victims.

He finds his subject among acquaintances, at a "cure" institution or perhaps by making inquiry of a preacher, a priest, or a doctor. He begins his talk with his new acquaintance by telling him the true nature of his disease and how remote are his chances for permanent cure.

When he has convinced the man that he is a true alcoholic and must never drink again, he continues:

"You had better admit that this thing is beyond your own control. You've tried to solve it by yourself, and you have failed. All right. Why not put the whole thing into the hands of Somebody Else?"

Even though the man might be an atheist or agnostic, he will almost always admit that there is some sort of force operating in the world—some cosmic power weaving a design.

And his new friend will say:

"I don't care what you call this Somebody Else. We call it God. But whatever you want to call it, you had better put yourself into its hands. Just admit you're licked, and say, 'Here I am, Somebody Else. Take care of this thing for me.'"

The new subject will generally consent to attend one of the weekly meetings of the movement. He will find twenty-five or thirty ex-drunks gathered in somebody's home for a pleasant evening. There are no sermons. The talk is gay or serious as the mood strikes.

The new candidate cannot avoid saying to himself, "These birds are ex-drunks. And look at them! They must have something. It sounds kind of screwy, but whatever it is I wish to heaven I could get it too."

One or another of the members keeps working on him from day to day. And presently the miracle. But let me give you an example: I sat down in a quiet room with Mr. B., a stockily built man of fifty with a rather stern, intelligent face.

"I'll tell you what happened a year ago." He said, "I was completely washed up. Financially I was all right, because my money is in a trust fund. But I was a drunken bum of the worst sort. My family was almost crazy with my incessant sprees."

"I took the cure in New York." (At the hospital we have mentioned.) "When I came out of it, the doctor suggested I go to one of these meetings the boys were holding. I just laughed. My father was an atheist and had taught me to be one. But the doctor kept saying it wouldn't do me any harm, and I went."

"I sat around listening to the jabber. It didn't register with me at all. I went home. But the next week I found myself drawn to the meeting. And again they worked on me while I shook my head. I said, 'It seems O.K. with you; boys, but I don't even know your language. Count me out.'"

"Somebody said the Lord's Prayer, and the meeting broke up. I walked three blocks to the subway station. Just as I was about to go down the stairs—bang!" He snapped fingers hard. "It happened! I don't like that word miracle, but that's all I can call it. The lights in the street seemed to flare up. My feet seemed to leave the pavement. A kind of shiver went over me, and I burst out crying."

"I went back to the house where we had met, and rang the bell, and Bill let me in. We talked until two o'clock in the morning. I haven't touched a drop since, and I've set four other fellows on the same road."

The doctor, a nonreligious man himself, was at first utterly astonished at the results that began to appear among his patients. But then he put his knowledge of psychiatry and psychology to work. These men were experiencing a psychic change. Their so-called "compulsion neurosis" was being altered—transferred from liquor to something else.

Their psychological necessity to drink was being changed to a psychological necessity to rescue their fellow victims from the plight that made themselves so miserable. It is not a new idea. It is a powerful and effective working out of an old idea. We all know that the alcoholic has an urge to share his troubles. Psychoanalysts use this urge. They say to the alcoholic, in basic terms: "You can't lick this problem yourself. Give me the problem—transfer the whole thing to me and let me take the whole responsibility."

But the psychoanalyst, being of human clay, is not often a big enough man for that job. The patient simply cannot generate enough confidence in him. But the patient can have enough confidence in God—once he has gone through the mystical experience of recognizing God. And upon that principle the Alcoholic Foundation rests. The medical profession, in general, accepts the principle as sound.

"Alcoholics Anonymous" have consolidated their activities in an organization called the Alcoholic Foundation. It is a nonprofit-making enterprise. Nobody connected with it is paid a penny. It is not a crusading movement. It condemns neither liquor nor the liquor industry. Its whole concern is with the rescue of allergic alcoholics, the small proportion of the population who must be cured or perish. It preaches no particular religion and has no dogma, no rules. Every man conceives God according to his own lights.

Groups have grown up in other cities. The affairs of the Foundation are managed by three members of the movement and four prominent business and professional men, not alcoholics, who volunteered their services.

The Foundation has lately published a book, called *Alcoholics Anonymous*. And if alcoholism is a problem in your family or among your friends, I heartily recommend that you get hold of a copy. It may very well help you to guide a sick man—an allergic alcoholic—on the way to health and contentment.

SIGNIFICANCE

As Markey points out in his article, Prohibition had not been an effective method of controlling excess drinking. Today, there are drugs and psychological therapies that can be used to treat the craving for alcohol, but there was nothing like this for the alcoholic in the 1930s. The time was ripe for a new approach to help those who were ruining their lives through alcohol. A.A. started small, but by the end of 1941, following an article in the *Saturday Evening Post*, membership stood at 6,000, and by 1950 it had grown to around 100,000. Today A.A. is truly global, helping over two million recovering alcoholics. The basic philosophy has not changed since the time of Markey's article. Alcoholism is seen as a disease. The only way out is for the alcoholic to hand over control of his or her life to a higher power (which some interpret as God) and to give up drinking completely. At the core of the A.A. philosophy is the so-called "Twelve Steps," which guide the alcoholic through his or her recovery.

As part of his or her recovery, the alcoholic is committed to helping others who wish to overcome a drinking problem. Contact is maintained through meetings where recovering alcoholics share experiences and support one another. The idea of anonymity is seen as important in freeing the alcoholics to work on their recovery. Meetings are free and open to all. A.A. does not support alcohol research of any kind, nor does it accept or seek financial support from outside sources. Its organizational structure is kept to a bare minimum. Its unique model of recovery has been adopted for other addictions, such as narcotics and gambling. It has been hard, however, to assess the success of A.A. from a scientific point of view, since the approach does not readily lend itself to clinical trials. Some people rely on A.A. alone to recover from an alcohol problem, while others use it with drug treatment or psychotherapy. Modern addiction theory has confirmed that alcoholism is a disease, arising from a dysfunction of the brain's reward pathways. For A.A., the scientific basis of this disease is not a barrier to improvement, as long as its members remain committed to the program.

FURTHER RESOURCES
Books

Ketcham, Katherine, et al. *Beyond the Influence: Understanding and Defeating Alcoholism*. New York: Bantam, 2000.

Web sites

Alcoholics Anonymous. "Fact File." <http://www.aa.org/default/en_about_aa.cfm?pageid=24> (accessed November 2, 2005).

Barefoot's World. "AA History—the 1939 Liberty Magazine Article." <http://www.barefootsworld.net/aalibertymag1939.html> (accessed November 2, 2005).

A worker monitors vodka bottles being produced at a distillery in Moscow, Russia. Addiction to vodka and other forms of alcohol is a major problem in Russia. AP/WIDE WORLD PHOTOS.

Conscious Control of our Sex Life

Book excerpt

By: J. Rutgers

Date: 1937

Source: J. Rutgers. *How to Attain and Practice the Ideal Sex Life: Ideal Sex and Love Relations for Every Married Man and Woman.* Translated by Norman Haire. New York: Falstaff Press, 1937.

About the Author: Dr. J. Rutgers wrote *How to Attain and Practice the Ideal Sex Life* before 1924, and it was translated into English from the German (*Das Sexualeben in Seiner Bioligishchen Bedeutung*) in 1937. It is an early example of a sexual "how to" manual that is typical of the early twentieth century.

INTRODUCTION

Some years before 1924, Rutgers attempted to write a comprehensive guide for married couples for attaining an ideal sex life. The resulting book is a fascinating mixture of tangentially relevant scientific observations, interesting personal views, and semi-scientific lore. He covered a wide range of topics ranging from masturbation to self-control of sexual desire. For Rutgers, marital sex was the only appropriate sex, and he advised against premarital sex because it was thought to provoke severe anxiety that could spoil sexual enjoyment after marriage.

On the other hand, Rutgers cast aspersions on marriage as a defective institution, citing that it promoted male superiority and the view of women and children as property of the husband. He condoned common-law marriage, believing that it preserved equality between partners and promoted love and mutual respect. He even promoted bigamy as a way to accommodate the desire of multiple sexual partners to live and have children together, and felt that such unions should not be subject to legal sanctions. His views on homosexuality were at variance with the prevailing views of his time. He thought that homosexuals and bisexuals can be moral people, are happy to be homosexuals, and are not eager to be "cured" of their sexual orientation. Perversions exist among homosexuals, he admitted, but probably less often than among heterosexuals. Rutgers mentioned that homosexuals also could have lifelong unions that are as beneficial and well-intentioned as those of heterosexual partners.

In keeping with his liberal sexual outlook, Rutgers disapproved of sexual abstinence as a way of life. He felt that it put people at risk for mental illness due to physical and emotional stress. Some of his observations are likely to promote mirth today, such as his speculation that circumcision increases sexual sensitivity and could account for a high birth rate among Jews, or his theory that rubbing insect bites causes people to become more familiar with their bodies and, hence, more sexually sensitive.

The following excerpt focuses on the issue of avoiding casual sexual contact on the spur of the moment. Rutgers recommends avoiding casual sex because it is likely to result in unforeseen, negative physical and mental consequences. The essence of Rutgers's strategy is to plan avoidance of tempting situations well in advance, since temptation most often results in seduction.

◼ PRIMARY SOURCE

So we have enquired into the practical means of controlling our sexual passions. Now if we only carry out that good advice . . . yes, if we behave accordingly, but here we are confronted by a great difficulty. Just in those very moments when a sexual stimulus occurs, we want to be thus excited, and at the very instant when we ought to avoid this excitation, we do not wish to avoid it.

Nowhere is our unwillingness so great as in sexual self control. Here we are only too glad to allow ourselves to drift. And if we have once given way, and especially if we have often given way, then it soon becomes so habitual that we no longer wish to do otherwise, and we no longer think of what we are doing. That which we did at first more or less consciously, in the course of time we do unconsciously, more and more automatically.

Thus it is with married people in marital intercourse, with youths in masturbation and with old bachelors in prostitution. If we once become the slave of passion, what can be done? And especially in a sphere that is already so full of animal impulse. Of course St. Anthony might as well have preached to the fishes, for they, at any rate, are cold-blooded.

Yes, if we wait without energy, idly, until the last moment, then good advice would come too late—it would always be too late. But if we are in earnest we can begin taking precautionary measures today, whereby our will can be rightly directed for tomorrow and for our whole future. We must begin with prevention, before the temptation has got hold of us. Everything depends upon our directing our own free will in the right path, in anticipation.

In our psychic sphere also, we can employ the same method which we have seen to be so effective in the control of the material functions. We can seek out cause and effect in order to intervene early before evil influences have become too strong for us; nay, before they have made themselves manifest at all, for the law of causality also exists in the psychic sphere. Only the expressions of our will seem here to be an exception. Happily this is not so. If our will were free in the sense that we could without cause act justly one moment and irresponsibly the next, be upright one moment, and rascally the next, then all continuity of the moral life would disappear; all training, practice and self-control would be useless; our conception of morality would be all a matter of chance, a mockery of all ethics. But this is in direct contradiction of our experience. We see how one man always makes his decision in a crisis in an orderly, self-conscious and deliberate manner, while other people always allow themselves to be led to foolish deeds by momentary impulses.

There is no such thing as an expression of our will without cause, but we are not in the habit of paying much attention to the motives for our will. Even the most significant unconscious acts have an adequate cause. Why is it that when we have lain on our right side in bed for a while we turn round and lie on our left? This decision of the will is actuated by the fact that any position becomes uncomfortable if maintained too long. All our lives long we cannot endure a perpetual rest-point or point of support, any more than a drop of water can remain steam on a red-hot plate. We are only absolutely at rest when we are dead. The whole series of manifestations of our will when, in the morning, we get up, wash, dress, breakfast and go to our work, every movement has its cause, only in the course of time through custom it has become automatic. The causality has still remained the same, only we gradually come to recognise it less or not at all.

Only in difficult cases does it cease to act, that is to say, when the motives for and against are equally strong. And then it enters our consciousness, that now our own intellectual motives must decide. We think it over, we weigh the various motives until at last the balance sinks on one side because it is overcharged. Then we speak about our free will, because the decision of our will is not now actuated by external influences, as it so often is, but only inner motives and inclinations influence the decision, of which we ourselves could at first say nothing, as to how the balance would finally be decided.

To make my meaning clearer I will quote as a concrete example an every day occurrence, not taken from the sexual life, but from one just as impulsive, alcoholic intoxication. In the police court news appears the following: "During a quarrel in a restaurant X . . . fractured his friend's skull with the leg of a chair . . . Homicide, with extenuating circumstances . . . two years' hard labour."

On that fatal Saturday night, when the guilty man was overcome with drink, he was no longer responsible, but the previous afternoon his will was perfectly free and open to reason. He was a most respectable man; all his companions liked him whether they met in the tavern or out in the country. He said to himself: "I have worked too hard all the week, (first mistake) it was really too bad; but now I have done good business and want to have a bit of fun, (second mistake). Now the weather is so fine I might take a brisk walk out in the country with some of my friends, that would be the best recreation." No sooner said than done. But as he was going along the street his friend and tavern companion, the one whom he struck down later, met him. He was quite sober and jolly and called to him from a distance: "God's truth, old chap, is that you? You look so tired out, come along and let's drink a pint together. All the other fellows are coming tonight, too, we shall have a fine time, that's the best way to pull yourself together." In reality the good man was a little annoyed at the unexpected meeting, which upset his plans for a quiet day in the country and would much rather have said "No," because it was such a fine day for a walk. Before he had pulled himself together, (third mistake), and because being so tired he did not feel in a mood to resist, he said: "Oh, all right, I can go for a walk any time," and went along with his friend. The first thought that in order to enjoy himself, he must do something foolish was more powerful than the hygienic idea of going for a walk, and so it won the day.

SIGNIFICANCE

Looking back on the early twentieth century from the early twenty-first century, it is easy to assume that people now enjoy far greater openness and sophistication about sexual matters than people did a hundred years ago. This is probably true when expressed as a percentage of the population knowledgeable about sexual matters and tolerant of diverse sexual behaviors.

It is also undoubtedly true that people today have a much better scientific understanding of sexual anatomy and physiology than did Rutgers and his contemporaries.

However, Rutgers's mistrust of where sexual desire and instinct may lead as well as his concern regarding how to consciously control one's sexual life still characterizes current thinking and social dialogue about sex. Controversies about homosexuality, bigamy, and masturbation also remain as lively today as in Rutgers's day. The U.S. Surgeon General Jocelyn Elders resigned under pressure in 1994 after daring to endorse the practice of and education about masturbation, even as a way of helping young people avoid risky sexual contact (the very objective of the Rutgers excerpt).

A contemporary reader's reaction to Rutgers's book might well be a mixture of surprise regarding his frankness and prescience in discussing unusual and controversial sexual topics, and smugness regarding his far-fetched theories about the mental and physical effects of various sexual practices. It is this very surprise and interest in his moral stance regarding sex that says most about how similar our age is to his. It seems remarkable that a how-to manual such as this one would sell enough copies in the Europe of its day to economically merit translation into English and publication in the United States. It is also, perhaps, reassuring to sexually liberal readers that some of the tolerant attitudes expressed in the book are of such long standing, not only among the intellectual elite of those days, but also among the middle class readers of such a manual.

Viewed in historical perspective, *How to Attain and Practice the Ideal Sex Life* was part of a significant wave of books and instruction manuals about sex that were published in the 1930s. Other examples include: *New Patterns in Sex Teaching*, by Francis Strain (1938); *Encyclopedia of Sexual Knowledge*, by A. Costler and A. Willy (1937); *Anthropological Studies of Sexual Relations of Mankind*, by Paolo Mantegazza; *A Study of Masturbation and the Psychosexual Life*, by J. F. W. Meagher (1936); *The Sexual Question*, by August Forel (1932); *The Doctor Looks at Love and Life*, by Joseph Collins (1926); and *Married Love: A New Contribution to the Solution of Sex Difficulties*, by Marie C. Stopes (1931). Most of these books were written by medical doctors and contained an unpredictable mix of pseudoscience and personal opinion, as well as of ultraconservative Puritanism and progressive, even open-minded, views on sexuality. The proliferation of books addressing sexual behavior was particularly significant because there was very little published about sex before the 1930s.

By the 1930s, science and the rise of modern medicine had begun to provide answers to questions about sexual behavior that had previously been the province of religious morality for most people. As twentieth century science and technology gained in influence on popular thinking, secular views of sex and marriage began to take hold, giving rise to the demand for the sex encyclopedias and advice books that continues to the present. The novelty of writing about sex and the dearth of real research into sexual behavior at the time allowed the writers of these books to inject their personal views into a supposedly scientific or clinical discussion of sexuality.

Respect for scientific methods and references to rigorous research characterize current books about sex, but the mysteries of marital love, masturbation, homosexuality, and other topics covered by J. Rutgers and his contemporaries have yet to be encompassed by any widely supported scientific theories about the nature of sexuality. The hoary controversies and scientifically unsupported personal opinions about sex found in the how-to manuals of the early twentieth century persist to the present day. Efforts, such as those by Alfred Kinsey (1894–1956) and others, to treat sex as a field for objective scientific study continue to meet resistance. Although official censorship of sexual topics weakened after Rutgers's time, many in the American population resisted sexual discussions and explorations until the sexual revolution of the 1960s, the women's movement of the 1970s, and beyond.

FURTHER RESOURCES
Books

Costler, A., and A. Willy. *Encyclopedia of Sexual Knowledge.* Edited by Norman Haire. New York: Eugenics Publishing Company, 1940.

Collins, Joseph. *The Doctor Looks at Love and Life.* Garden City, N.Y.: Garden City Publishing Co., 1926.

Mantegazza, Paolo. *Anthropological Studies of Sexual Relations of Mankind.* New York: Anthropological Press, 1932.

Stopes, Marie C. *Married Love: A New Contribution to the Solution of Sex Difficulties.* New York: Eugenics Publishing Company, 1932. (Originally published in 1918.)

Strain, Francis. *New Patterns in Sex Teaching.* New York: D. Appleton-Century, 1938.

Our Bodies, Ourselves

The Women's Liberation Movement and Women's Health

Book excerpt

By: The Boston Women's Health Book Collective

Date: 1976

Source: The Boston Women's Health Book Collective. *Our Bodies, Ourselves: A Book By and For Women.* 2nd edition. New York: Simon and Schuster, 1976.

About the Author: The Boston Women's Health Book Collective, now also known as *Our Bodies, Ourselves,* was an outgrowth of the women's movement in the United States. In the late 1960s, there was a workshop at a feminist conference in Boston that concerned women's experiences of their bodies. During the workshop, the participants (all female) began to discuss their perceptions and understandings of their own anatomy and physiology and discovered that there was a general lack of knowledge, especially about sexuality and reproduction. The participants realized that they had much to learn. Several of them decided to research the topics raised and put the collected knowledge together to create a women's study course. The book that became *Our Bodies, Ourselves* was the result of creating this women's study course, sharing information with the original workshop participants, and gathering further information. The twelve feminists that formed the research group evolved into the Boston Women's Health Book Collective, which, in addition to creating subsequent editions of *Our Bodies, Ourselves,* has published several other books by and for women and their families.

INTRODUCTION

The Boston Women's Health Book Collective (BWHBC) grew over time, shifting from a collaborative group of twelve volunteers who designed a course and wrote *Our Bodies, Ourselves* to a formal organization managed by a highly diverse board of directors. It is now a global organization, working to inform and educate women (and men) about issues concerning not only women's sexual and reproductive health, but also abortion rights and reproductive freedoms, universal availability of health care, humanistic and woman-centered childbirth, and women's rights in developing countries. The BWHBC also assisted in the development of the National Women's Health Network (NWHN).

The National Women's Health Network was created as another means of empowering women in the United States to positively influence the direction of their own health care. One of the hallmarks of the organization is its independence from corporate sponsorship; it accepts no financial support from pharmaceutical companies, the medical industry, tobacco producing and marketing companies, or alcohol manufacturers. Essentially, the NWHN is a diverse, multicultural, grass-roots activist and advocacy organization that supports the development of humane medical treatments that are driven by efficacy rather than profits. In addition, it supports universal access to high-quality medical care and seeks to empower people to be well-informed about all aspects of their own health care.

Although none of the founding members of the BWHBC were health care professionals, they became progressively more well-educated about women's health issues and have repeatedly engaged in dialogue with women's rights and women's health advocates and activists around the globe. They have formed a strong alliance with the American Medical Women's Association and have participated in many international conferences and forums on women's physical and reproductive health issues. They remain quite involved in the global women's health movement.

One of the central issues that spurred the development of the women's health movement was abortion. Many states had narrowly restrictive abortion laws governing location of abortion services providers, the stage of gestation during which abortions could legally be performed, and the circumstances under which it was possible to have a pregnancy medically terminated. The structure of the abortion system made it extremely difficult for women who were not financially independent to obtain legal and safe abortions. A reaction against the perceived male-dominated and oppressive medical system led to the development of women's self-help clinics, based on the idea that women could best be empowered to make informed decisions about their health care if they had some basic familiarity with their anatomy and physiology. Groups of women gathered together and used mirrors to examine their own genitals. The goal of the self-help movement was the widespread sharing of information through conferences, meetings, and workshops across the nation.

PRIMARY SOURCE

Experiences in the women's movement have drastically changed our thinking and feelings about our bodies. We've described to one another the ways in which we've felt weak, especially in getting medical care, because we knew so little about ourselves. We have given each other support to begin learning about our bodies so that we could act to make some changes.

> Recently, as I became more aware of my body, I realized I had pretended some parts didn't exist, while others now seemed made of smaller parts. I also discovered mental and physical processes working together. I realized that when my chest pulled down and felt collapsed I felt unhappy or depressed. When I felt sad my chest would start to tighten. When I became aware of some of the connections, I could start to change. Gradually I felt a new kind of unity, wholeness in me, as my mental and physical selves became one self.

Until we began to prepare this material for a course for women, many of us didn't know the names of parts of our anatomy. Some of us had learned bits and pieces of information about specific body functions (menstruation, for example), but it was not permissible to find out too much. The taboos were strongest in the areas of reproduction and sex, which is why our book concentrates on them. . . .

FINDING OUT ABOUT OURSELVES

Knowing the facts about our anatomy and physiology helps us become more familiar with our bodies. Learning this information has been very exciting for us. It's exhilarating to discover that the material is not as difficult as we once thought. Understanding the medical terminology means that we now can understand the things the doctors say. Knowing their language makes medical people less mysterious and frightening. We now feel more confident when asking questions. Sometimes a doctor has been startled to find us speaking "his" language. "How do you know that? Are you a medical student?" We heard again and again. "A pretty girl like you shouldn't be concerned about that."

But we are. Out of our concerns we are acquiring specific medical knowledge. In response to our questions, many doctors have become aware of women's growing interest in medical issues. Some are genuinely cooperative. Yet many others appear outwardly pleased while continuing to "manage" their patients with new tactics.

Equally important as learning technical facts, we are sharing our experiences with one another. From this sharing we develop an awareness of differences as well as similarity in our anatomy and physiology. We start to have confidence in our knowledge, and that confidence helps us change our feelings about ourselves.

> I used to wonder if my body was abnormal even though I didn't have any reason to believe it was. I had nothing

to compare it with until I started to talk with other women. I don't feel any more that I might be a freak and not know it.

We realized that we were doing a lot of talking about our sexual organs but that we were not as familiar with their appearance as we were with other parts of our bodies. We found that with just a mirror we could see how we look on the outside. We have been encouraged to look inside at our vaginal walls and cervix (lower part of the uterus) by the women's self-help movement. To do this we use a mirror, flashlight and a clean plastic speculum, an examining instrument which is inserted into the vagina and gently opened up. This is something we can choose to do alone or with others, once or often. With practice we can see how the cervix and vaginal walls change with our menstrual cycle or with pregnancy, and learn to recognize the various vaginal infections. . . .

Some of us have taken a while to get over our inhibitions about seeing or touching our genitals. . . .

We still have many bad feelings about ourselves that are hard to admit. We have not, of course, been able to erase decades of social influence in a few years. But we have learned to trust ourselves. We *can* take care of ourselves.

SIGNIFICANCE

Before the U.S. Supreme Court's *Roe v. Wade* decision legalized abortion in the United States on January 22, 1973, women had few safe options regarding abortion and reproduction rights. The women's self-help movement, along with the women's health and feminist movements, sought to empower women to take control of their health care by educating them both about their bodies and about their civil rights. Alternately called self-help, women's empowerment, and consciousness raising, women's groups—in different parts of the country, at different times, and with varied missions—gathered around the overall goal of ending oppression and discrimination and ensuring equality, particularly in the health care arena, for all people regardless of gender, socioeconomic status, or race. Much research into the safety and efficacy of current birth control methods resulted from the women's health movement, and much was written and published as a result.

The grass-roots women's health movement quickly expanded its scope to include global issues. Of particular concern was the lack of appropriate, safe, and efficient reproductive technologies in developing countries. In many areas, there were few safe or legal abortion options, women had few rights concerning their bodies and reproductive health, and many countries practiced either forced sterilization or utilized potentially unsafe or unproven birth control methods. A central tenet of the women's health movement held that both sexual partners should bear equal responsibility for reproductive choices and prevention of sexually transmitted diseases.

In addition to its strong advocacy for women's freedom of choice in matters of health care, the women's health movement placed a constant emphasis the importance of knowledge and education as means of making empowered choices. It has lobbied to make government and industry more responsible to the public by mandating that they provide comprehensive public information on health policies, procedures, legislation, and research studies, as well as the ways in which each of those areas affect everyday life. The Boston Women's Health Book Collective and *Our Bodies, Ourselves*—which has gone through three editions and sold over three million copies—have had an ongoing impact on the lives and health of women all over the world.

FURTHER RESOURCES

Web sites

Feminist Women's Health Center. "Welcome to the Feminist Women's Health Center Website." <http://www.fwhc.org/welcome.htm> (accessed December 29, 2005).

National Organization for Women. "Women and Abortions: The Reasoning Behind the Decision." <http://www.now.org/issues/abortion/12-13-05guttmacher.html> (accessed December 29, 2005).

National Women's Health Network: A Voice for Women, A Network for Change. "NWHN in Action." <http://www.womenshealthnetwork.org/action/index.php> (accessed December 29, 2005).

womenshealth.gov: The Federal Government Source for Women's Health Information. "The History and Future of Women's Health." <http://www.4woman.gov/owh/pub/history/hlthmvmtf.htm> (accessed December 29, 2005).

A Medical Student in 1867

Book excerpt

By: John Allen Wyeth

Date: 1914

Source: John Allen Wyeth. *With Sabre and Scalpel: The Autobiography of a Soldier and Surgeon.* New York: Harper & Brothers, 1914.

About the Author: John Allen Wyeth was a physician and the founder of the New York Polyclinic Medical School and Hospital, which was considered the pioneer organization for postgraduate medical education in the United States. He was the president of that facility, as well as the institution's surgeon-in-chief. Wyeth served as president of the American Medical Association, the New York Academy of Medicine, the New York State Medical Association, the New York Pathological Society, the New York Southern Society, and the Alabama Society of New York City. He was an attending surgeon at St. Elizabeth's and Mt. Sinai Hospitals. In addition, he was an honorary member of the Medical Society of New Jersey and the Texas State Medical Association. In 1876, Wyeth won the Bellevue Alumni Association Prize; in 1878, he was awarded the first and second prizes of the American Medical Association. He was the author of a textbook on general surgery as well as numerous other works, including biographies, historical monographs, and essays on political and military subjects.

INTRODUCTION

American medical education during most of the nineteenth century was neither rigorous nor standardized. There were no required entrance examinations, nor were there any prerequisite courses of academic instruction. There were three common types of medical education: an apprenticeship model, in which students worked directly with a local physician and learned by observation and practice, rather than by classroom study; a proprietary school model in which students attended lectures given by small groups of faculty, who also owned the school; and the university model, in which students received an education that was both didactic (lecture) and clinical (laboratory or clinical work in a university-affiliated hospital). The university medical school was typically affiliated with both a college or university and a hospital. The courses of study for the latter two models were typically brief, consisting of two four- to seven-month school sessions, with the university-affiliated students also having some combination of didactic and clinical experiences. Even at the "best" medical schools in America, there was minimal emphasis on laboratory work and only slightly more focus on practical clinical training. There was virtually no direct training in surgical or operative techniques.

The requirements for completion of a medical degree were minimal as well, even for university-affiliated schools. Typically, all a student needed to do was pass final examinations at the end of the second year of school. There were few states with licensure laws, and there were no standards for practica (demonstrable clinical skills). Since there were no overall standards for medical coursework content, no significant entrance requirements, and few licensure laws, medical school graduates covered the entire spectrum of relative competency, theoretical and practical knowledge of the human body, and aptitude to practice medicine.

For most of the nineteenth century, American medical students graduated with very little real knowledge of how to go about the actual practice of medicine. Students who possessed a strong desire, as well as ample means, to broaden their scientific or clinical experience, traveled to Europe for further study. In France, Germany, England, and Scotland, in particular, American students were able to pursue far more rigorous and detailed scientific and clinical medical education.

In an ideal scenario, those students who were not able to continue their studies abroad would join an established physician and have the opportunity to learn by observation. That quite often was not the case, however, particularly in rural and frontier areas of the country. In addition, many practicing country doctors lacked formal medical school training. Often, several generations of doctors followed the apprenticeship path. They learned by practical experience and had little, if any, actual knowledge of the principles of medicine and the anatomy of the human body.

PRIMARY SOURCE

The medical department of the university I attended was in 1867 one of the oldest and deservedly best known of the medical colleges in the United States. The course of study and the standard of requirements then prevailing at this school may be taken as typical of medical education in the United States at that period. There was no preliminary or entrance examination. Any white male who could read and write and who had mastered the rudiments of English was eligible. Neither Latin nor Greek was essential.

The requirements for graduation were a satisfactory examination at the end of two college terms of seven months each. The division of subjects was: anatomy, physiology, surgery, medicine, obstetrics, chemistry, and materia medica. Anatomy was thoroughly taught, and the didactic course was supplemented by dissecting-room work of a high class. While material was not over-abundant, there not then being the same liberal construction of the law relating to the disposition of the unclaimed dead which now prevails, the activity of our dissecting-room janitor kept us in a sufficient quantity of cadavers. How he got them we did not know, and it was probably just as well that no inquiry was instituted. His name was Peter. Students inclined to disrespect spoke of him as "old Pete," but those who had been brought up under the influence of the Westminster Confession baptized him "St. Peter," the rock upon which our anatomical church was founded, and to whom it was said the keys of Cave Hill Cemetery had been given. In physiology there were no laboratory exercises; no practical demonstrations of the living structures and of the functions of the normal organs.

The teaching of surgery and medicine was almost wholly didactic. When an operative clinic was given the students witnessed it at such distance from the subject and with so many interruptions of vision that it was impossible to follow closely the details of technique, without which the lesson of a demonstration is valueless. Not once in my two college years did I enter the ward of a hospital or receive instruction by the bedside of a patient.

This is not in the least a reflection upon our teachers, but upon the system then in vogue. The greatest names in medicine in our country had been or then were associated with this institution. In the lectures on medicine we were told that the cause of malarial and yellow fever was a miasm emanating from decaying vegetable matter subjected to a temperature of form eighty to ninety degrees Fahrenheit for about thirty days, and that those who slept upon the ground floors of buildings suffered most, while those who occupied the second, third, and higher floors escaped the baneful effects in the direct ratio of their elevation. The same comparison was used in the discourse upon yellow fever, citing the fact that in the Louisville epidemic few, if any, persons sleeping upon the upper floors of houses were affected. Knowing as we do now that the mosquito is not prone to fly high, that he infests the lower floors of houses, seldom reaching the third or fourth floor, we can understand readily the error in etiology on the part of our professor of medicine. The teaching of obstetrics was entirely didactic. In my two terms of study I examined only one gynecological case, while in chemistry and materia medica the instruction was in the lecture-room to the whole class instead of with working sections in the laboratory, and there was no course of study in microscopy or urinary analysis.

I was graduated in the spring of 1869. I had been looking forward to the day when I should received my diploma and start out on my career as a practising physician and surgeon; but I can never forget the sinking feeling that came over me when I unfolded this sacred document in the privacy of my own room and realized how little I knew and how incompetent I was to undertake the care of those in the distress of sickness or accident. However, like Macbeth who was so far advanced in blood that it was as easy to go ahead as to recede, I felt I might just as well do as my predecessors had done and let the world take its chances.

The possessor of a pair of doctor's saddle-bags which held two rows of medicine bottles, diminutive apothecary scales for weighing dosage, two forceps for extracting teeth, and a small minor surgical operating set of instruments, and last, but not least, a tin sign, I rented an office in my home town, and after dark one night in March, 1869, I tacked my sign to "the outer wall." It was the irony of fate that my first call was obstetrical. If there was anything in the world I didn't want it was this kind of a case; but I didn't have the courage to back out. I thanked God it was a normal labor, for I had nothing to do but tie and cut the umbilical cord and tell the mother it was a boy. A strapping young farmer with lobar pneumonia came next, and he survived. For my first surgical operation I rode twenty-three miles and back the same day. My preceptor, an ex-army surgeon, gave the chloroform, and looked on as I dissected out some sort of tumor from the shoulder-blade of an elderly lady, whose resistance enabled us to register it as successful.

As we were starting home, the appreciative and grateful husband told us he didn't have any money, but, pointing to his apple orchard, then in bloom, said he had a "still," and would send us a barrel of apple-brandy in the fall. He kept his word, and I realized twenty dollars for my share.

Then came my Waterloo in a case of diabetes mellitus which progressed rapidly to a fatal termination. I cannot describe my feelings nor measure the depth of my depression and despair as I watched this patient die. I was overwhelmed with the conviction that I was unfit to take the grave responsibility of the life and health and happiness of those who might be willing to place themselves under my care. I needed a clinical and laboratory training under teachers of experience, and I determined to give up my practice until I could secure this training. That night, two months after I had tacked it up, I took my sign down and put it in my trunk, where it reposed for several years.

SIGNIFICANCE

Even among those physicians who had received university-affiliated medical training, overall understanding of the functioning of the human body was limited. Anatomy was studied by dissecting cadavers in the laboratory, but the study of the disease process in living humans was quite limited. Most of the beliefs concerning medical treatments were based on folklore or trial-and-error, rather than on sound scientific method. At that time, there was no general understanding of bacteria or of the germ theory of disease. Among the more common medical practices and remedies used during the first half of the nineteenth century were bloodletting, calomel (mercury chloride, typically used as a purgative—its use sometimes resulted in death and almost always resulted in the patient becoming quite ill), quinine, jalap, Epsom salts, castor oil, cupping, sweating, diuretics, emetics (to induce vomiting), and poultices of hot flaxseed or mustard applied to the chest or neck to treat upper respiratory ailments. None of these techniques had any real curative value. Many made the symptoms worse or made the patient sicker in other ways by causing new, and more dire, physical problems. Sometimes the patient died not because of the original illness, but as a consequence of the "cure." Until the last quarter of the nineteenth century (and beyond, in some areas), there was a dominant belief among medical practitioners that almost anything could be cured by serious purging or bleeding.

Almost all medical treatment took place either in the doctor's office or in the patient's home; by 1873 there were only 149 hospitals in the United States. Most hospitals had very limited standards of care and cleanliness, were staffed by nurses with little or no formal training or education, and catered to the destitute or dying patient. In most areas of the United States, all aspects of medical care were provided by local physicians, although many towns had midwives, who also acted as practical nurses. In 1870, the U.S. population was over 39 million and there were 62,000 individuals who described themselves as practicing physicians (a ratio of one doctor for every 642 people). In contrast, there were 44,000 clergy (a ratio of 1 to 905), 41,000 lawyers (a ratio of 1 to 971), and 11,000 bankers (a ratio of 1 to 3,620). There were 110 medical schools in America at that time, and they graduated approximately 2,000 new physicians per year (about eighteen graduates per medical school). Quite often, physicians were paid "in kind" for their services. It was not uncommon for physicians to receive food, livestock, quilts, or handmade clothing as payment for services rendered.

There was a limited pharmacopoeia, and the most common drugs utilized were the quinine, calomel, and digitalis (for heart ailments). Because there was, as yet, no mass production of pharmaceuticals, these medications often were in short supply. As a result, many doctors collected herbs and wild plants—such as spearmint, peppermint, raspberry leaves, fleabane, and mustard—that contained similar ingredients to the commercially prepared medications. Even when using manufactured drugs, which were obtained in bulk quantities, the doctor had to mix his own doses and proportions.

Doctors' equipment was equally limited in the latter half of the nineteenth century. In their saddlebags (the typical means of carrying necessary tools from the office to the patient's house), physicians usually carried bottles of medicines in various strengths and dosages, forceps (for pulling teeth and sometimes for assisting in difficult deliveries), a catheter, a stomach pump, a heating iron, some syringes (the hypodermic needle was not yet available), and assorted splints and bandages. Stethoscopes and thermometers were not readily available; a doctor placed the inside of his wrist against the patient's forehead to check for fever and placed his ear against the patient's chest to listen to heart and lung sounds. Wounds were anesthetized by rubbing them with morphine or opium; morphine was also administered orally for pain. Limbs that were mangled or badly broken often were amputated. Contagious diseases were most effectively treated by isolating the sick from the healthy and cleaning the areas previously inhabited by the sick persons.

A revolution was underway in American medicine by the end of the nineteenth century. In the first quarter of the twentieth century, this revolution resulted in sweeping changes in the system of medical education and in rapid scientific and technological advances fueled by a clear understanding of the germ theory and of sanitary methods.

FURTHER RESOURCES
Books

Dunlop, Richard. *Doctors of the American Frontier*. Garden City, N.Y.: Doubleday, 1965.

Ludmerer, Kenneth M. *Learning to Heal: The Development of American Medical Education*. Baltimore: The Johns Hopkins University Press, 1996.

Rothstein, William G. *American Physicians in the Nineteenth Century: From Sects to Science*. Baltimore: The Johns Hopkins University Press, 1972.

Smith, James J. *Looking Back, Looking Ahead: A History of American Medical Education*. Chicago: Adams Press, 2003.

Steele, Volney. *Bleed, Blister, and Purge: A History of Medicine on the American Frontier*. Missoula, Mont.: Mountain Press Publishing Company, 2005.

Web sites

fredrickboling.com. "A Tribute to the Frontier Doctor." <http://www.fredrickboling.com/frontier%20medicine.html> (accessed November 10, 2005).

This I Believe

Family Planning and Contraception

Speech

By: Margaret Sanger

Date: November 1953

Source: Sanger, Margaret. "This I Believe." *Edward R. Murrow's This I Believe* radio program broadcast, November 1953.

About the Author: Margaret Sanger (1879–1966) led the American birth control movement. One of eleven children, she attributed her mother's early death to the difficulties of raising so many children on a very small income. Sanger worked as a nurse on the Lower East Side of New York City where she saw a great number of poor tenement dwellers die from improvised abortions. One death particularly disturbed her. Sadie Sachs, a truck driver's wife was refused contraceptive advice by a physician and instructed instead to have her husband sleep on the roof. Sanger often cited Sachs as her motivation for promoting "family limitation," a term that she preferred to birth control. Sanger founded Planned Parenthood and helped finance the development of the birth control pill.

INTRODUCTION

The birth control movement spanned a century from the time that it became illegal to provide contraceptive information in 1873 to the Supreme Court decision in 1972 that extended the right of birth control to unmarried individuals in all states. At the center of much of the controversy stood Margaret Sanger. She dedicated her life to the right of people to plan the size of their families.

Until 1873, Americans had little difficulty obtaining birth control information. The declining birth rate in the nineteenth century, especially among the white middle class, suggests that more and more Americans used some sort of contraception. This proliferation of contraceptive devices and information troubled Victorian moral reformers, including influential morals crusader Anthony Comstock (1844–1915). Convinced that ready access to contraceptive information threatened the home and drove men towards illicit sexual activity, Comstock convinced Congress to pass an anti-obscenity law that made it a federal crime to send contraceptive devices and information through the U.S. mails. Fighting for repeal of the Comstock

In late 1916 Margaret Sanger (left) opened the first birth control clinic in the United States. Arrested during a police raid at the clinic for allegedly creating a "public nuisance," she appeared in court with her sister, Ethel Byrne (right). AP/WIDE WORLD PHOTOS.

laws became a centerpiece in the battle to legalize birth control in the United States.

Against a backdrop in which scientists and politicians were voicing fears about "race suicide" if the white middle class continued to practice contraception, Margaret Sanger began to actively promote birth control in the 1910s. She believed that common contraceptive methods such as withdrawal and condoms were undesirable methods because women were dependent on men to use them. Searching for a woman-centered form of birth control, Sanger settled on the diaphragm, which needed to be fitted by a medical professional. In 1916, Sanger opened the first birth control clinic in the Unites States in Brooklyn, New York. As a nurse, she fitted women for diaphragms. The clinic operated for ten days before it was raided and closed by the police. Sanger was arrested, convicted for violating anti-obscenity statutes, and spent a month in prison.

Sanger lost an appeal on her conviction in 1918, but gained an important legal victory when the judge ruled that the distribution of physician-prescribed birth control for the prevention of disease was not illegal. This framing of the legality of birth control changed the playing field by making birth control a medical matter, as opposed to a free speech, matter. Sanger turned all of her energies towards to establishing birth control clinics, which she considered could be legal as long as they were staffed by medical doctors and served a public health purpose. Forty years after Sanger began her campaign for available birth control for women, she recounted her efforts during the following speech aired on the well-known journalist Edward R. Murrow's "This I Believe" radio program.

▇ PRIMARY SOURCE

This I believe, first of all: that all our basic convictions must be tested and transmuted in the crucible of experience—and sometimes, the more bitter the experience, the more valid the purified belief.

As a child, one of a large family, I learned that the thing I did best was the thing I liked to do. This realization of doing and getting results was what I have later called an awakening consciousness.

There is an old Indian proverb which has inspired me in the work of my adult life. "Build thou beyond thyself, but first be sure that thou, thyself, be strong and healthy in body and mind." To build, to work, to plan to do something, not for yourself, not for your own benefit, but "beyond thyself"—and when this idea permeates the mind, you begin to think in terms of a future. I began to think of a world beyond myself when I first took an interest in nursing the sick.

As a nurse, I was in contact with the ill and the infirm. I knew something about the health and disease of bodies, but for a long time, I was baffled at the tremendous personal problems of life, of marriage, of living, and of just being. Here indeed was a challenge to "build beyond thyself." Where was I to begin? I found the answer at every door. For I began to believe there was something I could do toward increasing an understanding of these basic human problems. To build beyond myself, I must tap all inner resources of stamina and courage, of resolution within myself. I was prepared to face opposition, even ridicule, denunciation. But I had also to prepare myself, in defense of these unpopular beliefs, I had to prepare myself to face courts and even prisons. But I resolved to stand up, alone if necessary, against all the entrenched forces which opposed me.

I started my battle some forty years ago. The women and mothers whom I wanted to help, also wanted to help me; they, too, wanted to build beyond the self, in creating healthy children and bringing them up in life to be happy and useful citizens. I believed it was my duty to place motherhood on a higher level than enslavement and accident. I was convinced we must care about people; we must reach out to help them in their despair.

For these beliefs I was denounced, arrested, I was in and out of police courts and higher courts, and indictments hung over my life for several years. But nothing could alter my beliefs. Because I saw these as truths, I stubbornly stuck to my convictions.

No matter what it may cost in health, in misunderstanding, in sacrifice, something had to be done, and I felt that I was called by the force of circumstances to do it. Because of my philosophy and my work, my life has been enriched and full. My interests have expanded from local conditions and needs, to a world horizon, where peace on earth may be achieved when children are wanted before they are conceived. A new consciousness will take place, a new race will be born to bring peace on earth. This belief has withstood the crucible of my life's joyous struggle. It remains my basic belief today.

This I believe—at the end, as at the beginning of my long crusade for the future of the human race.

▇

SIGNIFICANCE

Sanger enjoyed a key legal victory in 1936 when the Supreme Court ruled in *U.S. v. One Package of Japanese Pessaries* that the medical prescription of birth control for disease prevention or well-being was not illegal under the Comstock Act. One year later, the American Medical Association issued its support for birth control.

At the same time, birth control advocates began to identify their movement as one of family planning. This linguistic shift eliminated the idea that women should have the right to control their own reproduction. Sanger persisted in her search for an effective female-controlled contraceptive and helped finance the development of the first birth control pill. The U.S. Food and Drug Administration approved "the Pill," the first oral contraceptive, in 1960.

Even though the *One Package* case had eliminated federal restrictions on the prescription of birth control, many states still had laws that prevented physicians from prescribing birth control such as the Pill to

At the National Conference on Birth Control in 1934 in Washington, DC, women's rights activist Margaret Sanger (left) stands with reception committee chairperson Mrs. John F. Dryden and Professor Henry Pratt Fairchild. AP/WIDE WORLD PHOTOS.

married women. Following several failed legal challenges, the Supreme Court overturned all such laws in a 1965 decision, *Griswold v. Connecticut*. This case was additionally significant because it marked the first time that the Supreme Court identified the legal doctrine of a right to privacy. The court later extended the same rights to unmarried individuals in *Eisenstadt v. Baird* in 1972.

Other contraceptives have been developed since the introduction of oral contraceptives, including hormone patches, barrier methods such as the contraceptive sponge and the cervical cap, and new-generation intrauterine devices (IUDs). Even birth control pills themselves have undergone significant developments, including changes in the types and amounts of synthetic hormones each pill contains. There are now numerous types of oral contraceptives on the market, a testament to their efficacy and lasting popularity.

FURTHER RESOURCES

Books

Gordon, Linda. *Woman's Body, Woman's Right: Birth Control in America*. New York: Penguin, 1977.

Riddle, John M. *Eve's Herbs: A History of Contraception and Abortion in the West*. Cambridge, MA: Harvard University Press, 1997.

Tone, Andrea. *Devices and Desires: A History of Contraceptives in America*. New York: Hill and Wang, 2001.

Remarks on the Youth Fitness Program

Speech

By: John F. Kennedy

Date: July 19, 1961

Source: *JFK link*. "Remarks on the Youth Fitness Program, July 19, 1961." <http://www.jfklink.com/speeches/jfk/publicpapers/1961/jfk293_61.html> (accessed November 29, 2005).

About the Author: John Fitzgerald Kennedy (1917–1963), also known as JFK, was the thirty-fifth President of the United States. Kennedy was born in Brookline, Massachusetts, and lived there for several years before moving with his family to the New York City suburbs. He attended private, non-parochial elementary schools, and then spent four years at Choate in New Milford, Connecticut. After his high school graduation (from Choate) in 1935, JFK spent the summer studying at the London School of Economics before entering Princeton University. He suffered an attack of jaundice over Christmas break, and withdrew from classes. He transferred to Harvard University in the fall of 1936, and graduated cum laude in 1940. In 1939, he spent some time in the United Kingdom, where his father was serving as U.S. Ambassador to Britain. He stayed in American embassies, and spent much of his time talking with diplomats, political leaders, and members of the press. He used his experience as the basis of his senior thesis, later published under the title of "Why England Slept," concerning the Munich Pact of 1936. During World War II, Kennedy served as a lieutenant (junior grade), and was in command of a torpedo (PT) boat in the Solomon Islands. His boat was rammed by a Japanese destroyer, and sunk. He was able to gather the survivors of the crash and get them safely to a nearby island. He personally towed a wounded comrade for three miles through dangerous waters. He received the Purple Heart and the Navy and Marine Corps Medal for his bravery, and because his back was badly injured (the site of an old injury). After his discharge from the Navy in 1945, he spent several months as a reporter for the Hearst newspapers; he covered the conference in San Francisco that was to establish the United Nations. After a short time, he decided to devote his career to politics, and he returned to Boston. In January of 1960, he announced his candidacy for president; he won the Democratic nomination. His campaign was noteworthy for a series of televised debates against his Republican opponent,

Vice President Richard M. Nixon. He won the election by a rather narrow margin, and became the youngest elected president at age forty-three.

INTRODUCTION

President Dwight D. Eisenhower established the President's Council on Youth Fitness on July 16, 1956, after being presented with the results of a study in which American children obtained significantly lower scores on a battery of physical fitness tests than did European children. His goal was to encourage the children of America to lead physically fit, healthy, and active lives. The title was changed to *The President's Council on Physical Fitness* in 1960, by President John F. Kennedy, who sought the name to be emblematic of a commitment to enhance the health and fitness of all Americans, no matter what their ages. In 1966, President Lyndon Johnson created the *Presidential Physical Fitness Award*, which was later renamed the *President's Challenge Youth Fitness Awards Program*. The *Presidential Sports Award* program began in 1972. In 1968, President Lyndon Baines Johnson appended the *and Sports* to the title in recognition of the great importance of sports throughout the human lifespan. May was declared *National Physical Fitness and Sports Month* by Congress in 1983. The *Surgeon General's Report on Physical Activity and Health* was published in 1996, and the President's Council on Physical Fitness and Sports' report on *Physical Activity and Sport in the Lives of Girls* was made public in 1997.

Kennedy considered that physical fitness would greatly enhance the health and well being of the American people. In addition to changing the organization's name, he appointed Bud Wilkinson as head of the council. It was JFK's contention that, "we do not want in the United States a nation of spectators. We want a nation of participants in the vigorous life." Kennedy was candid in his expressions that Americans were less fit than their European neighbors, and needed to make some significant changes. Publishing an article in *Sports Illustrated* about his concerns, entitled "The Soft American," it was his contention that, "We are under-exercised as a nation; we look instead of play; we ride instead of walk." JFK prodded the federal government to increase its level of involvement in national fitness promotion, and encouraged it to pilot youth fitness programs.

◼ PRIMARY SOURCE

Remarks on the Youth Fitness Program, July 19, 1961

The strength of our democracy and our country is really no greater in the final analysis than the well-being of our citizens. The vigor of our country, its physical vigor and energy, is going to be no more advanced, no more substantial, than the vitality and will of our countrymen.

I think in recent years we have seen many evidences in the most advanced tests, comparative tests, that have been made that many of the boys and girls who live in other countries have moved ahead of younger people in this country in their ability to endure long physical hardship, in their physical fitness and in their strength.

This country is going to move through difficult days, difficult years. The responsibilities upon us are heavy, as the leader of the free world. We carry worldwide commitments. People look to us with hope, and if we fail they look to those who are our adversaries.

I think during this period we should make every effort to see that the intellectual talents of every boy and girl are developed to the maximum. And that also their physical fitness, their willingness to participate in physical exercise, their willingness to participate in physical contests, in athletic contests—all these, I think, will do a good deal to strengthen this country, and also to contribute to a greater enjoyment of life in the years to come.

This is a responsibility which is upon all of us—all of us who are parents—to make sure that we stress this phase of human life and human existence. It is also the responsibility of our schools— and our schools have been doing a great deal to meet this responsibility—of our school administrators and school committees, and communities, and states. And also, of course, it is a matter of vital interest to our national Government.

To members of school boards, school administrators, teachers, the pupils themselves, and their parents, I am directing this urgent call to strengthen all programs which contribute to the physical fitness of our youth.

I strongly urge each school in the United States to adopt the three specific recommendations of our National Council on Youth Fitness.

First, to identify the physically underdeveloped pupil and work with him to improve his physical capacity. And if he will work and the school will work together, a great deal can be done.

Two: Provide a minimum of fifteen minutes of vigorous activity every day for all of our school students, boys and girls alike.

Three: Use valid fitness tests to determine pupil physical abilities and to evaluate their progress.

The adoption of these recommendations by our schools will insure the beginning of a sound basic program of physical development, exercise, and achievement.

I want to urge that this be a matter of great priority. "A sound mind and a sound body" is one of the oldest slogans

Two fifth-grade students speak to Oklahoma lawmakers in February 2005 to ask for the creation of a voluntary physical activity program for children throughout the state. AP WIDE WORLD PHOTOS.

of the Western World. I am hopeful that we will place a proper weight on intellectual achievement, but in my judgment, for the long-range happiness and well-being of all of you, for the strengthening of our country, for a more active and vigorous life, all of you as individuals and as groups will participate in strengthening the physical well-being of young American boys and girls.

This is a matter of importance, and I am hopeful that we can move ahead in the coming months.

Thank you very much.

SIGNIFICANCE

The President's Council on Physical Fitness was created with the singular goal of promoting physical activity, sports, and fitness as means of strongly encouraging Americans to adopt and lead fit, active, healthy lifestyles. The council has always focused much of its attention on the youth of America, as healthy lifestyles choices that become habitual in childhood tend to persist throughout the lifespan.

Kenneth H. Cooper, a preventive medicine physician who is credited with being the father of aerobics, was a prominent figure in the public efforts to encourage all people to become fit and healthy through regular exercise in the 1960s. While in the military, Cooper was director of the Aerospace Medical Laboratory in San Antonio, Texas, where he worked with NASA (National Aeronautics Space Administration) to create fitness and conditioning programs for United States astronauts. He was the developer of the twelve minute fitness test and the Aerobics Point System, still in use by the Navy, the Army, the Secret Service, many public and private organizations, and more than 2,500 public schools and universities across America.

Kenneth Cooper was among the first American public figures to advocate wellness and disease prevention, rather than to simply focus on treatment of existing diseases. It was his contention that "It is easier to maintain good health through proper exercise, diet, and emotional balance than it is to regain it once it is lost." He was a strong proponent of gathering and utilizing sound epidemiological data as a means of illustrating the benefits of maintaining a regular exercise program and maintaining a healthy lifestyle. He gathered data from several thousand individuals to use as the basis for his widely popular 1968 book, *Aerobics*. The message inherent in the book is that the way to live a long and healthy life, and to prevent the development of chronic and degenerative diseases, is to participate in an ongoing program of aerobic and cardiovascular exercise, and to maintain a high level of fitness across the entire lifespan. His work continues to be influential in the field of preventive medicine and fitness.

The four-plus decades since President Kennedy made his speech have seen enormous changes in the American way of life. Technological advances have been exponential, but they have been accompanied by a decline in fitness levels and a striking increase in obesity statistics as a nation. The statistics on childhood obesity are particularly alarming: the results from the 1999–2002 National Health and Nutrition Examination Survey (NHANES IV) estimate that 16 percent of American children between the ages of six and nineteen are overweight. This represents a 45 percent increase from the overweight estimates when the survey was done between 1988–1994, when overweight was estimated at 11 percent. Far more striking, however, is the difference between the 1963–1970 and 1999–2002 data: roughly 4.5 percent (4 percent for ages six to eleven and 5 percent for ages twelve to nineteen) of children between ages six and nineteen were considered overweight in the 1960s, and 16 percent (percentage is identical for both age groups) were overweight in 1999–2002. That represents an increase in prevalence of obesity of 355 percent over a span of forty years. When the statistics were closely examined by year, it was determined that the degree of overweight remained comparatively stable from the early 1960s through 1980. However, between 1986 and 1994, the prevalence of overweight children nearly doubled, and then increased by 45 percent between studies in 1988–1994 and 1999–2002.

As children become progressively more overweight, their risk factors for heart disease, high blood pressure, and high cholesterol increase. Type II diabetes, once considered an adult disease, has sharply increased among children and adolescents, and is often associated with obesity. Overweight adolescents have a significantly increased risk of becoming overweight or obese adults, increasing their lifelong risk for all of the previously mentioned diseases as well as some forms of cancer.

Many schools have made budget cuts in physical fitness programs since the 1960s, so many children are less active at school than they were in the past. Many schools have also eliminated daily recess periods in favor of increasing instructional time, in an effort to accommodate curriculum demands. Children (and adults) have become more sedentary as the technology for self-entertainment has advanced: they spend progressively more time indoors watching television, playing electronic video games, and using computers (statistical estimates of at least two hours per day spent engaged by some form of electronic activity), and equivalently less time out of doors or being engaged in active or imaginative play.

In order to begin to reverse the current overweight and obesity trends, the Centers for Disease Control and Prevention recommends that Americans opt for healthy, freshly prepared foods rather than highly processed or fast foods, reduce the amount of time spent in sedentary activities, and use more of their leisure time for active sports and fitness-related activities.

FURTHER RESOURCES
Periodicals

Kennedy, John F. "The Soft American." *Sports Illustrated* 13, no. 26 (December 26, 1960): 15–17.

Web sites

National Center for Health Statistics. "Prevalence of Overweight Among Children and Adolescents: United States, 1999–2002." <http://www.cdc.gov/nchs/products/pubs/pubd/hestats/overwght99.htm> (accessed November 29, 2005).

The President's Council on Physical Fitness and Sports. "About PCPFS." <http://www.fitness.gov/aboutpcpfs/aboutpcpfs. html> (accessed November 29, 2005).

The President's Council on Physical Fitness and Sports. "Getting America Moving." <http://www.fitness.gov/history.pdf> (accessed November 29, 2005).

The Complete Book of Running

Book cover

By: Jim Fixx

Date: 1977

Source: Jim Fixx. *The Complete Book of Running.* New York: Random House, 1977.

About the Author: James F. Fixx (1932–1984) wrote the best-selling book, *The Complete Book of Running.* His book helped to launch the running and jogging boom in the United States and worldwide. In an ironic twist of fate, Fixx died at the age of fifty-two while jogging, only seven years after his famous book was published. The cause of death was a heart attack brought on by extensive coronary artery disease, a disease that also had killed Fixx's father at age forty-three.

INTRODUCTION

At the age of thirty-five Jim Fixx transformed his lifestyle by quitting smoking and starting to run for long distances. In an increasingly sedentary society, he became an articulate advocate for a healthy way of life focused on an improved diet coupled with intensive and prolonged aerobic exercise. His untimely death at fifty-two while pursuing his favorite activity had virtually no negative impact on the growing popularity of running and other aerobic activity. Many people saw his death while jogging as a coincidence that did not undermine the validity of Fixx's advocacy of this and other aerobic activities.

In 2005, 75,000 runners applied to enter the New York City Marathon, which accepts half of the applicants using a lottery system. From 1984 to 2003, the number of runners completing marathons in the United States increased from 170,000 to 400,000

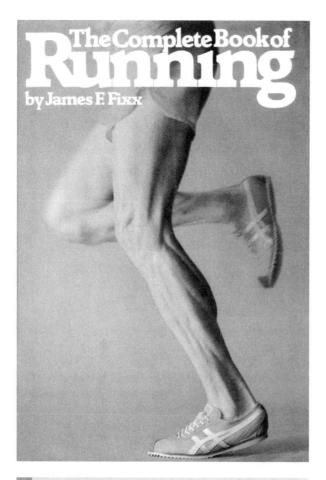

PRIMARY SOURCE

The Complete Book of Running. The cover of *The Complete Book of Running,* by James Fixx. This best-seller appeared in bookstores across America and inspired countless other guides to physical fitness and exercise in the late 1970s. "COVER," COPYRIGHT© 1977 BY RANDOM HOUSE, INC., FROM *THE COMPLETE BOOK OF RUNNING* BY JAMES FIXX. USED BY PERMISSION OF RANDOM HOUSE, INC.

according to the U.S. Track and Field association. The many runners seen daily on paths in city parks and alongside suburban streets illustrates that Jim Fixx had a lasting impact on the way that Americans use their leisure time and maintain health and fitness. Yet, the nation is still beset with rising rates of chronic disease related to obesity and a sedentary lifestyle.

PRIMARY SOURCE

THE COMPLETE BOOK OF RUNNING
See primary source image.

SIGNIFICANCE

Jim Fixx's death while jogging demonstrates a paradox about the risk of sudden death and exercise. Running poses some risks. Studies from Seattle and Rhode Island calculated that the number of persons who die annually from heart attacks while exercising is one out of 15,000. The Rhode Island study used data on all deaths during jogging from 1975 through 1980 in that state. Data analysis revealed that one death occurred annually for every 7,620 male joggers between the ages of thirty and sixty-five. When patients with known coronary artery disease were eliminated from the analysis, the annual incidence of sudden death was one death per year for every 15,240 previously healthy joggers. In spite of survey bias and other methodological limitations, the sudden death rate for healthy subjects was similar to a later estimate from Seattle of one death for every 18,000 physically active males.

The Seattle study also examined the sudden death rate based on accustomed activity levels. The authors observed that regular exercise both reduces the probability of sudden death during exercise and temporarily raises the risk of myocardial infarction (MI) even among individuals who regularly exercise, but men who spent more time during the week exercising had a lower risk of sudden death. Using these data and taking into account that active men exercise more hours and therefore have a lower risk per hour of exercise than sedentary men, the annual risk of sudden death during exertion is one death per 17,000 in men who spend 1–19 minutes per week in vigorous activities, one death in 23,000 for men who expend 20–139 minutes per week, and one death per 13,000 men who expend more than 140 minutes per week.

Both of these studies use old data and found very low total numbers of deaths: ten deaths in Rhode Island and nine in Seattle, indicating that statistical inference from these studies might not be highly reliable. A more recent study of runners in the Marine Corps and Twin Cities Marathons between 1976 and 1994 suggests one death per 50,000 participants.

While runners and others who engage in strenuous exercise appear to be more at risk during their training time, especially if they run marathons, they appear to have a much lower risk of death than the general population for the remainder of the day. Many studies suggest that rigorous aerobic training can actually extend peoples' lives and improve their overall health. A prospective study of Harvard University alumni concluded that people can live an extra two years or more by engaging in light exercise regularly. In this study, men who burned 2,000 kilocalories per week

Jogging became popular in the 1970s. Even President Jimmy Carter got into the act by jogging around the grounds of the White House during his term in office. ©BETTMANN/CORBIS.

performing cardiovascular exercises had a 25 to 33 percent lower death rate. Notably, the rate of coronary artery disease was decreased by 41 percent in the group that regularly exercised, compared to those who did not participate in cardiovascular exercise. Other studies indicate that regular exercise and a healthful diet may extend life spans by six to nine years.

The risk of MI also is related to an individual's usual fitness level. A study examined the relative risk of suffering MI during or within one hour of exercise. In this study the relative risk of MI during or just after exercise was at least 5.6 times greater than the risk during less vigorous activity. Common activities associated with MI included lifting or pushing (18 percent), isotonic activities such as jogging (30 percent) and yard work such as gardening and chopping wood (52 percent). In patients who were usually sedentary, the relative risk of MI was 107 times higher during exercise than it was at rest. Among those who regularly exercised at least five times a week, the relative risk was only 2.7 times higher than it was at rest. Patients with

diabetes had a relative risk of exercise-related MI that was 18.9 times higher than their risk at rest.

The best conclusion based on current information is that the additional risk of sudden death during exercise is proportional to the difference between a person's usual activity level and the transient activity level while exercising. Furthermore, there is a temporary period during and immediately after strenuous exercise in which an individual is at a significantly increased risk of sudden death. This risk is reduced by more regular exercise and a higher level of physical fitness. Jim Fixx's death while running could have been used to demonstrate the risks of exercise and its inability to reverse inexorable cardiovascular decline. Instead, his death seemed to spur an ongoing increase in research into the specific risks and health benefits of exercise.

Fixx was an evangelist for the beneficial effects and enjoyment of exercise, running, and a healthful diet. His message of improving personal fitness helped bring about significant changes in the average level of exercise in the U.S. population. However, it would be wrong to conclude that the running and fitness movement energized by Jim Fixx has converted America into a nation of physical fitness enthusiasts. The National Institute on Aging reports that only 58 percent of the U.S. population pursues a regimen of cardiovascular exercise as leisure time activity, and of those people, only 26 percent do so three or more times a week as part of a long-term fitness program.

It is tempting to blame Americans for sedentary habits and not heeding the scientific evidence that supports the benefits of healthier activity levels and diet. Yet, as prosperity and labor-saving technology spreads throughout the world and sedentary work replaces physical labor, it is increasingly difficult for people to carve out time for exercise in their busy lives. To do so places a premium on health risk awareness and discipline. The "running revolution" that Jim Fixx helped to start may not have eliminated the risk of chronic illness fostered by contemporary society, but it has promoted an "exercise ethic" that now helps keep cardiovascular and other lifestyle-related diseases at bay for millions of people.

FURTHER RESOURCES
Periodicals

Maron, B. J., L. C. Poliac, and W. O. Roberts. "Risk for Sudden Cardiac Death Associated With Marathon Running." *Journal of the American College of Cardiology* 28 (1996): 428–431.

Mittleman, M. A., et al. "Triggering of Acute Myocardial Infarction by Heavy Exertion: Protection Against

Triggering by Regular Exercise." *New England Journal of Medicine* 329 (1993): 1677–1683.

Thompson, P. D. "Cardiovascular Risks of Exercise: Avoiding Sudden Death and Myocardial Infarction." *The Physician and Sports Medicine* 29 (April 2001).

Thompson, P. D., et al. "Incidence of Death During Jogging in Rhode Island from 1975 through 1980." *Journal of the American Medical Association* 247 (1982): 2535–2538.

Americans with Disabilities Act

Speech

By: George H. W. Bush

Date: July 26, 1990

Source: U.S. Equal Employment Opportunity Commission. "Remarks of President George Bush at the Signing of the Americans with Disabilities Act." July 26, 1990. Available online at <http://www.eeoc.gov/abouteeoc/35th/videos/ada_signing_text.html> (accessed October 5, 2005).

About the Author: George H. W. Bush served as the forty-first president of the United States from 1989 to 1993. Born into a politically influential family, Bush was admitted to Yale University while still in his teens. However, when the United States entered World War II (1939–1945), Bush joined the Navy, where he became its youngest aviator. Bush became active in politics in the late 1950s. He joined the Republican Party, and after being defeated in his first bid for the United States Senate representing Texas (1964), Bush was elected in 1966, and served two Senate terms. During the 1970s, Bush was appointed to several high-profile jobs under Presidents Richard Nixon (1913–1994) and Gerald Ford (1913–), including ambassador to the United Nations (1971), and director of Central Intelligence Agency (1976). Before becoming president in 1989, Bush served as Ronald Reagan's vice president from 1980 to 1988.

INTRODUCTION

In 1990, the United States Congress passed landmark legislation that became known as the Americans with Disabilities Act of 1990 (ADA). The purpose of this law is simple—to prohibit discrimination and ensure equal opportunity for persons with disabilities in areas such as employment, education, transportation, and communication. The key objective of this law is to make all aspects of American society equally accessible to individuals with disabilities.

"Remarks of President George Bush at the Signing of the Americans with Disabilities Act" is a transcript of the speech given by President George H. W. Bush at the time he signed this legislation into law. The ADA, which is the world's first comprehensive civil rights law for people with disabilities, is considered by many to be one of the most significant achievements of the first Bush administration. In his speech delivered on the White House lawn before a large audience of activists, members of Congress, and disabled people, Bush highlighted the importance of the law, its implications, and its impact on the disabled community.

PRIMARY SOURCE

. . . This is an immensely important day, a day that belongs to all of you. Everywhere I look, I see people who have dedicated themselves to making sure that this day would come to pass: my friends from Congress, as I say, who worked so diligently with the best interest of all at heart, Democrats and Republicans; members of this administration—and I'm pleased to see so many top officials and members of my Cabinet here today who brought their caring and expertise to this fight; and then, the organizations—so many dedicated organizations for people with disabilities, who gave their time and their strength; and perhaps most of all, everyone out there and others—across the breadth of this nation are 43 million Americans with disabilities. You have made this happen. All of you have made this happen. To all of you, I just want to say your triumph is that your bill will now be law, and that this day belongs to you. On behalf of our nation, thank you very, very much.

Three weeks ago we celebrated our nation's Independence Day. Today we're here to rejoice in and celebrate another "independence day," one that is long overdue. With today's signing of the landmark Americans for Disabilities Act, every man, woman, and child with a disability can now pass through once-closed doors into a bright new era of equality, independence, and freedom. As I look around at all these joyous faces, I remember clearly how many years of dedicated commitment have gone into making this historic new civil rights act a reality. It's been the work of a true coalition, a strong and inspiring coalition of people who have shared both a dream and a passionate determination to make that dream come true. It's been a coalition in the finest spirit—a joining of Democrats and Republicans, of the legislative and the executive branches, of Federal and State agencies, of public officials and private citizens, of people with disabilities and without.

that wrong. But the stark fact remained that people with disabilities were still victims of segregation and discrimination, and this was intolerable. Today's legislation brings us closer to that day when no Americans will ever again be deprived of their basic guarantee of life, liberty, and the pursuit of happiness.

This act is powerful in its simplicity. It will ensure that people with disabilities are given the basic guarantees for which they have worked so long and so hard: independence, freedom of choice, control of their lives, the opportunity to blend fully and equally into the rich mosaic of the American mainstream. Legally, it will provide our disabled community with a powerful expansion of protections and then basic civil rights. It will guarantee fair and just access to the fruits of American life, which we all must be able to enjoy. And then, specifically, first the ADA ensures that employers covered by the act cannot discriminate against qualified individuals with disabilities. Second, the ADA ensures access to public accommodations such as restaurants, hotels, shopping centers, and offices. And third, the ADA ensures expanded access to transportation services. And fourth, the ADA ensures equivalent telephone services for people with speech or hearing impediments. . . .

SIGNIFICANCE

The Americans with Disabilities Act is a more complete version of prior laws, especially the Civil Rights Act of 1964 and the Rehabilitation Act of 1973. Any person who has a current condition that impairs a major life activity, such as walking, hearing, speaking, or executing physical tasks, is considered disabled under the law.

The Americans with Disabilities Act is divided into five sections or titles. Title I, which pertains to employment, states that all qualified individuals with disabilities cannot be denied jobs, equal wages and benefits, pay hikes, and other aspects of employment solely due to their disabilities. In other words, an employer must provide equal opportunity to all qualified candidates, including those with disabilities. In the workplace, the ADA brought the concepts of reasonable accommodation, essential functions, and essential tasks to the forefront. Employers are required to identify the physical characteristics necessary (essential functions) to perform major aspects of a job (essential tasks), then to make reasonable accommodation for a disabled person who is otherwise qualified to perform it. For example, an employer could provide a physically handicapped employee with a restructured computer workstation that allows the employee to operate the computer effectively.

After the passage of the Americans with Disabilities Act in the United States, more and more buildings were fitted with wheelchair ramps so that the disabled can gain access. ©ROYALTY-FREE/ CORBIS.

This historic act is the world's first comprehensive declaration of equality for people with disabilities—the first. Its passage has made the United States the international leader on this human rights issue. Already, leaders of several other countries, including Sweden, Japan, the Soviet Union, and all 12 members of the EEC, have announced that they hope to enact now similar legislation.

Our success with this act proves that we are keeping faith with the spirit of our courageous forefathers who wrote in the Declaration of Independence "We hold these truths to be self-evident, that all men are created equal, that they are endowed by their Creator with certain unalienable rights." These words have been our guide for more than two centuries as we've labored to form our more perfect union. But tragically, for too many Americans, the blessings of liberty have been limited or even denied. The Civil Rights Act of 1964 took a bold step towards righting

Title II, which relates to public services, states that public bodies, including local and state governments, as well as government-owned public transportation companies, cannot deny any service to individuals with disabilities that is being otherwise offered to a person without any disability. In other words, disabled people must have an equal opportunity to utilize all government programs and services, such as public education, employment, transportation, recreation, health care, social services, courts, voting, and town meetings. This law also requires governments to follow specific construction and design standards (for buildings as well as public transportation) to provide easy access and communication for disabled individuals.

Title III is similar to the Title II, but it pertains to other service providers. It requires all companies, both private and public, to follow construction and design standards (especially for new construction) that allow easy access to public facilities for disabled individuals. Public facilities include restaurants, retail stores, theaters, rest rooms, grocery stores, and privately owned transportation.

In 1998, the U.S. Congress passed another piece of legislation known as the Workforce Investment Act. Section 508 of this act pertains to individuals with disabilities and is often considered by many as an extension of Title III of ADA. This section states that all federal agencies are required to have their electronic and information technology designed so that they are easily accessible to people with disabilities (federal employees as well as the general public). For example, federal government Web sites must incorporate design standards that allow easy access to anyone with a disability.

Title IV of the Americans with Disabilities Act addresses telephone and television access for people with hearing and speech disabilities. It allows people with such disabilities access to telephone communication using special instruments, known as telecommunication devices for the deaf, or TDD, and a special service provided by telephone companies known as the telecommunications relay service (TRS).

Title V protects other individuals who have an association with a person known to have a disability, and even those who are subjected to retaliation for assisting people with disabilities in asserting their rights under the ADA.

The Americans with Disabilities Act was not without opposition. At the time the law was passed, many members of Congress predicted that the act would place a significant burden on the economy. Ten years after the law was enacted, however, businesses found that the cost of making the changes required by the ADA was far lower than expected. In addition, the ADA opponents assumed that the act would be responsible for generating a large number of lawsuits by disabled individuals. The huge spate of lawsuits never materialized. Also, more than 90 percent of the ADA discrimination cases brought to the Equal Employment Opportunity Commission (the agency that monitors the equal employment section of the ADA) between 1990 and 2000 were decided in favor of the employers.

The ADA has significantly changed the manner in which individuals with disabilities are viewed in society. For example, institutions and organizations now provide equal opportunities for individuals with disabilities, and many more students with disabilities are admitted to colleges and universities than were admitted before the ADA was passed. Additionally, public transportation, along with public and private businesses, must have easy accessibility for people with disabilities. Ramps, curb cuts, lifts on buses, and similar design modifications related to accessibility have become commonplace.

Although the Americans with Disabilities Act has achieved notable successes, including providing increased community access, there are many issues still facing the disabled community in America. President George W. Bush announced a "New Freedom Initiative" in 2002 that provides increased access to current assistive technology such as specialized computers, and funds research for the development of new assisted technologies. The initiative also provides more funds for education, especially in the early grades, and for promoting home ownership for disabled persons.

FURTHER RESOURCES
Books

Jones, Nancy Lee. *The Americans With Disabilities Act (ADA): Overview, Regulations, and Interpretations.* New York: Novinka, 2003.

U.S. Department of Justice. *Americans with Disabilities Act Handbook.* Anaheim, Calif.: BNI, 1992.

Web sites

Center for an Accessible Society. "The Americans with Disabilities Act." <http://www.accessiblesociety.org/topics/ada> (accessed October 5, 2005).

Job Accommodation Network. "ADA: A Brief Overview." March 2004. <http://www.jan.wvu.edu/links/adasummary.htm> (accessed October 5, 2005).

National Council on Disability. "Promises to Keep: A Decade of Federal Enforcement of the Americans with Disabilities Act." June 27, 2000. <http://www.ncd.gov/

newsroom/publications/2000/promises_1.htm>
(accessed October 5, 2005).

U.S. Department of Justice. "A Guide to Disability Rights Laws." March 27, 2003. <http://www.ada.gov/cguide.htm>(accessed October 5, 2005).

U.S. Equal Employment Opportunity Commission. "The Americans with Disabilities Act (ADA): 1990–2002." October 15, 2002. <http://www.eeoc.gov/abouteeoc/35th/thelaw/ada.html> (accessed October 5, 2005).

A Wake-Up Call

Americans and Sleep

Book excerpt

By: Stanley Coren

Date: 1996

Source: Stanley Coren. *Sleep Thieves: An Eye-Opening Exploration into the Science and Mysteries of Sleep*. New York: The Free Press, 1996.

About the Author: Stanley Coren is a psychologist. A prolific writer in his field, Coren has published scholarly texts, monographs, and several hundred journal articles. His areas of particular interest are sensation, perception, and neuropsychology. He has received numerous awards and honors by his peers as well as by professional organizations. Coren also wrote a best-selling series of books for dog owners.

INTRODUCTION

Both sleep researchers and the media describe the United States as a nation of people who, on the whole, fail to get enough sleep on a regular basis. Sleep is lost in an effort to balance the demands of work, family, assorted commitments, and the stresses of day-to-day living. Often as adults, and sometimes as children, there are too many time demands to fit into a normal day, and sleep time is sacrificed in an effort to meet responsibilities.

Numerous scientific and practical reports state that adults function best after receiving an average of eight hours of sleep nightly. Children require more sleep, and adolescents more still. However, most American adults sleep only about six hours nightly. People vary widely in their sleep needs, with some needing up to ten hours to feel at their best, others spontaneously awakening, and feeling sleep-satiated after only four or five hours. Sleep scientists have suggested that adequate sleep amounts (of seven to eight hours) per night offer some physiological protection against heart disease.

The ideal amount of sleep for an individual has been defined as the quantity that allows the person to awaken feeling refreshed, having an ample supply of energy to meet the demands of the day, and remaining generally healthy (not getting sick with excessive frequency). Another yardstick for sleep time is that amount that allows one to awaken spontaneously, without need of an alarm clock. Some researchers have written that a good way to determine optimal hours of sleep is to pay attention to patterns while on vacation, or in a situation in which there is no need to arise at a specific time. The number of hours slept is probably about what the body needs to feel optimally rested. However, it may take one a few days to accurately note the point at which this occurs.

There are a variety of factors that can interfere with getting enough sleep, or with experiencing high quality sleep. Individuals who sleep with pets, babies, or small children, or who sleep in beds too small or crowded for comfort, tend to lack quality sleep. People who work at or through the night, have rotating shift schedules, or have an infant or person who is very ill in the home tend to get sleep that is lower in quality and quantity than is ideal. Those who stay out late and have to get up early, or persons with very demanding lives, with stressful jobs, or large or highly time-intensive families, often experience sleep loss over prolonged periods. When that occurs, it is termed sleep deprivation. Sleep-deprived people tend on average to be more irritable, more prone to feelings of depression, and more emotionally labile; have less sustainable energy; have more erratic school, task, or work performance; have less efficient immune systems (and therefore get sick more often); and may even age (physiologically) at an accelerated rate. Several studies, in the United States and in Europe, have offered evidence suggesting that prolonged sleep deprivation may increase the likelihood of heart disease, type II diabetes, obesity, and hypertension.

Although sleep has been a subject of scientific research for decades, and of anecdotal study for as long as there have been curious humans, the specific and discrete reasons for its occurrence have not yet been determined. All living and mobile (that is, not rooted to a particular location) organisms have an innate need for sleep, and cannot survive without it for any prolonged period of time. Published research reports on the physiology of sleep have suggested that it aids in the maintenance of the immune system, allows the body time to repair and replace cells, facilitates metabolism, and allows the tired body to restore its depleted energy reserves. Some data has supported the possibility that sleep somehow facilitates the construction or strengthening of long-term memories.

There is a body of scientific evidence likening the biochemical and physiological effects of sleep deprivation to those of alcohol intoxication: both negatively affect gross and fine motor skills, hamper coordination, dull reflexes and response time, and impair judgment and critical thinking skills. Police and traffic monitoring agency statistics indicate that roughly 250,000 motor vehicle accidents per year result from drivers who fall asleep at the wheel. Lack of sleep slows reflexes, impairs coordination, and impacts judgment. It can, and does, lead to accidents—sometimes with tragic results. The National Commission on Sleep Disorders has estimated that sleep deprivation costs America $150 billion annually in increased stress and decreased work performance.

▉ PRIMARY SOURCE

The idea that one can go without sleep is wrong. The data seem to be quite clear about this. It is probably the case that we may need nine and one half to ten hours of sleep a day for optimal performance. This sleep can be had in one continuous nightly session, or it can be divided into something like 7 1/2 to 8 hours at night and 1 1/2 to 2 hours in the afternoon. With this amount of sleep we seem to be obtaining the quantity that evolution programmed us for. With this amount of sleep we also seem to be building up a bit of a reserve or a cushion, which will allow us to better handle times of stress and short-term sleep deprivation.

If we need 10 hours, why have we always seemed to be able to get along on the 8 hours of sleep that is traditional? Many of us can do fine on 8 hours of sleep for most purposes. As we pointed out earlier, what we lose is our safety margin. If we now encounter a short period of time when our sleep is restricted, we go downhill faster. Our normal efficiency, alertness, and creativity is not as good with 8 hours of sleep as it is with 10, and a significant segment of the population is still sleep and fatigued with this amount of sleep. So 8 hours of sleep is survivable, over the long term, but 10 is better.

When we try to sleep less than the 8-hour minimum, things start to deteriorate. First of all, the effects of less than 8 hours of sleep a night seem to accumulate as a sleep debt. If you lose 2 hours today and 2 hours tomorrow, on the third night your efficiency is as low as if you had lost 4 hours of sleep in one night. This is the way our sleep debt builds up. Eventually, if the sleep debt becomes large enough, we become slow, clumsy, stupid, and, possibly, dead. This is not an exaggeration. Remember, the

national death rate by accidents jumps 6 percent as a result of simply losing 1 hour more of sleep as we shift to daylight savings time in the spring.

Perhaps it is time for policymakers, health workers, and all the rest of us to wake up. The data is now quite clear that sleepiness, the direct result of not enough sleep, is a health hazard to individuals. It also may be a danger to the general public, because of the possibility that a sleepy individual might trigger a catastrophic accident such as those associated with Chernobyl, Three Mile Island, the *Exxon Valdez*, and the space shuttle *Challenger*.

As a society we attempt to exert controls on personal behavior that constitutes a personal health hazard or has the possibility of affecting the health and safety of others. Many places in society today restrict tobacco smoking because secondhand smoke may cause cancer in others. We restrict alcohol use because public drunkenness has been shown to be associated with outbreaks of violence and drunkenness on the highway may kill other drivers. We do, however, permit both drinking and smoking in private, where no harm can be done to anyone except the individual. At one time smoking was considered a sign of sophistication; later it was a sign of toughness. The ability to drink large amounts of alcohol has been viewed as a sign of strength and of self-control, especially in certain groups of males. Today, however, heavy drinkers and heavy smokers are not viewed very favorably in our society.

There are parallels between sleep deprivation and drinking or smoking. Today, the person who runs on little sleep is seen as mentally tough, ambitious, and admirable. Perhaps as society recognizes the harm that building up a sleep debt does to the sleep-deprived person and to those around him or her, this situation will change. Perhaps someday society will act to do something about sleepiness. It may even come to pass that someday the person who drives or goes to work while sleepy will be viewed as being reprehensible, dangerous, or even criminally negligent as the person who drives or goes to work while drunk. If so, perhaps the rest of us can all sleep a little bit more soundly.

▉

SIGNIFICANCE

David Dinges is a sleep expert working at the University of Pennsylvania. In his opinion, studies that looked at the timing of sleeping-driver-related-motor vehicle accidents across the course of the day suggest that there are large peaks (clusters of accidents) in the middle of the night and smaller peaks in the middle of the afternoon. He believes that the biological functions responsible for regulating brain activity

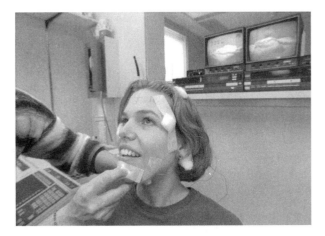

To determine why people have difficulty sleeping, scientists conduct sleep studies. Here, a researcher applies sensors to the face of a university student during a sleep study in 1995. AP WIDE WORLD PHOTOS.

also contribute to so-called "fall asleep" roadway collisions. In other words, humans have time periods during which their bodies rather critically need sleep, and people have a limited ability to fight off this physiological imperative.

The British Sleep Foundation has also targeted tired drivers, and likens driving while tired to driving while intoxicated. A study in Australia compared the relative effects on performance of alcohol and sleep deprivation, and found that severely sleep-deprived subjects performed as poorly as those with significant blood alcohol levels.

Among the most chronically sleep deprived individuals reported are night shift workers. British sleep researchers report that people who work at night and who try to sleep during the day are getting a poorer quality of rest, less deep sleep, and therefore fewer REM (rapid eye movement) cycles than those who work day shifts and sleep at night. Such chronic lack of sleep slows thinking and reaction time, making it more difficult for them to learn new skills or work efficiently.

A study conducted at the University of Chicago Medical Center concluded that cutting back significantly on required nightly sleep can produce large changes in glucose tolerance and endocrine functioning, comparable to what might be seen in the early stages of diabetes or of advanced age. This was a particularly important study, as it was much more like the real-world experience of people who are chronically sleep-deprived than studies in which subjects are entirely prevented from sleeping for prolonged periods. In the course of everyday life, people

are more prone to smaller but chronic sleep losses, than to routine bouts of complete lack of sleep. At the height of the sleep debt study, volunteers took 40 percent longer than normal to regulate their blood sugar levels following a high carbohydrate meal, and their ability both to secrete, and to respond to, insulin each decreased by roughly 30 percent—a pattern similar to early clinical markers for diabetes. Sleep debt also decreased production of thyroid stimulating hormone and increased afternoon and evening cortisol levels. Those results are typical in senescence, and are believed to be associated with age-related health problems, such as memory impairment and insulin resistance.

FURTHER RESOURCES

Books

Bush, Andrew J., et.al. *Epidemiology of Sleep: Age, Gender, and Ethnicity*. Mahwah, New Jersey: Lawrence Erlebaum Associates, 2004.

Web sites

BBC News: Health. "Lack of Sleep May Speed Ageing Process." <http://news.bbc.co.uk/1/hi/health/481340.stm> (accessed November 25, 2005).

BBC News: Health. "Sleep Deprivation Dangers." <http://news.bbc.co.uk/1/low/health/300940.stm> (accessed November 25, 2005).

CNNinteractive: Health Story Page. "Lack of Sleep America's Top Health Problem, Doctors Say." <http://www.cnn.com/HEALTH/9703/17/nfm/sleep.deprivation/> (accessed November 25, 2005).

Occupational Health & Safety. "Lack of Sleep Is Dangerous." <http://www.uaw.org/hs/01/02/hs03.html> (accessed November 25, 2005).

Home Diagnostic Tests: The Ultimate House Call?

Magazine article

By: Carol Lewis

Date: November/December 2001

Source: Lewis, Carol. "The Ultimate House Call?" *FDA Consumer* 35 (November/December 2001): 18–20.

About the Author: Carol Lewis is a staff writer for the *FDA Consumer*, the official magazine of the U.S. Food and Drug Administration (FDA). Now part of the Department of Health and Human Services, the FDA grew out of the work of a single chemist in the Department of Agriculture in 1862. The FDA's mission is "protecting the public health by assuring the safety, efficacy, and security of human and veterinary drugs, biological products, medical devices, our nation's food supply, cosmetics, and products that emit radiation. The FDA is also responsible for advancing the public health by helping to speed innovations that make medicines and foods more effective, safer, and more affordable; and helping the public get the accurate, science-based information they need to use medicines and foods to improve their health."

INTRODUCTION

Tests on body fluids, such as blood and urine, can yield a significant amount of information about an individual's health. Such diagnostic tests were once the preserve of the pathology lab, and doctors and patients had to wait for the results. Now, thanks to advances in chemistry, many tests are quick and simple. As a result, people can now perform many tests for themselves and get the results quickly and easily in the privacy of their own homes.

Home pregnancy tests were the first of the do-it-yourself diagnostic tests. First marketed in the 1970s, they are still the most popular product on the home diagnostic market. One-third of all women have used these tests at some time. Home pregnancy tests allow early access to highly sensitive and personal information. With today's tests, a woman can get a positive or negative result within days of a missed period, rather than waiting the traditional two weeks. The result also is available within minutes of performing the test, rather than having to wait for a doctor's appointment.

If all home diagnostic tests were like pregnancy tests, there would be few problems. Although a pregnancy test may give an incorrect result, either because of test limitations or because it was used improperly, the outcome is unlikely to be life-threatening. However, today there are many other home diagnostics on the market, some of which test for serious conditions such as HIV, hepatitis C, or drug use. The article that follows describes some of the key issues involved in the growth of home diagnostic tests.

▉ PRIMARY SOURCE

More and more Americans are playing doctor in the privacy of their own bathrooms, using a few drops of blood or a urine sample to test for cholesterol, blood glucose, or evidence of colon or rectal cancer. In fact, a snippet of a child's hair now can confirm the use of illicit drugs.

Often seen as a less expensive and a more convenient alternative to a trip to the doctor's office, self-testing diagnostic and monitoring devices are booming in sales. Devices such as blood-glucose tests and blood-pressure kits make it easier for people to self-monitor conditions such as diabetes and hypertension. However, this technology-driven trend is not without limits and could result in serious problems for those who rely on the tests instead of on the expertise of their health-care provider. A recent shift in the home diagnostics market—from monitoring chronic illnesses to diagnosing serious or potentially fatal diseases—is raising red flags among health professionals.

For years, pregnancy tests and ovulation predictors dominated the home test kit market. While these devices still generate large numbers of self-care sales, other tools of the medical trade are fast becoming available outside the doctor's office—no prescription needed. Spiraling health-care costs, increased interest in preventive health care, and a desire for privacy are paving the way for products that now include screening for the virus that causes AIDS and for drugs of abuse.

Screening tests often are used at home to check for symptoms of a disease when they may not be readily apparent. For example, people can measure their cholesterol and triglyceride levels—two types of fats in the blood—to help minimize the risk of cardiovascular disease.

BENEFITS AND LIMITATIONS

Home test kits are, in many cases, as inexpensive as a co-payment to a doctor and a lot less time-consuming. Some can provide speedy results. Women often use home pregnancy test (HPT) kits for these reasons, as well as for the convenience of testing at home. Some women prefer to know for sure that they are pregnant before visiting their physicians, and HPT kits can help confirm pregnancy earlier. An earlier confirmation provides an opportunity for health-care providers to counsel women about their options, and to discourage potentially harmful behaviors, such as smoking and use of alcohol or drugs.

Kidney disease is one of the most devastating complications of diabetes, but it's also detectable and treatable in its earliest stages. A home test kit allows people with diabetes to test for glucose and even small amounts of protein in their urine—an early sign of kidney dysfunction.

Jim Watson, R.Ph., a pharmacist at the CVS pharmacy in Gaithersburg, Md., says that in his experience, blood glucose monitoring systems and home pregnancy tests are among the most popular tests purchased for home use.

"Diabetics already know they have the disease and so they test their blood sugar levels several times a day," he says. By contrast, Watson says, although women may only use a pregnancy test once, they are still one of the most popular tests the store sells. Sales of both HIV and drug screening home tests are infrequent, according to Watson.

One sign of their overall increasing popularity is the fact that many pharmacists are moving home test kits from behind their counters onto free-standing displays. The lure of the Internet is also helping to make these devices more readily available.

Steven Gutman, M.D., director of the Food and Drug Administration's clinical laboratory devices division, says that consumers need to be wary about buying and using the kits on their own. "People need to carefully read the test-kit labeling and instructions, where important information and warnings about the product are listed," he says. Among other things, this information tells how a test works, and what to do when it doesn't. Home test kits are meant to be an adjunct to doctor visits, not a replacement for them. "Although the menu of home testing products has expanded," Gutman says, "the advice is still the same."

SEE YOUR DOCTOR, TOO

While convenience, confidentiality, and the cost-saving benefits of home testing cannot be overlooked, doctors are concerned about the availability of medical tests that encourage self-diagnosis because of the possibility that the results could be misinterpreted and treatment might be delayed.

For example, Sandy Stewart, Ph.D., a research biomedical engineer in the FDA's Center for Devices and Radiological Health (CDRH), says that blood pressure monitors should be used for tracking blood pressure readings between doctor's visits. "Users should never change their medications based on a home blood pressure reading." If there are significant changes, he says, the user should see his or her doctor immediately. "The blood pressure reading taken in the physician's office must be the final word."

In addition, the diagnostic value of home test kits can be affected by users who don't follow instructions carefully. In an effort to conceive a child, Donna Trossevin of Frederick, Md., bought from a local pharmacy an ovulation predictor that uses body temperature to help pinpoint a woman's most fertile time. Although the kit consisted of only a thermometer and special paper to chart her daily temperatures, Trossevin says it was difficult to get accurate readings because "if you don't hold the instrument just so, you can easily misread the numbers." And the half a degree increase from a person's normal temperature that a woman is looking for to predict ovulation "is such a small window of opportunity and easy to miss," says Trossevin. "I just never knew 100 percent whether I was ovulating or not."

Those who rely on home tests also miss out on pre- and post-test counseling, which offer information, support, competence, interpretation, and follow-up advice to consumers that only a health-care professional can give. The benefit of having a health-care professional involved in a test or screening procedure is that the results can be evaluated within the context of the whole health picture, not just one test. Furthermore, receiving news of potential pregnancy, illness, or infection over the phone, or from the color of a test strip, can be devastating.

"The first 72 hours following a positive result for an illness as serious as HIV is when people are most likely to hurt themselves," says Edward Geraty, a licensed clinical social worker with Behavioral Science Associates in Baltimore. Geraty says it's important to have a face-to-face relationship when delivering the news of a positive HIV test. Without it, he says, "there's a psychological component of the person's illness that is completely left out of the process."

Bob Barret, Ph.D., agrees. A professor of counseling at the University of North Carolina at Charlotte, Barret believes that home test kits, particularly for HIV, "are best used only by those who are well-educated about the disease, and who are in touch with their emotions and have a good support system around them."

FIND A REPUTABLE SOURCE

Accuracy, too, is an important consideration when it comes to home testing. False positive test results indicate that a condition is present when, in fact, it is not. False negatives are results that do not identify a condition that is present.

The Federal Trade Commission, which enforces consumer protection laws, recently reviewed results of several unapproved HIV test kits advertised and sold on the Internet for self-diagnosis at home. In every case, the kits showed a negative result when used on a known HIV-positive sample.

Similarly, the FDA recently tested a number of unapproved home HIV test kits sold on the Internet that were confiscated during a criminal investigation. None produced accurate results. In reality, the outcome could have had grave consequences for a user in terms of mental and emotional stress, access to proper medical treatment, and transmission of the disease to others. The FDA's Center for Biologics Evaluation and Research, which reviews all blood-related products, continues to investigate firms and people involved in the illegal sale of unapproved HIV home test kits in the United States.

FOLLOW THE DIRECTIONS

Home test kits, for the most part, involve relatively simple procedures. Some are as straightforward as one pregnancy test in which chemically treated test strips dipped in urine produce colored indicator lines. Others require a finger prick and the placement of a blood sample onto a reagent strip. The strip is inserted into a machine that measures blood glucose levels. Still others, like the only FDA-cleared HIV home sample collection kit, consist of multiple components, ranging from pre-test counseling information to a personal identification number for obtaining the test's results. In any case, the FDA requires that the kits be simple enough for an average consumer to use at home without a doctor's supervision.

Some home tests give their results as positive or negative. Performance of these is described in terms of sensitivity—the probability that the results will be positive when a disease or condition is present; and specificity—the probability that the results will be negative when a disease or condition is not present. Other home tests give numerical results. Performance of these is described in terms of precision—how reproducible the results are when a test is run over and over; and accuracy—how well the results compare to a laboratory test. All diagnostic tests have limitations, and sometimes their use may produce erroneous or questionable results. Test results obtained at home can often be clarified by a physician, who may recommend another test that is handled by a laboratory.

Gutman, whose office is within CDRH, says that home test kits should not be stored in places where they might be exposed to extreme temperatures, since this may cause product deterioration over time. He also stresses the importance of checking test-kit expiration dates—chemicals in an outdated test may no longer work properly, so the results are not likely to be valid.

While manufacturers of professional test kits used in clinics and hospitals or doctor's offices are required to include sensitivity and specificity information in their labeling, the FDA does not make manufacturers of home test kits do so. But Lori Moore of Maysville, Ky., thinks they should.

"As a consumer, I want to see the data that supports this being a good brand," she says. "For the average person, this information truly lets them know what they're purchasing." But Moore happens to be more familiar with sensitivity and related product information than most people, since she has worked as a registered laboratory technician. Still, she insists that today's consumer wants more information visible on the product's label than is currently available.

Dave Lyle, a medical technologist in the FDA's clinical laboratory devices division, explains that "the decision was made several years ago to exclude this information from over-the-counter kits because it might confuse the consumer." However, Lyle agrees that "in today's world, most consumers are very sophisticated and want as much information as possible to make an informed decision."

Complications of home testing may interfere with obtaining accurate results. Consumers may not be able to follow the instructions. Proper collection, storage and shipment of specimens are all critical for accuracy. Samples held too long, for example, or subjected to severe temperature changes could generate false positive or negative readings. Urine samples taken too early or too late in the day or foods eaten that mimic the metabolites being measured also can produce inaccurate readings.

And people need to beware of bogus tests—those not cleared by the FDA. Unapproved home test kits do not come with any guarantee of accuracy or sensitivity, nor do they have a documented history of dependability. Proper training to interpret results is not provided with the kits, and they do not have a validated record of precision. This means that unapproved tests may be inconsistent and inaccurate.

Approved tests, on the other hand, have undergone extensive study and review by the manufacturer of the product to satisfy the FDA's requirement that they are as safe and accurate for consumer use as their laboratory counterparts are for professional use. For any in-home test, the manufacturer must convince the FDA that the results of a test will benefit consumers and that consumers have the knowledge necessary to decide whether testing themselves is appropriate.

For example, Stewart says people purchasing blood pressure monitors should look for a statement in the label that says the device has been validated in a human study "where the statistics have been calculated to ensure that good accuracy can be demonstrated." Stewart says the label also should include a statement that says measurements obtained by the blood pressure monitor are equivalent to those obtained by a trained observer using a cuff and stethoscope.

"Indeed, reading the label is the most important thing," he says, "but it might also be useful to ask the pharmacist or one's doctor to get a recommendation."

POPULAR BUT NOT PERFECT

Amid sweeping changes in U.S. health care, the trend toward cost-effective self-care products used in the home emphasizes prevention and early intervention. The home test kit market is offering faster and easier products that lend themselves to being used in less-sophisticated environments to meet consumers' needs.

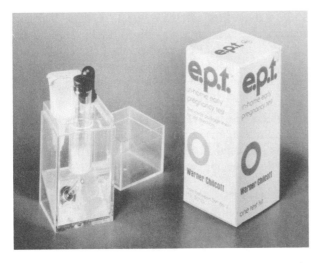

In 1978, Warner-Chilcott introduced the "E.P.T. in-home early pregnancy test" in the United States. The test helped women determine if they were pregnant before seeking the opinion of a doctor. ©BETTMANN/CORBIS.

However, Gutman emphasizes, "even the best screening tests are occasionally wrong. No tests, whether performed at the lab or in the home, are perfect."

SIGNIFICANCE

Today, patients are better informed, thanks to the Internet and other media coverage of health. Physicians also carry larger workloads. The increased use of home diagnostic tests appears to fit in with these trends. Prior to a doctor's visit, home diagnostic tests equip a patient with information that he or she would otherwise have had to wait for or might not have obtained at all. However, there is, as yet, no clear evidence that self-diagnosis is improving the nation's health and clear guidance is lacking as to the role of home test kits in health care.

For patients with a chronic condition, such as diabetes or high blood pressure, home monitoring would seem to be useful. However, this self-monitoring needs to be done in partnership with the doctor, because other checks are needed that cannot be done by the patients themselves. When it comes to self-diagnosis, there are self-tests for hepatitis, HIV, cholesterol, and fertility. Most of these self-diagnostic tests use a simple color test based on a rapid chemical reaction that occurs in blood or urine. The main issue with these tests is that the results still must be confirmed by a pathology laboratory, despite advances in the technology of the tests. This is standard scientific practice and often is explicitly stated on the product label.

The Internet has contributed to the growth of the home diagnostics industry since the article above was published. People can buy tests anytime and in complete privacy, which may be attractive to some consumers. Some of these tests are FDA approved and are the same as those sold in pharmacies. Others are not recommended and, as with many products available on the Internet, are hard to regulate. It may not be easy for a consumer to distinguish an approved from a non-approved test when they visit a Web site. Buying a test on the Internet guarantees privacy, but there is none of the face-to-face follow up which is so important in interpreting a result. For example, tests for prostate specific antigen (PSA) may indicate an increased risk of prostate cancer, but do not mean much in the absence of a physical exam and a confirmation test.

Home diagnostics probably will continue to expand as the technology becomes simpler and faster. For example, genetic tests for susceptibility to certain diseases will likely become available in the near future. Ideally, consumers will only use approved tests. If they do not, then they should remember that a do-it-yourself test is only a part of the diagnostic work-up and discussion with a doctor is still important.

FURTHER RESOURCES

Web sites

Center for Devices and Radiologic Health. "Buying Diagnostic Tests from the Internet: Buyer Beware!" <http://www.fda.gov/cdrh/consumer/buyerbeware.html> (accessed November 22, 2005).

Office of In-vitro Diagnostic Device Evaluation and Safety. "Home Use Tests." <http://www.fda.gov/cdrh/oivd/consumer-homeuse.html> (accessed November 22, 2005).

Deaths: Preliminary Data for 2003

Life Expectancy Reaches Record High

Report extract

By: Donna L. Hoyert, et. al.

Date: February 28, 2005

Source: National Center for Health Statistics. *National Vital Statistics Reports* 53, no. 15 (February 28, 2005).

Life expectancy and health status rose significantly during the twentieth century, allowing many senior citizens to enjoy an active lifestyle well past traditional retirement years. ©MARK A. JOHNSON/CORBIS.

About the Author: This article was written by staff from the Division of Vital Statistics in the National Center for Health Statistics (NCHS) a section of the Center for Disease Control and Prevention (CDC), part of the U.S. Department of Health and Human Services. CDC was founded in 1946 to help control malaria. Today its mission is to improve public health by preventing and controlling chronic disease, injuries, workplace hazards, disabilities and environmental health threats. The NCHS is the nation's leading health statistics agency and collects timely, relevant, and accurate data to help guide actions and policies to improve the health of the American people.

INTRODUCTION

Life expectancy at birth in the United States went up dramatically during the twentieth century and, according to the data collected so far, has continued to increase during the early years of this new century.

In 1900, male life expectancy was forty-eight years and female life expectancy was fifty-one. By 2000, these figures had increased to seventy-four and eighty years, respectively. The figures for 2003 show a further small increase to 74.8 years for men and 80.1 years for women.

There are two ways of looking at life expectancy, depending on how old the individual is at the time the data is collected. Life expectancy at birth will differ from life expectancy at a specific age. Thus in 2000, an American white male born that year would have a life expectancy of seventy-five, while a man aged sixty-five had a remaining life expectancy of sixteen years. The reasons why some people live longer than others probably depend on many factors. If someone has survived longer than the average life expectancy then they may (for biological reasons still not well understood) be aging more slowly than average and still have many years left to live.

The first half of the twentieth century saw a dramatic fall in the number of deaths from infection thanks to improvements in public sanitation, the introduction of antibiotics, and wider usage of vaccination. As people began to live longer, they became more prone to the diseases of aging and lifestyle such as heart disease, stroke, and cancer. As the abstract from the report below shows (an abstract is an overview), the death rates from some of these chronic diseases are now beginning to fall as well, probably because of earlier diagnosis and better treatments.

PRIMARY SOURCE

ABSTRACT

Objectives—This report presents preliminary U.S. data on deaths, death rates, life expectancy, leading causes of death, and infant mortality for the year 2003 by selected characteristics such as age, sex, race, and Hispanic origin.

Methods—Data in this report are based on a large number of deaths comprising approximately 93 percent of the demographic file and 91 percent of the medical file for all deaths in the United States in 2003. The records are weighted to independent control counts for 2003. For certain causes of death such as unintentional injuries, homicides, suicides, and respiratory diseases, preliminary and final data differ because of the truncated nature of the preliminary file. Comparisons are made with 2002 final data.

Results—The age-adjusted death rate for the United States decreased from 845.3 deaths per 100,000 population in 2002 to 831.2 deaths per 100,000 population in 2003. Age-adjusted death rates decreased between 2002 and 2003 for the following causes: Diseases of heart, Malignant neoplasms, Cerebrovascular diseases, Accidents (unintentional injuries), Influenza and pneumonia, Intentional self-harm (suicide), Chronic liver disease and cirrhosis, and Pneumonitis due to solids and liquids. They increased between 2002 and 2003 for the following: Alzheimer's disease, Nephritis, nephrotic syndrome and nephrosis, Essential (primary) hypertension and hypertensive renal disease, and Parkinson's disease. Life expectancy at birth rose by 0.3 years to a record high of 77.6 years.

SIGNIFICANCE

Americans are living longer, but the yearly increments in life expectancy are slowing down. This may suggest that there is a biological natural limit to how long humans can live. Reaching one hundred years is no longer uncommon, but there are a few who have survived to 110 and beyond. What is perhaps more relevant than increasing how long we can live is looking the quality of life remaining in later years. And this involves using the data to look at the trends in the diseases that cause death.

Increased rates of death were found in the most recent data, summarized above, for Alzheimer's and Parkinson's diseases and for complications of high blood pressure (hypertension). The first two are neurological diseases for which there is still an urgent need for early diagnosis and effective treatments. High blood pressure is treatable, but remains undiagnosed and uncontrolled in many individuals.

The statistics also look at ethnic differences in mortality and life expectancy. For the first time, life expectancy for all women in the United States exceeded eighty years. Overall, however, there were still ethnic differences, with white people having a life expectancy of seventy-eight years compared to seventy-three years for African Americans. Meanwhile, shortest life expectancy group was for African American males at less than seventy years.

The United States may, arguably, be the most developed nation on earth but it does not have the highest life expectancy. This belongs to Japan, where people can expect to live more than eighty years. An affluent lifestyle is not always beneficial for health. Some experts have said that the Unites States is vulnerable to a downward trend in life expectancy in coming years because of the increased incidence of obesity and related diseases such as diabetes, cancer, and heart

disease. Meanwhile, infectious disease, and HIV/AIDS in particular, continue to blight the life expectancies of developing countries. Collection of mortality and life expectancy data, such as that reported above, continues to be a vital tool in helping improve health and quality of life among people around the world.

FURTHER RESOURCES
Books

Bohan, Suzanne, and Glenn Thompson. *50 Simple Ways To Live A Longer Life: Everyday Techniques From The Forefront Of Science*. Naperville, IL: Sourcebooks, 2005.

Periodicals

Dwyer, J. "Global health and justice." *Bioethics* October 2005 19: 460–475.

Web sites

ElderWeb. "1900–2000:Changes in Life Expectancy in the United States." <http://www.elderweb.com/history/?PageID=2838> (accessed December 4, 2005).

Medical News Today. "Life Expectancy in USA Increases to 77.6 Years; Deaths from Heart Disease, Cancer Decline, Report Finds." <http://www.medicalnewstoday.com/newsletters.php> (accessed December 4, 2005).

National Center for Health Statistics. "Deaths: Preliminary Data for 2003." <http://www.cdc.gov/nchs/data/nvsr/nvsr53/nvsr53_15.pdf> (accessed December 4, 2005).

Obesity Trends Among U.S. Adults

Map

Date: 2004

Source: Centers for Disease Control and Prevention (CDC). <http://www.cdc.gov/nccdphp/dnpa/obesity/trend/maps> (accessed August 20, 2005). The map shows trends in obesity in the United States during 1991–2004.

About the Author: The Centers for Disease Control and Prevention is a federal government agency that provides health and safety information for U.S. citizens and international health professionals. It reports accurate and timely information regarding health issues, and develops and applies disease prevention and control measures. The CDC is also involved in health promotion and education.

INTRODUCTION

The surveillance of behavioral factors that increase the risk of chronic disease is a key epidemiological (the study and documentation of disease patterns) responsibility of the Centers for Disease Control and Prevention (CDC). Assessing trends in the prevalence of certain behaviors such as smoking and excess calorie consumption is an important surveillance activity for calculating and predicting the current and future burden of chronic illness in the United States.

In 1984, the CDC established the Behavioral Risk Factor Surveillance System (BRFSS) to help in the accumulation and statistical analysis of health and safety data using a telephone survey. The surveillance survey gathers reports on fifty-four different behavioral risk areas. The BRFSS is used by the states to generate policies and initiate disease prevention programs, often with the support of the CDC.

One of the major programs funded by the CDC is the National Nutrition and Physical Activity Program to Prevent Obesity and Other Chronic Diseases. The program provides assistance with training of health professionals, and community initiatives to encourage healthier eating and physical activity. The objective of this program is to assist nutritionists in counseling patients to establish healthy eating habits by reducing calorie intake, increasing the consumption of fruits and vegetables, establishing a balanced diet, and maintaining a healthy body weight.

▍ PRIMARY SOURCE

OBESITY TRENDS AMONG U.S. ADULTS

See primary source image.

SIGNIFICANCE

During the past twenty years, there has been a dramatic increase in obesity in the United States. In 1991, four states had obesity prevalence rates of 15 to 19 percent and no states had rates at or above 20 percent. In 2004, seven states had obesity prevalence rates of 15 to 19 percent; thirty-three states had rates of 20 to 24 percent; and nine states had rates greater than 25 percent.

The rapid increase in obesity rates between 1985 and 2004 has been blamed on a number of factors. The major contributors to these have been identified by the CDC and population health researchers as high-fat, high-calorie diets; reduced physical activity, due mainly to increased time spent watching television,

working on computers, or playing video games; and an increased dependence on automobiles for transportation, even for short distances. According to the CDC map, the most pronounced increase in obesity prevalence has been in the Southern and Midwestern United States. This could involve dietary patterns as well as racial composition and other lifestyle patterns. The prevalence of obesity is higher in the African American and Latino minority population.

The diets of people living in western nations, especially Americans, are characterized by an increased consumption of convenience and "fast" foods with a higher fat or sugar content than more traditional foods. These changes in eating habits are primarily attributed to longer working hours and to less time spent preparing meals at home. Along with the changes in type of food consumed, portion sizes have increased dramatically over the past twenty years, particularly in fast food outlets. This combination of factors has resulted in significantly increased calorie intake.

According to the CDC, based on body mass index (BMI) statistics, approximately 65 percent of Americans were classified as overweight and 30 percent of adults over twenty years of age were obese in 2004—about 60 million people. While BMI has shortcomings as a measure of obesity (e.g., the confounding of body fat and muscle mass), trends in BMI are generally indicative of obesity trends. Although the percentage of overweight people has not increased significantly over the past ten years, the level of obesity has nearly doubled, from 11.6 percent in 1995 to 22.1 percent in 2005. This increase has occurred in all age groups, although the highest percentage is among adults between fifty and sixty-four years of age. Disturbingly, 16 percent of children between six and nineteen years of age are overweight.

A significant consequence of the obesity epidemic is an increase in the level of chronic or life-threatening diseases, such as type 2 diabetes, hypertension, stroke, osteoarthritis, some cancers (endometrial, breast, and colon), high cholesterol levels, and respiratory problems. The percentage of people at risk for such conditions nationwide in the United States increased from 29.7 percent in 1995 to 58.9 percent in 2002. This increase in chronic or life-threatening diseases has led to a dramatic increase in direct and indirect medical costs. In 2000, these costs were estimated to be more than 117 billion dollars.

Because obesity results from reduced physical activity as well as increased calorie consumption, CDC campaigns also target physical exercise. According to CDC data from 2000, over 26 percent

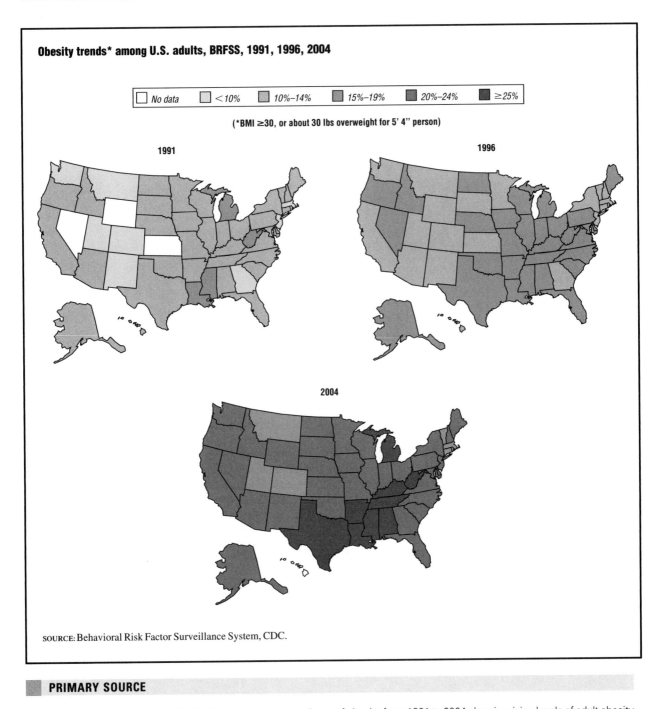

Obesity trends* among U.S. adults, BRFSS, 1991, 1996, 2004

No data   <10%   10%–14%   15%–19%   20%–24%   ≥25%

(*BMI ≥30, or about 30 lbs overweight for 5' 4" person)

1991

1996

2004

SOURCE: Behavioral Risk Factor Surveillance System, CDC.

PRIMARY SOURCE

Obesity Trends Among U.S. Adults State by state comparisons of obesity from 1991 to 2004 showing rising levels of adult obesity in the United States. CENTERS FOR DISEASE CONTROL AND PREVENTION

of Americans, including children and teenagers, are not getting enough exercise. The decrease in physical activity among people in younger age brackets, often ascribed to more time spent watching television or using computers, is particularly alarming because it multiplies the long-term population risk of the chronic diseases mentioned above.

The rise of obesity among children is of particular concern. According to the American Obesity Association (AOA), "Today's youth are considered the most inactive generation in history caused in part by reductions in school physical education programs and unavailable or unsafe community recreational facilities." The AOA calls the trend toward obesity in

Lilian Reyes, 37, makes meat pies for sale at her home in Santiago, Chile, April 29, 2004. Lillian is a member of the Chilean Movement of Morbid Obese People (MOM), an organization fighting to have the morbid obesity condition covered by public and private health insurance companies. AP/WIDE WORLD PHOTOS.

children "the major health care challenge for the twenty-first century." The AOA is an advocacy group that sponsors research into the treatment and cure of obesity and pushes for the coverage of obesity treatments under health insurance.

The extent of the emerging health crisis associated with childhood obesity is exemplified by several trends. About 30 percent of children aged six to eleven are considered overweight and 15 percent are classified by the CDC as obese. The figures for adolescents (ages twelve to nineteen) are similar. Excess weight in childhood and adolescence has been found to predict overweight status in adults, particularly when there is a familial pattern of obesity. In one study reported by the AOA, overweight children aged ten to fourteen with at least one overweight or obese parent were reported to have a 79 percent likelihood of becoming overweight or obese adults.

Numerous studies in the major chronic disease areas have demonstrated that excess weight during childhood and particularly adolescence is related to elevated morbidity and mortality in adulthood. Children and adolescents with moderate to severe asthma have a significantly higher prevalence of overweight status than a matched control group. The prevalence of type 2 diabetes has quadrupled in children and doubled in adolescents from 1975 to 2000. This increase is largely accounted for by a parallel increase in the prevalence of obesity in these age groups. Obese children have been found to have a prevalence of persistently elevated blood pressure that is nine times higher than the prevalence among non-obese children.

Growing evidence in obesity research indicates that obesity, and childhood obesity in particular, is a medical, social and economic time bomb for Western society. In recent years, the epidemic of obesity with a concomitant increase in the prevalence of diabetes and cardiovascular disease is spreading to emerging industrializing nations as well, notably China. All indications point to obesity becoming a condition that is as widespread and as lethal and expensive a risk factor for disease and death as smoking was in the twentieth century.

FURTHER RESOURCES

Periodicals

Calle, E. E., et al. "Body Mass Index and Mortality in a Prospective Cohort of U.S. Adults." *New England Journal of Medicine* 341 (October 7, 1999): 1097–1105.

Mokdad, A. H., et al. "The Continuing Epidemics of Obesity and Diabetes in the United States." *Journal of the American Medical Association* 286 (September 12, 2001):1195–1200.

———. "Prevalence of Obesity, Diabetes, and Obesity-related Health Risk Factors, 2001." *Journal of the American Medical Association* 289 (January 1, 2003): 76–79.

Web sites

American Obesity Association Web site. "AOA Fact Sheet." <www.obesity.org> (accessed February 1, 2006).

The Centers for Disease Control and Prevention. "Overweight and Obesity: Defining Overweight and Obesity." <http://www.cdc.gov/nccdphp/dnpa/obesity/defining.htm> (accessed May 10, 2005).

National Institute of Diabetes and Digestive and Kidney Diseases. "Understanding Adult Obesity." <http://win.niddk.nih.gov/publications/understanding.htm> (accessed May 10, 2005).

U.S. Department of Health and Human Services. "The Surgeon General's Call to Action to Prevent and Decrease Overweight and Obesity." <http://www.surgeongeneral.gov/topics/obesity/calltoaction/CalltoAction.pdf> (accessed May 10, 2005).

America Is Still Working on Its Abs

Newspaper article

By: Alex Williams

Date: March 27, 2005

Throughout the years, a variety of fitness tools have been developed to help people lose weight. Here, a woman uses a vibrating exercise belt in 1946. AP/WIDE WORLD PHOTOS.

Source: Alex Williams. "America Is Still Working on Its Abs.". *New York Times* (March 27, 2005): Section 9, Page 1.

About the Author: Since 1989, Alex Williams has worked as a newspaper reporter, magazine editor, television broadcast anchor, and online journalist. He holds a master's degree from the Medill School of Journalism at Northwestern University.

INTRODUCTION

According to the United States Centers for Disease Control and prevention, obesity is the second leading preventable cause of death in the United States. Excess weight has been linked to a variety of health problems, including diabetes, high blood pressure, and an increased risk of heart disease.

The quest to shed weight has spawned a multibillion dollar industry in the United States alone, encompassing nutritional and fitness-related approaches. Some exercise programs such as aerobics were designed primarily to improve cardiovascular fitness. Increased muscle strength and fat loss tend to be additional benefits of improved cardiovascular endurance. Other fitness programs, in particular weightlifting, focus on building strength and on toning the body.

The latter is associated with a flat stomach and prominent abdominal muscles (popularly dubbed "a six-pack", in recognition of the three pairs of abdominal muscles). Exercise regimens such as pilates and yoga, and the use of aids such as the medicine ball all target the abdominal muscles. This approach is known as core conditioning.

Core muscles are those attached to the spine or pelvis; these include the transversus abdominis—the muscles of the pelvic floor in the lower portion of the torso, and the lats and obliques in the middle and upper torso. The core is also called the powerhouse muscle group, as much of the power of movement and stability arise from here.

The premise behind core conditioning is that a strong midsection will increase both agility and the range of available physical activities. Stability as well as core strength (abdominal and lower-back muscles) are addressed using one-sided body weight exercises, balance boards, and stability balls. Properly accomplished, core conditioning mimics movements done in day-to-day living and sports. However, as with any popular fitness approach, core conditioning can be exploited for fast profit at the expense of negligible fitness gain and, even worse, the possibility of physical injury.

Fitness fads often arise from the participation of a recognizable celebrity. Examples include the aerobics approaches popularized by Richard Simmons and Jane Fonda in the 1970s. Related fitness fads include Jazzercise and Tae Bo (a combination of aerobics and martial arts movement). The presence of a charismatic and fit spokesperson helps a fitness regimen become popular. Similarly, celebrities like Chuck Norris and Christie Brinkley have helped popularize exercise equipment as an aid to achieving muscular and cardiovascular improvement.

PRIMARY SOURCE

Yes, it all seems so very mid-'90s. And since then the fitness industry, which depends on new fads to keep slothful Americans renewing health club memberships and buying workout videos, has introduced many novelties. There have been trampolines and spinning bikes, Soloflexes, Bowflexes, and gravity boots.

But the obsession of Americans with their abdominal muscles is apparently forever. For the latest trend at the gym, look to the past. Consider that the six fitness guides on the market four years ago with the word "abs" in their names have expanded to 28 today, according to the Books in Print database.

"Abs rule," said Kurt Brungardt, who wrote the best-selling *Complete Book of Abs* (1993) and just finished the manuscript for *The Complete Book of Core Training*, whose title includes one of the latest fitness buzz-words—describing a routine that is focused on the stomach.

Brungardt has tried for success with *The Complete Book of Shoulders and Arms* and *The Complete Book of Butt and Legs*. But nothing could match selling Americans ways to a well-defined set of rectus abdominus muscles. . . .

Besides core conditioning, another new fitness craze focuses on the abdominal region: Pilates, whose practitioners have increased more than fivefold over the past five years, according to SGMA International, a sporting-goods trade group. These days "all roads lead to abs," confirmed Dawn-Marie Ickes, an owner of a Pilates studio in Studio City, Calif.

A skeptic might wonder, why abs? Why not pectoral or gluteus muscles?

David Zinczenko, the editor in chief of *Men's Health*, whose current bestseller, *The Abs Diet: The Six-Week Plan to Flatten Your Stomach and Keep You Lean for Life* (Rodale, 2004), is in its 18th printing, explained: "Up until the 1960s or so, broad shoulders or biceps were features that made women swoon. Shoulders and biceps say, 'I can lift heavy things.' But society has changed. Men don't labor in the fields anymore, so those features are not as essential. Abs are the new biceps. Abs say: 'I'm in control of life, I've got it all together. I can work, play, and still build these.'"

Abs measuring stick Vicki Beck, an accountant who works in television in Los Angeles, is something of an abs measuring stick. Over the past decade, she has been through all the phases: clipping how-to diagrams for the latest crunches from *Self* magazine, buying an abs machine from a late-night infomercial.

Now she has turned to the more holistic approach of Pilates. "Abs, especially the deep, core abs," explained Ickes, her instructor, "are the cornerstone, the building block of every Pilates exercise you do."

Pilates, a workout regimen developed in the early twentieth century by a German boxer and acrobat named Joseph H. Pilates, was adopted in the United States by dancers for George Balanchine and Martha Graham. The number of American practitioners rose to 9.5 million from 1.7 million between 2000 and 2003, according to SGMA International. The workout emphasizes flexibility, strength and balance exercises, even breathing, all in the ultimate service of building strength through the abdomen and spine.

Pilates is not cheap. Beck pays up to $60 a session for the privilege of climbing at least twice a week onto the Wunda chair (basically, a spring-loaded stepladder) at Ickes' studio, which is also a physical therapy clinic called Core Conditioning.

For Beck's birthday this year her boyfriend bought her a Reformer, a Pilates machine with springs, pulleys, and sliding cushions. It looks like a cross between a beach chair and a crossbow.

Reformers sell for as much as $500. Beck keeps hers in a spare bedroom at home, next to her big white rubber stability ball—balls being the last big thing in the abs world—her foam tube roller and her Pilates Magic Circle. (That would be her big rubber ring.)

"The stomach is most important," she said. "We live in Southern California, we go to the beach. More skin does show."

A broader focus than Pilates, core conditioning targets the abs you see, the deeper abs, as well as the lower back and even the pelvic muscles, the so-called girdle of strength. (Pilates techniques are often a component of core programs.)

A term that emerged from physical therapists in the '90s, core has become perhaps the most marketable word in the fitness business, several trainers said. Reebok sells a core board for $149.99. It is a plastic disc, which teeters on an axis at its center. Standing on it roughly approximates the experience of trying to balance on a lurching subway train. "Core is where the value icon is now," Brungardt said. "It breathes new life into the ab craze. It's the next generation."

Then again, maybe the craze is already shifting. . . .

Forestalling an aging body The new approach appears more grown up. Fantasies of a Brad Pitt washboard (Kate Bosworth's in "Blue Crush" might be the female ideal) still inspire some younger absaholics, but particularly among baby boomers lurching through their 50s, abs mania can mean another way of forestalling the creaks of an aging body.

"It used to be this huge aesthetic push, how ripped can you be?" said Chris Imbo, a personal trainer in New York. "It was the classic six-pack everyone was chasing after. That was something that was a hard reach for most people."

You don't have to travel far in fitness circles to hear the conclusion that the "hard body" days are over. One need only track the success of the Curves International chain of gyms, intended for full-size women, or the Bally Total Fitness chain ads that featured regular people,

Jazzercise, a form of aerobics that combines exercise with jazz music, was created by Judi Sheppard Missett (center). It helps people improve their flexibility, reduce stress, maintain a healthy heart, and lose weight. ©DOUG MENUEZ/CORBIS.

including some with a few extra pounds and a few extra years on them.

Perhaps no one represents the shift to total-body health more than Zinczenko, the editor of *Men's Health*. His book, with its 120-decibel blaze-orange cover, has sold 350,000 copies, and that is before you get to "The Abs Diet Workout" DVD or the spinoff recipe guide, *The Abs Diet Eat Right Every Time Guide*.

Men's Health, which comes out 10 times a year, has published about 60 articles on abs in the past 2½ years.

Anyone would think the country was ripe for an abs overdose. But in one poll of more than 3,000 men conducted by Zinczenko's magazine, to be published in the June issue, respondents were asked which muscle group was their No. 1 priority for the beach season. Abdominals trounced the nearest challenger, pectorals, by 70 percent to 15 percent.

SIGNIFICANCE

Fitness fads, by definition, wane in popularity after a time. Some people may go on to try other fitness approaches or diet solutions, with varying degrees of success. However, what begins as a fitness fad can become the basis of a solid fitness program. Aerobics is one example. While the numbers of aerobics enthusiasts may have tapered from the millions of Americans who went to aerobics studios and health clubs in the 1970s and 1980s, the cardiovascular approach to fitness targeted by aerobics remains a solid mainstream fitness strategy. Thus, a fitness fad can be the beginning of a longer-term fitness program.

In addition to physical activities, diets can become a focus of a fitness campaign. Various popular diets have emphasized proteins or carbohydrates as a means to shed weight. Rigid diets can sometimes be successful in the short-term, but, for long-term fitness, a diet that is part of a healthier long-term approach to everyday food choices (such as Weight Watchers) tends to be more successful. Indeed, a report published in the January 2005 issue of *Annals of Internal Medicine* reported that of the ten most popular weight loss programs in the United States, only Weight Watchers could be proven to be a means of successfully losing weight while maintaining healthy eating habits.

Like any fad, fitness fads can be exploited by those seeking profit. Americans spent over fifteen billion dollars in 2004 seeking physical fitness, including almost ten billion dollars on gym memberships and about five billion dollars on home exercise equipment. Although few of the myriad of exercise products are tested for efficacy (effectiveness), the U.S. Consumer Products Safety Commission regularly tests exercise products for safety, issues recalls, and reports unsafe exercise products to the public.

FURTHER RESOURCES

Books

American College of Sports Medicine. *ACSM Fitness Book.* Champaign, Ill.: Human Kinetics, 2003.

Periodicals

Johnson, Dan. "Tracking Fitness: From Fashion Fad to Health Trend." *The Futurist* 32 (May 1998): 4, 8.

Web sites

American Council on Exercise. "Is the AB-DOer a Don't?" <http://www.acefitness.org/getfit/abdoerstudy.aspx> (accessed May 2, 2005).

U.S. Consumer Products Safety Commission. <http://www.cpsc.gov/index.html> (accessed January 20, 2006).

Fresh Faces

Cosmetic Surgery Boom

Magazine article

By: Sascha de Gersdorff

Date: May 2005

Source: Gersdorff, Sacha. "Fresh Faces." *Boston Magazine* (May 2005).

About the Author: Sascha de Gersdorff is lifestyle editor of the *Boston Magazine*, a monthly magazine about the city of Boston, Massachusetts, with a circulation of half a million.

INTRODUCTION

Plastic surgery can be used in both a therapeutic and in an aesthetic manner. Therapeutic surgery is about restoring the form and function of practically any part of the human body, while aesthetic plastic surgery is concerned with improving an individual's physical appearance. In practice, there is probably no strict dividing line between the two types of plastic surgery. People often assume the word plastic means artificial when in fact it comes from the Greek word *plastikos*, which means to mold or give form to. Using increasingly sophisticated tools, the plastic surgeon can perform tasks as diverse as reconstructing a woman's breasts after surgery for breast cancer, remodeling the nose and chin, or removing acne scars with a technique called dermabrasion.

There is evidence that plastic surgery was used more than 4,000 years ago to treat facial injuries. But it really came into its own during World War I (1915–1918), when plastic surgeons were called on to rebuild soldiers' faces that had been shattered by modern weapons. The 1960s saw many new scientific advances, such as the use of silicone for breast implants. Today, the aesthetic side of plastic surgery allows women and men alike to turn back the signs of aging and to remodel their facial and bodily features. Once seen as the province of the middle-aged, plastic surgery is now more common in younger age groups, as the article below illustrates.

PRIMARY SOURCE

... For more and more teens, achieving the ideal look means scheduling time under the plastic surgeon's knife.

Kristin wanted a new nose. A better nose. A resculpted, slightly smaller version of the original, with no bump on its bridge and a shorter, perkier tip. It wasn't that she was ugly, or that her nose was so terrible: Kristin just wanted her features to be symmetrical. But doctors said she would have to wait at least a year before considering cosmetic surgery. After all, she was only 14.

At 15, Kristin got her wish. A Boston plastic surgeon performed the long-awaited rhinoplasty during her school's spring break. The petite, blond Newton native couldn't be happier with the results. "It turned out exactly how I wanted it," Kristin, now 17, says, "I feel like my face finally fits together."

Others agreed. Most girls at her west suburban high school told her she looked pretty and praised her new look. And, influenced by a youth culture that is increasingly open to all things cosmetic, some did a little resculpting of their own. "My best friend just got her nose done last summer," says Kristin (whose name, like those of other young patients quoted in this story, has been changed).

"And my other best friend is planning on doing it as soon as she can."

Plastic surgery is a national hot topic, thanks in no small part to television shows like ABC's *Extreme Makeover*, Fox's *The Swan*, MTV's *I Want a Famous Face*, and a veritable bonanza of other media attention. Everywhere they look, young Americans are bombarded with promises of planned perfection. Ads for cosmetic procedures pepper magazines and newspapers, toned Hollywood actors sport wrinkle-free figures, and celebrity rags rave over young starlets with impossible combinations of tiny waists and huge breasts.

The pressure to look young and beautiful is at an all-time high, and more and more people are picking up the phone to schedule surgical enhancements. Americans spent $12.5 billion on cosmetic procedures last year, according to the American Society for Aesthetic Plastic Surgery. Since 1997, the number of both surgical and nonsurgical procedures performed annually has increased by a whopping 465 percent.

"The television shows have really captured the country's imagination and attention," says Dr. James May, director of plastic surgery at Massachusetts General Hospital. "The sensationalism of those programs has brought plastic surgery to the minds of young people and their parents. It's now a dinner-table conversation."

And the nation is changing its perspective. Whereas some Americans used to keep their tummy tucks and Botox shots a secret, they're now showing them off with pride. Today, 60 percent of women approve of cosmetic surgery, while 82 percent say they would not be embarrassed by other people knowing that they'd had some. And these aren't just aging narcissists: 34 percent of 18- to 24-year-olds say they would definitely consider surgery for themselves, the highest proportion of all age groups.

Many teens like Kristin already have. The plastic surgery society notes that Americans 18 and younger had 46,198 chemical peels, 17,233 rhinoplasties, 4,211 breast augmentations, and 4,074 Botox injections last year alone. All in all, teenagers underwent nearly a quarter million cosmetic procedures last year.

"Teenagers are the new market," says Sharlene Hesse-Biber, professor of sociology at Boston College. "Magazines have pushed the envelope on what it means to be beautiful, and surgery is now a way to deal with body issues. We're a very visual and quick-fix society. Young people are now getting that quick fix, that instant body."

When he was 16, Brian started thinking about enhancing his appearance. He had breathing problems and was unhappy with his nose. So he did something about it. A surgeon performed a rhinoplasty. That same year, Brian paid for a chin implant. "What's great about cosmetic surgery," says Brian, who went on to attend Boston University, is that "you have the ability to change what couldn't otherwise be changed." He says he'd recommend surgery to other young people as a "self-esteem boost."

"All you have to do is watch any television show, and you will see relatively uncovered, young, supposedly ideal-looking Americans," says Chestnut Hill's SkinCare Physicians co-director Dr. Jeffrey Dover. "Twenty years ago, liposuction didn't even exist, but now young women are coming in for it. They're looking at all the magazines, from *People* to *Vogue* to *Seventeen*. Large breasts with skinny bodies are very popular right now. Look at Christina Aguilera. She has very large breasts in a tiny body, and teenagers want to look like her."

It's not just girls feeling the pressure. Young men, inspired by the metrosexual movement, are also taking shortcuts to better looks. Dover says his practice has seen a dramatic increase in the number of 16- to 19-year-old males who come in for laser hair removal. He says they might be prompted by *GQ* and *Men's Health*, whose cover models sport nary a hair on their bodies.

Newbury Street surgeon Dr. Ramsey Alsarraf agrees that cosmetically enhanced celebrities' looks are affecting the way teenagers view themselves. "I've had young boys bring in 10 pictures of Brad Pitt and his nose from different angles and say 'I want to look like this.' Those are unrealistic expectations. Generally if someone says they want to look like Britney Spears or J.Lo, that puts up a red flag."

Lisa sees red flags, too. Now a 21-year-old college senior at the University of Maryland, Lisa had plastic surgery as a teenager. She, too, is pleased with the results of her rhinoplasty, which she'd been contemplating since middle school. But she says she's seen the cosmetic culture shift since then. Lisa thinks more people find surgery acceptable and that invasive procedures have become "easier than the alternatives, such as making an effort to accept yourself as beautiful or physically working hard to lose weight." Teenagers who want to look like models or celebrities they see should think again, she says.

That's what many plastic surgeons say, too. But all too often, they say, teenagers brush off any long-term implications in favor of immediate results. This blasé attitude, coupled with widening acceptance, helps young people gloss over the potentially ugly details of surgical procedures. Nor do many Boston doctors outright refuse to perform most such surgery on teenagers, though some ask the kids to wait a few years.

"I want a 17-year-old to understand that if she's going to have breast implants, she might need a new procedure at age 27," May says. "Then at age 47 she might have another revision. I would say the likelihood of her needing to have these other procedures is around 50 percent. It's very important to send the message loud and clear that surgery early in life is heading the patient down the pathway of having more operations."

Some wonder if even teenagers who have smaller, noninvasive procedures such as laser hair removal or microdermabrasion might become mentally predisposed to surgery. While there is no solid research to support this theory, the notion that kids can become "addicted" to cosmetic alteration doesn't come as a surprise to sociologist Hesse-Biber.

"We're entering this cultlike status," she says. "Every time we have a little wrinkle, we want to run in for some Botox. We're becoming addicted. I'm not saying that women shouldn't look beautiful, but when surgery becomes the fix and you still don't feel good about yourself, what then?"

Alarmed parents are asking similar questions in response to a perceived nationwide increase in teenage plastic surgeries. And the media is fueling the fire. Nearly every major American newspaper and magazine has run stories on teenage breast augmentations and liposuctions, or procedures gone horribly wrong.

The attention rose to such heights that in February the American Society of Plastic Surgeons released a statement attributing the teenage cosmetic surgery "epidemic" to overblown media hype. A recent study found that only 5 percent of college-aged women have had cosmetic surgery. But that same study revealed that more than 60 percent of the same group surveyed could see themselves having at least one procedure in their lives.

Back in Boston, teenagers' cravings for physical perfection appear not quite as high as those of teens in places like Miami and Los Angeles, where breast augmentations are reported to be popular high-school graduation gifts. Despite its liberal airs, Boston remains steeped in conservative tradition and shrouded by a hush-hush mentality about cosmetic surgery. Many people here still consider cosmetic procedures déclassé. But local doctors say they have many teenagers come in for rhinoplasties, hair removal, and Botox, though requests from teens for breast augmentation are rare. Even rarer are doctors who would perform the procedure the Food and Drug Administration does not approve for girls under 18.

"You'd have to look hard in Boston for someone who's pushing breast implants on 16-year-old girls," Alsarraf says. "If you can't vote or smoke, should you really be able to have a synthetic piece of plastic put into your chest? That doesn't make much sense to me."

It doesn't make much sense to Kristin either. But while her mother says she would be shocked by a high school student having a breast augmentation, Kristin seems nonplused. "At my school, it doesn't happen enough for

people not to be surprised," she says. "But it wouldn't be like 'Oh my God!'" Cosmetic procedures have simply become part of the culture, something she says her friends all talk about briefly before moving on to the next topic.

Kristin's mother admits she knows at least one parent who would let her own daughter get much-desired bigger breasts. And May says that although the media reports may be exaggerated, all the fuss does represent a fear that soon kids will be planning their dream bodies at an alarmingly young age.

Asked if she would consider having additional cosmetic procedures, Kristin nods enthusiastically. "Yeah, definitely," she says. She says there's nothing wrong with wanting to feel better about yourself. "I'm not going out searching for things to do, but if there was something I wanted to change, wanted to be different, I would do it."

SIGNIFICANCE

Young people are especially vulnerable to media images and may want to look like their favorite pop star or a famous model. But the desire for plastic surgery may not necessarily be immature or frivolous—treating, say, severe acne scars or remodeling a nose can lead to a great improvement in self-esteem and social skills that will genuinely enhance quality of life and psychological health. Since there has been an increase in plastic surgery procedures across the board in the last decade, it is hardly surprising that there has been an increase in the number of teens having these procedures. But the proportion of teens having plastic surgery has stayed roughly the same, at about 2.7 percent of the total.

Nose reshaping, known clinically as rhinoplasty, is the most commonly carried out surgical procedure on those aged eighteen and under, according to the American Society for Aesthetic Plastic Surgery. It can be performed once the nose has completed 90 percent of its growth, which happens at age thirteen or fourteen for girls and fifteen or sixteen for boys. Chin augmentation also may be carried out with rhinoplasty to make the face look more balanced. Breast reduction can be helpful for girls with overlarge breasts that are causing back and shoulder pain, but it should be delayed until the breasts are fully developed. Breast asymmetry also can be treated and breast implants are generally allowed for this indication and for posttrauma reconstruction in girls under the age of eighteen. Gynecomastia, a condition occurring in boys in which the breast area is overdeveloped, can be special considerations which a responsible surgeon must take into account. First, physical maturity must be assessed; operating before growth is complete could interfere with natural development, and the results of the surgery may be complicated by further growth in years to come. It is important to look at the young person's emotional maturity and their reasons for wanting surgery. If he or she has unrealistic expectations, then these must be corrected. The patient and the parents/guardians also must understand the risks involved and the length of recovery time. If all these issues are addressed, then plastic surgery may well be an appropriate solution in certain cases. Age alone should not be a barrier to a person benefiting from plastic surgery. Equally, however, it should not be performed for purely frivolous reasons. The data suggest that there is not exactly an epidemic of teens wanting to change their appearance. But as surgery becomes less invasive and more sophisticated, an increase in demand is likely.

FURTHER RESOURCES

Books

Libal, Autumn. *Can I Change the Way I Look?: A Teen's Guide to the Health Implications of Cosmetic Surgery, Makeovers, and Beyond.* London: Mason Crest, 2004.

Winkler, Kathleen. *Cosmetic Surgery for Teens: Choices and Consequences.* Hillside, N.J.: Enslow, 2003.

Web sites

American Society for Aesthetic Plastic Surgery. "Teenagers and Cosmetic Plastic Surgery." <http://www.surgery.org/press/news-release.php?iid=1> (accessed November 11, 2005).

American Society of Plastic Surgeons. "The History of Plastic Surgery." <http://www.plastic-surgeon.org/pshistry.htm> (accessed November 11, 2005).

Two contestants pose during a beauty pageant in China in 2004. Unlike other beauty competitions, this contest is only open to women who have had plastic surgery. AP/WIDE WORLD PHOTOS.

corrected by plastic surgery to give a more masculine body contour.

Plastic surgery should not be undertaken lightly at any age, especially for purely aesthetic reasons. All surgery carries a risk and, for teens, there are some

Alternative Medicine

Alternative medicine refers to the use of nontraditional remedies (at least in the context of Western medicine) or clinically unproven supplements or techniques to improve physical fitness or cure illness. These remedies include diet therapies, like vegetarianism; herbal and homeopathic medicines; physical and mental disciplines like yoga, meditation, and tai chi; and therapies like acupuncture and chiropractic.

Because the clinical benefits of most alternative therapies have not been established in peer-reviewed Western medical literature, their use has generated both medical and social debate. Indeed, many medications have been sold that have little medical value, but appeal to consumer fear and preconceptions. However, studies show that some forms of alternative medicine do prove beneficial.

The growing popularity of alternative forms of medicine reflects a social change in which individuals are increasingly assuming greater responsibility for their own health. One area that individuals can control most easily is their diet. Vegetarianism and other diets that emphasize fruits and vegetables and discourage meat consumption, almost unheard of in North America a generation ago, are today socially acceptable diet alternatives.

One popular herbal medicine is an extract of a North American perennial called echinacea. The extract—the most widely used herbal product in the United States—is claimed to strengthen a person's immune system, and so is used by many people as a means of preventing maladies such as the common cold or influenza. Studies of the remedy are mixed, though, with some showing benefits in taking echinacea, and others showing no benefit.

Yoga—a series of movements and controlled breathing exercises that emphasizes meditative behavior—has also become a popular form of relaxation and pain relief, as well as a fitness regimen. Meditation, which involves sitting quietly and focusing the mind, can also have positive effects on physical and mental well-being. Tai chi, a traditional Chinese practice that uses slow-moving series of movements, has been shown to help seniors gain balance and body awareness.

In acupuncture, an ancient Chinese remedy, the practitioner uses thin, solid needles that penetrate the skin at defined points. When manipulated by hand or used to conduct an electrical current, the treatment eases a variety of pain types, relieves nausea, and lessens the symptoms of asthma. Although it has been long regarded with some skepticism by the Western medical community, acupuncture is increasingly being accepted as a valid therapy. In fact, the National Institutes of Health and the U.S. Food and Drug Administration have endorsed its use for pain relief.

Manipulation of the body, particularly the spine, by a chiropractic physician can sometimes provide relief from health problems associated with muscular, nervous, or skeletal malfunctions. While as recently as the 1970s chiropractors faced opposition from traditionally trained doctors, the approach is now seen as an effective and relatively low-cost way to treat some disorders, particularly back injuries.

The National Center for Complementary and Alternative Medicine, a part of the U.S. National Institutes of Health, seeks to investigate the safety and effectiveness of alternative medical therapies and integrate effective alternatives into more traditional treatment regimens.

Yoga and Transcendental Meditation

Photograph

By: Genevieve Naylor

Date: 1962

Source: Corbis Corporation.

About the Photographer: Genevieve Naylor was a photo-journalist whose professional career spanned nearly 50 years. Her subject matter ranged from high fashion studio and field location work to coverage of political conflicts and global events for the Associated Press and for several commercial magazines.

INTRODUCTION

Jane Fonda was successfully able to be a proponent of cutting edge fitness and natural healing trends for several decades in America. In this particular case, however, she was somewhat ahead of the curve. She began practicing yoga during the 1960s, at the beginning of the natural health movement, when yoga, the natural and holistic health movements, and various relaxation techniques, such as transcendental meditation, were just beginning to be practiced in the United States. In the early 1990s, after releasing several tremendously successful aerobics and workout videos, Jane Fonda released a yoga practice video which harkened back to her practice of this spiritual, meditative, and healthful discipline some three decades earlier.

The origins of the terminology for yoga practice have been traced to Sanskrit words for the concept of focused attention and concentration upon a concept or practice that is to be applied (not a literal translation). The theoretical roots of the discipline of yoga lie in Indian philosophy, in which it is known as one of the six orthodox philosophical systems. One of the founding texts of the spiritual practice of yoga is the *Bhagavad Gita,* in which the discipline of yoga is described as a practice in which the individual consciousness is able to attain a connection to the universal consciousness. The modern practice of yoga consists of various poses, or asanas, which are precise and controlled body postures. The overall aim of the asanas is to achieve a state of physical, emotional, and spiritual harmony.

In the medical or rehabilitation context, the practice of therapeutic yoga has been tailored to promote healing from injuries, particularly those

■ PRIMARY SOURCE

Yoga and Transcendental Meditation. Actress Jane Fonda in a yoga pose in 1962. Yoga and meditation have again emerged as complimentary activities in maintaining a healthy lifestyle and in treating conditions ranging from lower back pain to anxiety disorders. ©GENEVIEVE NAYLOR/CORBIS.

involving the skeletal system. Yoga has also become an accepted form of complementary treatment for behavioral health conditions that can benefit from focused and controlled forms of relaxation. The principles of therapeutic yoga incorporate both the physical discipline of traditional yoga postures and the inner, body-mind of contemporary psychotherapy.

Natural or holistic (sometimes called wholistic) health care is based on a philosophical orientation that considers all aspects of the person, and conceptualizes the mind and body as a unified, integrated system. The focus is on the maintenance of wellness and the prevention of disease. Holistic practitioners look at the entire life circumstance of the individual in determining the appropriate regimen, and often suggest very subtle lifestyle changes, such as a dietary shift to include or exclude a certain type of food (for example, the elimination of wheat products from the diet), or the incorporation of a particular practice, such as yoga or meditation, into daily life.

Yoga is designed to harmonize the mind, body, and spirit. It helps people relax and become more flexible. Some forms also improve strength. ©MIROSLAV ZAJÍC/CORBIS.

PRIMARY SOURCE

YOGA AND TRANSCENDENTAL MEDITATION
See primary source image.

SIGNIFICANCE

In addition to the renewed popularity of the practice of yoga, the popularity of holistic and natural medicine practice began to gain recognition in America during the last half of the twentieth century. Various forms of meditation began to grow in popularity as well. Transcendental meditation (also called TM) was one form that gained early notoriety, in part because of its association with the stars of films and the popular music culture.

The basic practice of transcendental meditation involves brief periods of quietly focused attention, also called a state of restful alertness, in which the mind and the body are progressively quieted, achieving a deep state of physical and cognitive relaxation, called transcendental consciousness. Transcendental consciousness is described by TM practitioners as a unique state of consciousness, apart from waking, sleeping, and dreaming. The proponents of transcendental meditation purport that this practice encourages fuller activation of the brain's innate potential, increasing intellectual capacity, productivity, and overall mental and physical well-being, leading to a happier, healthier, more fulfilled life experience.

More mainstream practitioners of meditation (not TM), describe it as a discipline that involves the achievement of a state of profound relaxation of the body and mind. For those whose daily routines regularly involve the exercise of meditation, it is generally one part of a cohesive style of living, referred to by many practitioners of Buddhism as mindfulness. There are many varieties of meditation, and the successful practice of any of them has been associated with quantifiable health benefits. Meditation often decreases the subjective experience of stress. The relaxation associated with meditation lowers blood pressure, slows and deepens the breathing rate, and decreases the heart rate. Other measurable physiological changes associated with meditative states include some lowering of cortisol and lactate levels in the blood, lowered muscle tension, and often, increased serotonin production, which helps stabilize or improves mood.

There are also myriad emotional and psychological health benefits associated with the practice of meditation, such as improvement in overall mood, decreased experience of anxiety, depression, and emotional lability, diminished irritability, diminished experience of chronic (or temporary, such as postoperative) pain, increased focus and concentration abilities, enhanced receptivity to knowledge acquisition and learning, increased feelings of happiness and well-being, and increased experience (and objective expression, quite often) of creativity.

Therapeutic yoga, a less-intense form of yoga that focuses primarily on breathing techniques that help increase lung capacity and reduce stress, is the subject of several ongoing clinical studies sponsored by the National Institutes of Health. Results so far indicate that therapeutic yoga, practiced regularly and involving a variety of postures, deep breathing, and meditation exercises, can provide some relief for people with asthma, insomnia, chronic back pain, arthritis, and some obsessive compulsive/anxiety disorders, among other conditions. Other studies are examining potential benefits of yoga in persons with diabetes and multiple sclerosis.

FURTHER RESOURCES
Books

Kessel, Frank. Patricia L. Rosenfield, and Norman B. Anderson, eds. *Expanding the Boundaries of Health and Social Science: Case Studies in Interdisciplinary Innovation.* New York, NY: Oxford University Press, 2003.

Mitchell, Stephen. *Bhagavad Gita: A New Translation.* New York, NY: Three Rivers Press, 2000.

Web sites

The Transcendental Meditation Program. "The TM Program at a Glance." <http://www.tm.org/discover/glance/index.html> (accessed January 16, 2006).

Yoga, Health & Fitness. "Hatha Yoga Styles-Types of Hatha Yoga-Yoga Information." <http://www.yoga-for-health-and-fitness.com/yoga-styles.htm> (accessed January 16, 2006).

More People Trying Vegetarian Diets

Article

By: Dixie Farley

Date: October 1995

Source: *FDA Consumer,* (October 1995): 52–55.

About the Author: This article was written by a staff member of *FDA Consumer,* the official magazine of the U.S. Food and Drug Administration (FDA). Now part of the Department of Health and Human Services, the FDA began in 1862 as a single chemist working for the Department of Agriculture. Today, the agency regulates the production, sale, delivery, and storage of medicine and medical devices, and evaluates applications for new drugs, medical products, and food additives.

INTRODUCTION

In 1971 Frances Moore Lappé's *Diet for a Small Planet* reinvigorated the American vegetarian movement. A researcher into world poverty, Lappé showed that raising animal protein for food required wasteful amounts of energy, land, grain, water, and other natural resources. It would be kinder to the planet and its people, she said, to eat lower down the food chain. Though not a vegetarian herself, Lappé's words struck a chord; the book became a commercial success and the popularity of vegetarianism soared.

The term "vegetarian" was coined by the British Vegetarian Society in the mid-1800s. Around this time in Britain, many people were practically vegetarian by default as beef and pork were very expensive. Only with the introduction of effective refrigeration and freight transport in the early twentieth century did meat became a staple of Western diets.

Diet for a Small Planet was followed four years later by another influential work, *Animal Liberation: A New Ethics for Our Treatment of Animals,* by Australian philosopher Peter Singer. This book spurred the development of the U.S. animal rights movement and the group People for the Ethical Treatment of Animals (PETA), both of which strongly promote vegetarian eating as part of their campaign for animal rights.

The health effects of eating meat were analyzed by Dr. John McDougall in *The McDougall Plan for Super Health and Life-Long Weight Loss* in 1983. He advocated a vegan diet in which no animal products are consumed, a term and concept first espoused by British teacher Donald Watson in the mid-1940s.

In 1987 John Robbins combined the ethical and health arguments for vegetarianism in *Diet for a New America*, which fueled yet another resurgence of interest in vegetarianism. Recognizing the benefits of less meat consumption, the U.S. government revamped its "food pyramid" in the 1990s to emphasize the consumption of grains, vegetables, and fruits. The article below discusses the health benefits of the vegetarian diet.

■ PRIMARY SOURCE

MORE PEOPLE TRYING VEGETARIAN DIETS

Perceiving plant foods as beneficial because they are high in dietary fiber and, generally, lower in saturated fat than animal foods, many people turn to vegetarian diets.

Grain products, for instance, form the base of the U.S. Department of Agriculture and Department of Health and Human Services' Food Guide Pyramid, which recommends 6 to 11 daily servings of bread, cereal, rice, and pasta. Daily intakes advised for other foods are: 3 to 5 servings of vegetables; 2 to 4 servings of fruits; 2 to 3 servings of milk, yogurt, and cheese; and 2 to 3 servings of meat, poultry, fish, dry beans, eggs, and nuts. The guide advises using fats, oils, and sweets sparingly.

And, who hasn't seen signs in their grocer's produce section urging consumers to eat "5 a day for better health"? This slogan reflects a major government-industry campaign to help people eat more fruits and vegetables as part of a high-fiber, low-fat diet that emphasizes variety.

The campaign is consistent with the USDA–DHHS Dietary Guidelines for Americans (<www.cfsan.fda.gov/~lrd/nutguide.txt>), which states, "Most Americans of all ages eat fewer than the recommended number of servings of grain products, vegetables, and fruits, even though consumption of these foods is associated with a substantially lower risk for many chronic diseases, including certain types of cancer" Also noted: "Most vegetarians eat milk products and eggs, and as a group, these lacto-ovo-vegetarians enjoy excellent health."

But health benefits are not the only reason vegetarian diets attract followers.

Certain people, such as Seventh-day Adventists, choose a vegetarian diet because of religious beliefs. Others give up meat because they feel eating animals is unethical. Some believe it's a better use of the earth's resources to eat low on the food chain—that is, to eat plant foods, rather than the animals that eat the plant foods. And many people eat plant foods simply because they are less expensive than animal foods.

It's wise to take precautions, however, when adopting a diet that entirely excludes animal flesh and dairy products, called a vegan diet.

"The more you restrict your diet, the more difficult it is to get the nutrients you need," says John Vanderveen, Ph.D., director of the Food and Drug Administration's Office of Plant and Dairy Foods and Beverages. "To be healthful, vegetarian diets require very careful, proper planning. Nutrition counseling can help you get started on a diet that is nutritionally adequate."

If appropriately planned, vegan diets, though restrictive, can provide adequate nutrition even for children, according to the American Dietetic Association and the Institute of Food Technologists.

Plant Food Benefits Registered dietitian Johanna Dwyer, of Tufts University Medical School and the New England Medical Center Hospital, Boston, summarizes these plant food benefits:

"Data are strong that vegetarians are at lesser risk for obesity, atonic [reduced muscle tone] constipation, lung cancer, and alcoholism. Evidence is good that risks for hypertension, coronary artery disease, type II diabetes, and gallstones are lower. Data are only fair to poor that risks of breast cancer, diverticular disease of the colon, colonic cancer, calcium kidney stones, osteoporosis, dental erosion, and dental caries are lower among vegetarians."

According to Dwyer, vegetarians' longevity is similar to or greater than that of non-vegetarians, but is influenced in Western countries by vegetarians' "adoption of many healthy lifestyle habits in addition to diet, such as not smoking, abstinence or moderation in the use of alcohol, being physically active, resting adequately, seeking ongoing health surveillance, and seeking guidance when health problems arise."

Can Veggies Prevent Cancer? The National Cancer Institute <www.cancer.gov> in its booklet "Diet, Nutrition, & Cancer Prevention: A Guide to Food Choices," states that 35 percent of cancer deaths may be related to diet. The booklet states:

- Diets rich in beta-carotene (the plant form of vitamin A) and vitamin C may reduce the risk of certain cancers.
- Reducing fat in the diet may reduce cancer risk and, in helping weight control, may reduce the risk of heart attacks and strokes.
- Diets high in fiber-rich foods may reduce the risk of cancers of the colon and rectum.
- Vegetables from the cabbage family (cruciferous vegetables) may reduce the risk of colon cancer.

FDA, in fact, authorized several health claims on food labels relating low-fat diets high in some plant-derived foods with a possibly reduced risk of cancer.

While FDA acknowledges that high intakes of fruits and vegetables rich in beta-carotene or vitamin C have been associated with reduced cancer risk, it believes the data are not sufficiently convincing that either nutrient by itself is responsible for the association. Nevertheless, since most fruits and vegetables are low-fat foods and may contain vitamin A (as beta-carotene) and vitamin C, the agency authorized a health claim relating diets low in fat and rich in these foods to a possibly reduced risk of some cancers.

Another claim may relate low-fat diets high in fiber-containing vegetables, fruits and grains to a possible reduction in cancer risk. (The National Cancer Institute recommends 20 to 30 grams of fiber a day.) Although the exact role of total dietary fiber, fiber components, and other nutrients and substances in these foods is not fully understood, many studies have shown such diets to be associated with reduced risk of some cancers.

Lowering Heart Disease Risk FDA also notes that diets high in saturated fats and cholesterol increase blood levels of total cholesterol and LDL cholesterol, and thus the risk for coronary heart disease. (The National Cholesterol Education Program recommends a diet with no more than 30 percent fat, of which no more than 10 percent comes from saturated fat.) For this reason, the agency authorized a health claim relating diets low in saturated fat and cholesterol to a possibly reduced risk of coronary heart disease.

Another claim may relate diets low in fat and high in fruits, vegetables, and grain products that contain fiber, particularly soluble fiber, to a possibly reduced risk of coronary heart disease. However, the agency recognizes that it is impossible to adequately distinguish the effects of fiber, including soluble fiber, from those of other food components.

With respect to increasing fiber in the diet, Joanne Slavin, Ph.D., R.D., of the University of Minnesota, in 1990 in *Nutrition Today,* gives this advice: "The current interest in dietary fiber has allowed recommendations for fiber supplementation to outdistance the scientific research base. Until we have a better understanding of how fiber works its magic, we should recommend to American consumers only a gradual increase in dietary fiber from a variety of sources."

Precautions The American Dietetic Association's position paper on vegetarian diets states, "Because vegan diets tend to be high in bulk, care should be taken to ensure that caloric intakes are sufficient to meet energy needs, particularly in infancy and during weaning."

Dwyer and Suzanne Havala, also a registered dietitian, updated the paper in the 1993 issue of the association's journal.

It's generally agreed that to avoid intestinal discomfort from increased bulk, a person shouldn't switch to foods with large amounts of fiber all at once. A sensible approach is to slowly increase consumption of grains, legumes, seeds, and nuts. "Some may choose to eliminate red meat but continue to eat fish and poultry occasionally, and such a diet is also to be encouraged," said Jack Zeev Yetiv, M.D., Ph.D., in his book *Popular Nutritional Practices: A Scientific Appraisal.*

As with any diet, it's important for the vegetarian diet to include many different foods, since no one food contains all the nutrients required for good health. "The wider the variety, the greater the chance of getting the nutrients you need," says FDA's Vanderveen.

In its position paper on vegetarian diets, the American Dietetic Association states that, with a plant-based daily diet, eating a variety of foods and sufficient calories for energy needs will help ensure adequate intakes of calcium, iron and zinc.

The mixture of proteins from grains, legumes, seeds, nuts, and vegetables provides a complement of amino acids so that deficits in one food are made up by another. Not all types of plant foods need to be eaten at the same meal, since the amino acids are combined in the body's protein pool.

"Soy protein," the paper states, "has been shown to be nutritionally equivalent in protein value to proteins of animal origin and, thus, can serve as the sole source of protein intake if desired."

The Institute of Food Technologists also recommends careful diet planning for vegetarians. This is especially important when the diet excludes dairy foods, to ensure adequate intake of calcium, iron, riboflavin, and vitamin D. For these vegetarians, the institute recommends calcium supplements during pregnancy, when breast-feeding, and for infants and children.

The institute and the American Dietetic Association say a vitamin D supplement may be needed if sunlight exposure is limited. (Sunlight activates a substance in the skin and converts it into vitamin D.)

They also point out that vegan diets should include a reliable source of vitamin B12, because this nutrient occurs only in animal foods. Vitamin B12 deficiency can result in irreversible nerve deterioration.

The need for vitamin B12 increases during pregnancy, breast-feeding, and periods of growth, Dwyer says. In a recent issue of Annual Review of Public Health, she writes that elderly people also should be especially cautious

Processed tofu, made from soybeans, is prepared for shipment. ©MICHAEL S. YAMASHITA/CORBIS.

about adopting vegetarian diets because their bodies may absorb vitamin B12 poorly.

Unless advised otherwise by a doctor, those taking dietary supplements should limit the dose to 100 percent of the U.S. Recommended Daily Allowances.

With the array of fruits, vegetables, grains, and spices available in U.S. grocery stores and the availability of vegetarian cookbooks, it's easy to devise tasty vegetarian dishes that even non-vegetarians can enjoy.

However, the key to any healthful diet—vegetarian or non-vegetarian—is adherence to sound nutrition principles.

SIGNIFICANCE

In the ten or so years that have elapsed since the above article appeared, the food and health debate has narrowed to focus on the optimal balance of fat, protein, and carbohydrate in the diet.

The vegan diet is the most restrictive form of vegetarianism, for it excludes any kind of animal-based food. Lacto-vegetarians eat dairy products such as milk and cheese, but not eggs. Lacto-ovo-vegetarians include both dairy and eggs. There are even more "liberal" vegetarians who eat fish and chicken but avoid all red meat. These varied diets will, inevitably, have very different amounts of fat, protein, and carbohydrate.

When *Diet for a Small Planet* was published, some nutritionists were concerned that a meatless diet would not contain sufficient protein and could have an adverse effect on health. Lappé herself believed, at the time, that plant protein was not as complete, in terms of its amino acid content, as animal protein. To compensate, she advocated "protein complementarity"—in which plant foods are eaten in prescribed combinations (rice and beans, for instance) to get the proper balance of amino acids. This made the vegetarian diet a complicated prospect for many. However, the theory was later discredited and she retracted it in the 1981 edition of the book.

When considering protein content, foods must be evaluated in their own right, rather than as plant or animal derived. Experts disagree on how much protein is necessary to maintain health—estimates vary between 2 and 10 percent of daily dietary intake. Meat contains, on average, 50 percent protein, although bacon has only 5. Beans contain on average 28 percent protein, nuts 10, and fruit about 5. In general, a varied diet—vegetarian or not—provides a sufficient amount of protein. Strict vegetarians and vegans, however, must guard against vitamin B12 deficiency, since animal foods are the main source of this vitamin.

In 1999, the FDA highlighted the benefits of soy protein, which for many vegetarians many is a diet staple. Products with more than 6.25 grams of soy protein per serving were labeled "heart healthy," since many studies indicated that soy protein could lower the cholesterol profile which, in turn, lowers the risk of heart disease. Obtaining these health benefits, however, was thought to require a daily intake of at least 25 grams of soy protein. This can come from tofu or tempeh, both made from cooked soybeans; miso, a paste made from fermented soybeans; or soy milk. Many vegetarian versions of meat products like hamburgers and sausages also contain high amounts of soy protein. In January 2005, however, the American Heart Association backed away from its strong endorsement of soy protein as beneficial in reducing risk factors for cardiovascular disease. Based on data from twenty-two randomized clinical trials, the American Heart Association stated it found no measured benefit from soy protein in lowering LDL cholesterol, improving HDL cholesterol, or lowering blood pressure. Although there is still much to learn about what makes a nutritionally complete, healthy diet, the vegetarian trend is now considered a growing mainstream nutritional option.

FURTHER RESOURCES

Books

Lappé, Frances Moore. *Diet for a Small Planet.* Twentieth Anniversary Edition. New York: Ballantine, 1991.

Web sites

FDA Consumer Magazine. "Soy: Health Claims for Soy Protein, Questions About Other Components." <http://www.fda.gov/fdac/features/2000/300_soy.html> (accessed March 20, 2006).

Vegetarian Guide. "A History of Vegetarianism" <http://michaelbluejay.com/veg/history.html> (accessed January 8, 2006).

Consensus Statement on Acupuncture

Government report excerpt

By: David J. Ramsay, et. al.

Date: 1997

Source: D. J. Ramsay, et al. "National Institutes of Health Consensus Statement on Acupuncture." 15, no. 5 (November 3–5, 1997). Available online at: <http://www.healthy.net/LIBRARY/Articles/NIH/Report.htm> (accessed January 20, 2006).

About the Author: At the time that the NIH Consensus Panel issued its finding on acupuncture, David J. Ramsay, a physiologist, was President of the University of Maryland and chairman of the twelve-member panel.

INTRODUCTION

In November, 1997 a National Institutes of Health (NIH) consensus panel concluded that there was clear evidence that acupuncture treatment shows effectiveness in treating postoperative nausea, nausea and vomiting due to chemotherapy, nausea of pregnancy, and postoperative dental pain.

The NIH panel also concluded that there are other pain-related conditions for which acupuncture may be effective as an adjunct therapy, an acceptable alternative, or as part of a comprehensive treatment program. These conditions include, among others, addiction, stroke rehabilitation, headache, menstrual cramps, tennis elbow, fibromyalgia (general muscle pain), low back pain, carpal tunnel syndrome, and asthma.

The consensus panel called for further research to validate the findings with respect to acupuncture, and to explore ways in which traditional Chinese medical practice might be integrated into Western medicine, for example by elucidating the biological mechanisms that might account for acupuncture's efficacy. Although some of the panel members are reported to have dissented from the findings, the consensus statement conveyed the opinions of the majority of the panel members.

Acupuncture, which originated in China more than 2,500 years ago, involves stimulation of certain points on or under the skin, mostly with ultra-fine needles that are manipulated manually or electrically. Although there are other forms of acupuncture, the NIH panel focused particularly on needle acupuncture

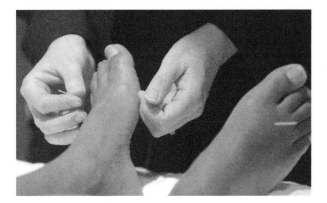

Licensed Acupuncturist Cynthia Ista places a needle in patient Victoria Zackery's foot during a therapy session at Abbott Northwestern Hospital's Institute for Health and Healing in Minneapolis. Zackery uses acupuncture treatments to help manage pain and nausea from chemotherapy. AP/WIDE WORLD PHOTOS.

because this was the form most widely researched and practiced in the United States.

PRIMARY SOURCE

1. What is the efficacy of acupuncture, compared with placebo or sham acupuncture, in the conditions for which sufficient data are available to evaluate?

Acupuncture is a complex intervention that may vary for different patients with similar chief complaints. The number and length of treatments and the specific points used may vary among individuals and during the course of treatment. Given this reality, it is perhaps encouraging that there exist a number of studies of sufficient quality to assess the efficacy of acupuncture for certain conditions.

According to contemporary research standards, there is a paucity of high-quality research assessing efficacy of acupuncture compared with placebo or sham acupuncture. The vast majority of papers studying acupuncture in the biomedical literature consist of case reports, case series, or intervention studies with designs inadequate to assess efficacy.

This discussion of efficacy refers to needle acupuncture (manual or electroacupuncture) because the published research is primarily on needle acupuncture and often does not encompass the full breadth of acupuncture techniques and practices. The controlled trials usually have only involved adults and did not involve long-term (i.e., years) acupuncture treatment.

Efficacy of a treatment assesses the differential effect of a treatment when compared with placebo or another

treatment modality using a double blind controlled trial and a rigidly defined protocol. Papers should describe enrollment procedures, eligibility criteria, description of the clinical characteristics of the subjects, methods for diagnosis, and a description of the protocol (i.e., randomization method, specific definition of treatment, and control conditions, including length of treatment, and number of acupuncture sessions). Optimal trials should also use standardized outcomes and appropriate statistical analyses. This assessment of efficacy focuses on high-quality trials comparing acupuncture with sham acupuncture or placebo.

Response Rate. As with other interventions, some individuals are poor responders to specific acupuncture protocols. Both animal and human laboratory and clinical experience suggest that the majority of subjects respond to acupuncture, with a minority not responding. Some of the clinical research outcomes, however, suggest that a larger percentage may not respond. The reason for this paradox is unclear and may reflect the current state of the research.

Efficacy for Specific Disorders. There is clear evidence that needle acupuncture is efficacious for adult post-operative and chemotherapy nausea and vomiting and probably for the nausea of pregnancy.

Much of the research is on various pain problems. There is evidence of efficacy for postoperative dental pain. There are reasonable studies (although sometimes only single studies) showing relief of pain with acupuncture on diverse pain conditions such as menstrual cramps, tennis elbow, and fibromyalgia. This suggests that acupuncture may have a more general effect on pain. However, there are also studies that do not find efficacy for acupuncture in pain.

There is evidence that acupuncture does not demonstrate efficacy for cessation of smoking and may not be efficacious for some other conditions.

While many other conditions have received some attention in the literature and, in fact, the research suggests some exciting potential areas for the use of acupuncture, the quality or quantity of the research evidence is not sufficient to provide firm evidence of efficacy at this time.

Sham Acupuncture. A commonly used control group is sham acupuncture, using techniques that are not intended to stimulate known acupuncture points. However, there is disagreement on correct needle placement. Also, particularly in the studies on pain, sham acupuncture often seems to have either intermediate effects between the placebo and 'real' acupuncture points or effects similar to those of the 'real' acupuncture points. Placement of a needle in any position elicits a biological response that complicates the interpretation of studies involving sham acupuncture.

Thus, there is substantial controversy over the use of sham acupuncture as control groups. This may be less of a problem in studies not involving pain.

2. What is the place of acupuncture in the treatment of various conditions for which sufficient data are available, in comparison with or in combination with other interventions (including no intervention)?

Assessing the usefulness of a medical intervention in practice differs from assessing formal efficacy. In conventional practice, clinicians make decisions based on the characteristics of the patient, clinical experience, potential for harm, and information from colleagues and the medical literature. In addition, when more than one treatment is possible, the clinician may make the choice taking into account the patient's preferences. While it is often thought that there is substantial research evidence to support conventional medical practices; this is frequently not that case. This does not mean that these treatments are ineffective. The data in support of acupuncture are as strong as those for many accepted Western medical therapies.

One of the advantages of acupuncture is that the incidence of adverse effects is substantially lower than that of many drugs or other accepted medical procedures used for the same conditions. As an example, musculoskeletal conditions, such as fibromyalgia, myofascial pain, and "tennis elbow," or epicondylitis, are conditions for which acupuncture may be beneficial. These painful conditions are often treated with, among other things, anti-inflammatory medications (aspirin, ibuprofen, etc.) or with steroid injections. Both medical interventions have a potential for deleterious side effects, but are still widely used, and are considered acceptable treatment. The evidence supporting these therapies is no better than that for acupuncture.

In addition, ample clinical experience, supported by some research data, suggests that acupuncture may be a reasonable option for a number of clinical conditions. Examples are postoperative pain and myofascial and low back pain. Examples of disorders for which the research evidence is less convincing but for which there are some positive clinical reports include addiction, stroke rehabilitation, carpal tunnel syndrome, osteoarthritis, and headache. Acupuncture treatment for many conditions such as asthma, addiction, or smoking cessation should be part of a comprehensive management program.

Many other conditions have been treated by acupuncture; the World Health Organization, for example, has listed more than forty for which the technique may be indicated.

3. What is known about the biological effects of acupuncture that helps us understand how it works?

Many studies in animals and humans have demonstrated that acupuncture can cause multiple biological responses. These responses can occur locally, i.e., at or close to the site of application, or at a distance, mediated mainly by sensory neurons to many structures within the central nervous system. This can lead to activation of pathways affecting various physiological systems in the brain as well as in the periphery. A focus of attention has been the role of endogenous opioids in acupuncture analgesia. Considerable evidence supports the claim that opioid peptides are released during acupuncture and that the analgesic effects of acupuncture are at least partially explained by their actions. That opioid antagonists such as naloxone reverse the analgesic effects of acupuncture further strengthens this hypothesis. Stimulation by acupuncture may also activate the hypothalamus and the pituitary gland, resulting in a broad spectrum of systemic effects. Alteration in the secretion of neurotransmitters and neurohormones and changes in the regulation of blood flow, both centrally and peripherally, have been documented. There is also evidence that there are alterations in immune functions produced by acupuncture. Which of these and other physiological changes mediate clinical effects is at present unclear.

Despite considerable efforts to understand the anatomy and physiology of the "acupuncture points," the definition and characterization of these points remains controversial. Even more elusive is the scientific basis of some of the key traditional Eastern medical concepts such as the circulation of Qi, the meridian system, and the five phases theory, which are difficult to reconcile with contemporary biomedical information but continue to play an important role in the evaluation of patients and the formulation of treatment in acupuncture.

Some of the biological effects of acupuncture have also been observed when "sham" acupuncture points are stimulated, highlighting the importance of defining appropriate control groups in assessing biological changes purported to be due to acupuncture. Such findings raise questions regarding the specificity of these biological changes. In addition, similar biological alterations including the release of endogenous opioids and changes in blood pressure have been observed after painful stimuli, vigorous exercise, and/or relaxation training; it is at present unclear to what extent acupuncture shares similar biological mechanisms.

It should be noted also that for any therapeutic intervention, including acupuncture, the so-called "non-specific" effects account for a substantial proportion of its effectiveness, and thus should not be casually discounted. Many factors may profoundly determine therapeutic outcome including the quality of the relationship between the clinician and the patient, the degree of trust, the expectations of the patient, the compatibility of the backgrounds and belief systems of the clinician and the patient, as well as a myriad of factors that together define the therapeutic milieu.

Although much remains unknown regarding the mechanism(s) that might mediate the therapeutic effect of acupuncture, the panel is encouraged that a number of significant acupuncture-related biological changes can be identified and carefully delineated. Further research in this direction not only is important for elucidating the phenomena associated with acupuncture, but also has the potential for exploring new pathways in human physiology not previously examined in a systematic manner.

4. What issues need to be addressed so that acupuncture may be appropriately incorporated into today's health care system?

The integration of acupuncture into today's health care system will be facilitated by a better understanding among providers of the language and practices of both the Eastern and Western health care communities. Acupuncture focuses on a holistic, energy-based approach to the patient rather than a disease-oriented diagnostic and treatment model.

An important factor for the integration of acupuncture into the health care system is the training and credentialing of acupuncture practitioners by the appropriate state agencies. This is necessary to allow the public and other health practitioners to identify qualified acupuncture practitioners. The acupuncture educational community has made substantial progress in this area and is encouraged to continue along this path. Educational standards have been established for training of physician and non-physician acupuncturists. Many acupuncture educational programs are accredited by an agency that is recognized by the U.S. Department of Education. A national credentialing agency exists that is recognized by some of the major professional acupuncture organizations and provides examinations for entry-level competency in the field.

A majority of States provide licensure or registration for acupuncture practitioners. Because some acupuncture practitioners have limited English proficiency, credentialing and licensing examinations should be provided in languages other than English where necessary. There is variation in the titles that are conferred through these processes, and the requirements to obtain licensure vary widely. The scope of practice allowed under these State requirements varies as well. While States have the individual prerogative to set standards for licensing professions, harmonization in these areas will provide greater confidence in the qualifications of acupuncture practitioners. For example, not all States recognize the same credentialing examination, thus making reciprocity difficult.

The occurrence of adverse events in the practice of acupuncture has been documented to be extremely low.

However, these events have occurred in rare occasions, some of which are life threatening (e.g., pneumothorax). Therefore, appropriate safeguards for the protection of patients and consumers need to be in place. Patients should be fully informed of their treatment options, expected prognosis, relative risk, and safety practices to minimize these risks prior to their receipt of acupuncture. This information must be provided in a manner that is linguistically and culturally appropriate to the patient. Use of acupuncture needles should always follow FDA regulations, including use of sterile, single-use needles. It is noted that these practices are already being done by many acupuncture practitioners; however, these practices should be uniform. Recourse for patient grievance and professional censure are provided through credentialing and licensing procedures and are available through appropriate State jurisdictions.

It has been reported that more than one million Americans currently receive acupuncture each year. Continued access to qualified acupuncture professionals for appropriate conditions should be ensured. Because many individuals seek health care treatment from both acupuncturists and physicians, communication between these providers should be strengthened and improved. If a patient is under the care of an acupuncturist and a physician, both practitioners should be informed. Care should be taken so that important medical problems are not overlooked. Patients and providers have a responsibility to facilitate this communication.

There is evidence that some patients have limited access to acupuncture services because of inability to pay. Insurance companies can decrease or remove financial barriers to access depending on their willingness to provide coverage for appropriate acupuncture services. An increasing number of insurance companies are either considering this possibility or now provide coverage for acupuncture services. Where there are State health insurance plans, and for populations served by Medicare or Medicaid, expansion of coverage to include appropriate acupuncture services would also help remove financial barriers to access.

As acupuncture is incorporated into today's health care system, and further research clarifies the role of acupuncture for various health conditions, it is expected that dissemination of this information to health care practitioners, insurance providers, policymakers, and the general public will lead to more informed decisions in regard to the appropriate use of acupuncture.

Conclusions and Recommendations Acupuncture as a therapeutic intervention is widely practiced in the United States. There have been many studies of its potential usefulness. However, many of these studies provide equivocal results because of design, sample size, and other factors. The issue is further complicated by inherent difficulties in the use of appropriate controls, such as placebo and sham acupuncture groups.

However, promising results have emerged, for example, efficacy of acupuncture in adult post-operative and chemotherapy nausea and vomiting and in post-operative dental pain. There are other situations such as addiction, stroke rehabilitation, headache, menstrual cramps, tennis elbow, fibromyalgia myofascial pain, osteoarthritis, low back pain, carpal tunnel syndrome, and asthma where acupuncture may be useful as an adjunct treatment or an acceptable alternative or be included in a comprehensive management program. Further research is likely to uncover additional areas where acupuncture interventions will be useful.

Findings from basic research have begun to elucidate the mechanisms of action of acupuncture, including the release of opioids and other peptides in the central nervous system and the periphery and changes in neuroendocrine function. Although much needs to be accomplished, the emergence of plausible mechanisms for the therapeutic effects of acupuncture is encouraging.

The introduction of acupuncture into the choice of treatment modalities that are readily available to the public is in its early stages. Issues of training, licensure, and reimbursement remain to be clarified. There is sufficient evidence, however, of acupuncture's value to expand its use into conventional medicine and to encourage further studies of its physiology and clinical value.

SIGNIFICANCE

News spread quickly in the final months of 1997 when the NIH panel of experts concluded that acupuncture was an effective therapy for certain medical conditions, particularly for nausea and pain. The idea that physicians should try to integrate traditional Chinese medicine into standard medical practice for these problems was simultaneously considered both remarkable and unlikely by many health care professionals, even when they were inclined to accept the panel findings.

In the spirit of Herodotus' admonition to "do no harm," the panel emphasized that acupuncture was comparatively safe, with fewer side effects than many well-established pain therapies, including opioids (medicines with opiate compounds such as codeine) and nonsteroidal anti-inflammatory medications. Current estimates of acupuncture use are that more than a million Americans rely on acupuncture to treat ailments ranging from headache and bowel disorders to arthritis and stroke.

The panel's findings encouraged more patients and physicians to consider acupuncture as an alternative or complementary treatment for some common health problems, including nausea associated with pregnancy and cancer chemotherapy, and pain following dental surgery. The report has fostered the use of acupuncture to treat chronic problems, like low back pain and asthma, for which standard treatments are inadequate or costly or may entail serious side effects. It also encouraged some medical doctors to become certified as medical acupuncturists and augment their practices by treating acupuncture patients themselves.

The report prompted health insurers, including Medicare and Medicaid, to begin covering the costs of acupuncture for conditions where the panel identified clear evidence of its benefits.

The positive recommendation of the panel came as a surprise to many health care providers and medical scholars. The medical establishment had been slow to accept acupuncture because the traditional Chinese explanations for its observed effects were based on unproved concepts of opposing forces called yin and yang, which, when out of balance, disrupt the natural flow of qi in the body.

However, the panel cited growing evidence of biological effects induced by acupuncture that might help to explain the benefits observed in scores of studies and in medical practice. For example, acupuncture is associated with the release of natural pain-relieving endorphins. Acupuncture also appears to alter the functioning of the immune system.

Thus, after evaluating seventeen presentations summarizing hundreds of studies conducted in recent years, primarily in Western countries, the panel recommended that acupuncture be integrated into medical practice. However, acupuncture critics said that the presentations were biased in favor of acupuncture's effectiveness and that experts wanting to testify against its efficacy were not invited to present their views. Wallace Sampson, a researcher who prepared the National Council Against Health Fraud's position paper on acupuncture (1991) pointed out that the best-designed studies of acupuncture tended to show the poorest efficacy results. This fact was also mentioned in several of the panel presentations.

Nevertheless, the panel represented multiple scientific disciplines and included some physicians who practice acupuncture or have been treated by it. The panel based its conclusions almost entirely on studies that meet criteria for well-designed research. It did not issue a forceful endorsement of acupuncture, but did find the procedure to be particularly effective for treating painful disorders of the musculoskeletal systems, such as fibromyalgia and tennis elbow, and possibly safer than currently accepted remedies for those disorders. Also, acupuncture might be a reasonable option for low back and post-operative pain, and showed some potential for use in drug addiction, stroke rehabilitation, carpal tunnel syndrome, osteoarthritis, headache, and asthma.

Although the panel cited the lack of well-designed clinical studies of acupuncture, it found that in many cases "the data supporting acupuncture are as strong as those for many accepted Western medical therapies." Many of these therapies are simply palliative. The long-term use of non-steroidal anti-inflammatory painkillers is known to have risk for deleterious effects, including hemorrhagic stroke and gastrointestinal bleeding. Still, the panel called for larger, better, and longer studies to properly establish acupuncture's therapeutic benefits and limitations. This is unlikely to happen independently of government funding, as the private sector is unlikely to support research on a technique that cannot be patented.

Although the panel focused on clinical studies that represented the gold standard of efficacy research, randomized placebo-controlled double-blind trials, these studies often had small numbers of patients. There is also controversy over whether "sham acupuncture," in which needles are placed in spots that are not recommended in traditional acupuncture, is a true placebo control. Sham acupuncture is also associated with some of the neurohormonal changes that have been found to result from regular acupuncture, so it is unclear whether sham acupuncture truly qualifies as "no treatment." This makes it difficult to determine the true benefit of real acupuncture.

The dependency of medical research on the economic incentives involved in patent protection is perhaps the most significant observation coming out of the consensus panel review process. This dependency has consequences far beyond the question of the efficacy of acupuncture. Private enterprise has been a huge source of dramatic and profound innovation in health care. However, the area of research pertaining to older and traditional therapies such as acupuncture that could potentially show as much effectiveness as some expensive innovations, is one in which the current research funding system is weak. Consequently, certain areas such as pain in which true innovations have been hard to achieve suffer from a paucity of well-designed, well-funded studies that could either usher in a new era of "high-touch" medical practice with less use of potentially harmful drug treatment, or finally put to rest contentions that this form of traditional

medicine can really benefit people who desperately seek better quality of life.

The NIH National Center for Complementary and Alternative Medicine is an attempt in the United States to address the underfunding of rigorous research in important alternative health care areas that do not promise large financial returns to private investors. The center is currently pursuing research in the efficacy and safety of herbal medicines; biologically based practices such as dietary supplements, some of which (e.g. quinine) have proved to be effective medical treatments; manipulation and body-based practices such as chiropractic; mind-body medicine; and whole medical systems such as traditional Chinese medicine, acupuncture, and homeopathy. Some of research could produce useful treatments that otherwise would be discarded or overlooked because they would not reward significant financial investment.

FURTHER RESOURCES
Books

Kidsin, Ruth. *Acupuncture for Everyone.* Rochester, VT: Healing Arts Press, 1991.

Periodicals

Cassileth, B. R. and G. Deng. "Complementary and Alternative Therapies for Cancer." *The Oncologist* 9 no. 1 (February 2004): 80–89.

Web sites

National Center for Complementary and Alternative Medicine. "Whole Medical Systems: An Overview." <http://nccam.nih.gov/health/backgrounds/wholemed.htm#tcm> (accessed January 31, 2006).

Manipulative and Body-Based Practices: An Overview

Therapeutic Massage and Chiropractic Care

Report excerpt

By: National Center for Complementary and Alternative Medicine

Date: October 2004

Source: National Center for Complementary and Alternative Medicine. "Manipulative and Body-Based Practices: An Overview." <http://nccam.nih.gov/health/backgrounds/manipulative.htm> (accessed January 17, 2006).

About the Author: The National Center for Complementary and Alternative Medicine (NCCAM) is part of the National Institutes of Health (NIH), which is one of the agencies under the administrative umbrella of the Department of Health and Human Services (DHHS) in the Public Health Service (PHS). The NCCAM has a threefold task: to support, conduct, and fund training and research in the areas of complementary and alternative medicine, to educate health-care professionals and the lay public regarding the utility and efficacy of complementary and alternative medicine, and to support education and professional development of future complementary and alternative medicine providers.

INTRODUCTION

The first therapeutic massage probably occurred when a very early human sustained an injury and instinctively rubbed the area, noticed that it made the injury feel better, and repeated the process with the next wound. The American Massage Therapy Association (AMTA) defines massage therapy as that process in which a (trained) provider employs any of a number of specific manual techniques, causing soft tissue movement or manipulation, either with or without the use of complementary or additional methodologies, with the goal of improving the overall feeling of wellness of the client.

In the United States prior to the last few decades of the twentieth century, massage was considered to be primarily a relaxation and stress reduction technique, typically performed in the context of a health spa setting, or as an adjunct to a physical or sports conditioning program. Historically, massage has been utilized much more as a therapeutic modality in Europe, Asia, and the Middle Eastern countries than in the United States.

Two of the most common forms of therapeutic massage employed elsewhere in the world (and now in America as well) are shiatsu and Swedish massage. Shiatsu is predicated upon the Chinese concept of the movement of subtle energy, also called chi or qi. One of the main premises of energy movement theory is that the body is divided into segments, called meridians, that encircle the body both horizontally and vertically (two separate sets of meridians). Specific points (identical for shiatsu, acupuncture, and acupressure) along the meridians control the totality of the functioning of the body's systems. By applying either deep tissue pressure, stretching, or other techniques, it is thought that the health of the entire body-mind can be maintained, in addition to achieving a profound sense of comfort and relaxation. It is a philosophical and aesthetic process, as well as a physical one.

Swedish massage is much more physiologically centered than is shiatsu. There are a variety of strokes and soft tissue manipulations inherent in the practice, each of which has a discrete function. Overall, the goal is to improve circulation, assist stretched or over exercised muscles in rapid recovery, enhance the functioning of the immune and circulatory systems, and maintain the integrity and high functioning of the muscles, tendons, ligaments, and joints. Like shiatsu, it is used for optimizing the physical well-being of the body, as well as for relaxation of the mind.

The use of massage in a medical scenario in America is relatively recent. It has sometimes been used in conjunction with physical or occupational therapy in order to relax or stretch muscles, resolve swelling or tissue inflammation, maintain muscle tone in fractured limbs that must be immobilized for prolonged periods, or in the limbs and extremities of persons with various types of paralysis or peripheral neuropathies.

In addition to shiatsu, Swedish, and the various medical massage techniques, there are several other modalities used frequently in the massage therapy setting. The most well-known among them are: reflexology, craniosacral, deep tissue, trigger point, myofascial release, sports massage, and reflexology.

The following excerpt from a government report issued by the National Center for Complementary and Alternative Medicine discusses the prevalence and efficacy of chiropractic care and massage therapy.

▊ PRIMARY SOURCE

Introduction Under the umbrella of manipulative and body-based practices is a heterogeneous group of CAM interventions and therapies. These include chiropractic and osteopathic manipulation, massage therapy, Tui Na, reflexology, rolfing, Bowen technique, Trager bodywork, Alexander technique, Feldenkrais method, and a host of others. Surveys of the U.S. population suggest that between 3 percent and 16 percent of adults receive chiropractic manipulation in a given year, while between 2 percent and 14 percent receive some form of massage therapy. In 1997, U.S. adults made an estimated 192 million visits to chiropractors and 114 million visits to massage therapists. Visits to chiropractors and massage therapists combined represented 50 percent of all visits to CAM practitioners. Data on the remaining manipulative and body-based practices are sparser, but it can be

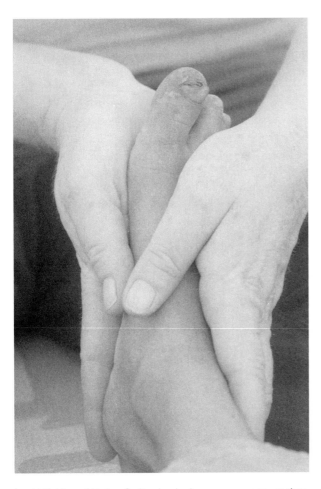

Ingrid Kohler, of Uster, Switzerland, gives an acupressure therapeutic healing massage to an injured orphan, Wednesday, Jan. 19, 2005, at a refugee camp in Banda Aceh, Indonesia. Kohler taught the art of massage to Indonesian volunteers as a way to help relieve the stress and trauma orphans are experiencing following the Dec. 26, 2004, tsunami. AP/WIDE WORLD PHOTOS.

estimated that they are collectively used by less than 7 percent of the adult population. . . .

Clinical Studies: Mechanisms Biomechanical studies have characterized the force applied by a practitioner during chiropractic manipulation, as well as the force transferred to the vertebral column, both in cadavers and in normal volunteers. In most cases, however, a single practitioner provided the manipulation, limiting generalizability. Additional work is required to examine interpractitioner variability, patient characteristics, and their relation to clinical outcomes.

Studies using magnetic resonance imaging (MRI) have suggested that spinal manipulation has a direct effect on the structure of spinal joints; it remains to be seen if this structural change relates to clinical efficacy.

Clinical studies of selected physiological parameters suggest that massage therapy can alter various neurochemical, hormonal, and immune markers, such as substance P in patients who have chronic pain, serotonin levels in women who have breast cancer, cortisol levels in patients who have rheumatoid arthritis, and natural killer (NK) cell numbers and CD4+ T-cell counts in patients who are HIV-positive. However, most of these studies have come from one research group, so replication at independent sites is necessary. It is also important to determine the mechanisms by which these changes are elicited.

Despite these many interesting experimental observations, the underlying mechanisms of manipulative and body-based practices are poorly understood. Little is known from a quantitative perspective. Important gaps in the field, as revealed by a review of the relevant scientific literature, include the following:

- Lack of biomechanical characterization from both practitioner and participant perspectives
- Little use of state-of-the-art imaging techniques
- Few data on the physiological, anatomical, and biomechanical changes that occur with treatment
- Inadequate data on the effects of these therapies at the biochemical and cellular levels
- Only preliminary data on the physiological mediators involved with the clinical outcomes . . .

Utilization/Integration In the United States, manipulative therapy is practiced primarily by doctors of chiropractic, some osteopathic physicians, physical therapists, and physiatrists. Doctors of chiropractic perform more than 90 percent of the spinal manipulations in the United States, and the vast majority of the studies that have examined the cost and utilization of spinal manipulation have focused on chiropractic.

Individual provider experience, traditional use, or arbitrary payer capitation decisions—rather than the results of controlled clinical trials—determine many patient care decisions involving spinal manipulation. More than 75 percent of private payers and 50 percent of managed care organizations provide at least some reimbursement for chiropractic care. Congress has mandated that the Department of Defense (DOD) and the Department of Veterans Affairs provide chiropractic services to their beneficiaries, and there are DOD medical clinics offering manipulative services by osteopathic physicians and physical therapists. The State of Washington has mandated coverage of CAM services for medical conditions normally covered by insurance. The integration of manipulative services into health care has reached this level despite a dearth of evidence about long-term effects, appropriate dosing, and cost-effectiveness.

Although the numbers of Americans using chiropractic and massage are similar, massage therapists are licensed in fewer than 40 states, and massage is much less likely than chiropractic to be covered by health insurance. Like spinal manipulation, massage is most commonly used for musculoskeletal problems. However, a significant fraction of patients seek massage care for relaxation and stress relief....

Patient Satisfaction Although there are no studies of patient satisfaction with manipulation in general, numerous investigators have looked at patient satisfaction with chiropractic care. Patients report very high levels of satisfaction with chiropractic care. Satisfaction with massage treatment has also been found to be very high....

SIGNIFICANCE

The use of therapeutic massage as a complementary medical modality has increased dramatically in recent years. One factor that led to its increase in the last two decades of the twentieth century was the prevalence of neuropathies; and tissue, muscle, and wasting syndromes associated with HIV and AIDS. Because the disease constellation was still quite new in America, little was known about the most effective ways in which to provide physical (and emotional) relief for patients experiencing a plethora of painful and debilitating symptoms throughout virtually their entire bodies. Because of the shortage of effective therapies, many people with HIV/AIDS turned to complementary and alternative treatments, including dietary manipulation, the use of herbal and botanical supplements, and the therapeutic use of massage—both for pain and symptom management and for stress reduction.

According to the AMTA and the NCCAM, research on the therapeutic benefits of massage has been going on for more than one hundred years. Based on both current and long-term research studies, massage has myriad medical and therapeutic benefits, among the most salient of which are to increase the flow of lymph and blood circulation, stimulate the release of endogenous endorphins (also referred to as the body's naturally occurring painkillers), lower heart rate and blood pressure, stretch and relax muscles, reduce the physical effects of stress on the body, increase a feeling of focus and alertness, and improve the range of motion in joints that are worked on. Among the myriad health benefits listed by consumers of therapeutic massage are improvements in chronic pain and degenerative joint syndromes (such as

rheumatoid and osteoarthritis), decreased sinus and allergy symptoms, improved circulation, decrease in number and intensity of headaches, decreased feelings of stress associated with neck, shoulder, and back pain, more rapid healing of strains, muscle pulls, and many types of sports injuries, and improvements in signs and symptoms associated with the experience of stress, depression, and anxiety.

Many physician's offices and health clinics have begun to utilize on-site massage therapists as well as to refer their patients to them. Natural food and some specialty stores have begun to set up massage chairs. Even American shopping malls have begun to set up therapeutic massage kiosks (generally for chair massages only). Employers have started offering the use of therapeutic massage as a standard health benefit, and some utilize on-site massage therapists in the workplace. Among those who do so, preliminary data have indicated an increase in productivity, a decrease in job site accidents, and a decrease in sick leave. However, it is still early in this research, and the results are not yet considered conclusive.

FURTHER RESOURCES

Books

Gordon, James S. *Manifesto for a New Medicine: Your Guide to Healing Partnerships and the Wise Use of Alternative Therapies.* Reading, MA: Perseus Publishing, 1996.

Websites

American Massage Therapy Association. "Manipulative Research Confirms Massage Therapy Enhances Health." <http://www.amtamassage.org/news/enhancehealth.html> (accessed January 17, 2006).

American Massage Therapy Association. "Massage Therapy Tips for Consumers." <http://www.amtamassage.org/news/massagefacts.html> (accessed January 17, 2006).

National Certification Board for Therapeutic Massage and Body work. "Consumers' Guide to Therapeutic Massage and Bodywork." <http://www.ncbtmb.com/consumers_guide.htm> (accessed January 17, 2006).

Echinacea Disappoints: There's Still No Cure for the Common Cold

Herbal Medicine

Journal article

By: Nathan Seppa

Date: July 30, 2005

An herbalist fills a prescription using traditional Chinese medicines in a Chinatown apothecary in San Francisco, California. Ca. 1989. ©PHIL SCHERMEISTER/CORBIS.

Source: Seppa, Nathan. "Echinacea Disappoints: There's Still No Cure for the Common Cold." *Science Service* 70, no. 1 (July 30, 2005).

About the Author: Nathan Seppa is a writer and magazine journalist specializing in the areas of biomedicine, science, and the social and behavioral sciences. He has been a staff writer for biomedical *Science News Online*, *Science*, and the *APA Monitor*.

INTRODUCTION

Herbal products and supplements are rarely well understood by the American public. There is an interesting dichotomy in that few people would take any form of prescription medication before being educated by their local pharmacist about its mechanisms of action and potential side effects, as well as its possible interactions with other medications currently being taken. However, many readily purchase and ingest herbal supplements based on media advertisements, suggestions of friends or colleagues, or the advice of a health or natural food store employee, without first researching the possible side effects and interactions of supplements. There is often a tacit assumption among the herbal and botanical supplement using public that natural substances are likely to be beneficial, and they cannot cause harm.

The Dietary Supplement Health and Education Act of 1994 defines any form of dietary supplement, whether herbal, botanical, enzyme, amino acid, vitamin or mineral, as a food substance, taken by mouth and intended to supplement the diet. Supplements are not considered medicinals, and are therefore not currently regulated by the Food and Drug Administration (FDA) with the same rigorous standards as are pharmaceuticals. The FDA only regulates supplements if complaints are made against particular manufacturers, or the specific substances that are created and marketed by them. The Federal Trade Commission (FTC) is the body that has oversight concerning whether the producers of supplements are advertising truthfully. However, the National Center for Complementary and Alternative Medicine (NCCAM) has significant jurisdiction over the production, product claims, safety and efficacy, and marketing statements made by the purveyors of dietary supplements, and they oversee extensive research in that area. These products fall under the general category of biologically based therapies.

■ PRIMARY SOURCE

Echinacea disappoints: there's still no cure for the common cold. A folk remedy touted as a cold treatment has failed its most recent—and possibly most exacting—test. Volunteers exposed to a cold virus and given the herbal supplement echinacea fared no better than did virus-exposed participants who received an inert substance, researchers report in the July 28 *New England Journal of Medicine*.

The U.S. study is the third in 3 years in which echinacea failed to alleviate colds in children or, as in this case, young adults. These findings run counter to earlier reports, most out of Europe, that echinacea revs up an immune response against cold viruses (SN: 3/27/99, p. 207).

For the new study, researchers recruited 399 young adults. Some received drops of Echinacea angustifolia extract and others got placebos. After a week, all volunteers received nasal sprays containing rhinovirus type 39, a common cold virus, and were sequestered in a hotel room for 5 days.

After exposure, volunteers getting echinacea continued to take it. Some participants getting the placebos were switched to echinacea, while others continued with the placebos.

None of it mattered, says study coauthor Ronald B. Turner of the University of Virginia in Charlottesville. More than 80 percent of the people in each group became infected with the virus, and roughly three-fifths of each group showed cold symptoms within a week. The severity of the symptoms also was the same across the groups.

Furthermore, blood tests showed no significant immune boost from echinacea.

"While this study tested only E. angustifolia, there is considerable overlap in the chemical constituents of the three purple cone-flower species from which echinacea is derived," says Benjamin Kligler of the Albert Einstein College of Medicine in New York.

Therefore, the new study's findings "might apply to the other Echinacea species as well," says herbal medicine specialist Wallace Sampson of Stanford University.

Echinacea formulations often contain more than one species of the plant (SN: 6/7/03, p. 359). Since the preparations are sold as dietary supplements and not drugs, the Food and Drug Administration doesn't regulate their effectiveness or content.

"Three big negative trials have now come out," says Bruce P. Barrett of the University of Wisconsin-Madison. In the study that he led, reported in 2002, college students with colds fared the same whether they got placebos or a mix of the Echinacea species. In a 2003 report, researchers at the University of Washington in Seattle found that Echinacea purpurea, a common ingredient in formulations, was no weapon against colds in children.

Barrett and Kligler, both physicians, say that they wouldn't discourage people currently using echinacea from continuing to do so, because the supplement is generally safe and may have a significant placebo effect. "But I sure wouldn't go out and tell people who don't believe in it to start taking it," Barrett says.

SIGNIFICANCE

The purchase and use of dietary supplements of all kinds has increased enormously in the United States since the 1970s. In keeping with the growing interest in promoting health, supplements are claimed to stave off the effects of aging (particularly among the "baby boom" generation) and naturally enhance physical abilities, such as energy, strength, and endurance (without the use of steroids). Among the largest consumers of supplements are people with chronic or life-threatening illness, athletes seeking to improve capacity or performance, and people who are trying to lose weight. Many also use vitamins, herbal preparations, or botanical supplements in an effort to treat common illnesses, such as the flu, other viral infections, or colds.

Although there have been many research studies concerning the safety and efficacy of various dietary supplements, much of it has lacked the precision and scientific rigor of the clinical trials undergone by the manufacturers of pharmaceuticals in the United States, so it has been challenging to accurately assess the claims made by manufacturers. Another significant issue is the lack of standardization in the manufacture and production of supplements: pharmaceuticals are produced according to specific formulations, and at standard (universal) dosages based on safety and efficacy studies. This is not the case for non-pharmaceutical biological preparations. Many herbal and botanical supplements are made of complex mixtures, comprised of several, or a great many, ingredients. It is very difficult to evaluate purity, quality, and consistency of formulation under those circumstances. When NCCAM and others have completed analyses of many multi-ingredient preparations, they have sometimes found significant differences between the amounts of each substance labeled and what was determined by chemical analysis. Dietary (used interchangeably with nutritional throughout) supplements are not subject to the standards set for medicinals by the FDA, referred to as good manufacturing practices, or GMPs.

Some of the nutritional supplements whose limited study has shown sufficient promise to warrant larger scale research, are: glucosamine hydrochloride and chondroiten sulfate for use with osteoarthritis, shark cartilage for use with lung cancer, Saint John's wort for mood disorder (although the current results regarding its use in treating depression are equivocal at best), black cohosh for treating symptoms associated with menopause, ginkgo biloba for use as a protection against the development of dementia, saw palmetto and vitamin E for use in disorders of the prostate, and melatonin or valerian root for use with sleep onset disorders. That these substances are being studied more closely does not imply that they will be proven efficacious. Several supplements have been shown to block or interfere with the mechanisms of action of prescription pharmaceuticals, such as Saint John's wort's capacity for neutralizing the effects of many prescription medications, and ginkgo biloba's capacity for potentiating the effects of anticoagulants, thereby increasing potential bleeding problems in some people who take them together. A potentially significant association was demonstrated between both kava extract and comfrey root and liver failure, so both are now sold with that warning on the label. Ephedra was discovered to cause potentially lethal side effects in some people and has been banned by the FDA. Many vitamins, herbal preparations, and botanical supplements interfere with the mechanisms of action of different chemotherapy drugs.

Both the National Center for Alternative and Complementary Medicine and the Federal Food and Drug Administration continue to explore herbal compounds for use in the treatment of disease and its symptoms through research and clinical trials.

FURTHER RESOURCES

Books

Robson, Terry, ed. *An Introduction to Complementary Medicine*. Crows Nest, New South Wales: Allen & Unwin, 2003.

Web sites

familydoctor.org. "Herbal Products and Supplements: What You Should Know." <http://familydoctor.org/860.xml> (accessed January 18, 2006).

Memorial Sloan-Kettering Cancer Center. "About Herbs: Black Cohosh." <http://www.mskcc.org/mskcc/html/11571.cfm?RecordID=405&tab=HC> (accessed January 18, 2006).

National Cancer Institute. "Thinking About Complementary And Alternative Medicine: A *Natural* Product Does Not Mean A *Safe* Product." <http://www.cancer.gov/cancertopics/thinking-about-CAM/page7> (accessed January 18, 2006).

Bioethics

The field of bioethics deals with the moral issues that arise from the use of new medical procedures or advances in biotechnology. Ethical issues are inherently social issues, and how bioethical debates are framed reflect a society's history, language, commonalities, and divisions.

A long-standing social issue rooted in bioethics is the right of a woman to terminate a pregnancy via an abortion. In the United States, the 1973 *Roe v. Wade* decision by the U.S. Supreme Court determined that abortion restrictions were a violation of the constitutional right to privacy. Opponents have long argued for the repeal of the decision, while proponents insist that a woman's right to choose should be maintained.

Issues related to the end of life, including the "right to die," withholding resuscitation, and physician-assisted suicide, provide an often volatile mixture of deeply held personal conviction, longstanding medical tradition, and law. Other evolving social issues involve the use of genetic and medical information, and a patient's legal rights versus expectations of privacy.

Another important facet of bioethics involves the use of animals in research. Although animals are a good model for medical research, the ethics of sacrificing animals or subjecting them to pain has spawned much discussion, and even the destruction of animal care facilities in research institutions by extremist groups opposed to such research.

A more recent ethical issue in medicine involves the use of stem cells, the cells present in human embryos, umbilical cord blood, and in adult bone marrow that have the potential to differentiate into a variety of specialized cells. While stem cells offer tantalizing research and clinical potential, the use of embryonic stem cells is contentious. Although many countries around the world allow regulated stem cell research, as of 2006, stem cell research in the United States was tightly restricted, especially with regard to the origin of cells.

Cloning (producing a genetic duplicate in a lab) has been possible with a number of animal species. Although there has not been any real success in human cloning, the potential of such cloning as a reproductive technology presents daunting technical and moral challenges. Critics contend that designer life could be created to supply parts to the living (see "Made-to-order Baby Created in Hopes of Saving Ailing Sister"), while others hail the technology for exactly the same reason.

As a result of genetic manipulation, gene therapies are being developed for specific diseases. Since drugs can be patented, this raises the issue of whether the genetic blueprints of living organisms used as gene therapies can be patented. The notion that life is patentable and a source of profit is hotly debated.

In 1953 James Watson and Francis Crick's discovered the structure of deoxyribonucleic acid (DNA). Thus began the era of molecular biology, a discipline that has made it possible to alter the genetic composition of humans and other creatures. This holds great potential for relief from diseases such as cystic fibrosis and spinal injuries. As technologies further advance, bioethical issues are going to continue to challenge humanity.

Eugenics and Sex Harmony

Foreword

Book excerpt

By: Winfield Scott Pugh

Date: 1947

Source: H. H. Rubin. *Eugenics and Sex Harmony*. New York: Pioneer. 1947.

About the Author: Winfield Scott Pugh was a physician and advocate of eugenics (controlled human breeding intended to better the human race), a belief system especially prominent in America in the period encompassing the two World Wars (1915–1945). Pugh, considered a medical expert on women's sexual health, wrote the foreword to the self-help booklet *Eugenics and Sex Harmony*, written by Herman H. Rubin to popularize and apply eugenics concepts to everyday management of marital relations.

INTRODUCTION

Eugenics and Sex Harmony was written in 1933 by Herman H. Rubin, MD, a prominent physician and eugenicist. The book was intended to explain basic concepts of sexual reproduction to Americans who, as Pugh's foreword noted, were largely uneducated about such matters. Rubin introduced readers to the ideas of sexual selection and eugenics, explaining his belief that physical and mental traits could be inherited, not just directly from parents, but from prior generations as well.

A large section of the booklet discussed the potential consequences of absorbing of the Black race into the Caucasian. Rubin, who considered stereotypical racial characteristics to be heritable traits, lamented the possibility that African-American folk culture would be lost to the world should such miscegenation occur, predicting that their genetic heritage would be diluted by Nordic genes.

The booklet advised readers to choose mates wisely: to examine their pedigree, channel sexual energy properly into matrimony, marry at the optimal age (20 for women and 30 for men), and avoid marrying relatives. It concluded by contrasting the positive life outcomes of people and their offspring when they followed eugenicist principles with the personal tragedy—including crime, exploitation, and poverty—that awaited the sexually "ignorant" who refused to delay gratification.

PRIMARY SOURCE

FOREWORD

For many years a veil of hypocrisy has surrounded everything associated with sex or eugenics and mere mention of such a word as 'venereal,' was sufficient to arouse consternation far and wide. We Americans still have with us many ideas inherited from our Pilgrim Fathers; particularly regarding all matters akin to sex and disease. These antiquated notions stick like leeches and in many localities greatly interfere with attempts at control of baneful maladies, or hinder other scientific progress.

Fortunately today, members of a rising generation are refusing to accept dogmas just because their forbears did so for centuries. The flowering youth wants to know and will insist on knowing—all censors or bans notwithstanding. Thus the clouds of ignorance and superstition are fading away before the radiant Sun of Knowledge and proving most helpful. . . .

In dealing with sex problems and eugenics, we must first of all be honest. Human anatomy and physiology must be taken as the Creative Force so constructed and not as we would like to see. In this connection, I must tell you observation of many writers on sexual topics reveals the fact they are writing for employers and moralists, not for the benefit of a suffering public. Many such gentry know full well what they say is not true, but find it necessary to misstate facts in order to hold their meal tickets.

In matters pertaining to eugenics and sex, we have been very much like the ostrich, but it is well nigh time we pulled our heads out of the sand. Currier Bell once said, "such annoyances as Society cannot cure, it usually forbids utterance on pain of its scorn; said scorn being only a tinseled cloak to its deformed weakness."

Among another group of facts we must not overlook, are first the sexual instinct is possessed by every human being, regardless of gender. There is great truth in Byron's statement, "Man's love is of man's life a thing apart; 'tis woman's whole existence." A very wise provision of Nature. Second, a well regulated sexual life is just as essential to the well-being of an individual as the other, but properly recognized physiological activities. In other words, the sexual function is not an instrument of the Devil, designed to drag men and women down to Sin, but is a God-given physiological function of Man and all animal kind. If not so intended, why were we so endowed? Nature is no respecter of man-made laws, therefore its dictates will be obeyed. In the constant conflict between socalled civilization and the primitive, the latter always wins. I repeat, always. Sex has existed from the beginning of Time and will continue to the end; or else there would be no world.

It is highly essential everyone have a thorough concept of sex and eugenics. This can readily be obtained by following the teaching so clearly outlined by Doctor H. H. Rubin, in Eugenics and Sex Harmony. In this connection, I deny that sex knowledge tends to make young folks inquisitive; while on the other hand, hiding from them the real facts of life renders them morbidly curious.

Birth control is becoming of increasing interest to all communities and has really ceased to be regarded as a crime. It is an economic factor that can no longer be ignored. You must know about it.

A knowledge of every-day psychology and the psychology of sex are of great importance as they influence our daily lives. They impart to us a feeling of tolerance for our less fortunate brothers and sisters upon whom Nature has played queer pranks. Many whom we formerly regarded as criminals, we now know to be sick; they are really more to be pitied than censured.

Folks so frequently say they are not interested in eugenics. This is an unintentional falsehood, as every sane parent wants to be proud of its offspring. This volume will be found of encyclopedic scope on Eugenics and so many other subjects, it is impossible to comment on all in a foreword. Eugenics and Sex Harmony is written in a language easily understood and will be found a valuable guide book for every household. It should have appeared long ago.

WINFIELD SCOTT PUGH, M.D.

New York City.

SIGNIFICANCE

Winfield Scott Pugh's introduction to *Eugenics and Sex Harmony* introduced readers to an unfamiliar aspect of the eugenics movement—open discussion of and enlightened attitudes about sex. Today eugenics is a discredited philosophy that advocates "improving" the human race for dubious racial and social ends through genetic selection. The Nazi movement in Germany borrowed its dream of a "master race" from the teachings of American eugenicists.

Eugenicists believed that applying science to human breeding would solve several vexing problems that faced American society in the early twentieth century. In pursuit of their goals, they advocated an agenda that is still considered important today—better public health, family planning, realistic preparation for marriage, and sex education. They saw these as ways to encourage reproduction of the "best and the brightest." Unfortunately, their belief that character and mental traits had a large, usually overwhelming heritable component also led them to promote the exclusion and even persecution of many groups they considered "undesirable" and "unfit": criminals, alcoholics, the mentally ill, retarded, paupers, racial and ethnic minorities, and those with chronic physical disabilities.

Many prominent Americans were eugenicists, and their views had broad support in public policy. Their goal was to insulate the American gene pool from "contamination." Unfortunately, their advocacy led to the forced sterilization of the mentally ill; antimiscegenation laws, which forbade marriages between people of different races; and immigration restrictions. At the height of the eugenics movement in the U.S., President Theodore Roosevelt warned that the American middle class was committing "racial suicide" by having too few children, a quote that reverberated for at least another generation thereafter.

Despite these disturbing objectives, eugenics was sold to the public as a method of family management. The Eugenics Record Office, a privately funded center for eugenics thought and "research" that was eventually annexed to the Carnegie Insititution, published several self-help manuals for life and marital management, of which *Eugenics and Sex Harmony* was a typical example. Eugenics was even presented as a mainstream science by most high school biology textbooks, and chairs for eugenics were established at prominent American universities.

After World War II and Nazi atrocities showed the terrifying extent to which eugenics could take mankind, the theory fell into disrepute among both scientists and the general population. The concepts of eugenics were disputed by geneticists, and its few testable predictions proved unfounded. The growing American civil rights movement and an expanding conviction that poverty and criminality had social and environmental causes revealed eugenicists' narrow, judgmental, and simplistic assumptions, and also challenged their view of social progress. The benign tone of the foreword to *Eugenics and Sex Harmony* belied the nefarious and coercive public policy tactics desired by eugenicists, including racial segregation, bans on interracial marriage, immigration restrictions, and the forced sterilization of "unfit" individuals.

Eugenics still casts a shadow on discussions of "nature" and "nurture" in the development of personality, intelligence, and social behavior. As humanity learns about the human genome and discovers ways to manipulate genetically based processes, it is possible that this knowledge might once again empower a cold and narrow view of humanity—this time supplying its advocates with real tools for selecting "ideal" human traits.

FURTHER RESOURCES

Books

Hankins, Frank Hamilton. *Birth Control and the Racial Future.* New York: People, 1931.

Rubin, Herman H. *Eugenics and Sex Harmony: The Sexes, Their Relations and Problems.* New York: Pioneer, 1938.

Periodicals

Eugenical News. "Commentary and Full Translation of the German Sterilization Statute of 1933: Eugenical Sterilization in Germany." 18, no. 5 (September-October 1933).

Kempton, J. H., "Sterilization for Ten Million Americans." *Journal of Heredity* 25, no. 10 (October 1934): 415–418.

New York Times. "A Critical Review of the Third International Eugenics Congress. 'Genes and Eugenics.'" (August 24, 1932) p. 16.

Web sites

Image Archive on the American Eugenics Movement. <www.eugenicsarchive.org/eugenics> (accessed November 13, 2005).

Nuremberg Code Establishes the Principle of Informed Consent

Legal document

By: Nuremberg Military Tribunal

Date: August 19, 1947

Source: Excerpt of the verdict in the case of *U.S.A. v. Karl Brandt et al.* ("Doctors Trial"), contained in *Trials of War Criminals before the Nuremberg Military Tribunals under Control Council Law No. 10* (Washington, D.C., U.S. Government Printing Office, 1949), vol. 2, pp. 181–183.

About the Author: After World War II (1939–1945), the Allied nations established a series of International Military Tribunals, mostly at Nuremberg, Germany, to try several high-ranking Nazis as war criminals. These trials sought to bring to justice those responsible for the atrocities of the Holocaust. Among the defendants were physicians who had either ordered or performed the torture or murder of prisoners in numerous Nazi concentration and death camps.

INTRODUCTION

Since ancient times, beneficence has been a key principle of the medical profession, enshrined in the Hippocratic Oath and subsequent codes of medical ethics. Beneficence entails that physicians must always put the needs and welfare of patients first. By extension, bioscientists must always put the needs and welfare of human research subjects first. However, until the verdict was handed down in the Nuremberg "Doctor's Trial," the specific rights of human subjects of modern biomedical research were not codified.

Twenty-three physicians, including Karl Brandt, Adolf Hitler's personal physician, were charged as defendants at Nuremberg. The most notorious offender, Josef Mengele of Auschwitz, escaped and was never brought to trial. The court found that the Nazi government had instituted a clear policy of performing cruel and unnecessarily painful experiments of dubious scientific merit on non-consenting prisoners, mostly Poles, Jews, Gypsies, homosexuals, and the handicapped. The trial, under judges Walter B. Beals, Harold L. Sebring, Johnson T. Crawford, and Victor T. Swearingen, all Americans, lasted from December 9, 1946, to August 20, 1947. Seven defendants were acquitted, sixteen were convicted; seven, including Brandt, were sentenced to be hanged.

One of the most important outcomes of the Doctor's Trial was the portion of the verdict subtitled "Permissible Medical Experiments," which defined the concept of informed consent and marked the beginning of international jurisprudence and regulation in this aspect of biomedical research ethics. Its ten enumerated principles became known as the "Nuremberg Code." Informed consent is what allows human research subjects to be active and voluntary participants rather than victims or unwilling tools of the scientific process.

▮ PRIMARY SOURCE

PERMISSIBLE MEDICAL EXPERIMENTS

The great weight of the evidence before us is to the effect that certain types of medical experiments on human beings, when kept within reasonably well-defined bounds, conform to the ethics of the medical profession generally. The protagonists of the practice of human experimentation justify their views on the basis that such experiments yield results for the good of society that are unprocurable by other methods or means of study. All agree, however, that certain basic principles must be observed in order to satisfy moral, ethical and legal concepts:

1. The voluntary consent of the human subject is absolutely essential.

This means that the person involved should have legal capacity to give consent; should be so situated as to be able to exercise free power of choice, without the intervention of any element of force, fraud, deceit, duress, over-reaching, or other ulterior form of constraint or coercion; and should have sufficient knowledge and comprehension of the elements of the subject matter involved as to enable him to make an understanding and enlightened decision. This latter element requires that before the acceptance of an affirmative decision by the experimental subject there should be made known to him the nature, duration, and purpose of the experiment; the method and means by which it is to be conducted; all inconveniences and hazards reasonably to be expected; and the effects upon his health or person which may possibly come from his participation in the experiment.

The duty and responsibility for ascertaining the quality of the consent rests upon each individual who initiates, directs or engages in the experiment. It is a personal duty and responsibility which may not be delegated to another with impunity.

2. The experiment should be such as to yield fruitful results for the good of society, unprocurable by other methods or means of study, and not random and unnecessary in nature.

3. The experiment should be so designed and based on the results of animal experimentation and a knowledge of the natural history of the disease or other problem under study that the anticipated results will justify the performance of the experiment.

4. The experiment should be so conducted as to avoid all unnecessary physical and mental suffering and injury.

5. No experiment should be conducted where there is an a priori reason to believe that death or disabling injury will occur; except, perhaps, in those experiments where the experimental physicians also serve as subjects.

6. The degree of risk to be taken should never exceed that determined by the humanitarian importance of the problem to be solved by the experiment.

7. Proper preparations should be made and adequate facilities provided to protect the experimental subject against even remote possibilities of injury, disability, or death.

8. The experiment should be conducted only by scientifically qualified persons. The highest degree of skill and care should be required through all stages of the experiment of those who conduct or engage in the experiment.

9. During the course of the experiment the human subject should be at liberty to bring the experiment to an end if he has reached the physical or mental state where continuation of the experiment seems to him to be impossible.

10. During the course of the experiment the scientist in charge must be prepared to terminate the experiment at any stage, if he has probably cause to believe, in the exercise of the good faith, superior skill and careful judgment required of him that a continuation of the experiment is likely to result in injury, disability, or death to the experimental subject.

Of the ten principles which have been enumerated our judicial concern, of course, is with those requirements which are purely legal in nature—or which at least are so clearly related to matters legal that they assist us in determining criminal culpability and punishment. To go beyond that point would lead us into a field that would be beyond our sphere of competence. However, the point need not be labored. We find from the evidence that in the medical experiments which have been proved, these ten principles were much more frequently honored in their breach than in their observance. Many of the concentration camp inmates who were the victims of these atrocities were citizens of countries other than the German Reich. They were non-German nationals, including Jews and "asocial persons," both prisoners of war and civilians, who had been imprisoned and forced to submit to these tortures and barbarities without so much as a semblance of trial. In every single instance appearing in the record, subjects were used who did not consent to the experiments; indeed, as to some of the experiments, it is not even contended by the defendants that the subjects occupied the status of volunteers. In no case was the experimental subject at liberty of his own free choice to withdraw from any experiment. In many cases experiments were performed by unqualified persons; were conducted at random for no adequate scientific reason, and under revolting physical conditions. All of the experiments were conducted with unnecessary suffering and injury and but very little, if any, precautions were taken to protect or safeguard the human subjects from the possibilities of injury, disability, or death. In every one of the experiments the subjects experienced extreme pain or torture, and in most of them they suffered permanent injury, mutilation, or death, either as a direct result of the experiments or because of lack of adequate follow-up care.

Obviously all of these experiments involving brutalities, tortures, disabling injury, and death were performed in complete disregard of international conventions, the laws and customs of war, the general principles of criminal law as derived from the criminal laws of all civilized nations, and Control Council Law No. 10. Manifestly human experiments under such conditions are contrary to "the principles of the law of nations as they result from the usages established among civilized peoples, from the laws of humanity, and from the dictates of public conscience."

Whether any of the defendants in the dock are guilty of these atrocities is, of course, another question.

SIGNIFICANCE

For two decades after the Nazi atrocities came to light, a false and self-satisfied optimism pervaded the Western world that such cruel mockeries of good science could only happen under dictatorships such as Hitler's. While indeed the Nazi abuses of human research subjects were the worst, other blatant and unjustifiable violations of the principle of informed consent continued to occur throughout the West. Two examples are the study of syphilis among African-American men in Tuskegee, Alabama, funded by the federal government from 1932–1972, and the study of hepatitis among children at the Willowbrook State School for the Retarded, Staten Island, funded by New York State from 1955–1972.

As these abuses were gradually exposed, various governmental and professional agencies, both national and international, moved to counteract them and to prevent future occurrences. The Helsinki Declaration of the World Medical Association in 1964, the U.S. National Research Act in 1974, the Belmont Report of the U.S. Department of Health, Education, and Welfare in 1979, and the Common Rule of the U.S. Department of Health and Human Services in 1991 can all be seen as corollaries to the Nuremberg Code.

FURTHER RESOURCES

Books

Baumslag, Naomi. *Murderous Medicine: Nazi Doctors, Human Experimentation, and Typhus.* Westport, Conn.: Praeger, 2005.

Lifton, Robert Jay. *The Nazi Doctors: Medical Killing and the Psychology of Genocide.* New York: Basic Books, 2000.

Schmidt, Ulf. *Justice at Nuremberg: Leo Alexander and the Nazi Doctors' Trial.* New York: Palgrave Macmillan, 2004.

Spitz, Vivien. *Doctors from Hell: The Horrific Account of Nazi Experiments on Humans.* Boulder, Colo.: Sentient, 2005.

Weindling, Paul. *Nazi Medicine and the Nuremberg Trials: From Medical War Crimes to Informed Consent.* New York: Palgrave Macmillan, 2004.

Periodicals

Kious, B. M. "The Nuremberg Code: Its History and Implications." *Princeton Journal of Bioethics* (2001): vol. 4, 7–19.

Marrus, M. R. "The Nuremberg Doctors' Trial in Historical Context." *Bulletin of the History of Medicine* (1999): vol. 73, no. 1, 106–123.

Web sites

United States Holocaust Memorial Museum. "Online Exhibitions: The Doctors Trial, Nuremberg Code excerpt."

<www.ushmm.org/research/doctors/Nuremberg_Code.htm> (accessed January 9, 2006).

University of Missouri–Kansas City, School of Law. "Nuremberg Trials: 1945–1949." <www.law.umkc.edu/faculty/projects/ftrials/nuremberg/nuremberg.htm> (accessed January 9, 2006).

Wilson Memorandum

Use of Human Volunteers in Experimental Research

Government document

By: Charles E. Wilson

Date: February 26, 1953

Source: Department of Energy. "DOE: Openness: Human Radiation Experiments." <http://www.eh.doe.gov/ohre/index.html> (accessed November 29, 2005).

About the Author: Charles E. Wilson (1890–1961) left the presidency of General Motors to serve as Secretary of Defense for President Dwight D. Eisenhower from 1953 to 1957. As a business executive of some note in the administration of a former United States Army general, Wilson was expected to concentrate on defense management rather than formulation of basic national security policy. Wilson reorganized the Department of Defense and attempted to run the Pentagon like a business corporation with much authority decentralized to allow for greater civilian control. He also implemented Eisenhower's New Look program for the military that reduced conventional weapons and increased the number of nuclear weapons in an effort to do more with less money. The Wilson-Eisenhower effort to curb defense expenditures provoked criticism from military leadership and Congress. In 1957, Wilson resigned his office and retired to Michigan.

INTRODUCTION

From 1944 to 1974, the U.S. government prepared for possible war with the Soviet Union by attempting to determine the effects of radiation on the human body. Military and government leaders assumed that as both the United States and the Soviet Union possessed nuclear weapons, any war between the countries would likely involve nuclear attacks on major cities with hundreds of thousands of people likely suffering heavy radiation exposure.

While radiation experiments were conducted in San Francisco, Chicago, and Rochester, New York, the experiments at Cincinnati General Hospital are perhaps the best known. For eleven years beginning in 1960, University of Cincinnati physicians at the hospital irradiated ninety unwitting patients as research for the Department of Defense. This project needed subjects who could be irradiated over their whole bodies as if for treatment of cancer. The radiation was given in one continuous dose in an effort to stimulate the exposure of soldiers in nuclear war. Twenty men and women died within a month of exposure.

The experience of Lula Tarlton was typical. Tarlton, an elderly African American domestic worker, had a recurrence of breast cancer. After receiving total body radiation in the basement of the hospital, she vomited profusely for weeks, then fell into convulsions and died. Like other patients in the experiment, Tarlton received no follow-up care, such as help with nausea or pain. Additionally, no consent form had been offered to Tarlton and no one in her family knew that she had participated in an experiment. According to the doctors, patients were told only that they were being treated for their disease.

In 1972, University of Cincinnati English professor Martha Stephens read an account in *The Village Voice* about radiation experiments. Wondering about possible tests done at her own school, she headed over to the University of Cincinnati medical school and convinced the director to share six hundred pages of files. Shocked, she helped author a report by the Junior Faculty Association that put an immediate halt to the experiments but the findings were almost completely ignored by the Cincinnati media. The researchers hotly denied any wrongdoing and the media regarded them as more credible.

PRIMARY SOURCE

26 February 1953
Memorandum for the Secretary of the Army
Secretary of the Navy
Secretary of the Air Force
Subject: Use of Human Volunteers in Experimental Research

1. Based upon a recommendation of the Armed Forces Medical Policy Council, that human subjects be employed, under recognized safeguards, as the only feasible means for realistic evaluation and/or development of effective preventive measures of defense against atomic, biological, or chemical agents, the policy set forth below will govern the use of human volunteers by the Department

of Defense in experimental research in the fields of atomic, biological and/or chemical warfare.

2. By reason of the basic medical responsibility in connection with the development of defense of all types against atomic, biological and/or chemical warfare agents, Armed Services personnel and/or civilians on duty at installations engaged in such research shall be permitted to actively participate in all phases of the program, such participation shall be subject to the following conditions:

a. The voluntary consent of the human subject is absolutely essential.

1) This means that the person involved should have legal capacity to give consent; should also be so situated as to be able to exercise free power of choice, without the intervention of any element of force, fraud, deceit, duress, over-reaching, or other ulterior form of constraint or coercion; and should have sufficient knowledge and comprehension of the elements of the subject matter involved as to enable him to make an understanding and enlightened decision. This latter element requires that before the acceptance of an affirmative decision by the experimental subject there should be made known to him the nature, duration, and purpose of the experiment; the method and means by which it is to be conducted; all inconveniences and hazards reasonably to be expected; and the effects upon his health or person which may possibly come from his participation in the experiment....

f) No experiment should be conducted where there is an a priori reason to believe that death or disabling injury will occur....

h) Proper preparation should be made and adequate facilities provided to protect the experimental subject against even remote possibilities of injury, disability, or death....

k) During the course of the experiment the scientist in charge must be prepared to terminate the experiment at any stage, if he has probable cause to believe, in the exercise of the good faith, superior skill and careful judgment required of him that a continuation of the experiment is likely to result in injury, disability, or death to the experimental subject.

l) The established policy, which prohibits the use of prisoners of war in human experimentation, is continued and they will not be used under any circumstances.

3. The Secretaries of the Army, Navy, and Air Force are authorized to conduct experiments in connection with the development of defenses of all types against atomic,

biological and/or chemical warfare agents involving the use of human subjects within the limits prescribed above. . . .

/signed/
C. E. Wilson
copies furnished:
Joint Chiefs of Staff
Research and Development Board
TOP SECRET
Downgraded to UNCLASSIFIED
22 Aug 75

SIGNIFICANCE

While the U.S. government had protections in place for the protection of human subjects since the issuing of the 1953 Wilson Memorandum, these protections were kept secret from the public. By the time that the government made the protections public in 1973, a number of Americans had received exposure to radiation, often in the form of injections of plutonium and uranium. Scientists claimed that the subjects were terminally ill anyway and would not survive the ten years required to be significantly affected by a small radiation dose.

In late 1993, Hazel O'Leary, Secretary of the Department of Energy in the administration of President Bill Clinton, became concerned about possible human rights violations in connection with Cold War-era radiation research experiments. Like all radiation research in the early Cold War, the results had been classified secret but the information was declassified and made generally available in the 1960s. However, the media missed the story and the research remained largely unknown to the general public. O'Leary formed the Presidential Advisory Committee on Human Radiation Experiments. In October 1995, the committee recommended that financial compensation be made to the surviving family members of the radiation subjects.

The families of radiation test subjects who received plutonium injections received a $4.8 million settlement from the U.S. government in 1996. Physicians were uncertain whether the deaths of the subjects were directly related to the experiments. However, plutonium exposure causes painful osteoporosis and autopsies on patients injected with plutonium revealed bones that "looked like Swiss cheese" according to a lawyer for the plaintiffs. Survivors and next-of-kin of the Cincinnati radiation subjects sued the University of Cincinnati, the researchers, and, as one-time owner of the hospital, the city of Cincinnati for fraud and violation of civil rights. In 1999, they won a $3.5 million settlement and

the erection of a small memorial on the college campus.

The Department of Energy established the Office of Human Radiation Experiments in March 1994 to address the government's role in radiation research. It is charged with identifying and cataloging 3.2 million cubic feet of records scattered across the country.

FURTHER RESOURCES

Books

Stephens, Martha. *The Treatment: The Story of Those Who Died in the Cincinnati Radiation Tests*. Durham: Duke University Press, 2002.

Web sites

Department of Energy. "DOE: Openness: Human Radiation Experiments." <http://www.eh.doe.gov/ohre/index.html> (accessed November 29, 2005).

World Medical Association Declaration of Helsinki

Ethical Principles for Medical Research Involving Human Subjects

Declaration

By: World Medical Association

Date: June 1964

Source: *World Medical Association Declaration of Helsinki: Ethical Principles for Medical Research Involving Human Subjects: Adopted by the 18th WMA General Assembly, Helsinki, Finland, June 1964, and Amended by the 29th WMA General Assembly, Tokyo, Japan, October 1975; the 35th WMA General Assembly, Venice, Italy, October 1983; the 41st WMA General Assembly, Hong Kong, September 1989; the 48th WMA General Assembly, Somerset West, Republic of South Africa, October 1996; and the 52nd WMA General Assembly, Edinburgh, Scotland, October 2000; Note of Clarification on Paragraph 29 Added by the WMA General Assembly, Washington 2002; Note of Clarification on Paragraph 30 Added by the WMA General Assembly, Tokyo 2004.*

About the Author: The World Medical Association (WMA), founded in Paris on September 17, 1947, describes itself as "the global representative body for physicians." Its earliest mission was to develop and promote the highest standards of medical ethics as a means to ensure that the kinds of crimes committed by Nazi physicians in World War II would never be repeated. Since then, it has worked more broadly through about eighty national medical associations to improve the professional lives of physicians and especially to safeguard their independence. The organization is a prolific author of policy statements on all aspects of medical ethics.

INTRODUCTION

The goal of the WMA 18th General Assembly in 1964 was to write a clear policy statement to help physicians and bioscientists navigate the increasingly complex issues and vocabulary of research ethics. Awareness had grown after the Nuremberg "Doctor's Trial" in 1947 that even when a certain research protocol is necessary to advance the cause of science, it cannot be justified when it puts unwitting human beings in jeopardy. The WMA responded not only to deliberate abuses such as the Nazi atrocities, but also to accidental or careless violations of medical and scientific ethics. The organization paid special attention to the plight of vulnerable populations of potential research subjects such as children, the terminally ill, the incompetent, the incapacitated, and the handicapped.

The WMA considered competence, a person's ability to think and act reasonably in general, and capacity, a person's ability to understand and judge a particular set of options, in terms of individual autonomy. It tied the well-being of each patient and research subject to the complementary concepts of informed consent and informed refusal—the free, uncoerced, and absolute right of every competent, capable individual, or guardian of an incompetent or incapacitated individual, to decide if a certain medical, surgical, or scientific procedure can be performed on him or her.

Because questions of how the biomedical research community recruits, educates, protects, and compensates the human subjects of its research continue to perplex ethicists, fund granting agencies, and government regulators, the WMA frequently updates the Helsinki Declaration. It adopted the following version on October 9, 2004.

PRIMARY SOURCE

A. INTRODUCTION 1. The World Medical Association has developed the Declaration of Helsinki as a statement of ethical principles to provide guidance to physicians and other participants in medical research involving human subjects. Medical research involving human subjects includes research on identifiable human material or identifiable data.

2. It is the duty of the physician to promote and safeguard the health of the people. The physician's knowledge and conscience are dedicated to the fulfillment of this duty.

3. The Declaration of Geneva of the World Medical Association binds the physician with the words, "The health of my patient will be my first consideration," and the International Code of Medical Ethics declares that, "A physician shall act only in the patient's interest when providing medical care which might have the effect of weakening the physical and mental condition of the patient."

4. Medical progress is based on research which ultimately must rest in part on experimentation involving human subjects.

5. In medical research on human subjects, considerations related to the well-being of the human subject should take precedence over the interests of science and society.

6. The primary purpose of medical research involving human subjects is to improve prophylactic, diagnostic and therapeutic procedures and the understanding of the aetiology and pathogenesis of disease. Even the best proven prophylactic, diagnostic, and therapeutic methods must continuously be challenged through research for their effectiveness, efficiency, accessibility and quality.

7. In current medical practice and in medical research, most prophylactic, diagnostic and therapeutic procedures involve risks and burdens.

8. Medical research is subject to ethical standards that promote respect for all human beings and protect their health and rights. Some research populations are vulnerable and need special protection. The particular needs of the economically and medically disadvantaged must be recognized. Special attention is also required for those who cannot give or refuse consent for themselves, for those who may be subject to giving consent under duress, for those who will not benefit personally from the research and for those for whom the research is combined with care.

9. Research Investigators should be aware of the ethical, legal and regulatory requirements for research on human subjects in their own countries as well as applicable international requirements. No national ethical, legal or regulatory requirement should be allowed to reduce or eliminate any of the protections for human subjects set forth in this Declaration.

B. BASIC PRINCIPLES FOR ALL MEDICAL RESEARCH 10. It is the duty of the physician in medical research to protect the life, health, privacy, and dignity of the human subject.

11. Medical research involving human subjects must conform to generally accepted scientific principles, be based on a thorough knowledge of the scientific literature, other

relevant sources of information, and on adequate laboratory and, where appropriate, animal experimentation.

12. Appropriate caution must be exercised in the conduct of research which may affect the environment, and the welfare of animals used for research must be respected.

13. The design and performance of each experimental procedure involving human subjects should be clearly formulated in an experimental protocol. This protocol should be submitted for consideration, comment, guidance, and where appropriate, approval to a specially appointed ethical review committee, which must be independent of the investigator, the sponsor or any other kind of undue influence. This independent committee should be in conformity with the laws and regulations of the country in which the research experiment is performed. The committee has the right to monitor ongoing trials. The researcher has the obligation to provide monitoring information to the committee, especially any serious adverse events. The researcher should also submit to the committee, for review, information regarding funding, sponsors, institutional affiliations, other potential conflicts of interest and incentives for subjects.

14. The research protocol should always contain a statement of the ethical considerations involved and should indicate that there is compliance with the principles enunciated in this Declaration.

15. Medical research involving human subjects should be conducted only by scientifically qualified persons and under the supervision of a clinically competent medical person. The responsibility for the human subject must always rest with a medically qualified person and never rest on the subject of the research, even though the subject has given consent.

16. Every medical research project involving human subjects should be preceded by careful assessment of predictable risks and burdens in comparison with foreseeable benefits to the subject or to others. This does not preclude the participation of healthy volunteers in medical research. The design of all studies should be publicly available.

17. Physicians should abstain from engaging in research projects involving human subjects unless they are confident that the risks involved have been adequately assessed and can be satisfactorily managed. Physicians should cease any investigation if the risks are found to outweigh the potential benefits or if there is conclusive proof of positive and beneficial results.

18. Medical research involving human subjects should only be conducted if the importance of the objective outweighs the inherent risks and burdens to the subject. This is especially important when the human subjects are healthy volunteers.

19. Medical research is only justified if there is a reasonable likelihood that the populations in which the research is carried out stand to benefit from the results of the research.

20. The subjects must be volunteers and informed participants in the research project.

21. The right of research subjects to safeguard their integrity must always be respected. Every precaution should be taken to respect the privacy of the subject, the confidentiality of the patient's information and to minimize the impact of the study on the subject's physical and mental integrity and on the personality of the subject.

22. In any research on human beings, each potential subject must be adequately informed of the aims, methods, sources of funding, any possible conflicts of interest, institutional affiliations of the researcher, the anticipated benefits and potential risks of the study and the discomfort it may entail. The subject should be informed of the right to abstain from participation in the study or to withdraw consent to participate at any time without reprisal. After ensuring that the subject has understood the information, the physician should then obtain the subject's freely given informed consent, preferably in writing. If the consent cannot be obtained in writing, the non-written consent must be formally documented and witnessed.

23. When obtaining informed consent for the research project the physician should be particularly cautious if the subject is in a dependent relationship with the physician or may consent under duress. In that case the informed consent should be obtained by a well-informed physician who is not engaged in the investigation and who is completely independent of this relationship.

24. For a research subject who is legally incompetent, physically or mentally incapable of giving consent or is a legally incompetent minor, the investigator must obtain informed consent from the legally authorized representative in accordance with applicable law. These groups should not be included in research unless the research is necessary to promote the health of the population represented and this research cannot instead be performed on legally competent persons.

25. When a subject deemed legally incompetent, such as a minor child, is able to give assent to decisions about participation in research, the investigator must obtain that assent in addition to the consent of the legally authorized representative.

26. Research on individuals from whom it is not possible to obtain consent, including proxy or advance consent, should be done only if the physical/mental condition that prevents obtaining informed consent is a necessary characteristic of the research population. The specific reasons for involving research subjects with a condition that

renders them unable to give informed consent should be stated in the experimental protocol for consideration and approval of the review committee. The protocol should state that consent to remain in the research should be obtained as soon as possible from the individual or a legally authorized surrogate.

27. Both authors and publishers have ethical obligations. In publication of the results of research, the investigators are obliged to preserve the accuracy of the results. Negative as well as positive results should be published or otherwise publicly available. Sources of funding, institutional affiliations and any possible conflicts of interest should be declared in the publication. Reports of experimentation not in accordance with the principles laid down in this Declaration should not be accepted for publication.

C. Additional Principles for Medical Research Combined with Medical Care 28. The physician may combine medical research with medical care, only to the extent that the research is justified by its potential prophylactic, diagnostic or therapeutic value. When medical research is combined with medical care, additional standards apply to protect the patients who are research subjects.

29. The benefits, risks, burdens and effectiveness of a new method should be tested against those of the best current prophylactic, diagnostic, and therapeutic methods. This does not exclude the use of placebo, or no treatment, in studies where no proven prophylactic, diagnostic or therapeutic method exists.

30. At the conclusion of the study, every patient entered into the study should be assured of access to the best proven prophylactic, diagnostic and therapeutic methods identified by the study.

31. The physician should fully inform the patient which aspects of the care are related to the research. The refusal of a patient to participate in a study must never interfere with the patient-physician relationship.

32. In the treatment of a patient, where proven prophylactic, diagnostic and therapeutic methods do not exist or have been ineffective, the physician, with informed consent from the patient, must be free to use unproven or new prophylactic, diagnostic and therapeutic measures, if in the physician's judgement it offers hope of saving life, re-establishing health or alleviating suffering. Where possible, these measures should be made the object of research, designed to evaluate their safety and efficacy. In all cases, new information should be recorded and, where appropriate, published. The other relevant guidelines of this Declaration should be followed.

Note of Clarification on Paragraph 29 of the WMA Declaration of Helsinki: The WMA hereby reaffirms its position that extreme care must be taken in making use of a placebo-controlled trial and that in general this methodology should only be used in the absence of existing proven therapy. However, a placebo-controlled trial may be ethically acceptable, even if proven therapy is available, under the following circumstances:

Where for compelling and scientifically sound methodological reasons its use is necessary to determine the efficacy or safety of a prophylactic, diagnostic or therapeutic method; or

Where a prophylactic, diagnostic or therapeutic method is being investigated for a minor condition and the patients who receive placebo will not be subject to any additional risk of serious or irreversible harm.

All other provisions of the Declaration of Helsinki must be adhered to, especially the need for appropriate ethical and scientific review.

Note of Clarification on Paragraph 30 of the WMA Declaration of Helsinki: The WMA hereby reaffirms its position that it is necessary during the study planning process to identify post-trial access by study participants to prophylactic, diagnostic and therapeutic procedures identified as beneficial in the study or access to other appropriate care. Post-trial access arrangements or other care must be described in the study protocol so the ethical review committee may consider such arrangements during its review.

SIGNIFICANCE

The medical profession consists of the "three-legged stool," research, education, and patient care. If any of these three legs breaks, then the stool collapses. The Helsinki Declaration, the Nuremberg Code, the Belmont Report, the Common Rule, and other essential modern documents in medical ethics, primarily address research. International ethics guidelines for research practices emphasize the importance of public confidence in the integrity and beneficence of biomedical science. The basic model of medical and bioscientific professionalism shifted in the late twentieth century from paternalism toward a general respect for the autonomy of patients and research subjects. Medicine shifted from doctor-centered to patient-centered and bioscience shifted from scientist-centered to subject-centered.

Influenced by the Nuremberg and Helsinki documents, and motivated in reaction to the cruelty of the Tuskegee Syphilis Study and the hepatitis experiments at the Willowbrook State School for the Retarded on Staten Island, theologian Paul Ramsey (1913–1988) founded the consumer health movement in 1970 with his book, *The Patient as Person*. Even though Ramsey's focus was on patients, he recognized that his words applied equally to medical research subjects. Both the WMA and Ramsey sought to empower patients and research subjects by law, education, and publicity.

FURTHER RESOURCES

Books

Faden, Ruth R., Tom L. Beauchamp, and Nancy King. *A History and Theory of Informed Consent.* New York: Oxford University Press, 1986.

Macklin, Ruth. *Double Standards in Medical Research in Developing Countries.* Cambridge: Cambridge University Press, 2004.

Periodicals

Levine, R. J. "International Codes of Research Ethics: Current Controversies and the Future." *Indiana Law Review.* vol. 35, no. 2 (2002): 557–567.

Rhodes, R. "Rethinking Research Ethics." *American Journal of Bioethics.* vol. 5, no. 1 (2005): 7–28.

Web sites

National Institutes of Health. "Regulations and Ethical Guidelines." <http://ohsr.od.nih.gov/guidelines/helsinki.html> (accessed January 15, 2006).

University of Nevada—Las Vegas, Division of Research and Graduate Studies, Office for the Protection of Research Subjects. "History of Research Ethics." <http://www.unlv.edu/Research/OPRS/history-ethics.htm> (accessed January 9, 2006).

The World Medical Association. "Policy." <http://www.wma.net/e/policy/> (accessed January 15, 2006).

Survivor of '32 Syphilis Study Recalls a Diagnosis

Newspaper article

By: James T. Wooten

Date: July 27, 1972

Source: James T. Wooten. "Survivor of '32 Syphilis Study Recalls a Diagnosis." *New York Times* (July 27, 1972).

About the Author: James T. Wooten was a staff writer for the *New York Times*, a daily newspaper with a circulation of more than one million readers worldwide.

INTRODUCTION

In 1932, the U.S. Public Health Service (USPHS) under Taliaferro Clark of the Venereal Disease Division began an experiment in Macon County, Alabama, to determine the natural course of untreated, latent syphilis in African American men. The experiment, known as the Tuskegee Syphilis Study, involved 400 men with syphilis, as well as 200 uninfected men who served as controls. The men were told that they were ill with "bad blood," a rural Southern colloquialism for syphilis and anemia, but were never informed that they were participants in a study. The USPHS was investigating the possibility that anti-syphilitic treatment was unnecessary.

Syphilis is a sexually transmitted disease. In pregnant women, the disease, if untreated, is transmitted to the baby. In the primary period of syphilis infection, which lasts from three to eight weeks, a painless sore appears at the point of infection with similar sores spreading throughout the groin area, on the fingers, and on the eyelids. The secondary stage of syphilis occurs at least forty-five days after the appearance of a red, hard lesion. This stage can last for two to three years and has numerous clinical symptoms, including aching in the bones and joints, rashes, mouth sores, fevers, and headaches. Symptoms of the third stage of syphilis appear a minimum of five years after infection, but sometimes do not arise until twenty or thirty years later. In the tertiary stage, rashes appear over the entire body, hair is often lost, mushroom-like growths appear over the genitals and rectum, eye disease often occurs, and parts of the body are damaged, especially the heart, brain, and bones. The long-term effects of syphilis can include hepatitis, meningitis, central nervous systems disease, and heart and blood vessel diseases, culminating in death.

Despite the fact that major medical textbooks in 1932 advocated treating syphilis at the latent stage, the USPHS actively prevented the men enrolled in the study from receiving treatment. They were never given a clear diagnosis. In 1934, the USPHS advised local black hospitals not to treat the study subjects, and when the Alabama Health Department took a mobile venereal disease unit into Macon County in the early 1940s, the USPHS advised the health officials to deny treatment to the test subjects. At the start of World War II (1941–1945), several of the men were drafted for military service and were told by the Army to begin anti-syphilitic treatment. Concerned about the continuation of the experiment, the USPHS gave the names of 256 study members to the Alabama state draft board and asked that they not be drafted and, thus, receive treatment in the military. The draft board complied with the request. When penicillin became widely available by the early 1950s as a cure for syphilis, the men enrolled in the study did not receive treatment.

No effort was made by the USPHS to protect the wives and families of the diseased men from syphilis. The officials in charge of the experiment presumed that syphilis existed naturally in the black community, presumed that African American men were promiscuous, and presumed they would not seek or continue treatment even if given the choice.

The first published report of the Tuskegee Syphilis Study appeared in 1936, with subsequent papers issued every four to six years throughout the 1960s. Each report noted the ravages of untreated syphilis. In 1969, a committee from the Centers for Disease Control decided that the study should be continued. However, by this time, some of the test subjects had received antibiotics for other illnesses, thereby compromising the syphilis study. Only in July 1972, when the Associated Press reported the story, did the Department of Health, Education, and Welfare (HEW) halt the experiment amid great public outrage. At that time, seventy-four of the test subjects were still alive. Many of the subjects had died from untreated syphilis with estimates of the dead ranging from twenty-eight to one hundred men. In August 1972, HEW appointed an investigatory panel, which subsequently found the study to be "ethically unjustified." HEW declared that penicillin should have been provided to the men. None of the physicians who participated in the study were ever prosecuted for any crimes, although the United States did settle a lawsuit brought by the survivors and their families for $10 million.

PRIMARY SOURCE

Tuskegee, Ala., July 26—They came around one day in 1932 and told Charles Pollard he could get a free physical examination the next afternoon at a nearby one-room school.

"So I went on over and they told me I had bad blood," the 66-year-old farmer recalled today. "And that's what they've been telling me ever since. They come around from time to time and check me over and they say, "Charlie, you've got bad blood."

Yesterday, Mr. Pollard learned that, for the last 40 years, he has had syphilis. He is one of 74 survivors of a United States Public Health Service experiment in which 400 local black men went without treatment for the disease and were used without their consent or knowledge in a study of its ultimate effects.

Dr. Donald Printz of the Center for Disease Control in Atlanta said that the Tuskegee Study, as the project has come to be known, was "almost like genocide." He said

that "a literal death sentence was cast on some of those people."

Today, the Department of Health, Education, and Welfare began a formal inquiry. And a spokesman for Gov. George C. Wallace said Alabama officials were attempting to determine whether state laws requiring mandatory treatment of venereal disease had been violated.

Under those laws, Mr. Pollard should have been given treatment, at public expense if necessary, as soon as the Public Health Service technicians discovered at the school that he was infected with the disease.

The Federal representative had placed him in a 200-man group of infected subjects who would not be informed of their condition or treated for it. A second group of 200 men, also infected, were to have received the best treatment available, but it was disclosed today that none of the 400 men who had syphilis was ever treated.

The third classification within the study was a 200-man group not infected.

While the study began a decade before penicillin was discovered and about 15 years before it was widely available to physicians, the Public Health Service maintained its no-treatment policy with its study subjects after the drug was determined to be effective against the disease.

The program's primary research techniques were periodic examinations and autopsies, both of which were attempts to determine what damage the untreated disease could do to the human body.

In return, the subjects were promised hospital care, free burial, and $100 for their survivors.

"But I never got into that much," Mr. Pollard said today on his 66-acre farm about three miles from Tuskegee, which is 40 miles east of Montgomery. "I've always been able to pretty much make my own way."

He was born, he said, half a mile from the little brick and frame house where he lives with his wife, Louiza. He inherited the land from his father, who was the son of a slave couple.

He appeared to be in excellent health and said he had not missed a day of working "in a long, long time." Dr. Ralph Henderson, of the Center for Disease Control, said that Mr. Pollard was probably among the one-third or so of those who contract syphilis in whom the organism either dies out or becomes dormant without medical intervention.

A newcomer to the Tuskegee Study, Dr. Henderson said that it was his understanding that the term "bad blood" was simply a synonym in the black community for syphilis.

"That could be true," Mr. Pollard said. "But I never heard no such thing. All I knew was that they just kept saying I had the bad blood—they never mention syphilis to me, not even once."

Mr. Pollard, who is described by his neighbors as a "fairly well-to-do man" was dressed today in the traditional garb of farmers in this area—faded blue overalls and a work shirt. He said he had no idea when he might have contracted the disease. He said that his only child, a daughter, was born in 1925.

"My wife hasn't had it—at least not that I know of—and I've been a clean-living man," he said in response to an inquiry about the possible infection of others.

Then he seemed weary of discussing the matter and climbed aboard his tractor. "I have to go to work now," he said. "I understand work. All of the rest of this mess I don't understand."

SIGNIFICANCE

The Tuskegee Syphilis Study was a blatant example of racial bias in medicine. In the early twentieth century, many medical authorities (who were mostly white) wrongly considered African Americans to be especially susceptible to venereal disease due to lust, immorality, unstable families, or other social tendencies. Physicians generally discounted socioeconomic explanations for the poor state of black health and argued that better medical care could not alter the evolutionary scheme. These arguments provided the underpinnings for an ethical lapse at the USPHS, and, as a result, the USPHS jeopardized the health of an entire community by leaving this communicable disease untreated.

The Tuskegee Syphilis Study led to new standards for experiments that employ human subjects. In U.S. Senate hearings on human experimentation held in the wake of publicity about the study, physicians were reminded that the goal of human experimentation must always be to advance the human condition and to improve the situation of the subjects of the study. Institutional review boards were established to guarantee that studies are grounded in scientific principles and that the rights of study participants are protected.

In May 1997, President Bill Clinton issued a formal apology for the Tuskegee Syphilis Study on behalf of the United States government. Surviving participants and families, along with members of the Tuskegee Syphilis Study Legacy Committee, were invited to the White House to witness the president's speech.

FURTHER RESOURCES

Books

Jones, James H. *Bad Blood: The Tuskegee Syphilis Experiment.* New York: Free Press, 1981.

Reverby, Susan M. *Tuskegee's Truths: Rethinking the Tuskegee Syphilis Study.* Chapel Hill: University of North Carolina Press, 2000.

Web sites

National Public Radio (NPR). "Remembering Tuskegee." <http://www.npr.org/programs/morning/features/2002/jul/tuskegee/> (accessed October 20, 2005).

The Pill: How Is It Affecting U.S. Morals, Family Life?

The Pill and the Sexual Revolution

Magazine article

By: Anonymous

Date: July 11, 1966

Source: "The Pill: How Is It Affecting U.S. Morals, Family Life?" *U.S. News & World Report* (July 11, 1966).

About the Author: This unattributed article was written by a staff writer for *U.S. News and World Report*, a weekly news and commentary magazine with a wide circulation.

Introduction

"The pill," the nickname given to an oral contraceptive for women, was the most effective form of birth control ever developed. It separated sexual intercourse from reproduction and made it possible for women to engage in strictly recreational sex. With the introduction of the pill, the sexual revolution of the 1960s became possible.

Created by the American physician Gregory Pincus (1903–1967) at the instigation of birth control pioneer Margaret Sanger (1879–1966), the pill could be taken as easily as an aspirin. A combination of synthetic progesterone and estrogen, it was approved for use as a contraceptive in 1960. By 1965, the two leading producers of the pill, Searle and Syntex, had respective annual sales of $89 million and $60 million. In that same year, it was estimated that one in four married American women under 45 either had used or was using an oral contraceptive. However, not all women could obtain the pill because some states prohibited the sale of contraceptives. In *Griswold v.*

Connecticut (1965), the Supreme Court struck down bans on the use of contraceptives by married couples on the grounds that the Constitution established a "zone of privacy." In 1972, it would extend the same protections to single people.

The availability, ease of use, and reliability of the pill permitted people to engage in sexual activity more freely. In the space of just a few years, sexuality became very open. Sexuality was affirmed as a value in itself, not only for married couples, but for single people as well. *The Human Sexual Response*, a 1966 book by scientists William H. Masters and Virginia E. Johnson, opened a public discussion of how sexual response could be heightened for greater enjoyment. Six years later, Alex Comfort's *The Joy of Sex* climbed the best-seller list.

The sexual revolution of the 1960s was not the first dramatic shift in sexual attitudes. In the 1920s, young people threw off the restraints of the Victorian era by dancing the tango, petting in the backseats of cars, and devising the idea of romantic sexual love. The sexual revolution of the 1960s lacked the innocence of the earlier era because the pill removed the fear of pregnancy as a major restraint on sexual behavior.

▮ PRIMARY SOURCE

An era of vast change in sexual morality now is developing in America.

Fear is being expressed that the nation may be heading into a time of "sexual anarchy."

Just six years ago the birth-control pill came onto the market. Today—

- College girls everywhere are talking about the pill, and many are using it. The pill is turning up in high schools, too.
- City after city is pushing distribution of the pill to welfare recipients, including unmarried women.
- Tens of thousands of Roman Catholic couples are turning to the pill as a means of practicing birth control.

These and other trends are expected to accelerate in times just ahead as laboratories perfect the long term "contraceptive shot" and the retroactive pill which wards off pregnancy even if taken after sexual intercourse.

Result: Widespread concern is developing about the impact of the pill on morality.

Being asked are these questions: With birth control so easy and effective, is the last vestige of sexual restraint to go out the window?

Will mating become casual and random—as among the animals? Recently, John Alexander, general director of the Inter-Varsity Christian Fellowship, which has its headquarters in Chicago, said: "I think it is certain that the pill will tear down the barriers for more than a few young people hitherto restrained by fear of pregnancy—and this will be even more true when the 'retroactive pill' comes on the market. I am very much afraid that sexual anarchy could develop."

The nation's Presbyterian leaders, at their 178th General Assembly, warned recently of increasing "confusion about the meaning of sex," which they ascribed, in large part, to new methods of birth control such as the pill.

Disquiet is voiced even by an official of Planned Parenthood-World Population, which actively promotes birth control. Dr. Donald B. Strauss said: "The two great supports of sexual morality in the past—fear of disease and fear of pregnancy—have now, happily, been largely removed. . . . This, I submit, leaves our generation of parents with a problem that largely remains unsolved."

EARLY PROMISCUITY

The dimensions of that problem are being outlined daily by signs of growing sexual promiscuity among America's young.

The Connecticut State Department of health recently estimated that one 13-year-old girl in every six in the State will become pregnant out of wedlock, before she is 20.

Almost countless incidents have been reported, across the U.S., of teen-age girls in high school carrying birth control pills.

In some cases, these have been supplied by their parents.

"Sex clubs" at high schools are reported from time to time.

On the East Coast, high school girls of the middle and upper income classes join a steady traffic reported among college girls who fly to Puerto Rico for legalized abortions.

Recently a freshman at one of the East's most exclusive girl's colleges told her parents that, when a group in her class visited an Ivy League university as a weekend guests, her classmates stayed the night at motels with boys—some whom they had never seen before and might never see again.

Such occurrences, she said, were commonplace and there were eight or nine pregnancies in her class during the past academic year. Girls declining to engage in sex relations were regarded as "squares," she said.

A different outlook. Seen as playing an important role in the form of "sexual anarchy" among youngsters is a new attitude towards morality. An official at Mills College in

Oakland, CA, reported that "there is less talk than there used to be about right or wrong—the question today is more, 'Is the individual making a wise decision for her future?'" . . .

One thing is clear: the pill, itself, now is becoming a major topic of conversation among students, and among faculty members, too, on nearly all the nation's campuses.

At Brown University, it was disclosed last autumn that the campus health director had prescribed the pill for two unmarried coeds at Pembroke College, the undergraduate school for girls. The health director pointed out that both girls were over 21, and said applicants were carefully questioned. "I want to feel that I'm contributing to a solid relationship and not contributing to unmitigated promiscuity," he said.

The health director's action was defended by Brown University's president and by the Pembroke student newspaper. The latter held that "the social system is geared to safety and efficiency and not to the ordering of the personal lives of its students, or to the legislating of chastity."

From Brown's chaplain, the Rev. Julius S. Scott, Jr., came this comment: "This situation patently documents the moral ambiguity of the contemporary college campus, the collapse of tight ethical systems."

To obtain the pill, most women students must turn to private physicians—or to a "black market" said to exist on a number of campuses.

One news report from Austin, Tex., quoted a gynecologist there as saying he prescribed the pill "without qualms" for eight to ten coeds a month. "I would rather be asked for the pills than for an abortion," this physician was quoted as saying.

In the medical profession, however, some uneasiness is beginning to be felt on the problem. It has been pointed out by some physicians that a doctor could be sued by a girl's parents—or charged with contributing to the delinquency of a minor—if he prescribes the pill without her parents' consent.

As a result, some physicians are prescribing the pills for unmarried girls only on a restricted basis. For example, a Washington D.C. gynecologist said: "If a young woman over 18 years old came in and told me that she wanted a prescription because she was getting married, I would be inclined to give it to her. But, of course, I would have no way of knowing for sure that she really was getting married."

Still other physicians are refusing prescriptions to unmarried girls on any basis. In San Francisco, one said: "I don't like to give pills to a girl without her parents' consent, although I do know that girls can get them freely and are doing so. Some girls get a big supply and pass them around. Some deterrent is needed, and having to tell their parents first is a deterrent."

Student action. Today, a movement appears to be developing among students to force colleges to make pills available to them at college health clinics.

At the University of Texas, a candidate for president of the student body proposed that the pill be dispensed at the student health center. He lost the election, but it was agreed that he had developed a "popular issue."

At Stanford University, students voted more than 2 to 1 in favor of authorities' making contraceptives available to students on an "individual basis," as once was the case. The practice was stopped in 1962 because of complaints from parents, religious groups, and alumni. The university administration has indicated that it has no intention of resuming the practice.

The student senate at American University in Washington D.C., recently called for dissemination of pills and other birth control materials at the school's health center. The matter was dropped, and it was found that coeds at this Methodist-sponsored institution are having no trouble in getting the pill from private physicians.

Much of the student demand is found to center in the metropolitan areas, where, it is pointed out, official policy now is to dispense the pill freely to growing numbers of welfare clients, including many with records of sexual promiscuity.

Changing attitudes. Until recently, church pressure was a curb on private, as well as public, clinics for birth control among the poor.

Today, however, welfare administrators everywhere are turning to the pill as a means of keeping women from producing large broods, many illegitimate, to be supported by the public treasury.

New York, Chicago and Washington D.C., at first limited birth-control services among the poor to married women. Now unmarried women, too, are getting the pill in those cities.

A number of officials and clergymen are voicing concern over this trend. Unchecked, they say, it could lead to official endorsement of the idea that sexual promiscuity is acceptable as long as pregnancy does not result. The Rev. Dexter L. Hanley, S.J., of Georgetown University's law school, told a Senate subcommittee on May 10: "There are those who sincerely feel that the distribution of information and supplies to the unmarried will encourage promiscuity and a breakdown of public morality. . . . If contraceptive advice is to be distributed to the unmarried, two things will be necessary. . . . [firstly] adequate counseling and increased attention to family values . . . secondly, doctors and counselors will have to be able to exercise discretion."

Still another moral dilemma is arising from use of the pill—this one involving Roman Catholic married couples.

Recently a Government-financed study showed that 21 percent of Catholic wives under the age of 45 have used, or are using, birth control pills despite the Church's ban on all unapproved means of family planning.

The comparable figure for Protestant wives was 29 percent.

A number of Catholic clergymen have held the pill to be morally acceptable—not an "unnatural" process as the Church has held earlier contraceptives to be.

Dr. John Rock, a leading Catholic layman and one of the pioneers of the birth control pill, said: "There have been several statements made by authoritative theologians that the method by which the pill works is not clearly against nature, and that there is justification for use of the pill by those who, in all conscience, feel they should practice family planning by this means. Until such time as authoritative instruction comes from the Pope, these theologians believe that the question of 'right or wrong' in regard to the pill is one to be decided by the parents." . . .

What sociologists think. Sociologists point out that the pill, itself, is only one element in the danger of moral anarchy.

Dr. Mary S. Calderone, executive director of Sex Information and Education Council of the U.S., said: "Society provides young people with far too many examples of sex irresponsibly used. High-school kids see sex used as a commercial come on, as an end in itself, presented to them. If the pill hadn't come along, we would be excited about whatever methods were being used."

Even so, the pill is becoming a major factor in the problem. Six million American women are using it. This sudden and overwhelming popularity has caused a few physicians to caution that physical effects over the long run are not thoroughly known. But neither these reservations nor the moral issues are dimming enthusiasm felt by many Americans. One social worker said: "The pill is so clean and simple, and sure, that everybody who hears about it wants it. And I tell everybody about it."

CRISIS AHEAD?

Less enthusiastic are many Americans who feel that the pill is making moral choices much more difficult for a lot of people, and could precipitate a crisis in sexual morality.

Recently the Right Rev. Richard S. Emrich, Episcopal Bishop of Michigan, said: "the existence of the pill opens up dangerous possibilities . . . . It provides an invitation to

premarital sex. There must be limitations and restrictions on the use of sex if we are to remain a civilized people."

SIGNIFICANCE

The sexual revolution made it acceptable to be open about sexual matters. Things that were once only whispered about or hidden behind closed doors suddenly were made public. The repercussions of this shift in attitude are still being felt at the beginning of the twenty-first century.

While the pill was not 100 percent effective, the fear of pregnancy largely vanished. Women, free to regard sex as another recreational activity, began pursuing sexual opportunities. Men, under increasing pressure to provide sexual pleasure to their partners, began purchasing widely advertised and readily available drugs to cure erectile dysfunction. While new freedoms were gained, the focus on sexual pleasure also led to a number of developments that are of questionable merit, including a rise in pornography and the sexual objectification of women.

Removing the taint from sexuality also made it possible to openly discuss such matters as rape. The anti-rape movement of the 1970s grew out of the women's movement and rape crisis centers were established as activists succeeded in shifting focus from the rape victim to the rapist, as sin was no longer attached to sex.

The sexual revolution also made possible the gay rights movement that began at the Stonewall Bar in New York City in 1969. Homosexuality became visible, and familiarity led to increasing acceptance of gays, lesbians, and bisexuals as well as the transgendered.

The pill began a celebration of sexuality that dramatically transformed culture and politics, and greatly impacted medicine. Despite the pill, a general increase in sexual activity among young persons led to increased rates of teenage pregnancy and unintended pregnancy among young adults in the United States. Elective abortion was made legal in the United States in the 1970s, and by 1990, the United States had one of the highest abortion rates in the Western world. One study sponsored by the National Research Council in the 1990s found that up to 60 percent of all pregnancies in the U.S. were unintended, and recommended increased availability, education about, and access to contraception, along with research to develop a new generation of contraceptives.

Another feature of the sexual revolution was a general increase in the number of sexual partners that a person had during his or her lifetime. This, in turn, facilitated the spread of sexually transmitted diseases, such as genital herpes, the human papilloma virus, and AIDS.

FURTHER RESOURCES
Books

Asbell, Bernard. *The Pill: A Biography of the Drug that Changed the World.* New York: Random House, 1995.

D'Emilio, John, and Estelle B. Freedman. *Intimate Matters: A History of Sexuality in America.* New York: Harper and Row, 1988.

Tone, Andrea. *Devices and Desires: A History of Contraceptives in America.* New York: Hill and Wang, 2001.

Roe v. Wade and the Abortion Debate

Legal decision

By: Henry A. Blackmun

Date: January 22, 1973

Source: *Roe v. Wade*, 410 U.S. 113 (1973).

About the Author: Harry A. Blackmun is best known as the author of the U.S. Supreme Court's *Roe v. Wade* decision. Born on November 12, 1908, in Nashville, Illinois, Blackmun grew up in St. Paul, Minnesota. Upon graduation from Harvard Law School in 1932, he joined a prestigious Minneapolis law firm. He became general counsel for the Mayo Clinic in 1950. This job allowed him to apply his legal skills to his lifelong interest in medicine. Blackmun took his seat on the Supreme Court on June 9, 1970. A modest man who publicly stated that he agonized over decisions, he took a year to write the *Roe v. Wade* opinion. Blackmun based his decision on research that he conducted at the Mayo Clinic library during the Court's summer recess. He concluded that abortion, at least in early pregnancy, was widely tolerated both under English common law and at the time of the adoption of the U.S. Constitution, with legal prohibitions becoming widespread only in the late nineteenth century.

INTRODUCTION

The *Roe v. Wade* decision legalized abortion in the United States. The case began when a young woman, who subsequently used the pseudonym Jane Roe, was prohibited by Texas state law from obtaining an abortion to end an unwanted pregnancy. Henry Wade, a Dallas County district attorney, bore the responsibility for enforcing the law banning abortion and, as a result, became the respondent in the case.

The Texas state law was typical of antiabortion legislation. Passed in 1854, it was part of a nineteenth-century push to protect women from the dangerous substances and techniques associated with the termination of a pregnancy. An estimated 20 to 25 percent of all pregnancies ended in abortion by midcentury. These abortions reduced the birthrate among white Protestant women in relation to the birthrates among poor, immigrant, and African American women. To protect women and to promote the birth of what were thought to be more desirable children, legislators banned abortion.

The legislation did not stop abortion. As time progressed, young white women beginning to enter the workforce, married women concerned about family size, and women of all sorts who could not afford a child continued to obtain illegal (so-called back-alley) abortions. By the 1950s, medical doctors began to form hospital abortion boards to review cases in which women sought permission to end pregnancies on medical grounds. Soon, women began to seek abortions on the psychiatric grounds that they were suicidal or unsuitable to be a mother, and physicians began to perform abortions because they believed that women should have access to the service. By the mid-1960s, national feminist organizations were focusing on abortion as a key to women's liberation. In the late 1960s and early 1970s, several state legislatures liberalized their abortion laws.

The *Roe v. Wade* decision was based on constitutional principles: 1) Women have a fundamental, constitutional right to reproductive control and privacy; 2) The government must remain neutral regarding a woman's decision to have or decline an abortion; 3) In the period before "viability" (the point at which a fetus can survive outside the womb), the government may restrict abortion only in the interests of protecting the woman's health or life. The *Roe v. Wade* decision also established a trimester concept of pregnancy, in which a woman has an unimpeded right to abortion only in the first three months of pregnancy. All of these principles have since come under heavy attack by opponents of abortion.

PRIMARY SOURCE

This right of privacy, whether it be founded in the Fourteenth Amendment's concept of personal liberty and restrictions upon state action, as we feel it is, or, as the District Court determined, in the Ninth Amendment's reservation of rights to the people, is broad enough to encompass a woman's decision whether or not to terminate her pregnancy. The detriment that the State would impose upon the pregnant woman by denying this choice altogether is apparent. Specific and direct harm medically diagnosable even in early pregnancy may be involved. Maternity, or additional offspring, may force upon the woman a distressful life and future. Psychological harm may be imminent. Mental and physical health may be taxed by child care. There is also the distress, for all concerned, associated with the unwanted child, and there is the problem of bringing a child into a family already unable, psychologically and otherwise, to care for it. In other cases, as in this one, the additional difficulties and continuing stigma of unwed motherhood may be involved. All these are factors the woman and her responsible physician necessarily will consider in consultation.

On the basis of elements such as these, appellant and some amici [friends] argue that the woman's right is absolute and that she is entitled to terminate her pregnancy at whatever time, in whatever way, and for whatever reason she alone chooses. With this we do not agree. Appellant's arguments that Texas either has no valid interest at all in regulating the abortion decision, or no interest strong enough to support any limitation upon the woman's sole determination, are unpersuasive. The Court's decisions recognizing a right of privacy also acknowledge that some state regulation in areas protected by that right is appropriate. As noted above, a State may properly assert important interests in safeguarding health, in maintaining medical standards, and in protecting potential life. At some point in pregnancy, these respective interests become sufficiently compelling to sustain regulation of the factors that govern the abortion decision. The privacy right involved, therefore, cannot be said to be absolute. In fact, it is not clear to us that the claim asserted by some amici that one has an unlimited right to do with one's body as one pleases bears a close relationship to the right of privacy previously articulated in the Court's decisions. The Court has refused to recognize an unlimited right of this kind in the past. *Jacobson v. Massachusetts*, 197 U.S. 11 (1905) (vaccination); *Buck v. Bell*, 274 U.S. 200 (1927) (sterilization).

We, therefore, conclude that the right of personal privacy includes the abortion decision, but that this right is not unqualified and must be considered against important state interests in regulation.

SIGNIFICANCE

The Supreme Court legalized abortion in a seven-to-two vote. The majority decision, as expressed by Blackmun, referred repeatedly to abortion as a

"choice." The dissenting justices, Byron White and William Rehnquist, defined the choice to have an abortion as an "extermination" based on a woman's "convenience," "whim," change of mood, "dislike of children," or "no reason at all." The negative characterization of some women who chose abortions reflected and stimulated the rise of the organized abortion movement immediately following the Supreme Court decision.

In the years since legalization, millions of American women have obtained safe abortions. These years also have been marked by a range of efforts by opposition groups to block the availability of abortions. These efforts have had some success, with the number of abortions declining to about 350 abortions for every 1,000 live births. Using demonstrations, clinic blockades, harassment of abortion-seeking women, judicial appointments, legal challenges, and violence such as bombings of clinics and the murder of abortion providers, various segments of the anti-abortion movement have expressed their anger with the *Roe v. Wade* decision. Congress and state legislatures have partially regulated access to abortions with parental notification laws, waiting periods, bans on particular types of procedures, and limits on abortion coverage in health plans. A changing Supreme Court has led some proponents of a woman's choice for abortion to consider that *Roe v. Wade* could be overturned.

Given the history of abortion, if *Roe v. Wade* is overturned, it is very unlikely that abortion will disappear in the United States. While outlawing abortion will block some women from obtaining one, other women will likely return to the strategies of pre-*Roe* days to end unwanted pregnancies. Since *Roe v. Wade* made it possible for women to obtain abortions in sanitary environments with care provided by licensed medical providers, medical complications and deaths were reduced. Before legalization, almost one million illegal abortions were performed and about 1,000 women died each year from substandard procedures and unhygienic conditions. Women of color were most at risk, constituting 75 percent of those who died in 1969 alone, because poverty made it difficult to afford quality care.

FURTHER RESOURCES
Books

Hull, N. E. H., and Peter Charles Hoffer. *Roe v. Wade: The Abortion Rights Controversy in American History.* Lawrence: University Press of Kansas, 2001.

Two activists—one advocating pro-life and the other supporting pro-choice—clash during demonstrations marking the 32nd anniversary of *Roe v. Wade* in San Francisco in 2005. AP/WIDE WORLD PHOTOS.

Joffe, Carole. *Doctors of Conscience: The Struggle to Provide Abortion Before and After Roe v. Wade.* Boston: Beacon, 1995.

Solinger, Rickie, ed. *Abortion Wars: A Half Century of Struggle, 1950–2000.* Berkeley: University of California Press, 1998.

Web sites

Touro Law Center. "Roe v. Wade." <http://www.tourolaw.edu/patch/Roe/> (accessed October 25, 2005).

On Death and Dying

Book excerpt

By: Elisabeth Kübler-Ross

Date: 1969

Source: Elisabeth Kübler-Ross. *On Death and Dying.* New York: Macmillan, 1969.

About the Author: Elisabeth Kübler-Ross (1926–2004) gained fame in the 1970s for developing a theory concerning the stages and psychological impact of death and grieving. Her ideas are credited with making possible the mainstream public acceptance of the hospice movement in the United States.

INTRODUCTION

In the course of her practice at major hospitals in New York, Colorado, and Chicago, Elisabeth Kübler-Ross was appalled by what she saw as the standard treatment of dying patients, who in her view were shunned and deceived. She began sitting with these patients, particularly pediatric cases, encouraging them to talk to her about their feelings and concerns. She observed that there were several common themes in the experiences and emotions of dying people, and started a series of lectures on her ideas and the theory of grieving that she developed based on her interviews with patients. She was able to persuade some of the terminally ill, such as the seventeen year-old girl with aplastic anemia featured in the excerpt, to discuss their experiences and thoughts in a group setting that included other medical professionals and students.

and possessions; and 5) acceptance of the inevitability of death and cessation of the emotional struggle against it.

The following excerpt from Elisabeth Kübler-Ross's book *On Death and Dying* is a transcription of one of her interviews with a terminally ill patient. In this interview, the patient described her most intimate feelings about the experience of dying.

Dr. Elisabeth Kübler-Ross wrote the groundbreaking work *On Death and Dying* in 1969. AP/WIDE WORLD PHOTOS.

Her work with and lectures about the dying were revolutionary, and brought about more inclusive and compassionate treatment of the terminally ill by the medical profession and society as a whole.

On Death and Dying, derived from her lectures and published in 1969, was a best-selling first book and secured her fame worldwide. It continues to be required reading in many medical, nursing, and psychology programs. The five psychological stages of dying that she described in the book (denial, anger, bargaining, depression, and acceptance) became part of the popular understanding of death and grieving across the world.

The stages of dying that Kübler-Ross formulated are: 1) denial and isolation, in which patients and families temporarily protest against the bad news of impending death; 2) anger at being singled out for death by God or at being singled out for death instead of others that might deserve death more; 3) bargaining, in which the patient hopes to postpone death until some goal is met; 4) depression characterized by mourning for the losses of relationships, profession,

PRIMARY SOURCE

DOCTOR: I think I'll make it a little easy on you, okay, and let us know please if you get too tired or are in pain. Do you want to tell the group how long you have been ill and when it all started?

PATIENT: Well, it just came on me.

DOCTOR: And how did it come on?

PATIENT: Well, we were at a church rally in X, a small town from where we live, and I had gone to all the meetings. We had gone over to the school to have dinner and I got my plate and sat down. I got real cold, got the chills and started shaking and got a real sharp pain in my left side. So they took me to the minister's home and put me to bed. The pain kept getting worse and I just kept getting colder and colder. So this minister called his family doctor and he came over and said that I had an appendicitis attack. They took me to the hospital and it seemed like the pain kind of went away; it just kind of disappeared by itself. They took a lot of tests and found that it wasn't my appendix so they sent me home with the rest of the people. Everything was okay for a couple of weeks and I went back to school.

STUDENT: What did you think you had?

PATIENT: Well, I did not know. I went to school for a couple of weeks and then I got real sick one day and fell down the stairs and felt real weak and was blacking out. . . . They ran a whole bunch of tests and that's when they found out that I was aplastic.

STUDENT: When was this?

PATIENT: That was about the middle of May.

DOCTOR: What did this mean to you?

PATIENT: Well, I wanted to be sure it was too, because I was missing so much school. The pain hurt quite a bit and then, you know, just to find out what it was. So I stayed in the hospital for ten days and they ran all kinds of tests and then they told me what I had. They said it was not terrible. They didn't have any idea what had caused it.

DOCTOR: They told you that it was not terrible?

PATIENT: Well, they told my parents. My parents asked me if I wanted to know everything, and I told them yes, I wanted to know everything. So they told me.

STUDENT: How did you take that?

PATIENT: Well, at first I didn't know and then I kind of figured that it was God's purpose that I got sick because it had happened all at once and I had never been sick before. And I figured that it was God's purpose that I got sick and that I was in his care and he would take care of me so I didn't have to worry. And I've just gone on like that ever since and I think that's what kept me alive, knowing that. . . .

STUDENT: Do you think you've got more faith during this time.

PATIENT: Uh huh. I really do.

STUDENT: Do you think this would be one way that you've changed? Your faith is the most important thing then that will pull you through?

PATIENT: Well, I don't know. They say that I might not pull through, but if he wants me to be well, I've got to get well.

STUDENT: Has your personality changed, have you noticed any changes each day?

PATIENT: Yes, because I get along with more people. I usually do, though. I go around and visit a few of the patients and help them. I get along with the other roommates, so I get someone else to talk to. You know, when you feel depressed it helps to talk to someone else.

DOCTOR: Do you get depressed often? Two of you were in this room before, now you are all alone?

PATIENT: I think it was because I was worn out. I haven't been outdoors for a week now.

DOCTOR: Are you getting tired now? Tell me when you get too tired, then we will finish this session.

PATIENT: No, not at all.

STUDENT: Have you noticed any change in your family or friends, in their attitude toward you?

PATIENT: I've been a lot closer to my family. We get along well, my brother and I were always close when we were small. You know he's eighteen and I'm seventeen, just fourteen months apart. And my sister and I were always real close. So now they and my parents are a lot closer. You know, I can talk to them more and they, oh, I don't know, it's just a feeling of more closeness.

STUDENT: It's deepened, enriched your relationship with your parents?

PATIENT: Uh huh, and with other kids, too.

STUDENT: Is this a sense of support for you during this illness?

PATIENT: Yes, I don't think I could go through it now without my family and all the friends. . . .

STUDENT: What is it that you do have to face, what's your vision of what death is like?

PATIENT: Well, I think it's wonderful because you go to your home, your other one, near to God, and I'm not afraid to die.

DOCTOR: Do you have a visual picture of this "other home," realizing, you know, all of us have some fantasies about it though we never talk about it. Do you mind talking about it?

PATIENT: Well, I just kind of think it's like a reunion where everybody is there and it is real nice and where there's someone else there—special, you know. Kind of makes the whole thing different.

DOCTOR: Is there anything else you can say about it, how it feels?

PATIENT: Oh, you would say you have a wonderful feeling, no more needs and just being there and never again alone.

DOCTOR: Everything just right?

PATIENT: Just right, uh huh.

SIGNIFICANCE

Elisabeth Kübler-Ross studied dying and grieving in the context of an American society often characterized as unwilling to face and accept death, and prone to avoiding contact with the dying. It should probably not be unexpected that this culture spawned such a systematic and empirical approach to the study of death and dying, which then opened the way to a more accepting emotional connection to terminally ill patients. Her practice of providing palliative treatment and companionship to dying patients also led to the widespread provision of hospice care to provide more dignified handling of patients' final hours.

Since Kübler-Ross's work became dominant in the study of death and dying, several other approaches to the field and critiques of her methodology and conclusions have arisen. Other investigators such as Robert Kastenbaum have questioned the assertion that people go through stages in the sense that an ordered set of conditions are present in coping with death. In reviewing Kübler-Ross's cases he found that while patients exhibited emotions that characterized the five stages, none of them went through all of the five stages in order. While he grants that Kübler-Ross's interview methodology was a good qualitative starting point for research, he maintains that it should have been followed up by more systematic and quantitative data gathering. Qualitative, open-ended interviewing is a useful exploratory research technique, but is subject to bias based on the relationship between the interviewer and subject as well as bias based on what a subject might choose to reveal.

That Kübler-Ross's theory became so famous is also problematic, because people came to see it as prescriptive rather than descriptive. Patients might feel pressured internally or by relatives to reach the final stage of acceptance of death, which might be seen as the only way to die properly. Also, the uniqueness and accomplishments of each patient's life could be overlooked and become subsumed in this rather generic sequence of stages that are supposed to take place in the final weeks or months of life. Critics have particularly focused on this tendency of Kübler-Ross's ideas to underestimate the extent to which the uniqueness of each individual tends to shape feelings, experiences, and personal development at and near the end of life.

From another perspective, William McDougall, founder of the field of social psychology, saw the process of dying as being one of personal growth rather than one of protest and resignation. In McDougall's view, dying is the last in a sequence of significant experiences in life that needs to be intellectually integrated into one's view of self and the world. His ideas appear to have influenced some of Kübler-Ross's later thinking and writing.

Kübler-Ross thrived on the pioneering aspect of her work and the notoriety that it gained her, and was a prolific writer and active with dying patients until she experienced a series of disabling strokes prior to her death in 2004. She was frustrated that disability intervened to prevent her from being in control of the circumstances of her own death after having helped so many patients to accept their deaths. Also, Kübler-Ross stated that the strokes prevented her from coming to grips with what she saw as the mystery of death and life after death.

In spite of its scientific shortcomings, the work of Kübler-Ross has had a profound impact on medical practice and the care of the dying by both health care professionals as well as by nonprofessional and family caregivers. It has been instrumental in helping Western society to face death squarely and stop avoiding it both as a topic of discussion and in resisting involvement with dying people. It is not clear, however, that society is any closer to an actual acceptance of death. This is, perhaps, what Kübler-Ross herself was attempting to find as she explored the experiences of resuscitated patients, including the "bright light"

and the "tunnel" toward which they reported being drawn as they were at death's door.

FURTHER RESOURCES

Books

Beauchamp, Tom, and Robert Veatch, eds. *Ethical Issues in Death and Dying*. 2nd edition. New York: Prentice Hall, 1996.

Kastenbaum, R. J. *Death, Society, and Human Experience*. 6th edition. New York: Allyn and Bacon, 1998.

Kübler-Ross, Elisabeth. *On Grief and Grieving*. New York: Scribner, 2005.

Kübler-Ross, Elisabeth, and David Kessler. *Life Lessons: Two Experts on Death and Dying Teach Us about the Mysteries of Life and Living*. New York: Scribner, 2000.

Web sites

Elisabeth Kübler-Ross. <http://www.elisabethkublerross.com> (accessed November 23, 2005).

Film Monthly. "Facing Death: Elisabeth Kübler-Ross (2004)," by Kristin Schrader. <http://www.filmmonthly.com/Video/Articles/FacingDeath/FacingDeath.html> (accessed November 23, 2005).

Practical Guidelines for Do-Not-Resuscitate Orders

Journal article

By: Mark H. Ebell

Date: 1994

Source: Mark H. Ebell. "Practical Guidelines for Do-Not-Resuscitate Orders." *American Family Physician* 50 (November 1, 1994).

About the Author: Mark H. Ebell is a physician who has practiced in Athens, Georgia, held a faculty position at Michigan State University College of Human Medicine, and has contributed several articles to *American Family Physician*. He also has written a number of "handheld" clinical guides for different medical topics and recently edited a book concerned with the use of handheld computers in the practice of medicine.

INTRODUCTION

Do not resuscitate (DNR) orders, along with medical advance directives, are designed to empower patients who are unlikely to derive long-lasting benefits from the use of extraordinary life-saving measures. Simply put, they allow patients to choose not to have

CPR or other resuscitative measures if their heart or breathing should stop. If there is no DNR physician's order present in a hospitalized patient's medical chart, the medical staff is bound (by medical and legal regulations, as well as professional ethical standards) to employ CPR, mechanical ventilation, and other life-saving techniques and equipment in the event of cardiac or respiratory failure. Several decades of research have shown that, for people who are critically or terminally ill, there is not always substantial recovery or quality of life benefit gained after cardiac cessation and prolonged resuscitation efforts.

During the 1960s and 1970s, there were relatively few decisions to be made in the care of terminally ill patients, as there was no real technology available to prolong life in the event of multiple organ or system failure. A simple order prohibiting the use of CPR was generally sufficient during that era. By the end of the twentieth century, life-sustaining technologies had reached such sophistication that the decisions had become far more complicated. They concerned not only CPR, but also in-dwelling nasal or gastric feeding tubes, prolonged intubation or the use of tracheotomy for the purposes of maintaining mechanical ventilation, ongoing mechanical suction to prevent choking on oral and nasal secretions, and the type and degree of cardiac resuscitation tools to be used in the event the heart stopped beating. In addition to those more mechanical process decisions, an entire gamut of other ethical issues arose. How far does a medical team go in order to prolong the life of a terminally ill patient? Where does one draw the line at attempting or continuing chemotherapy or radiation, or attempting surgery?

As medical technology has expanded exponentially, the educational level of patients also has increased. Many individuals now use the Internet to educate themselves about a wide range of health and disease topics. For the first time, patients are able to use outside sources and do not have to rely solely upon their own physicians or medical care providers for information. They can obtain realistic, real-time, cutting-edge data regarding the likely prognosis of their disease, as well as a comprehensive listing of the location, availability, and likelihood of positive outcomes with experimental or nontraditional interventions. Patients now have the ability to access information that allows them to make informed choices—both to direct their care and to plan their own end-of-life processes through the use of palliative care and pain control measures.

PRIMARY SOURCE

Do-not-resuscitate (DNR) orders are directives in the medical record that preclude the use of resuscitative measures such as chest compressions, artificial respiration, cardioversion and/or cardioactive medications in the event of cardiopulmonary arrest. DNR orders are widely used in the United States, with studies showing that the majority of hospitalized patients who die have had a DNR order written.

Because of the wide application of DNR orders, it is important that physicians understand the ethical, legal and medical implications of these documents. This article summarizes the historic background and ethical rationale for DNR orders and describes laws and policies regarding DNR orders in the context of their implications for clinical practice. This article also provides practical guidelines for the use of DNR orders, including specific information regarding prognosis, to help physicians carry out discussions with patients and families.

BACKGROUND

Like many medical technologies, cardiopulmonary resuscitation (CPR) became the standard of care without careful consideration of its effectiveness in different patient populations. Kouwenhoven and colleagues, first described the technique in 1960; they reported a 70 percent survival rate in a small group of perioperative patients. As experience with the technique grew and CPR was applied to other patient populations, it became clear that only a minority of patients who had CPR survived to hospital discharge. Also, resuscitative attempts in patients who had a period of hypoxia sometimes resulted in the loss of higher cortical function but the preservation of brainstem function, leaving patients in a vegetative state for varying amounts of time. Physicians became increasingly concerned that they could be doing harm to some patients by attempting resuscitation in all patients.

During this same period, patients were demanding an increased role in medical decision-making. This need was rooted in a rising awareness of individual rights and in dissatisfaction with the traditional paternalistic model of the physician-patient relationship. Thus, a desire to conform to the ethical principles of nonmalfeasance (not doing harm) and autonomy (the right of self-determination) resulted in the development and increased use of DNR orders. . . .

POLICY ISSUES

The most recent policy statement by the Council of Ethical and judicial Affairs of the American Medical Association supports the use of DNR orders and identifies futility and patient preference as the two primary reasons to withhold CPR. In addition, the joint Commission on Accreditation of Health Care Organizations requires that all acute care facilities have a formal institutional policy regarding advance directives and DNR orders. Finally, institutions must have a survey process that ensures compliance.

Specific types of DNR policies include recognition of only a single "no code" or "do-not-resuscitate" designation, as well as more comprehensive policies that recognize varying levels of care. The latter are preferable, since they allow physicians to tailor the DNR order to fit the patient's specific needs. It has been suggested that "do not attempt resuscitation" may be a more appropriate term than "do not resuscitate," especially given the low rate of survival in some patient populations. Also, the term "comfort-oriented care" is used by some facilities, since it reminds caregivers that for many terminally ill patients, fear of pain and abandonment are very important factors in a patient's decision to request resuscitation. . . .

Rationales for Writing DNR Order A number of rationales have been proposed for the use of DNR orders. These rationales include patient preference for any reason, poor quality of life before CPR, a perception that the burden of care imposed by the CPR process outweighs the benefit, the cost of medical care, religious preference and previous personal experience.

Although still somewhat controversial, a consensus is emerging that physicians may write a DNR order for a patient if they believe that resuscitation would be futile. In its statement on DNR orders, the Council on Ethical and judicial Affairs of the American Medical Association states that "when efforts to resuscitate a patient are judged by the treating physician to be futile, even if previously requested by the patient, CPR may be withheld. In such circumstances, when there is adequate time to do so, the physician should inform the patient or the incompetent patient's surrogate of the content of the DNR order, as well as the basis for its implementation, prior to entering a DNR order into the patient's record." In such a case, the physician should inform the patient or appropriate surrogate decision-maker of the decision and provide the opportunity for transfer of care if a conflict arises.

Timing of Discussion About DNR Order Most patients have discussed issues of resuscitation with their families and would like to discuss these concerns with their physician. However, only 10 percent of patients have discussed their wishes regarding CPR with a physician. Also, while approximately 75 percent of patients who receive a DNR order are impaired at the time that it is written, only 10 percent are impaired at the time of admission to the hospital. Thus, most patients are not given the opportunity to participate in discussions about their own resuscitation, although they would like to do so. . . .

Patients for Whom DNR Orders Should Be Addressed in the Outpatient Setting or Early in Hospitalization:

Patients with any terminal illness

Patients who may be considered to have a poor quality of life

Patients who may have an illness or disabling condition that is severe and irreversible

Patients who are at increased risk for cardiac or respiratory arrest

Patients who have suffered an irreversible loss of consciousness

Patients who are unlikely to benefit from CPR based on a single factor such as metastatic cancer, or a combination of factors such as sepsis and impaired renal function or advanced age and pneumonia

Patients in whom there is some reason to question the presumption of consent for CPR

(Adapted from "Guidelines on Cardiopulmonary Resuscitation" from the Hastings Center.)

Many approaches may be taken to initiating discussion about DNR orders, depending on the physician's individual style. It is often helpful to begin the conversation with a qualifying remark such as, "I routinely discuss CPR with my patients who are in the hospital. Do you know what CPR is?" The depiction of CPR in the mass media has resulted in significant misconceptions among patients about the length, intensity and possible outcomes of the CPR process. In order that patients give truly informed consent, it may therefore be necessary to describe the process in some detail.

It is also important to emphasize that DNR orders are a mechanism for expressing the patient's wishes for medical care. A physician could open the discussion by saying, "I think it is important to talk about (CPR, resuscitation, endotracheal intubation) because I want to make sure that I know what kind of medical treatment you want when you are not able to talk to me or tell me your opinion." Patients may respond by putting the decision-making burden on someone else, with a statement such as "Whatever you think, doc," or "Just talk to my family." If this happens, it is important that the physician reemphasize to the patient that it is the patient's opinion that is most important, while understanding that some patients may be more comfortable with a more paternalistic model of care.

Providing Prognostic Information When discussing DNR orders with patients, it is helpful to provide concrete prognostic information. Just under one-half of patients survive the code itself, even if only for a long enough period to be transferred to the intensive care unit; one-third survive for

24 hours, and approximately one-eighth survive to hospital discharge. In the most careful follow-up study to date, approximately 30 percent of patients who survived to discharge after CPR suffered a significant increase in dependence, requiring either extensive home care or institutionalization. A smaller percentage, approximately 2 to 5 percent, have severe mental impairment....

Involving Others in the Decision-Making Process If a conflict exists, or if a patient indicates a desire to discuss issues regarding resuscitation with family members, a family meeting may be an appropriate forum for discussion. Although most patients place the greatest value on the input of their spouse, physician and children, it is best to ask the patient exactly who should attend a discussion about DNR orders. It may be appropriate in some instances to include lovers, life companions, ministers, social workers and nursing staff.

In such a meeting, the physician serves as facilitator....

FINAL COMMENT

The appropriate use of DNR orders is an important way to prevent unnecessary suffering and the misallocation of scarce medical resources. Most patients will welcome an open and caring discussion of their alternatives regarding resuscitation with a physician who is prepared to discuss these issues.

SIGNIFICANCE

The concept of medical choice regarding the ending of an individual's life is relatively novel and has been fraught with ethical concerns for physicians and other senior health care providers. The American Medical Association's Council on Ethical and Judicial Affairs has smoothed the way considerably, and their guidelines have offered physicians a measure of ethical assurance and comfort, which should permit them to work in partnership with their patients in order to facilitate informed and well-considered individual choices about end-of-life care.

In the past, patients have frequently not been offered the full range of information that could impact their decision-making, when they still possessed sufficient mental clarity to be able to make good use of the data. Patients were often encouraged by well-meaning family members and caregivers to "fight to the end," rather than to make an informed choice to use only palliative (comfort) care or to stop treatments that might negatively impact their quality of life near the end. Not infrequently, family members historically chose to hide the truth of a terminal diagnosis from

their loved ones—particularly if the dying person was elderly or a child—out of a belief that this was a kind thing to do. The paradigm has shifted dramatically, and children and older adults are now being given honest information, as well as some say in the direction of their care, on a more frequent basis. Increasingly, patients (and significant others in their lives) are demanding the right to be knowledgeable members of the treatment planning team, and are afforded more opportunities to direct their own care, when those requests are reasonable and economically feasible. The key, for all concerned, is to have the physician or treatment team leader give the patient understandable and objective information, delivered in a sensitive and respectful manner, at a time that the patient is not too ill to be able to hear it. Ideally, the conversation should be initiated well before the patient needs to be in an inpatient setting. Medical schools and hospital programs are increasingly providing training for physicians in the art of initiating conversations with their patients about resuscitation efforts and advanced directives.

From the standpoint of the larger health care system, this is not only the most reasonable course, it is the most economically feasible, since the number of heroic and often unsuccessful (but very costly) treatments undertaken is likely to be considerably limited. Typically, the most extraordinary measures are also among the most expensive—and third-party payers (such as insurance companies) are not always as quick to either authorize or reimburse when the patient is terminally ill, moribund, or deceased. In addition, there are far fewer legal ramifications for all concerned if the patient is able to be an active participant in the end-of-life care plan, rather than leaving the treatment team with the responsibility for making those types of decisions under duress and in highly stressful and emotionally charged circumstances.

When patients are allowed and encouraged to be active participants in the care given at the end of their lives, they are able to make choices that allow them to increase the quality of their remaining time with loved ones, complete unfinished business, effectively control pain, and exert significant control over the timing and manner of their death. They can help to choose the methods by which their symptoms are managed, the manner in which they receive nutrition (or not), and elect not to have the disease progression altered at the end. The concept of the Do-Not-Resuscitate order allows patients to die with a far greater degree of dignity, with much less stress, and in a far more *natural* manner with the assistance of knowledge and ever-advancing technology.

FURTHER RESOURCES

Periodicals

American Academy of Pediatrics Committee on School Health and Committee on Bioethics. "Do Not Resuscitate Orders in Schools." *Pediatrics* 105 (April 2000): 878–879.

American Medical Association Council on Ethical and Judicial Affairs. "Guidelines for Appropriate Use of Do-Not-Resuscitate Orders: Patients' Preferences, Prognoses, and Physicians' Judgments." *Annals of Internal Medicine* 125 (1996): 284–293.

Web sites

American Academy of Family Physicians. "Advance Directives and Do-Not-Resuscitate Orders." <http://www.aafp.org/afp/20001001/1683ph.html> (accessed December 20, 2005).

Ethics in Medicine, University of Washington School of Medicine. "Do Not Resuscitate Orders." <http://eduserv.hscer.washington.edu/bioethics/topics/dnr.html> (accessed December 20, 2005).

familydoctor.org. "Advance Directives and Do Not Resuscitate Orders." <http://familydoctor.org/003.xml> (accessed December 20, 2005).

The Promised End

Constitutional Aspects of Physician-Assisted Suicide

Journal article

By: George J. Annas

Date: August 29, 1996

Source: George J. Annas. "The Promised End—Constitutional Aspects of Physician-Assisted Suicide." *New England Journal of Medicine.* vol. 335, no. 9 (1996): 683–687.

About the Author: George J. Annas is published in fields of bioethics, law, and public health. He received his *Juris Doctorate* and Masters in Public Health degrees from Harvard's schools of law and public health. Annas co-founded Global Physicians & Lawyers, a nongovernmental organization of lawyers and physicians who promote health and human rights around the globe. He is currently a professor of law and bioethics at Boston University.

INTRODUCTION

Physician-assisted suicide refers to the practice of a physician prescribing or regulating, upon a patient's informed request, a lethal dose of medication for the purpose of ending that patient's life. Both advocates and opponents of the practice dispute the term physician-assisted suicide. Some favor calling the practice physician-assisted dying to avoid negative social and religious connotations of the word suicide.

Physician-assisted suicide differs from euthanasia in that patients, and not physicians, ultimately control their own means of death. Under Oregon's legalized Death With Dignity scheme, physicians prescribe the lethal dose of medication, while patients themselves administer the lethal dose. A patient's informed refusal of life-saving treatment is neither assisted suicide nor euthanasia, and is generally permitted under United States law.

The first law legalizing physician-assisted dying was passed in the state of Oregon in 1994. After a series of court challenges, the Death with Dignity measure was later reaffirmed by statewide voter referendum. Between 1998 and 2005, approximatly two hundred terminally ill Oregonians relied on the act to end their life.

Under Oregon's Death with Dignity Act, a person who desires a physician-assisted death must be eighteen years of age or obtain parental consent. Furthermore, the person must be a resident of Oregon who was diagnosed with a terminal illness that is expected to lead to death within six months. The person must give informed consent and cannot desire to utilize the law amid depression or other mental disorder. Two physicians and two other witnesses must verify the person's terminal diagnosis and clarity of mental state.

Proponents claim Oregon's law is ethical and compassionate. Opponents argue that physician-assisted suicide laws undermine social perceptions about the sancity of life. The debate is certainly not limited to Oregon. The practice is widely debated in the United States and throughout the world. Neither the medical profession nor community of academic bioethicists are in agreement about the ethical implications of physician-assisted dying.

■ PRIMARY SOURCE

THE PROMISED END—CONSTITUTIONAL ASPECTS OF PHYSICIAN-ASSISTED SUICIDE

The debate over physician-assisted suicide has dramatically shifted to a discussion of constitutional issues. This spring, within a month of each other, U.S. Circuit Courts of Appeals on both coasts ruled that state prohibitions of assisted suicide are unconstitutional when applied to physicians who prescribe lethal medication for

Stacey Richter holds a sign outside a federal courthouse in Portland, OR, March 22, 2002, where a hearing opened to decide the fate of Oregon's physician-assisted suicide law. The hearing opened with arguments from the state's attorney, who said U.S. Attorney General John Ashcroft lacked the authority to overturn a state law twice approved by voters. AP/WIDE WORLD PHOTOS.

terminally ill, competent adults who wish to end their lives. The Ninth Circuit includes Alaska, Arizona, California, Hawaii, Idaho, Montana, Nevada, Oregon, and Washington, and the Second Circuit includes New York, Connecticut, and Vermont. Both courts reached the same conclusion but for different legal reasons.

In the Ninth Circuit, four physicians and three patients (one dying of AIDS, one of cancer, and another of emphysema) challenged a Washington law that prohibits aiding another person in committing suicide. In the Second Circuit, three physicians and three patients (two dying of AIDS and one of cancer) challenged New York laws that prohibit aiding another person in committing or attempting suicide. None of these patients were currently suicidal, but all wanted lethal drugs that they could take if their suffering became unbearable. All the physicians said that they felt unable to comply with the requests because of the laws

against assisting suicide (there are no laws against committing suicide). Both cases present the same two issues: Is there a constitutional right to the assistance of a physician in committing suicide? And if so, does the state nonetheless have a sufficient interest to prohibit the exercise of this right?

The Opinion of the Ninth Circuit Court The Ninth Circuit Court adopted the term "physician-assisted suicide" to describe "the prescription of life-ending medication for use by terminally ill, competent adult patients who wish to hasten their deaths" but was not happy with it, saying, "We have serious doubts that the terms "suicide" and "assisted suicide" are appropriate legal descriptions of the specific conduct at issue here." Instead of simply ruling that the assisted-suicide laws do not apply to the prescriptions of potentially lethal drugs, the court's ambitious eight-to-three opinion, written by Judge Stephen Reinhardt, relied on a substantive due-process approach (based on the due-process clause of the 14th Amendment) to create a new constitutional right: the right to determine "the time and manner of one's own death."

This new right is broadly worded, but the court ruled that only a narrow category of patients may lawfully exercise it: competent, terminally ill adults who have "lived nearly a full measure" of life and who want to die with dignity. For such patients, "wracked by pain and deprived of all pleasure, a state-enforced prohibition on hastening their deaths condemns them to unrelieved misery or torture." . . .

After this new constitutional right is defined, the only remaining question is whether the state has a sufficient interest to prohibit its exercise. The court concluded that it does not: "When patients are no longer able to pursue liberty or happiness and do not wish to pursue life, the state's interest in forcing them to remain alive is clearly less [than] compelling." The court did, however, call on states to regulate the practice, suggesting procedural safeguards—such as witnesses, waiting periods, second medical opinions, psychological examinations, and reporting procedures—to help avoid "abuse."

The Opinion of the Second Circuit Court One month later, in April, the Second Circuit Court summarily rejected the Ninth Circuit Court's entire substantive due-process analysis as a defensible way to discover a new constitutional right, concluding simply, "The right to assisted suicide finds no cognizable basis in the Constitution's language or design, even in the very limited cases of those competent persons who, in the final stages of terminal illness, seek the right to hasten death." But the Second Circuit Court nonetheless did find a new constitutional right underlying a doctor's lethal prescription, based on the equal-protection clause (rather than the due-process clause) of the 14th Amendment. The equal-protection clause requires states to treat people who are similarly situated in a similar manner. Although this is superficially a different constitutional approach from that of the Ninth Circuit Court, the Second Circuit Court also had to discover a new constitutional right before it could conclude that the right was being protected unequally by the state.

The Second Circuit Court did this by making two related assertions: the right to refuse treatment is the same as the right to "hasten death," and there is no distinction between a person who is dependent on life-support equipment and one who is not. Both assertions are problematic. As to the first, the court argued that New York treats similarly situated people unequally because its law permits people "in the final stages of terminal illness who are on life support systems . . . to hasten their deaths by directing the removal of such systems," but those not receiving life support cannot hasten their deaths "by self-administering prescription drugs." The primary cases cited for this proposition are *Cruzan* and *Eichner*, even though neither of the two patients involved, who were both in persistent vegetative states, was terminally ill, and neither had expressed any desire to commit suicide. The patient in the *Eichner* case, Brother Joseph Fox, was an elderly Catholic brother of the Society of Mary who had said to his friend, Father Phillip Eichner, before hernia surgery, "If I wind up like Karen Quinlan, pull the plug." Since suicide is a mortal sin in the Catholic Church, it is likely that Brother Fox would have been horrified at the notion that his refusal of a ventilator constituted suicide. As both *Eichner* and *Cruzan* make clear, the right at stake in these cases is the right to refuse treatment (even if refusal results in death), and there is no legal requirement that a person be either terminally ill or in pain to exercise this right. Americans have never been obligated to accept any or all manner of medical treatment available to prolong life; the essence of the legal right at stake is the right to be free from unwanted bodily invasions.

Even more striking is the court's second assertion, which is based on its acceptance of Justice Antonin Scalia's strange concurring opinion in the *Cruzan* case (an opinion that no other justice on the Supreme Court joined). Scalia argued that refusals of treatment that result in death are all suicides, and that any notion that the patient dies a "natural" death from the underlying disease is nonsense. The Second Circuit Court adopted Justice Scalia's position, concluding that death after the removal of a ventilator is "not natural in any sense"; rather, it brings about "death through asphyxiation." Likewise, the Second Circuit Court stated that the removal of artificially delivered fluids and nutrition causes "death by starvation . . . or dehydration." In the court's words, "The ending of life by these means is nothing more nor less than assisted suicide." Because it considered both refusing treatment and taking lethal drugs as equally constituting suicide, the Second Circuit Court concluded that giving citizens equal protection under the law means that the state must treat both acts in the same manner. The court argued that because doctors are permitted to "assist" patients being sustained by various life-support mechanisms to commit suicide by removing them, patients who do not need these medical interventions to continue to live should also be entitled to the assistance of a physician in committing suicide.

As to the state's possible interest in distinguishing between these acts, the court concluded that the state has no interest "in requiring the prolongation of a life that is all but ended." . . .

Physicians and Assisted Suicide The patients whose cases were presented to these two courts are all sympathetic, and it is not surprising that the courts wanted to help them. Cancer and AIDS often lead to "hard deaths," and patients dying of these two diseases make up the vast majority of patients in hospices, as well as of those who seek the assistance of physicians in committing suicide, probably because the final stages of these illnesses are relatively predictable. What is surprising is that the courts failed to acknowledge explicitly that it has never been illegal to prescribe pain medication that competent terminally ill patients *might* use to commit suicide, as long as the physicians' *intent* is to foster the patients' well-being by giving them more control over their lives and the drugs have independent legitimate medical uses. Such prescription can legitimately be seen as suicide prevention rather than assistance in suicide. Neither court could point to even one case of a physician ever being criminally prosecuted for the conduct they approve of, and both courts would have been on much stronger ground if they had simply acknowledged that intent matters in criminal law and that prescriptions under these very limited circumstances are not assisted suicide by definition.

In this regard, it should be noted that the Ninth Circuit Court's restatement of the principle of the double effect, which treats pain relief and death as equally intended, is false: the principle is that treating the patients' pain is acceptable even if the treatment hastens death (which it will, of course, not always do). Providing medication to control pain has always been a legitimate and lawful medical act, even if death or suicide is risked. There is a difference between an intended result and an unintended but accepted consequence. Thus, no physician should conclude on the basis of the opinion of the Ninth Circuit Court that providing pain medication that increases the risk of death is either assistance in suicide or homicide. . . .

I find it impossible to accept either court's logic about the cause of death after refusal of treatment. The failure to distinguish real causes of death from various medical tools and techniques that may temporarily substitute for particular bodily functions is fatal to the logic of both of these opinions. . . .

State Regulations Perhaps recognizing this weakness in their analyses, both courts called for states to regulate physician-assisted suicide, and the Ninth Circuit Court seemed to approve of Oregon Ballot Measure 16, which provides legal immunity to physicians who follow certain procedures when prescribing lethal drugs to terminally ill patients with the intent that they use them to commit suicide. . . .

By ignoring the past two decades of jurisprudence concerning the right to refuse treatment (including the rulings by state supreme courts that explicitly hold that refusals of treatment are neither suicide nor homicide), and by failing to make such basic distinctions as those between the right to refuse treatment and the right to die, between suicide and assisted suicide, between law and ethics, and between ends and means, these courts virtually guarantee that their decisions will not be the last word on the subject. . . .

There are real problems with the way patients die under physicians' care, and these rulings are important demonstrations of how a large number of judges view dying at the hands of modern medicine. . . .

Shakespeare changed the traditional ending of the legend on which he based his play [*King Lear*] to have both Lear and Cordelia die, rather than to have Lear restored to his throne and all live essentially happily ever after. Shakespeare's ending fits well with our postmodern intimations of disaster and apocalypse, just as assisted suicide seems a reasonable way out of our inability to control the decay of our bodies. Nonetheless, the more appropriate lines from *King Lear* in this context may be the questions of Kent and Edgar near the end of the play: "Is this the promised end?/Or image of that horror?"

SIGNIFICANCE

The debate over physician-assisted suicide is fervent and complex. Proponents of physician-assisted dying assert that the practice is ethical because it relies on established notions of compassion, individual liberty and personal freedom, and justice. It is argued that competent individuals have the right to make decisions about the course of their life, and in the event of illness, the course of their medical treatment. Individuals also have the right to control how and when their life will end.

Most proponents of physician-assisted suicide agree that the practice must be regulated by both law and the medical profession to prevent abuse and promote safety. Proponents assert that assisting some patients to hasten their deaths does not violate the ethical duty of physicians. In limited circumstances, such as those enumerated in Oregon's Death with Dignity statute, the act is a compassionate means of alleviating suffering.

Opponents of physician-assisted suicide assert that the practice undermines in society the value of individual life. Many disability advocates claim that physician-assisted suicide enforces negative social stereotypes about what people consider a valuable and meaningful existence. They claim that by giving terminally ill patients a means of avoiding debilitation physicians are reinforcing attitudes that debilitation makes life unbearable or less worthy.

Many opponents claim that the practice of physician-assisted dying has an innate potential for abuse. Some worry that elderly and disabled patients may be pressured into choosing physician-assisted suicide, or that these patients may not be presented with the full range of available palliative (pain-relieving) care. Others worry that physician-assisted suicide laws will become more lax or will eventually expand to permit euthanasia.

In 2006, the Supreme Court of the United States upheld Oregon's Death with Dignity Act. The Court rejected a challenge to the law that claimed that physicians who prescribed lethal dosages of medications, in line with Oregon's policy, violated federal laws regulating controlled substances. The Court stood by its 1997 ruling that there exists no constitutional "right to die." Their 2006 ruling in *Gonzalez v. Oregon* leaves open the possibility for other states to legalize physician-assisted dying. As of 2006, three additional states were considering enacting legislation similar to that in Oregon. However, the Court's ruling also permits state legislatures—and perhaps the U.S. Congress—to explicitly ban the practice. Several states have proposed legislation that would outlaw physician-assisted dying within their borders.

As of 2005, Switzerland, The Netherlands, Columbia, and Belgium legally recognized or limitedly permitted physician-assisted suicide.

FURTHER RESOURCES
Books

Annas, George J. *American Bioethics: Crossing Human Rights and Health Law Boundaries.* New York: Oxford University Press, 2004.

———. *The Rights Of Patients: The Authoritative ACLU Guide To The Rights Of Patients.* New York: New York University Press, 2004.

Periodicals

Longmore, Paul K. "Policy, Prejudice, and Reality: Two Case Studies of Physician-Assisted Suicide." *Journal of Disability Policy Studies*. vol. 16.1 (June 22, 2005): 38.

Web sites

Oyez. "*GONZALES V. OREGON* (04-623) 368 F.3d 1118, affirmed." <http://supct.law.cornell.edu/supct/html/04-623.ZS.html> (accessed February 7, 2006).

Tube Is Removed After a Chaotic Day

Right to Die Issues

Newspaper article

By: William R. Levesque, Anita Kumar, Chris Tisch, and Graham Brink.

Date: March 19, 2005

Source: Lesvesque, William R., Anita Kumar, Chris Tisch, and Graham Brink. "Tube Is Removed After a Chaotic Day." *St. Petersburg Times* (March 19, 2005).

About the Author: This article was written by four journalists for the *St. Petersburg Times*, a daily newspaper based in Florida with a circulation of more than 300,000.

INTRODUCTION

On February 25, 1990, twenty-six-year-old Terri Schiavo suffered a cardiac arrest thought to have been caused by a chemical imbalance triggered by an eating disorder. The oxygen supply to her brain was cut off for five minutes, causing irreversible brain damage and leaving the young woman in a persistent vegetative state (PVS). Neurological examinations revealed minimal brain activity, and it was necessary to provide artificial nutrition and hydration through a tube from then on to maintain Terri Schiavo's life.

According to Florida law, Michael Schiavo, Terri's husband, became her legal guardian. In 1998, he filed a petition to have the feeding tube removed so she could die naturally. This, he claimed, is what she would have wanted, since there was no hope for her recovery. The case might have ended there, except that Terri's parents, Bob and Mary Schindler, disagreed. They argued that she might recover. The feeding tube was first removed on April 24, 2001, but was reinserted only two days later. In 2002, a Florida trial court judge conducted

six days of hearings, including evidence from neurologists called by Michael Schiavo and the Schindlers. The latter relied on video evidence showing signs of apparent alertness and responsiveness on Terri's part; such signs are not uncommon in PVS and can appear somewhat deceptive, since there is still no meaningful brain activity.

Terri Schiavo's feeding tube was removed for a second time on October 15, 2003, but a few days later, Florida's lower house passed what became known as "Terri's Law," which gave Governor Jeb Bush the power to order doctors to reinsert the tube. On October 23, 2003, the tube was reinserted a second time and shortly thereafter, Michael Schiavo asked a Florida court to rule "Terri's Law" unconstitutional. On September 23, 2004, Florida's Supreme Court struck down the law. Jeb Bush and the Schindlers' supporters, including those in the U.S. Congress, fought on. Judge Greer, who had been involved from the start, rejected these appeals and ordered removal of the tube for the third, and final, time on March 18, 2005, as described in the article below.

■ PRIMARY SOURCE

Pinellas Park, March 19—The U.S. Marshals had delivered the congressional subpoena for Terri Schiavo.

As the clock ticked to 1 p.m.—the hour a judge had ordered Schiavo's feeding tube be removed—a leading House Republican appeared before television cameras and reassured the nation that "Terri Schiavo will not be forsaken."

Fifteen years after Schiavo collapsed and seven years since the start of a bitter battle between her family to remove her feeding tube, Congressional leaders thought they had saved her.

Minutes later it all changed, again.

Pinellas-Pasco Circuit Judge George Greer faced off with lawyers for the U.S. House seeking to delay removal of the feeding tube. He stood his ground, and wondered why the federal government had suddenly shown up after all these years.

"The fact that...your committee chooses to do something today doesn't create an emergency, sir," Greer said. "I'm sorry. My order will stand."

A lawyer standing by at the Hospice House Woodside where Schiavo lives asked if the order was effective immediately.

"The word was forthwith," the judge repeated. Now.

Demonstrators cover their mouths with tape during a news conference outside Woodside Hospice in Pinellas Park, Florida, where Terri Schiavo was a patient. Terri Schiavo had been in a coma-like state for fifteen years and Pinellas County Circuit Judge George Greer set March 18, 2005, as the date her husband, Michael Schiavo, could have her feeding tube removed. AP/WIDE WORLD PHOTOS.

At 1:45 p.m. a doctor uneventfully removed Schiavo's feeding tube. A crowd of over 200 protesters outside awaited word and prayed.

It was the climax of another remarkable day of legal and political intrigue in a case that has captured the attention of the world, from the halls of the Vatican to the chambers of both Congress and the Florida Legislature.

White House spokesman Scott McClellan said President Bush discussed the case with his brother, Gov. Jeb Bush, and members of the state's congressional delegation during his swing through Florida on Friday to discuss Social Security. "The president believes when there are serious questions or doubts in a case like this that the presumption ought to be in favor of life," McClellan said.

This is the third time Schiavo's feeding tube has been removed, and she is expected to die within two weeks unless her parents, Bob and Mary Schindler, find a way around court orders.

Even with the tube removed, few are willing to predict events in the coming days given a case whose unpredictable and complicated history is thought unprecedented for any right-to-die case.

Two previous times, the Schindlers have won orders to reinsert the tube, the last time in 2003 when state lawmakers passed a law to accomplish it. The courts declared it unconstitutional.

Lawmakers in the nation's capitol were shocked their 11th hour tactic to subpoena witnesses and win delay didn't work, and described the removal of Schiavo's feeding tube as barbaric.

"Mrs. Schiavo's life is not slipping away—it is being violently wrenched from her body in an act of medical terrorism," House Majority Leader Tom DeLay said.

This time, the Schindlers lawyers acknowledge they are nearly out of legal options. "We're now up against a very tight clock because Terri is in the process of being starved to death," David Gibbs III said. "It looks like she's going to have a hungry weekend."

George Felos, attorney for Schiavo's husband, Michael Schiavo, condemned political interference.

"It was odious. It was shocking. It was disgusting," Felos said. "They cannot walk over the dying body of Terri Schiavo for their own political gain."

But the Schindlers remain hopeful. Congress may yet pass a bill on Monday to keep their daughter alive. Michael Schiavo is just as hopeful the feeding tube won't be reinserted.

* * *

The day opened with The U.S. House Government Reform Committee issuing five subpoenas to Schiavo and her husband, two doctors and a hospice employee to appear at a hearing at the Pinellas Park hospice March 25 and to maintain "in its current operating state," the nutrition and hydration systems that have kept Schiavo alive.

A Senate committee sent a letter to Schiavo and her husband to appear at a March 28 hearing in Washington.

Congressional lawmakers had moved into action once it became clear the U.S. House and Senate wouldn't immediately draft new legislation to delay the removal of Schiavo's feeding tube.

"This is about getting all the facts," said Rep. Tom Davis, R-Va., chairman of the House Government Reform Committee, which issued the subpoenas. "The Senate and the House remain dedicated to saving Terri Schiavo's life," Senate Majority Leader Bill Frist said. The hearings are supposedly to review health care policies and practices of non-ambulatory persons or long-term care of incapacitated adults. But congressional leaders were not expected to go through with them since they were supposed to be used as a delay tactic only.

Federal criminal law protects witnesses called before official congressional committee proceedings from anyone who may obstruct or impede a witness attendance or testimony, and those who violates this law is subject to criminal fines and imprisonment.

Rep. Henry Waxman of California, senior Democrat on the Government Reform Committee, called the subpoenas a "flagrant abuse of power."

"The committee has no business inserting itself in the middle of an excruciating private family matter," he said.

In Tampa, the Schindlers' attorney filed a petition in U.S. District Court, a "last-ditch" effort to get the courts to stop removal of the feeding tube. Within hours, a judge tossed it out.

* * *

Schiavo was 26 when she suffered cardiac arrest on Feb. 25, 1990. Her brain went without oxygen for five minutes. Doctors believe she suffered a chemical imbalance possibly caused by an eating disorder.

While the court, based on doctors' testimony, ruled she is in a vegetative state, her parents say she isn't. People in a persistent vegetative state may sleep and wake, grimace or laugh. But such movements are involuntary. They are not conscious, have no awareness of their surroundings, and have no thinking abilities.

On Friday, the Government Reform Committee petitioned Greer to intervene in the case so it could ask for a delay. Greer called an emergency hearing in Clearwater.

As the legal drama unfolded, a hospice priest administered communion to Schiavo, a Catholic, through the tube, and the last rites.

With events breaking quickly, Greer, lawyers for the House, Michael Schiavo and the Schindlers along with reporters crowded into a conference room at the courthouse as a telephone conference was set up.

At 12:30 p.m., just a half hour to the planned tube removal, Greer hadn't called into the conference.

Pinellas-Pasco Circuit Judge David Demers, chief of the circuit, got on the line and said he was trying to get in touch with Greer, who was guarded at an undisclosed location. Demers temporarily barred removal of the feeding tube, but ordered everyone to remain on standby.

Minutes later, Greer contacted a bailiff by cell phone and the hearing began. Greer quickly dispensed with the House motion to intervene. As a House attorney explained why lawmakers wanted a delay to hold a hearing March 25 at the hospice, Greer cut him off. "How many other field trips are scheduled for people on feeding tubes?"

"I'm not aware that there are any others at this time," said attorney Kerry Kircher.

Minutes after Greer's confirmed his order, hospice staff asked family to leave Schiavo's room.

An unidentified representative of Michael Schiavo and a doctor, and hospice staff, were in the room before the tube was removed. They said a prayer, Felos said, and shed some tears.

"It was a very calm, peaceful procedure," he said. "Of course with a degree of emotion."

Michael Schiavo came to the room shortly after the tube was removed, Felos said.

Schiavo's brother-in-law, Michael Vitadamo, also was inside Terri's room when family was asked to leave. They were allowed back in about 4 p.m.

In that time, Schiavo had been moved from her bed to a chair. The room had been rearranged so a police officer could observe any visitors inside the room. The tube was gone.

The Rev. Patrick Mahoney, director of the Christian Defense Coalition, said protesters will try to bring bread and water into the hospice today. Mahoney said when police officers stop the protesters, they will say "I'm sorry, I must feed my sister."

***

Gibbs said he had one remaining legal option: an appeal to the federal 11th Circuit appeals court in Atlanta that he planned to file quickly.

And he hasn't given up hope that Florida lawmakers may yet step in. The Florida House has passed a bill, but few expect their measure to gain approval in the Senate.

The U.S. House appealed Greer's order to the Florida Supreme Court. The court quickly dismissed it. Late Friday, the House went to the U.S. Supreme Court and asked it to order the feeding tube to be reinserted while it pursues appeals to have its subpoenas recognized.

House and Senate leaders are meeting behind closed doors this weekend, and expect to return to the Capitol Monday afternoon to vote on a bill.

As of late Friday, the two chambers still had major differences.

Both bills sought the same result: moving the case to federal court, where a judge would hold a new trial to review the facts and determine whether Schiavo's rights were violated.

Late Friday, Republican House members were told to remain accessible throughout the weekend.

"We will fight for Terri's life and spend all the time necessary to do that," DeLay said. "For friends, family and the millions of people praying around the world this Palm Sunday weekend, Terri Schiavo will not be forsaken."

SIGNIFICANCE

Terri Schiavo died on March 31, 2005. The thirteen days between the final removal of her feeding tube and her death were marked by a further flurry of legal activity involving President George W. Bush himself. On March 20, the Senate passed an emergency bill calling for a review of the case. This was backed by the House of Representatives and the president signed it in the early hours of March 21 to bring the law into effect immediately. Next day, a Florida judge refused to order the resumption of feeding and appeal judges backed the decision. The Supreme Court then refused to hear an emergency appeal from the Schindlers and, over the next few days, five further appeals were rejected.

The Schiavo case caught the attention of the U.S. and, indeed, of the world. It is being seen as a landmark in the ethical, legal, and political debate over the right to die. Most cases of PVS do not attract this level of attention, because the family is usually united over

what the patient would have wanted. It also helps if the patient has left a living will, describing his or her wishes in the event of losing the ability and competence to make medical decisions. Terri had not left a living will, so it was up to her husband to decide. The breakdown in relationship between the husband and the parents—with so many "right to life" campaigners (including Governor Bush and the president himself) siding with the parents—made this an immensely complex case. Besides arguing that Terri could recover from PVS, the Schindlers pointed out that Michael had been living with a woman with whom he had two children and that this complicated his attitude towards his wife.

The case signifies that, under the U.S. Constitution, there is a limit placed on the ability of politicians to interfere in individuals' lives. It is up to judges to interpret the law. Of course, many still think the judges were wrong to order the removal of Terri Schiavo's feeding tube for the third and final time. The Vatican, for instance, strongly condemned the decision. But doctors largely agree that although Terri, technically, starved to death, she would not have suffered, since she had no conscious awareness. Many medical experts also agree that to prolong her life artificially would have been both unethical and illegal.

FURTHER RESOURCES
Books
Lynne, Dianna. *Terri's Story: The Court-Ordered Death of an American Woman*. Grants Pass, Ore.: WND, 2005.

Periodicals
Quill, Timothy E. "Terri Schiavo—A Tragedy Compounded." *New England Journal of Medicine* 352 (2005): 1630–1633.

Web sites
BBC News. "Schiavo Case Tests America." <http://news.bbc.co.uk/1/hi/programmes/from_our_own_correspondent/4400865.htm> (accessed November 11, 2005).

Remarks by the President on Medical Privacy

Speech

By: William Jefferson Clinton

Date: December 20, 2000

Source: *Department of Health and Human Services.* "Remarks by the President on Medical Privacy." December 20, 2000. <http://www.hhs.gov/ocr/whpress.html> (accessed September 22, 2005).

About the Author: William Jefferson Clinton (more popularly known as Bill Clinton) was the forty-second President of the United States. Clinton served two terms as president from 1993 to 2001, making him the first democratic president since Franklin D. Roosevelt (1882–1945) to win a second term. In his 2000 speech, Clinton urged Congress to take action to further strengthen regulations governing the privacy of individual medical records.

INTRODUCTION

With an increase in the dependence on information technology and the gaining popularity of electronic media, the issue of individual privacy rights for records came to the forefront of American society in the 1990s. The health care system relies heavily on medical information for making better-informed decisions about an individual's care. Until the 1990s, maintaining the confidentiality of medical records was not a major issue. However, with the advent of many fundamental reforms, such as third party insurance plans, bigger involvement of government agencies, and easy access to medical records by entities outside of the health care industry aided by the computer automation of the records, many Americans perceived medical privacy as under threat.

To partially counter this problem, Congress passed the Health Insurance Portability and Accountability Act in 1996 (more commonly known as HIPAA). HIPAA, which is monitored by the Department of Health and Human Services (HHS), was created mainly to enhance the access of health insurance coverage to the average citizen of America. Although the act mentioned some of the privacy concerns related to medical information, few specific initiatives were included. In 1997, HHS made specific medical privacy recommendations to Congress. These recommendations paved the way for the HIPAA Standards for Privacy of Individually Identifiable Health Information, also known as the Privacy Rule, issued by the Clinton administration in December 2000. The text titled "Remarks by the President on Medical Privacy," as the name suggests, is a transcript of remarks made by Clinton while issuing this rule. The HIPAA Privacy Rule went into effect on April 14, 2001.

PRIMARY SOURCE

...Look, we're having a good time today, but I want to take a moment to be very, very serious. We say that we are a free nation in a world growing increasingly free. And in so many ways, that is literally true. During the period in which I was President, I was fortunate enough to serve here at a time when, for the first time in all of human history, more than half the people on the globe live under governments of their own choosing.

Now, that's a wonderful thing. That's one manifestation of freedom. Then, there's free speech, the freedom of the press, the right to travel. And also, I might add, minority rights of all kinds, restrictions on the ability of government to compromise the fundamental interests and rights of those who may not agree with the majority.

But we must never forget, in this age of increasing interdependence, fueled by an explosion in information technology that is completely changing the way we work and live and relate to each other, that increasingly, we will have to ask ourselves: Does our freedom include privacy? Because there are new and different ways for that privacy to be restricted.

In 1928, Justice Brandeis wrote his famous words saying that privacy was "the right most valued by civilized people," and he defined it simply as the right to be left alone.

Nothing is more private than someone's medical or psychiatric records. And, therefore, if we are to make freedom fully meaningful in the Information Age, when most of our stuff is on some computer somewhere, we have to protect the privacy of individual health records.

The new rules we release today protect the medical records of virtually every American, they represent the most sweeping privacy protections ever written, and they are built on the foundation of the bipartisan Kennedy-Kassebaum legislation I signed four years ago.

This action is required by the great tides of technological and economic change that have swept through the medical profession over the last few years. In the past, medical records were kept on paper by doctors and stored in file cabinets by nurses; doctors and nurses, by and large, known to their patients. Seldom were those records shared with anyone outside the doctor's office.

Today, physicians increasingly store them electronically, and they are now obliged to share those records in paper or electronic form with insurance companies and other reviewers. To be sure, storing and transmitting medical records electronically is a remarkable application of information technology. They're cost-effective; they can save lives by helping doctors to make quicker and better-informed decisions.

But it is quite a problem that, with a click of a mouse, your personal health information can be accessed without your consent by people you don't know who aren't physicians, for reasons that have nothing to do with your health care. It doesn't take a doctor to understand that is a prescription for abuse.

So, the rules that we release today have been carefully crafted for this new era, to make medical records easier to see for those who should see them, and much harder to see for those who shouldn't. Employers, for instance, shouldn't see medical records, except for limited reasons, such as to process insurance claims. Yet, too often they do, as you just heard.

A recent survey showed that more than a third of all Fortune 500 companies check medical records before they hire or promote. One large employer in Pennsylvania had no trouble obtaining detailed information on the pre-scription drugs taken by its workers, easily discovering that one employee was HIV positive. That is wrong. Under the rules we released today, it will now be illegal.

There's something else that's really bothered me too, for years, and that is that private companies should not be able to get hold of the most sensitive medical information for marketing purposes. Yet, too often, that happens as well. Recently, expectant mothers who haven't even told their friends the good news are finding sales letters for baby products in their mailboxes. That's also wrong. And under these new rules, it will also be illegal.

Health insurance companies should not be able to share medical records with mortgage companies who might be able to use them to deny you a loan. That actually happens today, but under these rules, it will be illegal. Health insurance companies shouldn't be able to keep you from seeing your own medical records; up to now, they could. Under these rules, they won't be able to do that anymore.

Under the rules being issued today, health plans and providers will have to tell you up front who will and won't be allowed to see your records. And under an executive order I am issuing today, the federal government will no longer have free reign to launch criminal prosecutions based on information gleaned from routine audits of medical records.

With these actions today, I have done everything I can to protect the sanctity of individual medical records. But there are further protections our families need that only Congress can provide. For example, only new legislation from Congress can make these new protections fully enforceable, and cover every entity which holds medical records. So I urge the new Congress to quickly act to provide these additional protections....

SIGNIFICANCE

Medical records contain considerable personal information including an individual's complete medical history, details about his or her lifestyle, lab tests, medications taken in the past or present, and additional information such as health insurance numbers and Social Security number. Prior to the Privacy Rule, private companies could obtain these records from insurance firms and use them for their own marketing purposes. Employers were also often privy to detailed medical information about their employees. Under the HIPAA Privacy Rule, employers cannot access employee medical information unless they process the employee's insurance claims. Violation of these rights result in fines and/or prosecution.

The HIPAA Privacy Rule identifies all sensitive and confidential information within a medical record as Protected Health Information (PHI). In addition to the restricted access by organizations outside of the health care industry, any individual has the following rights under this rule (as stated by the HHS and Electronic Privacy Information Center (EPIC):

- Right to access, inspect, and copy PHI held by hospitals, clinics, health plans, and other entities
- Right to request amendments to PHI
- Right to request an accounting of disclosures that have been made without authorization to anyone other than the individual for purposes other than treatment, payment, and health care operations
- Right to request confidential communications of PHI
- Right to request restrictions on uses or disclosures, although the covered entity receiving the request is not obligated to accept it.

Portions of the HIPAA Privacy Rule were amended on August 14, 2002, in an effort to simplify and standardize requirements by health care providers and to allow medical records to be disclosed under certain conditions, including public health surveillance and law enforcement activities.

FURTHER RESOURCES

Books

Kennedy, Edward M. *Oversight On Medical Privacy: Hearing Before The Committee On Health, Education, Labor, and Pensions, U.S. Senate* Collingdale, Pa.: Diane, 2004.

Sullivan, June M. *HIPAA: A Practical Guide to the Privacy and Security of Health Data.* Chicago: American Bar Association, 2005.

Web sites

Electronic Privacy Information Center. "Medical Privacy." July 8, 2004. <http://www.epic.org/privacy/medical> (accessed September 23, 2005).

Privacy Rights Clearinghouse. "How Private is My Medical Information?" February 2004. <http://www.privacyrights.org/fs/fs8-med.htm>(accessed September 23, 2005).

Owning Genetic Information and Gene Enhancement Techniques

Why Privacy and Property Rights May Undermine Social Control of the Human Genome

Journal article

By: Adam D. Moore

Date: April 2000

Source: *Bioethics* 14 (April 2000): 97–119.

About the Author: Adam D. Moore is an assistant professor in the Philosophy Department and the Information School at the University of Washington. He specializes in philosophy of law, applied ethics, information policy, and political philosophy. Moore is the author of *Intellectual Property and Information Control*, and editor of *Intellectual Property: Moral, Legal, and International Dilemmas* and *Information Ethics: Privacy, Property, and Power*. His articles have appeared in many journals, including *American Philosophical Quarterly*, *Bioethics*, *The Journal of Value Inquiry*, *Business Ethics Quarterly*, *The Hamline Law Review*, *The Canadian Journal of Law and Jurisprudence*, and *Knowledge, Technology, and Policy*.

INTRODUCTION

In his classic 1932 book *Brave New World*, Aldous Huxley (1894–1963)—a renowned English novelist and essayist of the twentieth century—envisions a future world in which babies are created in test-tubes rather than in the womb. Before birth, the embryos are sorted into various classes of differing capabilities by "predestinators" who decide the future occupation of each embryo within the society. A more contemporary vision of the future is seen in the motion picture *Gattaca*. It depicts a near-future society in which personal and professional destiny is determined by genetic constitution. In this society, "Valids" (genetically engineered individuals) qualify for positions at prestigious corporations, such as Gattaca, which grooms its most

qualified employees for space exploration. "Invalids" (naturally born individuals) are deemed genetically flawed and destined for low-level occupations. In the society of Gattaca, genetics determine caste and social destiny. Although both stories are science fiction, their future dystopias have a firm foundation in current scientific fact. The human genome is now sequenced and medical and genetic knowledge continue to develop at a sometimes alarming pace. Therefore, ethical preparedness is crucial if we are to avoid the future as envisioned in *Brave New World* and *Gattaca*.

The prospect of human genetic enhancement conjures up both dreams of human progress and nightmares of a "new eugenics." Eugenics is the study of methods for improving the human race by controlled selective breeding. Although scientists are far from the ability to produce "designer babies," techniques enabling some forms of genetic enhancement are currently available. For example, scientists have successfully introduced the gene for IGF-1 into mouse muscle cells, which results in healthier, stronger, and more efficient muscles. This technique could be used either to cure diseases like muscular dystrophy or to improve musculature of athletes. In the future, genes that confer resistance to particular pathogens (disease-causing organisms, such as those that cause anthrax or smallpox) might be added to the human genome in an attempt to protect a population from attacks with biological weapons.

What are the ethical applications of, for example, human muscle enhancement by genetic means? On what basis would society distinguish between acceptable and unacceptable applications? Are these matters best left to the decisions of individual "customers," or should they be made and regulated by law? These are difficult questions. Most scientists believe that genetic variety is essential to the survival of any species, including humans, for long periods of time. If humans were to achieve genetic homogeneity (a genetic uniformity obtained by gene enhancement techniques), then a newly emerged disease could decimate the entire human population, since all individuals would be susceptible.

Adam D. Moore, professor of philosophy at the University of Washington, uses the argument that profound discoveries such as the human genome sequence that were built upon the foundation of previous discoveries should be shared and regulated by all humanity. He further uses the inequality argument in his article to illustrate potential flaws in allowing individuals to decide whether or not to undertake genetic enhancement procedures. Despite both arguments against genetic enhancement procedures, Moore concedes that the technology could possibly be wide-spread in future years, and suggests that individual property and privacy rights remain paramount and protected.

PRIMARY SOURCE

In recent years, the ethical issues surrounding genetic enhancement, gene therapy, cloning, and privacy rights have been hotly debated. With the human genome project accelerating and the advancement of gene therapy we stand on the cusp of a brave new world. In the near future it will be possible to alter one's own genetic profile—maybe a change of eye color or a loss of weight. It may also be possible to affect the genetic make-up of future generations. For instance we may be able to banish diabetes and similar diseases from the human genome....

In this article I will argue that intangible property of this sort can be owned—that the proper subjects of intangible property claims include medical records, genetic profiles, and gene enhancement techniques. Coupled with a right to privacy these intangible property rights allow individuals a zone of control that will, in most cases, justifiably exclude governmental or societal invasions into private domains. I will argue that the threshold for overriding privacy rights and intangible property rights is higher, in relation to genetic enhancement techniques and sensitive personal information, than is commonly suggested. Once the bar is raised, so-to-speak, the burden of overriding it is formidable. In the end, I am not so worried about the prospects of a brave new world brought upon us by gene manipulation—I am much more worried when societies, committees, and concerned citizens use the force of government to tell us what we can do to and in our own bodies....

PRIVACY, PROPERTY, AND GENETIC ENHANCEMENT TECHNIQUES

...My goal is simply to show that privacy rights and intangible property rights, once established, are not so easily swept aside as some might think. Thus many policy decisions that have been recently proposed or enacted—citywide audio and video surveillance, law enforcement DNA sweeps, genetic profiling, and national bans on genetic testing and enhancement of humans, to name a few—will have to be backed by very strong arguments.

Interference with Liberty and Privacy Argument ...Suppose that Ginger has discovered the genetic markers for diabetes and has developed a gene therapy technique that will correct this condition. In fact her technique will eliminate the gene or combination of genes that cause diabetes in mature cells (somatic cells) as well as cells that may be passed on to one's offspring (germ line cells). Fred, who

has been suffering from the complications of diabetes since childhood, contacts Ginger and arranges to have genetic therapy. Moreover, suppose that Fred has privacy rights that allow him a certain kind of control over personal information and body or capacities. Fred undergoes the procedure, pays Ginger, and forever alters the genetic profile of his descendants.

...Ginger's love of science and desire to help others drives her to burn the midnight oil and produce a revolutionary new technique. Fred's right to privacy allows him, within certain constraints, to decide what happens to and in his body. It would seem that there are no grounds for third party interference in this case—nothing that would override the presumptive rights already in place.

Now if Fred and Ginger had conspired to change his genetic profile in such a way that caused his descendants to have childhood diabetes, then surely interference or sanctions are warranted (assuming, of course, that Fred is going to go on to father children). I would hope that such activity would fall under the umbrella of child protection laws. Those individuals who do things that endanger the health and well being of dependents will have sanctioned interferences with private domains and ownership....

Top-down laws that seek to regulate genetic therapy will almost always interfere with individual liberty and privacy....

Moreover, with better technology and less invasive techniques undergoing genetic therapy may become as simple as getting a shot....

While it may be the case that certain types of genetic enhancement are immoral it does not automatically follow that they should be regulated. There are many actions, both moral and immoral that arguably fall outside of the domain of societal regulation. Lying and helping the poor are two obvious examples....

The Social Nature of Intangible Works ...Unesco's International Bioethics Committee has urged government regulation of all genetic research because the human genome is the common heritage of humanity. One view is that you may have the right to change your own genes but you may not make changes that will be inherited by future generations. "The draft Unesco resolution doesn't rule out somatic therapy, which alters the DNA only in mature cells. Germline therapy is the no-no, since it changes DNA in sperm or ova, and those changes will be passed on to every subsequent generation."...

...Individuals should not have exclusive ownership of the works that they create because these works are built upon the shared knowledge of society. Allowing rights to intangible works would be similar to granting ownership to the individual who placed the last brick in a public works dam. The dam is a social product, built up by the efforts of hundreds, and knowledge, upon which all intangible works are built, is built up in a similar fashion.

Similarly, the benefits of market interaction are social products. The individual who discovers crude oil in their backyard should not obtain the full market value of the find. The inventor who produces the next technology breakthrough does not deserve full market value when such value is actually created through the interactions of individuals within a society. . . .

Finally, it is obviously the case that the information found in the human genome is discovered rather than created. . . . The genetic enhancement techniques that will be built upon this information are created rather than discovered—alas, there may be infinitely many ways to modify human genetic structure. Thus, even if an argument could be marshaled that justified societal ownership of the information found in the human genome this would not automatically yield claims to control every subsequent invention based on this information. Thus if I am correct, the social nature of intellectual works argument will not undermine intangible property rights to creations like genetic enhancement techniques.

The Inequality Argument One argument commonly given against allowing individuals the liberty to undergo genetic enhancement procedures is that such technology is expensive and will only impact the rich. Those with the financial resources will genetically engineer their offspring to eliminate defects while the poor will be left what nature gives them by chance. This inequality in health care will lead to further economic and social inequalities. It may also lead to longer more healthy lives for some, ultimately creating a class based society and discrimination against those who are genetically challenged.

This view is subject to several decisive objections. Almost every medical advancement at its beginning was available only to the rich. By refining these advancements and techniques prices dropped which opened up new markets for those less financially fortunate. In the end, procedures that were once cost prohibitive are now available to everyone. . . .

One sort of reply to this view is given by The Council for Responsible Genetics which opposes germline modification unconditionally. "The cultural impact of treating humans as biologically perfectible artifacts would be entirely negative. People who fall short of some technically achievable ideal would be 'damaged goods.' And it is clear that the standards for what is genetically desirable will be those of society's economically and politically dominate groups. This will only reinforce prejudices and discrimination in a society where they already exist." Obviously I disagree. There is no reason to think that gene modification of any sort will necessarily lead to "treating humans as

biologically perfectible artifacts" or that those who don't live up to some ideal will be viewed as "damaged goods." Maybe genetically manipulated individuals will be labeled as "unnatural" rather than superior.

CONCLUSION

If I am correct there is a fairly strong presumption in favor of privacy and intangible property rights that will limit the kinds of legislation that have recently been offered concerning genetic research and gene therapy. Furthermore, two commonly cited arguments, the social nature of intellectual works argument and the inequality argument, fail to justify overriding these rights. While there is much more to be said concerning these issues I would urge caution in a different direction and put the burden of proof in a different place. Let property rights and privacy rights stand in the absence of strong overriding reasons. In the end, it seems that we are headed toward a world that includes clone farms, organ banks, and genetic manipulation. If so, let us at least face this future with our basic rights of property and privacy intact.

SIGNIFICANCE

In the article, Moore argues that the proper subjects of abstract property claims include medical records, genetic profiles, and gene enhancement techniques. Coupled with a right to privacy, these nonfigurative property rights allow individuals a zone of control that will, in most cases, justifiably exclude governmental or social invasions into private domains. Moore further argues that the threshold for overriding privacy rights and abstract property rights is higher, in relation to genetic enhancement techniques and sensitive personal information, than is commonly suggested. Once the bar is raised, so to speak, the burden of overriding it is formidable. Thus, many policy decisions that have been recently proposed or enacted, such as audio and video surveillance, law enforcement DNA sweeps, genetic profiling, national prohibition on genetic testing and enhancement of humans, will have to be backed by very strong arguments. Moore argues for facing a future that may include the wide availability of genetic manipulation techniques with our basic rights of property and privacy intact.

The perfecting of techniques for human genetic intervention has been driven largely by the desire to confront genetic diseases. Gene insertion and correction, however, are not limited to medicine. Genetic intervention has been explored, at least speculatively, for altering physical characteristics such as weight, strength, height, and longevity—in short, for genetic enhancement. All this makes the questions surrounding human genetic enhancement especially appropriate for investigation and moral reflection. Everett Mendelsohn, history of science professor at Harvard University, commented, "Solving the 'technically sweet' problems first (a phrase used by atomic scientists), and only then turning to deal with the moral and social consequences of the experiments, has in the past proved much too costly, and will again." The "sweet challenge" of sequencing the complete human genome was achieved in 2003. What to do with this information is not a task confronting only bioethicists, but it intimately involves society as a whole.

FURTHER RESOURCES

Books

Fukuyama, Francis. *Our Posthuman Future: Consequences of the Biotechnology Revolution*. New York: Picador, 2003.

Huxley, Aldus. *Brave New World and Brave New World Revisited*. New York: HarperCollins, 1932/1958.

Kass, Leon R. *Beyond Therapy: Biotechnology and the Pursuit of Happiness*. New York: Regan Books, 2003.

———. *Life, Liberty and the Defense of Dignity: The Challenge for Bioethics*. San Francisco: Encounter Books, 2002.

Moore, Adam D. *Intellectual Property and Information Control*. Somerset, N.J.: Transaction Publishers, 2001.

Moore, Adam D, ed. *Information Ethics: Privacy, Property, and Power*. Seattle: The University of Washington Press, 2005.

———. *Intellectual Property: Moral, Legal, and International Dilemmas*. Lanham, Md.: Rowman & Littlefield, 1997.

Stock, Gregory. *Redesigning Humans: Our Inevitable Genetic Future*. Boston: Houghton Mifflin, 2002.

Periodicals

Kolata, Gina. "Fertility Ethics Authority Approves Sex Selection." *New York Times* (September 28, 2001): 16.

Platt, Charles. "Evolution Revolution." *Wired Magazine (online version)* no. 5.01 (1997): 1–10.

Web sites

Genetics & Public Policy Center. "Genetics Information." <http://www.dnapolicy.org> (accessed April 14, 2005).

Human Genome Project Information. "Genetics Privacy and Legislation." <http://www.ornl.gov/sci/techresources/Human_Genome/elsi/legislat.shtml> (accessed April 14, 2005).

The President's Council on Bioethics. "Genetic Enhancement of Muscle." <http://www.bioethics.gov/transcripts/sep02/session7.html> (accessed April 14, 2005).

Audio and Visual Media

Gattaca, directed by Andrew Niccol (original release, 1997). Columbia Tristar, 1998 (DVD).

National Geographic. Clone. National Geographic Video, 2002 (VHS).

Nova. "Cracking the Code of Life." Available from <http://www.pbs.org/wgbh/nova/genome/program.html> (with video link; accessed November 29, 2005).

The Sixth Day, directed by Roger Spottiswoode (original release, 2000). Columbia Tristar, 2001 (DVD).

X-Men, directed by Bryan Singer (original release, 2000). Twentieth Century Fox Home Entertainment, 2000 (DVD).

Organ Donations Increase When Families Have Good Information about the Donation Process

Article

By: Agency for Healthcare Research and Quality

Date: July 3, 2001

Source: *Agency for Healthcare Research and Quality*. "Organ Donations Increase When Families Have Good Information about the Donation Process." <http://www.ahrq.gov/news/press/pr2001/organpr.htm> (accessed January 31, 2006).

About the Author: The Agency for Health Care Policy and Research was established in 1989 as part of the Public Health Service in the U.S. Department of Health and Human Services; it was reorganized in 1999 as the Agency for Healthcare Research and Quality. It supports research to improve the quality, safety, efficiency, and effectiveness of health care for all Americans.

INTRODUCTION

Organ transplantation has become almost routine, thanks to improvements in medical technology and surgical techniques. As the population ages and two major indicators for organ transplantation increase— diabetes and heart failure—the U.S. waiting list for donated organs increases each year.

Unfortunately, supply has not kept pace with demand, and many patients die while waiting for a transplant. When Secretary of State for Health and Human Services Tommy Thompson announced the Organ Donation Initiative on April 17, 2001, he noted that a transplant candidate dies every ninety-six minutes, because only about half of the potentially

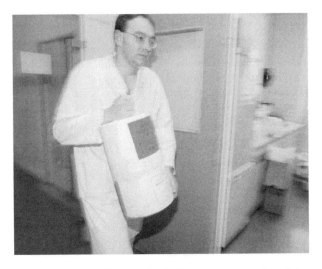

Saint Louis Hospital's organ bank. Emergency reception of the heart of a deceased donor. ©DUNG VO TRUNG/CORBIS SYGMA.

available organs are actually donated. This translates into thousands of lost lives.

Family members are approached about organ donation at a very difficult time—when they have just lost, or are about to lose, a loved one. While the medical staff who approach them have been specially trained to help them make this difficult decision, those involved must be informed of both the potential donor's wishes and the facts about in organ donation.

A patient's wishes can be indicated on a driver's license, by being listed on the donor registry, or by carrying a donor card. Ideally, however, such intentions should have been discussed with friends and family. Secretary Thompson's initiative included a national donor card, signed by witnesses, that would, ideally, include a family member.

Potential donors and their families should also be reassured that willingness to donate will not affect the patient's medical treatment. There are no costs to the family, and anyone, regardless of age or medical condition, can be a potential donor. The article below describes how increased awareness of the facts about organ donation has measurably improved the supply.

■ PRIMARY SOURCE

Organ Donations Increase When Families Have Good Information about the Donation Process Press Release Date: July 3, 2001

People often do not have all the information they need to make decisions about donating a family member's organs nor do they have a clear understanding of the donation process, according to a new study funded by the U.S. Agency for Healthcare Research and Quality (AHRQ)....

Almost 80,000 patients are waiting for organ donations for transplantation at a time when the U.S. is experiencing a critical shortage of organs. Evidence shows that families' refusal to consent to patient organ donation may be a factor in limiting the availability of organs.

"The need for donated organs continues to grow faster than the supply of available organs," said Health and Human Services Secretary Tommy G. Thompson. "This study clearly indicates that we need to further intensify our public awareness and education efforts to increase the number of organ donors. It also is a reminder that organ donors need to share their decisions to donate with their loved ones."

In the largest, most comprehensive study conducted to understand how family members make decisions about organ donations, researchers at Case Western Reserve University and the University of Pittsburgh conducted interviews with health care providers, organ donation professionals, and adult family members at nine trauma hospitals, including two pediatric hospitals, located in southwest Pennsylvania and northeast Ohio. Interviews were conducted over a 5-year period from January 1994 to December 1999; medical records were also reviewed.

The study found that:

- Families who knew about the patient wishes were seven times more likely to donate organs.
- Families who were kept updated about their loved ones' condition and got timely and detailed information on organ donation were five times more likely to donate.
- Families who met with organ donation professionals about the donation process were more than three times as likely to donate in spite of other negating factors such as sociodemographics or preconceived attitudes.
- Families who first met with the health care provider and then with an organ donation professional were almost three times as likely to consent to donate organs.

In addition, the authors conclude that the study supports regulations implemented in August 1998 by the Health Care Financing Administration, now known as the Centers for Medicare & Medicaid Services, requiring that only trained organ donation professionals approach families about donation requests.

Laura A. Siminoff, Ph.D., researcher at Case Western Reserve University, said, "Public education has been key in building the awareness of the success of organ donations and transplantation and improving the health of critically ill patients. As a result, the demand for organs has increased dramatically since 1988. However, the supply of organs has not kept pace with the demand. This research helps explain why."

Earlier this year, Secretary Thompson launched a national campaign to encourage Americans to agree to organ donation. In addition to a partnership with businesses and others to promote donation in the workplace, the Secretary unveiled a model national organ donor card which includes space for signatures of the donor and two witnesses. The purpose of the witness signatures is to help ensure that family members or others who may need to consent to donation will know the individual's wishes.

"We owe it to our loved ones to tell them our wishes and help them know they're making the right decision, in case they should have to speak for us," Secretary Thompson said. . . .

SIGNIFICANCE

Secretary Thompson's 2001 Organ Donation Initiative was designed to raise public awareness of the facts about and benefits of organ donation. The research described above suggests that this would help increase the supply of available donations, even as the waiting lists continue to grow.

Thompson's initiative may well be succeeding. In 2003, the number of transplants increased by about 2 percent, thanks to a greater supply of donated organs. In addition, from 2002 to 2003, better communication between centers with available organs and those that could handle a transplant increased referrals by 10 percent. This kind of communication is vital to increasing the supply, because the logistics of matching donor and organ are essential if the transplant is to take place.

The number of living kidney and liver donors has also increased. This helps further close the gap between supply and demand, but raises more complex issues of informed consent. The donor must be aware of potential health risks, and these must be balanced against the recipient's potential benefit.

In the future, mechanical heart and liver assist devices, which currently function as a support before transplant, may become longer-term solutions. Research is also exploring the possibility of xenotransplantion, in which organs from genetically modified animals could be used in humans. But these approaches are still on the medical horizon, and those awaiting organ transplants will depend on generous donors and their families for years to come.

FURTHER RESOURCES

Periodicals

Port, Friedrich K., Dawn M. Dykstra, Robert M. Merion, and Robert A. Wolfe. "Trends and Results for Organ Donation and Transplantation in the United States, 2004." *American Journal of Transplantation* 5 (April 2005): 843–849.

Web sites

Donate Life. "Frequently Asked Questions." <http://www.organdonor.gov/faq.html> (accessed November 24, 2005).

Made-to-order Baby Created in Hopes of Saving Ailing Sister

Assisted Reproduction and Preimplantation Diagnosis

Document

By: Margaret Taus

Date: 2000

Source: Margaret Taus. "Made-to-order Baby Created in Hopes of Saving Ailing Sister." Associated Press Archive. October 3, 2000.

About the Author: Margaret Taus is a journalist who has written for the Associated Press International and the *Seattle Post-Intelligencer*, among others.

INTRODUCTION

In the early days of research in the field of reproductive medicine, scientists attempted to understand the causes of infertility, and to correct them surgically or with drug therapies that corrected biochemical abnormalities. Among the earliest invasive and direct fertility enhancing procedures was artificial insemination, in which semen was placed inside the vagina, near the cervix, of a woman who was due to ovulate. As technology advanced, it was possible to use various techniques that could increase the number, or enhance the mobility of healthy sperm to be placed either inside the vagina, or directly into the uterus.

For many women experiencing infertility, which is defined by the Centers for Disease Control and Prevention (CDC) as the inability to become pregnant after a minimum of twelve continuous months of attempting to do so, artificial insemination did not solve their lack of fertility. In addition to the development of several fertility-enhancing pharmaceuticals (the most common first-line drug treatment for infertility is clomiphene citrate, also called Clomid), the procedure for fertilizing a human ovum (egg) outside the body was developed in the 1970s. Termed in vitro fertilization, or IVF, it involved the administration of medications to stabilize the woman's menstrual cycle, followed by medications that increased the number of mature ova (eggs) produced by a woman's ovaries during a particular cycle (typically, the female body releases only one mature egg per menstrual cycle). The eggs were then surgically harvested after ultrasound showed the follicles of the ovary had produced sufficiently mature eggs. Scientists then examined the eggs microscopically to determine their apparent health, and then exposed them to healthy, motile, sperm in a culture medium in the laboratory. The eggs were examined microscopically within a day, and fertilized eggs were allowed to incubate for about three days, in order to undergo successful cell divisions. Because relatively few fertilized eggs actually develop into viable embryos capable of completing a full gestational period, several embryos (often three) would be typically surgically implanted in the uterus, with the hope of a single healthy live birth. A similar procedure to IVF is called GIFT, or gamete intrafallopian transfer, where the harvested eggs and collected sperm are placed in the fallopian tubes immediately after egg harvest, and fertilization (if it occurs) takes place inside the woman's body.

Along with burgeoning technology in other realms came vast improvements in the field of reproductive technology. During the final two decades of the twentieth century, the obstetric subspecialty of assisted reproductive technology (ART) grew exponentially. For the first time, not only could previously infertile couples (frequently) achieve successful pregnancy, they could select for a specific gender, and screen out specific types of genetic abnormalities, assuring that any pregnancies carried to term would be free the genetic abnormalities for which screening techniques exist. This is especially crucial for parents who are known carriers of such heritable disorders as some muscular dystrophies, Tay-Sach's disease, sickle-cell anemia, or cystic fibrosis, among others. With a technology called pre-implantation genetic diagnosis (PGD), it is possible to accomplish detailed genetic screening on a single cell (sometimes two cells are used) from an early embryo that has divided enough times to have at least eight cells or be at the *blastocyst* stage. At this stage, cells have not yet begun to differentiate and each cell of the blastocyst is genetically identical. The removed cell is genetically mapped to determine whether there are any inherent chromosomal abnormalities indicating the expression of a genetic disorder for which there is a known genetic code. This is sometimes referred to as an embryo

biopsy. Those embryos having no evidence of genetic abnormalities (within the bounds of screening ability) are retained; those that are abnormal are destroyed. Of the remaining embryos, a selected number are implanted in the woman's uterus, and the remainders are frozen for potential later use.

A further advance of the use of ART is for screening and development of embryos that are genetically compatible with an older sibling afflicted with a disease, for which a stem cell transplant (typically from umbilical cord blood obtained shortly after birth) might provide a cure.

PRIMARY SOURCE

In the first known case of its kind, a Colorado couple created a test-tube baby who was genetically screened and selected in the hope he could save the life of his 6-year-old sister.

The sister, Molly Nash, has a rare genetic disease, Fanconi anemia that prevents her body from making bone marrow. But last week, doctors gave her an infusion of umbilical-cord blood from her newborn little brother, Adam, to try to correct the disease. Doctors should know in a couple of weeks whether the infusion is helping Molly develop healthy marrow cells.

Screening laboratory-created embryos for genetic diseases before implanting them in a woman is not new. But this is the first known instance in which parents screened and selected an embryo in order to find a suitable tissue donor for an ailing sibling.

"People have babies for lots of reasons: to save a failing marriage, to work the family farm," said Dr. Charles Strom, director of medical genetics at the Reproductive Genetics Institute in Chicago, where Adam was conceived. "I have absolutely no ethical problems with this whatsoever."

Molly was just beginning to show signs of leukemia, which is frequently associated with the disease, when she had the transplant, said Dr. John Wagner, her physician at the University of Minnesota. The infusion procedure between siblings has a 90 percent success rate.

"Molly's doing very well," Wagner said Tuesday, although she had a slight cold. She was playing on a computer, he said.

As part of her disease, Molly was born without thumbs, but surgeons built some from a finger on each hand. She also had no hip sockets but can now walk thanks to the use of heavy braces.

Her parents, Jack and Lisa Nash of Englewood, Colorado, wanted more children but were afraid to conceive because both carry a faulty version of the Fanconi gene, meaning each child would have a 25 percent chance of developing the disease.

The Nashes used a process called pre-implantation genetic diagnosis, or PGD: Embryos were created from Ms. Nash's eggs and her husband's sperm. Then fertilized eggs were analyzed, and when one was found to be disease-free and a tissue match, it was implanted. The couple had to try the procedure several times before she became pregnant.

Ms. Nash, who works as a neonatal nurse, said she and her husband could not knowingly bring another child into the world with the disease.

"We wanted a healthy child," she told the *Star Tribune* newspaper last month. "And it doesn't hurt him to save her life."

Adam was born Aug. 29. On Sept. 26, umbilical cord blood cells from Adam were given to Molly at the University of Minnesota.

If the transplant doesn't take, the next step could be to repeat the process with Adam's bone marrow.

Among the first couples to acknowledge publicly that they conceived a child as a transplant donor were Abe and Mary Ayala of Walnut, Calif. But they couldn't select an embryo a decade ago and had only a 1-in-4 chance that their daughter would be a suitable donor of bone marrow to fight her teen-age sister's leukemia. The baby, born in 1990, turned out to be a suitable donor, and her big sister recovered from the disease.

Arthur Caplan, director of the Center for Bioethics at the University of Pennsylvania, said he doesn't see anything morally wrong in the Nash case, but it raises interesting questions.

"The first issue is, is it right to design anybody as a tissue source?" he said. "And sometimes it can be. In this case, there's no harm or danger to a person."

But the practice can become a "slippery slope," Caplan said. "What about a parent who says, 'Hey, I'd like to do that for my child who needs a kidney, or a piece of lung?'"

The procedure also raises the question of whether children will be "designed" for specific traits.

"To what extent are doctors and parents going to be free to design whatever they want in their kids?" Caplan asked. "That's not going to happen tomorrow, but this is a baby step down that road."

When Molly is healthy, the Nashes plan to have more children through test tube fertilization, Strom said.

SIGNIFICANCE

Since the birth of Adam Nash in 2000, the use of assisted reproductive technology in order to create "made-to-order babies" has garnered much media attention. By the early twenty-first century, families around the globe sought PGD. The procedure is costly and time intensive, which is a deterrent for many parents. In addition, many countries have not yet developed the necessary technology.

The process is not without considerable controversy. For those groups whose religious belief it is that humanhood begins at conception, the destruction of fertilized embryos is anathema; they oppose the IVF process for the same reason. Some opponents would also say that simply possessing the gene for certain heritable disorders does not definitively guarantee that they will be expressed, and that humans should not interfere with the natural order of genetics. Bioethicists express some concerns about potential misuse of the burgeoning technology as a means of eliminating various characteristics that might be outside the desired norm, such as handedness, small stature, or sexual orientation. In all likelihood, the cost, the technology, the time, the risks, and the extreme unlikelihood of third-party payors authorizing large-scale use of PGD will prohibit those concerns from occurring in the near future.

Several genetic disorders, and some forms of cancer, are potentially life-threatening blood disorders that can sometimes be cured by transplants that result in rebuilding the host's immune system. Other disorders, if resistant to conventional therapies, may only be potentially cured by a bone-marrow transplant from a genetically compatible donor. A family with a biological child who has a life-threatening disorder may seek the use of PGD technology in order to conceive an infant who is a suitable donor. By using IVF and PGD, a genetically suitable embryo may be produced and implanted, and may develop into a healthy fetus who can donate stem cells from cord blood. In the case of the Nash family, Adam was born healthy, and was able to donate cord blood to his sister without being subjected to any risk to his health or safety. Molly Nash tolerated the procedure, made a full recovery and has remained healthy for more than five years.

FURTHER RESOURCES
Books

Henig, Robin Marantz. *Pandora's Baby: How the First Test Tube Babies Sparked the Reproductive Revolution.* Boston, MA: Houghton-Mifflin Company, 2004.

Web sites

CBS News. "British Couple Has Designer Baby." <http://www.cbsnews.com/stories/2003/06/19/tech/main559430.shtml> (accessed November 29, 2005).

Health & Medical News. "Test Tube Baby Donor a Parent's Right." <http://www.abc.net.au/science/news/health/HealthRepublish_195552.htm> (accessed November 29, 2005).

Lifeissues.net. "Lowering the Bar on Test-Tube Babies." <http://www.lifeissues.net/news.php?newsID=00013065&topic=> (accessed November 29, 2005).

MSNBC Health: Fertility Frontiers, the Future of Babymaking. "'Test-tube' Babies vs. Clones: Human Cloning Should Not Be Viewed in Same Light as IVF." <http://msnbc.msn.com/id/3076787/> (accessed November 29, 2005).

Reproductive Genetics Institute. "PGD: Preimplantation Genetic Diagnosis." <http://www.reproductivegenetics.com/genetics.html> (accessed November 29, 2005).

University of Minnesota Cancer Center. "The Nash Family Miracle Baby." <http://www.cancer.umn.edu/page/research/trsplant/cord6.html> (accessed November 29, 2005).

PCR machines such as this one in Walnut Creek, California, allowed the sequencing of the human genome due to its ability to amplify bits of genetic information at high speeds, essentially making huge numbers of a gene that serve as templates for sequencing. AP/WIDE WORLD PHOTOS.

Screening Creates Disease Free Baby

Genetic Selection, Ethical Issues

News article

By: Anonymous

Date: February 22, 2002

Source: *BBC News.* <http://news.bbc.co.uk/1/hi/health/1842932.stm> (accessed December 28, 2005).

About the Author: This news article was written by an unattributed author for the British Broadcasting System (BBC), the United Kingdom's public news service. The BBC provides interactive TV channels, radio networks, and an online news site, all providing local and national news and commentary.

INTRODUCTION

Genetics is one of the most rapidly growing specialties in medicine. Since 1980, research in genetics has added immeasurably to the understanding of the etiology of many diseases by identifying biologically important genes and disease-causing mutations. These data have generated large numbers of new clinical diagnostic assays, the majority of which are performed on peripheral blood or bone marrow of children or adults. The information obtained is used to make a specific diagnosis that leads to appropriate treatment for the patient. But when testing is done prenatally, other choices are possible. If the fetus is affected or potentially affected with a debilitating or life threatening disease, pregnancy termination is an option. Although it is not yet possible to create a "designer" baby (a baby with characters chosen by the parents), it is possible to perform prenatal testing for one or more defined characters. This raises concerns about when, and if, it is appropriate to select or deselect a fetus based on certain "desired" criteria.

■ PRIMARY SOURCE

A woman has chosen to have a genetically selected baby to ensure it does not develop early onset Alzheimer's disease which runs in the family.

The woman, who is 30 and has not been identified, may be unable to recognize or care for her daughter within 10 years.

She and her family carry a mutation which causes the onset of Alzheimer's disease before the age of 40.

However, the child, who is now about 18 months old, did not inherit the tendency to develop the disease.

Early onset Alzheimer's, a very rare condition, is defined as Alzheimer's—a form of dementia—that strikes before the age of 65.

Researchers at the Reproductive Genetics Institute of Chicago said the baby's birth marked the first time preimplantation genetic diagnosis, as the technique is called, has been used to weed out embryos carrying the defect that causes early onset Alzheimer's.

The little girl is thriving, said Yuri Verlinsky, chief author of the report in this week's *Journal of the American Medical Association.*

Verlinsky said genetic screening has been used more than three thousand times and is often employed to avoid inherited disorders like sickle cell anaemia.

His clinic was involved in a case last year where an embryo was chosen to provide stem cells to assist a sibling of the unborn child.

Ethical debate While the child's mother is still healthy, her sister developed early onset Alzheimer's at the age of 38, her father died at 42 after suffering psychological and memory problems and one of her brothers began having short-term memory problems at 35.

He said: "I can't speak for the public, but it's a decision of the family and not the public."

In a commentary published in the same journal, Dena Towner and Roberta Springer Loewy of the University of California said the study raised ethical questions.

They said: "Much like her sister, the woman in the report...most likely will not be able to care for or even recognise her child in a few years."

The two doctors said the mother acted responsibly by ensuring that her child will not have to live with the threat of developing early onset Alzheimer's.

However, they took issue with defining her ethical responsibility "solely in terms of disease prevention" without considering that she may not be able to care for her child.

"The differences between these two interpretations of ethical responsibility are stark, but both rest on assumptions made about reproduction—is it a privilege or it is an unquestionable and inalienable right?" they asked.

SIGNIFICANCE

Ethical issues arise in all areas of medicine, but special attention focuses on genetics, probably because this field explores the transmission of genes within families. In particular, issues associated with prenatal diagnosis seem to be problematic.

Prenatal genetic diagnosis can identify a large number of diseases by evaluation of placental and/or fetal cells. The studies are usually performed between ten and twenty weeks gestation, and the type of study used is based on the parents' age, medical history, and ethnicity. When a known disease or major malformation is identified, the parents have the option of terminating the pregnancy. For a more limited group of diseases, preimplantation genetic diagnosis can be performed. With this technology, eggs removed from the mother are fertilized *in vitro* by sperm from the father, and the resultant zygotes are cultured to the eight-to-sixteen cell stage. One cell from each is removed and tested, and only "normal" embryos are implanted in the mother's uterus. This technology eliminates the need for termination of an ongoing pregnancy and, thus, is more acceptable to many individuals. Either technique has the effect of selecting a fetus based on specific criteria.

Under what circumstances is this type of selection acceptable? Geneticists use the technology to obtain relevant clinical information on a patient. If the data shows the fetus has a lethal or severely debilitating disorder, termination of pregnancy is considered an acceptable option. Therefore, parents may be offered a choice between continuing or terminating a pregnancy with a confirmed diagnosis of terminal conditions such as anencephaly or trisomy thirteen, or an incapacitating disease such as Tay Sachs, sickle cell disease, or Duchenne muscular dystrophy.

A different dilemma is posed by diseases such as Alzheimer's disease, Huntington's disease, and breast cancer. These are classified as late onset diseases since affected individuals show no signs or symptoms until they are adults. Genetics professionals discourage the use of prenatal diagnosis to select against embryos or fetuses at risk for such disorders since most affected individuals can live a productive life before the disease strikes. However, these diseases are usually progressive, and watching a loved one slowly deteriorate can be devastating for families. Thus, some will chose prenatal diagnosis rather than bringing a child into the world knowing that he or she would have that fate.

An area of genetic selection that is considered unethical by genetics professionals is elective termination of a pregnancy solely because the sex of the fetus is not what the parents desire. This abuse of the system can occur since most prenatal testing provides the sex of the fetus as a courtesy to the parents.

Decisions on what testing to request and how to use the results are often difficult. Geneticists provide counseling, but the final choice rests with the patient. It is critical that all relevant factors be considered before a decision is made. For example, in the case cited above, a question was raised if the mother acted ethically in having a child whom she could take care of for only a few years. But, this should not be an issue if the woman has a partner or family member who participated in the decision to have the child and who will be able to raise the child after the mother becomes incapacitated.

As of January 2006, there are few rules governing genetic selection via prenatal diagnosis, creating a challenge for potential parents and geneticists alike.

FURTHER RESOURCES

Books

Magill, Gerard, ed. *Genetics and Ethics: An Interdisciplinary Study*. New York: Fordham University Press, 2003.

Verlinsky, Yury, and Anver Kuliev. *Practical Preimplantation Genetic Diagnosis*. New York: Springer, 2005.

Web sites

ADEAR. Alzheimer's Disease Education and Referral Center. National Institute on Aging. <http://www.alzheimers.org/generalinfo.htm> (accessed January 23, 2006).

The Genetics and Public Policy Center. <http://dnapolicy.org/index.jhtml.html> (accessed January 23, 2006).

Human Genetics in the Public Interest. The Center for Genetics and Society. <http://www.genetics-and-society.org> (accessed January 26, 2006).

PGD: Preimplantation Genetic Diagnosis. A Discussion by the Genetics and Public Policy Center <http://dnapolicy.org/downloads/pdfs/policy_pgd.pdf> (accessed January 23, 2006).

Patient Rights and Responsibilities

Web site

By: Johns Hopkins Media Relations Staff

Date: 2004

Source: Johns Hopkins Hospital and Health System. "Patient Rights and Responsibilities" <http://www.hopkinsmedicine.org/patients/JHH/patient_rights.html.> (accessed January 14, 2006).

About the Author: Johns Hopkins Media Relations Staff is the public relations department for the Johns Hopkins Hospital in Baltimore, Maryland.

INTRODUCTION

Many hospitals across the United States have statements of patient rights and responsibilities similar to Johns Hopkins's. These list ways in which patients can expect to be treated while at the hospital as well as ways in which they are expected to behave to facilitate care.

Such lists are usually tempered with caveats, often telling patients they can expect appropriate attention but that others might have greater or more immediate needs, that their privacy will be respected within the confines of the law, and that restraints will not be used unless clinically required. Patients are also assured of nondiscriminatory treatment, and told that they may refuse to participate in research studies. They are also informed about the Health Insurance Portability and Accountability Act of 1996, or HIPAA—legislation that prompted hospitals and clinics to explain patient rights and responsibilities in plain language.

HIPAA ensures that all medical records, medical billing, and patient accounts meet certain standards with regard to documentation, handling, and privacy. It requires that all patients be able to access their own medical records, correct errors or omissions, be informed about how personal information is shared, especially with insurance companies, and used by various third parties. Other provisions set standards for notification of health care providers and procedures for safeguarding patient privacy.

■ PRIMARY SOURCE

OUR RESPONSIBILITIES

As a patient at Johns Hopkins Hospital you can expect:

- Considerate, respectful, and compassionate care regardless of your age, race, gender, religion, national origin, sexual orientation, or physical or mental disability.
  - Attention when you request help, with the understanding that other patients may have more urgent needs.
  - To be addressed by your proper name.
  - Care provided in a safe setting.
  - Care provided by concerned staff committed to pain prevention and management.
  - Coordination of sign language or foreign language interpretation services, if you need them.
- To be told the names of the doctors, nurses, and other health team members directly involved in your care.

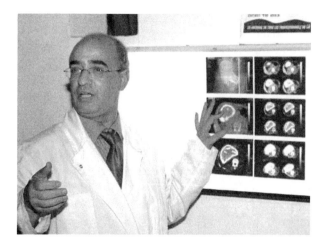

Chafferdine Ouazzani, head of the obstetrics and gynecology department of Rabat's Souissi Hospital, shows x rays of a 46-year-old calcified fetus that was removed from an unnamed woman's womb, during a press conference in Rabat, Oct. 25, 2002. At the operation, which took place in June, doctors said they removed a fully fossilized, 3.5-kilogram (7.7-pound) fetus which they believe had been lodged in the woman's abdominal cavity since an ectopic pregnancy in 1956. The case was not made public until for four months to allow the woman time to recover emotionally. AP/WIDE WORLD PHOTOS.

- Information about your diagnosis, treatment, and expected result to be provided by your attending physician.
  - Information on the planned course of treatment, including an explanation about procedures.
  - Information on the risks, benefits, and alternatives of your treatment.
  - Information about pain and pain relief measures.
  - Freedom from the use of seclusion or restraints in any form unless clinically required.
- To make decisions about your plan of care before and during treatment, when medically possible.
- To refuse a recommended treatment to the extent permitted by law, and to be informed of the medical consequences of your refusal.
- That you have the right to leave the hospital against the advice of your doctor. If you choose to do so, the hospital and doctors will not be responsible for any medical consequences that may occur.
- That if you are asked to participate in a research study related to your illness, you can decline to participate in or withdraw from that study at any time. Your refusal to participate will not affect your hospital care.
- Within the confines of the law, all communications and records pertaining to your care will be treated

as confidential. You have the right to review or obtain a copy of your medical record according to hospital policy, and to have the information explained as needed by a physician. You have the right to add additional information to your medical record by contacting Medical Record Services.
- To be able to make health care decisions in advance.
  - If you provide us with a copy of your advance directive, we will respect your wishes to the extent permitted by law and hospital policy.
  - If you do not have an advance directive, we will provide you with information about an advance directive, and assist you in completing one, if desired.
  - You may request evaluation for organ and tissue donation.
- To be informed of care options when hospital care is not indicated. We will help to coordinate options, as necessary.
- To question the accuracy of your hospital and physician bills. You have the right to request a summarized list of charges and to obtain information about those charges. You can expect to be informed about any payments made to your bills.
- Assistance from a patient representative in resolving complaints or grievances regarding your treatment.
  - You may forward complaints or grievances to the Patient Relations Department at 410-955-2273.
  - If your concern is not resolved to your satisfaction, you have the right to request a review by the Maryland Department of Health & Hygiene, Office of Health Care Quality, Hospital Complaint Unit, Spring Grove Hospital Center, Bland Bryant Building, Catonsville, Maryland 21228, 410-402-8016.
- Assistance with an ethical issue by contacting an Ethics Committee member at pager number 410-283-6104.
- To choose the home health agency that will provide for your care after you leave the hospital. A list of home care agencies is available for your use.

Your responsibilities

As a patient, you and /or your representative are expected to:

- Provide complete and accurate information about your health, including present condition, past illnesses, hospitalizations, medications, natural products and vitamins, and any other matters that pertain to your health.
- Provide complete and accurate information including your full name, address, home telephone

number, date of birth, Social Security number, insurance carrier, and employer when it is necessary.

- Provide your doctor or the hospital with a copy of your advance directive if you have one and want it to apply during your admission.

- Ask questions when you do not understand what your doctor or other member of your health care team tells you about your diagnosis or treatment. You should inform your doctor if you anticipate problems in following prescribed treatment. Inform your doctor if you are considering alternative therapies.

- Ask your doctor or nurse what to expect regarding pain and pain management, and work with them to develop a pain management plan. You should tell your doctor or nurse about any worries you have about taking pain medication.

- Keep appointments, be on time for your appointments, and call as soon as possible if you cannot keep your appointments.

- Leave valuables at home and bring only those items necessary during your hospital stay.

- Abide by all hospital rules and regulations.

  ◦ Comply with the No SMOKING policy.

  ◦ Comply with the visitor policies to ensure the rights and comfort of all patients. Be considerate of noise levels, privacy, and safety. Weapons are prohibited on premises.

  ◦ Treat hospital staff, other patients, and visitors with courtesy and respect.

- Provide complete and accurate information for insurance claims and work with the hospital and physician billing offices to make payment arrangements.

  ◦ Know your health insurance coverage and related policies concerning required pre-approvals, co-pays, covered services, admissions, and the hospital and doctors covered by your insurance provider.

  ◦ Pay your hospital and physician bills in a timely manner.

  ◦ Ask questions of your insurance company or hospital and physician billing departments if there is a financial issue that you do not understand.

SIGNIFICANCE

The patient rights movement was fueled by controversies that erupted during the rise of managed care, especially health maintenance organizations (HMOs), in U.S. health insurance. HIPAA was passed during the late 1990s, when Congress was under intense pressure from class action lawsuits from consumer and patient rights advocates. These groups maintained that there were financial incentives for patients to receive substandard medical treatment based on insurance agreements between doctors, hospitals, and HMOs.

In creating their health care provider networks, insurance companies entered into various types of contracts that put the providers at some financial risk, because the providers paid for care with insurance company funds that were fixed or limited in some way (e.g., a fixed amount per hospital admission, a fixed payment per patient per month or PMPM). If the care required was too costly, the health care provider could lose money, but the insurer didn't have to worry about its financial impact.

For example, insurers put hospitals at financial risk by setting fixed prices for inpatient stays for certain diagnoses and bundling surgical or other inpatient procedures together as diagnosis-related groups or DRGs. These are provider-reimbursement techniques first implemented in 1983 under the Medicare program. This system created an incentive for the hospitals to discharge patients quickly, because the longer the hospital stay, the greater the use of hospital services and resources, and the less likely the hospital would be to profit from a particular case.

At the physician level, health insurers developed contracts with "bonus" and "withhold" clauses that compensated physicians more for not prescribing particular "overused" diagnostic tests and surgical procedures. Insurers transferred almost all financial risk when they signed "capitation" contracts with physicians, paying them a fixed amount per insured patient/member per month (PMPM) regardless of how many services the doctors provided or prescribed. Such contracts required patients to designate a primary care physician to manage all of the health care financed under the insurance program.

Under this kind of contract, the physician became a gatekeeper who was financially responsible not only for his or her own services, but also for specialist, hospital, laboratory, and radiology services. While this may sound onerous, the probability of hospitalization and the PMPM cost were both low enough that capitation contracts were profitable for medical groups with adequate business management. Capitation contracts provided powerful financial incentives to keep patients out of the hospital and to avoid prescribing diagnostic tests. Prescription drugs are generally not included in such contracts, however, and insurers remained at financial risk to pay for these.

The question raised by consumer and patient advocates in the late 1990s (and still being debated) was whether these incentives were so compelling to providers that they perverted the quality of care and the physician–patient relationship. With the growing prevalence of HMOs and other managed care plans, patients began to fear their doctors would skimp on necessary care under the guise of avoiding "unnecessary" treatment. By agreeing to undertake financial risk, in fact, providers did align their financial interests with the insurers, and acquired the same incentives to profit from monthly premiums by keeping expenditures low.

Lawyers attacked capitation contracts by bringing a large class-action lawsuit (unsuccessfully) against Aetna in Texas, threatening one of the most powerful medical cost-containment tools available to insurers. HIPAA legislation partially defused this crisis by ensuring the "depersonalization" of patient information shared between providers and insurers. However a closer reading of the act reveals that Congress actually sidestepped the issues of whether transferring financial risk from insurers to health care providers is appropriate and if it could influence treatment. Instead, HIPAA simply codified the rules pertaining to the use of protected medical information about individuals and patient privacy while leaving the types of risk-transfer contracts that physicians and insurers can use intact.

The basic questions of patient rights advocates—such as whether physicians can be penalized financially for providing more expensive "appropriate" care, as well who decides what care is appropriate—thus remain unaddressed. In the early years of the twenty-first century, insurance companies, frightened by class action lawsuits and HIPAA legislation, considerably reduced their efforts to control medical costs by shifting the financial burden to providers.

The number of capitated physician contracts stagnated, and many subsequent provider contracts were issued as "fee-for-service" reimbursement plans, in which the more services physicians provide, the more they were compensated. Consequently, U.S. health care costs grew even while patients were granted increased privacy under HIPAA. As a result, patients pay ever-increasing out-of-pocket copayments and coinsurance premiums as their health insurance coverage gradually thins.

Advocates have shifted their focus from the insurance-related controversies that gave birth to the patients' rights movement to a wide range of critical and emotionally charged issues, including the right to die, informed consent in medical research, privacy rights, balancing free speech and patient rights, commitment of the mentally ill, sexual harassment/

intimacy between patients and providers, and reconciling religious beliefs and patient rights.

FURTHER RESOURCES

Books

Annas, George J. *The Rights of Patients: The Basic ACLU Guide to Patient Rights.* 2nd ed. Carbondale and Edwardsville, Ill.: Southern Illinois University Press, 1989.

Periodicals

Wakefield, Julie. "Withering Rights." *Washington Monthly* 33, September (2001).

Web sites

United States Department of Health and Human Services. "Office for Civil Rights—HIPAA. Medical Privacy—National Standards to Protect the Privacy of Personal Health Information." <http://www.hhs.gov/ocr/hipaa> (accessed December 8, 2005).

Human Cloning-Ethical Issues

General assembly adopts United Nations declaration on human cloning by vote of 84–34–37

Press Release

By: United Nations

Date: March 08, 2005

Source: United Nations. "General assembly adopts United Nations declaration on human cloning by vote of 84–34–37." March 3, 2005. Press Release GA/10333. Available online at <http://www.un.org/News/Press/docs/2005/ga10333.doc.htm> (accessed January 30, 2006).

About the Author: The United Nations (UN) is an organization established on October 24, 1945. The fifty-one founding countries (as of 2006, 191 member countries) were committed to the preservation of peace through international cooperation and providing collective security.

INTRODUCTION

Cloning is the creation of a creature using the genetic material of another creature. The genetic compositions of both are identical. Cloning leapt to public attention in 1997, with the cloning of the first mammal, a sheep named Dolly.

With the realization that cloning was achievable, public concern about the possibility that a human could be cloned grew. As of 2006, it is still in the realm of potential rather than reality, although in 2004, a sect known as the Raelians claimed to have accomplished the feat (no evidence has ever been provided to support the announcement). However, in 2001, a company called Advanced Cell Technology successfully cloned human embryonic cells, which were allowed to undergo several rounds of division before the growth was ended. While not yet recognizable as an embryo, the experiment demonstrated that the process was possible.

The prospects of human cloning has focussed concern on the use of humans for the therapeutic benefit of others. As two examples, cloned humans could be used as a source of donor organs and tissues, and offspring could be tailored. Such prospects have inspired calls for the banning of cloning research. However, others express the fear that this limits the pursuit of intellectual curiosity, and potential cures for diseases such as Parkinson's, Alzheimer's and diabetes.

Not surprisingly, many theologians and religious leaders support the banning of human cloning, with the view that a human is a human from the moment of conception.

In 2005, the UN adopted the Declaration on Human Cloning by a vote of eighty-four in favor, thirty-four against, and thirty-seven abstentions. The declaration prohibited all techniques of cloning, arguing that these violated human dignity and were not protective of human life. The lack of consensus and comments by some representatives that affirmed the right of cloning research made it clear that the passage of the non-binding declaration by no means settled the issue of human cloning.

■ PRIMARY SOURCE

ON HUMAN CLONING BY VOTE OF 84–34–37

The General Assembly this morning adopted the United Nations Declaration on Human Cloning, by which Member States were called on to adopt all measures necessary to prohibit all forms of human cloning inasmuch as they are incompatible with human dignity and the protection of human life.

Acting on the recommendation of the Sixth Committee (Legal), contained in its report A/59/516/Add.1, the Assembly adopted the text by a vote of 84 in favor to 34 against, with 37 abstentions.

By further terms of the Declaration, Member States were also called on to protect adequately human life in the application of life sciences; to prohibit the application of genetic engineering techniques that may be contrary to human dignity; to prevent the exploitation of women in the

application of life sciences; and to adopt and implement national legislation in that connection.

The Declaration adopted today was the product of a Working Group established by the Assembly to finalize the text of a United Nations declaration on human cloning, which met in New York last month. Last November, the Sixth Committee averted a divisive vote on the question of an international convention against human reproductive cloning by deciding to take up the issue as a declaration.

Regretting the failure to achieve consensus, several delegations said they had voted against the text today because the reference to "human life" could be interpreted as a call for a total ban on all forms of human cloning. The Assembly had missed an opportunity to adopt a convention prohibiting reproductive cloning, said the United Kingdom representative, because of the intransigence of those who were not prepared to recognize that other sovereign States might decide to permit strictly controlled applications of therapeutic cloning. Echoing the views of a number of speakers, he said the Declaration was a non-binding political statement, which would not affect his country's position on the issue.

Those in favor of the Declaration welcomed its adoption, saying it constituted an important step in the protection of human dignity and the promotion of human rights, as well as a stepping stone in the process towards a complete ban on human cloning. The text, noted Costa Rica's representative, sought to advance science in a clear framework of ethical norms. The text, added Ethiopia's representative, sent a clear message against unethical research which made human life the object of experimentation. . . .

Explanations after Vote . . . Having voted against the Declaration, the Chinese Government would continue to adhere to its position against reproductive human cloning, while maintaining strict controls over therapeutic cloning.

. . . India had voted against the political Declaration, as some of the provisions of the Declaration could be interpreted as a call for a total ban on all forms of human cloning. . . .

Belgium's representative regretted that it was not possible to find agreement on a Declaration that could have found consensus in the Assembly. . . . Rather than bringing States together, it had divided them. It was essential that reproductive human cloning be prohibited. However, it was reasonable to preserve, at the national level, the possibility of carrying out therapeutic cloning.

The representative of the United Kingdom said he voted against the Declaration, because the reference to "human life" could be interpreted as a call for a total ban on all forms of human cloning. He could not accept such an ambiguous Declaration, which might sow confusion about the acceptability of that important field of research. The Assembly had missed an opportunity to adopt a convention prohibiting reproductive cloning because of the intransigence of those who were not prepared to recognize that other sovereign States might decide to permit strictly controlled applications of therapeutic cloning. The Declaration voted on today was a weak, non-binding political statement that did not reflect anything approaching consensus within the Assembly, and would not affect the United Kingdom's strong support of stem cell research.

Hungary's representative said he voted in favor of the Declaration because it attached the utmost importance to sending a strong message that the birth of cloned human beings was not acceptable.... He hoped the Declaration was only one step in the consideration of human cloning, and not the final stage....

The representative of the Republic of Korea said his country had voted against the political Declaration, which had not achieved a political consensus. It was not binding and would not affect the Republic of Korea's future position on therapeutic cloning, which would reaffirm human dignity by relieving pain and suffering.

The representative of Thailand expressed regret that the General Assembly and the Sixth Committee had been unable to adopt a consensus Declaration.... In light of that, Thailand had voted against the Declaration and felt that it should be left to Member States to use their own interpretation as to whether or not to prohibit therapeutic cloning.

The representative of Spain said that the term "human life" contained in the text was confusing and should be replaced by the term "human being" as used in scientific texts.... Spain was opposed to reproductive cloning, but favored therapeutic cloning, which was looked upon positively by the scientific community....

Singapore's representative said he had voted against the resolution because it did not capture the diversity of views on the issue....

The representative of the United States, welcoming the adoption of the Declaration, recalled that his delegation had explained its position in the Sixth Committee and would not give a further explanation today....

The representative of Poland said his delegation had voted in favor of the Declaration and unequivocally opposed the cloning of human embryos....

The representative of Canada, emphasizing that his country's position was clear, said reproductive cloning was illegal in Canada in whatever form....

Norway's representative said that his Government opposed both reproductive human cloning and therapeutic cloning, as reflected in its domestic legislation.... He had voted against the Declaration, since it did not reflect the views of all States and did not enjoy consensus.

The representative of Costa Rica said the adoption of the Declaration today constituted a historic step to promote human rights and guarantee human dignity in all circumstances....

...France had voted against the Declaration, and regretted the inability of the Assembly to send a universal message on such a vital issue.

The representative of Nigeria regretted that he was not in the room when the voting took place. He was fully in favor of the Declaration.... It was an unconceivable paradox that proponents of therapeutic cloning would sacrifice the life of one in order to serve another.... Today's Declaration was only a stepping stone in the process towards a convention on a complete ban on human cloning....

The representative of the Russian Federation said that the question involved complex scientific and ethical issues and that his country had always been in favor of consensus. Regrettably, there had been no consensus. But, the Russian Federation had voted in favor of the Declaration, in order to send a message to the international community about the impermissibility of reproductive human cloning.

The representative of Uganda said that her country had voted in favour of the Declaration because it opposed the destruction of human embryos and believed in the protection of human dignity....

The representatives of the Netherlands said his country had opposed the Declaration because it could be interpreted as a total ban on all forms of cloning....

The representative of Ethiopia said he had voted in favor of the Declaration, which sent a clear message against unethical research, that made human life the object of experimentation. He hoped the funding for research into human cloning could be redirected towards research and development to find cures for those affected by HIV/AIDS, tuberculosis and malaria....

Libya's representative congratulated the international community for adopting the Declaration, which was a step forward in the process towards a future convention to ban all forms of human cloning....

In favor: Afghanistan, Albania, Andorra, Australia, Austria, Bahrain, Bangladesh, Belize, Benin, Bolivia, Bosnia and Herzegovina, Brunei Darussalam, Burundi, Chile, Comoros, Costa Rica, Côte d'Ivoire, Croatia, Democratic Republic of the Congo, Djibouti, Dominican Republic, Ecuador, El Salvador, Equatorial Guinea, Eritrea, Ethiopia, Georgia, Germany, Grenada, Guatemala, Guyana, Haiti, Honduras, Hungary, Iraq, Ireland, Italy, Kazakhstan, Kenya, Kuwait, Lesotho, Liberia, Liechtenstein, Madagascar, Malta, Marshall Islands, Mauritius, Mexico, Federated States of Micronesia, Monaco, Morocco, Nicaragua, Palau, Panama, Paraguay, Philippines, Poland, Portugal, Qatar, Rwanda, Saint Kitts and Nevis, Saint

Lucia, Saint Vincent and the Grenadines, Samoa, San Marino, Sao Tome and Principe, Saudi Arabia, Sierra Leone, Slovakia, Slovenia, Solomon Islands, Sudan, Suriname, Switzerland, Tajikistan, The former Yugoslav Republic of Macedonia, Timor-Leste, Trinidad and Tobago, Uganda, United Arab Emirates, United Republic of Tanzania, United States, Uzbekistan, Zambia.

Against: Belarus, Belgium, Brazil, Bulgaria, Cambodia, Canada, China, Cuba, Cyprus, Czech Republic, Democratic People's Republic of Korea, Denmark, Estonia, Finland, France, Gabon, Iceland, India, Jamaica, Japan, Lao People's Democratic Republic, Latvia, Lithuania, Luxembourg, Netherlands, New Zealand, Norway, Republic of Korea, Singapore, Spain, Sweden, Thailand, Tonga, United Kingdom. . . .

SIGNIFICANCE

The UN vote on the Declaration on Human Cloning is representative of the debate underway in the society at large. Opinions for and against human cloning are deep, passionate, and vocal. The debate goes to the very heart of what it means to be a human being and when human life begins.

The knowledge that adult stem cells also hold the potential to be manipulated into the tissue of choice holds some promise to resolve the use of stem cells, since adult cells could be obtained from donors without harm. As of 2006, the use of adult stem cells is in its infancy, with much work still to be done before these cells can be of therapeutic use.

Despite the fervor of the stem cell debate, the area remains a hot topic of research. In January 2006, for example, it was revealed that most of the groundbreaking stem cell research reported by South Korean researcher Dr. Hwang Woo Suk was fraudulent. Suk's actions speak volumes upon how important a breakthrough in stem cell research would be to the researchers accomplishing the feat.

FURTHER RESOURCES
Books

Cole-Turner, Ronald, ed. *Human Cloning: Religious Responses.* Phoenix: Westminster John Knox Press, 1997.

Kass, Leon R., and John Q. Wilson. *The Ethics of Human Cloning.* Washington, D.C.: American Enterprise Institute Press, 1998.

McGee, Glenn. *The Human Cloning Debate.* Berkeley: Berkeley Hills Books, 2002.

Naam, Ramez. *More Than Human: Embracing the Promise of Biological Enhancement.* New York: Broadway, 2005.

Nussbaum, Martha C., and Cass R. Sunstein, eds. *Clones and Clones: Facts and Fantasies About Human Cloning.* New York: W. W. Norton, 1998.

Waters, Brent, and Ronald Cole-Turner, eds. *God and the Embryo: Religious Voices on Stem Cells and Cloning.* Washington, D.C.: Georgetown University Press, 2003.

Periodicals

Annas, G. J. "Politics, Morals and Embryos." *Nature* no. 431 (2004): 19–20.

Vogel, G. "Scientists Take Step Toward Therapeutic Cloning." *Science* no. 303 (2004): 937–939.

Monitoring Stem Cell Research

Government Report

By: President's Council on Bioethics

Date: January 14, 2004

Source: "A Report of the President's Council on Bioethics". January 14, 2004. Available online at <http://www.bioethics.gov/reports/stemcell/index.html> (accessed January 22, 2006).

About the Author: The President's Council on Bioethics was convened on November 28, 2001, to advise President George W. Bush on the bioethical concerns that have arisen around the therapeutic use of stem cells.

INTRODUCTION

Stem cells are cells that have not differentiated into one of the variety of specialized cells in the body (such as smooth muscle cells and cells of various organs). Stem cells recovered from human embryos following the deliberate or calamitous termination of pregnancy can be manipulated in the laboratory to develop into a specialized cell of choice. Less frequently, the small population of stem cells that exists in human adults can be similarly manipulated.

The ability to use stem cells to create new tissue holds the promise of organ regeneration and limb replacement. As well, stem cell replacement holds the potential to cure a variety of diseases. For example, the replacement of cells that are defective in insulin production could cure diabetes. Similarly, replacement of cells that are defective in the transport of sodium and chloride could cure cystic fibrosis. Neurologically-based illnesses such as Parkinson's disease could be a target of stem cell therapy.

Tempering this promise has been the embryonic source of cells. The potential for the deliberate termination of pregnancy, or the specific creation of embryos for the purposes of stem cell acquisition, has raised great moral and ethical concerns.

■ PRIMARY SOURCE

INTRODUCTION

The monitoring report has its origins in President George W. Bush's remarks to the nation on August 9, 2001. It was his first major national policy address, and the topic was unusual: federal funding of human stem cell research. In his speech, the President announced that after several months of deliberation he had decided to make federal funding available, for the first time, to finance research involving certain lines of embryo-derived stem cells. At the end of the speech the President declared his intention to name a President's Council to monitor stem cell research, to recommend appropriate guidelines and regulations, and to consider medical and ethical ramifications of biomedical innovation.... This council will keep the population informed of new developments and give the nation a forum to continue to discuss and evaluate these important issues.

In keeping with the President's intention, the Council has been monitoring developments in stem cell research, as it proceeds under the implementation of the administration's policy. Our desire has been both to understand what is going on in the laboratory and to consider for ourselves the various arguments made in the ongoing debates about the ethics of stem cell research and the wisdom of the current policy. Although both the policy and the research are still in their infancy, the council is now ready to give the President and the public an update on this important and dynamic research area.

This report is very much an "update." It summarizes some of the more interesting and significant recent developments, both in basic science and medical applications of stem cell research and in the related ethical, legal, and policy discussions. It does not attempt to be a definitive or comprehensive study of the whole topic. It contains no proposed guidelines and regulations, nor indeed any specific recommendations for policy change. Rather, it seeks to shed light on where we are now—ethically, legally, scientifically, and medically—in order that the President, the Congress, and the nation may be better informed as they consider where we should go in the future.

I. What are stem cells, and why is there contention about them?

The term "stem cells" refers to a diverse group of remarkable multipotent cells. Themselves relatively undifferentiated and unspecialized, and they can and do give rise to

Elizabeth Blackburn poses by her microscope in her lab in San Francisco. She's best known as the outspoken human embryonic stem cell research and therapeutic cloning advocate the Bush administration fired from the President's Council on Bioethics. AP/ WIDE WORLD PHOTOS.

the differentiated and specialized cells of the body (for example, liver cells, kidney cells, brain cells). All specialized cells arise originally from stem cells, and ultimately from a small number of embryonic cells that appear during the first few days of development. ... all stem cells share two characteristic properties: (1) the capacity for unlimited or prolonged *self-renewal* (that is, the capability to maintain a pool of similarly undifferentiated stem cells), and (2) the potential to produce *differentiated* descendant cell types. As stem cells within a developing human embryo differentiate in vivo, their capacity to diversify generally becomes more limited and their ability to generate many differentiated cell types generally becomes more restricted.

Stem cells first arise during embryonic development and exist at all developmental stages and in many systems of the body throughout life. The best described to date are the bloodforming (hematopoietic) stem cells of the bone marrow, the progeny of which differentiate (throughout life) into the various types of red, white, and other cells of the blood. It appears that some stem cells travel through the circulatory system, from their tissue of origin, to take up residence in other locations within the body, from which they may be isolated. Other stem cells may be obtained at birth, from blood contained in the newborn's umbilical cord. Once isolated and cultured outside the body, stem cells are available for scientific investigation. Unlike more differentiated cells, stem cells can be propagated in vitro for many generations—perhaps an unlimited number—of cell-doublings.

Stem cells are of interest for two major reasons, the one scientific, the other medical. First, stem cells provide a wonderful tool for the study of cellular and developmental processes, both normal and abnormal. With them, scientists hope to be able to figure out the molecular mechanisms of differentiation through which cells become specialized and organized into tissues and organs. . . . Second, stem cells and their derivatives may prove a valuable source of transplantable cells and tissues for repair and regeneration. If these healing powers could be harnessed, the medical benefits for humankind would be immense, perhaps ushering in an era of truly regenerative medicine. . . .

Why then, is there public contention about stem cell research? Not because anyone questions the goals of such research, but primarily because there are, for many people, ethical issues connected to the means of obtaining some of the cells. The main source of contention arises because some especially useful stem cells can be derived from early-stage human embryos, which must be destroyed in the process of obtaining the cells. Arguments about the ethics of using human embryos in research are not new. They date back to the mid–1970s, beginning not long after in vitro fertilization (IVF) was first successfully accomplished with human egg and sperm in 1969. A decade later, after IVF had entered clinical practice for the treatment of infertility, arguments continued regarding the fate and possible uses of the so-called "spare embryos," embryos produced in excess of reproductive needs and subsequently frozen and stored in the assisted-reproduction clinics. Although research using these embryos has never been illegal in the United States (except in a few states), the federal government has never funded it, and since 1995 the Congress has enacted an annual legislation prohibiting the federal government from using taxpayer dollars to support any research in which human embryos are harmed or destroyed.

Although the arguments about embryo research had been going on for twenty-five years, they took on new meaning in 1998, when the current stem cell controversy began. It was precipitated by separate publications, by two teams of American researchers, about methods for culturing cell lines derived respectively from: (1) cells taken from the inner cell mass of very early embryos, and (2) the gonadal ridges of aborted fetuses. (In this report, we shall generally refer to the cell lines derived from these sources as, respectively, *embryonic stem cells* [or "ES cells"] and *embryonic germ cells* [or "EG cells"].) This work, conducted in university laboratories in collaboration with and with financial support from Geron Corporation, prompted great excitement and has already led to much interesting research, in the US and abroad. It has also sparked a moral and political debate about federal support for such research: Is it morally correct to withhold support from research that holds such human promise? Is it morally permissible to pursue or publicly support (even beneficial) research that depends on the exploitation and destruction of a nascent human life?

People interested in the debate should note at the outset that ES and EG cells are not themselves embryos; they are not whole organisms, nor can they be made (directly) to become whole organisms. Moreover, once a given line of ES or EG cells has been derived and grown in laboratory culture, no further embryos (or fetuses) need be used or destroyed in order to research with cells from that line. . . . Thus, there is a continuing scientific interest in developing new embryonic stem cell lines, and the existence of large numbers of stored cryopreserved embryos in assisted-reproduction clinics provides a potential source for such additional derivations. Complicating the debate has been another group of stem cells, commonly called "adult stem cells," are derived not from embryos but from the many different tissues in the bodies of adults or children—sources exempt from the moral debate about obtaining ES and EG cells. For this reason, we often hear arguments about the relative scientific merits and therapeutic potential of embryonic and adult stem cells, arguments in which the moral positions of the competing advocates might sometimes influence their assessments of the scientific facts. Further complicating the situation are the large commercial interests already invested in stem cell research and the competition this creates in research and development not only in the United States but throughout the world. The seemingly small decision about funding stem cell research may have very large implications.

SIGNIFICANCE

"Monitoring Stem Cell Research" provided a forum for discussion on stem cell research, with the diverse concerns of those who see the therapeutic value of stems cells and those who are concerned about the moral and ethical considerations of the research. The report revealed the deep divide that currently exists over the rights of the pre-embryonic collection of dividing cells that, depending on one's viewpoint, has the potential to develop into a human being or is already a human being.

Stem cells exist in sources other than embryonic cells. For example, hematopoieic stem cells, which form blood cells, are found in the blood, in bone marrow, and in umbilical cord blood. Retrieval of these cells is less ethically contentious. Blood can be withdrawn or umbilical cord blood collected after birth. Currently, these cells are used for transplantation; their use as the source of cells for organ and tissue replacement is still years in the future.

The process of directed differentiation of a stem cell into the desired cell (for example, a kidney cell) is still not clearly understood and is even more difficult to achieve. Without stem cell research, the necessary research may be slowed down, at least in countries such as the United States. Elsewhere in the world, such as in Singapore and South Korea, stem cell research has been embraced.

The zeal to advance knowledge of stem cells, and to reap resulting personal career rewards, has led one South Korean researcher to falsify data. In the early years of this century, Hwang Woo Suk, a veterinarian and prominent stem cell researcher in South Korea, had reported stunning success in cultivating stem cells in the laboratory. Unfortunately, in late 2005, after months of suspicion, he admitted that most of the data was fraudulent.

Whether this dampens enthusiasm of legislators in the United States and elsewhere to support stem cell research is as yet unclear. What is clear and real is the potential that stem cells offer for tissue replacement.

FURTHER RESOURCES

Books

Holland, Suzanne, Karen Lebacqz, and Laurie Zoloth, eds. *The Human Embryonic Stem Cell Debate: Science, Ethics, and Public Policy (Basic Bioethics)*. Cambridge: MIT Press, 2001.

Novartis Foundation. *Stem Cells: Nuclear Reprogramming and Therapeutic Applications*. New York: John Wiley & Sons, 2005.

Parson, Ann B. *The Proteus Effect: Stem Cells and Their Promise for Medicine*. Washington, D.C.: Joseph Henry Press, 2004.

Snow, Nancy E., ed. *Stem Cell Research: New Frontiers in Science and Ethics*. Bloomington, Ind.: University of Notre Dame Press, 2004.

Periodicals

Golden, F. "The Man Who Brought You Stem Cells/Stem Winder." *Time* no. 7 (2001): 27–28.

Lanza, R. "The Stem Cell Challenge." *Scientific American* no. 6 (2004): 92–99.

Web sites

Embryonic Stem Cells: Research at The University of Wisconsin-Madison. "Stem Cells in Culture." <http://www.news.wisc.edu/packages/stemcells/es_gpt.html> (accessed April 24, 2005).

NIH Stem Cell Information. "Frequently Asked Questions." <http://stemcells.nih.gov/info/faqs.asp> (accessed April 24, 2005).

PBS—Nova "Stem Cells/Watch the Segment." <http://www.pbs.org/wgbh/nova/sciencenow/3209/04.html> (accessed April 24, 2005).

Suffer the Children

Two Worlds: Health Care Standards in Developing Nations and the Developed World

Magazine report

By: Kit R. Roane

Date: December 10, 2001

Source: Kit R. Roane. "Suffer the Children." *U.S. News & World Report.* (December 10, 2001).

About the Author: Kit R. Roane is a senior editor for the news magazine *U.S. News and World Report*. Among his journalistic specialties is behind the scenes reporting in areas of conflict or political strife. In addition to his work as a writer, Sloane is a photojournalist and a still photographer, with an extensive gallery Web site.

INTRODUCTION

Every day, according to the World Health Organizaiton (WHO), thousands of people die, both children and adults, in the developing areas of the world. Their deaths often come as a result of lack of food or shelter, lack of drinkable water, and because of preventable infectious diseases. Tuberculosis, AIDS, and malaria are three of the biggest killers, resulting in as many as eight million deaths annually. In Africa, the four leading causes of death are AIDS, malaria, respiratory infections (including tuberculosis), and diarrheal diseases. According to statistics published by *Time* magazine on November 7, 2005, AIDS is the fourth most prevalent cause of death in the world.

Developing countries are besieged by enormous challenges: they are often rife with poverty; they typically lack an organized, sufficient, wide-ranging, and easily accessible public health care system; they experience famine and drought—leading to widespread malnutrition and dehydration; there is a lack of education about sanitation and preventive (or any) health care; there are frequently cultural biases, practices, norms, or beliefs that render it nearly impossible to prevent certain diseases (such as the spread of AIDS in sub-Saharan Africa); there is often an absence of social and political infrastructure. Coupled with the lack of philosophical infrastructure, there is often a dearth of physical infrastructure as well—there may be no hospital, clinic, or medical office system in many areas, coupled with a lack of basic medical and life-saving supplies and equipment (or a place to safely store those brought in by relief agencies); there is often a lack of centralized roadway systems and no form of public transit, making the transport of supplies and equipment by relief agencies nearly impossible; there may be no effective internal communication system, no set up telephonic electronic relays in place, rendering contact with the outside world virtually impossible—although this is becoming somewhat less so with the progressive advancement of satellite-based communication systems; there is great paucity of local, adequately educated or trained, health care workers or professional providers.

The cultural, social, and political practices and systemic beliefs that impede efforts at widespread education and behavior change aimed at prevention and transmission of infectious diseases are particularly insidious and challenging to eradicate, particularly in areas where belief systems are entrenched and access to personal health care information is grossly deficient. For example, it is nearly impossible to convince a culture that has never used condoms and has no ready access to HIV testing that their use will prolong or enhance lives, or prevent others from dying. In some cultures in far Southern Africa, there are prevalent beliefs that female genital mutilation and having sexual intercourse with a young (female) virgin will cure the disease constellation that the developed world knows as AIDS.

PRIMARY SOURCE

KABUL, AFGHANISTAN—Mohammad Daud leans against the wall inside the Indira Gandhi Hospital for children, waiting for his daughter to die. The doctors swarming about the intensive care unit could treat the meningitis that's causing the hemorrhaging in her brain and the sepsis that hollows the tiny, limp body resting in her mother's arms. But Daud has failed his little girl in too basic a way for the doctors to intercede. The forty-one-year-old manual laborer is jobless, and even though he has sold every appliance in his house, there is not enough money for the medicine that could ensure little Diba a life. "Maybe God will help me," Daud says, raising a hand toward heaven. "But if not, she will surely die." The doctors nod.

For Afghanistan's poor—and nearly everyone here is—a trip to the hospital is often a fruitless and dispiriting journey. The country's hospital system is a shambles. After decades of war, it struggles under burdens far beyond its limited capabilities. Malnutrition, disease, and injuries from land mines—these top the list of Afghan health woes. Afghans get little help without paying for it first.

That's true even for the Indira Gandhi Hospital, perhaps the best public hospital in the country and the only full-service facility to deal with children's needs. When the war allows, patients come from as far away as Herat, a full day's drive to the west. But until their families can scrape up the necessary funds, children lie listlessly in beds here waiting for treatment. They stare blankly into their mothers' eyes or cry themselves to sleep. "Many times we pay from our pockets to buy the medicine for these children; we do have a conscience," said Mujeeb, a doctor who works in the intensive care unit. "But there is only so much we can do with so little."

It is, perhaps, a miracle then that just fifteen percent of the children who come to this hospital die here. Many others die later, though, after their wounds become infected and their parents cannot pay for antibiotics.

Still, that hospital care is available at all in Afghanistan is something of a miracle. Surgeries, even in emergencies, are often delayed while doctors try to find forceps and scalpels. Many days there is no electricity, so pots of water boiled by wood or gas must substitute for sterilization machines. Film for X-rays is a luxury. Heat is intermittent, even in the dead of winter. Doctors work for months without being paid. How long has it been for the doctors at the children's hospital? Four months, the doctors agree; to get by, they support themselves by working in private clinics during off hours.

So, without money, the children at Indira Gandhi wait. Children like Taib. The frail ten-year-old, suffering from a testicular trauma, complains of pain. While his uncle runs around Kabul trying to borrow money for the anesthetics and drugs needed for surgery, Taib lies on a gurney. A doctor stands nearby. "The patient has to bring the drugs because we have nothing for the surgery," says Massood, a doctor who has worked at the hospital for two years. "All we can do is wait."

Tin-roofed shacks in Africa's largest slum, Kibera, where 600,000 Kenyans live with neither sewage nor public health care, 2005. AP/WIDE WORLD PHOTOS.

Blocked aid. The new government has promised salaries for the hospital's workers. One day, it says, it will also provide oil to run the hospital's generator. For now, though, there is nothing. And, ironically, the hospital has become an unintended casualty of the U.S. war on terrorism. An Arab charity, the Al Rashid Trust, built a new surgery ward for the hospital. Now that the trust has been added to a list of groups banned as suspected fundraisers for terrorism, however, the new wing sits empty. Humanitarian aid might help, but donors can be fickle. Aid organizations donate some medicine to the hospital and provide orthopedic limbs for amputees. But there are many diseases plaguing Afghans that aid organizations seem less willing to tackle. Tuberculosis, meningitis, and life-threatening intestinal diseases (caused by Afghanistan's unreliable water supply) don't seem to attract donations in the West the way photographs of children with limbs blown off by land mines do.

The picture isn't completely bleak, though. Two months ago, a boy named Salim, ten, was maimed by an explosion blamed on a bomb dropped by an American warplane. The onetime forward on a Kabul soccer team lost one leg up to his shin; his other foot was badly mangled. Today Salim is progressing rapidly, being swirled around the spartan hospital corridors in a wheelchair by a friend as he waits to be airlifted to Germany. An aid organization there has pledged to fix Salim up with orthopedic limbs. One day, Salim says, "I will be an engineer."

Salim's story, sadly, is the rare exception. Not far from his hospital room, Shaima sits in a room praying over her eighteen-month-old daughter. The toddler lies motionless in her lap, her brain hemorrhaging after she was pushed off the roof of her home by a rambunctious nephew. "I don't have much money to buy medicine," Shaima says, recounting how her brother had died of cancer just a week before. She talks about what a good man he was, hardworking and peaceful. Then she talks about how she wishes there was a treatment for the dreaded disease. The doctors standing nearby are not shocked. In Afghanistan, the doctors say, the idea of treating cancer exists only in dreams.

SIGNIFICANCE

In the developed world, with its modern sanitation, adequate nutrition, safe drinking water, and advanced health care systems, people live longer than ever before. That is not the case for areas mired in poverty, in drought, in famine, in political and economic instability, and struggling against the rising tides of epidemics of infectious diseases (some of which have been virtually eradicated in the western world). Some diseases, such as tuberculosis which had been well-controlled, have mutated into drug-resistant forms. New bacteria and microbial disease agents have emerged, such as Avian influenza and SARS, and could be transmitted globally by air travelers (as has occurred with HIV/AIDS and SARS).

Although the WHO and UNICEF report that early childhood survival rates (birth through age five) have increased dramatically since the middle of the twentieth century, more than 25,000 children below the age of five still die daily, from preventable causes, primarily dehydration resulting from diarrheal diseases, respiratory infections (such as pneumonia and tuberculosis), and malaria. A growing focus of the world's health care and relief agencies is on newborn care. *Save the Children* estimates that roughly 40 percent of the preventable deaths occurring annually (estimated by that agency as some ten million children under the age of five) occur among newborns. It is their belief that simple solutions, such as utilizing means of keeping underweight babies' skin sufficiently warm by encouraging skin-to-skin contact, making oxygen supplies available throughout labor and delivery, and providing clean means of severing and caring for the umbilical cord area after birth, would dramatically increase survival rates, as would the availability of effective antibiotics for treatment of respiratory infections, and providing mothers with adequate means of nutrition so as to ensure nutritionally enriched breast milk. Providing impoverished countries with a means of establishing maternal and infant health care would go a very long way toward decreasing infant mortality—in many places in the developing world, there is no infant care, no means of saving babies born prematurely or of low birthweight, or providing immunizations for infants.

UNICEF, other international aid organizations, and private relief agencies have been working steadily to control or eradicate disease in developing countries, and to ensure adequate health care for all of the world's citizens. Among their goals is the assurance of safe drinking water, appropriate shelter, and sufficient healthy food for all. By affording the foundation for health, they are attempting to further the goals attained by improving (or providing) health care, creating immunization and vaccination programs, developing oral rehydration systems for children affected by diarrheal and dehydration syndromes, providing high quality vitamin supplements, and establishing educational and occupational training programs, they are working to eliminate the multigenerational poverty cycle. By creating the conditions in which children can grow up with good health, they can gradually—at least physically—strengthen and heal the world.

FURTHER RESOURCES

Books

Marquez, L. *Helping Healthcare Providers Perform According to Standards. Operations Research Issue Paper 2(3).* Bethesda, MD: Published for the U.S. Agency for International Development (USAID) by the Quality Assurance Project, 2001.

Web sites

NHS in England. "About the NHS—How the NHS Works." <http://www.nhs.uk/England/AboutTheNhs/Default. cmsx#primarycaretrusts> (accessed January 18, 2006).

PhRMA. "Health Care in the Developing World." <http://world.phrma.org/index.html> (accessed January 4, 2006).

Roane Photography. "About the Photographer." <http://homepage.mac.com/kitroane1/about.htm> (accessed January 4, 2006).

The World Bank: News & Broadcast. "Corruption: How the World Bank Fights Corruption." <http://web.worldbank.org/WBSITE/EXTERNAL/NEWS/0, contentMDK:20040922%7emenuPK:34480%7epage PK:34370%7etheSitePK:4607,00.html> (accessed January 4, 2006).

Sources Consulted

BOOKS AND WEB SITES

Acierno, Louis J. *The History of Cardiology.* London: Parthenon Publishing, 1994.

Agency for Healthcare Research and Quality. "Agency for Healthcare Research and Quality." <http://www.ahrq.gov> (accessed March 15, 2006).

Agency for Toxic Substances and Disease Registry (ATSDR). "Agency for Toxic Substances and Disease Registry (ATSDR)." <http://www.atsdr.cdc.gov> (accessed March 15, 2006).

AIDS Research Institute (ARI). "AIDS Research Institute (ARI)." <http://ari.ucsf.edu> (accessed March 15, 2006).

Alabama Department of Public Health. *Manual for the Conduct of County Health Departments.* Wetumpka, Ala.: Wetumpka Printing, 1937.

American Association for the Advancement of Science (AAAS). "American Association for the Advancement of Science (AAAS)." <http://www.aaas.org> (accessed March 15, 2006).

American College of Cardiology. "American College of Cardiology." <http://www.acc.org> (accessed March 15, 2006).

American College of Sports Medicine. *ACSM Fitness Book.* Champaign, Ill.: Human Kinetics, 2003.

American Heart Association. "American Heart Association." <http://www.amhrt.org> (accessed March 15, 2006).

American Institute of Physics (AIP). "American Institute of Physics (AIP)." <http://www.aip.org/aip/> (accessed March 15, 2006).

American Journal of Preventive Medicine. "American Journal of Preventive Medicine." <http://www.elsevier.com/locate/amepre> (accessed March 15, 2006).

American Psychiatric Association. *Diagnostic and Statistical Manual of Mental Disorders,* Fourth Edition, Text Revision (DSM-IV-TR). Washington, D.C: American Psychiatric Association, 2000.

Anderson, Robert S., COL. MC. *Preventive Medicine in World War II, Volume IX.* Washington, D.C.: Office of the Surgeon General: U.S. Army, 1969.

Andreae, Christine. *When Evening Comes: The Evolution of a Hospice Volunteer.* New York: Thomas Dunne Books, 2000.

Annas, George J. *American Bioethics: Crossing Human Rights and Health Law Boundaries.* New York: Oxford University Press, 2004.

————. *The Rights of Patients: The Basic ACLU Guide to Patient Rights.* 2nd ed. Carbondale and Edwardsville, Ill.: Southern Illinois University Press, 1989.

Annual Review of Public Health. "Annual Review of Public Health." <http://arjournals.annualreviews.org/loi/publhealth> (accessed March 15, 2006).

The Arthritis & Autoimmunity Research Centre (AARC). "The Arthritis & Autoimmunity Research Centre (AARC)." <http://www.uhn.ca/foundations/aarc/site/pages/research/aboutresearch.htm> (accessed March 15, 2006).

Asbell, Bernard. *The Pill: A Biography of the Drug that Changed the World.* New York: Random House, 1995.

Baly, Monica E. *Florence Nightingale and the Nursing Legacy.* London: Croom Helm, 1986.

Bankston, John. *Frederick Banting and the Discovery of Insulin.* Hockessin, Del.: Mitchell Lane, 2001.

Barnett, Tony, and Alan Whiteside. *AIDS in the Twenty-First Century: Disease and Globalization.* Waynesboro: Marlowe & Company, 2003.

Barzansky, Barbara, and Norman Gevitz, eds. *Beyond Flexner: Medical Education in the Twentieth Century.* New York: Greenwood Press, 1992.

Baumslag, Naomi. *Murderous Medicine: Nazi Doctors, Human Experimentation, and Typhus*. Westport, Conn.: Praeger, 2005.

Beauchamp, Tom, and Robert Veatch, eds. *Ethical Issues in Death and Dying*. 2nd ed. New York: Prentice Hall, 1996.

Beck, Theodoric Romeyn. *Elements of Medical Jurisprudence, Volume I of II*. Albany, N.Y.: Webster and Skinner, 1823.

Beers, M. H., and R. Berkow, eds. *The Merck Manual of Diagnosis and Therapy*. Centennial Edition. Whitehouse Station, N.J.: Merck Research Laboratories, 1999.

Beigbeder, Yves, with Mahyar Nashat, Marie-Antoinette Orsini, and Jean-François Tiercy. *The World Health Organization*. The Hague: Martinus Nijhoff, 1998.

Bertolotti, Dan. *Hope in Hell: Inside the World of Doctors Without Borders*. Tonawanda, N.Y.: Firefly Books, 2004.

Bethard, Wayne. *Lotions, Potions, and Deadly Elixirs: Frontier Medicine in America*. Lanham, Md.: Roberts Rinehart Publishers, 2004.

Black, Kathryn. *In the Shadow of Polio: A Personal and Social History*. Reading, Mass.: Addison-West, 1996.

Blackwell, Elizabeth. *Pioneer Work in Opening the Medical Profession to Women: Autobiographical Sketches*. London: Longmans, 1895.

Bliss, Michael. *The Discovery of Insulin*. Chicago: University of Chicago Press, 1982.

————. *William Osler: A Life in Medicine*. Oxford: Oxford University Press, 1999.

The Boston Women's Health Book Collective. *Our Bodies, Ourselves: A Book By and For Women*. 2nd ed. New York: Simon and Schuster, 1976.

Bourke, Dale Hanson. *The Skeptics Guide to the Global AIDS Crisis: Tough Questions, Direct Answers*. New York: Norton, 2003.

The British Columbia Cancer Research Centre. "The British Columbia Cancer Research Centre." <http://www.bccrc.ca> (accessed March 15, 2006).

British Library. "British Library Images Online." <http://www.imagesonline.bl.uk/britishlibrary/> (accessed March 15, 2006).

British Medical Journal. "British Medical Journal." <http://bmj.bmjjournals.com> (accessed March 15, 2006).

Brock, Thomas. *Robert Koch: A Life in Medicine and Bacteriology*. Washington, D.C.: American Society for Microbiology, 2000.

Cambridge University. "Cambridge University, Institute of Public Health." <http://www.iph.cam.ac.uk> (accessed March 15, 2006).

Carbone, Larry. *What Animals Want: Expertise and Advocacy in Laboratory Animal Welfare Policy*. Oxford: Oxford University Press, 2004.

CDC (Centers for Disease Control and Prevention). "CDCSite Index A-Z." <http://www.cdc.gov/az.do> (accessed March 15, 2006).

Centers for Disease Control and Prevention. "Centers for Disease Control and Prevention." <http://www.cdc.gov> (accessed March 15, 2006).

Chronic Disease Prevention Branch. "Chronic Disease Prevention Branch." <http://www.cdc.gov/nccdphp> (accessed March 15, 2006).

Cirillo, Vincent J. *Bullets and Bacilli: The Spanish-American War and Military Medicine*. New Brunswick, N.J.: Rutgers University Press, 2004.

ClinicalTrials.gov. "Information on Clinical Trials and Human Research Studies: Search." <http://clinicaltrials.gov/ct/action/GetStudy> (accessed March 15, 2006).

Coan, Peter M. *Ellis Island Interviews: In Their Own Words*. New York: Facts on File, 1997.

Cole, Leonard A. *The Anthrax Letters: A Medical Detective Story*. Washington: National Academy of Science, 2003.

Cole-Turner, Ronald, ed. *Human Cloning: Religious Responses*. Phoenix: Westminster John Knox Press, 1997.

Cornell University, Department of Public Health. "Cornell University, Department of Public Health." <http://www.med.cornell.edu/public.health> (accessed March 15, 2006).

Cosmas, Graham A. *An Army for Empire: The United States Army in the Spanish-American War*. Columbia: University of Missouri Press, 1971.

Costler, A., and A. Willy. *Encyclopedia of Sexual Knowledge*. Edited by Norman Haire. New York: Eugenics Publishing Company, 1940.

Cowdrey, Albert E. *Fighting for Life: American Military Medicine in World War II*. New York: The Free Press, 1994.

Crisci, Madeline. *Public Health in New York City in the Late Nineteenth Century*. Bethesda: U.S. Department of Health and Human Services, 1990.

Crosby, Alfred W. *America's Forgotten Pandemic*. New York: Cambridge University Press, 2003.

Daniels, Geoff. *Human Blood Groups*. Cambridge, Mass.: Blackwell, 1995.

Dennis, Carina, and Richard Gallagher, eds. *The Human Genome*. New York: Palgrave Macmillan, 2002.

Desowitz, Robert S. *The Malaria Capers: More Tales of Parasites and People, Research and Reality*. New York: W. W. Norton, 1993.

Doyal, Len, and Jeffrey S. Tobias, eds. *Informed Consent in Medical Research*. London: BMJ Books, 2001.

Dubos, René. *Pasteur and Modern Science*. Berlin: Springer-Verlag, 1988.

Duncan, Kirsty. *Hunting the 1918 Flu: One Scientist's Search for a Killer Virus.* Toronto: University of Toronto Press, 2003.

Dunlop, Richard. *Doctors of the American Frontier.* Garden City, N.Y.: Doubleday, 1962.

Dunning, James M. *Dental Care for Everyone: Problems and Proposals.* Lincoln, Neb.: iUniverse, 1999.

Evans Schultes, Richard, and Siri von Reis, eds. *Ethnobotany: Evolution of a Discipline.* Portland, Ore.: Dioscorides Press, 1995.

Faden, Ruth R., Tom L. Beauchamp, and Nancy King. *A History and Theory of Informed Consent.* New York: Oxford University Press, 1986.

Federation of American Scientists. "Federation of American Scientists, ProMED Initiative." <http://www.fas.org/promed> (accessed March 15, 2006).

FedStats. "FedStats." <http://www.fedstats.gov> (accessed March 15, 2006).

Fenner, Frank, et al. *Smallpox and Its Eradication.* Geneva: World Health Organization, 1988.

Food and Drug Administration. "Food and Drug Administration." <http://www.fda.gov> (accessed March 15, 2006).

Freud, Sigmund. *The Interpretation of Dreams.* Oxford: Oxford University Press, 2000.

Frist, Bill. *When Every Moment Counts: What You Need to Know about Bioterrorism from the Senate's Only Doctor.* Lanham, Md.: Rowman & Littlefield, 2002.

Fukuyama, Francis. *Our Posthuman Future: Consequences of the Biotechnology Revolution.* New York: Picador, 2003.

Gamble, Vanessa Northington. *Making a Place for Ourselves: The Black Hospital Movement, 1920–1945.* New York: Oxford University Press, 1995.

GAO (Government Accountability Office). "Site Map." <http://www.gao.gov/sitemap.html> (accessed March 15, 2006).

Gebhard, Paul H., and Alan B. Johnson. *The Kinsey Data: Marginal Tabulations of the 1938–1963 Interviews Conducted by the Institute for Sex Research.* Philadelphia: W. B. Saunders Company, 1979.

Getz, Kenneth, and Deborah Borlitz. *Informed Consent: The Consumer's Guide to the Risks and Benefits of Volunteering for Clinical Trials.* Boston: CenterWatch, 2003.

Goldstein, Avram. *Addiction: From Biology to Drug Policy.* New York: W. H. Freeman, 1994.

Gordon, James S. *Manifesto for a New Medicine: Your Guide to Healing Partnerships and the Wise Use of Alternative Therapies.* Reading, Mass.: Perseus Publishing, 1996.

Gordon, Linda. *Woman's Body, Woman's Right: Birth Control in America.* New York: Penguin, 1977.

Gostin, Lawrence O. *Public Health Law and Ethics: A Reader.* Berkeley, Calif.: University of California Press, 2002.

Harvard University. "Harvard School of Public Health." <http://www.hsph.harvard.edu> (accessed March 15, 2006).

Hazardous Substances & Public Health. "Hazardous Substances and Public Health." <http://www.atsdr.cdc.gov/HEC/HSPH/hsphhome.html> (accessed March 15, 2006).

Health Resources and Services Administration (HRSA). "Health Resources and Services Administration (HRSA)." <http://www.hrsa.gov> (accessed March 15, 2006).

Hobhouse, Henry. *Seeds of Change: Five Plants That Transformed Mankind.* New York: Harper & Row, 1986.

Holmes, Chris. *Spores, Plagues, and History: The Story of Anthrax.* Dallas: Durban House Publishing, 2003.

Hopkins, D. R. *The Greatest Killer: Smallpox in History.* Chicago: University of Chicago Press, 2002.

Hull, N. E. H., and Peter Charles Hoffer. *Roe v. Wade: The Abortion Rights Controversy in American History.* Lawrence: University Press of Kansas, 2001.

Humphreys, Margaret. *Malaria: Poverty, Race, and Public Health in the United States.* Baltimore: Johns Hopkins University Press, 2001.

Huxley, Aldus. *Brave New World* and *Brave New World Revisited.* New York: HarperCollins, 1932/1958.

Imperial College School of Medicine, Epidemiology and Public Health. "Imperial College School of Medicine, Epidemiology and Public Health." <http://www1.imperial.ac.uk/medicine/about/divisions/pcphs/eph/default.html> (accessed March 15, 2006).

Institute of Medicine. "Topics." <http://www.iom.edu/CMS/2956.aspx> (accessed March 15, 2006).

International Astronomical Union (IAU). "FAQs." <http://www.iau.org/FAQs.56.0.html> (accessed March 15, 2006).

International Society for Infectious Diseases. "International Society for Infectious Diseases." <http://www.isid.org> (accessed March 15, 2006).

Joffe, Carole. *Doctors of Conscience: The Struggle to Provide Abortion Before and After Roe v. Wade.* Boston: Beacon, 1995.

Jones, James H. *Bad Blood: The Tuskegee Syphilis Experiment.* New York: Free Press, 1981.

Kass, Leon R. *Beyond Therapy: Biotechnology and the Pursuit of Happiness.* New York: Regan Books, 2003.

Kass, Leon R., and John Q. Wilson. *The Ethics of Human Cloning.* Washington, D.C.: American Enterprise Institute Press, 1998.

Kastenbaum, R. J. *Death, Society, and Human Experience.* 6th ed. New York: Allyn and Bacon, 1998.

Ketcham, Katherine, et al. *Beyond the Influence: Understanding and Defeating Alcoholism.* New York: Bantam, 2000.

Kidsin, Ruth. *Acupuncture for Everyone.* Rochester, Vt.: Healing Arts Press, 1991.

Kleinke, J. D. *Oxymorons: The Myth of a U.S. Health Care System*. San Francisco: Jossey-Bass, 2001.

Koop, C. Everett. *Critical Issues in Global Health*. Hoboken, N.J.: John Wiley & Sons, 2002.

Kramer, Peter. *Against Depression*. New York: Viking, 2005.

Kübler-Ross, Elisabeth. *On Grief and Grieving*. New York: Scribner, 2005.

Kübler-Ross, Elisabeth, and David Kessler. *Life Lessons: Two Experts on Death and Dying Teach Us about the Mysteries of Life and Living*. New York: Scribner, 2000.

Kuebler, Kim K. *End of Life Care: Clinical Practice Guidelines*. Philadelphia: W. B. Saunders, 2001.

Lappé, Frances Moore. *Diet for a Small Planet*. Twentieth Anniversary Edition. New York: Ballantine, 1991.

Lappé, Frances Moore, Joseph Collins, and Peter Rosset. *World Hunger: 12 Myths*. New York: Grove Press, 2001.

Lashley, Felissa R., and Jerry D. Durham. *Emerging Infectious Diseases: Trends and Issues*. New York: Springer Publishing Company, 2002.

Lawrence Berkeley National Laboratory. "Risk-Related Research at Lawrence Berkeley National Laboratory." <http://www.lbl.gov/LBL-Programs/Risk-Research.html> (accessed March 15, 2006).

Leavitt, Judith Walzer. *Typhoid Mary: Captive to the Public's Health*. Boston: Beacon, 1996.

Legal Information Institute, Cornell University. "Code of Federal Regulations." <http://www4.law.cornell.edu/cfr/> (accessed March 15, 2006).

Library of Congress. "Library of Congress Online Catalog." <http://catalog.loc.gov/cgi-bin/Pwebrecon.cgi?DB=local&PAGE=First> (accessed March 15, 2006).

Lifton, Robert Jay. *The Nazi Doctors: Medical Killing and the Psychology of Genocide*. New York: Basic Books, 2000.

Link, Kurt. *The Vaccine Controversy: The History, Use, and Safety of Vaccinations*. Westport, Conn.: Praeger, 2005.

L'Institut Pasteur. "L'Institut Pasteur." <http://www.pasteur.fr/english.html> (accessed March 15, 2006).

Lock, Stephen, John M. Last, and George Dunea, eds. *The Oxford Illustrated Companion to Medicine*. Oxford, UK: Oxford University Press, 2001.

Ludmerer, Kenneth M. *Learning to Heal: The Development of American Medical Education*. Baltimore, Md.: Johns Hopkins University Press, 1996.

———. *Time to Heal: American Medical Education from the Turn of the Century to the Era of Managed Care*. New York: Oxford University Press, 1999.

Macklin, Ruth. *Double Standards in Medical Research in Developing Countries*. Cambridge: Cambridge University Press, 2004.

Magill, Gerard, ed. *Genetics and Ethics: An Interdisciplinary Study*. Fordham University Press, 2003.

Marantz Henig, Robin. *Pandora's Baby: How the First Test Tube Babies Sparked the Reproductive Revolution*. Boston, Mass.: Houghton-Mifflin Company, 2004.

Médecins Sans Frontières, eds. *In the Shadow of Just Wars: Violence, Politics, and Humanitarian Action*. Translated by Fabrice Weissman and Doctors Without Borders. Ithaca, N.Y.: Cornell University Press, 2004.

MedWeb at Emory University. "MedWeb at Emory University search page." <http://170.140.250.52/MedWeb/> (accessed March 15, 2006).

Melosh, Barbara. *"The Physician's Hand": Work Culture and Conflict in American Nursing*. Philadelphia: Temple University Press, 1982.

Miller, Judith, Stephen Engelberg, and William J. Broad. *Germs: Biological Weapons and America's Secret War*. New York: Simon and Schuster, 2001.

Moore, Adam D. *Intellectual Property and Information Control*. Somerset, N.J.: Transaction Publishers, 2001.

Moore, Adam D., ed. *Information Ethics: Privacy, Property, and Power*. Seattle: The University of Washington Press, 2005.

Morbidity and Mortality Weekly Report. "Morbidity and Mortality Weekly Report." <http://www.cdc.gov/mmwr> (accessed March 15, 2006).

Nader, Ralph. *Unsafe At Any Speed, 25th Anniversary Edition*. Massachusetts: Knightsbridge Publishing Company, 1991.

NASA (National Aeronautics and Space Administration). "Jet Propulsion Laboratory." <http://www.jpl.nasa.gov/> (accessed March 15, 2006).

———. "Visible Earth." <http://visibleearth.nasa.gov/> (accessed March 15, 2006).

National Academies. "Environmental Issues." <http://www.nationalacademies.org/environment/> (accessed March 15, 2006).

———. "Health and Medicine at the National Academies." <http://www.nationalacademies.org/health/> (accessed March 15, 2006).

———. "The National Academies: Advisers to the Nation on Science, Engineering, and Medicine." <http://www.nationalacademies.org/> (accessed March 15, 2006).

National Academy of Sciences. "National Academy of Sciences." <http://www.nas.edu> (accessed March 15, 2006).

National Center for Biotechnology Information. "PubMed." <http://www.ncbi.nlm.nih.gov/entrez/query.fcgi?DB=pubmed> (accessed March 15, 2006).

National Commission for the Protection of Human Subjects of Biomedical and Behavioral Research. *The Belmont Report: Ethical Principles and Guidelines for the Protection of Human Subjects of Research*. Washington, D.C.: U.S.G.P.O., 1979.

The National Council for Science and the Environment (NCSE). "Congressional Research Service Reports." <http://www.ncseonline.org/NLE/CRS/> (accessed March 15, 2006).

National Human Genome Research Institute (NHGRI). "National Human Genome Research Institute (NHGRI)." <http://www.nhgri.nih.gov> (accessed March 15, 2006).

National Institute of Diabetes and Digestive and Kidney Diseases (NIDDKD). "National Institute of Diabetes and Digestive and Kidney Diseases (NIDDKD)." <http://www.niddk.nih.gov> (accessed March 15, 2006).

National Institute of Environmental Health Sciences (NIEHS). "National Institute of Environmental Health Sciences (NIEHS)." <http://www.niehs.nih.gov> (accessed March 15, 2006).

National Institutes of Allergy and Infectious Diseases, Division of AIDS. "National Institutes of Allergy and Infectious Diseases, Division of AIDS." <http://www.niaid.nih.gov/daids/default.htm> (accessed March 15, 2006).

National Institutes of Health. "National Institutes of Health." <http://www.nih.gov> (accessed March 15, 2006).

National Library of Medicine. "Environmental Health and Toxicology." <http://sis.nlm.nih.gov/enviro.html> (accessed March 15, 2006).

———. "History of Medicine." <http://www.nlm.nih.gov/hmd/index.html> (accessed March 15, 2006).

National Medical Society. "Library of the National Medical Society." <http://www.medical-library.org/> (accessed March 15, 2006).

National Program of Cancer Registries. "National Program of Cancer Registries." <http://www.cdc.gov/cancer/npcr> (accessed March 15, 2006).

National Public Health Institute. "National Public Health Institute." <http://www.ktl.fi/portal/english> (accessed March 15, 2006).

National Toxicology Program. "National Toxicology Program." <http://ntp-server.niehs.nih.gov> (accessed March 15, 2006).

National Tuberculosis Center. "National Tuberculosis Center." <http://www.umdnj.edu/globaltb/home.htm> (accessed March 15, 2006).

Nation's Health. "Nation's Health." <http://www.apha.org/tnh/> (accessed March 15, 2006).

Nature. "Nature." <http://www.nature.com> (accessed March 15, 2006).

Naval Health Research Center, Behavioral Science and Epidemiology. "Naval Health Research Center, Behavioral Science and Epidemiology." <http://www.nhrc.navy.mil> (accessed March 15, 2006).

Naythons, Matthew. *The Face of Mercy: A Photographic History of Medicine at War.* New York: Random House, 1993.

NCI - National Cancer Institute. "NCI - National Cancer Institute." <http://www.nci.nih.gov> (accessed March 15, 2006).

NEI - National Eye Institute. "NEI - National Eye Institute." <http://www.nei.nih.gov> (accessed March 15, 2006).

Ng, Rick. *Drugs From Discovery to Approval.* Indianapolis: Wiley-Liss, 2003.

NHGRI - National Human Genome Research Institute. "NHGRI - National Human Genome Research Institute." <http://www.nhgri.nih.gov> (accessed March 15, 2006).

NHLBI - National Heart, Lung, and Blood Institute. "NHLBI - National Heart, Lung, and Blood Institute." <http://www.nhlbi.nih.gov/index.htm> (accessed March 15, 2006).

NIA - National Institute on Aging. "NIA - National Institute on Aging." <http://www.nia.nih.gov> (accessed March 15, 2006).

NIAAA - National Institute on Alcohol Abuse and Alcoholism. "NIAAA - National Institute on Alcohol Abuse and Alcoholism." <http://www.niaaa.nih.gov> (accessed March 15, 2006).

NIAID - National Institute of Allergy and Infectious Diseases. "NIAID - National Institute of Allergy and Infectious Diseases." <http://www.niaid.nih.gov> (accessed March 15, 2006).

NIAMS - National Institute of Arthritis and Musculoskeletal and Skin Diseases. "NIAMS - National Institute of Arthritis and Musculoskeletal and Skin Diseases." <http://www.niams.nih.gov> (accessed March 15, 2006).

NIBIB - National Institute of Biomedical Imaging and Bioengineering. "NIBIB - National Institute of Biomedical Imaging and Bioengineering." <http://www.nibib1.nih.gov> (accessed March 15, 2006).

NICHD - National Institute of Child Health and Human Development. "NICHD - National Institute of Child Health and Human Development." <http://www.nichd.nih.gov> (accessed March 15, 2006).

NIDA - National Institute on Drug Abuse. "NIDA - National Institute on Drug Abuse." <http://www.nida.nih.gov> (accessed March 15, 2006).

NIEHS - National Institute of Environmental Health Sciences. "NIEHS - National Institute of Environmental Health Sciences." <http://www.niehs.nih.gov> (accessed March 15, 2006).

NIGMS - National Institute of General Medical Sciences. "NIGMS - National Institute of General Medical Sciences." <http://www.nigms.nih.gov> (accessed March 15, 2006).

NIMH - National Institute of Mental Health. "NIMH - National Institute of Mental Health." <http://www.nimh.nih.gov> (accessed March 15, 2006).

NINDS - National Institute of Neurological Disorders and Stroke. "NINDS - National Institute of Neurological Disorders and Stroke." <http://www.ninds.nih.gov> (accessed March 15, 2006).

NINR - National Institute of Nursing Research. "NINR - National Institute of Nursing Research." <http://ninr.nih.gov/ninr> (accessed March 15, 2006).

NLM - National Library of Medicine. "NLM - National Library of Medicine." <http://www.nlm.nih.gov/> (accessed March 15, 2006).

Nobel Foundation. "Nobelprize.org." <http://nobelprize.org/index.html> (accessed March 15, 2006).

Novartis Foundation. *Stem Cells: Nuclear Reprogramming and Therapeutic Applications.* New York: John Wiley & Sons, 2005.

Nussbaum, Martha C., and Cass R. Sunstein, eds. *Clones and Clones: Facts and Fantasies About Human Cloning.* New York: W. W. Norton, 1998.

Office of Global Health Affairs. "Office of Global Health Affairs." <http://www.globalhealth.gov> (accessed March 15, 2006).

Office of Public Health and Science. "Office of Public Health and Science." <http://phs.os.dhhs.gov/ophs> (accessed March 15, 2006).

Office of Research on Women's Health. "Office of Research on Women's Health." <http://www4.od.nih.gov/orwh> (accessed March 15, 2006).

Osler, William. *The Principles and Practice of Medicine.* 6th ed. New York: D. Appleton, 1906.

Palladino, Michael A., and Stuart Hill. *Emerging Infectious Diseases (The Benjamin Cummings Special Topics in Biology Series).* New York: Benjamin Cummings, 2005.

Pharma-Lexicon International. "MediLexicon." <http://www.medilexicon.com/> (accessed March 15, 2006).

Piantadosi, Stephen. *Clinical Trials: A Methodologic Perspective.* New York: Wiley Interscience, 1997.

Pinstrup-Andersen, Per, and Ebbie Schioler. *Seeds of Contention: World Hunger and the Global Controversy Over GM Crops.* Washington, D.C.: International Food Policy Research Institute, 2001.

Plotkin, Stanley A., and Walter A. Orenstein, eds. *Vaccines.* Philadelphia: W. B. Saunders, 1999.

Porter, Roy. *The Greatest Benefit to Mankind.* New York: W. W. Norton, 1999.

———. *Madness: A Brief History.* Oxford: Oxford University Press, 2003.

Porter, Roy, ed. *Cambridge Illustrated History of Medicine.* Cambridge: Cambridge University Press, 1996.

Preston, Richard. *The Demon in the Freezer.* New York: Random House, 2002.

———. *The Hot Zone: A Terrifying True Story.* New York: Anchor, 1995.

Project Gutenberg. "Online Book Catalog - Overview." <http://www.gutenberg.org/catalog/> (accessed March 15, 2006).

ProMED-mail electronic reporting system. "ProMED-mail electronic reporting system." <http://www.promedmail.org> (accessed March 15, 2006).

Publiclibraries.com. "National Libraries of the World." <http://www.publiclibraries.com/world.htm> (accessed March 15, 2006).

Quantitative Genetics Resources. "Quantitative Genetics Resources." <http://nitro.biosci.arizona.edu/zbook/book.html> (accessed March 15, 2006).

Reverby, Susan M. *Tuskegee's Truths: Rethinking the Tuskegee Syphilis Study.* Chapel Hill: University of North Carolina Press, 2000.

Rice, Emmett A. *A Brief History of Physical Education.* New York: A.S. Barnes, 1926.

Richelson, Jeffey T. *The U.S. Intelligence Community (4th Edition).* Boulder, Colo.: Westview Press, 1989.

Riddle, John M. *Eve's Herbs: A History of Contraception and Abortion in the West.* Cambridge, Mass.: Harvard University Press, 1997.

Ridley, Rosalind M., and Harry F. Baker. *Fatal Protein. The Story of CJD, BSE, and Other Prion Diseases.* Oxford: Oxford University Press, 1998.

Robson, Terry, ed. *An Introduction to Complementary Medicine.* Crows Nest, New South Wales: Allen & Unwin, 2003.

Rocco, Fiametta. *Malaria and the Quest for a Cure that Changed the World.* New York: HarperCollins, 2003.

Royal Society, (UK). "Science issues." <http://www.royalsoc.ac.uk/landing.asp?id=6> (accessed March 15, 2006).

Rutkow, Ira. *Bleeding Blue and Gray: Civil War Surgery and the Evolution of American Medicine.* New York: Random House, 2005.

Science Magazine. "Science Magazine." <http://www.sciencemag.org> (accessed March 15, 2006).

Sheen, Barbara. *Mad Cow Disease (Diseases and Disorders).* New York: Lucent, 2004.

Shepard, Philip S., and Christopher Dean. *Monoclonal Antibodies: A Practical Approach.* Oxford: Oxford University Press, 2000.

Shnayerson, Michael, and Mark J. Plotkin. *The Killers Within: The Deadly Rise of Drug-Resistant Bacteria.* New York: Little, Brown, 2002.

Simmons, Marie A. *Monoclonal Antibodies: New Research.* New York: Nova Biomedical Books, 2005.

Sinclair, Upton. *The Jungle.* New York: The Jungle Publishing Co., 1906.

Sizemore, Chris, and Elen Sain Pittillo. *I'm Eve.* Garden City, N.Y.: Doubleday, 1977.

Sloan, Frank A., et al. *The Price of Smoking*. Cambridge, Mass.: MIT Press, 2004.

Smith, James J. *Looking Back, Looking Ahead: A History of American Medical Education*. Chicago, Ill.: Adams Press, 2003.

Smith, Mickey, et al. *Pharmaceutical Marketing: Principles, Environment and Practice*. New York: Pharmaceutical Products Press (Haworth Press), 2002.

Snow, Nancy E., ed. *Stem Cell Research: New Frontiers in Science and Ethics*. Bloomington, Ind.: University of Notre Dame Press, 2004.

Spitz, Vivien. *Doctors from Hell: The Horrific Account of Nazi Experiments on Humans*. Boulder, Colo.: Sentient, 2005.

Standford University. "Stanford Center for Molecular and Genetic Medicine (CMGM) Bioinformatics Resource." <http://cmgm.stanford.edu> (accessed March 15, 2006).

Stanford University. "Stanford Prevention Research Center." <http://prevention.stanford.edu> (accessed March 15, 2006).

Starr, Paul. *The Social Transformation of American Medicine*. New York: Basic Books, 1982.

Steele, Volney. *Bleed, Blister, and Purge: A History of Medicine on the American Frontier*. Missoula, Mont.: Mountain Press Publishing Company, 2005.

Stock, Gregory. *Redesigning Humans: Our Inevitable Genetic Future*. Boston: Houghton Mifflin, 2002.

Substance Abuse & Mental Health Services Administration (SAMHSA). "Substance Abuse & Mental Health Services Administration (SAMHSA)." <http://www.samhsa.gov/index.aspx> (accessed March 15, 2006).

Sullivan, June M. *HIPAA: A Practical Guide to the Privacy and Security of Health Data*. Chicago: American Bar Association, 2005.

Thomson, Alison, and Jim McWhir, eds. *Gene Targeting and Embryonic Stem Cells (Advanced Methods)*. Oxford: BIOS Scientific Publishers, 2004.

Tone, Andrea. *Devices and Desires: A History of Contraceptives in America*. New York: Hill and Wang, 2001.

Townes, Charles H. *How the Laser Happened: Adventures of a Scientist*. New York: Oxford University Press, 2002.

Tracy, Kathleen. *Robert Koch and the Study of Anthrax*. Hockessin, Del.: Mitchell Lane Publishers, 2004.

UNAIDS. "UNAIDS Research." <http://www.unaids.org/en/Issues/Research/default.asp> (accessed March 15, 2006).

UNICEF Staff. *Emergency Field Handbook: A Guide for UNICEF Staff*. New York: UNICEF, 2005.

United Nations Drug Control Program. *World Drug Report 2000: United Nations Office for Drug Control and Crime Prevention*. New York: Oxford University Press, 2001.

United Nations/World Water Assessment Programme. *UN World Water Development Report: Water for People, Water for Life*. Paris, New York, and Oxford: UNESCO (United Nations Educational, Scientific and Cultural Organization) and Berghahn Books, 2003.

United States Census Bureau. "United States Census Bureau." <http://www.census.gov> (accessed March 15, 2006).

U.S. Department of Defense. *Emergency War Surgery*. Washington, D.C., 1975.

U.S. Department of Justice. *Americans with Disabilities Act Handbook*. Anaheim, Calif.: BNI, 1992.

University of Chicago, Environmental Medicine. "University of Chicago, Environmental Medicine." <http://www.uchospitals.edu/online-library/library.php?content=P00488> (accessed March 15, 2006).

University of Colorado Health Sciences Center. "University of Colorado Health Sciences Center, Department of Preventive Medicine and Biometrics." <http://www.uchsc.edu/pmb/pmb> (accessed March 15, 2006).

University of London. "University of London, Department of Public Health Sciences." <http://phs.kcl.ac.uk> (accessed March 15, 2006).

University of Toronto. "University of Toronto, Department of Health Policy, Management and Evaluation." <http://www.hpme.utoronto.ca/scripts/index_.asp> (accessed March 15, 2006).

University of Virginia. "University of Virginia, Division of Biostatistics and Epidemiology." <http://www.healthsystem.virginia.edu/internet/hes/biostat/biostat_home.cfm> (accessed March 15, 2006).

Walsh, Christopher. *Antibiotics: Actions, Origins, Resistance*. Washington, D.C.: ASM, 2003.

Waters, Brent, and Ronald Cole-Turner, eds. *God and the Embryo: Religious Voices on Stem Cells and Cloning*. Washington, D.C.: Georgetown University Press, 2003.

Weindling, Paul. *Nazi Medicine and the Nuremberg Trials: From Medical War Crimes to Informed Consent*. New York: Palgrave Macmillan, 2004.

Wellcome Library for the History and Understanding of Medicine. "The Guide to History of Medicine Resources on the Internet." <http://medhist.ac.uk/> (accessed March 15, 2006).

Westaby, Stephen. *Landmarks in Cardiac Surgery*. Oxford: Isis Medical Media, 1997.

Wheatley, Steven C. *The Politics of Philanthropy: Abraham Flexner and Medical Education*. Madison: University of Wisconsin Press, 1988.

World Health Organization. "WHO Bulletin." <http://www.who.int/bulletin/en> (accessed March 15, 2006).

———. *World Health Organization*. "WHO Statistical Information System (WHOSIS)." <http://www3.who.int/whosis/menu.cfm> (accessed March 15, 2006).

———. "WHO Weekly Epidemiologic Record (WER)." <http://www.who.int/wer/en> (accessed March 15, 2006).

———. "World Health Organization." <http://www.who.int/en> (accessed March 15, 2006).

Yale University. "Yale School of Public Health." <http://info.med.yale.edu/eph> (accessed March 15, 2006).

———. "Yale School of Public Health, Emerging Infections Program." <http://info.med.yale.edu/eph/eip> (accessed March 15, 2006).

Yam, Philip. *The Pathological Protein: Mad Cow, Chronic Wasting, and Other Deadly Prion Diseases.* Chichester, UK: Copernicus, 2003.

Yuwiler, Janice M. *Insulin.* Detroit: Lucent Books, 2005.

Index

Page numbers in **bold** indicate primary sources; page numbers in *italic* indicate images; page numbers in ***bold italic*** indicate primary source images; page numbers followed by the letter *t* indicate tables. Primary sources are indexed under the entry name with the author's name in parentheses.

A

A.A. (Alcoholics Anonymous), 370–373
AAAS (American Association for the Advancement of Science), 270
AAAS Resolution: Death of Dr. James Carroll from Yellow Fever Experiment (American Association for the Advancement of Science), **271**
Abortion, 376–378
   human stem cell research and, 486, 487
   prenatal diagnosis and, 478
   Roe v. Wade, 450–452, *452*
Acquired immune deficiency syndrome (AIDS), 36–39
Acupressure, *427*
Acupuncture, *254*, 420–425, *421*
AD (Alzheimer's disease), 177–180, *179*, 477–478
ADA (Americans with Disabilities Act), 390–393, *391*
Addiction, drug, *299*, 317–320
   See also Alcoholics Anonymous (A.A.)
Advertisements
   Bayer aspirin, *220*
   Bayer Pharmaceutical Products (Anonymous), *221*
   Dr. McMunn's Kinate of Quinine and Cinchonine, 118
   health care, 247–249, *248*
   Reliable Quinine (Anonymous), *117*
   tobacco and cigarette smoking, 300–303, *301*, *302*
Aeromedical transport, 245–247, *246*
AFMIC (Armed Forces Medical Intelligence Center), 196–198

African American doctors, 214–217
   See also Racism in medicine
Age First Premarital Petting (Kinsey), **212t**
Agency for Healthcare Research and Quality, 472–474
AIDS (Acquired immune deficiency syndrome), 36–39
Air pollution, 320–322
Airplane travel and disease, 333–337
Alabama Department of Public Health, 280–282
Alcoholics and God (Markey), **370–372**
Alcoholics Anonymous (A.A.), 370–373
Ali Maow Maalin Survives the Last Endemic Smallpox Case (Anonymous), ***306***
Alps Still Contaminated by Radiation from Chernobyl (DeLeo), **344**
Alternative medicine, 413–431
Alvarez, Nieves, *160*
Alving, Barbara M., M.D., 173–176
Alzheimer's disease (AD), 177–180, *179*, 477–478
America, Pull Up a Chair—We've Got Something Good to Talk About (Centers for Medicare and Medicaid Services), **256–258**
America Is Still Working on Its Abs (Williams), **405–407**
American Association for the Advancement of Science (AAAS), 270–272
Americans with Disabilities Act (ADA), 390–393, *391*
Americans with Disabilities Act (Bush, George H. W.), **390–391**

Amniocentesis, 54–57, *55*
Amy's Story-Anorexia (Amy), **160–163**
Anatomical nomenclature, *8*
Anatomical prints, 4–9
   Head and Upper Body: Anatomical Prints of the Human Body with Natural Dimensions (Antommarchi), *6*
Anatomy, 4–9
Anderson, Donald, *283*
Anderson, Robert S., 196–197
Anesthesia, 91–95, *94*
Animal research, 49–54, *50*
Animals and Medical Science: A Vision of a New Era (Wiebers), **50–53**
Annas, George J., 459–462
Anne, Princess, *292*
Anorexia nervosa, 159–163, *160*
Anthrax, 201–203, *202*, 329–330
Anthrax as a Biological Weapon: Medical and Public Health Management (Inglesby), **202–203**
Anti-smoking campaigns, *302*, 302–303
Antibiotics, 67–71, *71*, 192–196, *195*
Antibodies, monoclonal, 39–41, *41*
Antidepressants, 45–49, *48*
Antiseptic surgery, 100–103
Antiseptic Surgery: Method of Changing a Psoas Abscess Dressing (Cheyne), **103**
Antommarchi, Franceso C., 4, *5*
Anya, *344*
AP (Associated Press), 343–344
Armed Forces Medical Intelligence Center (AFMIC), 196–198
ART (Assisted reproductive technology), 474–477

Articles
  More People Trying Vegetarian Diets (Farley), 417–419
  Organ Donations Increase When Families Have Good Information about the Donation Process (Agency for Healthcare Research and Quality), 473–474
Artificial insemination, 474
Aspirin in Tablet Form: Bayer Aspirin, 220
Assisted reproductive technology (ART), 474–477
Associated Press (AP), 343–344
Avian influenza, *309*, 337, *362*
  strain H1N1, 308–309
  strain H5N1, 361–364
Ayala, Anna, 86–87

B

Baboon heart transplant, 41–45
Baby Fae Loses her Battle (Wallis), **42–44, *43***
Bacillus anthracis, 201–203, *202*, 329–330
Bacillus cereus, 329
Bacteria, antibiotic resistance, 67–71, 71, 195–196
Bacteriology, 17–20
Baird, Amy, 177–179
Balancing Act: The Health Advantages of Naturally-Occurring Hormone Replacement Therapy (Alving), **174–176**
Banting, Frederick Grant, 20–21, *21*
Barber, Amos Walker, 103–104, *105*
Barrionuevo, Alexei, 82–85
Bayer Company, *220*, 220–221, *221*
Bayer Pharmaceutical Products (Anonymous), **221**
Beck, Theodoric Romeyn, 186–189
Bellevue Hospital, New York City, 97–100
The Belmont Report (National Commission for the Protection of Human Subjects of Biomedical and Behavioral Research), **239–242**
Best, Charles Herbert, 20–21, *21*
Bigelow, Henry J., 91–95
Bioethics, 238–242, 433–491
Biomedical science, 1–87
Biopsies and cellular pathology, 11–13
Biosafety laboratory, *165*
Bioterrorism, 201–203, *202*, 328–330
Bioterrorism at the Salad Bar (Frist), **328–329**
Bird flu, 308–309, *309*, 337, 361–364, *362*

Birth control
  abortion, 376–378, 450–452, *452*
  movement, 382–384
  "the pill," 446–450
Birth defects, *55*, 282–284, 291–293, *292*
  See also Genetic diseases
Black lung disease, *164*, 164–165
Blackburn, Elizabeth, *486*
Blackmun, Henry A., 450–451
Blackwell, Elizabeth, *208*, 208–210, *210*
Blake, Francis G., *195*
Blalock, Alfred, 126–128
Blood, *25*, *73*, 488
Blood banks, 124–126
Blood groups, 23–26
Blood transfusions, 24–25, 124–126
"Blue baby"operations, 126–129
Blue Cross Blue Shield Association, 235
BMT (Bone marrow transplant), 129–131, *131*
Bob, I've Got Emphysema (Houston), *302*
Bone marrow transplant (BMT), 129–131, *131*
Book covers
  The Complete Book of Running (Fixx), *388*
Book excerpts
  Bioterrorism at the Salad Bar (Frist), 328–329
  Case II (Howard, Ripley), 90–91
  Conscious Control of Our Sex Life (Rutgers), 374–375
  On Death and Dying (Kübler-Ross), 453–454
  Disqualifying Diseases (Beck), 186–188
  A Doctor's Memories: The Spanish-American War (Vaughan), 190–191
  Don'ts in Removing Superfluous Hair (Hayes), 368
  Eugenics and Sex Harmony (Pugh), 434–435
  Gentlemen of the Class of 1878 (Summerville), 215
  Implementation of the Program (Kendrick), 124–125
  The Jungle (Sinclair), 224–226
  Medical Intelligence (Anderson), 197
  A Medical Student in 1867 (Wyeth), 379–380
  Not by Bread Alone (Wiley), 366–367
  Our Bodies, Ourselves (The Boston Women's Health Book Collective), 377–378
  Postoperative Insanity (Da Costa), 119–120
  Psychological Consultation Report: Mrs. White and Miss Black (Thigpen, Cleckley), 122–123

Report on Condition of Women and Child Wage-Earners in the United States (Neill), 272–273
Sanitation (Osler), 277–278
Sorting of Casualties (U.S. Department of Defense), 199–200
A Wake-Up Call (Coren), 394
Booklet excerpts
  Guide to Children's Dental Care in Medicaid (U.S. Department of Health and Human Services), 170–172
Borkan, Jeffrey M., 136–139
The Boston Women's Health Book Collective (BWHBC), 376–378
Bovine spongiform encephalopathy (BSE), 152–155, 226
Bradsher, Keith, 333–334
Brain, *34*, 177–180, *179*, 338–341
Breast augmentation, 409–411
Brink, Graham, 463–466
Brody, Howard, 142–147
Brown, John C., 67–71
Brown, Louise Joy, 34–35, *35*
Brown, Michael S., 132–136
BSE (Bovine spongiform encephalopathy), 152–155, 226
BSE Inquiry: The Report, Executive Summary, Key Conclusions (Committee of the BSE Inquiry), **153–154**
Bulletins
  Outbreak Notice (Centers for Disease Control and Prevention), 362–363
Bulman, Erica, 351–352
Bumper stickers, MADD, *333*
Burial, premature, 95–97, *97*
Burroughs Wellcome, 116–117
Bush, George H. W., 390–391
BWHBC (The Boston Women's Health Book Collective), 376–378

C

Calhoun, Archie S., Dr., 232–233
California Department of Health Services, 310–312
Camp Devens Letter (Roy), **307–308**
Can Gene-Altered Rice Rescue the Farm Belt? (Barrionuevo), **82–84**
Cancer
  cervical, 155–159
  Frederick III of Prussia, 11–13
  hormone replacement therapy, 174–176
  lung, 300–303
  radiation therapy, 110–112
  thyroid, *344*

Cardiac surgery, 126–129
Carrier of SARS Made Seven Flights Before Treatment (Bradsher), **335–336**
Carrol, James, 270–272
Carter, Jimmy, 78–80, *389*
Case II (Howard, Ripley), **90–91**
Casualties, sorting, 198–201
CDC. *See* Centers for Disease Control and Prevention (CDC)
Cellular pathology, 11–13
Centers for Disease Control and Prevention (CDC), 139–142, *165*, 347–351, 361, 401–404
Centers for Medicare and Medicaid Services (CMS), 255–256
Cervical cancer, 155–159
Cervical smears. *See* Pap smear
Chernobyl nuclear power plant explosion, 343–346, *344*
Cheyne, William Watson, 100–102
Children
    dental care in Medicaid, 169–173
    health and sanitation standards, 488–491, *490*
    immunization campaigns, 310–313, *312*
    infant mortality rates, 272–274
    iodine deficiency disorders, 338–341
    lead poisoning, 295–297, *296*
    obesity, 402–404
Chinese medicines, *429*
Chiropractic care, 426–428
Cholera, 106–110, *108, 109*, 266–268, *267*
Cholesterol, 131–136, *135*
Cholesterol and Heart Disease (Nobel Assembly at the Karolinska Institute), **132–134**
Chorionic Villus Sampling and Amniocentesis (Olney), **54–57**
Chorionic villus sampling (CVS), 54–57
Cigarette smoking, 300–303, *301, 302*
Circular Letter No. 36 (Standlee), **193–194**
Clark, Matt, 129–131
The Clean Air Act, Title 1: Air Pollution Prevention and Control (U.S. Environmental Protection Agency), **321**
Cleckley, Hervey C., 121–123
Clinical medicine, 89–183
Clinton, William Jefferson, 467–468
Cloning, human, 482–485
CMS (Centers for Medicare and Medicaid Services), 255–256
Coal worker's pneumoconiosis, *164*, 164–165
Cocaine, crack, 317–320, *319*

Commission of the World Health Organization, 284–285
Committee of the BSE Inquiry, 152–155
Common cold, 429–430
Communicable disease transmission, 333–337
Community Mental Health Centers Construction Act of 1989 (U.S. Congress), 313, **314–316**, 317
The Complete Book of Running (Fixx), *388*
Computerized tomography (CT) scanning, 32–34
Conditions at Bellevue Hospital (Anonymous), **99**
Congenital abnormalities. *See* Birth defects
Congenital heart defects, 126–129
The Connecticut Hospice, Inc., 148–149
Conscious Control of Our Sex Life (Rutgers), **374–375**
Consensus Statement on Acupuncture (Ramsay), **421–424**
Constitution of the World Health Organization, Chapters I and II (The Commission of the World Health Organization), **285–286**
Construction of the Panama Canal, 271
Contraception. *See* Birth control
Cord blood, *73*, 488
Coren, Stanley, 394
Cosmetic surgery, 252–255, 408–411, *411*
Cowley, Geoffrey, 45–47
COX-2 inhibitors, 341–343
Crack cocaine, 317–320, *319*
Crash tests, 323–324
Crazy all the Time: On the Psych Ward of Bellevue Hospital, 100
Creutzfeld-Jakob disease, 152–155
Crick, Frances Harry Compton, 29–31
Crops, genetically modified (GM), *82*, 82–85
Cross-cultural medicine, 136–139
CT (Computerized tomography) scanning, 32–34
CVS (Chorionic villus sampling), 54–57

D

Da Costa, John Chalmers, 118–120
Death
    COX-2 inhibitors and risk of, 341–343
    Do-Not-Resuscitate orders, 455–459
    exercise and, 387–390
    motor vehicle safety, 322–325, *323, 324*

physician-assisted suicide, 459–463, *460*
premature burial, 95–97, *97*
psychological aspects, 452–455
right to die, 463–466, *464*
statistics, 272–274, 399–401, *400*
Deaths: Preliminary Data for 2003 (National Center for Health Statistics), **400–401**
Declarations
    World Medical Association Declaration of Helsinki (World Medical Association), 441–443
DeLeo, Maryann, 343–344
Delirium, postoperative, 118–120
Dempster, 293–294
Dental care
    children, 169–173
    medical tourism and, 252–255
    water fluoridation, 347–351, *350*
Deoxyribose nucleic acid (DNA), 29–32, 61–65
Department of Defense (U.S.), 198–201
Department of Health, Education, and Welfare (HEW), 295–296
Department of Health and Human Servies (DHHS), 166–172
Depression, treatment of, 45–49
A Developmental Model of Ethnosensitivity in Family Practice Training (Borkan, Neher), **136–138**
DHHS (U.S. Department of Health and Human Services), 166–172
Diabetes, 20–23
Diagnostic tests
    home, 395–399, *399*
    pre-implantation genetic diagnosis, 475–476, 477–479
    prenatal diagnosis, 54–57, *55*, 477–479
Diana, Princess, *150*
DID (Dissociative identity disorder), 120–124
Diet for a Small Planet (Lappé), 416, 419
Dietary supplements, 338–341, 428–431
Diets, vegetarian, 416–420, *419*
Disabilities, 390–393, *391*
Disasters
    Hurricane Katrina, 260–264
    Indian Ocean Tsunami of 2004, 351–353, *352, 357*
    response and aid delivery, 353–358, *357*
Disqualifying Diseases (Beck), **186–188**
The Dissociation of a Personality (Prince), 121
Dissociative identity disorder (DID), 120–124
Djokomoelyanto, Kodyat B., 338

DNA (Deoxyribose nucleic acid), 29–32, 61–65

DNA sequenator, *64*

Do-Not-Resuscitate (DNR) orders, 455–459

A Doctor's Memories: The Spanish-American War (Vaughan), **190–191**

Doctors Without Borders (Médecins Sans Frontières), 203–205, *204, 357*

Doctors Without Borders (Médecins Sans Frontières) (Healing), *204*

Documents
  Made-to-order Baby Created in Hopes of Saving Ailing Sister (Taus), 475–476
  Don'ts in Removing Superfluous Hair (Hayes), **368**

Drawings, anatomical. *See* Anatomical prints

Drinking and driving, 330–333, *333*

Drug abuse, 297–300, 317–320

Drug addiction, *299*, 317–320

Drug manufacturers, 220–223, 249–253, 341–343

Drug recalls, 341–343

Drunk driving, 330–333

Dubois inhaler, *94*

Dudley Board of Health, *109*

Dying
  Do-Not-Resuscitate orders, 455–459
  hospice movement, 147–150, *150*
  life-sustaining treatment, 142–147
  palliative care, 146–147
  physician-assisted suicide, 459–463, *460*
  psychological stages of, 452–455
  right to die, 463–466, *464*

E

E-mail from Hurricane Katrina (Montgomery), **260–263**

E-mails
  E-mail from Hurricane Katrina (Montgomery), 260–263

Eating and nutrition, 366–368, 428–431

Eating disorders, 159–163, *160*

Ebell, Mark H., 455–458

Ebola virus, *50*, 61, 139–142, *141*

Echinacea Disappoints: There's Still No Cure for the Common Cold (Seppa), **429–430**

Education, medical. *See* Medical education

Education on Palliative and End-of-Live Care (EPEC), 132

Electrolysis, 368–370

Electrosurgery, 368–370

Elizabeth Blackwell, First Female Physician (Lee), **208–209**

Ellis Island, *268*, 268–269, *269*

Embryos, 474–479, 485–488, *486*

Emphysema, 300–303

Encephalopathies, 152–155, 226

End-of-life care
  Do-Not-Resuscitate (DNR) orders, 455–459
  hospice movement, 147–150, *150*
  life-sustaining therapy, 142–147
  physician-assisted suicide, 459–463, *460*
  psychological stages of death, 452–455

End-of-Life Issues (Flatow), **148–149**

Environmental protection, 320–322

Environmental Protection Agency, 320–321

EPEC (Education on Palliative and End-of-Live Care), 132

Epidemiology of cholera, 266–268, *267*

Essays
  On the State of Rural Hygiene (Nightingale), 288–290

Estrogen, 173–177

Ethics in medicine, 238–242, 433–491

Ethnobotany, 249–253

Ethnosensitivity training, 136–139

Eugenics, 434–436, 469–472

Eugenics and Sex Harmony (Pugh), **434–435**

Eulogy for Mattie Stepanek (Carter), **78–81**

Exercise, 387–390, 404–408, *405, 407*

Experimental research
  on animals, 49–54
  on human subjects, 238–243, 436–438, 438–440, 440–443
  United States public health systems, 2–4

F

Family practice, ethnosensitivity training, 136–139

Famine and Public Health (Dempster), *294*

Famines, 293–295, *294*

Farley, Dixie, 416–420

Females. *See* Women

Fitness, 384–387, *386*, 404–408, *405, 407*

Fixx, Jim, 387–388

Flatow, Frederick, 147–150

Fleming, Alexander, *195*

Flexner, Abraham, 214, 227–229

The Flexner Report (Flexner), 215, **228–229**

Flu
  avian, 308–309, *309*, 337, 361–364, *362*
  Spanish, 306–309

Fluoridation, water, 347–351, *350*

Fluoridation of Drinking Water to Prevent Dental Caries (Centers for Disease Control and Prevention), **348–350**

Fluoxetine, 45–49

Foli, Ray, 34–35

Fonda, Jane, *414*

Food, Drug, and Cosmetic Act of 1938, 232–233, 367

Food and Drug Administration, 325–327

Food poisoning, 328–329, *329*

For a Few Pennies More (Television Trust for the Environment), **338–340**

Forensics, 85–87

Fresh Faces (Gersdorff), **408–410**

Freud, Sigmund, *113*, 113–116

Frist, Bill, 328–329

Frontier medicine, 103–106

G

Galle, Sri Lanka, *352*

Gamete intrafallopian transfer (GIFT), 475

Gene therapy, 65–67, *66*

Gene Therapy: Promises and Problems (Pfeifer, Verma), **65–66**

Genetic diseases, 78–82, 475–476, 477–479

Genetic enhancement, human, 469–472

Genetically modified (GM) crops, *82*, 82–85

Genetically modified soybean seeds, *82*

Genetics, 469–472, 482–485

Genomes, human, 61–65, 469–472

Gentlemen of the Class of 1878 (Summerville), **215**

Germ theory of disease, 101–102, 191

Gersdorff, Sascha de, 408–410

GIFT (Gamete intrafallopian transfer), 475

Global Outbreak Alert and Response Network (GOARN), 337

Globalization and health, 333–337

GM (Genetically modified) crops, *82*, 82–85

GOARN (Global Outbreak Alert and Response Network), 337

Goiters, 338–341

Goldstein, Joseph L., 132–136

Goodman, Phyllis, *248*

Gottlieb, Michael S., 35–36

Gottlieb, Nicole, 155–159

Government documents
  *America, Pull Up a Chair—We've Got
    Something Good to Talk About*
    (Centers for Medicare and
    Medicaid Services), 256–258
  The Belmont Report (National
    Commission for the Protection of
    Human Subjects of Biomedical and
    Behavioral Research), 239–242
  *BSE Inquiry: The Report, Executive
    Summary, Key Conclusions*
    (Committee of the BSE Inquiry),
    153–154
  Circular Letter No. 36 (Standlee),
    193–194
  *Community Mental Health Centers
    Construction Act of 1989* (U.S.
    Congress), 314–316
  Consensus Statement on Acupuncture
    (Ramsay), 421–424
  Monitoring Stem Cell Research
    (President's Council on Bioethics),
    486–487
  Preliminary Survey and Current Data
    (Alabama Department of Public
    Health), 280–281
  *Stem Cells; Scientific Progress and
    Future Research Directions*
    (Kirchstein, Skirboll), 73–74
  *Trends and Results for Organ Donation
    and Transplantation in the United
    States, 2004* (U.S. Department of
    Health and Human Services),
    167–168
  Wilson Memorandum (Wilson),
    439–440
  See also Legislation
Graffiti, *319*
Graft-versus-host disease (GVH),
  130–131
Graham, David J., 341–343
Grubbe, Emil H., 110–112, *112*
Gsell, Laurent-Lucien, 9, *10*
*Guide to Children's Dental Care in
  Medicaid* (U.S. Department of
  Health and Human Services),
  170–172
GVH (Graft-versus-host disease),
  130–131

H

Hair removal, 368–370
A Hand and a Home for Pregnant Addicts
  (Wyss), **318–320**
Hand with Ring (Roentgen), **13–14**, *14*
Handbook of Systematic Human Anatomy
  (Henle), 7

Hantavirus pulmonary syndrome
  (HPS), *60*, 60–61
Harper's Weekly, 99
Has Your Child Had a Lead Test Yet?
  (U.S. Department of Health,
  Education, and Welfare), **296**
Hayes, Plymmon Sanford, 368
Hazardous substances warning sign, *321*
He Never Gave Up (Klugar), **76**
*Head and Upper Body: Anatomical Prints
  of the Human Body with Natural
  Dimensions* (Antommarchi), *6*
Healers and ethnobotany, 249–253, *251*
Healing, Lionel, 204
Health care
  advertising, 247–249, *248*
  Health Insurance Portability and
    Accountability Act, 466–469, 479,
    480, 481–482
  herbal medicine, 428–431, *429*
  Hurricane Katrina, 260–264
  Indian Ocean Tsunami of 2004,
    351–353, *352*, *357*
  patient rights and responsibilities,
    479–482
  public health, 265–364
  standards in developing nations,
    488–491, *490*
  wellness and health, 365–411
  women, 376–378
  See also specific topics
Health insurance
  Health Insurance Portability and
    Accountability Act, 466–469, 479,
    480, 481–482
  Medicare, 236–238
  Medicare Part D Prescription Drug
    Coverage for seniors, 255–260
  private, 233–236
Health Insurance Portability and
  Accountability Act (HIPAA),
  466–469, 479, *480*, 481–482
Heart attacks, 341–343, 387–390
Heart defects, congenital, 126–129
Heart disease, cholesterol and,
  131–136, *135*
Heart surgery, 126–129
Heart transplants, 41–45, *168*
Helicopter medical transport,
  245–247, *246*
Helicopter Rescue of Air Crash Victims
  (Anonymous), **246**
Hemorrhagic fever, *50*, 139–142, *141*
Henle, Friedrich Gustav Jakob, 7, 101
Herbal medicine, 428–431, *429*
Herko, Robert J., 150–151
HEW (U.S. Department of Health,
  Education, and Welfare), 295
Hill-Burton Act of 1947, 290–291

HIPAA (Health Insurance Portability
  and Accountability), 466–469, 479,
  480, 481–482
HIV (Human immunodeficiency virus),
  36–39, *38*
HLAs (Human leukocyte antigens),
  129, 131
Home diagnostic tests, 395–399, *399*
*Home Diagnostic Tests: The Ultimate
  House Call?* (Lewis), **396–399**
Hormone replacement therapy,
  173–177, *174*
Hospice movement, 147–150, *150*
Hospital Survey and Construction Act.
  See Hill-Burton Act of 1947
Hospitals, 479–482, 488–491
Houston, Scott, 300–301
*How Many Immunizations Does It take
  To Protect Your Child?* (California
  Department of Health Services),
  312
*How to Attain and Practice the Ideal Sex
  Life* (Rutgers), 375
Howard, Horton, 90–91
Hoyert, Donna L., 400–401
HPS (Hantavirus pulmonary
  syndrome), *60*, 60–61
Hypercholesterolemia, 134–136
Human cloning, 482–485
Human embryos, 474–477, *477*–479,
  486
Human genetic enhancement, 469–472
The Human Genome Project, 62,
  63–64, 65
Human genomes, 61–65, 469–472, *477*
Human immunodeficiency virus (HIV),
  36–39
Human leukocyte antigens (HLAs),
  129, 131
Human medical research subjects,
  238–243, 436–438, 438–440,
  440–443
Human stem cell research, 72–74,
  485–488, *486*
Hunger and famines, 293–295, *294*
Hurricane Katrina, 260–264
Hygiene, rural, 287–291

I

IDD (Iodine deficiency disorders),
  338–341
IHR (International Health
  Regulations), 337
Illustrations
  *Antiseptic Surgery: Method of Changing a
    Psoas Abscess Dressing* (Cheyne), 103

Conditions at Bellevue Hospital (Anonymous), 99

Imaging, medical, 32–34, *33, 34*

Immigrant Girl Receives Medical Exam at Ellis Island (Anonymous), **268**

Immigrants, *268,* 268–270

Immunization campaigns, 310–313, *312*
  See also Vaccines and vaccinations

Implementation of the Program (Kendrick), **124–125**

In-vitro fertilization (IVF), 34–35, 475

Indian Ocean Tsunami of 2004, 351–353, *352, 357*

Industry and medicine, 207–264

Infant mortality rates, 272–274, 282–284

Infantile paralysis, 282–283, *283,* 358–361, *360*

Infarctions, myocardial, 341–343, 387–390

Influenza
  avian, 308–309, *309,* 337, 361–364, *362*
  Spanish, 306–309

Informed consent, 436–438

Inglesby, Thomas V., 201–202

Inhalation of anesthesia, 91–94, *94*

The Initial Assessment: A Quick Checklist (UNICEF), **354–356**

Insanity, postoperative, 118–120

Insemination, artificial, 474

Insensibility During Surgical Operations Produced by Inhalation (Bigelow), **92–94**

Insulin, 20–23

Insurance, health. *See* Health insurance

The Internal Secretion of the Pancreas (Banting, Best), **21–23**

International Health Regulations (IHR), 337

The Interpretation of Dreams (Freud), 115

Iodine, 344–345, *345*

Iodine deficiency disorders (IDD), 338–341

Iodized salt, 338–341

Is There a Doctor in the House? (Anonymous), **248–249**

Ista, Cynthia, *421*

IVF (*In-vitro* fertilization), 34–35, 475

J

Jazzercise, *407*

Jogging, 387–390, *389*

John Snow's Map (Snow), **267**

Johns Hopkins Media Relations Staff, 479–481

Johnson, Lyndon B., 236–238

Journal articles
  Anthrax as a Biological Weapon: Medical and Public Health Management (Inglesby), 202–203
  Chorionic Villus Sampling and Amniocentesis (Olney), 54–57
  Constitution of the World Health Organization, Chapters I and II (The Commission of the World Health Organization), 285–286
  A Developmental Model of Ethnosensitivity in Family Practice Training (Borkan, Neher), 136–138
  Echinacea Disappoints: There's Still No Cure for the Common Cold (Seppa), 429–430
  Fluoridation of Drinking Water to Prevent Dental Caries (Centers for Disease Control and Prevention), 348–350
  Gene Therapy: Promises and Problems (Pfeifer, Verma), 65–66
  Insensibility During Surgical Operations Produced by Inhalation (Bigelow), 92–94
  The Internal Secretion of the Pancreas (Banting, Best), 21–23
  The Lancet (Wakely), 2–3
  Owning Genetic Information and Gene Enhancement Techniques (Moore), 470–471
  Pneumocystis Pneumonia—Los Angeles (Gottlieb, et al.), 36–37
  Practical Guidelines for Do-Not-Resuscitate Orders (Ebell), 456–458
  The Promised End—Constitutional Aspects of Physician-Assisted Suicide (Annas), 459–462
  Radiation Used to Treat Tumors (Grubbe), 111
  The Sequence of the Human Genome (Venter), 63
  A Structure for Deoxyribose Nucleic Acid (Crick, Watson), 30–31
  Telemedicine (Yousef), 181–182
  Withdrawing Intensive Life-sustaining Treatment (Brody), 143–145
Journal of the American Medical Association, 4

The Jungle (Sinclair), **224–226**

K

Kasmauski, Karen, 60

Katrina, Hurricane, 260–264

Kendrick, Douglas B., 124–126

Kennedy, John Fitzgerald, 384–385

Keyhole surgery. *See* Laparoscopic surgery

Kinsey, Alfred C., 210–213

Kirchstein, Ruth L., 72–74

Klugar, Jeffrey, 75–77

Koch, Robert, 17–20

Köhler and Milstein Develop Monoclonal Antibodies (Wigzell, Presentation Speech for the Nobel Prize in Physiology or Medicine, 1984), **40–41**

Kramer, Peter S., Dr., 47–48

Kryptonite (Baird), **178–179**

Kübler-Ross, Elisabeth, Dr., 452–455, *453*

Kumar, Anita, 463–466

L

Laboratory animals, 49–54, *50*

The Lancet (Wakely), **2–3,** *4*

Landau, Robert, 300

Landsteiner, Karl, 23–24, 124

Laparoscopic surgery, 150–152, *152*

Laser surgery, 150–152, *151, 152,* 360

Lasers and Fiber Optics Enable Microsurgery and Keyhole Surgery (Herko), *152*

Lead poisoning, 295–297, *296*

Lectures
  On Individual Differences in Human Blood (Landsteiner), 24–25
  Origin and Development of Psychoanalysis, First Lecture (Freud), 114–115

Lee, Charles Alfred, 208–209

Legal decisions
  Roe v. Wade (*Roe v. Wade,* 410 U.S. 113 [1973]), 450–451

Legal documents
  Permissible Medical Experiments (Nuremberg Military Tribunals), 436–437

Legionella pneumophilia (Legionnaires' disease), *41*

Legionnaires' disease (*Legionella pneumophilia*), *41*

Legislation
  The Clean Air Act, Title 1: Air Pollution Prevention and Control (U.S. Environmental Protection Agency), 321
  See also specific acts

Lehigh County Tuberculosis Society, 26–29

Letter by Dr. A. S. Calhoun to Franklin D. Roosevelt (Calhoun), **232–233**

Letter to Lord Chamberlain Hugo Radolinski (Virchow), **11–13**

Letters

　Camp Devens Letter (Roy), 307–308

　Letter by Dr. A. S. Calhoun to Franklin D. Roosevelt (Calhoun), 232–233

　Letter to Lord Chamberlain Hugo Radolinski (Virchow), 11–13

　A Strong Nation Is a Healthy Nation (Lehigh County Tuberculosis Society), 27–28

　Thalidomide and Congenital Abnormalities (McBride), 292

Levesque, William R., 463–466

Lewis, Carol, 395–396

Lewis, Jerry, *81*

Library of Congress, 313–316

Life expectancy, 399–401, *400*

Lister, Joseph, 89, 102

Lithographs

　Rabies Vaccination in Pasteur's Clinic in Paris (Gsell), *10*

Liver transplant, *166*

Louise Brown and her Parents (Foli), *35*

Lung cancer, 300–303

M

Mad cow disease, 152–155, 226

MADD (Mothers Against Drunk Driving), 330–333, *333*

Made-to-order Baby Created in Hopes of Saving Ailing Sister (Taus), **475–476**

Magazine articles

　Alcoholics and God (Markey), 370–372

　Animals and Medical Science: A Vision of a New Era (Wiebers), 50–53

　Baby Fae Loses her Battle (Wallis), 42–44, *43*

　Fresh Faces (Gersdorff), 408–410

　A Hand and a Home for Pregnant Addicts (Wyss), 318–320

　He Never Gave Up (Klugar), 76

　Home Diagnostic Tests: The Ultimate House Call? (Lewis), 396–399

　Is There a Doctor in the House? (Anonymous), 248–249

　Matthew's New Marrow (Clark), 129–131

　The Pill: How Is It affecting U.S. Morals, Family Life? (Anonymous), 447–449

　The Promise of Prozac (Cowley), 45–47

A Revised System for Reporting Pap Test Results (McNeil, Gottlieb), 157–159

　Suffer the Children (Roane), 489–490

Magnetic resonance imaging (MRI), 33–34, *34*

Malaria, 15–17, 116–118, *271*

Mallon, Mary ("Typhoid Mary"), 274–276

Manipulative and Body-Based Practices: An Overview (National Center for Complementary and Alternative Medicine), **426–428**

Manipulative therapies, 425–428

Manson, JoAnn, Dr., *174*

Manual of Rational Pathology (Henle), 7

Maps

　John Snow's Map (Snow), *267*

　Obesity Trends Among U.S. Adults (Centers for Disease Control and Prevention), *403*

March of Dimes, 282–284, *283*

Markey, Morris, 370–372

Marlboro Man (Landau), *301*

Mary Elizabeth Inn, San Francisco, *314*

Massage, therapeutic, 425–428, *427*

Maternal deaths, 272–274

Matthew's New Marrow (Clark), **129–131**

McBride, W. G., 291–292

McClintock, Barbara, *85*

McDonald's Restaurant, London, *155*

McNeil, Caroline, 155–159

MD (Muscular dystrophy), 78–82

Meat inspection, 223–226, *226*

Meat Inspection Act of of 1906, 223–224, 226

Médecins Sans Frontières (Doctors Without Borders) (Healing), *204*

Médecins Sans Frontières (MSF), 203–205, *204*, *357*

Medicaid and children's dental care, 169–173

Medical education, 227–229, 378–381

　Blackwell, Elizabeth, *208*, 208–210, *210*

　minorities, 214–217

　standards, 227–230

Medical exams, *187*, *268*

Medical imaging, 32–34, *33*, *34*

Medical industry, 207–264

Medical intelligence, 196–198

Medical Intelligence (Anderson), **197**

Medical privacy, 466–469

Medical research

　on animals, 49–54, *50*

　on human subjects, 238–243, 436–438, 438–440, 440–443, 444–446

　United States public health systems, 2–4

A Medical Student in 1867 (Wyeth), **379–380**

Medical tourism, 252–255, *254*

Medical Tourism Companies Luring Americans Abroad with Surgery-Vacation Trips (Parotin), **252–254**

Medical transport, air. *See* Aeromedical transport

Medicare, 236–238, 255–260

Medicine

　alternative, 413–431

　Chinese, *429*

　clinical, 89–183

　cross-cultural, 136–139

　ethics in, 433–491

　frontier, 103–106

　herbal, 428–431, *429*

　industry and, 207–264

　military, 106, 124–126, 191–196, 196–198, 198–201

　racism in, 136–139, 434–436, 444–446

　reproductive, 474–477

　telemedicine, 180–183, *181*

　war and, 185–205

　See also specific diseases and treatments

Medicine men, *137*, 249–253, *251*

Medics, 199

Meditation, 415–416

Meeting minutes

　End-of-Life Issues (Flatow), 148–149

Memoirs

　Memories of Polio (Pernick, Mohanty), 358–360

Memoranda

　Risk of Acute Myocardial Infarction and Sudden Cardiac Death in Patients Treated with COX-2 Selective and Non-Selective NSAIDS (Graham), 342–343

Memories of Polio (Pernick, Mohanty), **358–360**

Menopause, hormone replacement therapy and, 173–177

Mental illness

　Bellevue Hospital, New York City, 99–100

　Community Mental Health Centers Construction Act of 1989, 313–317

　dissociative identity disorder, 120–124

　postoperative insanity, 118–120

　psychoanalysis, 113–116

Merck & Company, 341–343

Microsurgery, 150–152, *152*

Midwifery, 90–91

Military medicine, 106

　blood banks, 124–126

　medical intelligence, 196–198

penicillin, 191–196
triage, 198–201
Military service, 186–189, *187*
Milk pasteurization, 325–328
Miller, Anne, *195*
Minorities and medical education, 214–217
Missett, Judy Sheppard, *407*
Mohanty, Alakananda, 358–360
Monitoring Stem Cell Research (President's Council on Bioethics), **486–487**
Monoclonal antibodies, 39–41, *41*
Montgomery, James T., 260–263
Moore, Adam D., 469–471
More People Trying Vegetarian Diets (Farley), **417–419**
Mortality rates, 272–274, 400–401
Mosquito larvae, *16*
Mothers Against Drunk Driving (MADD), 330–333, *333*
Motor vehicle safety, 322–325, *323, 324*, 330–333, *333*
Motor Vehicle Safety and Public Health (Wright), *323*
MPD (Multiple personality disorder). *See* Dissociative identity disorder (DID)
MRI (Magnetic resonance imaging), 33–34, *34*
MSF (Médecins Sans Frontières), 203–205, *204, 357*
Multiple personality disorder (MPD). *See* Dissociative identity disorder (DID)
Muscular dystrophy (MD), 78–82
Myocardial infarctions, 341–343, 387–390

N

Nacke, Chuck, 163–164
National Center for Complementary and Alternative Medicine (NCCAM), 426–429
National Center for Health Statistics (NCHS), 400
National Commission for the Protection of Human Subjects of Biomedical and Behavioral Research, 238–242
National Institutes of Health (NIH), 4, 72–73
Navajo medicine man, *137*
Naylor, Genevieve, *414*
NCCAM (National Center for Complementary and Alternative Medicine), 426–428

NCHS (National Center for Health Statistics), 400
Neher, Jon, 136–139
Neill, Charles P. ("C.P."), 272–274
Neuropharmacology, 45–49, *48*
New York Board of Health, 106–108
Newspaper articles
Alps Still Contaminated by Radiation from Chernobyl (DeLeo), 344
America Is Still Working on Its Abs (Williams), 405–407
Amy's Story-Anorexia (Amy), 160–163
Can Gene-Altered Rice Rescue the Farm Belt? (Barrionuevo), 82–84
Carrier of SARS Made Seven Flights Before Treatment (Bradsher), 335–336
Medical Tourism Companies Luring Americans Abroad with Surgery-Vacation Trips (Parotin), 252–254
Screening Creates Disease Free Baby (Anonymous), 477–478
Shaman Loses Its Magic (Anonymous), 250–251
Survivor of '32 Syphilis Study Recalls a Diagnosis (Wooten), 445–446
Tube Is Removed After a Chaotic Day (Levesque, Kumar, Tisch, Brink), 463–466
Typhoid Mary Has Reappeared (Anonymous), 275
Water, Sanitation Key to Disaster Response, Long-Term Development (Bulman), 351–352
Woman Finds Human Finger in Wendy's Chili (Reed), 86
Niger, *346*
Nightingale, Florence, 217–220, 287–291, *290*
Nightingale Home and Training School for Nurses, St. Thomas Hospital (Anonymous), *219*
NIH (National Institutes of Health), 4, 72–73
Nixon, Richard Milhous, 297–299
Nobel Assembly at the Karolinska Institute, 131–136
Nomenclature, anatomical, *8*
Normandy Invasion, World War II, *199*
Nose jobs, 405–411
Not by Bread Alone (Wiley), **366–367**
Nuremberg Military Tribunals, 436–437
Nursing, 217–220, *219*, 230–232
Nutrition, 366–368, 428–431
Nutritional supplements, 338–341, 428–431

O

Obesity, 401–408, *403, 404, 405, 407*
Obesity Trends Among U.S. Adults (Centers for Disease Control and Prevention), *403*
Occupational safety and health, 163–166, *164, 165*
Official documents. *See* Government documents
Olney, Richard S., 45–57
On Death and Dying (Kübler-Ross), **453–454**
On Human Cloning By Vote of 84—34—37 (United Nations), **483–485**
On Individual Differences in Human Blood (Landsteiner), **24–25**
On the State of Rural Hygiene (Nightingale), **288–290**
Online articles
What the Heck Is Antibiotic Resistance? (Brown), 68–70
Operation: November 29, 1944 (Blalock), **127–128**
Oral contraceptives, 446–450
Ordinance excerpts
Pasteurization and Aseptic Processing (U.S. Food and Drug Administration), 326–327
Organ donation, 166–169, 472–474, *473*
Organ Donations Increase When Families Have Good Information about the Donation Process (Agency for Healthcare Research and Quality), **473–474**
Organ transplants
bone marrow, 129–131, *131*
heart, *168*
liver, *166*
organ donation for, 472–474, *473*
trends and results, 166–169
Origin and Development of Psychoanalysis, First Lecture (Freud), **114–115**
Osler, William, 277–279
Ouazzani, Chafferdine, *480*
Our Bodies, Ourselves (The Boston Women's Health Book Collective), **377–378**
Outbreak Notice (Centers for Disease Control and Prevention), **362–363**
Outbreak of Ebola Viral Hemorrhagic Fever—Zaire, 1995 (Centers for Disease Control and Prevention), **140–142**
Owning Genetic Information and Gene Enhancement Techniques (Moore), **470–471**

P

Packaging, tamper-resistant, *243*, 243–245
Paintings
  The Premature Burial (Wiertz), 97
  Rabies Vaccination in Pasteur's Clinic in Paris (Gsell), *10*
Palliative care, 146–150, *150*
Pamphlets
  Priority Traffic Safety Laws (MADD—Mothers Against Driving Drunk), 332
Panama Canal, *271*
Pancreas, 20–23
Pap smear, 155–159
Papanicolaou, George N., Dr., *156*
Parkinson's disease patient, *66*
Parotin, Maria M., 252–254
Pasteur, Louis, 9–10, 101–102, *327*
Pasteurization and Aseptic Processing (U.S. Food and Drug Administration), **326–327**
Pasteurization of milk, 325–328
Pathology, cellular, 11–13
Patient rights, 479–482
Patient Rights and Responsibilities (John Hopkins Media Relations Staff), **479–481**
Patient Undergoing a CT Scan (Anonymous), *33*
PCR machines, *477*
Pediatric cardiology, 126–129
Penicillin, 191–196, *195*
Permissible Medical Experiments (Nuremberg Military Tribunals), **436–437**
Pernick, Martin, 358–359
Personality disorders, 121–123
Pettersson, Ralf F., 57–59
Petting, premarital, *212t*, *213*
Pfeifer, Alexander, 65–67
PGD (Pre-implantation genetic diagnosis), 475–476, 477–479
PH-MHS (Public Health and Marine Service), 3–4
Pharmaceutical manufacturers. *See* Drug manufacturers
Photographs
  abortion protest, *452*
  acupressure, *427*
  acupuncture, *254*, *421*
  Ali Maow Maalin Survives the Last Endemic Smallpox Case (Anonymous), *306*
  anthrax, *202*
  bird flu, *309*, *362*
  Blackburn, Elizabeth, *486*

  Bob, I've Got Emphysema (Houston), *302*
  Carter, Jimmy, *389*
  Famine and Public Health (Dempster), *294*
  food poisoning, *329*
  Galle, Sri Lanka, *352*
  health care advertising, *248*
  heart transplant patient, *168*
  Helicopter Rescue of Air Crash Victims (Anonymous), *246*
  herbal medicine, *429*
  HIV positive patient, *38*
  Immigrant Girl Receives Medical Exam at Ellis Island (Anonymous), *268*
  Indian Ocean Tsunami Disaster of 2004, *357*
  jazzercise, *407*
  John Snow's Map (Snow), *267*
  Lasers and Fiber Optics Enable Microsurgery and Keyhole Surgery (Herko), *152*
  Louise Brown and her Parents (Foli), *35*
  Manson, JoAnn, Dr., *174*
  Marlboro Man (Landau), *301*
  Mary Elizabeth Inn, San Francisco, *314*
  meat inspection, *226*
  Médecins Sans Frontières (Doctors Without Borders) (Healing), *204*
  medical exam, *187*
  Motor Vehicle Safety and Public Health (Wright), *323*
  Nightingale Home and Training School for Nurses, St. Thomas Hospital (Anonymous), *219*
  Normandy Invasion, World War II, *199*
  obesity, *404*, *405*
  organ donation, *473*
  Patient Undergoing a CT Scan (Anonymous), *33*
  penicillin, *195*
  physician-assisted suicide, *460*
  plastic surgery, *411*
  polio vaccination, *360*
  Portrait of Donald Anderson (Anonymous), *283*
  Private Health Insurance Originates with Blue Cross and Blue Shield (Blue Cross Blue Shield Association), *235*
  Product Tampering: The Tylenol Scare (Anonymous), *243*, *244*
  Rabies Vaccination in Pasteur's Clinic in Paris (Gsell) (photograph of lithograph), *10*
  right to die, *464*
  Rules for the Prevention of Cholera (New York Board of Health), *108*

  safety belts, *324*
  Sanger, Margaret, *382*, *384*
  shamans, *251*
  Sisters of Notre Dame, *179*
  sleep studies, *395*
  slums, Kibera, Kenya, *490*
  Surgeon Amos Walker Barber, Wyoming Territory (Anonymous), *105*
  thalidomide victim, *292*
  thyroid cancer, *344*
  trash collection, *277*
  vodka distillery, *373*
  World Water Crisis (Sanogo), *346*
  X Ray of the Lungs of a Coal Miner (Nacke), *164*
  Yoga and Transcendental Meditation (Naylor), *414*
  Zoonosis (Kasmauski), *60*
Physical fitness. *See* Fitness
Physician-assisted suicide, 459–463, *460*
Physiology, 6–8
"The pill," 446–450
The Pill: How Is It affecting U.S. Morals, Family Life? (Anonymous), **447–449**
Planches anatomiques du corps humain exécutées d'après les dimensions naturelles (Antommarchi). *See Head and Upper Body: Anatomical Prints of the Human Body with Natural Dimensions* (Antommarchi)
Plastic surgery, 252–255, 408–411, *411*
Pneumocystis carinii, 35–37
Pneumocystis Pneumonia—Los Angeles (Gottlieb, et al.), **36–37**
Poems
  Kryptonite (Baird), 178–179
  Stepanek, Mattie, 80
  This Day Relenting God (Ross), 16
Polio, 282–283, *283*, 358–361, *360*
Pollution, air, 320–322
Poor Law Commissioners, 287–288
Portrait of Donald Anderson (Anonymous), **283**
Posters
  Has Your Child Had a Lead Test Yet? (U.S. Department of Health, Education, and Welfare), *296*
  How Many Immunizations Does It take To Protect Your Child? (California Department of Health Services), *312*
  March of Dimes *Portrait of Donald Anderson* (Anonymous), *283*
  McDonald's, *155*
Postoperative insanity, 118–120
Postoperative Insanity (Da Costa), **119–120**
Poverty, 293–294
Practical Guidelines for Do-Not-Resuscitate Orders (Ebell), **456–458**

Pre-implantation genetic diagnosis (PGD), 475–476, 477–479

Pregnancy
assisted reproductive technology, 474–477
drug addiction and, 318–320
maternal deaths, 272–274
prenatal diagnosis, 54–57, *55*, 477–479
tests, 395–399, *399*
See also Abortion; Birth control

Preliminary Survey and Current Data (Alabama Department of Public Health), **280–281**

Premarital petting, *212t, 213*

Premature burial, 95–97, *97*

The Premature Burial (Wiertz), **97**

Prenatal diagnosis, 54–57, *55*, 477–479

Prescription drug benefits, 255–260

President Lyndon Johnson Signs Medicare Bill (Johnson), **237–238**

President Nixon Declares "War" on Drugs (Nixon), **298**

President's Council on Bioethics, 485–487

Press releases
Cholesterol and Heart Disease (Nobel Assembly at the Karolinska Institute), 132–134
On Human Cloning By Vote of 84—34—37 (United Nations), 483–485

Preventive dentistry, 169–172, 347–351

Prince, Morton, 121

Princess Anne, *292*

Princess Diana, *150*

Prions, 57–59, *59*

Prions: Newly Identified Infectious Agent (Pettersson, Presentation Speech for the Nobel Prize in Physiology or Medicine, 1997), **58–59**

Priority Traffic Safety Laws (MADD—Mothers Against Driving Drunk), **332**

Privacy, medical, 466–469

Private Health Insurance Originates with Blue Cross and Blue Shield (Blue Cross Blue Shield Association), **235**

Product tampering, 243–245

Product Tampering: The Tylenol Scare (Anonymous), *243, 244*

Professional society resolutions
AAAS Resolution: Death of Dr. James Carroll from Yellow Fever Experiment (American Association for the Advancement of Science), 271

Progesterone, 173–177

The Promise of Prozac (Cowley), **45–47**

The Promised End—Constitutional Aspects of Physician-Assisted Suicide (Annas), **459–462**

Prozac, 45–49, *48*

Psychiatric care, 99–100
See also Mental illness

Psychoanalysis, 113–116

Psychological Consultation Report: Mrs. White and Miss Black (Thigpen, Cleckley), **122–123**

The Psychopathology of Everyday Life (Freud), 115

Psychopharmacology, 45–49, *48*

Public health, 3–4, 107–109, 265–364, 488–491, *490*

Public Health Act of 1848, 290

Public Health and Marine Service (PH-MHS), 3–4

Public health notices
Rules for the Prevention of Cholera (New York Board of Health), 107–109, **108**

Pugh, William Scott, 434–435

Pure Food and Drug Act, 366

Q

Quarantine, 275–276, *276*

Quinine, 116–118, *117, 118*

R

Rabies vaccination, 9–11

Rabies Vaccination in Pasteur's Clinic in Paris (Gsell), **10**

Racism in medicine, 136–139, 434–436, 444–446

Radiation
Chernobyl nuclear power plant, 343–346, *344*
human experiments, 438–440
tumor treatment, 110–113
X rays, 13–15, *14*, 110–113, *164*

Radiation oncology, 110–112

Radiation Used to Treat Tumors (Grubbe), **111**

Radolinski, Hugo, Lord Chamberlain, 11–13

Ramsay, David J., 420–424

Recalls, drug, 341–343

Reed, Dan, 85–86

Reeve, Christopher, 75–77

Registration of nurses, 230–232

Reliable Quinine (Anonymous), **117**

Remarks by the President on Medical Privacy (Clinton), **467–468**

Remarks on the Youth Fitness Movement (Kennedy), **385–386**

Report on Condition of Women and Child Wage-Earners in the United States (Neill), **272–273**

Reports
Deaths: Preliminary Data for 2003 (National Center for Health Statistics), 400–401
The Flexner Report (Flexner), 228–229
Manipulative and Body-Based Practices: An Overview (National Center for Complementary and Alternative Medicine), 426–428
Outbreak of Ebola Viral Hemorrhagic Fever—Zaire, 1995 (Centers for Disease Control and Prevention), 140–142

Reproductive medicine, 474–477

Research, medical. *See* Medical research

Research laboratories, animals in, 49–54

A Revised System for Reporting Pap Test Results (McNeil, Gottlieb), **157–159**

Reyes, Lilian, *404*

Rhinoplasty, 405–411

Richter, Stacey, *460*

Right to die, 463–466, *464*

Ripley, William, 90–91

Risk of Acute Myocardial Infarction and Sudden Cardiac Death in Patients Treated with COX-2 Selective and Non-Selective NSAIDS (Graham), **342–343**

Roane, Kit R., 488–490

Robert Koch Identifies the Bacteria that Cause Anthrax, Tuberculosis, and Cholera (Mörner, Presentation Speech for the Nobel Prize in Physiology or Medicine, 1905), **17–19**

Roe v. Wade (Roe v. Wade, 410 U.S. 113 [1973]), **450–451**, *452*

Roentgen, Wilhelm Conrad, 13–14

Rofecoxib, *342*, 342–343

Ross, Ronald, Sir, 15–16

Roy, 307–308

Rules for the Prevention of Cholera (New York Board of Health), **107–109, 108**

Running, 387–389

Rural hygiene, 287–291

Rutgers, J., 373–375

S

Safety belts, *324*

Salad bars, 328–329

Salmonella typhimurium, 328–329

Salt, iodized, for iodine deficiency prevention, 338–341

Sanger, Margaret, *382*, 382–383, *384*

Sanitation, 276–279
disaster response and aid delivery, 353–358, *357*
Indian Ocean Tsunami of 2004, 351–353, *352*, *357*
rural hygiene, 287–291
standards in developing nations, 488–491, *490*

Sanitation (Osler), **277–278**

Sanogo, Issouf, *346*

SARS (Severe acute respiratory syndrome), 269, 335–336

Saunders, Cicely, Dame, 147–148

Schiavo, Terri, 463–466

SCID (Severe combined immune deficiency) treatment, 129–131

Scientific Registry of Transplant Recipients, Organ Procurement and Transplantation Network, 166–169

Screening Creates Disease Free Baby (Anonymous), **477–478**

Selective serotonin reuptake inhibitors (SSRIs), 45, 48

Selective service system, 188

Seniors and Medicare Part D Prescription Drug Coverage, 255–260

Seppa, Nathan, 429–430

The Sequence of the Human Genome (Venter), **63**

Severe acute respiratory syndrome (SARS), 269, 335–336

Severe combined immune deficiency (SCID) treatment, 129–131

Sexual behavior
eugenics and, 434–436
and "the pill," 446–450
premarital petting, *212t*, *213*
sexuality and casual sex, 373–376
studies, 210–214
syphilis and, 444–446

Sexual Behavior in the Human Female (Kinsey), 211

Sexual Behavior in the Human Male (Kinsey), 211

Shaman Loses Its Magic (Anonymous), **250–251**

Shaman Pharmaceuticals Company, 249–253

Shamans, 249–253, *251*

Sinclair, Upton, 223–226

Sisters of Notre Dame, *179*

Sizemore, Christine Costner, 121–123

Skirboll, Lana, 72–74

Sleep, 393–395, *395*

Slums, Kibera, Kenya, *490*

Smallpox, 303–306, *305*, *306*

Smoking, 300–303, *301*, *302*

Snow, John, 266–267

Sorting of Casualties (U.S. Department of Defense), **199–200**

Soybean seeds, *82*

Spanish-American War, 189–191

Spanish flu, 306–309

Speeches
Americans with Disabilities Act (Bush, George H. W.), 390–391
Elizabeth Blackwell, First Female Physician (Lee), 208–209
Eulogy for Mattie Stepanek (Carter), 78–81
Köhler and Milstein Develop Monoclonal Antibodies (Wigzell, Presentation Speech for the Nobel Prize in Physiology or Medicine, 1984), 40–41
President Lyndon Johnson Signs Medicare Bill (Johnson), 237–238
President Nixon Declares "War" on Drugs (Nixon), 298
Prions: Newly Identified Infectious Agent (Pettersson, Presentation Speech for the Nobel Prize in Physiology or Medicine, 1997), 58–59
Remarks by the President on Medical Privacy (Clinton), 467–468
Remarks on the Youth Fitness Movement (Kennedy), 385–386
Robert Koch Identifies the Bacteria that Cause Anthrax, Tuberculosis, and Cholera (Mörner, Presentation Speech for the Nobel Prize in Physiology or Medicine, 1905), 17–19
State Registration of Trained Nurses (Welch), 230–231
This I Believe (Sanger), 383

Spinal cord injuries, 75–78

SSRIs (Selective serotonin reuptake inhibitors), 45, 48

Standlee, Earle G.G., 191–196

Staphylococcus bacteria, *71*

Starzl, Thomas, Dr., 166, *166*

State Registration of Trained Nurses (Welch), **230–231**

Statin drugs, 134–136

Stem cell research, 72–75, 485–488, *486*

Stem Cells; Scientific Progress and Future Research Directions (Kirchstein, Skirboll), **73–74**

Stepanek, Mattie, 78–81

A Strong Nation Is a Healthy Nation (Lehigh County Tuberculosis Society), **27–28**

A Structure for Deoxyribose Nucleic Acid (Crick, Watson), **30–31**

Suffer the Children (Roane), **489–490**

Suicide, physician-assisted, 459–463

Summerville, James, 214–215

Surgeon Amos Walker Barber, Wyoming Territory (Anonymous), **105**

Surgery
anesthesia, 91–95
antiseptic, 100–103
"blue baby" operations, 126–129
cardiac, 126–129
cosmetic surgery, 252–255, 408–411, *411*
electrosurgery, 368–370
laparoscopic surgery, 150–152, *152*
laser surgery, 150–152, *151*, *152*, 360
medical tourism and, 252–255
microsurgery, 150–152, *152*
plastic surgery, 252–255, 408–411, *411*
postoperative insanity, 118–120
surgery-vacation trips, 252–255

Surgical notes
Operation: November 29, 1944 (Blalock), 127–128

Survivor of '32 Syphilis Study Recalls a Diagnosis (Wooten), **445–446**

Syphilis, 444–446

T

Tables
Age First Premarital Petting (Kinsey), *212t*

Tamper-resistant packaging, *243*, 243–245

Tattoos, *299*

Taus, Margaret, 475–476

Taussig, Helen Brooke, 126–128

TB (Tuberculosis), *19*, 26–29, *137*

Telemedicine, 180–183, *181*

Telemedicine (Yousef), **181–182**

Television transcripts
For a Few Pennies More (Television Trust for the Environment), 338–340

Television Trust for the Environment, 338–340

Testimony excerpts
Balancing Act: The Health Advantages of Naturally-Occurring Hormone Replacement Therapy (Alving), 174–176

Tetralogy of Fallot, 126–129

Thalidomide, 291–293, *292*

Thalidomide and Congenital Abnormalities (McBride), **292**

Therapeutic massage, 425–428, *427*
Thigpen, Corbett H., 121–123
This Day Relenting God (Ross), **16**
This I Believe (Sanger), **383**
Three Essays on the Theory of Sexuality (Freud), 115
The Three Faces of Eve (Thigpen, Cleckley), 121, 123
Thyroid and iodine deficiency, 338–341
Thyroid cancer, *344*, 344–345
Tisch, Chris, 463–466
TM (Transcendental meditation), *414*, 415–416
Tobacco advertising, 300–303, *301*, *302*
Tofu, *419*
Tourism, medical, 252–255, *254*
Traffic safety, 330–333
Transcendental meditation (TM), *414*, 415–416
Transfusions, blood, 124–126
Transmissible spongiform encephalopathies (TSEs), 152–155
Transplants
   bone marrow, 129–131, *131*
   heart, *168*
   liver, *166*
   organ donation for, 472–474, *473*
   trends and results, 166–169
Transportation
   aeromedical, 245–247, *246*
   spread of disease and, 333–337
Trash collection, *277*
A Treatise on the Complaints Peculiar to Females Embracing a System of Midwifery (Howard), 90
Trends and Results for Organ Donation and Transplantation in the United States, 2004 (U.S. Department of Health and Human Services), **167–168**
Triage, 198–201
TSEs (Transmissible spongiform encephalopathies), 152–155
Tsunami, Indian Ocean, 2004, 351–353, *352*, *357*
Tube Is Removed After a Chaotic Day (Levesque, Kumar, Tisch, Brink), **463–466**
Tuberculosis (TB), *19*, 26–29, *137*
Tuleremia, 61
Tumors, X ray treatment of, 110–113
Tuskegee Syphilis Study, 444–446
Tylenol product-tampering scare, *243*, 243–245, *244*
Typhoid, 274–276
Typhoid Mary Has Reappeared (Anonymous), **275**
"Typhoid Mary" (Mallon, Mary), 274–276

U

Umbilical cord blood, *73*, 488
UN (United Nations), 482–485
UNICEF (United Nations International Children's Emergency), 353–356, 491
United Nations documents
   The Initial Assessment: A Quick Checklist (UNICEF), 354–356
   See also Government documents
United Nations International Children's Emergency Fund (UNICEF), 353–356, 491
United Nations (UN), 482–485
United Nations World Water Assessment Program (WWAP), 346–347
U.S. Department of Defense, 198–201
U.S. Department of Health, Education, and Welfare (HEW), 295–296
U.S. Department of Health and Human Servies (DHHS), 166–172
U.S. Environmental Protection Agency, 320–321
U.S. Food and Drug Administration, 325–327

V

Vacations, medical tourism and, 252–255, *254*
Vaccines and vaccinations, 9–10
   immunization campaigns, 310–313, *312*
   polio, *360*, 360–361
   rabies, 9–11
   smallpox, 304–306, *305*, 305–306
   tuberculosis, *19*
Variant Creutzfeld-Jakob disease (vCJD), 152–155
Variola virus, 303–306, *305*, *306*
Vaughan, Victor C., 189–191
VCJD (variant Creutzfeld-Jakob disease), 152–155
Vegetarian diets, 416–420, *419*
Venter, J. Craig, 61–64, *62*
Verma, Inder M., 65–67
VHF (Viral hemoraggic fever), 139–142
Vibrio choleraa, 106–110, *108*, *109*, 266–268, *267*
Video consultations, *181*
Vioxx, *342*, 342–343
Viral hemoraggic fever (VHF), 139–142
Virchow, Rudolf, *11*, 11–13
Vodka distillery, *373*

W

A Wake-Up Call (Coren), **394**
Wakely, Thomas, 2–3
Wallis, Claudia, 41–44
War and medicine, 185–205
War on Drugs, 297–300
Warning signs, hazardous substances, 321
Water
   crisis, *346*, 346–347
   fluoridation, 347–351, *350*
   Indian Ocean Tsunami of 2004, 351–353, *352*
Water, Sanitation Key to Disaster Response, Long-Term Development (Bulman), **351–352**
Watson, James Dewey, 29–31, *30*
Web sites
   Patient Rights and Responsibilities (John Hopkins Media Relations Staff), 479–481
Weight problems, 401–404, *403*, *404*, 404–408, *405*, *407*
Welch, William Henry, 230–231
Wellness and health, 365–411
Wendy's chili hoax, 85–87
What the Heck Is Antibiotic Resistance? (Brown), **68–70**
Wheelchair ramps, *391*
WHI (Women's Health Initiative), 174–176
WHO (World Health Organization), 284–287, 304–307, 337, 491
Wiebers, David O., 49–53
Wiertz, Antoine, 95–96
Wigzell, Hans, 39–41
Wiley, Harvey Washington, 366–367
Williams, Alex, 405–407
Wilson, Charles E., 438–440
Wilson Memorandum (Wilson), **439–440**
Withdrawing Intensive Life-sustaining Treatment (Brody), **143–145**
WMA (World Medical Association), 440–443
Woman Finds Human Finger in Wendy's Chili (Reed), **86**
Women
   abortion, 376–378, 450–452, *452*
   birth control movement, 382–384
   first female physician, *208*, 208–210, *210*
   health movement, 376–378
   hormone replacement therapy, 173–177
   iodine deficiency disorders, 338–341
   Mary Elizabeth Inn, San Francisco, *314*
   mortality rates, 272–274

physicians, 208–210
and "the pill," 446–450
pregnancy and crack cocaine,
    318–320
sexual behavior, 211–213
thalidomide and congenital
    abnormalities, 291–293, *292*
Women's Health Initiative (WHI),
    174–176
Wooten, James T., 444–446
World Health Organization (WHO),
    284–287, 304–307, 337, 491
*World Medical Association Declaration of
    Helsinki* (World Medical
    Association), **441–443**
World Medical Association (WMA),
    440–443

World Water Crisis (Sanogo), ***346***
Wright, Tim, 322–323
WWAP (United Nations World Water
    Assessment Program), 346–347
Wyeth, John Allen, 379–380
Wyss, Dennis, 317–320

X

X Ray of the Lungs of a Coal Miner
    (Nacke), ***164***
X rays, 13–15
    calcified fetus, *480*
    hand, *14*
    lungs, *164*
    tumor treatment, 110–113

Y

Yellow fever, 270–272, *271*
Yoga, *414*, 414–416, *415*
Yoga and Transcendental Meditation
    (Naylor), ***414***
Yousef, Jasemian, 180–183
Youth fitness program, 384–387, *386*

Z

Zackery, Victoria, *421*
Zoonosis (Kasmauski), ***60***, 60–61